Basic Pathophysiology
A Holistic Approach

Basic
Pathophysiology
A Holistic Approach

Maureen W. Groër, R.N., Ph.D.
Professor and Director of Doctoral Program,
College of Nursing,
University of Tennessee at Knoxville,
Knoxville, Tennessee

Maureen E. Shekleton, R.N., D.N.Sc.
Assistant Professor of Nursing,
Department of Medical-Surgical Nursing,
College of Nursing
The University of Illinois at Chicago;
Complemental Faculty
Rush University College of Nursing,
Chicago, Illinois

Third edition

with 331 illustrations

The C. V. Mosby Company
ST. LOUIS • BALTIMORE • PHILADELPHIA • TORONTO 1989

 Mosby

Editor: William Grayson Brottmiller
Senior developmental editor: Sally Adkisson
Project manager: Patricia Gayle May
Production editor: Barbara Merritt
Design: Liz Fett
Cover design: Elise Stimac

Third edition

The C.V. Mosby Company
11830 Westline Industrial Drive, St. Louis, Missouri 63146

Library of Congress Cataloging-in-Publication Data

Groër, Maureen Wimberly
    Basic pathophysiology: a holistic approach / Maureen W. Groër,

  Maureen E. Shekleton.—3rd ed.
       p.   cm.
    Includes bibliographies and index.
    ISBN 0-8016-2452-5
    1. Physiology, Pathological. I. Shekleton, Maureen E.
  II. Title.
    [DNLM: 1. Disease. 2. Pathology. 3. Physiology.   QZ 140 G869b]
  RB113.G67 1989
  616.07—dc19
  DNLM/DLC
  for Library of Congress   89-2962
                                    CIP

C/VH/VH 9 8 7 6 5 4 3 2 1

Contributors

Kay Bultemeier, M.S.N., M.A.
Family Nurse Practitioner in Private Practice;
Assistant Professor,
University of Tennessee, College of Nursing,
Knoxville, Tennessee

MaryAnn Colletti, M.S., R.N.
AIDS Clinical Nurse Specialist,
Rush-Presbyterian-St. Luke's Medical Center,
Chicago, Illinois

Peggy Covey
Senior Research Specialist in Health Science,
University of Illinois, College of Nursing,
Chicago, Illinois

Charlotte A. Curtis, M.S.N., C.E.N., R.N.
Trauma Nurse Coordinator,
St. Mary's Medical Center,
Knoxville, Tennessee

Kimberly L. Davis, M.S.N.
Pediatric Clinical Instructor,
University of Tennessee, College of Nursing,
Knoxville, Tennessee

Patricia G. Droppleman, Ph.D., M.S.N.
Associate Professor,
Coordinator, Parent-Child Graduate Track,
University of Tennessee,
Knoxville, Tennessee

Mildred M. Fenske, Ph.D., M.N.
Associate Professor,
University of Tennessee, College of Nursing,
Knoxville, Tennessee

Ben Francisco, B.S., A.D.
Education Coordinator, Pediatrics,
University of Tennessee Medical Center,
Knoxville, Tennessee

Mark S. Gaylord, B.S., M.D.
Assistant Professor,
University of Tennessee Medical Center,
Knoxville, Tennessee

Nan M. Gaylord, B.S.N., M.S.
Instructor, Pediatrics,
University of Tennessee, College of Nursing,
Knoxville, Tennessee

Cynthia Gronkiewicz
Pulmonary Clinical Specialist,
Chest Medicine Consultants,
Chicago, Illinois

Lois Halstead, Ph.D., R.N.
Assistant Professor of Nursing,
Assistant Chairperson,
Department of Maternal Child Nursing,
Coordinator, Parent Child Nursing
Rush University College of Nursing,
Chicago, Illinois

Lynda Harrison, Ph.D., R.N.
Director, Nursing Research Center,
University of Alabama,
Tuscaloosa, Alabama

Lisa Hopp, M.S.N., R.N.
Staff Nurse, Medical ICU,
Rush-Presbyterian-St. Luke's Medical Center,
Chicago, Illinois; Doctoral Candidate,
University of Illinois, College of Nursing,
Chicago, Illinois

Katie Lemley, M.S.N., R.N., C.
Nurse Practitioner,
Health Care for the Homeless,
Chicago, Illinois

Sarah Naber, Ph.D., C.N.M.
Coordinator, Nurse Midwifery Program,
Assistant Professor of Nursing,
Associate Chair, Department of Maternal Child
Nursing,
Rush-Presbyterian-St. Luke's Medical Center,
Chicago, Illinois

Judith Paice, M.S., R.N.
Assistant Professor,
College of Nursing, Rush University,
Acting Coordinator of Oncology,
Nursing Program,
Chicago, Illinois

Margaret S. Pierce, M.P.H., M.S.N.
Assistant Professor,
University of Tennessee,
Knoxville, Tennessee;
Oncology Clinical Nurse Specialist,
St. Mary's Medical Center,
Knoxville, Tennessee

Xavier Smith, M.S., R.N.
Practitioner-Teacher,
Department of Medical Nursing,
Rush-Presbyterian-St. Luke's Medical Center,
Rush University College of Nursing,
Chicago, Illinois

Ingrid Stram-Doll, B.S., R.N.C., F.N.P.
Family Nurse Practitioner,
San Jose, California

Judy Trufant, M.N., R.N.
Assistant Professor and Practitioner-Teacher,
Department of Pediatric Nursing,
Rush-Presbyterian-St. Luke's Medical Center,
Chicago, Illinois

Candice Vitalo, B.S.N., R.N.
Research Specialist in Health Science,
University of Illinois, College of Nursing,
Chicago, Illinois

Elizabeth Wharton, M.S.N., B.S.
Oncology Nurse Manager,
Durango, Colorado

Susan Wright, D.N.Sc., R.N.
Clinical Assistant Professor,
University of Illinois, College of Nursing,
Champaign-Urbana, Illinois

Preface

Since the first edition of *Basic Pathophysiology* was published in 1979, the nursing profession has undergone some fairly revolutionary changes. There have been substantial changes in the roles nurses are adopting. Increasing independence has been assumed by nurses in almost every role. Many nurses have developed private nursing practices and expanded their functions to include many new settings. Members of the nursing profession have begun the development of an independent, diagnostic nomenclature for defining the problems nurses address and solve. More and more nurses are prepared at the baccalaureate and graduate levels. To respond to these exciting changes in nursing, and in answer to suggestions received by faculty and students who have used *Basic Pathophysiology*, we have reorganized the content of the book within a different framework. We believe that this approach will enhance the usefulness of the book in most nursing curricula. There have been no substantive changes in the depth and scope of the pathophysiology reviewed, other than expansion in some areas and presentation of the most recent research in each area. We have retained a strong systems theory approach, viewing pathophysiologic mechanisms as a breakdown in negative feedback, or development of positive feedback. However, stronger emphasis has been placed on coping and adaptation, which we see as the normal human response to potential or actual health problems. We have also presented recent views of the tremendous importance of mind-body interactions in the development of deviations from wellness.

A major change in the book is the organization of the content within a framework similar to functional health patterns. Since nursing is the diagnosis and treatment of human responses to potential or actual health problems, we believe that pathophysiologic mechanisms should be organized to facilitate the process of nursing diagnosis and treatment. Using this classification framework, the content is grouped within units and titled according to the appropriate pattern. There will be crossover of the content from one pattern to another. For example, the human response to cancer will sometimes involve self-perception and self-concept (as might many other diseases), but we have classified it more appropriately in the unit that refers to individual-environmental interactions. There are other examples of this type of crossover that we believe further emphasize the holistic nature of the human responses to actual and potential health problems.

An additional approach that will facilitate application of students' understanding of pathophysiology is the use of case studies throughout the book. The case studies include analysis of the objective and subjective data, an explanation of the biologic bases of the data, and extension of the analysis to include nursing diagnoses. Many of these case studies have been contributed by students and colleagues; they represent actual cases that have been altered when appropriate to protect the identity of the client.

The reader may wonder about the change to the title, *Basic Pathophysiology: A Holistic Approach* from *Basic Pathophysiology: A Conceptual Approach*. We have not abandoned the conceptual approach and in fact have added more concepts (for example, pain). The holistic approach incorporates the concept that mind-body interactions are important in disease mechanisms and that coping and adaptation operate at both levels to restore wellness whenever possible. Many disease mechanisms are now presented much more holistically, and the important influence of psychoneuroimmunology in disease is integrated throughout the text. We have provided more in-depth discussions of coping responses, and have expanded our previous concept of a healthy "steady state" to one of "wellness," a much more positive process in our view. Using this approach, we can also develop discussions of lifestyle factors, health habits, personality, behavior, risk factors, and potential, as well as actual, health problems.

The authors appreciate the very favorable responses to the previous two editions of this book and hope that the changes we have made will further enhance the use of this book in nursing curricula.

We would like to express our appreciation to colleagues who reviewed new sections of the third edition:

Marilee Donovan, PhD, RN
Professor and Chairperson
Department of Medical Nursing
Rush-Presbyterian-St. Luke's Medical Center
Chicago, Illinois

Ginger Evans, MSN, RN
Assistant Professor
College of Nursing
University of Tennessee at Knoxville
Knoxville, Tennessee

Joanne Maklebust, MSN, RN, CS
Clinical Nurse Specialist
Ostomy/Wound Care
Harper Hospital
Detroit Medical Center
Detroit, Michigan

Johnie Mozingo, PhD, RN
Professor and Associate Dean of
Undergraduate Studies
College of Nursing
University of Tennessee at Knoxville
Knoxville, Tennessee

Margaret Pierce, MSN, RN
Assistant Professor
College of Nursing
University of Tennessee at Knoxville
Knoxville, Tennessee

David Rubin, MD
Attending Physician
Department of Pulmonary Medicine
Rush-Presbyterian-St. Luke's Medical Center
Chicago, Illinois

We also wish to express our gratitude to our children and husbands for their continuing support and sacrifice, and we appreciate the editorial assistance of Bill Brottmiller and Sally Adkisson throughout the development of this third edition.

Maureen W. Groër
Maureen E. Shekleton

Contents

UNIT I

Introduction

1

Deviations from wellness

Wellness can be disrupted through a variety of pathophysiologic processes. These processes are usually viewed as biologic aberrations and the resultant disease as a measurable physicochemical phenomenon. For example, if a person inhales an irritant gas, the physical properties of the gas cause a predictable sequence of physical effects and biologic responses that act to decrease the irritant effects. Inflammation may result as an adaptation and ultimately may act to remove the irritants and heal the affected tissues. However, there are situations in which the expected response does not occur. These cases appear to contradict the purely physical or biologic nature of the agent-host interaction. Some aberrant cases might result in a chronic irritation and inflammation. Others might not yield the same degree of inflammation, and if the irritants move to other areas of the respiratory tree, a different type of damage may ensue. There are individual, and sometimes unpredictable, aspects of the response of human beings to exogenous agents capable of causing disease.

As another example, let us consider a headache. Many different mechanisms can result in headache, but there is probably one common denominator, such as the presence of a pain producing chemical or perhaps a disruption in pain and anti-pain chemicals such that pain endings become stimulated. Is it proper to assume that each person is the same in this response, or is the behavioral component of a phenomenon such as pain important to consider? Is there an individual pain threshold, based on genetics, physiology, social and psychologic history, and personality? How can these very plausible influences be integrated into pathophysiologic processes?

It is just such individualized responses that necessitate consideration of a mind-body interaction as well as the disease process itself. Another situation brings to mind the tremendous importance of mind-body interactions in the production of disease. People can "think themselves sick" and produce the stigmata of just about any disease through purely psychologic influences. Is this disease any less real than one with a demonstrable cause? Are the symptoms as reflective of disordered physiology, and can they be treated in the same way as a person with the "real" disease? How influential is this psychologic component in pathophysiology in general, and can it be a useful adjunct to healing?

A view of pathophysiology that excludes the tremendous importance of mind-body interaction in the production and development of disease is sterile and unrealistic. Traditionally, disease has been viewed within the dualistic framework of modern medicine, rather than within the monistic approach of holism. We, as authors of two editions of this textbook, have been as guilty as others in using a systems approach to pathophysiology without regard to the mind-body system. In fact, a systems approach can lead to a machine-like view of health and disease. Presumably, if all the parts of a system are operating well in open interaction, then the result must be considered health. If one part of a system breaks down, then the effects on all the other systems will resonate through all interacting networks to cause disruption. Coping mechanisms will be activated immediately to adjust to the perturbation and to restore the dynamic equilibrium of the steady state. Yet, if the body is viewed as such a machine, then many phenomena of disease and wellness can not be explained. Consider the individual with a stress-related disorder, such that there exists an inherent weakness in the immune system. It could be predicted that all types of adaptation to the disturbance will occur. For example, there might be a compensatory response of reticuloendothelial cellular enzymes, an elevation in the production of bone marrow and lymphoid-stimulating substances, or a change in certain hormone levels. Although all of this is somewhat predictable, an additional component can neither be predicted nor measured. The individual may have an inherent capacity, through intensive imagery, positive thinking, real hope, or other self-directed, introspective techniques of the mind, to actually produce a state of immunocompetence. How can we know if this has occurred, since this phenomena assumes a link between the mind and body that cannot currently be explained?

It suggests that the mind and body are a single entity rather than two separate entities and that there is a real oneness of mind and body. It at first appears to be a mystical linkage, since science currently can not explain it. Some have suggested that the modern scientific paradigm is inadequate to explain this unity and that new paradigms of holism are needed. This belief assumes that the current scientific measurements and statistical tools are inadequate to deal with these holistic phenomena. There are others who are seeking empirical explanations that rely on determinism and science to discover how the mind and the body may be physically linked. There are studies showing, for example, receptors on immune cells that respond to central nervous system neurotransmitters, providing a pathway for sending messages between the brain and the immune system. This approach assumes that the mind is in the substance of the brain and that all of "personhood" resides ultimately in the physical material of the central nervous system. For those who espouse holism entirely, this is not an acceptable paradigm. They would rather see the body-mind-soul as the whole, and the individual, reflecting in their own personhood and existence, the wholeness of the universe. Any disturbance in the wellness of an individual reverberates throughout the universe, distorting the whole to some degree, affecting all of the parts of the whole, and existing forever. Such ideas of personhood are certainly not foreign to nursing, and much nursing theory draws heavily on concepts of holism.

We see disease as a disturbance of the whole. We also view wellness as more than the absence of disease and as a process that continues throughout life. Disease can seriously disturb wellness, but it does not always do so. We see wellness as an integrated state of body, mind, and spirit. Therefore a physical disease or the process of senescence, with its usual decrements and decline, are perturbations of only one aspect of the whole. In fact, for some individuals, aging and death are the ultimate processes of self-actualization and therefore represent a high level of wellness. Nevertheless, most pathophysiologic processes threaten wellness and are deviations from the ideal. As we present pathophysiologic mechanisms in this book, we will always attempt to view the processes within a holistic framework. Current examination, speculation, and research of the mind-body relationship will be examined. We will not personally refute the more mystical notions of such interactions. However, where evidence exists of biologic, chemical, or physical links between the body and the mind, we will present it and attempt to make sense of these relationships in explaining pathophysiology.

NURSING DIAGNOSIS

Like all other clinical practice disciplines, nursing uses the clinical, problem-solving method, which incorporates the steps of assessment and diagnosis and the planning, delivery, and subsequent evaluation of care. The term "diagnosis" is used here to refer to the recognition and labeling of a pattern within the data derived from assessment. The focus of nursing practice is the human response to actual or potential health problems. Many of these health problems have a pathophysiologic basis, and in order to understand, diagnose, and treat the concomitant human response, a sound knowledge of pathophysiology is required (Titler, 1986).

We have organized the discussion of pathophysiologic mechanisms into a functional health patterns framework. Nursing diagnoses are discussed as potential responses to the pathophysiologic mechanisms that can lead to disease and deviation from wellness. Specific diagnoses are listed in each case study. This approach will help the reader link the pathophysiologic concepts with the potential human responses, and it seemed most consistent with the definitions of pathophysiology and nursing that we espouse. In previous editions we defined pathophysiology as the study of mechanisms by which disease occurs in living organisms, the response of the body to the disease process, and the effects of these pathophysiologic mechanisms on normal function. Nursing has been defined by the American Nurses' Association (1980) as "the diagnosis and treatment of human responses to actual or potential health problems."

Currently there is controversy within nursing as to the appropriateness of physiologic diagnoses within a nursing diagnostic taxonomy. Kim (1984) has summarized the issues surrounding the use of physiologic nursing diagnoses. These issues are related to differing philosophical stands on the nature and scope of nursing practice. First, is the belief that the focus of nursing is on patterns related to health rather than illness and that physiologic diagnoses connote only the latter. Second is the stance that physiologic diagnoses fall primarily within the realm of medicine. Third is a view linking the concept of nursing autonomy with that of nursing diagnosis; the only nursing diagnoses accepted as "legitimate" are those that the nurse can diagnose and treat independently of other health care professionals.

It seems apparent from this that the nursing diagnosis movement has been entwined with an attempt to sort out what nursing is and what it is not. The nature and scope of nursing practice is not static;

it reflects the dynamic nature of science, health care, and the ever changing needs of society. The nature and scope of practice cannot be defined solely by the content of that practice. On the other hand, the content of practice does help to define and delineate that practice. Incorporation of the biophysical with the psychosociocultural and spiritual domains is necessary if a holistic perspective is to be achieved in practice. Dismissing diagnoses that are physiologic in nature or that require collaborative or interdependent nursing interventions would result in delineation of a scope of practice that is too narrowly circumscribed to reflect actual, present day practice let alone future practice as multidisciplinary, collaborative, practice models grow.

Because nursing is a professional practice discipline, the nature and scope of practice will change in response to the changing needs, demand and capacities of society, and expansion of the scientific base of practice. The boundaries of a discipline will shift to reflect these changes as well. The boundaries of nursing reflect a truism stated in the A.N.A. Social Policy Statement (A.N.A., 1980): "All of the health care professions interact, share the same mission, have access to the same published scientific knowledge, and in some degree overlap in their activities." The physiologic domain is one area where this overlap is most apparent and thus has become a focal point in an unrealistic attempt to clearly and completely separate nursing and medical practice. As long as the scientific base of practice is a shared one there will be overlap. Carnevali (1984) sums this up most succinctly, "It is a fact of life that nurses must diagnose regularly in both the biomedical and nursing domains as part of their professional role."

The view of nursing autonomy as synonomous with independent nursing action is a narrow one. Autonomy seems more directly related to the exercise of clinical judgment, which incorporates choice of action as only one component of a very complex process. Diers (1985) describes clinical judgment as an artful and scientific process whereby clinical decisions about diagnosis and treatment are made based on the available assessment data and diagnostic resources, using theories and knowledge that enable the clinician to predict outcome with a given probability. Tanner (1983) describes the process as one of identifying alternatives, gathering information to reduce uncertainty about the alternatives, and selecting the most likely diagnosis or optimal treatment plan. This process, she continues, requires consideration of the probabilistic relationships between assessment and diagnosis and between diagnosis and management strategies. Clinical judgment requires more than mere application of knowledge to a particular phenomenon. It requires that the clinician move from the observed to the conceptual, consider multiple explanations for the occurrence of the phenomenon and the most appropriate treatment related to each explanation, and estimate the probability of success for each. The clinician is required to reason inductively and to sort out competing hypotheses. This thought process is required even when the interventions are prescribed within a medical regimen, including standing orders. This is consistent with Kim's (1984) definition of an interdependent nursing intervention as "that which the nurse makes on the basis of independent judgment and decision making to carry out medical orders or to implement the medical regimen."

It is a fallacy that a physiologic diagnosis precludes independence on the part of the nurse. Dougherty (1985), as one exam-

NANDA-APPROVED NURSING DIAGNOSES

Activity intolerance
Potential activity intolerance
Impaired adjustment
Ineffective airway clearance
Anxiety
Potential for aspiration
Potential altered body temperature
Constipation
Diarrhea
Bowel incontinence
Ineffective breastfeeding
Ineffective breathing pattern
Decreased cardiac output
Chronic pain
Pain
Impaired verbal communication
Colonic constipation
Perceived constipation
Family coping: potential for growth
Defensive coping
Ineffective denial
Ineffective family coping: compromised
Ineffective family coping: disabling
Ineffective individual coping
Decisional conflict (specify)
Potential for disuse syndrome
Diversional activity deficit
Dysreflexia
Altered family processes
Fatigue
Fear
Fluid volume deficit (1)
Fluid volume deficit (2)
Potential fluid volume deficit
Fluid volume excess
Impaired gas exchange
Anticipatory grieving
Dysfunctional grieving
Altered growth and development
Altered health maintenance
Health seeking behaviors (specify)
Impaired home maintenance
Hopelessness
Hyperthermia
Hypothermia
Functional incontinence
Reflex incontinence
Stress incontinence
Total incontinence
Urge incontinence
Potential for infection
Potential for injury

Potential for poisoning
Potential for suffocation
Potential for trauma
Knowledge deficit (specify)
Impaired physical mobility
Noncompliance (specify)
Altered nutrition: less than body requirements
Altered nutrition: more than body requirements
Altered nutrition: potential for more than body requirements
Parental role conflict
Altered parenting
Potential altered parenting
Post-trauma response
Powerlessness
Rape-trauma syndrome
Rape-trauma syndrome: compound reaction
Rape-trauma syndrome: silent reaction
Altered role performance
Bathing/hygiene self-care deficit
Dressing/grooming self-care deficit
Feeding self care deficit
Toileting self care deficit
Body image disturbance
Personal identity dusturbance
Self esteem disturbance
    Chronic low self-esteem
    Situational low self-esteem
Sensory/perceptual alterations (specify) (visual, auditory, kinesthetic, gustatory, tactile, olfactory)
Sexual dysfunction
Altered sexuality patterns
Impaired skin integrity
Potential impaired skin integrity
Sleep pattern disturbance
Impaired social interaction
Social isolation
Spiritual distress (distress of the human spirit)
Impaired swallowing
Ineffective thermoregulation
Altered thought processes
Impaired tissue integrity
Altered oral mucous membrane
Altered (specify type) tissue perfusion (renal, cerebral, cardiopulmonary, gastrointestinal, peripheral)
Unilateral neglect
Altered patterns of urinary elimination
Urinary retention
Potential for violence: Self-directed or directed at others

ple, has demonstrated through research that the majority of nursing interventions for the diagnosis, decreased cardiac output, are independent in nature. Jacoby (1985) states that while nurses do diagnose and treat independently physiologic dysfunction, more often are potential physiologic alterations diagnosed and treated independently. This is consistent with the views expressed by other authors (Titler, 1986; Kim, 1984).

It is hoped that the presentation of nursing diagnosis in this manner will assist the nursing student and the practicing nurse in applying pathophysiologic concepts in clinical practice. The list of nursing diagnoses that have been approved by for clinical use and validation by the North American Nursing Diagnosis Association (NANDA) is presented on the preceding page. It should be obvious to the reader that this list is neither complete nor comprehensive but rather in a state of evolution. Diagnostic categories are developed and described, validated through research, and approved through the accepted NANDA process.

BIBLIOGRAPHY

American Nurses' Association: Nursing: a social policy statement, Kansas City, Mo, 1980, American Nurses' Association.

Carnevali D: The diagnostic reasoning process. In Carnevali D, et al., editors: Diagnostic reasoning in nursing, Philadelphia, 1984, JB Lippincott Co, pp 25-56.

Diers D: Preparation of practitioners, clinical specialists and clinicians, J Prof Nurs Jan-Feb, p 41-47, 1985.

Dougherty C: The nursing diagnosis of decreased cardiac output, Nurs Clin North Am 20(4):787-800, 1985.

Jacoby M: The dilemma of physiological problems: eliminating the double standard, AJN 85:281 and 285, 1986.

Kim M: Physiologic nursing diagnosis: its role and place in nursing taxonomy. In Kim MJ, McFarland G, and McLane A, editors: Classification of nursing diagnoses: proceedings of the Fifth National Conference, St Louis, 1984, The CV Mosby Co, pp 60-62.

Kim M: Without collaboration, what's left? AJN 85:281 and 285, 1985.

Tanner C: Research on clinical judgment. In Holzemer W, editor: Review of research in nursing education. Thoroughfare, NJ, Slack, Inc, pp 2-32, 1983.

Titler M: Baccalaureate nursing education: teaching pathophysiology with a nursing diagnosis framework. In Hurley M, editor: Classification of nursing diagnoses: proceedings of the Sixth National Conference, St Louis, The CV Mosby Co, pp. 233-244, 1986.

UNIT II

Individual-environmental interaction pattern

2

Host factors: inflammation, immunity, and infection

The human body has been called the 3 million-year-old healer. Many regulative, protective, and self-preserving mechanisms act vigilantly to guard and maintain wellness. Much of modern medicine's pharmacopeia relies on drugs that mimic the body's own chemicals. To act, drugs often bind to cellular receptors that normally are available for interaction with the body's own hormones, biogenic amines, neurotransmitters, immune-modulating substances, and other molecules. Protective barriers and defenses work in concert with these biochemical mechanisms.

The major categories of human protective mechanisms include the stress response, the system of white blood cells and tissue phagocytes, the inflammatory reaction, immunity, blood coagulation, and many discrete enzymatic and cellular reactions. Certainly there are also physical barriers presented by the integument and its accessories and the mucous membrane linings of the respiratory, digestive, and genitourinary tracts. This chapter will explore major aspects of host defense that involve the white blood cells, namely inflammation, immunity, and infection. Other chapters in this book are devoted to the other barriers. The body defenses and barriers are illustrated in Fig. 2-1.

White Blood Cells

The blood and tissue neutrophils, monocytes, and eosinophils can nonspecifically kill many pyogenic bacteria and fungi by using a variety of mechanisms. These include chemotaxis, adhesion, opsonization (a labeling of the bacterium by antibody and complement), phagocytosis, and intracellular microbial lysis. Very few specific recognition phenomena are required for these cells to attack and destroy microbes. However, some recognition is necessary for these cells to function optimally. The immune system, in cooperation with these cells and with macrophages, constantly stands guard and surveys all material that enters the body through the skin and mucous membrane barriers.

INFLAMMATION

Inflammation is not a pathophysiologic mechanism. Rather it is a defense that, in interaction with the immune system, causes the removal of dead cells, microbes, debris, and exudate formed by trauma or by the interaction of environmental agents that have penetrated the mucous membranes or skin barriers or when trauma has occurred. Normally these barriers are extremely competent, allowing people to defend against literally millions of biologic

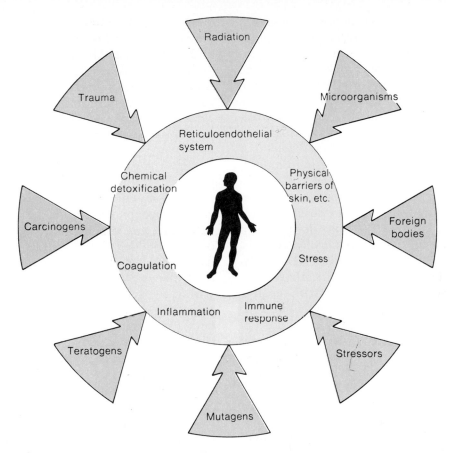

Fig. 2-1. Human lines of defense. Humans are constantly assaulted by environmental factors. In healthy state an organism is able to respond through the many defense mechanisms.

organisms in the environment and constant physical and chemical threats to wellness. Inflammation is a containment mechanism, acting to isolate a reaction of an outside agent with body cells, permitting damage and cell destruction to localize, and ultimately providing a healing environment.

IMMUNITY

Inflammatory and immunologic mechanisms act to preserve a person's safety and equilibrium in the presence of constant environmental threats. Immunocompetence is one of the greatest protections that hu-

man beings have. More than any other body system, the integrity of the immune system is necessary for the maintenance of wellness. Yet, it is the immune system that is most profoundly affected by the hormones released by the adrenal cortex during chronic stress states. Stress is almost always a concomitant condition of any serious illness and is a natural consequence of many people's life-styles. Therefore the possibility of both transient and constant immunodeficiency states in many people must be considered fundamental to pathophysiologic theories. Immunodeficiency resulting from the stress of any acute or chronic physical or psychologic illness will weaken a person's ability to maintain wellness. Other pathophysiologic processes and positive feedbacks will become established, creating further disruption. One of the most important things nurses do is help their patients cope with stressors and alleviate potential stressors that would compromise the patient.

This chapter will review basic immunology and inflammation and then discuss inflammatory and immunologic deviations. Normal immunology is reviewed for two reasons. First, many students do not learn immunology in basic physiology courses. Second, the field is changing so rapidly, with frequent new discoveries, that many students will need some updating even if they have studied immunology before.

It is difficult to describe the functions of the immune system, the macrophages, and the granulocytes as separate, because there is extremely well-coordinated cooperation between these as they deal with foreign antigen material. Since the most biologically significant foreign material is bacterial, with a failure of the body defenses resulting in a clinical infection, much of the discussions will be framed around penetration and reactivity of microbes with body tissue. However, the surveillance system will also screen out other foreign materials, such as airborne, waterborne, and foodborne foreign matter, foreign cells, and aberrant cells. For these functions to occur, the surveillance and defense systems must be able to recognize nonself materials, carry or direct the materials to cells that are capable of reacting with and destroying the materials, and provide a clean-up and healing process that will restore the human being to a well state. Most of the time, this process is so efficient that people have no evidence that it is happening. Only when the system gets overwhelmed or has suffered some sort of deficiency or weakness do the symptoms and signs arise. Allergic responsiveness is an example of an immunologic weakness that gives rise to symptoms. Loss of immunologic strength and later infection are certainly seen after profound stress and perhaps even after relatively minor stress experiences. Bacterial invasion and secondary infection are observed in a person made immunologically weak by cancer therapy. Even something as simple as a streptococcal infection of the tonsils indicates that the organisms responsible have penetrated the throat's mucosal barriers, have invaded the mucous membranes of the throat, and are even multiplying within the lymphoid tonsillar tissue. However, the soreness, swelling, redness, and heat produced by this invasion are good signs that indicate that the body is actively producing an inflammatory response within the throat, limiting the spread of the microbes from the throat, and producing a reaction that will eventually, in almost all cases, destroy the microorganisms and restore the throat to its former state of health. Susceptibility to infection is related to sleep and rest state, stress, nutrition, attitude, concurrent infection, circadian factors, and many other influences.

IMMUNOLOGIC MECHANISMS

The immune system is not isolated but is an open system that communicates with other cellular defense systems. It is also becoming apparent that this system is not isolated from the nervous system and may in fact network with every system of the body through a complex array of receptors and mediators. Immune cells may serve as messengers, through membrane receptor signaling, carrying information from the brain to other parts of the body. Lymphocytes are the cells of the immune system and are mobile cells found in the blood, the thymus gland, lymph nodes, spleen, and tissue spaces. They require interaction with macrophages, and many authorities actually classify the macrophages as immune cells. Secretions of macrophages are called monokines, and it is through release of monokines that macrophages signal lymphocytes. Macrophages are also very phagocytic and are capable of being transformed into extremely lethal cytolytic cells, phagocytizing nonspecifically and finally lysing themselves in the process. For an initial immune response to occur, macrophages must somehow recognize foreign antigen, which causes them to secrete monokines that recruit and activate T-lymphocytes. Through a poorly understood process of internalization and processing of the antigen material by the macrophage, the antigen is marked for lymphocyte recognition. The antigen is then extruded from the macrophage and presented to the lymphocytes on the cell surface (Fig. 2-2). Lymphocytes are of two major classes, B and T cells. There are several subclasses identified in the T cell category. Both cell types, however, respond to antigen by secretion. In the case of B cells, the antigen stimulates the B cell to secrete immunoglobulin specific to the antigen, thus creating a serum titer of antibody capable of humoral reaction with antigen. T cells also secrete in response to antigen, but their products, known as lymphokines, act locally to amplify the immune response, and the type of immunity produced is called cellular immunity.

Cells of the immune system

B cells. B cells are known to acquire identity in the bursa of Fabricius in the chicken, an animal that has provided us with a wealth of information about the im-

mune system. Within the bursa the B cells develop during embryonic life and begin to produce immunoglobulins, and if chicken embryos are "bursectomized," the chickens will develop a variety of immunodeficient states. The development of these immunoglobulin-producing cells is not dependent on the introduction of any foreign antigenic material and thus must be considered genetically programmed. Once the immunoglobulin-producing B cell is formed in the bursa, further expansion of these compartments of cells requires stimulation by foreign antigens. The human analogue to the bursa of the chicken has been identified as the fetal liver and bone marrow.

B cells cannot be morphologically distinguished from T cells except under close examination by electron microscopy. (Scanning electron microscopy of T and B cells shows that the B cells have longer microvilli.) Within the peripheral blood smear there are no obvious differences, however. These cells have been identified in the 9-week-old human embryo, and thus the differentiation of this immune component occurs very early in intrauterine life. Both B cells and T cells are found in greatest abundance in the lymphoid tissue, which is found throughout the body in lymph nodes or in other structures such as tonsillar tissue, spleen, bone marrow, and thymus. They are also in the peripheral blood, constituting about 35% of the leukocytes, and they are also present in the tissue spaces. B cells appear to be responsible for immunity to most pyogenic pathogens. The production of immunoglobulins by B cells is termed humoral immunity.

T cells. T cells, or thymus-derived lymphocytes, originate in the fetal hematopoietic tissue (as do all the blood cells) and then migrate during embryogenesis to the

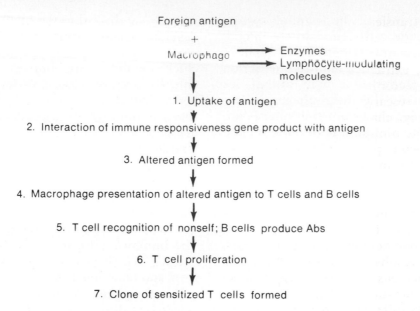

Fig. 2-2. Macrophage processing of antigen. It is believed that macrophages "process" antigen, preparing it in some unknown manner, before presenting it to lymphocytes. After interaction with macrophages, antigen is then ready to be identified by immune lymphocytes. *Abs,* antibodies.

bone marrow. Those lymphocytes that will become committed as T cells leave the bone marrow and pass from the bone marrow through the thymus before passing on to seed the lymphoid tissues of the body, a process that takes several days. This system was originally described in chickens but is known to also occur in humans. The thymus gland is located in the mediastinum and is large in infancy and childhood, involuting greatly during adult life.

The thymus gland is known to have at least two functions. The first is differentiation of primitive lymphocytes into immunocompetent T cells. The second is the further expansion of antigen-stimulated T cells, perhaps by the production of extracts or hormonal substances such as thymosin.

T cells can be identified by their ability to respond to certain chemicals known as *mitogens*. Mitogens such as phytohemagglutinin, a kidney bean extract, cause T cells to transform and divide. T cells also can be identified by their ability to form "rosettes" with sheep erythrocytes. Other differentiating markers of T and B cells are related to biochemical differences between the cells. T cells are long lived, as compared to B cells, which live 5 to 7 days. The type of immunity produced is cellular or delayed hypersensitivity immunity.

T cells attack bacterial, viral, parasitic, and mycotic microorganisms, (2) are responsible for autoimmune phenomena, and (3) participate in rejection of malignant cells and transplant tissue. One important characteristic of the T cell response is the ability of a cell-free leukocyte extract to transfer cellular immunologic reactivity to an antigen from one host to another. The nature of the component in the cell-free extract remains obscure, but this elusive factor has been named transfer factor, and research has been dedicated to identifying, characterizing, and therapeutically administering transfer factor. Transfer factor preparations have been used clinically in the treatment of many diseases; the first disease so treated was chronic mucocutaneous candidiasis. Since then immunodeficiency diseases such as thymic hypoplasia and Wiskott-Aldrich syndrome have been treated with transfer factor. The results of this treatment were transitory increases in delayed hypersensitivity, as measured by skin testing, and resistance to infection. Chronic viral, fungal, and certain facultative bacterial infections are extremely common in individuals with depressed T cell immunity, and treatment of these infections with transfer factor has occasionally been successful.

Antigens and T and B cells

Antigens are generally protein or protein-bound macromolecules, exceeding molecular weights of 10,000. These molecules are usually complex and their stereochemistry confers on them a specific identity. This molecular configuration is important because it elicits the release of specific antibodies. Foreign antigens are soluble in body fluids and are different in structure than self-antigens. The immune system tolerates self-antigens except in diseases of autoimmunity.

Lymphoid macrophages are initiators of much of the T cell responsiveness, by releasing monokines on being stimulated by antigen. Interleukin 1 (Il-1) is the monokine that causes T cells to produce interleukin 2 (Il-2). However this monokine may also play a central role in many other phenomena, including sleep, pain, and inflammation. It is the major endogenous pyrogen responsible for febrile reactions in inflammatory responses. Another monokine is fibronectin, which opsonizes foreign antigen to make it more digestible by immune cells. The macrophage must be physically present for T cell stimulation, and it appears to interact initially with antigen by phagocytosing the antigen and reacting it with a protein product of the immune responsiveness (IR) gene. This gene is linked to the major tissue compatibility antigen genes, known as the HLA system. The gene product interacts with the antigen, altering it, and then the macrophage presents the altered antigen to T cells, actually physically contacting the lymphocytes, which then recognize it as nonself. However most of the antigen is destroyed intracellularly by the macrophage, so that less than 1% of the antigenic material becomes expressed on the cell surface for presentation to the lymphocytes. At this point T cells and B cells that are committed (a term that defines mature clones of cells that react with single, specific antigens) bind the antigen. A cascade of events ensues whereby the T helper cells help the committed, antigen-stimulated B cells produce specific immunoglobulin to the antigen material. This antibody will bind the antigen that is circulating and remove it. Of course, some of these B cells become memory cells and will continually divide and maintain a clone of B cells capable of reacting in the future to the same antigen. For B cells to optimally function, the T cells must interact first with stimulated macrophages and then with the B cells.

T cells can be classified as either effectors (e.g., cytotoxic [killer] cells) or regulators (e.g., T suppressor cells, T helper cells). Within each group of T cells are several subsets that have different functions. When T cells become stimulated by the binding of antigen material to the cell surface, they usually react by producing lymphokines that then act locally or at a distance to amplify or modify immunoresponsiveness. For example, an important lymphokine, Il-2, acts on other T cells, causing them to become T helper cells. T helpers also release other lymphokines and act to help B cells respond to antigen. T helper cells secrete vasodilatory materials, which cause increased circulation and increased cell numbers within the lymph nodes, thus causing them to swell. T cells stimulated by Il-2 release interferon, which acts on macrophages, causing them to become extremely cytotoxic, and stimulates production of T cytotoxic cells. T cytotoxic cells specifically attack and destroy the particular antigen that has provoked the immune response, while the killer macrophage is nonspecifically phagocytic and cytolytic. Il-2 is also a B cell growth factor, and thus a B cell clone that makes appropriate immunoglobulin to the antigen will be stimulated to expand. These T cell interactions are illustrated in Fig. 2-3.

Another important immune cell is the natural killer (NK) cell, which is believed to be derived from the lymphocytic line. The NK cell is activated by Il-2 and interferon and is an extremely cytotoxic cell type, which does not require specific antigenic recognition to attack and lyse antigenic material on cell surfaces. NK cells are believed to be of great importance in the immunologic attack that the body mounts against malignant cells.

The T suppressor cell series is poorly understood, but it is possible that these cells are responsible for the usual lack of immunologic attack against one's own cells.

They suppress B cells from reacting to antigenic material. The antigen must bind to the T suppressor cells to activate them, and T helper cells are also probably needed. Exactly how the T suppressor cells stop immunoglobulin production is unknown. They may act directly on B cells, or they may act by inhibiting the T helper cells that would normally aid the B cells. It is also possible that the T suppressor cells release substances that bind the antigen that is on the T helper cells' surface, paralyzing T helper cell function.

Antibodies (immunoglobulins)

There are five classes of immunoglobulins in humans: IgG, IgM, IgE, IgA, and IgD. Only the functions of the first four classes are known. Immunoglobulins are comprised of heavy and light chains of protein (Fig. 2-4). The active binding site of the antibody molecule is part of a region of variable amino acid composition, which gives the antibody its specificity. Amino acid composition of the heavy and light chains has been delineated for some immunoglobulins and has been shown to differ from one immunoglobulin to another. *Multiple myeloma* is a malignancy of the plasma cells (Fig. 2-5) that results in tremendous overproduction of immunoglobulins, sometimes of one particular type and sometimes of a number of different types. These immunoglobulins are usually of the IgG class. Individuals with multiple myeloma often excrete Bence Jones proteins, which are light chains of immunoglobulin molecules. Thus a source of light chains for study is provided by the blood and urine of these individuals. Heavy chains are also produced in a specific disease state known as *heavy chain disease*, which is another neoplasm of the plasma cells.

IgA (immunoglobulin A). IgA makes up

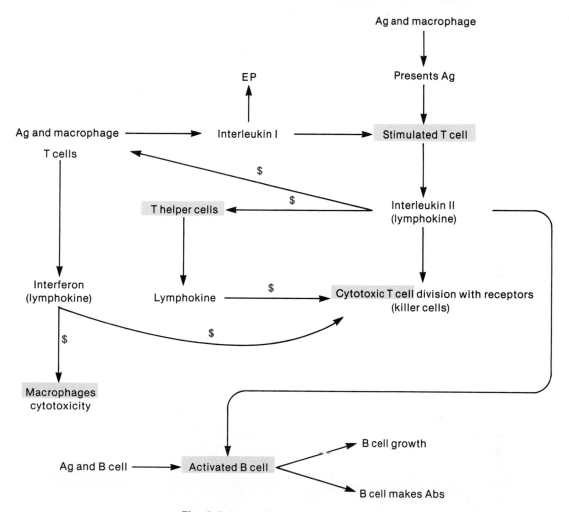

Fig. 2-3. Interactions among immune cells.

only 5% to 10% of the serum immunoglobulins and has a half-life of 7 days. It is comprised of two light and two heavy chains. IgA is concentrated in the respiratory and gastrointestinal tracts, namely, in saliva, tears, and gastrointestinal secretions. When it is found in the exposed surfaces of the respiratory and gastrointestinal tracts, IgA has a specific configuration, which differs from its structure in the interstitial tissues. The specific config-

uration results from the attachment of a *secretory component*, thought to be synthesized in epithelial cells. This allows IgA to attach to exposed surfaces and to withstand the harsh environments where it is usually found.

IgG (immunoglobulin G). IgG is the major immunoglobulin of the blood. It is found in high concentrations within the lymphoid follicles, where it is secreted by B-lymphocytes. The structure of IgG is ex-

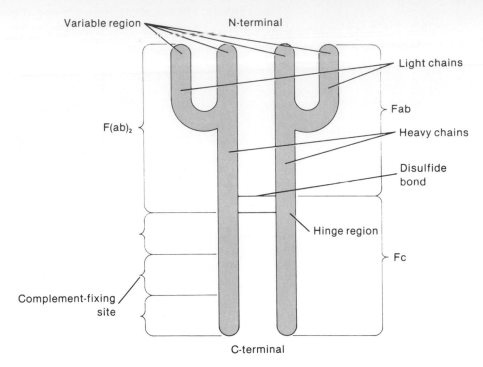

Variable region   N-terminal

Light chains

Fab

Heavy chains

Disulfide bond

F(ab)₂

Hinge region

Fc

Complement-fixing site

C-terminal

Fig. 2-4. Immunoglobulin molecule. Immunoglobulins are proteins made up of heavy and light chains of amino acids. Regions of variable amino acid composition are indicated. This determines which antigens immunoglobulin will bind to. Complement-attaching (-fixing) site also exists (Fc region).

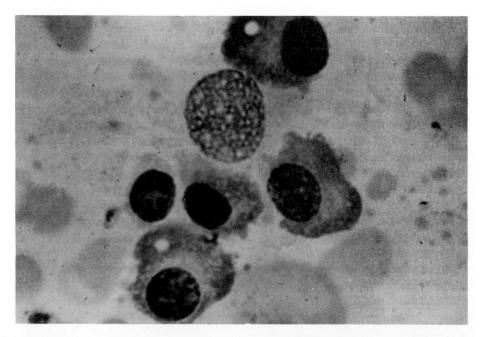

Fig. 2-5. Multiple myeloma cells are found in abundance in blood and lymphoid tissue of patients. They produce Bence Jones proteins and are malignant plasma cells.

(Courtesy Department of Pathology, University of Tennessee, Memphis.)

tremely similar to IgA, with two light and two heavy chains. It plays its major role in recognizing microorganisms and facilitating the removal of these invaders by phagocytes. IgG also has the ability to activate complement, a series of cell surface bound proteins that lyse cells. It is able to pass from the blood into the interstitial space and also to pass quite easily through the placenta, thus providing the fetus and newborn with maternally acquired immunity until the infant is able to produce sufficient immunoglobulins to render it safe in a germ-filled world. It is present in high concentrations in colostrum.

IgE (immunoglobulin E). IgE (formerly known as reagin) is the immunoglobulin involved in allergic, anaphylactic, and atopic reactions.

IgM (immunoglobulin M). IgM makes up about 10% of the serum immunoglobulins. Its structure has been postulated to be made up of ten heavy and ten light chains. Its size prevents it from traversing through capillary barriers, and it reacts therefore with foreign antigens in the bloodstream. It is also capable of activating complement. IgM is believed to be the major immunoglobulin produced during infancy, with colostrum and breast milk providing maternal immunoglobulins of the other classes.

IgD (immunoglobulin D). Although IgD has been described in human serums, its function remains unknown at this time. It comprises about 1% of the total immunoglobulins in the serum and has an extremely short half-life.

Nature of the antigen-antibody reaction. The extraordinary ability of the immune system to react with at least 1 million different possible antigens during a human's lifetime is thought to result from the production (by about 15% of the total DNA) of immunoglobulin molecules, which have the distinct capability of reacting with specific antigens. This specificity is the most striking characteristic of the immune system.

Antibody diversity

An important key to understanding diseases of the immune system is to understand the generation of all the diverse reacting immunoglobulin to all the potential antigens. Immunoglobulins bind to antigens with varying degrees of affinity. This specificity of antibodies occurs by random mutations and genetic reshufflings of the immunoglobulin coding genes during the development of B cells, resulting in committed cells that react only with specific antigenic determinants. As noted in Fig. 2-4, the variable regions of each immunoglobulin chain, which consist of about 110 amino acids, form the part of the antibody that will combine with the antigen in a highly specific way. The variable regions produce a folded configuration that will bind antigen. There are five genes that code for the variable regions on the heavy and light chains of immunoglobulins. With the known genetic diversity that exists at these variable region gene sites, the diversity that can occur at the variable regions is close to 5×10^7 (Nossal, 1987). The variability is generated during immunogenesis by apparently random translocations of the many minigenes that originally exist at each genetic locus, such that each clone of B cells produces an immunoglobulin with a genetic mix of variable region amino acids. Furthermore, B cells are unique in their mutation rate. Mutations occur very frequently in these cells as compared to other cells, so further diversity of antibodies continuously occurs. It is also important to note that an antigen can react weakly with an immunoglobulin or a B cell at first, but as the B cells undergo mutations, selection of cells producing immunoglobulin with higher affinities will occur, so that there is some degree of "induction" of the best immunoglobulin by the antigen.

Serologic responses. A number of possible phenomena may result from the combining of antigen with antibody in the blood. These include (1) neutralization, (2) agglutination, (3) complement fixation, and (4) precipitation (Table 2-1).

These serologic reactions in Table 2-1 are now explained at the molecular level in terms of immunoglobulin reactions, cell surface phenomena, and complement activation. They can occur in the test tube, in which case they are used as a diagnostic aid. For example, neutralization forms the basis of the antistreptolysin O (ASO) test; agglutination is observed in various antibody titration tests (e.g., Widal's test, Weil-Felix test); complement fixation is the basic phenomenon occurring in the Wasserman test; and precipitation occurs in the VDRL test and in the *Streptococcus* grouping.

Agglutination. Agglutination is a type of antigen-antibody reaction that can occur in blood incompability reactions.

Blood transfusion reactions. Agglutination is the basis of blood group incompatibilities, which are experienced by newborns and by patients receiving incompatible blood transfusions. There are four major blood antigen types: A, B, AB, and O. Individuals with erythrocytes bearing A antigens have antibodies of the IgG type, which react with B antigens, and normally there would be no B antigen–containing erythrocytes present in this blood. However, if a transfusion of type B blood were received, the donor erythrocytes would react with the serum antibodies of the recipient, causing a massive agglutination or clumping of the donor cells. The reverse process is observed in patients with blood group B who receive a transfusion of type A blood. The type O designation is reserved for individuals whose erythrocytes bear neither A nor B antigens. This blood, called the universal donor, is therefore acceptable blood for emergency transfusion since it does not often elicit a transfusion hemagglutination reaction. Individuals with type O blood have antibodies for both

Table 2-1. Major serologic reactions involving the immune system

	Neutralization	Agglutination	Complement fixation	Precipitation
Reaction	Toxin-antitoxin reactions: bacterial exotoxin (powerful poisonous enzyme released from bacterial cells) reacts with specific antitoxin obtained from immune animal when both injected into host animal	Complexing of *insoluble* antigens to antibody	Complexing of antigen with antibody with result that complement is activated	Complexing of *soluble* antigen with immune antiserum At optimal ratios of antigen to antibody, a precipitate forms in the body
Example	Tetanus antitoxin administered to patients infected with *Clostridium tetani* neutralizes the exotoxin	Erythrocytes are hemagglutinated by antibodies against the erythrocyte's surface antigens	Arthus reaction and immune complex disease	Certain forms of glomerulonephritis

A and B antigens in their blood serum, but these antibodies are usually so diluted by the recipient's blood that no reaction occurs. The AB blood type contains no antibodies to A or B antigens, but the erythrocytes contain A and B antigens. Therefore AB blood is considered the universal recipient.

The antigens are produced as gene products, and the blood group is inherited from the parents as either the homozygous (OO, AA, BB) or heterozygous (AO, BO) state. It has been shown that type O blood does contain an antigen that appears to be a precursor to the A and B antigens. This antigen is known as H substance, and thus the blood group genotypic system is referred to now as the ABO(H) system.

Agglutination of incompatible blood results in a reaction that can be immediate and dramatic. The clumped red blood cells can obstruct vessels, resulting in ischemia and necrosis. Patients experience pain and dyspnea; shock may occur. Renal failure may also result from obstruction of the glomerular vessels, leading to necrosis of the tubules and renal damage.

Erythroblastosis fetalis. An analogous situation to blood transfusion agglutination is the disease erythroblastosis fetalis, or hemolytic disease of the newborn. In this disease the presence of an Rh antigen on the erythrocytes of the fetus and the absence of this antigen on the erythrocytes of the mother lead to immunization of the mother such that she produces antibodies to the Rh antigen, which can traverse the placenta and react with and result in lysis of the fetal erythrocytes. The fetus attempts to compensate for the excessive hemolysis by erythropoiesis, which results in an increased number of primitive erythroblasts in the blood. These cells are not as capable of oxygen transport as normal blood cells, the blood is more viscous, and the hemolysis of the cells leads to jaundice and kernicterus (the deposition of bilirubin in the nervous tissue), which can lead to irreversible neurologic damage. Many of these infants are spontaneously aborted or are stillborn. (If children with erythroblastosis fetalis do survive birth, they are usually at high risk and may have to undergo exchange transfusion a number of times.)

Since immunization of the mother with the infant's blood takes place during the first pregnancy and especially during the birth process itself, the first child is not at risk. It has been possible to prevent the development of this condition in susceptible families by the administration of RhoGAM to Rh negative mothers after the birth of the first Rh positive child. RhoGAM is anti-Rh_0 gamma globulin, which acts to destroy any Rh-positive fetal cells that enter the mother's circulation before they can produce an antibody response to the Rh antigen. Thus subsequent infants usually are protected from erythroblastosis fetalis.

Complement

Immunologically mediated cellular destruction is an obvious outcome of immune mechanisms. Viruses and virally infected cells, cancer cells, bacteria and other microorganisms, and foreign proteins and cells are all targets of immune destruction through a variety of mechanisms. For example, cells may be removed through the reticuloendothelial system after being tagged by the immune system. *Opsonization* is the attachment of complement molecules that the reticuloendothelial system recognizes, with the result that the cell is engulfed through phagocytosis. Complement is a mechanism used by the body defenses to both opsonize cells and promote inflammatory changes and to ultimately actually destroy cells, lysing them and thus removing them from the body. Complement refers to a series of inactive proteins that are produced by liver cells and monocytes.

Complement's role is to continuously clean out the system of antigens that the immune system has identified and to aid the immunologic defense mechanisms in their many functions. The antigen-antibody recognition and amplification mechanisms we have described require continual positive reinforcement from complement activity and vice versa.

Complement, a system rather than a single entity, is the name given to a cascade of activation of nine major normally inactive proteins, in which the preceding activation of a component is required in order for a subsequent activation of a component to occur. This domino-like effect results in activated complement factors that have the ability not only to activate other complement factor, but also to exert specific biologic effects of their own. Fig. 2-6 shows the components of the classical complement pathway. Activated components as well as biologically active fragments are produced along the cascade, with the ultimate result being production of C9, which causes cell lysis. A cell membrane–bound antigen-antibody reaction is generally required for the initial activation to occur. There are probably 25 complement factors involved in the system (Frank, 1987).

Complement usually plays an active role even in simple acute inflammation. C-reactive protein, found in the serum of patients with an acute inflammation, can activate the first component of the complement cascade by binding to the carbohydrate of microorganisms. This reaction takes the place of the usual antigen-antibody reaction in the complement cascade. Complement can also be activated through Hageman factor activation, which is the first initiating step in blood coagulation. A complement factor of importance in inflammation is C3a (anaphylatoxin), which is chemotactic for polymorphonuclear leukocytes and can also release histamine from mast cells, leading to vasodilation and increased vascular permeability. A cleavage product of $C\overline{3}$ may stimulate the release of granulocytes from the bone marrow. Complexes of antigen-antibody are initially fixed by C1, at a point on the immunoglobulin molecule known as the Fc region. This is shown in Fig. 2-4. From

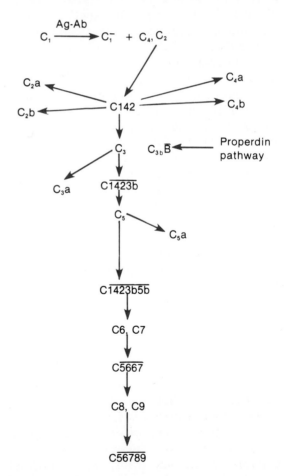

Fig. 2-6. Classical and alternate complement systems.

Table 2-2. Known functions of complement factors and fragments

Factor/Fragment	Function
C$\overline{14}$,* C $\overline{1423}$ *	Neutralization of virus
C3a	Dilation of capillaries
C5a	Dilation of capillaries; chemotaxis
C2a, C4a	Kinin-like
C3a, C3c, C3b	Opsonization
C3, C5 fragments	Chemotaxis of leukocytes
C3a, C3c	Immune adherence; phagocytosis
C5b67	Chemotaxis
C1-9	Cell lysis

*Bar signifies activation.

that initial reaction cascade activation and fixation of C4 and C2 by activated C1(C$\overline{1}$) occur. One consequence of this fixation is the fragmenting of C4 and C2 into small, biologically active molecules, which play important roles in promoting removal of foreign material and bacteria from the body. Table 2-2 lists the known functions of complement factors and fragments. C5a is released by the action of C$\overline{1423}$ on C5 and acts as a potent leukocyte chemotactic factor. C5b acts on C6, which then fixes C7 to form a complex, C5b67. C8 and C9 become fixed to this complex, and the last component of the cascade known as the membrane attack complex is thus formed, able to effect cell lysis. This entire sequence is often extremely localized to a cell or a group of cells, ultimately lysing these cells. The C3b and C$\overline{1423}$ complex formed on the cell's surfaces cause opsonization and ultimately phagocytosis of the cell. This is particularly important in the destruction of bacterial cells. Phagocytic cells have C3b receptors, so that once the target cell is opsonized, C3b can act as a bridge between it and the phagocytic cell, enhancing phagocytosis. Widespread complement activation is pathophysiologic

and may occur in diseases such as disseminated intravascular coagulation (DIC). These local effects tend to provoke typical inflammatory changes in the process of the actual cell destruction. Thus if the complement fixation should take place along a blood vessel, local inflammatory changes here might produce vasculitis, which is a pathophysiologic process.

In addition to the classical complement cascade, another pathway is operative. The *properdin* (or alternate) *pathway* also generates complement factors and fragments. It differs from the classical system in that nonprotein antigenic material such as polysaccharide or endotoxin may initiate the first activation step. The properdin factors are lettered, with P and D becoming activated, $\overline{D}$ then acting on B in the presence of C3b. A resultant complex forms that can then enter the classical pathway at the level of C3.

The significance of complement in immunopathology is a matter of much research. There are certain genetic defects associated with deficiencies in specific complement factors. Such disorders generally cause a decrease in the ability of the individual to defend against infection and in some cases cause vasculitis syndromes such as systemic lupus erythematosus. Another group of complement-related disorders is diseases in which cells are peculiarly sensitive to complement. Paroxysmal nocturnal hemoglobinuria is a disorder of erythrocytes, which are lysed by complement when the affected individual is sleeping. This is conceivably related to the drop in plasma pH that occurs in deep sleep, precipitating the hemolytic tendency.

Diseases associated with immune complex formation and deposition are another class of disorders in which complement plays a central role in the pathophysiology. Such diseases include systemic lupus crythematosus (SLE), a nephritis that may occur in patients with subacute bacterial endocarditis, and a nephritis and arthritis associated with hepatitis B infection. The mechanism of complement-mediated destruction in these disorders is believed to be attachment of immune complexes to the vessel walls and subsequent complement fixation, resulting in vasculitis, which may, through self-perpetuating inflammatory processes, become chronic. An autoimmune etiology is speculated to be at the heart of the initial vascular attack. Other autoimmune diseases that are pathologic through complement activation are autoimmune hemolytic anemias and idiopathic thrombocytopenic purpura. Complement is also instrumental in the massive cell lysis that may take place during transfusion of incompatible blood. In many autoimmune diseases, complement levels in the blood drop as the factors are used up in complement-fixing inflammatory reactions.

NATURE OF INFLAMMATION

Found only in vertebrates, inflammation is a complex, integrated host response to a great variety of threats from the internal and external environment. It is a nonspecific response to any cell and tissue injury or death. In other words it is not a response to an irritant per se, and the nature of the response does not depend directly on the causative agent. Chemicals, heat, microorganisms, foreign bodies, irradiation, trauma, immune complexes, and many other agents and threats to the wellness state may stimulate an inflammatory response. An acute reaction is an immediate response to these stressors. This type of inflammatory process usually resolves itself entirely if no complicating circumstances interfere with healing. Normal simple acute inflammation has a usual

time course of 8 to 10 days between the onset of the acute response and the ultimate healing of the inflamed site. Inflammation that does not follow this pattern but instead pursues a course of weeks, months, or even years is considered chronic inflammation.

While the inflammatory response itself is nonspecific in nature, any agent that causes it may also cause a specific response in the host. For example, radiation causes inflammatory changes, which are essentially the same as those that arise from chemical trauma, heat, or infection. Radiation also causes very specific effects in the host, such as alopecia, bone marrow depression, and nausea and vomiting. Thus there is superimposed on any injury that causes an inflammatory response a wide variety of other possible interacting factors that may contribute to the development of pathophysiologic mechanisms.

Essentially there are three broad categories of inflammation: (1) simple acute, (2) chronic, and (3) immunologically mediated delayed hypersensitivity. The simple acute type involves the typical signs of inflammation: pain, redness, and swelling. Chronic inflammation is also characterized by pain, redness, and swelling; however, it differs from the acute form in that it does not subside in a period of days but may instead have a relentless, damaging course of weeks, months, or years. Certain acute inflammatory responses appear able to develop into chronic inflammation, while other forms of inflammation appear to have been destined to be chronic from the beginning. Chronic inflammation seems to be a process in which healing becomes impaired.

The third type differs from simple acute inflammation in that it is directly caused by an antigen-sensitized lymphocyte reaction, so that the inflammation is a direct response to this interaction and thus takes longer to develop. The delayed hypersensitivity reaction is a typical inflammatory response; that is, it also is characterized by pain, redness, and swelling. The major difference between simple acute and delayed hypersensitivity inflammation lies in the initiating factors.

However, it is unlikely that any type of inflammatory response is completely devoid of an immunologic component. For example, in trauma there is much cell destruction and death, with a resultant release of millions of previously hidden self-antigens. Some believe that the exposure of these antigens results in an immunologic response, which then would cause an inflammatory reaction through macrophages, lymphocytes, and complement.

Acute inflammation

Simple acute inflammation is characterized by three major phenomena, which occur in the following order: (1) increased vascular permeability, (2) leukocytic cellular infiltration, and (3) repair.

An inflammatory tissue exudate is formed because of the increased permeability of the blood vessels at the inflammatory site and the leukocytic infiltration that occurs secondary, to a degree, to the increased permeability. This exudate is rich in protein and has a high specific gravity. As the inflammatory process proceeds, the exudate changes from a clear serous fluid to a thick, creamy fluid, which contains necrotic debris. The exudate formed during the course of the common cold illustrates this change and is well known to all of us. The exudate in the tissue increases the tissue pressure, and sensitive pain nerve endings are stimulated. Furthermore, chemicals found in the inflammatory exudate can directly stimulate these nerve endings, so that pain usually accompanies acute inflammation. Another sign of inflammation is increased

temperature and a reddish coloration of the inflamed site. These properties are caused by vasodilation and stasis of blood at the site.

The signs of inflammation are *rubor* (redness), *calor* (heat), *dolor* (pain), *tumor* (edema), and *loss of function*. Loss of function occurs as the aftermath of acute inflammation and can actually result in more debility and deformity than what would have been produced by the original irritant had the inflammatory process not occurred! There are certain clinical conditions for which pharmacologic agents are administered to suppress the inflammatory response. These drugs include the corticosteroids, penicillamine, NSAIDS, and aspirin. The inflammation associated with rheumatoid arthritis can cause so much joint destruction, pain, and disability that a normal life is impossible without the aid of these medications.

Vascular permeability increase. In 1927 Lewis described the triple response to a firm stroking of the skin. This can best be seen in very light-skinned individuals but occurs in everybody. The initial response is a very transient vasoconstriction, which is immediately followed by dilation of small blood vessels along the line. The second response is thought to result from the local axon reflex; it occurs because of a dilation of neighboring arterioles. The third response is a whealing of the skin. Lewis identified *histamine* as the cause of the triple response that results from vasodilation and increased vascular permeability. The result of these blood vessel alterations is stasis of blood at the inflammatory site, hemoconcentration, increased viscosity, and decreased colloid osmotic pressure of the capillary blood. Inflammatory exudate is formed entirely because fluids and proteins leak through the capillary walls into the inflamed tissue site. The mechanism

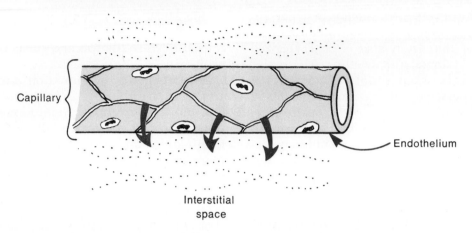

Fig. 2-7. Fluid movement in inflammation. Capillary permeability is vastly increased during acute inflammation, mainly because of a widening in gaps between adjacent endothelial cells.

by which the permeability increase occurs is through a widening of the junction between adjacent endothelial cells (Fig. 2-7). More fluids as well as proteins and blood cells can filter into the tissue, resulting in tissue edema that contains a highly cellular exudate. Furthermore, *hyperemia* may be obvious. Hyperemia is the engorgement of tissue with blood; it may be active or passive. Active hyperemia occurs when the blood flow to a tissue increases dramatically as, for example, in exercising muscle. Passive hyperemia, on the other hand, could be the result of venous stasis in a tissue, which then, of course, leads to hypoxia of the tissue and a reflex vasodilation of arterioles. The increased volume of blood at the inflammatory site, coupled with vasodilation, hemostasis, capillary engorgement, increased vascular permeability, and the resultant decreasing colloid osmotic pressure of the blood as protein leaks into the tissue, all act to promote formation of the exudate.

Recent research has indicated that histamine alone is not responsible for the increased permeability that accompanies early inflammation. Many other substances have been identified, but the most important agents appear to be kinins and prostaglandins. Two distinct phases of increased permeability, which appear to be different in nature and cause, have been well characterized.

Early phase. The increased permeability of blood vessels at an inflamed site has two phases; the first appears almost immediately after the application of an irritant, such as a toxin or heat, and disappears 30 minutes later. The second phase of permeability increase occurs 2 to 4 hours later and lasts for approximately 10 hours. The first phase appears to involve mainly venules. The increased leakiness of these minute postcapillary vessels is probably caused by histamine, which is formed by the enzymatic decarboxylation of histidine, an amino acid, and is stored primarily in mast cells. These are basophilic tissue cells that release histamine into the inflammatory site soon after inflammation begins. Antihistaminic drugs, if given at this time, reduce the first phase of the increased permeability response. They act by preventing histamine from combining with its receptors. These drugs are substituted ethylamines, which mimic the molecular configuration of histamine and may be able to combine with histamine receptors and thus block histamine attachment. Serotonin is another mediator released during this early phase.

The phenomenon of increased permeability is also a tissue response rather than solely a vascular reaction. Events occur in an apparently coordinated manner in the blood vessels, interstitium, and lymphatics.

Delayed phase. The delayed or second phase of the permeability increase, which involves small venules and capillaries, occurs by the same mechanism as that illustrated in Fig. 2-7 but is of much longer duration. The nature of this response is different from the first phase, and it is not clear what chemical mediators are involved and in what sequence. There is evidence that first bradykinin and then prostaglandin E (PGE) may play roles, but both of these mediators do not seem to have a long enough duration of action. The changing nature of the tissue at the inflamed site may itself play a major role in the development of the second permeability increase. For example, the pH of the tissue changes from neutral to acidic during the acute inflammatory response as venous stasis leads to hypoxia, and this may indirectly affect local blood vessel permeability.

When injury is extremely severe, such as might occur with deep burns of the skin or extensive traumatic injury that results in tissue death and blood vessel destruction, the biphasic nature of increased permeability is lost. Excessive permeability results from total destruction or great damage to blood vessels. Loss of blood from the damaged vessels into the tissue spaces will continue until a clot forms and closes off the vessel.

Mediators. *Bradykinin* is considered by many authorities to be a major vasodilator in the inflammatory process. The extent of its involvement in the later increased permeability phase remains unclear. It is known to transiently increase the permeability of microcirculation. In addition, bradykinin is now known to stimulate pain nerve endings at the inflamed site and is responsible for the "dolor" of inflammation. It also participates with PGE in leukocyte chemotaxis. It is a nine amino acid peptide produced in the plasma by the action of *kallikrein* on a precursor substance, *bradykininogen*. The origin of kallikrein is through the action of activated Hageman factor, the same factor responsible for the coagulation cascade. Blood clotting at the inflamed site, which helps to wall off the area with a mesh of fibrin strands, creating a minienvironment, also aids in the bradykinin action, as a peptide formed in coagulation (fibrinopeptide B) potentiates bradykinin's permeability effect. Fibrinopeptide B is also a chemotactic substance that attracts leukocytes into the site.

Notice in Fig. 2-8 the role activated Hageman factor plays in a variety of body defenses. It appears that this factor, previously associated only with blood coagulation, has a more central, unifying role in many biologic responses. True compartmentalization of the different body defenses does not occur, as any inflammatory agent provokes an integrated, holistic reaction so that many responses and feedbacks will act to restore the disrupted steady state.

Prostaglandins (PGs) are also suspected to be important in causing the increased permeability of inflammation, as well as causing vasodilation and pain responses.

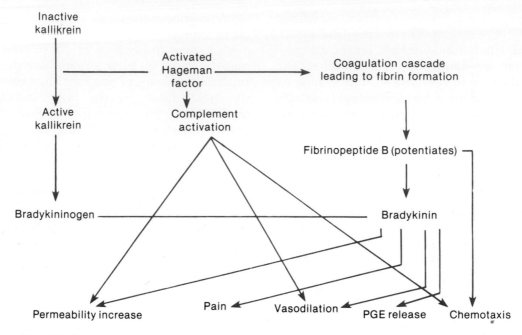

Fig. 2-8. Formation and role of bradykinin. Bradykinin is a major mediator of inflammatory response and is formed through action of activated kalikrein. Its action is further potentiated by fibrinopeptide B, formed in coagulation process.

Prostaglandins are compounds derived from arachidonic acid, a fatty acid that forms various PGs when enzymatically oxygenated. PG precursors are released from cell membranes under a variety of conditions through the action of many different stimuli, including certain hormones, mechanical disturbances, and inflammatory and immune reactions. Once released, the type of PG formed depends on the particular tissue microenvironment that dictates which enzymes are available for synthesis of PGs. Fig. 2-9 shows the synthesis of major PGs and PG-like compounds of importance in inflammation. The roles of these various substances are subject to research at this point, but PGEs appear to be the most prominent in inflammation.

The first step in all prostaglandin synthesis is oxygenation of arachidonic acid by the enzyme cyclooxygenase. Inhibition of this enzyme would result in a depression in the synthesis of all types of prostaglandins. Interestingly, nonsteroidal antiinflammatory drugs such as aspirin and indomethacin inhibit cyclooxygenase, and this appears to be their major mode of antiinflammatory action. In contrast, steroids act on cellular precursor formation of arachidonic acid from cellular phospholipids so that a decreased amount of arachidonic acid is formed. Steroids also act in many other ways to inhibit inflammation.

The PGs involved in inflammation (PGE_2, PGF_2, and PGI_2, and TXA_2) may only be transiently present in some cases, but they may nevertheless be extraordinarily potent. PGEs produce vasodilation, pain, and edema. Together with PGIs they

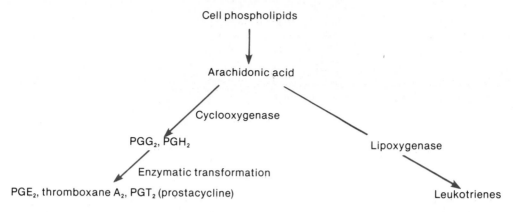

Fig. 2-9. Enzymatic formation of prostaglandins. All prostaglandins and prostaglandin-like compounds are derived and then released from the cell upon certain perturbations or chemical interactions. The type of prostaglandin that forms from the arachidonic acid that is released depends on the enzymes available extracellularly. This in turn depends on many complex factors.

also act to potentiate the effects of histamine and bradykinin. Furthermore, bradykinin itself can stimulate the release of arachidonic acid from cells. The cells that release PGEs include synovial, interstitial, and monocytic cells, with very little being produced by the polymorphonuclear leukocytes, which are the first cell type found in inflammatory exudates. Arachidonic acid may be acted on by a different enzyme, lipoxygenase, which is insensitive to nonsteroidal antiinflammatory drugs. This metabolic path leads to the production of hydroxy fatty acids and leukotrienes. A leukotriene is extremely chemotactic (see below) for polymorphonuclear granulocytes (PMNs), the first inflammatory cell type. There is other evidence that supports the concept that leukotrienes have mostly pathophysiologic effects. For example, SRS-A (slow reacting substance of anaphylaxis) is a leukotriene. The substance causes bronchoconstriction and vasodilation during an acute allergic reaction.

Leukocytic cellular infiltration. The second major hallmark of inflammation is the migration and proliferation of leukocytes. Leukocytes, which are derived from the blood and ultimately the bone marrow, race to an injured area almost as soon as the tissue damage occurs. The increase in permeability that occurs almost simultaneously probably plays a major part in facilitating the escape of these cells from the bloodstream, but cellular infiltration is not merely a passive phenomenon. The leukocytes initially appear to stick to the endothelial lining of the capillaries and marginate (or line up around the circumference of the vessels) before moving through the wall. This process occurs independently of the permeability changes of the vessels.

Generally the first cell type that is found in great abundance at the inflamed site is the neutrophil, a polymorphonuclear granulocytic cell with great phagocytic capabilities. These cells appear to be especially attracted to the injured tissue through *chemotaxis*, a chemical attraction of tissue substances for the leukocytes.

Chemotaxis. Chemotaxis is an important

aspect of inflammation in that certain substances are produced by inflamed tissues that are chemotactic for particular cell types. Numerous substances have been identified as chemotactic for neutrophils and macrophages and possibly for lymphocytes. Lymphocytes, rather than neutrophils, may be the first inflammatory cell type to enter virally infected tissue, and occasionally eosinophils may predominate in allergic or parasitic inflammation. The neutrophils that typically enter the inflamed site are accompanied by mononuclear phagocytes, but neutrophils are the major cell type present during the first 12 hours of the inflammatory response. They are actively phagocytic at that time and may eventually leave the site; more commonly they rupture (lyse) and die, releasing their cytoplasmic lysosomal enzymes into the interstitium. These lytic enzymes digest the connective tissue matrix and help to excavate the inflamed site in preparation for healing. Furthermore, these enzymes act as an additional chemotactic stimulus for monocytic infiltration. The major chemotactic agents for neutrophils appear to be the breakdown products of complement, particularly C5a, which becomes chemotactic through the action of a serum peptide, *cocytotoxin*. Other known chemotactic factors may actually require that complement be present for maximal activity.

Neutrophil function. The major role of the neutrophil at the inflamed site is to dispose of invaders, foreign bodies, and cellular debris through phagocytosis (Fig. 2-10) and enzymatic dissolution. Phagocytosis is a mechanism that requires energy input from the cellular metabolism.

Before a neutrophil can phagocytose a microorganism *opsonization* must occur. During the process of phagocytosis of the microbe the neutrophil activates a special-ized, oxygen-consuming metabolic pathway, resulting in the "oxidative burst," which produces large amounts of hydrogen peroxide and oxygen-free radicals, which then cause peroxidative killing of the microorganisms. The importance of this process is demonstrated by chronic granulomatous disease, in which the affected patients are subject to recurrent pyogenic infections. It has been shown that there is defective phagocytosis in these patients so that phagocytosed microbes persist and proliferate inside neutrophils and other phagocytic reticuloendothelial cells. It appears that this results from a defect in the cellular metabolic pathway that generates hydrogen peroxide.

In the normal cell, once the material is encapsulated by a phagosome inside the cytoplasm, the membrane fuses with the lysosomal membrane, and the hydrolytic enzymes of this organelle spill into the phagosome. These enzymes can break down bacterial cell walls and dissolve other materials. Certain organisms and foreign bodies are not destroyed very well by the neutrophils and macrophages and may persist intracellularly in giant cells that form at the site. The causative organisms of tuberculosis and leprosy typify this reaction, which will perpetuate a chronic inflammation. Occasionally microscopic bits of wool or steel remain inside giant cells as part of a foreign body reaction.

Phagocytosis may be inhibited in certain disease conditions, as described above, or by immunosuppressant drugs.

Monocyte function. The monocytic series of cells begins to predominate within inflamed tissue after 12 hours as the neutrophils die off. The major cell type is the macrophage, which appears to rise from the monocyte. If the inflammatory lesion becomes subacute or chronic, then the cel-

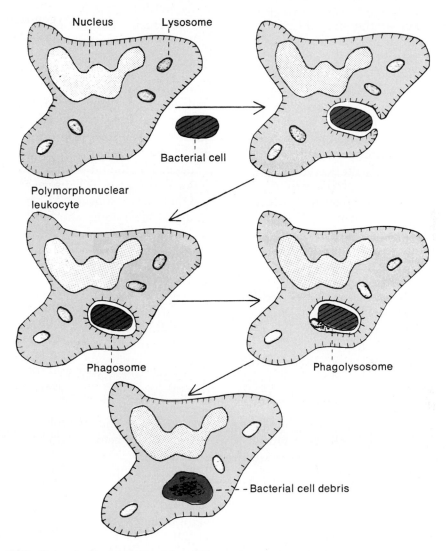

Fig. 2-10. Stages in phagocytosis of bacterial cell by neutrophil. Chemotoxins elaborated by cell attract neutrophil, which then begins to surround bacterium. After engulfment, bacterium is retained in a phagosome. On contact of phagosome with lysosomes, enzymes from lysosomes are released into structure, which is now termed a *phagolysosome,* or *phagolysome.* Undigested debris from bacterium is eventually egested.

(From Barrett JT: Textbook of immunology: an introduction to immunochemistry and immunobiology, ed 3, St Louis, 1978, The CV Mosby Co.)

lular infiltrate remains high in macrophages throughout the life of the inflammation. Activation of the macrophage appears to occur at the site and probably is the result of immune mechanisms. Once activated the macrophage is an extremely phagocytic, mobile cell. It secretes enzymes such as collagenase and elastase, which may allow it to pave its way through connective tissue to reach the inflamed site. The role of macrophage in processing antigen and recruiting lymphocytes has previously been described.

While the character of the cell type is thought to be dependent on the nature of the tissue at a specific time and on the release of appropriate chemotactic substances, the circulating blood leukocyte composition and concentration may also play a major role. Fluctuations in the blood neutrophil concentration occur during the inflammatory response, which coincides with the concentration of these cells at the inflamed site.

Delayed hypersensitivity inflammation. Inflammation caused by a delayed hypersensitivity response differs from acute inflammation in that the inflammatory response is dependent upon an *antigen-sensitized lymphocyte reaction*, and the initial cellular infiltrate is predominantly lymphocytic. Simple acute inflammation may have an immune component but is not directly caused by a reaction of antigenic material with the lymphocytes of the blood and tissue. The positive tuberculin skin test is a good example of delayed hypersensitivity inflammation. When tuberculin is injected into the skin, specific lymphocytes in the skin and in adjacent lymph nodes that bear receptors for this particular antigen are attracted to the tuberculin, react with it, begin to divide, and produce *lymphokines*. Known inflammatory lymphokines include (1) *chemotactic factors*, which act to attract lymphocytes, neutrophils, and macrophages to the inflamed site, (2) *mitogenic factors*, which stimulate leukocyte division, and (3) *macrophage inhibiting factor*, which acts to inhibit the movement of macrophages away from the inflammatory site, thus prolonging their action.

Cellular infiltration is a hallmark of all inflammation, including the delayed hypersensitivity reaction. The positive tuberculin test is a swollen, red, itchy, and sometimes painful induration. The classic signs of acute inflammation (redness, heat, swelling, and pain) are all evidenced by the tuberculin reaction. This reaction reaches a peak between 48 and 72 hours and then slowly subsides. Tuberculin is a readily digestible irritant, and young macrophages and granulocytes can ingest and destroy this material quickly. When the tuberculin is removed from the skin by the macrophages, the irritation is also removed, the inflammation subsides, and repair begins. The delayed hypersensitivity reaction, typified by the positive tuberculin test, is thus a localization of antigenic tuberculin material through (1) recognition by T-lymphocytes and (2) the resultant recruitment by lymphokines of more sensitized lymphocytes and macrophages, which migrate into the skin and react with the tuberculin at the site. Thus the tuberculin can be destroyed in situ before it can enter the systemic circulation.

The macrophages are chemotactically attracted to the site by lymphokines, becoming activated by interacting with T-lymphocytes that have been previously sensitized by tuberculin. These T cells appear to be able to transfer antigen receptors from their surface to the surface of macrophages and other lymphocytes. This activated macrophage then becomes an extremely potent killer cell that can phagocytose a variety of antigenic materials (Fig. 2-11). The process of phagocytosis by macrophages involves the encapsulation of the antigenic material by a mem-

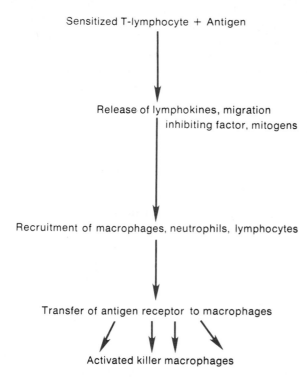

Sensitized T-lymphocyte + Antigen

Release of lymphokines, migration inhibiting factor, mitogens

Recruitment of macrophages, neutrophils, lymphocytes

Transfer of antigen receptor to macrophages

Activated killer macrophages

Fig. 2-11. Production of delayed hypersensitivity inflammation. Activation of killer macrophages in delayed hypersensitivity inflammation is believed to be caused by a transfer of antigen receptors from T-lymphocytes to macrophages.

brane contiguous with the cell membrane. This forms a vacuole, which enters the cell and fuses with a lysosome, which then pours its hydrolytic enzymes into the vacuole and breaks down the foreign material into its components. The macrophage can then either cytolyze (break apart or lyse) at the inflammatory site or travel away from the site through the lymphatics. Eventually the macrophage may be destroyed by the RES.

The delayed hypersensitivity inflammatory reaction is responsible for the rejection of foreign tissue transplants, which is a serious problem accompanying heart, kidney, and other organ transplants. The T-lymphocytes recognize the transplanted organ cells as foreign and react with them, becoming activated and capable of killing all cells that carry the foreign antigens. The cell killing may be direct killing or may be caused or augmented by the release of lymphokines, which would attract other cells to the inflammatory site. Rejection of cancer cells is also a T cell response.

Tumor patients generally show cellular immunity to their tumor antigens, but this is blocked by factors in their serums. These factors are thought to be antigen-antibody complexes.

DiGeorge's syndrome is a condition in which the patient is born without a thymus gland. These individuals do not possess T cells but are able to produce immunoglobulins quite adequately. Because of this, the significance of the T cell helper function is not clear at this time, at least in humans. T cell-suppressor function has also been described and appears to be involved in the development of self-immunity. Suppressor T cells may inhibit the production of certain immunoglobulins by B cells.

Systemic responses. Although the acute inflammatory process appears to result in a localized phenomenon, there are many systemic changes observed during the acute phase. There are changes in the blood levels of certain proteins, which may in turn result from altered synthetic rates of these proteins by the liver. For example, albumin may decrease in the plasma during the acute response, while α_1-acid glycoprotein may increase to 20 times its normal concentration. Antiinflammatory plasma protein, which appears to be produced by the liver, rises in concentration after an injury; these proteins are called *acute phase reactants*. The functions of many of these proteins are known. For example, fibrinogen functions in clotting and repair, and α_2-acid acute phase glycoprotein is antiinflammatory. Kininogen and kininogenase allow the release of bradykinin, and complement fragments C3 and C5 play major roles in immune processes and chemotaxis. The functions of other proteins are not so well characterized.

The changes in plasma proteins may affect the outcome of drug therapy in an individual with an acute inflammation. Aspirin, for example, binds to albumin, and only the unbound fraction is responsible for the drug action. A decrease in albumin may allow for more aspirin becoming available to the inflamed site, but it also increases the possibility of toxicity.

Certain disorders have been traced to abnormal acute phase reactant concentrations. Patients deficient in an antitrypsin are subject to pulmonary emphysema. Hereditary angioneurotic edema may be associated with a decrease in a C1 esterase inhibitor.

The erythrocyte sedimentation rate is increased in inflammatory states, because of the presence of these acute phase reactants. Erythrocyte rouleaux formation is enhanced and the cells settle more quickly, indicting a clinical inflammation is present.

Other systemic effects of inflammation include fever (pyrexia), malaise, increase in the white blood cell count (leukocytosis), fibrinolysis, shock, and endocrine and metabolic dysfunctions.

Fever. Fever is defined as a hyperthermic state in which core body temperature rises because of a storage of excessive heat. The steady state of temperature control is disrupted, and heat gain exceeds heat loss until a higher core temperature is reached. A new, usually transient steady state, defined as fever, results. The hypothalamic thermostat, consisting of centers regulating heat loss and heat gain, apparently readjusts during febrile states to the new higher set point for body temperature. Biochemical messengers act to readjust neurons regulating the set point. These substances are known as pyrogens, and their major site of action is at the preoptic anterior hypothalamus. Pyrogens are both exogenous and endogenous; however, in most cases exogenous pyrogens act by producing endogenous pyrogen (EP). The major EP is Interleukin-1 (Il-1). Known exogenous pyrogens include microorganisms and their products (e.g., endotoxins), certain drugs (e.g., bleomycin, colchicine), and a few steroids (etiocholanolone, lithocholic acid). Il-1 in contrast is a substance that is actively produced by human cells through the action of many different fever-producing substances and febrile states. Many cells can produce Il-1 upon appropriate stimulation, but the major sources in inflamed tissue are neutrophils and monocytes. Lymphocytes themselves do not respond during inflammation by producing Il-1. However, lymphokines produced by lymphocytes can act as pyrogens. It can be seen that a variety of activating inflammatory stimuli such as exogenous pyrogens cause phagocytic leukocytes to actively produce Il-1, which is quickly released and not stored. This molecule then moves into the circulation and on to the neural control centers. Very minute amounts of EP are biologically amplified into a body temperature elevation and the Il-1 molecule is very quickly destroyed. Thus in order for a febrile state to be maintained a continuous supply of Il-1 is necessary.

The mechanism by which Il-1 resets the hypothalamic set point is unknown. There is strong evidence for PGE being the

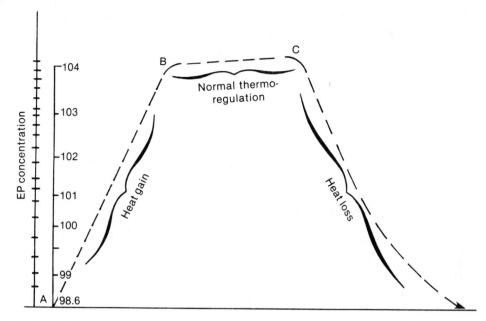

Fig. 2-12. Thermoregulation in febrile states. Fever production is dependent on EP resetting the hypothalamic neurons involved in temperature control. When a higher set point is present, heat gain mechanisms will become activated. However, once the febrile state is achieved, thermoregulation acts to defend the higher value. Removal of EP results in heat loss, and the normal temperature is once again achieved.

neural mediator of fever. The action of antipyretic drugs such as aspirin is possibly related to a decrease in arachidonic acid metabolism. As noted previously, prostaglandins are produced through cyclooxygenase action on arachidonic acid. Other arachidonic acid metabolites might theoretically also be involved in the production of fever.

The behavioral response to fever in humans consists usually of actions aimed at preserving the higher temperature. The febrile individual often curls up into a knee-chest position and seeks a warm environment. There is a shivering response, which is an indication that the heat gain mechanisms are active, since shivering produces a large heat load. These psychologic and physiologic heat-gaining mechanisms are active during the first phase of the fever while the temperature is rising. In Fig. 2-12 the contrast between the normal set point and the set point in a febrile state can be observed. The heat-gain mechanisms are active at the onset of the state. During the second phase of the fever the new core temperature reaches the altered set point temperature. The body acts at this point to conserve the heat that has been gained. Bascially, thermoregulation is not disturbed and heat can be gained or lost at this point (for example, through exercise) in a normal manner. However, the set point is higher and the higher core temperature is physiologically defended.

The third phase of fever is sometimes described as a "breaking" of the fever. The production of Il-1 presumably halts, the hypothalamus resets to normal core temperature, and the heat sensors recognize the hyperthermic state. Heat loss mechanisms are activated. There is diaphoresis, which is a major heat loss mechanism, and the individual seeks a less warm environment. The body temperature gradually returns to normal through these mechanisms.

These phases of fever must be considered when therapeutic approaches to fever control are employed. Approaches that act to remove the heat load through external cooling are often inappropriate or may be greatly resisted by patients. This is particularly true in ice water or alcohol sponging. Children may respond by crying and shivering, both of which will promote further heat gain and higher body temperature. Furthermore, the skin vessels will vasoconstrict, and this will prevent heat loss. Resetting of the hypothalamus by antipyretic drugs is usually the appropriate treatment in most fevers. Aspirin is thought to act by returning the hypothalamic set point to a more normal value. Heat loss mechanisms—mainly sweating—are then stimulated and temperature drops.

Some diseases are associated with a particular type of fever such as a relapsing fever (syphilis), a single daily fever spike (septicemia), sustained fever (many infectious diseases), or low-grade fevers (malignancies). It is likely that all of these responses are associated with Il-1 fluctuations.

Although it is extremely rare for a fever to persist or exceed a level that is dangerous to normal anatomic or physiologic integrity (greater than 106° F [41.4° C] in adults), there is a controversy about whether fever is a beneficial phenomenon. Most people with a fever feel uncomfortable, achy, dry, and hot, yet their thermo-regulation and behavior act to protect the higher temperature. It is also rather hard to imagine that preservation of the febrile response in most vertebrates through evolutionary history is without benefit. Presumably there must be a beneficial action of fever as a response to inflammation and infection. Before the discovery of antipyretic drugs, medical practice commonly accepted fever as natural and sometimes promoted fever production in ill patients. Kluger (1986), Blatteis (1986), and Dinarello (1986) have reviewed research on fever and pointed out the following findings. Ectothermic and endothermic vertebrates develop fevers in response to pyrogens. Those animals that use the environmental temperature to raise or lower body temperature, such as reptiles and some fish, can produce a "behavioral" fever by seeking a hotter environment. These animals have increased survival and recovery from infection, when compared to animals who are restricted from developing the behavioral fever or are given antipyretics. If reptiles "choose" to develop fever, it is argued that this might be an adaptive response, and therefore human fever must also be beneficial. This is a debatable point among researchers in the field. Concrete evidence of augmented immunologic response in the presence of fever has been found for mammals, however. Il-1, the endogenous pyrogen, produces many biologic responses other than fever. For example, the activation of T cells produced by Il-1 is an essential step in cell-mediated immunity. This is apparently enhanced in the presence of elevated body temperature. Neutrophil migration and phagocytosis are also accelerated by fever. Interferon, an essential antiviral and anticancer chemical, has enhanced function in the presence of fever. Lastly, Il-1 also appears to inhibit bacterial growth by decreasing serum iron. For all of these examples, there are experiments calling into question the generally beneficial action of fever. However, clinical studies of humans do support moderate fever as enhancing recovery and decreasing morbidity and mortality.

Although the question has not been definitively answered, there appears to be enough evidence to support the nontreatment of moderate fever (1.5° to 2.25° C) in patients who would not suffer ill effects. The development of fever produces a high metabolic demand; therefore, any person with heart disease, cachexia, limited metabolic reserves, or a history of febrile seizures or who is pregnant should probably be treated with antipyretics. High fevers (40° C and greater) can produce damage, including delerium, dehydration, wasting, and focal lesion and brain hemorrhages, and should always be avoided.

Leukocytosis. Fig. 2-13 shows the origin of granulocytic and monocytic leukocytes involved in inflammation. These cells originate from stem cells in the bone marrow, which are termed CFU-C (colony forming unit in culture). This name relates to the ability of this stem cell to form mixed colonies in culture, which is a method for assaying this stem cell in bone marrow specimens. The regulation of these leukocytes during inflammation is not understood. Many factors are postulated to stimulate the initial polymorphonuclear cell response and then the monocyte proliferation during an inflammatory episode. It is likely that the inflamed tissue somehow sends either a cellular or biochemical signal to the bone marrow. In a culture system the granulocyte-monocyte stem cell (CFU-C) requires a substance known as CSF (colony stimulating factor) to proliferate. CSF or a substance like it may be released from acutely inflamed tissue, or the damaged cells may release a substance

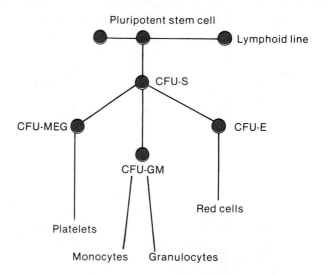

Fig. 2-13. Origin of blood cells. All blood cells are derived from the pluripotent stem cells of the bone marrow. However, in the differentiation of this cell, some cells become irreversibly committed to development of a particular cell line, as illustrated. *CFU-S,* colony forming unit–spleen; *CFU-GM,* colony forming unit–culture; *CFU-E,* colony forming unit–erythroid; *CFU-MEG,* colony forming unit–megakaryocyte.

that stimulates CSF release from other cells. CSF is released by human monocytes when these cells are stimulated by endotoxin. Other cells known to release CSF include lymphocytes, macrophages, and endothelial cells. The release of CSF during inflammation ensures that an adequate supply of inflammatory leukocytes will be available through bone marrow proliferation of stem and precursor cells. Obviously, the control of this entire process is extremely complex and the subject of continuing research.

Chronic inflammation

Occasionally acute inflammation does not become fully resolved, and healing is not evidenced, even after a period of weeks. It is not known whether an inflammatory process, by its nature, is destined in certain cases to become chronic, or whether any acute inflammation has the potential to become chronic. The nature of a chronic inflammation is certainly different from the acute type, and the systemic effects on the host are not the same. An acute inflammatory response is protective and immediate, and when the source of the injury is removed by the inflammatory process, healing restores structure and function in many cases, or repair with scar formation will at the very least result in structural integrity. A chronic inflammatory process, whether local or systemic, is debilitating and damaging and has long-term, far-reaching effects on the host's well-being.

Chronic inflammation can be caused by a great variety of agents, such as infection by bacteria and viruses, physical factors such as trauma, irritation, or the actual size or solubility of a foreign body, and biochemical factors, such as an unresolved immune reaction. Many investigators believe that prolongation and chronicity of any inflammation are ultimately the result of aberrant immunologic mechanisms. Rheumatoid arthritis is characterized by a chronic inflammatory course and is thought to be of an autoimmune nature.

Cellular infiltrate. The nature of the inflammatory site changes as the inflammation becomes chronic. The macrophage becomes the major cell type, although plasma cells and lymphocytes are also found. It functions as an activated phagocyte that contains microbicidal substances and hydrolytic enzymes. Activated macrophages also release a number of enzymes, such as plasmin activator, collagenase and pyrogens, that will cause a febrile response. Occasionally the inflammation is best characterized as subacute rather than chronic, and this usually occurs when an irritant remains at the inflammatory site after the acute response has passed. Con-

tinuous migration of macrophages occurs into the area, and these cells may divide at the site. They are eventually killed by the irritant and spill cytoplasmic enzymes into the site. Some vaccines, namely, BCG (bacille Calmette Guérin), pertussis, and typhoid, will produce a subacute lesion, which will be resolved only when the vaccine material is either destroyed, removed, or effectively sequestered by cells.

A chronic inflammation, on the other hand, has a *slow* macrophage turnover. The cause is often a fairly nontoxic but not readily digestible irritant. The macrophages may react to the substance by forming multinucleated giant cells. The irritant may cause the macrophages to release biologically active substances, which act to further perpetuate the inflammatory process.

Chronic inflammation is more *proliferative* than exudative, as compared to acute inflammation, and necrosis commonly occurs and recurs. Granulation tissue will form in response to this, and then connective tissue will follow. Increasing amounts of fibrous scar tissue will characterize a persistent, long-term chronic process.

Types of chronic inflammation. Two types of chronic inflammation have been characterized, *granulomatous* and *banal*. A granulomatous inflammation is highly cellular and destructive and is typified by tuberculosis, leprosy, syphilis, sarcoidosis, or rheumatoid arthritis. The first three diseases are all characterized by infection of the host by large, facultative, intracellular bacteria, while sarcoidosis and rheumatoid arthritis are of unknown origin. Many fungi, minerals, and foreign bodies will stimulate a granulomatous reaction, and antigen-antibody hypersensitivity reactions themselves may also be important causes.

The granulomas may be of a high or low

turnover type with regard to the recruitment, division, and death of macrophages, which are found in great numbers at the site. Fibroblasts can form part of the cell population in both types, particularly at the periphery of the granuloma where organization and attempts at repair are occurring. This may be observed, for example, at the border of a tubercle or in silicosis, which stimulates a fibrogenic response by itself. The tubercle is the characteristic pulmonary lesion of tuberculosis (Fig. 2-14). The granuloma consists of macrophages and epithelioid giant cells at the center of the lesion, the core of which is often necrotic. Lymphocytic infiltration can be seen at the periphery of the lesion, which is further edged by fibroblasts and connective tissue. The tubercle reaches a size of approximately 1 mm, and as the disease advances the tubercles begin to merge, and extensive fibrotic changes in the tissue further complicate the disease process.

Granulomatous infection may or may not be marked by the typical focal lesions that have been described. The systemic effects of the disease may be the more obvious clinical manifestation of the inflammation. Furthermore, the granulomatous histology for any given disease varies.

Banal chronic inflammations are generally not highly cellular and produce relatively smaller lesions. They may produce severe illness in the affected individual, however. Examples of banal chronic inflammation include chronic glomerulonephritis, cholecystitis, and many skin inflammations.

In general, a chronic inflammation is caused by the persistence of an irritant after the acute response. That irritant may be of a biologic, physical, or chemical nature. The irritant remains at the site because the macrophages are unable to di-

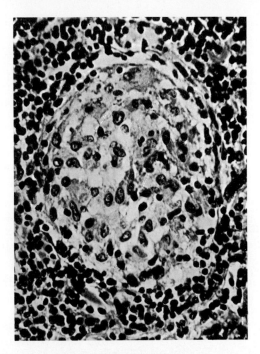

Fig. 2-14. Chronic tuberculosis. Macrophages in tubercle, which is circumscribed ovoid focus in center. Peripheral cells mostly lymphocytes. Caseous necrosis subsequently developing at center of tubercle. (×510.)
(From Anderson WAD and Kissane JM, editors: Pathology, ed 7, St Louis, 1977, The CV Mosby Co.)

gest it. The cycle of cellular infiltration, necrosis, and fibrosis will continue as long as the irritant remains. Very often there is a delayed hypersensitivity response associated with the chronic irritation and inflammation, and there is also a great variety of systemic responses (fever, lymphoplasia, leukocytosis), which may contribute to the debility and further susceptibility of the host to other diseases.

HEALING AND REPAIR

The processes of healing and repair at the inflamed site begin with the removal of the agent that caused the original pertubation, usually through the already described mechanisms of phagocytosis and enzymatic dissolution. Healing will be uneventful if the inflammatory process does not become complicated by excess necrosis, hemorrhage, ulceration, abscess formation, or cellulitis.

Necrosis is always part of the inflammatory picture in that individual cells die and remain at the site. Certain infections are particularly characterized by necrosis caused by bacterial toxins. Gas gangrene, a clostridial infection, is an anaerobic process characterized by overwhelming local sepsis and tissue destruction. The affected part, often a limb, becomes extremely edematous, discolored, and noxious smelling and may have to be amputated.

When the necrotic debris in the exudate at the inflamed site is purulent and very localized so that the pus is confined to a space in which hydrostatic pressure can increase, an *abscess* forms. The pressure eventually will result in a track forming in the area of least resistance, and the pus will drain out in this direction. Rupturing of the abscess in this manner results in the formation of a fairly large defect, and scarring may be marked. Many times this can be partially eliminated if the abscess is drained surgically.

Ulceration at an inflamed site can occur, particularly when the inflammation is complicated by vascular obstruction or infection. The inflammation then may be chronic. An example of this process is a peptic ulcer, which is an excavation in the lining of the stomach or duodenal mucosa, surrounded by inflamed, infiltrated tissue. Continuous irritation of the site perpetuates the inflammation.

Healing can be accompanied by *regeneration*, which is repair of the defect left by an injury or by the aftermath of the inflammatory process; this repair is accomplished through replacement of the tissues with cells of the same type as those that were destroyed. However, more commonly healing is accompanied by *replacement* of the lost cells with connective tissue cells, a process that results in scar formation.

Regeneration

The ability of cells to regenerate is dependent on whether they are labile, stable, or permanent cell types. Labile cells, which divide constantly during their life span, such as the cells lining the gastrointestinal tract, epithelial cells of the skin, or cells of the bone marrow, are less specialized than the permanent cell types, such as nerve cells. They are more capable of regeneration than nerve cells, and injury to the skin epithelium can be followed by regeneration and healing without scar formation. The liver and kidney parenchymal cells do not divide constantly as part of their normal physiology, but nevertheless they do retain the capacity to regenerate when the organ becomes damaged or lost through injury or disease. Lower animals have the capacity in certain instances to replace an entire limb, and theoretically every cell in the human body has the memory within its nuclear DNA to replace an amputated limb, but this code is suppressed or somehow lost in the cells of higher animals.

Replacement

Most injuries heal by connective tissue repair and second intention. *First intention* healing occurs when wound margins are nicely apposed, such as in surgical repair of a surface wound. Little scar formation occurs if there is no secondary infection, trauma, or vascular obstruction. *Second intention* connective tissue repair occurs when the wound is large and exudative, with a large amount of necrotic tissue formed as part of the inflammatory process. The site first fills in with a highly vas-

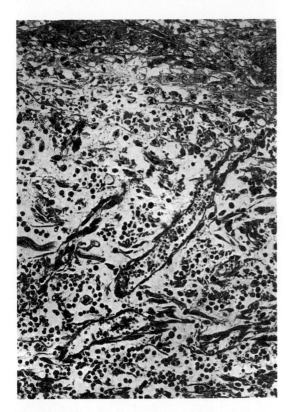

Fig. 2-15. Granulation tissue in pericarditis. Newly formed blood vessels are supported by loosely arranged connective tissue, in interstices of which lie inflammatory cells. Fibrinous exudate *(top)* obscures outline of serosal pericardium. (×170.)

(From Anderson WAD and Kissane JM, editors: Pathology, ed 7, St Louis, 1977, The CV Mosby Co.)

cular, pinkish tissue known as granulation tissue (Fig. 2-15). Fibrin, which was formed in the initial inflammatory exudate, serves as a scaffolding for migrating fibroblasts from the neighboring connective tissue and a matrix on which the granulation tissue is laid down. Fibrin eventually undergoes fibrinolysis (or liquefaction) through the action of fibrinolytic agents released by the lysosomes of leukocytes, or more usually through the action of *plasmin*, which is a blood protease. The fibroblasts move into the granulation tissue and lay down an initially disordered array of collagen fibrils, which later become remodeled into an organized structure that will form a scar. Granulation tissue receives an excellent blood supply from capillary buds that form new vessels, which bend and loop into the defect. This vascular supply later regresses, so that the final scar *(cicatrix)* is less vascular than normal tissue (accounting for its whitish coloration). Collagen formation by the fibroblasts is dependent on adequate amounts of vitamin C (ascorbic acid), which is required in the hydroxylation of lysine and proline, subunits of the collagen molecule. Granulation tissue not only is a compact sealer of the wound but is also resistant to infection and contains macrophages that assist in the removal of debris and necrotic cells. It later contracts greatly in the healing process, and this allows the wound edges to move together, facilitating the repair.

Gout: an inflammatory model

Inflammation is a sign of a great many disorders that would not ordinarily be classified primarily as inflammatory disorders. Inflammation accompanies any injury or insult to vascular tissue and thus is seen in conditions ranging from acute appendicitis to cirrhosis of the liver to a herpetic cold sore. Indeed, in all these conditions the inflammation secondary to the cellular damage wrought by the pathogen or toxin causes the greatest discomfort to the patient.

Gouty arthritis is classified as an inflammatory disorder, a metabolic error, a genetic disease, and an arthritis. This typifies the manner in which many diseases can be classified, and an understanding of pathophysiology must be underscored by a knowledge of these interrelationships.

Gouty arthritis is a complication of prolonged uric acid elevation in the blood, which ultimately results in the deposition of uric acid deposits in the joints, kidneys, and subcutaneous tissue. The basic cause of the hyperuricemia may vary from patient to patient, but the primary form is an inborn metabolic defect in purine metabolism or in uric acid excretion. The disease is typified by acute attacks, which are precipitated by such factors as trauma, drugs, and possibly overeating. The first attack of gout involves only the great toe in most patients, 90% of whom are male. Later attacks may involve other joints.

The inflammation that characterizes gouty arthritis is immediate and results in great pain, swelling, and redness. It is treated medically, usually by the administration of salicylates, allopurinol, or colchicine, or it may resolve spontaneously. The mechanism of action of colchicine is obscure, in that it relieves the pain of only this condition. It does not act by increasing the urinary excretion of blood concentration of uric acid, as do the salicylates. It does not alter the function of xanthine oxidase as does allopurinol, nor does it reduce the amount of uric acid that is formed through purine metabolism. The most plausible mechanism for colchicine action is through interruption of the leukocytic response to the uric acid crystals, so that the characteristic inflammation is halted.

The inflammation of gouty arthritis is initiated by the precipitation of uric acid crystals, which occurs at lowered pH levels in the acidic joint capsules. This results when the serum uric acid increases above 6.5 mg/100 ml. The uric acid crystals can activate Hageman factor and the kinin system, which have previously been described; an acute effusive inflammation in the joint ensues. Repeated attacks of gout lead to the collection of large crystals, which initiate a chronic granulomatous response. These granulomas, known as *tophi*, can seriously impair joint function and if formed in the kidney may result in obstruction and renal damage. Tophi can often be demonstrated in the earlobe of the gouty individual and may ulcerate in any location. Thinning of the cartilage and pitting of the bony surfaces may result when chronic inflammation characterized by tophi formation occurs.

Pathophysiologic States

Now that we have looked at the processes by which the white blood cells interact to protect humans from environmental threats, we can begin to understand inflammatory and immunologic diseases. The models presented here illustrate various mechanisms of pathophysiology. It is important to note, however, that the white blood cells interact not only with each other but also are affected by endocrine and neurologic control. The lymphocytes for example are profoundly affected by stress (Chapter 7). The neutrophils and monocytes may be capable of receiving neurally mediated signals through their membrane receptors. Imagery in which an intense visual image of the white blood cells attacking malignant or infected cells has many proponents who believe cure to be as much a matter of mind and willpower as a purely biologic phenomenon. Allergic manifestations are often affected by the mind. Evidence of "learning" by the immune system has been recently accumulating. The placebo effect is so powerful a response that great biologic changes may occur in response to placebos. If the immune system and the networks of eosinophils, neutrophils, and monocytes are capable of this type of manipulation, then surely many disease mechanisms must be looked at in the framework of mind-body, rather than body alone. As will be discussed in Chapter 7 stress can lead to real physical illness. It makes sense that a positive life-affirming mental outlook can lead to wellness.

The first disease model presented is that of infection.

INFECTION: AN IMMUNOLOGIC AND INFLAMMATORY MODEL

It is assumed that students using this book have had a college level course in introductory microbiology. Therefore little emphasis will be placed on agents of infectious disease but rather on the response of the body to infection, both pathophysiologic and restorative.

It has been implicit in the discussions concerning immunity and inflammation that the infectious process may trigger the responses that have previously been detailed. Any infection will elicit both an inflammatory and an immune reaction. However, for the infection to be clinically apparent these defense mechanisms must be overcome by the agent causing the infection. The susceptibility to infection and the manifestation of infection within the host depend on a great number of possible interacting factors. These factors include the virulence, invasiveness, and organ preference of the infecting organism; the health and age of the host; the presence of other infection, which would increase the host's susceptibility to additional infection; the general integrity of the host's natural defenses and barriers, the nutritional status of the host; and other factors such as gender, occupation, race, drug ingestion, radiation exposure, temperature, fatigue, and stress.

Infection can be defined as the successful attack and growth of microorganisms in a particularly suitable host. Survival of microbes demands that these living organisms find an appropriate environment in which to invade, divide, and multiply. Thus a parasitic relationship has developed between the microorganisms and the human body. In the vast majority of instances this parasitic relationship can be thwarted in its early development by human defenses, such that the microorganisms do not overwhelm and destroy cells and tissues. In fact, many infections are inapparent in that no overt signs and symptoms ever develop. As the severity of the parasitic attack increases, so also do the signs and symptoms in the host. The human body serves as a limited reservoir in which microorganisms grow, producing progeny, which can leave one host and attack another. The evolution of both human beings and microbes has proceeded in such a way that most invasions of human tissue do not cause significant damage to the host but yet allow the continued propagation of the various species of microorganisms that attack humans.

Major infecting organisms of humans

Briefly, those organisms that are responsible for infection in humans are the bacteria, mycoplasmas, rickettsiae, viruses, chlamydiae (bedsonia), fungi, protozoas, and larger parasites such as roundworms and flatworms. The process of infection differs for each of these classes. Some can infect directly; others require animal vectors or reservoirs. A great many environmental factors must operate together for an actual infection to occur, and thus infection must be considered multicausal.

Pathophysiology of infection

When infection is clinically apparent there are several fairly common findings. Each organism will, of course, cause specific symptoms, such as the rash of measles, the tubercle of tuberculosis, or the parotitis of mumps. The acute inflammatory response and the immune system will predictably react and cause certain phenomena, such as fever, leukocytosis, general malaise, and lymphadenopathy. Of course, not all infections will result in all these signs, but these four responses are the most common signs and symptoms of infection. Most of the damage wrought by infectious organisms is related to the production of endotoxins and exotoxins. Other effects may be produced by obstruction of vital structures, bacterial enzymes, invasion, virulence, and organ preference.

Fever. This sign of infection is variable and may appear at any stage of an infectious process, depending on the agent and the host. Generally, however, infection causes fever, and fever does not appear until the infecting organisms have caused an acute inflammatory reaction and cellular necrosis has occurred. Different infections may produce different fever patterns.

Leukocyte changes in infection. Several changes occur in the white blood cells as a response to infection.

Neutrophilia. An increase in the percentage of circulating white blood cells is found in many infections. All leukocytes are produced in the bone marrow and probably originate from a single progenitor or stem cell. The continuing process of leukopoiesis provides for renewal of the various cellular populations when cells are depleted, usually through cell death, from the circulating blood and tissue spaces. It is believed that the neutrophils, which make up approximately 55% of the total leukocytes of the blood, are the major phagocytic cells of the blood, and they are known to increase early in the infectious process. The stimulus to neutrophil production is secretion of mediators such as CSF, which are released from infected, ne-

crotic tissue and macrophages. Neutrophils are granulocytic, polymorphonuclear cells, which can freely move from the blood to the tissue and back. They are mobilized early in an acute inflammatory reaction. Neutrophils mature into their adult multilobulated nuclear structure from cells with only slightly indented nuclei. Thus the presence of these immature, or *band*, cells in the bloodstream indicates that neutrophil production has been stimulated and the juvenile neutrophils are being released from the bone marrow in response to the infection. The term *shift to the left* has arisen to describe an increase in the immature neutrophils in comparison to the normal percentage, which is about 7.9%. This term is used because the table of cells used for differential counting of blood smears indicates the immature neutrophils toward the left of the table and the mature forms toward the right. The term *neutrophilia* indicates an increase in the percentage of neutrophils and is usually accompanied by some degree of shift to the left in acute infections, particularly infections of the pyogenic type.

Pyogenic, or pus-producing, infections are the result of infections by microbes that kill the neutrophils that phagocytose them. This cytolytic property results in the accumulation of cellular debris, which forms as pus. Infections caused by organisms that persist within macrophages and do not form pus differ from infection by pyogenic organisms. The former do not result in white blood cell lysis, and cause result in chronic, low-grade infections. Examples of pyogenic microbes are the cocci bacteria such as *Streptococcus*, *Staphylococcus*, and *Pneumococcus*; nonpyogenic organisms include the *Mycobacterium*, *Salmonella*, and *Brucella*.

Other causes of neutrophilia include certain fungal *(Actinomyces)*, viral (rabies, poliomyelitis, herpes zoster), and parasitic (liver fluke) infections. Neutrophilia is particularly common in localized infection, such as in an abscess, furuncle, osteomyelitis, tonsillitis, and otitis media, and in certain generalized infections, including rheumatic fever, scarlet fever, chickenpox, diphtheria, septicemia, appendicitis, peritonitis, meningitis, and gonorrhea. Noninfectious processes, including intoxications, hemorrhage, surgery, thrombosis, neoplasms, hemolysis, leukemias, and exercise can also cause neutrophilia; neutrophilia is also present physiologically in the normal newborn.

Generally, the degree of neutrophilia in an infection indicates the degree of resistance of the host. It is critical to determine the absolute number of neutrophils, the percentage increase, and the percentage of immature forms that are found. Neutrophilia is the normal physiologic response to certain infecting organisms and certain types of infections. It is only when the demands of the infection are so great that the bone marrow is unable to effectively respond that pathophysiologic mechanisms are perpetuated. A severe infection that is well handled by the host is indicated by a neutrophilia, leukocytosis (increase in the total number of leukocytes), and a moderate shift to the left, which could be as much as 25% immature forms.

The presence of toxic granules in the immature neutrophils is another important indicator of the adequacy of the bone marrow response to the infection. These large or small granules indicate that the cell is an inadequate phagocyte and may in fact be a damaged cell. Some toxic granulation is still compatible with an effective response, but if an increase in toxic granulation is accompanied by a fall in the total leukocyte count and a great increase in the number of immature neutrophils, it indi-

cates that the neutrophils' response is probably inadequate to handle a severe infection. Some extremely severe infections such as septicemia are in fact accompanied by a leukopenia, indicating that the bone marrow has been overwhelmed. The actual mechanism for the production of this phenomenon is not known, however.

Leukopenia. Leukopenia may be the normal response to certain infecting agents, especially the viruses and rickettsiae, in which leukocytosis may not occur unless bacterial infection occurs along with the viral process. Again, the cause of the leukopenia is obscure but is an important aid in the differential diagnosis of an infection.

Lymphocytosis. An increase in the normal percentage (35%) of lymphocytes occurs in response to certain acute infections, such as pertussis and infectious mononucleosis, in some exanthem-causing diseases, such as rubella, in a large number of chronic infections, in leukemias, in infancy, and during the recovery stage of an acute infection. The role of the lymphocyte in inflammation and immunity has previously been discussed.

Monocytosis. Mononuclear cells may increase above normal values (6.5%) in infections such as tuberculosis. They are also commonly elevated in rickettsial infections such as Rocky Mountain spotted fever and typhus. The monocyte is the chief cell in the formation of the tubercle of tuberculosis.

Eosinophilia. The role of the eosinophil in atopy has been described, and it is therefore not surprising that these granular polymorphonuclear cells increase in percentage value above normal (3%) in allergy, such as asthma, hay fever, and eczema. They are also increased in skin diseases, such as pemphigus and dermatitis herpetiformis, and in parasitic infestations, such as trichinosis and ascariasis. Certain infections, such as scarlet fever, are also characterized by eosinophilia, and eosinophilia may be present in chorea.

Basophils. The function of the basophils, which make up about 0.5% of the total leukocyte count, is not known, and variations of basophils with disease states and infections are not noteworthy.

Summary of white cell responses. In general, infection can be characterized by three phases. The first phase is progressive and acute and is accompanied by neutrophilia, a shift to the left, and some toxic granulation. During the stage of recovery from an acute infection the monocytes begin to reappear and increase in number while the neutrophilia decreases. Eosinophils also reappear at this time. During the convalescent stage of acute infection the lymphocytes begin to increase in number, the neutrophils drop to their normal percentage, and the shift to the left disappears. Different organisms may produce different patterns as have been described; this is therefore only a general picture of the stages of the leukocyte response to all infection.

General malaise. General malaise is a nonspecific but extremely common symptom of many infections. It is difficult to trace pathophysiologically. The feeling of "sickness" may be the result of the stress response (see Chapter 7). It may also be produced through the release of various substances by necrotic cells that can act on many organ systems of the body. In a sense malaise serves a useful purpose, since the individual is forced to be confined to bed, not having the inclination or the stamina to engage in daily activities. Thus the organism's myriad defenses can be recruited in one major direction, that of combating the infection. However, there is little research in the area of general malaise, albeit the most common symptom of any sickness, and there is little that can be done to alleviate it.

Lymphadenopathy. Most moderate to severe infections are accompanied by some degree of palpable enlargement of the lymph nodes. Often the involved nodes drain the infected areas of the body, but they may also be enlarged generally, as in a systemic infection. Nodular enlargement may be so severe that pain and impairment of mobility are serious side effects. Lymphadenopathy indicates immune responsiveness to the infecting agents and is therefore a reassuring sign of an adequate response. It can also be a pathophysiologic sign in certain malignant diseases, such as Hodgkin's disease. During an inflammatory response there is an increase in the flow of lymph, which is carried in the lymphatic channels from the inflammatory site. The lymph nodes then mount a response to the agents that may be carried in the lymph. However, if there is not an effective response, the lymph itself may be the major mechanism by which an infection is carried from one site to another. Reticuloendothelial phagocytes line the lymphatic channels and are also found in the lymph nodes, liver, spleen, bone marrow, lung, and tissues throughout the body. Thus the liver and spleen may also be significantly enlarged in an acute infection. The hypertrophy of lymph nodes, liver, and spleen is the result of the presence of increased numbers of lymphocytes, histiocytes, and other cells.

Disease models of acute infection: otitis media

Suppurative infection of the middle ear is common in the young child because of the high incidence of nasopharyngeal infections in this age group and because of the structure of the eustachian tube infants and toddlers. Because the eustachian tube is much shorter and straighter in the child than in the adult, infecting organisms have an easier transit to the middle ear. The fact that an infant or young child is often in the supine position increases the probability of infection as does feeding in the supine position. Milk or formula can actually drain into the middle ear cavity.

The development of otitis media is often preceded by a respiratory tract infection. The child complains of pain or may pull on the affected ear. The child is irritable, anorexic, febrile, and may appear to have pain on swallowing. Often the fever will be as high as 40° or 41° C (104° or 105° F), and the infant must be carefully watched for the development of febrile convulsions. There is usually a leukocytosis with neutrophilia. Physical examination often reveals lymphadenopathy, and otoscopic examination of the tympanic membrane indicates the presence of inflammation and exudate behind the membrane. There can be perforation of the tympanic membrane caused by a buildup of exudate and therefore pressure. The membrane, which is normally pearly gray, may be swollen, reddish or yellow when infected. The light reflex may be lost in otitis media, and the normal landmarks are obscured.

Pathogenesis of otitis media is thought to require blockage of the eustachian tube. This may occur in any respiratory tract infection that causes mucosal swelling. When the tube is obstructed any microorganisms present can multiply and thus become a potent localized source of infection. It is interesting to note that the most common agents of otitis media are components of the normal bacteria of the respiratory tract and under normal circumstances are nonpathogenic. These include *Streptococcus pneumoniae*, *S. pyogenes*, and *Hemophilus influenzae*.

Treatment of otitis media is with decongestants and antibiotics, usually broad-spectrum types such as ampicillin.

Treatment rationale. As in the disease model just described, treatment of infection is aimed at alleviating specific signs and symptoms (for example, use of myringotomy), but whenever the microorganism is susceptible, antibiotics are also used. Most bacterial but few viral infections can be treated with antibiotics; drugs also exist to treat rickettsial, fungal, and other types of infection. Briefly, the mechanism of action of the various types of antibiotics includes inhibition of the synthesis of the bacterial cell wall, alteration in the bacterial cell membrane permeability, inhibition of the genetic coding of bacterial proteins, and inhibition of the synthesis of essential metabolites. Table 2-3 lists various antibiotics according to these modes of action.

The efficacy of antibiotic therapy in a

Table 2-3. Model of action of antibiotics*

Mode of action	Representative antibiotics
Inhibition of bacterial cell wall synthesis	Penicillins
	Cephalosporins
	Bacitracin
Alteration of membrane permeability	Polymyxin B
	Amphotericin B
	Nystatin
Inhibition of microbial DNA translation and transcription	Erythromycin
	Tetracyclines
	Streptomycin
	Lincomycin
	Kanamycin
	Chloramphenicol
Inhibition of essential metabolite synthesis	Para-aminosalicylic acid
	Sulfonamides
	Isoniazid

*Adapted from Wehrle PF and Top FH: Communicable and infectious diseases, ed 9, St Louis, 1981, The CV Mosby Co, p 40.

given host with a specific infection depends on a great many variables, including the host's defenses and barriers. Simply stated, the more severe the infection, the more difficult to cure with appropriate antibiotics. Furthermore, many microorganisms have become resistant to certain antibiotics. A strain of gonorrhea has been described, supergonorrhea, that is resistant to most known antibiotics. There are many other resistant strains of common microorganisms, and the mechanisms of resistance development within microbes is dependent on natural selection of the hardiest, most enduring strains of microorganisms in the environment. Thus those strains least affected by antibiotics will be the most likely to survive and propagate, creating a large population of resistant organisms capable of infecting humans. New antibiotics to destroy the new strains of microbes must continually be developed.

There is also some evidence that certain antibiotics themselves can alter the cell wall of certain bacteria, making them resistant. Some instances in which antibiotics actually stimulated the growth of colonies of bacteria have also been described.

Superinfection is a problem that can affect the efficacy of antibiotic treatment. In this process the normal flora of the respiratory tract, gastrointestinal tract, vagina, and perhaps other systems is disrupted by the bactericidal activity of the antibiotic, and normally small populations of potential pathogens are then allowed to grow rapidly, since the competition for nutrients has been decreased. Removal of the normal flora may allow resistant strains that are present to flourish, making the treatment of infection extremely problematic.

Chronic EBV infection

Another interesting model of infection is chronic mononucleosis caused by the Ep-

stein-Barr virus (EBV). It is associated many times with the diagnosis of chronic fatigue syndrome. EBV is a herpes virus and, like other herpetic infections, appears capable of residing in the host after an acute infection and reactivating at certain times in the host's life. Acute infectious mononucleosis is a disease of childhood and adolescents and has as a typical course: fever, fatigue, pharyngitis, lymphadenopathy, hepatomegaly and splenomegaly, lymphocytosis and atypical lymphocytes, and a usual time course of about 3 weeks. However, in many patients, especially young children, unusual variations of the disease, and even death, can occur. Recently the syndrome of chronic EBV infection has been described (Welliver, 1986). This syndrome has nonspecific symptoms such as sore throat, swollen glands, fevers, fatigue (that may be profound), depression, and myalgia and has been recently termed the "chronic fatigue syndrome." Some cases of severe depression and debilitating fatigue have been found to be the result of EBV although other viruses may be implicated. There is a significant increase in the incidence of allergies in those afflicted, but the relationship between EBV and allergy is not clear. EBV may sensitize the host to develop atopy. On the other hand, allergy may create the immunologic environment for reactivation. Other immunologic deficiencies, such as that caused by severe stress, may reactivate the virus, which is believed to reside in the latent state, inside B lymphocytes. It is clear that history of acute mononucleosis should be evaluated in all patients with chronic fatigue or depression.

Immunologic disease models

The most common immune deficient condition is immunoglobulin A (IgA) deficiency, which occurs in about one in every

600 people. Fortunately the majority of those affected are asymptomatic. IgA deficiency may be the result of vitamin B_{12} deficiency or may occur following severe viral infections, such as acute infectious mononucleosis. There may be an autoimmune etiology, since antibodies are commonly found to IgA in people affected. When symptoms are present they are related to an increased incidence of infections, particularly of the upper respiratory tract.

When hypogammaglobulinemia (decreased IgG) occurs, susceptibility to infections (particularly bacterial infections) is the predominant finding. Such states are more common in children, with boys being five times more frequently affected. Developmentally, adult levels of both IgA and IgG are not achieved until between 6 and 10 years of age. Transient hypogammaglobulinemia can develop during infancy. Adults between the ages of 20 and 30 acquire common variable hypogammaglobulinemia. Since IgG is the major immunoglobulin protective against bacterial infection, upper respiratory tract infections, particularly bronchiectasis, and diarrheal infection are the common findings. Individuals with this deficiency also have a greatly increased risk of malignancy occurring (16% develop cancer in 1 to 30 years). The defect does not arise as a result of a drop in B cells but rather as a dysfunction of B cell secretion or possibly as a result of T suppressor cell disturbance.

IgA and IgG deficient states, as described, are the most common immunodeficiencies. However, the increasing incidence of acquired immune deficiency syndrome (AIDS) from human lymphotropic viral infection has become a much more serious threat. Before considering this syndrome in depth, we will review other, rare, genetic immunodeficiency states. Although these are extremely uncommon, these immunodeficiency states are important to understand because they have taught immunologists a great deal about the basic function of the immune system.

The first well-described immunodeficient state was X-linked infantile agammaglobulinemia, in which patients lack B cells but have apparently normal T cell reactivity. Since that discovery, more than 20 immunologic disorders have been described. These disorders can be classified according to which cell type is affected and at what point in the development of the cellular system the disease process has intervened. Stem cell, B cell, T cell, and combined B and T cell immunodeficiency diseases have been discovered in humans.

Stem cell immunodeficiency. Over 200 cases of a condition known as severe combined immunodeficiency (SCID) have been described. These children have a striking lymphopenia and overwhelming susceptibility to infections; this condition is now thought to be the more common genetic immunodeficiency disease. It is believed that the disease process usually results from the early lack of a stem cell, which would normally give rise to lymphocytes in the bone marrow. Thus the bone marrow contains very few lymphocytes, and the thymus is dysplastic, contains no or few lymphocytes, and is located in the neck rather than the mediastinum. There is an absence of cellular immunity and antibody synthesis, and there is very little immunoglobulin in the blood. Lymphopenia may be profound, and the lymphocytes that are present are immature. This overwhelming disease invariably is associated with fatal infection. Half those affected with SCID have a marked deficiency in the enzyme adenosine deaminase. It is possible that the lack of this enzyme results in the accumulation of adenosine, which may then act to inhibit T and B cell differentiation during early development.

Treatment rationale. Treatment of these infants has been difficult. The hereditary nature of the condition is known, and certain infants have been isolated from birth in germ-free (gnotobiotic) chambers that protect them from the environment. Such measures are aimed at maintaining these children until appropriate treatment can be instituted. The most practical treatment is bone marrow transplantation, which is the intraperitoneal injection of bone marrow containing immunocompetent stem cells. The major difficulty in bone marrow transplantation is the need to use completely histocompatible cells. Histocompatibility antigens of the HLA system are a major basis for determining the tissue type of a donor and a recipient. These are cellular antigens, which are, of course, genetically determined, and therefore the possibility of two individuals possessing the same or similar HLA antigens is greatly increased in relatives.

Occasionally SCID patients have been treated with thymus transplants, and some have received fetal liver or bone marrow cells. Again the major problem is graft versus host reactions, leading to severe disease and eventual death. Another form of therapy for patients with this disease who have not had transplants because of a lack of a suitable donor is the use of thymosin, a hormone produced by the thymus gland, and transfer factor. The use of these agents requires that some lymphoid precursor cells be present.

B cell immunodeficiency. When the production of adequate numbers of B cells is disturbed, humoral immunity is impaired. The best example of this condition is infantile X-linked agammaglobulinemia. There is a delay between birth and the onset of signs and symptoms of this immunodeficient state because of the retention of maternal immunoglobulins by the child. By about 9 months of age, however, these children begin to develop severe infections caused by pyogenic organisms such as *staphylococcus, pneumococcus, streptococcus,* and *Hemophilus influenzae.* The children are not unusually susceptible to viral or enterobacterial infections. The disease affects boys only, and in addition to recurrent infection a variety of collagen-like symptoms and signs are observed. There is also a high incidence of hemolytic anemia, eczema, and allergy.

The response of these patients to infection is often bizarre. Delayed hypersensitivity is either slightly reduced or normal, yet the blood lymphocyte count is normal. The diagnostic criterion for this condition is the absence of plasma cells in antigen-stimulated lymph nodes. The lymphoid tissue is also often disorganized, and frequently tonsils are atrophic or absent.

Treatment of these patients is replacement of the missing immunoglobulins, particularly IgG. Gamma globulin is therefore given regularly, with antibiotics also occasionally being administered prophylactically. Commercially prepared IgA, IgE, and IgM are not presently available, and therefore a source of immunoglobulins of all classes is donor plasma infusion.

Several variants of infantile X-linked agammaglobulinemia have been described. One such situation appears to be agammaglobulinemia caused by a block in the maturation of B-lymphocytes so that they never actually release immunoglobulins into the blood.

Other B cell disorders have been described in which there is a selective loss of some and retention of other immunoglobulin production capabilities. An example of this is IgA deficiency, in which there is a normal or increased number of lymphocytes, but the concentration of IgA in the blood and other secretions is minimal, and there is an absence of IgA-synthesizing plasma cells. There appears therefore to be a maturation block in the development of IgA-synthesizing plasma cells. IgA deficiency is often found in normal individuals with no signs of disease (in fact, IgA was discovered by two healthy immunologists to be absent in their own blood). Some cases are associated with steatorrhea and nontropical sprue (see Chapter 21). The lack of IgA in the gastrointestinal tract may play an important role in the etiology of these conditions. There is also a lack of IgA in ataxia-telangiectasia, which is a hereditary disease associated with a defect in cellular immunity. Ataxia begins during infancy, but the typical skin lesions do not appear until childhood.

T cell immunodeficiency. The best described disease that results from a defect in T cell–mediated immunity is DiGeorge's syndrome. In this rare condition there is a congenital anomaly that results in the partial or total absence of the parathyroid and thymus glands. Both of these structures are derived from the embryonic pharyngeal pouches, and both glands arise simultaneously during embryogenesis. It is therefore believed that this syndrome results from the action of teratogenic influences on these developing structures. It is interesting to note in this regard that congenital heart disease, most commonly tetralogy of Fallot, is usually found as well. These infants are hypocalcemic and extremely susceptible to infection. There is normal B cell humoral immunity, but cellular immunity is absent. In cases where some thymic and parathyroid tissue is present, the disease may follow a relatively less morbid course, and some T cell capability is acquired in both the severe and mild forms of the disease if the children survive to 4 or 5 years old.

Treatment rationale. Fetal thymic transplants have been used to treat children with T cell immunodeficiency; even in children with 10% to 20% of the normal amount of thymic tissue, tiny amounts of fetal thymus can result in the production of a state of immunocompetence in the previously immunodeficient child. Therefore it is apparent that the absolute amount of thymus gland tissue is not the sole criterion for the production of adequate T cell–mediated cellular immunity.

T and B cell immunodeficiency. Another category of immunodeficiency encompasses a large number of disease states that are associated with impairment of both B and T cell immunity. A disease model that illustrates this spectrum of complex disorders is the Wiskott-Aldrich syndrome. The immunologic defect that produces this disease appears to result from an inability of the immune system to initiate a response to antigen, rather than a primary defect in the immune cells' capability. There is usually a normal number of B and T cells, and in vitro tests indicate that the cells are able to launch an immune response to antigen. Therefore the disease originates somewhere in the so-called afferent limb of the immune response. The afferent limb consists of the processing of antigen by lymphoid and accessory phagocytic cells before the antigen is presented to immunocompetent cells with which it then combines and initiates the typical immune response. (The efferent limb is that part of the immune response in which T and B cells are activated to react normally to antigen.)

The signs and symptoms of the Wiskott-Aldrich syndrome include thrombocytopenia, eczema, and repeated episodes of many different types of infection. There is also an increased incidence of malignancy in these patients. The condition is genetically transmitted as an X-linked trait and is therefore found only in males. This disease has been successfully treated with transfer factor, the effects of which may last as long as a year.

Acquired immune deficiency syndrome. Acquired immune deficiency syndrome (AIDS) is a devastating viral infection of the T4 subset of the lymphocytes, (which includes the T helper cells) and the macrophage. This ultimately results in both T cell–, B cell–, and natural killer cell–mediated deficiency. The virus has been shown to also infect other cells including cells of the brain and muscle cells. The monocyte/macrophage is believed to be the reservoir of the virus in the infected person. The virus responsible is the human, T cell, lymphotropic virus-III, known as HIV (human immunodeficiency virus). HIV-1 is an insidious RNA retrovirus capable of hiding inside infected cells, escaping immune surveillance, and producing a latent state that is very difficult to detect or predict. The lymphotropic virus family is responsible for other human diseases, the most notable being human T cell leukemia. HIV-2, recently discovered, and possibly a new form, HIV-3 causes an AIDS-like illness. (Marx, 1988). The more these retroviruses are investigated, the more they are seen to be involved with various clinical syndromes. One aspect that is most disturbing is the capability of these viruses to undergo constant genetic change in the infected host. This variation produces a continual baffling of the immune system, as new viral antigens are produced that have not been previously recognized by the immune system. Furthermore, infected macrophages sequester the virus from immunological recognition.

AIDS is transmitted through anal and vaginal intercourse and by infected blood, needles, and transplant tissue. It can also be transmitted from an infected mother to a fetus. The disease is predicted to kill 50,000 Americans each year. Over 1.5 million Americans are now infected with the virus, and about 270,000 cases of AIDS are expected by 1991. AIDS has been primarily spread through homosexual male contacts in the United States, but the incidence of heterosexual spread is increasing. In central Africa the disease infects men and women equally, and the number of children acquiring AIDS is steadily increasing. It is possible that hundreds of thousands of African infants will die of AIDS in the next 10 years (Baum, 1986).

To understand the pathophysiology of AIDS, it is necessary to examine how retroviruses generally infect their hosts. All viruses require living cells to proliferate. Retroviruses infect cells and transcribe their genetic material, RNA, into DNA through the enzyme reverse transcriptase, which is carried by the virus (Fig. 2-16). Once the viral genes are coded as DNA, viral proteins can be made through the use of the cellular endoplasmic reticulum, amino acids, and enzymes that are normally used for protein synthesis. Viral proteins can then function to reassemble new infectious viral particles, which collect inside the cell, and can then bud off from the cell or leave through cell lysis. When infected T cells die, they form giant cells that are the result of fusion of many other cells. This would result in depletion of the T cells, as they fuse, and ultimately die. Retroviruses can also become latent inside infected cells. Once the viral RNA is transcribed into DNA, the viral DNA can insert itself into the host cell DNA and remain there in an inactive state. Mitotic activity of the cell or other stimulatory signals would then cause the viral DNA to become activated, to code for viral proteins, and to make new viruses. Eventually, in either case, an end result of retroviral infection is death of the cells. In AIDS, a profound deficiency develops in the T4 cells. In healthy

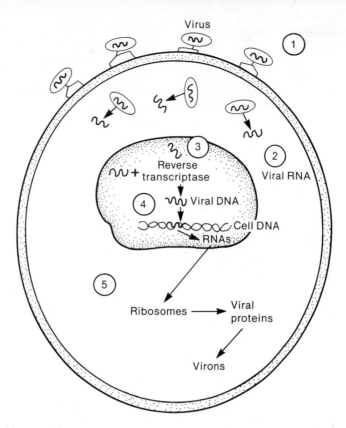

Fig. 2-16. *1*, Virus attaches to cell. *2*, Virus inside cell "uncoat" to reveal RNA. *3*, RNA and viral enzyme reverse transcriptase, enter nucleus and transcribe strand of viral DNA. *4*, Viral DNA codes for RNAs to produce viral RNAs that will then use cells' protein synthesizing; *5*, to produce new infectious virus particles (virons).

individuals the ratio of helper to suppressor cells is 2:1, but in AIDS the ratio changes to 1:2, as the helper cells are depleted. As previously discussed, helper T cells help B cells produce immunoglobulins and help other T cells, including T killer cells, in their functions. Thus a deficiency of this cell type has profound repercussions throughout the immune system.

When the AIDS virus infects a human being, it seems to have a preference for the T4 cells. However, it initially infects macrophage and may infect other cells. Some individuals show muscle weakness as their first symptom, indicating involvement of muscle cells. Once inside lymphocytes, the virus may remain latent. Initially only about 10% of the T4 cells are infected. However, T cells, in contrast to individual B cells, are long lived, and so these virus-containing cells may be present for years. This is also true for macrophages. For the host's immune system to destroy the virus, it must be able to recognize it. Low-level viral infection does in time result in enough expression of viral antigens to cause the host immune system to produce immunoglobulins against them. This results in conversion of a host, following infection, to a seropositive state. It is thought that once antibodies are found in the blood, the person has been infected. From 5% to 50% of those infected will ultimately develop AIDS.

There is, in the natural progression of this disease, an intermediate stage seen in some patients, known as AIDS-related complex (ARC). This is characterized by seropositivity and symptoms such as fever, diarrhea, infections, lymphadenopathy, and weight loss. It is believed to be either an early or mild form of the full-blown AIDS infection. Some research suggests another viral form, such as HIV-2 or HIV-3 may cause ARC. Once a person is classified as having AIDS, the fatality rate is 100%. It is not known if ARC patients will all eventually develop AIDS.

AIDS virus is not destroyed by the host's immune system because it is an infection of the immune system. However, there is evidence that the immune system makes an attempt to act against the virus. Evidence for this is seen in the antibody titer that is produced and in the recent finding that monocytes/macrophages may contain the virus. Presumably the macrophages have engulfed viral particles in their normal phagocytic capacity. However, because macrophages are the primary presenting cells, it is probable that the initial cell type containing virus is the macrophage. These are mobile cells, which could then carry the virus to many sites within the body. The immune system is also constantly being baffled by the AIDS virus, as the virus is known to undergo genetic change within the infected host, and the immune system cannot keep up with the genetic variability that occurs. There are at least seven genes in the HIV-1 virus, and small mutations in these genes, occurring with a high frequency within an infected person, could result in inadequate immune response to the virus.

Besides undergoing mutation, the AIDS virus further perpetuates its existence by containing within its genetic material a base sequence that is similar to long terminal repeat sequences for Il-2 and gamma interferon (Marx, 1986). Thus, whenever T cells are stimulated to produce these lymphokines, a consequence would also be viral replication stimulation. The T cells containing the virus do not appear to become active virus producers until they are activated by antigen. However, there is no way to predict what types of antigens would stimulate those cells containing HIV-1, and thus protect the latently infected host. Antigen stimulation is just a natural consequence of living, and as the cells are activated and produce the virus, the viral infection involves more and more cells, eventually producing the characteristic overwhelming depletion of the T4 cells.

When cellular immunodeficiency of this sort develops, protection against fungal, protozoal, and viral agents is decreased as is cancer cell surveillance. Patients with AIDS have a greatly increased susceptibility to opportunistic infections such as *Candida* yeast infections, *Pneumocystis carinii* infection (a protozoal pneumonia), and herpetic infection. AIDS patients also contract a rare skin cancer, Kaposi's sarcoma. The infections that develop are severe, extremely difficult to treat, and usually atypical. There are also multiple effects on other physiologic systems, such as cachexia, anorexia, anemia, thrombocytopenia, arthralgia, sleeplessness, diarrhea, and neurologic symptoms. It is now known that as many as 70% of AIDS patients develop dementia as the disease progresses (Barnes, 1986). This is possibly a result of actual infection of the brain with the AIDS virus, although secondary opportunistic infection of the brain also can occur. The brain becomes atrophic, and patients can become profoundly demented and manifest a range of neuropathies.

There is currently little hope for the patient with AIDS, although research into the nature of the virus, the pathophysiologic mechanisms by which it causes the disease, and the risk factors for AIDS has proceeded at remarkable speed. Prototypes for vaccines are currently being devised, and some antiviral agents appear to hold promise for treatment. Without a cure for AIDS, this disease is without question the most severe infectious disease that threatens the world population in the Twentieth Century.

CASE STUDY: ACQUIRED IMMUNE DEFICIENCY SYNDROME

History

JI is a 32-year-old, white, homosexual male with a history of hepatitis, gonorrhea, proctitis, and allergies associated with recurrent bouts of sinusitis. Because of his life-style, recent unintentional weight loss, and persistent fatigue, he was tested for HIV antibodies 3 weeks ago; the results were positive.

Aside from current complaints, he has no other history of infections and/or malignancies associated with HIV infection.

JI denies any history of drug abuse or occupational HIV exposure. In addition, he denies ever having received a blood transfusion. He has never traveled to countries beyond the United States.

Objective and Subjective Data

JI was admitted to the hospital via the emergency room. He has been experiencing dyspnea at rest, and temperatures up to 103.8° F for 3 days.

General appearance: Thin, white male,

Contributed by MaryAnn Colletti.

sitting upright in bed; a nasal cannula is in place; he is somewhat restless, but cooperative

Vital signs

Temperature: 104.0° F (orally)

Pulse: 132 (apical, regular)

Respirations: 36 (somewhat labored)

Blood pressure: 90/56 (sitting, left arm)

Height: 6′0″

Weight: 154 lbs

Skin: Warm, dry, flushed; nailbeds mildly dusky; no skin lesions, rashes, or alopecia; lips are dry and cracked; skin turgor is good

Head and neck: Oral thrush; PERRLA; no lymphadenopathy, alopecia, cranial nerve signs, neck rigidity, or nasal flaring

Respiratory: Regular, somewhat labored breathing without intercostal retractions or use of accessory muscles; good excursion; breath sounds decreased two-thirds of the way up bilaterally; non-productive cough with exertion

Cardiovascular: Normal sinus tachycardia; without pedal edema or jugular venous distention

Abdomen: Scaphoid; mild tenderness in right upper quadrant; bowel sounds are hyperactive throughout

Neurologic: Alert and oriented to time, place, and person; mood anxious; attention, recent and remote memory, and abstract thinking are intact; speech is normal; sensation, proprioception, and cerebellar function are intact, deep tendon reflexes 2+ throughout; no gait disturbance

Laboratory data

WBC with differential: Leukepenia; marked lymphopenia

Hemoglobin/hematocrit: 6.8 gm/dl/22.5%

Arterial blood gases: ph: 7.40; Po_2: 65 mm on 3L/oxygen by nasal cannula

Blood cultures: Gram stain: negative

Chemistries: Slightly elevated SGOT, SGPT, and alkaline phosphatase; BUN/creatinine: slightly increased; Albumin/TP: decreased

Treatment

Following admission to the unit, JI is treated empirically with trimethoprim-sulfamethoxazole (TMP/SMX) (Bactrim, Septra) intravenously. Supportive treatment includes oxygen therapy, fluids, and a transfusion of 2 units of packed red blood cells. The day following admission, JI undergoes a bronchoscopy that results in the diagnosis of *Pneumocystis carinii* pneumonia (PCP). He does well on therapy as evidenced by a decreased temperature and resolution of dyspnea when not receiving supplemental oxygen. However, approximately 6 days after admission, JI develops a diffuse, macular, erythematous rash that is attributed to the drug therapy. The TMP/SMX is discontinued, and JI is switched to pentamidine isethionate (Lomidine) intravenously. He continues to receive this drug for 3 more days and responds well. JI is discharged and will complete the full 21 days of therapy by receiving the pentamidine on a daily basis at home via a "heparin lock."

Discussion

This patient is in one of the high risk groups for developing HIV infection. A history of gonorrhea and hepatitis are indicative of past sexual activity, and a more detailed sexual history should be elicited to determine (1) if he has been exposed to other persons with HIV infection, (2) the types of sexual practices he engages in (with anal sex considered the least "safe"), and (3) his knowledge level regarding "safe sex" practices. The HIV status of his current partner may also be important, especially with regard to future teaching.

In addition to obtaining a sexual history, it is necessary to also screen the patient for any other risk factors for HIV infection, such as the receipt of blood or blood product transfusion, sexual activity in countries where widespread transmission of HIV occurs (such as Haiti, Africa), and/or intravenous drug abuse.

Dyspnea in an HIV infected host may be caused by several infectious agents, including *Cryptococcus neoformans*, *Mycobacterium avium* or *tuberculosis*, and cytomegalovirus. Other organisms, such as *Streptococcus pneumoniae* or *Hemophilus influenzae*, which are not considered opportunistic organisms, may cause pulmonary disease in HIV-infected patients. Herpes simplex virus, *Coccidiodes immitis*, *Histoplasma capsulatum*, other fungi, *Toxoplasma gondii*, cryptosporidium, and *Legionella* are identified occasionally as a cause of pneumonia. Other etiologies of dyspnea include invasive Kaposi's sarcoma, lymphoma, and non-specific, interstitial pneumonitis (when no pathogen is identified).

In addition to dyspnea, another manifestation of pulmonary problems may be a non-productive cough. (If a cough that is productive of purulent sputum is manifested, a pyogenic bacterial infection should be ruled out.) Systemic signs and symptoms include fever, weight loss, and malaise and may antedate or coincide with respiratory symptoms. Oral thrush is often present and is another clue indicative of weakened cell-mediated immunity. Malnutrition and anemia may also contribute to the subjective experience of dyspnea.

Pneumocystis carinii pneumonia (PCP) is an opportunistic infection and is the most common cause of respiratory disease in patients with AIDS. Because PCP is so common in this patient population, specific, empiric, antimicrobial therapy is usually initiated before more definitive and invasive diagnostic tests are conducted to determine the exact cause of interstitial infiltrates on chest x-ray examination. Induced sputum examination with special stains are performed in some institutions. If such examinations are not or can not be done, the next diagnostic step is usually fiberoptic bronchoscopy with transbronchial biopsy and/or bronchoalveolar lavage.

The drugs most commonly used for the treatment of pneumocystis pneumonia are TMP/SMX and pentamidine isethionate. Both have been found to be equally efficacious and do not differ in frequency of adverse reactions (Wharton, 1986). It is important to note, however, that side effect profiles differ, and depending on the patients' response to either drug, the alternative may be used.

Side effects associated with pentamidine therapy include pancytopenia (especially neutropenia), impaired renal function, and hypotension that may be sudden and severe after a single dose. Hypoglycemia has been associated with pancreatic islet cell necrosis, leading to inappropriately high, plasma insulin concentrations. Hyperglycemia and diabetes with or without preceding hypoglycemia have also occurred, sometimes several months after the initial therapy.

Pentamidine may also be given in an aerosolized form that appears to be less toxic since major organs affected during systemic therapy (bone marrow and kidneys) are bypassed. Administered in aerosol form, pentamidine may also prove to be an effective prophylactic therapy over the course of HIV infection.

In addition to TMP/SMX and pentamidine, several other drugs have been used with some success: difluoromethylornithane (DFMO), dapsone-trimethoprim, and pyrimethamine-sulfomethoxazole (Fansidar). One agent in particular, trimetrexate, has received a great deal of recent attention because of its low, side effect profile. Some researchers have concluded that, in combination with leucovorin, trimetrexate is "safe and effective for initial treatment of PCP . . . and for treatment of patients with intolerance or lack of response to standard therapies" (Allegra, 1987). This drug is currently in clinical trials.

In addition to antimicrobial therapy to directly eradicate the *Pneumocystis* infection, supportive care, including oxygen therapy, pulmonary hygiene, nutrition, fluids to combat dehydration, and transfusions to correct underlying anemia, are usually indicated. Corticosteroids have also been used with some success during the acute stages of illness to decrease the inflammatory process that accompanies pulmonary infestation with *Pneumocystis carinii*.

Nursing Diagnoses

1. Impaired gas exchange.
2. Activity intolerance related to dyspnea, anemia, wasting syndrome
3. Potential for infection
4. Fluid volume deficit related to fever, poor intake, hyperventilation, diaphoresis post fever, etc.
5. Anxiety related to dyspnea, new diagnosis, hospitalization, etc.
6. Sleep pattern disturbance related to dyspnea, anxiety, depression, etc.
7. Knowledge deficit related to AIDS and its implications

Allergy

An allergic condition is a pathophysiologic response of the immune system. Even among susceptible individuals, the pathophysiologic presentation of an allergic reaction differs remarkably, a phenomenon that in part may be a result of inherent circadian (daily) rhythms in susceptibility. Many asthmatic patients, for example, suffer acute attacks at night. The manifestation of allergy in susceptible individuals varies, ranging from chronic rhinitis (inflammation of the nasal cavities) and sinusitis to sudden death from acute anaphylactic shock. The symptoms of all allergic disorders are, nevertheless, related to the release of substances such as histamine and slow-reactive substance of anaphylaxis (SRS-A). These mediators are released primarily as a result of mast cell and basophil stimulation by an allergen. The discovery of the importance of immunoglobulin E (IgE) in the allergic response has opened up new areas in research and treatment of allergies. IgE is present in only tiny amounts in the blood, but this concentration is increased in allergic diseases such as hay fever and asthma.

Mechanism of IgE-produced allergy. The role of IgE in normal, nonallergic individuals is not clear, but it would be surprising that nature has allowed this gene-determined antibody to persist unless there was some selective advantage to it. It has been suggested that IgE and the immune allergic response it provokes in susceptible people is pathophysiologic in most societies. However, in present-day primitive tribes, as in humans' early ancestors, IgE plays a role in controlling parasitic, especially helminthic, infestations. This protective IgE-mediated reaction takes place mainly in the gut mucosa. An IgE reaction also results in the release of heparin from mast cells; heparin is involved in protection of the host against certain infections, snake venoms, and microbial metabolites. Thus atopic sensitivity is the bothersome expression of a potentially useful mechanism in certain environments. Humans as a species have not been freed from these types of parasitic and microbial threats long enough for natural selection mechanisms to operate in the elimination of the IgE reaction.

The term "atopy" implies a susceptibility to develop immediate hypersensitivity reactions, or allergies. Four factors are usually present in the atopic individual: (1) signs and symptoms, (2) a family history of atopy, (3) skin reactivity (usually a weal and flare) to injected allergens, and (4) eosinophilia. The atopic individual reacts to antigens in the environment by sensitization rather than immunization. Instead of producing an immune reaction that removes the antigen from the blood and tissues by an antigen-immunoglobulin G (IgG) complex, which can be phagocytosed or otherwise eliminated, the atopic individual continuously combines certain antigens, or allergens, with IgE, which is produced upon the first exposure to the allergen. This IgE then remains fixed to the membranes of basophils, which are leukocytes, and to mast cells, which are cells found along the walls of blood vessels and scattered throughout the tissues. Allergen attaches to this IgE upon subsequent exposure, and the cells respond by degranulation, or exocytosis of their large intracellular granules. The granules are believed to contain histamine, heparin, and other substances, and the degranulation process involves intracellular microtubules in a step that requires Ca^{++}. These mediators are then free to exert their effects. Histamine, for example, causes weal formation, itching, bronchoconstriction, and hypotension. SRS-A is also released during the degranulation process, although probably not from the granules per se. This mediator is believed to be the major substance in intrinsic asthma, and evidence suggests that it may also be released from polymorphonuclear leukocytes. SRS-A is produced in great quantities by lung mast cells during an allergic respiratory reaction, and it is a potent bronchoconstrictor, which could account for wheezing, the major pathophysiologic manifestation of asthma. Various prostaglandins are also released with SRS-A; their role was previously discussed. It is believed that during allergic reactions these compounds may sensitize nerve endings to bradykinin, thus causing itching and pain.

The molecular events surrounding degranulation of the mast cells (Fig. 2-17)

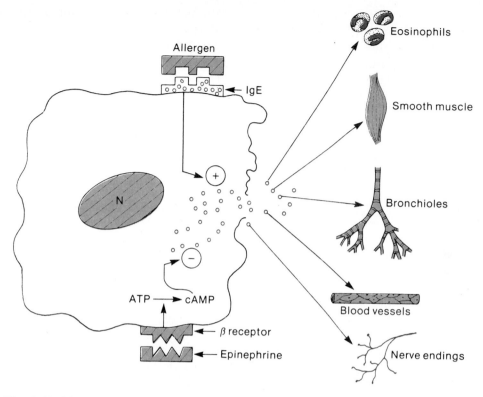

Fig. 2-17. Mast cell degranulation in allergy. Mast cell is target cell of allergen that combines with membrane-bound IgE and initates events in mast cell that lead to degranulation. Granules contain histamine, slow-reactive substance of anaphylaxis, and perhaps other mediators, which act on nerve endings, blood vessels, bronchiolar and other smooth muscle, and eosinophils. Effects produced on these targets cause allergic responses such as eczema and asthma. Epinephrine acts in an inhibitory manner on degranulation by stimulating cAMP formation.

and basophils have not been completely described, but evidence that cyclic AMP is involved has come from a number of sources. The target cells of the allergic reaction appear to have a number of different cell membrane receptors, one of which is a beta-adrenergic receptor for epinephrine. When epinephrine combines with the beta-receptor, there is a rise in cyclic AMP concentration and a subsequent block in degranulation. Thus a mode of action for epinephrine and other antiallergic agents in acute allergic reactions is suggested at

the cellular level, in addition to their well-known bronchodilator and vasoconstrictor effects. Cyclic AMP is the "second messenger" for a number of hormonal actions. It is converted from ATP by the action of membrane-bound adenyl cyclase, an enzyme that is activated by the "first messenger," which is the hormone. Cyclic AMP signals the cell that hormonal stimulation is present, and a variety of phenomena, depending on the hormone and other factors in the cellular environment, takes place. In the case of mast cells and basophils, activation of adenyl cyclase by epinephrine blocks degranulation. Binding of the IgE-allergen complex to the cell membrane conversely causes a fall in adenyl cyclase, which appears to be associated in an unknown manner with initiation of degranulation.

Histamine itself, which is released in large amounts from the mast cells and basophils, may exert an autoregulatory influence on the degranulation process by acting in a negative feedback manner on these cells, inhibiting degranulation, when present in sufficient quantities. Histamine cell membrane receptors may exist on these cells.

Mast cells and basophils also release a substance that is chemotactic for eosinophils, and eosinophilia is a characteristic of atopy. This substance (ECF-A, eosinophil chemotactic factor in anaphylaxis) not only attracts eosinophils but also causes these cells to release the enzyme aryl sulfatase, which inactivates SRS-A. Other factors present in eosinophils may inhibit histamine release and function. Eosinophils then are thought to act as a "switch off" mechanism to the acute hypersensitivity response of allergen and IgE. Eosinophils are also mildly phagocytic, and their true function in allergy is just being discovered. They are increased in concentration in the blood of individuals with parasitic, particularly helminthic, infestations. This is an interesting corollary to the role of the IgE response to helminthic infections, which was previously described.

Theories of atopy. While the basic mechanism of atopy is the combining of particular antigens to IgE, it is not at all clear why certain individuals are more prone to atopy than others. About 20% of the United States population suffers from some form of allergy. Four major theories of atopy are presently being investigated.

The first theory is that susceptible individuals are more prone to produce skin-sensitizing antibodies of the IgE type in response to repeated low doses of antigens. The second theory suggests that the atopic individual has an intrinsic enzyme deficiency or defect such that antigens that penetrate the body barriers are retained for longer periods than in normal people, and there is increased antibody formation in response. The third theory suggests that there is an enhanced reactivity to the mediators that are released from mast cells and basophils during an IgE-mediated reaction. The fourth theory implicates the local defenses of the body, suggesting that an increased concentration of antigen is absorbed into the body across mucous membranes.

It is possible that no single theory will be found to encompass all possible atopic reactions. The mechanisms involved in asthma, for example, appear to be somewhat different from those involved in allergic atopic dermatitis or eczema. There is some evidence to suggest that atopic individuals respond to antigens by secreting IgE, while the normal individual produces protective types of antibodies, such as immunoglobulin A (IgA) and IgG. Others believe that everyone has the possibility of developing atopy, but there is a genetically programmed threshold of antigen for each person, above which an allergic reaction will ensue. Another possibility is that the atopic response results from a primary deficiency in the IgA system, which then causes an overstimulation of the IgE antibodies. Furthermore, it has been shown that IgG antibodies play some role in the regulation of the IgE response, as IgE falls when IgG rises, so that the primary defect may rest in the gamma globulins. The thymus may be involved as well in IgE regulation.

Whatever theory is finally accepted,

medical management of atopy will always focus on prevention of damaging symptoms, such as wheezing, skin rashes, swelling, and hay fever.

Treatment rationale. Common allergens for those who are atopic include pollens, certain foods, drugs, dust, insect venoms, molds, and animal dander. The most common allergic condition, hay fever, affects 20 million persons in the United States. It has an hereditary background in that at least the susceptibility to hay fever is apparent within families. Hay fever is seasonal, being most related to the environmental concentration of ragweed pollen. Treatment of hay fever involves the careful administration of antihistaminic drugs, which compete with histamine for specific cell membrane receptors, displacing the histamine molecule and preventing its action. Another approach to severe allergy, including hay fever, is immunotherapy. The individual is desensitized to the allergen by repeated injections of minute amounts of ragweed pollen extract. The antigen present in the extract causes the development of specific IgG over time, which can then function as a "blocking" antibody to the IgE-allergen combination, preventing target cell degranulation. Suppressor T cells may also be stimulated during long-term immunotherapy.

Although hay fever, with its accompanying swollen nasopharyngeal mucosa, rhinitis, sinusitis, headache, and general malaise, is the purest model of immunologic allergy, three other conditions, which are in reality complex disorders, serve as good models of allergic processes: atopic dermatitis, asthma, and anaphylaxis.

Atopic dermatitis. Atopic dermatitis is allergic in nature and is caused by environmental allergens that are either ingested or inhaled. Most infantile eczema can be classified this way, but the condition can develop at any time in life. Lesions are often located in the skin creases and folds, on the face, genitalia, and antecubital and popliteal areas. They are scaly, dry, itchy lesions, which can be either nummular or diffuse. These lesions are susceptible to superinfection, particularly with vaccinia virus, herpes, and bacteria such as *Staphylococcus*. In infants, widespread, disseminated, infected skin lesions can develop after a smallpox vaccination, and the disease that results can be serious enough to cause death.

Although allergic mechanisms are known to operate in the development of atopic dermatitis, it is certainly possible that contributory factors play just as important a role. For example, the atopic individual often perspires more than normal, and the sweat is less able to solubilize oil. The skin is often very dry as well. These factors may combine to produce a state in which the sebaceous glands become plugged with oil, resulting in local areas of skin breakdown at which eczematous lesions arise. Wool is extremely irritating to the skin of the atopic individual and provokes the typical lesions of atopic dermatitis. The increased incidence of exacerbations of the disease in the winter months is thought to be caused both by dryness of heated indoor spaces and the heavy clothing required in the colder months.

Eczema that develops in infancy often follows an irregular course characterized by periods of quiescence and then sudden flare-ups, which are thought to occasionally be caused by emotional stress. In up to half of those children with persistent childhood eczema, respiratory manifestations of allergy develop later in childhood and adolescence.

The penetrance of the genetic factors that control atopy are probably greatly influenced by environmental factors. For example, avoidance of certain notorious allergens in early infancy, such as chocolate, eggs, and even cow's milk, may prevent both skin and respiratory manifestations in the potentially atopic individual. An autosomal dominant gene or groups of genes with weak penetrance are postulated in most cases. There is evidence that the X chromosome carries these genes, which influence IgE synthesis. There is also further evidence of genetic factors as the atopic individual has increased levels of certain histocompatibility antigens, primarily HLA-3 and HLA-9. The general association of autoantigens and disease will be discussed later in this chapter. It should be mentioned that contact dermatitis caused by chemical irritants can be atopic.

Asthma. Asthma is either extrinsic (caused by factors outside the body) or intrinsic in nature. More than half of the adults with asthma wheeze in response to intrinsic factors, usually mediated by the autonomic nervous system. Excessive parasympathetic activity may be caused by laughing, sneezing, coughing, or exposure to cold air. Efferent parasympathetic fibers release acetylcholine, which initiates bronchospasm in susceptible people. The attacks are often more severe than those seen in allergic asthma. The etiology is speculated to be either an increased sensitivity to acetylcholine or the result of partial beta-adrenergic blockade or increased alpha-adrenergic stimulation.

Allergic asthma is based on the allergen-IgE reaction and will be described in the next section. Evidence is accumulating to implicate various neurologic factors also in this type of asthma. The role of personality has been difficult to document, although there is a tendency for some asthma patients to be dependent and to use their condition for secondary gain. There are many stories of asthma patients wheezing in response to fake or imagined substances. For example, patients allergic to flowers may wheeze when exposed to an artificial flower. One quarter of asthmatics wheeze in response to injections of normal saline, when they believe that the injection contains allergens. Conditioned learning of allergic response has been shown in experimental animals. For example, guinea pigs reacted to an odor alone by allergic manifestations when they had been conditioned by previous pairing of the odor with an allergen. There is undoubtedly a reactivity to stress in asthmatics, but the relationship is not well understood.

Infectious asthma is particularly common in children. Many infants and children respond to upper respiratory infections by wheezing, but it would be a serious misnomer to label these children as asthmatics. The bronchospasms that occur in infection may be the responses to bacterial antigens, and some viruses (respiratory syncytial virus) appear to cause increased respiratory tract cell-bound IgE.

Atopic asthma. Atopic asthma is a respiratory distress disorder manifested within minutes after a second or subsequent exposure to a particular allergen. It is characterized by bronchial and bronchiolar constriction, which leads to acute dyspnea in which expiratory stridor or wheezing is the major sign. SRS-A and histamine are thought to cause vasodilation, subsequent edema, and bronchoconstriction, producing symptoms of wheezing, itching, sneezing, and coughing. Bronchospasm, increased secretions and accumulation of secretions, aggravates the asthmatic attack.

The first exposure to the offending allergen usually is not noticeable, as it results only in sensitization of the individual. This process causes the immune system to be stimulated to secrete IgE antibodies, which will rise in titer over time, and when the second exposure occurs, the IgE is then available to combine with the allergen and cause the classic allergic response just discussed. Asthma in children is usually atopic in nature, but adults may have intrinsic or infectious asthma, which may not be accompanied by an elevation of serum IgE. The individual with allergic asthma nature exhibits the four major signs of atopy (see p. 58) in contrast to those with infectious or intrinsic asthma. The atopic reaction is localized to the respiratory tree and occurs in response to inhalants or ingested allergens. Allergens to which the atopic individual is hypersensitive may be determined by skin testing and thus avoided if possible. Generally, however, an atopic individual is allergic to many different substances, and the number of possible allergens tends to increase as the individual gets older.

Delineation of the underlying pathophysiology of intrinsic asthma, in which no allergen can be found, is more difficult. It has been suggested that under normal circumstances SRS-A and histamine may function to maintain normal respiratory tree muscle tone, and their effects may be held in check by epinephrine, as discussed previously in terms of cell membrane control of adenyl cyclase in mast cell degranulation. If the beta-adrenergic receptor response was inadequate, epinephrine regulation would be lost, and all the signs and symptoms of atopic asthma would be present in the nonatopic individual. This is the beta-blockade theory of intrinsic asthma, and there is good experimental support for this theory. Intrinsic asthma is characterized by hyperreactivity of the bronchial muscle tone.

Treatment rationale. An acute asthmatic attack is serious and requires medical intervention. The aim of therapy is prevention of the effects of the mediators respon-sible for the symptoms. Thus epinephrine or drugs that mimic epinephrine are usually given. Aminophylline, for example, is a bronchodilator that is thought to inhibit the enzyme that breaks down cyclic AMP, which then inhibits degranulation. Various inhalant sprays are also available so that the asthmatic may be able to control an impending attack through bronchodilation. Another aspect of therapy for the asthmatic is identification of the allergen(s) by skin testing and desensitization. The results of desensitization are often questionable, but research into the chemistry and ultimate purification of antigenic material may eventually result in effective prophylaxis against asthma and other atopic reactions. Another possible area of treatment may result from research into the role of the central nervous system in asthma, as it has been shown that there is interplay of nervous as well as hormonal and cellular aspects in the bronchospasm of acute asthmatic wheezing. Biofeedback, hypnosis, relaxation, and other mind–body approaches are gaining recognition as an important adjunct to asthma therapy.

Anaphylaxis. The most dramatic and life threatening of all allergic manifestations is anaphylactic shock. This results from the second or subsequent exposure to an allergen, usually in an individual known to be atopic. Common allergens that promote the attack are drugs, particularly penicillin, and insect venoms. Within minutes after exposure to the allergens, the individual becomes acutely ill, experiencing profound bronchoconstriction and vasodilation. The latter may be so severe as to result in shock characterized by decreasing cardiac output and falling blood pressure. There may or may not be skin urticaria, or "hives," which are skin manifestations of the IgE-allergen reaction. The mechanisms of anaphylaxis do not differ from those already described in asthma and atopic dermatitis. The manifestation of the allergic reaction is just much more immediate and severe, and treatment is aimed at life-saving restoration of vasomotor tone and bronchial tree patency.

Clinical ecology. In recent years a field of specialization dealing with allergy, clinical ecology, has arisen. The foundation for this field is the belief that environmental chemicals and most man-made materials, foods, and chemicals have the ability under certain circumstances of provoking immune system destruction, allergic responses, or autoimmune disease. An example of such an alleged chemical that has received much attention is dioxin. Dioxin was a contaminant of Agent Orange, a defoliant used in Vietnam. Other populations in the United States have been accidentally exposed to this chemical. Clinical ecologists point out immune cell disturbances in exposed populations. An extreme case of immune system disturbance from chemicals in the environment are those few individuals who appear to have acquired hypersensitivity to nearly all man-made matter and must live in highly protected environments. Whether allergy can occur to this extreme and whether the immune system is susceptible to this kind of environmental perturbation is yet to be determined.

Immune complex disease

This category of immune system diseases includes serum sickness, systemic lupus erythematosus, and certain forms of glomerulonephritis. The diseases are associated with a precipitation reaction to a foreign protein and deposition of antigen-antibody complexes in the blood, kidney, and other organs to a sufficient degree that symptoms result. There is a typical allergic component to the disease, except that the reaction, which is characterized by hives or skin rashes, edema, fever, and joint pains, usually does not appear for 7 to 10 days. The most common cause of serum sickness is the injection of bovine or horse antitoxins or penicillin, particularly of the long-acting type.

The systemic inflammatory nature of serum sickness is interesting. Aside from the deposition of immune complexes in joints, blood vessels, kidneys, and the heart, activation of complement also occurs in serum sickness. Complement activation is sufficient to produce the pathophysiologic alterations that result in tissue damage. A variety of possible processes could interact to cause the inflammation and necrosis associated with immune complex disease. Platelet aggregation is induced by the collection of immune complexes and complement along the blood vessel walls. Platelets are then stimulated to release vasoactive amines such as serotonin and histamine. Furthermore, coagulation may occur as the result of the platelet aggregation. Activation of platelet histamine and serotonin release can also be accomplished by the action of *anaphylatoxins,* which are released during the activation of the complement system. It has recently been realized that anaphylatoxins play an important role in the tissue destruction so often associated with inflammation. They are thought to be released as fragments of C3 and C5 and are therefore known as C3a and C5a. These mediators are 10 times more potent than bradykinin, and thus their role in inflammation should be appreciated. Their biologic activity includes histamine release from basophils and mast cells, although the mechanism is not known; smooth muscle contraction; leukotaxis, particularly for neutrophils, eosinophils, and monocytes; and stimulation of the release of lysosomal enzymes from human neutrophils. The action of complement and the production of anaphylatoxins, along with the mechanical effects of immune complex formation and deposition, are probably sufficient to cause the pathophysiologic alterations associated with immune complex disease.

Autoimmunity

The development of tolerance to self-antigens is believed to occur very early in embryonic life, although the basic mechanisms by which this occurs have not been completely described. It is obvious that individuals tolerate their own cells and tissues. When autoantibodies arise, a pathophysiologic process ensues that impairs function and ultimately destroys the individual's own cells.

Some examples of diseases considered to be primarily autoimmune in nature include systemic lupus erythematosus (SLE), Hashimoto's thyroiditis, autoimmune hemolytic anemia, juvenile diabetes, rheumatoid arthritis, and myasthenia gravis.

The basic pathophysiology involves the production of autoantibodies to DNA, RNA, red blood cell membrane, platelets, muscle cells, gamma globulin, thyroglobulin, and brain tissue. These autoantibodies can be formed in the blood and tissues. Complexing of these autoantibodies to self-antigens results in several manifestations, depending on which type of antigen-antibody reaction occurs and which tissues are involved. Hemolysis of red blood cells occurs when the autoantibody-antigen reaction occurs on the surface of the erythrocyte. Thrombocytopenia may result if this occurs on the surface of the platelet. Chronic thyroiditis develops when the autoantibody reacts against thyroglobulin.

Self-tolerance

To understand the development of autoimmune disease, the normal development of self-tolerance should be reviewed. This is a complex and theoretic area of research. Several possible mechanisms for the development of self-tolerance have been suggested. One theory, originally put forth by Burnet, is the *forbidden clone theory*, which explains tolerance on the basis of events in early embryonic life that destroy or inactivate any lymphocytes that produce immunoglobulins against or are capable of reacting with self-antigens. Thus self-antigens are permitted to exist within the adult. This is the classic theory of self-tolerance, and while there is much experimental evidence to support it, there are also conflicting findings in the literature. It is clear, however, that self-tolerance develops during embryonic and early neonatal life, and foreign antigens that are presented to the fetus can "fool" the primitive immune system so that they are subsequently treated as self-antigens by the adult immune system. When the animal is exposed to the same antigen later in life it does not produce antibodies against it.

It has been shown that the T cell system is extremely important in the development of self-tolerance. Long-lived T suppressor cells, which are capable of inhibiting B cell production of immunoglobulins, particularly IgG, are thought to be produced during early life.

Other mechanisms of immune inhibition include the production of blocking factors, which are known to exist in the serum and are probably complexes of antigen and antibody. They may compete for membrane receptors on immune cells and thus suppress certain immune responses. Their presence and the presence of unblocking factors are suggested to be important in carcinogenesis as well. These suppressive and inhibitory phenomena are thought to involve mainly cell-bound antigen reactions.

Soluble antigens in the blood and other body fluids are also recognized as self-antigens in the normal individual. Two types of tolerance may develop in response to soluble antigens injected into experimental animals, and these same types may also occur in the development of self-tolerance during the ontogeny of the immune system. These are low-dose and high-dose tolerances, both of which are mediated by the cells of the immune system.

Low-dose tolerance appears to involve only the T cells, but both T and B cells are implicated in the development of high-dose tolerance. It has been observed that when antigens are injected they are sometimes immunogenic only within a narrow dose range. Repeated injections of low doses of soluble antigenic material or administration of very high doses induces a tolerant state, such that no specific antibodies are produced in response to subsequent injection of the antigen. The low-dose effect is thought to result from the elimination of T helper cells so that specific immunoglobulin production by B cells is inhibited. Low doses of certain antigens also result in small amounts of IgG being produced, which is thought then to act in a negative feedback manner on the production of further specific IgG. It is possible too that low doses of certain antigens may not be sufficient to produce a significant immunoglobulin production stimulation.

High doses, on the other hand, may result in paralysis of both T and B cells and may form aggregates in the body fluids, which then are not able to bind with receptors and initiate an antibody response. High-dose tolerance is often characterized by the presence of antigen in the serum, which is continually being removed by an-

tibody. In some cases the tolerance is reversible once the antigen is eliminated by the body. It is believed that the affinity of lymphocyte receptors for different antigens may be important in low- and high-dose tolerance. Lymphocytes with high-affinity receptors are more easily stimulated by low concentrations of antigen than are lymphocytes with low-affinity receptors, but they can be inactivated by extremely high doses of antigen. In self-tolerance the lymphocytes with high-affinity receptors to self-antigens may be eliminated or inactivated, while the low-affinity lymphocytes may actually persist. Certain high-dose tolerance to a protein such as serum albumin (normal value 40 mg/ml) can be understood in this framework as a high-dose switch off. Low-dose tolerance to a protein such as thyroglobulin, which is present in the minute concentration of 100 ng/ml, can also be explained in terms of elimination of T helper cells.

Theories of autoimmunity. Autoimmune diseases are those in which the immune system turns against self-antigens in an overwhelming and destructive way, a process of heightened recognition. This occurs through the production of autoantibodies and possibly cytotoxic T cells. To understand this process, it is necessary to explore how in health the normal self-antigens are tolerated by the immune system. All human cells have protein membrane antigens on their surfaces, which are immunologic markers. These antigens also provide other discrete functions. Transplantation antigens, for example, are matched by identifying a system of membrane antigens known as the major histocompatibility complex (MHC) class I antigens. If there is sufficient compatibility between donor and recipient, then rejection of the transplanted tissue cells will be less profound than if the antigens were completely dissimilar. Genetically, only identical twins would produce a perfect match of these cellular antigens, but the chance of good compatibility increases between family members and close relatives. Nevertheless, even when compatibility is very good, transplant patients usually receive immunosuppressive drugs throughout life to dampen the immune rejection of these foreign antigens.

Why is it then that people do not produce antibodies against self? The phenomenon of "clonal anergy" may produce the suppression of anti-self B cells during embryonic development. This is a kind of paralysis of immune cells when they are exposed to very large amounts of antigen. The cells are then nonresponsive to antigen when they are exposed later in life. However, the cells still exist throughout life and could theoretically be provoked under certain circumstances to release self-immunoglobulins. Suppressor T cells are also known to be capable of inhibiting anti-self B cell clones.

Another mechanism of autoimmunity is the production of self-antibodies after tissue damage. When significant tissue damage occurs, such as after a myocardial infarction, normally hidden self-antigens are released from the heart muscle and the immune system reacts to them, becoming stimulated to produce antiheart immunoglobulins. A modification of this process occurs after a vasectomy. Sperm are absorbed into the bloodstream since the usual route for loss is now absent. There is no self-tolerance at all for these sperm antigens, and so antisperm antibodies are produced. Brain tissue also shares these characteristics with heart and sperm. Further research has indicated people actually do have low-level titers of low-affinity autoantibodies, including antiDNA immunoglobulin, which apparently are not harmful. Some have a physiologic function. Old red blood cells become

coated with anti-RBC immunoglobulins and this then marks them for phagocytosis by the cells of the spleen. While anti-self B cells may be present, much less T cell activity appears. Another consideration, when examining the possible causes of autoimmune diseases, is to recognize the phenomenon of cross-reactivity. Viral and bacterial antigens may fool the immune system of the infected person, because they may be structurally similar to self-antigens, and the immunoglobulins specific to them may also react with self-antigens. Thus autoimmune disease could result from exposure of masses of sequestered self-antigens through tissue injury, by production of excessive autoantibodies, or by cross-reactivity. Virus might also produce autoimmunity by producing excessive expression of sequestered cell antigen through the process of viral cell membrane budding.

An important theory of immune regulation was first proposed by Jerne (1974). According to this network theory, idiotypes (Ab0), which are the unique antigenic determinants of a molecule (Colvin and Olsen, 1985), produce the initial antibody response (Ab1). However, the Ab1 also contains particular idiotypes, and thus a second wave of immune response occurs producing anti-idiotype antibodies (Ab2). (This implies the production of immunoglobulin to immunoglobulin, a common phenomenon in autoimmune disease.) The effect of Ab2 would be to suppress the function of Ab1 and thus down regulate the system of immune responsiveness. The next obvious step would be the production of anti–anti-idiotype antibodies (Ab3) to act against Ab2, and so forth (Ab4, Ab5, etc.). Ab3 appears to act and look like Ab1, thus providing a circular control loop (Fig. 2-18). Cytotoxic T cells reacting against idiotype would also be a part of this model, producing immunity. Tolerance to

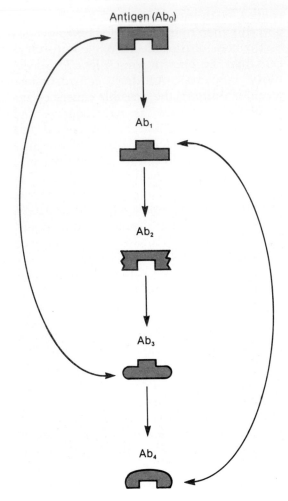

Antigen (Ab$_0$)

Ab$_1$

Ab$_2$

Ab$_3$

Ab$_4$

Fig. 2-18. The network theory of idiotypes and anti-idiotypes.

stimulate antibody production further. Normally self-antigens are somehow silent and do not provoke immune response. If mutations occur in the idiotype region of the self-antigen, the result would be an escalating production of anti-idiotype immunoglobulins. (Suciu-Foca et al., 1985). This theory thus suggests that autoimmune diseases occur as a result of mutations of the genes which code for self-antigens and that these antigens function as initial idiotypes for an escalating cascade of anti-idiotypes.

General features of autoimmunity. Autoimmune diseases share some characteristics. There is an increased incidence with aging, possibly from a senescent decline of immunocompetence. These diseases also have an apparent genetic basis, sometimes running in families and appearing more frequently in females. There is an association of HLA antigens with the appearance of autoimmune diseases. This is a striking association, with more than 87% of people afflicted with ankylosing spondylitis and 37% of those with Reiter's disease carrying the B27 antigen (Cruse and Lewis, 1985).

There is a frequent association of viral infection and the appearance of symptoms, which may be a result of expression of normally sequestered self-antigens by viral infection, complexing of virus with cell surface antigens and increasing their antigenicity, or a nonspecific activation of the immune system, resulting in expansion of many B cell clones, including autoantibody-producing clones.

There are some drugs capable of producing autoimmune disease (hydantoin, hydralazine, procainamide, and alpha-methyldopa), but features of the disease vary.

Autoimmune diseases may have widespread effects on all types of cells and tissues (systemic lupus erythematosus [SLE]) or may be largely confined to a single or-

idiotype, on the other hand, might be produced by production of a population of anti-idiotype suppressor T cells. In this network model, all of immune interaction would be based on networks of idiotype and anti-idiotype immunoglobulins and T cells. Autoimmune disease is conceived of as arising from production of anti-idiotype autoantibodies. Note in Fig. 2-18 that Ab2 conformationally is similar to the original antigen and thus could perhaps weakly

Table 2-4. Major autoimmune diseases

Disease	Possible etiologic characteristics
Class A	
Systemic lupus erythematosus	Autoantibodies against altered self-antigens; atypical response to normal self-antigens
Autoimmune thyroiditis	
Rheumatoid arthritis	
Myasthenia gravis	
Type I diabetes mellitus	
Class B	
Rheumatic fever	Cross-reacting antigens
Glomerulonephritis	
Class C	
Hereditary angioedema	Excessive complement activation
Class D	
Encephalomyelitis	Defective immune response to a specific exogenous agent

Adapted from Smith and Steinberg, 1983.

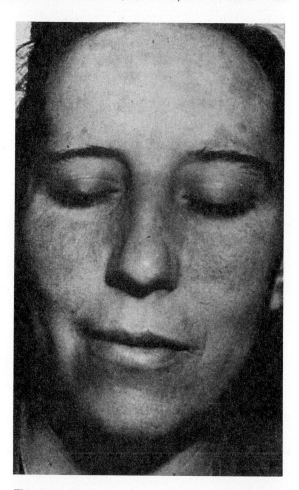

Fig. 2-19. "Butterfly" rash of SLE. Skin manifestations, including butterfly-shaped rash over cheeks and nose, are extremely common in SLE.
(Courtesy Department of Pathology, University of Tennessee, Memphis.)

gan (Type I diabetes). Autoantibodies to both intracellular and extracellular components may be produced. Many autoimmune diseases produce immune complexes, aggregates of antigen and antibody, which are capable of causing complement activation and inflammatory reactions. Tissue damage may occur in the target organ or may be widespread, resulting in vasculitis or dermatologic manifestations. Table 2-4 lists the major autoimmune diseases.

Models of autoimmune disease

Systemic lupus erythematosus. Systemic lupus erythematosus, rheumatoid arthritis, and myasthenia gravis will be discussed as models of autoimmune disease. Systemic lupus erythematosus (SLE) is primarily a disorder of young women, and in many cases it is associated with a sun-sensitive butterfly-shaped rash on the nose and cheeks, the sign of the "red wolf" (lupus erythematosus) (Fig. 2-19). This rash is but one of many possible manifestations of the basic pathophysiology. Although the disease is autoimmune in nature, it can also be considered an immune complex disorder. Deposition of complexes of autoantibodies and self-antigens in tissues such as the kidneys, joints, blood vessels, and central nervous system occurs.

Central to the diagnosis of SLE is the presence of LE cells (Fig. 2-20). LE cells are neutrophils containing one or more LE bodies, structures that may occasionally be found free in the blood as well. The LE body is formed from anti-DNA antibody to the IgG class of immunoglobulins. Thus the immune system is activating an autoantibody against its own nucleoprotein, forming a structure that the phagocytes of the blood attempt to remove, as evidenced by LE cells. These immune complexes cannot be totally removed from the blood by phagocytosis, and they cause an immune complex disease pattern. SLE is associated with the presence of autoantibodies of all types. The antigenic stimulus for the development of these autoantibodies is not known, but many investigators have suggested that a viral infection may precede and cause SLE. A disease that is likely viral in a specific strain of mice appears to be identical to SLE in humans. Furthermore, viral-antiviral complexes have been identified in the cytoplasm of glomerular endothelial cells from SLE patients. Certain drugs are also known to induce an SLE-like syndrome, which is usually reversible when the drug is withdrawn. Procainamide in particular has been implicated in the development of serologic abnormalities usually found only in SLE.

The virus or the drug that might cause SLE could act by altering self-antigens and thus provoking the production of autoantibodies. The virus could also presumably act by antigenically combining to antibodies, attaching to cells, at which site the immune reaction then causes cell lysis and release of intracellular constituents, which react with autoantibodies. The production of self-antigen–autoantibody complexes would then ensue, causing immune

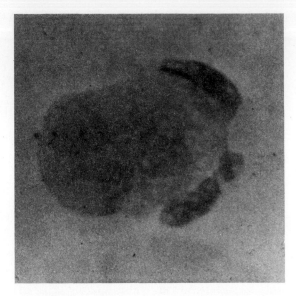

Fig. 2-20. LE cells, which contain inclusions and abnormal nuclei, are found in SLE. They are considered evidence of an autoimmune pathogenesis.
(Courtesy Department of Pathology, University of Tennessee, Memphis.)

complex deposition, complement activation, cell destruction, and lesion formation. Thus SLE results in inflammation and necrosis throughout the body. Another theory of pathogenesis of SLE suggests that T suppressor cells, which normally suppress clones of B-lymphocytes capable of reacting with self-antigens, are inactivated. It has been reported that patients with SLE have a decreased number of T cells and an increased number of null cells. Also present in SLE serum is a substance toxic to lymphocytes. These factors may then contribute to a depletion in available T suppressor cells and allow B-lymphocytes to recognize and react with self-antigens, causing an autoimmune disorder. The disease is characterized by B cell hyperactivity.

The autoantibodies found in SLE include antibodies to nucleoprotein, cell cy-

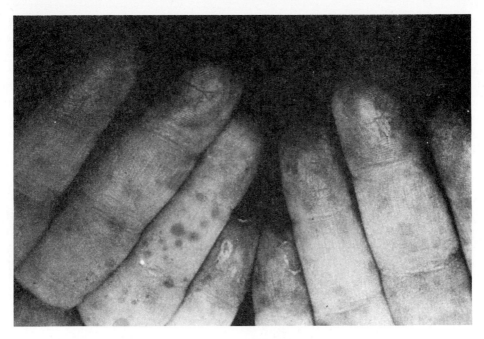

Fig. 2-21. SLE rash. Skin lesions on fingers of patient with SLE.
(Courtesy Department of Pathology, University of Tennessee, Memphis.)

toplasmic protein, red blood cell and platelet membranes, and plasma proteins, including some of the factors involved in the coagulation cascade. The deposition of the immune complexes formed by the reaction of these various autoantibodies with self-antigens and the diverse number and nature of the autoantibodies lead to the major characteristic of SLE—its protean nature and course. This has led to the name "the great imitator," for many tissues of the body may be involved, and the course is generally characterized by remissions and exacerbations. Often SLE is not diagnosed for years, because the signs and symptoms may be vague in the early stages of the disease. Only when renal and cardiovascular involvement becomes severe is the disease recognized. The presence of rheumatoid factors and LE cells is then determined, and treatment is insti-

tuted. Much of the serious pathophysiology that develops in these patients can be related to the deposition of immune complexes in the renal glomeruli and blood vessels. In this regard SLE greatly resembles serum sickness. Serum complement levels are decreased during the acute stages of the disease, suggesting that complement has been used up in the development of the lesions in susceptible tissues.

SLE affects many different organs and tissues and causes serious pathophysiologic interruptions in mobility, oxygenation, and elimination through involvement of the joints, kidneys, heart, and serous membranes throughout the body. Skin involvement occurs in 80% of the patients but in most cases is not disfiguring (Fig. 2-21). One remarkable aspect of the skin involvement is the photoreactive nature of the skin rash. Exposure to sunlight often precipitates the development of the typical SLE rash. The rash may develop into discoid rashes, which are elevated erythematous patches that can occur anywhere on the body.

Involvement of the heart and blood vessels is extremely common. Blood vessels of involved organs are usually inflamed (acute vasculitis), which appears to be caused by immune complex deposition and activation of complement. Occasionally this will proceed to necrosis and scarring, with great damage to the hypoxic organ occurring over time. Renal failure is the major cause of death in SLE and results from glomerulonephritis, which ultimately arises from capillary necrosis caused by immune complex deposition. The heart is involved in about 50% of SLE cases and shows signs of lesion formation, resulting in small growths on the valves and endocardium. The inflammation may subsequently produce scar formation. The vessels of the heart may be involved as well, and cardiac signs and symptoms may become severe as the disease progresses. Serous membranes such as the pleura and pericardium can be involved, with exudation and effusion causing symptoms. Joint involvement is common but unlike rheumatoid arthritis is not associated with great pain and deformity. The synovial membranes of the joint capsules are most particularly affected.

Neuropsychiatric symptoms are present in 33% to 76%, and include depression, psychoses, confusion, seizures, and cranial nerve symptoms (Grade and Zegans, 1986).

The general course of SLE is variable, and treatment is based on the stage of the disease and the severity of organ involvement. Generally the corticosteroids form the major arsenal against SLE, and immunosuppressive drugs are also used. Rest and relaxation is often advised. Since stress is often cited as a precipitant of SLE symptoms, SLE is considered by some as a model for mind-body interactions (Grade and Zegans, 1986). Newer strategies for SLE might include psychoneuroimmunological strategies such as biofeedback, imagery, visualization, and hypnosis. Mice have been manipulated by conditioned response paradigms, and a strain with lupus was able to reduce their symptoms. These New Zealand Black mice had significantly decreased proteinuria and mortality when conditioned to respond to injections of saccharine as if they were receiving cyclophosphamide (an immunosuppressant drug) (Ader and Cohen, 1982).

The following case study illustrates some typical clinical features of SLE.

CASE STUDY: SYSTEMIC LUPUS ERYTHEMATOSIS

History

HV is a 28-year-old white female, diagnosed with systemic lupus erythematosis (SLE) 6 years ago, after having been symptomatic for approximately 4 years. Her symptoms consisted of skin lesions, and for this reason she avoided the sun. She presently has no exacerbation of skin lesions, other than some rash on the nasal bridge. She stated that approximately 1 year ago she noticed marked hair loss, which has since grown back. She also has had a long-standing history of low back and left-sided hip pain with numbness extending down the lateral aspect of her leg into her foot. The pain is worse when she sits. Her last ophthalmologic examination was 7 months ago and was normal. She has also had a history of depression and has been on 75 mg amitriptyline hydrochloride (Elavil) but stated that it makes

Contributed by Ingrid Stram Doll.

her drowsy. Her medications include 15 mg prednisone per day, taken in one dose. She has in the past taken alternating daily doses of 10 and 15 mg daily, but on this regimen she had a flare-up of arthritic pain and skin lesions. She was also treated in the past with hydroxychloroquine sulfate (Plaquenil Sulfate), 200 mg per day. Her back pain had been controlled with naproxen (Naprosyn) initially, but it did not relieve the pain, so she was switched to 800 mg ibuprofen three times a day. She had heartburn with this and doesn't get much pain relief. She also has a history of intravenous cocaine use and has attempted suicide, although she presently denies any suicidal ideation. She smokes a quarter pack of cigarettes a day, denies alcohol use, and has no known allergies. She states her last antinuclear antibody (ANA) was 1:320. She is a gravida I para I and had a C-section 9 years ago. The family history is noncontributory.

Medications:

Ibuprofen (Motrin) 800 mg three times a day

Prednisone 15 mg each day

Subjective and Objective Data

Physical examination
  Weight: 172
  Pulse rate: 84
  Blood pressure: 130/80
  Respiratory rate: 20
  Temperature: (not taken)
  General: Moderately obese female in no acute distress.
  Head: Normal; no areas of balding
  Ears: Normal; there is a small patch of eczematoid rash or discoid lupus on the tragus of the right ear
  Nose: Clear
  Oropharynx: Significant for a white-coated tongue, showing hyphae on microscopic examination; no other oral lesions.
  Eyes: Pupils equally reactive to light and accommodation; fundi normal in appearance; there are areas of scarring over both cheeks and a lupus-like rash over the bridge of the nose
  Neck: Supple without lymphadenopathy, thyromegaly, jugular venous distention
  Chest: Clear bilaterally
  Heart: Regular rate and rhythm without murmur; S1 and S2 are normal
  Breasts: Nontender; no masses, nipple discharge, or lesions
  Abdomen: No organomegaly; bowel sounds normally active all quadrants; no masses or tenderness
  Back: Spine midline; tender to palpation over the 5th lumbar spine and the left sacroiliac joint; sciatic notch is slightly tender; no CVA tenderness
  Extremities: No clubbing, cyanosis, or edema; distal circulation appears intact without signs of digital ischemia or thrombosis; no rashes are noted
  Neurologic examination: DTRs 1 to 2 +/ 4, symmetrical; cranial nerves are grossly intact, and Babinski is negative
Laboratory findings
  Sedimentation rate: 22 (elevated) and ANA titer positive; LE prep positive
  WBC: 6.6×10^3
  Segs: 82%
  Bands: 1%
  Lymphs: 15%
  Monos: 2%
Assessment
1. SLE
2. Oral thrush
3. Depression

Pathophysiology

SLE is a chronic inflammatory disease of unknown origin that affects many different organs. The clinical manifestations include fever, an erythematous rash, polyarthralgia and arthritis, pleurisy and pericarditis, anemia, thrombocytopenia and renal, neurologic, and cardiac abnormalities. SLE has a strong predilection for women, especially adolescents and young adults; females are affected about eight times as often as males. The disease affects all races, with a rate in the United States for black females nearly three times that for white females. The disease can be fulminating and rapidly fatal. In most cases the course is chronic and irregular with episodes of activity interspersed with long periods of near complete remission. Although SLE may exist in a mild form, some patients eventually die from vascular lesions affecting the kidneys or central nervous system, whereas others die of complicating secondary infections. The pathogenesis of SLE is deposition of immune complexes consisting in part of DNA, anti-DNA (IgG), and complement components. These deposits occur in the basement membrane of the kidney, blood vessels of the spleen, heart, lung, liver, choroid plexus of the central nervous system, and dermoepidermal junction of the skin. These deposits make SLE an autoimmune disease, as DNA is not normally antigenic, but becomes so in SLE. Genetically, there is a prevalence in the first degree relatives of SLE patients and in monozygotic twins. Hormones, especially estrogen, may also play a role in SLE. In SLE, the B cells proliferate and secrete a large amount of immunoglobulin, and there is poor T cell proliferation in response to antigen stimulus.

Most SLE patients have immunopathologic abnormalities of their kidneys. Patients without urinary abnormalities may have small deposits of immunoglobulins in the kidney without any changes on light microscopy. There are four main types of lupus nephritis: (1) minimal lupus nephritis, with nearly normal glomeruli, (2) mild lupus nephritis, with segmental proliferation of some glomerular tufts, (3) diffuse proliferative nephritis, with abnormalities of more than 50% of the glomeruli, and (4) membranous nephritis, which is unlike other forms of lupus nephritis.

Immune complexes comprised of autoantigen and autoantibodies that activate the complement cascade are major pathogenic agents for the lesions in the skin, kidneys, lungs, and synovial membranes. Autoantibodies may predispose to immune complex–related injury, and neutrophils and macrophages may generate toxic oxygen metabolites that contribute to tissue injury.

In the skin, active lesions may contain circulating immune complexes. Ultraviolet (UV) radiation from sunlight causes the formation of immune complexes in which a DNA antigen has been modified by the UV radiation. SLE patients are therefore instructed to avoid sunlight.

There is no real pattern of clinical features at the onset of SLE and the course of the illness is not consistent. SLE may start with a single organ or with many organs. The first symptoms may be general: fever, fatigue, weakness, or weight loss. The appearance of the characteristic butterfly rash across the cheeks and nose and arthritis or nephritis make the diagnosis more obvious. Joint involvement is the most common manifestation of SLE, and joint pain or swelling may precede the multisystem disease for many years. The joints most commonly involved are the proximal interphalangeal joints (first finger joints), knees, wrists, and metacarpophalangeal joints. The joint involvement is symmetrical.

Skin, hair, or mucous membrane involvement is the second most common manifestation of SLE. These discoid lesions usually are on the scalp, external ear, and face.

Vasculitic lesions with ulceration may occur in a variety of places on the extremities. This patient is free of this type of lesion, and skin manifestations of SLE are varied.

The American Rheumatology Association (ARA) has developed criteria for the classification of SLE. The presence of four or more of the 11 criteria either serially or simultaneously is considered diagnostic. These criteria are:

1. Malar rash
2. Discoid rash
3. Photosensitivity
4. Oral ulcers
5. Arthritis (nonerosive of two or more peripheral joints)
6. Serositis—pleuritis or pericarditis
7. Persistent proteinuria with 0.5 gm/day, or cell casts
8. Seizures or psychosis
9. Hemolytic anemia, leukopenia, lymphopenia, or thrombocytopenia
10. Positive LE cell prep antiDNA or antiSm, or a false positive serologic test for syphilis
11. Antinuclear antibody (ANA)

This patient meets several of the ARA criteria for SLE diagnosis. She has a discoid rash, photosensitivity, and oral ulcers in the form of oral thrush, which can be associated with lupus, possibly secondary to her decreased lymphocyte count of 15 (normal is 25) and her chronic use of steroids, which can also suppress the lymphocytes. She has a positive ANA. The onset of her disease at age 18 is typical of SLE, which is more common in adolescent females. She does not have a family history of SLE although there is sometimes a genetic component. The onset of this patient's disease was characterized by skin lesions, for which she has been on several medications, including hydroxychloroquine sulfate and corticosteroids. She states a history of hair loss with full regrowth 1 year ago, which is typical of exacerbation-remission of SLE. She has arthritic pain, but it is typical of SLE arthritis, which is usually nonerosive, bilateral, and in peripheral joints. She also has a history of depression, intravenous drug use, and attempted suicide. She has been on a high dose of corticosteroid for a long period, which itself can cause behavior changes. She has discoid skin lesions of her right ear, which are thick and dry in the center, atrophic with a loss of dermal appendages, follicular plugging, and circumscribed with a central loss of color and hyperpigmentation at the margin.

The dermoepidermal junction of these lesions is widened and homogenous and has deposition of immune complexes. Skin that is free of lesions will also show this deposition. The typical butterfly rash over her nose with evidence of a healed rash on her cheeks is typical of SLE, although it is seen less commonly now than in the past. This rash may be a nonspecific maculopapular rash, and there may be scattered macules on the palms, fingers, or soles of the feet. This patient does not have rash in these areas. She stated that she avoids the sun because it exacerbates her symptoms. The mechanism of this is believed to be the formation of immune complexes in which DNA antigen has been modified by the UV radiation, causing the outbreak of rash.

The ANA is positive in approximately 95% of SLE patients and indicates that antibodies capable of destroying the nucleus of the patient's own cells are present. The pattern of the ANA antibodies and the specific antibodies are also evaluated. Serum complement levels are usually depressed in SLE, especially when the disease is active. This patient shows depression of her C4 level, which is typical of mild disease.

This patient's kidney function is unimpaired, as evidenced by her normal BUN, creatinine, urine creatinine clearance, indicating ability of the kidney to excrete creatinine. There are no RBCs, WBCs, or casts in her urine, and her urine protein is low. In mild SLE there is still deposition of immune complexes on UV light microscopy; however, renal problems are not severe in mild SLE. She has no signs of anemia at present. She has gained 50 pounds, which is more typical of SLE than weight loss.

HV's complain of lower abdominal pain could be a manifestation of her SLE, or it could be resulting from a urinary tract infection, although there was no bacteria in her urinalysis. It is also important to note her cardiac examination, because pericarditis is the most frequent cardiovascular manifestation of SLE. It is important to listen for a transient friction rub on each visit. Tachycardia may also indicate myocardial ischemia.

Nursing Diagnoses

1. Powerlessness related to unpredictable course
2. Ineffective individual coping, related to unpredictable course and altered appearance
3. Social isolation related to embarrassment and the response of others to appearance
4. Knowledge deficit related to pharmacologic therapy
5. Potential fluid volume excess, related to sodium and water retention
6. Altered nutrition: more than body requirements

Rheumatoid arthritis. Rheumatoid arthritis is a chronic, systemic, inflammatory disease involving tissues throughout the body. Although there is little question that the inflammation itself appears to perpetuate both the disease process and the resultant deformity, much research on the basic mechanisms of inflammation is needed before the nature of the abnormality in rheumatoid arthritis is known. Rheumatoid arthritis may strike people of all ages. Its cause is unknown, but much evidence has accumulated to indicate an autoimmune etiology, which may be precipitated by a severe infection, a drug reaction, or stress. Epstein-Barr virus has most recently been implicated, but the evidence for a causative role is equivocal (Pope and Talal, 1985). The presence of *rheumatoid factors* (RFs) in almost all patients is the most striking evidence in this regard. RFs are antibodies (of the IgG and IgM classes of immunoglobulins) to

gamma globulin. It is speculated that antibodies to one's own proteins may occur if the structure is altered so as to "fool" the immune system. Such a configurational change might be caused by a viral infection, an abnormal metabolic reaction, or a previous antigen-antibody reaction.

Rheumatoid arthritis may be caused by a mechanism similar to that operative in SLE or may, like chronic glomerulonephritis and rheumatic fever, be the possible result of a cross-reactivity of human antigens with bacterial antigens. Some bacterial antigens such as those of the *Streptococcus* might be so similar in structure to the human antigens that immunoglobulins specific to the bacterial antibodies could also attack and destroy certain human antigen-bearing cells. It is also possible that the immune phenomena are only the result of the disease process of rheumatoid arthritis, rather than initiating causes of the disease; however, the disease appears to be self-perpetuating, once initiated.

Complement is activated as part of the initial inflammation in rheumatoid arthritis, and consequently leukocyte infiltration ensues. These cells, as well as the synovial membrane cells of the joint capsule, then release lysosomal enzymes, which themselves act to perpetuate a chronic synovitis, leading to eventual destruction of the articular cartilage, and the typical pain, stiffness, and loss of function. Serum complement often is not decreased in rheumatoid arthritis, but the synovial complement concentration may be decreased, possibly indicating that it has been used up in the activation of the complement cascade. Immune complexes are found within the synovial tissues, presumably the result of RFs being released into the synovium.

In this condition it would seem that the

inflammation itself, which normally serves a protective and self-limiting function, leads to the disease process and is in a sense a protective mechanism gone awry. The major pharmacologic treatment for this disease is suppression of the inflammatory process with both nonsteroidal antiinflammatory agents and glucocorticoid steroids. The physiology of corticosteroid treatment in inflammatory disease is based on the fact that corticosteroids increase the vasomotor activity of the vascular bed so that capillary dilation is decreased and sensitivity to epinephrine-induced vasoconstriction is increased. These effects would oppose the normal increases in vascular supply and permeability during inflammation. Corticosteroids also alter the permeability characteristics of blood vessels directly. Therefore inflammatory edema and tissue swelling are decreased by the administration of these drugs. Corticosteroids inhibit polymorphonuclear chemotaxis, decrease granulocyte adherence, and decrease fibroblast proliferation collagen production, and blood vessel growth at the inflamed site.

The onset of symptoms of rheumatoid arthritis is often preceded by an infectious illness. The precipitating cause leading to persistent inflammation may be a transient infection of the joint lining by an organism such as a latent virus or mycoplasma. This results in the conversion of gamma globulin to a form that then stimulates autoimmunization. RFs certainly appear to play an important role in the pathophysiologic propagation of the rheumatoid disease process. The RFs themselves may provoke tissue damage, causing vasculitis, histamine release, and kinin activation. Phagocytosis may be enhanced or depressed in the presence of RFs, and complement fixation to RFs also has been reported.

Rheumatoid arthritis may be characterized by an initial attack, which is then followed by a complete disappearance of symptoms or by a course characterized by remissions and exacerbations and occasionally by a relentless, progressively destructive, and irreversible destruction of the joints. Synovial membranes are the most commonly affected tissues, but blood vessels, pericardium and pleura, and subcutaneous tissue can all show inflammatory changes. Connective tissue nodules occur in at least 15% of the cases and may themselves cause pain and disability, depending on location. These nodules are granulomatous inflammatory reactions of the connective tissue of the derma. Gradual deformation and contracture of the joints can occur, particularly without early and continued treatment.

The principal symptoms begin usually as morning stiffness, often of the fingers (although one or many joints can be initially involved), which gradually clears with movement. The involved joints become red, hot, and swollen, and the individual is usually fatigued and debilitated during the acute stages of the disease. The swelling of the fingers is described as fusiform, or spindle shaped, and is quite characteristic. In addition, muscular atrophy may develop and become quite marked. Further diagnostic criteria include an elevated erythrocyte sedimentation rate, a positive test for rheumatoid factor, and a variety of systemic symptoms such as fever, anemia, and lymphadenopathy. On x-ray examination a thinning of the cartilage may be seen, as well as the presence of small punched-out areas of bone.

The tendency to avoid movement of a painful joint may lead to contracture and ankylosis of the joint, and this coupled with progressive synovitis and joint damage may lead to severe deformity. In the

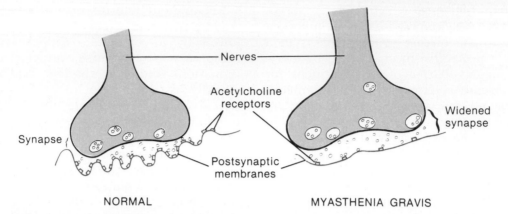

Fig. 2-22. In myasthenia gravis the postsynaptic membrane appears flattened and less folded, with a widening of the synaptic cleft occurring and fewer postsynaptic acetylcholine receptors being present to bind with neurotransmitter molecules.

most severe forms of the disease, vasculitis can lead to tissue anoxia, necrosis, and gangrene. In the acute form of rheumatoid arthritis pulmonary and cardiac inflammation may also produce overt signs of distress.

Often rheumatoid arthritis follows a relatively benign course with periods of long remission. Treatment with rest and moderate exercise, physiotherapy, and administration of drugs such as the salicylates, penicillamine, and corticosteroids often allows the arthritic individual to function optimally in spite of the disease. Joint surgery may be required when severe deformity leads to pain and loss of function.

CASE STUDY: RHEUMATOID ARTHRITIS

History
Objective and Subjective Data

MF is a 46-year-old registered nurse who works on a medical unit of a local hospital. She reports that following a bunionectomy of her left foot 3 months ago, she developed diffuse joint pain in her fingers,

Contributed by Mildred M. Fenske.

shoulders, ankles, wrists, and knees. She has had some swelling and prolonged aching of her right shoulder and wrists and she has stiffness in her joints. She is exhausted and has lost approximately 10 pounds since her surgery.

Present illness: Increasing severity of joint pain the past 2 days. Morning stiffness interferes with dressing for work. Her fatigue overwhelms her.

General appearance: Alert, well-dressed, cooperative

Vital signs

Temperature: 100° F

Blood pressure: 130/84

Pulse: 96 per minute

Respirations: 20 per minute

Neuromuscular: MF reports joint stiffness that is most acute in the morning and that lasts 45 minutes to 1 1/2 hours. Mid and proximal interphalangeal joints of both hands are warm, tender to touch, and thickened, especially the third finger of the left hand. There is no limitation of movement. There is an absence of subcutaneous or subperiosteal nodules in the olecranon bursa and ulnar shafts. The right shoulder is warm, tender, but soft with increased pain on adduction. The left shoulder is warm, tender. There is an absence of atrophy of deltoid, shoulder girdle muscles. MF states that it is now difficult to walk barefoot and that she can no longer tolerate wearing high heels.

Laboratory values

Hgb: 11.0 g/100 ml
Hct: 34%
WBC: 11,500
  Bands   03%
  Segs   69%
  Eos   04%
  Lymphs   20%
  Monos   04%

Sed Rate: 110 mm/h (Westergren)

Urinalysis:

pH: 6.38
Sp. gravity: 1.025
Protein: negative
Sugar: negative
Ketone: negative
Nitrites: positive
Leucocyte esterase: trace
WBC: 7-8/HPF
RBC: 0

X-ray report

PA, oblique, and lateral films of the hand and wrist were taken. There is articular soft tissue swelling, uniform narrowing of the interosseous spaces, and bilateral metacarpophalangeal joint erosion. The navicular spaces are rotated into the hollow of the distal radii with erosion in the mid-portions. There is slight distal displacement of the ulna bilaterally.

Treatment

MF was diagnosed as having rheumatoid arthritis. She was instructed to take sulindac 200 mg, orally, twice a day, with food. She was also instructed to immerse her hands in a paraffin bath twice daily, to acquire adequate rest, and to receive instructions from physical therapy regarding range of motion of all joints after 1 week of sulindac therapy.

Discussion:

Rheumatoid arthritis is a chronic, systemic disease characterized by inflammation of the synovium. It causes painful, deformed joints. Exacerbations (flares) and remissions characterize the disease.

On admission, MF was experiencing a rheumatoid arthritic "flare." Persons with rheumatic disease have aching, soreness, and stiffness lasting at least 30 minutes. Inflammation is an early sign of rheumatoid arthritis; limitation of motion occurs later.

Usual radiologic findings include soft tissue swelling that involves both sides of the joint, uniform narrowing of the cartilage space, and marginal erosions.

Immune mechanisms thought to activate rheumatoid inflammation begin when IgG-IgG, and IgM (rheumatoid factor) attract polymorphonuclear leukocytes into the articular cavity where they ingest immune complexes and form rheumatoid arthritis (RA) cells. The enzymes formed by the neutrophils after phagocytosis produce the proliferative and destructive changes of rheumatoid arthritis.

An increased erythrocyte sedimentation rate reflects an increase in plasma globulins or fibrinogen causing cells to adhere to each other and fall faster than normal. In nonpregnant states, an elevated sedimentation rate usually indicates infection, malignancy, or a collagen vascular disease. Inflammatory processes are associated with increased segmented white cells. MF may, in addition to rheumatoid arthritis, have a urinary tract infection; however, ascorbic acid may invalidate both urine nitrite and WBC leukocyte esterase tests. Smokers tend to have higher WBC counts than do non-smokers.

Rheumatoid factor results indicate abnormal serum proteins. Although present in other disease states, 75% of persons with rheumatoid arthritis have positive rheumatoid factor tests, and the highest titers are found in persons with rheumatoid arthritis.

Sulindac, a non-narcotic, non-steroidal,

anti-inflammatory agent, provides symptomatic relief of rheumatoid arthritis. Warm paraffin baths decrease joint discomfort. Physical therapy that is begun after the acute joint pain subsides maintains joint mobility and decreases the incidence of joint contractures.

Nursing Diagnoses

MF has been newly diagnosed with rheumatoid arthritis. She will therefore require education regarding the disease and its anticipated remissions and exacerbations. In addition, the following nursing diagnoses are suggested:
1. Activity intolerance related to joint inflammation and stiffness
2. Body image disturbance related to difficulties in performing self-care
3. Potential anxiety related to unknown course of the disease
4. Pain related to disease process

Myasthenia gravis. Myasthenia gravis is an autoimmune disease that is currently being investigated with the monoclonal antibody technique. (This disorder will be more fully characterized in Chapter 10, since it is a disease associated with alteration of neuromuscular synaptic transmission.) A recent development in scientific technology is the process in which normal immune cells are fused with certain malignant cells, creating essentially immortal cultures of cells known as hybridomas. The hybridoma cells are like self-perpetuating factories releasing the gene products of the immune cell with which it originally fused. Each immune cell that forms a hybridoma produces a single type of antibody, thus the term *monoclonal* (coming originally from one cell). Growing hybridomas in tissue culture is a way of collecting, measuring, and characterizing immunoglobulins against all sorts of antigens.

Monoclonal antibodies to components of the acetylcholine receptor have been produced.

In myasthenia gravis the intersynaptic cleft is widened and the postsynaptic acetycholine receptors are both fewer and less sensitive to the neurotransmitter (Fig. 2-22); therefore the predominant symptoms are muscle weakness and marked fatigue following movement. The postsynaptic membrane is much less folded in myasthenia than normally, having less surface area available for interaction with acetylcholine. It appears that the basic cause of this postsynaptic membrane destruction is an autoimmune mechanism, largely mediated through complement fixing of acetylcholine receptor components and subsequent destruction.

The acetylcholine receptor is itself a very large complex structure comprised of subunits. It has been possible to make monoclonal antibodies against many of the acetylcholine receptor subunits and subunit fragments. These immunoglobulins are then tested in vivo in experimental animals for possible effects on neuromuscular transmission. Furthermore, blocking antibodies to these immunoglobulins can be made, and their effects on experimental myasthenia gravis are also being studied. This approach has led to some new ideas about myasthenia. First, the disorder appears to be a polyclonal response to several acetylcholine receptor components. In other words, the disease may have several causes. Second, the treatment of this disease may eventually be the administration of antibodies directed against the immunoglobulins that are destroying the postsynaptic membrane.

Association of HLA antigens and disease

It has long been suspected and recently confirmed that immune responsiveness and general resistance to certain diseases is genetically determined. With the advent of techniques to identify certain human tissue antigens to match donor and recipient in transplant procedures, a great number of tissue or histocompatibility antigens have been described. The vast majority of these make up part of the HLA system of tissue antigen genes. These are genetic determinants located on chromosome 6 at four different loci. The HLA complex is made up of many different alleles and is genetically polymorphic. The nomenclature of the four linked loci of the HLA system is described in order on the chromosome as HLA-A, HLA-C, HLA-B, and HLA-D. Making up these four loci are many genes, which code for tissue antigens.

Fifty tissue antigens of the HLA system are now known. These tissue antigens can be identified in vitro and used to match donor organs and recipient tissues, thus preventing major graft versus host reactions after organ transplant. The actual function of these tissue antigens in normal physiology is not known. Besides coding for the histocompatibility antigens, the HLA complex also appears to be involved in immune responsiveness to a variety of antigens and also may play some role in the complement system.

The HLA pattern is extremely variable in any given individual, but patterns of similarities exist within ethnic groups and in geographic areas. Within groups of individuals with certain patterns of HLA antigens it has been noted that some disease states are much more prevalent than in the population as a whole. This phenomenon has been observed in laboratory animals and has now been confirmed in humans.

The disease that has the best correlation to a given HLA antigen is ankylosing spondylitis. It has been shown that about 90%

of these patients have the histocompatibility antigen HLA-B27, while the frequency of this antigen among the general population is only 9%.

Other diseases that have been correlated to specific HLA antigens include multiple sclerosis, SLE, myasthenia gravis, juvenile diabetes mellitus, Addison's disease, chronic hepatitis, celiac disease, and herpes labialis. Other associations are continually being made, particularly with regard to various malignant diseases. There is great optimism among researchers in this field that early and better differential diagnoses as well as possible prevention of diseases may result from this research.

The actual mechanism whereby the association exerts its effect on resistance or susceptibility to various diseases is unknown. It is speculated that immune responsiveness genes are linked to various HLA determinants, and these genes in turn exert a regulatory effect on the T cell immune system. Another possibility is that certain disease agents are antigenically similar to the HLA antigens and thus are not aggressively attacked by the immune system if they infect an individual. Another suggestion is that the HLA antigens may themselves be involved in the mechanisms of various diseases. HLA antigens may function as complement receptors on certain cell membranes. Furthermore, the Epstein-Barr virus, which causes infectious mononucleosis and Burkitt's lymphoma, binds to the C3 receptor of lymphocytes, suggesting that HLA antigens may actually be important in the propagation of certain diseases, including certain viral diseases, autoimmune diseases, and cancer. Another possible explanation for the association of HLA antigens with various diseases is that infecting viruses that cause a given disease act to alter the HLA complex and modulate its genetic expression in terms of antigenic types.

Whatever mechanism or mechanisms are finally shown to be important in the pathophysiologic functioning of this association, there is no doubt that they will shed much light on a great variety of human diseases.

BIBLIOGRAPHY

Ader R and Cohen N: Behavioral conditioned immunosuppression and murine systemic lupus erythematosis, Science 215:1534, 1982.

Allegra CJ, et al: Trimetrexate for the treatment of *Pneumocystis carinii* pneumonia in patients with AIDS, N Engl J Med 317:978-985, 1987.

Barnes D: AIDS-related brain damage unexplained, Science 236:1091-1093, 1986.

Baum RM: AIDS researchers make in roads in understanding a complex virus, Chemistry and Engineering News, December, p 7-12, 1986.

Blatteis CM: Fever: is it beneficial? Yale J Biol Med 59:107-116, 1986.

Colvin RB and Olson KA: Idiotypes in autoimmune diseases. In Torrenco P, editor: Biological response modifiers, New York, 1985, Academic Press.

Cruse JM and Lewis RE, Jr, editors: Autoimmunity: basic concepts, systemic and selected organ-specific diseases, New York, 1985, S. Karger.

Dausset J: The major histocompatibility complex in man, Science 221:1469-1473, 1981.

Dinarello C, Conti P, and Mier, J: Effects of human interleukin-1 on natural killer cell activity: is fever a host defense mechanism for tumor killing? Yale J Biol Med 59:97-106, 1986.

Frank M: Complement in the pathophysiology of human disease, N Engl J Med 316:1525-1529, 1987.

Grade M and Zegans L: Exploring systemic lupus erythematosis, autoimmunity, self-destruction, and psychoneuroimmunology, Advances 3:16-45, 1986

Jerne NK: Towards a network theory of the immune system, Ann Immunol 125C:373-389, 1974.

Johnston M: Basic concepts of immunity. In Torrence P, editor: Biological response modifiers, New York, 1985, Academic Press.

Kluger MJ: Is fever beneficial? Yale J Biol Med 59:89-95, 1986.

Marshall E: Immune system theories on trial, Science 234:1490-1492, 1986.

Marx J: Chemical signals in the immune system, Science 221:1362-1364, 1983.

Marx J: The slow, insidious nature of the HTLVs, Science 231:450-451, 1986.

Marx J: Tracking variations in the AIDS virus family, Science 241:659-660, 1988.

Milstein C: From antibody structure to immunological diversification of immune response, Science 231:1261-1268, 1986.

Moldofsy H, et al: The relationship of interleukin-1 and immune functions to sleep in humans, Psychosom Med 48:309-318, 1986.

Nossal G: The basic components of the immune system, N Engl J Med 316:1320-1325, 1987.

Pope R and Talal N: Autoimmunity in rheumatoid arthritis, Concepts Immunopath 1:219-250, 1985.

Smith HR and Steinberg AD: Autoimmunity—a perspective, Ann Rev Immunol 1:175–210, 1983.

Suciu-Foca N, et al: Autoimmunity and self-antigens. In Torrence P, editor: Biological response modifiers, New York, 1985, Academic Press.

Wharton JM, et al: Treatment for pneumocystis pneumonia in AIDS, Ann Int Med 105:37–44, 1986.

Welliver RC: Allergy and the syndrome of chronic Epstein-Barr virus infection, J Allergy Clin Immunol 78:278-281, 1986.

3

Hematopoietic and coagulation disorders

This chapter describes the more common hematologic disorders, including anemias, white cell disorders, and coagulopathies. As with all disorders that humans can develop, hematologic disorders are physiologically stressful and in some cases can actually be precipitated by physical and psychologic stress, as we shall describe. Furthermore, red blood cells are essential for oxygenation, and hypoxia can lead to disregulation of many adaptive mechanisms. Functions and disorders of white cells have been described in Chapter 2, thus only a small elaboration is needed here. Coagulation disorders may lead to inadequate body defense against injury or ischemia as a result of obstruction of the vasculature. The importance of normal hematologic function is appreciated when we consider that blood flow is essential for every cell, tissue, and organ to function, and potential for disruption of every physiologic function exists when disorders of the cellular components of the blood are present.

It is necessary for the student to recall the stages and sequences of normal hematopoiesis. Hematopoiesis is established very early in the embryonic yolk sac and then is taken over by the fetal liver and bone marrow, providing mature cells to populate the blood. The blood cells are constantly being replaced throughout life by hematopoiesis, which after birth occurs only in the bone marrow. The bone marrow is a stem cell compartment, and early progenitor cells give rise to cells that differentiate through a set sequence of maturational stages into the mature erythrocytes, leukocytes, and platelets. Stemcells also divide to form new stem cells, so that hematopoietic potential is present throughout life. It can be seen from Fig. 3-1 that the earliest stem cell in the hematopoietic series is called the CFU-S (colony-forming unit–spleen), which is so called because of the ability of these cells to establish colonies in the spleen if they are injected into animal models, demonstrating blood cell–forming pluripotential. This early cell has never been actually identified under the microscope, and its existence has only been proved experimentally. The CFU-S divides very early to produce cell lines that will give rise to the erythrocyte population, through the CFU-E (colony-forming unit–erythrocyte), the lymphocytes through the CFU-L (colony-forming unit–lymphoid), and granulocytes and monocytes through the CFU-GM (colony-forming unit–granulocyte macrophage), and the platelets through the CFU-MEG (colony-forming unit–megakaryocyte). If a disturbance in cell growth or maturation occurs at the level of the CFU-S, then all blood cell lines are potentially

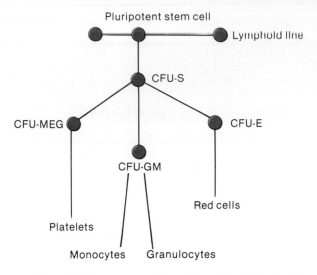

Fig. 3-1. The hematopoietic series with all blood cells originating from the CFU-S.

disturbed. If a later cell in the differentiation process is affected, then perhaps only a single line of cells becomes disturbed. Some of the aplastic anemias apparently involve all of the blood cells, so it is speculated that a drug, virus, or toxic chemical damages the CFU-S population, essentially obliterating all hematopoiesis. On the other hand, a particular leukemia, such as acute lymphocytic leukemia, involves only lymphocytes in the initial pathogenesis.

For hematopoiesis to successfully continue to supply the blood with mature cells, some essential conditions must be met. There must be adequate perfusion of the bone marrow and adequate amounts of oxygen and energy sources made available to continue this energy-demanding process. Essential substrates are also required, such as iron, folic acid, and vitamin B_{12} for erythropoiesis. Deficiencies in some or all of these substrates and nutrients can occur in many specific diseases and most chronic diseases. Another requirement is that there be adequate space for hematopoiesis. If the bone marrow is infiltrated with cells or fat, there will be

deficient production of cells resulting from competition for nutrients and space. Lastly, hematopoiesis is regulated through multiple stimulating factors (poietins) produced outside of the bone marrow that carry messages to the stem cells to increase or decrease division and expansion of certain cell compartments. Erythropoiesis is regulated largely through the hormone erythropoietin, a secretion of the kidney, in response to hypoxia. Colony-stimulating factors for the various other cell compartments are produced by macrophages and other cells. Feedback regulation is, therefore, another requirement for hematopoiesis.

ANEMIAS

Anemias are common disorders that may be classified in many different ways. Anemias can be a result of blood loss, excessive erythrocyte destruction, or impaired production of erythrocytes. This is a very general categorization. Anemia means a loss in the oxygen-carrying capacity of the blood either through inadequate numbers of functional cells or cells that are inadequate in their physiologic function. Anemia is diagnosed by examining various indices of red cell function and number. Some anemias may be associated with small pale cells, others with macrocytic cells, and others with abnormally shaped cells. The amount of hemoglobin inside each individual cell, measured by the mean corpuscular hemoglobin concentration (MCHC), is decreased in some cases and actually increased in others. Causes of anemia can range from clearly hereditary disease (such as the thalassemias) to acquired disease (such as iron deficiency anemia from an inadequate diet). On the other hand, some anemias may have both a genetic and an acquired component (pernicious anemia). This chapter will describe the major forms of anemia in each classification and the specific symptoms associated with it. Before this, however, we will examine the general physiologic effects of anemia, no matter what the cause.

General physiologic effects of anemia

As with many other disorders, the symptoms of anemia depend to a great degree on how quickly the anemia has developed. Acute anemias, such as those resulting from hemorrhage, lead to very serious signs and symptoms, yet chronic forms, such as might be a result of a slowly bleeding colon lesion, lead to vague or even absent symptoms, until the hemoglobin and hemocrit values reach really critically low levels. This exemplifies the adaptive and coping capacity of the human being. Most of the symtoms of anemia are related to the tissue hypoxia that results from a lack of adequate oxygen carriage and delivery. Symptoms are also related to the degree in change of total blood volume that may accompany the anemia and any underlying disease that may be present. The critical factor is whether or not there has been adequate compensation for the anemia.

The major mechanisms of compensation are (1) shifting to the right of the oxyhemoglobin dissociation curve, resulting in increased oxygen extraction at the tissue capillary; (2) redistribution of the blood flow to supply adequate oxygen to the brain, heart, and muscles; (3) increased cardiac output, even though the blood volume may be decreased; and (4) increased velocity of blood flow through the tissues. When the hemoglobin level drops to below 7.5 gm/dl, there is increasing cardiovascular compensation, which may lead to loud systolic murmurs, venous bruits, and a humming sensation in the head that the person subjectively experiences. These symptoms result from increased blood flow and decreased blood viscosity. Tachycardia is present, and there is usually moderate exertional dyspnea. Patients may complain of faintness, vertigo, headaches, and profound fatigue. Pallor accompanies anemia and may be assessed most easily in the conjunctiva, nailbeds, and mucous membranes. Chronic anemic conditions may be associated with early graying of the hair, thinning and brittleness of the nails, and vague gastrointestinal and neurologic symptoms.

Types of anemia
Disturbances in erythropoiesis

This classification of anemia includes aplastic anemia, megaloblastic anemias, and the anemia associated with chronic disease or renal disease. Each of these types will be considered separately.

Aplastic anemia. Aplastic anemia may follow exposure to chemicals (benzene, insecticides), x-rays, viruses (human parvovirus), or drugs (chloramphenicol, phenylbutazone, penicillin). It involves a rapidly progressive decline in the formation of the formed elements of the blood, with fatty infiltration of the marrow and apparent loss of the earliest stem cell compartments. Very few islands of bone marrow hematopoiesis can be observed, and the peripheral blood is remarkably low in red cells, white cells, and platelets in many cases, although purely red cell hypoplasia can occur. The appearance of anemia is not always well correlated with the amount of, or time of exposure to, the disease-causing agent. Aplastic anemia can appear after hepatitis for as long as 26 weeks after the hepatitis has resolved (Thorup, 1987). A form of aplastic anemia, Fanconi's ancmia, occurs congenitally and is associated with a syndrome of hypogonadism, skeletal defects, short stature, hyperpigmentation, and pancytopenia. This is a rare disease, and most cases of childhood aplastic anemia are acquired, not genetic.

The course of this disease is usually progressive pancytopenia and marrow hypoplasia, and during this time the patient's immune system is essentially missing, oxygenation is threatened, and coagulation is impaired. There is a very high mortality associated with aplastic anemia, but some patients do recover and repopulate their bone marrow over time, producing essentially normal blood on recovery, although coagulation deficits may persist. Others are treated aggressively with cortisone, testosterone, and immunotherapy. A bone marrow transplant can be curative if histocompatible marrow is available.

Megaloblastic anemia. Megaloblastic anemia is a macrocytic anemia caused by a disturbed erythropoiesis as a result of abnormal DNA synthesis. This results from vitamin B_{12} deficiency, which causes pernicious anemia or folic acid deficiency. An extremely deficient diet would be required to produce megaloblastic anemia. It is most commonly caused by lack of absorption of these nutrients or increased utilization states, such as pregnancy. It can be observed in patients with fish tapeworm disease, with alcoholic cirrhosis, after a gastrectomy, and in cases of small bowel bacterial flora overgrowth. The peripheral erythrocytes are normochromic but have an increased mean corpuscular volume. The cells are often oval in shape but may assume bizarre shapes. The reticulocyte count may be high, and the reticulocytes are also macrocytic. The hemoglobin is often less than 6 or 7 gm/dl. The polymorphonuclear leukocytes are also affected in this disease and have many nuclear lobes. This may be the earliest sign of the disease. At the bone marrow level, a *megaloblastic* process rather than a normoblastic is observed. The cells that are produced are inadequate erythrocytes, which are poor oxygen carriers and subject to decreased survival in the peripheral blood.

Pernicious anemia is the most common form of megaloblastic anemia. This is the result of vitamin B_{12} deficiency, which usually results from atrophy of the gastric mucosa and loss of gastric secretions, including hydrochloric acid, enzymes, and most importantly, intrinsic factor. Fig. 3-2 shows how intrinsic factor acts to bind vitamin B_{12} and carries it to the ileum where it is normally absorbed. In the absence of intrinsic factor, there is decreased vitamin B_{12} availability to the bone marrow, even though the diet may be adequate. The cause of the disease is unknown, although it increases in incidence with aging and is often historically associated with acute gastritis, leading to chronic gastritis and then to atrophic gastritis. The disease may have an immunologic basis since circulating antibodies to intrinsic factor are found in some patients with pernicious anemia.

The manifestations of pernicious anemia develop insidiously and are often vague. Weight loss, fevers, gastrointestinal complaints, a sore and glossy tongue, paresthesias, and difficulty with gait occur. The cause of the neurologic symptoms is still unknown, but 80% of patients report sensory changes, areas of numbness and tingling (often in a glove and stocking distribution), lack of coordination, and hyperflexia. The dorsal and lateral columns of white matter and the peripheral nerves seem to be affected by the vitamin B_{12} deficiency.

Anemia of chronic illness. Many chronic illnesses including malignancies, traumatic injuries, burns, and rheumatoid arthritis have an associated chronic anemia, which is generally mild and appears to be related to iron deficiency. It is possible that this is not nutritional but rather a result of competition for available iron by inflammatory and reticuloendothelial cells, which are increased and activated in

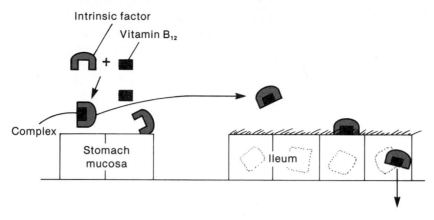

Fig. 3-2. Normal binding of vitamin B_{12} and intrinsic factor, without intrinsic factor vitamins B_{12} is not absorbed in ileum.

such situations. There is also decreased red cell survival in many chronically ill patients, a result of the presence of a more highly active splenic reticuloendothelial system, destroying older cells sooner than normal. Erythropoietin responsiveness of the marrow may be depressed, so that increased loss of cells unaccompanied by matching erythropoiesis leads to anemia. Interleukin 1 has been suggested as a mediator in several of these mechanisms (Thorup, 1987) since its production is increased in inflammatory and malignant diseases.

Iron deficiency anemia. The most common anemia results from inadequate iron intake or absorption, leading to depressed erythropoiesis. It is prevalent in underdeveloped countries, but it is also seen very frequently in the United States among children of all socioeconomic groups. Hypochromia and microcytosis are associated with lowered hemoglobin and hematocrit values. There are several contributing factors to the more frequent appearance of anemia during childhood. Red cell survival is less, nearly 50% less in the infant. Hemoglobin concentration is normally lower than adult norms throughout childhood, and therefore anemia develops more readily. The major cause is dietary, often as a result of inordinate milk consumption, with lack of other nutrient intake in toddlers. The development of the anemia occurs in three stages (Monzon, 1985). First, the iron stores are depleted, which are indirectly measured by the serum ferritin concentration. Ferritin is the iron transport molecule that brings iron to the bone marrow from the intestinal mucosal cells and iron stores (liver, reticuloendothelial cells, and skeletal muscle). Second, iron transport deficiency occurs as measured by decreased serum iron and increased serum capacity to bind iron. Finally, decreased hemoglobin production occurs, resulting in the production of small, pale erythrocytes. As in other anemias, the reticulocyte count is often increased, reflecting the release of immature red cells from the stressed bone marrow.

Although the usual cause is directly nutritional, it is common during pregnancy, where the fetal iron demands may exceed the available supply. The treatment in any case is administration of oral supplements of iron salts.

Disturbances in erythrocyte survival

Anemia may occur when red cell survival is threatened in the peripheral blood;

genetic and acquired disorders comprise this classification of anemia and include hemolytic anemias, hemoglobinopathies, and metabolic derangements of the erythrocyte.

Hemolytic anemias. The hemolytic anemias include several types of hereditary disorders. Defects in the integrity of the erythrocyte cell membrane or abnormal red cell metabolism can produce fragile cells with limited life span and susceptibility to lysis in the hypoxic and somewhat hostile environment of the spleen. Also included in the hemolytic anemias are the various hereditary hemoglobinopathies, such as the thalassemias and sickle cell anemia. Abnormal hemoglobins can lead to lysis because they disturb the normal architecture of the red cell and usually interfere with many aspects of physiologic function. Acquired hemolytic anemia occurs when red cells are destroyed by outside agents, i.e., snake venom or the malarial protozoan, or by immunologic destruction, such as occurs after the transfusion of incompatible blood. This anemia occurs also when damaged or inflamed blood vessels trap and sequester red cells, and when prosthetic valves produce traumatic injury to blood components. The anemia that is produced may be normochromic and normocytic, if there is no intrinsic red cell disease. The signs and symptoms of hemolytic anemia are mild anemia, splenomegaly, jaundice, decreased hemoglobin and hematocrit, and reticulocytosis.

Hemoglobinopathies

Sickle cell anemia. Sickle cell anemia is present in about 0.2% of the North American Black population, whereas the frequency of the sickle cell trait is about 8%. The genetic basis for sickle cell anemia will be described in Chapter 4. The anemia is a result of a point mutation resulting in the substitution of valine for glutamic acid at the sixth amino acid position from the N terminal in beta globulin. If a person is homozygous at the genetic loci, then essentially 100% of the hemoglobin will be hemoglobin S (Hb S). The presence of heterozygosity (sickle cell trait) does not usually produce symptoms, because adequate amounts of normal hemoglobin are present in the erythrocytes; in many people, presumably resulting from selection pressures, less than 50% Hb S is actually present. Hb S is a molecule with vastly different properties than the normal hemoglobin A2. Fig. 3-3 shows the abnormal shape of sickled cells. The erythrocytes assume these bizarre shapes whenever they are stressed by hypoxia or acid pH. Their presence on a peripheral blood smear is diagnostic of sickle cell anemia. Under physiologic conditions sickling is reversible up to a point. When the cell becomes irreversibly sickled it will lyse. Sickling occurs when the misplaced valine residues on the β chain of one hemoglobin molecule reacts with corresponding complementary sites of the α chain of another hemoglobin molecule, forming hydrophobic bonds.

Fig. 3-3. Sickled erythrocytes showing bizarre sickle formations.

In general, sickle cells have a shortened life span, since sickling is likely to occur in the spleen, which normally removes damaged and senescent red cells. Another common site for sickling is in the renal vasculature, where the 1300 mOsm environment causes osmotic stress for even normal cells. The solubility properties of Hb S cause the cells to sickle. Hb S polymerizes forming an insoluble molecular mass that distorts the cell, making the usual passage through the microvasculature difficult and increasing its chance of lysis. Masses of sickled cells can obstruct blood vessel lumens. Furthermore, there is a general tendency for blood flow to decrease, and the irreversibly sickled cells tend to stick to endothelium, further perpetuating the vaso-occlusive event. As hemoglobin sickles, the erythrocytes begin to leak potassium and water, presumably from some membrane alterations induced by the polymerized hemoglobin. This causes the cells to become dehydrated, and the already increased cellular mean corpuscular hemoglobin concentration will become even more concentrated (Embury, 1986). This increases the tendency of the cells to be stiffer and more fragile, and sickling becomes irreversible, promoting further vaso-occlusion. In a normal capillary bed, as a result of vasomotion, periodic occlusions may be occurring frequently in patients with sickle cell anemia. However, deobstruction occurs as perfusion pressure changes, so that symptoms of ischemia may not appear. When vaso-occlusion of a larger vessel or of many small vessels occurs ischemic pain results (Nagel et al, 1985). This pain is the hallmark of sickle cell crisis and presages possible tissue infarction if blood flow is not restored. Crises, which are more common during childhood and in the late 20s and early 30s, are precipitated by atmospheric pressure changes, exercise, infections, fevers, and many other stressors. Even emotional stress has been reported to precipitate repeated crises in susceptible patients (Charache and Zohoun, 1987). If tissue becomes infarcted, chronic damage to essentially all organs of the body can occur.

Sickle cell anemia is a disabling and debilitating affliction. Frequent infection, gallbladder disease, bone degeneration, blindness, and a host of other pathophysiologic complications occur. Prevention of sickle cell crisis is important when possible, by avoiding stressful or hypoxia-producing events, and treatment is supportive during a crisis. No effective antisickling drug is currently available.

CASE STUDY: SICKLE CELL ANEMIA

History

BN is a 9-month-old female with sickle cell anemia; the diagnosis was made 1 month ago. She is an only child. Her mother stated that she was a carrier of the sickle cell trait before becoming pregnant. She did not know that the father was also a carrier of the trait. Because of the impact of the disease on BN's life, her mother does not plan to have any more children. BN's mother reports periodic swelling of and discomfort in her child's joints during the past 6 to 7 months.

BN remains asymptomatic until an upper respiratory tract infection, virus, or otitis media develops. She has experienced several infections during the past 2 months. When infection is present, BN becomes irritable, cries unconsolably, has swollen joints, refuses to stand, and has a decreased oral intake.

BN has been in the hospital for 1 day. She was admitted after experiencing vomiting and diarrhea for 1 week. Her mother stated that BN had been crying constantly and had swollen joints.

Contributed by Kim Davis.

Subjective and Objective Data

BN is febrile (100° F), has bibasilar rales and upper airway congestion, a nonproductive cough, swollen feet and hands, and is irritable. She will not stand and prefers to be held by her mother.

Vital signs

Temperature: 98.7° to 100° F

Pulse: 120 to 140

Respiration: 28 to 32

Blood pressure: 96/104 to 68/86

The complete blood count shows the following

WBC: 13.0×10^3 cells/mm^3

RBC: 3.41×10/mm^3

Hgb: 8.9 g/dl

Hct: 27.6%

Plt: 664×10^3/mm^3

2+ oat-shaped cells—indicative of sickle cell shapes

Weight: 15½ lb (there has been a loss of 1½ lb within past 2 weeks)

Serum iron: 19 μg/dl

Reticulocyte count: 14.2%

Intake (24 hour): 1395 ml

Output (24 hour): 1032 ml

Urine specific gravity: 1.004 to 1.012

Skin turgor: Fair

Treatment

BN is diagnosed as experiencing a vaso-occlusive crisis and is treated with intravenous antibiotics and fluid replacement as follows:

Ampicillin: 350 mg intravenously, every 6 hours

Claforan: 220 mg intravenously, every 6 hours

D5 1/4 NS @ 50 ml/hr

Pathophysiology

BN's case is typical of sickle cell disease. The disease is transmitted genetically through two parents carrying the sickle cell trait. Sickle cell crisis is initiated by increased oxygen demands on the body, infection, or stress. Under these conditions erythrocytes sickle. The sickled cells become enmeshed and therefore increase blood viscosity. Because of increased viscosity, circulatory flow slows, capillary stasis occurs, and vaso-occlusion results, causing ischemic pain.

At present there is no cure for sickle cell anemia and treatment of the disease focuses on prevention. Nursing care of the patient should focus on minimizing oxygen demands to prevent tissue hypoxia, promoting hydration to prevent sickling of erythrocytes and a vaso-occlusive crisis, promoting an infection-free state, promoting comfort during a crisis, and providing support to family members.

Nursing Diagnoses

1. Altered tissue perfusion related to sickling of erythrocytes, vaso-occlusion, and hypovolemia
2. Potential fluid volume deficit related to decreased oral fluid intake and inability of kidneys to concentrate urine
3. Pain related to tissue ischemia
4. Altered family processes related to guilt and recurrent hospitalizations of the child

The treatment of the child with sickle cell anemia is largely symptomatic at the present time and directed toward relief of pain that can be excruciating and alleviation of the anemia. The degree of anemia varies; the affected child may have delayed growth and development, cardiac insufficiency, weakness, cold intolerance, susceptibility to infection, episodes of swelling of hands and feet, back and abdominal pain, and occasionally pain elsewhere. The child with sickle cell anemia suffers not only from the debilitating effects of anemia but also from progressive ischemic damage in many organ systems (kidneys, lungs, liver, and brain) caused by recurring sickle cell crises. The child requires excellent preventive care to increase both the quality and the length of life.

When possible, hypoxemia should be avoided or at least predicted beforehand. For example, if a child requires general anesthesia for a surgical or dental procedure, a partial exchange transfusion will help dilute the Hb S–containing red cells. Exchange transfusion is also done during a crisis. Current studies are focusing on the evaluation of several antisickling agents. The most commonly used drug is sodium cyanate, which unfortunately has many undesirable side effects.

Identification of the cause of the crisis is also essential to treatment, since there are other forms of crisis besides the occlusive hypoxic sickling. A crisis can occur when there is an acute infection, and bone marrow failure may follow, which is characterized by a rapid drop in erythrocytes and other cells. The child will require blood transfusions and careful medical and nursing care. Another form of crisis is the result of the rapid development of splenic hypertrophy. Normally the spleen removes aged and damaged red cells but it is often inadequately functioning in sickle cell anemia. In splenic sequestration crisis the spleen becomes tremendously engorged with sickled cells and blood, is very tender, and is subject to rupture. The removal of these blood cells from the general circulation can be significant enough to cause the development of hypovolemic shock.

Thalassemias. The thalassemias are a group of hemoglobinopathies in which there are genetic disturbances in the production of either the alpha or beta chains of hemoglobin. There are homozygotes and heterozygotes for these disorders; the disease is seen with highest frequency in people of Mediterranean origin, but Blacks and Asians may have certain thalassemia variants. α-Thalassemias involve deletion or disturbed function of the genes that code for the α chains, whereas the more common β-thalassemias affect β chain production. In fact, the patient with β-thalassemia major has mostly fetal hemoglobin (two α chains and two γ chains), because no or very limited β chains are produced. There is increased α chain production in the β-thalassemias, and the α chains tend to stick together, which causes membrane damage to developing cells in the bone marrow. The thalassemias are characterized by splenomegaly, hepatomegaly, pallor, reticulocytosis, decreased hemoglobin and hematocrit, and small, pale cells. Furthermore, the hemoglobin is not as functional in oxygen carriage and dissociation, and so hypoxic damage to organs develops. This is especially marked during the growing years, and a typical facies and skeletal growth disturbance characterize many patients.

Metabolic derangements of the erythrocytes. There are many genetic diseases that disrupt the normal metabolic functions of erythrocytes and several specific membrane defect diseases, all of which cause hemolytic anemias. Perhaps the most interesting of these relatively rare disorders is glucose-6-phosphate dehydrogenase deficiency. This is a hereditary decrease in an enzyme that is important in the anaerobic metabolism of erythrocytes, and for the cells to be protected from oxidative damage, this metabolism must be intact. Without protection, cells that are exposed to oxidative stress will lyse. This deficiency is an ancient disorder and Pythagoreas reportedly advised his followers to avoid the fava bean fields. Fava beans contain a chemical that can oxidate unprotected red cells, and exposure to the air of a fava bean field, or smoke from burning its foliage, may cause a hemolytic crisis in afflicted people. Since hemolysis occurs only on exposure to oxidants, the treatment is aimed toward prevention of exposure. The antimalarial drugs and other chemicals are the most common oxidants of concern. The defect is found in persons of Mediterranean, African, Southeast Asian, and Far Eastern descent.

Blood loss (anemia)

The anemia associated with blood loss depends on whether acute hemorrhagic loss or chronic blood loss is present. With an acute bleeding episode, the anemia is a result of a loss of circulating blood cells. The true degree of anemia is initially difficult to discern as dilution by water movement into the vascular space occurs as a compensatory response to the blood loss. The lowest hematocrit is not usually reached for 24 hours after the hemorrhage, and the reticulocyte count does not increase until 3 to 5 days later. Of course, the anemia itself is normocytic and normochromic. In chronic blood loss, the anemia that develops is associated with iron deficiency, so microcytosis and hypochromia develop. The most common cause of chronic blood loss is gastrointestinal bleeding, although menstrual bleeding can be excessive and can lead to this form of anemia.

Polycythemia

Polycythemia refers to a condition in which red blood cell production is excessive and the hematocrit, hemoglobin, and erythrocyte count are elevated above normal values. Since hematopoiesis is stimulated by hypoxia-induced erythropoietin release, conditions accompanied by tissue hypoxia may produce a polycythemic response. For example, congenital heart disease, chronic obstructive pulmonary disease, and congestive heart failure often have an accompanying polycythemia. An acquired disease, polycythemia vera, is not associated with hypoxia but appears to arise from a stem cell disturbance and is associated with excessive production of all the blood cells. It may be the result of an unresponsive stem cell proliferative system or lack of dependency on erythropoietin. This is a chronic condition that is usually treated by periodic blood letting, as there may be considerable pathophysiology associated with this hypercellularity. For example, the high hematocrit will increase the blood viscosity and slow its flow, which increases cardiac demand. Thromboses are possible, and dyspnea and symptoms of decreased cerebral flow may develop. Splenomegaly is the result of reticuloendothelial activity, which is activated by the need for enhanced red cell removal.

WHITE BLOOD CELL DISORDERS

The importance of the white blood cell in inflammation and immunity has been described at length in Chapter 2. The box below lists the granulocyte disorders. A short case study illustrates a genetic neutropenic disorder that serves as a model of white cell dyscrasia.

DISORDERS OF THE GRANULOCYTES

Neutrophils

Maturational disorders—aplastic anemia, pernicious anemia

Phagocytic and secretory disorders—chronic granulomatous disease

Neoplasias—granulocytic leukemias

Neutropenias—cyclic neutropenia, cachexia, cirrhosis, lupus

Eosinophils

Eosinophilia—allergic disease, skin disorders, parasitic infestations

Eosinopenia—stress

Basophils

Increased production—myxedema

Decreased production—hyperthyroidism

CASE STUDY: CYCLIC NEUTROPENIA

History

Tommy is a 14-year-old boy with a disorder known as cyclic neutropenia. He is the second child in his family to inherit this disorder; another brother died in adolescence from complications associated with the disease. Tommy's mother also appears to have a variant of the defect but has minimal symptoms at this point. She reports, however, that during childhood she was frequently ill but had never been diagnosed with cyclic neutropenia. Tommy develops neutropenia and occasionally catastrophically low white cell counts on a fairly regular 60-to-90-day cycle. Between the episodes of neutropenia, he remains essentially symptom free. When neutropenic, he develops fevers, night sweats, and bacterial infections, and on occasion he has become septic and morbidly ill. The illness appears to have worsened since Tommy entered puberty.

Subjective and Objective Data

Tommy is seen during an acute neutropenic episode. He is febrile (103° F) and pale and has rales in both lungs, a cough with purulent blood-streaked sputum, and moderate cervical lymphadenopathy. There is mild splenomegaly and hepatomegaly. The complete blood count shows the following:

White blood cells	2,450
Neutrophils	7%
Eosinophils	0%
Basophils	2%
Lymphocytes	72%
Monocytes	19%
Hemoglobin	11 gm/dl
Hematocrit	36%

Radiographic studies and sputum cultures indicate bilateral pneumococcal pneumonia.

_____
Contributed by Maureen Groër.

Pathophysiology

This defect is a genetic disturbance in hematopoiesis, probably related to regulation of the cell division, and disrupted feedback control, probably at the membrane level. An animal model, the gray collie dog, has regular cycles in all blood cell components, and this may also occur in humans, although the decline in neutrophils produces the most symptoms. The disease often becomes less severe with age, although cycles may continue through the life span.

This is a rare disease but is probably not diagnosed as frequently as it occurs, because the cycles of neutropenia are somewhat variable and may range in severity. Tommy's mother still has neutropenic cycles, but they are so mild that no symptoms are produced. On the other hand, Tommy's neutropenia is severe and to the point of producing serious infections. Stressed by the memories of the loss of Tommy's brother, Tommy's family is very fearful about his apparently worsening disease.

Nursing Diagnoses

The nursing diagnoses for this patient and his family center on protection from infection and management of the psychologic stress experienced:

1. Impaired gas exchange related to pneumonia
2. Potential for infection related to inadequate body defenses
3. Fear related to death of sibling and worsening disease process
4. Self-concept disturbance related to frequent illnesses impeding the completion of adolescent developmental tasks

DISORDERS OF COAGULATION

Platelets and blood and tissue factors work together in coagulation. The process of

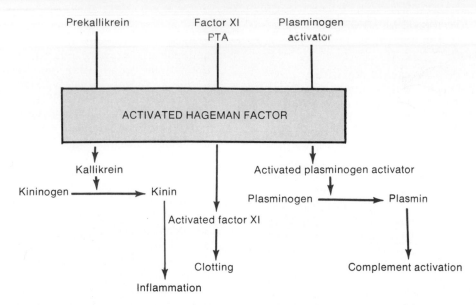

Fig. 3-4. Interrelationships between inflammation, coagulation, and complement. Activated Hageman factor is believed to be involved not only in coagulation cascade but also in formation of kallikrein and activated plasminogen. Thus, kinins, which are involved in inflammation, plasmin, which is involved in fibrinolysis and complement activation, and the coagulation cascade are linked through Hageman factor activation.

blood coagulation is a normal defense of the body that functions to confine and contain the blood and seal off injured blood vessels. Coagulation does not occur independently from the other operating defenses and barriers. The activation of Hageman factor results not only in the blood coagulation cascade but also sets into play other important responses to injury (Fig. 3-4). Hageman factor initiates the conversion of prekallikrein to kallikrein, which then causes the formation of kinin from kininogen. The importance of kinins in inflammation has been described previously. Contributing also to the inflammatory response is activation of complement by Hageman factor–dependent formation of plasmin from plasminogen. Plasmin also plays a major role in fibrinolysis, or clot dissolution. It can be seen that there is a tremendous interaction between coagulation, fibrinolysis, and acute inflammation.

Normal coagulation

Blood coagulation is a complex and multifactorial process. A currently plausible scheme is shown in Fig. 3-5, which diagrams the requirements and interactions responsible for coagulation. Two major systems operate in coagulation, an intrinsic and an extrinsic system, along with the blood platelets. The ultimate result of these reactions is the formation of strands of fibrin, which form the actual meshwork of a clot. The initiation of coagulation by Hageman factor activation sets off a cascade of events that results eventually in fibrin formation. Once the first event occurs, other events follow as if they were irrevocably "programmed," much like falling dominoes. The factors involved in co-

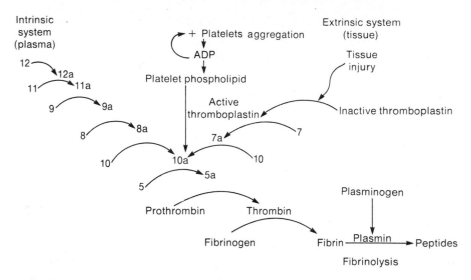

Fig. 3-5. Blood coagulation. Intrinsic and extrinsic systems of coagulation, in concert with effects of platelet aggregation, yield activated factors, which produce a cascading effect, ultimately leading to formation of strands of fibrin. Fibrin is broken down through action of plasmin. Both coagulation cascade and process of fibrinolysis require activated Hageman factor, as shown in Fig. 3-4.

agulation are normally present in the blood and tissues as inactive precursors. The initiating event, that of Hageman factor activation, is not well understood. It is believed that this activation is surface dependent. Hageman factor is a protein that becomes activated upon contact with negatively charged materials (kaolin, glass, silicates) and biologic material (e.g., collagen, endotoxin, uric acid, and various crystals). This activation seems to be quite slow but is accelerated by other activated factors as they form and thus is a positive feedback phenomenon.

Arterial and venous thrombi

Changes in the vascular endothelium can result in surface activation of Hageman factor. Atherosclerotic plaque formation demonstrates this quite well. Such plaques are often observed to cause localized coagulation, or thrombus formation. The thrombus may obstruct a vessel, causing local tissue ischemia, or may dislodge from the vessel wall and travel through the blood to other

sites in the body such as the lungs or brain. Such traveling clots are known as *emboli* and can cause sudden death if they lodge in critical organs such as the lungs (pulmonary embolism), the heart (myocardial infarction), or the brain (cerebrovascular accident). Thrombin formation appears to occur predominantly in the arterial side of the circulation and is mainly caused by roughened endothelium and collagen exposure, resulting in platelet aggregation and activation of the intrinsic and extrinsic coagulation cascades.

Venous thrombosis appears be a response to different pathophysiology. Most commonly such thromboses develop in the deep veins of the leg and are associated with venous stasis. The veins can hold large quantities of blood in their function as capacitance vessels, but normally the blood moves through these vessels by the action of muscular contraction, which acts as a pump. Furthermore, the veins contain valves that do not permit backflow of blood distally through the vein. When immobilization of a part of the body occurs with loss of muscle pumping activity, the blood may remain and stagnate in the veins. Increased viscosity of the blood, such as occurs in high hematocrit states, also may result in sluggish flow through all the vessels. This stasis creates a local environment in which thrombin is concentrated. Thrombin itself can initiate platelet aggregation and thrombus formation. The intimal endothelium in a thrombosed vein is usually normal, and it is believed that the thrombin is generated elsewhere in the body at sites of arterial injury or microinjury. Normally this endogenously formed thrombin would be removed by the liver and inactivated, but in conditions of venous stasis the thrombin may be concentrated by the stasis, sequestered from the liver, and not destroyed adequately. Thus it can initiate local venous coagulation, which typically can spread, sometimes the entire length of the involved vein, obstructing blood flow and creating a situation in which multiple emboli may arise. There is also some evidence that fibrinolysis is inadequate in individuals prone to venous thrombosis and may result from impaired plasminogen activation. In susceptible patients there appears to be a shift toward clot formation rather than dissolution. Some researchers believe that a small amount of natural clotting occurs continuously, but in normal individuals these activated coagulation factors and clots are rapidly removed. In the patient prone to venous thrombosis these control mechanisms may be lost, setting up a situation for thrombus formation whenever venous stasis occurs. Causes of venous stasis include immobility, surgery, childbirth, injury, estrogen-containing oral contraceptives, and systemic illnesses. These factors may interact in very complex ways with other factors in the environment. Of interest, for example, is the finding that patients with blood group A who take oral contraceptives are more at risk for venous thrombosis formation than are persons with other blood groups. Furthermore, humans are peculiar among the animal kingdom with regard to the formation of venous thrombosis; no animal system exists in which to study the process. Therefore the understanding of thombosis in humans is limited by the lack of experiments on the basic process and the interaction of factors.

Disseminated intravascular coagulation

Disseminated intravascular coagulation (DIC) is a serious major complication of a variety of conditions, including childbirth, abruptio placentae, transfusion reactions, endotoxin shock, infection, surgery, metastatic cancer, necrotizing enterocolitis, snake bite, and severe tissue damage from trauma. In this condition massive coagulation occurs, mostly in the small vessels, because of activation of the intrinsic coagulation cascade. The process by which this activation occurs is not clear. It is believed that its occurrence in obstetric patients results from the intravascular invasion of thromboplastic material, perhaps from the placenta. Immune mechanisms are also known to operate, and it is thought that immune generation of tissue thromboplastin may be responsible for activation of clot formation. Widespread complement activation may also be responsible for the symptoms. Certain malignant tumors may release substances that digest fibrin or otherwise interrupt normal coagulation. DIC may be acute, subacute, or chronic. The subacute form is less common and is associated with disseminated cancer or retention of a dead fetus in utero for 3 or more weeks. The rare chronic form occurs in certain vascular deformities.

Although the pathogenesis of DIC is not clearly understood, one common characteristic is defibrination. The defibrination, or extremely prolonged clotting time, is thought to result from the utilization of the coagulation factors in the disseminated coagulation, so that hemorrhage follows, since the coagulation cascade becomes delayed. Fibrinogen levels are usually extremely low, and fibrinolytic digestion products (FDP) are found in the blood. FDPs are formed by the action of plasmin on fibrin and have been shown to inhibit clotting by inhibiting the thrombin-fibrinogen reaction and platelet release of ADP. Thus the depletion of the coagulation factors and the accumulation of FDPs appear to be responsible for DIC-induced hemorrhage.

The treatment of DIC is complicated by the fact that coagulation and hemorrhage, two opposite phenomena, have occurred in the same patient. The usual treatment is heparin given intravenously at a slow rate. In many patients this will result in cessation of bleeding and be life saving, while in other patients heparin infusion may accentuate the bleeding. Further treatment must also be aimed at the underlying cause of DIC in each individual patient. Attention must be directed to the effects of hypoxia on organs as the result of intravascular fibrin deposition. Gross alteration in function of any organ may result. The reticuloendothelial system's capacity to phagocytose foreign or particulate matter may be overwhelmed, leading to alteration in the body's defenses and barriers. Multiple organ failure is a possible end result.

Effects of increased viscosity on coagulation

Viscosity is affected by many variables, including metabolic disease, cancer, infections, trauma, smoking, and blood diseases, all of which may result in the high viscosity syndrome, leading to aggregation and concentration of blood cells. This, in turn, results in localized vascular stasis and hypoxia, conditions that promote platelet aggregation. These effects set up potent positive feedbacks or vicious cycles, which act to further potentiate the effects of high viscosity. Stress and hypoxia lead to necrosis, intravascular coagulation, and thromboembolism, which may then be overtly manifested as a variety of thrombotic disease states.

High viscosity is usually indicated by a high blood hematocrit (percentage of erythrocytes per 1 dl whole blood). The movement of high-hematocrit blood through capillaries of critical radius leads to sludging and stasis. This always leads to a reduction in the oxygenation of tissues, a phenomenon that may result in damage to the capillary walls so that the permeability of the endothelium is increased. Such an effect leads to increased net filtration from the capillary into the tissue space and further hemoconcentration of the blood. This is but one example of the many positive pathophysiologic feedbacks perpetuated in conditions of increased blood viscosity. Hematocrit itself may not always be elevated when blood viscosity is increased. Conditions that cause the erythrocytes to aggregate (viral infections, fever, excess fibrinogen, toxins) may have the same ultimate result as high-hematocrit blood. The red cell aggregation makes the blood more viscous and difficult to transport through the capillaries, and ultimately stasis and hypoxia are produced.

Disorders of platelets
Properties of platelets

Platelets are unique structures formed from giant cells, megakaryocytes, which are normally found only in the bone marrow. Platelets, although not possessing nuclei and therefore not true cells, nevertheless are metabolically active and capable of phenomena such as exocytosis and active transport. They are extremely small bits of megakaryocytes and are surrounded by a true cell membrane. Platelets undergo a process known as viscous metamorphosis when they are activated. Major changes in shape and morphology occur in this process before the platelets undergo ultimate dissolution. Activation of viscous metamorphosis is through contact with foreign surfaces such as exposed collagen, antigen-antibody complexes, thrombin, proteolytic enzymes, endotoxins, ADP, and viruses.

Once the platelet is stimulated through contact via probable receptors on its cell membrane surface, an immediate shape change ensues. This is then followed by a change in the character of the membrane; it becomes sticky, the platelets adhering to surfaces such as collagen and the basement membrane, spreading out pseudopods such that a maximal degree of contact between the platelet and the surface occurs.

The next major phenomenon is platelet aggregation, a process by which platelets adhere to each other, causing a platelet plug, and because of early aggregation, the release phenomenon results. ADP, in particular, is released from platelets at this time, and a positive feedback occurs in which ADP itself causes further platelet aggregation. Aggregation requires Ca^{++} and some fibrinogen to be present. The release of ADP and other factors from platelets is by a process of extrusion of the contents of granules inside the platelet cytoplasm and through the membrane. Substances known to be released by activated platelets include ADP, ATP, serotonin, Ca^{++}, possibly an antiheparin substance, lysosomal enzymes, a permeability factor, fibrinogen, and platelet factor 3, or

platelet phospholipid. The latter factor is believed to activate a prothrombin-to-thrombin reaction as does thromboplastin and thus stimulate blood clotting.

The formation of a plug of platelets is a different process from the actual formation of a blood clot. Although the ultimate result of platelet aggregation is release of substances that aid in the clotting mechanism, blood clotting can occur without platelets being present, and platelet aggregation can theoretically occur in the absence of blood clotting, although thrombin is required in small amounts for platelet release to occur. Platelets "bridge the gap" between vascular contraction and clotting in an injury. They form a hemostatic plug, which acts to seal the vessel so that the intrinsic and to some degree the extrinsic system can operate to form fibrin strands.

Vascular contraction, which is the result of many factors (e.g., nervous, mechanical, and myogenic reactions) operating in an injury also is aided by the release of serotonin by the platelets. This amine stimulates the local vessel contraction, which then allows platelets to anchor, aggregate, and form a seal upon which fibrin strands will be laid down. Typically platelets will disappear from a blood clot by 24 hours, to be totally replaced by fibrin. The clot, or thrombus if this is the result of the injury, is then invaded by polymorphonuclear phagocytes and later by monocytes in an acute inflammatory reaction to the clot. By 11 days after the injury the lesion formed is full of new muscle cells and fibroblasts and is covered with endothelium, and the integrity of the vessel is restored.

Platelet aggregation

The phenomenon of platelet aggregation is interesting in that it is affected by many drugs and disease states and may be fundamental to conditions that were formerly believed to be entirely immune in nature. Platelet aggregation is increased in patients with high triglycerides but not in those with hypercholesterolemia. It is a process that is tremendously enhanced by epinephrine; the possible effects of constant stress in susceptible individuals (which results in increased activity of the sympathetic nervous system) upon coagulation-dependent phenomena (e.g., strokes, myocardial infarctions) are important to consider. Platelet aggregation is greatly inhibited by aspirin. The acetyl group appears to be responsible for this effect. A 0.5 mM blood concentration of aspirin, which could result from the ingestion of two to four tablets, causes a mild bleeding tendency. Furthermore, a single dose of aspirin produces an effect that remains for days, long after the aspirin has been metabolized and excreted. An increased bleeding time can be measured after aspirin ingestion in normal individuals, and in the hemophiliac aspirin can cause severe impairment of hemostasis. The mode of action is believed to result from a surface-active effect of the drug on platelet ADP release. Inhibition of the release will result in loss of positive feedback stimulation of platelet aggregation. Prophylactic aspirin use is now common in patients who are at high risk for myocardial infarction or stroke. Other drugs that are known to inhibit platelet aggregation include PGE_1 (prostaglandin E_1), dipyridamole, and nitroglycerin. Heparin also has some inhibitory effect on platelet aggregation, although this is not its main physiologic action in coagulation disorders.

The interaction of platelet aggregation with immune responses is of great interest. It has been demonstrated that when antigen-antibody complexes are injected into rabbits they are found in the pulmonary vessels, where they cause obstruction. It has also been shown that the platelet count drops in such an immune reaction, and platelet plugs are also found in the pulmonary vessels. The development of shock in response to the injection of endotoxins in the rabbit does not occur when pretreatment aspirin is given. The development of platelet plugs is inhibited, and pulmonary vessels do not become obstructed with either immune complexes or platelets. Immune complex disease and the Shwartzman phenomenon may be intimately involved with activation of platelets by immune complexes, antigens, and microorganisms, and aggregation of platelets in the microvasculature.

Disease models of platelet dysfunction

Idiopathic thombocytopenic purpura and von Willebrand's disease will be discussed as models of platelet disorders.

Idiopathic thrombocytopenic purpura (ITP). Most thrombocytopenia (or decreased production of platelets) is idiopathic, that is, its etiology is unknown. The bone marrow production of megakaryocytes is depressed, sometimes as the result of certain drugs, radiation, or exposure to chemicals. ITP may also have an autoimmune nature as evidenced by the presence of IgG autoantibodies to platelet proteins in this disease. Quinine and quinidine both can cause ITP, and autoantibodies are also found in this form. Platelet deficiency is manifested by a prolonged bleeding time, ecchymoses, petechiae (minute hemorrhages of the skin and mucous membranes), epistaxis, and low platelet count. In children the disease may undergo spontaneous remission with medical treatment, which nearly always includes the administration of corticosteroids. If the bleeding tendency becomes extremely severe, splenectomy may be done. The spleen is the organ that removes damaged or aged erythrocytes and platelets; it also may be important in the synthesis of autoantibodies. Two thirds of the patients with ITP who undergo splenectomy are cured. However, there is considerable risk in the surgery itself because of the bleeding dyscrasia.

von Willebrand's disease. This hereditary disorder is manifested by an increased bleeding time and a basic defect in the ability of platelets to aggregate in the presence of a normal platelet count. This condition represents a bleeding dyscrasia that is intermediate between the platelet disorders such as ITP and the disorders of the intrinsic and extrinsic systems of coagulation such as hemophilia. Along with the decreased ability of the platelets to aggregate, there is a deficiency in factor VIII that results from the absence of a plasma factor that normally stimulates the formation of factor VIII. Patients with von Willebrand's disease usually do not bleed into joints as do classic hemophiliacs. These patients are able to produce factor VIII when given transfusions of normal plasma. The disease also occurs in females and often improves with age and during pregnancy.

Other platelet disorders. Platelet deficiency states may arise in conditions characterized by aplasia or hypoplasia of the bone marrow or in conditions in which paltelet survival is decreased, or they can be acquired as the result of transfusions of platelet-poor blood. Platelet function may be impaired in other conditions that are not as yet well characterized. The best example of this is von Willebrand's disease, but other conditions are known to exist (Glanzmann's disease, Bernard-Soulier syndrome, albinism, Wiskott-Aldrich syndrome). These conditions are all hereditary, but acquired disorders of platelet function may be present in uremia, in diseases in which fibrin or fibrinogen degradation products are found (liver disease, DIC, fibrinolysis), in certain myeloprolif-erative disorders such as polycythemia vera, in scurvy, in glycogen storage disease, and in the presence of certain drugs.

Disease model of coagulation deficiency: hemophilia

At least 11 factors are known to be required for the normal coagulation cascade to proceed. A deficiency of any of the nine particular factors (I, II, V, VII, VIII, IX, X, XI, and XIII) results in a bleeding tendency. The type of bleeding tendency associated with various factor deficiencies differs from that associated with platelet abnormalities. In the latter case the bleeding that follows an injury is often profuse, usually immediate, and once it stops, it generally does not recur. With coagulation defects the amount of bleeding after an injury is not usually excessive, but rather it is prolonged and tends to recur. Bleeding into joints, muscle, and subcutaneous tissue characterizes these factor deficiencies, while purpura, ecchymosis, gastrointestinal bleeding, epistaxis, and menorrhagia are the most common forms of bleeding that take place in platelet or hemostatic disorders.

Hemophilia is the most common factor-deficiency disease, although still extremely rare, occurring in 1 out of 25,000 persons in the general population in its severe form. Milder variants are more common. Hemophilia is transmitted as a sex-linked recessive trait (see Fig. 4-8). It is also possible for the hemophilia trait to arise from a mutation, as nearly 30% of the affected males cannot demonstrate the disease in the family tree. Carriers of the trait often show some slight tendency toward bleeding following trauma.

The classic hemophilia is characterized by a deficiency in factor VIII, seen in 80% of the patients. Factor IX deficiency, or Christmas disease, clinically resembles hemophilia in every way and is found in 13% of these patients, while factor XI (PTA) deficiency is observed in 6%. Other factor deficiencies make up less than 1% of all hemophilias. Classic hemophilia no longer can be described as an absolute deficiency in factor VIII, since evidence that this factor is present in the blood is compelling. It would appear, however, that factor VIII consists of two subunits, and one subunit deficiency is responsible for classic hemophilia deficiency while an absence or decrease in the other subunit occurs in von Willebrand's disease. In classic hemophilia, factor VIII may be present as only one subunit, and therefore the coagulation cascade is interrupted at this point.

The signs and symptoms of classic hemophilia are related to the severity of the disease, but the most common problem is, of course, bleeding with or without trauma, which often occurs into joints. Such joint hemorrhages, which are painful and debilitating, are called hemarthroses. The hemarthrosis itself is damaging to the synovial lining of the joint, but it also causes distension of the joint and resultant ischemia that can progressively result in more and more thickening and scarring of the joint. Ankylosis of the joint may eventually develop with resultant deformity and muscular atrophy from immobility. Bleeding also may occur in the gastrointestinal tract and into the urine, and the hemophiliac patient may exasanguinate in severe traumatic injury or major surgery.

Treatment is based on the qualitative absence of factor VIII. Factor VIII concentrate, which is prepared by cryoprecipitation, is usually given for bleeding episodes, and of course supportive therapy to the joints, muscles, and other involved areas must also be carried out.

SUMMARY

This chapter has examined disturbances in the formation of and physiologic function of the blood cells. Since the various blood cells have differing functions, the dyscrasias produce a wide variety of signs and symptoms. Considering the enormously important transporting functions of the blood, when disruption of the cellular components occurs, many coping strategies must be employed. A person with anemia, for example, will tend to conserve energy because hypoxic stress may occur with activity. Fatigue is a real problem not only for the anemic patient but also for those with deficient platelet or white cell function when crises occur. The person with a bleeding disorder may not be able to carry out the activities of daily living without assistance. When coping itself becomes so fatiguing and stressful, many other aspects of wellness become disturbed. It is often a nursing goal to support coping and assist in conserving energy so that life will have higher quality as a person learns to tolerate chronic illness or to recover from acute problems.

BIBLIOGRAPHY

Biggs R, editor: Human blood, coagulation, haemostasis, and thrombosis, ed 2, Oxford, England, 1976, Blackwell Scientific Publications Inc.

Charache S and Zohoun I: Pathogenesis of painful sickle cell crises. In Nagel R, editor: New York 1987, Pathophysiological Aspects of Sickle Cell Vasoocclusion. Alan R Liss Inc.

Embury S: The clinical pathophysiology of sickle cell disease, Ann Rev Med 37:361, 1986.

Hocking W, editor: Practical hematology, New York, 1983, John Wiley & Sons.

Monzon C: Anemia in infancy and childhood, Postgrad Med 78:275, 1985.

Nagel R, et al: Sickle cell painful crisis: a multifactorial event. In Nagel R, editor: Pathophysiological Aspects of Sickle Cell Vasoocclusion New York 1987, Alan R Liss Inc.

Thorup O: Fundamentals of clinical hematology, ed 5, Philadelphia, 1987, WB Saunders Co.

Wintrobe M: Clinical hematology, ed 8, Philadelphia, 1981, Lea & Febiger.

4

External factors: developmental pathophysiology

This chapter will describe the influence of development on pathophysiologic phenomena. Because of maturational factors during infancy, childhood, and adolescence and senescent changes during adult life, development dictates risk for many pathophysiologic processes. The fetal period, for example, is fraught with danger from internal and external teratogens that can impede normal organogenesis. Congenital defects develop during this period that have long-lasting effects throughout life. During infancy and childhood, the immune system develops and the child may suffer various disease processes as a result of lack of immunocompetence. Growth may result in skeletal disturbances. In adolescence, puberty may cause endocrine and dermatologic problems. Adulthood is associated with cumulative disease processes such as cardiovascular disease and cancer, and aging has an associated host of pathophysiologic declines in every organ system. The goal of this chapter is to point out how developmental physiologic and psychologic phenomena increase the risk for certain types of pathophysiologic processes. The first section of this chapter focuses on the teratogenic and genetic mechanisms of disease responsible for fetal pathophysiology.

The Fetal Period

HUMAN GENE POOL

Each individual's appearance, body structure, intellectual capacity, and biochemistry is controlled in large part by the up to 40,000 possible gene pairs on the 23 pairs of human chromosomes. Every living species can be considered to have a pool of possible genes, and the combination of these genes through reproduction allows for the incredible variety that is observed in all the individuals of the species. Nevertheless, there is a constancy in the gene pool so that the characteristics of the species itself are preserved from one generation to the next. The expression of the *genotype*, which is the individual's unique set of genes, through the transcription of deoxyribonucleic acid (DNA) into ribonucleic acid (RNA) and finally into proteins, results in a specific *phenotype* for each member of the species. Each individual, while possessing traits that are species specific (e.g., fur, limbs, hemoglobin), has the possibility for great variety in the nature of these traits through mutations that have occurred during the course of evolution and that have been retained by the species and form part of the gene pool.

Mixing of the parents' genes also allows

for individual variation and occurs during the processes of oogenesis and spermatogenesis through meiosis. Meiosis is a type of cellular division in which the normal, or *diploid*, chromosomal number (46 in the human) is reduced to half, or to the *haploid* number. The basic difference between mitosis and meiosis is that in meiosis the centromeres do not divide as in mitosis, so that whole chromosomes move to the poles of the cell and then into the daughter cells. This process is illustrated in Fig. 4-1. The final result of spermatogenesis and oogenesis is the production of four haploid gametes, which have the potential to unite with gametes from the opposite sex and form diploid embryos. In the case of oogenesis only one haploid gamete, the ovum, is produced, the three other products of meiosis forming *polar bodies*, which cannot be fertilized. The process of meiosis, when considered in light of the tremendous number of possible gene combinations from the species gene pool, ensures that no two individuals can ever be exactly the same except, of course, in the case of *monozygotic* (from one ovum) twins.

Mutations

Mutations are alterations in the sequence of bases in the DNA molecule, which forms the genetic code. They may be caused by such agents as viruses, radiation, chemicals, and the aging process. Some mutations are lethal, some sublethal, some beneficial, and probably most are inconsequential. The cell has an elaborate and efficient system of enzymes that repair DNA damage in most cases. An additional factor is the tremendous redundancy of information that is contained within the genetic code. A set of three bases in DNA makes up a "codon," which is specific for a particular amino acid. However, up to six different codon sequences can code for the same amino acid.

Individuals inherit genetic material from both parents and for many traits a set of *alleles* exists (alleles are genes coding for the same trait and are identically placed on homologous chromosomes, since one is inherited from each parent). There are, of course, some traits that are sex linked and carried on only the X chromosome. In this case, a male individual has only one gene for that trait whereas a female, having two X chromosomes, would have two genes for the trait.

Mutations that occur in somatic (body) cells, if not repaired, may cause damage or change in that organism's functional integrity, but the mutation will not become part of the human gene pool, because it is lost when the individual dies. Mutations in germ (sex) cells that are retained can be passed on to viable progeny and could eventually become part of the gene pool.

During the course of the millions of years of evolution, mutations constantly occurred within the genetic material of all species and were, in fact, necessary for speciation and survival. The possibility of mutation is required by Darwin's theory of natural selection. Mutations will cause a change in either the nature or the amount of the protein coded for by the DNA segment that has mutated. Fig. 4-2 illustrates the normal coding of DNA for RNA and protein. A change in a protein may not affect the protein's function to any measurable degree, and many minor differences in amino acid composition of particular proteins have been discovered. Amino acid variations of the same proteins among different species represent mutations that occurred in the distant past and have been retained as part of the gene pool. Generally speaking, a mutation that results in a deformity or a disease confers a selective

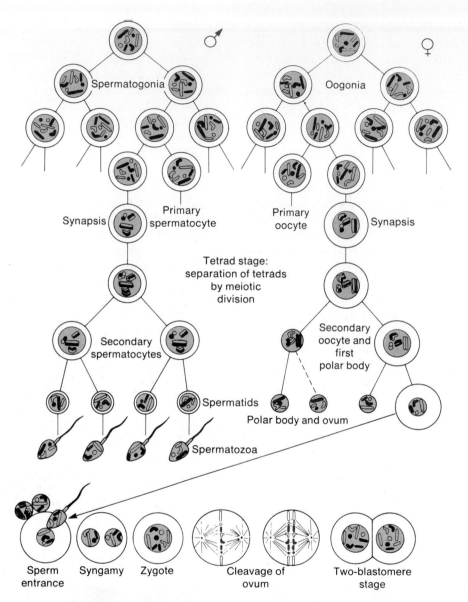

Fig. 4-1. Meiosis. Process of spermatogenesis and oogenesis involves meiotic division, during which whole chromosomes move to daughter cells. Primary spermatocyte and oocyte undergo synapsis, in which pairs of chromosomes line up and bits of genetic material may be exchanged between chromosomes. Chromosomes line up on spindle (tetrad stage), and then each member of a pair of chromosomes moves to a daughter cell of division. In this way, diploid number of chromosomes is reduced to half (haploid) in spermatozoa and ovum. Result of sperm entrance (fertilization) is indicated with fertilized egg containing diploid number of chromosomes. In humans, the second meiotic division occurs only after sperm penetration.

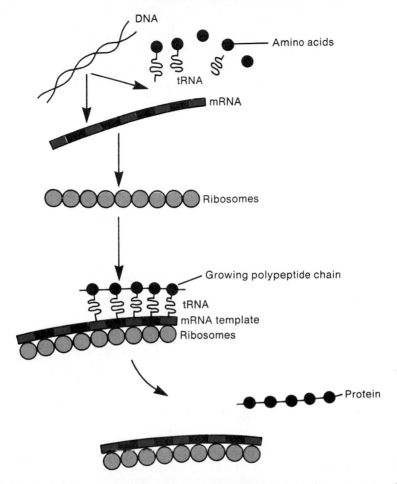

Fig. 4-2. Protein synthesis. Proteins are synthesized on ribosomes, and component amino acids are assembled according to sequence dictated by the code on mRNA. Sequence of mRNA is determined by transcription of nuclear DNA code. Amino acids are brought to ribosomes by the tRNA, which attaches via complementary bases, to mRNA, ordering amino acids in proper sequence.

disadvantage upon the individual, which in the competitive struggle for survival will make it more difficult for that individual to find food, shelter, and a mate. Thus through the process of natural selection, undesirable traits are weeded out, and the strongest and healthiest of the species will continue to survive, bearing the most offspring for the further propagation of the species and parent-specific traits. Muta-

tions that confer a selective advantage upon the individual will also be retained through the same process.

Natural selection is extremely slow, however, and many deleterious mutations within DNA presently exist and form part of the human gene pool. The reasons for this are obscure and complex. Theoretically, any disease-causing mutation should be eliminated by natural selection, unless it somehow confers a selective advantage. For example, certain areas of the world, the endemic malaria belts, coincide with the distribution of the sickle cell anemia trait. It has become apparent that the presence of the sickle cell trait, which is the asymptomatic heterozygous state of the mutated gene that codes for the abnormal hemoglobin of sickle cell disease, confers a resistance to malarial infection that results in a selective advantage in the carrier. Thus the sickle cell trait has persisted in 10% of the black population in the United States in spite of the fact that the homozygous condition, sickle cell anemia, is a serious and often fatal disease (see Chapter 3).

Most perfectly healthy people probably have three to five mutated genes for which they are heterozygous and which cause no symptoms of disease. If found in the homozygous state these genes would result in an inborn error of metabolism that could seriously affect the individual's potential for a healthy and productive life. The majority of genetic diseases are the result of point mutations. A problem facing modern medicine lies in the treatment of people with hereditary conditions who live a long and healthy life, bearing offspring who may inherit the trait if not the disease. The mechanisms by which natural selection operates in nature can no longer ensure that the members of a species who survive are the strongest and most well adapted to the environment. This alone has implications for the future of mankind, and the science of DNA technology presages an entirely new direction for evolution in the future.

NORMAL DIFFERENTIATION

The human being develops from a single fertilized ovum into an incredibly complex, multicellular organism. The fertilized ovum, or zygote, is diploid and begins to divide by mitotic division shortly after fertilization. Mitosis (Fig. 4-3) produces two identical daughter cells with the same amount and type of DNA. Very early in the division or *cleavages* of the ball of embryonic cells, certain cells begin to differentiate into different tissues, and three primitive germ layers are formed: the ectoderm, mesoderm, and endoderm. The ectoderm will further differentiate into major structures such as the skin and nervous system. The mesoderm differentiates into structures such as bone and muscle, whereas the endoderm will form the gastrointestinal tract and major abdominal organs. This process is known as *organogenesis* and takes place primarily in the first 3 months (trimester) of the human gestational period. The sequence and extent of organogenesis are precisely "programmed" in all animals. The first trimester as a whole is considered to be a critical period in terms of organ structure and function in that the developing human embryo is most susceptible to the damaging effects of agents known as *teratogens*. Teratogens cause developmental or *congenital* anomalies when put in contact with differentiating and growing embryonic tissues. Major teratogens include physical agents (trauma, irradiation), chemicals (drugs such as thalidomide), and microorganisms (rubella virus: German measles). The basic processes of teratogenesis will be discussed later.

HEREDITARY MECHANISMS

Basic laws of mendelian inheritance require that any trait be governed by pairs of genes, which are located on pairs of chromosomes.

The 46 human chromosomes consist of 22 pairs of autosomes and 1 pair of sex chromosomes. One member of each of the 23 chromosomal pairs was initially contributed by the father's haploid sperm and

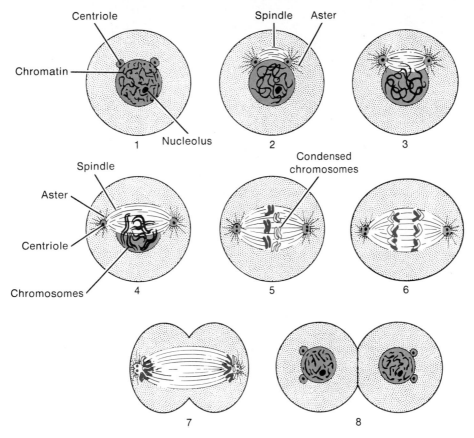

Fig. 4-3. Mitosis is process by which somatic cells divide. In mitosis individual chromosomes are pulled apart at centromere when cell divides, with chromatids moving to opposite poles and ultimately to daughter cells. Chromatids eventually duplicate, thus preserving diploid number of chromosomes.

one by the mother's haploid ovum. The individual chromosomes can be identified from prepared slides of certain cells such as stimulated leukocytes in metaphase, and a karyotype (a photograph of the matched chromosome pairs, Fig. 4-4) allows the geneticist to categorize the 46 chromosomes into seven groups, which are based on size, shape, and certain special characteristics.

Human karyotyping has become more accurate in recent years. Techniques for *banding* the individual member of each chromosome pair with Giemsa stain or fluorescent dyes have been developed. This banding is characteristic. Large numbers of syndromes and abnormalities have now been linked to chromosomal defects, some of them identifiable only by banding, and now geneticists believe that every human chromosome can be structurally altered, producing various defects in the offspring.

Genetic loci

The technology for ascertaining the location of certain genes on particular chromosomes is becoming available but is ex-

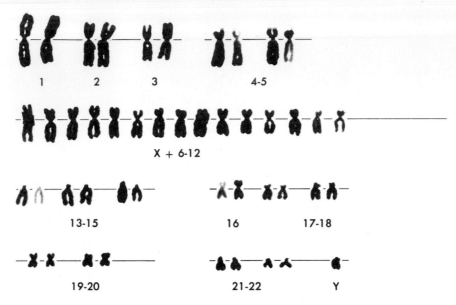

Fig. 4-4. Normal karyotype. Chromosomes are grouped according to size and centromere position.
(From Reisman LE, and Matheny AP: Genetics and counseling in medical practice, St Louis, 1969, The CV Mosby Co.)

tremely complex. It, along with the technology involved in the construction of DNA in the laboratory, has opened a scientific frontier that is both awe inspiring and frightening in its possibilities. Basic research into cell *hybridization* has led to the identification of the loci for 50 genes on 18 chromosomes controlling various enzymes; for example, enolase, adenylate kinase, phosphoglucomutase, and peptidase genes have all been localized to chromosome 1 in the human. The gene for malate dehydrogenase has been identified on chromosome 2, and the gene coding for glucose 6-phosphate dehydrogenase is on the X chromosome. Elegant experiments involving human cells and other species cells in hybridization result in fusion of cells in tissue culture and the resultant production of hybrid cells, which contain the genetic material of both cells (Fig. 4-5). Experiments in which human fibroblasts and mouse hepatoma cells were fused re-

sulted in cells containing between 41 and 55 chromosomes. All 40 mouse chromosomes were invariably present; the human chromosomes that were present in different hybrid cells were variable and appeared to be present on a random basis. Identification of the mouse and human chromosomes can be carried out by Giemsa or fluorescent staining and by electrophoresis of the protein gene products. The amino acid composition of proteins of mice and humans is sufficiently different to allow separate identification. When genes coding for different proteins are either lost together or expressed together in hybridization experiments, it can be assumed that these genes are *syntenic* or on the same chromosome. Thus through careful study of the karyotype and the proteins coded for by the hybrid cells, the location of various genes has been elucidated. Refinement of these basic techniques is leading to exciting discoveries in

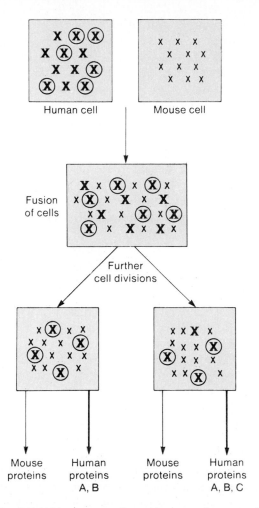

Human cell   Mouse cell

Fusion
of cells

Further
cell divisions

Mouse   Human   Mouse   Human
proteins   proteins   proteins   proteins
             A, B   A, B, C

Fig. 4-5. When mouse cells and human cells are made to fuse under experimental conditions, cells that are formed contain both human and mouse chromosomes. These cells therefore produce both human and mouse proteins. All mouse chromosomes are retained, but a *variable* number of human chromosomes can be found in hybrid cells. Study of karyotype and protein products of fused cells has led to localization of genes on chromosomes.

both the basic biology of genetics and in the understanding and treatment of diseases. It is now known, for example, that the polio virus receptor protein is coded by chromosome 5 and that the antiviral

substance *interferon* requires two genetic loci for its production.

Maligant transformation may also be studied using these hybridization techniques. It has been demonstrated that genes can be repressed by repressor proteins and derepressed if present in the proper environment. Normally, human leukocytes do not produce albumin. If hybrids of these cells and mouse hepatoma cells are made, some of the hybrids produce human albumin (as well as the normally produced mouse albumin). This would indicate that factors from the mouse hepatoma cells can possibly unmask the repressed gene for albumin in the human leukocyte chromosome. This experimental result has great implications for medical research. Gene expression and modulation in human cancer cells and in fetal cells derived from amniotic fluid may be studied, yielding knowledge that can be applied to the prevention and treatment of acquired and congenital diseases.

Recombinant DNA experiments are similar to the hybridization experiments, but biologic combination takes place at the molecular level, with the production of strands of DNA made up of pieces of DNA from different species. Researchers have produced bacterial cells that contain *plasmids* made up of the bacteria's own DNA and foreign DNA from another species. Plasmids are extrachromosomal pieces of DNA found in bacterial cells; plasmids sometimes participate in the exchange of genetic material between bacterial cells. The recombinant DNA produced by the enzymatic fusion of the different segments of DNA is able to code for the proteins of both types of DNA. Furthermore, when the bacterial cell divides, the plasmids containing the recombinant DNA are retained in the daughter cells, producing a new *clone* of cells. Such genetic engineering opens many possibilities for the treatment of disease. Manipulation of bacterial DNA so that certain synthetic capabilities are guaranteed and the insertion of this genetic material into the cells of individuals with various deficiency diseases (diabetes mellitus being only one of many examples) is one future possibility.

Genetic engineering also carries potential danger. The possibility of creating organisms that could play microbiologic and ecologic havoc on the planet has not been overlooked by scientists and concerned citizens. Careful control and regulation of recombinant DNA research is now legislated.

GENETIC EXPRESSION

Traits inherited as *dominant* are the expression of either the homozygous or heterozygous state. Homozygous genes are present in two copies, one on each member of the chromosomal pair, while heterozygous genes are present only on one chromosome. *Recessive* inheritance requires that the homozygous condition of the gene be present. Therefore, the possibility of a homozygous individual's being born to heterozygous parents is one in four; the chance of a heterozygous child is one in two. Certain traits are carried on the sex chromosomes and are either *X*-linked recessive or dominant traits. Since males have only one *X* chromosome and females have two, the presence of an *X*-linked gene is only expressed in the female if she is homozygous for the particular recessive gene.

The *penetrance* of a gene refers to the degree with which that particular trait occurs in the general population. Penetrance of hereditary disorders may be greatly influenced by environmental factors.

Potential genetic diseases may not be apparent in affected individuals if the diseases require that other genes be inactive or altered, and it certainly is true that many traits are controlled by multiple genetic loci. The actual genetic cause of a disease may also be obscured by compensatory mechanisms that take place. For example, a genetic deficiency in a particular protein might be so well compensated for by the overproduction of an alternate protein that no actual disease appears. Another factor, particularly in diseases that result in the accumulation of a potentially toxic substance in the body, is the concept of a *threshold*. A threshold is a critical value above which a substance will cause disease but below which disease is inapparent. For a number of genetic diseases, for example, galactosemia and phenylketonuria, the threshold value is reached over a period of time, and symptoms are absent until it is reached.

A fetus with an inherited disorder has not been directly affected by a teratogen during embryogenesis but rather has had an altered genetic code from the moment of conception. Diagnosis of a hereditary disease is based primarily on study of the individual's family tree. The appearance of the disease in ancestors and relatives with a mendelian pattern is convincing evidence of a genetic basis. Some diseases previously thought to be purely genetic are now believed to arise from de novo mutations at certain allelic sites. Asymptomatic individuals may pass traits on to their offspring. Many such disease conditions require that the affected individual carry the altered genes in the recessive *homozygous* state. For this to occur the individual must be born of heterozygous parents. In many cases the heterozygous parent will have no symptoms of the disease or will have symptoms only during the unusual circumstances. For example, heterozygote carriers of the disease *thalas-*

semia are asymptomatic unless they become subject to severe hypoxia, such as might occur at high altitudes. The homozygote, on the other hand, suffers anemia, growth retardation, jaundice, and a great variety of other debilitating effects of the disease regardless of environmental conditions. Many laboratory tests have been developed for the detection of heterozygous states of hereditary diseases, which is of great importance in genetic counseling.

Hemoglobinopathies

The hemoglobinopathies or abnormal hemoglobin conditions provide an excellent illustration of the pathophysiologic mechanisms whereby an inherited genetic disorder eventually produces the signs and symptoms of disease. To understand these conditions the normal genetic control of hemoglobin synthesis will be discussed.

Hemoglobin, a protein molecule containing iron, is produced by immature red blood cells. Mature erythrocytes cannot produce any protein molecules. These corpuscles lack the necessary nuclear and cytoplasmic protein-synthesizing machinery, having lost it during maturation from the reticulocyte stage. Hemoglobin is a buffer molecule; it plays it major physiologic role in the carriage and transport of oxygen in arterial blood. The hemoglobin molecule actually consists of four polypeptide strands, two alpha (α) chains and two beta (β) chains. This form of hemoglobin is the predominant form in most people and is called hemoglobin A_1 (Hb A_1). A minor fraction of hemoglobin, hemoglobin A_2 (Hb A_2), is also normally present. Hb A_1 is commonly notated as $\alpha_{21}^{A} \beta_{21}^{A}$, which indicates that it is Hb A_1 and consists of two alpha chains and two beta chains. Fetal hemoglobin, which is normally present only in fetal life and early infancy, is notated as $\alpha_2^{A} \gamma_2^{F}$, indicating that two alpha

chains and two gamma chains (rather than beta chains) make up its composition. The differences between the types of polypeptide chains lie in the sequencing and kinds of amino acids that make up the protein strand. Great differences in physiologic functioning of hemoglobin occur when even a single amino acid is altered on a strand.

Sickle cell anemia is one hereditary hemoglobinopathy, thalassemia is another. Many other conditions are caused by the great variety of possible abnormal hemoglobins. It is also quite common for an individual to have a mixture of several abnormal hemoglobins. Conditions such as these have allowed geneticists to speculate on the location and types of genes that control the ultimate configuration of the hemoglobin molecule. The genetic control of alpha and beta chains appears to be entirely separate, and genes that regulate the production of hemoglobin chains (operons) also have been suggested.

Sickle cell anemia. Sickle cell anemia is caused by the substitution of valine for glutamine at position 6 on the beta chain. It is thought that this is the result of a single mutated gene, which is responsible for the coding of the amino acid at this particular position on hemoglobin. Fig. 4-6 shows the production of the abnormal hemoglobin in a cell containing such a mutated gene. The valine substitution greatly alters the ability of this hemoglobin, called hemoglobin S (Hb S), to transport oxygen. Erythrocytes that contain Hb S have a shorter life span, are more fragile than normal erythrocytes, and tend to form a sickle shape, particularly under hypoxic conditions. The sickling process can be observed in vitro when red blood cells containing Hb S are observed under a coverslip with a microscope.

The signs and symptoms of sickle cell

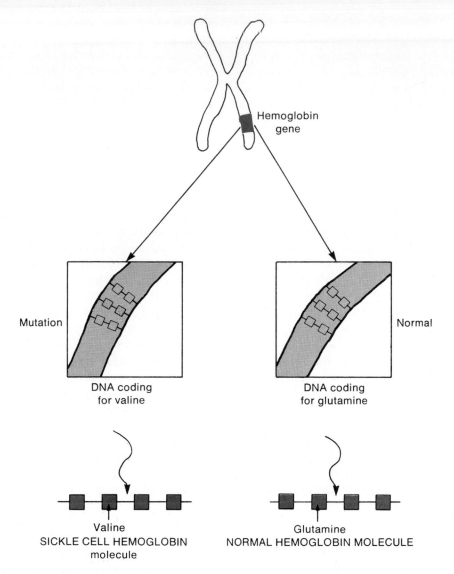

Fig. 4-6. In sickle cell anemia, gene coding for normal amino acid (glutamine) at position 6 of beta chain is substituted for by valine, leading to altered and abnormal hemoglobin (Hb S).

anemia can be explained by the physiologic disturbances caused by the abnormal hemoglobin and are described in detail in Chapter 3. Chronic anemia, arthralgia, and episodes of acute pain are the most striking symptoms of this disease. Hb S has a low solubility at low oxygen tension and thus tends to form a gelatinlike mass *(tactoid)* inside the erythrocyte when the oxygen concentration is reduced, and the red blood cell thus becomes deformed into the sickle shape. The sickling of the erythrocytes increases the blood viscosity, and eventually stasis of the blood occurs within capillaries, decreasing oxygen and nutrition supply to the involved tissue and thus producing anoxic pain.

The course of the disease is marked by episodes of acute crisis that may follow infection or a stressful situation but that often are without an identifiable precipitating cause. The crisis is usually caused by hypoxia and vascular occlusion and is identified by severe, often excruciating pain in the limbs or abdomen. If the circulating blood volume is significantly reduced by the removal of the sickled red blood cells by the reticuloendothelial system, shock may ensue and cause death. Children with sickle cell anemia often die during the first 10 years of life because of infection, heart or kidney failure, or complications of crisis.

Carriers of the sickle cell trait usually show no signs of disease in normal circumstances other than perhaps a mild anemia but can be identified from the general population since there is a mixture of Hb A_1 and Hb S in their circulating red blood cells. Carriers of the trait and those affected by the disease are almost always of the black race, although there is evidence that the trait originated outside of Africa, perhaps in India. It is thought that the sickle cell gene persists because of the resistance it affords against a certain virulent strain of malaria. When the falciform parasite enters the red cells of individuals either carrying the trait or actually having the disease, the erythrocytes sickle and make an environment nonconducive to the parasite.

Thalassemia. Thalassemia may result from a mutation of an operon gene that normally controls the rate of chain synthesis. Either alpha or beta chains may be involved, leading to α- or β-thalassemia.

The α thalassemias are characterized by defective synthesis of alpha globin chains.

Two alpha globin genes are known to occur on chromosome 16, and therefore from one to four globin genes may be involved. The degree of the thalassemia is correlated to the number of genes involved. The homozygous α-thalassemia appears to be incompatible with life.

In one type of β-thalassemia, Hb A_1 concentration is very low or absent, and fetal hemoglobin (Hb F) and Hb A_2 are the chief hemoglobins found. These hemoglobins are physiologically inferior to HB A_1 in the adult individual, and anemia and other signs and symptoms of the disease are present. Different types of thalassemia have been described, but the classic Cooley's anemia is β-thalassemia major and is a homozygous condition that causes impaired beta chain synthesis and a blood level of as much as 90% Hb F, which is distributed unevenly in the erythrocytes. β-Thalassemia minor is the heterozygous condition, and these individuals have few symptoms but can be identified by examination of the blood. The thalassemias appear to affect persons of Mediterranean origin primarily and may also confer a selective advantage with regard to malarial resistance when present in the heterozygous state.

The molecular genetics of thalassemia are complex. The DNA that codes for the mRNA copy contains not only the code for the amino acid sequence of the globin, but also sequences of bases that appear to separate individual genes on the DNA molecule. These "intervening sequences" are transcribed onto the mRNA molecules coded by the DNA. Before these mRNA copies of the gene can function in the synthesis of β globin, the intervening sequences must be enzymatically spliced. It now seems that there is a mutation in the intervening sequences in some forms of β-thalassemia. Long strands of RNA accumulate inside the cell, and globin synthesis is either absent or incomplete. The degree of anemia in thalassemia may be correlated with the type of mutation occurring in the intervening sequences and the resultant inability of the cells to make enough β globin.

The treatment of the individual with thalassemia is directed toward correction of the anemia, which varies according to the type and degree of thalassemia present. Children affected with β-thalassemia suffer the general effects of profound anemia, and are usually growth retarded, have hepatomegaly and splenomegaly, and a variety of skeletal problems. A characteristic facies is associated with thalassemia caused by compensatory hyperplasia of the facial bone marrow in the profoundly anemic child. Because of this increase in the bone marrow, the bones become wider and flatter, and the child usually has a pronounced malocclusion, a protruding maxilla, a broad, flat nose, a bossing of the frontal bone, and a mongoloid slant to the eyes. The skin is usually a characteristic bronze color.

The child generally requires repeated frequent blood transfusions to survive. If the hemoglobin values are maintained by frequent transfusions at a level only slightly lower than normal, the child usually has fewer problems. A result of frequent blood transfusions is an accumulation of iron within the body tissues, a problem that already exists in thalassemia because of the pathophysiology of the disease. Iron may deposit in many structures and interrupt vital functions; iron also deposits in the skin and contributes to the peculiar skin coloration. Excess iron may actually be a major cause of death in thalassemia, and treatment may include the chronic administration of drugs that remove iron (e.g., desferrioxamine with as-

corbic acid). Patients with thalassemia are also subject to infection and splenic damage and hypertrophy. Common causes of death include iron toxicity, infection, and cardiac failure. Most patients with β-thalassemia major do not survive beyond childhood.

Other known genetic diseases

The hemoglobinopathies are perhaps the best characterized genetic diseases in that the expression of the altered gene is a protein molecule that can be easily discerned by laboratory techniques such as electrophoresis. Furthermore, this group of diseases is fairly common, and many patients are available for study. Phenylketonuria (PKU), another genetic disease, is notable in another regard. Through modern methods of mass screening of newborn infants the serious side effects of this disease can now be nearly totally prevented. PKU is an inborn error of metabolism in which the affected individual is unable to metabolize phenylalanine. It is inherited as an autosomal recessive trait, so that both parents are heterozygous for the defective gene. The gene that is defective normally controls the formation of an enzyme, *phenylalanine hydroxylase,* which is responsible for the hydroxylation of phenylalanine to tyrosine. Without treatment, which is simply restriction of phenylalanine in the diet, the infant accumulates phenylalanine in the blood and excretes phenylpyruvic acid and phenylketones. Eventually, neurologic damage occurs, resulting in severe mental retardation.

The pathophysiology of PKU is extremely interesting in that the infant is normal at birth, and the signs and symptoms develop as phenylalanine accumulates and causes damage over the first year of life. The parents may be the first to observe abnormalities in the child, such as a peculiar odor in the urine and sweat and slow development. The major damaging effect of excessive phenylalanine is deficient myelination of the nervous tissue during the first year of life. The brain is still developing during that time and must construct proteins from the amino acids that are available in the blood and tissue fluids. Because of the liver enzyme deficiency phenylalanine concentration increases tremendously, and the general amino acid pattern of the blood and cellular and cerebrospinal fluid is distorted, and the maturation of the brain may be irreversibly impaired as a consequence. Fig. 4-7 describes the pathogenesis of phenylketonuria in the untreated individual.

Other possible genetic diseases that can result in abnormalities at birth or later in life include disorders of carbohydrate, protein, lipid, purine or pyrimidine, and mineral metabolism. Diabetes mellitus is an example of a condition with a striking hereditary background, which often requires the presence of environmental factors in order for penetrance of the genetic disorder into a phenotypic abnormality.

Hemophilia is an X chromosome–linked recessive trait. The pattern of inheritance is diagrammed in Fig. 4-8. It is usual for the hemophiliac to be male, having inherited the gene on the X chromosome from his mother. The other X chromosome in the carrier mother is able to code for sufficient antihemophiliac factor for her, but in the male the Y sex chromosome does not contain genes coding for this factor. Thus the coagulation cascade is inter-

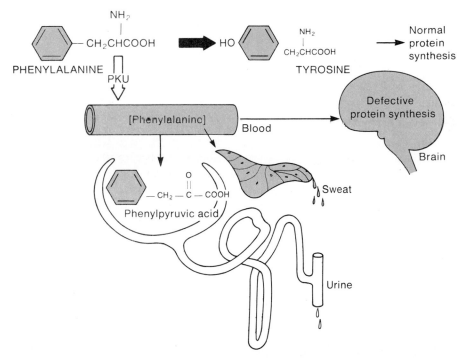

Fig. 4-7. When phenylalanine accumulates in phenylketonuria (PKU), increased concentration of this amino acid results in defective protein synthesis in developing brain. Large amounts of phenylpyruvic acid are excreted in sweat and urine.

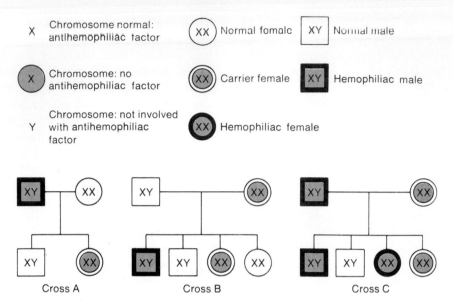

Fig. 4-8. Transmission of hemophilia, which is generally carried in recessive state by female. Hemophiliacs are generally male (cross B) since the Y chromosome does not code for antihemophiliac factor. If a hemophiliac male marries a hemophilic carrier female, both male and female offspring may have hemophilia (cross C).

rupted in the hemophiliac, and excessive bleeding following injury is likely to occur.

Cystic fibrosis

As new technologies develop and older ones are refined, genetic mapping of the entire human genome seems a future possibility. Recombinant DNA technology and cell hybridization experiments have provided information on human gene sequences and chromosomal locations. Analysis of DNA "fingerprints" is a new approach to identifying a specific individual by the gene map of certain highly variable DNA sequences. These methods have recently led researchers closer to the gene for the most common, lethal, recessive genetic disease of Caucasians. The cystic fibrosis (CF) gene is present in 4-5% of the white population, and when two carriers marry, every pregnancy has a 25% chance of producing a child with this disease. CF is characterized by the production of vis-

cus mucus in the lungs, intestines, and pancreatic ducts that leads to chronic respiratory disease, malabsorption, and pancreatic dysfunction. There is an increased amount of chloride present in the sweat and it is through the "sweat test" that this characteristic is used to make the diagnosis. Children usually have failure to thrive, frequent respiratory infections, diarrhea, and chronic pulmonary disease (see Chapter 16), which lead eventually to a high mortality rate. Many children die during childhood or adolescence, although survival into adulthood does occur more commonly as supportive therapies have improved.

Prenatal diagnosis of CF has been attempted, as have genetic experiments that have attempted to locate the gene for CF and to determine its function. It is believed that CF is a disease that may be amenable to approaches whereby a normal gene is introduced into the DNA and

GENETIC DISEASES

Disorders of carbohydrate metabolism

Diabetes mellitus
Pentosuria
Glycogen storage diseases
Galactosemia

Disorders of lipid metabolism

Familial lipoprotein deficiency
Familial lecithin-cholesterol acyl-transferase (L-CAT) deficiency
Tay-Sachs disease
Gaucher's disease

Disorders of protein metabolism

Familial goiter
Phenyketonuria
Albinism
Alkaptonuria
Tyrosinosis

Disorders of purine and pyrimidine metabolism

Gout
Lesch-Nyhan syndrome

Disorders of metal metabolism

Wilson's disease
Hemochromatosis

Disorders of connective tissue, bone, and muscle

Familial periodic paralysis
Muscular dystrophies
Mucopolysaccharidoses

Disorders of the hematopoietic system and blood

Sickle cell anemia
Glucose 6-phosphate dehydrogenase deficiency
Thalassemias
Hereditary spherocytosis

Disorders of exocrine glands

Cystic fibrosis

the defective gene bypassed. Gene therapy is a method of introducing such genes into cells. It is performed through the use of viral probes that carry the normal gene, "infect" the cells, and inject the normal gene into the cell's DNA. Of course, there are many potential problems that currently exist in the use of this technology, but it seems to hold great future promise. The gene for CF may be involved in chloride channel regulation, and this defect may be the underlying pathophysiology for all of the disruptions that occur. The CF gene is now known to be located on chromosome 7, and the region of the chromosome is believed to contain only several hundred thousand base pairs (5 to 50 genes) (White, 1986). Precise localization of the gene, base pair analysis, and analysis of the protein product of the gene are goals of future research. Currently, amniotic fluid sampling and measurement of certain enzymes is the only method for diagnosis in a pregnancy at risk for CF, but chorionic villus sampling and genotype analysis could be performed much earlier in a pregnancy. Furthermore, gene mapping will eventually provide a way for determining the carrier state, something that is impossible to determine conclusively at this time.

It is clear that many genetic diseases will be explored and eventually treated by the sophisticated genetic technology of the future. The box at the top of the page gives a partial listing of other diseases known to be caused by hereditary factors. These diseases are classified as to the metabolic pathways that they most profoundly affect.

TERATOGENIC MECHANISMS

While the importance of heredity in determining conditions at birth and susceptibility to diseases throughout life cannot be underestimated, many of the obvious structural organ and tissue defects and many syndromes of the newborn are caused by unknown external factors acting on the dividing cells of the developing embryonic tissue in utero. For 60% to 70% of human congenital anomalies, the definite cause is unknown.

There are some general principles regarding the process of teratogenesis:

1. There are critical periods during organogenesis when damage occurs. The preimplantation period (days 1 to 10 following conception) is the time during which damage to the conceptus will interfere with implantation of the embryo into the uterine wall. The embryonic period (until the end of the first trimester) is the period of major organogenesis. Teratogens will cause a great variety of structural defects during this period. The fetal period, which spans the time between the end of the first trimester and birth, is a time of major growth, and teratogens may interfere with this process as well. Physiologic abnormalities may also result.

2. Many teratogens appear to have a proclivity for certain tissues. The rubella syndrome, which will be discussed later, illustrates this phenomenon.

3. Teratogenesis is a process involving not only the teratogen and fetus but also the mother. The mother's health, nutrition, and prenatal care are of great importance in determining the final outcome of teratogenesis on the fetus.

4. It is often impossible to identify the teratogen that caused a deformity in a newborn. Furthermore, many conditions may be hereditary rather than acquired (about 25%).

Congenital anomalies range in severity and occasionally result in death of the infant before or shortly after birth. It is likely that many embryos with gross genetic errors and developmental defects do not survive and are aborted early in the pregnancy. It has been reported that at least 40% of all embryos spontaneously aborted during the first trimester have chromosomal abnormalities.

Many defects that are present in newborns may be repaired surgically with total recovery and a normal life span possible. It is quite common, however, for congenital anomalies to occur together, indicating that the teratogen affected different developing structures during embryogenesis. The care of an infant with several anomalies may be extremely complicated and challenging.

It is possible to categorize congenital defects into those associated with gross chromosomal abnormalities of either autosomes or sex chromosomes, those associated with structural defects of tissue and organs, and those associated with syndromes (a group of specific sign and symptoms observed in relationship to a particular pathogenesis).

CHROMOSOMAL DEFECTS
Autosomal trisomies

Defects of the autosomal chromosomes are identified on the basis of both karyotype and phenotype. Such anomalies appear to occur at the result of improper separation of chromosomes during meiosis. The most common example of a gross autosomal anomaly is a *trisomy*, which is the presence of three rather than two chromosomes at one of the 23 possible pair positions in the human karyotype. The most common trisomy is at the G group of chromosomes at 21 and results in Down syndrome, occurring at a general incidence of 1.0-1.2 per 1000 live births. The phenotypic expression of a chromosome 21 trisomy is very characteristic, as are the facies (Fig. 4-9) and karyotype of such an individual (Fig. 4-10). The condition is always characterized by mental retardation and accounts for 10% of the institutionalized retarded people. Down syndrome individuals suffer not only mental retardation but also disordered bone growth, altered dermatoglyphics (as exemplified by the presence of the simian crease), and anomalies of other organs and tissues;

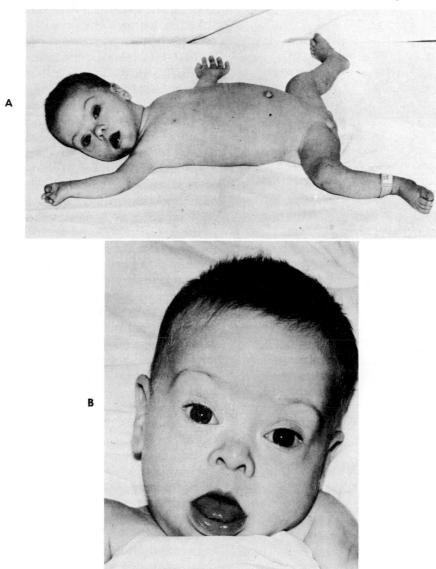

Fig. 4-9. Down syndrome in newborn. **A,** Floppy, hypotonic newborn. **B,** Small square head with slanted eyes, flat nasal bridge, and protruding tongue.

(From Reisman LE, and Matheny AP: Genetics and counseling in medical practice, St Louis, 1969, The CV Mosby Co.)

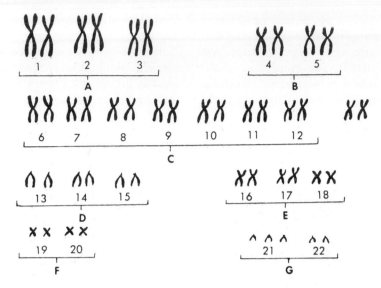

Fig. 4-10. Karyotype of "classic" trisomy of chromosome 21. There is an extra chromosome 21 in Down syndrome probably due to nondisjunction during meiosis.

(From Whaley LF: Understanding inherited disorders, St Louis, 1974, The CV Mosby Co.)

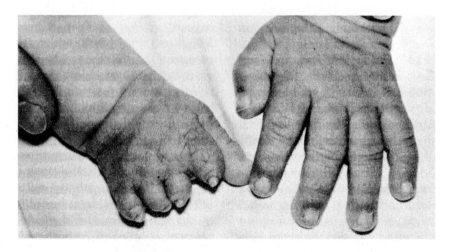

Fig. 4-11. Micromelia in child with Down syndrome. Various types of such birth defects are commonly found in Down syndrome.

(From Reisman LE, and Matheny AP: Genetics and counseling in medical practice, 1969, The CV Mosby Co.)

they are usually susceptible to upper respiratory infection and have a significantly decreased life span. Furthermore, the incidence of leukemia in these children is 15 times the normal. Other congenital abnormalities are also found in Down syndrome. Micromelia is illustrated in Fig. 4-11.

The pathogenesis of Down syndrome is probably the result of a *nondisjunction* during the second division of meiosis, so that a whole chromosome rather than a chromatid moves into a gamete (Fig. 4-12). The resulting gamete, if fertilized, will have 47 rather than 46 chromosomes, with three chromosomes at the chromosome 21 position (trisomy). Younger women who give birth to a child with Down syndrome sometimes show a *translocation* of an extra chromosome 21 onto chromosomes 14, 21, or 22, so that the normal diploid number appears to be retained, but in essence an extra chromosome 21 is present. This occurs in less than 6% of Down syndrome individuals.

Down syndrome may be the result of a teratogen's acting on the ovum before fertilization or aging of the ovum may cause the *meiotic efficiency* of the cell to be impaired. The incidence rises with maternal age and is reported as occurring in 1 in 50 births in women over the age of 45, compared to 1 in 2,300 for women between the ages of 15 and 19. The increased incidence of Down syndrome with maternal age indicates that ova from older women are subject to an aging effect or to hormonal alterations. This appears to be the cause of the meiotic abnormality; however, in 20% to 30% of the cases, paternal nondisjunction is responsible for the trisomy. Down syndrome is not as highly related to paternal age as it is to the maternal age effect (Levine, et al, 1983). The exact aging effect is not known, but most research points to multiple causes.

Down syndrome and many other genetic diseases can be detected by amniocentesis. Cells from samples of amniotic fluid that has been withdrawn from the pregnant uterus can be examined as early as the third month of gestation. The cells can be karyotyped, and the presence of abnormal numbers or structure of chromosomes can be determined with great accuracy.

Trisomies of other autosomes, such as of groups D and E, have been well documented in the literature and produce characteristic phenotypes, but by far the most common viable autosomal trisomy is Down syndrome. Trisomy E has been labeled as Edwards' syndrome, and chromosome 18 appears to be involved. The majority of these infants are postmature girls with low birth weights; they generally have round faces with small eyes, mouths, and jaws, low-set or poorly formed ears, altered dermatoglyphics, and extra skin folds on the neck and back. Congenital heart disease is also often present.

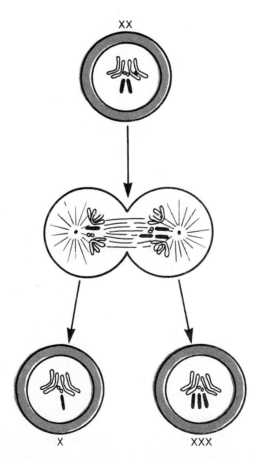

Fig. 4-12. Nondisjunction. During the first cell division of meiosis, chromosome pairs do not move equally to daughter cells. In this case, one cell contains three chromosomes, whereas other contains only one.

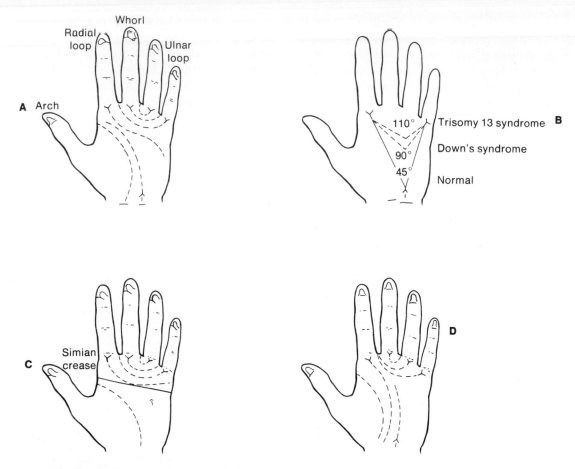

Fig. 4-13. Abnormal palm prints. **A,** Dermatoglypnic pattern of normal hand. **B,** Angles in normal person and in patients with Down syndrome and trisomy 13 syndrome. **C,** Dermatoglyphic pattern in a patient with Down syndrome. **D,** Dermatoglyphic pattern in a patient with trisomy 18 syndrome. (From Porter IH: Heredity and disease. Copyright 1968 McGraw-Hill Book Co. Used with permission of McGraw-Hill Book Co)

Most E trisomy infants die during fetal life. Many trisomies and other congenital anomalies are associated with altered dermatoglyphics; patterns of these abnormalities are illustrated in Fig. 4-13.

Other autosomal defects

Deletions of short or long arms of chromosomes have been described in association with various syndromes. However, deletions of the D group chromosomes can be found in 2% of the normal population. The cri-du-chat syndrome appears to be the result of a deletion of the short arms of the chromosome 5 pair of the B group. The syndrome is so named because of the characteristic mewing cry during infancy, which accompanies other phenotypic expressions such as microcephaly, failure to thrive, mental retardation, epicanthal folds, abnormal ears, and strabismus.

Duplication of chromosomal material

results in a lengthening of the chromosomal arms. These defects also cause mental retardation and other anomalies.

Translocation of one chromosomal segment to another chromosome has already been described for one type of Down syndrome.

Ring chromosomes sometimes form and replace a normal chromosome. Again retardation and abnormal dermatoglyphics are often part of the clinical picture.

Additional small metacentric chromosomes have been found in human karyotypes and have not been clearly identified as members of any specific karyotypic group.

These abnormalities of the autosome usually are studied in an obviously malformed or atypical-appearing segment of the population, and thus the true incidence of such defects is not known. Most embryos with chromosomal abnormalities are aborted before implantation takes place, and many times the woman never realizes that a conception had occurred.

Abnormalities of the sex chromosomes

A number of fairly common disorders of both males and females can now be traced to abnormalities of the sex chromosomes. In the karyotype the human female sex chromosomes are designated as XX and the male as XY. The presence of at least one X chromosome is required for viability, and no sex chromosome disorders have been identified in living individuals in which the X chromosome was absent. However, a large number of disorders that involve either the *absence* or *multiplication* of the additional X or Y chromosome do occur. As in the abnormal autosomal defects, each of these disorders usually involves a specific karyotype.

The indifferent gonad. The normal embryogenesis of the gonad should be reviewed before disorders of sexual identity are discussed. Briefly, the gonad in the male or female embryo is *bipotential*, that is, it is capable of forming either male or female genitalia and internal organs, independent of the karyotype of the embryo. The major factor in sex determination is the hormonal environment of the embryo at the time of differentiation of the gonad. It has indeed been argued that all individuals are "basically" female, in that a karyotypically male embryo, if deprived of male hormones during gonadal differentiation, will develop as a female.

The early human gonad consists of a cortex and medulla. Both contain primitive germ cells that have migrated into the structure during very early embryonic development. These cells will eventually give rise to either ova or sperm. If the gonad is destined to become a testis, producing male spermatogonia, the cortex regresses, and the medulla of the gonad differentiates into seminiferous and rete tubules, which are lined with epithelium containing the primordial sperm cells. If an ovary is to form, the cortex becomes germinal epithelium, which hypertrophies and produces follicles within which the primordial ova lie.

The usual sources of the hormones in the developing embryo are the organs and glands of the embryonic reproductive and endocrine systems. This production is under the control and regulation of both the sex chromosomes and autosomes. Without the proper hormonal balance as the gonads develop in the embryo, the indifferent gonad will differentiate in a direction that is not apparently dictated by the sex chromosome complement it has received at conception. The importance of hormonal influence is shown by numerous animal studies. The freemartin that is produced in cattle twinning has been shown to result from the effects of male sex hormone on the developing female embryo. When cattle twins of different sexes share the same fetal circulation, so that the male sex hormone from the male twin can pass to the genotypically female twin, the female will develop into a basically male but sterile calf. Other evidence for the importance of the hormonal environment comes from hens. If the hen's ovary is removed at an early age or is destroyed by disease, the hen will develop testes and become a rooster. The same effect is observed in the adreogenital syndrome in humans.

The influence of the genotype is, of course, profound. The presence of a Y sex chromosome will stimulate the indifferent gonad to form testes, even in the presence of multiple X chromosomes. Without a Y chromosome present to exert its masculinizing control on the immature gonad, the normal course of development will be to produce female structures. There is evidence that elements on other chromosomes, possibly the X chromosome, may be additionally required to produce this male determination, but the controlling genetic element is itself regulated by the Y chromosome.

In the female, while only one X chromosome is necessary for the production of female characteristics, including the development of an ovarian gonad, a second X chromosome appears to be required for later normal development of an ovary. In *Turner's syndrome*, which is characterized by the presence of only one X chromosome, germ cells and ovarian tissue are present in fetal life and after birth, but by puberty all signs of ova and normal ovarian tissue have disappeared.

Turner's syndrome. Turner's syndrome, found in its pure form only in females, is caused by the absence of the second X sex chromosome and is therefore expressed karyotypically as 45, XO. It occurs in 0.45 of 1,000 live births. This disorder is characterized by *ovarian dysgenesis*, which is the absence of germ cells and mature ovaries, resulting in primary amenorrhea (absence of menstruation). A variety of somatic aberrations often accompany the sexual sterility and absence of secondary sexual characteristics. These include short stature, webbed neck, broadly spaced nipples, occasionally mild mental retardation, abnormal dermatoglyphics, an increased incidence of kidney anomalies, and coarctation of the aorta. Variants of ovarian dysgenesis syndromes have been described, and occasionally *mixoploidy* is observed. This is sexual mosaicism in which some cells of the body follow an XO cell line, whereas other cells may have an XY karyotype, and XX, or even XYY or XXX. In the case of mixoploidy the proportion of cells containing XY sex chromosomes to those with only X is crucial in determining whether the individual will be of male or female phenotype. Females with ovarian dysgenesis also may have an abnormally shaped second X chromosome rather than a complete absence of it as in the classic Turner's syndrome. The pathogenesis of Turner's syndrome appears to be the loss of the paternal sex chromosome in the zygote. The vast majority of such fetuses die in utero, and those that do survive may develop life-threatening cardiac or renal disease.

Klinefelter's syndrome. Klinefelter's syndrome is a eunuchlike condition found in males with one or more extra X chromosomes; it has an incidence of 2.13 per 1,000 live births. Phenotypically these individuals have small testes, enlarged breasts, a feminine distribution of pubic hair, and frequently mild mental retardation. Moreover, these boys grow rapidly after puberty and have proportionately long legs. This disorder is associated with advanced maternal and paternal age. Klinefelter's syndrome is characterized by a 47, XXY sex chromosomal complement in 82% of the cases. Mixoploidy occurs in 11%, and 7% have either 48, XXYY, 48, XXXY, or 46, XX chromosomal complements. As in a normal female only one X chromosome remains genetically active within all cells, so that multiples of X chromosomes do not result in multiple copies of the genes that are present on the X chromosome. Multiple Y chromosome disorders also do not confer a great redundancy of genetic information, since the Y chromosome's only apparent function is to regulate embryonic sexual differentiation. In about two thirds of the cases the origin of the XXY sex chromosomes in Klinefelter's syndrome appears to be the result of *maternal meiotic nondisjunction* (Fig. 4-12).

The occasional Klinefelter's syndrome patient with an XX or female karyotype but with external and internal male genitalia represents an interesting case. The origin of such individuals remains a matter of speculation. It is possible that these males began from a mixoploid cell line that contained a Y chromosome, which was able to exert its masculinizing effect on the embryo before being entirely lost in the individual. It is possible too that the missing Y chromosome becomes translocated onto the X chromosome and is thus not identifiable. One intriguing possibility is that the XX Klinefelter's male is the result of a sex-linked autosomal recessive gene that could lead to complete sex reversal by stimulating the medulla of the indifferent gonad to differentiate into a testis. Animal studies bear out this possibility.

Sex chromosome polysomies. A number of situations have been described in which the X or the Y chromosome becomes duplicated. For example, polysomy 47, XXX females have been found in chromosomal surveys, and the incidence of this condi-

tion is about 0.65 per 1,000 live births. Such females have no particular phenotypic anomalies or congenital defects and are often fertile. An even rarer polysomy is 48, XXXX, of which five cases have been reported. All of these females are severely retarded but show no common phenotypic abnormality or aberrations of sexual developments. The origin of X chromosome polysomies may be correlated with advanced maternal age. The most common origin is the fertilization of an XX ovum by an X-bearing sperm, or in the case of 48, XXXX, successive meiotic nondisjunction during oogenesis.

Among males, duplication of the Y chromosome has been reported and implicated in behavioral and phenotypic abnormalities. The origin of these males is probably *paternal nondisjunction*, which results in fertilization of X-bearing ovum with a YY sperm. The frequency of XYY males among tall, violent, and criminal or psychopathic individuals may be as high as 24%. The general portrait of the XYY male is a person who is mentally deficient, tall, tending toward antisocial or criminal behavior, often suffering from acne, and often alcoholic. General sexual development and maturity seem unimpaired.

Intersexuality. XX males with Klinefelter's syndrome and XY females are examples of individuals with complete reversal of their sexual genotype. *Hermaphroditism* represents partial sex reversal. These conditions are described as intersexual. True hermaphrodites are classified on the basis of sexual mosaicism (gynandromorphism), in which both male and female cell lines can be found. Male and female cell clones may also be present in the gonadal tissue. Ovarian and testicular structures are both found in true hermaphroditism, while in *pseudohermaphroditism* the gonads are of one type only. The male pseudohermaphrodite has testes, but the internal geni-

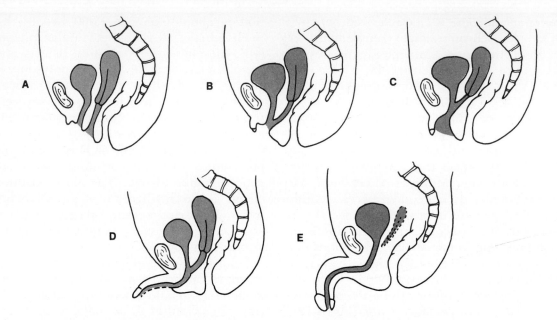

Fig. 4-14. Abnormal sexual development. **A,** Normal female. **B** to **C,** Deviations in structure of external genitalia. **B** and **C,** Rudimentary penis is present along with female structures. **D,** Penis is large, and bladder and vagina merge to form male-type urethra. **E,** Uterus is rudimentary.

talia are ambiguous; the external genitalia are male but poorly developed or feminized. The female pseudohermaphrodite usually has ovaries but rudimentary and masculinelike external genitalia and often a male phenotype. The common intersexual urogenital systems are diagramed in Fig. 4-14.

It should be mentioned that virilization of a female fetus could be effected by external sources. Tumors of the adrenal gland in the fetus or ovary in the mother might result in over-production of male androgens, which in turn could act on the indifferent gonad. Administration of male androgens to the pregnant mother may also result in the same phenomenon.

GROSS STRUCTURAL ORGAN DEFECTS

It is beyond the scope of this book to describe in detail the many types of organ malformations and the pathophysiologic mechanism operating in these conditions. Other chapters in this book deal with various mechanisms of disease in the different organ systems, and these principles can be applied to the pathophysiology of defective organ structure. Birth defects have been catalogued in atlases, and detailed descriptions can be found in medical textbooks of pediatrics. This chapter's task is to define the pathogenic mechanisms through which such defects occur during embryogenesis.

Congenital anomalies

Fig. 4-15 lists various structures and organs and the times during embryogenesis at which these structures are most susceptible to the action of teratogens. Although it is theoretically possible for any organ to be malformed, those that are most com-

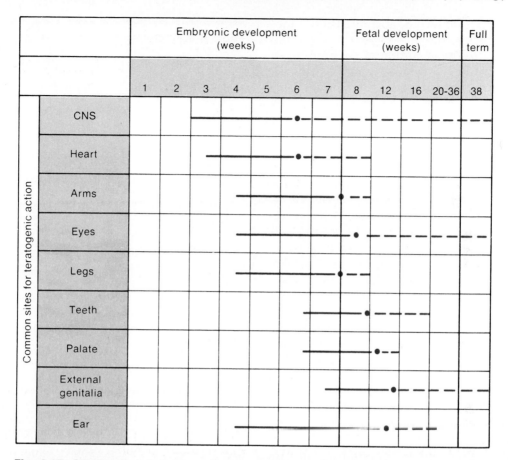

Fig. 4-15. Critical periods in human embryogenesis. Teratogens may act on a developing embryo at any time, but for any given teratogen, different tissues exhibit different sensitivity. For example, CNS anomalies in general are more likely to occur between the third and fifth weeks than at other times in embryogenesis.

monly seen are defects in the fusion of the lips and palate, abnormalities in the formation and rotation of the heart, central nervous system defects in brain, spinal cord integrity, and cerebrospinal fluid circulation, abnormalities in kidney structure, and defects in the formation of the gut.

Modes of action of teratogens

The end result of teratogens acting on developing embryonic tissue is either death,

malformation, retardation of growth, or functional disturbance. The vast majority of anomalies that an infant may be born with are caused by unknown factors acting during pregnancy. For a great variety of animal and human disorders it would appear that multiple interacting factors may be required before the abnormality occurs. For example, a teratogen known to cause cleft lip and palate may only do so in certain strains of mice and then only when the maternal diet is altered. Thus genetic, teratogenic, maternal, and nutritional factors must operate together at a very specific time in the gestation of the embryo in order for the congenital anomaly to appear in the progeny. Developmental disorders in humans that appear to follow this multifactorial threshold model include congenital hypertrophic pyloric stenosis, various congenital heart diseases, anencephaly and spina bifida, and Hirschsprung's disease. It can be said that for disorders with a known genetic background, such as cleft palate, the penetrance of the disease may be greatly affected by modifiers in the environment.

Most of our knowledge of the mechanisms of action of teratogens is derived from animal studies in which the processes of normal and abnormal embryogenesis can be followed very carefully. Extrapolation to humans is often made but has been shown many times to be invalid. Powerful teratogens in mice may have no effect on the human embryo and vice versa. The well-known thalidomide tragedy, in which a tranquilizer given to pregnant women resulted in lack of limb development and other anomalies in the offspring, is a case in point. Human teratogenesis presents an enormous problem for scientific investigation, and the application of the multifactorial threshold model to human anomalies has been made on the basis of the frequency of the disorder generally, in the families of those affected, and mathematical fit to the model, based on these studies.

Table 4-1 lists some of the known human teratogenic substances. No common underlying similarities can be found among these agents at first glance. It would appear that the mode of action can be different with the end result in the fetus being the same. A number of theoretic mechanisms have been summarized by

Table 4-1. Common teratogenic agents

Teratogens	Effects
Chemicals	
Alcohol	Fetal alcohol syndrome
Androgens	Masculinization of female fetus if administered to mother
Antibiotics (e.g., tetracycline)	Tooth defects
Cancer chemotherapy (e.g., aminopterin)	Central nervous system defects
Thyroid drugs (e.g., potassium iodide)	Congenital goiter
Tranquilizers (e.g., thalidomide)	Limb and other organ defects
Microbes	
Rubella	Rubella syndrome
Cytomegalovirus	Central nervous system and ophthalmic disorders
Toxoplasma gondii	Ophthalmic disorders
Radiation	
Therapeutic and possibly diagnostic radiation	Central nervous system and skeletal system abnormalities

Wilson and Clarke in *Handbook of Teratology* (1977). There is some experimental evidence to support each of these mechanisms in malformation induction.

1. *Mutation* has been discussed as the original cause of all defects known to be hereditary; mutation can also be acquired through the action of some teratogens, such as irradiation, viruses, and a number of chemicals. Mutations in germ cells are usually implied when speaking of teratogenesis, although mutations in somatic cell lines are possible.
2. *Chromosomal nondisjunction and breaks* also have been discussed and are often related to maternal age and aging of spermatozoa in the genital tract as well.

3. *Mitotic interference* can be effected by a large number of teratogens, which can delay mitosis, prevent the spindle apparatus from functioning normally, or induce abnormalities in the formation or separation of the chromatids. Cells so interfered with usually cannot follow the developmental pattern of their particular cell line and thus delay or alter normal structure formation.

4. *Altered nucleic acid integrity or function* is the fourth possible mechanism by which developing embryonic cells can be affected. Drugs such as antibiotics and cancer chemotherapeutic agents are known to induce malformations in this manner and act basically by inhibiting purine or pyrimidine synthesis, cross-linking DNA, or binding with DNA to block RNA synthesis.

5. *Lack of precursors and substrates needed for biosynthesis* is another mechanism of teratogenesis, which has been well described for vitamin deficiency–induced malformations. Drugs that mimic required nutritional factors, thus taking their place in metabolic processes, may result in developmental abnormalities. Furthermore, the role of the placenta is important in that the fetus must receive all nutrients from the mother's bloodstream through the extremely permeable placenta. Azo dyes and tissue antiserums in the placenta of experimental animals are able to interfere with the absorption of metabolites and nutrients into the fetus. However, this mechanism has not been documented for humans.

6. *Altered energy sources* may be an important mechanism of teratogenesis. Cells deprived of energy sources will not be able to generate ATP, which is required for all synthetic processes, and such phenomena common to the embryonic cell as division, differentiation, and motility.

7. *Enzyme inhibition* is the seventh possible mode of action by which teratogens affect growing embryos. Certain teratogenic drugs inhibit the function of a number of critical enzymes, such as DNA polymerase or carbonic anhydrase.

8. *Osmolar imbalance* has been defined as a teratogenic mechanism based on the edema that results in chick embryos subjected to hypoxia. The accumulation of abnormal amounts of fluids and electrolytes in developing tissue could not only mechanically distort the tissue but also interfere with physiologic function. Osmotic changes could, of course, be secondary to a variety of teratogenic insults.

9. *Alteration in membrane characteristics* is the last conjectured mechanism and, while probably rare, is a theoretic mode of action. Ultrastructural membrane damage caused by vitamin A hypervitaminosis has been reported to be teratogenic in rodent embryos.

Although the mechanisms described above may have different results in developing tissue, a search for a single, common, unifying process in teratogenesis would appear to implicate cellular necrosis in almost all teratogenic phenomena. Cellular necrosis at any age stage of embryogenesis could interfere with normal formation, development, resorption, and growth. Cell death is one of the most common aspects of teratogenisis, no matter what mechanism has initiated the process. The pathophysiology of teratogenesis is shown in Fig. 4-16.

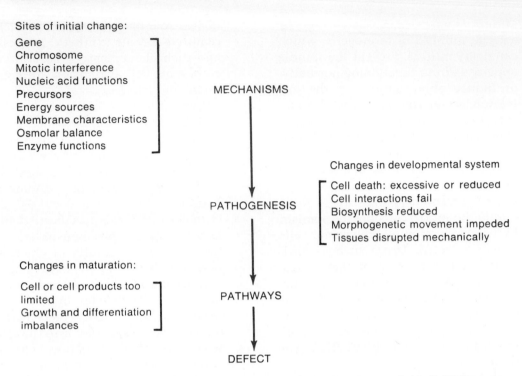

Sites of initial change:

Gene
Chromosome
Mitotic interference
Nucleic acid functions
Precursors
Energy sources
Membrane characteristics
Osmolar balance
Enzyme functions

MECHANISMS

Changes in developmental system

Cell death: excessive or reduced
Cell interactions fail
Biosynthesis reduced
Morphogenetic movement impeded
Tissues disrupted mechanically

PATHOGENESIS

Changes in maturation:

Cell or cell products too
limited
Growth and differentiation
imbalances

PATHWAYS

DEFECT

Fig. 4-16. Pathophysiology of developmental defects resulting from teratogenic insult. While teratogens may act at many possible sites, pathogenic pathways leading to defect are relatively few.

Maternal factors in teratogenesis

The interruption of pregnancy by childbirth must be considered as just another landmark in human development. Indeed, the first postnatal year is in many ways an extension of the fetal period as many organs and tissues are still developing and maturing during that time. Many congenital anomalies may not be evident at birth but certainly will be by the first birthday. A major difference between prenatal and postnatal life is the maternal influence on development while the fetus is in utero. There are two major ways that teratogens may affect the embryo. The first is directly, by crossing the placenta and interacting with embryonic cells at critical stages of development. The second mechanism is often given little attention but may ultimately prove to be just as important as the first. Teratogens may do their damage by altering the maternal physiology, so that the fetal development is impeded in a much more indirect way. For example, the degree and ease of the placental transfer of certain teratogens may be greatly affected by the maternal physiology, and it is one of the principles of embryology that a teratogenic effect is often dose dependent.

Malnutrition during pregnancy, while not directly related to major congenital anomalies, does result in low birth weight infants, and these infants have a higher incidence of perinatal mortality and developmental defects. Some authorities consider low birth weight to be a congenital anomaly in itself, and it has been associated with maternal viral infections. Smoking is directly correlated with low birth weight and prematurity in off-spring. Also, a simian crease, a characteristic of Down syndrome and often found in association with congenital heart defects and other anomalies, has been found in some children of heavy smokers.

Fetal alcohol syndrome. There is an association between drinking alcohol during pregnancy and a triad of growth deficiency, specific facial features, and mental retardation in the newborn. Alcohol causes a continuum of effects with the most severe cases being referred to as fetal alcohol syndrome (FAS). Alcohol may be the major cause of preventable mental retardation in newborns. At all teratogenic doses, alcohol appears to have an effect on the developing nervous system. Some children may have learning disabilities, hyperactivity, or communication disorders, whereas others may show profound retardation (Levine et al., 1983).

Growth disturbances, both during fetal life and in childhood, are also observed. Small for gestational age infants do not display catch-up growth and are often classified later as failure to thrive infants. Alcohol also appears to impair the morphogenesis of the facial features. The characteristic facies consist of short palpebral fissures, a short nose with a flat nasal bridge, a small jaw, and thin lips with a smooth philtrum. Fig 4-17 shows the characteristic appearance of a child with fetal alcohol syndrome. Other effects of alcohol on the fetus include cardiac malformations, abnormal palmar creases, limited joint mobility (especially in the fingers and elbows), and many other cardiovascular and skeletal aberrations (Levine, 1983).

The dosage of alcohol required to produce an effect is not known, although animal studies indicate that all amounts may produce some potential fetal damage. Clearly, alcoholic mothers are much more likely to have a child with fetal alcohol

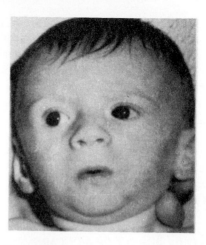

Fig. 4-17. The facial features of a child born with fetal alcohol syndrome.
(From Seidel HM, et al., Mosby's guide to physical examination, St. Louis, 1987, The CV Mosby Co.)

syndrome, but the accepted and cautious approach is generally advocated and it is recommended that no alcohol be consumed during pregnancy.

Drug abuse. Drugs commonly abused by humans easily cross the placenta and enter the fetal bloodstream. All types of drugs, including narcotics, barbiturates, tranquilizers, analgesics, nicotine, caffeine, cocaine, and amphetamines, have been observed in fetuses as the result of placental transfer. The fetal metabolism and toxic effects from drugs differs markedly from the maternal mechanisms in many cases. Many of these drugs enter the fetal nervous system, have endocrine consequences on fetal development (such as the altered sexual differentiation induced by opiates), disturb fetal nutrition, and lead to fetal and perinatal addiction. Cocaine use among women of all socioeconomic classes is currently one of the greatest addictive problems of the perinatal period. Often mothers who use cocaine also use marijuana and alcohol during pregnancy (Braude et al., 1987). Women who use cocaine have more complications during pregnancy, and their infants are smaller and have more respiratory distress syndrome, genitourinary tract anomalies, small intestinal infarctions, and cerebral infarctions. The infants of cocaine-abusing mothers are generally jittery, easily startled, have disturbed infant sleep states, increased startle reflex, and decreased interest in interactions.

The following case study will illustrate the neurobehavior and problems associated with an infant born of a cocaine-addicted mother.

CASE STUDY: INFANT OF A COCAINE ADDICTED MOTHER

History

JH, a 22-year-old, gravida 1, para 0, black female was admitted to the labor and delivery suite at 36 weeks' estimated gestation. She was admitted with vaginal bleeding that followed the inhalation of approximately 5 gm of cocaine the night before admission. A previous pregnancy ended at 20 weeks' gestation with the spontaneous abortion of a female child secondary to a massive abruption following a week of heavy (4 to 6 gm/day) cocaine abuse. The current pregnancy has been complicated by minimal prenatal care (this was only her second visit to a medical facility; her first visit was at diagnosis of the pregnancy at 22 weeks). Substance abuse has been significant, including 2 to 6 gm of cocaine per day (primarily "snorted" or smoked as "crack"), 2 to 4 marijuana cigarettes per week, alcohol intake of 1 to 2 beers per day with occasional intoxication, and smoking one and one-half packs of cigarettes per day. For the past 24 hours, JH had experienced abdominal cramping and dark red vaginal bleeding. On admittance, she was tremulous and in early spontaneous la-

Contributed by Mark Gaylord.

bor, her blood pressure was 140/95, and she had an obviously tender uterus. In the past 24 hours she had soaked approximately 15 vaginal pads. Ultrasound examination revealed an approximate 36-week gestation, small for gestational age (SGA) infant. There is a 3 × 5 cm echo dense pocket retroplacental that was consistent with an abruption. The placenta is grade 3, small, and heavily calcified. Placement of an external fetal monitor revealed a flat, fetal heart rate baseline with poor beat-to-beat variability and an occasional late deceleration. Examination of the cervix revealed several dark clots of blood and only 1 cm dilation with 70 effacement.

The decision was made by the attending obstetrician to deliver the child by way of emergency caesarean section under spinal anesthesia because of the fetal distress and the mother's inability to tolerate labor. A viable, SGA, male infant was delivered with Apgar scores of 7 and 8.

Physical examination

Weight: 1800 gm

Height: 42 cm

Occipital frontal circumference: 29 cm

Heart rate: 150 Respiratory rate: 64; BP: 55/32

Gestational age: Appropriate for 36 weeks, SGA

General—SGA, 36-week-male, slightly tremulous, no acute distress

  Head: Normocephalic—sutures approximate, anterior fontanelle 2 × 2 cm

  Eyes: PERRLA, red reflex present bilaterally

  Ears: Normal placement, canal patent

  Nose: Patent, no septal deviation

  Mouth: Palate intact

  Heart: Regular rate and rhythm; S1 and S2 WNL, Gr 1/6 murmur, upper left sternal border; normal pulses, femorals present

  Lungs: Slight increased respiratory rate, clear to auscultation, no retractions

Abdomen: Liver palpable 2 cm below right costal line, three-vessel small umbilical cord, no masses, hyperactive bowel sounds

Rectal: Patent

Extremities: Decreased subcutaneous fat

Genital: Normal uncircumcised male, testes in scrotum

Neurologic: Cranial nerves intact; tone appropriate to increased for 36 weeks gestation; infant obviously tremulous, jittery with periods of frantic crying: appeared to be ravenously hungry, then refused to eat; deep tendon reflexes increased with 5 to 6 beats ankle clonus bilateral; very short periods of quiet sleep observed.

Laboratory results: Dextrostix—40 mg%; Hct—63 mEq%; Ca—8.4 mEq/L; Na—135 mEq/L; K—4.2 mEq/L

Discussion

A 36-week, SGA, male infant born by way of an emergency caesarean section because of fetal distress caused by an acute placental abruption following heavy cocaine abuse. The infant's size was secondary to chronic cocaine abuse, cigarette smoking, poor prenatal care, and advanced placental age. The infant now has signs and symptoms of early cocaine intoxication manifested by jitters, franticness, difficulty in feeding, inability to sleep for long periods of time, and increased tone and deep tendon reflexes. The child is at risk for seizure activity, hypoglycemia secondary to poor feeding and SGA, cerebral infarction secondary to transplacental cocaine injestion, and long-term developmental delays.

Pathophysiology

The use of cocaine in the United States has reached epidemic proportions; 22 million, or 1 in 10, Americans report using cocaine at least once, and 5 million report regular use. With such a large number of Americans using cocaine on a regular basis, it can be assumed that a large number of women have used cocaine while pregnant. As the prevalence of cheaper cocaine ("crack") has dramatically increased in our cities, so have medical reports of the effect of cocaine on pregnancy, the fetus, and the newborn.

Cocaine is a central nervous system stimulant and, in addition, acts peripherally to inhibit nerve conduction by blocking the reuptake of norepinephrine at the nerve terminals. This action produces increased norepinephrine levels with subsequent vasoconstriction, tachycardia, and hypertension (Chasnoff et al, 1987). Placental vasoconstriction also occurs (Sherman and Gautier, 1972), decreasing blood flow to the fetus. With increased norepinephrine levels, an increase in uterine contractility has been reported (Lederman, 1978). Not only are these pharmacologic properties of cocaine the probable cause of the complications seen in pregnancy, but a direct teratogenic effect has also not been eliminated. Urogenital abnormalities have been described in infants exposed to cocaine (Chasnoff et al, 1985). However, it could easily be theorized that increased uterine vascular resistance and decreased uterine blood flow, accompanied by fetal hypoxia and hypertension, could affect almost any developing organ system, depending on the time of exposure.

Relatively little data are available on the fetal or neonatal pharmacokinetics of cocaine. At relatively low levels it is metabolized by the plasma cholinesterase system in the pregnant woman, the fetus, and the neonate (Oro and Dixon, 1987). Toxicologic urine studies have shown that cocaine and its metabolites persist in the urine of an adult for as long as 60 hours after intranasal use (Ambre, 1985). Studies in neonates whose mothers have used cocaine 1 to 2 days before delivery have revealed slow excretion of its metabolites for up to 5 days after delivery (Chasnoff et al, 1986). Since cocaine is a highly lipid-soluble compound and readily crosses biologic membranes, it is reasonable to assume that it will pass into human milk and affect the breast-fed infant (Chasnoff et al, 1987). Cocain intoxication (as evidenced by irritability, tremors, hypertension, dilated pupils, and hyperactive deep tendon reflexes) has been reported secondary to breast-feeding with a mother who has used cocaine (Chasnoff et al, 1987).

The complications seen in the pregnancies of women who use cocaine are consistent with the pharmacologic properties of the drug. Increased rates of prematurity, intrauterine growth retardation (IUGR), abruptio placentae, premature delivery, and stillbirths are observed (Chasnoff et al, 1985; Oro and Dixon, 1987). Dose-related morbidity may exist, with prolonged exposure coupled with poor prenatal care having the worst outcome. Combined exposure with other drugs (narcotics) significantly increases the incidence of IUGR and fetal distress.

Neonates exposed in utero to cocaine are often of low birth weight and demonstrate neurobehavioral abnormalities with marked tremulousness, irritability, abnormal sleep patterns, poor feeding, and deficiencies in mood control and interactive behavior (Oro and Dixon, 1987). These behaviors may be a result of the cocaine rather than withdrawal from it, since they are present immediately after birth. Until the drug is metabolized, these infants may be hyperirritable; after metabolization they may become extremely drowsy and require tube feeding. Focal seizures have been reported secondary to an in utero, cerebral infarction in an infant born following a 5 gm, intranasal, maternal cocaine ingestion (Chasnoff et al, 1986). Cocaine is rapidly becoming the recreational "drug-of-choice" of all socioeconomic groups in the United States because of its relatively low cost and easy accessibility, and we will continue to learn more of its effects on the fetus and newborn.

Treatment

Infants exposed to cocaine in utero need to be observed closely. This may often require an intensive care nursery or a level II facility. Since these infants are often of low birth weight and premature, they need to be followed metabolically (serum glucose, electrolytes, and calcium). They may experience the common problems of prematurity (respiratory distress, temperature instability, feeding difficulties) and require the appropriate intervention for those conditions. Since their condition is primarily associated with marked irritability, they should be nursed in a calm, relaxed environment with minimal external stimuli. They respond best to being wrapped with a blanket and lowering of the nursery lighting. As their drug levels abate, they may become very drowsy and require nasogastric tube feeding. Close observation for seizure activity should be maintained, and a computerized axial scan should be obtained to rule out a cerebral infarction. These infants should be breast-fed only if their mothers are abstaining from cocaine use. As in all substance abuse cases, the mothers should be counseled toward programs to eliminate her drug habits. Since cocaine addiction is often associated with multiple drug abuse, lower socioeconomic status, nutritional deficiencies, and criminal (drug seeking) activities, these infants are at high risk for significant social and family problems. Their developmental progress should be followed closely. Although there are major concerns about these children's school performance, the problem of cocaine abuse is too new for adequate long-term data to have been obtained.

Nursing Diagnoses

1. Altered nutrition, less than body requirements related to SGA and cocaine abuse
2. Sleep pattern disturbance related to cocaine abuse

3. Sensory—perceptual alteration: total CNS dysfunction related to cocaine abuse
4. Altered development, related to SGA and cocaine abuse
5. Potential altered parenting related to maternal drug abuse and negligence
6. Potential for injury related to seizures
7. Potential for aspiration related to drowsiness.

Other external factors. The incidence of anencephaly and spina bifida has also been shown to be above average in countries such as Ireland and states such as Maine possibly because of the mother's consumption of blighted potatoes. The antibiotic produced by the potato in response to blight has been particularly implicated as the teratogen responsible. Stored potatoes with any trace of blight should be scrupulously avoided by pregnant women particularly during the first 4 weeks of pregnancy.

Maternal vitamin deficiencies and excesses have been reported to be teratogenic in many animal species, but little information is available on these effects in humans. Vitamin A excess has been the best described vitamin teratogen in experimental animals. Other maternal nutritional factors that have been studied include the effects of undernutrition during the prenatal periods on subsequent brain development and behavior. Whether humans are subject to *permanent* changes in brain function as the result of maternal undernutrition has not been clearly established.

Increased maternal age has been established in association with Down syndrome, as previously discussed. The incidence of other congenital anomalies may be increased in younger women. An example is anencephaly and spina bifida, which occurs with an incidence of 1 in 1,000 total births in the United States. Its occurrence in miniepidemics is interesting, but no true relationship with environmental agents has as yet been established, although folic acid deficiency is suspected. The incidence of children with this defect is higher in short mothers than among the general population, and it is possible that malnutrition during the mother's childhood resulted in damage to germ cells or reproductive tract integrity, which was then later expressed as teratomas in the offspring. Anencephaly and spina bifida are also found with a higher frequency among infants of mothers of lower socioeconomic status, among blacks, and in infants of low birth weight.

Maternal ingestion of potentially teratogenic drugs may result in defective offspring if the mother's own detoxification or metabolism of the drug is abnormal. The liver metabolism of thalidomide differs greatly among species, and this may account for the wide disparity of teratogenicity among species. Two drugs, isotretinoin and valproic acid, have been recently found to be extremely teratogenic in humans (Holmes, 1987).

Although not conclusively established, many case histories of mothers who have borne children with congenital abnormalities include maternal stress and psychologic imbalance, suggesting that maternal psychosocial well-being is somehow related to normal growth and development of the fetus.

Maternal rubella. The disease model for teratogenesis in this chapter is the rubella syndrome, which is the sequela of maternal rubella during pregnancy. The relationship between congenital malformations and maternal rubella was first suggested by Gregg in Australia in 1941, following a rubella epidemic. Children born of mothers who had contracted rubella (which is itself a mild, self-limiting illness) during pregnancy were observed to have an increased incidence of congenital cataracts, deafness, microcephaly, mental retardation, congenital heart defects, and evidence of chronic infection in many organs. The association of these signs with a history of maternal rubella came to be known as the rubella syndrome.

The risk of rubella syndrome in the offspring of an infected mother is greatly increased during the first trimester of the pregnancy, but it has recently become apparent that long-range sequelae from rubella infection in utero can occur even when the infection occurred later in the pregnancy. For fetal damage during organogenesis to occur, several events must proceed in an orderly fashion. An initial maternal viremia that may be so mild as to be undetected by the pregnant mother is followed by infection of the placenta with rubella virus. The fetus then becomes infected, and fetal viremia ensues. Many organs and tissues can become sites of local rubella infection with subsequent inflammation and necrosis. The virus often persists in these structures long after damage has occurred, and the virus has been cultivated in the eye of a child with congenital rubella-induced cataracts after 3 years. Live virus may be shed through the nasopharynx and urine of infants born with congenital rubella syndrome for many months after birth and may be a source of infection for others. The pathophysiologic mechanism whereby the fetal rubella infection subsequently causes the characteristic organ malformations may be an arteritis, which leads to hypoxia of developing parts. Of course, direct cell necrosis may play an important role. Often, too, the infection persists in the fetal cells and becomes chronic, and development can be interfered with on a long-term basis. Statistical likelihood of malformations in the offspring is highest among mothers infected during the first month of pregnancy, with an estimated risk of 50%. The probability decreases to 22% during the second month, and to 6% to 8% in the third through fifth months of gestation.

It should be mentioned that fetal rubella infection is not always associated with congenital anomalies and that a certain percentage of rubella-infected fetuses survive and appear to be normal. Table 4-2 tabulates data from a major study (at Johns Hopkins) on maternal rubella and risk to offspring.

The long-range effects of maternal rubella infection on the affected offspring are becoming apparent continuously as these children are identified and followed over their lifetimes. IQ is definitely affected, and children with normal IQs frequently experience a variety of learning disorders. Many children have hearing difficulty, the organ of Corti being the auditory structure most often infected with the rubella virus. Little improvement has occurred with age in the children in the Johns Hopkins' study. Growth retardation, which is evident at birth in these children, is maintained during the early years of childhood. Recent reports also suggest that rubella syndrome children are subject to a variety of late onset diseases, particularly during the first year of life. These include chronic rashes, thrombocytopenia, failure to thrive, persistent diarrhea, and generalized interstitial pneumonia. Another condition that is appearing in the second decade of life in these children is a chronic panencephalitis, which is progressive and degenerative. Rubella virus has been isolated from the central nervous system in one of the four reported cases.

In 1969 a rubella vaccine was licensed for use, and massive immunization of children and women at risk for rubella was carried out. It is routine in many states to determine the rubella antibody titer be-

Table 4-2. Teratogenic effects of rubella virus by gestational age of fetus*

Gestational age	Congenital anomalies				No congenital anomalies		Deaths
	No.	Severe	Moderate	Mild	? Normal	Normal	
Preconception	5	1					4
0-4 weeks	23	11	6				6
5-8 weeks	28	7	3	7	1	1	3
9-12 weeks	14	3	3	7	1		0
13-16 weeks	10	2	3	1	2		2
17-20 weeks	7	1		1	1	3	1
21-30 weeks	11	1	2	2	2	4	0
31-45 weeks	4			1	2	1	0

*From Hardy JB: Immediate and long-range effects of maternal viral infection in pregnancy. In Bergsma D, and Schimke RN, editors: Cytogenetics, environment and malformation syndromes. The 1975 Birth Defects Conference, New York, 1976, Alan R Liss Inc for the National Foundation—March of Dimes.

fore marriage and subsequently to carry out prophylactic vaccination. A decline in the incidence of rubella and rubella syndrome has been occurring since the widespread vaccination program was begun.

The Neonatal Period

The neonate is at risk for a variety of disorders as a result of its developmental immaturity. If difficulties during the birth period occur, the infants is vulnerable to hypoxia, respiratory complications, and metabolic and nutritional disturbances. Infants born prematurely (24 to 38 weeks gestation) may develop jaundice, difficult feeding, respiratory distress, infection, and neurologic impairments.

Infants who are small or large for gestational age are also vulnerable to disorders. If an infant is full term but small (less than 2500 gm), fetal malnutrition during the intrauterine period is indicated. Causes include genetic factors, chromosomal defects, multiple gestation, maternal malnutrition, maternal drug abuse (including smoking, alcohol, and narcotics), high altitude, placental defects, preg-

nancy-induced hypertension, and infection. These children remain small and underweight, tend to have neurologic problems, and may have problems in school, but are likely to have a normal IQ (Rossetti, 1986).

Large for gestational age infants are overnourished and also have special problems. These infants are most frequently the children of diabetic mothers. The mechanism for fetal overgrowth in diabetes is apparently related to maternal hyperglycemia, which produces fetal hyperglycemia. The fetal pancreas responds with insulin output, and the lipogenic activity of insulin produces excess fat storage and increased protein synthesis. The result is not only an increase in body weight, length, and adiposity but also in organ size. The same phenomenon is occasionally observed in infants of prediabetic mothers or in mothers with gestational diabetes (Naeye and Tafari, 1983).

The maternal risk factors described above must be assessed to prepare for the possibility of an at-risk infant. Additionally, young adolescent mothers (under the age of 16) and older mothers (over the age of 36) are more likely to have premature babies or babies that are small for their gestational age. A comprehensive discussion of neonatal disturbances is out of the scope of this book. However, to highlight the mechanisms by which pathology may occur and to stress how important the immaturity of the infant is in these pathologic processes, we will discuss one common problem in premature or small gestational age infants, ineffective breathing pattern.

The breathing pattern of a newborn infant may fall into any one of four categories: regular, irregular, periodic, or apneic. The usual breathing pattern of a normal, full-term infant is regular with occasional irregularities. There are equal breath-to-breath intervals interspersed with an occasional unequal breath-to-breath interval. This is in contrast to the usual and ineffective breathing pattern seen in a preterm infant (gestational age of less than 37 weeks), which is characterized by irregular breath-to-breath intervals interspersed with periodic and/or apneic events. This difference can be attributed directly to the lack of maturity, coordination, and integration of the neurochemical regulatory controls, the lung tissue and airways, and thoracic musculoskeletal function (see Chapter 16) (Dulock, 1986). Volpe and Hill (1987) hypothesize that periodic breathing is the result of incomplete development of a system that modulates respiration in the cerebral hemispheres and/or, possibly the diencephalon. Both of these areas of the brain undergo great maturational change during the latter part of the gestational period.

Apnea is the cessation of breathing for a period of 20 seconds (10 seconds if accompanied by bradycardia and cyanosis) and is followed by hypotonia and unresponsiveness. Periodic breathing is a patterned cessation of breathing effort alternating with normal respirations. It is not accompanied by heart rate changes or significant hypoxemia. The incidence of these altered breathing patterns is inversely related to the gestational age (Hodson and Truog, 1987), and they usually develop toward the end of the first week and during the second week of life (Usher, 1987). The sim-

---

CHARACTERISTICS OF PERIODIC BREATHING

Common characteristics

Occurrence inversely related to gestational age

Rarely occurs after 36 weeks' gestational age

Rarely occurs during first 24 to 48 hours of life

Frequency may increase during first weeks(s) of life, depending on degree of immaturity

May be initiated by conditions that reduce functional residual capacity or that produce hypoxemia

May be abolished by increasing functional residual capacity or by maintaining normal arterial oxygenation

Tends to recur

Differentiating characteristics

Periodic breathing

- Cessation of respiration for 3 seconds or longer, separated by respiratory periods of less than 20 seconds
- Not associated with changes in heart rate, arterial oxygenation, or cyanosis
- Thought to be a benign condition, especially if not intermixed with recurrent periods of apnea that require intervention

Apnea

- Cessation of respiration for 10 to 20 seconds or longer
- Frequently accompanied by bradycardia, fall in blood pressure, hypoxemia, and cyanosis
- Occurrence of repeated episodes of hypoxia resulting in CNS damage or death

From Dulock H: Apnea, 1986, pp. 137-159. In Carrieri V, Lindsay A, and West C, *Pathophysiological phenomenon in nursing:* WB Saunders Co, Philadelphia, PA.

ilarities and differences between these two ineffective breathing patterns are summarized in box on p. 138. These two breathing patterns could be viewed on a continuum of increasing pathologic severity since they share many common characteristics with one another. Premature infants with periodic breathing tend to develop apnea (Rigatto and Brady, 1972), indicating that they share a common developmental pathophysiologic cause as well.

A variety of pathologic conditions may also alter the breathing pattern of a premature infant, including respiratory distress syndrome, CNS hemorrhage, sepsis, and patent ductus arteriosus. However, this most often occurs in response to the immature development of the nervous and respiratory systems. Incomplete neuronal myelination and dendritic development, undeveloped chemoreceptor responses, lack of fatigue resistant muscle fibers in the diaphragm, and the greater percentage of time spent in REM sleep (Gabriel et al, 1976) make the premature infant susceptible to apnea of prematurity. Situational stressors that compound this risk include ambient temperature changes and extremes and care giving activities such as suctioning, feeding, handling, and diagnostic and therapeutic treatments (Speidel, 1978). Noises may also cause a startle response. Crying is known to cause a decrease in transcutaneous oxygen pressure, and infants respond to many of these situational factors by crying and then develop hypoxemia as a result. Physiologic stressors such as hypoxemia, hyperthermia or hypothermia, hypoglycemia, nutritional deficits, acidosis, abdominal distention, anemia, or alterations in fluid volume and composition also place the premature infant at risk.

Although periodic breathing may be considered relatively benign, it does indicate an increased risk of experiencing apnea. Apnea of prematurity may lead to significant hypoxemia, bradycardia, and all the sequela of tissue hypoxia. This can include disruption of organ function and further impairment of development, especially of the central nervous system. Death may even occur as a result of an apneic episode.

There has been much speculation about the relationship of apnea to sudden infant death syndrome (SIDS). Apnea is only one of many mechanisms that have been proposed to be pathogenetic in SIDS, and this continues to be an area of speculation and study. It has been proposed that the terms *apnea of infancy* or *infantile apnea* be used to describe a "near miss" or aborted SIDS event, in which an infant is found to be not breathing and is successfully resuscitated (editorial correspondence, 1981; Brooks, 1982 and 1984; Shannon and Kelly, 1982). This new terminology does imply a disorder of respiratory drive that is a different clinical entity than apnea of prematurity (Ariagno, 1984; Task Force, 1985).

The goals of treatment include prevention of apneic episodes and their sequelae and restoration of an effective, regular breathing pattern. The heart and respiratory rates and the transcutaneous oxygen pressure should be monitored continuously. Interventions to maintain a regular breathing pattern are based on the theory that disruption of the breathing pattern is related to lack of afferent stimulation of the respiratory control center as a result of immaturity of the nervous system and can be countered by an increase in afferent stimuli. Cutaneous stimulation has been used to prevent and resolve apneic episodes (Kattwinkel et al, 1975). Oscillating water beds have been used to stimulate the vestibuloproprioceptive responses in much the same way as would the uterine environment (Korner et al, 1978). The situational and physiologic stressors that can precipitate an alteration in the breathing pattern must be avoided. Pharmacologic therapy with respiratory stimulants such as caffeine, aminophylline, and theophylline may also be used to prevent apnea when apneic episodes have been recurrent (Hodson and Truog, 1987).

Should an apneic episode occur, treatment must be immediate and the goal is to prevent significant development of hypoxemia and subsequent tissue hypoxia. Mechanical ventilation, continuous positive airway pressure (CPAP), artificial ventilation, and/or the use of supplemental oxygen may be necessary. Oxygen must be used with care since it can have toxic effects when used in higher concentrations or for prolonged periods (see Chapter 16).

Infancy and Childhood

The pathologic problems common to this stage of the lifespan are related largely to immaturity of the developing body systems and to psychosocial factors. The most common causes of morbidity during childhood are (1) infections, (2) dental caries, (3) accidents, (4) school and behavior problems, (5) visual problems, (6) allergies, and (7) hearing problems.

INFECTIONS DURING CHILDHOOD

Any system of the body is potentially vulnerable to infection, although age-related influences in organ size or physiology may play important roles in infectious processes. An average child has 3.5 infections per year, and infection is the major health problem of childhood. The underlying pathophysiologic mechanism is that the immune system grows and matures during childhood by a process of recognition and amplification. Unfortunately this is accompanied by frequent bouts of infection as the various pathogens invade. Infants are born with the capacity to respond immunologically, but the major antibody is IgA. Maternal immunoglobulins of the IgA type provide most of the immunity during the first months of life, but with a half life of about 21 days, the infant's immunity is required to respond very soon after birth. IgG levels are at their lowest value when the infant is about 6 months of age. This is therefore a very vulnerable period. Adult levels of IgG are usually attained by 5 years of age and for IgM by 10 years.

The portal of entry for most childhood infections is the upper respiratory tract and therefore children develop many colds, coughs, pharyngitis episodes, ear infections, and pulmonary disorders. Their immune systems "learn" to recognize these microbes and expand B cell clones, which are capable of recognition and efficient destruction of them on subsequent exposures. Another important type of infection is infection of the gastrointestinal tract, with diarrheal diseases being particularly serious and potentially devastating. The earlier a child is introduced to sources of infection (i.e., other children and adults), the quicker the immunologic development. Children who are protected and isolated may not have many infections until they enter school. Infants brought to day care centers from a very early age suffer these consequences earlier, but they also develop their immunocompetence earlier.

Upper respiratory infections and meningitis

The risk of upper respiratory infections during infancy and early childhood is related to anatomic structure and immune system influences. Infants are obligatory nose breathers, and when nasal congestion occurs, great distress may occur if the obstruction is severe. The frontal and sphenoid sinuses are absent or very underdeveloped in the newborn, and are not pneumatized until middle childhood. Therefore when children develop nasal infections, it is initially confined to the nasal passages, and the small sinuses become inflamed and swollen. The rhinitis is severe, and because children usually do not blow their noses efficiently, the drainage is constant. Another problem is related to middle ear anatomy. The eustachian tube is short and straight in the infant, and nasal drainage and even formula can drain through the tube into the middle ear. Inflammatory responses lead to edema, and in this environment many pathogenic microorganisms can thrive and cause middle ear infection. Once a child develops an acute otitis media, recurrent bouts of both infection and serous otitis media can occur. The underdeveloped bony structures and immature immune system, along with frequent upper respiratory infections, lead to an increased risk of meningitis in infants and toddlers. Meningitis is one of the most serious complications that can occur from ear, nose, throat, or pulmonary infections. Since the mastoid process is not present at birth, middle ear infection can result in meningitis. Infection of the meningeal membranes leads to inflammation, edema, cellular necrosis, and potential destruction of brain cells. Early diagnosis and antibiotic treatment has greatly decreased the morbidity and mortality of meningitis.

The most common respiratory infection of childhood is pharyngotonsillitis, most commonly a result of viral infection. Important respiratory viruses include adenovirus, Epstein-Barr virus, influenza, parainfluenza, herpes simplex virus, and enterovirus. The bacterial infection of greatest concern is streptococcal pharyngotonsillitis. Streptococcal sore throat requires treatment not only for the inflammation but also to prevent antigenic stimulation leading to cross reactivity and subsequent kidney or cardiac problems. Children with streptococcal pharyngitis typically have fever, sore throat, red exudative tonsils, enlarged and tender peritonsillar lymph nodes; they may have abdominal pain, loss of appetite, and a scarlatiniform rash.

Children also commonly suffer from various obstructive respiratory disorders, such as laryngotracheobronchitis (croup), asthmatic bronchitis, and asthmatic attacks. Croup is a reactive, inflammatory response usually to a viral infection. It is seen in infants and toddlers and produces a hoarse voice, cough, and marked inspiratory stridor resulting from edema of the vocal cords and subglottic area. Typically the stridor becomes most severe at night, and children appear acutely ill. This disease must be differentiated from acute epiglottitis, which is a bacterial inflammation of the epiglottis and which can lead to life-threatening respiratory obstruction. (See Chapter 16.)

Other obstructive respiratory diseases are infectious or bronchospastic in nature. Many children who do not have allergic asthma respond to infection and inflammation with bronchoconstriction. This may be the result of inflammatory edema of the bronchioles, but the effect is an asthmatic like expiratory wheezing. True acute asthmatic attacks in children are a result of exposure to allergens, exercise, or cold and are the result of bronchoconstriction from smooth muscle spasm.

Because of their smaller respiratory passages and higher numbers of respiratory infections, children frequently develop pneumonia, which impairs respiratory function and can lead to problems in oxygenation. Children are more likely than adults to become bacteremic from any nidus of infection and may yet appear much less sick than an adult would.

When children become ill there is a greater need to supply them with comfort, support, nutrition (which can quickly become inadequate), fluids, and rest. They are adaptively less able to handle the stress of infection, fever, and fluid imbalance, and they may not be able to understand why they feel unwell and listless.

Adolescents are also prone to infections, particularly during times of stress, fatigue, accelerated growth, and exposure to microorganisms. Two common types of infections in this age group include infectious mononucleosis and sexually transmitted disease. Adolescents also develop childhood diseases, if they have not been adequately immunized.

Gastrointestinal disturbances

Although gastrointestinal diseases and diarrhea are described in detail in Chapter 21, there are some aspects of developmental physiology that help us to understand the pathophysiology of these problems in children. Children are susceptible to diarrheal disease as a result of their general lack of concern over cleanliness. Microorganisms are transmitted usually through the fecal-oral route in diarrheal diseases of childhood. Viruses, enteropathic *Escherichia coli*, *Shigella*, and *Salmonella* are important causes. The major responses that can occur, especially in infancy, are alterations in fluid volume and composition, nutritional deficiency, and a vicious cycle of diarrheal disease that leads to chronic problems. The fluid and electrolyte problems are related to developmental physiologic factors, such as the decreased ability of the young kidneys to excrete concentrated urine and save water, the larger surface area to volume ratio, the proportionately increased extracellular fluid to intracellular fluid compartments, and the difficulty a child has communicating thirst. Nutritional deficits develop rapidly since many children do not have great energy reserves and tend also to have higher fevers, which also increase fuel use. Fluid intake is usually the major source of calorie intake for infants, and if the child vomits formula or has repeated bouts of diarrhea, energy sources will not even be absorbed. Chronic diarrhea is a particular problem in underdeveloped countries, but can also occur in other children. The inflammatory and infectious process responsible for the initial attack of gastrointestinal disease alters the mucosa of the small intestine, which then becomes incapable of the normal reabsorptive properties that allow for fluid balance and food molecule uptake. The diarrhea continues and sets up a vicious cycle by which the child becomes more and more depleted. The bowel must rest to recover, and food and fluid must be supplied by other than oral means.

Growth disturbances

Infancy, childhood, and adolescence are periods of amazing growth. The processes governing growth are complex, involving both internal and external influences. Nutrition, rest, environmental factors, psychosocial phenomena, and hormonal function are necessary for adequate growth in children. Early malnutrition, fetal influences, and socioeconomic class all contribute to stature and weight. Disturbed growth is therefore a problem of the early years, since it is essentially completed by late adolescence. The rate of growth varies during childhood with the most rapid rate observed during infancy. Birth weight is usually doubled by the age of 5 months, and birth length is increased 50% by the age of 1 year. During toddlerhood and the school-age years, growth rate is steady and slower, but preadolescent growth spurts occur in both boys and girls between the ages of 10 and 12. At adolescence, growth and maturation accelerate, more quickly in girls than in boys, but in both sexes, pathophysiologic problems associated with growth may occur. A common problem observed in boys more frequently than girls is Osgood-Schlatter's disease. This is a painful knee problem in which rapid epiphyseal growth creates a bony overgrowth that is palpable below the knee cap. Other growth centers may show similar rapid growth disturbances, including the heels (calcaneal apophysitis). These conditions may lead to necrosis, alter mobility, and cause discomfort, which may seriously impair the child's ability to engage in physical activity. However, the problems usually disappear with time. The following case study describes the problems associated with Osgood-Schlatter's disease.

CASE STUDY: OSGOOD-SCHLATTER'S DISEASE

History

This 14-year-old, white, male patient had been seen at the clinic for well-child care and minor acute illnesses. Past illness history includes: otitis media (3X), strep throat (2X), chicken pox, and conjunctivitis. The patient received sutures at 12 years of age on his right arm after falling out of a tree. His immunizations are up to date, with the last diptheria-tetanus given at age 12.

The family history is negative for arthritis, degenerative joint disease, cancer, or knee problems, except for the patient's

Contributed by Nan Gaylord.

father. He had knee surgery after "tearing all the ligaments in his right knee" while playing football.

The patient is now present in the pediatric outpatient clinic for the complaint of bilateral knee pain for the past 2 months. He is concerned about his ability to continue competing on the school basketball team. The pain is episodic and increases after exercise; it does not interfere with normal activities and has not made him fall. There is no history of recent or past trauma. There are no complaints of pain in any other joint. The patient has not reported an elevation in temperature nor any bacterial/viral infections within the past 3 months.

Physical examination
  Height: 174 cm (90th percentile)
  Weight: 55 kg (60th percentile)
  Oral temperature: 37° C
  Pulse rate: 70/min
  Respiratory rate: 14/min
General: Cooperative, friendly; well-developed musculature
Skin: Small erythematous papules on nose. No rashes.
Eyes: PERRLA. CLR equal. EOM's 180°.
Ears: TM's clear and mobile. Canals clear.
Nose: No drainage.
Throat: No erythema or exudate.
Mouth: Mucous membranes clear. Sixteen permanent teeth without caries.
Heart: S_1 and S_2 clear and distinct. No murmur.
  No brachial-femoral lag.
Lungs: Clear in all lobes. No rhonchi or rales.
Abdomen: Bowel sounds present. No masses. No organomegaly.
Musculoskeletal
  Knees: Full flexion and extension without discomfort. Knee pain bilaterally when resistance applied while full extension is attempted. No tenderness on patella. Patella not ballotable. No crepitus. All collateral liga-

ments in tact. Negative drawer sign. Point tenderness bilaterally at tibial tuberosity with redness, warmth to touch and 1+ edema.

Other: All other joints without redness or warmth. Full range of motion present without discomfort.

Genitalia: Tanner III. Circumcized male. Both testes descended.

Neurologic: DTR's 2+ and equal bilaterally (knee reflex omitted bilaterally)

Pathophysiology

In 1903 Osgood and Schlatter first described this entity. Osgood-Schlatter disease occurs primarily in adolescent males between 10 and 15 years of age but is also seen in adolescent females between 8 and 13 years of age. The exact cause of this condition is not completely understood, but it appears to be an overuse injury of the quadriceps muscle that stresses the patellar tendon at the attachment site on the tibial tuberosity. Either there is a microtearing of the fibers in the tendon from the bony epiphysis or the lesion is a partial separation through the growth plate. This condition is most often a very benign one but may be episodic with recurrences throughout adolescence. Most cases cease to be symptomatic once the proximal tibial growth plate closes, at approximately 15 years of age.

Nursing Diagnoses

1. Impaired physical mobility related to Osgood-Schlatter's disease
2. Altered role performance related to effect of disease on growth and development
3. Alteration in comfort
4. Knowledge deficit related to disease state

• • •

Another frequent musculoskeletal problem, scoliosis, is observed more commonly in girls than in boys and is a lateral curvature that develops in the spine during growth. Ten percent of American children develop some degree of scoliosis during their growing years. Severe scoliosis requires treatment, and surgical intervention may be required.

A growth anomaly that is present during childhood is small stature. Pituitary dwarfism is an endocrinopathy that results from hypopituitarism. Short stature is much more common and is related to inadequate secretion of growth hormone and is unrelated to genetic regulation of height. Since children with very short stature often develop psychologic feelings of inadequacy and isolation, there are recent attempts to treat this problem with growth hormone extracts. Although the cause of short stature is known to be decreased growth hormone, it is not clear why this occurs.

Bone cancer is another potential skeletal disease that occurs with higher frequency in children than in adults. Osteogenic sarcoma is a tumor that develops in long bones, and that causes initial pain and eventual osteolytic destruction and lung and brain metastases. Often the limb must be amputated, which to a child may be a more devastating event than the diagnosis of cancer. Osteogenic sarcoma has a high mortality rate and is one of the most common solid tumors that can occur in childhood.

One of the most difficult problems of growth is the failure to thrive syndrome (FTT). This disorder is an excellent model of mind-body interaction. Psychosocial factors interrupt growth apparently by inhibiting growth hormone release—a deprivation dwarfism. Failure to thrive is defined as chronic growth deficit, with weight persistently below the third percentile for age. There are organic and nonorganic causes that must be explored in any infant with this disorder. Any chronic severe pediatric disease carries the potential of growth deficit. Disturbances in gastrointestinal function, such as malabsorption syndromes, will also impair nutrition and thus growth.

Infants with severe feeding difficulties, such as in cleft palate, also are at risk. Many times it has been noted that a child with a particular organic problem will be regarded unfavorably by the caregivers and develop failure to thrive from both organic and nonorganic causes. The nonorganic causes include the following four areas of disturbance: (1) the child is perceived as difficult and sickly and the family is disturbed, with an overwhelmed and isolated mother and unavailable father; (2) there is severe interactional deficit between the mother and infant; (3) feeding is inadequate with irregular feeding, feeding problems, and lower caloric intake; and (4) there is a constellation of psychosocial factors such as poverty, marital disruption, loss, and stress (Levin et al., 1983).

Infants with failure to thrive have characteristics indicative of both their deprived growth and their psychosocial stress. They are severely underweight (in terms of weight for height), their head circumference is within the normal range, they have decreased skin fold thicknesses, and they may be hypoalbuminemic and anergic. Their affect is often flat and little attention is given to environmental stimuli and people. They rarely smile or fixate their eyes on another's face. Their posture may be similar to decorticate posture, and their developmental maturation is severely delayed. These infants do not cuddle when held and are actually rigid. Their posture, interactions, and poor feeding all point to an infant who is emotionally starved and unable to engage in the most elementary social responses. The infant may also engage in rumination and volitional vomiting. The infant may be rejecting food because, in terms of infancy, food and love are inseparable.

Although calories are inadequate most of the time, this is not enough to explain the failure to thrive. Deficient secretion of growth hormone is possibly a cause, as is vomiting and diarrhea, which are often present. The disease can be treated only by assessment and treatment of the family and their interactional problems. This is often very difficult, and persistence of the problem is common. Although children may eventually experience catch-up growth, the developmental outcomes on cognition and psychologic health are dismal. The incidence of mental retardation and behavioral problems have been high in all of the follow-up studies of failure to thrive (Berwick, 1980).

Accidents

Although infections and growth problems are common, accidents are the leading cause of morbidity and mortality in the United States, outweighing by far other causes of death in children under 4 years of age. The types of accidents that cause injury and death are closely related to developmental factors and psychosocial factors. Falls, electrical injuries, poisoning, drowning, and aspiration of a foreign body are the most common types of accidents in younger children, but automobile accidents also claim many lives. As children get older and during the teenage and young adult years, motor vehicle accidents become more common and are the leading cause of death during adolescence and young adulthood. The risk of accidents is related to parental stress, highly active, dare-taking children, fatigue, time of day (late in the afternoon or on Saturday morning are common times for children to have accidents in the home), and lack of anticipation by the parents for developmental advances that increase a child's risk. Anticipatory guidance would help prevent many accidents, such as accident-proofing the home by placing objects out of reach and safeguarding against electrical shock. Seatbelt use and child restraints clearly have been responsible for fewer highway deaths.

Adolescence

The problems of adolescence are complex, and adolescent medicine is now a subspecialty dealing with these complex problems. Developmentally, growth and pubertal maturation are the major phenomena, but psychosocially, adolescence is a time of turmoil as identity is more firmly established and important career decisions are being made. Adolescent stress should not be underemphasized in the etiology of adolescent disorders. The establishment of life-styles and health habits is also important. For example, smoking, which is a major risk factor for many diseases of adulthood, usually starts during adolescence. Thomas and Groer (1986) found that smoking was related to blood pressure levels in young adolescents, as was body size and urban residence. Adolescent hypertension appears to be an incresingly common problem, and obesity and sedentariness are unfortunately also common. Drug abuse is another serious problem of adolescence, and there are many health problems that are influenced by drug and alcohol abuse. The leading cause of death for this age group is motor vehicle accidents, and alcohol intoxication often plays a major role in these accidents.

Other problems of adolescence include infections (with infectious mononucleosis and sexually transmitted diseases being important) depression, school problems, menstrual problems, and pregnancy.

Adulthood

Most of the chapters in this book deal with the pathophysiologic processes of adult life. Many of these mechanisms start incipiently; there may be no signs and symptoms for many years, yet there are many pathologic changes taking place. Coronary artery disease is the best example of such a process. A mortality table for Americans over the age of 40 indicate that the leading causes of death are largely life-style related. The top ten causes of death are listed in Table 4-3. Other causes of morbidity include infections, hypertension, periodontal disease, sexually transmitted diseases, hypercholesterolemia, and obesity. Most of these problems are either partially or completely preventable through life-style modification. Many of these pathophysiologic phenomena contribute to longevity and the quality of old age, as

Table 4-3. Ten leading causes of death (total population 1+ years of age)

Cause	Rate per 100,000
Heart disease	336
Cancer	181
Cerebrovascular disease	85
Accidents (not including motor vehicle)	25
Influenza and pneumonia	23
Motor vehicle accidents	23
Diabetes	15
Cirrhosis of liver	14
Arteriosclerosis	14
Suicide	13

Compiled from The Center for Disease Control, U.S. Department of Health and Human Services.

will be discussed in Chapter 9. The role of stress continues to be emphasized in the pathophysiology of all of these disease processes of the adult years. The adoption of deleterious habits, such as smoking or excessive food consumption leading to obesity, may be the direct result of stress and inadequate coping in adults.

BIBLIOGRAPHY

Ambre J: The urinary excretion of cocaine and metabolites in humans J Anal Toxicol 8:241-245, 1985.

Ariagno RL: Evaluation and management of infantile apnea, Pediatr Ann 13:210-217, 1984.

Baer C, and Williams B, editors: Clinical pharmacology and nursing, Springhouse, PA, 1988, Springhouse Corp.

Bergsma D and Shimke RN: Cytogenetics, environment and malformation syndromes. The 1975 Birth Defects Conference, New York, 1976, Alan R Liss Inc.

Berwick D: Rev. Nonorganic failure to thrive, Pediatrics 1:265, 1980.

Braude M, et al: Perinatal effects of drugs of abuse, Fed Proc. 46:2446, 1987.

Brent RL: Environmental factors in the causation of birth defects, Frontiers in genetic medicine. Ross Conference on Pediatric Research, Ross Laboratories, 1987.

Brooks JG: Apnea of infancy and sudden infant death syndrome, Am J Dis Child 136:1012-1023, 1982.

Brooks JG: Relationship of apnea of infancy to SIDS, Perinatol Neonatol 8:15-18, 1984.

Chasnoff IJ, et al: Cocaine use in pregnancy N Engl J Med 313:666-669, 1985.

Chasnoff IJ, et al: Perinatal cerebral infarction and maternal cocaine use, J Pediatr 108:456-459, 1986.

Chasnoff IJ, Lewis DE, and Squires L: Cocaine intoxication in a breast fed infant, Pediatrics 80:836-838, 1987.

Corbett J: Laboratory tests and diagnostic procedures with nursing diagnoses, Norwalk, CT, 1987, Appleton & Lange.

Dulock H: Apnea. In Carrieri VK, Lindsey AM, and West CM: Pathophysiological phenomena in nursing: human responses to illness, Philadelphia, 1986, WB Saunders Co, pp 137-159.

Editorial correspondence, Statement on terminology from the National SIDS Foundation, J Pediatr 99:664, 1981.

Farrell PM and Palta M: Bronchopulmonary dysplasia. In Bronchopulmonary dysplasia and related chronic respiratory disorders. Ross Conferences on Pediatric Research, Ross Laboratories, 1986.

Gabriel M, Albani M, and Schulte FJ: Apneic spells and sleep states in preterm infants, Pediatrics 57:142-147, 1976.

Hodson WA and Truog WE: Special techniques in managing respiratory problems. In Avery GB, editor: Neonatology: pathophysiology and management of the newborn ed 3, Philadelphia, 1987, J.B. Lippincott Co, pp 460-492.

Holmes LB: Environmental factors, Frontiers in genetic medicine. Ross Conferences on Pediatric Research, Ross Laboratories, 1987.

Isher JM, Estes M III, and Thompson PD: Acute cardiac events temporally related to cocaine abuse, N Engl J Med 315:1438-1443, 1986.

Kattwinkel JB, et al: Apnea of prematurity: comparative therapeutic effects of cutaneous stimulation and nasal continuous positive airway pressure, J Pediatr 86:588, 1975.

Korner AF, et al: Reduction of sleep apnea and bradycardia in preterm infants on oscillating waterbeds: a controlled polygraphic study, Peidatrics 61:528, 1978.

Lederman RP, et al: The relationship of maternal anxiety, plasma catecholamines and plasma cortisol to progress in labor, Am J Obstet Gyncol 132:495-500, 1978.

Levin MD, et al: Developmental-behavioral pediatrics, Philadelphia, 1983, WB Saunders Co.

Lovell W and Winter R, Editors: Pediatric orthopedics ed 2, vol. II, Philadelphia, 1986, JB Lippincott Co. p 890.

Naeye R and Tafari N: Risk factors in pregnancy and disease of the fetus and newborn, Baltimore, 1983, Williams & Wilkins.

Oro AS and Dixon SD: Perinatal cocaine and methamphetamine exposure: maternal and neonatal correlates, J Pediatr 11:571-578, 1987.

Reisman LE and Methany AP: Genetics and counseling in medical practice. St. Louis, 1969, The CV Mosby, Co.

Rigatto H and Brady JP: Periodic breathing and apnea in preterm infants: hypoxia as a primary event, Pediatrics 50:219-228, 1972.

Rodman G, McEwen C, and Wallace S: Primer on the rheumatic diseases, New York, 1973, The Arthritis Foundation.

Rossetti L: High risk infants, Boston, 1986, Little, Brown & Co Inc.

Shannon DC and Kelly DH: SIDS and near miss, N Engl J Med 306:959-965, 1982.

Sherman WT and Gautier RF: Effect of certain drugs on perfused human placenta. X. Norepinephrine release by Bradykinin, J Pharm Sci 61:878-883, 1972.

Speidel DB: Adverse effects of routine procedures on preterm infants, Lancet 1:864-865, 1978.

Task Force on Prolonged Infantile Apnea, American Academy of Pediatrics: Prolonged infantile apnea, Pediatrics 76:129-131, 1985.

Taussig LM: Long term management and pulmonary progress in bronchopulmonary dysplasia in bronchopulmonary dysplasia and related chronic respiratory disorders. Ross Conferences on Pediatric Research, Ross Laboratories, 1986.

Thomas and Groer 1986

Usher R: Extreme prematurity. In Avery GB, editor: Neonatology: pathophysiology and management of the newborn, ed 3, Philadelphia, 1987, J.B. Lippincott Co, pp 264-331.

Volpe JJ and Hill A: Neurologic disorders. In Avery GB, editor: Neonatology: pathophysiology and management of the nerwborn, ed 3, Philadelphia, 1987, J.B. Lippincott Co, pp 1073-1132.

Whaley LF: Understanding inherited disorders, St. Louis, 1974, The CV Mosby Co.

White R: The search for the cystic fibrosis gene, Science, 234:1054, 1986.

Wojtys E: The lower extremity and the knee, Orthop Clin North Am **18**(4) 1987.

5

Chemical and physical agents

Wellness is often maintained in the midst of great adversity. Physical and chemical threats are always present in the environment, and there are many mechanisms by which people respond and cope. Chemical exposure can be ubiquitous or self-induced—drug or alcohol abuse. There is the potential for physical trauma every time a person chooses to drive an automobile. Accidents are the leading cause of morbidity and death in children and young people. Children may injure themselves through chemical ingestion, falls, burns, and drowning. This chapter will discuss the pathophysiologic mechanisms through which chemical agents and physical factors disturb wellness. Several disease models for chemical and physical mechanisms will be provided, as well as a case study that illustrates how the effects of chemical poisoning can be extremely difficult to diagnose.

CHEMICAL AGENTS
The nature of chemical injuries

Chemicals that are toxic to the body generally have specific effects on certain susceptible cells, which result in characteristic signs and symptoms. One common underlying result of chemical injury is cellular necrosis. Cell death can result from many pathophysiologic mechanisms. Necrosis that occurs in inflammation may be the result of direct physical injury to the cells, may be produced by toxins and injurious chemicals, may result from autocatalytic reactions by which the cell destroys itself, or may occur through hypoxia. The latter cause of necrosis is an important one generally, in that hypoxia may be the result of myriad disease mechanisms. Whenever cell hypoxia occurs, however, a predictable sequence of events ensues. Hypoxic cells are not able to metabolize effectively and must switch to anaerobic glycolysis, which is not an efficient energy-yielding pathway. If the hypoxia does not irreversibly damage the cell, the cell may be able to revert to aerobic metabolism and survive when normal oxygenation is returned.

The effects of inefficient anaerobic glycolysis at the cellular level are manifold (see Chapter 16). Lactic acid is the end product of the Embden-Myerhof pathway in a hypoxic cell. The lactic acid accumulates, with the result that the pH may become more and more acidic. Furthermore, the lack of adenosine triphosphate (ATP) generated by anaerobic glycolysis results in inefficient membrane active transport, such that sodium accumulates inside the cell as potassium leaks out. Cellular swelling is the ultimate result of a breakdown in the Na^+-K^+ pump. Cells that have undergone hypoxic changes are characterized as having "cloudy swelling." Osmotic swelling and acid pH changes have many effects on cell function. One important result is interference with various enzyme activities, which can produce a cascading effect of further derangement until cell function ceases and necrosis appears. Interference with nuclear function seems to be the point at which damage becomes irreversible. Thus it is difficult to say at what point a dying cell is truly dead!

The process of necrosis takes time and, as we have seen previously, involves the interaction of the tissue in an acute inflammatory response. Progressive functional and structural changes are usually observed unless cell death has been caused by an extremely rapidly acting agent (e.g., formaldehyde).

It is also possible for chemical agents to cause reversible changes in the cell that do not always lead to necrosis. These changes are termed degenerative. Degenerative changes usually occur in the cytoplasm and may consist of swelling, formation of cytoplasmic vacuoles, and deposition of lipid in certain tissue cells (e.g., the liver in chronic alcoholism; see Chapter 21).

One important concept to keep in mind is the remarkable ability of cells to adapt to the conditions imposed by the presence of potentially injurious agents. The responses of metaplasia and hyperplasia will be discussed in Chapter 6. Other responses include atrophy and hypertrophy of cells in the presence of toxic agents or stressors. Atrophy of cells often leads to pathologic processes. Hypertrophy may be pathologic or physiologic, depending on the degree and tissue involved. For example, the heart hypertrophies in response to the stressor effect of an increased work load, which might occur in hypertensive dis-

ease. While this is an adaptive response it will eventually result in pathophysiology, since there is a definite limit to the degree that myocardial fibers can grow and be stretched. At this point the adaptation becomes pathophysiologic.

A number of disease models of cell injury caused by chemical agents will be discussed in this chapter. They are intended to illustrate various mechanisms of injury. It would be impossible to describe the effects of all the chemicals that may injure cells or cause damage to the human body. However, the reader is encouraged to consider the basic pathophysiologic concepts that are presented in relation to the disease models and to apply these concepts to the possible damage wrought by other chemical agents.

Pathways of detoxification

The body has elaborated many complicated mechanisms of defense. One defense mechanism is that of cellular detoxification of environmental chemicals that would normally be extremely toxic to the organism. The study of the human response to these agents is the science of toxicology. Toxicology studies the effect of toxic substances on the body and the physiologic and pathophysiologic responses to toxic agents. Such study has become increasingly more important in our time, since the environment is becoming more and more polluted with foreign gases and synthetic chemicals to which humans have never before been exposed (xenobiotic substances). Evolutionary mechanisms that would ultimately lead to cellular detoxification processes for these agents cannot operate in a 20-year or even a 100-year period. Our only hope therefore is that science will be able to predict the responses of the body to these agents and prevent them by manipulation of the environment or medical pretreatment of the population at risk. Of course, the former possiblity is much more attractive but is less likely to occur. Therefore, effort must be expended in the area of cellular toxicology, so that a basic understanding of the cellular responses can be achieved. Furthermore, the effects of these agents on the biosphere in general and on the ecologic environment cannot be ignored. Thus humans may be affected directly by toxicants or indirectly through effects on the food chain and environment.

Of course, there are other chemicals in the environment that have been present throughout the course of evolution but to which humans have not evolved adequate detoxification mechanisms. For example, elements such as lead and arsenic were present in the early environment but probably not to a degree that they represented any serious threat to survival of the human species. Oxygen, on the other hand, was present in the earliest environment, and all living creatures appear to have evolved from organisms that were able to detoxify oxygen through oxidative processes such as the metabolism of glucose. Clearly this metabolic pathway, which is essential for human survival, may also be viewed as a process that removes oxygen from the cell environment. The effects of high concentrations of oxygen, even in the presence of these detoxification mechanisms, are extremely pathologic. Oxygen can directly damage cells, causing for example, *retrolental fibroplasia* or *bronchopulmonary dysplasia* in the premature infant treated with high concentrations of oxygen.

The liver is the major organ involved in detoxification of potentially harmful chemicals that are taken into the body. Other tissues also have the capacity to detoxify various substances, but their roles are secondary to that of the liver, at least in mammals. The major site for detoxification in the liver cells is at the cytoplasmic microsomes, which are that subcellular fraction of the cytoplasm containing the endoplasmic reticulum obtained by ultracentrifugation. The membranes of the endoplasmic reticulum contain various enzymes that function in detoxification. Microsomal electron transport chains, similar to those found in the mitochondria (see Chapter 16), appear to play an extremely important role in the detoxification process, involving the introduction of one atom of oxygen into both endogenously produced and xenobiotic toxins, which may be a first step in their ultimate detoxification. By changing the chemical nature of the toxin, the body protects itself against detrimental effects.

As in the mitochondria, these electron transport chains involve various types of cytochromes, NADH, NADPH, and flavoproteins. The enzymes that make up these electron transport chains are known as *mixed function oxidases*. The terminal oxidase in the mixed function oxidase chain is *cytochrome* P_{450}, a protein- and heme-containing enzyme that can bind oxygen. This cytochrome accepts electrons, binds oxygen, and finally delivers the oxygen to the substance that is being detoxified. Along with oxidation of the toxic substance, water is generally produced in this reaction. A general scheme of the reaction sequence is presented in Fig. 5-1.

A characteristic of the mixed function oxidase system is that its activity can be induced by many different endogenous and xenobiotic chemicals, which are ultimately oxidized by the reactions of the system. The mixed oxidase system also appears to be linked in many cases to the conjugation of the toxic substance by glucuronic acid after it has been oxidized. This results in the production of a water-solu-

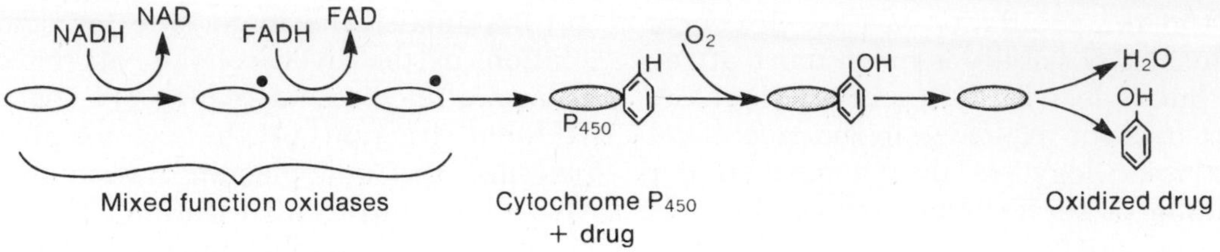

Fig. 5-1. Drug detoxification occurs via electron transport system comprised of enzymes known as mixed function oxidases. Drug is oxidized and rendered inactive.

ble complex, which can then be excreted either into the bile or the bloodstream.

The mixed function oxidase system also can be inhibited by certain toxic substances. Lead and other heavy metals in particular exert toxic effects in this manner.

In addition to oxidation of the chemical toxin other possible modes of detoxification include reduction, hydrolysis, and conjugation. Fig. 5-2 shows various ways in which toxic substances can be converted to harmless substances by the action of liver detoxification mechanisms. All these processes are mediated by microsomal or nonmicrosomal enzymes. The latter process involves the attachment, or conjugation, of the chemical agent to a naturally produced molecule such as glucuronic acid (produced by carbohydrate metabolism), glycine (an amino acid), or acetyl groups, which act to acetylate the chemical agent. The conjugation results in inactivation of the compound, and usually this is then excreted as a waste product from the body. These compounds are excreted primarily through the bile and kidneys.

Certain toxins can induce formation of the appropriate enzymes that detoxify them. This is a major mechanism in developing tolerance to a toxic agent through chronic exposure. Drug tolerance may develop in this manner. The enzymes are induced by low doses of the drug; then more and more of the drug is needed to produce the desired effect, since much of the drug

is immediately detoxified when it is taken into the body and thus is inactivated before it can produce the desired effect. This phenomenon is typified in chronic barbiturate users. The chronic user can tolerate extremely high doses, creating a barbiturate level that would kill the nonaddicted person. Also, enzyme induction by one chemical may affect the metabolism in the liver of other substances, often detrimentally. For example, carbon tetrachloride (CCl_4) is an extremely potent toxin; its toxicity is greatly enhanced in the chronic barbiturate user because of its interaction with the barbiturate-induced enzymes.

Individual variation in tolerance to toxic agents is apparent, resulting from the maturity of the individual and genetic differences in the amount and nature of the detoxification enzymes. This effect is most striking in infants. The newborn infant is not capable of the same degree of detoxification as the child or adult and thus is much more susceptible to damage by toxic chemicals than is the older child or adult. This is exemplified by the toxicity of chloramphenicol in infants. This drug produces the "gray baby syndrome" because liver detoxification and conjugation enzymes are deficient. The drug accumulates within the tissues and causes hypoxia, leading to dyspnea, cyanosis, and shock. Certain drugs (e.g., barbiturates and morphine) can also pass through the placenta and affect the fetus, accumulating there

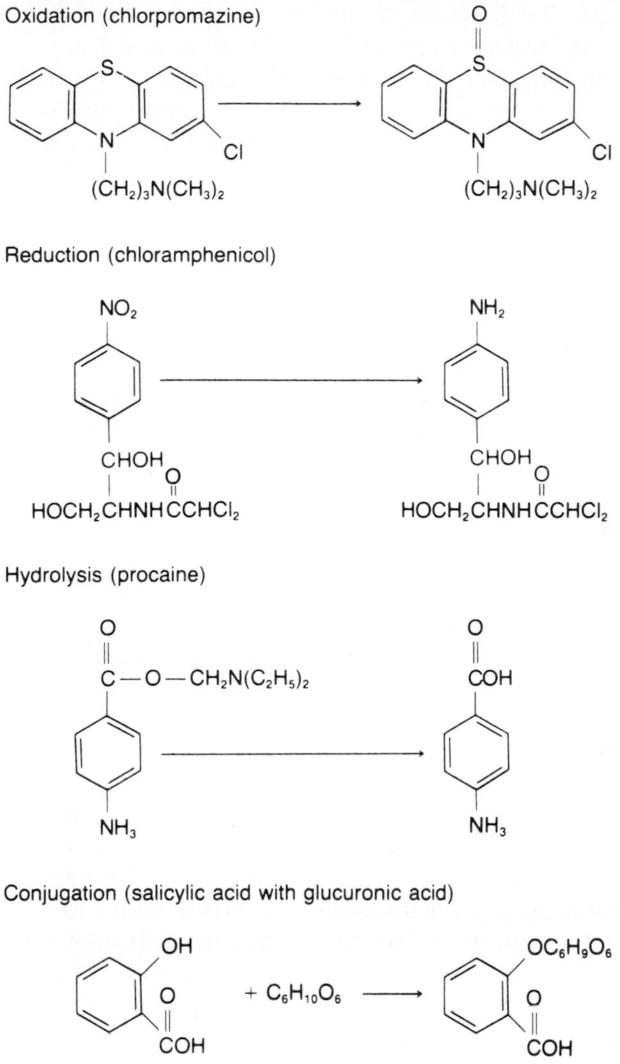

Oxidation (chlorpromazine)

Reduction (chloramphenicol)

Hydrolysis (procaine)

Conjugation (salicylic acid with glucuronic acid)

Fig. 5-2. Pathways of detoxification and removal of drugs. Toxic chemicals are either oxidized, reduced, hydrolyzed, or conjugated by liver mechanisms, which act to alter and remove toxic substance.

and causing respiratory depression resulting from the fetal immaturity of detoxification.

Genetic influences may also be important in the ability of one individual to withstand a drug or chemical that would have extremely adverse effects on another person.

Pathophysiology caused by chemical agents

Those agents that cause the most profound effects on human physiology are agents against which the body has not evolved elaborate defenses. Naturally, synthetic compounds in particular would be most likely to disturb normal physiology. Drugs are common examples of substances that can cause serious side effects resulting from pathophysiologic mechanisms they promote. Such effects are usually entirely apart from the therapeutic aspects of drug treatment. There is a definite difference among individuals in the manner in which they respond to a particular drug and the degree to which specific side effects may be manifested. The dosage of a chemical agent, such as a drug, is important in determining the pathophysiologic effect.

Other chemicals that cause serious effects in humans are the heavy metals and metallic salts, including lead, mercury, ferrous sulfate, cobalt, cadmium, nickel, thallium, uranium, and platinum. A general pattern of heavy metal poisoning is the deposition of the metal or salt in various tissues so that with continued exposure, large concentrations of the substance accumulate in the body, causing chronic disease. (Lead poisoning will be discussed later in this chapter as a disease model of heavy metal poisoning.)

Gases may also be considered chemical poisons. Many gases are produced by industrial and automobile pollution of the environment, for example, carbon monoxide and ozone. Other hazardous pollutants include acids, polycyclic hydrocarbons, insecticides, and pesticides.

Many people have occupations that expose them to substances not normally found in the environment. For example, both asbestos and silica dust cause chronic pulmonary disease; exposure to asbestos may result in mesothelioma (see Chapter 6). Other dusts that can cause disease are coal dust, iron oxide, soot, and kaolin. Accumulation of dust in the lungs of exposed workers results in pneumoconiosis. The disease process involves a chronic inflammatory response by the lungs to the inhaled and deposited dust, ultimately resulting in decreased lung function, which may progress to severe, chronic, interstitial lung disease.

Certain chemicals may irritate the lungs, resulting in chemical pneumonia. This condition predisposes the individual to pulmonary edema, which develops as a direct result of damage by the chemical to the alveolocapillary epithelium. Such a situation sets up pathophysiologic mechanisms, leading to the development of right-sided heart failure caused by pulmonary hypertension.

Other chemical poisons include various alcohols. Ethyl alcohol (ethanol) and methyl alcohol (methanol) are the two most commonly ingested alcohols that result in serious disease in humans.

Disease models of chemical injury

Alcohol. Ethanol is a unique chemical poison in that it is purposefully ingested and may lead, of course, to addiction as described in Chapter 11. Alcohol is a potent teratogen. Chronic alcohol ingestion may lead to cirrhosis of the liver in the susceptible person. It is a direct hepatotoxin but also causes damage to other organs (see Chapter 21).

While many organs and tissue changes are often present in the alcoholic, the effects of ethanol itself must be separated from the effects of various contaminants that are commonly found in liquor. These include toxic substances such as lead, cobalt, ethylene glycol, and methanol.

The major effects of ethanol include fatty infiltration of the liver, which proceeds in the chronic alcoholic to Laennec's cirrhosis. The cirrhotic process involves necrosis of liver parenchymal cells, which eventually results in fibrotic changes throughout the liver and loss of liver function. To understand the gross morphologic evidence of liver cell damage, the effects of alcohol on liver cell metabolism and function must be examined.

Ethanol is a calorie-yielding substance (7 calories/gm) that is readily absorbed through the stomach and intestinal wall. Once absorbed into the bloodstream, almost all the ethanol is removed by the liver, 5% being excreted by the lungs, kidney, and skin. In the liver, ethanol is metabolically degraded to acetaldehyde, which then forms CO_2 and H_2O. In many alcoholics this metabolism is the major source of calories since poor nutritional intake is common. Alcohol directly decreases appetite by causing gastritis, and also may interfere with the activation of vitamins in the liver, and since many alcoholics have a poor diet because of the cost of their habit, malnutrition is common. For many years it was assumed that the development of liver disease in the alcoholic was the direct result of this malnutrition. However, more recent work indicates that ethanol can cause direct damage to liver cells.

Cellular metabolism of ethanol. There are three pathways for the oxidation of ethanol in liver cells: the alcohol dehydrogenase system, the microsomal oxidizing system, and the enzyme catalase. The first pathway appears to be the most significant involving the enzymatic breakdown of ethanol in the presence of NAD to acetaldehyde.

Alcohol dehydrogenase is thought to exist in order to remove small amounts of alcohol produced through fermentation in the gut (Lieber, 1984). The alcohol dehydrogenase system requires NAD and zinc to function. Thus NADH must be oxidized to NAD before the reaction can proceed. In the chronic alcoholic the NAD→NADH reaction is speeded up tremendously, so that the metabolism of ethanol to acetaldehyde is also increased, evidence of an adaptive response to the ethanol. The NADH generated by the reaction shown above is then utilized by the liver cell in the mitochondrial electron transport chain. The excess NADH levels achieved by ethanol metabolism block the utilization of fatty acids, so that these accumulate and are not used for energy. Lactate production is increased in the liver, and blood pH drops. Because the general metabolism of alcohol is so active, many alcoholics (when they are sober) are able to tolerate large doses of drugs such as barbiturates and sedatives, since the enzymatic detoxification machinery is available. However, this does not occur when the alcoholic is drinking. Ingestion of sedatives at this time may produce a lethal depression of the brain because the sedative is poorly detoxified due to competition between the sedative and the alcohol. This action of alcohol and sedatives is termed *synergistic*.

While the NADH produced by the oxidation of alcohol is utilized for energy, there appears to be a qualitative difference between the calories generated by alcohol and those generated by carbohydrate metabolism. As NADH accumulates, the Kreb's cycle is depressed, as is fatty acid oxidation. Diets supplemented with equivalent amounts of calories, one from ethanol and the other from carbohydrates, produce entirely different patterns of weight gain. Chocolate supplementation causes a fairly linear increase in weight over time, whereas alcohol supplementation shows an irregular pattern of weight gain and loss with little or no net gain over time. An explanation for this phenomenon might be related to the fact that the microsomal oxidizing system, which is induced in chronic alcoholism, does not generate ATP but rather results in heat production, which is essentially wasted energy in terms of the body's needs. Thus the calories in ethanol are to a large degree "wasted" or incomplete calories.

The effects of alcohol on physiologic function are related to dosage. The classic signs of intoxification (stupor, sensory and motor disturbance, slurred speech, etc.) occur when the blood level of ethanol is 100 to 150 mg/100 ml. A lethal level of ethanol is about 500 mg/100 ml blood. This is rarely achieved, however, because most people lapse into a deep stupor before being able to imbibe enough to reach this blood level.

Both ethanol and acetaldehyde are considered toxic to many tissues, such as the heart, bone marrow, and brain. Acetaldehyde may bind to proteins and impair the structure and function of cell microtubules, cause intracellular protein trapping, and cause cell enlargement (Lieber, 1984). Acetaldehyde and ethanol are also teratogenic. The difficulty in definitively ascribing the noted changes to a direct effect of alcohol is related to the fact that malnutrition so commonly accompanies chronic alcoholism. In the liver cells it has been reported that both ethanol and acetaldehyde can injure mitochondria. Ethanol easily traverses the placental barrier, and there is an increased incidence of skeletal abnormalities in the offspring of alcoholic mothers. Acetaldehyde may also be involved in the phenomenon of addiction at the level of brain metabolism, by interfering in such ways that psychogenic compounds are formed, or by forming neurotransmitter-like compounds in the brain, which have chemical structures similar to morphine. Persons with inborn defective acetaldehyde metabolism might be more prone to alcohol addiction since these compounds build up in the blood and tissues more readily. This has led to the concept of the "alcogene." The brain appears generally less sensitive to the effects of alcohol in the chronic alcoholic.

Alcoholic cardiomyopathy develops in chronic alcoholics and leads to congestive heart failure. This condition typically develops in men 30 to 55 years of age with a long history of alcohol ingestion. The heart becomes dilated, and areas of necrosis contribute to conduction delays. The cardiac muscle is diffusely hypertrophied, and the clinical manifestations include arrhythmias, emboli, congestive heart failure, and sudden death (Segal, et al., 1984). When the cardiomyopathic effects of alcohol are combined with the typical, severe, nutritional deficiencies, heart disease is likely to develop.

Alcohol in small amounts and taken regularly is reported to have a beneficial effect on heart disease risk. The mechanism of action is obscure, but it may be the result of alcohol induction of increased high density lipoproteins, increased fibrinolytic activity, or psychologic relaxation. The multiple other effects of alcohol as well as the potential for addiction, prohibit recommendation of frequent alcohol ingestion as a "health" habit.

Alcohol is also responsible for skeletal muscle myopathy, which may be acute (in binge drinkers) or chronic. Chronic alcohol myopathy is associated with denervation and atrophy. Muscle disease may be present in association with Wernicke's encephalopathy, an alcohol-induced, neurologic disease. The syndrome is the result of thiamine deficiency, which is the result of malnutrition associated with alcoholism. Alcoholic polyneuropathy and cerebellar degeneration are other possible outcomes of chronic alcohol ingestion.

Whatever mechanisms are involved in chronic alcoholism, the pattern of pathophysiology once it appears is fairly uniform. Excess alcohol causes a variety of liver abnormalities such as fat accumulation, hepatitis, necrosis, and decreased liver function, blood flow, and vitamin activation. Profound changes in the blood are indicative of chronic alcoholism, and the effect of these changes on various organs produces the symptoms typically seen in this disease process. These include hepatic coma, ascites, esophageal varices, kidney disease, gout, heart and muscle disturbances, and brain disruption. Many of these effects are related to Laennec's cirrhosis, which has a complex pathophysiology (see Chapter 21).

The effects of alcohol on the fetus appear to depend on the amount of alcohol ingested, with growth retardation occurring in infants whose mothers ingest two or more alcoholic drinks per day during pregnancy. The fetal alcohol syndrome appears in newborns of mothers with heavy alcohol usage during pregnancy, and is characterized by abnormal facies, mental retardation, small size, and psychomotor abnormalities. The mechanism of teratogenicity is not known, and whether the alcohol itself or metabolic products such as acetaldehyde are responsible for the damage is also not clear at this time. Certainly, the developing nervous system seems to be particularly vulnerable to the effects of alcohol. For example, alcohol-fed mother rats produce offspring with multiple biochemical and morphologic alterations in the nervous tissues. Fetal alcohol syndrome is described further in Chapter 4.

Lead poisoning. Another disease model that illustrates the concept of chemical injury is lead poisoning. Lead poisoning is common among children exposed to lead-base paint on furniture, woodwork, and walls. Children who practice pica (the eating of nonfood substances) are particularly at risk to develop lead poisoning. Small children are more likely to become poisoned than adults, even by low environmental concentrations of lead because gastrointestinal absorption of lead is much more efficient in the very young. Present statistics still indicate the possible hazard of lead poisoning; as many as 10% of all children in the United States under the age of 6 have abnormally elevated levels of lead in their blood. Once lead is ingested it is stored in the body and exerts its toxic actions for many months or even years after ingestion. Thus lead poisoning is a chronic environmental disease.

Lead is absorbed into the blood through both the respiratory and digestive tracts. Then it may either be excreted or deposited in various tissues. Lead is the oldest environmental pollutant to which human beings as a species have been exposed. It has been used by humans since about 250 BC, when large stockpiles of it began to accumulate as humans separated out the valuable silver contained in lead sulfide ore. The lead was used in many ways as it is today. Pipes, cisterns, eating and drinking vessels, salves, ointments, and paints were but a few of the early uses for lead.

Sources of environmental lead are manifold. More than 3.5 million tons of lead are produced industrially every year. This lead pollutes oceans and the atmosphere. Drastic increases in atmospheric lead have occurred because of the increased utilization of lead-burning automobile fuel. Lead is concentrated in the urban areas, which are centers of industrialization. People living in these contaminated atmospheres have higher blood levels of lead, one third of which is derived from leaded gasoline exhausts. Some workers are exposed to particularly high levels of lead (e.g., traffic policemen, automobile inspectors, garage workers, and Boston Sumner Tunnel workers) and thus show the highest blood levels (25 to 31 μg/100 ml).

According to Settle and Patterson (1980) Americans breathe air containing from 500 to 10,000 nanograms of lead per cubic meter; the Environmental Protection Agency's maximum "safe" level is 1500 ng/m^3. It is believed that the lead concentration in the air as well as lead contained within the food chain has drastically increased since prehistoric times, during which an air lead value of 0.04 ng/m^3 is speculated. Settle and Patterson suggest that lead pollution of humans is widespread and unrecognized, and that lead toxicity is probably extremely common. The lead concentration within air, food, and water, which has been considered to be the normal standard background level, may in fact indicate heavy environmental contamination of lead. When background levels are determined in ultraclean laboratories using materials and procedures free from lead contamination, background levels are thousands of times smaller. There are many biochemical pathways and reactions that are disturbed by lead concentrations at the so-called "background" level. It is possible that lead poisoning to some degree exists in all Americans. Lead-soldered cans and some processed foods are the major sources of this environmental lead contamination, and individuals eating many types of canned foods are those most at risk. Lead-soldered cans are used to package even some infant formulas; thus lead contamination begins very early in life. Recently, lead poisoning in children has become more common, especially in very deprived home situations. Peeling paint can expose the paint underneath and if this is old paint, it is often lead-based.

Cellular effects of lead. Most of the lead stored in the body is found in bone where it replaces calcium in the apatite crystalline structure of mineralized bony tissue. Some of this lead contacts and is freely exchangeable with the hematopoietic tissue and bloodstream. Large deposits are present in the epiphysis and may be seen radiographically. Tissues most affected by lead poisoning are those of the hematopoietic, gastrointestinal, and nervous systems.

Lead has marked effects on the erythropoietic process and on the circulating cells. It appears that lead is a specific inhibitor of the enzyme δ-amino-levulinate dehydrase as well as other enzymes. This enzyme is required in the biosynthesis of hemoglobin by precursor cells of the erythrocyte series. The enzyme catalyzes the conversion of δ-aminolevulinic acid into porphobilinogen. When the enzyme is inhibited, aminolevulinic acid accumulates in the body and may be excreted in the urine. One test for determining lead poisoning is the excretion of this acid. Erythrocytes are often smaller than normal, and their hemoglobin concentration is also less than normal. Thus anemia is often present in lead poisoning. The red blood cells also show an unusual basophilic stippling, which is thought to result from agglutination of ribosomes in the precursor cells. The cells may also appear to be coated with lead salts, which are present in the blood. The fragility of these cells is increased, leading to hemolysis, which also may contribute to anemia.

Other cellular effects of lead appear to be related to damage to cytoplasmic organelles such as mitochondria. Lead is bound by mitochondria and can actually be actively transported by mitochondria. It appears that lead competes with calcium on the ion carrier in these organelles, thus inhibiting the uptake of calcium and causing, in this manner or in other more direct ways, swelling and interruptions in the normal ionic distribution across the mitochondrial membrane. Lead is also known to enter the cell nucleus and accumulate there in inclusions.

Lead poisoning involves the gastrointestinal tract, causing nausea, vomiting, diarrhea, distention, and wandering abdominal pain. Gastritis and peptic ulceration are common in lead poisoning. Although the cause of these effects is unknown, it has been suggested that lead may cause spasms of the capillaries of the pyloric and upper duodenal area. Lead has been reported to cause vascular spasm throughout the body. This could result in ischemia and atrophic or ulcerative changes. Lead has also been reported to decrease acid secretion in the stomach. One characteristic of chronic lead poisoning in adults is the presence of the "lead line," a dark line of accumulated lead sulfide in the gingiva lining the teeth.

In chronic lead poisoning the central nervous system is the most dramatically affected of all the systems. The major effets appear to be deposition of lead with resultant degeneration and necrosis of the neurons of the brain and demyelination of the peripheral nerves. Edema usually occurs extensively throughout the brain as well and may cause acute life-threatening symptoms from increased intracranial pressure. The signs and symptoms are related to the degree of involvement. Children manifest central nervous system signs more frequently than do adults. Convulsions, delirium, and coma may occur, or changes in behavior may be the only signs. Lead encephalopathy is associated with a high mortality rate in children and may often be followed by retardation in the child who survives. Peripheral nerves that

become involved may have impaired function. Thus neuritis is a frequent sign in the adult; footdrop, wristdrop, and paralysis may be present.

Other organs susceptible to damage in long-term lead poisoning include the kidney, the liver, and the myocardium. Lead sulfide may also be deposited in the retina, where it is often found even in early cases.

Treatment rationale. Obviously the best form of treatment is to remove the individual from the source of lead. A disturbing factor in our times is that many children may have subacute forms of chronic lead poisoning caused by environmental pollutants, the effects of which may be considered minor and insidious but are not without significance. Lead has been shown to cause developmental anomalies, particularly growth retardation in the fetus, and the young child appears to be generally more susceptible to the effects of lead. Thus body burdens of lead of a certain level may cause cumulative damage in the child but be without effect in the adult.

When lead poisoning has been identified, one approach to treatment is aimed at removal of the lead by chelating agents. These chemicals act to bind metals such as lead. However, most lead is found in the bone, and chelating agents are not able to reach this site. Chelating agents such as calcium disodium edetate (Calcium Disodium Versenate) may be administered to remove the lead from soft tissue, but removal from the bone is more or less a time-dependent process, which can be speeded up by administration of vitamin D, increased body temperature, and acidosis. An important observation is that in the presence of an increased body burden of lead in the bone, an infection, fever, or other stress may cause increasing amounts of lead to essentially demineralize from the bone, enter the soft tissues and bloodstream, and cause acute signs and symptoms of lead poisoning.

Iatrogenic chemical poisoning. Iatrogenic chemical poisoning results from the use and abuse of drugs. Some general principles regarding iatrogenic effects are that many drugs have known and expected toxicity, that some individuals manifest allergic reactions or are susceptible to toxicity, and that overdosage and polypharmacy (the combining of many drugs) are important contributing factors. Some systems are extremely susceptible to the toxic action of drugs. The blood, for example, is a sensitive tissue and may often manifest signs of disturbance. Aplastic anemia is caused by many drugs and continues after the drug is discontinued. Leukopenia (a decrease in the white blood cell count) is the result of drugs such as the sulfonamides, thiouracil, barbiturates, and phenothiazide derivatives. Hemolytic anemia can be caused by penicillin, and thrombocytopenia (a fall in the platelet count) is seen after administration of streptomycin, meprobamate, and barbiturates. These are only a few examples of drugs that affect the hematopoietic system.

The liver is also a sensitive organ, as it is the major site of drug detoxification and can be directly injured by certain drugs. The kidney is the major organ involved in drug excretion and thus is also at risk (e.g., analgesic nephropathy). Other organs that often show signs of drug toxicity are the gastrointestinal tract (e.g., peptic ulcers after chronic aspirin ingestion), the respiratory tract (e.g., alveolar damage caused by high concentration of oxygen), and the nervous system (e.g., extrapyramidal tract damage caused by phenothiazines).

Many factors appear to interact within any given individual to determine the response to a drug and the possibility of toxicity of the drug. The very young and the very old both appear most likely to develop toxic drug reactions, perhaps for the same reason. In the infant various detoxification enzyme systems may not have reached an appropriate level of efficacy, whereas in the aged a decline in absolute amounts and activities of these enzymes renders them susceptible to drug toxicity. An altered elimination pattern related to deficient excretory function may also contribute to increased drug toxicity in both the young and the old.

Drugs and the degenerative changes of old age may act together to cause toxic reactions. The use of young animals for the vast majority of toxicologic testing may provide results that are not applicable to the treatment of the geriatric patient.

The effect of temperature on drug toxicity has also not been determined for humans. The sympathomimetic amines in particular have been shown to have increased acute toxicity with increased ambient temperature. It has also been reported that treatment with the phenothiazines can result in hyperthermia if the ambient temperature is high. Any drug that affects thermoregulation may have toxic effects if the ambient temperature is changed and perhaps even if it is not.

The phenomenon of polypharmacy also deserves mention in relation to the iatrogenic effects of drugs. The administration of many different drugs to a patient at one time is common, particularly in the aged, a group least able to tolerate it. In most cases the combination of drugs is used to treat many different symptoms, although drug combination may be used to treat one symptom. The degree of adverse drug reactions in patients treated by polypharmacy is not as high as one would expect. Nevertheless, the problem among certain groups is probably significant. Those who are having great difficulty maintaining wellness because of disease- or age-related deterioration may suffer further loss when certain drug combinations produce toxic effects. For example furosemide enhances the nephrotoxicity of cephalosporin; if a patient with kidney damage combines these two drugs, renal failure can result.

The disease model chosen to illustrate iatrogenic toxicity demonstrates one important concept: a drug may occasionally be administered to a wide population for many years before its iatrogenic effects are discovered.

Disease model: hexachlorophene poisoning. Hexachlorophene is an antiseptic agent that was used for nearly 30 years in many different products such as soaps, baby powders, and deodorants. In 1971 toxicologic experiments were done to study a possible use of the chemical in foods. These experiments showed that hexachlorophene had a direct neurotoxic effect. The compound caused cerebral edema and an encephalopathy of the white matter, which led to the development of multiple large cysts throughout the brain in experimental animals.

One year after these studies were done, several infants in France developed severe encephalopathy. It was discovered that they all had been exposed to baby talc containing 5% hexachlorophene (soap containing hexachlorophene may have as much as 3%). Several infants died as a result of the effects, which included convulsions, vomiting, spasms, and coma. The damage wrought by the drug in the central nervous system appears to be reversible over a long period of time. Nevertheless, continued exposure to rather high concentrations of hexachlorophene in soap leads to high blood levels, as it is readily absorbed through the skin. Use of the drug on burned skin leads to high blood levels. Neurotoxic effects, although not observed in the population exposed at large, may nevertheless have occurred at a subclinical (nondetectable) level.

Hexachlorophene's mechanism of action is unknown, but it has been reported that mitochondrial metabolism is disturbed in its presence. In rats the white matter and the peripheral nerves are the tissues chiefly affected.

Hexachlorophene is available only in prescription products in the United States now, and these products are not recommended for babies or for use on burned or broken skin. This drug is one example of a chemical with potentially lethal effects that was present in many products and in fact was highly recommended for disinfection purposes in hospitals. The sophistication of toxicologic testing has improved tremendously since the first appearance of the drug on the market.

The following demonstrates how chemical poisoning can be very difficult to diagnose, especially in children who may not be able to give a reliable history of ingestion.

CASE STUDY: SALICYLATE TOXICITY

History

At 9:40 PM, a 27-month-old, white female was brought to the emergency room with tachypnea, high fever, and vomiting of 3 hours duration. No cough, drooling, or diarrhea was reported. A rash was present across her cheeks and trunk. The patient's mother stated that the rash had appeared only that afternoon. The child had been well that morning with only slight, clear, nasal drainage. Previous medical history included a birth weight of 4 lb, 3 oz and a 7-day hospitalization with respiratory

Contributed by Ben Francisco.

distress syndrome. She responded well to short-term ventilatory support and was discharged from the intensive care nursery without complications. Three months prior to the present admission, she was treated for otitis media without recurrence. Growth and development appeared to be normal. There were no known allergies.

Physical examination: Physical examination revealed a generally pale, toxic-appearing child with hyperpnea and inspiratory stridor. She lay supine, did not cry, and was totally compliant to examination. Her respiratory effort is marked with moderate intercostal retractions. Her skin was pale and warm. Pupils were equal and responsive to light and tympanic membranes were not inflamed. Mucous membranes are moist. Anterior cervical nodes were firm and mobile—approximately 5 mm in diameter. Chest auscultation revealed coarse rhonchi with inspiratory stridor. No rales were heard. The rash extended across the chest and back. The lesions were macular and pink to darker color. The chest x-ray was essentially unremarkable.

CBC:

WBC:	24,000
Segs:	77%
Hgb:	12 gm/dl
Hct:	35%

Serum electrolytes:

Na:	137 mEq/L
K:	4.0 mEq/L
Ca:	8.0 mEq/L
Mg:	1.7 mEq/L

Urinalysis

pH	5
Specific gravity	1.014
Large acetone	
Glucose:	120 mg/dl

Arterial blood gases:

pH:	7.45
P_{CO_2}:	12 mm
P_{O_2}:	130 mm
HCO_3:	8.5 mEq/L
BE:	−10.4

The initial clinical impression of the managing physician was respiratory distress secondary to acute epiglottis versus laryngotracheal bronchitis with probable sepsis and attendant respiratory alkalosis. The initial plan was to:

1. Obtain a lateral neck x-ray to rule out epiglottitis and retropharyngeal abscess
2. Culture cerebrospinal fluid, blood, and tracheal aspirate with Gram's stain.
3. Consult anesthesiology for operative visualization of the epiglottis and possible intubation or tracheotomy should respiratory distress become more marked
4. Begin intravenous fluids and antibiotic therapy after cultures are obtained

The lateral neck x-ray indicated no soft tissue masses and failed to define the epiglottis. Lumbar puncture was attempted twice unsuccessfully. Tracheal aspirate gram stain was negative. At 1:00 AM, the toddler remained febrile (rectal temperature: 102.4 °F), tachycardic (pulse: 180), tachypneic (50 breaths per minute); blood pressure was stable (92/60). Her pupils were equal and reactive and she could be aroused with tactile stimulation. Her breath sounds were equal, but her respiratory effort was greater and the intensity of stridor more pronounced. She was transported to the operating room for visualization of the epiglottis. Laryngoscopy disclosed a patent airway with slight inflammation of the epiglottis and upper trachea. During visualization of the airway, the child exhibited generalized seizures. She was subsequently treated with succinyl choline and intubated. After being returned to the critical care unit, she received a loading dose of 10 mg/kg phenobarbital over 15 minutes. Her rectal temperature was 105.2°F. She was placed on a cooling blanket, given 120 mg aspirin rectally and sponged with tepid water. Her pupils were pin-point, equal, and responsive. Because of the high fever, convulsions, and apparent lack of significant airway obstruction, central nervous system infection was considered as a probably cause. Chloramphenicol 275 mg IV was administered. The intravenous fluids were increased to 55 ml/hr with D_5E75. Spinal tap was attempted by a second physician unsuccessfully. Repeat arterial blood gases, were little changed—PH: 7.46; Pco_2: 17; Po_2: 98:HCO_3: 12.9; and BE -7.8.

By 3:30 AM, her rectal temperature had fallen to 102.8 °F. Generalized clonic-tonic seizures recurred twice for brief intervals. She responded to voice and touch by brief movement of her extremities. Pupils were pin-point, equal, and reactive. She remained hyperpneic. Urinary output since admission was 240 ml, approximately 45 ml/hr. In the next 4 hours, her temperature returned to normal (on the cooling blanket). Respiration was unchanged, and seizure activity ceased. A salicylate level drawn at this time was 83, indicating severe salicylate toxicity.

Pathophysiology

The foregoing case study of a 27-month-old patient admitted for "respiratory distress" is, in fact, a classic picture of salicylate poisoning. A review of the pathogenesis of severe aspirin overdose will highlight the salient clinical findings.

Aspirin poisoning has long been the most common cause of poisoning in children. Accidental ingestion by toddlers, suicide attempts by adolescents, and inadvertent overdosage in long-term therapy are primary problems. Recent concern about the role of aspirin in the cause of Reye's syndrome has resulted in markedly reduced use in the treatment of fever in children. However, aspirin has enjoyed increased popularity in adult medicine and continues to be widely available. Non-aspirin sources of salicylates are also important, especially oil of wintergreen (methyl salicylate). A level teaspoonful of the oil equals 5 gm of salicylate and re-

mains a dangerous source for "accidental" ingestion. Toxic effects of aspirin occur with acute ingestion of 200 to 300 mg/kg of body weight. The severity of salicylate poisoning is determined by the magnitude and duration of blood levels. Peak levels occur approximately 90 minutes after ingestion and may reach 50 mg/dl without symptoms. A plateau is established by 2 hours after ingestion and blood levels gradually decline thereafter. Plateaus of greater than 30 mg/dl invariably result in symptoms. The normal half-life of aspirin is 24 hours. The kidney is the key organ of excretion. Excretion of salicylate by the kidney is enhanced by an alkaline pH in the renal tubular fluid. A change of urine pH from 6.5 to 7.5 produces a tenfold increase in salicylate elimination. The half-life of aspirin under alkalotic urine conditions is less than 6 hours.

The pathophysiology of salicylate toxicity is best explained by two basic mechanisms:

1. Direct stimulation of the respiratory center of the brain
2. Uncoupling of oxidative phosphorylation

A number of additional mechanisms interplay to influence the altered steady states seen in salicylate poisoning. These pathways will be discussed as they relate to this case, focusing on the observed symptoms. The primary action of salicylate as it is absorbed in toxic amounts into the bloodstream is on the respiratory center of the medulla. Initially, a direct medullary stimulation occurs resulting in an increased rate and depth of respiration. The resultant alveolar hyperventilation is reflected in a fall in arterial Pco_2. A commensurate reduction in hydrogen ion concentration occurs. The known effects of respiratory alkalosis include enhanced urinary retention of H^+ with excretion of K^+ and bicarbonate. These are compensatory mechanisms that tend to restore steady state. General vasoconstriction is another effect of alkalosis. Persistently severe, toxic levels of salicylate in the blood eventually exhaust respiratory drive and precipitate respiratory failure.

The second major effect of salicylate overdose is the uncoupling of oxidative phosphorylation. Two important consequences of this action are a reduction in the formation and availability of ATP to fuel cellular metabolism and increased heat production as free energy is liberated by oxidation. A reduction in the availability of ATP has an impact on many cellular systems, however. The Na-K pump is of critical importance in the pathogenesis of salicylate poisoning. Enhanced membrane permeability to K^+ and impaired pump action result in a depletion of intracellular K^+. In the face of renal compensation for alkalosis, potassium losses are rapid. *Serum* potassium levels may or may not reflect the real losses that are occurring. Compensation for reduced availability of ATP to body cells occurs by an increased rate of catabolism and gluconeogenesis. Blood glucose may be elevated initially as glycogen stores are mobilized, but a late hypoglycemia is threatened. An increased rate of oxygen consumption occurs, markedly increasing cellular demands for respiration. Increased levels of tissue CO_2 accumulate. An important circumstance influencing increased catabolism is that the set point—ATP availability—cannot be reached because of uncoupling of oxidative phosphorylation. Free energy is expressed as heat gain—hyperpyrexia. The vasoconstriction of alkalosis may exacerbate the problem, impairing the exchange of heat with the environment. Insensible water loss is *dramatically* increased. Dehydration becomes a major factor in salicylate poisoning because of hyperpyrexia, increased renal excretion of solute, and altered intake and output. Ingestion of salicylate promotes primary water loss by inducing nausea and vomiting. Reduced oral intake and vomiting occur as a result of stimulation of the medullary emetic center and gastric mucosal irritation.

A final major action of salicylate warrants discussion in this case. In toxic doses salicylate also acts as an inhibitor of dehydrogenase and aminotransferase. The effect is incomplete metabolism and accumulation of acid intermediates. Elevated plasma organic anions in turn deplete buffers and result in metabolic acidosis superimposed on a respiratory alkalosis. An organic aciduria ensues with the appearance of ketones in the urine.

The classic symptoms of salicylate poisoning are hyperventilation, severe vomiting, hyperthermia, convulsions, and coma. An explanation of the pathogensis of CNS disturbances is more elusive than the other symptoms. Possible mechanisms for convulsions include hyperthermia, hypoglycemia, hypercapnea (late in the course of intoxication as respiratory failure develops), and the inhibition of glutamate decarboxylase activity by salicylate in brain tissue. Experimental and clinical evidence exists to support a primary role for salicylate in CNS toxicity. These findings link the late acidosis commonly seen in poisoning to enhanced uptake of salicylate into the brain and the onset of major CNS disturbances.

Returning to our case study, let us review the preliminary findings in light of the pathophysiology of salicylate poisoning. On admission to the emergency room, the child exhibited hyperpnea, fever, and a history of vomiting. Inspiratory stridor and a "toxic" appearance simulated a presentation of epiglottitis. However, subsequent neck x-ray and laryngoscopy discounted this hypothesis. An elevated white count also complicated the clinical picture. The possibility of a CNS infection and inability to obtain a spinal tap to rule out this question further confused the issue. Lack of antecedent events suggesting an ingestion and the presence of fever biased the examiners to seek infectious causes. The admission arterial blood gases and urinalysis proved to be diagnostic (pH: 7.45; Pco_2: 12; Po_2: 130; HCO_3: 8.5; and BE; -10.4. These levels indicated profound alveolar hyperventilation. A deceptively normal pH is explained by a coexistent metabolic acidosis, secondary in this case to increased bicarbonate excretion and accumulation of organic intermediates. The urinalysis reinforces this finding with 3^+ ketone and a pH level of 5. Traditional methods of treating the febrile child suspected of having a CNS infection and exhibiting convulsions are antipyretics, antibiotics, and an anticonvulsive agent. In this case administration of rectal aspirin and intravenous phenobarbital was deleterious. Phenobarbital is known to potentiate salicylate toxicity.

Nursing Diagnoses

1. Impaired gas exchange related to alveolar hyperventilation
2. Hyperthermia related to salicylate-produced uncoupling of oxidative phosphorylation
3. Fluid volume deficit related to hypermetabolism
4. Potential for injury related to seizure activity
5. Impaired home maintenance management related to safety

Summary

Chemical toxins are ubiquitous, having many environmental and endogenous sources. Exposure to these agents is increasing at a tremendous rate yearly, and evolution has not provided humans with effective mechanisms to deal with many of these chemicals. A human being's detoxification mechanisms are mainly hepatic and generally are fairly nonspecific. Many abnormal metabolites, drugs, and chemi-

cals can be detoxified by these enzymatic processes. Many agents on the other hand are not efficiently detoxified and can cause serious pathophysiologic effects. It is a continual challenge to discover the cellular actions of these agents in order to devise ways that they may either be made safe in the environment or inactivated in the body. The signs of toxicity are multiple and often specific to the agent. Many factors enter into the response of any given individual to a potentially toxic chemical agent.

PHYSICAL AGENTS

Human defenses to stressors that injure the body through their physical properties are not as finely regulated and complex as those that protect us against chemical agents. Obviously the sheer mass of the body helps to prevent physical injury from trauma, but this protection is not particularly effective when severe forces are experienced.

The skin functions as a major thermoregulatory organ and as a protective coating against extremes of heat and cold. Nevertheless, humans are easily injured by such extremes, and the defenses are not very effective even when variation is small.

Radiation is another physical force that can greatly damage human cells and tissues. Carcinogenesis is but one subtle effect of radiation. Radiation also can have gross effects such as burns, necrosis, ischemia, vascular damage, and systemic sickness.

Near-drowning produces various pathophysiologic effects on the body. The fluid and electrolyte changes differ depending on whether immersion occurred in salt or fresh water.

Human response to physical injury includes not only specified physiologic reactions but also a marked stress response.

Emotional state, social support systems, hopefulness, and outlook are all contributing factors.

This section of the chapter will describe various forms of physical insults to the body's normal physiology and the pathophysiologic mechanisms that may result from such interferences.

Trauma

Multiple trauma is a common occurrence and is an extremely complex situation involving physiologic adaptations and pathophysiologic disruptions in virtually every system. It is accompanied by profound physical and emotional stress, disbelief, confusion, and family and social disruption. Organ failure and sepsis are the most common problems associated with morbidity and mortality in people who survive a multiple trauma event.

Most traumatic injuries are accompanied initially by some degree of shock, in which the human system conserves energy, heat, and oxygen. This is followed by a catabolic phase 3 to 7 days after the injury. Hypermetabolism and an increase in oxygen consumption occur during this phase. Hyperglycemia ensues as proteins are broken down for energy needs; hyperglucagonemia, hypercortisolism, and insulin resistance are present; gluconeogenesis is accelerated. These hyperdynamic responses preserve serum glucose. However, protein synthesis, and thus tissue repair, will suffer since the amino acids are used for gluconeogenesis. The need for extra calories is obvious in the trauma victim. There is a 25% increase in caloric expenditure in patients who have experienced mild to moderate trauma and a 50% increase in patients who have experienced severe trauma. When traumatic injury occurs, recovery depends on the degree of injury, myocardial function, cardiac output, blood volume, ventilatory function, protein synthesis, immunologic and antibacterial functions, and wound healing. All of these factors depend on adequate nutrition (Gusberg, 1986). Unfortunately, it is very difficult to meet the nutritional needs of trauma patients. The injury, state of consciousness, loss of appetite, and severe stress confound adequate, nutritional intake, which often must be supplied intravenously. Malnutrition in hospitalized patients is a serious problem, with 33% to 65% of generally hospitalized patients suffering significant malnutrition (Apelgren et al., 1986). Malnutrition leads to immunodeficiency through decreased phagocytosis and chemotaxis, decreased lymphocyte count and function, hypogammaglobulinemia, and decreased complement. Iatrogenic malnutrition is so common that nutritional assessment of all hospitalized patients should be routine. Adding the accelerated caloric demands of the hyperdynamic state associated with trauma, sepsis, burns, and inflammation only compounds the problem.

Another early response to trauma has been termed the "sick cell" syndrome (Trunkey, 1987). Cellular alterations include changes in electric membrane potential, swelling, altered cell transport, and impaired cell secretion or excitation. Depending on the number of cells and on the importance of the organ, organ failure can occur early. Other complications that occur fairly early following multiple trauma include right-sided heart failure, adult respiratory distress syndrome, disseminated intravascular coagulation, cerebral edema, small bowel obstruction, acute renal failure, and immunologic deficiency. Cerebral edema may be the result of shock-induced hypoxia and/or hypovolemia, as well as direct injury to the brain tissues. If orthopedic injuries are extensive and involve the long bones, the patient is also at risk for fat embolism.

The case study that follows this discussion illustrates this aspect of organ failure associated with multiple trauma. Later organ failure is often the result of sepsis, which many times is nosocomial in origin.

Sepsis, if it occurs after an injury, will further threaten energy balance. Trauma patients are very likely to develop infection and possibly sepsis due to the high likelihood of introduction of microorganisms at the time of traumatic injury, the nature of the injury itself, as well as the many invasive measures that are required in treating traumatic injury. Wound healing itself requires increased caloric expenditure. If an infection occurs, the demands of the inflammatory and immune systems must be considered. The rising count of white blood cells, while responsive to the infection, requires glucose as a major source of metabolic fuel for anaerobic metabolism. Sepsis that is accompanied by fever will further increase oxygen consumption and glucose use, and protein breakdown may continue to further provide fuel, but at the expense of immunocompetence and repair. Provision of calories in the form of dextrose in water is totally inadequate for such patients. Three liters of 5% dextrose in water supplies only 600 calories, which may be less than a tenth of what is required.

Patients who have experienced multiple trauma may suffer multiple organ failure secondary to sepsis, ARDS, and disseminated intravascular coagulation (DIC). After a serious traumatic injury, the coagulation cascade is quickly activated, which may lead to thromboemboli. Thromboemboli can contribute to respiratory distress and possibly to adult respiratory distress syndrome (ARDS). The mechanism of cascade activation is probably through exposure of tissue collagen and is accompanied by decreased fibrinolysis 2 to 5 days following trauma. At that point fibrin removal is impaired and may contribute to the incidence of DIC, thrombosis, and ARDS. ARDS may also develop in consequence to complement activation, which also occurs after multiple trauma.

CASE STUDY: MULTIPLE TRAUMA

History

LG is a 26-year-old male with no known allergies and no significant contributory medical history.

Present illness: LG was transferred from a small community hospital via a medical helicopter following a motor vehicle accident, in which he was thrown approximately 50 feet from the vehicle, landing on his head. He was admitted to the emergency department 4 hours after the accident. Initial examination revealed the following.

Physical examination:

General appearance: Unconscious

Vital signs

Temperature:	98.0° F
Pulse:	112
Respirations:	30 (via Ambu)
Blood pressure:	142/90

Respiratory: Mechanical ventilations via tracheotomy tube: clear bilateral breath sounds: normal chest expansion: no spontaneous respirations

Cardiovascular: Sinus tachycardia without ectopy, murmur, or gallop: bounding peripheral pulses: two peripheral intravenous lines: isotonic saline solution and lactated Ringer's solution

Neurologic: Unconscious; decerebrate posturing in response to pain; pupils: left—2 mm in diameter and reacts sluggishly to light; right—5 mm in diameter and shows no reaction to light

Skin: Pale, cool, and dry: avulsed right eyelid: two, large, chin lacerations; abrasions on right cheek and forehead;

Contributed by Charlotte A. Curtis.

deep, soft tissue avulsion on right hand with exposed tendons; abrasions on left hand; deep bilateral knee abrasions

Gastrointestinal: Loose and broken teeth; nasogastric tube in left nostril with minimal clear liquid drainage; absent bowel sounds

Genitourinary: Indwelling urethral catheter with clear, straw-colored urine

Musculoskeletal: Immobilized with a rigid cervical collar and long spine board

Significant laboratory values

ABG

P_{CO_2}:	30 mm Hg
HCO_3:	17.5 m Eq/L
P_{O_2}:	463 mm Hg

CBC

RBC:	4.33
WBC:	25.0
Bands:	12
Segs:	73
Lymphs:	11

SMA-18

Gluc:	294
LDH:	373
SGOT:	102

Coag

PTT:	24.8

Additional diagnostic findings

An x-ray of the cervical spine indicates a questionable fracture of C-2. A computed tomography (CT) scan of the head and neck indicates the following:

1. Epidural hematoma of the right temporal lobe and intracerebral hematoma
2. Shift of the ventricles from right to left
3. Fracture of the right temporal skull
4. Fracture through the arch and body of C-2

Treatment

LG was taken to surgery following the CT scan. The following surgical procedures were performed: (1) craniotomy with evacuation of the epidural hematoma, (2) debridement and repair of the facial, hand, and knee injuries, and (3) cervical immobilization with a halo vest. Post-operatively the patient was admitted to the neurologic intensive care unit for treatment and constant monitoring.

Pathophysiology

Prior to the patient's transfer to the neurologic ICU, a tracheostomy was performed to ensure maintenance of the airway and to facilitate mechanical ventilation. The presence of severe facial injuries and swelling, the loose and broken teeth, and the need to maintain cervical spine immobilization necessitated a tracheostomy rather than endotracheal intubation. The patient's obvious head trauma, unconsciousness, and loss of spontaneous respirations suggested the presence of cerebral edema with resultant increased intracranial pressure. The injury caused damage to the cerebral capillaries, with a resultant increase in capillary permeability and leakage of fluid from the vascular compartment into the interstitial spaces of the brain. This leakage decreases circulation and tissue perfusion to the affected areas, causing hypoxia and carbon dioxide (CO_2) retention, with an increase in hydrogen ion (H^+) concentration. This increase leads to a compensatory cerebral vasodilation, in an attempt to increase oxygenation and decrease CO_2 and H^+. However, this vasodilation only serves to perpetuate the cerebral edema, because of the altered capillary integrity and subsequent osmotic gradient. The edema also prevents the normal reabsorption of cerebrospinal fluid into the vascular bed, which results in an increase in intracranial pressure (ICP). In order to interrupt this detrimental positive feedback cycle, the patient was hyperventilated with a high concentration of oxygen via his tracheostomy tube to decrease P_{CO_2} and H^+ and increase P_{O_2}. Although pH was normal on admission, respiratory alkalosis was achieved within 6 hours with the following values:

pH:	7.53
P_{CO_2}:	20.9 mm Hg
HCO_3^-:	17.6 m Eq/L
P_{O_2}:	460 mm Hg

These relative values were maintained by controlled hyperventilation on the respirator throughout treatment. Additional vascular damage resulted in epidural hematoma. Although no active bleeding of the middle meningeal artery was found at the time of surgery, this is frequently the source of epidural hematomas and is commonly associated with injuries to the temporal skull.

Mannitol, a hyperosmolar solution, was administered intravenously to help pull fluid back into the vascular compartment and reduce cerebral edema, ultimately resulting in an osmotic diuresis. To avert a decrease in the plasma osmotic pressure, which would also perpetuate the cerebral edema, the patient was given isotonic saline solution in one IV line. Lactated Ringer's solution was infused through the second IV line to help replace the fluid and electrolytes being lost through wound drainage.

A nasogastric tube was inserted to check for gastric bleeding and to decompress the stomach and prevent vomiting, which would increase ICP and contribute to the cerebral edema. The patient had no gag reflex in response to insertion of this tube, indicating ischemia of this reflex center in the medulla oblongata. The initial gastric aspirate was bloody, clearing with minimal irrigation. This suggests that he may have had reflex swallowing of blood from the oral cavity, indicating some remaining function of this portion of the medulla. However, there may have simply been a gravitational drainage of the bloody secretions into the stomach.

The indwelling catheter was inserted to provide ongoing assessment of renal function, as well as to assess possible renal contusion. No blood was found in the urine. The patient maintained an adequate volume of output with a normal urine specific gravity and a normal blood urea nitrogen (BUN). Also, the reduced HCO_3^- was indicative of the successful attempt of the kidneys to maintain a normal blood pH by excreting bicarbonate ions.

The response of the patient's left pupil indicated some remaining function of the pons, although there was probably some ischemia as evidenced by the slow response. The lack of response of the right pupil was the result of the pressure and ischemia caused by the epidural hematoma and resultant right to left shift of the ventricles. The patient had no blink reflexes, indicating damage to this portion of the pons. He did have some occasional spontaneous respiratory efforts, indicating some residual function of the pons and medulla. Painful stimuli elicited decerebrate posturing (rigid extension of all extremities), indicating an intact portion of the reticular formation of the brainstem without the inhibitory function of the damaged basal ganglia and cerebral cortex. The abnormal presence of Babinski's reflex indicates loss of all but the lowest motor functions of the cerebral cortex. In response to oral care, the patient made smacking movements of his lips and tongue similar to the suckling reflex seen in infancy, also indicating the presence of only lower, cortical, motor functioning. During suctioning, the patient demonstrated a cough reflex, again illustrating some remaining function of the medulla.

The slight decrease in red blood cells (RBCs) represents blood loss from the injured tissues. Two days of moderately heavy serosanguinous drainage from operative sites plus the drainage from open wounds led to a significant blood loss. No other sources of blood loss were identified. By the third day of hospitalization, the patient's hematocrit (Hct) was 28.6%

and his hemoglobin (Hgb) was 9.9gm/dl. He was transfused with 2 units of packed RBCs, and the following day showed a Hct of 32.1 and a Hgb of 11. The leukocytosis with the left shift of the differential represents the normal inflammatory response to the acute, traumatic event. The decrease in the lymphocytes is an indication of the body's stress response.

The stress response is also responsible for the elevated glucose. Stress stimulates the release of adrenocorticosteroids, which leads to gluconeogenesis and makes more glucose available for energy to respond to the stress. Predictably, as more proteins are mobilized for gluconeogenesis, the serum protein level decreases. Two days after admission, the patient's total protein was 5.3gm/dl; the level of albumin, the major protein, was at 3.2gm/dl. This decrease was probably partially due to the loss of protein in the exudate of the injured tissues. The sympathetic nervous system's discharge of epinephrine, which was stimulated by the stress response, accounts for the patient's tachycardia (with pulse ranging from 110 to 160), bounding peripheral pulses, borderline hypertension, and bouts of fever (100° to 103°F). The fever may also represent damage to the temperature regulating center of the hypothalamus. Hyperthermia causes an increase in metabolic demands, which subsequently aggravates the cerebral edema. A cooling blanket was used in an attempt to attain a normal temperature but was not consistently effective.

On the patient's second day in ICU, his calcium level was slightly decreased at 8.5 mg/dl. This is the result of the decreased ionization of Ca^{++} that occurs in the presence of alkalosis. With a Ca^{++} deficit, hyperactivity of the nervous system would be anticipated. On the fourth and fifth days, with a Ca^{++} of 8.1 and 8.4 respectively, the patient was noted to have isolated episodes of twitching of his tongue and lower lip. These are the same muscles involved in his response to stim-

ulation of the oral cavity that was described previously. The elevated LDH and SGOT are an expected result of his injuries as these enzymes are released from damaged muscles. Likewise, the slightly shortened PTT is a normal coagulation response to the bleeding wounds.

The patient was continued on a low-dose, mannitol infusion and his serum sodium and potassium levels were maintained within normal limits by intravenous administration of 5% dextrose in one half-strength saline with added postassium chloride. This also maintained a high, normal serum osmolality (around an average of 290 mOsm/L), which minimized the perpetuation of cerebral edema.

By the fourth day, LG began to deteriorate. Painful stimuli evoked decorticate posturing (rigid flexion of the upper extremities accompanied by extension of the lower extremities). This was indicative of lessening cerebral function and was more ominous than the previous decerebrate posturing. By the morning of the fifth day, he had no pupillary response to light, no cough reflex with suctioning, no response to oral care, no Babinski reflex, no spontaneous respirations, and completely flaccid muscle tone with no response to pain, indicating a terminal progression of his cerebral edema. A repeat CT scan showed generalized cerebral edema. Brainstem, auditory evoked potentials demonstrated preservation of conduction along the auditory nerve but no conduction of auditory responses through the brainstem. Thus the cerebral functions that had survived the accident were now absent. His blood pressure and heart rate began to decline, indicating the deterioration of the most basic brainstem functions. His neurosurgeon was called regarding possible organ donation. The representative from the organ retrieval program was contacted and met with LG's family and obtained permission to proceed. The patient was started on vasopressive agents (dopamine and norepinephrine bitartrate [Levophed]) to maintain perfusion of the organs to be donated. By the end of the fifth day following the accident, LG was pronounced dead, and his organs were donated to promote the lives of others.

Nursing Diagnosis

LG's prognosis was poor from the time of his injury. However, he deserved every chance possible for recovery or rehabilitation. In providing this, many needs must be addressed simultaneously. These needs are represented in the following nursing diagnoses:

1. Ineffective airway clearance secondary to brain ischemia and unconsciousness
2. Ineffective breathing patterns related to brainstem injury
3. Impaired gas exchange secondary to ineffective airway clearance and breathing patterns
4. Altered cerebral tissue perfusion secondary to injury and cerebral edema
5. Altered nutrition: less than body requirements related to the increased demands during stress and healing, and to decreased intake in the comatose state
6. Impaired physical mobility related to the comatose state and cervical immobilization
7. Impaired skin integrity related to the open wounds
8. Potential for disuse syndrome related to cervical immobilization
9. Sensory-perceptual alterations: all senses, related to severity of brain injury
10. Impaired verbal communication related to brain injury and presence of tracheostomy
11. Total self-care deficit related to coma

In view of the severity of this patient's condition and his eventual death and organ donation, the following diagnosis should be considered in assessing the response of his family.

12. Potential for infection, related to multiple skin abrasions and tracheostomy
13. Ineffective family coping: compromised, related to grief

Many of the physiologic responses to trauma also are apparent in the burned patient.

Thermal injury

Thermal injury to living tissue is one of the most acute physical injuries that humans can suffer. Burns not only produce traumatic cutaneous wounds of varying thickness but also set the stage for many other disruptions of wellness. Destruction of large areas of the skin results in the loss of one of the major body defenses—the integrity of the skin. Thus body fluids can be easily lost through the broken barrier, and microorganisms can enter. Furthermore, a burn represents an acute stressor, causing the typical alarm stress reaction of sympathetic nervous system activation and hypothalamic-adenohypophyseal-adrenocortical axis activation. Due in part to these responses and to other as yet unknown mechanisms a unique, hyperdynamic, metabolic state exists in the postburn patient.

The body of a patient who has sustained a thermal injury has been subjected to an insult that ultimately affects every system. The early effects of extreme heat range from physical carbonization of cells to lesser degrees of cellular injury, such that enzyme systems are disrupted, mainly through protein denaturation. Change in the metabolic activity of the cells begins to occur with heat exposure of approximately 49° C (107.6° F). The temperature and length of exposure to the heat source are the major determinants of the degree of cellular injury. The cell may essentially burn away, the cellular machinery may be greatly interrupted such that necrosis develops, or the cell may be minimally affected with recovery possible. The extent of the burn is the single criterion upon which prognosis is based. This is determined by various computations of the percentage of the total body surface area that has been burned. The most frequently used assessment is based on the "rule of nines" (Fig. 5-3), in which the body surface is divided into areas of 9% or multiples of 9%. The rule of nines is modified for infants and children.

The former classification of burns as first, second, and third degree has been replaced with the classification of partial- and full-thickness burns. The new classification is based on the presence or absence of epithelializing elements. In partial-thickness burns (Fig. 5-4) there is a possibility of reepithelialization of the burned area without skin grafting. This is true for burns in which even the stratum germinativum, the innermost layer of dividing epithelial cells, is destroyed, as other epithelial structures lie deeper in the dermis (e.g., hair follicles and sweat glands). These structures can then supply epithelial cells to heal the burned area. In full-thickness burns this is not possible, as even the dermal epithelial elements have been destroyed. Such burns usually require skin grafting to achieve some degree of normal structure and function. It is also possible that a partial-thickness burn of a deep dermal nature may become a full-thickness burn through infection. Infection can cause necrosis of the epidermal ele-

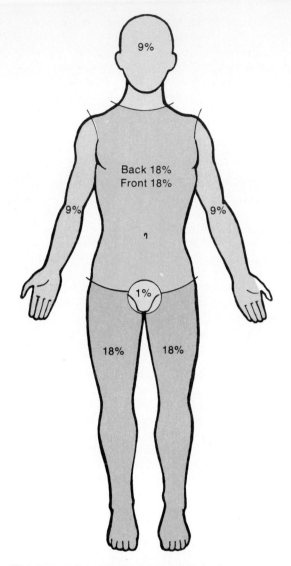

Fig. 5-3. Rule of nines for estimating percentage of body surface areas burned.

ments that had originally survived the burn, resulting in the development of a full-thickness injury. Such responses of partial-thickness burns are now often avoided through the use of topical antibacterial ointments.

Full-thickness burns, which involve the

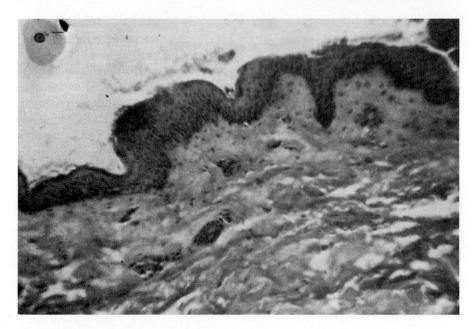

Fig. 5-4. This partial-thickness burn affected epithelium, causing some epithelial damage. Stratification of cells and integrity of epithelium are preserved. Edema is present as sign of inflammatory response.

(From Department of Pathology, University of Tennessee, Memphis.)

epidermis, dermis, and subcutaneous tissue, result in the formation of a tough, dark, dry eschar, which often contains thrombosed veins. The eschar is usually without sensation, as the sensory nerve endings in the dermis are destroyed by the burn. Sensation may never return or may return gradually over a long period of time. The total burned area often consists of patches of burns of varying depths. Diagnosis of the total depth is then based on the physical examination and the cause of the burn. For example, electrical burns are usually deeper than first suspected, and substances not readily washed off, such as grease, oil, and certain chemicals, will remain on the skin, continuing to cause damage until adequately diluted or removed.

The anatomic area burned must also be considered. Burns of the head and neck region may be accompanied by respiratory distress because of damage of the upper airway. Inhalation of smoke, chemical fumes, and hot gases (even without actual surface burns) may result in laryngeal edema and obstruction of the airway, which requires that a tracheostomy be performed. Respiratory damage is most likely when the individual was exposed to fire in an enclosed space. Because of its nonresilient nature, eschar on the chest and trunk may also aggravate respiratory burns by restricting expansion of the chest cavity. When this occurs a procedure known as an escharotomy is performed to relieve constriction. Other anatomic sites to consider are the perineum and hands and feet. Burns around the perineal area are more susceptible to contamination by fecal material. Burns of the hands and feet restrict mobility and the patient's ability to care for himself.

Preexisting disease states may present special problems in terms of management and recovery during the postburn period. For example, underlying cardiac or renal diseases will complicate fluid management. The diabetic is more susceptible to the development of infection and is more prone to problems with wound healing. The stress of the burn may aggravate an underlying endocrine problem.

The fluid and electrolyte problems and treatment of the severely burned patient are complex (see Chapter 17). This chapter will deal with thermal injury as a stressor that affects many systems of the body, causing a variety of pathophysiologic mechanisms to develop. We will therefore consider the acute stage of the burn and the stages after the burn during which many responses and complications can arise that may aggravate these pathophysiologic mechanisms.

The first 24 hours. The acutely burned patient is nearly always alert, anxious, and talkative. While the burned area may appear white, yellow, red, or even black if there has been significant tissue carbonization, the usual pattern is of an immediate blanching followed by reddening as the arterioles dilate. This is a typical inflammatory response, and within 24 hours after the burn, cellular infiltration and inflammatory exudate move into the burned area. By 24 hours the burned area becomes grossly edematous, and blisters may be obvious. Erythrocytes in skin vessels are destroyed by the burn, and this destruction may be massive enough to cause hemolysis and anemia. Other tissue elements may also be destroyed, and the blood vessels may be grossly visible in the burned skin as darkened, thrombosed structures.

Because of the massive shift of isotonic fluid from the vascular compartment into the interstitial space, a major problem in the acute stage is hypovolemic "burn" shock. Fluid therapy (see Chapter 17) is absolutely essential. Treatment for hypovolemia may lead to massive tissue edema. This may be due to inflammatory edema and to a colloid osmotic force generated by the burned tissue (Demling, 1987).

Although the respiratory complications associated with severe burns usually do not develop immediately, many patients hyperventilate during the acute postburn stage because of fear and anxiety. Many times true respiratory complications, if they do appear, will be noticeable by about 24 hours, when edema becomes significant. Of severely burned patients, 3% to 15% have inhalation injuries. Aspiration is also a potential complication in burn patients, since vomiting is a frequent problem. The presence of respiratory involvement and edema dramatically increase mortality.

The initial endocrine response to injury is widespread sympathetic nervous system arousal with increased heart rate being a noticeable effect. This, combined with fluid shift from the vascular space, may be severe enough to cause a drop in glomerular filtration rate and decreased renal output with possible kidney failure. Antidiuretic hormone (ADH) is also released, as are the adrenal corticoids in a typical stress response. These reactions can lead to other long-term problems.

Burn patients often do not complain of pain until several hours after the injury. Then increasing tissue pressure as fluid accumulates is probably the most significant factor causing pain. Many times in acute traumatic injury of all types no sensation of pain is recalled during the early stage. This may be caused by a selective blocking of afferent pain fiber messages by the nervous system or stress induced release of endorphines.

Shock may develop in the first 24 hours after the burn either because of fluid shift from the plasma to the interstitial fluid, or the trauma itself, which causes neurogenic shock. Septic shock may develop later in the postburn period. Accurate measurement of blood pressure and pulse pressure is critical in determining which type of shock is present. In neurogenic shock a complete loss of vascular tone results in tremendous vasodilation throughout tissues such as the splanchnic bed and muscles. In hypovolemic shock caused by fluid shift, the mean arterial pressure falls, the pulse pressure is usually decreased because of the effects of the sympathetic nervous system on pulse rate and arteriolar diameter, and central venous pressure is low.

Second stage. We have divided the response of a patient to thermal injury into an acute stage and a second stage, which occurs after the first 24 hours. Nevertheless, the burn patient will experience many acute problems for many days and even weeks after the initial injury.

The burn patient's general metabolic state is altered greatly from the normal, a factor that must be considered at all times. While the response of many organs and systems to a burn is unique, superimposed on these responses is the change in metabolism, which may then act synergistically with specific responses to cause pathophysiology.

Hypermetabolism. The basal metabolic rate (BMR) increases dramatically in the burn patient. Increases to 100% of normal may be sustained for long periods of time. The hyperdynamic state supports accelerated circulatory and respiratory function, wound healing needs, and nitrogen balance. It was always assumed that in-

creases in the BMR resulted from the demand caused by increased evaporation of water from the surface of the burned tissue. For every gram of water that evaporates from the human body, 0.58 kcal of heat is produced. This is the normal response of the body to heat stress: an increased evaporative rate and heat loss from perspiration. Even under normal conditions, 25% of the heat lost from the body is in the form of evaporative water lost through the skin and lungs. It has been shown, however, that the burn patient's hypermetabolism is not a response to heat loss through evaporation. When a waterproof film was applied to burns a decrease in evaporation and weight loss was observed, but no change in the BMR occurred.

This state of hypermetabolism may result from other effects of the burn on the normal physiology. One theory of hypermetabolism in burns implicates catecholamine release. Catecholamines are released when the sympathetic nervous system is aroused. The release of catecholamines appears to be sustained at a high level even during the second stage of the burn injury. Blockade of both alpha and beta receptors in the hypermetabolic burn state causes a drop in the BMR, whereas administration of exogenous epinephrine increases it. In Wilmore and associates (1974) classic studies of the hypermetabolism of burn patients, they noted that the BMR increased with the size of the burn, and that when the ambient temperature is increased to 32° C, a decrease in the metabolic rate results. However, the patients' core temperature and skin temperature were both increased above normal levels at all ambient temperatures studied. Research indicates that the burned human being has a normal physiologic response to a warm environment but an adverse and pathophysiologic response to a cold environment; cold appears to augment the hypermetabolic state.

Temperature regulation is further disturbed in burn patients because of the normal inflammatory hyperemia that occurs in the burned skin. Large amounts of blood are shunted into the skin as a result. Thus the burn patient cannot reduce the skin temperature in response to cooling as adequately as can the normal individual, and the skin stays warmer at all ambient temperatures. This suggests that a burn victim is not capable of thermoregulation with the same efficiency as normally occurs, and that evaporative losses to the environment do not account for the state of hypermetabolism. Evaporative loss that does occur is simply a route of heat loss produced by the increased metabolism. It is conjectured that this state results from an alteration in metabolism caused by catecholamine release. Catecholamines, which have a direct effect on cellular heat production, are increased in burn patients. Catecholamines are, of course, released in many stress situations, and the hypermetabolic state they produce, with its associated increase in heat production, may be an underlying survival mechanism common to many stress states, including burns. The beta receptors are those receptors stimulated by catecholamines to cause calorigenic (heat-producing) activity. Glucose metabolism, oxygen consumption, and catabolism are all increased through the effects of catecholamines. The hypermetabolic effect is greater for burns than for any other type of stress-producing injury.

The hypermetabolic response requires that adequate amounts of catecholamines be available. Depletion of these stores or tissue refractoriness to them is a possibility in severe burns. The severely burned patient may not be able to elaborate additional catecholamines in response to further stressors in the environment. Thus the effects of all types of stressors may be greatly aggravated by potential catecholamine depletion. Infection, a serious problem in the burn patient, can be viewed as a stressor to which the patient is unable to adequately respond. The burn patient who is not able to maintain the hypermetabolic state because of infection or other stressors undergoes a progressive hypothermia and appears to have a tissue refractoriness to catecholamines. Contributing to the hypermetabolic state is Interleukin-1 (IL-1), which is released by monocytes and other cells. IL-1 is the major endogenous pyrogen and can produce marked increases in energy expenditure and protein catabolism (Pasulka and Wachtel, 1987).

The hypermetabolic state of the burn patient is associated with great demands on the cardiovascular and pulmonary systems. Exercise, even so mild as limited ambulation, may cause severe stress in patients with preexisting circulatory or ventilatory problems. The caloric demands of the burn patient are obviously very high, and weight loss is common. Often there will be nausea, vomiting, or anorexia, which make adequate caloric intake impossible. Total parenteral nutrition may be required in order to meet the excessive body demands for calories.

The net increase in catabolism that is associated with catecholamines and with the state of postburn hypermetabolism leads to a state of *negative nitrogen balance*. All types of traumatic injury can produce this response. The cause of the negative nitrogen balance is cell breakdown and net increases in proteolysis, gluconeogenesis, and urea-genesis. In burn patients, losses of greater than 200 gm/day, of protein can occur during the first week after injury (Pasulka and Wachtel, 1987). It appears that the catecholamines and the insulin:glucagon (I:G) ratio are the major agents producing this state. Catecholamines stimulate glucagon production and inhibit insulin release. Thus the I:G ratio is decreased. The normal I:G ratio is 3.27 ± 0.2. This can drop to values as low as 1.1 ± 0.4 during catabolic states associated with severe stressors such as burns, infections, starvation, or trauma. A low ratio means that more amino acids are being utilized for gluconeogenesis and urea production at the expense of protein synthesis. It is possible that the amino acids released through the process of tissue breakdown stimulate the pancreatic alpha cells directly, resulting in the production and release of glucagon.

Nondiabetic patients who were studied in the postburn stage showed an increase in circulating glucagon, even when exogenous intravenous administration of glucose was carried on. Therapeutic measures for treatment of the catabolic state might therefore be aimed at the production of an anabolic state by the administration of exogenous insulin and glucose when necessary. This might become particularly important in the individual with either overt or latent diabetes. These people are susceptible to infection and are deficient in wound healing. Furthermore, the catabolic state that follows severe injury such as trauma or burns can produce a pathophysiologic aggravation of the diabetes, leading to severe symptoms.

Infection. Hypovolemic shock must be avoided if the patient is to survive the immediate postburn period. Prevention of infection is the major need of the patient during healing, as infection is the major cause of death. Depressed immune function is characteristic of the post-burn period. Infection not only can interrupt the healing process but also can result in massive tissue destruction, septicemia, and septic shock. The organisms that commonly infect burns are microbes that make up the normal flora; they are gram-negative organisms such as *Pseudomonas* and *Escherichia coli*, which tend to invade blood vessels. Another factor in the high incidence of infection in burn patients appears to be a general immunodepression, which therefore makes infection more likely to occur. The inflammatory reaction that occurs immediately after the burn appears to be less effective in burn wounds than in other forms of injury. When sepsis does occur, organisms often invade other portals of entry, such as catheters and tracheostomies.

Infection is prevented in part by maintenance of either a sterile or a clean environment. While the philosophy of care varies from one burn center to another, a major goal is always to reduce the possibility of infection. Environmental cleanliness is but one means. Care of the skin, eschar, and graft are all essential measures. Removal of the eschar presents the greatest problem in this regard. As the eschar dries and sloughs away, debridement of the dead tissues can be done. Escharotomy may also be necessary; dermabrasion, which abrades the surface of the eschar, thus removing necrotic debris, is another possible approach. The eschar must be kept dry during the healing process. Open exposure treatment of the burn, which is most commonly done today, appears to accelerate the drying and eventual cracking and sloughing of the eschar. Most burns are also treated with antibacterial ointment application. The major ointment in use is Sulfamylon Cream. This drug is a carbonic anhydrase inhibitor, and thus a possible side effect, especially in the patient with respiratory disease, is acidosis.

A major problem in the use of this most effective cream is the pain that many patients experience upon its application. Since the drug inhibits bacterial growth, the inflammatory response is retarded, and the eschar takes longer to slough away than in the untreated patient.

Major burns have recently been treated by excision and cadaver skin grafting, which markedly reduces pain and infection. The survival rate is also greatly improved when grafting is done immediately (Heimbach, 1987).

Organ and organ system effects of burns. Virtually every organ and organ system is affected by a severe burn. Much of this effect may result from sympathetic nervous system activation, which over a prolonged period of time can lead to hypoxia and ischemia of various organs because of vasoconstriction of the major blood supplies. Other effects of burns on organ structure and function are most likely related to the hypermetabolic state of the postburn patient and to specific mediators released from the burned necrotic tissue.

The respiratory system is often affected by the direct effects of heat on the tissues or by the inhalation of smoke and other toxic fumes during exposure to the fire. Respiratory disease aggravates any effects that the burn might have on pulmonary function. Of course, if shock has occurred, the possibility of ARDS must also be considered. Another complication that may occur in the lungs or elsewhere is embolism caused by the thrombosis of vessels in the burned tissue. Most burn victims are immobilized for long periods of time, and this factor can contribute to the formation of pulmonary embolism.

The cardiovascular system is also often compromised in the burn patient. Some of the changes that have been observed are probably the result of fluid overhydration in the treatment of the burn.

The high incidence of stress or Curling's ulcers in acutely burned individuals is probably related to the effect of sympathetic nervous system–induced gut ischemia. Other effects of burns include paralytic ileus, which may be the result of splanchnic vasoconstriction, infection and sepsis, fear, pain, and hypokalemia.

There is also a high incidence of osteoporosis in burn patients. This is probably related to the catabolic, hypermetabolic state and the patient's immobility. Both calcium and phosphorus are depleted in these patients, and replacement therapy is usually ineffective; thus renal calculi are a possible result of therapy.

Renal changes are extremely common in burn patients and may result from renal ischemia caused by prolonged sympathetic nervous system activation. Another possible cause is the hemoconcentration observed in burn patients as the result of fluid shifts from the vascular space. The sludging of blood leads to occlusion of minute vessels and hypoxia. It also predisposes the patient to coagulation, which can lead to thrombi and emboli formation in any organ. Another possible factor contributing to renal damage in the burn patient is the nephrotoxic effect of some common systemic antibiotics. Also important can be the effects of hemoglobin released from lysed erythrocytes, which may clump in the tubules, causing obstruction. Acute tubular necrosis can lead to renal failure, which presents grave problems for the burn patient who has a limited ability to respond to any stress.

The blood is also affected by a thermal injury. All circulating elements may be harmed, but the erythrocytes and platelets in particular are subject to heat induced lysis. Therefore coagulation deficiencies and anemia are common in the burn patient. One interesting phenomenon is the increased fragility of surviving erythrocytes, which may be caused by either heat damage to the membranes or the catabolic state of the burn patient. There is high intracellular sodium and low potassium levels in the circulating erythrocytes, which return to normal values within 3 to 5 days after a diet of 6,000 cal per day. Thus it would seem that these alterations in erythrocyte cations reflect the patient's nutritional status and catabolic state and indicate that erythrocyte active transport is inhibited. Damage to all aspects of immunologic and nonspecific defense mechanisms occur as well. Polymorphonuclear cell function, complement levels, and T and B cell functions are all disturbed. The thermally injured patient is subject to many possible pathophysiologic interactions caused by the injury itself, the metabolic state, and the normal stress response. Treatment must therefore be aimed at the conditions manifested in the patient, and those that can be anticipated should be prevented if possible. The burn patient who survives the first few days following the injury is nevertheless continuously subject to further pathophysiologic mechanisms, which develop through the interaction of many systems that become disordered as the result of the burn, the patient's response, or even occasionally the treatment. The major needs of the patient througout the postburn period are related to fluid and electrolyte balance metabolism, prevention or treatment of infection, and maintenance of a positive, hopeful attitude in the presence of many possible decompensating pathophysiologic effects.

Psychosocial aspects of burn injury. When a severe burn injury is sustained, the person is shocked, stressed, and often fighting for life. He will need support and reassurance to sustain him in the early postburn phase. Feelings of guilt may arise since many burns are the result of preventable accidents. This may be even more apparent if other people have been injured or killed in the fire. All resources of the body and mind will be called on in the hypermetabolic state following injury. Realization of the extent of disfigurement or disability may cause serious depression and the patient may become unwilling to cooperate with caregivers. Pain may be so severe as healing ensues that nothing can divert attention from it. Infection is greatly feared, and the burn patient may become physically and emotionally isolated in response. The burn patient represents a challenge to supportive, long-term, rehabilitative, physical and emotional support. Involvement of the family or other loved ones in the patient's recovery is important. Acceptance of deformity and the need for years of reconstructive surgery are long-term stressors.

The effects of temperature extremes

Heat. Humans are exposed to great swings in ambient temperature in accordance with climatic, seasonal changes. Evolution has provided humans with mechanisms with which to adjust to sudden changes in temperature and to adapt over longer periods of time to temperature extremes. The degree of compensation and adaptation is limited, however, and various pathophysiologic mechanisms can occur when humans are exposed to environmental temperature extremes. States of hyperthermia and hypothermia can result when the ability to adequately adjust to heat and cold stressors is insufficient or overwhelmed.

Hyperthermia. The hyperthermic state is characterized by an elevation in core temperature. Humans respond to many infections by hyperpyrexia, or fever. Humans also may respond to other conditions or situations by hyperthermia. It will be recalled that heat is normally produced in the body through metabolism of food, and the major organ sources of heat are the liver and the skeletal muscles. The heat is used to maintain the body core temperature at a species-specific, genetically determined set point, which appears to be regulated by the hypothalamus. Various thermoreceptors throughout the body "inform" the hypothalamic heat-regulating center of the temperature, and the hypothalamus, through a variety of negative feedback mechanisms, acts to either activate heat-gaining or heat-losing mechanisms. In states of hyperthermia either these mechanisms are impaired or the hypothalamus itself is not responding to the elevation in temperature. Thermoreceptors must, of course, also be intact and functional if the hypothalamus is to receive temperature information from various parts of the body.

Heat stroke. While other responses to heat produce symptoms, for example, heat cramps and heat exhaustion, these are not characterized by an elevation in body temperature. Heat stroke, or heat pyrexia, is associated with a greatly elevated core temperature and a significant (10% to 80% mortality. The core temperature in heat stroke is greater than 40.6° C (105° F), which will result in neurologic damage. Heat stroke develops in people in humid, hot environments in which cooling by evaporation cannot be accomplished because of the absence of an evaporation gradient from the skin to the air. The temperature cannot be regulated and increases to the point that collapse occurs. Heat stroke occurs more readily in the elderly or in persons who are already debilitated be-

cause of preexisting disease. It is one of the leading causes of death in athletes. Hyperpyrexia can result in increased heart rate and cardiac output, and generalized vasodilation, which will cause the diastolic pressure to fall. In the elderly, end diastolic pressure and cardiac output may be significantly reduced, so that shock ensues. Initially the pulse and respiratory rates are rapid, but both fall as the patient deteriorates. The erythrocytes may be affected by heat, and their increased permeability leads to increased leakage of potassium into the extracellular fluid, causing a state of hyperkalemia. The effects of heat are in a sense similar to those observed in cells that have been mildly burned. The metabolism and enzyme functions are impaired, and cells may swell and undergo necrosis. Wide degenerative changes occur throughout the tissue in patients surviving prolonged periods of hyperthermia. The incidence of myocardial infarction and other acute ischemic or hemorrhagic processes is high following recovery from heat stroke. Patients also may be hyperglycemic, acidotic, hypokalemic, and hypophosphatemic.

In hyperpyrexia, treatment is aimed initially at restoration of the body temperature by cooling the individual rapidly (ice water immersion is best). The skin should be vigorously massaged following the drop in temperature to stimulate the return of the cooler peripheral blood to the hotter internal organs. Close observation of the patient is essential, as the dangers of a return to a hyperthermic state, cardiac failure, and hemorrhage are imminent in the acute stage of the disease process.

Heat exhaustion. Heat stroke is to be contrasted with the effects of heat in healthy individuals. Sweating may occur in heat stroke but often the water and electrolytes lost through sweating are not replaced adequately. Ingestion of water alone further dilutes the extracellular fluid, leading to signs of hyponatremia. These individuals are able to maintain their core temperature but suffer signs of salt depletion, a condition known as *heat exhaustion*. Stoker's cramps may develop in muscles because of salt depletion, but the collapse, weakness, dizziness, and headaches that are found in heat exhaustion are related to excessive sweating that leads to hypovolemia. Thus these patients show the signs of widespread sympathetic nervous system activation that characterizes hypovolemic shock. The skin is cold and moist, the pupils are dilated, the heart rate is increased, and the pulse pressure is narrow. Nevertheless, the core temperature is maintained. Treatment is aimed at the restoration of electrolytes and water and treatment of shock.

Malignant hyperthermia. Hyperthermia may result from exposure to anesthetic agents or drugs (see Chapter 13). Malignant hyperthermia is associated with exposure to potent, volatile, anesthetic agents, such as halogenated agents, or to depolarizing muscle relaxants, such as succinylcholine. Anesthetic agents lead to increased skeletal muscle metabolic activity, a morbid rise in body temperature, and neurologic damage. Malignant hyperthermia is the result of a multifactoral, genetic susceptibility. The defect in the skeletal muscles is postulated to be related to accumulation of calcium ions in the sarcoplasm, leading to a hypermetabolic, hypercontractile state associated with an increase in oxygen consumption (Nelson and Flewellen, 1983). Early signs of this state in susceptible patients include tachycardia and hyperpnea, which occur in response to developing metabolic acidosis and decreasing Po_2. Limb muscle rigidity, which is associated with rising body temperature, usually follows rapidly.

The defect can be diagnosed through family history and muscle biopsy before administration of anesthesia. Muscle tissue from susceptible individuals shows abnormal contractions in response to caffeine or halothane exposure.

Hyperthermia may also be associated with drug toxicity (Rosenberg et al., 1986). This may occur through a rise in body temperature or interference with heat loss. Drugs known to produce hyperthermia include sympathomimetic agents, epileptogenic agents, salicylates, which increase heat production, and anticholinergics and phenothiazines, which decrease heat dissipation.

Hypothermia. Hypothermia may be a pathophysologic response of the body to cold stress, although occasionally it is accomplished therapeutically during surgery. A decrease in body temperature to values ranging from 35° to 25° C (95° to 77° F) constitutes hypothermia. The effects of temperature drop on the human physiology are manifold and both local and systemic effects may occur. Metabolism in general is temperature dependent and will be greatly depressed in hypothermia. Cell ischemia and necrosis in various organs may also occur. An important effect of hypothermia appears to be cold-induced injury to the capillary endothelium, which in turn results in increased capillary permeability and loss of plasma into the interstitial space. Hypovolemia may result. If chilling of the tissues is accomplished very rapidly, edema may not occur until after the individual is rewarmed. The degree of vascular injury is related to the extent and length of the exposure to cold. In frostbite, for example, the vascular effects are so profound as to cause first occlusion and then ischemia leading to necrosis and gangrene of the affected part. In systemic hypothermia there is tissue ischemia, but it is usually not as profound. The most common cause of systemic hypothermia is exposure. Particularly susceptible are mountain climbers at high altitudes and the elderly at normal altitude during the winter months.

The hypothermic individual has an extremely low rectal temperature (usually off the scale of the thermometers commonly used in the hospital) and appears pale, cold, and stiff. Respiratory rate, heart rate, and blood pressure are usually decreased markedly. Edema is also often present. There may be signs of cardiac failure, and the patient is either extremely lethargic or unconscious.

Treatment is not rapid rewarming, since this will act to dilate only peripheral vessels and thus decrease the blood supply to the critical internal organs. The plasma volume must be expanded to aid cardiac function and prevent the effects of hemoconcentration and resultant ischemia. The administration of warm fluids and the utilization of either hemodialysis or peritoneal dialysis with warmed blood or dialyzing fluid acts to restore core temperature. Even after recovery from the acute hypothermic episode, there are generally pathologic changes throughout the tissues, which may lead to further disease.

Adaptation to a chronic cold environment is necessary for a person to maintain a normal body temperature and not suffer the effects of hypothermia. While humans usually respond to a cold ambient temperature by heat production through shivering and heat containment by peripheral vasoconstriction, the cold-adapted person produces required extra heat through a process called *nonshivering thermogenesis*, which is characterized by increased oxygen consumption, BMR, and caloric requirements. The mechanism for nonshivering thermogenesis may be uncoupling of

ADP from the electron transport chain in the cellular mitochondria. Thus if the constraint of the ADP concentration, which limits the speed of the electron transport, is removed, electron movement can be increased, and heat production would also increase. The thyroid gland activity is also increased in the cold-adapted animal, and there are increased concentrations of circulating catecholamines.

Humans with decreased function of the endocrine system would be less able to adapt to a cold environment. Exposure of infants to either acute or chronic cold will lead to deterioration. Newborns are unable to shiver and thus must rely on their supply of *brown fat*, which is present in significant amounts in humans only during fetal and neonatal life. Brown fat is found normally in hibernating mammals and is rich in mitochondria. Its particular biochemistry allows it to participate in nonshivering thermogenesis. It allows some degree of cold adaptation in the infant, but it is not able to keep up with the heat requirements of the small, nonshivering infant who is suddenly exposed to a cold ambient temperature. Preterm infants lack significant brown fat deposits and therefore are especially susceptible to the development of hypothermia.

It is conceivable that inability to adapt to cold may lead to significant pathophysiology among the human population in the future, as humans slowly and purposefully change their environment and deplete it of all available heat-producing fuel. Therefore an understanding of this process is necessary in order to develop possible biochemical means for manipulating the response of humans to cold.

Radiation

Ionizing radiation has been present in the environment since life began. Many believe that without it no life could have evolved, since mutation is necessary in order for diversity to exist, and ionizing radiation is a powerful mutagen. As our technology becomes more and more complex, the peaceful utilization of nuclear energy for energy production, diagnosis and treatment of disease, and food preparation is becoming increasingly widespread. Questions are continually being raised as to what is a "safe" level of radiation in the environment and what are the dangers of accidental exposure to human physiology.

Some basic questions in radiation biology are related to the effects of low doses of radiation on humans. It must be realized that half of all the radiation exposure of the average individual comes from natural, rather than man-made sources. Fig. 5-5 illustrates the contribution of different sources to the total radiation dose of the average person. In man-made sources only a small percentage is derived from fallout and occupational exposure, the remainder coming from medical usage. The most biologically acceptable concept of low-dose effects is that of a threshold to radiation. This is in contrast to the linear hypothesis, which basically implies that there is dam-

age to living organisms from all exposures to radiation, down to even the most infinitesimal amount. The threshold theory, on the other hand, suggests that there is a threshold dose, below which no damage occurs and above which damage dependent on dosage occurs. These two theories are illustrated in Fig. 5-6.

Research into the cellular mechanisms of repair is a basic approach to studying the effects of low doses of radiation. These enzymatic processes appear to be highly efficient at low doses of radiation but may be "swamped" by the damage caused by larger doses. Large doses may also produce irreparable damage. As discussed in Chapter 6, radiation-induced carcinogenesis is a process that appears to require certain events to happen over time (the latent period) before the cancer is diagnosed. These events do not necessarily have to be the result of radioactivity. They could result from the effects of chemicals, viruses, or immune phenomena. Thus radiation as an agent that can cause damage to living cells must be viewed in perspective. Many

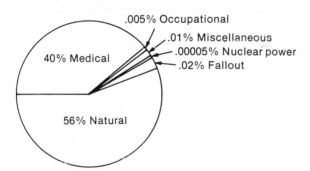

Fig. 5-5. Contributions of various sources to annual radiation dose. Total dose per year: 182 millirems.

Adapted from: Federal research on the biological and health effects of ionizing radiation, 1981, National Academy Press, Washington, DC.

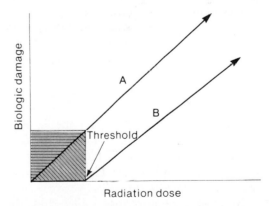

Fig. 5-6. Linear and threshold dose—response curve theories of radiation damage. Linear theory *(A)* holds that some damage occurs at all doses, whereas threshold theory *(B)* states that a threshold dose exists below which no damage occurs and above which damage of a linear nature with dose occurs.

other phenomena are concurrently interacting and competing with each other to cause damage to the cell.

The effects of radiation may not be manifested in certain cells until other events occur that disrupt the cell. On the other hand, a cell exposed to radiation may never develop damage either because efficient repair occurs so that no deleterious effects of the radiation remain or other factors damage or kill the cell before radiation-induced damage can be manifested.

Ionizing radiation exists in many forms. Examples are alpha particles, which are helium nuclei; beta particles, which are energetic electrons emitted formed from the atomic nucleus; gamma rays, which are a very energetic form of electromagnetic radiation like visible light, ultraviolet light and x-rays; and neutrons, which carry no charge, are about the same mass as protons, and can be produced in reactors. Other particles can be made highly energetic in accelerators. Alpha particles are heavy, charged, and can be stopped by the skin. Beta particles can move through the skin and tissue, and gamma rays of sufficient energy can penetrate the human body; lead shielding must be used to protect humans who are exposed to gamma or x-rays.

The term *ionizing* implies that these forms of radiation can cause the ejection of electrons from the outer shells of an atom, thus forming an ion. The electrons so produced are of sufficient energy to cause further ionization (Fig. 5-7). The energy of these particles or waves can result in direct damage to molecules that they impinge upon. For example, if a particle strikes a DNA molecule, the energy transferred by the reaction may be sufficient to cause abnormal structural configurations of the DNA, and mutations may be formed in the DNA. It is thought that if the mutation is not repaired, it may be lethal and kill the cell. If it is sublethal, the mutation may cause abnormal coding for proteins, and it may also be passed on to daughter cells if the damaged cell divides.

The presence of oxygen permits ionizing radiation to do more damage to biologic material because free radicals can be formed through the interaction of ionizing radiation and water. Since water is present in high concentrations inside cells and tissue, this interaction assumes great importance because the free radical formation results in molecules that can produce secondary effects. Free radicals, for example, can peroxidate biologic molecules such as membrane lipids. Sulfhydryl groups can be oxidized so that disulfide bonds may ultimately form between adjacent molecules. Large molecules may be degraded into smaller fragments, thus losing their chemical specificity. Cross-linking of molecules can also result, so that two or more molecules will be held in a rigid configuration. These effects are all produced by the free radicals formed by the radiation in the aqueous solution and thus are termed *secondary effects. Primary effects* of radiation are direct hits of molecules with damage produced by this interaction.

Radiation repair. When biologic molecules are damaged either directly or indirectly by ionizing radiation, the cell may protect itself against the effects of the damage in a variety of ways. Certain enzymes such as catalase or peroxidases act to protect the cell, in that peroxides that are formed are removed through the action of these enzymes. Nuclear damage to DNA molecules is also repaired through enzymatic reactions. When ionizing radiation breaks a single DNA strand, repair enzymes exist to patch the DNA together.

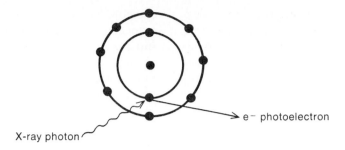

X-ray photon

e⁻ photoelectron

Fig. 5-7. Ionization is a process by which orbital electrons are ejected. A low-energy x-ray photon, which is a "packet" of x-ray energy, "hits" an atom and interacts with an orbital electron, transferring its energy to the electron and knocking it out of orbit. This produces a photoelectron, which can cause further ionization, and leaves behind a charged atom, or ion.

When both strands of DNA are broken by the radiation, repair is less likely to occur. Radiation can produce minute point mutations in DNA or can result in gross structural damage to the chromosome, which is observable upon microscopic examination of the cell. Radiation can also interrupt the normal division patterns of the cell and can affect cells in various ways, depending on the stage of the cell cycle the cell is in at the time of the radiation. If the genetic damage is in germ cells, there exists a possibility that the DNA damage will be handed down to subsequent generations. When the damage occurs in a somatic cell, there is no possibility of its becoming part of the gene pool. As we have previously discussed, the more immature or undifferentiated a cell, the more radiosensitive it is. The germ cells are generally more sensitive to the effects of radiation than are most somatic cells.

Radiation sickness. So far we have described the effects of radiation on specific cells. The teratogenic and carcinogenic properties of radiation have been described in previous chapters. The therapeutic aspects of radiation have been discussed in terms of cancer radiotherapy. Another effect of radiation occurs with exposure of the whole body, either intentionally or by accident. There are groups of individuals who have been exposed to large doses of whole-body radiation, and it is from these people that we have learned the most about the effects of radiation on humans. These include the survivors of the atomic bombings of Hiroshima and Nagasaki, the radium watch dial painters, early radiologists, people treated for a variety of conditions with either large doses of radiation or radium, and more recently, workers in contact with radioactivity who have been accidentally exposed. Confirmation of the effect of whole-body radiation on animals has been obtained in humans.

Radiation sickness, the acute result of large doses (greater than 50 rads) of whole-body radiation, consists primarily of changes in three major organ systems: the hematopoietic, gastrointestinal, and central nervous systems. Of course, alterations in any of these systems will have effects on other systems as well. The effects of radiation on these three systems is related to dose. While radiation sickness may occur after acute exposures greater than 50 rads, specific central nervous system damage is not seen unless the exposure has been to a very high dose. The central nervous system syndrome is an early effect of very high doses of radiation.

When exposures high enough to cause signs of central nervous system damage have occurred, death is inevitable. With doses of acute radiation between 500 and 2000 rads the signs and symptoms are related to damage in the gastrointestinal tract. Symptoms begin to appear 3 to 5 days after the exposure and consist of nausea, vomiting, anorexia, and diarrhea. These can then progress to gastrointestinal hemorrhage, which may lead to severe anemia. The body becomes extremely susceptible to infection under these circumstances. With radiation doses under 500 rads, or in individuals surviving the effects of the gastrointestinal syndrome, the hematopoietic syndrome appears with 10 to 15 days after the exposure. This is caused by the effects of radiation on sensitive blood-forming elements, and once there is depletion of the red cells, white cells, and platelets, signs appear in the patient. Blood cell depletion results in great susceptibility to infectious disease at this

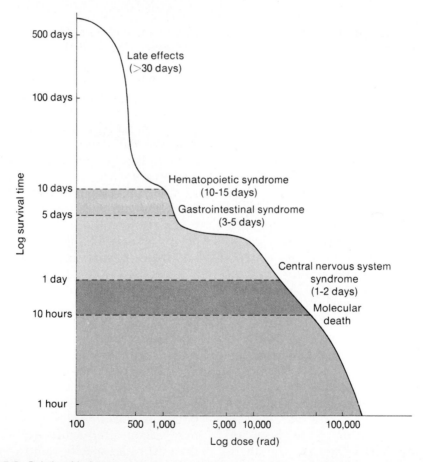

Fig. 5-8. Relationship between dose and survival time for adult rats following a single total-body exposure of x-rays. Radiation damage produces many alterations, leading to breakdown of steady state.

(From Casarett, AP: Radiation biology, © 1968, pp 222 and 223. Reprinted by permission of Prentice-Hall, Inc, Englewood Cliffs, NJ.)

time. Fig. 5-8 illustrates this relationship of dose and survival.

If recovery from the hematopoietic syndrome occurs, diseases may develop later in the individual's lifetime as the direct result of the radiation. Cancer is, of course, a major risk. There may be disorders of growth, and hair loss that occurs during the hematopoietic syndrome may be permanent. The aging process may be accelerated. permanent sterility may result, and radiation-induced cataracts may appear many months or even years after the exposure. Fig. 5-9 shows the pathophysio-

logic interactions of the systems most affected by radiation.

Treatment rationale. The treatment of an individual with radiation sickness is aimed at prevention of infection, hemorrhage, and fluid and electrolyte imbalances. Each case of radiation exposure must be handled on an individual basis. Transfusions, antibiotics, and bone marrow transplantation are all possible modes of treatment.

While radiation sickness of the degree just described is rarely encountered clinically, many patients receiving radiation therapy do experience minor variants of

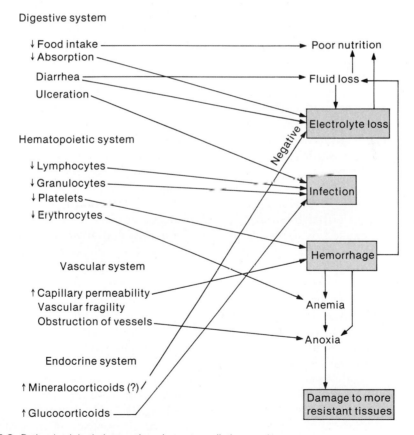

Fig. 5-9. Pathophysiologic interactions in acute radiation syndrome.

(From Casarett, AP: Radiation biology, © 1968, pp 222 and 223. Reprinted by permission of Prentice-Hall, Inc., Englewood Cliffs, NJ.)

the radiation sickness syndrome. Nausea, vomiting, hair loss, skin and mucous membrane lesions, and hematopoietic depletion are all commonly experienced. Furthermore, the target tissue of the radiotherapy may be damaged significantly, and if the tissue is radiosensitive, the patient will show signs and symptoms related to this damage.

Various chemicals and drugs have been described as radioprotective, in that they may diminish some of the damage caused by radiation when administered before and sometimes after the radiation exposure. These include sulfhydryl-containing compounds such as cysteine, a naturally occurring amino acid. These compounds may act as free radical "scavenger" molecules removing the highly reactive compounds before they can damage biologic molecules. Radioprotective drugs include those that produce tissue hypoxia, such as histamine, epinephrine, and carbon monoxide. Pentobarbital, morphine, heroin, and central nervous system depressants also protect against radiation damage to some degree.

Drowning

Death by drowning in either fresh and salt water is primarily caused by asphyxia and brain hypoxia leading to neuronal death. However, other pathophysiologic alterations contribute to the cause of death during drowning and are of great significance in cases of near-drowning. Much recent attention has been directed toward the phenomenon of cold water near-drowning. An understanding of all the changes that are taking place in the body during a potential drowning event are important to understand in order to rationally treat the near-drowning victim; these will be described in this section.

Physiologic effects of immersion. It is natural to assume that drowning results

from the unavoidable aspiration of water into the lungs. However, this is not always the case. Several physiologic reflexes are stimulated by prolonged submersion. The initial reflex is choking, gasping spasms of the larynx caused by involuntary breathing attempts made under water, which results in some water entering the trachea. The oxygen starvation that follows will eventually cause relaxation of the larynx, which permits further entry of water into both lungs and the stomach. In about 15% of the drowning victims, the laryngospasm continues to allow significant amounts of water to enter the lungs, and the victim dies of asphyxia.

Another physiologic effect of submersion is the diving reflex, which is most pronounced in infants and toddlers. This reflex is instantly initiated by placement of the face into cold water. Both fear and the temperature of the water are factors involved in the degree of response. Initially, there is a bradycardia, and a shunting of blood into the cerebral and coronary circulations. This factor combined with cold water immersion, which produces a profound hypothermia, leads to a much greater potential for complete recovery even in a child or adult who appears clinically dead upon removal from the water. Hypothermia that develops rapidly in water of a temperature less than 5° C and more slowly in water temperatures of less than 20° C decreases basal metabolic rate, energy demands, and oxygen requirements of all tissues, including the nervous system. This protective effect can prolong potential for life even when a cardiopulmonary arrest has occurred. A report from Norway of a 40-minute submersion in icy cold water with complete recovery occurring after resuscitation dramatizes this possibility (Siebke et al., 1975). Children are even more likely to be protected from the effects of cerebral hypoxia since they tend to cool down more quickly in the water because of a relatively greater surface area and a lesser amount of subcutaneous adipose tissue, and because of the diving reflex. The heart may continue to beat for up to 10 minutes after submersion during infancy, continually supplying some oxygen to the brain and helping to preserve function.

Fluid and electrolyte changes. The osmotic effects of fresh and salt water within the lungs is of great importance not only in determining the etiology of the drowning, but also in treating sequelae should the victim be successfully resuscitated. Fresh water has much less osmotic pressure than the body fluids and will be drawn through the alveolar membranes into the plasma. The result will be a drop in overall plasma osmotic pressure, which the osmotic forces throughout the body will attempt to equalize by movement of water through the capillary membranes and into the interstitial spaces. The falling osmotic pressure of the blood will also have a profound effect on the erythrocytes, causing hypotonic lysis of these cells. The imbalance in the body fluids and electrolytes can quickly become so great that cardiac irregularities and ventricular fibrillation occur even before the asphyxia causes death. In individuals who recover from fresh water drowning, fluid and electrolyte balance assumes as much importance in treatment protocols as does pulmonary edema and central nervous system integrity.

Salt water drowning has virtually the opposite osmotic effects. Because of the hypertonicity of salt water in the lungs, body fluid is drawn into the alveolar spaces. In fact, up to one fourth of the blood volume may move osmotically into the lungs, leading, of course, to intravascular dehydration and shock. If successful resuscitation of the salt water drowning victim occurs, the pulmonary complications can be severe and life-threatening afterward, with a state of pulmonary edema often developing, which can predispose to pulmonary infection.

With both fresh and salt water drowning, the potential for resuscitation depends upon the length of time of immersion, the temperature of the water (as previously discussed), the age of the individual, and the rapidity with which resuscitation takes place. The latter is such a crucial factor that, if possible, resuscitation should begin while the victim is still in the water.

Recovery and treatment rationale. The near-drowning victim may be able to walk away from the scene after resuscitation (although naturally this is not advised), or may be comatose and basically unresponsive to stimuli. In either case, the victim requires hospitalization for observation and oftentimes very vigorous treatment. According to Conn (1979), five problem categories can be observed in the near-drowning victim; hyperhydration, hyperventilation, hyperpyrexia, hyperexictability, and hyperrigidity. Hyperhydration results from the intake of large amounts of fresh or salt water, as well as the iatrogenic effects of intravenous fluids and plasma expanders that may be administered. Two target tissues are the most affected during recovery, the lungs and the brain. Pulmonary and cerebral edema can both lead to serious problems, and diuretics and fluid restriction should be employed. Continuous monitoring of intracranial pressure will lead to prompt treatment if one of the most common complications, cerebral edema, occurs.

Hyperventilation is the reflex response to hypercapnia and hypoxia, which most near-drowning victims experience. The result of hypercapnia can be fatal, as the cerebrovascular bed responds to elevated P_{CO_2} by vasodilation, which can potentiate increased intracranial pressure. The victim's blood gases must be carefully monitored during the initial recovery period, while the P_{CO_2} is kept at a value lower than normal.

An additional response, hyperpyrexia, can lead to further brain damage following near drowning; therefore body temperature must be reduced to around 30° C through the use of a cooling mattress. Neuronal recovery is aided by a lower core body temperature, and the possibility of cerebral edema is lessened by cooling.

Central nervous system damage can lead to either hyperexcitability or, in profound cases, decerebrate rigidity. This may be controlled by the administration of muscle relaxants such as curare derivatives. Careful nursing and continuous monitoring will further contribute to the prevention of increased intracranial pressure, brain swelling, and neuronal death.

The recognition that complete recovery from near drowning is possible, particularly in cases of cold water drowning, even with prolonged submersion, provides a rationale for aggressive treatment of these victims. Rescue personnel should immediately institute resuscitation whenever a drowning is witnessed and vigorously continue resuscitation while transporting the victim to the nearest emergency department.

SUMMARY

Described in this chapter are pathophysiologic effects of chemical and physical agents. It has related the specific effects of various agents to the general, nonspecific effects of stressors of all types in the body. The agents that can cause pathophysiologic processes are agents that have penetrated, overcome, and overwhelmed the normal body defenses and barriers. All of the defenses and barriers act in cooperation with each other to protect wellness. Although we have discussed these defenses and barriers separately in the preceding chapters, they are mutually interactive at all times in the healthy person. When pathophysiology of one defense system develops, often the structural and functional integrity of the other defenses also breaks down. All pathophysiology can be viewed in some sense as a breakdown in the normal body defenses and barriers. As we will discuss various disease mechanisms in the organ systems of the body in the following chapters, it is well for the reader to keep this concept in mind: regardless of which tissue or organ system is involved, injury will always provoke defense reactions such as inflammation and immune responsiveness. When studying the process of peptic ulceration, for example, we must keep in mind not only the effects of peptic ulceration on normal gastrointestinal physiology; ulceration must also be viewed as an inflammatory, necrotic, ulcerative process, which has resulted from a breakdown in normal barriers and has further perpetuated a state in which the normal defenses are depressed. This example typifies pathophysiology, for it is important not only to understand a disease mechanism but also to relate the disease process to normal physiology as a whole, and always in relationship to the individual's ability to protect and maintain wellness.

BIBLIOGRAPHY

Apelgren KN, et al: Malnutrition in Veterans Administration surgical patients, Arch Surg 116:1059-1061, 1981.

Cassaret A: Radiation biology, Englewood Cliffs, NJ, 1968, Prentice-Hall.

Conn AW, Edmonds JF, and Barker GA: Cerebral resuscitation in near drowning, Pediatr Clin North Am 26:691-701, 1979.

Demling R: Fluid replacement in burned patients, Surg Clin North Am 67:15-30, 1987.

Gusberg R: The multiple trauma victim: a nutritional cripple, Yale J Biol Med 59:403-407, 1986.

Heimbach D: Early burn excision and grafting, Surg Clin North Am 67:93-107, 1987.

Jernigan E, editor: Lead poisoning in man and animal, New York, 1973, MSS Information Corporation.

Lieber C: Metabolism and metabolic effects of alcohol, Med Clin North Am 68:3-31, 1984.

Nelsen TE and Flewellen EH: The malignant hyperthermia syndrome, N Engl J Med 309:417-418, 1983.

Pasulka P and Wachtel T: Nutritional considerations for the burned patients, Surg Clin North Am 67:109-131, 1987.

Rosenberg J, et al: Hyperthermia associated with drug intoxication, Crit Care Med 14:964-969, 1986.

Segal L, et al: Alcohol and the heart, Med Clin North Am 60:147-161, 1984.

Settle D, and Patterson C: Lead in albacore: guide to lead pollution in Americans, Science 207:1167-1176, 1980.

Shires GT: Principles of trauma care, New York, 1985, McGraw-Hill, Inc.

Siebke H, et al: Survival after 40 minutes' submersion without cerebral sequelae, Lancet 1:1275-1277, 1975.

Trunkey D: Multiple organ failure: early and late, Proceedings of the Symposium on Critical Care Medicine, March 1987, Las Vegas, Nevada.

Wilmore DW, et al: Hyperglucagonaemia after burns, Lancet 1:73-75, 1974.

Wilmore DW, et al: Catecholamines: mediator of the hypermetabolic response to thermal injury, Ann Surg 180:653-668, 1974.

6

Cancer

Cancer is one of the most dreaded diseases and, unfortunately, also one of the most common. Even today, when 50% of cancer is curable, the diagnosis is usually overwhelming to most people. Cancer often connotes pain, loss of dignity, financial destitution, dependence, and death. When the war against cancer was declared in the 1960s, most people thought that if enough time and money were invested a cure for cancer could be attained. Nearly 30 years later people still suffer from this disease and the overall incidence has not changed significantly. Treatment has become more sophisticated and efficacious and it is now possible for patients who cannot be cured to survive for many years. For cancers such as acute childhood leukemia and Hodgkin's disease, cure is a real goal. Cancer research has certainly helped increase our knowledge of the disease and has provided an enormous amount of information about basic cellular biology that has aided us in understanding many other diseases. Still, one out of every three people in the United States will be diagnosed with some form of cancer in their lifetime. The incidence of some cancers appears to be increasing (e.g., lung, pancreas, and breast) while that of others is decreasing (e.g., stomach and uterus). Another aspect to cancer is the unreliability of the 5-year

survival rate, which formerly indicated cure. Now we know that some cancers (breast, prostate, kidney) can metastasize and set up new growths many years after the initial diagnosis (Levy, 1985). For the most part, cancer has become a group of long-term illnesses, rather than an acute, short-term, morbid disease.

The roles of life-style, culture, diet, various carcinogens, and psychosocial processes in the development of cancer are currently being widely studied. This chapter will review much of this research and will discuss the mechanism by which cancer is believed to arise.

NATURE OF CANCER

No single definition of cancer has been universally accepted, and no common unifying theory of cancer causation has been scientifically validated. The nature of cancer appears to be one in which a genetic change in normal somatic (body) cells produces an abnormal cell type, which perpetuates itself. The cell loses normal regulatory constraints on mitotic division and generally appears immature and poorly differentiated. The diagnosis of cancer can be made by examination of these cellular changes. This is usually done by examination of the cells taken by biopsy from the tissue that is suspect. The morphologic cellular changes and the processes by which cancer causes disease and death are known and occur in a characteristic manner—regardless of the actual cause of the original change in the cells.

As more is learned about the process whereby a normal cell undergoes carcinogenic transformation and about the pathophysiology of malignant cells, the less likely it appears that a single basic biologic phenomenon will be described for all cancers. The diseases classified as cancer probably result from many factors interacting in the host at the biochemical, cellular, tissue, organ, and organism levels, and all factors interact again within the host's particular environment.

The recognition of cancer as a group of chronic diseases of primarily environmental origin has been the single most important common result of cancer research and has provided various rationales for the prevention, detection, and treatment of certain kinds of cancer. Much further research needs to be carried out on the basic mechanism of carcinogenesis throughout the animal and plant kingdoms and on the natural history of the disease process in humans, in order to aid both the scientist and the health care provider in approaching cancer from phenomenologic and practical aspects.

The common pathophysiologic mechanisms that appear to operate in all cancer cells are (1) the loss of regulation of mitotic rate, (2) the loss of specialization and differentiation of the cell, (3) the ability of the cancer cell to move from the original or *primary* site and establish new malignant growths at other tissue sites *(metastasis)*, and (4) the capacity to invade and destroy normal tissue in which the cancer grows.

Cancer can be found diffusely, as in leukemia, in which leukemic cells are widely dispersed, or in cellular associations called *tumors*, which form actual masses within tissues. Tumors or neoplasms (new growths) can be benign or malignant and can arise in any tissue or organ of the body. The tissue of origin of the primary tumor can be determined from tumor nomenclature, the Greek root for tumor being *oma*. For example, a sarcoma is derived from connective tissue, a carcinoma from epithelial tissue, an adenoma from glandular tissue, and a teratoma from embryonic tissue. Malignant tumors are distinguished from benign tumors by the morphology of the cells in the mass and the fact that benign tumors are generally noninvasive and encapsulated within a membrane and never metastasize. It is important to realize, however, that a benign tumor can be extremely pathologic to the host if it obstructs critical vessels, ducts, or tracts within the body, interfering with normal oxygenation, nutrition, or elimination, or if it has functional activity, such as excess hormone production, which would disrupt the normal feedback regulation of the endocrine system. Conversely, occasional malignant tumors grow so slowly that there is little effect on the host for a considerable period. Many tumors do not have to reach a certain critical size before cells begin to break away and metastasize, however.

A typical example that characterizes the natural history of the malignant disease in humans is one in which the affected individual presents initially to the physician with malignant, metastatic, and invasive cancer, usually accompanied by vague generalized symptoms. The development of *cachexia* may be apparent, which is a syndrome characterized by muscle wasting, weakness, fatigue, anorexia (loss of appetite), and anemia. It is less common for a malignancy to be discovered early in the disease process by a physician or screening clinic when the mass is small, locally confined (in situ), and no metastatic dissemination has occurred. It is obvious that the detection of cancer in the early stages plays an important role in the efficacy of therapy and control of the advancement of the malignant disease process. Early detection of many tumor types results in a greater survival rate, and the possibility of cure is much more real when treatment is initiated early.

CANCER CELLS
Predisposing factors

The cancer cell shows morphologic and physiologic deviations from normal. The anaplastic (without form) nature of the malignant cell is characterized by immaturity and lack of differentiation of the dividing cells. It may be difficult to distinguish structurally the cell type from which the malignancy was originally derived. Frequently hyperplasia and metaplasia precede the conversion of the normal tissue into neoplastic tissue. For example, the incidence of endometrial cancer is significantly increased in females who have a history of endometrial hyperplasia. *Hyperplasia* is a process in which cells respond to a stress by increasing in number through increased cellular division. The endometrium may respond to an increased concentration of estrogen, for example, by hyperplasia. The incidence of uterine cancer in postmenopausal women who received excessive replacement therapy with estrogen compounds has been established and may be related to this hyperplastic process. It is conceivable that hyperplasia predisposes to neoplasia by merely increasing the statistical likelihood of a cellular neoplastic transformation in that many more cells are dividing much more rapidly than in normal tissue and may

therefore generally be more sensitive to carcinogens.

Metaplasia is the process whereby one cell type changes to another cell type in response to stress and generally assists the host to adapt to the stress.

Dysplasia is another type of nonmalignant cellular growth, which again may precede neoplastic changes in the tissue. It is associated with chronic irritation of a tissue by a chemical agent, such as cigarette smoke, or by inflammatory irritation of a chronic nature, such as chronic cervicitis (inflammation of the cervix). The dysplastic tissue appears somewhat structureless and disorganized and may consist of atypical cells.

Dysplasia, hyperplasia, and metaplasia are intrinsically reversible in nature when the stress that initiates the changes is removed. Malignant neoplastic growth, on the other hand, is not reversible when the carcinogenic stress is removed but appears to be a permanent alteration in the transformed cell, which is inherited by all the daughter cells from every division of the neoplastic cell. One school of thought suggests that all malignancy proceeds through a benign stage and that all benign growths have some potential for malignant transformation.

Cellular pathophysiology of malignancy

Cancer appears to arise from an originally normal cell that is transformed. This transformation, according to the Berenblum theory, probably involves at least two steps: *initiation and promotion* (Fig. 6-1). Agents that initiate and later promote transformation are termed *carcinogens*. Carcinogens may be chemical agents, viruses, radiation, hormones, and perhaps physical irritation. Cocarcinogens may be required for the carcinogen to effect transformation or perhaps for promoting the

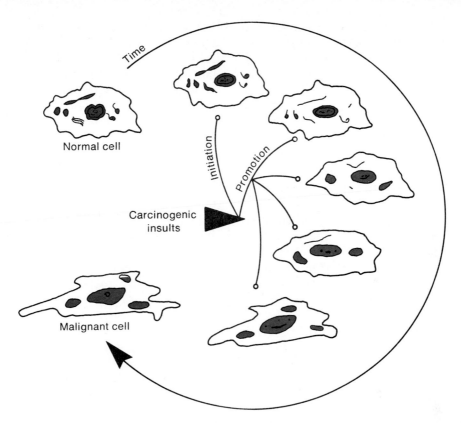

Normal cell

Time

Initiation

Promotion

Carcinogenic
insults

Malignant cell

Fig. 6-1. Berenblum's theory of carcinogenesis: initiation and promotion. Several events are required for a normal cell to become transformed into a cancer cell. Initial event, initiation, will not cause cancer unless several promoting events occur over time.

growth of the cells once they are transformed. Promoters may act at the membrane once a cell is irreversibly initiated, changing growth characteristics by influencing membrane sensitivity to various growth factors. All initiating carcinogens appear to act ultimately at the nuclear level of the cell and are able to damage or somehow alter the normal nucleic acids. It is not known whether carcinogenesis directly results from this type of damage, but it appears highly likely that the DNA of neoplastic malignant cells is altered as the malignant properties of the transformed cell are inherited by the daughter

cells of every mitosis of the originally transformed cell.

It has been shown experimentally that the cancer process can originate in animals when a single malignant cell is injected. Nevertheless, cancer cells are not necessarily autonomous in nature but may require considerable immunologic, nutritional, chemical, and hormonal support from the host to flourish. This is demonstrated by the occasional reports of long intervals between the surgical excision of a primary tumor and the appearance of secondary metastases. This phenomenon may result from the anoxic environment created at the surgical site that suppresses growth and metastasis of malignant cells left behind after surgery. Over a period of years the surgical site becomes revascularized and normoxic, and the cells are no longer suppressed by the host's hostile environment.

It is interesting to note that transmission of information through cellular mitosis in cancer cells is magnified not always by a rapid division rate but by the further division of every daughter cell of every mitosis, which is in contrast to the normal mitotic pattern. It has been shown that a single cell cycle, consisting of division, rest, and growth, is not shorter in many tumor cells and may, in fact, be longer than in the normal cell. Tumor formation may result when a normal pattern of division and growth within a tissue renewal system is altered. Many normal tissues renew themselves constantly as cells are lost from that tissue. This process occurs continuously in the skin, the gastrointestinal tract, the testes, and the blood.

The originator of the new tissue replacement cells is an undifferentiated, unspecialized, immature cell known as the *stem cell*. This primitive cell is committed to divide and develop a new population of like cells through a progression of (1) mitosis and (2) differentiation of daughter cells. The stem cell divides a certain number of times, and then it appears that only one daughter cell continues to divide further, while the other daughter cell will differentiate into a specialized cell type. Malignant cells may not follow this pattern but will divide continuously without differentiation into very specialized or functionally integrated cells. The cells remain anaplastic and immature. Stem cells are themselves in general sensitive to the mutagenic effects of radiation. Malignancy may occur when a carcinogen, such as ra-

diation, acts upon the sensitive stem cell, which then divides and propagates the initial transformation of the cell into a malignant tumor mass (Fig. 6-2).

The growth of a tumor may also be influenced by the rate of cell loss from the growing cell mass whether or not the cell cycle is changed in duration. Some skin cancers grow extremely slowly over a period of years without a significant increase in size. This is probably the result of rapid and constant *exfoliation* (loss of skin cells from the surface of the epithelium) from the malignant mass. Many solid tumors, as well, generally appear to grow to a defined size, which may, in fact, be maintained only by metastasis of cells away from the tumor rather than by a decrease in the actual growth.

The degree of malignancy produced by a given carcinogen may be dependent on the stage of differentiation of the target cell of the carcinogen. It is theorized that a benign tumor might be the result of a carcinogenic stimulus acting on the matured cells in a tissue renewal system (such as skin, gut, or blood), whereas the same carcinogen acting on a stem cell could give rise to a potently malignant cell. Tumors can generally be classified by biopsy into four grades of malignancy:

Grade 1 Tumors in which 75% or more of the cells appear well differentiated
Grade 2 Tumors in which 50% to 75% of the cells appear differentiated
Grade 3 Tumors in which 25% to 50% of the cells appear differentiated
Grade 4 Tumors in which 0% to 25% of the cells appear differentiated

Tumors of higher grade would consist largely of anaplastic cells and would in general have the poorest prognosis for the patient.

Considerable evidence exists that cer-

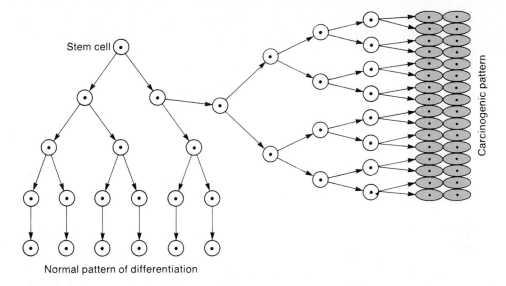

Stem cell

Carcinogenic pattern

Normal pattern of differentiation

Fig. 6-2. Carcinogenesis. Carcinogen acts on sensitive stem cell, which then produces malignant tumor through a loss of normal mitotic pattern and differentiation of daughter cells.

tain tumors are derived from transformed undifferentiated stemlike cells. Tumors originating from embryonic tissues (teratocarcinomas) in particular seem to have this characteristic. Indeed, carcinogenesis in the adult organism may be a pathophysiologic caricature of the normal histogenesis observed in the developing embryo as it differentiates toward a mature form. A carcinogen would then be seen to act by derepressing (i.e., unmasking) certain genes that are usually active only during embryonic life and repressing others. The activated genes would then code for a certain protein profile, which would characterize the cell as malignant.

The search for particular embryonic proteins in cancer tissue is an important part of the research into carcinogenesis. Cancer of the colon and liver appears in many cases to produce embryonic proteins, which may be detected early in the disease process. Such cancer markers may aid in early cancer screening and detection.

If cancer can be regarded as a return of a differentiated cell to a state somewhat like the embryonic one, then the question arises, "Are embryonic cells similar in any way to malignant cells?" Certain characteristics of cancer are reminiscent of the embryo. The anaerobic metabolism and motility of cancer cells, anaplasia, production of fetal antigens, release of angioblastic (blood vessel–forming) substances by tumors, decreased contact inhibition, and invasiveness of cancer cells (which can be compared to the extraordinary invasive penetration of the endometrium by the trophoblast of the embryo) all point to certain similarities.

It has also been shown that prenatal exposure to radiation, stilbesterol therapy, and certain viral diseases, especially parainfluenza and chickenpox, increases the subsequent risk of cancer in the child. Furthermore, there is an observed association between congenital malformations and cancers in the fetus. These observations would lend credence to the theory that cancer develops more readily in undifferentiated tissue and may in fact represent a mimicking of embryogenesis, albeit uncontrolled and pathologic.

Morphology

The degree of malignancy of a tumor is positively correlated with the degree of anaplasia. Anaplastic cells themselves are of abnormal size and shape, and the nuclei are usually large and contain grossly abnormal nucleoli. The nucleolus, a nuclear organelle that contains DNA and RNA, is not only pleomorphic (abnormally shaped) in malignant cells but also is subsequently altered by cancer chemotherapeutic agents such as actinomycin D, which causes the nucleolus in cancer cells to change both its shape and activity. The role of the nucleolus in both the transformation of a cell and the maintenance of the neoplastic processes has not been determined.

Malignant cells also contain *abnormal chromosomes* and unusual mitotic spindles, which produce bizarre cell divisions. It appears likely that the abnormalities of the nucleus and chromosomes are secondary to the intrinsic loss of regulation of cell mitosis and other physiologic processes rather than the direct result of carcinogenic injury or insult to the nucleus. The many cells of a given tumor do not usually exhibit absolutely identical karyotype and phenotype, although it is believed that a tumor develops from an initial single cell.

Metabolism and protein synthesis

The cancer cell exhibits a general loss of the capabilities to synthesize specialized protein that would identify it as a differentiated cell type. For example, a differentiated liver cell synthesizes only liver cell enzymes. Highly anaplastic cells from a hepatocarcinoma might synthesize few of these normal enzymes, and in fact a *fetal* liver protein may be produced. It seems that the enzymes and other proteins that cancer cells do produce allow only for the tumor cell mass to grow rapidly, and the "frills" of differentiated and specialized protein production are eliminated in this process.

The biochemical metabolism of neoplastic cells is usually more anaerobic than that of normal non–rapidly dividing cells and is greatly accelerated. Malignant cells may be able to withstand hypoxic conditions for prolonged periods. Cancer cells have high levels of hexokinase, which increases their glucose utilization.

Nuclear changes

The chromosomes that constitute the *karyotype* (the chromosomal number, sizes, and shapes) of neoplastic cells generally are altered, and many of the known carcinogens are *mutagens* (i.e., able to cause mutations in the cellular DNA). Carcinogens therefore might act by causing direct mutations in the chromosomes of the cell, and this may constitute transformation. Carcinogens might also act in other ways, by membrane damage, for example, or by altering the general characteristics of the tissue in which the neoplasm is destined to arise. They may act by promoting complex intracellular relationships that result in genetic expression of repressed bits of DNA. The kinds of chromosomal aberrations that are commonly observed in the malignant cell are *nonspecific* in nature, except for a few cancer types. Chronic myelogenous leukemia is usually characterized by the appearance of an extra chromosome, known as the Philadelphia chromosome, in certain blood cells of the individual. There is also an increased incidence of leukemia in Down syndrome, a condition that results from a trisomy of the chromosome 21 pair in humans (see

Chapter 4). A genetic marker accompanying cancer seems to be the deletion of the long arm of chromosome 13 in retinoblastoma and a deletion in the short arm of this chromosome in children with Wilms' tumor (a pediatric nephroblastoma). Other tumors, such as osteogenic sarcoma, a tumor of bone, also appear in these individuals, thus indicating an association of a chromosomal defect with malignancies (Kolata, 1986).

The presence of chromosomal aberrations by themselves does not indicate that cancer is the result of faulty DNA. Clearly, factors other than the DNA code itself are involved in the expression of genetic traits in both normal and malignant cells. This is exemplified by an experiment in which two populations of malignant cells were fused, with a resultant mixing of the cellular DNA. The cells produced by the fusion were not malignant. Certain genes may be repressed in normal cells and expressed in cancer cells by cytoplasmic and nonnucleic acid nuclear factors.

Membrane changes

There are conflicting reports regarding the nature of the cancer cell membrane (the membranes of cancer cells have been variously reported to have increased passive and active permeability and drastically decreased permeability). Cancer cells in tissue culture usually have increased glucose and amino acid uptake. There may be an altered calcium ion concentration in the malignant cell membrane, which may in part be responsible for the lack of *contact* (or density-dependent) *inhibition* and cohesiveness in neoplastic cells (Fig. 6-2). In tissue cultures of cancer cells, the transformed cells clump together and pile up on one another instead of forming the typical cellular monolayer usually seen in tissue cultures. This can be viewed as an in vitro microtumor. Normally, cell division

in a population of cells is impeded by cell surface-to-surface contact.

Cellular membrane communication appears lost in cancer cells, so that movement of materials and cell membrane–mediated transmission of biologic information is impaired, and cellular cohesion is interrupted as well. The malignant transformation process may be accompanied by the revelation of normally masked membrane components, such as antigens, channels, or binding sites. The membranes of neoplastic cells also do not turn over the lipoprotein components with the same rapidity as normal cells. This may indicate that the membrane is the site of initial carcinogenic insult and injury. Disruption at the membrane could be magnified by a cascade of events throughout the cell, eventually resulting in modifications of DNA synthesis, protein synthesis, and cell mitosis.

Electron microscopy of cancer cells has shown that the cell membrane, surface coat, and cytoplasmic projections may be abnormal, and cancer cells are known to be intensely phagocytic and mobile. Cancer cell surfaces may have an increased surface electric charge, decreased surface glycolipid, and decreased surface fibronectin (a large glycoprotein).

Invasion

Cancer cells have increased motility and decreased stickiness, both of which are factors in the property of invasion and infiltration of normal tissue by malignant tissue. Invasion may be aided by the production of lytic enzymes, which are increased in neoplastic cells. Invasion is not well understood, but experiments indicate that there is a preferential destruction of the normal tissue by the malignant cells, as has been demonstrated in vitro. Invasion is defined as the penetration of adjacent local tissue by a neoplasm. Normal

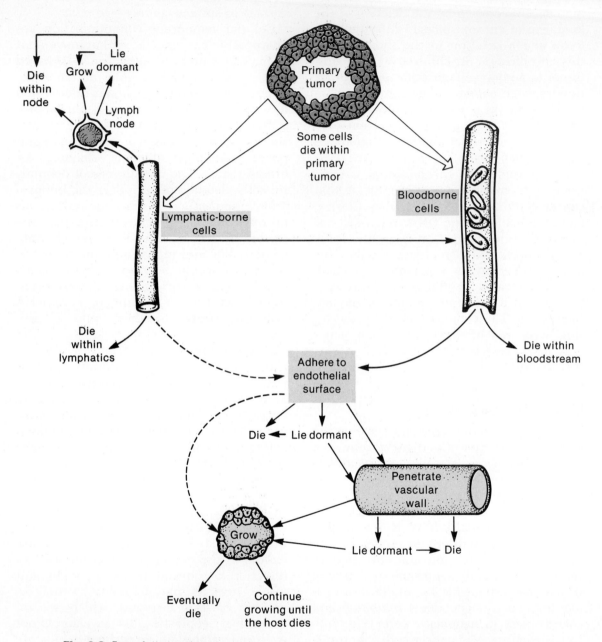

Fig. 6-3. Fate of metastatic cancer cells.

(Redrawn from Kupchella C and Burton R: Cellular biology of cancer, Cancer Nursing. Groenwald S, editor: Boston, 1987, Jones & Bartlett.

invasion of a tissue by another tissue can occur and is characteristic of implantation of the zygote in the uterine wall. Neoplastic invasion appears random and unchecked, however. It has been shown that normal tissue interactions that maintain histologic structure are disturbed in malignant invasion. Invasion of epithelial malignant tumors into the underlying connective tissue is accompanied by structural and functional changes in the cell surfaces, which allow the malignant cells to more easily penetrate the dermal tissue. Tumor invasion may also be enhanced by the elaboration of angioblastic substances by malignant cells, which promote vascularization of the infiltrating tumor. The property of invasion of normal tissue can account for much morbidity in the cancer patient and in part can explain the development of cachexia (severe wasting) in terminally ill individuals with cancer.

Metastasis

Fifty percent of newly diagnosed, cancer patients with tumors have occult metastases that are not readily identifiable. Metastasis from a secondary site is also possible, so that these malignant growths may already be shedding cells into the bloodstream even as the primary tumor is being identified.

Metastasis is the dissemination of clumps of malignant cells from the primary cancer site to other tissues in the body and the establishment of secondary malignancies that have many of the same characteristics as the primary tumor. Cells or tissue fragments from a malignant growth can break away at any time from the primary tumor and travel through lymphatic vessels and veins, or interstitially through the tissue spaces. Lymphatics appear to be the most common method of metastatic spread. The presence of cancer cells or cancerous tissue fragments in

the circulating blood does not constitute metastasis. There is no correlation between the presence of these cells in the bloodstream and the ultimate prognosis of the cancer patient. Many millions of cells may break off a primary tumor and never set up any new growths. Most cancer cells die in the bloodstream.

The malignant cells that leave the primary tumor must find a favorable tissue environment in which invasion and growth is facilitated. It is well known that certain primary tumors metastasize preferentially to specific organs. Such spread does not seem related to such known tissue characteristics as location or vascularity. Establishment of secondary cancer in a tissue is also aided by the elaboration of an angioblastic substance that promotes a microcirculation in the growing tumor mass. The *selective affinity theory* of metastasis describes the spread of the neoplastic cells to certain organs that are particularly favorable for the growth of that cell type. Some unknown character of the tissue is therefore involved in establishing a favorable environment for the primary tumor cells. The *mechanical theory* of metastasis relates metastasis only to factors such as metastatic cell size, pressure, vessel size, and other purely physical factors. The *transformation theory* of metastasis correlates cancer cell spread with the transformation of secondary tissue cells by cancer cell DNA. Generally, most metastatic invasion can be described by the selective affinity theory, but mechanical factors do seem important in some cases.

Examination of the histology of a primary tumor often reveals a marked heterogeneity of cell types, even though it is believed that the tumor originally came from a single cell. This phenomenon is known as phenotypic drift (Welch and Bhuyam, 1986). The metastases that develop at different sites, which originally arose from a primary tumor, also exhibit differences from each other. It may be that metastatic cells are sorted out and that there are selective differences in which secondary sites are seeded.

Metastasis occurs most commonly to the lymph nodes, lungs, liver, bones, kidneys, and adrenal glands. Individual cells can travel through the lymph or blood, or actual cancer cell thrombi can seed an organ. These tissue fragments often become coated with fibrin, and anticoagulant therapy has been used for the prevention of metastasis. Cancer cells can metastasize to areas that have been physically injured. Growth of cells along the puncture wound of a needle biopsy site has been described. Secondary carcinoma has also been observed along the suture line of a surgical incision resulting from cancer surgery. The trauma of surgical manipulation has been shown to release a shower of malignant cells into the tissue spaces and bloodstream. The release of cancer cells from a primary tumor has even resulted from manual diagnostic examination of a tumor.

Certain tumors are more likely to metastasize than others. For example, the basal cell carcinoma of skin rarely metastasizes. Metastasis generally moves away from the primary tumor via the lymphatic vessels. These vessels end in blind, thin-walled, and highly permeable capillaries. Lymph is filtered by the lymph nodes, which are dispersed along the lymphatic channels. The lymph nodes are thought by many authorities to be an important barrier to cancer spread, and the routine removal of lymph nodes during cancer surgery is now being questioned by some. Degenerating and necrotic cells can sometimes be found in these nodes, as well as *histiocytes* (macrophages that act to phagocytose debris and foreign material), indicating that a defense reaction of the body occurs in response to the neoplastic cells. Cancer cells

can grow in the lymph nodes, however, resulting in localized hard and painful tumor masses that must be removed. The presence of malignant cells in the lymph nodes surrounding and draining a malignant cancer indicates that metastasis has begun, and the extent of lymph node involvement can often be correlated with the patient's ultimate prognosis.

To establish secondary growths in organs or body cavities, the malignant cells must leave the bloodstream. The cells invade the vessel wall and destroy the blood vessel. These cancer cells then extend directly into the tissue. Sometimes the cells seem to escape from the blood vessel through a type of ameboid diapedesis (Fig 6-3).

Malignant cells usually infiltrate through veins, whereas arterial invasion is rare. The tumorous tissue erodes into the veins and propagates by growing along the endothelium. Vessels can actually become obstructed with plugs of neoplastic cells. The tumors of higher grade are more anaplastic and show the greatest incidence of venous spread.

Metastasis is the most lethal property of cancer cells and ultimately causes death in patients with incurable cancer. Much cancer therapy is aimed toward preventing or retarding this process.

CARCINOGENESIS
Models

The known carcinogens, the populations they affect, and the pathophysiologic processes that occur in carcinogenesis all lead to several theories of cancer.

Berenblum's two-stage initiation and promotion theory is one of the most widely accepted and unifying theories (Berenblum, 1978), but little is known about the actual molecular mechanisms by which a cell is transformed. The prevalent notion is that genetic changes must take place for a cancer to appear in previously normal tissue, and there is controversy concerning the actual number of sequential mutational events that must occur before a cell can be considered malignant. Mathematic models of chemical carcinogenesis suggest that three steps are involved in malignant transformation. Radium-induced human tumors also may occur when three nuclear "hits" by radioactive emission from the bone-incorporated radium transform a bone cell (Marshall and Groer, 1977).

Burch's model of carcinogenesis suggests that every cell has several restraining genes that act independently to prevent the development of cancer in the cell. When all these genes are inactivated by carcinogenic insults, the cell is released from the effects of these genes and becomes malignant. Thus all carcinogens would act by a common mechanism, that of inactivation of the restraining genes. The probability that all the restraining genes in a given cell will become inactivated would naturally be a function of how long the cell has been subject to carcinogenic threats. For many cancers this would depend on the individual's age. When a mathematic plot of cancer incidence and age of appearance of the cancer is done, the slope of the plotted line suggests that five mutations must occur during the individual's life span before a malignancy will develop. Thus cancer can be considered to have an "incubation period" that begins with the first mutation, which is the initiating step, and ends with the fifth, which precludes the onset of a malignant growth. This theory not only explains the increased incidence of cancer with age but also elucidates the long latency period that characterizes many cancers. Furthermore, it suggests that by middle age, many individuals will have small nests of potentially neoplastic cells in many tissues and organs. Rampant malignancy may

never occur in these sites because of the long latency of the tumor and the limitations imposed by the life span in the host. The theory also implicates environmental factors in the causation of cancer, which are potentially avoidable threats to the human organism.

COMMON CARCINOGENS

Research and epidemiologic investigations have resulted in a number of prominent theories of carcinogenesis. Most theories recognize that as much as 85% of all human cancers are of environmental origin. Known environmental carcinogens include radiation, chemicals, diet, viruses, hormones, and irritation. Table 6-1 describes the influences of common carcinogens.

Chemical carcinogenesis

Pott described cancer of the scrotum in chimney sweeps over 200 years ago. Since then many other naturally occurring and synthetic compounds have been shown to have carcinogenic potential, and the list

Table 6-1. Carcinogens and their varying influences

Carcinogen	Estimated percentage of cancer causation
Tobacco	30
Alcohol	3
Nutritional factors	35
Food additives	< 1
Reproductive behavior	7
Occupation	4
Pollution	2
Industrial chemicals	< 1
Medical care and medicines	1
Geophysical factors	3
Infection	?
Unknown	?

Adapted from Doll R and Peto R: The causes of cancer, New York, 1981, Oxford University Press Inc, p 1256.

grows constantly. The identification of chemicals that are carcinogenic in humans is sometimes complicated by long latent periods between exposure and the first appearance of cancer. We may now be exposed to carcinogens that may ultimately result in cancer 20 years hence. The ubiquity of latency in neoplastic development is a poorly understood phenomenon. The length of the latent period appears to be a function of the carcinogen as well as the host; it may be the time required for a transformed committed cell to form a clone of critical size or for a sequence of promoting events to occur that ultimately result in cancer. The latter possibility has the most experimental support.

Carcinogens or the metabolites of carcinogens are often mutagenic, but it is not known if all carcinogenesis proceeds from an initial mutational change in the host cell DNA. However, alkylating agents are mutagens as well as carcinogens, and the degree of carcinogenesis is directly correlated with the degree of binding of the agent to DNA. A number of known carcinogens bind covalently to DNA and RNA. All chemical carcinogens have an *electrophilic* (electron-loving) nature in common or will produce electrophilic compounds in vivo. These structures contain electron-deficient atoms, are highly reactive, and can interact with DNA, RNA, and certain cellular proteins. The postulated mechanisms by which chemical carcinogens transform normal cells include (1) *mutations* in the host cell DNA or modifications of RNA, (2) heritable changes in the *expression* of the host cell DNA, (3) *activation* or release of part or all of a latent integrated viral genome, and (4) *selection* of a latent tumor cell.

One of the most useful laboratory tests for carcinogenic potential involves testing the mutagenicity of the substance in a bacterial culture. This is the Ames test and is a good indicator of carcinogenicity, thus suggesting that most chemical carcinogenesis proceeds through mutagenesis.

Chemical carcinogenesis is dose-dependent. Many substances that are components of the atmosphere, soil, and food and drink have been shown to induce tumors in experimental animals when used in high concentrations. Some of these agents are listed on pp. 205 and 206. Little is known about the effects of these carcinogens when humans are exposed to minute amounts in the environment over a period of many years. The same is true for the effects of very low doses of ionizing radiation. There is controversy about the threshold for biologic damage by carcinogens, below which the damage is repaired and above which irreparable injury occurs.

The mechanism by which chemical carcinogens cause neoplastic transformation is not known. It is clear that for cancer to occur, the host cells themselves must interact with most carcinogens causing enzymatic activation of these compounds. For example, the derivatives of human metabolism of the polycyclic hydrocarbons (chemicals found in oxidizing smogs of the Los Angeles type) yield cancer-inducing entities, as do the aromatic amines. Individuals vary in their abilities to activate chemical carcinogens, and this genetically determined difference may be correlated with cancer susceptibility.

The process of activation requires cellular enzymes, which are induced by the carcinogen. However, there is variability in the amount of enzyme that can be induced by the carcinogen, which has led to the idea that genetic susceptibility to cancer may have its basis in the degree of inducibility of the activating enzymes. One system of enzymes is the aryl hydrocarbon hydroxylase system, which converts the

CHEMICAL CARCINOGENS AND REPRESENTATIVE MOLECULES

Carcinogen	Representative molecule	Effect
Aklylating agents (e.g., nitrogen mustard)	 Nitrogen mustard	Experimental skin tumors and sarcomas
Polycyclic aromatic hydrocarbons (e.g., methylcholanthrene, soot tar, cigarette smoke)	 Methylcholanthrene (potent carcinogen: has been prepared from desoxycholic and cholic acid)	Lung tumors
Food additives (e.g., azo dyes)	 p-Dimethylaminoazobenzene "butter yellow"	Experimental liver tumors
Metals (e.g., arsenic, asbestos) Molds (e.g., aflatoxin B)	 Aflatoxin B₁	Skin cancer, mesothelioma Possible hepatic carcinoma in humans
Nitrosamines	 Dimethylnitrosamine	Experimental liver and kidney tumors
Urethan		Lung adenomas in mice
Aromatic amines (e.g., benzidine, 2-naphthylamine)	 2-Naphthylamine	Bladder cancer in humans

Continued.

CHEMICAL CARCINOGENS AND REPRESENTATIVE MOLECULES—cont'd

Carcinogen	Representative molecule	Effect
Hormones (e.g., diethylstilbestrol)		Genital cancers

$$CH_3$$
$$|$$
$$CH_2$$
$$|$$
$$HO-\bigcirc-C=C-\bigcirc-OH$$
$$|$$
$$CH_2$$
$$|$$
$$CH_3$$

Diethylstilbestrol

carcinogen benzo(a)pyrene, a component of cigarette smoke, into its ultimate carcinogenic form. Individuals with lung cancer appear to have a higher level of inducibility of this enzyme system than both smokers and nonsmokers without lung cancer. Perhaps those smokers who never develop lung cancer have a genetically lower concentration of aryl hydrocarbon hydroxylases, and this accounts for their resistance. Cigarette smoke is one of the most potent carcinogen-carrying agents known, containing nearly 7000 chemical substances including many different types of carcinogens. Smoking contributes to cancer not only of the lung, but also at several different sites including the bladder and esophagus. The risk of developing lung cancer in smokers increases if there are other environmental perturbations that can act as cocarcinogens with the cigarette smoke. Thus air pollution contributes significantly to the risk of lung cancer in smokers who live in urban areas. Similarly, workers who smoke and who are exposed to irritants such as coal dust or asbestos are much more likely to develop lung cancer than are similar workers who do not smoke. The incidence of lung cancer appears to be increasing in "passive smokers," people who are constantly ex-posed to smoke from cigarette smokers around them (Trichopoulos, 1981).

Other chemical carcinogens include aniline dyes (bladder cancer), polycyclic hydrocarbons (skin cancer), asbestos (mesothelioma), and amphetamine sulfate (leukemia). Chemical carcinogens commonly found in the environment include nitrites, coal tar, aromatic amines, and aflatoxin B (a product of a common food mold).

Occupational groups at high risk for the development of certain forms of cancer include furniture workers, electoplaters, cannery workers, book binders, jewelers, zinc mixers, and tanners. The list is lengthy, indicating the prevalence of chemical carcinogens within the industrial environment. The general population's exposure to carcinogens is more difficult to quantitate, but some generalizations can be made. Food preservatives and food additives that are in common usage have been shown to be carcinogenic in laboratory animals when used at high concentration.

There is evidence implicating chlorination of water with the development of rectal, colon, and bladder cancer. Chlorine is very commonly used as a purifying agent for drinking water, particularly in urban settings. It is not the chlorine itself, but the action of chlorine on organic compounds such as humic acid, carried in soil, that produces the carcinogens that have now been identified in drinking water. Since November 1981 the government has taken steps to control the concentration of some of these carcinogens to levels below 100 parts per billion for cities with populations greater than 75,000 (Maugh, 1981). In 1984 the same standards were applied to cities with a population between 10,000 and 75,000. Rural dwellers are comparatively protected since many of them drink water that has not been subjected to chlorination.

Commonly used food preservatives and additives have been found to be carcinogenic when used at high concentration in experimental animals. Even food itself may have some carcinogenic potential, depending upon how it is stored and its age when consumed. Several different food molds are capable of producing extremely potent carcinogens. The most well known example is aflatoxin B, produced by the mold *Aspergillus flavus*, which grows in high carbohydrate foods under hot, moist conditions.

Cooking may release or produce carcinogens in food. Charcoal broiling, a common American practice, causes polycyclic hydrocarbons to be formed in the food. Any burnt food, including coffee, has some potential carcinogenic effect.

Nitrites and nitrates are also possible carcinogens and are found in many naturally occurring foods and foods that have been preserved, such as bacon and smoked meats. Nitrate is converted into nitrite in the body to some degree, and nitrite forms nitrosamines, which are carcinogenic. This conversion can be inhibited by vitamin C, leading to the claim that vitamin C is protective against cancer.

There is also evidence that a high fiber, high bulk diet decreases the incidence of colon and rectal cancer by increasing the number and frequency of bowel movements. This prevents prolonged contact of the gastrointestinal tract wall with degradation products of bile acids, which may be carcinogenic in humans. Other research describes an association of a low cholesterol diet with an increased incidence of colon and rectal cancer.

The presence of many chemical carcinogens in the food, air, and water is an indisputable fact. There are many experts who claim that 90% of the known cancers result from environmental causes, over which we presumably have some control. Cancer is the product of chemical carcinogenesis in a host in which other factors interact. This includes the immune system, the psychologic state, the body's defenses and barriers, and numerous genetic factors. Before we can unequivocally accept that cancer is an environmental disease, these phenomena need to be more clearly understood. However, we do need to be tremendously concerned with the quality of our environment. Since the process of carcinogenesis is commonly characterized by a period of latency between the initial carcinogenic exposure and the appearance of actual malignant disease, one can only speculate on the incidence and types of future cancers caused by environmental carcinogens presently acting on human cells.

Many substances have been shown to be carcinogenic in the laboratory. Chemically transformed cells injected into an animal host cause malignant disease in the animal, but such an experiment, of course, cannot be done in humans. Although transformation of human cells in tissue cultures has been shown for many chemical carcinogens, much of the evidence for chemical carcinogenesis in humans has been gathered from epidemiologic investigations, which can only infer a cause-and-effect relationship from statistical evaluation. It must also be mentioned that transformation in vitro by a chemical agent does not always imply carcinogenesis, as many cell lines, human and otherwise, that are grown as tissue cultures in laboratories all over the world commonly undergo spontaneous transformation into neoplastic cells. It is not known why this process occurs, but it could theoretically be because of cell age, reactivation of a latent virus within the tissue culture cells, or exposure of the cells to the essentially abnormal in vitro environment, which is, of course, devoid of the normal hormonal, physiologic, and chemical regulation by the total organism.

Radiation carcinogenesis

Ionizing radiation is mutagenic in all living organisms, and almost from its earliest use radiation was correlated with an increased incidence of cancer among those exposed. The carcinogenic effects of radiation in all its high-energy forms (ultraviolet, x-ray, alpha, beta, and gamma) have been demonstrated both in tissue culture and in whole animals. The most common cancer, skin cancer, unquestionably results from sunlight exposure. Human radiation carcinogenesis has been studied in groups of people accidentally or purposefully exposed to high levels of radiation. These include the survivors of the atomic bombings of Hiroshima and Nagasaki, groups of patients who received radiation therapy for a variety of conditions, and groups of individuals who ingested radioactive materials, such as the radium watch dial painters who ingested radon when they tipped their paint brushes with their lips.

The incidence of leukemia, particularly myeloid leukemia, was greater in the Hiroshima and Nagasaki populations than in the nonexposed Japenese populations. This correlated with the distance of the exposed individual from the hypocenter of the bomb and therefore with radiation dosage. Thyroid tumors also appeared in this population and were characterized by a latency period of 15 to 20 years after exposure. The increased thyroid cancer may have been caused by radioactive iodine fallout after the bombing, which was taken up by the thyroid gland, as is normal iodine, when it was absorbed into the body. Another observation in the exposed Japanese population is the presence of one or more abnormal chromosomes in the circulating blood cells in certain groups. It is not possible to correlate this directly with carcinogenic transformation, however.

Individuals treated with therapeutic irradiation for conditions such as ankylosing spondylitis in general appear to develop leukemia with greater than average frequency. The incidence peaks 4 to 8 years following the irradiation and then falls in incidence to a relatively low level after 15 or more years. Another group of radiation-exposed individuals received thymus gland and tonsil irradiation as children. They have been identified as having a high risk for thyroid tumors, both benign and malignant.

Ingestion or therapeutic injection of bone-seeking radioactive isotopes such as ^{224}Ra also leads to a high incidence of cancer, most commonly osteogenic (bone-forming) tumors.

The degree of radiosensitivity in terms of carcinogenesis differs among the organ systems. The four most common sites for radiation-induced cancer are the lymphoid system, the thyroid, the female breast, and the lung. Background levels of radiation caused by fallout, medical use, and cosmic and naturally occurring radiation is, on the average, 0.2 rads per year. Theoretically, such a dose is responsible for 30 cancer deaths per million people per year (Reif, 1981). This assumes that radiation damage is a linear response to dose received, rather than there being a threshold for radiation damage. This controversy is discussed in more detail in Chapter 5.)

In summary, radiation is a potent carcinogen in humans. Its mechanism of action in carcinogenesis is related to its mutagenic property. In support of this theory is the frequent occurrence of multiple skin tumors in individuals with xeroderma pigmentosum (Fig. 6-4), a rare hereditary defect in which the cellular enzymes that repair ultraviolet light–induced mutations within cellular DNA are missing. Reduced repair of DNA from xeroderma pigmentosum cells has also been observed following

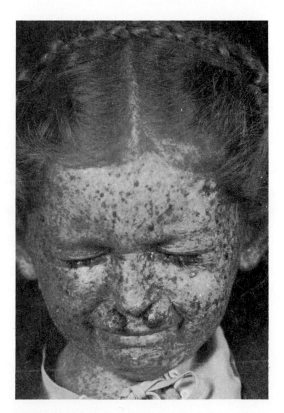

Fig. 6-4. Child suffering from xeroderma pigmentosum. Such a patient inevitably dies of multiple skin carcinomas.

(From del Regato JA and Spjut HJ: Ackerman and del Regato's cancer: diagnosis, treatment, and prognosis, ed 5, St Louis, 1977, The CV Mosby Co.)

exposure to a chemical carcinogen. The etiology of this disease supports the concept that cancer is the result of mutations in the host cell DNA. In xeroderma pigmentosum cells it may be that the initial irreparable mutation allows further transforming events to occur, leading to neoplasia.

Further support also comes from the high incidence of cancer in individuals affected with *Fanconi's anemia*, a hereditary disease characterized by a defect in DNA repair and in which many spontaneous and chemically induced chromosomal breaks have been identified in the cells.

It is probable that radiation damages biologic macromolecules such as DNA through the formation of highly reactive oxygen-free radicals that are formed in cells and that have the further capability of peroxidating other cellular molecules. Since cells are mostly water, this kind of radiation effect is enhanced. Radiation with sufficient energy could also cause carcinogenesis by direct hits on the nuclear DNA, causing mutation, or possibly activating cancer-causing viral DNA sequences present within the genetic code of the individual. This possibility is further discussed in the following section on viral carcinogenesis.

Viral carcinogenesis

Viruses identified as causative agents in the production of tumors are known as *oncogenic viruses*. Many of these have been implicated in animal cancers, but the identification of tumor viruses in humans has been extremely difficult. Oncogenic viruses can transform cells in tissue culture, including human cells, but this is not adequate evidence for viral oncogenicity in the total organism. When viruses have been observed by electron microscopy inside cancer cells, it has not been possible to show whether the viruses caused the malignancy or were merely nonintrusive passengers in the cell. Other means of identification of oncogenic viruses include biochemical determination of viral antigens (proteins specifically coded for by viral DNA), which can be considered as "footprints" of viral presence, or viral nucleic acids, isolation of the virus from the cancer cell, and experimental demonstration of oncogenicity in cell cultures or whole animals.

Only one human cancer has been unequivocally shown to be a result of a retroviral infection. Adult T-cell leukemia, a relatively rare cancer, is caused by a C type RNA viruses, Human T-lymphotropic virus, type I and type II. HTLV-I and II are members of the same family as the virus that causes AIDS (HTLV-III or HIV). Retroviruses contain *reverse transcriptase*, an enzyme that allows RNA to transcribe for DNA, thus permitting exogenously introduced viral RNA to act as a template for the formation of DNA. The viral DNA can then code for specific viral proteins, using the host cell protein-synthesizing machinery. The retroviruses have been implicated in the cause of feline leukemias and appear to be infectious, that is, horizontally transmitted rather than vertically transmitted from parents to offspring through the genes. Retroviruses are also associated with leukemias, sarcomas, and carcinomas of chickens and mice.

While C-type RNA viruses have been identified in human cancer cells, no clear-cut relationship between their presence and the general carcinogenic process has yet been established. All RNA viral transformed cells produce changes in the antigenic makeup of the cell surface. Furthermore, human cancer cells produce virus-specific antigens. Identification of C type viruses in human leukemic cells grown in tissue culture and the observation that leukemic cells contain DNA and RNA with base sequences identical to known primate and murine leukemic viruses have further implicated retroviruses in human leukemia.

Other RNA retroviruses are oncogenic because they carry a particular nucleic acid sequence known as a viral oncogene. These viruses are either nonreplicative and highly transforming or infective and very minimally transforming. Because these viruses cannot replicate inside the cell they are often associated with helper viruses that assist in their replication.

Viruses are often suspected in cancer causation because a nonspecific viral-like illness characterized by fever, malaise, leukocytosis, and upper respiratory symptoms sometimes precedes the onset of acute leukemia. This infectious insult may initiate the leukemic process directly or may simply decrease the immunologic competency of the individual, allowing cancer to occur. Hodgkin's disease also appears to have an infectious, possibly viral, background. The Epstein-Barr virus has been particularly implicated. Clustering of cases of Hodgkin's disease within families, schools, and communities has been reported, further substantiating the viral theory.

Human breast cancer is another malignancy for which evidence has accumulated to implicate viral involvement, specifically a B-type RNA virus (Bittner factor). This virus has been identified in mouse mammary gland carcinoma and can be transmitted through the mother's milk to the suckling mice or vertically from parents to offspring through the gametes. If virus-free mice of a certain strain are injected with the Bittner factor, the virus concentrates in the mammary gland, which then proceeds to produce virus particles in large quantities. When these mice eventually lactate at 8 to 10 months of age, many will have developed mammary tumors. Identification of a similar virus in association with human breast cancer has been attempted, and a small amount of Bittner factor can be found, but human milk also contains factors that destroy it. A virus like the Bittner factor has been found replicating in a line of tissue-cultured cells derived from a human breast cancer. Human milk also contains an RNA-directed DNA polymerase, which is perhaps of viral origin. An oncogene is amplified in breast cancer tissue, and the degree of activity is strongly correlated with prognosis (Kolata, 1987). Additional evidence for a viral origin in human breast cancer is provided by the discovery that there are nucleic acid base sequences in human breast cancer that are nearly identical to those of the murine mammary tumor virus. It has also been shown that the leukocytes from many human breast cancer patients are immunologically sensitized to their own tumors and to *other* breast cancer patients' tumors. As a further note, immunization of many strains of laboratory mice by formalin-inactivated mouse mammary tumor virus has been carried out successfully with a resultant dramatic drop in the incidence of mammary tumors among the mice.

DNA viruses have also been linked with human cancers. The best documented relationship is between *Burkitt's lymphoma*, a malignancy of the jaw region found with striking predominance in malarial belts of Central Africa, and the Epstein-Barr virus (EBV), the causative agent of infectious mononucleosis. EBV is a herpeslike virus that infects only B lymphocytes and may remain in a latent state in the cells after the initial infection. Some environmental factors may then interact with the latent virus, causing it to become oncogenic. The EBV can transform lymphocytes in vitro,

and continuous lymphoblastoid cell lines can be easily established in vitro from Burkitt's tumor tissue. Nucleic acid like that from EBV has been detected in 98% of African Burkitt's lymphoma biopsies. The antibody titer against the viral antigen falls and rises with tumor regression and recurrence.

Other herpesviruses have also been strongly implicated. The herpes simplex virus is well known as the causative agent of cold sores and fever blisters in humans and is highly prevalent among the human population, existing in a latent state that is subject to reactivation by a variety of agents, such as exposure to high temperature or radiation. Another member of the herpesvirus family, herpesvirus II, also infects humans and can lie dormant subject to reactivation. The virus can cause genital infection, which has been shown in females to be associated with the later development of cervical cancer. Patients who develop malignancy have a high titer of antibodies to the virus, and the malignant cells contain viral DNA, RNA, and proteins. Preinvasive cervical cancer cells have also been reported to contain herpesvirus antigens.

Hepatitis B infection of the liver is associated with an increased incidence of liver cancer, as is chronic hepatitis. It seems likely that the viral infection per se does not cause cancer, but rather depresses the immune capability of the liver to handle other types of carcinogenic insults. Because it is the liver that does the major work of detoxification of chemicals, including chemical carcinogens, such as assumption seems reasonable.

Oncogenes

RNA tumor viruses (retroviruses) are responsible for many animal tumors, and the sequence of nucleic acid that determines oncogenicity is known for many of them. Such sequences have been genetically mapped and termed "viral oncogenes" or "v-oncs." The first identified v-onc (the src gene) was linked to tumors in chickens and found to be part of the Rous sarcoma virus. Since then, 20 viral oncogenes from various tumor viruses have been identified. Many of these RNA sequences have also been discovered in human cells, as part of the normal human genome. These are termed "proto-oncogenes," and these nucleic acid sequences code for normal human proteins. Expression of these proto-oncogenes does not change the phenotype of the cell, or in and of itself, cause malignant transformation. When the initial homology between viral oncogenes and cellular proto-oncogenes was discovered, there was great excitement in the cancer research community. It was belived that cellular proto-oncogenes were the cancer genes, and the proteins that they coded for must be transforming proteins. Furthermore, it was suggested that all carcinogens might act by derepressing these cellular oncogenes, turning on activity of a normally repressed gene. These genes were believed to be developmentally important genes that participated in embryogenesis or tissue growth, but when activated in the mature organisms led to the uncontrolled growth of cancer.

More recent understandings of proto-oncogenes suggest that this is too simplisitic a picture (Duesberg, 1985). Viral oncogenes are not as strikingly homologous with proto-oncogenes as was initially suspected, although the origin of the nucleic acid in the oncogenic virus is clearly animal. The virus picks up ("rescues") and incorporates part of the cellular proto-oncogenic material into its RNA, a process known as transduction, and the result is implanted cellular RNA with tremendously altered function once in the viral particle environment. The piece of proto-oncogene comes under the control of viral regulatory genes and is now a v-onc. Because the isolation of oncogenic viruses has been only from tumorous tissue, it seems that the virus in the process of infecting a cell undergoes a rare recombinational event, producing a virus that is transforming rather than infective. Oncogenic viruses are newly arisen particles incapable of self-replication (because they are not infective), unless assisted by the presence of helper viruses. These oncogenic changes do not become a permanent part of the viruses' genetic code, because they are not necessary for virus survival and are quickly eliminated. Presumably then such oncogenic events arise de novo from viral and proto-oncogenic combinations that are accidental and unusual events. When these viral particles are isolated from human or animal neoplasms and then put into tissue cultures, they are extremely efficient in transforming the cells. A single gene introduction causes cancer in this situation. For most cancers though, a multi-stage model of carcinogenesis is accepted. Oncogene activation and viral involvement would only be part of the carcinogenic process under most circumstances, probably acting as initiating factors.

Because the transduction confers carcinogeneity on the virus, it is speculated that the human proto-oncogenes, under other than normal circumstances, might develop carcinogenic potential. For example, if retroviral DNA becomes inserted directly into the human cellular DNA, the viral genes could begin to regulate the expression of the proto-oncogene. If proto-oncogenes become translocated they might end up next to inappropriate regulatory genes that could alter their normal function. Proto-oncogenes and/or their normal regulator genes might be mutated by chemical carcinogens, viral infection, or radiation and produce altered proto-oncogenes. A frequent human cellular proto-oncogene is "c-myc" (which has been localized to human chromosome 15). However, other mutated, inappropriately amplified, or translocated proto-oncogenes have been identified (Bishop, 1987). Altered c-myc is associated with Burkitt's lymphoma, small cell carcinoma of the lung, and breast cancer; altered c-abl with chronic myelogenous leukemia; altered c-erb with squamous cell cancer and glioblastoma; and altered c-ras with several other cancers. Some cancers may have several proto-oncogenes involved, and a cascade of sequential oncogene activation may be necessary (Slamon, 1984).

There are subtle ways by which oncogenes influence carcinogenesis. Overt chromosomal breaks and translocations are associated with certain malignancies and many of these have been shown to occur at chromosomal sites of oncogenes. Oncogene activation, alteration, or mutation may result in an excessive, unregulated, or chemically-altered gene product.

These proteins have functions in gene regulation and growth. C-sis codes for platelet-derived growth factor, c-erb for epithelial growth factor, and c-abl and c-ras codes for embryonic proteins (Welch and Bhuyan, 1986). All proto-oncogenes thus far identified code for proteins that act in only four ways (Bishop, 1987). They phosphorylate proteins, bind GTP, control mRNA production, or influence DNA replication. Nevertheless, as the research on oncogenes evolves, the long hoped for single origin of cancer is still elusive, although the importance of the cellular DNA in initiating carcinogenesis is confirmed.

Interesting ideas for treatment based on oncogene function included blocking of the gene, blocking of the gene product, or genetic activity modulation. Some experimental attempts to genetically manipulate human cancers through these mechanisms are currently being attempted.

Hormones and physical injury

Hormones and physical injury have both been implicated in neoplastic transformation. Estrogen may play a role in the development of both male and female breast cancer. Progesterone acts as a cocarcinogen with viruses or chemicals in the production of murine mammary tumors. In 1975 evidence suggested that endometrial cancer was associated with postmenopausal hormone replacement therapy, suggesting a role for female sex hormones in carcinogenesis. A decrease in use of hormonal therapy since then has been associated with a drop in endometrial cancer incidence. Another hormone, *diethylstilbestrol*, administered to prevent threatened abortion, has been linked to an increased incidence of vaginal and testicular cancer in the children of the women on whom it was used as these children reach puberty.

It is difficult to imagine that physiologic levels of hormones can be carcinogenic. It seems more likely that hormones act indirectly when elevated, by enhancing normal cellular proliferation until neoplastic transformation occurs. When depleted, they may act by failing to inhibit target cells so that uninhibited cells proliferate and become neoplastic. Hormones may also potentiate the conversion of normal cells to malignant cells when carcinogenesis has been initiated by another agent. Lastly, hormones may support the growth and spread of an established tumor.

Irritation and physical injury may also

play a role in carcinogenesis. The early experiments on tar-induced skin cancer in the rabbit demonstrated that cancers developed frequently around injured areas of the skin. Some investigators have suggested that the neoplastic process itself is a response to injury and represents an uncontrolled "overhealing" reaction. Continuous irritation of a premalignant lesion may result in transformation. For example, the development of malignant melanoma from a previously benign pigmented mole that has been subject to prolonged irritation supports this concept of carcinogenesis. Ulcerative colitis, polyposis coli (a familial disease characterized by polyps of the colon that frequently become malignant), and a high meat diet all predispose to cancer of the colon, and all may act by continual irritation. When *20-methylcholanthrene* is applied to animal skin, followed by weekly treatment of the site with an irritant, neoplasia may result in malignancy. However, 20-methylcholanthrene alone does not cause cancer. The irritant may act by promoting the malignant change initiated by the chemical. Lung cancer, therefore, could theoretically be initiated by chemical carcinogens in the environment and promoted by the highly irritating as well as carcinogenic components of cigarette smoke.

Mind-body relationships in cancer

Although we have focused on environmental, genetic, and cellular phenomena in the preceding discussions, we cannot negate the powerful influences of the behavioral state, degree of stress, and personal belief system on the development and morbidity of cancer (psycho-oncology). For many years researchers have been examining the contribution of these "soft" influences and the "hard" (biologic and chemical) influences. Early literature suggested that there was a particular cancer personality,

one characterized by repression and hopelessness. Although these latter characteristics may interface with other phenomena to produce the setting in which cancer arises and grows, a particular personality syndrome probably does not exist. What does appear to be important is stress in all its manifestations. The unifying link between the mind and the body is the influence of psychoneuroimmunology (see Chapter 2 for a more in-depth discussion). Briefly, recall that various arms of the immune system are involved in cancer cell surveillance, identification, and removal. The helper T cells, NK cells, and macrophages are most directly involved in this process. Stress is known to suppress the immune system, through corticosteroid action, central mechanisms, and autonomic nervous system secretions. Decreased immunologic strength results in increased susceptibility to infection, autoimmune diseases, and malignancy. An essential element of this theoretical explanation is that cancer cells have recognizable and altered cell surface antigens, which are recognized by the immune system and reacted against (Fig. 6-5). There are two schools of thought with regard to this, and the evidence for unique cancer antigens is still accumulating and not definitive.

More important than the presence of stress is the ability of a person to cope with the stressor. Coping includes psychologic and physiologic mechanisms to adapt to the stressor and to limit its pathophysiologic effects. Let us review the studies that support a relationship between psychosocial factors, coping, and cancer.

There is a link between cancer and depression, although depression is a state that is stressful in and of itself and associated with hypercortisolism (see Chapter 11). Certainly, people who are diagnosed

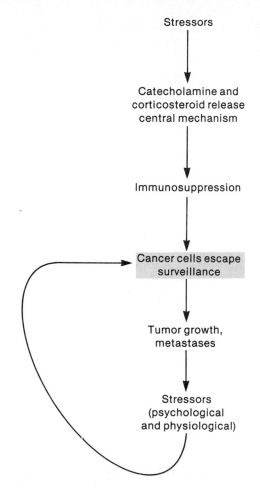

Stressors

↓

Catecholamine and
corticosteroid release
central mechanism

↓

Immunosuppression

↓

Cancer cells escape
surveillance

↓

Tumor growth,
metastases

↓

Stressors
(psychological
and physiological)

Fig. 6-5. The relationship between stress, immuno-supression, and cancer.

with cancer usually have some depression associated with this diagnosis. Preceding pathologic depression may predict incidence and mortality from cancer, as reported recently for a 20-year study (Persky, 1987). However, a general state of chronically mild distress may be more important. Loss and cancer development is another potential feature of the carcinogenic process. Loss of a loved one leading to bereavement is the greatest social readjustment factor on the Holmes-Rahe scale (see Chapter 7), and research supports the

notion of such loss producing prolonged immunosuppression and increased incidence of cancer risk. Many of the studies on life events and cancer have been criticized for methodologic reasons and refuted by other studies, so this research is not definitive. However, there is enough information available about stressful life events and increased cancer incidence to generally accept the relationship.

An important intermediary in this relationship appears to be social support. For those without strong family and friendship relationships, life events appear more stressful and more likely to cause cancer. A person probably at greatest risk for developing cancer would be a grieving widow or widower, lonely, isolated and without a social support network to offer him solace and comfort. Feelings of hopelessness and helplessness seem to provide the soil in which malignant cells flourish.

Many animal studies show that both acute and chronic laboratory stressors increase cancer likelihood, enhance tumor growth and metastases, and decrease survival from cancer. If the animals have been exposed to a stressor that is inescapable, the effect is enhanced, and if the animals have some coping abilities, the effect is diminished (Bieliauskas, 1984). Coping in humans is also probably important in cancer survival. Studies summarized by Dreher (1987) on breast cancer and malignant melanoma patients indicated that a fighting spirit and denial were two coping strategies associated with longer survival, whereas stoicism and hopelessness were linked to shorter survival. For most people with cancer, the disease progression is marked by further immunosuppression, resulting from chemotherapy, radiation, cachexia, and stress. It is an uphill battle for an individual to maintain a strong immune system in these circumstances. If malignant growth is being held in check by immune mechanisms, it is likely that such control is tentative and easily threatened once a patient is diagnosed and treatment begun. Cancer patients suffer many potentially avoidable psychosocial stresses (Feldman, 1984). People may suffer from the reactions of others to their diagnosis or to disabilities that they have. They may be rejected, isolated, and dismissed from employment. Depression is common, and they may suffer uncertainty about their disease and the treatment that is prescribed. Thus if the precepts of behavioral immunology hold true, stress may be involved not only in cancer development, but also in continuing tumor growth, morbidity, and mortality.

PATHOPHYSIOLOGY OF MALIGNANT DISEASE IN HOST
Immunologic responses to cancer cells

The provocation of an immunologic response by the host to cancer cells growing within the body has been well documented. Cancer cells produce proteins, known as antigens, some of which are specifically associated with the tumor cell membranes and which appear to elicit a cellular and humoral response by the immune system, with antibodies produced in response to the tumor-specific antigens. Two antigen groups that have been well characterized are the carcinoembryonic antigens (CEA) and alpha fetoprotein. Malignancies produced by oncogenic viruses appear to produce the same groups of viral antigens in a variety of hosts, whereas tumors that result from chemical- or radiation-induced carcinogens produce nonspecific antigens that are different in every host. A normal immunologic surveillance system would recognize the tumor-specific antigens as abnormal proteins and react against them. Up to 10 million cancer cells could be totally destroyed by the normal host defense response. However, a clini-

cally detectable neoplasm, 1 cm in diameter, contains approximately 1 billion cells. Thus even in individuals with apparently in situ palpable lesions of a barely detectable size, the immune system has likely been overwhelmed by the malignant mass.

Tumors constantly shed antigens that circulate in the bloodstream as antigens or antigen-antibody complexes. The soluble antigens may block the recognition and destruction of the malignant cells by T-lymphocytes.

Helper T cells along with macrophages participate in the effective destruction of the tumor cells by cytotoxic T killer cells. Suppressor T cells block the function of B cells and other T cells. Malignant cells may stimulate the generation of more suppressor cells. The continuous production of tumor cell antigens by the growing tumor over time may be a significant factor in stimulating the development of a large population of suppressor cells. Thus while cells that have the immune capacity to destroy a tumor are most certainly produced in cancer, it is possible that many more suppressor cells also are produced, essentially overwhelming the first response.

Another possibility is that B-lymphocytes may produce blocking antibodies that block the cells from attack by T cells and protect them from immunologically mediated destruction. This is depicted in Fig. 6-6. Tumor growth may be further enhanced by the generalized state of immunodepression that is commonly seen in patients with advanced cancer. This is a result of the generalized cachexia that is present and the usual modes of therapy for cancer. Most cancer treatments depress the body's ability to produce an immune reaction.

Suppression of the immune system can result in increased tumor incidence or enhancement of an existing tumor's growth, as has been reported for a number of on-

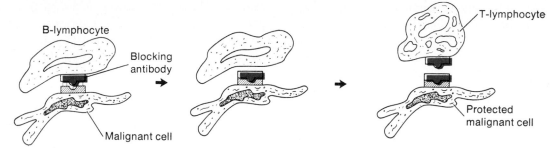

Fig. 6-6. Blocking antibodies and malignancy. Tumor cells may be protected from immune recognition by and interaction with T-lymphocytes by an initial B-lymphocyte reaction with malignant cell. B-lymphocyte may transfer blocking antibody to malignant cell as illustrated. T-lymphocyte receptor thus is blocked and cell protected.

cogenic virus-induced cancers. Furthermore, individuals with immunodepressive diseases or those treated with immunosuppressive drug therapy have an extraordinarily high rate of cancer. Depression of the immune system by such things as a simple viral infection in a normal individual may allow a transient loss of immunocompetence that is sufficient to permit cancer cells previously held in check to grow and spread. When immunologic suppression occurs, the T-lymphocyte killer cells' surveillance becomes inadequate, and malignant cell antigens will drain into the bloodstream. Cancer therapy initiated at this time may reduce the number of tumor cells to a number manageable for the immune system, and the malignant disease may be eradicated. However, a second immunodepressive event occurring before the dissemination of the malignant cells has been controlled might result in an overwhelming release of the cells from immunologic surveillance and control, and widespread metastasis would then occur.

It is also possible that carcinogens themselves, by being *intrinsically* immunodepressive, enhance their cancer-producing effects. There have been reports of depressed cellular immunity in patients with cancer. It may also be that the individual who develops cancer may not be able to launch a sufficiently great enough immune response to tumor antigens, a phenomenon that could perhaps be genetically determined.

Immunotherapy, combined as an adjuvant with other forms of cancer therapy, has been used successfully with many patients in the last 10 years. The incidence of spontaneous regressions of neuroblastomas, Burkitt's lymphomas, and choriocarcinomas and the relationship of such regressions to reported immunologic reactions in the host certainly justify further exploration and expanded use of immunotherapy in cancer. Four major types of immunotherapy are currently in use. A general stimulation of the immune system, a response that is nonspecific and poorly understood, by BCG (bacillus Calmette Guerin), a bacterial material used for the prevention of tuberculosis for many years, has resulted in clinical improvements in patients with malignant melanoma and leukemia. *Passive immunization*, or immunization of an individual with material from another host previously immunized with cancer-specific antigens, has not been successful in human recipients, but animal studies have shown that passive immunization with antiserums or lymphoid cells is possible. *Active immunization* in humans with certain tumor vaccines that have been inactivated by such techniques as irradiation, heat, or treatment with mitomycin C so that the tumor cells contained in the vaccines cannot proliferate in the recipient also holds considerable promise in cancer therapy. A drawback to immunotherapy is the possible transfer of antibodies to the individual with cancer, which can inhibit the host's own immune response to tumor antigens, resulting in a stimulus to tumor growth.

Recent immunotherapeutic approaches have attempted to use the body's own natural antitumor chemicals to attack malignant cells. A patient's own immune cells can be made more cytotoxic, by treating them with substances such as interferon and interleukin 2. The patient, usually one with advanced cancer, has blood withdrawn and a suspension of lymphocytes is obtained and treated with I1 2. The cells are injected back into the patient. Patients are also administered I1 2 parenterally as part of this treatment. The interleukin bolsters the anticancer activity of the lymphocytes and in early studies has produced remissions and tumor shrinkage (Marx, 1985). I1 2 appears to be most effective against solid tumors, whereas alpha interferon works against leukemias and lymphomas. The experience with interferon as an immunologic adjuvant has been more extensive than I1 2, which is still experimental. Nevertheless, manipulation of the body's natural defenses as an anticancer therapy is very promising.

Anorexia-cachexia syndrome

Cancer provokes many responses in the host apart from an immunologic one. Most systemic and organ-specific responses are poorly understood. The most damaging and debilitating systemic response to cancer is the development of cachexia, which is observed in at least two thirds of all cancer patients. Cachectic wasting is the most common cause of death in patients with cancer of the breast, stomach, and colon or rectum. It is, nevertheless, not exclusively a terminal symptom but may actually be the reason that an individual with undiagnosed cancer consults a physician. Weight loss of unexplained origin is often the first recognized sign of cancer. Cachexia is manifested by weight loss, wasting, weakness with resultant loss of mobility, anemia, fluid and electrolyte disturbances, malnutrition, increased basal metabolic rate, and anorexia. It appears that anorexia is so intimately related to the development of cachectic wasting that together they comprise the *anorexia-cachexia syndrome* (Fig. 6-7). It has long been thought that cachexia results from special nutritional demands of the tumor that compete with the host for those specific nutrients. It is also believed that tumors release specific anorexigenic substances that can act directly on the hypothalamic satiety and feeding center. The evidence for a specific competitive uptake of substances by malignant tissue or specific lack of nutrients in the host is sketchy. The evidence for a direct hypothalamic effect is also controversial.

Voluntary food intake declines in the cancer patient, and this anorexia appears to be the major cause of the cachexia. Many patients have altered taste sensations and marked aversions to certain foods.

When a person becomes nauseated, during chemotherapy or radiation therapy for example, there is a possibility of conditioned responses occuring while the patient is ill. Sensory stimuli, such as foods and certain odors, might become nega-

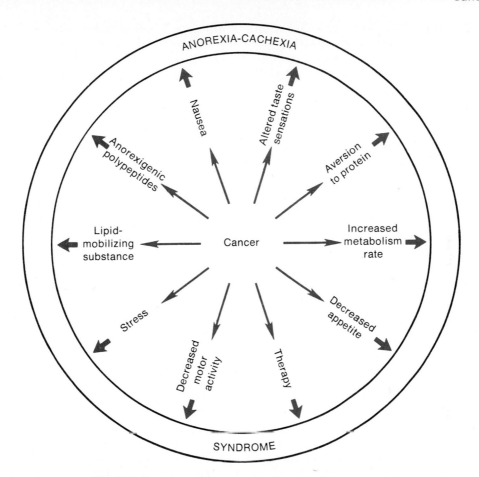

Fig. 6-7. Factors contributing to anorexia-cachexia syndrome.

tively associated with the feelings of nausea if they were present at the time of the therapy. This may lead to conditioned, prolonged food and taste aversions. This kind of conditioning paradigm may be important in producing the typical taste aversions of cancer patients, which then contribute to cachexia.

The anorexia is probably caused by a multifactorial disturbance in the host's metabolism. The anorexia not only contributes significantly to the development of cachexia, but also the cachexia appears to act in a positive feedback manner to reinforce the anorexia. Anorexia-cachexia develops as the result of many interacting factors. Metabolic abnormalities may play a major role, since many biochemical pathways are disturbed. Early in the disease process, many cancer patients have abnormal glucose metabolism, which is characterized by a syndrome that resembles diabetes mellitus. There is hyperinsulinemia, hyperglycemia, and an abnormal glucose tolerance test. Some patients with early malignancies have actually been initially diagnosed as having diabetes mellitus. Substances released by malignant tissue have been implicated in this alteration. Other factors may also be responsible, but the result is an increase in the metabolic utilization of the *Cori cycle*, which produces glucose from amino acids (gluconeogenesis). Cancer cells rely more on anaerobic metabolism and preferentially use glucose as a fuel. Normally there is protein sparing, even during starvation, but in cancer there is equal utilization of protein and lipid for energy early in the disease. The amino acids that fuel the Cori cycle come from tissue protein, and muscle and blood proteins become depleted, leading to a negative nitrogen balance. The typical wasting of anorexia-cachexia is the end result of this process.

The glucose that is produced from amino acid is not efficiently used since there is a state of cellular insulin resistance. Some authorities have suggested use of insulin in the cachectic patient, so that glucose will be more normally utilized. This may also slow down glucose production from the Cori cycle. There are efforts to detect exactly what is the initiator in the carbohydrate and protein metabolic abnormalities, since this could possibly eventually be blocked by other chemicals and could serve as a new nutritional therapy regimen for the cancer patient.

The development of cachexia is enhanced by other pathologic processes disturbing the normal physiology of the cancer patient, such as obstruction of the gastrointestinal tract by a malignant mass, hemorrhage, necrosis, ulceration, infection, nausea, and impaired tissue or organ function from tumor invasion and destruction. It is also further reinforced by the physiologic and psychologic stress that is so common in the patient with cancer and that may initiate a nonspecific stress alarm syndrome, which may result in anorexia. The tumor may also produce amino acids and polypeptides that inhibit food intake, such as those seen in patients with uremia. Furthermore, the chemotherapy and radiation given for the malignant disease may itself cause an aversion to protein foods in the cancer patient, enhancing and perpetuating the anorexia-cachexia syndrome.

Summary

Many patients with anorexia-cachexia are aided by a form of feeding known as total parenteral nutrition (TPN), if enteral feeding is not possible. Intravenous nutrient solutions containing all the necessary dietary requirements are infused, resulting in an increase in nutritional status. The effect often is multiple, with the patient feeling better and tolerating treatment regimens so that the tumor burden may decrease. Immune function is also enhanced by a positive nutritional balance. Although the person's nutritional status improves on TPN, there is some evidence that the tumor uses these nutrients for its own growth (Dewys, 1985). The general effect of nutrition on cancer morbidity and mortality appears to be small.

The major effect of the host on the tumor appears to be the attempt by the immune system to destroy the tumor, which for most individuals with cancer is an inadequate response. The major effect of the tumor on the host is the development of cachexia, immunologic suppression, and specific symptoms related to the type of tumor and its location in the body.

TUMOR TYPES

It is common to consider cancer as a group of often chronic diseases. The specific signs and symptoms of each cancer are related not only to the basic pathophysiology of the cancer cell and the host's response but also to the tumor type. Great variability exists among both individuals and tumor types. The following discussion will present some common forms of cancer as disease models. An understanding of these disease processes must be underscored by a knowledge of the pathophysiology of malignancy as previously presented.

While an exhaustive description of the common malignant diseases of humans is not possible in a book of this type, some tumor types will be described as illustrative models of cancer. The reader is referred to textbooks of clinical oncology for further reading.

Skin cancer

Skin carcinomas arise from the epithelium and are of two basic types: basal cell carcinoma and epidermoid or squamous cell carcinoma. These represent the most common form of all cancers, increasing in incidence with age. These malignancies rarely metastasize, and cause damage mainly through invasion of underlying structures. They respond extremely well to treatment, with a 90% or higher cure rate. Skin cancers usually occur more frequently on exposed surfaces such as the hands, head, and face. A number of factors predispose to the development of skin cancer. These include a history of chronic sun, radiation, or arsenic exposure, particularly in fair-skinned people. A long latency period before the cancer appears is characteristic. Fig. 6-8 shows the effects of radiation carcinogenesis on the skin. *Senile keratosis* (a thickening and pigmentation of the skin that occurs with age) also predisposes to skin malignancy.

Basal cell carcinoma usually begins as a painless, pearly gray nodule, often on the face. It almost never metastasizes but can grow and ulcerate and eventually invade underlying tissue, bone, and cartilage.

Squamous cell carcinoma appears initially as a slow growing, scaly, raised lesion resembling a wart. The tumor usually

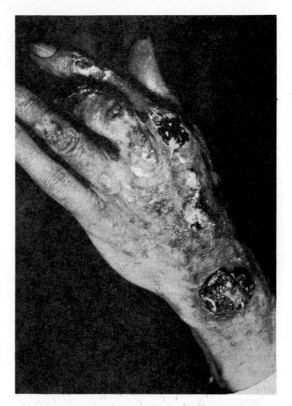

Fig. 6-8. Skin cancer and radiation. X-ray dermatitis and multiple carcinomas of 5 years' duration in 83-year-old male physician after 15 years of repeated small exposure to x-ray irradiation.

(From Anderson WAD and Kissane JM, editors: Pathology, ed 7, St Louis, 1977, The CV Mosby Co.)

arises from a previously hyperkeratotic patch on the hands, cheeks, or ears. The lesion will eventually ulcerate and become painful and invasive. Metastasis can occur through the lymphatics but does so only rarely.

The treatment is excision of the lesion and occasionally radiation. There is always a possibility of recurring skin cancer after treatment as well as the appearance of new primary tumors in susceptible individuals. Follow-up of patients treated for skin cancer should therefore be done on a regular basis.

Another form of skin cancer is *malignant*

melanoma, which arises from melanocytes (pigment cells) in a previously benign pigmented nevus. This mole is usually present for many years before malignant transformation takes place, and it has been suggested that exposure to sunlight and chronic irritation may play precipitating roles in the transformation. Malignant melanoma is the rarest form of skin cancer and by far the most pathologic. It is most common in whites between 40 and 70 years of age. The usual history is a sudden increase in the growth of a mole on the head, neck, or lower limbs, which becomes elevated and more pigmented and often bleeds. The gross appearance of the melanoma is of a heavily pigmented, firm, ulcerated lesion, which may be surrounded by elevated satellite nodules or dark fingerlike projections. The malignant cells have often infiltrated the lymphatics before the diagnosis is made and treatment instituted. The 5-year survival rate ranges from 70% to 0% depending on the size, depth, and location of the lesion and the extent of local and distant metastasis. The treatment of malignant melanoma is wide, local, surgical excision of the tumor and surrounding lymphatics, and this is often followed by chemotherapy and immunotherapy.

Other forms of skin cancer do occur, but over 90% of all skin malignancies are of the three types that have been discussed. Aside from malignant melanoma, skin cancer represents the most curable form of cancer and one in which the disease process is best understood.

Cancers of the gastrointestinal tract

Malignancy can occur in all parts of the gastrointestinal tract, but the most common types are cancer of the colon, rectum, and anus. It can be stated generally that the prognosis for gastrointestinal tract cancer improves for cancers of the lower part of the tract as compared with the upper alimentary canal. For example, cancer of the esophagus carries with it a 5 year survival rate of only 4%, whereas cancer of the colon has a 50% 5-year survival rate, and this could be vastly improved with earlier diagnosis.

Stomach cancer. Cancer of the stomach has been decreasing markedly in incidence over the last 30 years. No explanation for this phenomenon has been forthcoming, but some unknown dietary factor may be responsible. The decrease in incidence has been most noticeable in the United States. A diet that is high in starch and low in fresh fruits and vegetables may cause stomach cancer. Japan has a much higher death rate from stomach cancer, and the incidence is high among the American Japanese ethnic group. In general among all races and countries, there is a 2:1 male prevalence of occurrence.

There are a number of predisposing conditions, which include chronic gastric ulcers, pernicious anemia, and polyposis (multiple stomach polyps). Almost all cancers of the stomach arise from glandular cells and are adenocarcinomas. The signs and symptoms of this type of cancer are often vague and include epigastric pain, weight loss, anorexia, iron-deficiency anemia, and melena (blood in the stool). It is common for the symptoms to be so mild as to warrant no concern on the part of the patient until liver and peritoneal metastasis has occurred.

Ulcers that do not respond to the conventional forms of treatment should be suspected of malignancy. Diagnosis is made by barium studies of the upper gastrointestinal tract, gastroscopy and biopsy, and laparotomy. The usual treatment is surgical excision of the tumor and a large part of or the entire stomach, procedures known as subtotal and total gastrectomies. The prognosis for patients with cancer of the stomach is not good, as approximately 42% will be inoperable at the time of surgery. Of the remaining, the 5-year survival rate ranges from 8% to 25%. Distant metastases to the liver (Fig. 6-9), peritoneum, lung, and bone are the most common sites. When the regional stomach lymph nodes show no evidence of malignant cells, the 5-year survival rate may reach 67%, but with positive lymph nodes the chances for survival are small.

Cancer of the colon, rectum, and anus. Colon and rectal cancers carry with them the second highest death rate of any cancers in the United States and are the most prevalent internal cancers in this country. Both men and women are equally affected. Remarkably low incidence among the general population is reported in Japan and Finland.

This type of cancer generally appears after the age of 50, except in individuals who have been predisposed to this malignancy by ulcerative colitis or familial polyposis coli. *Chronic colitis* (inflammation of the colon, often associated with ulceration and bleeding) places individuals at a definite risk for colon cancer. This is particularly true if the chronic colitis began in adolescence. *Familial polyposis coli* is an hereditary condition that is inherited by mendelian dominant transmission. Polyps develop in the colon of affected individuals, and over a period of years the colon becomes a virtual bed of polyps, which have a marked tendency to undergo malignant transformation, the incidence of occurrence being nearly 100% as the affected individuals grow older.

Diet has been implicated as a major fac-

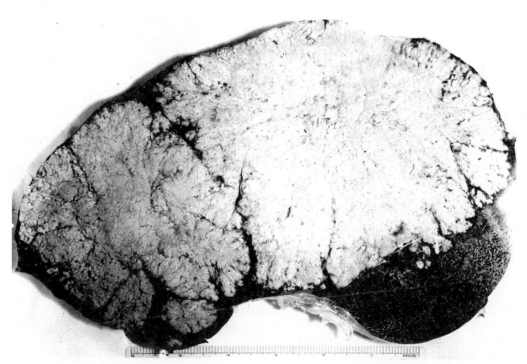

Fig. 6-9. Section of liver showing almost complete replacement of parenchyma by metastatic carcinoma. Primary tumor was in colon.

(From Anderson WAD and Kissane JM, editors: Pathology, ed 7, St Louis, 1977, The CV Mosby Co.)

tor in cancer of the colon. The incidence of this cancer is high in countries that have diets high in meat and low in undigestible cellulose. It is thought that the length of time of contact of fecal material with the colonic wall may be an important etiologic factor. Breakdown products of bile may be carcinogenic, and long exposure to these products may initiate carcinogenic transformation.

The signs and symptoms of lower gastrointestinal tract tumors depend upon the location and size of the tumor. Generally, rectal bleeding is the first sign and is often attributed to hemorrhoids, which are often present concurrently. A change in the normal bowel habits is another significant sign, and many patients also report abdominal cramping or pain. A small percentage of patients have no symptoms at all. Bowel obstruction can occur (Fig. 6-10) but may be so well compensated for by hypertrophy of the muscular lining of the large intestine that tumors may reach a fairly large size before producing significant symptoms, particularly if the tumor is located in the right colon. Many patients with colonic cancer develop a profound anemia, which may be the first sign of the disease.

It is important to note that 50% of all cancers of the colon and rectum can be detected by digital examination through the anus, and two thirds can be diagnosed through the use of the sigmoidoscope. This procedure should be part of the routine physical examination for all patients in high-risk groups. Diagnosis of cancer is made by sigmoidoscopy, barium enema, and biopsy. It is believed that this tumor grows quite slowly in situ, and early detection before metastasis and invasion have occurred would result in an excellent prognosis. The usual treatment for colonic cancer is removal of the colon segment containing the cancer and subsequent

Fig. 6-10. Constricting carcinoma of colon with dilation of bowel proximal to tumor. Pedunculated polyp is incidental finding.

(From Anderson WAD and Kissane JM, editors: Pathology, ed 7, St Louis, 1977, The CV Mosby Co.)

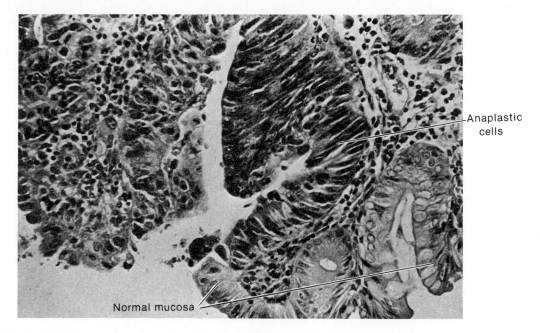

Anaplastic
cells

Normal mucosa

Fig. 6-11. Cancer of colon. Area of malignant anaplastic cells is found adjacent to normal mucosa.
(Courtesy Department of Pathology, University of Tennessee, Memphis.)

anastomosis of the adjacent ends of the intestine. A permanent colostomy may be necessary if the tumor is low and involves the rectum. The 5-year survival rate ranges from 25% to 50%. Fig. 6-11 shows the contrast of malignant cells with normal cells in the colonic mucosa.

Cancer of the pancreas. Cancer of the pancreas should be mentioned, as its general incidence is increasing rapidly, and it now can be considered among the five major sites of cancer and the most common gastrointestinal gland cancer. No known etiologic factors have been found for this carcinoma except possibly excessive coffee drinking. The presenting symptoms are often pain, anorexia, weight loss, indigestion, and nausea. The tumor may invade other abdominal structures such as the duodenum and cause obstructive disease with enlargement of the gallbladder and jaundice. Metastasis to the liver is common, and the disease process is extremely

morbid and rapid, so that only 10% of these patients are still alive 1 year from the time of first diagnosis. The treatment is surgical and palliative chemotherapy.

Reproductive tract cancers

Cancer of the prostate. Cancer of the prostate gland is the most common form of cancer in men over the age of 50 aside from skin cancer. It is most common in the United States, and the etiology is unknown but may be hormonal in nature. Most prostatic tumors are adenocarcinomas and almost always involve the posterior lobe of the gland. The early symptoms of this malignancy are easily confused with benign prostatic hypertrophy, which is common in older men. These symptoms include dysuria, hematuria, dribbling, and retention of urine in the bladder, which may cause cystitis. Pain may also be present and is referred to the bladder, urethra, rectum, perineum, and occasionally to the sacrum and legs, when it may be confused with sciatica. This cancer can be diagnosed by rectal examination followed by biopsy. Treatment is radical prostatectomy, which may be followed by radiation therapy. Patients may be treated nonsurgically if the stage of the malignancy or the general age and condition of the patient warrant it. This involves the administration of estrogens as a palliative measure. The metastasizing cells apparently require male hormonal support, which is masked by the administration of estrogen. Estrogen therapy often significantly relieves pain and anorexia-cachexia in patients with incurable advanced disease.

The 5-year survival rate ranges from 25% to 70%, depending on the stage of advancement of the disease at the time of diagnosis. The most common sites of metastases for prostatic cancer are the bone and lungs.

Cancers of the cervix and uterus. Cancer of the cervix represents that rare carcinoma that can be easily detected while in situ, before invasion or metastasis can take place and by a relatively simple and inexpensive screening procedure known as the *Papanicolaou smear*. Cytologic examination of the cells obtained by this smear of the cervix can detect not only carcinoma but also premalignant dysplasia, a condition that may be present 5 to 10 years before frank invasive carcinoma develops. It is thought that the natural progression of this cancer is from cervical epithelial dysplasia, to carcinoma in situ (of the squamous cell variety), to invasive carcinoma. Treatment of cervical carcinoma in situ yields a nearly 95% cure rate, and therefore the importance of regular Papanicolaou smears in all women over 21 years of age cannot be stressed enough. The general incidence of this cancer is high, making up 20% of all female cancers.

Known predisposing factors include frequent and early coital experiences, low socioeconomic class, and a history of venereal disease. The low incidence of this type of cancer among Jewish women has been attributed to genetic factors rather than circumcision among the males. The role of previous herpes infection has not as yet been clearly elucidated, but much evidence indicates that this virus is etiologic.

The early signs and symptoms of cervical carcinoma are often considered inconsequential by affected women and may be ignored until frank invasion occurs. These signs and symptoms include heavy menstruation, watery discharge, postcoital bleeding, and occasionally menstrual-type pain. Later symptoms include hemorrhage, pain, foul discharge, leakage of urine and feces from the vagina, anorexia-cachexia, nausea and vomiting, and signs of uremia when compression of the ureters occurs. The growth of the cervical tumor is into the vagina, toward the pelvic wall, and into the bladder and rectum. Metastasis occurs through the lymphatic channels and frequently involves the bone lungs, or liver. Treatment is surgical removal of the cervix and uterus and frequently other pelvic organs that have become involved. In stage 0 (early carcinoma in situ), surgical intervention is generally the only form of treatment. With stages I, II, III, and IV (the stages indicating increasing levels of invasion and lymph node metastasis) the preferred method of treatment is radiation therapy, which may be delivered externally or by insertion of a radioactive source such as radium into the cervical cavity.

Cancer of the uterus is much less common than cervical carcinoma. It is more frequent in postmenopausal women and among Jewish women. Etiologic factors may involve hormonal imbalance. Estrogen therapy in postmenopausal women may be associated with an increased incidence of endometrial uterine cancer. Ninety percent of these cancers are adenocarcinomas. The major presenting symptom of uterine cancer is postmenopausal bleeding, and the major form of treatment is hysterectomy or intracavitary radiotherapy for inoperable patients. Chemotherapy may be used in women with advanced carcinoma and in debilitated patients. It often includes the use of specific hormone regimens.

Cancer of the breast

Carcinoma of the breast is the most common form of cancer among women over the age of 40 and the leading cause of death from all causes in women between the ages of 40 and 44 years. The incidence appears to be increasing, and the prevalence (number with breast cancer in a given year) is approximately 100 per 100,000 women. About 1 in 10 women in the United States is now likely to develop breast cancer. It is more common in single, divorced, or widowed women than in married women and also more prevalent in women who have given birth for the first time at the age of 35 or over. The incidence is low among Japanese women, and this disparity is retained among Japanese ethnic groups who have emigrated to other countries with a higher incidence of breast cancer. Breast cancer does occur in males but is 100 times less frequent. It is more common among women whose mothers and maternal aunts have had breast cancer.

Chronic cystic mastitis is believed by some to predispose the affected individual to breast cancer. Cystic mastitis is seen with higher frequency in the breasts of women with diagnosed carcinoma, but this is, of course, not definitive proof that benign cystic mastitis tissue undergoes malignant transformation more readily than does normal breast tissue. The presence of multiple cysts in the breasts makes the early detection of a malignant tumor extremely difficult. Ninety-five percent of all breast cancers are discovered by the woman herself, either accidentally or by routine breast self-examination. Early masses are poorly movable, hard, painless lumps, half of which occur in the upper outer quadrant of the breast. Possible etiologic factors in breast cancer include viruses, hormonal factors, particularly estrogen levels, genetics, and immunologic abnormalities.

Breast cancer is diagnosed by a number of techniques that utilize x-ray films (mammography, xerography) and by thermography (which can detect "hot spots" of tissue, the increased temperature being a result of increased metabolic activity and mitotic index of tumor). Biopsy confirms carcinoma and may be done by excision or aspiration of the mass.

Most breast carcinomas arise in the epithelium of the glandular ducts of the breast and give rise to lesions with infiltrating edges, which invade the normal breast tissue. They can become large enough to cause nipple retraction such that the skin overlying the breast resembles the skin of an orange. Ulceration and hemorrhage of the breast is common if the tumor is not treated.

The major pathophysiologic mechanism whereby breast cancer causes morbidity and death is through metastatic dissemination of the malignant cells, usually through the axillary lymphatics. Prognosis is vastly better when regional lymph nodes show no evidence of metastasis, but 50% of those tumors that have been detectable for a period of 1 month will have spread to the lymph nodes. Some undetectable or barely detectable lesions may, on the other hand, remain small and non-metastatic for up to 2 years. The 5-year survival rate is 84% when no lymph node involvement is found at surgery and on the average 56% when lymph node involvement does occur. The more lymph nodes positive for malignant cells at the time of operation, the less favorable the prognosis.

Treatment of breast cancer is by removal of the lesion (lumpectomy), the breast (simple mastectomy), or most commonly the breast, lymphatic drainage, and underlying pectoral muscles (radical mastectomy). A complication of radical mastectomy is *lymphedema* of the shoulder and arm on the affected side, which results from the removal of the normal channels for lymphatic drainage. Radiotherapy is also frequently used postoperatively in an attempt to kill any tumor cells left at the site, thus preventing metastasis. Radiotherapy is also used in the treatment of metastasis to the bone, which is common with breast cancer. Dramatic relief of pain, prevention of fractures, and prolongation of life can be achieved with radiotherapy.

Hormone therapy is also a mode of treatment in metastatic breast cancer. These malignant cells appear to have cytoplasmic hormone receptors that allow an initial binding to hormone molecules to take place, which then causes cellular division and growth to ensue. The type of endocrine therapy carried out is dependent on the nature of the tumor cell receptors, as some are androgen dependent and some are estrogen dependent. Estrogens may be administered if the cells are androgen dependent so as to compete with and mask the effects of androgen and inhibit tumor cell growth and vice versa. Irradiation and surgical removal of the ovaries (oophorectomy) may also be done, and occasionally even the pituitary gland may be extirpated (hypophysectomy) so that estrogen production is blocked entirely.

Chemotherapy has been used in metastatic breast cancer (cyclophosphamide [Cytoxan], 5-fluorouracil, adriamycin) with patients who are not helped by hormonal treatment. Drugs are administered as part of a treatment regimen but have not been as successful in the treatment of breast cancer as they have been in some other forms of cancer.

Breast cancer mortality has not been changed dramatically with the advent of the treatments presently at hand, but the duration of life has increased for those individuals with metastatic disease.

Lung cancer

Lung cancer is a highly malignant, morbid disease that has been increasing dramatically in incidence over the past 60 years, with men being affected four to five times as frequently as women. There are 80,000 deaths per year from lung cancer, and bronchial cancer is the leading cause of cancer death among American men.

Most lung cancers arise from the main bronchus and are therefore termed *bronchogenic carcinomas* (Fig. 6-12). They may be of the squamous cell, oat cell, anaplastic, or adenocarcinoma type. The relationship of cigarette smoking to the development of both squamous cell and oat cell carcinomas has been demonstrated repeatedly in epidemiologic studies, the most notable being Doll and Hill's study of 40,000 British physicians. The 1964 US Surgeon General's report on smoking and health supported the belief that cigarette smoking is the most important etiologic agent in the causation of lung cancer among men and probably also among women. The risk of lung cancer is 60 times greater for a man who smokes two packages of cigarettes per day as compared to a man who has never smoked.

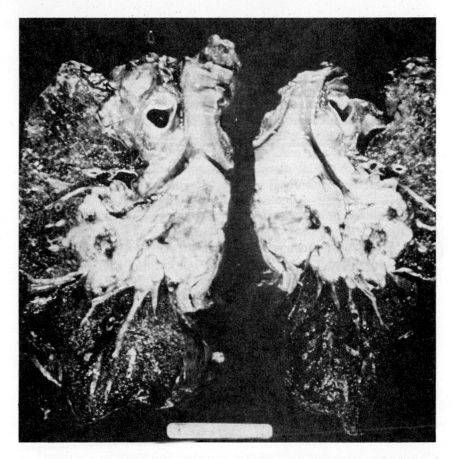

Fig. 6-12. Bronchogenic carcinoma. Extensive malignancy of bronchial tree is observed. (Courtesy Department of Pathology, University of Tennessee, Memphis.)

A number of carcinogenic components of smoke have been isolated and shown to cause cancer in laboratory animals. These include various hydrocarbons, among them the benzopyrenes. Other factors in the environment appear to increase the incidence of lung cancer among smokers by acting synergistically with cigarette smoke. Environmental pollution and exposure to radon, asbestos, and coal tar have been linked to lung cancer.

The lower incidence of lung cancer among women has been attributed to their past smoking habits—not only a smaller number of smokers but also fewer women who actually inhaled the cigarette smoke into the lungs. However, women who live with a smoker and therefore are passive smokers, have an incidence of cancer three times higher than the rate for women not exposed to cigarette smoke. Lung cancer incidence in women is rapidly approaching that of male incidence.

The mortality rate for lung cancer is around 90%. Half of the cancers are inoperable by the time the patient is first seen by a physician. The early symptoms are often ignored or interpreted by the patient as the symptoms of a prolonged cold. These symptoms include a heavy cough, particularly at night, hemoptysis (coughing up of blood), loss of weight, and sometimes chest pain. The symptoms progress to dyspnea, dysphagia, clubbing of fingers, pleural effusion, and sometimes signs of superior vena cava obstruction. Often the first signs of lung cancer are related to metastatic spread, particularly to the brain. Other common sites of metastases include endocrine glands, skin, and bones. The route of metastasis is through the lymphatic channels, and scalene node biopsy is often performed to determine if metastasis has occurred once lung cancer has been diagnosed. The usual diagnostic tools for lung cancer include x-ray films, bronchoscopy, sputum cytology, and bronchial brush or needle biopsy. Surgical exploration of the thorax (thoracotomy) is done when no evidence of metastatic spread is evident. Removal of a lobe of the lung (lobectomy) or an entire lung (pneumonectomy) is carried out.

If the tumor is inoperative, various chemotherapeutic regimens and radiation therapy may be carried out as palliative measures. The drugs most commonly used are alkylating agents, but generally the response of metastatic lung cancer to chemotherapy has been disappointing. Radiation therapy is successful in the alleviation of symptoms in the inoperable lung cancer patient, and some cures of bronchogenic carcinomas that have been treated by supervoltage radiation have been reported.

Leukemias and lymphomas

Leukemias and lymphomas are classified as malignant proliferative diseases of the hematopoietic system, particularly the bone marrow and lymph nodes. This is based on the fact that abnormal proliferation of one cell type occurs, often at the expense of the normal production of other hematopoietic cells. In leukemias incredibly high numbers of immature cells are found in the bloodstream and bone marrow, while in lymphomas the abnormal cells tend to remain more confined to the lymphoid organs rather than being disseminated into the circulation.

Fig. 6-13 indicates the pattern of hematopoiesis in humans and shows that all blood cells (erythrocytes, white blood cells, and platelets) are ultimately derived from a single cell, the stem cell, which then differentiates into different cell lines entirely distinct from each other. Erythroid, platelet, and leukocytic diseases could theoretically arise through a number of possible mechanisms operating at any stage in hematopoietic differentiation. The leukemias are disorders mainly of leukocytes and can be either acute or chronic in nature and lymphocytic or myelogenous in origin. The abnormal cell type that appears in the bone marrow and bloodstream identifies the cell of origin of the leukemia.

The pathophysiology of all forms of leukemia is very similar, with duration of survival and severity of symptoms being the most common variables between the acute and chronic forms. All leukemias cause an extensive infiltration of leukemic cells into the hematopoietic organs. This is a major cause of the various decreases, or *cytopenias*, that invariably accompany leukemia. Normal hematopoiesis is interfered with, resulting in an often profound anemia and thrombocytopenia. These account for the pallor and easy bruisability of the leukemic patient. Often the cause of death in leukemia is hemorrhage into a vital organ such as the brain. The mechanism whereby the leukemic cells prevent normal hematopoiesis is not clear at the present time. It may be caused by an actual mechanical overcrowding of the marrow spaces or by unknown inhibitory factors released by the leukemic cells.

The leukemic cells infiltrate the liver and spleen as well as other organs, giving

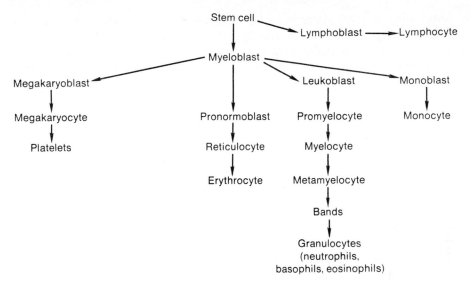

Fig. 6-13. Blood cell differentiation. All blood cells are produced from bone marrow stem cell, which differentiates into lymphoblasts and myeloblasts, primitive cells that are precursors for lymphocytes, granulocytes, monocytes, erythrocytes, and platelets.

rise to tremendous hypertrophy of these structures, signs that are often the first evidence of leukemia in the patient. Leukemic infiltration, no matter at which site it occurs, may interfere with the normal function of the tissue or organ, giving rise to particular signs and symptoms. Furthermore, the leukemic cells themselves may be either too immature to assist the organism in fighting infection or may be immunologically incompetent, as is the case in the lymphocytic leukemias.

Acute leukemia. *Acute lymphocytic leukemia* is the form of leukemia common in children, accounting for the most frequent cancer of childhood. The cell type that is abnormal is a leukemic lymphoblast (the suffix "blast" indicates that it is an immature form of lymphocyte). The carcinogenic transformation probably takes place in a bone marrow stem cell, which then gives rise to the malignant proliferation. The lymphoblasts cannot be identified as T cells or B cells in the majority of the cases. The leukemic cells crowd the bone marrow, bloodstream, and lymph nodes; anemia, granulocytopenia, and thrombocytopenia all are side effects of the disese process. The onset of this disease is usually abrupt, with a rapid course lasting about 4 months until death, unless treated. The early symptoms are fever, lymphadenopathy, pallor, fatigue, purpura, and general malaise. It is common for the leukemia to have run one third of its typical course before the disease is diagnosed.

Acute myelogenous leukemia is more common in adults than in children and involves the proliferation of immature blast cells derived from the bone marrow. Commonly the disease process involves the granulocytes (neutrophils, basophils, and eosinophils). Occasionally erythroid or monocytic blood elements become leukemic, thus confirming the concept of a stem cell transformation in the carcinogenic process. As with acute lymphocytic leukemia, the onset is abrupt, and the symptoms are similar. It is more common for splenomegaly to occur with this form of acute leukemia, while hepatomegaly and lymphadenopathy are generally more pronounced in the acute lymphocytic variety. Although the total white blood cell count is enormously elevated, the immature blast cells provide inadequate defense against infection, and a major complication of acute leukemia is infection. Thrombocytopenia and anemia are also often pronounced, thus contributing to susceptibility to infection. Leukemic cells infiltrate normal tissue and may cause severe disorders related to the site of infiltration.

Both acute forms of leukemia are considered fatal, although treatment of the childhood form has recently yielded some long-term remissions and possible cures. Treatment consists of intensive chemotherapy and bone marrow transplants when possible.

Chronic leukemias. Chronic leukemias are also of two major categories: lymphocytic and myelogenous. Both forms have slower onset than acute leukemia and are initially characterized by general malaise and loss of weight. Anemia is often the first presenting symptom, and the leukocytosis is discovered at that time. The course of the disease is much more prolonged than in the acute forms, with the median survival time being from 3 to 4 years.

Chronic lymphocytic leukemia occurs in individuals usually over the age of 35. The cell type involved in most patients is the immunoglobulin M–secreting B-lymphocyte, which appears to be immunologically incompetent and which does not seem able to give rise to mature immunologically competent cells. The carcinogenic transformation that occurs in chronic lymphocytic leukemia apparently occurs after the stem cell has differentiated into an identifiable B-lymphocyte. The leukemic process is similar if perhaps not identical in etiology to lymphosar-

coma, except that in the latter disease the malignant cells are predominantly confined to lymphoid tissue, while in leukemia the white blood cell count in the peripheral blood is often greatly increased. The cells do invade the lymphoid tissue in the leukemic process, however, and thus may present a pathology similar to that of lymphosarcoma, which is classified as a lymphoma. The lymph node enlargement and splenomegaly that can accompany the leukemia are often great, and patients with these signs and symptoms may be treated with chemotherapy and radiotherapy. Patients who are apparently well (even though the circulating lymphocytes may be increased to levels close to 1 million WBC/mm^3) are generally not submitted to any form of cancer therapy until the symptoms become indicative of more acute disease.

Chronic myelogenous leukemia is nearly always associated with the presence of a small acrocentric chromosome (derived from the long arm of chromosome 22) in the malignant leukocytes of the bone marrow and peripheral blood. Known as the *Philadelphia chromosome*, it has been detected in blood smears of individuals who subsequently developed chronic myelogenous leukemia many years later. The origin of the chromosome is entirely unknown, but there is no question that it is somehow associated with the carcinogenic process. The cells usually affected in this form of leukemia are the granulocytes and sometimes the megakaryocytes, and the cell of origin for this cancer is thought to be a stem cell. These cells present a more mature morphology than do those cells in the acute form of this leukemia.

Patients with chronic myelogenous leukemia have early symptoms that may have been present for many months before the diagnosis is made. Very often the spleen is greatly enlarged, and the patient complains about a dragging, full abdomen. The typical course of the disease runs about 3½ years and is controlled by chemotherapy. As the disease progresses, the leukemic process becomes more typical of acute myelogenous leukemia, and a blast crisis invariably occurs. The immature blast cells also contain the Philadelphia chromosome, and these cells may actually be lymphoblasts rather than myeloblasts. Once the blast crisis occurs, the response to chemotherapy may be poor, and survival is usually only a matter of weeks or months. Wellness can no longer be maintained as the body defenses and barriers are overwhelmed in the crisis.

Malignant lymphomas and Hodgkin's disease. Malignancy of the lymphoreticular system can take many forms. Hodgkin's disease was formerly classified as a malignant lymphoma but is now considered to be a different neoplastic process and will be discussed separately.

Malignant lymphomas arise initially in the lymph nodes and may then involve other organs of the reticuloendothelial system. The pattern of the disease may be either nodular or diffuse, and the involved cell type is used to categorize these lymphomas into lymphocytic, histiocytic, or reticular stem cell. It has been speculated that the origin of these malignancies involves some type of interference with the normal feedback regulation of lymphocyte proliferation, so that immature and poorly functioning lymphocytes are produced. Many patients with lymphomas have impaired B-lymphocyte (humoral) immunity and general hypogammaglobulinemia. Occasionally the disease will change into a typical lymphocytic leukemia, and there is some thought that the two disease processes involve the same mechanisms, with chronic lymphocytic leukemia being a disseminated form of lymphocytic lymphoma. The role of the Epstein-Barr virus in Burkitt's lymphoma has been discussed previously. All lymphomas may have a viral or infectious cause either with the virus producing an immune system depression that then allows a secondary carcinogenic transformation to ensure or with the virus itself acting as the carcinogen. The usual treatment of lymphomas involves radiotherapy and chemotherapy.

Hodgkin's disease also may have an infectious origin. The epidemiologic evidence for this has been previously presented. It is further supported by the pattern of morphologic and pathophysiologic disruption of the lymph nodes and other tissue that appears to present both an inflammatory and malignant picture. The diagnostic criterion for Hodgkin's disease is the presence of Reed-Sternberg cells in the lymphoid tissue. These cells may be found in other disease conditions, but they are always found in Hodgkin's disease. There are several histologic patterns to Hodgkin's disease. These are characterized by (1) lymphocyte predominance, (2) nodular sclerosis, (3) mixed cellularity, and (4) lymphocyte depletion. All forms of Hodgkin's disease, while probably arising at a single origin, may eventually result in invasion of any organ in the body.

The disease is thought to arise in the thymus gland or thymus-dependent areas of the lymph nodes and may be a T cell disease. HLA-A$_5$, a component of a system of leukocyte antigens, is increased in Hodgkin's disease, perhaps linking the presence of an altered histocompatibility gene to the oncogenic process. Cellular immunity is definitely impaired.

The course of the disease varies, depending often on the histologic type. The form characterized by lymphocyte predominance has the best survival rate, with the 5-year survival greater than 50% and the

15-year survival over 45% when adequate high-voltage radiation has been used as the principal form of treatment. The disease often begins as a painless swelling in one node, which may be accompanied by night sweats, fever, and weight loss. The progression of the disease may result in invasion of other lymphoid tissue and organs such as the bones and lungs, with the symptoms then being related to the extent of involvement of these organs. Hodgkin's disease patients may have long periods of disease-free remissions, and cures are possible with adequate treatment at every clinical stage of the disease. Occasionally the disease manifests itself as either an acute or chronic process, but most cases are of an intermediate variety.

Summary

The tumor types that have been discussed in this section represent those forms of primary cancer that are most commonly seen clinically. Metastatic cancer has not been discussed in great detail, but it should be noted that cancers of the brain, bone, and liver are often the sites of metastases from primary tumors at other origins. The signs and symptoms of cancer in these or any organ or tissue affected are often easily predictable if the normal physiology of that organ or tissue is understood. The pathophysiologic manifestations of disease in an organ or tissue can also be predicted once the student has gained a knowledge of the principles of pathophysiology both generally and for each organ system. Thus uremia may be a complication of obstruction, no matter what the actual cause of the obstruction in the urinary tract (malignant growth, heavy metal deposition, glomerulonephritis, hemorrhage, etc.).

The following discussion will present some principles that underlie the usual treatment of malignancy.

TREATMENT RATIONALE

The major treatment modalities used for malignant disease are surgery, radiation therapy, chemotherapy, and immunotherapy. The physiologic bases of these treatments will be discussed in this section, but it should be recognized from the outset that for most cancers no one mode of treatment is used exclusively. Rather, a combined interdisciplinary approach is followed, using methods and techniques from each area of treatment. The aim of all treatment is to reduce the tumor load and to assist the patient in restoring and maintaining the steady state. The oncology team usually consists of specialists from a number of disciplines: oncologist, surgeon, pathologist, radiologist, biochemist, nurse, social worker, etc.

Surgery

The rationale for the use of surgery may seem quite obvious at first. However, surgery may not always be the best treatment for the patient. The effects of a pneumonectomy on a patient with metastatic lung cancer do not warrant this surgery in this particular situation, and other forms of treatment are used. Although for many years surgery was the only treatment widely used for cancer, basic research into areas such as cell biology, the pathophysiology of cancer, chemotherapy, radiation therapy, and immunology has led to other forms of treatment that can be used instead of or along with surgical excision.

Some principles that govern the use of surgery in cancer are related to the extent of surgical excision when surgery is done. Normally a tumor and surrounding tissues are removed, along with the primary lymphatic drainage of the tissue involved (block dissection). The extent of this type of surgery is governed by whether the tumor is localized or has invaded the tissue, fixing tissue to the tumor; by whether or not widespread inflammation is present; and by whether or not palpable tumor can be felt in the lymph nodes. Local excision of the tumor alone may be done if the tumor is not highly malignant or metastatic, such as for skin carcinomas. Special surgical techniques are also used in cancer therapy. These include cryosurgery, lasers, and surgical isolation of vessels for perfusion or infusion.

Radiation therapy

One of the basic laws of radiation biology is that the more undifferentiated or immature a cell is, the more susceptible it is to the damaging effects of ionizing radiation. Thus compartments of cells constantly undergoing renewal and therefore containing populations of stem cells and cells in various stages of differentiation and maturity are affected by radiation at much lower doses than are mature and fully differentiated cells. Radiation acts basically on cellular targets, causing death of the cell when a critical number of targets have been hit by radioactive particles or waves. "Hits" of the targets are theoretic requirements of this target theory of radiation damage, and it is not known exactly what cellular components correspond to the targets, but DNA is suspected. There is no question that the genetic material of the cell is vulnerable to radiation damage and can be altered by a number of well-described mechanisms. Furthermore, the stage of the cell cycle during which the radiation is applied is also critical. These properties of radiation are considered when radiation is used in the treatment of cancer.

When a malignant tumor is irradiated, the radiologist hopes to kill cancer cells as selectively as possible, relying on the fact that the malignant cells are more radiosensitive than are the normal tissue cells around the tumor. The aim of radiation therapy is to kill cancer cells selectively, with as little damage as possible to underlying tissue and blood vessels, although in practice this may be difficult to achieve. Tumor cells are generally more radiosensitive than is the tissue around them, and also malignant cells are not as well able as normal cells to repair radiation-induced damage. This is also true at the tissue level, in that fibrous repair of normal tissue is very effective, whereas it is not in tumorous tissue.

The determination of the radiosensitivity of a tumor and thus of the dose of radiation required is related to three major factors. The various tissues of the body have different degrees of radiosensitivity, which is reflected also in tumors that may arise in these tissues. For example, one of the most radiosensitive tumors is testicular cancer, and one of the most radiosensitive compartments of cells is the spermatozoan series. Another factor is the cellular radiosensitivity itself, which is related to such things as cell type, cell cycle, mitotic rate, age, differentiation, and DNA synthesis rates. The third factor is the tissue environment. The *oxygenation* of tissue is an important factor, in that radiation causes the formation of oxygen and peroxide free radicals, which are highly reactive and can peroxidate lipids and other molecules in the cell, thus causing radiation damage indirectly. It should be recalled that tumors are often quite hypoxic in comparison to other tissues, and modification of radiosensitivity may be attempted by methods that increase tumor oxygen tension. The vascularity of the tissue also is important in regard to oxygenation and radiosensitivity in that blood vessels can become very permeable at fairly low doses of radiation.

Radiation can be curative for a number of malignant tumors provided the selection of the dose, the way the radiation is administered and focused on the tumor, the fractionation of the dose over time and the type of radiation used are all optimal.

It is a striking observation that radiation not only cures but also causes cancer. The radiation dose that is usually administered to malignant tissue is extremely high and is administered at very high voltages. The radiation is directed to a small area of tissue, so that maximum cell death occurs in that focus. It is nevertheless possible that normal cells around an irradiated tumor may receive carcinogenic doses of radiation, and although the original tumor may be completely eradicated, a second and entirely different tumor may appear at the site years later. The tumor's source is likely to have been a carcinogenically transformed cell that originated at the time of the therapeutic radiation.

Both the cell-killing and the cell-transforming effects of radiation probably reflect the ability of radiation to damage nucleic acids. The concept of a threshold of radiation dose below which no irreparable damage occurs to cells and above which damage accumulates and causes effects such as cancer or teratogenesis is a much debated matter in radiation biology. There is evidence that even very low doses of radiation can be carcinogenic, and some would extrapolate down to the background and zero levels of radiation dose. The incidence of leukemia in the offspring of mothers pregnant at the time of diagnostic radiation to the abdominopelvic area has been shown to be significantly higher than the normal incidence. Leukemia in the offspring of pregnant women irradiated by the bombing of Hiroshima has been linearly related down to very low doses with distance from the hypocenter.

Very low doses of diagnostic radiation received by women at the time of mammography have recently been correlated with a slight risk of later appearance of breast cancer.

While radiation is an extremely potent and effective tool in the arsenal of weapons against cancer, it is one that should be handled with extreme care. Knowledge of both the immediate and long-term effects of radiation is necessary to health care workers who are assessing patients undergoing radiation therapy. The most obvious effect may be the erythema of the overlying skin at the site of the radiation therapy. Vasodilation causes the skin to become red and warm, simulating a severe sunburn. It eventually becomes very hard and brown. Many patients undergoing radiation therapy also have severe gastrointestinal symptoms. The epithelium of the gut is a tissue renewal system that turns over rapidly and is therefore highly sensitive to radiation damage. Depending on the extent and area of radiation therapy, some gastrointestinal tract damage and symptoms may occur if the gastrointestinal tract is irradiated. The hematopoietic system is another tissue renewal system and is the most radiosensitive system. Exposure of the bone marrow and lymph nodes to very low doses will result in a depression of hematopoiesis. The lymphocytes particularly are radiosensitive, but erythrocyte, granulocyte, and platelet precursor cells are all affected by radiation. Therefore, anemia, leukopenia, and thrombocytopenia may all develop as the result of radiation to the bone marrow. This greatly increases susceptibility to infection, a process that may be life threatening in the cancer patient. The male reproductive tract is another tissue renewal system that is profoundly sensitive to radiation; the cells most easily damaged by radiation are the spermatogonia, particularly type A spermatogonia, which are the most primitive. Sterilization can occur as the result of radiation exposure to the testes. Ova are radiosensitive as well, and sterility can occur with radiation of the ovaries.

All the preceding effects of radiation on the patient are potentially reversible, however, with time. Some permanent changes in the organ systems mentioned may occur, such as might be caused by ischemia and necrosis resulting from any cause. The effects of radiation on different organ systems are more fully discussed in Chapter 5. It is important to realize that radiation damage to an organism is dependent on a number of factors. These include the dose of radiation, the volume of tissue irradiated, and the time over which the radiation is administered. A much larger dose of radiation can be administered to a patient if it is distributed over time (fractionated) so that the patient can recover between doses. The volume of tissue can be extremely small if the radiation is focused on a tiny area, and therefore very high dosages can be given. For example, 10,000 rads over a period of 1 month might be given to an organ. A dose of 450 rads given at one time as whole body irradiation (from a bomb or accidental exposure) would cause death within 30 days to 50% of those humans exposed to it.

The long-term effects of radiation may not be manifested for many years after the exposure. Carcinogenesis has been discussed before. Radiation is also known to affect life span by either accelerating the aging process or producing deleterious degenerative changes in the previously irradiated tissues, which increase the possibility of a variety of disease processes taking place. Other long-term effects of radiation include infertility, inhibition of bone growth, and cataractogenesis.

Chemotherapy

Only rarely can drugs be considered curative measures for cancer. For most patients the drugs are given to relieve discomfort and prolong life. Chemotherapeutic agents can be generally classified into four main groups: alkylating agents, antimetabolites, hormones, and antibiotics and plant alkaloids. Use of these drugs is in large part experimental, and recent research has indicated that combining and spacing drugs rather than giving them singly as part of a drug regimen may be more effective for many cancers. A major problem with chemotherapy is the fact that a drug can usually only be given in one course of therapy. Tumor cells apparently are subject to the same laws of natural selection and survival of the species that apply to all living organisms. Selection of tumor cells resistant to the action of the chemotherapeutic agent occurs, and the drug being used then becomes ineffective against the growth and metastasis of the malignancy. A new drug must then be initiated, until the same process occurs all over again (Fig. 6-14). Resistance develops more readily when single drugs or inadequate amounts of drugs are used. Often cells become multiply resistant. It now appears that the mode of resistance is through amplification of from one to five genes. These genes code for transport proteins, which pump the drug out of the cell as soon as it enters (Kolata, 1986).

The alkylating agents, plant alkaloids, antimetabolites, and antibiotics used to combat cancer all have profound side effects, which are primarily related to the mechanism of action of these drugs at the cellular level. These drugs interact in some way with the DNA, RNA, and protein-synthesizing machinery of the cell (Fig. 6-15). Such interruptions will inhibit either division or protein synthesis of the cell,

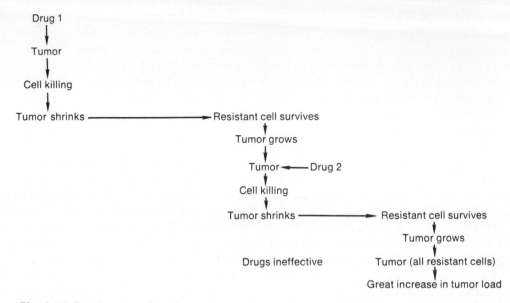

Fig. 6-14. Development of resistance to cancer chemotherapeutic agents occurs through a process of natural selection in which resistant cells are selected in presence of drug, grow, and produce clones of resistant cells.

eventually resulting in cell death. These drugs act not only on cancer cells but on all rapid turnover cell compartments (much as radiation does), and the side effects in some ways mimic the effects of radiation sickness. These include bone marrow depression, nausea, vomiting, diarrhea, lesions and hemorrhage of the mucous membranes, and alopecia. The reproductive tract may be affected, and liver toxicity may occur. The active chemotherapeutic agents have a further specificity of action, in that some are cell-cycle specific, perhaps acting only during mitosis (vincristine) or only at the S (synthesis) phase of the cell cycle (arabinosylcytosine, hydroxyurea). Table 6-2 lists major cancer drugs, their uses, dosages, and toxicities. Fig. 6-16 shows the molecular structure of some chemical agents used to treat cancer.

Immunotherapy

The field of cancer immunotherapy has been undergoing rapid growth in recent years. The reader is referred to the discussion in the early part of this chapter on the host's immune response to malignancy.

Manipulation of the immune response underlies immunotherapy, and there are three major modes of action of immunotherapy intervention. The first method is by active immunization of the host by tumor cells that have been first irradiated. The irradiated tumor cells may invoke a stronger immune response, thus destroying both injected and native tumor cells. Often this therapy is done in conjunction with chemotherapy and radiotherapy. It is possible also to separate leukocytes from peripheral blood samples, activate them with mitogenic chemicals, and then reinject the cells. A second method of immunotherapy is through passive immunization, with antilymphocyte serum in chronic lymphocytic leukemia, with lymphoid cells from donors who have previously submitted to grafting of the host's tumor, and with transfer factor, a sub-

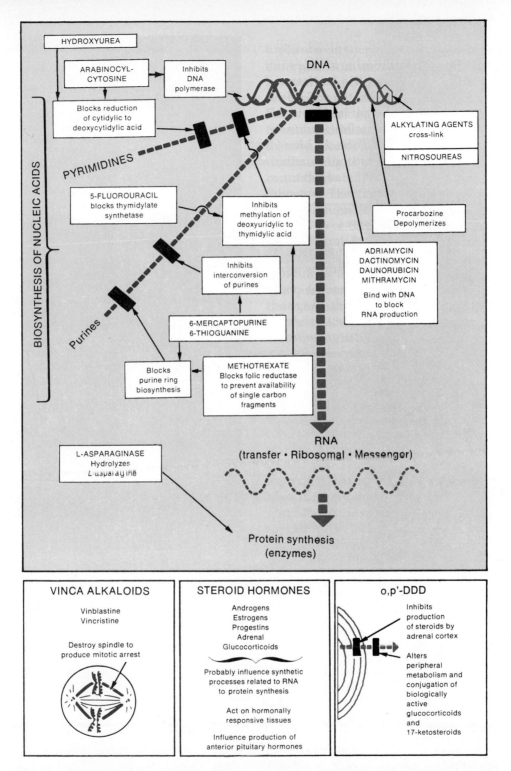

Fig. 6-15. Cancer chemotherapeutic agents act on DNA-RNA protein-synthesizing mechanism in various ways. Other agents act at different levels on cellular division or metabolism as indicated.
(From A Cancer Journal for Clinicians 23:208, 1973.)

Table 6-2. Cancer chemotherapy*

Drug	Common dosages	Examples of use	Signs of toxicity
Antimetabolites			
Methotrexate	PO 2.5-5.0 mg/day; IV 25-50 mg once or twice a week	Acute lymphocytic leukemia; cancers of testes, cervix; lymphosarcoma; choriosarcoma	Mouth and gastrointestinal tract ulcerations; hematopoietic depression; more toxic in patients with decreased kidney function
6-Mercaptopurine	PO 2.5 mg/kg/day	Leukemia	Nausea; vomiting; hematopoietic depression
5-Fluorouracil	IV 12 mg/kg/day for 3 days	Colon, pancreatic, ovarian, and breast cancers	Nausea; vomiting; hematopoietic depression
Alkylating agents			
Chlorambucil	PO 0.1-0.2 mg/kg/day	Chronic lymphocytic leukemia; Hodgkin's disease; lymphomas	Hematopoietic depression with decreased leukocyte, erythrocyte, and platelet counts; alopecia; cystitis; dermatitis; hepatotoxicity; nausea and vomiting
Cyclophosphamide	IV 40-60 mg/kg/day for 10 days; PO 50-200 mg/day	Acute leukemia, chronic lymphocytic leukemia; lung cancer; multiple myeloma	
Antibiotics			
Adriamycin	IV 50-75 mg/m² every 3 weeks	Bone, breast, lung, ovarian, bladder, and thyroid cancers; acute leukemia; Hodgkin's disease	Stomatitis; alopecia; hematopoietic depression; cardiac toxicity
Dactinomycin	IV 0.01 mg/kg/day for 5 days	Osteogenic sarcoma; Wilms' tumor; testicular cancer	Stomatitis; gastrointestinal disturbances; acne; alopecia; hematopoietic depression
Vinca alkaloids			
Vincristine	IV 0.02-0.05 mg/kg weekly	Acute lymphocytic leukemia; Hodgkin's disease; neuroblastoma	Peripheral neuritis; areflexia, weakness paralytic ulcers; hematopoietic depression
Vinblastine	IV 0.1-0.2 mg/kg weekly	Hodgkin's disease; lymphomas	Nausea; vomiting; areflexia; hematopoietic depression
Steroids			
Androgens		Breast cancer	Masculinization
Estrogens		Breast cancer	Sexual impotence in males
Progestins		Endometrial, prostate, kidneys, and breast cancer	Edema; altered menstruation
Adrenocorticoids		Hodgkin's disease; multiple myeloma; leukemia; breast cancer	Salt and water retention; edema; ulcers; diabetes, infection
Other drugs			
L-Asparaginase	IV 200 to 1,000 IU/kg 3 to 7 times weekly for 28 days	Acute lymphoblastic leukemia	Nausea; vomiting; anorexia; weight loss; abnormal liver metabolism; hyperglycemia; hyperlipidemia
Hydroxyurea	PO 20-40 mg/kg/day	Malignant melanoma; chronic granulocytic leukemia	Hematopoietic depression

*Modified from Krakoff IH: Cancer 23:209, 1973.

POLYFUNCTIONAL ALKYLATING AGENTS

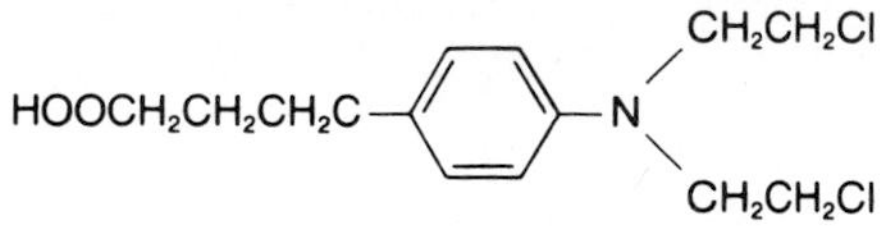

4-(p-[Bis(β-chloroethyl)amino]phenyl)
butyric acid

CHLORAMBUCIL

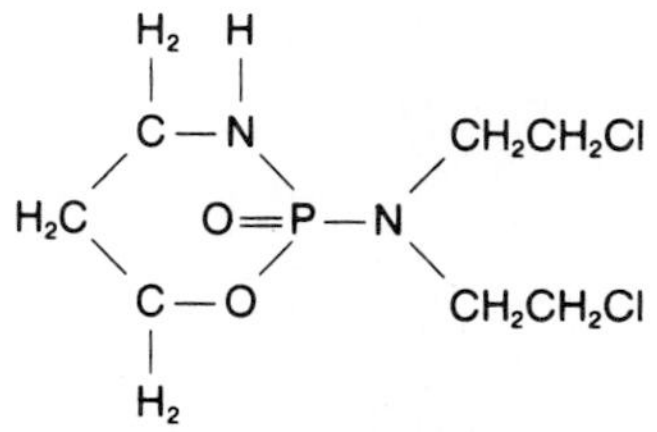

2-[Bis(β-chloroethyl)amino]-2H-1,3,2-
Oxazaphosphorinane, 2-oxide

CYCLOPHOSPHAMIDE

ANTIMETABOLITES

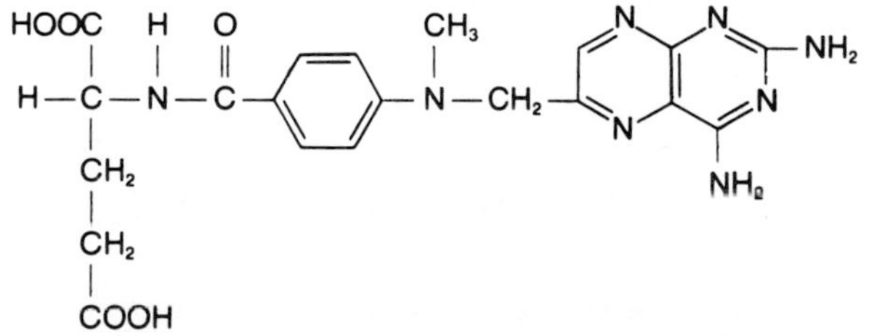

4-Amino-N^{10}-methylpteroyglutamic acid

METHOTREXATE

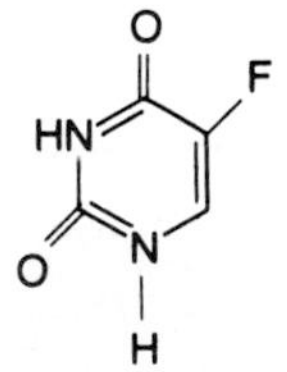

5-Fluorouracil

5-FU

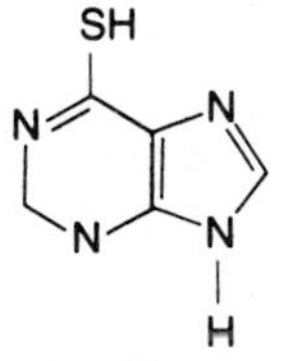

6-Mercaptopurine

6-MP

Fig. 6-16. Selected common chemotherapeutic agents used in treatment of cancer.

Continued.

ANTIBIOTICS

ADRIAMYCIN

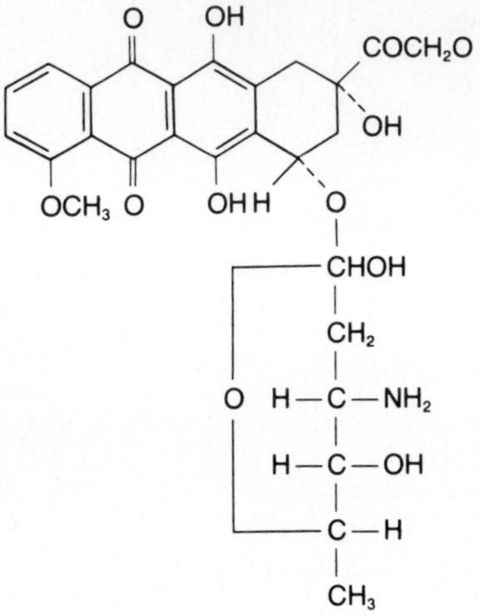

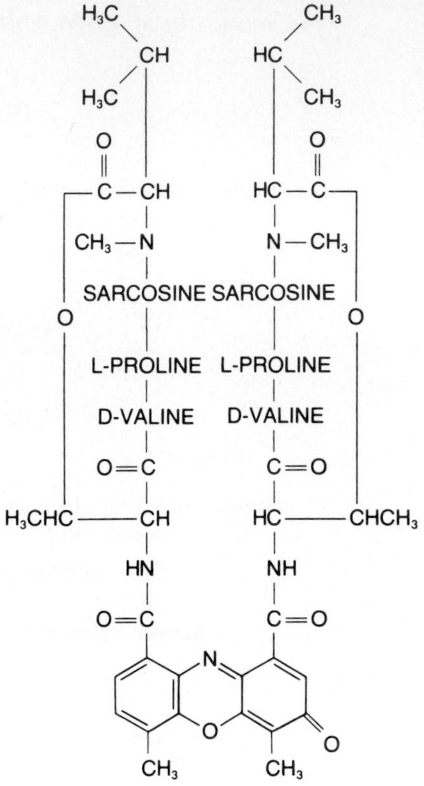

DACTINOMYCIN

MISCELLANEOUS DRUGS

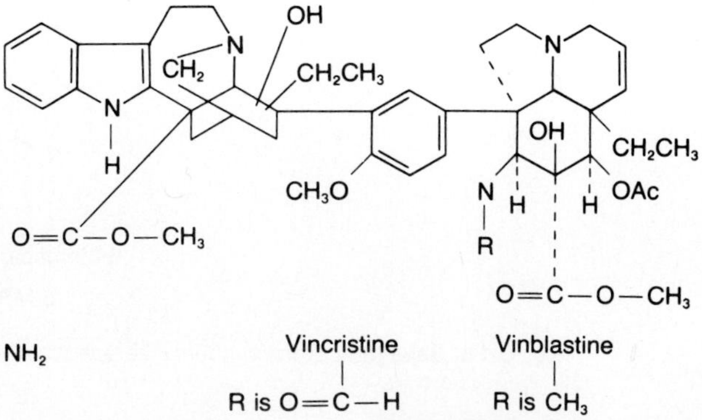

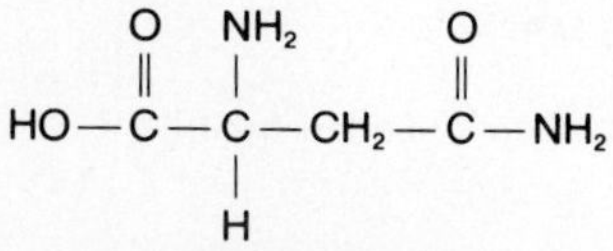

L-ASPARAGINE

Vincristine   Vinblastine

R is O=C—H   R is CH₃

VINCA ALKALOIDS
VINCRISTINE
VINBLASTINE

Fig. 6-16, cont'd. Selected common chemotherapeutic agents used in treatment of cancer.

stance produced by leukocytes, which can transfer delayed hypersensitivity reactivity from one person to another. The third mechanism of immunotherapy is through the use of agents known as immunologic adjuvants (BCG, *Corynebacterium parveum*), which appear to act nonspecifically but have been successful in the treatment of malignant melanoma.

The following illustrates the clinical features of a common cancer. Behavioral approaches such as imagery and visualization, social support, laughter and humor therapy, and other unique strategies have earned a part in the cancer treatment plan.

CASE STUDY: COLON CANCER

Objective and Subjective Data

Mr. M is a 72-year-old, white male who was diagnosed as having rectal carcinoma, stage Dukes C. He reported having had intermittent bleeding from the rectum for 6 months, which he attributed to hemorrhoids. He also noted a change in bowel habits with increasing constipation and increasing rectal pain over the last 6 months. When he sought medical attention, a palpable mass was found in the rectum. He underwent an abdomen-perineal resection with colostomy. Pathology revealed a moderately well-differentiated adenocarcinoma of the rectum with extension into the perirectal area and multiple nodal metastases. He has had slow healing of the perineal incision with a residual small amount of serous drainage persisting 6 weeks after surgery. He was admitted for initiation of chemotherapy with 5-fluorouracil and mitomycin and radiation to the lower pelvis in an attempt to eradicate any residual disease.

General appearance
  Vital signs
    Blood pressure: 142/76

Contributed by Margaret Pierce.

Pulse rate: 76
Respiratory rate: 20
Weight: 141 lbs
Height: 5 ft 8 inches
Body surface area: 1.76 M^2
Temperature: 98.6

Physical assessment
  Skin: Warm, dry and pink
  Pupils: Equal, round, and reactive to light
  EOMS: Intact
  Neck: No palpable nodes
  Thyroid: Not enlarged
  Lungs: Clear
  Heart: Regular without significant murmurs, rubs or gallops
  Abdomen: Soft, no palpable hepatosplenomegaly; no abdominal masses or tenderness; colostomy is present on left side of the abdomen; no femoral nodes present.
  Male genitalia: Normal
  Surgical absence of the rectum. The perianal tissues are well-healed.
  Extremities: Are intact.
  Neurologic examination: Is within normal limits.

Laboratory values
CBC
  WBC: 6000 cells/mm^3
  Hgb: 11.4 gm/dl
  Hct: 33.9%
  RBC: 3.98 × 10 cells/mm^3
  MCV: 85
  MCH: 29
  MCHC: 34
Platelets: 248,000
Differential WBC:
  Segs: 70%
  Band: 1%
  Lymph: 29%
  Mono: 0%
  Slight anisocytosis
Urinalysis-WNL

SMA		
	Glucose	81 gm/dl
	Na	141 mEq/L
	K	4.5 mEg/L
	CO_2	30 mm
	Ca	8.8 mEq/L
	PO4	4.1 mEq/L

Total protein	6.1 gm/dl
Albumin	3.6 gm/dl
Cl	106 mEq/L
BUN	15 mg/dl
Creatinine	0.9 mg/dl
Uric acid	7.1 mg/dl
LDH	198 μ/L
Total bilirubin	0.4 mg/dl
SGOT	21 μ/L
Alkaline phosphatase	102 μ/L
Carcinoembryonic antigen (CEA)	2.2 (nl 0-2.5) ng/ml
(pre-op CEA	88 ng/ml)

Treatment

Mr. M. was begun on a course of chemotherapy that included 5-flourouracil 1760 mg over 24 hours for 4 days (total dose 7040 mg) and mitomycin C 17 mg. Both drugs were given intravenously. Prior to the mitomycin, antiemetic therapy was given that included atavan 2.0 mg IV and compazine 10 mg IM. For the remainder of this course of chemotherapy, he was given compazine spansules 30 mg BID.

On the same day that his chemotherapy was initiated, he also began a course of radiation therapy to the pelvis. This involved a total dose of 5000 rads to the pelvis given in 28 fractions with a planned respite 2 weeks into treatment.

Discussion

Mr. M exemplifies many common characteristics of people with colon-rectal cancer. He is 71 years of age, which puts him in the age range where the peak incidence of this malignancy is found. He experienced increasing constipation and rectal pain along with intermittent gross rectal bleeding for several months before his diagnosis.

The most common symptom of colon cancer is a change in bowel habits. Blood in the stool is another common symptom; frequently the bleeding is occult and only detected by an occult blood test however.

Rectal pain also occurs but usually indicates a more advanced malignancy.

It is believed that most colon cancers originate from an adenomatous polyp emerging from the mucosa into the lining of the bowel. It is thought that malignant transformation occurs over several years. Dietary habits are thought to be a significant factor in the development of colon cancer with the "American" diet consisting of low fiber, high fat, and high protein—a diet having strong etiologic significance in this malignancy.

Epidemiologists today suggest that diets high in fiber and low in fat and protein may decrease the risk of colon cancer by reducing transit time of food in the bowel thereby decreasing the length of time of exposure of the bowel to carcinogens found in food. Dietary fiber may also dilute the concentration of carcinogens in the bowel.

The fact that Mr. M attributed his symptoms to hemorrhoids is also not unusual. However, any patient with rectal bleeding should undergo a rectal examination promptly to rule out other causes of bleeding. His 6 month delay in seeking treatment was unfortunate; perhaps making a difference in this extensiveness of his disease at diagnosis.

Colon cancers are staged utilizing the Dukes classification system. This system was developed by Cuthbert Dukes, a pathologist, in 1932. The general categories of this classification are:

Dukes A	The tumor has not penetrated through the bowel wall
Dukes B	The tumor has penetrated the bowel wall, but no lymph nodes are involved
Dukes C	The tumor involves regional lymph nodes
Dukes D	Distant metastasis is present

Patients with Dukes A and B tumors are often treated with surgery alone. Patients with Dukes C or D tumors often receive radiation, chemotherapy, or both, in an attempt to cure or delay recurrence of disease.

Because of the prolonged period of intermittent bleeding and surgery, Mr. M is moderately anemic. This is another common finding in colon cancer. In fact, anemia is often the first recognized sign leading to the workup and diagnosis of colon cancer.

The other laboratory value of significance in this case is the CEA (carcino embryonic antigen). This is a fetal antigen thought to be normally present in the fetus during cellular differentiation. Initially it was thought that the only time this was found to be elevated in an adult was when colon cancer was present. However, abnormal levels have also been found in patients with other types of cancer, with a variety of other chronic illnesses, and in smokers. If elevated at the time of diagnosis, the CEA is useful in monitoring patients with colon cancer. A decreasing CEA would suggest that treatment is successful, and an increasing value would indicate that the disease is recurring or advancing.

Nursing Diagnoses

Mr M's history reveals several areas of needed nursing intervention. Not only is he recovering from surgery, but he is also adapting to a diagnoses of cancer and functional change and the initiation of two potentially toxic treatment regimens. Possible nursing diagnoses include:

1. Altered in tissue perfusion related to anemia
2. Knowledge deficit related to side effects of radiation and chemotherapy
3. Potential altered in nutrition: less than body requirements, related to treatment side effects
4. Personal identity disturbance related to surgical change
5. Fear related to uncertain future

CONCLUSIONS

Cancer still remains a mysterious, elusive group of diseases, but the carcinogenic process is slowly becoming understood and newer treatment approaches offer hope where once there was none. Cancer involves multiple, interacting physiologic, psychologic, and social influences. This appears true for the etiology, morbidity, and mortality. Cancer must be viewed holistically, from an integrative biobehavioral approach, since body and mind are equally involved.

BIBLIOGRAPHY

Berenblum I: Established principles and unresolved problems in carcinogenesis, J Natl Cancer Inst 60:723, 1978.

Beutler B, Milsark I, and Cerami A: Passive immunization against cachectin/tumor necrosis factor protects mice from lethal effects of endotoxin, Science 229:869-871, 1985.

Bishop JM: The molecular genetics of cancer, Science 235:305-311, 1987.

del Regato JA and Spjut HJ: Ackerman and del Regato's cancer: diagnosis, treatment, and prognosis, ed 5, St Louis, 1977, The CV Mosby Co.

DeWys W: Nutritional problems in cancer patients: overview and perspective. In Burish T, Levy S, and Meyerowitz B, editors: Cancer, nutrition, and eating behavior, New Jersey, 1985, Lawrence Earlbaum Associates.

Doll R and Peto R: The causes of cancer, New York, 1981, Oxford University Press, Inc, p 1256.

Dreher H: Cancer and the mind: current concepts in psycho-oncology, Advances 4(3):27-43, 1987.

Duesberg P: Activated proto-onc genes: sufficient or necessary for cancer? Science 228:669-677, 1985.

Everson T and Cole W: Spontaneous regression of cancer, Philadelphia, 1966, WB Saunders Co.

Feldman F: Wellness and work. In Cooper CL, editor: Psychosocial stress and cancer, New York, 1984, John Wiley & Sons, Inc.

Gori GB: The regulation of carcinogenic hazards, Science 208:256-261, 1980.

Groer M and Pierce M: Guarding against cancer's hidden killer: anorexia-cachexia, Nursing 81 11:39-43, 1981.

Klein G, editor: Viral oncology, New York, 1981, Raven Press.

Kolata G: Why do cancer cells resist drugs? Science 231:220-221, 1986.

Kolata G: Two disease-causing genes found. Science 234(4777), 669-670, 1986.

Kolata G: Oncogenes give breast cancer prognosis, Science 235:160-161, 1987.

Krakoff IH: Cancer chemotherapeutic agents, Cancer 23:209-219, 1973.

Kupchella C and Burton R: Cellular biology of cancer. in Groenwald S, editor: Cancer nursing, Boston, 1987, Jones & Bartlett Publishers Inc.

Levy S: Behavior and cancer, Jossey-Bass Publishers, San Francisco, 1985.

Marshall J, and Groer P: A theory of the induction of bone cancer by alpha radiation, Radiat Res 71(1):149-192, 1977.

Marx J: Burst of publicity follows cancer report, Science 230:1367-1368, 1985.

Maugh TH II: New study links chlorination and cancer, Science 211:694, 1981.

Miller E: Some current perspectives on chemical carcinogenesis in humans and experimental animals, Cancer Res 38:1479-96, 1981.

Morrison SD: Generation and compensation of the cancer cachectic process by spontaneous modification of feeding behavior, Cancer Res 36:228-233, 1976.

Persky VW, Kempthorne-Rawson J, and Shekelle RB: Personality and risk of cancer: 20-year follow-up of the Western Electric Study, Psychosom Med 49:435-439, 1987.

Reif A: The causes of cancer, Am Sci 69:437-447, 1981.

Reddy B, et al: Nutrition and its relationship to cancer, Adv Cancer Res 32:237-345, 1980.

Rich R: Regulatory mechanisms in tumor immunity, Fed Proc 40:36-38, 1981.

Slamon D: Expression of cellular oncogenes in human malignancies, Science 224:256-262, 1984.

Theologides A: Cancer cachexia, Cancer 43:(supp): 2004, 1979.

Trichopoulos D, et al: Lung cancer and passive smoking, Int J Cancer 27:1-4, 1981.

Weiss N, and Sayvetz A: Incidence of endometrial cancer in relation to the use of oral contraceptives. N Engl J Med 302:551-554, 1980.

Welch DR, Bhuyan B, and Liotta LA, editors: Cancer metastases: experimental and clinical strategies, New York, 1986, Alan R Liss, Inc.

UNIT III

Coping-stress-tolerance pattern

7

Pathophysiology of stress

Stress is a term used frequently to describe the way people feel about physical, psychologic, and even spiritual disturbances. However, stress is actually a biologic response. It often produces physical signs and symptoms that people recognize as signs of stress. Some people may react with headaches and others with muscle pain or nausea. Wellness is a continuum on which various states of distress and eustress might be superimposed, and the ability to recognize and handle stressors is an attribute of a well person. Stressors evoke a stress response, which is not a pathophysiologic state but a coping mechanism to preserve wellness. However, as this chapter will describe, human stress often produces a loss of wellness, perpetuates pathophysiologic mechanisms, and ultimately reduces coping and resistance to other stressors.

THE NATURE OF THE STRESS RESPONSE

The general response of the body to stressors was first described by Hans Selye (Selye, 1976) who as a medical student observed that ill patients appeared to have two sets of symptoms, one that characterized the disease process and one that they described as the feeling of "just being sick." Further investigation with animals allowed identification of a group of responses that seemed to result whenever the animals allowed were stressed, the responses occuring in a uniform and characteristic manner no matter what the original stressor. Several phenomena were reported. The most prominent result of a stressor was release of adrenocorticosteroids and hypertrophy of the adrenal cortex. This was seen within hours after the stressor was applied. The other aspects of this stereotyped response to stressors were involution of the thymus, spleen, and lymph nodes, a decrease in the circulating eosinophils and lymphocytes, erosion of the gastric mucosa, and a general antiinflammatory reaction throughout the body. These characteristics make up what Selye described as the general adaptation syndrome (GAS). An important aspect of the GAS is that either an acute or chronic reaction is possible, and the chronic response, which follows continual and prolonged application of the stressor, leads to the stage of resistance, which theoretically allows the organism to adapt to the stressor. However, resistance may not be adequate enough and Selye believed that adaptation diseases would occur. The final stage in the stress response is exhaustion, in which the ability of the organism to respond further to stressors is totally depleted, and there is failure of adaptation (Fig. 7-1).

One further concept of Selye's theory is

248

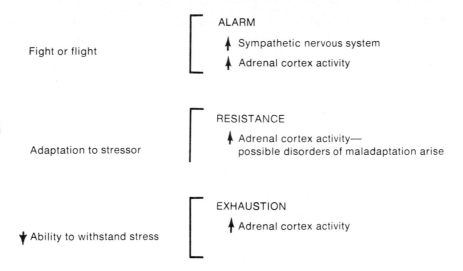

Fig. 7-1. General adaptation syndrome (GAS) consists of three stages: alarm, resistance, and exhaustion.

the concept of *eustress*. Selye believed that a certain amount of normal stress is necessary for an active, healthy life, and in fact it is eustress that offers protection from disease. Stress as a maladaptive process, causing diseases of maladaptation, is termed *distress*. These responses are considered inappropriate or excessive, and may perhaps eventually lead to peptic ulcers, cardiovascular disease, psychosomatic disease, and allergic disorders.

Superimposed on the acute stress response is sympathetic nervous system activation and generalized adrenergic vigilant responses that are typical of acute stress states in animals. Autonomic nervous system arousal leads to the state of alarm, in which the individual is physiologically prepared to deal with the stressor by "fight or flight." The adrenal cortex activation component leads to a later, more metabolic, adaptive resistant phase. Nevertheless, at the time of acute stress during the alarm phase, both reactions are occurring in the animal.

The mechanism of action for stress-induced responses is obscure. Whatever the stressor is, some mechanism by which it can activate the nonspecific hypothalamic arousal that ultimately leads to the GAS must exist. This does not appear to be primarily neural, as deafferentation (total severing of the afferent nerves to the area of the hypothalamus that stimulates the hypophysis) does not prevent the stress response, and adrenocorticotropic hormone (ACTH) release is above normal, as is the plasma corticoid concentration. Therefore it is believed that blood-borne factors must exist, which are liberated by the body whenever stressors act. Once the activation of the hypothalamus is achieved, corticotropin releasing factor (CRF) is released into the portal bloodstream, which supplies the adenohypophysis. Activation of the hypothalamus also results in sympathetic nervous system activation and the release of epinephrine from the adrenal medulla; many times antidiuretic hormone (ADH) is also released. CRF acts on the adenohypophysis, stimulating it to produce and release ACTH. This hormone then acts to stimulate the release of glucocorticoids and, to a much lesser degree, mineralocorticoids, from the adrenal cortex (Fig. 7-2). A state of acute stress alarm is typified by an increase in norepinephrine, epinephrine, ACTH, glucocorticoids, glucagon, growth hormone, and mineralocorticoids. A second effect of stressors appears to be an increase in the release of ADH from the posterior hypophysis, a phenomenon particularly important after surgical stress.

Although high levels of glucocorticoids are typical of the stress response during the alarm stage, blood levels decrease somewhat during the resistance stage of the GAS. The function of the glucocorticoids during alarm is probably related to their syntoxic effects. A syntoxic hormone is one that allows an individual to adapt to the stressor. Opposed to this are catatoxic hormones such as androgens, which actively "attack" the stressor. The glucocorticoids act in an antiinflammatory and antiimmune manner (see Chapter 2). These actions essentially permit the individual to coexist with the stressor. These hormones appear to have "permissive" as well as direct effects. They act to produce a favorable environment in which other

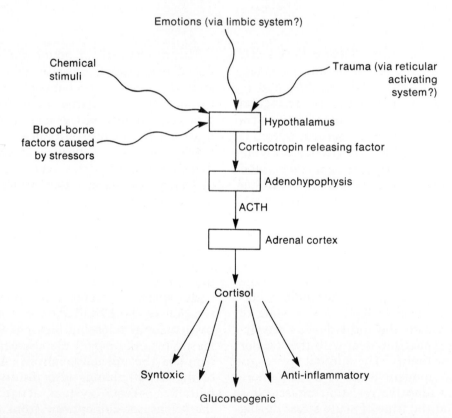

Fig. 7-2. Cortisol production. Hypothalamic—hypophyseal—adrenal cortex pathway. Effects of cortisol are broadly categorized.

factors may then act to cause a maximal effect. An example of this permissive action is the enhancement of the arteriolar response to catecholamines, which occurs in the presence of cortisol. An example of a direct effect of glucocorticoids is the inhibition of the enzyme hexokinase, which is required in the catabolism of glucose. Thus cortisol can inhibit glucose breakdown as it acts in other ways to enhance gluconeogenesis. Cortisol then acts to permit adaptation to the stressor, so that its effects will be minimized.

The net metabolic effect of these hormones is to increase the availability of fuel for energy production. There are increases in glycogenolysis, gluconeogenesis, lipolysis, and protein catabolism. Aldosterone, ADH, catecholamines, and glucocorticoids also act in ways that preserve the fluid volume of the body. The stress response is generally characterized by a hypermetabolic state, which has the potential of depleting body glucose reserves, breaking down fat, and wasting protein, if the stress state persists. An exaggeration of these metabolic effects is observed in patients with Cushing's syndrome or in patients receiving pharmacologic doses of steroids in the treatment of certain diseases. These metabolic effects are accompanied by antiinflammatory and antiimmunologic effects that persist as long as the glucocorticoid output from the adrenal cortex remains high.

HUMAN STRESS

The stress response is an ubiquitous phenomenon, an adaptive mechanism that allows a person to have available a ready supply of fuel, an adequate fluid volume, and a diminished inflammatory and immune reaction. The response allows for an acute defense and coping reaction in the face of a stressor. Unfortunately in our modern world and because of our unique ability to imagine and worry, human beings often react inappropriately, perceiving or imagining threats that do not exist. The stress response is an "old world" response that increases survival in an environment that was once filled with real stressors, such as temperature extremes, physical dangers, and uncertain food supplies. The modern environment is filled with other stressors, such as daily hassles (traffic, quarrels, and parking), unrealistic performance expectations (often self-imposed), interpersonal conflicts (marital separations and divorces), chemicals (alcohol, drugs, environmental toxins, and smoke), and self and family maintenance issues (salaries and cost of living). The physiologic response to these types of stressors is still essentially the same response that would occur if attacked by a snarling, angered, wild beast. Perhaps there is not the extreme fight or flight reaction, but sympathetic nervous system arousal is provoked, producing real physical changes and symptoms (perceived or not perceived) in the stressed person. Unlike a wild beast that will eventually leave, a stressor such as poverty or interpersonal conflict with a mother-in-law persists and is often accompanied by feelings of hopelessness and helplessness. In these modern situations the physical changes produced by the stress response are not adaptive, but pathophysiologic. These are important concepts since stress is considered etiologically important in many modern "lifestyle" diseases. It is difficult to determine exactly how important stress might be since most of these diseases are caused by many factors, but there are few today that would argue against a role for stress in hypertension, coronary artery disease, type II diabetes, peptic ulcers, mental illness, and immunologic dysfunctions.

The way that a stressor is perceived, considered, evaluated, and reacted against involves central nervous system processing. The brain itself is an endocrine organ of first importance, secreting hormone-like substances that may act at a distant part of the body or within the brain itself. The nervous system and the endocrine system are no longer conceptualized as distinct from each other but as connected in a *neuroendocrine* system that sends and receives information from all over the body. Stressors can be external events, such as a very cold environment, or internal phenomena, such as fear and worry over a pending examination. In both cases the central nervous system circuitry results in perception of the stressor through afferent input into the brain, association of the stressor with brain memories through the association cortex, and arousal and alerting through the sympathetic nervous system. Activation of hypothalamic centers also occurs, whereby the hypothalamus secretes releasing hormones that act on the anterior pituitary gland to stimulate it to release trophic hormones. These pathways are essentially independent of the type of stressor. Once the brain "decides" that the input is a stressor, the physiologic response is a nonspecific defense response.

Stress mediation

The role of the brain in mediating the afferent, potentially stressful input and determining the degree of biochemical and physiologic output required in the stress state is essential. This mediation is often equivalent to what we commonly call "coping." Cognitive processing and appraisal of the stressor, self-talk, denial, and optimism are all aspects of this mediation response. The brain also appraises whether the stressor is a short-term event or whether it is chronic, enduring, and inescapable. In many animal experiments, the aspect of inescapability from the stressor produces the greatest stress response. If the animal is given no hope of control over the stressor (hopelessness) or no possible escape from the stressor (helplessness), the stress response produced is greater. Even when no escape or control is available, if an animal has the opportunity to engage in *displacement* activities, the stress response is reduced. For example, if animals that are deprived of food and consequently stressed are able to gnaw and nibble on objects, their stress hormone output is less. Exercise is also used as a displacement activity in many animal stress studies. Clearly human beings also engage in displacement activities when stressed. These activities may actually reduce the pathophysiologic disturbances that the stress response can evoke. People faced with a social stressor, such as a divorce, may displace the stress with an activity such as alcohol abuse, cigarette smoking, or overeating. Unfortunately, all of these displacement activities have separate pathophysiologic effects. A displacement activity such as exercise may be more beneficial.

Sources of stress

Both animal and human research has identified unanticipated changes and novel situations as significant stressors. The Holmes and Rahe scale is predictive of illness and hospitalization in the year following assessment and is based on accumulated points derived from weighted social readjustments that a person experienced within the prior year. The most significant social readjustments are the death of a spouse, divorce, and marital separation.

Other very human stressors have been termed "daily hassles." Research has found that a significant number of daily hassles can produce all types of somatic complaints, and these little, annoying, persistent stressors can be even more important than a major life event.

Personality and behavior also play major mediating roles in the stress response. There are people who are fatalistic, always expect the worse, and chronically suffer from the effects of even small stressors. Others confound health care professionals with their cheerful, life-affirming optimism, even in the presence of grave illness. The cognitive appraisal systems that interpret the stressors are obviously very different in these two types of individuals. Consequently, the biochemistry of their separate stress responses also differs. The concept of "hardiness" helps us to understand these reactions. The three characteristics that confer hardiness and thus protection from serious illnesses, are commitment, control, and challenge (Kosaba and Pucetti, 1983). Committed people are committed to their tasks and involved deeply in their activities. Control implies an ability to manipulate situations and have power over situations and people. Challenge is the aspect of welcoming and positively anticipating novel situations. Executives, who typically live in a highly stressed environment, have fewer serious illnesses when they possess these hardiness attributes than when they do not.

A behavioral characteristic that is important in stress responsiveness is the type A behavior pattern. This behavior pattern is characterized by impatience, hurrying, polyphasic thinking and acting, and in some cases, anger and hostility. Anger and hostility appear to be the most significant in terms of cardiovascular disease. Presumably, such type A people are in a tonically greater stress state than their placid, relaxed, type B opposites.

Other influences

The preceding discussion focused on how the neurologic mechanisms and internal coping processes differ. People also differ greatly in their social support systems, and clearly stressors produce greater changes and pathophysiologic damage in lonely, isolated, or friendless people. Coping mechanisms that allow for adaptation are often reinforced by social support. Other external factors that may play a role in the stress response include ecologic influences that may impede, exacerbate, or disrupt the stress response. For example, a crowded, polluted, or noisy environment is itself stressful, and if additional stressors are added to this situation, there is often an exaggeration of the stress response.

Although the stress response produces fairly nonspecific, predictable, physiologic changes, people may differ in their end-organ responsiveness to the hormones of stress. This is best exemplified by the attribute of *autonomic nervous system reactivity or lability*. According to this theory, there are important differences in receptor sensitivity to the catecholamines that are typically released during the alerting, alarm phase of the stress response. Such individuals would therefore have an exaggerated heightening of smooth muscle, cardiac muscle, and glandular responses to circulating catecholamines. This theoretical framework also speculates that some people may produce excessive or inappropriate bursts of catecholamines when faced with stressors and thus the responses mediated by the autonomic nervous system tend to be exaggerated.

Stressors

A key concept of the stress-adaption response is that there is great individualization of stressors. Every person differs in what is stressful for him or her, and whether or not something is stressful is based on factors such as history, coping skills, presence of other exacerbating stressors, time, and emotional state. The stress response to the same stressor may also differ from day to day. There are some common stressors to which everybody reacts, such as temperature extremes, surgery, anesthesia, starvation, and trauma. Even when exposed to these uniform stressors, however, there will be some individual gradation of response. The unifying thread among these stressors is that they activate the hypothalamic–hypophyseal–adrenocortical axis and result in an outpouring of adrenocorticosteroids into the blood and body fluids. Each of these stressors also cause a specific response in the body. For example, heat can burn, drugs can sedate, trauma can result in tissue destruction. Nonspecific or specific external factors affecting humans produce many responses superimposed on each other.

Local adaptation syndrome

Another aspect of the stress theory is that certain topical stressors can produce a local adaptation syndrome (LAS), which involves responses at the vicinity of the injury. Selye believed that local stress and general stress are interacting phenomena. They are both characterized by three phases: alarm, resistance, and exhaustion; both are nonspecific and sensitive to ACTH, corticoids, and STH; and finally they both may influence each other. Of course, the LAS predominantly involves inflammatory and immune reactions to the local stressor, although local thrombosis, calcification, and necrosis are possible.

Selye's work also suggests that both local and general adaptation syndromes are subject to modification. In particular, "conditioning" an animal by various forms of pretreatment results in a qualitatively different stress response than if no pretreatment is done. From this work has come the idea that certain responses of the body may be caused by a single stressor or by a combination of several stressors distributed through time. For example, necrosis may occur in a tissue as the result of hypoxia and ischemia. Necrosis might also occur if a toxic material that normally does not produce necrosis is applied to tissues pretreated with substances that interfere with vascular absorption of the toxic substance. Thus the toxic substance is concentrated in the tissue at risk. In the living system it is possible that environmental stressors may act together to produce different local reactions, thus explaining why the lesions produced in different individuals by the same agent may take many different forms. Disease under these circumstances must be considered multifactorial.

Competing risks

An important concept is that of *competing risks*. Any given disease process may not occur in an individual because at all times during the individual's life span other disease processes are "competing" for that individual and causing pathophysiologic conditions. For example, an individual who is afflicted with cancer and may die from the disease process may also be at risk for atherosclerosis or diabetes. These processes may not have developed because insufficient time was available, assuming that disease processes are independent. The great complexity of pathophysiology leads us to speculate, however, that a disease process such as carcinogenesis is probably not independent of the effects of hypoxia that may occur in atherosclerotic disease. If both pathogenic mechanisms are occurring together in the same individual, it seems extremely likely that one process will have an effect on the other. Perhaps we may even go so far as to say that one disease process would never develop in a given individual unless the second (or third or fourth, or combination thereof) were also present and contributory.

This idea of dependence of pathophysiologic mechanisms leads us to the realization that morbidity and mortality, as usually expressed by public health statistics, are entirely misleading. Cause of death may be listed as hypertensive heart disease, but in reality, superimposed upon this disease process, would be many variables such as the effects of the stress response, hypoxia, inflammation, and calcification, which are widespread throughout the body. The cause of death per se is not sufficient information for us to make a judgment about the true pathophysiology. It has been shown repeatedly in autopsy studies that death from one particular cause is difficult to ascertain. Furthermore, many times one pathophysiologic mechanism is fully developed in the deceased, but evidence of other disease processes can also be found. If the individual had lived long enough, these mechanisms probably would have become pathologic enough to cause severe signs and symptoms or result in death.

Synchronizers

Innate biologic rhythms are another variable superimposed on the response of the body to stressors. Many of these rhythms are circadian (24 hour) in nature. They exist in almost all functions of the body from output of hormones to cellular enzymatic processes. Although these circadian rhythms are intrinsic to the organism, they are influenced by environmental variables called *synchronizers* or Zeitgebers (timekeepers). The most important synchronizer appears to be the daily light-darkness cycle. However, if the predominant synchronizer is removed, other synchronizers can be introduced that will continue to elicit the circadian rhythm pattern. Mice, for example, are synchronized by the dominant stimulus of the light-dark cycle (which is reversed from humans since mice are nocturnal animals) and secondarily by the modifying synchronizer of the feeding time. The secondary synchronizer may become dominant, however, if the mice are subjected to constant light or constant dark or to a 50% dietary caloric restriction.

Many physiologic rhythms can be reversed if the light-darkness cycle is reversed. The presence of circadian rhythms results in many important physiologic and pathophysiologic phenomena. The time in the cycle in which a drug is introduced to a given individual may play an important role in the efficacy of that drug or its possible toxicity. The response to ionizing radiation is somewhat dependent on the time of day at which it is received. The times at which susceptible individuals usually have brain seizures is also circadian dependent. Indeed, the time of death of terminally ill people also appears to depend on circadian rhythm, commonly occurring between 2 and 3 AM. Myocardial infarctions typically occur at 9 AM (Kolata, 1986). Fig. 7-3 shows an endogenous circadian rhythm of adrenal cortex activity, as measured by eosinophil count, ACTH, and 17-hydroxyketosteroid secretion. The body's ability to maximally withstand stress may be circadian dependent, as the activity of the adrenal cortex has an endogenous rhythm, with peak secretion occurring during early morning sleep.

Immunologic effects of stress

Much of the research in this area has been done using animals, and only in the past

CIRCADIAN RHYTHMS

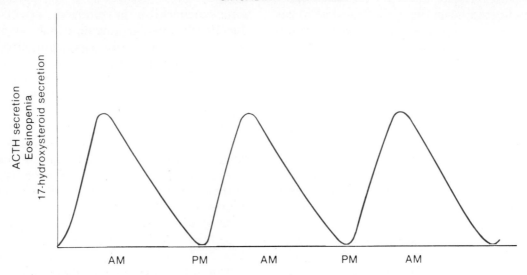

Fig. 7-3. Endogenous circadian rhythms exist as cellular, tissue, and organism level. Shown here are peaks of ACTH, corticosteroid secretion, and eosinopenia, indicating that an endogenous internal rhythm of stress exists.

10 years have human studies existed to corroborate the animal research. There is now overwhelming evidence of decreased immunocompetence resulting from stress in both animals and humans, and the implications of this phenomena are currently being explored. The mechanisms by which stress produces immunoincompetence are multiple and include effects on regulator cells, effector cells, and neurohumoral mechanisms. Stress is also antiinflammatory, decreasing the vascular and cellular response of both acute and chronic inflammation. The antiimmune and antiinflammatory characteristics of the stress response are generally considered adaptive, allowing the persistent stressor to exist within the host without causing damage and disruption.

This theoretically protective effect of the glucocorticoids tend to stretch the imagination. One hypothesis is that the reaction permits tolerance to massive amounts of normally-sequestered, cellular antigens that are suddenly released into the humoral fluids whenever stress-produced, tissue injury occurs. By suppressing the usual inflammatory and immunologic response, the deleterious effects of widespread reaction to these antigens are avoided. In this way, the stress response is seen as a biologic buffer, holding down waves of antibody responses and checking the inflammatory and immunologic reactions.

Munck and Guyre (1986) have proposed that the glucocorticoids, rather than being adaptive, provide a mechanism by which defense reactions produced by stress are counteracted. Their belief is that the glucocorticoids protect against an overshooting of the stress-produced, inflammatory, immunologic, neurochemical, fluid and electrolyte, and metabolic reactions that, if excessive, could lead to bodily damage themselves.

Regardless of the reason for the antiimmune and the antiinflammatory actions of the glucocorticoids, when stress becomes a chronic, unremitting state, the dominant effect on the physiology is pathophysiologic rather than adaptive. The presence of persistent human stress has been shown to lead to increased risks for autoimmune disease, infection, and malignancy. Some of these effects will be explained once the exact mechanisms by which glucocorticoids act are understood. One general effect on the immune system appears to be inhibition of the production or action of lymphokines, monokines, and inflammatory mediators such as prostaglandins and bradykinin. Cortisol is known to act at the membrane of cytoplasmic lysosomes, inhibiting rupture and decreasing lysosomal output by inflammatory cells. There are also effects on some hormones and neuropeptides involved in immunity and inflammation. Glucocorticoids act on immune cells and are capable of lysing them. During an acute stress response in rodents, the blood lymphocytes (which are mostly T cells) become profoundly depressed within a few hours. Thymocyte lysis also is marked, and cellular immunity is quickly depressed (Riley, 1981). The cells particularly sensitive to corticosteroid destruction are the natural killer (NK) cells. Recall that these cells are an important host defense against malignantly transformed cells and are constantly screening for cancer. There is evidence that institutionalized psychiatric patients, who presumably experience chronically high stress, have an increased cancer mortality. Other arms of the immune system are also depressed, including B cells. There is a decreased immunoglobulin production by the B cells under the influence of glucocorticoid hormones.

Human studies of stress and immune function have examined many of the aspects of immunologic integrity. Kiecolt-Glaser et al. (1984, 1985, 1986) have pioneered such studies and have shown that even the stress of an examination will decrease NK cells and helper cells and increase immunoglobulin titers to herpes viruses (indicating decreased resistance). Other studies have shown that salivary IgA decreases in acute stress situations, such as examinations (Jemmott et al., 1983) and childbirth (Annie and Groer, 1988). Sleep deprivation is also a stressor affecting immune function, as is bereavement, loneliness, and depression. It is probable that as this research in psychoneuroimmunology continues, a theme will be that whatever is perceived as stressful to an individual has the capability of suppressing immune function, particularly cellular immunity, significantly. Once the stressor is removed, the immune system is capable of repair, and there is an overshoot phenomenon in which immunoenhancement occurs after the stress state (Riley, 1981). Chronic stress appears capable of provoking sustained immunoincompetence, and it is likely that an already threatened or fragile immune system (such as that in childhood, old age, or during illness) will be more sensitive to these effects of stress.

Adrenergic mechanisms

Acute stress produces activation of the hypothalamic–hypophyseal–adrenocortical axis as has been described. However, adrenergic arousal, also mediated through the hypothalamus, is important in pathophysiologic mechanisms. Stressors that are most provoking of a catecholamine response include hypoglycemia, public speaking, harassment (especially in type A individuals), temperature extremes, exercise, surgery, hemorrhage, hypoxia, and myocardial infarction (Axelrod and Reisine, 1984). These responses are for the most part appropriate arousals and warnings of events that threaten the individual's wellness. However, even such appropriate responses can lead to pathologic sequelae. For example, acute renal failure may follow an episode of hemorrhage as a result of the vasoconstrictive and hypoxia-producing effects of massive sympathetic arousal. Another example is seen in stressed animals that develop gastric ulceration within hours, and the same phenomenon has been observed in humans. The ulcerogenic mechanism appears to be associated with adrenergic discharge and circulating catecholamines that vasoconstrict splanchnic vessels and decrease blood supply to the gastric mucosa. An important note is that the catecholamines and corticosteroid hormones act permissively with each other. That is, the action of one is enhanced by the other. It is also probable that there are multiple feedback, regulatory loops between the adrenergic and the glucocorticoid systems in stress. For example, it has been shown that epinephrine may modulate the secretion of corticotrophin releasing factor (CRF) from the hypothalamus.

Autonomic nervous system hyperreactivity has been suggested as an important component of the cause of cardiovascular disease, leading to atherosclerosis and arteriolar smooth muscle changes. The autonomic nervous system may also participate in immunologic regulation. Enkephalins (a type of endogenous opiate) are released by the adrenal medulla along with catecholamines. Endogenous opiates may modulate the immune response and are secreted both centrally and peripherally in stress. The lack of pain sensation noted by people who recall anesthesia while experiencing a severe and traumatic stress (such as a wound received on the battlefield) is probably accounted for by the release of these opiates. Endogenous opiates may participate in many of the behavioral aspects of the human stress response by affecting neurochemistry.

The contribution of the sympathetic nervous system to pathophysiologic mechanisms is based on the physiologic actions of the catecholamines. The vasoconstrictive effects can lead to arteriolar smooth muscle degeneration or sclerosis, Raynaud's phenomenon, migraine, tissue hypoxia; the myocardial effects can result in arrhythmias and angina; the platelet-aggregating effects could potentiate thrombotic phenomena; and the metabolic effects could contribute to hyperlipidemia and hyperglycemia. Many alterations in normal physiology are therefore possible when excessive catecholamines are released, when catecholamines are released at inappropriate times, or when a receptor is extremely sensitive to these hormones.

Parasympathetic mechanisms

We have focused on adrenergic arousal as a predominant force in the arousal and alerting typical of the alarm phase of the stress response. However, there are situations in which parasympathetic activation dominates during stressful states. Furthermore, there are some individuals who are more predisposed to parasympathetic responses compared to sympathetic responses. Parasympathetic responders might therefore respond to emotional stress with increased gastrointestinal motility and severe diarrhea, whereas a sympathetic responder would suffer the opposite effect. In some stress states, both arms of the automonic nervous system may be activated. A good example of this is psychogenic fainting. Witnessing an unpleasant event, or in some individuals, the sight of blood (Asterita, 1985) could result in this response. The vasovagal response of fainting is usually preceded first by sympathetic arousal, which shunts blood centrally, vasoconstricts peripherally, and increases muscle blood flow. This, combined with immobility and increased parasympathetic arousal, will result in a decreased venous return, decreased end-diastolic volume, and decreased cardiac output and blood pressure, followed by fainting.

Other aspects of parasympathetic response to stress include blushing (a phenomenon that is very poorly understood) and weeping in response to emotional distress. Individuals, therefore, differ in both their parasympathetic output and probably also in their end-organ sensitivity to the various neurohumoral mechanisms involved in the stress response.

One clinical aspect of stress is sudden death resulting from acute myocardial infarction (AMI), which is observed in people with and without underlying coronary atherosclerosis. It is mediated by the stress hormones, which have the potential of causing coronary artery vasospasm. The following exemplifies a typical history of AMI followed by sudden cardiac death.

CASE STUDY: SUDDEN CARDIAC DEATH

Objective and Subjective Data

MB, a 51-year-old male, was admitted to the emergency room via an ambulance after collapsing. He had just been informed of the sudden death of his wife; he became pale, clutched his chest, and fell to the floor.

History

MB had been obese, hypertensive, and hypercholesterolemic for many years. He

Contributed by Maureen Groër.

smoked 2 packs of cigarettes a day, had a family history of heart disease, and was in a high stress job environment. He had been ill with a severe respiratory influenza during the weeks preceding his collapse.

Physical Examination

This patient received immediate cardiopulmonary resuscitation, but was nonresponsive. His pupils were dilated, and there were no vital signs. He was declared dead on arrival.

Pathophysiology

In this case AMI was preceded by some significant risk factors. The patient had a long history of poorly controlled hypertension, smoked, was sedentary, could be classified as having a type A behavior pattern, and was obese. His serum cholesterol was in the high risk category (300 mg). Nevertheless, his AMI was precipitated by what was, in his frame of reference, a highly significant, stressful event. In fact, the literature is replete with case histories in which people experience sudden death after hearing news of the death of a loved one. The mechanism involved here is related to several integrated events. The alarm phase of the stress response leads to a sudden elevation in sympathetic nervous system activation and high levels of circulating catecholamines. In this susceptible patient, these produced a coronary vasospasm, which immediately raised coronary resistance. Blood flow to the myocardium was disturbed, cells became hypoxic, and many damaged cells eventually lysed, releasing their intracellular contents into the myocardial cytoplasm. Zor et al. (1985) have suggested that AMI results not only from the stress-associated catecholamine burst, but also from an immunologic release of leukotrienes. These substances are released from certain cells when intracellular calcium is increased. Both neurotransmitters and cellular immune reactions can result in increased intracellular calcium and leukotriene release. The leukotrienes are a class of compounds that are metabolites of arachidonic acid, as are the prostaglandins. The most well known leukotriene is a slow-reacting substance of anaphylaxis (see Chapter 2). A major effect of the leukotrienes is smooth muscle contraction, and thus they are potentially vasospastic. Immunologic mechanisms are known to release leukotrienes from cells, including cardiac cells. Thus an individual with a viral illness, may be immunologically "ready" for AMI, provided the acute stress reaction occurs. In this case, the patient had influenza during the week preceding his sudden cardiac death and was still convalescing. This can be viewed as an infection-stressor capable, through antibody-antigen activation, of damaging cardiac muscle and releasing leukotrienes. Combined then with the psychologic stressor of the death of his spouse, this patient suffered an acute vasospastic process that lead to further leukotriene release, further vasospasm, hypoxia, and myolysis. Because the cardiac integrity in this individual was already compromised by some atherosclerosis and combined with viral illness and sudden stress, the patient's heart was unable to maintain function and failed.

BIBLIOGRAPHY

Annie C and Groer M: Salivary immunoglobulin secretion in prepared and unprepared primagravidas at childbirth, 1988, in manuscript.

Asterita M: The physiology of stress, New York, 1985, Human Sciences Press Inc.

Axelrod J and Reisine T: Stress hormones: their interaction and regulation, Science 224:452, 1984.

Day S, editor: Cancer, stress, and death, ed 2, New York, 1986, Plenum Medical Book Co.

Jemmott J, et al: Academic stress, power motivation, and decrease in secretion rate of salivary secretory immunoglobulin A, Lancet 1:1400, 1983.

Kiecolt-Glaser J, et al: Psychosocial modifiers of immunocompetence in medical students, Psychosom Med 46:7, 1984a.

Kiecolt-Glaser J, et al: Urinary cortisol, cellular immunocompetency, and loneliness in psychiatric inpatients, Psychosom Med 46:15, 1984b.

Kiecolt-Glaser J, et al: Distress and DNA repair in human lymphocytes, J Behav Med 8:311, 1985.

Kolata A: Heart attacks at 9:00 AM, Science 233:417-418, 1986.

Kosaba SC and Puccetti MC: Personality and social resources in stress resistance, J Pers Soc Psychol 42:168, 1982.

Munck A and Guyre P: Glucocorticoid hormones in stress: physiological and pharmacological actions, News in Physiolog Sci 1:69, 1986.

Selye, H: Forty years of stress research, Can Med Assoc J, 115:53-56, 1976.

Riley V: Psychoneuroendocrine influences in neoplasia, Science 212:1100, 1981.

West L and Stein M: Critical issues in behavioral medicine, Philadelphia, 1982, J B Lippincott Co.

Zor U, et al: Immunological stress induces severe cardiac myolysis: mediation by leukotrienes. In McKerns K and Pantic V, editors: Neuroendocrine correlates of stress, New York, 1985, Plenum Publishing Corp.

8

Endocrine pathophysiology

The endocrine system was historically considered to be a rather discrete group of ductless glands which, when appropriately stimulated, poured their secretions, the hormones, into the blood. Recent discoveries of endocrine function by many different tissues and organs has led to an expansion of this former concept. For example, cells within the gastrointestinal tract and throughout the nervous system have been discovered to secrete the same or similar small peptides, which function as messengers. When a messenger molecule is secreted at one site, absorbed into the bloodstream, and acts at a different site, the molecule is considered a hormone. Hormones produced by both the gut and the nervous system include cholecystokinin (CCK), substance P, somatostatin, vasoactive peptide, endorphins, enkephalin, neurotensin, and gastrin (Snyder, 1980). Other molecules produced by many different tissues that are now characterized by the term "hormone" include prostaglandins and other substances produced during an inflammatory reaction. Thus endocrine cells that secrete hormones are widely dispersed throughout the body, as well as being located within the endocrine glands.

Because of discoveries of over forty separate, dispersed cell types in both the central nervous system and peripheral tissues, a distinct neuroendocrine system is now recognized. Neuroendocrine secretions can function as neurotransmitters, or they can modify or regulate neurotransmission. These secretions fit the definition of a hormone since they are released by neurons and other cells and then travel humorally to act at a distance on their target cells.

All nutritional, metabolic, growth-related, and developmental processes occur in the presence of particular optimal environments. Hormonal influences or interactions regulate those environments in precise ways. Hormones are also required for "on off" signaling, as many processes will not be initiated, even in the presence of adequate substrates, enzymes, and cofactors, without receiving some external "message." The controlled regulation of hormone concentration is obviously essential for metabolism and growth, and negative feedbacks operate to maintain the appropriate secretion of the hormones. A key end product of a hormone-stimulated reaction increases in concentration in the blood and eventually reaches a value that exerts negative feedback on the hormone secretion. This value is a set-point, sensed by critical tissues that play roles in the production of the hormone. This includes not only the endocrine cells themselves, but usually also cells in the nervous system or pituitary gland that secrete appropriate releasing or tropic hormones. Essential to the idea of feedback regulation of hormone release is the concept of cellular receptors. Receptors are involved in the set-point recognition of the end product produced through the hormone action. Receptors are also present on or within hormone-responsive cells. An understanding of the molecular events that ensue upon hormone-receptor interaction is essential, as pathophysiologic disturbances in these processes are often a cause or consequence of many endocrine diseases.

RECEPTORS IN HORMONE ACTION

All hormones interact with target tissue by an initial recognition by the cell. Only certain cells have receptors for certain hormones, and it is largely on this basis that hormone responsiveness occurs. This recognition is believed to take place through hormone-receptor binding. Receptors themselves are either membrane bound, cytoplasmic, or intranuclear. A receptor is defined as a cellular molecule that interacts with high selectivity and affinity with a particular hormone. Upon binding with the hormone, a predetermined sequence of events ensues, leading to a process that the hormone regulates. The hormone itself is usually not a participant in the process, but rather an initiator.

Membrane receptors

Membrane receptors for hormones occupy only a tiny proportion of the total cell surface area. Furthermore, for most hormone action, even this tiny proportion is redundant, often with only 10% occupancy of the receptors required for maximum activity. The receptors are specific, in that the hormone binds with high affinity. However, other molecules (agonists) may bind to them, as may antagonists. Agonists activate, producing the hormone-sensitive response. Many chemical and pharmaco-

logic agents act as either agonists or antagonists at the cell membrane receptor level. Hormone membrane receptors act to transduce the "first" message, the hormone, into the "second" message, the hormone-responsive event taking place in the cell. In order for this to occur, in some systems a second messenger molecule is released into the cell upon hormone-receptor interaction. Two second messenger molecules, cyclic adenosine monophosphate (cAMP) and cyclic guanosine monophosphate (cGMP) have been characterized. cAMP is generated by receptor-mediated responses in many cells and in a wide variety of situations; thus it is the receptor-hormone binding that is specific to the cell, rather than the second messenger. Only certain hepatic cells are endowed, for example, with glucagon receptors. Once glucagon molecules bind with a specific number of membrane receptors, the hormone-receptor complex activates membrane adenyl cyclase. This enzyme is present and moving rapidly and laterally within the fluid mosaic structure of the cell membrane. Upon binding with the glucagon-receptor complex, an alteration in the membrane stereochemistry occurs at the site of interaction. At this site adenyl cyclase becomes enzymatically active. ATP is acted upon, and ADP and cAMP are generated from it. cAMP is removed, once produced, by phosphodiesterases, enzymes that are activated by Ca^{++}. Thus increased intracellular Ca^{++} is associated with decreased cAMP. Up until this point all hormones acting by a second messenger proceed in the described manner. How the cAMP affects intracellular responses is cell specific. The major mechanism of cAMP and cGMP action is activation of cell protein kinases. For example, in the liver cell the production of cAMP activates a protein kinase that causes glycogen phosphorylase to form. This eventually results in the breakdown of glycogen and the subsequent release of glucose molecules. Glucagon from the alpha cells of the pancreas acts in opposition to insulin, causing a rise in blood glucose. After a meal high in protein, for example, its release is stimulated, and the blood glucose level is maintained through its action in the absence of dietary carbohydrate. The intracellular glycogenolysis is produced through enzymatic activations, which are diagrammed in Fig. 8-1. The stepwise production of active phosphorylase results in glycogen breakdown.

In another type of cell cAMP generation might activate an entirely different chain of enzyme reactions with perhaps a particular effect on cell division or fat metabolism. The universality throughout the animal kingdom of cAMP release in response to many different membrane receptor signals is an example of biologic conservation of energy, which is such an essential part of steady state kinetics. Some hormones appear to act by *reducing* the intracellular concentration of cAMP and in this way produce their desired effect. In some systems there may be release of cGMP through a hormone-receptor interaction. Some authorities believe that metabolic balance is achieved through the ratio of cAMP and cGMP, since often cGMP appear to act in opposition of cAMP, a

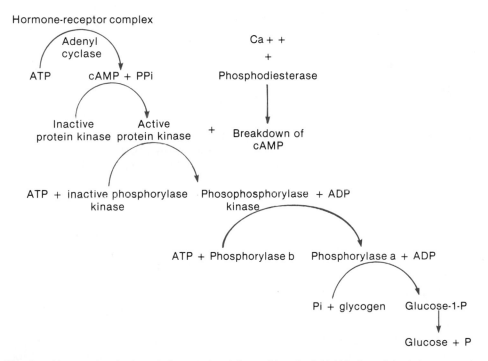

Fig. 8-1. Hormonal activation of glycogen breakdown. After the initial binding of the hormone to the receptor, adenyl cyclase is activated causing the formation of cyclic AMP. A chain of events then ensues, causing sequential activation of phosphorylases, until an active enzyme that splits glucose-1-phosphate from glycogen is formed. Cyclic AMP is quickly inactivated by phosphodiesterase in the presence of calcium.

kind of yin-yang theory of hormone action.

Hormones that bind to membrane receptors may act in ways other than stimulation or inhibition of cAMP or possibly cGMP release. A change in the permeability of the membrane to a certain substance may result from a hormone-receptor interaction. Such is thought to be the case for insulin, which in certain cells acts to facilitate glucose entry into the cells. Insulin has many other metabolic effects as well, which are described elsewhere.

Intracellular receptors

Receptors to certain hormones are present within the cytosol or in the nucleus. Thyroid hormone receptors, for example, appear to be present within the nonhistone protein fraction of sensitive cells' nuclei. Perhaps the hormone-receptor interaction there triggers a regulatory protein that acts to induce transcription of a specific genetic sequence of the cell's DNA, resulting in production of a particular protein. It is now believed that for both thyroid and steroid receptor responses, an initial cytoplasmic receptor binding occurs. This complex gains the ability to move into the nucleus and interact with nuclear proteins, and ultimately new genetic transcription ensues.

Intracellular binding of hormones to receptors depends on many factors. It is likely that the hormones involved in these types of interactions freely move into most of the cells of the body. However, only those cells endowed with appropriate receptors would respond to the hormone. The hormone-receptor interaction might also be dependent on modulating factors, such as other hormones.

Most intracellular hormone-receptor interactions are reversible and concentration dependent and have a limited period of effectiveness.

ENDOCRINE PATHOPHYSIOLOGIC MECHANISMS

Rather than present a cataloging of the endocrine glands and the many possible alterations in function, we will present a more conceptual approach. It should be recognized at the outset that endocrinologic disturbance can occur at the following levels: feedback sensitivity, tropic hormone or neurotropic control, output capability of the gland, carriage of the hormone in body fluids, target tissue hormonal sensitivity, disorders of the cellular machinery that is normally regulated by the hormone, and degradation.

Endocrine disease represents a profound threat to the maintenance of wellness. Endocrine responsiveness to internal and external environmental change is a major component of the organism's ability to quickly or more chronically adapt and adjust. We shall describe endocrine disease in that framework. Endocrinopathy that primarily disrupts metabolic pathways will be discussed first. Second, those disorders that interfere with the ability to react and adapt to stressors will be elaborated upon. Next, growth and developmental disturbance caused by endocrine imbalances will be described. See pp. 290-297 for a discussion concerning reproductive endocrinopathy.

ENDOCRINE DISTURBANCES OF METABOLISM

Many endocrine secretions regulate and direct metabolic intracellular pathways. Hormones can act directly by initiating a series of biochemical events or in synergism with other hormones to create a suitable environment in which a biochemical reaction is favored. They can, of course, also antagonize other hormone actions. Thus hormonal *balance* is really the key to metabolic balance. It is artificial to talk about the effect of one hormone upon metabolism without looking at the whole hormonal milieu. We shall examine those aberrations that primarily affect metabolism, with an appreciation of the complexity of the system. Disorders of the pancreas (diabetes mellitus, hypoglycemia) are not included here as they will be discussed in Chapter 19.

Thyroid gland disorders

The hypothalamic-hypophyseal-thyroid axis should be recalled from the study of normal physiology. Briefly, thyrotropin-releasing hormone (TRH) is produced by the hypothalamus, which stimulates the anterior pituitary gland to release thyroid-stimulating hormone (TSH). TRH is produced in response to nervous input and probably to endogenous levels of thyroid hormone. TSH acts on the cells of the thyroid gland, stimulating both the synthesis and secretion of thyroid hormones, T_3 (triiodothyronine) and T_4 (thyroxin). These hormones are synthesized by the thyroid gland from iodine and thyronine, the latter being formed by the pairing of two tyrosine molecules. Iodine is required therefore for adequate synthesis of thyroid hormone (T_3 and T_4 are known collectively as thyroid hormone). Most of the dietary iodine is efficiently trapped by thyroid tissue, the rest being excreted. The hormone circulates in the body fluids in equilibrium with several thyroid hormone–transporting proteins, but only the free hormone is effective. While most of thyroid hormone is made up of T_4, it is converted to the much more biologically active T_3, in peripheral tissues.

Thyroid hormone appears to exert its major effects by first entering responsive cells and binding to nuclear receptors in the active T_3 form or, less significantly, to cytoplasmic receptors that then enter the nucleus. This hormone-receptor complex becomes associated with DNA, which results in an enhancement of the ability of the receptor to further bind T_3. In addition, this association causes certain genetic sequences to be transcribed and subsequently translated to synthesis of particular proteins. T_4 and T_3 are major regulators of the basal metabolic rate. The mechanism of action for this important effect involves several biochemical systems. Thyroid hormone is believed to act directly at the level of mitochondrial oxidative phosphorylation, since oxygen consumption increases rapidly in most hormonally sensitive tissues when thyroid hormones are present. The actual mechanism for mitochondrial stimulation of metabolism by thyroid hormone is not known, but several major speculations are well accepted. One idea is that the thyroid hormone "uncouples" oxidative phosphorylation, that is, increases electron transport and oxygen utilization by eliminating the dependency of electron transport upon the normally rate-limiting concentration of adenosine diphosphate (ADP). Thus oxidative phospyhorylation would occur more rapidly, more heat would be generated, and more oxygen consumed. Another possible mode of action for thyroid hormones is through stimulation of nuclear or mitochondrial DNA to produce enzymes or other proteins that increase mitochondrial metabolism through some type of direct stimulation.

While mitochondrial effects of thyroid hormones have traditionally been considered important, more recent work has described an effect of thyroid hormones on transport systems, which is probably of major significance. In many tissues thyroid hormones increase the rate of sodium efflux and potassium influx through either a direct or indirect stimulation of the classic sodium pump (Smith and Edelman 1979). Calcium pumping is also stimulated (Dillman, 1985). These active transport mechanisms are characterized by a dependence upon cellular metabolism, since they are fueled by adenosine triphosphate (ATP), a high energy molecule that is produced through an efficient aerobic glycolysis, Krebs' cycle, and electron transport system. In order for the Na^+-K^+ pump or the Ca^{++} pump to operate efficiently. ATPase is required, which is synthesized by the nucleus. Thyroid hormones may act by stimulating the production of this enzyme by the nucleus. Increasing the availability and amount of the enzyme causes increased sodium-potassium–linked and calcium pumping, which results in increased ATP utilization and ADP production. Remember that for every ATP molecule that is used by the pump, an ADP and inorganic phosphate molecule are produced. Thus the extra ADP produced would stimulate cell metabolism, since under normal circumstances the amount of ADP is a major control on the rate of substrate metabolism within a cell. The excess metabolism also generates more heat and increased oxygen utilization, as would be expected. This phenomenon, is probably the major way that thyroid hormones increase the basal metabolic rate.

T_3 and T_4 also control lipid metabolism, increasing cholesterol synthesis. However, the hormones also increase the rate of turnover of cholesterol, possibly by stimulating the rate of catabolism of cholesterol, and in actuality the overall effect of the hormones is to decrease serum cholesterol. T_3 and T_4 may accomplish this by increasing the production of hepatic enzymes catabolizing low-density lipoproteins, cholesterol, and triglycerides.

Thyroid hormones also function in the regulation of normal differentiation and development during embryonic and fetal life. This effect depends on the hormonal milieu, and there is interaction of thyroid hormones with growth hormone and others. In particular, the maturation of the skeletal system and central nervous system is extremely sensitive to thyroid hormone deprivation. The developmental effects of thyroid hormones are probably related to the nuclear receptor transcription and translation control of protein synthesis.

Hyperthyroidism. When excessive thyroid gland secretion occurs, a state of hyperthyroidism is present. Approximately 1% of women in the United States will develop hyperthyroidism during their lifetime. The most typical form of hyperthyroidism is Graves' disease. In order to understand the pathophysiology of this disease, it is necessary to review the normal regulation of thyroid hormone release. In order for the thyroid gland to function normally, there must be adequate dietary iodine and normal release of thyroid-stimulating hormone (TSH) from the anterior pituitary gland. Normally TSH stimulates the thyroid gland to produce thyroid hormone and secrete it into the extracellular fluid. When a set-point level of thyroid hormone is reached, the brain and pituitary gland respond by decreasing the output of TSH. This is a very common negative feedback control of hormone release seen in endocrine function.

In hyperthyroidism there is an extremely elevated serum concentration of thyroid hormone, and often a decreased release of TSH. It appears that the normal balance is disturbed by either an abnormal brain and anterior pituitary response or by a change in the thyroid gland in terms of its responsiveness to TSH. The etiology of most secondary hyperthyroid disease is thought to be an autoimmune mechanism in which the body reacts inappropriately to its own thyroid tissue. In the known autoimmune thyroid diseases, there are autoantibodies against thyroglobulin, microsomal protein, and TSH receptors, T cell immunity against thyroid-antigen, and immune complex formation in the blood and tissues (Groot and Sridama, 1983). An immunoglobulin that is involved is known as LATS (long-acting thyroid stimulator). LATS is now known to be a TSH antibody. LATS has a long-term stimulating effect on the thyroid gland, and it is a molecule with the properties of an immunoglobulin. It binds to the TSH receptors present in thyroid gland tissue and stimulates intracellular production of cAMP. LATS has been demonstrated to be increased in the blood of individuals with Graves' disease. However, this is not consistently seen. It is nevertheless possible that LATS is released abnormally in Graves' disease and then acts as a blocker of TSH, a stimulator of thyroid gland activity, and an autoantibody. There is histologic evidence for an autoimmune process in the thyroid gland in Graves' disease. Immunoglobulins and complement are deposited, and the gland gives the appearance of toxic enlargement and inflammation. Furthermore, the thymus gland is often enlarged in Graves' disease, and numerous other autoantibodies to TSH, thyroglobulin, and thyroid gland antigens are often present.

Signs and symptoms. Hyperthyroidism can become suddenly exacerbated by stress or infection into *thyroid storm*, which is a life-threatening condition. Chronic hyperthyroidism often leads to cardiac changes, which are also very severe. Thus this is a serious disease in both chronic and acute forms and must be adequately treated. The clinical syndrome of hyperthyroidism is one in which all the normal metabolic effects of thyroid hormone become exaggerated and excessive. Since thyroid hormone has multiple effects throughout the body, the individual with Graves' disease often has many different symptoms (Table 8-1). Diagnosis is made on the basis of elevated T_3 and T_4 levels, increased protein-bound iodide (PBI), and the clinical history and picture. At the cellular level excessive thyroid hormone appears to accelerate metabolism and heat production and increase the rate of sodium-potassium–linked pumping. An exaggeration of beta receptor–mediated responses is also very typical. Thyroid hormone appears to increase either the sensitivity or the number of the beta receptors to catecholamines. Thus excessive thyroid hormone results in symptoms that are very similar to excessive catecholamine

Table 8-1. Clinical manifestations of hyperthyroidism

Causative mechanisms	Signs and symptoms
↑ Catabolism and heat production	Muscle wasting (negative nitrogen balance); weight loss; increased appetite; fatigue (at first ↑ physical stamina); heat intolerance
↑ Sensitivity to catecholamines	Sweating; heat intolerance; tachycardia and palpitations; warm hands and feet; ↑ nervousness and irritability; tremors and ↑ Achilles reflex time; increased susceptibility to infection
↑ Cardiovascular activity	Tachycardia and palpitations; ↑ cardiac output and ↑ blood pressure; congestive heart failure (high output)
↑ Gastrointestinal activity with ↑ motility	Diarrhea; weight loss; nausea and vomiting
Speech	Rapid speech; hoarseness
Mental status	Emotional instability
Reproductive activity	Oligomenorrhea or amenorrhea

or sympathetic nervous system stimulation. Specifically, cardiovascular symptoms such as tachycardia, elevated blood pressure, nervousness, sweating, tremor, palpitations, and electrical arrhythmias of the heart are present.

Cardiac symptoms are the most common result of hyperthyroidism. High-output cardiac failure may occur in chronic, untreated hyperthyroidism. In this condition, the cardiac output, although tremendously increased, is inadequate to respond to the oxygenation needs of the hypermetabolic peripheral tissues. Through normal autoregulation there is a drop in peripheral resistance caused by the accumulation of vasoactive metabolites such as adenosine, CO_2, and ADP. In order to perfuse the tissues adequately under these conditions the output must increase. Eventually a point is reached when this becomes impossible. Heart failure is the result of the tendency of catecholamine-stimulated heart toward abnormal electrical conduction and arrhythmia. Beta blocking drugs (e.g., propranolol) may be used to reverse the effects of the hyperthyroid-stimulated heart.

Other symptoms related to catecholamine sensitivity are neurologic and can be very disturbing to the individual. Hyperthyroid patients are often very restless, anxious, irritable, and nervous. Excessive activity is often the complaint of the individual (and also of those who live with the person). There is difficulty falling and staying asleep. The deep tendon reflexes are hyperactive, and there may be a fine tremor. Excessive activity and increased metabolic rate cause wasting and weight loss. In order to keep up with the great metabolic demand imposed by the disease, the appetite is increased dramatically.

Other systems that are disturbed by hyperthyroidism include the gastrointestinal and reproductive systems. Thermoregulation is also altered, with heat intolerance and excessive perspiration occurring. Gastrointestinal tract symptoms include abdominal pain, diarrhea, vomiting, hepatomegaly, and jaundice. The female with hyperthyroidism often becomes amenorrheic. Another common and disturbing sign of hyperthyroidism is exophthalmia (Fig. 8-2). The cause of this unusual condition is basically unknown. One speculation is that EPS (exophthalmos-producing substance), a fragment of TSH, is responsible for the exophthalmic changes. Recent work suggests that there are cross-reacting antibodies acting against both thyroid tissue and eye muscle proteins (Wall and Kuroki, 1985). The condition can occur in the absence of thyroid excess, and hyperthyroidism is not universally accompanied by exophthalmia. The changes that occur in the orbit of the eye include muscular degeneration and edema with infiltration of the affected muscles so that they bulge forward and cause the characteristic staring, nonblinking appearance of exophthalmia. The fatty tissue around the orbit also hypertrophies and contributes to the bulging of the eye. Even with treatment, some degree of exophthalmos usually remains in the hyperthyroid individual.

In Graves' disease the thyroid gland itself is overstimulated and becomes hypertrophied, or "goitrous." This enlargement is palpable during swallowing through the anterior neck or may even be visible to the eye. It appears round and feels quite firm. There is increased vascularity to the point that a murmur may be heard when the gland is auscultated.

Graves' disease possibly has a strong genetic background, occurring with high incidence in certain families and in identical twins. Furthermore, the HLA antigens HLA-B8 and DRw3 occur with greater frequency in individuals with Graves' disease compared to the normal population. It is

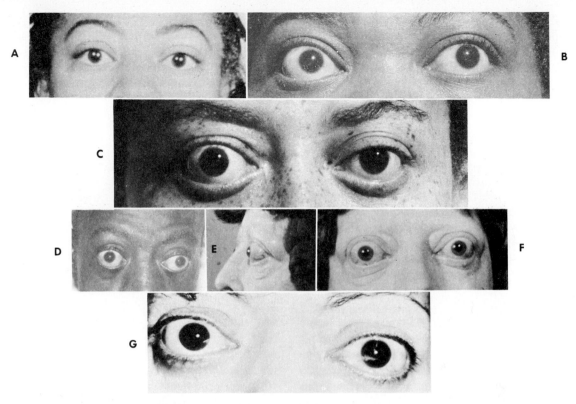

Fig. 8-2. Ophthalmopathy in Grave's disease. **A,** Minimal retraction of lower lids, no exophthalmos. **B,** Lid retraction with mild exophthalmos. **C,** Asymmetric exophthalmos. **D,** Ophthalmoplegia. **E** and **F,** Infiltrative ophthalmopathy with severe exophthalmos. **G,** Residual corneal scar in left eye after unilateral malignant exophthalmos.

(From Schneeburg, NG: Essentials of clinical endocrinology, St Louis, 1970, The CV Mosby Co.)

four times more common in women than men.

Treatment rationale. Graves' disease is best treated by efforts that oppose the hyperactivity of the gland. While surgery is one option, the drugs propylthiouracil or methimazole are often used initially. The mode of action of these drugs is to block the production of thyroid hormone by inhibiting the binding of iodine. A euthyroid state can often be maintained by drugs alone. Subtotal thyroidectomy is avoided if possible because of the possibility of creating a permanent hypothyroid state or of injuring the recurrent laryngeal nerve.

The following case study illustrates the clinical features of thyroid storm.

CASE STUDY: THYROID STORM

History

KL is a 50-year-old woman. She is married and the mother of two grown children. She is an elementary school teacher, active in both school and community activities, and is a competitive tennis player. She describes herself as always active, busy, and "hyper." She has never had any serious illnesses but recalls being

Contributed by Maureen Groër.

treated for a thyroid problem for a short period of time as an adolescent. During her second pregnancy she also experienced an "overactive" thyroid gland and remembers feeling agitated, nervous, and shaky during that time. After the pregnancy, the problems appeared to go away.

About 1 month ago, KL began to experience weight loss, nervousness, sleeplessness, and "hot flashes" that she attributed to menopause. She noticed that her neck looked a little "swollen" but thought that she probably had swollen glands.

KL was admitted 2 days before this evaluation for emergency surgery. She had been involved in an automobile accident that resulted in multiple contusions and a complex fracture of the tibia, which required surgical intervention. Shortly after surgery, while still in the recovery room, the patient developed signs and symptoms of thyrotoxic crisis. She was then transferred to the intensive care unit.

Subjective and Objective Data

KL appears flushed, is perspiring heavily, is extremely restless, confused, and agitated, is moaning in apparent pain, and does not seem able to coherently express her needs. She has vomited twice and has had profuse diarrhea three times in the last 4 hours.

Weight: 110 lbs
Height: 68 inches
Vital signs
   Temperature: 103°F
   Pulse: 112
   Respiratory rate: 30
   Blood pressure: 160/94
ECG: Frequent, bigeminal, premature atrial complexes
Serum:
   Glucose   88 gm/dl
   Na   140 mEq/L
   K   3.8 mEq/L
   Cl   90 mEq/L
   T3 uptake,
   percent of control   160

T4   20 μg/100 ml
PBI   19 μg/100 ml
Physical examination
Skin: Moist and hot to the touch; multiple bruises and abrasions on the chest and legs
HEENT: Eyes do not exhibit exophthalmos but do give a staring impression; pupils hyperreactive to light; several muscle tics of the external eye musculature noted during the examination; firm, enlarged, nodular thyroid tissue palpable and visible to inspection
Cardiorespiratory: tachycardic and hyperpneic; carotid bruit 2+ bilaterally; soft systolic murmur +2/5; pulse of large bounding amplitude in all arteries
Abdominal: Hyperactive bowel sounds; tenderness to palpation diffusely; liver, spleen, and kidneys not palpable
Nervous: Hyperactive +4 DTRs (biceps, triceps, right knee, and ankle; left leg casted); +2 abdominal reflex; negative Babinsky; difficult to assess cranial nerve function due to patient's condition; difficult to assess motor or sensory components
Musculoskeletal: Cast is dry, with no drainage; circulation, sensation, and motion intact; patient appears to have surgical pain related to recent setting of fracture

Pathophysiology

This patient is experiencing a life-threatening thyroid storm that was precipitated by the trauma and surgery she recently experienced. Although it is not possible to determine the duration of her preceding hyperthyroid state, it has probably been significant, although she does not show classical signs of exophthalmos. Her general metabolic state now is at a highly critical level, as evidenced by the fever, central and peripheral nervous system hyperactivity, cardiorespiratory acceleration, and atrial arrhythmia. These states could easily precipitate atrial fibrillation and cardiac failure if treatment is not instituted. The T3 and T4 levels are at very high levels, twice the normal values. The nodular thyroid tissue, probably a toxic adenoma, is probably autonomous T3-, and T4-producing tissue, not requiring TSH to function. Treatment must both be life supporting at this time (fever reduction, nutritional, fluid, and electrolyte treatment, digitalization, steroids) and be aimed at decreasing thyroid activity (usually by administration of large doses of antithyroid drugs such as propylthiouracil, followed by iodine administration). Some patients are also given adrenergic antagonists to decrease sympathetic nervous system activity.

Nursing Diagnoses

1. Pain related to injuries and surgical setting of fractured leg
2. Impaired verbal communication related to altered sensorineural state
3. Potential fluid volume deficit related to fever, diarrhea, vomiting, and diaphoresis
4. Hyperthermia related to thyroid storm
5. Altered nutrition, less than body requirements related to increased metabolic rate
6. Potential altered tissue perfusion, all organs, related to inadequate supply and increased demand

Hypothyroidism. A decreased output of thyroid hormone is caused by a variety of different conditions. All of the symptoms can be predicted from a knowledge of normal thyroid gland function. The adult form of hypothyroidism (myxedema) will be discussed in this section, since the major effects are related to depressed energy metabolism. The fetal and childhood form of hypothyroidism (cretinism) causes severe growth and development problems and will be discussed later in this chapter. Myxedema is either the result of a dis-

turbance in neurologic or anterior pituitary gland stimulation of thyroid gland function or a disease of the thyroid gland itself. The latter is best characterized by Hashimoto's thyroiditis, which is an autoimmune inflammatory destruction of the thyroid gland that often leads to hypothyroidism. Another cause of hypothyroidism is inadequate production of thyrotropin-releasing hormone from the hypothalamus. The gland may become small and scarred over time if a chronic deficiency of thyroid stimulation is present.

A much less common cause of hypothyroidism in these times is iodine deficiency. When iodine intake is inadequate, the response of the gland is to hypertrophy (become goitrous) in response to increased stimulation in the attempt to maintain a euthyroid state.

Signs and symptoms. As would be expected, basal metabolic rate in hypothyroidism is decreased, sometimes to 40% of the normal value. Cold intolerance is marked, and a major precipitant of acute myxedema coma is exposure to cold. Coma, which is often fatal, is marked by a drop in temperature as low as 75° F (24° C), and yet shivering often does not occur. The lowered basal metabolic rate results in other expected effects such as weight gain and sluggishness. The hypothyroid individual is often easily fatigued, sleeps a great deal, is apathetic, and usually has altered mental status. The deep tendon reflexes, sensation, and motor nerve function are all often disturbed. Hypothalamic regulatory centers appear disturbed. Myxedema is also associated with characteristic serum lipid changes that appear to be related to effects on cholesterol metabolism. Although the effects have not been clearly elucidated, it seems that there is a decreased rate of utilization of cholesterol in hypothyroidism, which leads to markedly increased serum cholesterol levels. This leads to a high incidence of atherosclerosis.

The term myxedema refers to the skin changes that are seen in chronic hypothyroidism. The skin and hair are typically dry and scaly, the nails are very soft and break easily, and there is a subcutaneous infiltration of a mucopolysaccharide substance that is hydrophilic and causes water accumulation in the skin. This substance also accumulates in organs other than the skin, such as the heart, muscle tissue, and intestinal tract. Cardiac muscle may become inefficient and flabby, leading to cardiac failure. The effect on the physical appearance of the myxedematous individual can be significant. Accumulation of pouches under the eyes is common, the facial features are often coarse, and the patient appears puffy. The skin may become yellow-tinged because of the accumulation of carotenoid pigments that are present as the result of inadequate hepatic conversion of carotene to vitamin A. Steroid metabolism is also disturbed.

Other features of the disease include anemia, which may be related to the absence of the usual thyroid hormone stimulation of hematopoiesis. Decreased metabolic rate also causes depression of normal gastrointestinal tract activity with resultant constipation. In children and adolescents growth is usually impaired. Table 8-2 summarizes the clinical manifestations of myxedema.

Treatment and rationale. The usual treatment is administration of L-thyroxin so that normal metabolic rate is restored. The hypothyroid individual on medication has to be alert to the effects of infection, fever, anemia, and stress in general, or any increased metabolic need for thyroid hormone. There is also a danger of too great a dose, leading to a hyperthyroid state (often measured by the resting pulse rate), or even to hyperthyroid crisis. Use of hormone preparations will, with time, sup-

TABLE 8-2. Clinical manifestations of hypothyroidism (myxedema)

Causative mechanisms	Signs and symptoms
↓ Energy production due to decreased metabolic reactions	Weakness; lassitude and easy fatigability, lethargy
↓ Heat production	Cold intolerance
	↓ Body temperature
	↓ Cardiac output and rate
↓ Oxygen requirements	↓ Blood pressure
	↓ Respiratory effort
	Dyspnea on exertion
↑ Blood lipids	
↑ Cholesterol due to depressed liver function	High incidence of atherosclerosis and coronary artery disease
↓ Tissue synthesis	Capillary fragility with bruising; dry, flaky skin: dry, brittle nails; dry, sparse hair; anemia (↓ bone marrow metabolism)
↓ Reproductive function	↓ Libido and fertility
Fluid shift due to accumulation of protein and electrolytes in interstitial space	Puffy appearance of face; edema
↓ Mental status	Apathy; speech slow
↓ Gastrointestinal activity	Weight gain; constipation, decreased appetite

press any remaining glandular function (disuse atrophy) so that dependence on hormone administration becomes lifelong.

Goiters and other thyroid diseases. Goiters are any enlargement of the thyroid gland caused by hypertrophy or benign or malignant tumors. Most are acquired, but some are congenital, caused by maternal thyroid disease or drug ingestion. Acquired goitrous enlargement can have the following possible common causes:

1. Thyroiditis (inflammation)
2. Neoplasia (benign modules; malignancy)
3. Iodine deficiency (endemic)

4. Excessive ingestion of certain goitro-genous foods (e.g., cabbage, turnips, kale, soybeans) or drugs (sulfon-amides, iodides, cobalt)

5. Colloid goiter (cause unknown; more common in females)

Adrenal cortex hypersecretion

The ability of people to adjust to environmental perturbations is largely dependent upon the hypothalamic-hypophyseal-adrenal cortical axis. It will be remembered from the study of normal physiology that the adrenal cortex secretes glucocorticoids, aldosterone, and androgens in response to stimulation by adrenocorticotropic hormone (ACTH), which is secreted by the anterior pituitary gland. The release of ACTH in turn is controlled by corticotropin-releasing hormone (CRH), which is produced in certain neurons of the hypothalamus and is carried through a portal blood system into the anterior pituitary gland. There is finely regulated negative feedback by the level of circulating cortisol on the release of both CRH and ACTH. Cortisol is a glucocorticoid hormone with innumerable effects on nearly every system—and perhaps every cell. While it allows people to adapt physiologically to a stress state, hypersecretion causes mainly metabolic effects. These metabolic effects are amplifications of the normal results of cortisol secretion during stress. We will therefore describe hypersecretion of cortisol in this section since we are describing endocrine disease with mainly metabolic effects.

Cushing's syndrome. Cushing's syndrome is characterized by excessive adrenal cortical output. While there are many metabolic effects of excessive corticosteroid output, there are also effects on the individual's ability to respond to stressors. Cushing's disease is, by definition, hyperplasia of the adrenal cortex caused by ex-cessive ACTH secretion, in most cases the result of a pituitary gland basophilic adenoma. However, Cushing's syndrome, which is the name given to the set of signs and symptoms produced by excessive secretion of cortisol (and to some degree androgen), may be caused by the following: (1) Cushing's disease, (2) ectopic ACTH secretion, (3) adrenocortical tumor, (4) excessive alcohol intake, or (5) ACTH or corticosteroid administration. All of these possible causes must be investigated when a patient presents with typical cushingoid symptoms and signs.

The syndrome may be produced by excessive ACTH secretion, no matter what the source, as is evidenced by ectopic ACTH secretion by certain tumors. The major types of tumors that secrete ACTH are oat cell carcinomas of the lung and carcinoid tumors. However, the patient with malignant disease, even when plasma cortisol levels are extremely high, rarely becomes truly cushingoid, a condition characterized by weight gain; rather, these patients usually become cachectic as is typical in highly malignant cancers. Adrenocortical tumors are rare causes of Cushing's syndrome in adults, but they cause the majority of cases of Cushing's syndrome in children. These tumors may be either benign or malignant and must be examined microscopically.

Alcohol ingestion is another quite common cause of Cushing's syndrome. It is possible that hepatic damage caused by chronic alcoholic cirrhosis results in a delay in the removal of cortisol from the blood, and this results in the elevated cortisol level. However, this is only speculation and further research is required to determine the mechanism. This cause of Cushing's syndrome is probably not recognized as frequently as it occurs.

Iatrogenic Cushing's syndrome is seen in patients receiving high doses of steroid drugs, usually for a chronic, inflammatory condition. Cushing's disease is the most common cause of Cushing's syndrome. The excessive ACTH secretion is usually the result of a pituitary tumor, although histologically this may be very small. An etiologic role for CRH has been frequently suggested, but no definitive data have accumulated to implicate it clearly in the disease. Neurotransmitters appear to be involved intimately in the ACTH release, including L-DOPA, serotonin, and catecholamines. One treatment for the disease in fact is administration of Bromocriptine, which is a dopamine agonist. The adrenal hyperplasia is the direct response to excessive stimulation by a constantly high level of ACTH.

Signs and symptoms. In order to understand the effects of excess cortisol on normal metabolism, it is necessary to review cortisol's action. This is summarized in Table 8-3. This is nevertheless a simplistic representation as corticosteroids affect, in one way or another, nearly every system.

In Cushing's syndrome the signs and symptoms largely reflect exaggerations of the normal metabolic effects of the hormones of the adrenal cortex. However, the effects of excessive ACTH on adrenal androgen and aldosterone secretion are variable, but all patients have elevated serum cortisol levels. One early phenomenon in the pathogenesis of the disease is a loss in the normal circadian rhythmicity of ACTH and cortisol secretion. Such individuals, while having very high baseline serum cortisol levels, are unable to respond adequately to stress by increased ACTH secretion. Insulin-induced hypoglycemia, a potent stressor, does not provoke an appropriate rise in either ACTH or cortisol. Another phenomenon usually considered in making the diagnosis is lack of suppression of ACTH secretion by the low-dose dexamethasone (Decadron, a synthetic steroid) suppression test. This is the result of the absence of the normal regulatory negative feedback of corticosteroids on the pituitary gland and hypothalamus. Negative feedback does exist, but the set-point for ACTH suppression is much higher than normal.

The cushingoid appearance is typically seen in severe cases (Fig. 8-3). This is marked by abnormal centripetal fat deposition. Since cortisol results in fatty acid mobilization, this effect is partly explained. However, the localization of fat in the face ("moon face"), the back of the neck ("buffalo hump"), and the abdomen is quite typical of this disease, and it is not clear why the excess fat so collects. Weight gain is commonly seen as well, and cortisol seems to increase appetite. In contrast to the fat deposition is the peripheral limb wasting, which is significant. It is believed that the increased protein mobilization for

Table 8-3. Summary of the action of cortisol

Liver	Muscle	Adipose tissue	Other
Increased gluconeogenesis	Increased protein catabolism	Increased free fatty acid	Permissive action on epinephrine, growth hormone
Increased glycogenesis		Increased plasma glucose	Antiimmune, antiinflammatory
Increased plasma glucose			

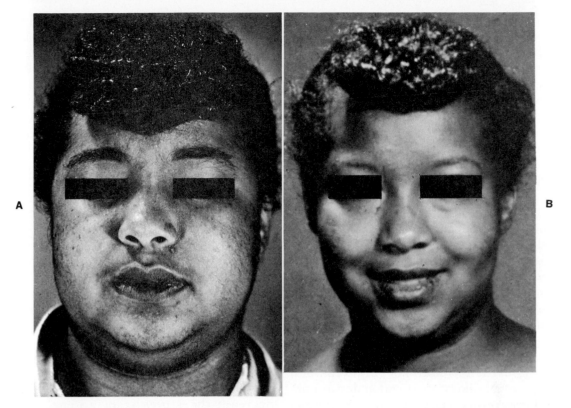

Fig. 8-3. Cushing's syndrome resulting from chronic excess glucocorticoids. **A,** Preoperatively. **B,** Six months postoperatively.

(Courtesy Dr. William M. Jefferies, Cleveland, Ohio. From Anthony CP and Thibodeau GA: Textbook of anatomy and physiology, ed 12, St Louis, 1987, The CV Mosby Co.)

gluconeogenesis caused by cortisol results in this effect. Protein catabolism occurs in other areas as well. The collagen network of the dermis of the skin can become undermined by protein mobilization, leaving the skin weak. Stretch marks, or striae, appear most prominently on the abdomen and can be extensive. This is a key feature of the disease, which is helpful in making the diagnosis. Protein breakdown also may occur in the perivascular sheaths of blood vessels. This causes weakening of the microvasculature to the point that the patient bruises easily. Thus the skin is thin and atrophic, often marked by deep purple striae. Multiple ecchymoses are typically seen in the Cushing's syndrome patient. The skin may also be deeply pigmented if excessive ACTH secretion is etiologic in the disease. The oral mucosa, knuckles, scars, and areas exposed to friction or light are most susceptible. The same phenomenon may be present in Addison's disease, again caused by excessive ACTH secretion resulting from physiologic feedback stimulation. Protein wasting contributes also to the weakness that is typically observed in patients with Cushing's syndrome. The microstructure of the muscle is disturbed and the sarcolemma and mitochondria are swollen and disrupted. Therefore the muscle tone and strength are both diminished, as well as the size of the muscles, and the patient exhibits generalized, bilateral muscle weaknesses.

Another common effect of excessive cortisol is osteoporosis. Glucocorticoids oppose the action of vitamin D on calcium absorption from the intestine. Furthermore, loss of collagen perpetuates bony weakness. Thus the patient responds to the decreased serum calcium level by secondary hyperparathyroidism, which results in demineralization of the bone, subsequent weakness, and finally fractures. Bone fractures can occur in response to relatively minor trauma. Compression fractures of the vertebrae are quite common and most patients with chronic, long-term Cushing's syndrome will actually shrink several inches because of osteoporotic collapse of the vertebral column. The patient with this disease is therefore not only weak but is also more likely to be off balance and fall because of disproportionate distribution of fat and enlarged abdomen. Fractures of the bones may result.

Gastrointestinal complications also occur in Cushing's syndrome. Peptic ulceration is the most common problem and may result from antagonism of prostaglandins in the gastrointestinal tract by glucocorticoids. Prostaglandins normally inhibit gastric acid secretion. Another phenomenon is the result of the antiinflammatory and antiimmune nature of the corticosteroids. Patients with severe Cushing's disease are more susceptible to infection, and will have fewer signs of an acute inflammation than normal people. Therefore gastrointestinal inflammation may go undetected until an acute peritonitis or other infection has become rampant. This is similarly true of inflammation and infection in other parts of the body.

Type II diabetes mellitus commonly develops in Cushing's syndrome because of insulin antagonism of cortisol, increased gluconeogenesis, inhibition of peripheral glucose utilization, and increased glucagon secretion. In fact, the patient with Cushing's syndrome is metabolically similar to a starved individual who is physiologically in a highly stressful situation. All of these responses in the cushingoid individual are inappropriate and pathophysiologic.

Psychiatric disturbances are extremely common in Cushing's syndrome, particularly in individuals with a predisposition to emotional problems. The incidence is approximately 40%, and is significantly decreased by appropriate treatment. This is to be contrasted to the euphoria and sense of well-being that some patients receiving steroid therapy report.

There is a variety of different effects on sexual function and reproductive integrity in Cushing's syndrome. Since ACTH may increase the secretion of adrenal androgens, the female patient may exhibit amenorrhea, because these hormones may contribute to suppression of the hypothalamic release of FSH and LH. Therefore the menstrual cycle may be abolished, and infertility results. Furthermore, the adrenal androgens may also increase the production of testosterone and in the female acne and some degree of hirsutism result. The effects on the male are minimal, although there is sometimes loss of both libido and potency. In some patients there are signs of hyperaldosteronism (see Chapter 18). It will be recalled that the normal release of aldosterone occurs in response to the renin angiotensin mechanism or to plasma potassium ion concentration, as well as to ACTH stimulation. The latter mechanism is probably the least important regulator of aldosterone release.

Cushing's syndrome patients will occasionally have electrolyte and fluid imbalances because of excessive aldosterone release. The result will be hypernatremia, hypokalemia, and metabolic alkalosis. The excessive secretion of aldosterone will upset electrolyte balance and may cause the patient to be overhydrated, hypertensive, and even edematous.

Treatment rationale. The first step in the treatment protocol is proper identification of the cause of the syndrome. Cushing's syndrome is the result of pituitary disease in most cases, but the disease can be treated by bilateral adrenalectomy. Such a patient would then be in a state of hypoadrenalism and would require life-long maintenance with exogenous steroid administration. This operation has an associated high mortality rate and postoperative morbidity. Another approach is to block the adrenal glands' production of corticosteroids by administration of drugs that inhibit the enzymatic synthesis of cortisol (metyrapone, aminoglutethimide). A third approach in Cushing's disease is pituitary implantation with yttrium 90 or pituitary irradiation. Alternatively, microsurgery to the pituitary gland may be carried out by an expert surgeon. Bromocriptine, which is a dopamine agonist, is occasionally able to completely control the excessive cortisol secretion of Cushing's disease, and other neurotransmitter antagonists and antagonists are being tried with some limited success.

The prognosis in Cushing's syndrome depends on the cause. Obviously, patients with malignant tumors are less likely to survive. However, well managed patients with Cushing's syndrome may have a normal life expectancy. This is particularly true of patients who understand their disease and the necessity for proper regulation of their plasma cortisol levels.

Disorders of the adrenal medulla

Pheochromocytoma. A pheochromocytoma is a tumor that secretes catecholamines. Most are derived from adrenal medullary tissue and therefore secrete epinephrine, but some are ectopic and may secrete either epinephrine or norepinephrine. A pheochromocytoma secretes catecholamines in an autonomous manner. The effects of excessive catecholamines on metabolism are hypermetabolism and hyperglycemia. Furthermore, bursts of paroxysmal hypertension are seen in epinephrine-secreting tumors. This may seem paradoxic at first, since epinephrine has little effect on peripheral vasoconstriction and acts primarily on the heart and skeletal muscle vessels, causing vasodilation. It is thought that a sudden increase in epinephrine would drop the total peripheral resistance initially, but that this would result in compensatory burst of norepinephrine through the sympathetic nervous system. The norepinephrine so released would dominate and be unopposed by the usual epinephrine antagonism, since the supply of endogenous epinephrine would have become depleted. The result would be a tremendous and sudden increase in arterial blood pressure.

In contrast are pheochromocytomas that secrete norepinephrine. In this case there is a continuously high blood pressure rather than paroxysmal hypertension. The patient with paroxysmal hypertension will complain of sudden attacks characterized by headache, blurred vision, sweating, nervousness, palpitations, ringing in the ears, heat intolerance, blanching or flushing, and blood pressure elevations, which may be in the range of 220/140. These attacks are extremely dangerous, and there is the possibility of cerebrovascular accident or of heart failure since the myocardium becomes very irritable and arrhythmias are likely to develop.

The treatment of pheochromocytoma is usually surgical excision of the tumor, which is usually benign, or pharmacologic sympathetic blockade.

ENDOCRINOLOGIC DISTURBANCES OF THE STRESS-ADAPTATION RESPONSE
Addison's disease

As was discussed in Chapter 7, the stress response, through the hypothalamic-hypophyseal-adrenocortical (HHA) axis, is essential for the maintenance of wellness. Certain endocrinologic diseases are most noteworthy for their effects on this response. Diseases involving output or responsiveness at any point in the HHA axis may disturb the ability of the open system to handle stressors. For example, inadequate corticotropin-releasing hormone (CRH) from the hypothalamus will ultimately result in decreased cortisol levels during stress. Another possibility would be normal CRH and ACTH output but a diseased adrenal cortex, such that its output of corticosteroid hormones is depressed. However, any increase or decrease in these hormones will have major effects on metabolism as well as on the stress response.

Addison's disease is the name given to a condition in which the output of the adrenal cortex is inadequate to maintain balance and meet the stress demands of the person. Addison's disease is either primary or secondary. Primary Addison's disease results from adrenal gland infection (tuberculosis) or atrophy (possibly an autoimmune response), whereas secondary disease is the result of pituitary disease or iatrogenically caused dysfunction. An understanding of the pathophysiology of Addison's disease can be gained if one imagines the effect of bilateral adrenalectomy. In this case both the adrenal cortex and medulla would be removed and a major

component of the sympathetic responsiveness to stress would be deleted. However, a person usually is able to tolerate this loss because of the widespread sympathetic nervous system capability to secrete catecholamines in response to "fight or flight" emergencies. The major manifestations of adrenal loss and Addison's disease will be those involving hormones of the adrenal cortex, namely glucocorticoids, mineralocorticoids, and sex steroids.

The symptoms are largely categorized as stress and metabolic effects, fluid and electrolyte effects, and in some cases sexual function effects. In the first category are symptoms of muscle weakness; weight loss; hypotension (with a standing blood pressure rarely rising above 110 systolic); anxiety and depression; gastrointestinal disturbances such as nausea, vomiting, diarrhea, cramping, and decreased secretion of the GI enzymes; and often severe hypoglycemic reactions. There is increased insulin sensitivity because of the loss of the insulin antagonism normally exhibited by cortisol. Cortisol has a permissive action on glucagon's stimulation of gluconeogenesis within hepatic cells. Without gluconeogenesis, the serum glucose is not maintained at steady state levels but rather fluctuates severely, leading to hypoglycemia attacks and postprandial reactive hypoglycemia. In addition, the normal sympathetic nervous system response to hypoglycemia is not as effective; in that cortisol also has a permissive effect on catecholamine action. Peripheral muscle and lymphoid protein seems not to be as readily available in adrenal insufficiency as it is normally, and this also causes decreased gluconeogenesis. Numerous experiments have been performed on the adrenalectomized animal, and it appears that the hepatic cell's ability to produce cyclic AMP in response to hormones (glucagon and epinephrine) is not altered, but rather the ability of the cell to respond to the hormones is depressed.

Another prominent feature of Addison's disease is hyperpigmentation. This is often the first clear sign of the disease, but is seen only in primary Addison's disease. Vitiligo is also common and is a condition of patchy depigmentation surrounded by areas of increased pigmentation. The accumulation of melanin in the patient with Addison's disease leads to the pigmentation of areas of the body that are normally exposed to light, pressure, or friction. It is seen in scars, skin creases, at the areolae, on the face, neck, knuckles, knees, and elbows. It may also occur in the oral and vaginal mucosa. Individuals may appear to be deeply tanned and therefore give an appearance of good health. The summer tan becomes deeper and lasts longer, and this may precede the development of overt Addisonian symptoms by many years. The cause of the pigmentation is a matter of scientific controversy. Since it is seen only in primary Addison's disease, it is thought that a normal feedback loop is responsible. When the adrenal cortex is diseased and is not producing the normal set-point levels of the hormones, the hypothalamus reacts to the low output of steroids by secreting excessive CRH and the anterior pituitary gland then responds by elevated levels of ACTH. Since these tropic influences do not increase the ability of a diseased adrenal cortex to produce hormones, the levels of CRH and ACTH are perpetually high. It will be recalled from the study of normal physiology that ACTH is produced by the cleavage of a larger molecule produced by pituitary basophils. Another cleavage product is β-lipotropin (β-LPH). This substance appears to be broken down to smaller peptides, which have melanocyte-stimulating activity. Since ACTH concen-

tration is increased so greatly, so also is β-LPH, and therefore pigmentation is seen in 90% of all cases of primary Addison's disease.

One last metabolic effect of cortisol deficiency is seen only in the young person. Cortisol has a permissive action on growth hormone and therefore growth will be decreased in juvenile forms of the disease.

The symptoms that are related to the inadequate mineralocorticoid secretion are largely due to sodium wasting and potassium retention. Normally, aldosterone acts to preserve sodium and excrete potassium through linked pumping in the distal convoluted tubules. In its absence hyponatremia and hyperkalemia can be severe. Fluid loss will also result leading to intravascular dehydration. Acid-base balance will be disturbed with a resultant metabolic acidosis, since the high potassium ion concentration will cause intracellular hydrogen ion shifts into the extracellular fluid. Hydrogen ion secretion into the distal tubule, which normally competes with potassium ion secretion, will be diminished. Because of these alterations in fluid volume and composition, especially when they are combined with the metabolic and stress-related problems, the patient will usually have orthostatic hypotension, muscle aches, weakness, gastrointestinal disturbances, and electroencephalographic abnormalities, sometimes associated with a tendency for seizures.

The deficiency in sex hormones may cause loss of body hair, amenorrhea, and lack of libido.

Acute adrenal crisis. Individuals suffering from Addison's disease are unable to withstand stress and are subject to life-threatening crises. Generally a patient presenting in acute adrenal insufficiency crisis has had chronic Addison's disease that has not been properly controlled with hormone replacement therapy, or has suffered a major trauma, hemorrhage, or stress such as an infection. Individuals with Addison's disease are so susceptible to stressors that the corticosteroids that they routinely take for replacement purposes must be increased in times of stress.

Individuals who are receiving pharmacologic doses of corticosteroids for conditions other than Addison's disease (e.g., rheumatoid arthritis, asthma) are also subject to Addisonian crisis. In this case suppression of the HHA axis occurs because of the physiologic negative feedback of the serum corticosteroid levels on the hypothalamus and adenohypophysis. Decreased levels of CRH and ACTH result, so that the adrenal glands receive no tropic stimulation. The response of the adrenal glands is therefore disuse atrophy. The adrenal cortex is then unable to respond to stressors in an appropriate manner, so that an iatrogenic Addison's disease is caused, leading to the susceptibility to crisis. Such an individual would be initially very difficult to diagnose as being in addisonian crisis, since there is often a typical cushingoid appearance from the steroid therapy. In fact, the stressor that has precipitated the addisonian crisis may actually *be* the result of the steroid therapy. Included in these effects are the very potent stressors of gastrointestinal ulcer perforation and hemorrhage. A telltale sign in such a situation is the absence of pigmentation, but this is, of course, not pathognomonic, since not all patients with primary Addison's disease have pigmentation nor is it seen in secondary Addison's.

Addisonian crisis can appear suddenly in a person who was previously well. This is seen most frequently in cases of septicemia. In children with meningococcemia, it constitutes a well described syndrome of rapid deterioration known as the Water-house-Friderichsen syndrome. The adrenal glands become infected and infarcted, and usually there is a resultant atrophy of the glands if the patient survives, necessitating hormone replacement therapy.

The signs and symptoms of addisonian crisis include weakness, hypotension, vomiting, diarrhea, and hypoglycemia. The patient is in danger of shock and collapse, and treatment must be instituted as soon as the diagnosis is made. Treatment is the administration of intravenous cortisol and fluid replacement to correct both dehydration and to provide glucose, with identification of the underlying stressor and appropriate treatment for it.

Treatment rationale. Addison's disease is a chronic, usually incurable condition that necessitates life-long hormone replacement therapy. Most patients do not require mineralocorticoid or sex hormone replacement, but all will require corticosteroid replacement. Since cortisol has some mineralocorticoid activity, usually it will correct the hyponatremia, hyperkalemia, and resultant problems. The administration of the corticosteroids should mimic the normal diurnal pattern of cortisol secretion, and thus a larger dose is given in the morning and a smaller one in the evening. The normal secretion of cortisol is 20 to 25 mg/day, and the replacement dose in Addison's disease need not be too much greater than this daily amount. The patient with Addison's receives far less drug than the patient being treated with pharmacologic doses for conditions in which the desired effect is antiimmune and antiinflammatory. One essential component of the replacement therapy is the need for individuals to at least double the usual amount of corticosteroids taken during infections, dental work, surgery, and other stress. It is also important for these individuals to carry some form of identification such as Medic-alert bracelets so that they will be quickly identified in case of crisis. Individuals with Addison's disease are extremely sensitive to morphine, and this drug should rarely, if ever, be administered. During pregnancy, the need for increased hormone replacement is most evident during the last trimester.

There is a definite increase in incidence of other endocrinologic disease in patients with Addison's disease. It is thought that an underlying autoimmune disorder may be responsible for idiopathic, primary Addison's disease. Pernicious anemia and type I diabetes mellitus are increased in incidence in patients with idiopathic Addison's disease, and there may be a basic common problem in the suppressor T cells' ability to regulate self-immunity.

The prognosis in Addison's disease is generally good as long as patient compliance with treatment is good. Of course, when there are other pathophysiologic disturbances, such as diabetes or pernicious anemia, the morbidity becomes greater and the patient's wellness is more difficult to maintain.

ENDOCRINOLOGIC DISTURBANCES OF GROWTH AND DEVELOPMENT
The phenomenon of growth

The remarkable rates of growth of the fetus, infant, and preadolescent demonstrates the capacity to respond to internal genetic cues. Yet many outside factors affect growth, and there are many causes for failure or interruption of growth. A most dramatic example is deprivation in which growth hormone release appears to be inhibited in neglected infants deprived of parental affection. Somehow the lack of love is sensed by the central nervous system, which reacts by depressing hypothalamic and anterior pituitary gland growth-promoting activity. The infant fails to grow and thrive and in fact may die, even while provided with adequate nourishment. There are other less bizarre examples of environmental effects on growth patterns. Malnutrition disturbs optimal growth, as does serious illness or great stress during childhood. Normally children gain height in the spring and weight in the fall. Growth is greatest when food, love, light, and rest are in abundance. There has been a secular trend toward increase in size over the last 200 years, which now appears to have leveled off. Genetic factors are a major determinant of growth; prenatal factors play a role as well. Smoking, multiple birth, teenage parity, malnutrition, and prematurity all may cause small infants who have a decreased potential for survival. Under optimal conditions such infants can "catch-up" during the first year of life.

Growth is a phenomenon of childhood. Repair and restructuring occur throughout the life cycle, but parts do not normally increase in size except during childhood. Endocrine secretions are in rapid flux during periods of growth, and there are many possible deviations. Many of the endocrine disturbances to be discussed in this section begin to alter growth during early fetal life. The effects of disruption at that time may, however, be manifested throughout the life cycle. Other disturbances arise later in life. It is not surprising to learn that many different types of endocrinopathies affect growth, since the phenomenon obviously requires incredibly well regulated, sequential events normally under the control of many endocrine glands. Just one example is the requirement of growing tissue for adequate nutrition and blood supply, both of which require endocrine integrity. The following section will describe in detail the major endocrine disturbances in growth.

Normal growth and development are the result of complex sequences of very carefully regulated events occurring at appropriate times and in appropriate ways. Ultimately the nuclear DNA is responsible for patterns of growth and maturation, but the hormonal milieu is essential to the proper regulation and function of the DNA. As has been discussed, some hormones produce their effects by entering the cell, moving to the nucleus as a receptor-hormone complex, or moving alone to later bind with a nuclear receptor and complexing with the DNA. Thyroid hormone is one hormone that appears to exert all of its effects on growth and development through nuclear T_3 receptor-binding. One of the most immediate effects of thyroid hormone in experimental situations is an increase in the synthesis of all types of RNA. Later effects of thyroid hormone also are related to synthesis of RNA. Of course, when RNA synthesis is stimulated, the end effect of this process of transcription is ultimately translation of the RNA sequences into certain proteins. Proteins produced under the influence of thyroid hormone during growth and development are thought to influence may of the metabolic processes of the developing child while others function as enzymes and perhaps structural proteins.

Cretinism

The importance of thyroid hormone in fetal growth is best demonstrated by the effects produced in its absence. Intrauterine development of fetal hypothyroidism leads to the development of a typical syndrome, congenital cretinism. This is a rare condition, occurring in approximately 1 in 4,400 births. The causes of congenital cretinism include abnormal or absent thyroid gland development (most common), decreased iodine intake in the mother, disease of the hypothalamus or pituitary gland, intake of excessive amounts of goitrogenous foods or drugs by the mother, disorders of the thyroid gland in the synthesis of hormone, or refractoriness of thyroid hormone–sensitive tissues to the hormone. The infant born with congenital hypothyroidism has a typical set of signs and symptoms, but the nurse or physician caring for the infant often has to be alert in order to distinguish them. The infant has many of the signs and symptoms of adult hypothyroidism such as dry, cold skin, constipation, and lethargy. There is often present an umbilical hernia, a large, protruding tongue, sparse dry hair, mottled skin, and poor feeding. As the child grows, presuming he or she is untreated, other features of the disease will begin to appear. A peculiar facies is very typical with a short forehead, broad nose, and widely spaced eyes. The stature of the child is short, with proportionately short legs and short, broad hands and feet. There is delay in the closures of both the posterior and anterior fontanelles. The child is often characterized as exhibiting failure to thrive, and will appear sleepy, listless, and apathetic. The untreated child will develop mental retardation, which is usually severe. The nervous system and skeletal system (particularly the skull, vertebral bodies, and long bones) seem to be most affected by thyroid deficiency during intrauterine life. Without treatment, epiphyseal bone growth centers are absent and long bone growth is diminished.

So devastating is this disease that even though its incidence is low, some centers perform routine neonatal screening of cord blood for T_3 and T_4 levels. There is evidence that detection and treatment within the first few weeks of life result in a vastly improved prognosis, particularly with regard to neurologic impairment. Treated infants with congenital hypothyroidism have normal development at the age of 1 year. The treatment of neonates with hypothyroidism is basically no different from that used with adults. L-thyroxine is administered and blood levels of T_4 are carefully monitored. The child must also be observed for the development of iatrogenic hyperthyroidism, as is true also with the adult. Treatment may produce normal neurologic development as well as adequate growth of the skeletal system. Some of these children will eventually be able to produce adequate endogenous thyroid hormone for their needs, but this is usually not the case.

Pituitary gland pathophysiology

The adenohypophysis, or anterior pituitary gland, is often referred to as the master gland, since it produces several tropic hormones that stimulate other target glands to produce their hormonal secretions, or to produce various effects within target tissues (see Table 8-4). One tropic hormone elaborated by the adenohypophysis is growth hormone, also called somatotropin. Growth hormone (GH) is a tropic hormone that is regulated by a GH-releasing hormone from the hypothalamus. There is evidence that GH produces its effects through liver somatomedins (SMs). SMs are effector molecules that act on GH target organs, causing cell division, tissue growth, and metabolic regulation of an insulinogenic nature (Laron, 1984). They appear to act through adenyl cyclase systems in target tissues as with most tropic hormonal systems, negative feedbacks regulate the hypothalamic-hypophyseal output (Fig. 8-4). GH has multiple target sites and is a large polypeptide containing many active fragments. Growth hormone is normally secreted during sleep, particularly during REM (rapid eye

movement or dreaming) sleep. It is responsible for stimulating growth during childhood and maintaining organ size during adulthood. While most hormones are present within the blood and endocrine tissue in extraordinarily small amounts, human GH is found in the pituitary gland in milligram amounts (8 mg may be present). It is possible that human GH is a complex of many different hormones, each having a specific function within different target tissues. For example, one fragment might have diabetogenic activity, whereas another might be growth promoting. Different activities appear to cause elevations in the concentrations of fragments of human growth hormone. Lewis (1980) has shown an increase following aerobic exercise. However, the diabetogenic fragment was not elevated by exercise. Stress and hypoglycemia also stimulate GH release. There appears to be a human growth hormone cleaving enzyme, but it has not yet been identified. Certain pituitary disorders could theoretically be associated with altered release of particular fragments of the human GH. However, recent research has shown that GH release in humans is regular, pulsatile, and largely unregulated by outside influences.

Hypersecretion of growth hormone. Most causes of hyperpituitarism are benign adenomas of the gland, usually involving the acidophil cell type, which is responsible for secretion of growth hormone, or chromophobe cells, which are cells that are actively secreting hormone and are difficult to identify as being originally either acidophilic or basophilic. Basophilic tumors are rarely large enough to produce signs or symptoms of endocrine pathophysiology. The basophil cells secrete ACTH, TSH, FSH, LH, and MSH. Most tumors of the pituitary gland result in excessive growth hormone secretion and quite

Table 8-4 Pituitary hormones: target tissues and actions

Hormone	Target tissue	Action
Anterior lobe		
ACTH (adrenocorticotropic hormone; also called corticotropin)	Adrenal cortex	Stimulates synthesis and release of corticosteroids and adrenocortical growth
TSH (thyroid-stimulating hormone; also called thyrotropin)	Thyroid gland	Stimulates synthesis and release of thyroxine and triiodothyronine (thyroid hormone)
GH (growth hormone)	Nonspecific (has a generalized effect)	Promotes growth through protein anabolism, insulin antagonism, and lipolysis
Prolactin (also called lactogenic hormone)	Mammary glands	Stimulates production of breast milk
LH (luteinizing hormone; also called interstitial cell-stimulating hormone [ICSH])	Follicle (female)	Stimulates ovulation, progesterone secretion, and luteinization of ovarian follicle
	Testes (male)	Stimulates secretion of testosterone
FSH (follicle-stimulating hormone)	Follicle (female)	Stimulates maturation of follicle and secretion of estrogen
	Testes (male)	Stimulates spermatogenesis
Intermediate lobe		
α-MSH and β-MSH (α and β melanocyte-stimulating hormones)	Melanocytes	Promotes pigmentation (secretion increased in pregnancy and may have a retarding effect on normal cycle)
Posterior lobe*		
Vasopressin (ADH or antidiuretic hormone)	Collecting ducts of kidney	Promotes water retention by increasing permeability of collecting ducts to water
Oxytocin (release is stimulated by infant's suckling of breast)	Mammary glands; uterus	Ejection of breast milk; stimulates uterine contraction (exogenous oxytocin used to induce labor in full-term pregnancy)

*Synthesized in hypothalamus and stored in posterior pituitary; transported between hypothalamus and posterior pituitary bound to neurophysines.

often increased ACTH secretion. The other pituitary tropic hormones may or may not be involved in hyperpituitarism although there may be hypersecretion of these hormones. Occasionally the pressure of an enlarging tumor results in necrosis of surrounding cells, which eventually causes hyposecretion, with a state of hypothyroidism and hypogonadism developing. Since growth hormone excess is the major problem in hyperpituitarism, and since excesses of the other tropic hormones are discussed elsewhere in this and other chapters, we will concentrate on the effects of excess growth hormone. To understand the effect of excess, it is necessary to review the biologic activity of growth hormone. This is summarized in Table 8-5.

As is true for most polypeptide-type hormones, target cells for growth hormone possess cell membrane–associated receptors. How the membrane binding of the hormone results in specific alterations in biochemical activity inside the cell is not known at this time. Under the influence of growth hormone, responsive cells react to the hormone in both general and specific ways. There is an increase in DNA, RNA, and protein synthesis. Increased transport of amino acids across cell membrane oc-

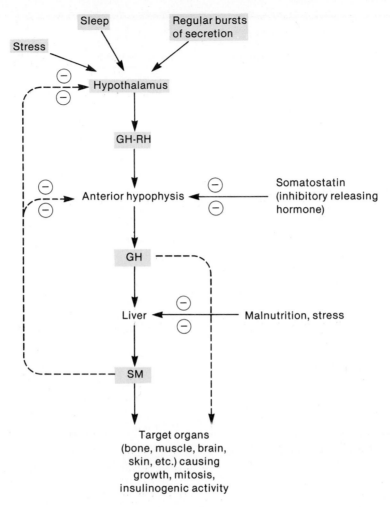

Fig. 8-4. Trophic hormonal system. Negative feedbacks regulate the hypothalamic-hypophyseal output.

Adapted from Laron Z: Growth hormone and somatomedin deficiencies in special topics in endocrinology and metabolism, 1984, New York, Alan R Liss, Inc.

curs and specific proteins such as somatomedins are induced to be formed.

Although human growth hormone seems to be required for normal growth, there are cases reported in which absence of the hormone or the presence of very low concentrations did not impair normal growth. Perhaps other factors can compensate for the lack of the hormone in certain cases. Nevertheless, in the majority of cases an absence of human growth hormone produces dwarfism during childhood, while an excess results in giantism. In the adult excessive growth hormone stimulates hypertrophic growth of flat bones and organs and produces a condition of acromegaly. Both of these results of hypersecretion will be described.

Giantism. Excess growth hormone during childhood results in increased growth

Table 8-5. Growth hormone effects on metabolism

Carbohydrate metabolism	Lipid metabolism	Protein metabolism	Electrolytes
Stimulates gluconeogenesis and glycogenolysis; causes rise in serum glucose Causes insulin release (in response to elevated serum glucose) Excess growth hormone may result in hyperglycemic state or even overt diabetes mellitus	Lipid mobilization from adipose tissue to liver; generalized lipolytic effect	Generalized protein anabolic effect Positive nitrogen balance Increased amino acid uptake across cell membranes	Increased intracellular levels of electrolytes Loss of bone calcium Decreased excretion of phosphorus, potassium, sodium

of bones and organs that are normally under the influence of the hormone. The increased growth is proportional but may be extremely great (heights of 8 feet) compared to the normal, leading to the condition *giantism*. The epiphyseal plates of children so affected have delayed closure. Most of these cases result from adenomas of the pituitary gland and therefore there may be signs of excess secretion of thyroid gland, adrenal glands, or gonads. Just as frequently an adenoma will cause no effect; in long-standing cases, there may actually be hyposecretion of the other tropic hormones caused by pressure of the tumor. In the adolescent there may be signs of delayed pubescence as a result of this. The life expectancy for the patient with untreated giantism is only about 21 years.

Acromegaly. Hyperpituitarism in the postpubertal period also leads to disordered growth. The box on p. 287 shows the categories of clinical manifestations of the disease. Acromegaly is a condition in which unusual and increased growth occurs in the flat bones, particularly the face and skull bones, the vertebral bodies, and the phalanges and tarsals. A characteristic

facies occurs, which develops so slowly that little attention is usually paid to the changes by either the individual or the family. These changes are usually very dramatic, however, when successive photographs are viewed. Other effects of acromegaly include enlargement of the vertebrae to the point that the individual has difficulty bending. There is a visceromegaly that occurs in this disease as well. Organs that particularly undergo hypertrophy include the liver, spleen, and kidneys, but all organs increase somewhat in size. Cardiomegaly can lead eventually to heart failure.

Frequently associated with acromegaly is hyperglycemia and tissue insulin resistance. The ability of the pancreas to actually secrete insulin is not impaired, but the patient has many of the signs and symptoms of adult onset of diabetes mellitus. Many times the patient with acromegaly will suffer severe headaches and may also have visual disturbances because of the pressure of the pituitary tumor upon the optic chiasm. Most of the time this pressure results in bitemporal hemianopia. Enlargement of the sella turcica may

CLINICAL MANIFESTATIONS OF ACROMEGALY

Increased tissue growth due to excessive growth hormone secretion

1. Bones (especially flat bones) disproportionately widened, which results in enlargement of the hands and feet, lengthening of the lower jaw, causing it to protrude (prognathism), and widening of the bridge of the nose; teeth separate, and malocclusion occurs secondary to the growth of the jaw
2. Arthropathy due to bone overgrowth around the joints and predisposes to osteoarthritis
3. Skin thickened with deep creases and folds; oversecretion of glands
4. Palpable enlargement of visceral organs, especially liver and kidneys
5. Enlargement of tongue, vocal cords, laryngeal cartilage, and lips causes speech to become disarticulate and voice to be deep and rough

Endocrine interactions

1. Decreased carbohydrate tolerance due to antagonistic effect of growth hormone on insulin
2. Hypermetabolism without hyperthyroidism, although thyroid may be enlarged and hyperthyroidism may occur in 20% of the patients
3. Hyperadrenocortical effects
4. Hyperlibido and hypertrophy of genitalia; hyperfunction is characteristic of early stages of acromegaly; this changes to hypofunction with all the signs and symptoms of hypopituitarism later in the course of the disease
5. Secretion of prolactin causing gynecomastia in the male and galactorrhea in the female

Psychologic effects

1. Emotional lability
2. Psychologic disturbances

---

be visualized by roentgenogram, and diagnosis is often confirmed by direct measurement through radioimmunoassay of serum human growth hormone, which may be 100 times normal concentration in the patient with acromegaly. Many pituitary tumors also secrete increased amounts of prolactin. This leads to a suppression of gonadotrophin releasing hormones and a resultant hypogonadism. Galactorrhea and amenorrhea are common signs in the female patient, and gynecomastia and decreased libido are common in the male patient.

Treatment rationale. The usual treatment of hyperpituitarism is surgical or laser ablation of the tumor. This may result in a lessening or complete disappearance of all the symptoms. In many patients it

will take several years for facial features and skeletal changes to become normal.

Hypopituitarism in childhood (dwarfism). When inadequate secretion of growth hormone occurs during early life, dwarfism may result. The presence of dwarfism is defined by an attainment of maximum stature that is 40% below the normal and by chronic disease that may be associated with inadequate growth. When stunted growth is caused by hypopituitarism, the pituitary dwarf is recognized as physically proportionate but usually having delayed or even absent sexual maturation, some degree of mental retardation, and accelerated aging. The causes of pituitary dwarfism may be hereditary or may be associated with lesions of or damage to the anterior gland. For example, breech birth may result in trauma due to traction on the pituitary stalk. A deficient secretion of growth hormone, or possibly some abnormality in the target organs' ability to generate somatomedins, is thought to be the major cause. It should be noted that hypothalamic disease may result in hypopituitarism. However, such cases are usually associated with decreased production of only one of the tropic hormones, such as TSH or ACTH. In hypopituitarism, dwarfism is usually the major sign, but other hormones are usually deficient as well. There are certainly effects on sexual maturation that may reflect deficiencies in FSH and LH. Most cases of hypothalamic-hypophyseal GH deficiency can be treated if diagnosed early. Human GH is available for therapy, and when GH is administered to children with pituitary dwarfism, liver SMs will increase. This arm of the endocrine pathway is usually intact, but requires adequate GH stimulation. One type of dwarfism is refractory to GH treatment. It involves defective GH receptors so that liver SMs are not produced; however, this is a rare cause of dwarfism.

Hypopituitarism during adult life. If growth has been completed and some pathologic process interferes with the ability of the anterior pituitary gland to produce its tropic hormones, either selective tropic hormone output may be decreased or a state of panhypopituitarism can occur. In the latter case all tropic hormones are absent from the gland. The possible causes of adult hypopituitarism are:

1. Sheehan's syndrome (infarction of the pituitary gland in the postpartum period caused by shock and hypotension)
2. Pituitary tumors or craniopharyngiomas
3. Chronic infections, such as tuberculosis

4. Partial or total ablation of the gland from trauma or radiation therapy
5. Suppression of the tropic hormone output by target gland hormone excess (such as is seen in patients being administered corticosteroid drugs over long periods of time)

CLINICAL MANIFESTATIONS OF HYPOPITUITARISM

1. Inhibited growth and development (in children) due to lack of growth hormone
2. Manifestations of adrenocortical (except aldosterone) and thyroid hormone deficiencies due to lack of tropic hormones (see Table 8-4); aldosterone secretion continues due to its regulation by factors other than ACTH
3. Hypogonadism; loss of secondary sex characteristics, oligomenorrhea or amenorrhea, and decreased spermatogenesis due to deficiency of tropic hormones, which affect reproductive functions
4. Paleness due to lack of MSH and subsequent reduction in pigmentation
5. Central diabetes insipidus due to vasopressin deficiency; polyuria and decreased specific gravity of the urine are manifestations

---

The signs and symptoms of hypopituitarism will, of course, depend on which hormones are deficient. When a state of panhypopituitarism results, as from trauma or a tumor, Simmond's cachexia is usually present. This term refers to a clinical syndrome associated with muscle and organ wasting and both digestive and metabolic disruption. Lack of growth hormone is thought to cause the decrease in organ and muscle size. The condition is also marked by absent ACTH secretion, so that the individual has a decreased ability to tolerate stress. Furthermore, there is hypoglycemia, since the steroid hormones from the adrenal gland that normally promote gluconeogenesis are not present. Thyroid-stimulating hormone is absent; therefore the thyroid gland is not able to produce sufficient thyroid hormone for normal metabolism and thermogenesis. There is usually some degree of myxedema as a result. Lack of melanocyte-stimulating hormone (MSH) results in pallor because of decreased pigmentation of the skin. Lastly, the gonads atrophy in the absence of gonadotropins, and there is loss of libido, body hair, and sexual function, with amenorrhea occurring in females.

All of these deficiencies upset the steady state of the affected individual to the point that a small crisis may prove to be life threatening. Since there is marked adrenal insufficiency, the stress response will be totally inadequate. This latter aspect is the most life-threatening acute situation that can arise in hypopituitarism, and untreated patients will die in acute adrenal insufficiency. Other acute manifestations include hypoglycemia, hypotension, hyponatremia, and general signs and symptoms of hypothyroidism.

The treatment for both the acutely and chronically ill individual with hypopituitarism is replacement therapy. Most important to the maintenance of the steady state is corticosteroid replacement, which, of course, is continuous. It is essential that affected individuals recognize that corticosteroid requirements may change with stressful situations such as surgery or infection.

Other causes of growth retardation. Growth retardation caused by endocrinopathy must be considered in any child whose growth is below the fifth percentile, or in a child with a very slow rate of growth or an unusually young bone age. Growth hormone deficiency is usually investigated first by challenging the child's hormonal responsiveness by insulin-induced hypoglycemia, L-dopa administration, or arginine tolerance. These tests produce an elevation in serum growth hormone in the normal child. If the results of these tests are normal in the child with extremely short stature, other causes are sought. An obvious cause in an older child is hypothyroidism. The growth impairment in this case is characterized by punctuate, irregular calcifications in the femoral epiphyses and a decreased bone age. Bone-age is an important measurement to determine the degree of skeletal ossification and maturation. It is evaluated by examining radiographs of the bones of the hands and wrists. These are scored independently in terms of the degree of ossification that has been achieved. However, bone age may be decreased in other endocrine disturbances other than childhood hypothyroidism, and if thyroid hormone level is normal, other causes must be investigated. Children with genetically short stature do not have a growth hormone deficit but instead secrete bursts of hormone of lower amplitude as compared to taller children (see Chapter 4).

Juvenile diabetes mellitus can be associated with overall growth retardation. The etiology of the growth impairment in diabetes is obscure but may be related to the nutritional deficiency at the cellular level that occurs in this disease. Another possible cause of growth retardation is corticosteroid deficiency, but excess corticosteroids can also have the same effect. It is thought that in the latter situation cortisol or steroid drugs inhibit growth by interfering with the action of tissue somatomedins. Children on long-term steroid therapy are therefore often extremely small in stature. Other possible causes of growth retardation include renal disease, chronic malnutrition, malabsorption syndromes, gonadal dysgenesis, genetic short-ness, achondroplasia, and chronic disease in general.

ENDOCRINOLOGIC DISTURBANCES OF REPRODUCTION

The control of normal reproductive capacity in men and women is carefully regulated by hormonal influences from the pituitary gland. Tropic hormones stimulate the gonads, and to some degree the adrenal glands, to produce the sex hormones. In the woman this is accomplished in a cyclical pattern known as the menstrual cycle. The onset of puberty brings about many changes that are the direct result of the major male and female sex hormones. These hormones and their normal physiologic control are diagramed in Figs. 8-6 and 8-7. This section of the chapter will discuss those disorders of reproductive capacity and identity that are the result of endocrinologic pathophysiology. The following chapter deals with other abnormalities of reproductive function.

Sexual identity during childhood

Adrenogenital syndrome. There are several pathophysiologic causes of ambiguous genitalia (see Fig. 4-14). In the female child the most common cause is congenital adrenal hyperplasia, but the adrenogenital syndrome and maternal ingestion of androgenic drugs during pregnancy also can cause this condition. This cause of ambiguous genitalia is the result of maternal overproduction of androgens during pregnancy. It is well known that the hormonal influence is as important as the genotype in determining the direction of sexual identity in the fetus. When an XX (female) fetus is subjected to high levels of adrenal androgens during development of the reproductive tract, the external and internal organs of reproduction may develop in a male direction producing some degree of pseudohermaphroditism. It is also believed that brain development is profoundly influenced by the embryonic, hormonal milieu either appropriately or inappropriately masculinizing or feminizing the brain.

The mother produces excessive androgens because of an abnormality in enzymatic synthesis of the hormone cortisol. The result of the defect is not only inadequate secretion of cortisol, but also oversecretion of androgens. Normally androgens are weakly active in terms of virilization capacity, but are produced in such great quantity in this disease that they are able to exert a marked effect. The mother herself is usually hirsute, and the fetus, if female, becomes masculinized during development. The fetal virilization is essentially irreversible in that the reproductive structures are fully formed at birth. Since it is typically only external genitalia that are masculinized in the female child, reconstructive surgery may produce a satisfactory result, even to the degree that the female individual will eventually be able to have sexual relations and bear children. However it is possible that brain development has been irrevocably affected directing the essentially female brain towards a "masculine" pattern and orientation.

Congenital adrenal hyperplasia. The most common cause of ambiguous genitalia is congenital adrenal hyperplasia. This is an autosomal recessive deficiency in one of the five possible enzymes necessary for the synthesis of cortisol by the adrenal gland. The pathophysiologic and morphologic effects of these enzyme deficiencies differ depending on the location of the block in cortisol production. All have the effect of producing a pediatric Addison's disease, in that there is a decreased absolute production in cortisol. The physiologic response to the decreased cortisol production is excessive stimulation of the hypothalamus and anterior pituitary gland with the result that ACTH not only stimulates cortisol production, but also inappropriately stimulates mineralocorticoid and adrenal androgen synthesis. If no enzymatic deficiencies are blocking it, there will be excessive production of these hormones in the absence of normal cortisol synthesis. The effects on the developing fetus are the same as those observed in the adrenogenital syndrome. The female becomes masculinized, and in some deficiencies the male becomes feminized during fetal development.

In order to understand these effects, the reader should refer to Fig. 8-5. Here the normal biosynthetic pathways of all the adrenal cortex hormones and the various key enzymes are illustrated. It can be seen that interruption in an early stage of bio-synthesis of cholesterol desmolase interrupts the synthesis of all the hormones. These children are unable to produce cortisol, aldosterone, and androgens. The female fetus with this defect will produce normal genitalia, since adrenal hormones are not required for female differentiation. The male fetus has ambiguous genitalia because of the lack of the required androgens. Furthermore, neither sex will undergo puberty, since the sex hormones will not be produced in adequate amounts. These children are unable to conserve sodium and are not able to deal with stress, as in Addison's disease. Other enzymatic blocks are also depicted in Fig. 8-5. A deficiency in 17-hydroxylase has effects on the conversion of both 5-pregnenolone and progesterone to their hydroxylated derivates. The usual deficiency is in androgen

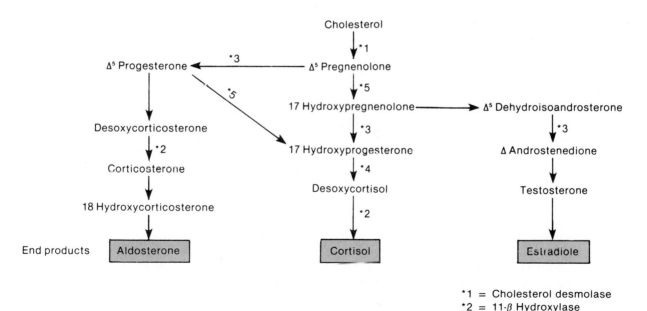

Fig. 8-5. Biosynthesis of steroid hormones. The various stages of steroid hormone synthesis are shown, and points of blockage are indicated by starred numbers.

and estrogen synthesis in both the adrenal glands and gonadal tissue since the enzyme deficiency affects both types of tissue. Aldosterone secretion will be excessive, so that there is usually hypertension.

A deficiency in β-hydroxysteroid dehydrogenase blocks progesterone synthesis. However, production of dehydroepiandrosterone will be greatly increased, since its synthetic pathway is still intact, and there is an excessive ACTH stimulation. This hormone is weakly androgenic, so that it will cause ambiguous genitalia in the female fetus. Therefore both sexes will usually have ambiguous genitalia. Furthermore, mineralocorticoid production is inadequate so that sodium reabsorption will be decreased and the child will have a tendency to lose salt.

A deficiency in 21-hydroxylase blocks aldosterone and cortisol production. The resultant excessive ACTH release as a negative feedback response causes overproduction of androgens. This results in female sexual ambiguity and precocious puberty in both males and females. The 21-hydroxylase deficiency is the most common cause of congenital adrenal hyperplasia. There appears to be two variants of the deficiency, one in which aldosterone deficiency is severe and the child suffers acute hyponatremia and dehydration early in life, and a non–salt-wasting form. The latter form usually requires some amount of mineralocorticoid therapy, however.

A deficiency in the enzyme 11-β hydroxylase also has two major variants and two enzyme systems appear to be involved, thus implicating a genetic defect involving two separate genes. ACTH overstimulation again causes excessive production of hormones. 11-Desoxycorticosterone increases because of a damming up or overflow production of hormones produced before the block. This substance has a strong mineralocorticoid effect, so that such individuals may have severe hypertension.

Treatment rationale. The treatment of children and the occasional adult who was previously undiagnosed depends on which enzyme is deficient. The major problems that can arise are ambiguous genitalia with resultant difficulties in gender assignment, salt-wasting, and hyponatremia, leading occasionally to episodes of hypovolemic shock, hypertension, precocious puberty, and hirsutism in females. Along with these problems can appear excessive growth during childhood, so that these children are often very tall. However, the epiphyses of the long bones may in fact close earlier than normal, resulting in shortness in the adult. Reconstructive surgery, mineralocorticoid therapy, sodium supplementation, and corticosteroids may be required depending on the effects of the block. It is desirable to inhibit the excessive production of ACTH in these deficiencies. This is done by the administration of corticosteroid drugs, which in and of themselves can have many unwanted side effects. Thus there must be very careful titration of the dose required to suppress ACTH and to avoid cushingoid side effects of the drug.

The prognosis for normal growth and reproductive function are all good if the child is treated early and managed well throughout childhood and puberty. Certainly there is a chance that psychologic problems may arise in children and teenagers if the question of sexual identity is not approached early, and usually with professional help for the parents. Once a gender assignment is made, it must be carried through by all who deal with the child and parents. Often times surgery will be undertaken in stages, and the child and parents will need a great deal of education, guidance, and counseling in order to handle the implications of the defect.

Endocrinologic causes of infertility

Normal production, maturation, and release of both spermatozoa and ova require hormonal regulation. Within the female, fertilization and implantation of the fertilized ovum are both dependent upon the hormonally regulated milieu. Examination of the graphs in Figs. 8-6 and 8-7 will remind the student of the normal hormonal control of oogenesis and spermato-

genesis. It is apparent that endocrinologic imbalances would seriously disrupt normal fertility in both the male and female.

Female infertility

Many structural impediments to normal female fertility are not endocrine dependent. The patency of the tubes of the entire reproductive tract is a requirement of both normal fertilization and delivery of a fertilized ovum to the uterine endometrium. In most cases of female infertility, the structural integrity of the reproductive

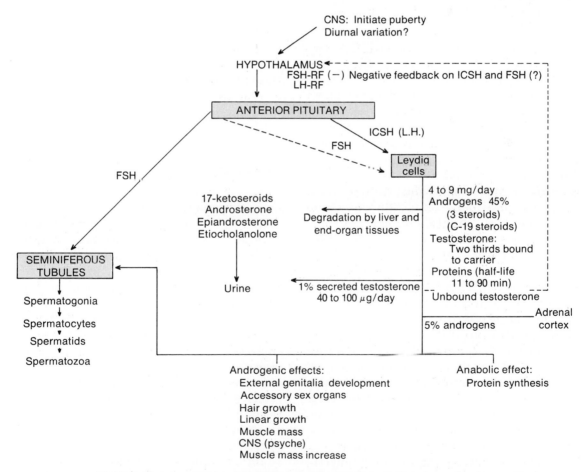

Fig. 8-6. Testes: control and function, including testosterone secretion and action.

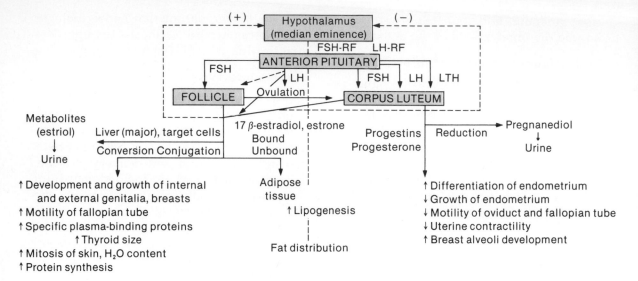

Fig. 8-7. Ovaries: control and functions of female reproductive hormones.

tract must be determined first. Where no obvious structural problem is apparent, an endocrine cause may be sought. Endocrine disorders of reproductive function can arise at any point in the neurologic hypothalamic-hypophyseal-ovarian axis. An essential event to monitor in the female is successful ovulation, which can be measured by basal body temperture elevation at the time of ovulation. Other measures are an increase in urinary gonadotropins before ovulation at the middle of the menstrual cycle, an increase in urinary estrogen before ovulation, the presence of increased viscosity of the cervical mucus, the appearance of estrogen-stimulated epithelial cells from the vagina at the time of ovulation, and an increase in pregnanediol excretion after ovulation has occurred. Of course the only absolutely certain indicator of ovulation is a subsequent pregnancy, but the measures listed above, when considered together, give an accurate indication of the ovulatory event.

Endocrinologic causes of female infertility include excessive or inappropriate ex-traovarian estrogen production, thyroid disease, and anovulation caused by hypothalamic pathophysiology. Anovulation resulting from primary ovarian failure is an additional but relatively rare possibility.

Extraovarian estrogen production

Production of estrogen by tissues other than the gonads is normally quite small. Sites of extraovarian estrogen production include adipose tissue and the liver. Obesity is sometimes associated with amenorrhea and anovulation since adipose tissue is capable of converting androstenedione to estrogen. The percent of conversion of this androgenic precursor, which is normally produced by the adrenal cortex, is therefore increased proportionately in the obese state.

Extraovarian estrogen production is increased in a number of diseases and disordered states. Included in this category are Cushing's disease, congenital adrenal hyperplasia, polycystic ovaries, thyroid disorders, obesity, and senescence. The extraovarian estrogen production is high and acyclic, and interferes with feedback regulation of FSH release from the hypophysis. Without cyclical variation in estrogen release, the normal menstrual cycle does not take place, since the tropic hormone release is sensitive to the serum concentration of the estrogen, and to a minor degree progesterone, produced by the ovaries.

There is a well-known association of stress with amenorrhea, which may be the result of high levels of extraovarian estrogen production. Stress is associated with an increase in adrenocortical activity. Increased androgenic precursor substances may be released by the adrenal cortex, and these are in turn converted to estrogens at extraovarian sites. The high estrogen levels will thus mask ovarian cyclical estrogen production and block FSH release.

Thyroid-gonadal disturbances. Disorders in thyroid hormone release are implicated in some cases of infertility. Both hyperthyroidism and hypothyroidism can cause ovarian dysfunction and interruptions in estrogen metabolism. In *hypothyroidism* there is often a delay in menarche or, quite commonly, amenorrhea and anovulation. A deficiency in thyroid hormone may cause the hypothalamus and pituitary to respond by an increased secretion of prolactin along with TSH. This may lead to galactorrhea in some young hypothyroid patients, as well as occasional cases of precocious puberty. The general slowing down of metabolism that is seen in hypothyroidism and myxedema may certainly interfere with normal reproductive function. Another effect of decreased thyroid hormone is a decrease in the synthesis of a sex hormone–binding globulin. An increase in free estrogens and androgens therefore occurs. High levels of estrogen result in interruption of the normal menstrual cyclicity, as has been previously described.

Hyperthyroidism increases the metabolism generally and will increase metabolism of the sex hormones. Furthermore, synthesis of the binding globulin will be increased and the effect will be a decrease in blood concentration of the sex hormones and therefore of their bioavailability. Young hyperthyroid girls usually have menstrual cycle irregularities, a decrease in the duration and amount of menstrual flow, and occasionally early menarche.

Anovulatory infertility associated with low gonadotropin levels. About 15% of all cases of infertility are caused by anovulation or oligoovulation (very infrequent ovulation). Of these a small number will have primary ovarian failure. There may be a decrease in the total number of oocytes or a resistance of the ovary to endogenous gonadotropins. However, the majority of cases of anovulatory infertility are the result of some abnormality originating in the brain or pituitary gland, with an essentially normal reproductive tract being present. One possibility is a decrease in secretion of gonadotropin-releasing hormone by the hypothalamus. This occurs in a variety of physical and psychologic stress states, as exemplified by the amenorrhea and infertility of Jewish women in German concentration camps. It is seen in women athletes who have a decreased total body fat composition, and in severe weight loss conditions such as anorexia nervosa. It may also appear in women regularly taking tranquilizers, such as reserpine, or in those inbibing large amounts of alcohol. Since follicular development hardly occurs in these women because of inadequate tropic stimuli from the pituitary gland, the production of estrogen is decreased and estrogen-mediated proliferation of the uterine endometrium is minimal. Obviously, then, amenorrhea is a common occurrence in these groups. This condition requires correction by administration of human gonadotropins. (Interestingly, these are usually prepared from the urine of pregnant women, who produce excessive amounts of FSH and LH due to absence of the normal feedback.) Follicular development results and is further perpetuated by injections of human chorionic gonadotropin, which will cause subsequent ovulation and possible pregnancy.

Anovulatory infertility associated with normal gonadotropin levels. It is possible to have normal amounts of gonadotropin released from the anterior pituitary gland and still have infertility. Patients with this disorder appear to have a defect in the sensitivity of the hypothalamic set-point to the feedback stimulation of gonadotropins by estrogen. A much lower than normal concentration of estrogen therefore shuts off gonadotropin-releasing hormone secretion, and thus inadequate amounts of FSH and LH are released. Treatment is quite successful by administration of weakly estrogenic compounds, such as clomiphene. Clomiphene stimulates FSH and LH production above the basal level in these women and ovulation may occur.

Anovulatory infertility associated with normal gonadotropin levels may occasionally be seen in the presence of prolactin-secreting chromophobe adenomas and in other states of hyperprolactinemia. Galactorrhea will be commonly observed in such women, and any female with amenorrhea and galactorrhea should be examined for a pituitary tumor. When the hyperprolactinemia is not associated with a tumor, the cause is usually hypothalamic, and may involve a decrease in the secretion of prolactin-inhibiting factor (PIF). Another possibility is a defect in the normal pattern of release of gonadotropins, which in the human is normally pulsatile. Thus gonadotropin plasma levels may be normal but there may be infertility present. The treatment for this form of infertility is, of course, surgical removal of a tumor, if present, or administration of the drug bromocriptine in the hyperprolactinemic patient without a pituitary tumor. Bromocriptine is a dopamine agonist and will substitute for dopamine on postsynaptic neuronal receptors in the pituitary gland. This causes a decrease in prolactin secretion, and over time the patient will regain menstrual periodicity and fertility.

Ovarian failure. The clinical disorder known as *Stein-Leventhal syndrome* is characterized by obesity, disturbed menses, hirsutism, and polycystic ovaries. This condition may be primarily an ovarian disease, or may have a strong adrenocortical dysfunction component associated with it. In the latter case there is a related elevation of 17-ketosteroid secretion. In Stein-Leventhal syndrome there is variability in the degree of hirsutism, menstrual irregularity, and obesity. However, all patients have bilaterally enlarged ovaries that are marked by multiple cysts. There is evidence that abnormal steroid metabolism is a major biochemical cause, with the enzymatic defects leading to an increased production of testosterone. In many cases the ovaries do not secrete estrogen, but only androstenedione and testosterone. Estrogen production by conversion of androgen is very high in extra-ovarian sites, so that there may be large amounts of estrogen produced. This, along with the excessive androgen produced by the ovaries and in some cases the adrenal cortex, causes a loss of normal feedback control of menstrual cyclicity. The secretion of FSH is very low, while LH secretion may be increased. LH acts to further stimulate the production of the androgens in the female patient, so that the disease is pathophysiologically perpetuated. The treatment of Stein-Leventhal syndrome is administration of clomiphene or wedge resection of the ovaries. Clomiphene acts by stimulating secretion of FSH. Wedge resection, while usually very effective in reducing androgen secretion, acts in an as yet unknown manner.

Ovarian integrity can be disturbed in a great number of chromosomal abnormalities, the classic example being Turner's syndrome in which there is ovarian dysgenesis. Some autoimmune disorders (e.g., Hashimoto's disease) are characterized by ovarian failure. In some individuals there may be an inadequate number of primordial follicles present within the ovaries. Ovarian tumor, infection, and trauma can result in refractory ovaries that do not respond to normal gonadotropins. Ovarian failure can be essentially present at birth or may develop later in life after menstrual cycles have been established.

Male infertility

Endocrinologic causes for male infertility are rare. In contrast to female infertility, it is extremely unusual for hypothalamic or hypophyseal failure of gonadotropin release to be etiologic. There is, of course, a direct tropic relationship of FSH and LH on spermatogenesis, and the values of these hormones do change in infertile men. For example, when there is a decreased sperm count resulting from seminiferous tubular epithelial disease, the concentration of FSH is increased. This is due to the absence of feedback control of FSH by the damaged testicular cells. In fact, FSH levels are determined diagnostically in men with infertility, since the inverse relationship of FSH with sperm count is useful as a tool to establish untreatable infertility. This method is now used in place of testicular biopsy.

Occasionally male infertility is associated with elevated prolactin levels, in which case there may be a pituitary tumor present. Hypothyroidism is sometimes implicated in male infertility, but is more likely to be associated with loss of libido and impotence rather than infertility.

Endocrine-based treatment of male infertility has been used on occasion, even when there is no direct evidence for an endocrinologic cause. Clomiphene, human chorionic gonadotropin, and gonadotropin-releasing hormone have all been tried, but the success rate is extremely low. One other endocrinologic manipulation is testosterone rebound therapy. Testosterone is given for several months to the infertile male, which suppresses spermatogenesis. After it is discontinued, a rebound increase in sperm count may occur, and the male may be able to successfully impregnate during that period of time, before the sperm count drops again.

SUMMARY

This chapter has presented endocrinologic pathophysiology as related to major phenomena such as metabolism, growth, adaptation, and reproduction. Selected disease models are represented here and in other chapters. Reproductive disorders that are not primarily endocrine in origin will be presented in Chapter 15.

BIBLIOGRAPHY

Baird DT: Endocrinology of female infertility, Br Med Bull 35:193-198, 1979.

Carlson H, editor: Endocrinology, New York, 1983, Wiley Medical Publications.

de Kretser DM: Endocrinology of male infertility, Br Med Bull 35:187-192, 1979.

Dillman WH: Mechanism of action of thyroid hormone in thyroid disease. In Kaplan M and Larsen R, editors: Med Clin North Am, September, 1985.

Dussault J and others: Preliminary report on the psychological development at age one of treated hypothyroid infants detected by The Quebec Network for Metabolic Disease, Pediatr Res 12:412A, 1978.

Groot L and Sridama V: Development of thyroid autoimmunity, new concepts in thyroid disease. In Soto R, Sartoria G, and deForteza I, editors: New York, 1983. Alan R Liss, Inc.

Hoffenberg R: Thyroid emergencies, Clin Endocrinol Metab 9:503-512, 1980.

Hurwitz LS: Nursing implications of selected pediatric endocrine problems, Nurs Clin North Am 15:525, 1980.

Laron Z: Growth hormone and somatomedin deficiencies. In Special topics in endocrinology and metabolism, New York, 1984, Alan R Liss, Inc.

Lewis U and others: Human growth hormone: a complex of proteins, Recent Prog Horm Res 36:477-508, 1980.

Ratzenhofer M, Hofler M, and Walker G, editors: Interdisciplinary neuroendocrinology, Basel, 1984, S Karger.

Snyder S: Brain peptides as neurotransmitters, Science 29:976-983, 1980.

Wall J and Kuroki T: Immunologic factors in thyroid disease, Med Clin North Am, September, 1985.

Williams R, editor: Textbook of endocrinology. Philadelphia, 1981, WB Saunders Co.

9

Senescence

It is important to understand the physiologic changes that occur with normal aging and the pathophysiologic alterations that are more likely to occur in the elderly. The prevalent lifestyle diseases of Americans steadily increase in incidence with age. Furthermore, the median age of Americans is increasing. More people survive into old age than ever before, and the number of elderly is increasing so that by the year 2050, one quarter of the population will be over 65 (Rodin, 1986). The health care costs of the elderly are expected to rise as the numbers increase. The elderly may suffer fairly minor health problems, such as arthritis, hearing impairments, and visual problems. In fact, the majority of elderly people feel well and report no health problems of great concern. Oftentimes this is an older person's perception in the face of physical evidence to the contrary. Elderly people tend to underreport symptoms and often care for themselves rather than seeking health care. The idea of elderly hypochondriasis is a myth (Riley, 1981). Encouragement and services that will help the elderly to maintain a high level of wellness for as long as possible are critical to the quality of life. Aging is invariably accompanied by fragile coping mechanisms, which can be quickly overwhelmed by even small threats to wellness. This is especially true

for frail, elderly persons; those who are already weak and very old. One example is osteoporosis, which may not cause severe physical disability but increases susceptibility to bone fractures. Once a hip is fractured many other coping mechanisms can fail to preserve the delicate balance that preserves wellness. Immobility, depression, loss of control, nutritional problems, elimination problems, and respiratory disturbances, may ensue after the initial hip fracture. Although an elderly individual may feel and often appear very healthy, it may take only one adverse event to trigger a domino-like effect of pathophysiologic mechanisms.

The diseases that cause mortality are chronic diseases that are the result of a lifetime of unhealthy habits and risk factors. Longevity is believed to increase in those who live a healthy, wellness-oriented lifestyle, a phenomenon influenced by physical, psychologic, spiritual, and social factors. Health professionals have a responsibility toward promoting high-level wellness for clients of all ages, and one result of this will be to decrease morbidity in the elderly and to provide the elderly with an opportunity to maintain a high quality of life. In this chapter we will discuss theories of aging and biologic mechanisms associated with the process of senescence. One of the goals of this chapter will be to integrate material from many other chapters and to examine the reasons why many mechanisms culminate in disease and disability in the aged. In keeping with the framework of this book, we will also examine the aging phenomena from the mind-body perspective, noting how aging and its associated disabilities mean different things to different people.

Aging is an irreversible, cumulative, predictable, universal process in all known multicellular living creatures.* Senescence is part of development and must be viewed as a point on a continuum. The rate at which it proceeds is species specific, and humans have the longest life span among the mammals. Aging and death appear to be genetically programmed in each individual, at least according to the most popular theory of aging; that is, cellular DNA determines the rate and pattern of senescence that is unique to every person. This leads to the question, "Is aging normal?" Is it intrinsic, or is it the result of exogenous factors that act on tissues and cells, causing them to undergo aging as we know it? To answer this question it is necessary to examine the normal pattern of senescence, both in general and in specific organs and tissues. We must also look to gerontologic research to answer basic questions about aging.

PATHOPHYSIOLOGIC MECHANISMS OF SENESCENCE

It will be recalled that cell death is a phenomenon that begins during embryogenesis and continues throughout the life of the organism. In no way can cell death per se be considered equivalent to the aging process. Cell death in many cell compartments results in cell renewal through differentiation of other cells. This has been well described in the gastrointestinal tract, epithelium, the hematopoietic series of cells, and the spermatozoa. Other compartments of cells do not renew at these rapid rates. Connective tissue, for example, has a slow turnover rate, and cell death in this compartment may lead to signs of aging, such as a decrease in elasticity. With aging there is a decrease not only in cell function but also in actual cell number, leading to atrophy of various tissues and organs. Connective tissue in general shows many more pathophysiologic signs of aging than does the epidermis of the skin, the lining of the gut, or the hematopoietic system, although all these systems are affected by senescence. Connective tissue also is ubiquitous, and therefore changes in this tissue will have far-reaching effects on organ function. The vasculature, for example, consists of tubes made patent by a lining of connective tissues; therefore, these vessels and the tissues they supply may be interfered with if the connective tissue becomes rigid and sclerosed.

The consideration that cell death is part of normal development and that rapid cell renewal systems are important in "saving" compartments of cells from senescence is verified by many studies. In terms of normal embryogenesis, growth of a new part, followed by its destruction and necrosis, is part of the normal development of organs thus setting the stage for growth of newly developing tissue and can be reversibly interfered with by transplantation of embryonic parts to other sites. This suggests that cell death is influenced by environmental factors. Further support for this comes from research showing a hormonal reliance for cell death during embryogenesis, at least in some species. Environmental

---

*The only multicellular organism that does not age is the sea anemone, which constantly regenerates itself.

factors such as surrounding tissue, nervous supply, and hormones that have been shown to influence cell senescence and death are termed *epigenetic* factors. However, much of the normal sequence of development both in the embryo and in the organism as it grows and matures appears to be genetically programmed and only modulated by epigenetic factors.

It is believed that there is tremendous redundancy in the genetic information contained in DNA and that only a small portion of the total DNA is switched on at any given time. The pattern of inactive and active DNA during embryogenesis, growth, and senescence makes up the program that ultimately determines both the quality and quantity of life. Epigenetic factors can influence the expression of this genetic program greatly by accelerating or slowing down senescence and death, such as through disease. Nevertheless, aging itself appears to be an irrevocable outcome of inherited genetic mechanisms.

There is evidence that the aging mechanism is extremely complex and subject to a central time regulator or biologic clock, which could be nervous, hormonal, or metabolic. For example, the hypothalamus has been suggested as the site that governs the aging rate of all body cells. Another possibility is that senescence is intrinsic to the aging cells themselves. As the cells age they accumulate mutations, which are not efficiently repaired. These mutations may themselves affect cell function, which then results in the changes associated with aging. Thus the biologic clock could be the irrevocable accumulation of mutations with time, which alters cell function and causes deterioration.

In an attempt to determine whether genetic or epigenetic factors are most important in aging, cell cultures have been studied as model systems of aging.

Maintenance of cell populations collected from animals at various stages in development has inevitably led to the same result. Cells in tissue culture have a finite survival capability, and characteristic changes and declining reproductive capacity invariably occur. Another method of studying cell survival is by transplanting cells into young hosts and retransplanting the same cells into new young hosts when the original hosts age. These studies also show that there is a limitation on cell survival even in the most optimal environment. They indicate that there is a definite limit on the number of times a human cell can divide (about 50), and this limitation in turn determines the ultimate survival of the organism. It is interesting to note that the number of population doublings of cultured normal embryo fibroblasts from the Galapagos tortoise is more than twice that of human fibroblasts under the same conditions. The Galapagos tortoise is the longest-lived organism, surviving for 175 years. This correlation should seem to indicate that there is a relationship between in vitro and in vivo aging, which is, of course, the central question in applying the results of laboratory studies to humans. Senescence is much more complex than aging of cells in vitro, with many interactions causing specific changes. Furthermore, different tissues age at different rates in the intact organism, and there is no question therefore that reduced division capability is only one part of the whole phenomenon of aging. It is interesting, however, to note that patients with *progeria* or *Werner's syndrome*, diseases that seem to be associated with accelerated aging, have cells with reduced proliferative capacity.

Some cells, particularly of a lymphoid line, that are grown in tissue culture, appear to be immortal and do not age and die. These are abnormal cells that have undergone *carcinogenic transformation*. In other words, perhaps cell survival requires complete dedifferentiation and anaplasia, in a sense a return to an early evolutionary state. Indeed, the earliest cells in the course of evolution (and possibly modern unicellular organisms) must be considered "immortal" in that their reproduction was asexual, so that no protoplasmic material was lost through cell necrosis. Old age and death are the prices that multicellular organisms pay for the pleasures of sexual reproduction.

One of the major cytopathologic changes observed in cells as they appear to age in cell culture is the accumulation of *lysosomes*. These cellular organelles are involved in inflammatory reactions and in autocatalysis, often being described as the digestive system or "suicide bags" of the cells. Not only do these structures increase in number, but their enzymatic contents change as well during aging. Such changes are not observed in cell cultures that have been carcinogenically transformed and propagating indefinitely. Some of the normal lysosomal enzymes may be able to cause breaks in the chromosomes of cells, and the activity of these enzymes increases with the age of the cells. Thus the lysosomal changes and accompanying enzymatic changes may share a cause-and-effect relationship with cellular senescence. Other observations regarding subcellular events that are associated with aging include an increase in the RNA accumulation with a decrease in RNA synthesis. Also the heterogeneity of the total cell population increases.

Environmental factors in a cell culture can alter the pattern of senescence and death. For example, hydrocortisone is known to greatly increase the life span of cells grown in culture when added to cells.

This effect is entirely dependent on serum being added to the cultures, which implies that hydrocortisone acts to potentiate the effect of some serum growth factor. The action of hydrocortisone seems to be to increase the number of cells that are rapidly proliferating. Research shows that aging cells lose cell receptors that bind to glucocorticoids, and this may play a role in the characteristic decline in reproductive capacity of cells both in vivo and in vitro as part of the aging process. The production of these cell receptors is apparently a function of the cell cycle stage, and as the population of cells consists of more cells that are nonreplicating, less and less responsiveness to glucocorticoids is evidenced. The action of hydrocortisone is apparently to increase the actual proportion of cells that are duplicating and therefore to increase the number of cells with an adequate number of receptors to hydrocortisone.

Nutritional composition of the medium in which the cells are grown can affect the pattern of senescence, as can certain additives. However, research concerning the types of additives, the nutritional requirements of aging cells, and the effects of deprivation or excess is in a preliminary stage. The ultimate effect for diploid animal cells, regardless of their environment, is senescence and death. It would appear from many studies that cells are genetically programmed to age and die, and the environment can act only to alter the rate at which this inevitable process occurs.

Although cell cultures are relatively easy to maintain and study with regard to aging, the process of senescence in intact mammals is much more difficult to study. Such studies require that suitable experimental animals be studied throughout their life span in a single experimental design. Studies on rodents therefore last about 2 years, but larger animals such as monkeys and dogs require continual investigation for as long as 12 years in dogs and 24 years in rhesus monkeys. The difficulty in maintaining large experimental and control groups is obvious. Therefore most of the whole animal research in aging has been done with mice, rats, insects, and fish, and very little has been done with larger mammals with longer life spans. As always, the assumption that what is true for the rat must also be true for humans cannot be made with confidence.* Some studies of aging in humans have also been made, but they are not the longitudinal types of studies that are being done with laboratory animals. Nevertheless, such studies are extremely valuable, particularly when viewed in light of similar animal studies. A current study, the Baltimore longitudinal aging and longevity study, is yielding human data as are the Duke longitudinal studies of aging.

Two concepts arise out of such studies. The average human life span of 71 to 74 years of age has increased significantly over historical time, and is now at its highest average. Life span is significantly affected by environmental factors, such as disease, food supply, and climatic conditions. The maximum life span is the life span that is possible for a species—the age reached by the longest-lived survivor. For humans, the maximum life span is 110 to 115 years (conservatively) (Walford, 1985). The maximum life span is largely controlled by genetic, fixed factors but may be subject to modification by environmental influences such as nutrition.

---

*The late George Sacher of Argonne National Laboratory pointed out in a personal communication that if the data for carcinogenesis in rodents are applied unequivocally to humans, then humans should theoretically have 50 times the incidence of cancer than that which is observed.

No single paradigm of aging has emerged from gerontologic research. It is generally agreed that understanding aging requires an interdisciplinary perspective. From a biologic point of view, aging is considered innate and genetic, but clearly from a sociologic or psychologic framework, aging is perceived in terms of environmental, cultural, and interactional influences. The first section of this chapter will examine the biologic theories of aging.

THEORIES OF AGING
Programmed theory

The programmed theory of aging implies that genes are turned on and off during the whole spectrum of development and that certain "aging" genes exist, which act to cause senescence. The mechanism of action for such genes is largely a matter for speculation, but possibly there could be errors in protein synthesis as the cell ages, with the eventual impairment of cell function. Accumulation of error-containing protein macromolecules affects both intracellular and extracellular events in such a way as to further impair DNA transcription of RNA and RNA translation into protein. Thus the more errors that are made in the protein products of the cell, the more enhanced and propagated is the initiating cause, namely, disturbances in DNA function. Of course, the inevitable result is death of the cell.

Another possibility supporting the programmed theory of aging is that DNA contains great redundancy of information and that mutations are continuously occurring in DNA. Furthermore, only a fraction of 1% of the DNA is active at any given time, the remainder being repressed. The redundant DNA information is called forth when changes or errors accumulate in the active genes. It is only when the mutations have caused such accumulated damage and no more reserve DNA is able to function that aging takes place. Such an accumulation is obviously time dependent and species specific, since the amount of linear sequencing and redundancy of DNA is characteristic of the species, with little variability among the individual species' members. It has been observed that older cells have a decreased number of copies of certain highly repetitive DNA sequences and extrachromosomal circular DNA pieces (Rothstein, 1986).

Further support for the programmed theory of aging comes from the suggestion that aging is the result of macromolecular effects caused by repression of certain sequences of DNA, which code for certain sequences of RNA and then for certain proteins. Environmental accidents can be particularly damaging to such cells that have genetically programmed malfunctioning DNA codons or errors in the transcription of DNA.

There is experimental evidence for all these hypotheses that support the programmed theory of aging. It is, nevertheless, difficult to explain why, in the evolutionary sense, DNA-directed, inevitable programmed aging came about. Presumably there must be some selective advantage for the species in the process of senescence and death. The most plausible explanation is that aging and death remove competition for food, sexual partners, and shelter for the young. This is, of course, epitomized by spawning salmon but is difficult to rationalize for other species, such as humans.

Research further substantiates the concept that biologic limits on survival are dictated by the nucleus. For example, when the nuclei of cells are removed by a variety of new laboratory procedures, the remaining cytoplasts can be fused with nuclei from cells of different ages. These experiments confirm the idea that the biologic time clock is associated with the nucleus, and therefore most probably resides in sequences of the cellular DNA.

Stress theory

In contrast to the programmed theory of aging are other theories, such as the stress theory, which implicates epigenetic factors as most important in the pathogenesis of aging and death. Death therefore is the result of the ultimate "wearing down" of the organism as a result of accumulated wear and tear beyond the capacity of the organism to repair. Those compartments of cells that undergo rapid turnover and renewal are least affected by wear and tear, since the cells are short lived. Cells that do not turn over frequently or at all, such as connective tissue, muscle, and nerve, are most affeted by stressors in the environment ultimately wearing down the organism. Thus the stress theory of aging suggests that aging occurs in tissues with slow or no turnover and that these tissues indirectly damage other compartments of cells. The classic stages of the stress response are alarm, adaptation, and exhaustion. Thus the stressed animal over the life span should enter the stage of exhaustion with its associated decreased resistance to further stress.

Experimental evidence for this theory of aging is not convincing. The aged adrenal cortex can respond to stressors by secreting large amounts of corticosteroids, and the response is only slightly reduced as compared to young individuals. Furthermore, when the values are corrected for the decreased muscle mass in the aged, one finds that the elderly can respond to stressors with great efficiency in terms of adrenocorticosteroid response. Of course, a physiologic decrease in the effectiveness of corticosteroids in response to stress might occur if the target tissues of the hormones were unresponsive or refractory, regardless of the level of hormones in the blood. This has been suggested not only for the adrenocorticosteroids but also for thyroid hormone, insulin, epinephrine, vasopressin, ACTH, aldosterone, norepinephrine, gonadotropic hormone, and testosterone. Furthermore, in the rare syndrome of progeria, which is characterized by extraordinarily accelerated aging such that senescence and death occur in the early teens, there is a decreased tissue response to hormones generally. It is difficult to determine whether this tissue phenomenon is the cause or the effect of aging.

One important belief of the stress theory is that exposure to stressors accelerates aging. This has been demonstrated for some but not all stressors and only when these stressors are continually applied. These include exposure to cold, repeated breeding, high altitude, radiation, and psychologic stress. Each individual, according to the theory, possesses a certain amount of *adaptation energy*, which is in part determined by genetic makeup and in part by the degree of stress the body is subjected to. Certainly there is evidence that chronic stress plays a role in the pathogenesis of certain cardiovascular diseases, especially arteriosclerosis and myocardial infarctions, and the incidence of these conditions does not increase with age. Whether this is the result of decreased adaptation energy is not known, since, as mentioned earlier, the aged generally have a good adrenocorticosteroid response to stress. Thus the role of stress in the aging process is not clear, but it would seem logical that the expression of genetically programmed sequential changes can be modified by the external environment, which includes many stressors that elicit the general adaptation syndrome. This in turn could ultimately lead to a stage of resistance and then exhaustion and act in positive feedback pathophysiologic ways to enhance the expression of the genetic program.

Error catastrophe theory

This theory correlates the aging process with random, irreparable, catastrophic mutations in DNA. Such mutations in somatic cells then lead to changes, which are characteristic of aging, in the cells and tissue. Mutations can lead to alterations in the structure, function, and absolute amount of enzymes produced by individual cells. There are many reports describing a loss in the enzymatic activity of cells as they age.

As deficient enzymes are produced, they could tend to perpetuate further deficient enzyme production if they are at all involved in the process of protein synthesis (Rothstein, 1986). This would produce a catastrophic cascade of deficient proteins, leading to error after error until the cell dies. Altered enzymes are reported to occur with aging, but the majority of enzymes that have been studied are perfectly normal and functional. This theory is still tenable, but most recent research does not support it as an important mechanism in the aging process. Enzymatic deficiency could play a role in disturbing hormone responsiveness in the elderly. The capacity to regulate enzymatic responses to hormonal stimulation is depressed in the aged.

Hormonal responsiveness has been particularly studied for insulin and corticosteroids. This changing ability to respond to hormones may reflect the biochemical pathology of tissue resistance that has previously been mentioned with the stress theory of aging. Accumulated mutations could conceivably alter enzymatic responsiveness, but certainly other mechanisms are equally likely to do so. Radiation-induced life shortening is a phenomenon that may be correlated with mutations in critical tissues, which lead to secondary alterations in other tissues. Radiation-induced senescence differs from normal aging, however, since the connective tissue does not appear to show an acceleration of the inelasticity and sclerosis normally found with age. Although it is not questioned that humans, and all biologic organisms, accumulate genetic damage during their life spans and that gross chromosomal aberrations increase in frequency with age and may be associated with senile changes, it is still not clear if such changes are the actual cause of aging. Rather they could reflect inability to adequately repair damage, which in turn could be part of the intrinsic genetic program, which would dictate a loss in repair enzymes with age.

Free radical theory

Free radicals are reactive atoms or molecules with highly excited electrons. The superoxide free radical, $O_2{}^{\cdot-}$, is generated through many normal biologic processes. Such free radicals are therefore able to oxidatively attack certain molecules, such as lipids, which may undergo lipid peroxidation. Radiation certainly promotes the formation of peroxide free radicals, which are known to damage biologic membranes through oxidative attack of the membrane lipids. A decrease in enzymes that normally remove free radicals (e.g., superoxide dismutase, peroxidase) may occur with age and may result in an increased concentration of these compounds but there is little evidence of such deficiencies. Free radicals can also be formed through the action of drugs and chemicals in the environment, and biologic systems can be protected from the attack of free radicals by chemicals known as *antioxidants*. Vitamin, (vitamin E) and many food additives function this way. Vitamin E (α-tocopherol) is a normal constituent of most cells, where it appears to act as a scavenger for free radicals and thus to protect membranes and cytoplasmic organelles from peroxidation.

Lipid peroxidation can lead to the formation of certain pigments, which have been identified with senescence. *Lipofuscin* is the most commonly deposited pigment in the nervous system, and its concentration there increases markedly with age. Lipid peroxidation produces malonaldehyde, which could then react with proteins and nucleotides. It has been suggested that an initial peroxidative event at cellular organelle membranes occurs and is followed by cellular repair efforts. The cellular mechanism for repairing or removing the damaged structure is through the autophagocytic organelle, the lysosome. The lysosome is able to combine with cellular constituents, other membranes, and lipids to form a new structure that is then able to digest these structures. The great importance of lysosomes in brain physiology is apparent when one recalls that the neurons have no cell turnover at all and are therefore fixed and stable throughout the life span. Excellent reparative mechanisms must exist to ensure the functional and structural integrity of the nervous system. Lysosomes eventually become structures known as *residual bodies* when they have completed their hydrolytic autophagic digestion of whatever they originally combined with. Lipofuscin pigments, or age pigments, are in reality residual bodies formed from lysosomes that have reacted with peroxidated lipids, proteins, and other molecules.

Although there is no question that these pigments do accumulate in aging, it has not been conclusively established that they are harmful or that they in any way interfere with the cell function of the aged human neuron. Some investigators believe that the accumulation of lipofuscin pigments merely indicates that the neuronal reparative processes are functioning normally, and the innocent end product of this process is the lipofuscin residual body. It is nevertheless possible that accumulation of these pigments with age aggravates pathologic damage caused by other agents of disease, and thus the aged's precarious steady state can be explained in light of such possible interactions. Much further research is required before the role of peroxidation and free radical formation, aging, lipofuscin pigment accumulation, and possible naturally occurring antioxidant defenses can be clearly described.

Slow virus infection theory

Since the advent of early electron microscopy the identification of viruses inside most cells has been considered evidence that many viruses may be present as passengers inside cells without causing pathologic damage. Further work has shown that some viruses present inside cells may be capable of remaining in either a latent state, which is subject to reactivation, or capable of producing a chronic subacute slow infection. Slow viruses have therefore been implicated as possible agents of aging. Their ubiquitous presence in all animals would lead to ultimate degeneration and disease of the infected cells, and thus senescence would be a viral infection with an ultimately fatal outcome.

Another consideration that might be more meaningful is that although not causative, slow viruses could nevertheless be involved in some of the degenerative changes associated with aging. Experimental backing for this possibility is found in the observations that certain slow virus infections of the central nervous system produce changes in the brain substance and vasculature that are extremely similar to the changes noted with normal senescence. The disease *kuru* is transmitted in primitive human tribes through the eating of infected nervous tissue of relatives as part of a mourning ritual. The agent is a slow virus that produces progressive brain degeneration. The symptoms develop insidiously, but once they are apparent, death usually occurs within 2 years. Another slow virus may be involved in Creutzfeldt-Jakob disease. These diseases have been transmitted experimentally from humans to chimpanzees and their viral nature proved. A number of other degenerative nervous system diseases have also been tentatively identified as caused by slow or latent viral infections. Some of these latent viruses have been successfully grown in tissue culture, and their cytopathic effects have been demonstrated in vitro. This may indicate that similar cellular damage occurs in their presence in vivo. It has been suggested that these latent viruses are normally present within human cells and that they are slowly activated with aging, resulting in chronic degenerative-tissue changes that characterize senescence. Silent viral infection is well described in humans for herpes simplex. Varicella (chickenpox) virus can cause herpes zoster lesions along sensory nerve roots in later life. These viruses all can be reactivated under appropriate environmental conditions. Herpes simplex can be reactivated by sunlight, radiation, trauma, and stress, causing the familiar coldsore, or fever blister. Herpes zoster causes the painful disease shingles, which also can be repeatedly reactivated by environmental stimuli. Epstein-Barr virus, which has been implicated in the serious infectious response that occurs in some patients after open heart surgery for cardiac bypass or heart transplantation, is considered to be silent or latent in many normal individuals. Epstein-Barr virus is also the causative agent of infectious mononucleosis and Burkitt's lymphoma and is present in an apparently latent form in most human leukocytes but can be activated to pathogenicity by immune suppression. Rubella virus also can persist in human tissues without causing further apparent damage to the host, as observed in children with rubella syndrome. The same property has also been described for measles virus and for a papovavirus in a disease that is associated with immunosuppression and progressive multifocal leukoencephalitis. Thus latent viruses do exist in human tissues and are capable of slow infection or reactivation. Their role in aging, however, remains obscure.

Autoimmune theory

Another theory of aging suggests that aging is an autoimmune disease, with the production of autoantibodies leading to cell damage and necrosis and producing the changes of senescence. There is evidence that autoantibodies increase with age, as does the incidence of known autoimmune disorders. Furthermore, the changes associated with autoimmune phenomena can be viewed as senescentlike. Also, if development, growth, and aging are all part of the same process, then the process of self-recognition that occurs in early life through poorly understood but probably ultimately genetic means could occur in reverse in senescence. Thymic involution occurs with age and may result in the organisms's depending on IgM anti-

bodies rather than IgG, with the result that autoimmune phenomena are more likely to occur in the absence of the more highly specific IgG. Both T cell– and B cell–mediated immunity decrease with age, and this is associated not only with autoimmune diseases but also with cancer and general susceptibility to infections. T suppressor cell function declines during senescence. There also appears to be a qualitative difference in the T cells between young and old animals. Implantation of old T cells into young mice results in a reversible state of immunodeficiency that is characteristic of the aged mice. This is perhaps one of the best pieces of evidence for cellular aging in vivo. It is thought that certain extrinsic factors may be involved in the development of autoimmunity with age. One such splenic factor is believed to cause the immune cells to respond less well to antigen. In light of this it is interesting to note that splenectomy has been one of the most effective life-lengthening measures in experimental animals.

Although certainly interesting and provocative, the autoimmune theory probably will help explain only some of the changes that are found in senescence, rather than identifying the ultimate cause of aging.

EARLY CALORIC RESTRICTION AND DELAYED AGING

The most striking experimentally induced delay in aging and death in the laboratory rodent and in many other animals is caused by early restriction of food intake. This phenomenon was first demonstrated by McKay in 1939 and has been confirmed many times. The mode of action of early caloric restriction is obscure, but the absolute amount of food, the time of restriction, and the nature of the diet all appear to be important in determining the life-lengthening effect. The amount of protein, carbohydrate, and total calories varies in different studies and in different animals. Caloric restriction of about 60% of the normal intake in a diet relatively low in protein and high in carbohydrate fed ad libitum to rats in the postweaning period had the greatest effect. Calorie restriction to control the obesity that usually results in rats fed ad libitum was essential although not severe enough to interfere with sexual vigor and development. Absolute growth was decreased in these animals. They were generally more active, sleeker, and leaner and appeared much younger than control rats of the same age. The major effect of early caloric restrictions on delayed senescence and death may be related to the absence of obesity in the animals, which acts to protect them from the diseases normally associated with advancing age in the rat. These include cardiovascular, muscular, renal, and malignant diseases that appear to be similar to the diseases of old age in humans.

Another interesting possibility is that early caloric restriction inhibits potentially tumorigenic cells early in the growth period, so that ultimate carcinogenic transformation of these cells is delayed significantly. Rats (and people) do not die of old age per se but from the ravages of the many diseases that are associated with normal senescence. A major disease of the aged is cancer, and its incidence is increasing as the proportion of elderly individuals among the general population also increases. Malignancy in this population might well be correlated with obesity or accelerated growth during certain critical periods, either of which acts to promote or initiate carcinogenesis. In this regard it is interesting to note that calorie-restricted rats do not develop tumors with the same frequency as control rats. Furthermore,

age and calorie intake in the rat are the two major determinants of ultimate tumor development during the rat's life span. The incidence of certain tumors can actually be predicted by the rat's weight at 70 days of age.

The relationship of growth in the early stages of life to ultimate senescence and death are major areas of research at the present time. It does appear that rapid early growth is associated with a shorter life span; growth rate and longevity are negatively correlated. Among mammals, humans have the longest growth and development period and the longest life span as well. Whether this relationship indicates a fundamental expression of the genetic sequencing and timing program is a matter for speculation. It is interesting to examine the theoretic life spans attainable for different species as measured in calories dissipated per gram of tissue. This would be in a sense a measure of the "living efficiency" of an organism. Data appear to indicate that caloric life span increases as the brain-to-body ratio increases, as well as with the length of the somatic growing period and brain maturation period. Ultimately, the size attained may be less than that determined genetically. The effects of early caloric restriction may produce eating patterns that persist throughout the life span. The smaller organism needs fewer nutrients to meet its energy requirements, consumes less, and is possibly even more metabolically efficient.

One interesting corollary to this experimental work is the greater longevity of the female of the human species. Possibly this is related to the usually smaller size of the female and therefore a longer caloric life span. Male mortality is greater throughout most of the life cycle for most diseases, a fact that may be attributable at least in part to the increased growth and therefore nutritional demands of the male organism (Stini, 1981).

It may be that early caloric restriction allows for ultimately more effective utilization of calories throughout the life span. The body in a sense "learns" to conserve energy very early during the critical growth periods. Critical periods for humans have not been defined, but the post-weaning period in the laboratory animal seems to be the time at which restriction produces the greatest life lengthening. Prenatal restriction in all animals, including humans, sets up pathologic changes in the developing fetus. Immediate postnatal restriction is not effective in life-lengthening experiments. If it can be presumed that there is some degree of applicability of this work to humans, the suggestion is that the prevention of childhood obesity carries with it the possibility of a healthier and longer life.

Other agents that have been shown to prolong life in experimental animals include immunosuppression, a germ-free environment, hypothermia, antioxidants, anti-cross-linking agents, prednisolone, and posterior pituitary extract. None of these agents are comparable or strikingly additive with the effects of early caloric restriction, however.

AGENTS THAT DECREASE LIFE SPAN
Radiation

Ionizing radiation has been reported to significantly shorten life span by accelerating aging. Part of this effect appears to be the carcinogenic effect of radiation, as tumors increase in incidence in irradiated populations of mice. Irradiation also causes increased body weight and fat deposition, conditions associated with premature onset of various diseases and early death. The types of pathologic lesions associated with irradiation include nephrosclerosis and infection. Single exposure of young mice to whole-body radiation produces essentially the same pattern as that produced by cumulative, spaced, low doses. Whether these effects of radiation truly mimic natural aging or are the specific pathologic effects of radiation on cells and tissues is not known. As has been mentioned before, radiation does not cause certain characteristics of normal senescence such as connective tissue sclerosis and collagen cross-linking. It is doubtful that normal senescence can proceed without these phenomena, at least in humans.

Nutrition

It would seem logical that aging can be accelerated by a poor, unbalanced diet and retarded by a good diet. It has been difficult to verify this experimentally, however, no matter how logical it seems. Certainly the relationship of obesity to various diseases associated with senescence (diabetes, cardiovascular disease) has been well demonstrated (see Chapter 12). The effects of early caloric restriction may in fact result from the prevention of obesity. Even genetically obese rats, which have a very high incidence of disease and early senescence, can be made to live longer and are healthier when they are calorically restricted and their obesity prevented. Nevertheless, the composition of the diet itself in retarding aging appears to be dependent on the species and strain of animal; no information is available for humans. The changes in dietary requirements throughout the life span are not well described, and essentially nothing is known about the changes that may occur in the requirements of the aged human. Table 9-1 shows the decrease in nutrient intake with age; only calcium is well below recommended allowances, but the in-

Table 9-1. Mean nutrient intake per day for men*

	Age in years			
	35-54	**55-64**	**65-74**	**75 +**
Calories (kcal)	2,643	2,465	2,051	1,866
Protein (g)	107	99	82	72
Fat (g)	133	124	100	90
Carbohydrate (g)	244	228	204	191
Calcium (g)	0.77	0.70	0.67	0.60
Iron (mg)	16.9	16.2	13.4	1.3
Vitamin A (IU)	6,650	9,740	5,640	4,720
Thiamine (mg)	1.4	1.4	1.2	1.1
Ascorbic acid (mg)	75	78	67	54

*From US Dept of Agriculture, Household Food Consumption Survey, 1965-1966.

Table 9-2. Recommended dietary allowances for persons over 50 years*

	Women	Men
Calories (kcal)	1,800	2,400
Protein (g)	46	56
Vitamin A (IU)	4,000	5,000
Vitamin E (IU)	12	15
Ascorbic acid (mg)	45	45
Niacin (mg)	12	16
Riboflavin (mg)	1.1	1.5
Thiamine (mg)	1.0	1.2
Calcium (mg)	800	800
Iron	10	10

*From Recommended Dietary Allowances, 8th rev ed, National Academy of Science, Washington, DC, 1974.

take of all nutrients decrease with age. Table 9-2 shows the recommended daily dietary allowances for older adults. Caloric allowance is decreased about 10% from that recommended for a mature adult. Other nutrients are not decreased, indicating that nutrient enrichment of diet per calories recommended should be carried out. Little experimental data exist on the changing nutritional needs of the elderly.

It is believed that since general metabolism is decreased in the aged there is a need for fewer calories and vitamins. Certainly the aged eat less and at irregular intervals more than do young or middle-aged adults. However, the social pressures associated with eating may change with age and may account for these differences.

One concomitant of aging that essentially is universal over the age of 80 is the development of *osteoporosis* (see Chapter 13). This process begins in middle adulthood and is most common in women. Some nutritionists believe that the osteoporotic process can be delayed by dietary factors before it has actually begun. According to some studies, bone density is significantly increased in vegetarians, but more work needs to be done to confirm these results. It is conceivable that a meat-rich diet can cause acid overloading, which is associated with a withdrawal of calcium from the bones. High-protein diets may also cause the same phenomenon. There is some evidence that osteoporosis can be partially prevented by water fluoridation, protein restriction, and increased calcium intake during childhood and early adulthood.

GENERAL CHANGES WITH AGE

Before the various changes that characterize senescence in the different organ systems are discussed, a description of the general structural and functional changes that occur with aging will be given.

Atrophy and involution

A general characteristic of aging is atrophy and involution of many structures. Accompanying these changes in size are also characteristic changes in function. The sexual organs involute markedly, particularly in women, a process that begins during the menopausal middle years. Accompanying the involution of these organs and glands is a decrease in the secondary sexual characteristics and for some women a decline in sexual appetite. The body fat distribution changes in women, and the muscular bulk and strength decline markedly in men. One exception to the atrophy is the high incidence of prostatic hypertrophy that occurs in men as they age.

Other organ systems undergo involution as well. The incidence of obesity declines from its peak incidence during the middle years. Height diminishes on the average 2 inches because of kyphosis and thinning and softening of the cartilaginous intervertebral discs. Loss of pigmentation of the hair is a nearly universal characteristic, and the hair itself often becomes thin and sparse.

Sclerosis

Connective tissue throughout the body undergoes a process of hardening and loss of elasticity, leading to sclerosis. This may be marked in structures such as arteries, which are supported by connective tissue, and in the skin. The dermis rather than the epidermis is affected, giving the skin its characteristic wrinkled appearance. The sclerotic process appears to involve increased fibrous content of connective tissue, as well as increased cross-linking of collagen molecules. As a result of this widespread process many organs and tissues can be affected. The contribution of this to the decline in function that accompanies senescence is difficult to measure but may be one of the major ways that secondary aging changes in tissues occur.

General organ function

Although the aged person may be maintaining a steady state, it is done so in the presence of much functional decline. Thus the steady state is precarious, and pathologic damage to one organ or organ system will therefore have far-reaching effects on other systems. Furthermore, the incidence of disease increases with age, and not only will this contribute to the senescent process, but also in many cases it will lead to death. The aged person thus is not able to cope effectively with environmental changes that threaten wellness.

Some notable functional declines that occur with aging are in glomerular filtration rate, cardiac index, respiratory function, fluid and electrolyte balance, basal metabolic rate, nerve conduction velocity, and memory. The aged person often has some sensory and motor deficits, and the special senses such as hearing and eyesight undergo diminution with age. There is an increased incidence of mental illness as well, much of which may go unreported and untreated because of the general tolerance of most cultures toward peculiar or deviant behavior in the elderly. Depression is extremely common, and the highest incidence of suicide among men occurs after age 75.

Loss of adaptability

Wellness requires that a person be able to adapt to changing environmental conditions to preserve a constant internal environment. There is a marked decrease in adaptive ability as the human ages, the result of a variety of interacting factors. One phenomenon that appears to be a universal concomitant of senescence is a decline in the ability of the organism to produce enzymes in an adaptive manner. Another related effect is the decreased responsiveness at the cellular level to many circulating hormones. Both are potential perturbers of the adaptive capacity. One example of these effects is the decreasing ability of the liver to produce adaptive levels of the enzyme glucokinase in response to blood glucose concentration. However, insulin is necessary to produce this adaptation in liver cells. It has been discovered that insulin release is decreased in aged rats. Thyroxin is another hormone required for an optimal liver glucokinase response to glucose. Both insulin and thyroxin decrease in concentration as a function of aging in rats and may reflect age-related changes in the glands that produce them. It is possible that pancreatic islets cells lose the capacity to secrete adequate amounts of insulin as a result of immunologic destruction of the beta cells.

The decreased adaptive abilities of the elderly to respond to various threats to wellness has been termed *homeostenosis*, a narrowing of the adaptive reserves. For example, there is decreased ability of the vascular system to modify peripheral resistance when necessary to adjust blood flow to various organs, diminished renal regulatory capacity to adjust sodium and water balance, less responsive thermoregulatory mechanisms, and decreased ability to adjust cardiac output in response to metabolic demands (Davis and Zenser, 1985). Thermal sensitivity and regulatory responses may be so impaired in the elderly as to account for many deaths. In hot environments hyperthermia is much more

likely to occur and cause death in people over the age of 60. Hypothermia may occur much more commonly than has ever been previously diagnosed (Kenney, 1985).

Although physiologic adaptation is diminished in the elderly and probably accounts for much morbidity, psychologic coping also appears to be decreased (Dye, 1985). This is related not only to central nervous system and neuroendocrine declines, but also to psychosocial factors, such as financial problems, loss of social support systems, bereavement, loss of control, physical changes, and changes in living conditions. All of these situations act additively to produce stress and deplete adaptive energies.

MIND-BODY INTERACTIONS IN AGING

Aging must be viewed as a holistic process that involves sociologic and cultural expectations, psychologic influences, and physiologic events. The history of each aging cohort is another consideration, since those who are 70 years old today have an entirely different biopsychosocial background than those who are 60 or 80 years of age. Studies that are being performed currently may have limited relevance for the aged in the year 2000. Although the genetic aging program is the timekeeper for aging, there are important psychologic and sociologic influences that can modify the program. A person's sense of control appears to be one of those factors that is highly related to health, particularly in the elderly (Rodin, 1986). Generally it is observed that social isolation, losses, and perceived loss of control are associated with ill health, probably through immune system suppression. Since immunologic function is significantly decreased by the biologic process of aging, there is less adaptive margin, and thus the relationship between these factors and immunodeficiency becomes stronger. However, the elderly may often have different views and interpretations of loss as compared to younger people. Therefore the meaning of the loss of control, isolation, or bereavement is the critical determinant in producing health effects. Nevertheless, loss of control is an adverse situation for people of all ages. It is associated with helplessness, hopelessness, and ultimately, physiologic disruptions such as immunosuppression, catecholamine release, and corticosteroid secretion, all of which contribute to pathophysiologic processes. Cardiac problems, increased blood lipids, hypertension, infections, and cancer could all be produced through such mechanisms in the elderly. Society often seems to restrict the older persons' sense of control by imposing retirement age, living conditions, and expectations of behavior. Assumptions about the abilities and health status of old people are made a priority, and these assumptions can significantly impact the potential for wellness. Long-lived societies tend to honor the elderly and value their contributions. There are many lifestyle factors that contribute to longevity, but social status, perceived value and control, and active involvement are also important.

COMMON DISEASES OF SENESCENCE

In senescence there is a tendency to develop infections more easily, because the immune system is less functional. The gastrointestinal tract is the most common area of complaint in the elderly, with constipation, diverticulosis, and gallstones being extremely common. Diabetes mellitus also increases with age. Cardiovascular disease is nearly universal, although its severity may vary among individuals. Malignancies increase in incidence in the aged population. Osteoarthritis and osteoporosis are considered normal pathologic

changes that occur with age; they are nearly universal, often causing severe disability. Chronic obstructive lung disease also is often present in the elderly.

These are all disease conditions that result in part from the functional impairment of many systems (Fig. 9-1). Nevertheless, only about 10% of the elderly population is seriously incapacitated with disease. Being old does not mean being sick, only more fragile and less adaptive. This next section will describe the various deficits that develop with senescence that can compromise wellness or increase risk of disease. It should be pointed out, however, that most elderly people do not feel handicapped by functional loss, since it has developed slowly over time and becomes barely noticeable. A wellness-oriented lifestyle, a positive attitude, activities and interests, a social support system, and a sense of control all contribute in many ways to slowing down some of these processes of decline and to allowing the elderly person to live a high-quality life in spite of any functional losses.

Integumentary system

The skin is comprised of a stratified epithelium separated by a basement membrane from a connective tissue dermis. The connective tissue is made up of fibroblasts, tissue cells, and fibers such as collagen, reticulin, and elastin. Collagen and elastin are proteins elaborated by the connective tissue cells and found in all connective tissues. The functions of connective tissues are related to transport, deposition of materials, and support. The nature of collagen is such that a variety of possible cross-linkages between collagen molecules can occur, thus altering the nature of the connective tissue. The collagen molecule is diagramed in Fig. 9-2, and the nature of possible cross-linkage is indi-

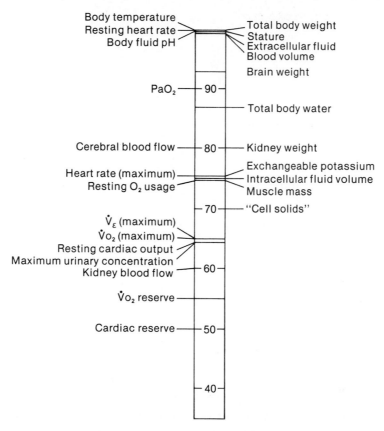

Fig. 9-1. Anatomic and functional variables in a 70-year-old man expressed as a percentage of values in a young adult.

(From Kenny R: Physiology of aging, 1985, Clinics in Geratric Medicine, 1:37-59.)

cated. Cross-linkage is not a pathologic process in all circumstances. It occurs in healthy human collagen under the influence of the tissue environment and various hormones. Thus it is a phenomenon that can be regulated in response to the needs of the organism. One type of cross-linkage of collagen might facilitate transport of substances through the tissue matrix, whereas another might give the connective tissue more tensile strength and facilitate the supportive function.

Senescence is accompanied by an increase in the cross-linking of collagen molecules within the connective tissue throughout the body. Thus molecular changes occur with aging of the organism. The collagenous fibers are not frequently renewed. Therefore they can accumulate errors with age, and repair of these errors is not efficient. The types of cross-linkages that occur when collagen ages are conversion of intramolecular aldol cross-links into stable cross-links of both an intramolecular and intermolecular nature. The second type of linkage is the Schiff base, which is formed as covalent bonding of the aldimine type. Cross-linkage of collagen confers more rigidity on the connective tissue in which the collagen is found. Such

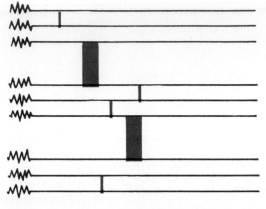

$$P - (CH_2)_3 - CHO + NH_2 - (CH_2)_4 - P = P - (CH_2)_3 - CH = N - (CH_2)_4 - P$$

Fig. 9-2. Collagen cross-linkage. Collagen may be cross-linked intramolecularly as indicated by thin bands connecting protein strands or intermolecularly as shown by thick bands holding molecules of collagen together. This cross-linkage causes a rigidity of structure, leading to eventual sclerosis of all connective tissues. Nature of molecular bond formed by a common type of cross-linkage is indicated at bottom. (*P*, Protein strand.)

cross-linked collagen is less soluble than normal collagen and physically stronger. The increase in collagen number and cross-linkage is accompanied by an increase in elastin fiber formation as compared to the relative amount of connective tissue matrix. The hexosamine:collagen ratio is highest in the newborn and declines with age. It is also low in the chronically ill. Thus with advancing age the amount of connective tissue ground substance and the number of cells decrease, whereas the collagen fiber formation, strength, and insolubility all increase. Calcium salts are also deposited in connective tissue with age, causing calcification. These changes cause the dermis of the skin to fold and buckle; the overlying epidermis also folds mechanically as the dermis changes. The epidermis itself undergoes very little change with age, being comprised of a rapid turnover compartment of epithelial cells, which constantly desquamate and are replaced. It is believed that the epithelium has the potential to far outlive the organism itself. The skin does wrinkle with age, but this effect results entirely from dermal changes rather than any properties of the epidermis.

The pigmentation of the skin changes with aging, and age spots (senile lentigo) are commonly found. The source of pigmentation in the human skin is melanocytes, which are under the influence of hormonal and environmental factors. Skin turgor is nearly universally lost to some degree, and the skin often has a lax appearance. The most common skin lesions associated with senescence are seborrheic keratosis characterized by irregular round or oval lesions that are brown and often warty, comedones (blackheads), dermatophytosis (a fungal infection), and dry, scaly skin. Both oil and skin glands decrease in number and activity. Nevi also occur often in the aged group. Cherry angiomas are commonly present, increasing in incidence after the third decade.

Musculoskeletal system

Bone and joints. Profound changes occur in the musculature and the skeleton, some of which have been previously described. Bone is an extremely active and dynamic tissue. It is constantly undergoing remodeling according to the stresses put on it so as to serve its major function, *support* (see Chapter 13). The microstructure of bone consists of cells and a mineralized matrix, which form a complex array of haversian canals and osteons. The matrix of the bone is mainly composed of calcium hydroxyapatite crystals, which form a latticelike structure. A portion of the calcium in bone is exchangeable with the blood; this is influenced by the activity of calcitonin and parathyroid hormone. This exchangeable pool of calcium diminishes with age, and thus the bone becomes demineralized or less dense. The bone becomes brittle and is subject to fracture when stressed. Demineralized bone does not provide adequate support for musculature and viscera. Fibrous and fatty infiltration of the haversian canals contributes to the instability of the demineralized bone. The microvasculature of the bone also may be compromised by arteriosclerotic changes that occur with age, and this adversely affects bone healing following fractures in the aged. Minute foci of necrosis and microfractures characterize the increasingly porous bone of old age.

Osteoclasts, which are giant resorptive bone cells that break down bone in preparation for new bone formation or growth and healing, are thought to be increased in number with senescence. Osteoclastic activity is also influenced by parathyroid hormone and is one mechanism by which calcium is removed from bone.

The initiating factors in osteoporosis are not known, although osteoporosis seems to be an intrinsic part of the aging program.

There is a fundamental dimorphism in osteoporosis with a much higher incidence in women than in men. Women at the age of 70 have lost about 50% of their skeletal mass to osteoporosis, compared to 70- to 80-year-old men who just begin to show the process. The two syndromes of osteoporosis related to aging are described in Chapter 13. This is basically a result of different total bone mass and density in males compared to females. The smaller, thinner female is the most at risk (Gordon and Genant, 1985). There are several ways in which the rate of osteoporosis development can be altered, some of which have been described. It has been suggested that somatotropin, gonadal insufficiency, hyperactivity of the adrenal cortex, sedentariness, and diet all increase the rate of osteoporosis. The osteoporotic process in women appears to begin after menopause. Loss of bone mass is most rapid in the first 8 to 10 years after menopause. Osteoporosis and bone atrophy and softening are all signs of senile changes, which increase the risk of fracture.

Cartilage also changes with age, as evidenced by softening of the fibrocartilaginous intervertebral discs, which then may invade the bodies of the vertebrae, contributing to kyphosis and decrease in stature. The cartilage in general, like other connective tissues, becomes calcified with age, and hard bone may actually form in the cartilage of very old persons. Degeneration of the cartilage also accompanies calcification and thus contributes to the decreased general elasticity of the skeleton. The articular cartilage is not spared these changes, and the joint capsules erode with age. As cartilage degenerates it appears that reparative efforts ensue, which result in bony overgrowth, causing "lipping" of the bone around the joint or the formation of bone spurs, which may project into the joint. Osteoarthritis is one of the most common disabling afflictions that occur normally with senescence (see Chapter 13). The joints themselves are hypertrophied, and there is a decreased flexibility, which leads to stiffness, pain, and limitations of motion. Crepitus, or noise in the joints on movement, is common, and loose bodies (joint mice) may also be present.

Muscle. As do most structures, muscles atrophy with age. There is associated with this a loss of muscular strength and decreased capacity for muscular work. It should be recalled that muscle is a tissue with very slow or no turnover and thus may reflect aging changes more markedly than other tissue. The microstructure of the muscle changes with age, accumulating collagen and elastin fibers. The cells themselves lose nuclei, the myofibrils lose their striations, and cellular degeneration results in atrophy and replacement of muscle fibers with adipose and connective tissue. These changes may be prevented to some degree by exercise, nutrition, and genetic factors. The changes observed in muscle with age may be caused by a lack of activity and use of the muscles and by the skeletal changes that also occur. A primary aging process in muscle seems likely as well, as hand grip strength declines markedly with age, although the use of the hand does not decrease with age.

Cardiovascular system

The myocardium, a muscle, is subject to the aging changes that have been described. Furthermore, it is composed of excitable cells capable of automaticity. Some studies indicate that ionic movement across the cardiac cell membrane is disrupted with aging of the myocardium. Fatty and connective tissue infiltration, degeneration and atrophy of individual fibers, and accumulation of lipofuscin pigments in the heart all occur with aging. These changes in the heart muscle are accompanied by senile changes in the epicardium and valves of the heart and in the conduction system. The endocardium thickens diffusely in the left atrium, causing left atrial hypertrophy. The other chambers of the heart undergo some hypertrophy, fatty infiltration, and sclerosis. The valves become thickened and fibrotic with advancing age, and the mitral valve in particular is subject to some degree of calcification. There are increases in the elastic fiber content and fat in the nodes and conduction system of the heart. It can be seen then that there are macroscopic and microscopic changes in the heart that must cause some derangement of function and also increase the susceptibility of the heart to injury under circumstances such as hypoxia or infarction. Furthermore, it has been demonstrated that coronary flow is decreased significantly in the aged, and the older animal does not appear to be as able to increase oxygen extraction during hypoxia as does the younger animal.

Other physiologic parameters of cardiac function decrease with age. The length-tension relationship, which is the basis of the Frank-Starling mechanism by which stroke volume is determined through end diastolic volume, is disturbed in the elderly. The stiffer ventricle has a higher filling pressure, or left ventricular end diastolic pressure, than does the younger ventricle. Therefore sudden stress in the older animal, which would require operation of the Frank-Starling mechanism, results in the maintenance of a higher left ventricular pressure for a longer period of time, thus contributing to an elevated end diastolic pressure. This in turn can contribute to development of congestive heart failure and pulmonary edema. In general, however, the mechanical properties of the heart are adequate in the well elderly, except when seriously stressed or pharmacologically challenged (Klausner and Schwartz, 1985).

Another parameter that changes with age is the duration of isometric relaxation and contraction in the older heart. These alterations may reflect intrinsic changes in contractile properties with age or may be a result of catecholamine depletion or decreased calcium removal from the actin and myosin of the myofibrils. When the heart rate increases for various reasons, the effects of prolonged relaxation and contraction could compromise ventricular filling such that incomplete relaxation occurs between contractions, causing higher left ventricular end diastolic pressure and higher pulmonary venous pressure, contributing to the development of pulmonary edema and congestive heart failure.

Cardiac output may decline to half of normal by age 80; if this is expressed as cardiac index (liter/min/m^2), total cardiac function declines with declining cardiac output.

The vascular system is also profoundly affected by the aging process. The total peripheral resistance increases as a function of age so that some degree of hypertension is considered a normal concomitant of senescence. The heart must pump blood through sclerotic vessels.

With each year of aging the peripheral resistance has been reported to increase 1%. Blood pressure elevation with age occurs in men in response to the rising peripheral resistance. Both systolic and diastolic pressures increase up to the age of 60, at which point the systolic pressure increases and the diastolic pressure actually may decrease. Women generally have both higher systolic and diastolic pressures than men by the age of 70.

There have been many studies done on the incidence of atherosclerosis with age and the influence of factors such as obesity, diet, activity, and habits. These have been discussed elsewhere in this book as has the basic process of atherosclerosis. Atherosclerosis is the most important cause of arteriosclerosis, and although atherosclerosis is multifactorial in its determination, age appears to be the most common cause.

Although many authorities consider atherosclerosis to be a multifactorial group of diseases, the pathophysiologic changes that occur with age in various arteries in the body must be examined in terms of senescent changes, since the process of atherosclerosis appears to be directly influenced by life span. The atherosclerotic process appears to preferentially involve certain parts of the arterial tree more frequently than others (e.g., coronary arteries, arterial branches, and the distal abdominal aorta). It appears that there are intrinsic properties of these vessel walls that predispose them to atherosclerotic plaque formation. It is conceivable that senescent changes in the arterial walls themselves may lead to plaque formation. It has been suggested that an initial lesion must occur before the atherosclerotic plaque formation ensues, namely, a myointimal cellular proliferation. This cellular proliferation may occur as the result of a number of possible processes, including endothelial injury and platelet factors, neoplastic changes in the arterial wall, and clonal senescence. Clonal senescence might occur as part of normal aging in which a clone of intimal smooth muscle cells has a limited life span and therefore undergoes an irreversible aging process, leading to decreased replicative ability.

Some experiments have been described in which cell cultures of various segments of the arterial tree were shown to have a diminished capacity for replication with age of the donor animal. This indicates that intrinsic aging of the smooth muscle cells of the arterial walls may occur. When the differentiated cells are not replaced adequately, the feedback regulation of cellular division is interrupted. This causes a compensatory proliferation at sites where the cells have aged and have not been replaced by differentiated cells from the intimal, smooth-muscle, stem-cell compartment. Cells stimulated to replace the aged differentiated cells are atypical and produce the early myointimal lesions that are the forerunners of atherosclerotic plaque formation.

Other explanations for intimal proliferation are possible, an important one being the effects of endothelial injury and platelet activation on the development of early lesions. Certainly it is conceivable that both processes can contribute to the development of atherosclerosis with aging.

It is well known that serum cholesterol levels increase with age, and cholesterol is believed to play some etiologic role in the increasing incidence of atherosclerosis that routinely occurs with aging. There are many other factors that also act to increase serum cholesterol levels, including smoking, obesity, high blood pressure, lack of exercise, and high uric acid levels. On the average, serum cholesterol levels increase from a mean of 111 in the average 25-year-old man to 227 in the 75-year-old man. Research has implicated not only the absolute level of serum cholesterol in atherosclerosis, but also the way that the cholesterol is carried in the blood on lipoproteins. It will be recalled that the liver produces lipoproteins, which bind lipid and transport it within the body fluids. High-density lipoproteins (HDLs), low-density lipoproteins (LDLs), and very-low-density lipoproteins (VLDLs) are the major serum lipoproteins, carrying varying amounts of cholesterol, triglycerides, and phospholipid. The HDLs are the smallest in terms of particulate size, and carry proportionately the greatest amount of lipid. Atherosclerotic deposition on the walls of the aorta and other vessels appears to be accelerated in the presence of an increased concentration of LDLs and decreased in incidence when HDLs predominate. Although there is some genetic control over the ratio of HDLs to LDLs, the concentration of HDLs in the blood can be increased through nutritional modifications, aerobic exercise, and weight loss. A natural decrease in the HDLs is associated with the aging process. This may play some role in the atherosclerosis of aging. Another alteration in lipid metabolism is the generally increased deposition of lipid and particularly cholesterol with age. Most tissues show this effect. The aged rat adipose tissue appears to be less active metabolically and therefore less able to participate in steady state regulation of fat metabolism.

Other changes in the vessels commonly occur with senescence. Connective tissue aging leads to hardening and loss of elasticity of the tissue. Blood vessels have a fibrous wall of connective tissue, containing ground substance, collagen and elastic fibers, and fibroblasts. With aging this tissue is subject to sclerosis, which leads to narrowing of the vessel lumen and increased rigidity and resistance to blood flow. The increase in collagen fiber deposition and cross-linkage, as well as calcium deposition that occurs in the dermis, may also be observed in the blood vessels. It is a change that is noninflammatory and not necessarily associated with atherosclerotic plaque formation. Obviously these connective tissue changes that occur with senescence can lead to a number of pathophysiologic processes, a prime one being tissue hypoxia, the effects of which may be quite profound (see Chapter 16). The brain function depends greatly on oxygenation, and senile vascular changes can lead to microfoci of tissue ischemia, or in the case of large vessel atherosclerosis, large areas of infarction with brain tissue necrosis. Thus the effects of hypoxia with age-related vessel changes may be minor, such as memory lapses, or profound, such as paralysis, coma, and death. Other tissues are subject to hypoxia, most particularly the renal, hepatic, and splanchnic beds. Indeed, when the decreasing cardiac output distribution of the aged is examined, it is apparent that the cerebral, coronary, and muscular blood flow are all maximally maintained at the expense of the visceral circulation. In fact, with advancing age it may be that the cerebral circulation receives a proportionately greater percentage of the cardiac output than in the younger person.

There is abundant evidence that cardiovascular decline with age may be associated with intellectual impairment. The effects of cardiovascular disease appear to act together with the intrinsic aging changes in the nervous system.

Respiratory system

The bronchial tree and lungs undergo changes with age that result not only in decreased respiratory function but also in chronic obstructive pulmonary disease (COPD) such as emphysema. The connective tissue of the bronchial tree undergoes characteristic age-related changes, and the lungs themselves also develop changes that are emphysematous in nature but that may not be correlated with the clinical signs and symptoms of COPD. The alveoli are often enlarged and the bronchial ducts dilated. The enlargement of the al-

veoli appears to be a result of weakening and stretching of the alveolar septal membranes, which have the tendency to rupture. When this occurs the membranes of the ruptured alveolus immediately fuse to an adjacent alveolus, thus preventing the escape of air into the intrapleural space. Furthermore, the adjacent alveolar membrane may also be stretched and may rupture. The two fused alveoli then form a new alveolar sac. This dilation, rupture, and fusion are processes that can be considered emphysematous. Corresponding to the alveolar changes are capillary defects. The acinar capillary network may become crowded and disorganized. Thus not only is the integrity of the alveoli decreased by the aging process, but also the gas exchange capabilities of the alveolocapillary membrane may be severely limited. Such changes would contribute to the decreased vital capacity, PaO_2, and maximum breathing capacity, and to the increased residual volume that are all associated with old age. Also important in the pathophysiology of these phenomena are the changes in the thoracic cage that occur with senescence. There is a reduction in thoracic cage volume resulting from kyphosis and osteoporotic changes in the vertebral column and ribs.

The respiratory alterations that are normal in old age increase the elderly person's susceptibility to severe pathophysiology when infections, stresses, and cardiac problems develop. The steady state is precarious at best in old age, and a minor pulmonary infection may set off a variety of responses that can lead to eventual pulmonary hypertension, respiratory failure, and cardiac decompensation.

Genitourinary system

As explained previously, renal circulatory perfusion is decreased during the aging process, and subsequently, the glomerular filtration rate and kidney function both decline. There is a steady loss of functional nephrons from the kidneys, which begins at the age of 40, such that by 75 years of age only 60% of the nephrons are functional. This may predispose the kidney to development of disease, which does occur with increased incidence in the aged. The aged kidney is not able to concentrate urine as effectively and is also less sensitive to the action of ADH. The kidney is able to maintain acid-base and fluid-electrolyte balance under normal circumstances, but these functions may be impaired in the aged kidney during stress. The kidney changes during senescence may be caused by infection or vascular disease. Many elderly people have significant pyuria in the absence of any clinical signs of pyelitis. Furthermore, the vascular changes in aging result in decreased renal plasma flow, decreased kidney perfusion, and often afferent arteriolar atrophy. It is possible also that renal senescence is intrinsic to the kidney cells, being accelerated or retarded by environmental factors. The process of renal senescence is difficult to evaluate since it does not occur in germ-free rats. Therefore the relative contribution of latent infection and arteriosclerosis in the aged must be further assessed.

The kidneys may also be implicated in the pathogenesis of hypertension, and both nephrosclerosis and hypertension are increased in incidence during senescence. The loss of nephrons with age and the declining kidney function are situations in which environmental factors may again act as a threat to the steady state in that the kidney's normal excretory, acidification, and base conservation processes are inadequate when the organism is severely stressed. Thus if heart failure and compensatory vasoconstriction occur, resultant renal ischemia could have a more pro-found effect in the older person, and renal failure would be the more likely sequela in the aged.

The reproductive systems of both the male and female undergo involution. It appears that the ovaries and the testes are affected by hormones, but whether their aging process is through intrinsic primary degeneration or by refractoriness to the hormones that stimulate them is not known.

Male reproductive system. Although atrophic changes occur throughout the male reproductive system and are often accompanied by degeneration, pigment deposition, and fibrosis, the capacity to produce viable sperm is retained in many men over the age of 60.

Nevertheless, many men do gradually lose sexual drive and capacity to produce viable sperm. Hormonal influences on male reproductive tract senescence have not been studied in detail, but it has been suggested that the hypothalamus in both men and women may play the most important role in determining the aging process, through the hypothalamic-hypophyseal-gonadotropic hormones. Testosterone levels decline progressively after the age of 50. Also important to consider are cultural expectations regarding sexuality, that may have an even greater influence than biological changes.

The cause of prostatic hypertrophy is not known other than that it is definitely linked to the aging process. It appears that the connective tissue component of the prostate is affected primarily, and this in turn causes the glandular epithelium to undergo morphologic changes.

Female reproductive system. The remarkable changes that occur in the structures of the female reproductive system throughout the life span have been the subject of much research. The 28-day cycle of the uterus occurs in most women for about

30 years and then becomes irregular, finally ceasing during the female climacteric or menopause. The ovarian hormones no longer are produced in sufficient quantities, and women at menopause begin to show signs of senescent pathology such as atherosclerosis and osteoporosis. It appears that estrogen protects women from these processes in the premenopausal period.

It had previously been thought that the determining factor in the timing of the menopause was the final loss of all ova from the ovaries through the repeated cyclic ovulation of the menstrual period. Thus the ovary was considered to age by primary means, having an inherent biologic clock, the timekeeper for which was the total number of viable ova. There are still many proponents of this theory. However, others believe that the ovary itself is theoretically capable of function long after the time of menopause but that hormonal factors influence its activity and result in its aging. The hypothalamus has been implicated as the major regulator of all endocrine activities and the site of the human biologic aging clock through its own intrinsic senescence. Its mode of action might be the development of decreased sensitivity to circulating steroids with aging, such that its regulatory functions on hormonal production become progressively disturbed.

A further effect would be glandular hyperactivity, since the negative feedback system is operating at a higher set point or threshold to the gland product. While the steady state is thus maintained, an imbalanced internal environment can easily be provoked by secondary factors that set up pathophysiologic mechanisms, which result in age-associated changes in many organ systems.

Whatever mechanism is responsible, at about the age of 50 the ovaries begin to atrophy, producing less and less estrogen.

The uterus also involutes, with the cessation of menstruation and loss of fertility. Corresponding to the fall in estrogen secretion is a rise in pituitary gonadotropin release. This is seen as the result of the loss of negative feedback inhibition of estrogens on pituitary gonadotropin production and release. Both FSH and LH are elevated throughout the postmenopausal period. The theory of hypothalamic elevation of threshold to feedback inhibition proposes that the female menopause would occur by the following mechanism. The hypothalamus becomes less sensitive to the negative feedback inhibition of estrogen on releasing factors for FSH and LH. This is determined by some sort of genetic program in the cells of the hypothalamus. As a result the hypothalamus produces FSH and LH, which act to stimulate the ovaries. The hypersecretion process eventually results in exhaustion of ovarian capacity to produce estrogen and permit ovulation. This is diagramed in Fig. 9-3.

When the menopause becomes established, a variety of changes occur, most of which are partially preventable by the administration of estrogen preparations. The estrogens do not, however, retard the basic aging process. Furthermore, the use of these hormones in postmenopausal women must be carefully monitored.

The atrophic changes that occur after menopause in the female reproductive tract may cause problems. Thinning of the vaginal membrane appears to predispose elderly women to chronic infection, and the vulva and vagina may be extremely irritable, disturbing sexual relations. Estrogen administration may result in alleviation of these problems through promotion of vaginal wall hypertrophy.

Endocrine system

The interaction of the hypothalamic-hypophyseal-hormonal circuit has previously

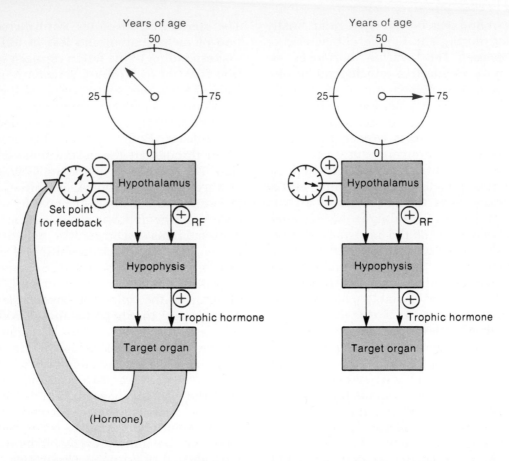

Fig. 9-3. Hormonal feedbacks in aging. With age, target organs such as ovaries can no longer produce hormones when stimulated. This leads to loss of negative-feedback inhibition on tropic hormone source, resulting in continuous outpouring of tropin, which has no effect on target gland. (*RF,* Releasing factor.)

been described, and it has been speculated that the same type of mechanism, that of elevated threshold to feedback inhibition, may operate at all levels of endocrine function and cause the secondary changes of senescence in target organs.

Metabolism is closely regulated by hormonal influences. Anabolic processes predominate during the growth and developmental periods and catabolic processes predominate during the maturation and senescent periods. The environment in which a tissue functions is also closely cor-

related with hormonal influences, and it is therefore reasonable to suggest that the endocrine system, by altering the tissue environment and the net catabolism of the organism, may serve as the ultimate time keeper or biologic clock, determining the rate of senescence of the various tissues. It is also reasonable to suggest that certain critical tissues are most affected by these endocrine mechanisms and thus show senescence as a primary phenomenon. These tissues then can exert a great variety of effects on other tissues, causing them to undergo a secondary or induced senescence.

Adrenocorticosteroids. No consistent changes in plasma cortisol occur with aging, and in fact the aged appear to have an adequate adrenocorticosteroid response to stress. However, it has been suggested that target organs of the steroids are less sensitive to the actions of these hormones.

According to Selye's stress-adaptation theory, chronic stress in an individual eventually leads to a stage of exhaustion, in which further stress cannot be tolerated because of ultimate depletion of the adrenocorticosteroid reserves. This has been considered equivalent to a process in which "adaptation energy" is decreased by constant stress. Life is accompanied by many stresses, and theoretically aging may occur as the adaptation energy stores are depleted. Primarily implicated in the loss of "adaptation energy" are the catabolic steroids, which may normally function in a protective manner and which may become deficient in senescence.

Thyroid hormone. Thyroxin, triiodothyronine, and thyrocalcitonin are hormones released by the thyroid. The first two act to stimulate metabolism, and the third acts on calcium and phosphate metabolism. The thyroid gland atrophies during senescence as do many organs and glands. However, thyroid nodules do appear quite frequently in older people. Thyroid function also declines with age, which may be the result of a decreased need for the hormone by the aged tissues. Basal metabolic rate (BMR) is decreased in the elderly, and some of the normal senescent changes in a sense mimic hypothyroidism, although a cause-and-effect relationship between these signs and hypothyroidism in the aged has not been shown. In fact, myxedema in the aged can be successfully treated with thyroid hormones. It would appear, however, that in times of stress, such as with an acute febrile illness, the thyroid gland is able to respond equally well in the old individual as in the young. Thus the gland itself does not appear to be functionally impaired in senescence, but rather the peripheral utilization of the hormone by target tissues is depressed in the aging process.

Pituitary hormones. The pituitary gland undergoes atrophy and degenerative changes with age. It appears that some depression of function is likely. It has been suggested that growth hormone secretion decreases during senescence. Administration of growth hormone to young animals may result in prolongation of life, but this effect is not observed in older animals. It will be recalled that this hormone increases anabolic pathways of metabolism in many tissues, including bone, muscle, and liver. Excess secretion of growth hormone may also accelerate aging. Excess growth hormone results in giantism in humans, and many pathologic growth processes appear to be accelerated by excess growth hormone in the laboratory animals. These include nephrosclerosis, periarteritis nodosa and hypertension, and various malignancies, all diseases associated with senescence. In general, decreased growth hormone secretion occurs.

ACTH release from the hypophysis does not appear to decrease with age, and TSH release also appears to remain normal or actually increase with age. Gonadotropin output is increased after menopause, and this also occurs in a slight degree in men.

The pituitary gland itself appears capable of producing hormones throughout the life span. In general the pituitary production of hormones does not seem to be a major cause or accompaniment of aging.

Tissue sensitivity. Target tissues of hormones may become less and less sensitive to the hormones with advancing age. The hormone production occurs therefore at a high rate because of negative feedback, and the target tissue begins to show signs of pathologic changes because of the relative lack of the hormone, which may be manifested as age-related diseases or merely as normal senescent processes. Much experimental research has indicated the validity of this concept, but conclusive evidence for most tissues is still lacking.

One intriguing theory pertaining to tissue unresponsiveness to hormonal stimulation with age is related to the increasing calcification of many soft tissues with senescence. Calcium also appears to accumulate in the cell membranes and might interfere in many ways with membrane function and membrane receptors, such as those that are believed to exist for hormone interactions. Increased membrane calcium may interfere with the adenyl cyclase system, which is involved in producing cyclic AMP, the second messenger for many hormone-mediated responses. Calcium in the membrane may inhibit the rate of turnover of membrane lipoproteins and thus favor the accumulation of alterations in the membrane such that the membrane "ages," and the tissue is also adversely affected.

Another possible mechanism for tissue unresponsiveness might be the actual effect of the hormones that act on the tissue over a period of many years. Thus repeated stimulation of the target tissue by the hormone itself produces changes that accumulate with age and cause signs of senescence.

Digestive system

The digestive system above all others appears to cause disturbing problems in the elderly. Splanchnic bed hypoxia may occur in the arteriosclerotic process that accompanies aging, as it does in the kidney. Therefore the gut, like the kidney, is a common site for age-related pathology. By far the most common complaint of the elderly is constipation, but it is difficult to ascertain if this results from primary GI tract atony, from decreased mobility of the aged person, or from repeated use of laxatives, which ultimately damage the bowel's capability to perform the defecation reflex.

The salivary glands' activity is decreased in the elderly, accounting for the dryness of the mouth and mucous membranes. The atrophy of the chewing and swallowing muscles and lack of teeth impair the elderly's ability to eat, and this of course may contribute significantly to the poor nutrition that is characteristic of the elderly population in general.

The esophagus and stomach both may have a thinning of the mucous membrane lining; atrophic gastritis is common and may be associated with vitamin B_{12} deficiency and pernicious anemia. There is also an associated risk of gastric carcinoma.

The small and large intestines also change with age and may show degenerative changes, pigment deposition, and calcification. Furthermore, in the large intestinal wall the increased incidence of diverticulosis indicates that the muscular lining may become weakened with age.

The pancreas has also been reported to show histologic senile changes. The liver, on the other hand, rarely shows fibrosis and the other degenerative changes of senescence. The individual parenchymal cells may occasionally show signs of aging such as large and unusual nuclei and cytoplasmic organelle variation. Other studies on aged human livers have shown no gross morphologic or functional alterations in the liver with aging. Enzymatic activities of the liver have in fact been reported to remain at a normal level throughout the life span.

Nervous system

Changes in the brain, spinal cord, and peripheral nerves can occur through hypoxic changes resulting from age-related vascular disease or through intrinsic properties of these tissues. The nervous system consists of highly differentiated cells that do not divide after approximately the first 18 months of life. Thus damage in these cells cannot be compensated for by cell replacement. Damage is either repaired or it accumulates. Aging of the nervous tissue has far-reaching effects on normal physiology and behavior and may lead to pathology. Although there is no question that neuronal cells are lost with aging, research has shown that neurons are capable of repair and in fact are constantly turning over components of the cell membrane as well as most of the cellular organelles. The chromosomes are not as well repaired as other cytoplasmic and nuclear components because of perhaps a repressing protein, which has been found in both neurons and spermatozoa.

Many theories of aging have ascribed a central role to the brain, in which the brain functions as the timekeeper or biologic clock for the entire organism. Certainly it is obvious that changes in the brain would effect the functioning of many organs. Whether this implies a biologic clock control function of the brain is debatable, however.

The rate of senescence is related to various factors that have been described previously. Positive correlations include brain size, neuron:glia ratio, and perhaps early environmental factors that tend to increase the size and connections of neurons and glial cells. Environmental factors include sensory stimulation and an enriched social and learning environment. It would also appear that neuronal circuits that are very active are more likely to be retained and have a longer life span. Of course, all these factors are dependent on the integrity of the vascular perfusion and microvasculature of the brain, and it is conceivable that the function of the brain in old age is intimately connected to blood supply rather than to intrinsic properties of neurons. Characteristically it appears that those neuronal structures that develop first during brain formation and maturation are the last to be affected by senility. These later areas are primarily in the association cortex, with loss greater in the left than in the right hemisphere.

Changes in the brain with age. The EEG (electroencephalogram) changes slightly with age in the human. These changes have an earlier onset and a slower decline than other waning physiologic functions, such as renal or respiratory function. They are possibly caused by age-related cellular impairments of neurons in the brain. The role of lipofuscin pigments, which accumulate so strikingly in brain tissue with age, is still not clear. Possible changes in the normal neurotransmitters may occur with aging. These alterations include decreases in levels of acetylcholine, dopamine, norepinephrine, serotonin, γ-aminobutyric acid, and glutamine. These declines of various neurotransmitters in certain parts of the brain may be associated with changes in the enzymes that normally regulate their concentration.

Neurofibrils also appear to become tangled and disoriented in the aged neurons. These structures transport neurotransmitter and other substances down the axon to the synapse.

Plaques may form, which consist of amyloid surrounded by degenerated nervous tissue cells. Amyloid is believed to be antigen-antibody complexes that have been degraded by neuronal phagocytes. This may implicate a role for the immune system in senile brain changes.

The brain weight declines, and calcification of the meninges may occur. The lateral ventricles may be enlarged, and the cerebral cortex atrophies. These changes are usually most striking in individuals with senile dementia (chronic brain syndrome), a disorder of old age associated with mental deterioration, cerebral cortex and basal ganglia atrophy, and accelerated senescence. The syndrome may appear in individuals as young as 45 years old, in which case it is usually correlated with cerebral arteriosclerosis and is known as Alzheimer's dementia which is discussed in detail in Chapter 10. Changes in the brain vessels rarely occur alone, and systemic pathology therefore is often present. The onset of the acute disease, which then develops into a chronic process, often follows a severe stress such as a cerebrovascular accident, a drug reaction, cardiac failure, or renal disease. This disorder progresses and ultimately ends in death from within 1 year to occasionally over 10 years after the onset of symptoms. The signs and symptoms of senile dementia include loss of memory, confusion, delirium, impaired intellectual function, and lack of judgment. While the neurologic status of the elderly does change with age these alterations appear to be greatly exaggerated in senile dementia. Changes in the sensorium, gait, muscular tremors, reflexes, and special senses (taste, olfaction, sight, pain) are all frequently found in the aged.

Signs of impaired short-term memory are often found in the aged, whereas long-term memory often appears unaffected. The permanence of long-term memory appears to be correlated to the DNA of the neuronal cells involved in the memory circuits. It is speculated that the aged suffer a loss of ability to learn and remember because of the accumulation of defects in the brain system that processes and stores memory and that involves DNA changes (the hippocampus). Short-term memory can be influenced by such factors as electroshock therapy, direct electrical stimulation of the brain, and drugs, whereas long-term memory is not affected by these factors. Thus it would appear that each learning experience must go through a process of becoming a permanent tracing in the brain, and this process may be interfered with in the aged brain. Memory processing involves mediation by hormonal and neurochemical substances, and these may be affected by aging.

Brain lipid content and turnover both decrease with age and may be related to declining enzymatic activity of the brain. The enzymes produced in the brain tissue may be altered in form and thus inactive. Another possibility is that the DNA of the aged brain cell is subject to inactivation by cross-linkage. The association of DNA with histone proteins may be involved in the cross-linking property. Cross-linkage of essential segments of DNA would act to functionally remove information from the organism.

As has been discussed, pigment accumulates strikingly in the brain as it ages. This is a nonspecific sign of aging, as pigment accumulation occurs throughout the body during senescence. The accumulation is most marked in fully differentiated cells, which are not believed to divide during adult and senescent life. Whether the accumulation of these pigments results *in* aging or is the result *of* aging is unknown. However, certain clinical syndromes known as *neuronal ceroid-lipofuscinoses* are associated with the accumulation of lipopigments in brain cells and to some degree in body cells. Lipopigments accumulate in these rare genetic conditions and cannot be removed by any known cellular mechanism. It appears that they are polymers of biologic molecules cross-linked with dialdehydes. Dialdehydes are produced by lipid peroxidation in many cells and thus are available to cross-link with molecules and in a sense to serve as a physiologic fixative.

Patients with these syndromes show signs of diffuse neuropathy, but cells containing large amounts of the pigment appear to be able to function normally. It is theoretically possible that age pigments may not chemically interfere with the functioning of the cells, as the residual bodies act to sequester the pigments inside a membrane-limited compartment. However, the effect of accumulation may ultimately be distention and mechanical impairment of the cell. In the neuronal ceroid-lipofuscinoses the rate of pigment accumulation appears to be greatly accelerated above that of the normal individual, such that the pigment accumulation approximates that of an aged person during the first years of life. The neurologic effects of pigment may be manifested in both the diseased child and the elderly individual when normal biosynthetic pathways are not able to compensate for the increased pigment production. The cells in this case undergo morphologic changes and eventually die.

Although there are from 10 to 12 billion neurons in the human brain, there are about five times as many supporting glial cells. The effects of aging on these latter cells, although largely unknown, cannot be ignored. Furthermore, the complex array of interacting fibers from myriad different nerve cells in the brain forms a suprastructure on the brain matrix, which also may be altered by the aging process. In addition, astrocytes are interposed between the nervous tissue and capillaries of the vascular system, forming the blood-brain barrier. Also the Schwann cells and oligodendrocytes that form the myelin layers of the nerves are intimately involved in providing the normal structural integrity of the brain and may be affected by the senescent process. Therefore, it is not only the tremendous complexity of the brain function that must be dealt with in aging research but also the topographic diversity.

There is considerable controversy over whether neuronal cells are actually lost as a routine part of the aging process. Diamond (1978) argues against any significant loss of cells, both neuronal and glial. Glial cells seem to actually increase in number. However, a parameter that does change is neuronal density, which differentially decreases in certain areas of the cortex in the rat. Cells projecting downward from the lower areas of the occipital cortex decrease in density much more markedly than cells in the upper occipital cortical layers. However, most of this change in density takes place early in the life of the rat. Diamond suggests that the change in density reflects cell death. She argues that there is tremendous redundancy within the brain, with millions more neurons being present than are necessary to carry out the basic processes of life. The key as to which cells survive may be the amount of stimulation these cells receive. Cells that are not stimulated are selectively removed from the brain through cell death, whereas cells receiving continual stimulation continue to thrive and form circuits ultimately involved in phenomena such as memory and learning. This certainly leads to some interesting insights into the importance of stimulation throughout the life span. It is known that early stimulation in the rat leads to an increase in dendritic growth and branchings. Further research is called for on the effects of environmental stimuli in older animals with regard to dendritic growth and cell death. It seems ironic that in elderly human beings with early signs of senility the trend is to institutionalize such people, and often the environments in which they are placed are drab, dull, and unchanging. This may lead to further decline.

The cause of age-related decrements in brain function do not have to reside in neuronal or even glial decline. It is conceivable that the ground substance of the brain, through which neurotransmitter precursors and nutrients must travel, undergoes biochemical alterations.

Nerves. The motor nerve must always be viewed in relationship to the muscle it innervates and the motor unit it forms. It has been found that the conduction velocity and neurotransmitter substance release are decreased in the motor nerves of the aged. This is not associated with degeneration of the nerve per se, but the effects of these alterations on the muscle are profound, resulting in or contributing to the atrophy that is common in senescence. It is of interest that physical training of muscles in the young may retard the basic process of muscular atrophy, in that the nerves are kept in a tonically active state. This has great implications for the care of the elderly, who have a need for preservation of mobility for as long as possible.

The sensory nerves are also affected by senescence, and a decline in special sensory acuity is nearly universal. It has been noted that the aged, like the very young, are likely to develop sensory deprivation, a phenomenon that is associated with a wide variety of physiologic and psychologic abnormalities. The deficits that occur in vision and hearing have been studied in regard to the aging process, but other special sensory changes are not well researched. These include vestibular, olfactory, taste, somesthetic and kinesthetic, pain, and touch sensitivities.

Neurotransmitter changes. Finch (1976) has suggested that neurologic decline during senescence is the result of altered catecholamine metabolism within the nervous system, particularly affecting the hypothalamic monoaminergic pathways. Finch believes that the biologic clock controlling the rate of senescence ultimately lies in the brain. The role of nutrition in senescence may play a key role within the constructs of this theory, since brain development and neuroendocrine function are both greatly influenced by the quality and quantity of the diet. Thus the neuroendocrine system, if altered by diet or other factors, may become less viable over the life span.

DISEASE MODEL: PROGERIA

The rare and impressive disorder of *progeria* (Fig. 9-4) has been implicated as a disease of accelerated aging. In this condition there is a cessation of growth and appearance of many signs suggestive of senescent pathology. The hair becomes gray, the skin wrinkled, generalized fibrosis and atrophy develop, premature atherosclerosis and connective tissue tumors are common, and death occurs early in life. Adult progeria develops in later life and is known as *Werner's syndrome*, which seems to be inherited in an autosomal recessive manner. It is characterized by processes similar to those occurring in the juvenile form, which is known as *Hutchinson-Gilford syndrome*. The people afflicted with these conditions have a bizarre senile appearance, which may coexist in the juvenile form with features of childhood. The primary teeth, for example, are often retained. Less than 100 cases of the juvenile progeria syndrome have been described in the literature. Thus it has been difficult to study the pathologic changes in progeria in an attempt to understand if the

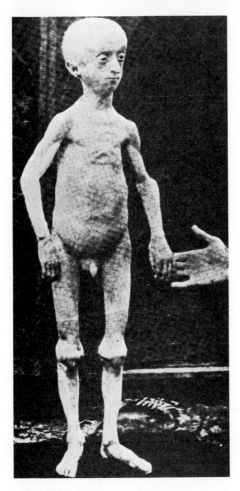

Fig. 9-4. Progeria. Teenage male with progeria. Similarities between changes observed here and those associated with normal aging are obvious.

(From Burgess J, and Everett A, editors: Hypothalamus, pituitary, and aging, 1976, Courtesy Charles C Thomas, Publisher, Springfield, Ill.)

condition is in reality accelerated aging.

Some observations have been made on cells from patients affected with progeria that indicate that the cells are antigenically and biochemically abnormal and in some respects similar to cells of aged people. Pathologic examination of progeria tissue indicates that collagen cross-linking, fibrosis, and lipofuscin accumulation

occur, as in senescence. Ninety percent of the patients examined appear to have coronary or aortic atherosclerosis. Serum cholesterol and lipoprotein levels are also often elevated. Patients with Werner's syndrome show many of these changes even more markedly. Werner's disease is thought to be the result of a single gene defect. These individuals usually die of coronary or cerebrovascular occlusion. An endocrine cause has been investigated in progeria, and the incidence of diabetes is reported to be very high. However, the pituitary gland appears to be normal in these conditions.

Good evidence would indicate that the processes of accelerated senescence, or progeria, bear a superficial relationship to those of normal aging, but important differences appear to exist, and progeria as a disease model of aging cannot be unequivocally accepted.

TREATMENT RATIONALE

The goal of gerontologic research is not only to gain an understanding of the basic cellular processes that occur in aging but also to ultimately delay or prevent aging and death and to improve the quality of life by the prevention of age-related diseases. Thus many therapeutic approaches to senescence have been suggested. Many are based on various theories of aging. For example, antioxidant therapy might prevent the cross-linking of biologic molecules and thus retard the aging process. Infusions of RNA have been attempted in the elderly to restore learning capabilities and memory. A drug known as *Gerovital H₃* has been used, mostly in Europe, for the treatment of senescent pathology. This drug is a monoamine oxidase inhibitor that has proved to be clinically effective in the treatment of depression, hypertension, arthritis, and angina pectoris. It has been shown that monoamine oxidase, an enzyme involved in the breakdown of catecholamines, is markedly elevated in humans after the age of 50. Other treatment modalities that have been used for senescent changes include procaine, stimulants such as amphetamines, vasodilators, hyperbaric oxygen, huge doses of vitamins, and hormones. The general effectiveness of these forms of treatment is difficult to measure, although most treatment has resulted in short-term therapeutic benefits.

The modern gerontologic approach to the treatment of senescent deterioration is based on three major phenomena: (1) free radical formation, (2) tissue hypoxia, and (3) macromolecular disorders, particularly of the polyribosomes, on which protein synthesis proceeds.

Therapy for free radical formation

The approach to treatment of pathology related to free-radical formation is based on the supposition that these highly reactive compounds damage biologic membranes and molecules through such processes as lipid peroxidation and cross-linking of large biologic molecules with each other. Free radical formation is a prominent result of radiation and is further enhanced in the presence of oxygen. It can be partially prevented by certain antioxidant free radical "scavenger" drugs such as vitamin E, vitamin C, and butylated hydroxytoluene (BHT). Addition of these agents to the diet of mice increases their life span, whereas feeding of polyunsaturated fats, which cause the formation of free radicals, shortens life span. Other studies refute this effect, however (Rothstein, 1986). The addition of antioxidants to the diet may eventually be shown to increase longevity in humans. Vitamin E is a naturally occurring antioxidant that should be present in the diet of the older person at the recommended daily allowance level.

Therapy for hypoxia

Hypoxia as a result of age-related vascular disease may be a major agent in promoting pathophysiologic changes that occur in aging. Cerebral hypoxia in particular is suspected of inducing most if not all of the neurologic manifestations of senility. Cellular hypoxia leads to abnormal function and structure, and necrosis and ischemia are ultimately inevitable. Thus therapy to reduce the effects of cerebral hypoxia in the aged has been attempted through the use of hyperbaric oxygen chambers. Significant improvement in many of these patients has been reported. Of course, as previously mentioned, oxygen increases the possibility of free radical formation, which may limit the efficacy of oxygen therapy. It has been found that the improvement in function, such as in learning and memory, is retained long after the period of maximum hyperoxygenation; therefore it is believed that the period of increased oxygen tension of the tissues results in some changes that are therapeutic and maintained. A possibility is that RNA and protein synthesis occurring during the period of oxygenation results in long-lived proteins that are involved with intellectual function.

Therapy for molecular disorders

It is generally believed that long-term memory requires the synthesis of specific RNA and protein. The actual changes in DNA, RNA, and protein during learning are probably extraordinarily complex. Thus disturbances in this macromolecular system may impair memory and learning. The polyribosomes of aged human cells are abnormal both structurally and functionally. These cytoplasmic organelles may be the site of action of many drugs that are therapeutic in senility, including phenytoin, procainamide, pemoline, and amphetamines. Procaine has been used for many years in Europe, as has Gerovital H$_3$, which is a derivative of procaine.

Summary

Although it is obvious that death cannot be prevented, certainly it appears that many of the changes that occur with senescence may be delayed by diet, exercise, healthy lifestyle, and certain vitamins and medications. Identification of the actual pathophysiologic mechanisms that perpetuate the aging process is in the preliminary stage, yet this research has resulted in several concepts that can be applied to the prevention of age-related pathology and the treatment of such conditions. It is likely that research will provide us with information that can be used to significantly increase longevity and health. Certainly some humans are capable of living to well over 100 years, as evidenced by certain populations of individuals in isolated areas in different parts of the world. Attainment of this life span is conceivable for all humans once the basic pathophysiology is well defined.

CONCLUSIONS

Although this chapter has reviewed physiologic declines that occur with aging and how these changes can produce pathophysiology, the reader should keep the following in mind. The physiologic decrements that occur do so very slowly and therefore are barely noticeable to the aging individual. Most of the systems of the body, although definitely less functional than in youth and middle age, are very capable of maintaining wellness as long as severe threats and stressors are not pres-

ent. Acute physical stress, pharmacologic challenges, and serious psychosocial disress can produce disequilibrium as a result of the limited adaptive functions and decreased physiologic reserves and capacities. As long as the well elderly are not threatened in these ways, homeostasis is usually very well maintained. The importance of psychologic attitude, social support systems, sense of control, activities, and purpose are equally important in maintaining wellness in the elderly individual.

BIBLIOGRAPHY

Anders TF, Carskadon MA, and Dement WC: Sleep and sleepiness in children and adolescents, Pediatric Clinic North America 27:29-43, 1980.

Boisson M and Chalazonitis N: Abnormal neuronal discharge, New York, 1978, Raven Press.

Candy J, et al: Aluminosilicates and senile plaque formation in Alzheimer's disease, The Lancet, February 15th 1986, 354-356.

Cashman N, et al: Late denervation in patients with antecedent paralytic polimyelitis, N Engl J Med 317:7–12, 1986.

Cervos-Navarro J and Ferszt R: Brain edema, Advanced Neur vol 28, 1980.

Cruz Martinez A, Perez Conde MC, and Ferrer MT: Chronic partial denervation is more widespread than is suspected clinically in paralytic poliomyelitis: electrophysiological study, Eur Neuro 22:314-321, 1983.

Cristofalo V and Rosner B: Modulation of cell proliferation and senescence of WI-88 cells by hydrocortisone, Fed. Proc. 38:1851-1956, 1979.

Dalakas M, et al: A long term follow-up study of patients with post-polimyelitis neuromuscular symptoms, N Engl J Med 314:959-963, 1986.

Davis B and Zenser T: Biological changes in thermoregulation in the elderly. In Davis B and Wood W, editors: Homeostatic function and aging, New York, 1985, Raven Press.

Diamond M: The aging brain: some enlightening and optimistic results, American Science, 66:66-71, 1978.

Dye C: (1985). Role of psychosocial factors in coping with homeostatic illness. In Davis B and Wood W, editors: Homeostatic function and aging, New York, 1985, Raven Press.

Faden A, Jacobs T, and Holaday J: Opiate antagonist

improves neurological recovery after spinal injury, Science 211:493-4, 1981.

Fahn S, Davis J, and Rowland L: Cerebral hypoxia and its consequences, Advanced Neuro vol 26, 1979.

Finch C: Physiological changes of aging in mammals, Rev Biol 51:49-83, 1976.

Fox, J: The brain's dynamic way of keeping touch, Science 225:820-822, 1984.

Goldgaber D, et al: Characterization and chromosomal localization of DNA encoding brain amyloid of Alzheimer's disease, Science 235:877-880, 1987.

Gordon G and Genant H: The aging skeleton, Clinics in Geriatric Medicine 1:95-118, 1985.

Gorelik P: Pathophysiology and diagnosis in nursing clinics of North America, Cerebrovascular Disease 21:275-288, 1986.

Hallstead L, Wiechers D, and Rossi C: Part II: Results of a survey of 210 polio survivors, Southern Medical Journal 78:1281-1287, 1985.

Holden C: Behavioral medicine: an emerging field, Science 209:479-481, 1980.

Kenny R: Physiology of aging, Clinics in Geriatric Medicine 1:37-59, 1985.

Klausner S and Schwarts A: The aging heart, Clinics in Geriatric Medicine 1:95-118, 1985.

Klein R and Armitage R: Rhythms in human performance: 1½ hour oscillations in cognitive style, Science 244:1326-1327, 1979.

Kolata G: Reys syndrome: a medical mystery, Science 70:1453-1454, 1980.

Kopin IJ: Toxins and Parkinson's disease: MPTP Parkinsonism in humans and animals, Advanced Neuro 45:137-144, 1986.

Kwentus J, et al: Alzheimer's disease, American Journal Medicine 81:91-96, 1986.

Lewin R: Is your brain really necessary? Science 210:1232-1234, 1980.

Mann D: The neuropathology of Alzheimer's disease: a review with pathogenetic, aetiological, and therapeutic considerations, Mechanisms of Ageing and Development 31:213-255, 1985.

Merskey H: Pain and emotion: their correlation in headache, advances in neurology, 33:135-141, 1982.

Muggleton-Harris A and Hayflict L: Cellular aging studied by the reconstruction of replicating cells from nuclei and cytoplasms isolated from normal human diploid cells, Exp Cell Res 103:321-330, 1976.

Pomara N and Stanley M: The cholinergic hypothesis of memory dysfunction in Alzheimer's disease-revisted, Psychopharmacology Bulletin 22:1986.

Price D, et al: Neurobiological studies of transmitter systems in aging and in Alzheimer-type dementia, Ann NY Acad Sci 457:35-52, 1985.

Prince, D: New perpectives on Alzheimer's disease, Ann Rev Neuroscience 9:489-512, 1986.

Riley M: Health behavior of older people: toward a new paradigm, in health, behavior, and aging, Washington, DC, 1981, National Academy Press.

Rodin J: Aging and health: effects of the sense of control, Science 233:1271-1276, 1986.

Rothman E and Collins R: Seizures in neurological pathophysiology, ed 3, New York, 1987, Oxford University Press.

Rothstein M: Biochemical studies of aging, Chemical & Engineering News, pp 26-39, 1986.

Selkow D, et al: Conservation of brain amyloid proteins in aged mammals and humans with Alzheimer's disease, Science 235:874-877, 1987.

Sinex FM and Myers R: Alzheimer's disease, Down's syndrome, and aging: the genetic approach, Ann NY Acad Sci 396:3-14, 1982.

Snyder S: Brain peptides as neuotransmitters, Science 209:976-983, 1980.

St. George-Syslop, P, et al: The genetic defect causing familial alzheimer's disease maps on chromosome 21, Science 235:885-890, 1987.

Stini W: Association of early growth patterns with the process of aging, Fed Proc 40:2588-2594, 1981.

Tanzi R, et al: Amyloid protein gene: cDNA, mRNA distribution, and genetic linkage near the Alzheimer locus, Science 235:880-884, 1987.

Torlak R: The pathologic physiology of dementia, New York, 1978, Springer.

Woodbury D and Kemp J: Basic mechanisms of seizures: neurophysiological and biochemical etiology. In Psychopathology of Brain Disfunction, New York, 1977, Raven Press.

UNIT IV

Cognitive-perceptual pattern

10

Neurologic and sensory pathophysiology

The human brain and the peripheral nerves comprise the most complex system of the human body. Without normal neurologic function, people are often considered less than human. The brain is regarded by many to be equivalent to the mind. Our understanding of how the brain works is so primitive in comparison to other systems that some still think of it as a "black box," with input producing output in essentially mysterious ways. Neurophysiologists dissect the functioning nervous system, piece by piece, in hopes of eventually understanding the whole. It is questionable whether the brain is the sum of its parts, as is a computer, or if it is something greater. The brain may be a hologram, and function may be so diffusely distributed that complete understanding may never be possible. Although stimulation of a discrete functional unit may produce a specific and discrete response (e.g., a muscle twitch), stimulation of another functional unit may produce a repertoire of memories and associations of incredible complexity (e.g., recollection of a person, with all the attendant historic and emotional facets involved in knowing that person). The brain is also wonderfully responsive or "plastic," especially in early life. Injuries to an infant's brain may produce an incredible, anatomic deficit but no

functional deficit. John Lorber, a British pediatrician, reported cases of hydrocephalic children with massive brain loss who had normal or even gifted intelligence (Lewin, 1980). The Savant syndrome (formally called idiot savant) is another example in which markedly "retarded" individuals develop a skill that is beyond the natural capability of even the most intelligent human. These people may be able to play musical instruments and remember musical pieces after hearing them one time; they may be capable of mathematical computation that is lightening fast; or they may be capable of data recollection throughout historical time. It appears that although these individuals suffer a neurologic deficit, other parts of their brain are capable of developing beyond "normal." These individuals perhaps give us a glimmer of the inherent, untapped capability of the human brain. Yet they are considered deviants by most of us. Extraordinary mathematical giftedness, on the other hand, is something we all admire. Many studies indicate that this ability may be a result of mistakes or abnormalities in fetal development, such as the presence of testosterone. A triad of mathematical giftedness, left handedness, and immunologic disorders appear together with a frequency that suggests that there was a pathophysiologic disturbance during fetal life that caused these aberrations.

Environmental influences on the development of the nervous system are extremely important. We will explore this in Chapter 11 as we look at psychopathologic deviations from wellness. In terms of the maturation and adaptation of the brain, these influences play a great role. Animal studies indicate that the nervous system is anatomically and functionally altered by experience, variety, injury, and stimulation. This happens even in aging animals. Sprouting, growth, increasing synaptic connections, and dynamic shifting of neuronal control are normal responses to stimuli (Fox, 1984). This research helps us to understand the pathophysiologic effects of sensory deprivation in infants and children and provides a rationale for infant stimulation as part of normal nurturance.

Finally the brain as an entity separate from the rest of the body is an artificial construct that has no functional meaning. We now know that the brain itself is an endocrine organ, an immunologic integrator, and only part of a network. When we say that our heart aches for someone or that we feel something in our gut, these may be feelings that truly represent the function of the nervous system. No organ functions in isolation from the brain or from other organs and systems. If pathophysiology is really to be understood, we must have an appreciation for the complex interaction that is possible.

In this chapter we will discuss deviations from normal neurologic function, focusing on major mechanisms by which disease occurs. Many times the manifestations of a particular disease process help us to understand the normal function of the diseased part. This is especially true in the brain. A person with temporal lobe epilepsy may have inappropriate emotional affect during seizure activity. This tells us that the temporal cortex is involved in emotions. A tumor of the hypothalamus may cause excessive eating, and this again is a clue to how the normal appetite is controlled. Many times, however, the signs and symptoms are less easily understood, and the disease process may be very diffuse, as in Alzheimer's disease. The student is reminded that it is necessary to review normal nerve cell function to understand many of the pathophysiologic processes. We will begin our description of nervous system pathophysiology by examining mechanisms through which normal nervous transmission is disrupted.

NERVE CELL DAMAGE

To understand the effects of disease on the function of neurons within the central nervous system, the student should be familiar with the normal anatomy and physiology of the nervous system. These topics will not be discussed in detail in this chapter, but this knowledge is required for good understanding. Some basic principles with regard to the effects of damage to nerve cells are the following: (1) Neurons have a very limited capacity for repair or regeneration. This is particularly true if the cell body of the neuron has been destroyed, but limited axonal regeneration can take place. (2) Within the first year of life there is still significant growth and differentiation of brain tissue. Injury during this time may be more readily repaired than at any other time in extrauterine life. (3) There is tremendous redundancy within the brain. Humans can learn to use other pathways for cognitive, autonomic, sensory, and motor function to some degree. The maximum extent to which this is possible is not known at this time. (4) Neuronal maturation and synaptic connection is a function of different phenomena, such as nutrition, early experience, genetics, and many other environmental factors. In this section we will look at disrupted transmission at the levels of the upper and lower motor neurons and in spinal cord injuries resulting from different types of nerve cell damage.

Upper motor neurons

The student will recall that the motor cortex is located in the frontal lobe of the cerebrum anterior to the central sulcus. Motor control is exerted through two systems arising in the motor cortex, the *pyramidal system* and the *extrapyramidal system*. The motor fibers of the pyramidal system extend from giant pyramidal cells in the motor cortex, through the internal capsule of white matter, and finally down into the spinal cord. The fibers course through the columns of white matter in the cord until they reach the appropriate anterior horn cells with which they then synapse. Fibers from the anterior horn are sent out from the cord in the spinal nerves to the various muscles of the body. Most of the neurons from the pyramidal cells cross over to the opposite side of the spinal cord before they synapse with anterior horn interneurons, so that the left side of the brain controls the muscles of the right side, and vice versa.

Extrapyramidal tracts arise in the motor cortex, but most of the fibers travel to the basal ganglia. Basal ganglia include the following structures: caudate nucleus and putamen (sometimes known collectively as the striatum), globus pallidus, substantia nigra, and red nucleus. These are all islands of gray matter with which extrapyramidal fibers synapse. The interconnections of the basal ganglia with each other and with other parts of the brain are very complex. There are, for example, connections between the basal ganglia and

the cerebellum, thalamus, and midbrain. The function of the basal ganglia appears to be related to posture and the planning of large movements. The pyramidal system seems to be involved with the initiation and coordination of fine movements. The effects of upper neuron loss depend on which system is diseased and at which point in the relay the neuron is damaged. Pyramidal fibers originating in the motor cortex may be destroyed by injury, tumor, or cerebrovascular accident (described later in this chapter). Disorders associated with extrapyramidal symptoms are:

1. Parkinson's disease, a disease of the basal ganglia
2. Huntington's chorea, a severe, hereditary, atrophic, neurologic disease involving the caudate nucleus and other brain structures
3. Hemiballismus, a disorder associated with purposeless and extreme muscle movements of an upper extremity, associated with damage to the subthalamic nuclei
4. Wilson's disease, a genetic disorder of copper metabolism, associated with hepatic cirrhosis, deposition of pigment in the eye, and degeneration of the basal ganglia
5. Athetosis, sometimes seen in cerebral palsy or following a cerebrovascular accident, associated with hemiplegia and writhing movements; characterized by degeneration of basal ganglia or areas around the basal ganglia near the internal capsule
6. Tardive dyskinesia as the result of drug-induced alterations in extrapyramidal function; occurs usually after phenothiazine use; associated with movements of the head, neck, face, and tongue

Disease model: Parkinson's disease. A model of upper motor neuron dysfunction is Parkinson's disease, a movement disorder, which appears with increased incidence among the elderly but may be associated with influenza, phenothiazine use, and cerebrovascular disease in other age groups. Parkinson's disease has only a slight genetic risk component and is probably caused by stable environmental factors. The incidence is approximately 20.5 people per 100,000 cases and has not significantly changed over the last 35 years. The disorder is associated with difficulties in starting and stopping movements (akinesia), tremor at rest, cog wheel rigidity, and a general overall decrease in muscle use. The latter leads to a mask-like facies, peculiarities in gait, and absence of gestures. The rigidity within the muscles makes it very difficult for an examiner to flex a limb because there is so much resistance. Three fourths of people affected also have cognitive and personality changes, phenomena that seem to be associated with the advanced age of the individuals, the stress associated with the disease, and the disease process itself.

Parkinson's disease is associated with a loss of melanin-containing neurons in the nigrostriatal system—the neural tract connecting the striatum and the substantia nigra of the basal ganglia. The initiating, pathophysiologic mechanism appears to be a very specific loss of pigmented dopaminergic neurons, resulting in a decreased ratio of dopaminergic to cholinergic neurons. It is not clear at this time if the disease is caused by a primary loss of these neurons or whether these neurons are destroyed as the result of some other pathologic process in the brain, which then affects the nigrostriatal neurons.

The cells of the substantia nigra actually produce dopamine for use by higher brain centers; as cells degenerate, the remaining cells attempt to increase dopamine production. The biochemical degradation of dopamine in these cells itself may produce peroxides that result in free radicals that can further damage nerve cells, thus accounting for the specificity of the disease to dopaminergic neurons. The dopaminergic and cholinergic systems within the basal ganglia are antagonistic to each other, and movement control is achieved partly through a steady state balance. When the dopaminergic neurons are lost as in Parkinson's disease, there is a proportionate excess of acetylcholine. Dopamine is generally inhibitory whereas acetylcholine is excitatory. The major form of treatment for Parkinson's disease for many years was the administration of anticholinergic drugs, which decreased the symptoms of the disease. Other neurotransmitters are also decreased in this disease, including gamma aminobutyric acid (GABA), serotonin, and norepinephrine. There is also decreased dopamine in the limbic forebrain of patients with Parkinson's disease, possibly accounting for the affective disorders that are seen.

A contaminant of synthetic heroin, known as MPTP (1-methyl-4-phenyl-1,2,3,6-tetrahydropyridine), produces a Parkinson-like syndrome in heroin abusers. Isolation of this contaminant and experimental studies have provided important new information about the pathophysiology of Parkinson's disease. MPTP is converted to a derivative, MPP+, by a monoamine oxidase B enzyme in the brain, the natural substrate of which is dopamine. MPP+ is highly toxic, as are metabolites produced through this enzymatic reaction. Furthermore, the toxicity is directed toward substantia nigra cells, as in Parkinson's disease. If monoamine oxidase B is inhibited, MPTP neurotoxicity does not occur. MPTP produces some of the same progressive symptoms seen in Parkinson's disease (rigidity, mutism, tremors, bradykinesia [Kopin, 1986]). There are also similar intellectual impairments. The disease is now treated by administering a dopamine precursor, L-dopa. Dopamine itself cannot cross the blood-brain barrier. L-Dopa often causes a marked decrease in symptoms. Other experimental forms of treatment are now developing as the mode of MPTP neurotoxicity begins to be understood.

Disease model: Decorticate rigidity. Many conditions produce damage of the upper motor neurons of the cerebral cortex. Most striking are diseases in which hypoxia of the brain has occurred, such as after infection, in cerebral edema, or during a cardiopulmonary arrest. The resultant posture that is produced by the motor neuron loss is known as decorticate rigidity. The legs are rigidly held in a position of extension, and the arms are flexed. This positioning results from destruction or damage of the area of the motor cortex that sends out fibers inhibiting stretch reflexes. Without these inhibitory signals, there is pronounced hyperactivity of gamma efferent neurons. The result is spasticity, hyperactive and pathologic reflexes, and muscle weakness but no muscle atrophy at first, since they are still innervated. The presence of decorticate rigidity is usually an ominous sign, indicating that the cerebral cortex is severely damaged.

Lower motor neurons

The lower motor neuron cell bodies are located in the anterior horns of the gray matter of the spinal cord. When upper motor neuron problems exist, as was just discussed, these neurons still function, but without the usual higher motor controls. These tonic upper motor neuron controls act to modulate and coordinate movements, and when lost there will be a resultant muscle spasticity caused by exaggerated stretch reflexes. When the spinal cord itself has been damaged and the lower motor neurons are interrupted, the result will be a flaccid paralysis. From the lower motor neurons arise the final common pathway for motor impulses to reach the muscles. Lower motor neuron disease is therefore associated with denervation of the muscle. In general the consequences of this denervation include flaccidity, atrophy, fasciculations, and fibrillations within the muscles.

Poliomyelitis. One model of lower motor neuron disease is poliomyelitis. This disease is viral, infectious, and was once the major crippler of children. Immunization is now given routinely during childhood, but occasional epidemics among nonimmunized groups have been reported.

When the lower motor neurons are infected with the poliomyelitis virus, the muscles innervated by these neurons become paralyzed. As the viral inflammation progresses, there is actual tissue destruction and resultant necrosis within the motor neurons. The same pattern observed in the spinal cord can also be seen in the brainstem and cerebellar and precentral gyrus motor nuclei.

There are three types of polio: nonparalytic; bulbar, which involves the brainstem and therefore respiratory function; and spinal, which affects skeletal muscle function. The muscles involved may undergo atrophy with time, since innervation is necessary to keep muscle tone and size.

Postpolio syndrome. Those readers who can recall the polio epidemic of the 1950s know most acutely the terror associated with this disease. In the United States today there are about 300,000 survivors of the disease, most of whom contracted the disease during childhood. Typically, these survivors have conquered the acute respiratory and muscular effects of polio and have survived to adulthood with minimal weakness. Many have had no neuromuscular impairment. In the past few years, however, a new problem, the postpolio syndrome, has been observed in many of these survivors. The median time of appearance of the symptoms of the syndrome is 26 years after the acute polio episode (Hallstead, Wiechers, and Rossi, 1985), and about 25% of the polio survivors are affected. This syndrome is characterized by new muscle weakness, fasciculations, pain, and atrophy. The severity of the syndrome is related to age of onset of polio, degree of paralysis, and ventilator dependency during the acute stage and in convalescence. The degree of impairment is usually mild, with approximately 1% decline in function per year (Dalakas, et al., 1986). Some people are more severely affected and have bladder function problems, impotence, sensory changes, and require the use of a wheelchair and ventilator. Some persons are able to maintain adequate respiratory function using nocturnal ventilation to rest the respiratory muscles and increase pulmonary reserves.

The pathophysiologic basis for postpolio syndrome is not completely understood, and various theories have been proposed. Reactivation of latent poliovirus has been suggested, but the virus has not been recovered, and there is no immunologic evidence of reactivation. Hormonal factors, normal aging changes, and immunologic mechanisms have also been suggested. One mechanism that has support relates to the pathologic changes that occur in the muscle fibers. Evidence of both chronic and recent denervation is seen, and nerve terminals themselves seem to be lost, causing the muscle to atrophy. After polio, some motor units enlarge to compensate for the polio-provoked denervation. Nerves actually sprout to produce more fibers, which innervate these other motor units, which respond by hypertrophy (Cashman,

et al., 1987). Over time these new motor units produce a stress on the cell bodies of the supplying nerves, so that eventually they cannot keep up with the demand. In some cases postpolio syndrome appears to be associated with strenuous exercise and an active life-style, which may produce further stress on the involved cell bodies. When these cell bodies begin to degenerate, muscles begin to show denervation atrophy, weakness, pain, and fasciculations. Polio survivors may in general be advised therefore to avoid excessive muscular work and to rest appropriately to perhaps retard the denervation process.

CASE STUDY: POSTPOLIO SYNDROME

History

Mr. L is a previously healthy, 45-year-old, married accountant, who is active in community activities, including youth soccer and track. He suffered from polio in 1953 and recalls a 2-week illness with a high fever followed by a period of paralysis of the lower limbs. The paralysis "cleared up" a great deal, there was never any breathing difficulty, and braces and crutches were never needed. However, Mr. L remembers considerable lower leg weakness and attending weekly physical therapy sessions for over 2 years. He remembers that his legs were not "strong" but is not sure if there was significant atrophy. As he entered his teenage years, Mr. L participated in many sports and "built up his legs" with weight training and physical exercise.

Present illness: Over the last year Mr. L has noticed increasing fatigue after exercise, some new lower limb weakness, possibly a decreased muscle mass in his legs, muscle pain, and frequent widespread muscle twitches, which can sometimes

Contributed by Maureen Groër.

be observed but are usually just subjectively felt. He states, "I can't keep up with the kids any more, and sometimes I just have to rest. I seem tired all the time. I'm not as strong as I used to be. I've even stopped my daily walks and jogging."

Physical Examination

Mr. L is a well-nourished, well-developed, middle-aged, adult male of normal weight. He appears generally healthy, and signs of damage from acute paralytic polio are not readily observed. He appears neuromuscularly intact, with normal deep tendon reflexes (DTRs), superficial reflexes, and sensation in all extremities. Visual examination of the extremities showed many fasciculations bilaterally in leg and foot musculature and occasional fasciculations in trunk and arm muscles. Lower leg and upper and lower back muscles are tender to deep palpation. Mild muscle wasting of the legs is present, more obvious on the right than the left. Gait is normal, but Mr. L walks slowly, and he prefers being seated to standing. Assessment of muscle strength revealed bilaterally diminished grip strength, decreased strength of shoulder shrug, decreased strength of leg muscles to produce flexion, extension, and abduction against resistance.

Electromyogram and muscle biopsy show evidence of both chronic and new denervation, without group atrophy. Fibrillation potentials were observed, as were an increase in the duration of motor unit potentials. Weaker muscles had higher motor unit fiber densities.

Discussion

Mr. L exemplifies a typical course for postpolio syndrome. His symptoms are related to denervation of previously enlarged, compensatory fibers, which over time have been unable to keep up with demand due to limitations placed on the capacities of motor neuron cell bodies.

The fasciculations are commonly seen in many lower motor neuron diseases, including amyotrophic lateral sclerosis (ALS). ALS has a rapid and pernicious course associated with atrophy and weakness, usually ending in death through respiratory muscle function loss. This is part of the differential diagnosis for Mr. L and should be carefully evaluated. The rather insidious process of postpolio syndrome and the absence of group atrophy (which would indicate loss of entire motor units) on the muscle biopsy decreases the likelihood of ALS. There is, however, some evidence that a history of polio is a risk factor for later development of ALS. Mr. L should be generally encouraged to pursue a less active life-style and to rest more when he does exercise. Fatigue is a very common problem and can become debilitating if the patient does not get extra rest.

Nursing Diagnosis

1. Activity intolerance related to muscular weakness and atrophy, and easy fatigability
2. Fatigue related to postpolio syndrome.
3. Potential impaired adjustment related to life-style change
4. Potential for diversional activity deficit related to life-style change
5. Body image disturbance related to physiological changes
6. Impaired physical mobility related to progressive muscle weakness and atrophy
7. Potential for disuse syndrome related to activity intolerance and impaired physical mobility

Spinal cord injuries: pathophysiologic mechanisms

Injuries to the spinal cord are among the most tragic accidents that can befall individuals. Most of the time such people were well and active, as many of these injuries occur during sports activities or as the result of automobile accidents. Once an injury to the spinal cord has occurred there are two mechanisms by which damage occurs: (1) the initial insult to the nervous pathways themselves that course through the spinal cord, and (2) the secondary, progressive ischemic damage caused by inflammation, edema, and decreased perfusion of the spinal cord tissue as a result of systemic hypotension at the time of the accident. Some of these latter changes appear to be mediated by endorphins, since the opiate antagonist naloxone appears to improve neurologic recovery greatly after spinal injury experimentally produced in cats (Faden, et al., 1980). The initial insult may be a contusion injury, a whiplash injury, or a partial or complete transection of the spinal cord.

It is important to recall the distribution of spinal nerves and the pathways and crossover points of the nerve tracts within the cord itself. Fig. 10-1 shows the distribution of the dermatomes that correspond to the areas innervated by the separate spinal nerves. When there has been a complete cord transection, those dermatomes innervated by spinal nerves below the transection will lose all nervous sensation and motion. Those innervated by nerves leaving the cord above the complete transection will be preserved.

Within the spinal cord the nerve fibers may synapse with interneurons and other neurons, or they may course up the spinal cord before the first synapse. Sensory touch neurons send fibers up the cord on the same side as they entered the cord, crossing over to the opposite side when they reach the medulla, after synapsing with the second neuron in the pathway and then ascending to the thalamus. At the thalamus, there is a third synapse and the neuron carries information from there to the appropriate sensory areas of the cortex. Some sensory pathways (pain and temperature) carry neurons that cross over to the opposite side of the cord not far from their point of entry rather than at the medulla. From there the pathway is to the thalamus and the sensory cortex.

The motor pathways from the motor cortex consist of nerve tracts that cross over and then traverse the spinal cord in specific tracts, which are descending. Thus the white matter of the cord consists of descending motor tracts and some ascending sensory nerve tracts. It is only when the anatomic organization of the spinal cord is understood that the results of cord injuries can be predicted and understood.

After an initial injury to the spine a usual state of *spinal shock* ensues, which generally lasts 2 to 3 weeks or longer. At this time there is loss of vasomotor control, with a drop in blood pressure. A flaccid, muscular paralysis is present, with loss of sensation, and bladder and bowel control, areflexia, and a drop in central venous pressure (CVP) as venous stasis occurs in the legs. Stasis occurs because the normal muscular pump produced by the contractions of skeletal muscle forcing blood up the venous system toward the heart is no longer operative. All of these effects are the result of loss of higher brain and spinal cord influences on neurons located lower in the spinal cord. As the spinal shock period ends, some reflexes return, and possibly also some sensation and motion depending on the location and type of the injury to the cord. Compression injuries, whiplash, and partial transection have different patterns from that of complete transection. The extent of deficit is, of course, dependent on which nerve tracts have been injured.

In a cord injury that is not a complete

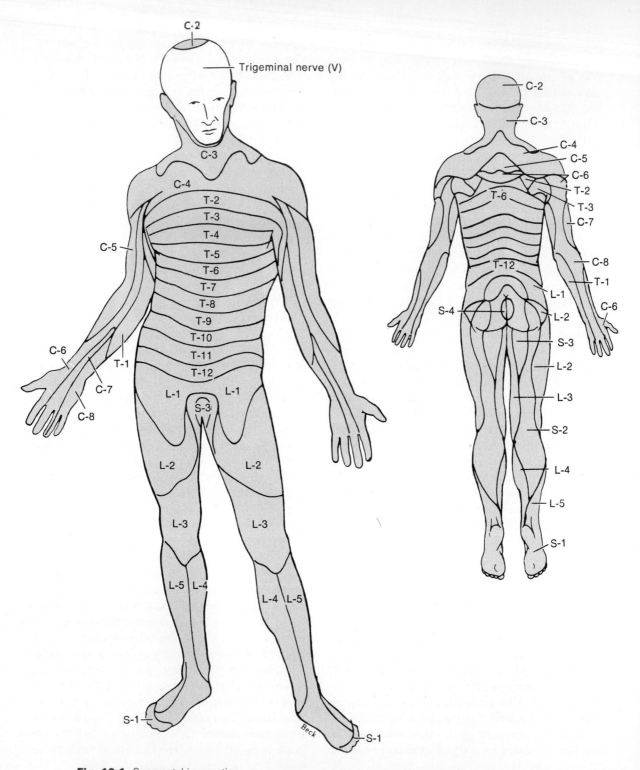

Fig. 10-1. Segmental innervation.

(From Anthony CP, and Thibodeau GA: Textbook of anatomy and physiology, ed 11, St Louis, 1983, The CV Mosby Co.)

transection, the motor losses on one side of the body are the result of injury to that same side of the spinal cord, since the motor pathways do not cross over in the cord. Some sensory pathways do cross over immediately whereas others travel up the cord on the same side before crossing over at the medulla. Thus the pattern of loss and the type of loss will indicate the location of the lesion. One model of spinal cord injury is the Brown-Sequard syndrome, which is the result of a hemisection (half-cut) of the spinal cord. Of course, the presence of some type of lesion or tumor would cause the same pattern of loss if it occupied and interrupted half the cord at the same segment. The pattern of sensory loss and paralysis is asymmetrical in the Brown-Sequard syndrome, since some pathways are left intact. For example, the motor and fine touch pathways are lost only on the side of the hemisection, so that the opposite side of the body has normal muscular function. However, because of crossover, there is a loss of pain and temperature sensations on the opposite side of the body with retention of these sensations on the same side as the lesion. These patterns are present below the level of the lesion; those areas innervated by higher segments of the cord have normal sensation and motion.

If a compression injury has occurred, the posterior columns of white matter at the level of the injury are usually involved. These nerve tracts carry the sensory fibers involved in proprioception, and when damaged an individual loses the sense of body position in space. Because muscle tone and movement require that the brain be constantly informed of proprioceptive factors, normal muscle movement cannot be accomplished and paralysis is present.

The problems that an individual with a spinal cord injury may experience depend on the location and extent of the injury. After the spinal shock period, the spinal reflexes reappear with flexor reflexes appearing first, followed by the extensor reflexes, superficial reflexes before deep reflexes, and more distal ones before the proximal reflexes. Paraplegia refers to the resultant paralysis and sensory loss that occurs when a cord injury is present in spinal cord segments T-1 to L-2. The upper half of the body is normally innervated, but the lower half has been denervated. This includes not only limb function but also bowel and bladder control and lower back and abdominal muscle function. The individual may have a flexor or extensor type of paralysis. The mass reflex is usually elicited by stimulation of the lower part of the body and is a mass withdrawal movement of the affected limbs. It indicates a spinal reflex that is intact even though a cord transection has taken place. The presence of a positive Babinski reflex is a common finding as well.

A quadriplegic injury is the result of cervical cord injury and involves all four extremities. A C-4 injury is also associated with respiratory difficulty, since the diaphragm and intercostals do not receive normal innervation. A cervical injury occurring higher than C-4 can be fatal. The patterns of sensory and motor loss resulting from cord injury can be predicted by looking at Fig. 10-1.

Spinal reflexes in the normal person do not operate in isolation from higher brain control, since descending pathways synapse with the neurons involved in the spinal cord and exert regulation over these reflexes. However, in the paraplegic and quadriplegic such control is lost. This accounts for the above reflexes being present and also for the phenomenon of autonomic hyperreflexia or dysreflexia. This is the result of reflex vasoconstriction of vessels innervated below the level of the lesion. Normally the higher autonomic centers are the prime regulators of the state of vasomotor constriction or dilation, but this is lost below the level of the lesion in cord transection. Therefore any noxious stimulus, such as a full bladder or the pressure of stool in the rectum, can elicit the unregulated spinal reflex in a person with a spinal cord injury at T7 or above. There is widespread and sometimes unremitting vasoconstriction, and the carotid sinus senses the rising blood pressure and attempts to control it, but the neurologic pathways are interrupted. There may be bradycardia and hypertension, and the face is often flushed. Massive sweating may also be present. Dysreflexia is a life-threatening, uninhibited, sympathetic response. This response must be recognized and the stimulus eliciting the reflex removed, or the patient is at risk for the neurologic sequelae of severe hypertension.

Treatment rationale. The spinal cord–injured individual may require surgical intervention if a fracture has occurred, but most need immobilization and extensive nursing care during the spinal shock period. Research on the role of endorphins may provide some new forms of early pharmacologic therapy. Cold and corticosteroids are often used to decrease swelling. There may be return of some function to points of intact innervation as long as 2 years following the injury. Some rehabilitation centers are currently conducting research on the use of electrical stimulation to elicit motor movement in paralyzed muscles.

Multiple sclerosis

Nerve cell damage can occur at any point along the nerve processes, dendrites, cell body, or axons. Another category of disorders characterized by nerve cell damage that results in disrupted transmission are the demyelinating diseases. The most common disorder within this category is multiple sclerosis.

Multiple sclerosis (MS) is a fairly common disorder (about 125,000 Americans) that affects mostly young adults. Epidemiologic studies show that the incidence is much higher in inhabitants of the Northern Hemisphere. Studies of people who have moved from one hemisphere to another at different points in their lives indicate the possibility that an early viral infection is responsible for the disease. The infection remains latent for many years before appearing in the form of the lesions of MS. Viruses that have been implicated include rubella, measles, and mumps. More recently, the RNA retrovirus, which causes adult T cell leukemia and possibly also non-Hodgkin's lymphoma, has been implicated. Because there is much research to support the presence of immunologic abnormalities in MS, the viral involvement may be related to a perturbation of the immune system. There is also evidence of a genetic predisposition, as determined by twin studies, in which the concordance is high.

Multiple sclerosis (MS) is a fairly common disorder (about 125,000 Americans) that affects mostly young adults. Epidemiologic studies show that the incidence is much higher in inhabitants of the Northern Hemisphere. Studies of people who have moved from one hemisphere to another at different points in their lives indicate the possibility that an early viral infection is responsible for the disease. The infection remains latent for many years before appearing in the form of the lesions quency of the HLA-B7 and HLA-A3 genotype, and with a decreased frequency of the HLA-A12 genotype. The genes of the major histocompatibility complex have an important role in immunologic responsiveness and regulation, and particular genotypes are associated with particular diseases (see Chapter 2 for further information).

Immunologic abnormalities of many different types have been demonstrated in MS. There is decreased suppressor T cell function (especially when the disease is active) and possible enhancement of B cell function, both of which lead to hyperimmunity. MS patients also appear to have a more competent immune system in response to many common viruses. Excessive immunologic responsiveness may thus be at the heart of the defect, with B cells being released from suppression and secreting autoimmunoglobulins to myelin. The antibodies then react with nerve cell myelin, causing the inflammatory, destructive lesions that are characteristic of MS.

MS is characterized by multiple lesions that appear throughout the central nervous system. These lesions are the result of initial demyelination followed by inflammation and later scarring. The lesions may occur in any part of the brain or spinal cord, and the disease pursues a relapsing and remitting course. Sixty percent of the patients experience visual disturbances such as blurring or diplopia. Other functions that may be impaired include motor functions, sensation, and coordination. The initial attack may last only a few days, and when the disease relapses there may be different nerves involved and therefore different symptoms. Long-term problems that usually develop include constipation, urinary problems, and muscle spasticity, characterized by exaggeration of the stretch reflexes and hyperreflexia of the deep tendon reflexes. There also may be painful spasm of the muscles, and the muscles are stiff and sore most of the time. With time many affected individuals suffer increasing debility and loss of function and may require increasing amounts of care. With each attack new areas of demyelination appear as patches along the nerves. There is inflammation and hyperemia along these patches and with healing there is some scarring, which interrupts transmission along that fiber. Thus the damage becomes cumulative over time.

Treatment rationale. The major form of treatment at the present time is corticosteroid administration, which is used on a short-term basis during an acute exacerbation. Laxatives are usually required, and prevention and treatment of urinary tract infections are also important. Measures to alleviate muscle spasticity and to provide as much mobility as possible to the patient are also required. Many people who develop MS are in the prime of life, having just reached young adulthood and starting families and careers. Therefore the psychologic problems of such individuals in dealing with such a devastating diagnosis and its implications may assume as much importance in the therapeutic plan as the physical care.

ELECTROCHEMICAL ABNORMALITIES: EPILEPSIES

The nervous system functions through the process of synaptic transmission, which depends on the establishment of electrochemical gradients across cell membranes and firing of cells by depolarization. These mechanisms should be familiar to the student; they are covered in all standard textbooks of human physiology. Nervous system disorders that arise through abnormalities in these processes include the epilepsies.

Epileptic seizures indicate a functional impairment of neuronal activity and as such may have many complex causes. In general, when deep subcortical structures are involved, the seizures that occur are generalized grand mal seizures; when cortical areas are involved the seizures are more commonly focal or produce initially focal symptoms that may become generalized. Predisposing factors are multiple, the most common being head injury (especially in young people and children), brain tumors, infections, toxins, metabolic factors, cerebrovascular disease, congenital causes, and possible genetic factors. It seems that damage and scarring are not always necessary for seizure disorders to develop. Also all brain scars do not result in seizure activity (Kutt and McDowell, 1979). The classification of seizure disorders is presented in Table 10-1. This classification is the result of work done by the International League Against Epilepsy and is commonly accepted nomenclature (Gastaut, 1970).

The following section will deal with the pathophysiology of epilepsy, which is a chronic seizure disorder. Many of the principles underlying abnormal neuronal excitability in the epilepsies can be applied to seizures that are not considered epileptic in origin, that is, those that occur only once or twice in conditions such as cerebral edema, poisoning, or fever in children. A brief discussion of the latter will be included at the end of this section, but the other disorders are discussed separately elsewhere in this and other chapters.

Pathophysiology

Within nervous tissue information is sent via action potentials, which are transmitted across synapses from neuron to neuron. There is normally directionality of the impulses and specific patterns of transmission determined by anatomic and functional connections. The electrochemical activity of the brain produces potential differences that can be measured by electroencephalography (EEG). Of course, the potentials measured are summated action potentials of many thousands of neurons but information about the brain's structural and functional integrity can be obtained through analysis of the EEG. In in-

Table 10-1. Major seizures classification

Partial seizures			
Elementary	**Complex**	**Secondary generalized**	**Generalized seizures**
Consciousness unimpaired	Consciousness lost	Initially partial, becomes generalized	Bilateral, and generalized from beginning
Types of symptoms	**Types of symptoms**		**Types**
Motor	Cognitive		Absence
Sensory	Affective		Myoclonus
Autonomic	Psychosensory		Infantile spasms
Compound	Psychomotor		Clonic
	Compound		Tonic-clonic (grand mal)
			Atonic
			Akinetic
			Tonic

Adapted from Gastaut H: Clinical and electroencephalographic classification of epileptic seizures, Epilepsia 11:102-113, 1970.

dividuals with epilepsy, the EEG is abnormal, the characteristic wave forms being altered by the appearance of spikes of electrical activity. These spikes are generated by a focus of cells known as the epileptogenic focus. The focus is morphologically altered, with an abundance of glial cells being present and alterations occurring in the dendritic processes of the neurons. Neurons appear bare and spineless. These changes are characteristic of *deafferentation*. When lack of normal afferentation is present, a denervation type of injury current occurs in which the cells are chronically depolarized and therefore hyperexcitable. It is thought that an epileptogenic focus is partially denervated or receives less input from other areas of the nervous system than in the normal individual. Whether this is cause or effect of epilepsy is not known.

In order for a seizure to occur, it must be triggered by some event. For some seizures the triggering activity is obvious, as in the generation of seizures in susceptible people by bursts of light flashed in a repetitive pattern into the eyes. Hypoglycemia may generate seizure activity, as can certain other metabolic changes. Other seizures appear to be generated by endogenous factors that are not easily detected. The triggering events probably differ from one individual to the next. It is apparent by EEG examination that an epileptogenic focus is discharging rhythmic bursts of depolarization many times during a day, but only very rarely does an actual ictal (convulsive) event take place. The type of EEG activity seen in epilepsy is known as the spike wave, is paroxysmal in occurrence, and may consist of a frequency as high as 1000/second. The activity is present only some of the time. The spike activity is considered to be the summated, synchronized electrical activity of a group of disordered neurons at an epileptogenic focus, which is known as a paroxysmal depolarization shift (PDS). This appears to be giant excitatory postsynaptic potential (EPSP). An EPSP is a depolarization in the postsynaptic neuron, which is normally small, and is produced by a burst of neurotransmitter at a local area of membrane causing the postsynaptic membrane to depolarize slightly. When there is enough area of membrane depolarized, there will be summation of the impulses to produce a spike. There can also be temporal summation, in which the bursts of presynaptic activity are so rapid that the membrane depolarizes and does not have time to fully recover before another action potential reaches the presynapse and causes neurotransmitter release. It would seem that in epilepsy the latter mechanism probably contributes most to the PDS.

There is evidence that spikes at synapses within an epileptogenic focus are not only conducted forward across the synapse in the normal manner (orthodromic transmission) but also are conducted backward (antidromic transmission) back up the presynaptic axon. Normally antidromic activity is not significant as the membrane becomes resistant to depolarization after the impulse travels past it and undergoes recovery. During the repolarization-recovery process, it is first absolutely and then relatively refractory. Within epileptogenic neurons, extra spikes often appear, with the epileptic activity being indicated by double-humped spikes. Thus it appears that the antidromic transmission reaches an area of membrane when it is excitable, having fully recovered from the first depolarization, and is therefore discharged again by the antidromic wave.

This pattern of activity may set up the constant depolarization of epileptogenic neurons and may explain the rhythmic pacemaker-like discharging of an epileptogenic site during ictal episodes. Initially, when a PDS is generated it is surrounded by a developing area of hyperpolarization known as *surround inhibition*. This serves to limit the spread of the PDS. In most epileptogenic spike activity the discharge is well confined and never goes beyond the epileptogenic focus. These spikes can, of course, be observed on the EEG. When cells at the seizure focus fire, they normally excite inhibitory interneurons, which release gamma aminobutyric acid (GABA). This inhibitory neurotransmitter causes the focus to turn off and also inhibits the surrounding cells. When seizure activity does occur, some mechanisms seem to override the surround inhibition and decrease the degree of hyperpolarization that usually occurs after the PDS. The normal checks and balance system on this activity probably involves excitatory and inhibitory systems, the latter of which becomes less effective during a seizure. When an ictal episode occurs there is spread of the depolarization and transmission of the excessive neuronal activity to other sites within the brain. A single neuron may have as many as 100,000 connections to other neurons through synaptic networks. Thus there is both a primary focus and secondary foci.

In many epilepsies a "mirror" secondary focus occurs on the opposite side of the brain in the homologous area of the primary focus. This opposite hemispheric focus is reached by nerve tracts through the corpus callosum. Cells within the secondary focus have some but not all of the morphologic and functional changes of the primary focus. It is interesting that both sites are neurologically normal when epileptogenic activity is not occurring. In some individuals with epilepsies epileptogenic activity may occur over 50% of the time, however. During epileptogenic activity the secondary foci will exhibit abnormal depolarization. Secondary foci may develop in subcortical structures also, such as in the limbic system. There are synaptic connections between the primary and the secondary foci in both cases. The effect of the excessive repeated depolarization of the primary focus is to produce secondary epileptogenic foci in these areas, but the mechanism through which this pathophysiologic effect takes place is not known. Once the primary focus is removed, the secondaries cannot incite seizure activity.

Along with the production of spontaneous PDSs, kindling of secondary foci, and morphologic changes, there are a great many biochemical alterations within the neurons of epileptogenic foci. Secondary foci also reflect the same types of differences, but the degree of alteration is much less. Briefly, there seems to be inhibition of protein synthesis, uncoupling of glucose oxidation and amino acid metabolism, and a decrease in GABA. Because GABA is a major inhibitory neurotransmitter, any decrease in its synthesis would lead to a generally more excitable brain. The GABA decrease is seen not only at the epileptogenic focus but throughout the brain tissue. There may also be defective membrane enzyme systems, particularly the Na^+-K^+-ATPase system, which maintains electrochemical gradients across cell membranes.

During repetitive firing of a group of neurons, such as occurs in an epileptogenic focus, ionic events occur that may play a role in the propagation of PDS into actual seizure activity. One contributing factor appears to be the calcium ion permeability, which increases when neuronal cells are fired. Excessive firing thus would cause an increased calcium ion influx into the cells, decreasing the level of extracellular calcium. A subsequent effect of this is an increase in potassium efflux from the cells into the extracellular space. Increasing the extracellular potassium depolarizes the cells even further, causing them to be generally more excitable. During epileptogenesis the extracellular potassium increases from 3 mM to as high as 10 mM within the extracellular fluid of the epileptogenic focus. Calcium ion decreases from 1.3 mM to 0.5 mM at the same time. These changes in calcium and potassium ions are enough to alter further the state of excitability of the neurons in the area of the focus. It is possible that actual seizure activity occurs when sufficient potassium ion accumulation in the extracellular space and calcium ion entry into the cells occurs to set off a sufficient number of hyperexcitable rhythmically discharging cells to cause spread. Such groups of neurons act in a sense like a pacemaker, but of course in a pathophysiologic manner.

Other factors that contribute to the development of seizure activity from a depolarizing epileptogenic focus may be metabolic factors such as blood glucose concentration, fluid and electrolyte balance in general, temperature, and nutritional status (Lothman and Collins, 1984). The local spread of depolarization may be confined, but in most cases the neurons will send traveling waves of depolarization through neurons with which they have synaptic connection. Multiple sites of excessive depolarization are then set up in the brain and the reticular activating system itself, once stimulated, will produce a generalized spread of activity throughout the brain and spinal cord. Loss of consciousness always occurs. Hypoxemia metabolic acidosis and hypercarbia also occur.

The duration of the seizure is variable, but on the average a generalized grand mal major motor type of seizure lasts from 5 to 10 minutes. There are many different processes that interact to halt the seizure activity in the brain. Presumably, as the excessive activity of the neurons and the extreme muscular activities occur, metabolic end products increase and through feedback inhibition slow down and finally stop the excessive discharge. The increasing extracellular potassium level eventually reaches a point where the cells will become hyperpolarized and refractory. An additional phenomenon that probably helps to limit the seizure activity is the supply of neurotransmitter that obviously must be rapidly depleted by the massive electrochemical discharge of the brain and spinal cord. The more frequent the seizures are the more easily they can continue to occur. This may be a result of swellings of interneurons and ultimately some of these cells, which normally contribute to surround inhibition.

Types of seizures

Partial seizures. Partial seizures, as indicated in Table 10-1, can have either fairly straightforward symptomatology or can be quite complex in effects. The first group includes partial seizures that occur without loss of consciousness and that have one category of symptoms. Those with motor symptoms usually involve the motor cortex and are usually unilateral. When bilateral, consciousness is lost and the patient has a more classic ictal episode with a postictal period. One type of focal partial seizure is the jacksonian march seizure, in which the spread of epileptogenic activity through the neuronal tissue is clearly indicated by the symptoms. As the seizure activity in the brain spreads, the areas of twitching progressively increase in a stepwise fashion. Thus the seizure is said to march along as successive parts become involved. Usually this is a unilateral type of seizure, but it can spread and become generalized.

Other types of partial seizures can have mainly sensory or somatosensory effects. The sensory symptoms that an individual with this disorder experiences can be quite bizarre. There may be sensations of lights and colors, or the individual may have transitory sensations in a focal area of the body. Partial seizures with complex symptoms include a group of epilepsies that in the past were often characterized as psychomotor. The separation of these seizures into four groups indicates that the symptoms of the seizures are sufficiently different from each other to categorize them in this manner. The classical *psychomotor seizure* is the result of temporal lobe epilepsy. There is no loss of consciousness during the seizure but there is a postictal phase. The manifestations of the seizure are multiple. For some individuals there will be peculiar yet purposeful motor activity such as chewing or swallowing, whereas others will have essentially purposeless activity. It is not unusual for other seizure types to occur in the individual with psychomotor epilepsy; thus there are often very complex symptoms and different types of seizures. Psychomotor seizures are the most common partial seizure type, occurring with highest frequency in children over the age of 3 years. When the symptoms are largely affective, the limbic system may be the epileptic site. These seizures are characterized by very peculiar and bizarre behaviors, which may be antisocial. The patient does not recall the behaviors after the seizure.

Generalized seizures. This group of seizures includes those epilepsies in which the seizure activity occurs immediately as a generalized seizure. The absence type of seizure (formerly called petit mal) is quite uniform in symptomatology from one patient to another and consists of symptoms such as brief staring episodes, momentary disturbances in cognitive function that may actually be true losses of consciousness, rolling of the eyeballs in an upward direction, nodding of the head, or blinking. The affected individual does not usually fall down and the seizures are often extremely short, lasting just a few seconds, although many hundreds may occur in a single day. Occasionally children with absence seizures will develop the grand mal type of seizure activity during the adolescent years.

Myoclonic and akinetic jerks are another type of generalized disorder. There are sudden attacks characterized by muscle jerks, similar to the myoclonus all people occasionally experience when falling asleep. The infantile form is known as infantile spasm and is characterized by the adoption of a "salaam" position during the seizure; the affected infant flexes and extends the head, trunk, and limbs as if nodding. Many hundreds of these myoclonic spasms may occur in a day, and there is usually severe brain damage associated with their presence. The infantile spasms are usually replaced with another form of epilepsy as the child gets older.

Grand mal epilepsy. This convulsive disorder, which appears to have some genetic predisposition, is characterized by generalized seizure activity that begins with an aura. The aura is usually a sensory or emotional phenomenon such as dizziness, a smell or taste, a peculiar abdominal sensation, or a feeling. In some cases the nature of the aura can help to identify the actual location of the epileptogenic focus in the brain. The aura is very transient and is quickly followed by sudden collapse and loss of consciousness. It is typical for both eyeballs to roll upward and the person to cry out. This is followed by a period of apnea, in which the pupils are dilated and there is cyanosis. Tonic contraction of the body occurs in which the back is arched and all muscles are rigid. The jaw may become tightly clenched after 5 to 15 seconds, and the contractions become clonic in which rhythmic and usually bilateral severe muscle twitching is present. The entire seizure generally lasts about 5 minutes, but seizures lasting up to 30 minutes have been observed. During this time there is loss of voluntary muscle control so that urination, excessive salivation, and defecation routinely occur. This latter effect is a useful guideline to use in determining whether or not a true tonic-clonic, grand mal seizure has taken place, since children with convulsive disorders can be quite skilled in simulating an epileptic convulsion. The seizure activity results in hypoxia, hypercapnea, and metabolic acidosis. The blood gas changes may result in cerebral vasodilation, thus compensating for the period of cerebral hypoxia. A condition known as *status epilepticus* can develop during seizure activity. In this case the seizure activity becomes continuous, with only short periods of quiet occurring between violent and nearly uninterrupted clonic contractions. There is great danger that an individual with this condition will succumb to hypoxia, acidosis, hypoglycemia, hyperthermia, and exhaustion if the convulsive activity is not halted.

Grand mal epilepsy is a major motor form of convulsive disorder, which probably originates in an epileptogenic focus in the gray matter of the diencephalon. The epileptogenic focus itself is unable to carry on its normal function and, secondarily, multiple synaptic connections to motor centers are suddenly bombarded with excessive bursts of depolarizations. If the seizure activity continues long enough, secondary foci may themselves become epileptogenic.

Febrile seizures. Children under the age of 2 years are particularly susceptible to seizure activity during times of high fever. Some children respond with seizure activity when the temperature rises to only 102° F, but a fever of greater than 103° F is more likely to generate seizure activity. Usually these seizures are generalized tonic-clonic in nature and have a characteristic postictal state of drowsiness. When the fever rises rapidly, the likelihood of febrile seizures occurring increases. A child's temperature must be carefully monitored during infancy and toddlerhood to prevent febrile seizures from occurring, since serious neurologic sequelae can result. Some children with a febrile seizure will actually have an underlying convulsive disorder, but most are neurologically normal and will suffer only one convulsive episode.

The mechanism by which temperature elevation results in seizure activity is unknown. There is a gender difference, with males being twice as likely as females to suffer such seizures. Heating of the brain tissue may cause increased excitability of certain (or perhaps all) neurons and lower the threshold for seizure activity to occur. Most of the time febrile seizures are fairly short but it is so frightening to the parents that they generally report that the seizure lasted much longer than it actually did. The child with a febrile seizure is usually not placed on anticonvulsant drug therapy if the EEG is normal and only one seizure has occurred.

SYNAPTIC DYSFUNCTION
Myasthenia gravis

Some nervous system diseases originate as a result of alterations in neurotransmitter release, supply, or postsynaptic membrane effect. Many central nervous system poisons act at the level of the synapse. Curare, for example, blocks acetylcholine binding at neuromuscular junctions by binding with the acetylcholine receptors of the postsynaptic membrane. Many other toxic substances such as insecticides produce their effects through similar mechanisms.

One disease model of altered synaptic transmission is *myasthenia gravis*. This disease was briefly described in Chapter 2. It is believed to be autoimmune in origin and is characterized by reduction of the miniature end plate potentials at the myoneural junction. There may not be enough acetylcholine receptors in the postsynaptic membrane, and the synapic cleft is also widened. The net result of this is that the muscle fatigues easily, since neurotransmission is limited by the paucity of acetylcholine transmitters and the delay in transmission. Muscle weakness and easy fatiguability characterize the myasthenia patient. Most cases involve only the ocular muscles, with the result that diplopia occurs, especially after the eyes have been used extensively, as in reading for long periods, or at the end of the day. A more serious form involves other muscles, with the distal muscles usually being more affected.

The incidence in the population is between 0.01% to 0.05%, and in those afflicted there seems to be some genetic predisposition. The disease is often characterized by periods of remissions and exacerbations. Treatment is by administration of anticholinesterases, which block the acetylcholine-destroying enzyme at the synapse, thus allowing for a longer action of the available acetylcholine. Thymectomy may allow considerable relief from symptoms, and often immunosuppressive drugs are used as well as the anticholinesterases. The ocular form of myasthenia gravis causes serious disruptions in the normal life-style but is not associated with shortening of the lifespan. The generalized form can eventually lead to cardiac and respiratory muscle weakness and death.

Botulism

Clostridium botulinum produces a deadly exotoxin, which can be lethal to human beings. It is usually the result of improper home food preserving and canning. The toxin produces its characteristic effects of blurred vision, paralysis, abdominal distention, and urine retention by acting at the neuromuscular synapse. Botulism toxin appears to decrease the ability of the presynaptic neuron to release sufficient neurotransmitter. The postsynaptic potentials are insufficient for the membrane to reach threshold and fire, and thus muscle depolarization is unable to occur.

ALTERED TISSUE PERFUSION: CEREBROVASCULAR DISEASE

The development of some degree of cerebrovascular disease as a concomitant of normal aging is well known. The elderly are more at risk than younger individuals for the development of occlusive processes in the brain vessels. The production of brain ischemia and hypoxia is the pathophysiologic manifestation of severe cerebrovascular occlusion as manifested by transient ischemic attacks (TIAs) and cerebrovascular accidents (CVAs, strokes). Each of these problems will be described, but we will first discuss the general problem of cerebral hypoxia.

Hypoxia

Neuronal hypoxia, like other forms, can be of anoxic, anemic, histotoxic, or stagnant origin. Those are described in detail in Chapter 16. Whatever the origin, the end result is that the brain is deprived of oxygen, and aerobic metabolism is diminished while the Embden-Meyerhoff pathway of anaerobic glycolysis is accelerated. Lactate production ensues, and the extracellular fluid pH drops as a state of metabolic acidosis is produced within the brain tissues. The local response of the cerebral arterioles to the drop in pH is dilation, which will compensate to some degree for the hypoxia by increasing the cerebral blood flow. Of course, adequate cardiac function and circulatory integrity are required for the compensatory effect, and in cases of cardiac arrest without cardiopulmonary resuscitation being immediately instituted, this will not be so. The neurons of the brain respond to the hypoxic state in a pathophysiologic manner, with altered membrane potential, excitability, and metabolism, so that brain function and the EEG will become grossly abnormal. The state of consciousness is lost or disturbed very quickly as the EEG changes. When the EEG waves, after first slowing, finally stop, the brain is considered irreparably damaged and not capable of sustaining life. This occurs after oxygen and glucose supplies are exhausted. Neurological recovery after a complete cardiac arrest depends on how quickly resusitation is instituted; recovery can occur after an arrest time of as long as 6 minutes.

We have been describing a generalized state of hypoxia and how it affects the entire brain. When dealing with arteriosclerotic cerebral disease, we are usually concerned with small portions of the brain tissue. Areas that become hypoxic suffer the same changes as described above but in a local manner. In addition the effects of hypoxia are superimposed upon the effects of damage or loss of functional neuronal tissue. This consideration becomes paramount in the infant who has suffered intrauterine or birth hypoxia, in which the damage to the brain may cause life-long neurologic consequences. In the older individual the possibility of permanent neurologic damage after hypoxic episodes becomes even more likely, since the ability to repair damage or to learn to use different parts of the brain in much more difficult as the organism matures.

Pathogenesis of cerebrovascular disease

The pathogenesis of arteriosclerosis is discussed in Chapter 17. The effects of occlusive atherosclerotic disease on the brain tissue are magnified by the central importance of the brain in all functions of the body. Several principles need review for the student to understand the problems associated with cerebrovascular disease. First, the brain is remarkably able to regulate its own blood supply in order to meet changing metabolic needs. The ability to regulate the blood vessel diameters independently of systemic blood pressure is effective only in the range of mean arterial blood pressures between 60 and 140 mm Hg. Obviously, this ability of the cerebral vasculature to autoregulate is a survival mechanism in times of severe physiologic stress to the organism, helping to preserve the function of the brain. Furthermore, as the metabolic needs of the brain tissue increase or decrease there are vasomotor controls over the blood vessels. The oxygen extraction capability of the brain is quite high so that many survival mechanisms interact to oxygenate the brain at nearly any cost.

The anatomic organization of the cerebral vasculature is also important to understand when studying the pathophysiology of arteriosclerotic disease. Fig. 10-2 illustrates the blood supply to the brain and the circle of Willis, as depicted in a lateral view. The effects of occlusive processes will depend upon which vessels are involved and which areas of the brain these vessels supply.

Anterior cerebral artery. Supplies blood to medial and superior surfaces of frontal and parietal lobes (includes motor and somatosensory control centers of cortex)

Middle cerebral artery. Supplies blood to inferior surface of frontal lobe and lateral surface of cerebrum (includes most of mo-

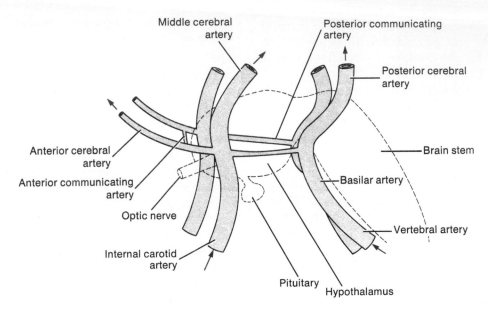

Fig. 10-2. Blood supply to brain and circle of Willis.

tor cortex and somatosensory cortex), speech area (in left hemisphere), and auditory areas

Posterior cerebral artery. Supplies blood to medial and upper surfaces of temporal lobe (includes some of limbic system and the visual cortex)

The anterior and middle cerebral arteries receive most of their blood supply from the internal carotid arteries; the posterior cerebral arteries are largely supplied by the basilar artery.

Transient ischemic attacks (TIAs)

Many people who experience a cerebrovascular accident have a history of preceding TIAs. These are momentary episodes having a very rapid onset, lasting from 2 to 15 minutes, and resolving within 24 hours. The TIA is a result of a neurologic deficit of vascular occlusive origin, and generally may be classified in terms of the brain's blood vessels. TIAs arising from occlusion in the carotid system usually cause transitory motor impairment such as weakness

or paralysis on one side of the body, with both the arm and leg possibly being affected. There may also be alterations in sensory function on that side. Some patients may have difficulty in speaking, writing, or calculating, and occasionally there will be unilateral blindness of an episodic nature.

TIAs arising from occlusion in the vertebral basilar arteries often have motor and sensory disturbances, but these are not sharply delineated, being sometimes present in all the extremities or moving from one to the other. Visual disturbances are also likely to be bilateral. As seen in Fig. 10-2, the basilar system provides blood to both sides of the brain via the posterior cerebral arteries while the carotids provide blood to separate sides of the brain. In patients showing symptoms of carotid artery TIAs there may be evidence of arteriosclerosis in the retina of the eyes, and a bruit may be heard over the carotid artery in the neck.

Many of the patients suffering TIAs have

hypertensive disease, and the presence of the TIA is a warning that even more serious occlusion of vessels, already greatly compromised by long-standing hypertension, is very possible. Up to 40% of individuals suffering a TIA will have a major cerebrovascular accident (CVA) within 5 years. Many people will have recurrent TIAs before the actual stroke takes place. Generally the TIA causes no permanent neurologic sequelae and so may be ignored as unimportant by the affected individual. Some strokes have no neurologic deficit and are now being classified by some authorities as a form of TIA. Therefore the most important difference between a TIA and a CVA is the reversible nature of the effects in TIA.

Cerebrovascular accident (CVA)

A CVA or stroke can be the most devastating insult that an individual experiences. Most of the affected people are elderly, hypertensive, and have elevated serum lipid levels; many smoke. Diabetes is also a risk factor. Because of the risk factors and hypertension there is usually an associated ischemic cardiac disease.

The most common type of stroke results from progressive cerebral ischemia and leads eventually to infarction, as a result of atherosclerosis. Common sites for atherosclerotic plaque in the cerebral circulation are at the origin of the internal carotid artery, at the convergence point of the basilar and vertebral artery, and in the middle and posterior cerebral arteries. When occlusive disease develops, there is usually some collateralization that provides the brain with adequate perfusion. Therefore the symptoms of a stroke depend on how well-collateralized the circulation has become. TIAs occur frequently, preceding the stroke usually by about 1 month. Other symptoms are headache, transient numbness and weakness, carotid

artery bruit, and retinal vessel changes.

The second most common cause of CVA is cerebral embolism. A cerebral embolism results from debris breaking off from atherosclerotic, thrombotic material in the cerebral arteries of the head and neck. Emboli may also arise in the heart. Activity or exercise often precipitates cerebral embolism. The embolism lodges in a smaller, distal cerebral vessel, causing hypoxia and eventual infarction. The embolism gradually dissolves or is actively removed by phagocytic cells, but fragmentation into smaller particles may occur during this process, with new emboli traveling into more distal vessels. The vessel may bleed out into the brain tissue during this time as well.

The third cause of stroke is hemorrhage into the brain. Hemorrhagic stroke is also a very sudden event, often preceded by a very severe headache and vomiting and less frequently by seizure and collapse. The causes of cerebral hemorrhage include a ruptured aneurysm (most of which are in the carotid arteries) and hypertensive hemorrhage (a result of progressive degeneration of arterial smooth muscle by the hypertensive process).

The effects of thrombosis and hemorrhage produce clinical symptoms, which are often identical so that the differential diagnosis must be made by computerized axial tomography scan (CAT scan). In general a hemorrhage may have a more rapid onset, which is characterized by headache and vomiting.

The mortality rate from an intracerebral hemorrhage is ten times higher than that from cerebral thrombosis, and most hemorrhages are in the cerebrum.

The signs and symptoms of a CVA depend on the extent of involvement of neuronal tissue and the side of the cerebrum that is affected. Most CVAs cause some degree of hemiplegia, and of course the side involved is opposite the side of the brain that is affected because of crossing over of sensory and motor nerve tracts. There is also a unilateral sensory deficit in most patients, and there may be the same visual disturbances that are observed in TIAs. An additional symptom is language disturbance in the patient with a left hemisphere CVA, because the language area is located on this side for nearly all right-handed and most left-handed people. The disturbance may take the form of *dysphasia* or *aphasia* that is either receptive or communicative.

The pathophysiologic effects and the prognosis for recovery are entirely different in right-sided versus left-sided CVAs. When the lesion occurs in the left hemisphere, a right-sided hemiplegia is present. The individual has good awareness of what has happened and has little cognitive disability, but may be extremely disturbed and depressed about the aphasia that is present. Perseveration may be present, in which the individual engages in repetitious acts or speech. The overall prognosis for recovery is better for right-sided hemiplegia, because of the ability of these patients to understand and realistically confront the situation. The left-sided hemiplegic has suffered damage to the right side of the brain and will therefore have no language dysfunction. However, these patients may have major deficits in visual-spatial functions, and they often show short attention span and poor judgment and do not really understand what has happened. These individuals may appear cheerful and optimistic, but because of their denial they often show much less potential for recovery than those with right-sided hemiplegia. They often forget about the affected side, and therefore are subject to accidents such as burns or cold injuries.

Treatment rationale. The best form of treatment for the CVA patient would have been preventive measures. After the stroke has occurred, most of the initial treatment is directed toward maintaining life support systems. Afterward, excellent nursing care and physical and speech therapy may make the difference in optimal recovery of function and acceptance of the deficits that remain. Delination of risk factors and their contribution to the CVA is important, because there is a likelihood of another CVA occurring. Control of hypertension is critical, and diet, smoking, and exercise factors should all be part of the rehabilitative plan.

Headache

One of the most common human experiences is headache. We describe it as beating, throbbing, and blinding, and attribute it to stress, sinus problems, fatigue, fluid, premenstruum, or allergy. In reality, for the common, garden variety headache, the pathophysiologic alterations are not known. For specific types of headaches, such as migraines, more information is available. Headaches can be classified clinically as the migraine and cluster, tension-vascular, muscular contraction, or depressive type.

Migraine is associated with both headache and systemic disturbances. The pain is usually unilateral and associated with anorexia, nausea, and vomiting. Some patients have a prodrome characterized by mood disturbances or neurologic symptoms. Transitory visual disturbances such as central vision impairment on the affected side are also common. Patients describe a scintillating scotoma extending from the blinded area. Some migraines persist for days, and patients frequently are depressed and fatigued during the attack. The origin of migraine is vascular, with intracranial vasoconstriction initially causing the prodromal and early symptoms. The vasoconstriction produces some degree of cerebral ischemia. The second phase is one of vasodilation of the scalp arteries, and this causes the headache. A bounding temporal pulse is frequently observed. It is likely that vasoactive substances are released that contribute to an increased vascular permeability of the dilated arteriolar trees and a localized, temporary inflammation occurs. The cause of the unilateral aspect of the migraine symptoms is not known. Precipitants of migraine attack include alcohol and certain food substances, menstrual cycle stage, stress, fatigue, and gastric disturbances. There is little evidence of a true "migraine personality," as early literature had reported. Rather, a relationship between migraine and anxiety, depression, and stress may produce the headache in susceptible people. This relationship may involve serotonergic pathways in the brain (Merskey, 1982). Another consideration is the effect of pain itself on personality and on recurrence risk. Fear and worry over a migraine attack may actually precipitate the attack. The misery and impairment of function in the person afflicted with migraine is often very severe.

INCREASED INTRACRANIAL PRESSURE

Intracranial pressure (ICP) is usually measured by inserting a needle into the cerebrospinal space of the lower spinal cord. The cerebrospinal fluid (CSF) pressure provides an overall picture of pressure within the ventricular system of the brain and the spinal canal and of the brain tissue. It is also a good indicator of the cerebral vascular perfusion since blood flow through the brain is dependent upon the usual pressure gradients operating throughout the circulatory tree, and the CSF pressure must be maintained at a value less than the brain's blood pressure for flow to occur normally.

There are three categories of increased ICP—that caused by obstruction of the flow of the cerebrospinal fluid or to its absorption, that caused by a space-occupying lesion, and that caused by cerebral edema. The first category constitutes the processes that produce *hydrocephalus*.

Hydrocephalus

To understand the mechanisms involved in the production of increased ICP from hydrocephalus, the student should be able to recall the normal pattern of CSF production, circulation, and absorption within the ventricular system of the brain and the canal of the spinal cord. The cerebrospinal fluid acts as an intermediary between the blood and the brain, and there is significantly decreased permeability of the brain capillaries compared to capillary beds elsewhere in the body. This decreased permeability serves as a barrier and is protective of the brain (the blood-brain barrier), acting to preserve the steady state even when major physiologic changes occur elsewhere in the body. Because neurons are so dependent for normal functioning on the ionic composition and substrate supply of the extracellular fluid, small changes in these produce major effects upon neuronal excitability. The extracellular fluid of the brain has the same composition as cerebrospinal fluid, and there is an equilibrium exchange between these two compartments. This results in two major phenomena: (1) the extracellular fluid of the brain is kept remarkably constant in both quantity and quality, and (2) pressure in either system will result in pressure in the other system. If there is a primary brain edema, there will be a flow of fluid and an increase in pressure within the CSF, conversely, a rise in CSF pressure may increase the pressure of the brain's extracellular fluid.

Hydrocephalus can either be congenital or acquired and refers to a condition of increased CSF pressure and fluid resulting from obstruction in the CSF drainage preventing its flow or absorption. The ventricles of the brain will be dilated and the heads of children born with the disease will be enlarged. The latter effect occurs when the fluid pressure causes expansion of the cranial compartment when the skull is soft and the sutures and fontanels are not closed. In the older child or adult the cranium is a rigid, closed box, and head enlargement will not occur. In the infant born with hydrocephalus, the pressure is accommodated much more readily than in the adult. Eventually pressure effects on the infant are sometimes devastating, but many infants with hydrocephalus have no brain damage if the condition is recognized early and a shunt is inserted into the cerebrospinal system to drain off the excessive fluid.

The causes of hydrocephalus include the following: obstruction caused by congenital malformations of the aqueduct of Sylvius; obstruction resulting from vascular injuries, tumors, or trauma; excessive secretion of CSF caused by a tumor of the choroid plexus; and decreased ability of the brain capillaries to absorb the CSF.

The ventricular system of the brain is illustrated in Fig. 10-3 so that the student can recall the position and relationship of these structures to the rest of the brain.

Cerebral edema

Cerebral edema, or an increase in the fluid content of the brain, is an effect of many pathophysiologic processes within the central nervous system. The term merely implies that there is an increase in the extracellular fluid of the brain; many times it is a reaction to other phenomena. The pathophysiologic effects of cerebral edema are related to the fact that it is a space-occupying process and will cause pressure upon the brain. In addition, it will produce a tissue pressure increase that eventually may exceed the vascular capillary pressure, thus impeding perfusion and circulation of the brain by a mechanical effect. The edema fluid pressure will cause bulk flow of the fluid into the other areas of the brain. The resultant neuronal hypoxia will cause positive feedback loops that aggravate the pathophysiologic state even further. For example, hypoxia at the neuronal and glial cellular level interrupts aerobic glucose metabolism, and less ATP is made available for maintenance of the osmotic gradients across the cell membranes. The cells will swell, and there will be an increase in extracellular potassium, interfering with normal neuronal excitability. There will also be an osmotic effect that is additive with production of lactate and other osmotically active molecules within the hypoxic tissue. The effect will be to further perpetuate the cerebral edema by osmotic transfer of water from the vascular compartment into the extracellular fluid.

Cerebral edema is one of the major causes of increased intracranial pressure. The tissue pressure of the brain becomes greater than that of the cerebrospinal fluid, which then acts as a "sink" draining the fluid from the brain and increasing the CSF pressure as a result. Some areas of the brain are more likely than others to accumulate edema fluid. The white matter is generally softer and looser, and thus edema fluid preferentially moves into the white matter. There appears to be no particularly damaging effects of the edema fluid on the neuronal cells, and most effects are the result of pressure.

In most cases of cerebral edema, there is a vasogenic cause. This means that the vascular bloodbrain barrier becomes opened up, or more permeable. The hypoxia previously described occurs as a result of the edema and aggravates the increased capil-

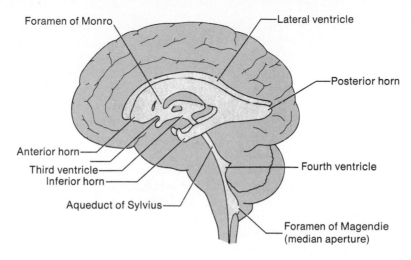

Fig. 10-3. Ventricular system of the brain and spinal cord.

lary permeability even further, since the capillary endothelium may become hypoxic and "leakier" than usual. Some conditions that produce a vasogenic cerebral edema as part of the initial insult to the brain are brain tumors, infections, radiation, and head injuries. Brain tumors also may perpetuate the edema formation by the production of proteinaceous molecules that have an osmotic effect as they increase in the brain extracellular fluid. Tumors that are very small may have as profound an effect as larger tumors.

Another obvious cause of cerebral edema is massive tissue damage such as might occur in a cerebral infarction and traumatic and penetrating injuries. There will be both vascular damage and an acute inflammatory reaction to the damaged tissue. The accumulation of blood also will increase intracranial pressure. Cerebral edema also occurs on occasion after a collection of subdural or epidural blood has been surgically removed. This edema occurs rapidly, and very little can be done to treat it. Such a situation was described in the case study in Chapter 5 on pp. 167.

The last type of cerebral edema is that which follows any ischemia-producing process in the brain. The mechanism by which hypoxia leads to cerebral edema has already been described. This latter form may occur secondarily to any of the other forms of cerebral edema.

Signs and symptoms. The effects of swelling of the brain are profound but in many cases reversible with prompt identification and treatment of the condition. There are changes in the sensorium and the alertness of the individual in early cerebral edema, which may then progress to lack of responsiveness and deep coma. When the ICP rises rapidly, such as might occur after head injury with subsequent hemorrhage into the brain, the symptoms are often very severe. Epidural hematomas, for example, usually caused by temporal bone fractures or tears of the middle meningeal artery, produce massive arterial bleeding with subsequent rapid development of symptoms. There may be violent vomiting, an excruciating headache, personality changes, alterations in the level of consciousness, and a variety of visual disturbances and eye changes. The light reflex may be absent, and one pupil or both may be widely dilated. The optic disc swells, a condition known as *papilledema*, which can be observed by ophthalmologic examination. Another problem is hyperthermia, and as the body temperature rises the metabolic demands on the brain increase. However, the brain may already be compromised by pressure and hypoxia, and pathophysiologic feedback loops will result.

Other more variable symptoms associated with increased ICF depend upon which areas of the brain are involved, the rapidity in the rise of the pressure, and the existing health of the affected individual. If untreated, increased ICP will eventually cause cardiovascular and respiratory pathophysiologic feedbacks, which act to further perpetuate the loss of brain integrity. These disruptions occur when the rising intracranial pressure reaches and then exceeds the blood pressure within the brain. Obviously, when this occurs, circulatory stasis become profound, and ischemia of vital life support centers occurs.

Treatment rationale. The rationale behind all forms of treatment for both cerebral edema and hydrocephalus is to somehow decompress the excessive pressure and fluid. With hydrocephalic conditions reconstruction of the ventricular system through surgical intervention (i.e., removal of tumor) is attempted when possible. However, most cases are treated with shunting of the CSF via plastic tubes that may empty into the peritoneal space or venous blood of the right atrium.

Cerebral edema is usually treated by physiologic shunting of blood out of the brain ECF through osmotically active medication. Hyperosmolar solutions of mannitol or urea have been used to osmotically pull the fluid from the brain into the vascular compartment. These solutions will have an immediate effect, and can be life saving, but will also produce a diuresis that may be great enough to reduce plasma osmotic pressure and result in a rebound movement of plasma fluid back into the brain interstitium. Other treatment includes administration of dexamethasone (Decadron), which appears to decrease the edema in some patients. There may also be attempts to decrease the amount of total body water by fluid restriction and diuresis. To decrease the metabolism of the brain, hypothermia and metabolic inhibitors have been tried.

DEMENTIAS
Alzheimer's disease

Alzheimer's disease is the most common, degenerative, progressive dementia, increasing in incidence with age so that 20% of the population over the age of 80 are afflicted. It contributes significantly to mortality. It is the fourth leading cause of death in the United States, according to some estimates (Kwentus, 1986). The current age-dependent incidence rate is 127 cases per 100,000 people per year. There is an incredible burden placed on those with the disease and their families in terms of emotional, social, and financial costs. Alzheimer's disease is irreversible, unremittingly progressive, and generally causes death of its victims within 2 to 10 years after diagnosis. There appear to be at least two forms of the disease. One form affects people in their middle years and the other form affects the very old. There is accumulating evidence that the form that appears in early ages is inherited and caused by a defective gene on chromosome 21 (Barnes, 1987). The late-onset form may also be influenced by genetics. This research will be reviewed later.

Alzheimer's disease usually begins with

memory lapses that become increasingly severe. Progressive cognitive and emotional deficits then develop. The following stages of this disease have been defined (Sinex and Myers, 1982);

0. Changes not associated with symptoms
1. Early disease associated with memory losses (recent and long-term), loss of judgment, mood changes, loss of spatial orientation
2. Intermediate disease characterized by irritability, anxiety, lack of cooperation, increased physical activity, inability to communicate, sleep disturbances, and night wandering
3. Late disease associated with apathy, unresponsiveness, incontinency; progresses to late neurologic problems such as seizures, dysphagia

The time intervals characteristic of each stage are extremely variable, and the diagnosis is difficult in the early stages. Other conditions that can cause similar symptoms include other progressive brain syndromes, such as Creutzfeld-Jacob syndrome, Pick's disease, demyelinating diseases, viral and fungal infections, brain tumors, normal-pressure hydrocephalus, and inflammatory or arteriosclerotic vascular diseases. Depression, a common problem in the elderly, can also produce symptoms very much like early Alzheimer's disease.

Genetics of Alzheimer's disease. A familial risk for Alzheimer's disease has been recognized for many years, with various theories of genetic penetrance being propounded. Autosomal, dominant inheritance with variable penetrancy has been suggested for those cases in which the onset is between the ages of 35 and 50. There is also evidence for a genetic basis to the late-onset form. It has been estimated that about 12% of the population carries the Alzheimer gene (Heston et al., 1981). Factors that would influence the expression of the gene could include environmental factors (nutrition, life-style, ecology). There may be lack of expression of the disease as a result of death from other causes (competing risk phenomena). Other circumstantial evidence for a genetic involvement comes from a study of surviving adult Down syndrome victims. Because better control of the cardiovascular and infectious disease problems associated with Down syndrome has been achieved, many are living into adulthood. Those who survive into their forties and fifties almost uniformly develop premature aging and dementia that in many ways is classic Alzheimer's disease. There is an increased appearance of Alzheimer's disease among relatives of Down syndrome patients (Heston et al, 1982). However, the most convincing evidence has come out of studies of chromosome 21 and gene mapping and genetic linkage analysis. Chromosome 21 is the site of the classic trisomy of Down syndrome. Down syndrome patients have an extra copy of this chromosome and presumably all of the genes on this chromosome. Recent research (St Georg-Hyslop et al., 1987) using genetic linkage analysis with DNA markers has strongly implicated chromosome 21 as the site of the gene for Alzheimer's disease. The region of the chromosome involved appears to be near the centromere in the long-arm region mapped as 21q11.2—21q22.2. This is not the same region for which trisomy dictates the full phenotypic expression of Down syndrome. Association of Down syndrome with Alzheimer's is not contradicted because trisomy of the whole chromosome is usually present in Down syndrome. Localization of a gene involved in Alzheimer's is a great step in the direction of both understanding the pathophysiology of the disease and in perhaps some-

being able to identify carriers and treat the disease in its earliest stages.

Other recent evidence (Tanzi et al., 1987) implicates the gene coding for amyloid protein. Amyloid is a protein substance found in the brain, and it deposits in the brain during both normal aging and in Alzheimer's disease. In Alzheimer's disease, however, there is an association of degree of cognitive impairment with plaque formation in the brain, and the plaques of Alzheimer's disease contain a core of amyloid. Other deposits of amyloid are also observed in the brain blood vessels. Amyloid deposits and plaques are also seen in the brain of Down syndrome patients. In the fetal Down syndrome brain there is evidence that excessive amyloid is produced. The normal function of amyloid, which can theoretically be produced by every cell, is currently unknown. The gene coding for the amino acid sequence of β amyloid has been localized to chromosome 21 and is in the same region as the Alzheimer gene. In Alzheimers's there may be excessive amyloid or an abnormal response to amyloid may occur. Amyloid may itself be a toxic substance when found extracellularly.

Pathologic characteristics

Gross brain changes. Many of the anatomic changes reported to occur in Alzheimer's disease also are present in the normal aged brain. There is not a striking correlation between these changes and the degree of deficit. In general the gross alterations that do occur are more striking in the younger victims of Alzheimer's disease. There is a cerebral cortical atrophy (reflected by an overall decreased brain weight) associated with cell loss, particularly in layers III and IV of the hippocampal cortex and outside the cortex in the nucleus basalis, septal nucleus, and locus caeruleus. Cell shrinkage is also seen in these areas, and there is an overall decreased cerebral blood flow, glucose metabolism, protein synthesis, and oxygen uptake. There is sometimes a dilation of the lateral ventricles of the brain, and the gyri are narrowed and the sulci widened. Although some normal elderly patients will have these same patterns, most of the research indicates that cell loss in particular is more severe in Alzheimer's disease, with some areas of the brain having nearly a 50% loss of neurons (Mann, 1985). What causes the loss and shrinkage of cells is not known. There appears to be a process of degeneration of nerve cells that primarily and initially involves the dendritic tree of neurons. The loss of dendritic surface area would impair synaptic transmission and nerve conduction in the central nervous system, and the cells themselves may undergo a kind of denervation atrophy as dendritic connections are lost.

Granulovacuolar degeneration. Granulovacuolar degeneration is a neuronal cytoplasmic process in which membrane-bound granules collect within the nerve cells as part of the degenerative process. This process is accelerated in Alzheimer's disease. Accumulation of lipofuscin pigment in the brain cells is also a feature of the disease, but this is seen in the normal aged brain and its pathologic significance is not clear. The changes may reflect the accumulation of materials by nerve cells and the way in which the material is packaged into granules and acted on enzymatically. The longer a person lives, the more materials might accumulate within the nerve cells, since these cells do not turn over at all, and there may be no particular damage wrought by these granules and pigment bodies.

Neurofibrillary tangles. Neurofibrillary tangles are an important feature of Alzheimer's disease, even though the normal, aged brain does contain them to a much lesser degree. There are other nervous system diseases that are associated with tangles, but their appearance in an Alzheimer brain is an important diagnostic criteria at autopsy. Neurofibrillary tangles are found within the cytoplasm of nerve cells and are most commonly found in the temporal cortex, hippocampus, and amygdala. The number and extent of tangles correlate with the clinical symptoms of dementia. The tangles are composed of highly insoluble filaments, which are present in pairs, and each filament is a tightly wound helix. Usually they are tightly packed masses, which can take up almost all of the cytoplasm of the neuronal cell. This may lead to damage to cytoplasmic organelles such as mitochondria and endoplasmic reticulum. The exact nature of the filaments is not known, but most researchers agree that they are ultimately formed from components of the cytoskeleton. The neurofilamentous material that accumulates may be the result of abnormal protein synthesis by the cell or may more likely represent a response of the cell to injury. For example, at the dendritic ending some sort of damage might obstruct neuronal flow through cytoskeletal tubules, leading to damage to the cytoskeleton as reflected by the development of tangles. Because tangles do appear in other diseases, the latter is a reasonable hypothesis.

Senile plaques. Senile plaques, although present to a small degree in the normal, aged brain, are many times more frequent in patient's with Alzheimer's disease. These plaques are composed of destroyed dendrites, terminal axons, synapses, glial cells, and a core of amyloid, as previously described. The neuronal cell material that is present often contains neurofibrillary tangles. The plaques are generally round, microscopic structures. They are often found close to blood vessels and are most prevalent in the frontal and temporal cortex. The senile plaque could represent a brain response to injury. In injury swollen, damaged nerve endings provoke a response from the microglial cells, which surround the damaged neuritic material. The source of the deposits of excessive amyloid protein is probably neuronal cells, but brain vascular endothelial cells could also be involved. There may be a large circulating amyloid precursor that deposits into the walls of the cerebral blood vessels or leaks into the brain through a damaged blood-brain barrier in Alzheimer's disease. Thus the defect may be abnormal amyloid, excessive amyloid, or a combination of either with some agent that damages the vascular endothelium, leading to amyloid deposition. Some researchers believe that amyloid is the end product of an antigen-antibody reaction (Mann, 1985).

Electroencephalogram changes. Many studies have shown that there are nonspecific EEG changes in Alzheimer's disease. In general there is increased, slow wave activity and increased latency in evoked potentials. These changes would generally reflect a general diminution of brain activity, synaptic transmission, and conduction, indications of overall brain cell loss, and decreased metabolic activity.

Neurotransmitter changes. Much of the neuritic damage in Alzheimer's disease appears to involve cholinergic neurons, although other systems (dopaminergic, catecholaminergic) are affected but not to the same degree. There is a 20% reduction in choline acetyltransferase in Alzheimer's disease. This would indicate a deficit in presynaptic cholinergic neurons, because this enzyme is required for acetylcholine synthesis (Kwnetus et al., 1986). The nucleus basalis of Meynet is particularly affected in Alzheimer's disease, showing a marked loss of cholonergic neurons. This structure is part of the basal forebrain cholinergic system, the neurons of which project to many areas of the brain, including the hippocampus, amygdala, and neocortex. Marked cholinergic denervation could help explain the loss of memory, attention, and behavioral function that occurs in Alzheimer's disease. Some patients with Parkinson's disease have an associated dementia, and this may be due to a loss of cholinergic neurons, similar in cause to that occuring in Alzheimer's disease. Plaque formation has been reported to be increased in the brains of such patients.

It has been speculated that the loss of cholinergic neurons in the nucleus basalis participates in the development of cortical plaques (Price et al., 1985). Cholinergic neuritic processes are present in some plaques, and plaques appear to develop in the areas of the brain to which the nucleus basalis projects. The exact mechanism by which the neuronal loss could lead to senile plaque formation is not known. It is also possible that retrograde factors from other parts of the brain cause the deficit in the nucleus basalis, rather than the deficit originating at this locus.

Pathophysiologic considerations. Genetic theories of Alzheimer's disease have already been described. Whether the disease will eventually be traced to a single defective gene or whether many genes are involved is a matter for speculation. In cases where a familial basis is not readily apparent, it may be that genetic variability at particular genetic loci could produce a susceptibility to exogenous agents and result in the disease. Some of the exogenous agents that have been proposed as important in the cause of Alzheimer's include viruses, metal ion exposure (particularly aluminum), and autoimmunologic factors.

Viruses. Speculation exists that Alzheimer's disease could be caused by a slow virus infection of the brain. Slow viruses include the agents that cause the disease scrapies in sheep, and Creutzfeld-Jacob disease and Kuru in human beings. Creutzfeld-Jacob disease is associated with dementia and rapidly developing motor symptoms and occurs with the highest frequency among Libyan Jews. However, it is generally thought that genetic background would predispose to infection with a transmissable agent, rather than it being a true genetic disease. Kuru, which is spread by cannibalism of nervous tissue, is chiefly a disease of the Fore tribesmen of New Guinea. It was believed that the eating of a dead relative's brain would confer special properties upon the partaker. Unfortunately if the deceased died of kuru, the viral agent spreads to the brain, producing eventual dementia and death. The latency for kuru can be as long as 20 years. All of these diseases share a long latency period, during which the viruses are present in the brain. Symptoms develop slowly, eventually resulting in dendritic degeneration and, in some cases, plaque formation and amyloid deposition. The infectious agents in these diseases are not believed to be conventional viruses. They are smaller and are thought to be DNA in nature. The genetics of Alzheimer's disease might interact with an exogenous virus, in terms of immunologic resistance or blood-brain barrier integrity. In this model of Alzheimer's disease, the nonfamilial form would be a result of slow virus infection. This theory of causation was popular 10 years ago, but little experimental support has been gathered to favor it.

Metal ions. The popular press has certainly expounded on the research that suggests a role for aluminum in the development of Alzheimer's disease. However, the experimental evidence is questionable. There is evidence that aluminosilicates accumulate in the center of the senile plaque (Candy et al., 1986). Aluminosilicate could possibly initiate the development of the senile plaque, or it could accumulate there as a result of the disease itself. Aluminum salts can induce neurofibrillary tangles, and the metal can be found localized to neurons containing tangles. Acute aluminum toxicity is associated with neurologic symptoms. Evidence opposing the metal ion hypothesis is that there is no greater incidence of Alzheimer's disease in aluminum workers and that aluminum and other metal ion concentrations in the brain increase in many neurologic diseases. Thus the presence of the metal may merely reflect the disordered pathophysiology of the diseased brain, rather than being etiologic. Aluminum is present in food and water sources and in cosmetic products such as antiperspirants. Until a role for metal ions in the development of the disease is clearly available, caution should be used in attributing Alzheimer's to metal ion intoxication.

Treatment rationale. Current treatment for this disease is largely supportive for both the patient and the family. Patients may live 10 years or longer with this disease, and they usually require close custodial care, even in early stages of the disease. Manipulation of the cholinergic systems of the brain through pharmacologic agents has been tried but with largely disappointing results. However, research continually explores possible psychopharmacologic strategies in an effort to halt the progress of this deadly disease. In early disease, there is the future possibility of using fetal brain cell transplants, once this approach is perfected. Brain cell transplants of adrenal tissue have already been used in Parkinson's disease, but with limited success.

INFECTIOUS DISORDERS OF THE NERVOUS SYSTEM

Infection within nervous tissue does not differ dramatically from the infectious process in other tissues, as was outlined in Chapter 2. However, the aspect of repair following acute inflammation and infection is pathophysiologic, because repair is mostly by connective tissue replacement with scar formation. Neuronal loss obviously becomes magnified into functional loss of the body parts innervated or controlled by that part of the brain or spinal cord that has become infected. Cognitive function, memory, learning, and even emotions may all be disrupted if the corresponding parts of the brain are disturbed. Therefore it is imperative to recognize central nervous system infections early and to treat them promptly and aggressively. Such approaches have markedly reduced both mortality and long-term sequelae in meningitis during infancy and childhood. Two models of brain and spinal cord infection will be presented in this section, meningitis and encephalitis.

Meningitis

Meningitis is bacterial infection of the meninges covering the brain and spinal cord. It usually follows an upper respiratory infection in infants and children, although occasionally adults may develop meningitis. The infection may spread from the middle ear through the mastoid bone to the meninges or from the nasal cavity through the sinuses and into the meninges. Usually the onset is sudden and characterized by high fever, irritability, stiff neck, and other signs of increased intracranial pressure. The child may vomit, appear lethargic, and refuse food. If the meningococcal form of meningitis is present, a purpuric rash will be visible, which is readily identifiable. The major causative organisms of bacterial meningitis are *Hemophi-*

lus influenzae, Diplococcus pneumoniae, Neisseria meningitidis, Escherichia coli, and β-hemolytic streptococcus In infancy the diagnosis may be difficult to make, since infants under 3 months of age may not have the typical fever and stiff neck, but signs of increased intracranial pressure are present. A particularly valuable sign is a bulging, tense fontanelle or a sudden increase in head circumference. The spinal fluid pressure is increased with increased levels of protein and polymorphonuclear leukocytes and a decrease in glucose appearing in the cerebrospinal fluid. The fluid will appear cloudy and turbid. The increase in cerebrospinal fluid pressure results from inflammatory exudate and the effects of swelling on the brain volume and perfusion. There may be seizures, especially in infants, that are related to the increased pressure and possibly also to focal brain infection and necrosis. Some patients also develop thrombi within the cerebral vessels and will have focal signs such as hemiplegia or weaknesses. The treatment is appropriate, prompt, and vigorous therapy with antibiotics, and supportive care to prevent fever and dehydration. Most children with meningitis can recover without any long-term effects such as mental retardation or paralysis if they receive adequate antibiotic therapy.

A particularly virulent form of meningitis is meningococcal meningitis caused by Neisseria menigitidis. This form often occurs in epidemics in crowded, unsanitary places. There may be a septicemia preceding the infection of the meninges, with a purpuric rash that results from disseminated intravascular coagulation. The coagulopathy can lead to infarction of the pancreas, producing a state of profound shock (Waterhouse-Fridrichsen syndrome). The areas involved in the skin rash often undergo necrosis, which may necessitate amputation of distal parts such as fingers and toes. The patient with this form of meningitis requires constant, expert care by both physicians and nurses in order to prevent complications and control the disease. The mortality rate is about 15%.

Encephalitis

Although meningitis is a bacterial disease, encephalitis is considered to be viral in origin, although both processes may be present in the patient with a brain infection, and some bacterial encephalitic diseases do exist. Encephalitis involves infection of the brain matter itself, and usually there is infiltration into the meninges as well. The damage is caused by neuronal invasion, infection, and death, and there are generalized inflammmatory changes within both the gray and white matter. Causes of viral encephalitis in humans include arthropod-carried virus, such as St. Louis encephalitis or Western equine encephalitis (commonly called sleeping sickness), mumps virus, herpes simplex, Epstein-Barr virus, and rabies, polio, and Coxsackie viruses.

An encephalitis syndrome can occur after many different viral diseases of childhood, but it appears to be the result of process that is secondary to the viral illness and may involve an immune response.

The signs and symptoms of encephalitis develop fairly gradually and include headache, fever, and signs of increased intracranial pressure and meningeal irritation. Most patients develop some changes in the sensorium, with the most dramatic being coma, which can last several weeks. The most common form of viral encephalitis is that following mumps infection in children. Usually the encephalitis appears concomitantly with the signs of mumps (i.e., swelling of the parotid gland and fever). This form does not usually have a very high mortality rate, nor is there serious neurologic damage as a sequela, but nerve deafness can occur and is usually permanent. The Western equine encephalitis may occur in epidemic form and is carried from its primary host, the horse, to humans through a mosquito vector. In many cases there also appears to be an intermediate bird vector. Control of the epidemic is through elimination of mosquito breeding places, which usually are small puddles in residential areas. This form of encephalitis can result in marked changes in sensorium and behavior, and coma can be quite prolonged, but complete recovery is usually possible.

Treatment is supportive, because there are no antiviral agents that effectively destroy the viruses, except in the case of herpes simplex encephalitis, which is treated with adenosine arabinoside.

Reye's syndrome

One of the most devastating complications of viral illness in children occurs from 10 to 14 days after the child has apparently recovered. This is a type of encephalopathy known as Reye's syndrome. One of the most common viral illnesses with this sequela is chickenpox. Some believe that the incidence of this syndrome is increasing, whereas others feel that identification of the condition has improved while the incidence has remained stable. Reye's syndrome is a virally produced encephalopathy involving many systems of the body, including the central nervous system.

The earliest sign of the disease is vomiting, which is followed by behavioral changes, confusion, and shouting. The child lapses into coma, the treatment of which is incredibly complex. Reye's syndrome appears to affect the liver as one of its target organs. There is a typical accumulation of lipid in the liver and disturbed architecture of the hepatic mitochondria and other cellular organelles.

The hepatic function becomes extremely poor; as a result, the liver becomes unable to detoxify ammonia, which accumulates in the blood. A type of hepatic coma ensues as a result of ammonia toxicity. However, the brain cells of the patient with Reye's syndrome show the same characteristic changes in mitochondria and there is cerebral edema, neither of which is the direct result of ammonia toxicity. The cerebral edema causes most of the pathophysiologic effects in Reye's syndrome; liver damage is reparable.

One third of the children who develop Reye's syndrome either die or have permanent brain damage. Because of a possible association between aspirin usage during an influenza-chickenpox infection and the ultimate development of Reye's syndrome there is a general recommendation to treat children's fever during viral illnesses with a nonsalicylate antipyretic such as acetaminophen. Early recognition of the condition, public education about it, and very aggressive treatment of children with the full-blown condition may decrease the morbidity now associated with Reye's syndrome. In the meantime it remains a very mysterious and deadly killer of children.

Another syndrome associated with suspected viral causation is Guillian-Barré syndrome. The following case study illustrates an unusual presentation of this polyneuritis, the development of the disease during pregnancy.

CASE STUDY: GUILLIAN-BARRÉ SYNDROME DURING PREGNANCY

History

CS is a 19-year-old married female with a past history that is unremarkable except

Contributed by Pat Droppleman.

for several episodes of bronchitis. She is a gravida, para 0 who was 18-weeks pregnant on admission to the emergency room at a local hospital.

Present illness: CS was admitted to the hospital via the emergency room complaining of nausea and vomiting and headache for 5 days duration. She experienced generalized weakness of all extremities for 2 days. The weakness began in her legs; the following day it had progressed to her upper arms, and it continues to worsen. She was unable to eat any food for 4 days before admission. She has no history of recent viral illness, diarrhea, or fever, nor has she been exposed to lead, chemicals, or insecticides. Initial examination revealed the following.

General

Well developed; 5 feet, 7 inches; 128-pound female who is mildly lethargic, reonsive, coherent, and pregnant.

Vital signs:

Temperature: 98° F

Pulse rate: 78/minute

Respiratory rate: 16/minute

Blood pressure: 110/62

Physical examination:

Skin: clear

PERRLA

Neck: nuchal rigidity positive, no bruits

Respiratory: diminished breath sounds in right lung; rales in left base; bilateral tenderness in lower back

Cardiovascular:

NSR without murmur

Abdominal:

Bowel sounds present in all quadrants

Neurologic:

Cranial and motor testing reveal generalized weakness in all muscle groups of the upper and lower extremities; decreased sensation to pin pricks in both lower extremities from hip to toe and decreased sensation in upper extremities with sensory deficit decreased proximally. Deep tendon reflex response in the biceps muscle is absent bilaterally. Patellar response is minimal. Babinski sign is negative.

Initial laboratory values

WBC: 11,100 HPF

Lumbar puncture: 2 WBCs

3 RBCs

0 Gram

Protein: 56

Glucose: 65

Blood glucose: 108

Chest x-ray: normal

Laboratory values 24 hours after admission

PH: 7.3

Pco^2: 46.4

Po^2: 13.8 with 99% saturation

FIo^2: 30% with 7.5 cms PEEP

CBC: 18,400 cells/mm^3

Hgb: 10.3 gm/dl

HCT: 30%

Platelets: 396,000 mm^3

Segs: 33%

Bands: 6%

Lymphs: 29%

Monos: 3%

BUN: 12 mg/dl

Creatinine: 0.5 mg/dl

SGOT: 103

Diagnosis

Guillain-Barré syndrome during pregnancy

Treatment

CS was admitted to the respiratory floor under close observation. Within 2 hours she developed metabolic acidosis and respiratory alkalosis and was moved to the intensive care unit. Because of decreased ability to maintain spontaneous ventilation and falling Po^2 the patient was intubated and within 24 hours she was unable to move anything voluntarily below her neck. She had sensory deficits and was areflexic. She could not blink, swallow, or talk. An ultrasound to assess fetal age and status revealed a single fetus, a normal amount of amniotic fluid, and fetal measurements consistent with an 18- to 19-week old gestation. The diagnosis of Gullain-Barré syndrome was confirmed. CS had a long, difficult medical course. She experienced atelectasis, right lower lobe pneumonitis, recurrent urinary tract infections, and recurrent bradycardia. She required a tracheostomy because of difficulty ventilating and discomfort from the endotracheal tube resulting from continued muscular paralysis. CS was apathetic, lethargic, chronically depressed, anxious and had recurrent insomnia.

She was required to stay in the intensive care unit for 2 months. An endotracheal tube was in place for 80 days. She had IV therapy via subclavian line and was tube fed. Caloric requirements were adjusted according to the stage of pregnancy and the increasing needs of the fetus. CS received prenatal vitamins and iron via a nasogastric tube. Three weeks after admission, CS was able to swallow occasionally. By the end of the first month she began some spontaneous breathing and minimal movement of the upper right shoulder. Following discharge from the intensive care unit, CS was sent to a respiratory floor for 7 days; physical therapy was begun at this time. Nearly 3 months after admission she was sent to an OB-GYN floor. She had been followed routinely by the obstetric resident staff since admission, but this care was now accelerated. Ultrasound examination to determine fetal growth and organ activity were conducted every 2 weeks; fetal heart tones were evaluated daily; fundal height measurements were taken daily. Nonstress tests were performed every 7 to 8 days. Excellent fetal movements were noted, fetal growth remained consistent with dates, and there was no evidence that the fetus was affected by the Guillain-Barré syndrome. CS continued to regain muscular strength.

Four months after admission CS spontaneously initiated labor at 6:00 a.m. The patient was moderately anxious during contractions but did not appear to have much pain. (She did not have control of

muscles so could not tense them.) She was working with contractions and using Lamaze breathing techniques. She held the hands of both her support persons. The first stage of labor lasted 2.75 hours. After 20″ pushing the patient appeared exhausted and was taken to the delivery room. The second stage of labor lasted 30 minutes. After a 3-hour labor, she delivered a 7 pound, ¾ ounce male with Apgar scores of 8 and 9 at 1 and 5 minutes. Pudendal block was used as anesthesia, and low forceps were used to assist delivery.

CS and baby son were discharged from the hospital 1 week later. A hospital bed, reclining chair, and wheelchair were sent home with her. Nursing care was provided by the hospital's home health agency. CS returned to the hospital weekly for physical therapy and follow-up by the obstetric staff for 2 months. Five weeks after discharge, CS was able to move from a lying position to a sitting position but continued to require assistance with the majority of activities of daily living. Abduction and adduction of thighs was evident as well as some spontaneous movement of lower legs. Fine motor coordination in both hands was still impaired. Bladder control was intact; the patient needed enemas for bowel control.

Pathophysiology

Guillain-Barré syndrome (GBS) is an acute polyneuritis of unknown etiology, although viral and immunologic causes are suspected. It may occur following influenza immunization in rare cases. It is a disorder of the peripheral nervous system that involves both sensory and motor components. It is the most commonly occurring neuropathy (incidence is 1.7 cases per 100,000 individuals). It rarely occurs in pregnancy. In fact, in a review of the world literature only 30 cases were documented. This is case no. 31. GBS patients diagnosed in the first or second trimester have an excellent prognosis for normal vaginal delivery at term. Efficient uterine contractions occur spontaneously despite the neurologic deficit.

About 50% of people with GBS have histories of mild febrile illnesses preceding the onset of symptoms by 1 to 3 weeks. One week before hospitalization this patient had a slight fever, anorexia, nausea, and malaise 3 days before admission. There is some evidence for an etiologic role for herpes viruses in GBS, Epstein Barr Virus (EBV), and cytomegalovirus (CMV) being particularly implicated (Adams and Victor, 1985). The disease is a demyelinating polyneuritis, affecting the more heavily myelinated fibers, and there is evidence of T lymphocyte mediated segmental destruction of the myelin. This patient had a positive CMV titer on admission, indicating exposure or possibly reactivation of the virus. The T cell attack may be precipitated by the viral infection, but in most cases it is a temporary immunological aberration. Some people do have recurrences of the disease after apparent full recovery, and some develop a chronic, severe peripheral polyneuritis.

Nursing Diagnosis

1. Impaired physical mobility related to neurologic deficit
2. Ineffective breathing pattern related to neurologic deficit
3. Powerlessness related to disability and pregnancy
4. Potential for disuse syndrome related to immobility
5. Potential altered parenting, difficulty in attachment resulting from limited ability to care for infant
6. Constipation related to neurological deficit
7. Self-care deficit: activities of daily living
8. Anxiety related to ability to care for self and infant

DISORDERS OF CONSCIOUSNESS AND SENSATION

Many of the disorders described in the preceding sections have some associated degree of altered consciousness or sensation. We have described pain in detail in Chapter 12. In this section we will specifically address phenomena such as sleep disorders, coma, and alterations in the function of the special senses. There are certain primary disorders that cause disturbances of consciousness and sensation, but many other disorders have these problems as secondary effects.

Decreased level of consciousness is seen in many different types of neurologic disorders, yet it is important to understand the pathophysiologic processes involved in coma, since such information may be necessary to care for and communicate with a patient suffering a decreased level of consciousness.

Sleep disorder represents another common category of problems in neurologically impaired patients and even more importantly, in hospitalized patients in general. Although sleep deprivation is common in such patients, its role in perpetuating pathophysiologic disruptions of the steady state is not well recognized. The physiology and pathophysiology of sleep are areas of much new and exciting research having great implications for the care, nurturing, and treatment of ill people.

Sleep disorders

The necessity for sleep is common to the entire animal kingdom, and disorders of sleep are one of our most common and most disturbing ailments. The quality and quantity of sleep are good indicators of the general state of wellness of an individual. Wellness cannot be preserved in the absence of adequate sleep, and without this the person becomes unable to adapt to change and to handle stressors appropriately. There are both physiologic and psychologic perturbations in the sleep-deprived subject, and these symptoms are well known to any student who has stayed up all night studying for an examination.

It has been known for many years that there are four stages in human sleep. Stage 1 is known as REM (rapid eye movement) sleep; stages 2 through 4 are non-REM (non-rapid eye movement) sleep. Health requires that both types of sleep be experienced in any given night's rest. Compared to non-REM sleep, REM sleep is characterized by low voltage, faster EEG activity. Furthermore, during these periods of sleep, the eyeballs move rapidly back and forth in scanning motion. Other physiologic phenomena occurring during REM sleep include inhibition of muscle activity and a faster heart and respiratory rate, which may also be irregular. Non-REM sleep is marked by higher voltage, slower EEG activity, regular, slow respiratory and cardiac rates, and tonic muscle activity. The eyes are still, and the person appears to be deeply asleep.

Dreaming takes place during both REM and non-REM sleep, but the content and nature of the dreams differ. During REM sleep dreams are irrational and bizarre, whereas non-REM dreams are generally more structured and logical. There are cycles of REM and non-REM sleep, which in the adult last from 80 to 120 minutes. During REM sleep the left cerebral hemisphere appears to be more active according to the EEG, whereas the reverse is true for non-REM sleep. It will be recalled that for righthanded people the right cerebral hemisphere is involved in visual, spatial, artistic, and intuitive types of approaches, whereas the left is the side involved in mathematical, logical, analytical, and language processes. Use of first one side of the brain and then the other during sleep also appears to occur during the waking hours, constituting what is known as the basic rest and activity cycle (BRAC). It has been found that healthy adults have an approximately 90 minute cycle in which cognitive style changes from more verbal to more spatial, (Klein and Armitage, 1979). This type of activity is important to note when studying nervous system pathophysiology, since damage to the left or right cerebral hemispheres may occur in cerebral vascular accidents, trauma, tumors, and infections. Optimal recovery for such patients is therefore dependent on cognizance of their normal capabilities, cerebral dominance, and the BRAC as another perhaps striking variable.

The nature of sleep changes with growth and development and is an index of relative maturation of the human organism. Generally the amount of REM sleep decreases as the child grows. The ratio of REM to non-REM sleep goes from 50:50 in a young child to 20:80 in the adult. Sleep patterns appear very early in the human fetus, and REM sleep is relatively greater in the fetus compared to the neonate. The cycles of REM and non-REM sleep are shorter in the infant, and the distribution of REM sleep throughout the sleep period is quite uniform, whereas in the adult the REM state occurs predominantly in the last third of the night. The importance of this maturational difference is appreciated when examining some of the sleep disorders of the infant and young child.

Sleep apnea. Periods of cessation of breathing lasting for longer than 10 seconds during sleep are classified as sleep apnea. These episodes occur more frequently in premature or small for gestational age infants, but can also occur in full-term and older infants. Incidence of sleep apnea is increased in times of respiratory infections in infants, and some believe that sleep apnea is etiologic in the sudden infant death syndrome (crib death). The period of apnea is accompanied by bradycardia and even cardiac arrhythmias and may occur during REM sleep, at which time it becomes more difficult to arouse the infant. These periods occur more frequently in cases of sleep deprivation regardless of age. Obviously, if an apneic episode continued when arousal mechanisms were diminished, the brain could become subject to hypoxia and further depression, leading to sudden death.

Identification of high risk infants is an important mechanism for preventing sudden death in these infants. The respiratory centers involved in sudden infant death may be either immature or defective. Many of these infants have near-misses but are resuscitated. Many newborns who have been observed to experience sleep apnea while in the intensive care nursery are now being sent home with monitors that will detect a sleep apneic episode and sound an alarm to arouse both the parents and infant.

Sleep apnea in infants appears to be related to immaturity of the respiratory control mechanisms at the nervous system level. However, sleep apnea may also occur in older children, adolescents, and adults. The results of sleep apnea in these populations are excessive sleepiness during the day and other signs of sleep deprivation, such as irritability and difficulty paying attention. Such individuals usually experience very noisy inspiratory snoring followed by an apneic episode that usually lasts a little longer than 20 seconds. On the average individuals with this disorder have as many as 300 episodes per night. These apneic episodes result in disturbances in the normal stages of sleep and length of sleep in the different stages.

There may be long-term sequelae in patients with sleep apnea. Young people often suffer such sleep deprivation that they are classified as mentally retarded or learning disabled. Adults and older children may suffer the long-term effects of chronic alveolar hypoventilation, such as cor pulmonale, pulmonary hypertension, and essential hypertension. In these individuals, the maturity of the respiratory control mechanisms during sleep may be impaired. However, the usual cause is related to upper airway obstruction, such as by enlarged tonsils or adenoids. Sleep apnea may also be associated with the pickwickian syndrome (Chapter 16), with Pierre Robin syndrome (in which there is a very underdeveloped chin), and the Arnold-Chiari syndrome.

Dysomnia and insomnia. Disturbed sleep (dysomnia) or inability to sleep (insomnia) plague people throughout the life cycle. Very often these problems are related to emotional trauma that cause great stress to the individual with the result that neuroendocrine balance may be upset. This factor may be etiologic in the disruption of sleep that follows. Although there are a few individuals who reportedly have no or very little need for sleep, most adults require a minimum of 6 hours per night. When sleep deprivation occurs, experiments show bizarre and uncharacteristic behaviors developing in the sleep-deprived subjects. These include hallucination and feelings of paranoia, inability to concentrate, irritability, and anxiety. Early research seemed to indicate that REM sleep deprivation led to acute psychiatric disruption, but later research indicates that there are no long-term sequelae of REM sleep deprivation. The biologic role of REM sleep is currently being investigated in many laboratories, as is the role of sleep in general. There seems to be an association of serotonergic influences on sleep, and in individuals suffering from insomnia or dysomnia it is certainly possible that some problem in brain monoamine metabolism is present.

Narcolepsy. Narcolepsy is an uncommon disorder in which individuals fall subject to sleep attacks during the day and have disturbances in REM sleep during the night. The waking EEG of such individuals shows that there are sleep episodes occurring throughout the day indicated by bursts of stage 1 non-REM sleep lasting a few seconds. Severe narcolepsy may be associated with sudden paralysis and collapse in some patients. More commonly there are attacks of inability to perform voluntary movements that involve only certain muscle groups. It is thought that narcolepsy, which has a familial basis in many cases, is the result of a disturbance in the mechanisms that regulate REM sleep. The usual time of onset of the condition is in the adolescent or early adult years, and little can be done to treat the problem other than prescription of stimulants and recommendation of frequent napping.

Coma

One of the most massive alterations in consciousness and sensation is the comatose state. The degree of consciousness can be graded according to the responsiveness of the patient:

stuporous Lethargic but arousable; can perform purposeful acts when requested
semicomatose Extremely lethargic; will not perform purposeful acts when requested; withdraws from painful stimuli; shows some spontaneous motor activity
comatose Unresponsive; not arousable; exhibits no withdrawal to painful stimuli; shows decerebrate, decorticate, or opisthotonic positioning of the body and extremities.

In deep coma the normal arousal of the cortex by the reticular activating system is interrupted. However, this does not imply that the patient cannot perceive environmental stimuli. Studies have shown that patients in coma who eventually recover can recall events that occurred while they were supposedly unconscious. The sense of hearing may remain in the unresponsive patient, and it should never be assumed that the comatose patient cannot hear and understand. Comatose patients show signs of autonomic nervous system arousal to particular environmental cues, for example, the entrance of a loved one into the room. Heart rate and blood pressure show increases, which indicate that the patient has some awareness. Although coma is a response to many different pathophysiologic processes that have been described in this chapter, the comatose state should be considered as an entity in itself in any therapeutic plan of care. The effects of immobility will be at a maximum in the comatose patient.

Alterations in the special senses

Visual disturbances. The eyes are in many ways extensions of the brain. The ending of the optic nerve within the retina can actually be visualized with an ophthalmoscope. The eye itself is a very complex structure, and there are many possible disruptions of the eye's function. Rather than attempt to review all of them here, we will focus on one very common disorder of the eye, glaucoma. The reader is referred to the section on diabetes mellitus (Chapter 19) for diabetic retinopathy, and to the section on atherosclerosis (Chapter 17) for hypertensive changes in the eye. Other problems of the eye are covered in more specialized texts.

Glaucoma. Glaucoma is the result of increased intraocular pressure that occurs when there is blockage of the canal of Schlemm. It can be either acute or chronic. The chronic form is the most common, and is known as open angle glaucoma. It occurs more frequently after the age of 30 years, and usually has no associated symptoms until later when vision has been seriously impaired.

The mechanism by which increased intraocular pressure is produced is through obstruction to the normal outflow of aqueous humor, which bathes the lens, the cornea, and the iris. It is formed by the ciliary body and then flows into the anterior chamber (Fig. 10-4). It is drained from the anterior chamber through the canal of Schlemm, which is located at the junction of the sclera and the cornea. From here the fluid is emptied into the venous blood drainage of the eye.

Whether acute or chronic, the end result of glaucoma is visual impairment and even blindness resulting from pressure on the retina and optic nerve. When glaucoma occurs in the acute, congestive form, it is typical for the individual to suffer severe pain and headache, with blurred vision, swelling of the eye, and an irregularly shaped pupil. The patient will often report seeing halos around lights, which may occur during the weeks before the acute attack. The pressure is easily measured by a procedure known as tonometry. Normal pressure is about 20 mm Hg; in acute glaucoma the pressure may exceed 50 mm Hg.

The patient with acute glaucoma must be treated immediately, as this is an emergency situation in which blindness is almost inevitable without treatment. Intraocular pressure can be reduced through

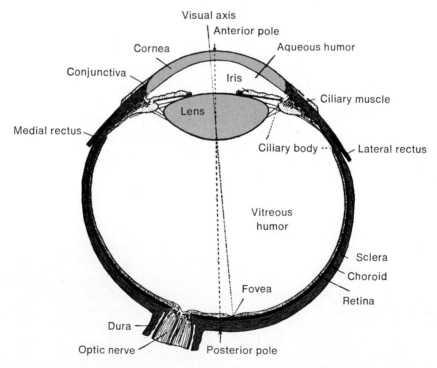

Fig. 10-4. Horizontal meridianal section of right eye.
(Adapted from Bevelander G, and Ramaley JA: Essentials of histology, ed 8, St. Louis, 1979, The CV Mosby Co.)

administration of Pilocarpine drops, Diamox to induce diuresis, and mannitol. After the patient is stabilized peripheral iridectomy is performed. Surgery is usually performed on the other eye also, because in glaucoma the anatomic structure of the anterior chamber is shallow in both eyes, allowing for the eventual possibility of blockage of the canal of Schlemm.

Auditory disturbances. The special sense of hearing is extremely complex, involving many different structures working in harmony within the ear apparatus to achieve audition. Pathophysiologic disruption can of course occur at any point in this pathway. Fig. 10-5 shows the anatomy of the normal ear.

Disruption commonly occurs in infants and children at the level of the middle ear, because of the high incidence of otitis media in this age group (see Chapter 2). Fluid and inflammation in the middle ear impedes the vibration of the ear ossicles and disturbs hearing at this point. Inner ear disorders may be caused through otosclerosis in which overgrowth of bone causes the stapes to be attached to the oval window. Nerve damage to the eighth cranial nerve will also result in deafness. Many drugs have particular toxicities for this nerve; streptomycin is the best known. Loud, continuous noise will also damage this nerve.

Meniere's disease. Meniere's disease is believed to be caused by circulatory disturbances in the vessels supplying the in-

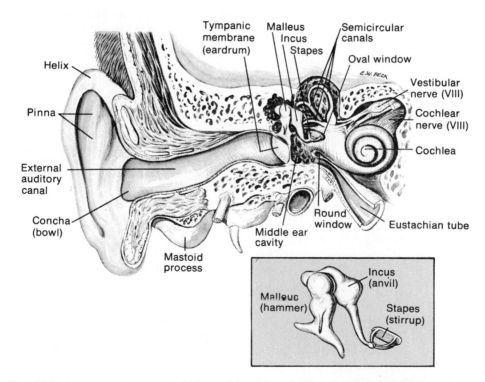

Fig. 10-5. Anatomy of external, middle, and inner ear. Auditory ossicles are shown enlarged in box.

(From Schottelius BA, and Schottelius DD: Textbook of physiology, ed 18, St Louis, 1978, The CV Mosby Co.)

ner ear. The initiating cause of the microcirculatory disturbance originates in the autonomic nervous system leading to dilatation of the membranous labyrinth. Some authorities believe it may be an allergic manifestation.

The symptoms of Meniere's disease are a sense of fullness in the ear, vertigo, tinnitus, hearing loss usually in the low frequency range, nystagmus during the attacks, and nausea and vomiting. This disorder is presented as a model of ear dysfunction because there are both vestibular and auditory problems in Meniere's disease. Some patients will have only vertigo without hearing loss. Meniere's disease often recurs, even after successful treatment. Treatment consists of diuresis, vasodilators, and in some cases allergic desensitization.

SUMMARY

This chapter has examined disorders of the nervous system from a holistic approach, keeping in perspective the tremendously important role that this system has on the maintenance of wellness. It has not been possible to present every condition that affects the central and peripheral nervous systems. By explaining common pathophysiologic mechanisms, we hope that the reader will be able to apply these concepts to any disorders that might be encountered in clinical practice. The disease models that have been described serve to illustrate the pathophysiologic mechanisms and are the most common types of nervous system problems that will be encountered. The view of the nervous system as a "black box" about which we can know nearly nothing is rapidly being discarded as neurophysiology continues to provide new basic information that can be applied to pathophysiologic processes. The discovery of psychoneuroimmunologic pathways and mechanisms is one illustration of this phenomenon. In the near future there should be many new findings of great interest and importance to practitioners of nursing and medicine in the arena of neuroscience.

BIBLIOGRAPHY

Adams RD, and Victor M: Principles of neurology, ed 3, New York, 1985, McGraw-Hill Book Co.

Anders TF, Carskadon MA, and Dement WC: Sleep and sleepiness in children and adolescents, Pediatric Clinic North America 27:29-43, 1980.

Boisson M, and Chalazonitis N: Abnormal neuronal discharge, New York, 1978, Raven Press.

Candy J, et al: Aluminosilicates and senile plaque formation in Alzheimer's disease, The Lancet, February 1986.

Cashman N, et al: Late denervation in patients with antecedent paralytic polimyelitis, N Engl J Med 317:7-12, 1986.

Cervos-Navarro J, and Ferszt R: Brain edema, Advanced Neuro, vol 28, 1980.

Cruz Martinez A, Perez Conde MC, and Ferrer MT: Chronic partial denervation is more widespread than is suspected clinically in paralytic poliomyelitis: electrophysiological study, Eur Neuro 22:314-321, 1983.

Dalakas M, et al: A long term follow-up study of patients with post-polimyelitis neuromuscular symptoms, N Engl J Med 314:959-963, 1986.

Faden A, Jacobs T, and Holaday J: Opiate antagonist improves neurological recovery after spinal injury, Science 211:493-4, 1981.

Fahn S, Davis J, and Rowland L: Cerebral hypoxia and its consequences, Advanced Neuro vol 26, 1979.

Fox, J: The brain's dynamic way of keeping touch, Science 225:820-822, 1984.

Goldgaber D, et al: Characterization and chromosomal localization of DNA encoding brain amyloid of Alzheimer's disease, Science 235:877-880, 1987.

Gorelik P: Pathophysiology and diagnosis in nursing clinics of North America, Cerebrovascular Disease 21:275-288, 1986.

Hallstead L, Wiechers D, and Rossi C: Part II: Results of a survey of 210 polio survivors, Southern Medical Journal 78:1281-1287, 1985.

Holden C: Behavioral medicine: an emerging field, Science 209:479-481, 1980.

Klein R, and Armitage R: Rhythms in human performance: 1 ½ hour oscillations in cognitive style, Science 244:1326-1327, 1979.

Kolata G: Reys syndrome: a medical mystery, Science 70:1453-1454, 1980.

Kopin IJ: Toxins and Parkinson's disease: MPTP Parkinsonism in humans and animals, Advanced Neuro 45:137-144, 1986.

Kwentus J, et al: Alzheimer's disease, American Journal Medicine 81:91-96, 1986.

Lewin R: Is your brain really necessary? Science 210:1232-1234, 1980.

Mann D: The neuropathology of Alzheimer's disease: a review with pathogenetic, aetiological, and therapeutic considerations, Mechanisms of Ageing and Development 31:213-255, 1985.

Merskey H: Pain and emotion: their correlation in headache, advances in neurology, 33:135-141, 1982.

Pomara N, and Stanley M: The cholinergic hypothesis of memory dysfunction in Alzheimer's disease-revisted, Psychopharmacology Bulletin, 22:110-116, 1986.

Price D, et al: Neurobiological studies of transmitter systems in aging and in Alzheimer-type dementia, Ann NY Acad Sci 457:35-52, 1985.

Prince, D: New perspectives on Alzheimer's disease, Ann Rev Neuroscience 9:489-512, 1986.

Rothman E, and Collins R: Seizures in neurological pathophysiology, ed 3, New York, 1988, Oxford University Press.

Selkow D, et al: Conservation of brain amyloid proteins in aged mammals and humans with Alzheimer's disease, Science 235:874-877, 1987.

Sinex FM and Myers R: Alzheimer's disease, Down's syndrome, and aging: the genetic approach, Ann N Y Acad Sci 396:3-14, 1982.

Snyder S: Brain peptides as neuotransmitters, Science 209:976-983, 1980.

St. George-Syslop P, et al: The genetic defect causing familial Alzheimer's disease maps on chromosome 21, Science 235:885-890, 1987.

Tanzi R, et al: Amyloid protein gene: cDNA, mRNA distribution, and genetic linkage near the Alzheimer locus, Science 235:880-884, 1987.

Torlak R: (1978). The pathologic physiology of dementia, New York, 1978, Springer.

Woodbury D, and Kemp J: Basic mechanisms of seizures: neurophysiological and biochemical etiology. In Psychopathology of brain dysfunction, New York, 1977, Raven Press.

11

Psychopathology

Theories about the cause of mental illness have ranged from possession by an evil spirit to the well known psychoanalytical model. There has always been, even in Freud's view, the realization that psychologic processes have a neurochemical substrate. This view became better defined as the profound effects of psychotropic drugs on behavior were observed. A swing toward the belief in a neurochemical basis for all mental illness has gradually occurred. This has been buttressed by genetic studies, biochemical research, and pharmacologic studies. With so much evidence that the chemistry of the brain influences behavior, it might be possible to ignore the alternate process, by which experience and environment alter neurochemistry. A holistic view of mental illness would encompass not only the effect of brain biology on mental function, but also the effect of experiences, interactions, and social influences on brain biology. Many cases of the latter exist, and a striking example is seen in the failure to thrive (FTT) syndrome. In FTT syndrome, infants and young children fail to gain weight, do not mature or develop appropriately, and suffer serious emotional consequences that could lead to behavioral disorders. These infants have no inherent biologic or genetically determined defect of brain chemistry to start with. They are usually children who have suffered profound maternal deprivation and abuse or maternal separation. In many cases, if these children are moved to a loving, supportive environment, they will start to gain weight and catch up developmentally and socially. If the environment can produce so profound an effect that children do not grow, even when they are fed (this is possibly the result of neuronal inhibition of growth hormone release), then obviously physiologic brain function also can be altered. Alterations in brain function could possibly occur as a result of impairment of brain development in the early years, changes in certain brain cell functions, loss of brain cells, and changes in neurotransmitter supply, distribution, and responsiveness. Incredible plasticity of brain function is present in early life. Rosenzweig, Bennett, and Diamond (1972) have shown that early experience and stimulation results in real anatomic changes in rats and that this effect occurs to some degree throughout life. They report increased synaptic connections between neurons and brain growth in response to stimulation. Recent research has also revealed that nerve cell growth potentially occurs in the human brain, throughout life under the influence of nerve growth factor (Marx, 1986). A new concept is that the brain is modeled and remodeled during a person's lifetime in response to endogenous and exogenous influences. The shaping of behavior is not only dependent on genetic factors but is strongly consequent on environmental stimuli.

Neurotransmitters appear to be most important in the etiology of the major mental illnesses—depression, schizophrenia, and anxiety. These diseases may occur as the result of excesses, deficiencies, or imbalances of neurotransmitters or through biochemical pathways that are aberrant, producing abnormal neurotransmitters. This chapter will focus on the pathophysiologic foundations of these disorders and will examine neurotic conditions, drug and alcohol addiction, and anorexia nervosa within a holistic, mind-body framework. This is a difficult task because the biologic substrates of behavior are not well known. The complexity of the brain is so overwhelming that to even begin to pick out possible points of disruption is a formidable task. We shall start with the most common mental illness—depression.

DEPRESSION

In a recent survey, the National Institutes of Mental Health found that one American in five has some type of mental illness (Fox, 1984). Depression is probably the most common psychiatric disease and is a precursor to suicide in most cases. Suicide is the tenth leading cause of death in the overall population, and in certain groups and at certain ages it ranks as the second leading cause of death.

The average age at which depression appears is the mid-twenties. Women have a 25% and men a 10% possibility of experiencing a major depression during their lifetime. It is now clear that the majority of depressive illnesses tend to recur.

General characteristics of the truly depressed state include extreme and hopeless sadness with little relief afforded by the usual activities that had formerly brought pleasure. There is a typical feeling of worthlessness and pessimism, and the individual often has difficulty performing tasks, maintaining a job, and relating to other people. There are physical changes in severe depression such as anorexia, weight loss, decreased motor activity, and a variety of aches and pains. Most depressed individuals experience sleep deprivation, since they are unable to sleep for 8 hours at a time, commonly waking in the early morning hours and being unable to return to sleep. About 20% of depressed people have a bipolar disorder in which the depressed episodes alternate with manic episodes. In the latter case the behavior appears to be diametrically opposed to depression, as the individuals appear agitated, excited, restless, and optimistic.

Depression can be classified as situational (i.e., provoked by a life event) or endogenous. Endogenous depression appears to have a biologic basis. Situational depression may also be biochemical in nature but may require a trigger to provoke the neurochemical brain changes. Unipolar depression is not clearly genetic, in contrast to bipolar (manic depression) disease. In studies on twins it has been found that the chance of developing manic depression is 80% in the unaffected twin. Recent studies of the Amish in Pennsylvania have further confirmed a genetic basis to manic depression. This group of individuals provided an excellent way to study the hereditary nature of the disease; detailed family records have been kept for generations and the symptoms of depression are easily observed in this population. The pattern of inheritance indicates that a single gene may be responsible, and the disease appears to be autosomal dominant with incomplete penetrance (Kolata, 1986). With this pattern, about 25% of the children of an affected parent develop manic depression during their lifetime. Exogenous factors are obviously important in allowing full expression of the genotype. It is of interest to note that the presence of the disease does not necessarily incapacitate an individual. Extraordinary creativity in poets, writers, and artists may coexist with bipolar disease and in fact may enhance aspects of that creativity (Holden, 1986).

Although bipolar disease may appear at first to be quite distinct from endogenous depression, one third of endogenous depression may actually be bipolar under certain circumstances. For example, "switching" from the depressive state to a manic state may occur when the person is given antidepressive medications.

Depression appears to be associated with monoamine concentration or availability in the brain. Fig. 11-1 illustrates the biochemical pathways involved in monoamine synthesis within the brain. These catecholamines are major, central neurotransmitters. Their concentrations are carefully controlled by reuptake into presynaptic membranes, by enzymatic removal through enzymes such as monoamine oxidase and catechol-o-methyl transferase, and by postsynaptic receptor binding. Fig. 11-2 illustrates these mechanisms for a dopaminergic neuron. The monoamines can be stimulatory or inhibitory, depending on the location and interactions of the neurons. The monoamine hypothesis of depression implicates primary deficiencies of dopamine (particularly in depressives with profound motor retardation) and serotonin (5-HT) and probably secondary deficiency of norepinephrine in the brain (Wood and Coppen, 1980). This theory is supported in several ways. First, many of the drugs (mono-amine oxidase inhibitors and tricyclics), which are effective in treating endogenous depression, act to increase brain catecholamines. Second, metabolic end-products of catecholamine breakdown can be measured in the urine; they are decreased during depression and increased during mania. This effect is not uniformly seen however. In some cases levels may actually be increased during depression, possibly indicating that the brain is unable to use the monoamines. Finally, the symptoms of depression have occasionally been produced in people treated for hypertension with the drug reserpine. Reserpine inhibits the reuptake of monoamines and eventually causes a decreased amount of brain monoamine neurotransmitter.

Some of the biologic markers of depression are (1) electroencephalograph evidence of decreased REM latency, such that the person develops REM sleep much earlier than normal, (2) impaired growth hormone release during sleep, and (3) loss of normal limbic system control of the hypothalamic-hypophyseal-adrenal cortex axis, such that an excessive amount of cortisone is produced. A test for depression is the dexamethasone suppression test. A synthetic corticosteroid, which normally suppresses the release of cortisone via inhibition of ACTH release by the anterior hypophysis, is administered. However, if hypothalamic drive, which is strongly affected by cortical innervation and normally inhibited through a noradrenalin pathway, overcomes dexamethasone suppression, this is evidence of abnormal neurologic regulation. The presence of hypercortisolism with early escape from dexamethasone suppression is therefore an important marker of endogenous depression. Not only is cortisone secretion increased, but the normal circadian rhythm of its secretion is lost.

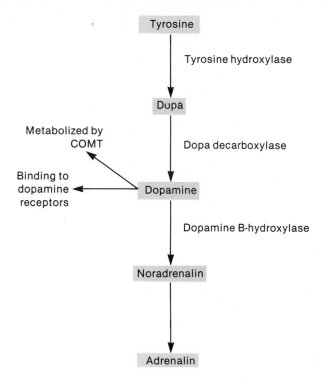

COMT = catechol-o-methyltransferase

Fig. 11-1. Synthetic pathway for monoamines in the brain. (*COMT,* Catechol-o-methyl transferase.)

Another type of depression may yield clues to the cause of depression generally. With *seasonal affective disorder,* people become profoundly depressed during the winter months and are normal during the summer. This type of depression is sometimes cured by moving to the southern hemisphere. It appears that the cause of seasonal depression involves light exposure—there is insufficient light during the short winter days. The role of the pineal gland in this disease is probably important; this gland has direct connection to the ocular apparatus and secretes mela-

tonin (which may have an effect on ACTH). Circadian rhythmicity is timed in part by the operation of this gland. Using artificial lights to increase light exposure by several hours during the early morning in winter can produce dramatic affective changes in these patients.

A current theory of depression postulates that the adrenergic receptors in the brain are altered. This theory suggests that the alpha and beta adrenergic receptors exhibit hypersensitivity or hyposensitivity (up and down regulation) in the states of mania and depression. The anti-

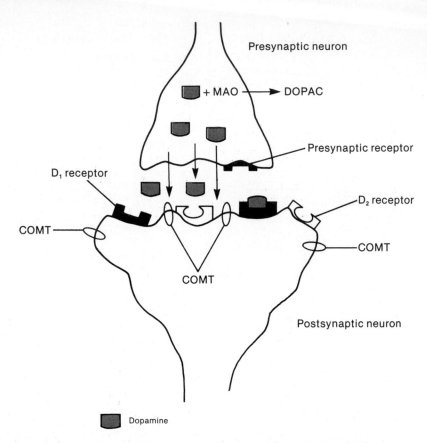

Fig. 11-2. Dopamine is synthesized in the presynaptic neuron and is either enzymatically destroyed (MAO and COMT) or binds to D_1 and D_2 receptors on the post-synaptic neurons membrane (*COMT*, Catechol-o-methyl transferase; *MAO*, monoamine oxidase; *DOPAC*, dihydroxyphenyl acetic acid.)

depressant medications have been shown to affect these receptors, and the defect in this disease may therefore be one of the membrane receptors to different neurotransmitters. Other possible membrane receptors that may be involved according to new research are the cholinergic and the histamine (H-2) receptors. Obviously, no clear answers to the problem of the pathophysiology of either the unipolar depressed state or the bipolar condition of manic-depression have as yet been arrived at, but many new research approaches are being tried. Lithium administration signif-

icantly decreases the number of manic episodes in manic-depressive patients and appears to also lessen the severity of the depressive state. The mode of action of lithium is not known, as it affects many systems of the body in many different ways, but it is possible that it alters the catecholamine concentration of the brain or cell membrane–bound adenyl cyclase activity. Lithium may substitute for calcium or increase its influx into cells upon depolarization; calcium is needed for neurotransmitter release.

Depression is characterized by neurochemical deficits in monoamines, although it is likely that depletion in specific tracts and locations is more important than generalized deficiency. Depression is a brain state, but it is necessary to ask whether situations and events can actually cause this brain state to develop. Little research has been done on this important question, but some evidence indicates that the neurobiologic effects of prolonged stress are similar to those changes found in depression (Gilbert, 1984). This includes hypothalamic changes and probable changes in higher centers. The depressed person appears in some ways to have a deficit in coping. In animal models studied, the response to inescapable stress included a decreased noradrenalin concentration in the dorsal bundle pathway. This neurologic structure appears important because lesions here cause deficits in an animal's ability to extinguish behavior that is not rewarded. Certainly there is some analogy here to the way depressed patients handle information and make decisions, as well as being of behavioral import (Weingartner et al., 1981).

Further research will expand our understanding of the neurochemical changes that occur in depression. Research will also help us to understand the neurochemical responses of the brain to inescapable and escapable stress, separation, isolation, lack of social support, helplessness, and other social and psychologic factors important in the human experience.

CASE STUDY: POSTPARTUM DEPRESSION

History

MC is an 18-year old female who comes to the office for her 6-week postpartum

Contributed by Kay Bultemeier.

examination. She is accompanied by her mother. Mary had an uneventful pregnancy and vaginally delivered a 7 lb 11 oz male child. She is single, but the father of the child is quite involved in the care of the child. Mary lives with her natural mother and father. Since delivery, Mary complains that she has not felt well. She is totally unable to care for her child and cries all day. She states that she eats "okay" but sleeps almost all the time or just lies in bed. She has not resumed any of her predelivery interests or activities. When she was asked how we could help, her response was, "just make me feel better."

Subjective and Objective Data

Physical examination
Weight: 127 lbs
Temperature: 98.6°F
Blood pressure: 110/62
Hemoglobin: 12.6 gm/dl
Urine: Negative
General appearance: Crying, dejected-appearing female in no acute distress
Neck: Thyroid not palpable, no lymphadenopathy
Lungs: Clear to auscultation
Heart: Regular rhythm without murmur
Abdomen: Soft, scattered striae, no organomegaly, no tenderness
Genitalia: Episiotomy well healed, no lesions
Vagina: Pink, ruggated, no discharge
Cervix: Multip, no erosion or bleeding
Uterus: Anteverted, nontender, normal size
Adenexa: Ovaries without enlargement

Treatment

It was determined that MC was suffering from postpartum depression. She was referred to a psychiatric social worker and subsequently placed on antidepressants for 4 months. Her symptoms completely resolved within 3 weeks of beginning the antidepressants. Symptoms did not return after discontinuation of the medication.

Pathophysiology

Very few studies have been made on postpartum depression. It is estimated that 50% to 70% of women will notice slight mood changes in the first 10 days after delivery. These are believed to be related to personal insecurity factors and to adapting to the maternal role model. When the concerns are short-lived, no psychiatric intervention is needed. In MC's case, we have classic symptoms of depression, including alteration of mood, apathy, negative self-image, isolation, change in appetite, and hopelessness. The chronicity of the problem is the concern.

Some investigators believe that the drastic reductions of estrogen and progesterone postpartum are the cause of depressive symptoms. Patients more likely to be affected are those with lower estrogen levels postpartum and those with the largest drops in progesterone. These hormonal levels may explain the mood changes in the first 2 weeks after delivery.

In Mary's case, her symptoms persisted too long to be considered hormonally mediated. Some investigators have found that major depression is more common in women at various stages in their reproductive lives, most noticeably near menarche, after childbirth, and perimenopausally.

Nursing Diagnosis

1. Diversional activity deficit related to depression
2. Alteration in parenting related to depression
3. Impaired physical mobility related to inactivity and excessive sleep

SCHIZOPHRENIA

Schizophrenia is a syndrome in which the patient has difficulty distinguishing reality and fantasy. There is usually some type of motor derangement ranging from increased disordered activity to greatly diminished activity, a state called catatonia. Other characteristics of the disease include feelings of depersonalization, paranoia, delusions, and hallucinations. Schizophrenia appears in young adults who usually have a history of being introverted and withdrawn. Schizophrenics find it difficult to focus on one thing at a time and to express appropriate ideas or emotions. It occurs in about 150 per 100,000 individuals each year.

The genetic background for schizophrenia is much less clear cut than that for manic depression, and it is believed that most schizophrenia is polygenic and multifactorial. The general estimates for risk are 20% to 75% for monozygotic twins, 40% to 68% for children of two affected parents, and less than 10% for children of one schizophrenic parent (Rosenthal, 1980).

An interesting marker of risk for schizophrenia has been reported as abnormal eye tracking (Holzman, 1985), which is seen in schizophrenic individuals and their first degree relatives. There is difficulty in smoothly following a moving object with the eyes, and a series of interrupted, jerky eye movements are found. Since this risk factor has an apparent genetic basis, it is used as evidence for a single, dominant gene controlling the expression of schizophrenia.

There are two main theories of biochemical causation for schizophrenia. The best documented theory implicates an imbalance in the dopaminergic transmission in certain areas of the brain (Spokes, 1980). There are three main nerve tracts within the brain in which dopamine appears to be the main neurotransmitter. These are the mesolimbic, the nigrostriatal, and the tuberoinfundibular tracts. The precise functions of these three areas in the brain are not known in humans, although the tuberoinfundibular system has cell bodies in the hypothalamus, which is a critical area for hormone release, autonomic nervous system function, temperature regulation, hunger, and many other functions. The nigrostriatal tract is thought to be involved in Parkinson's disease and contains 75% of the total dopamine. L-Dopa is the drug of choice for Parkinson's disease, and it is a precursor to dopamine. (Parkinson's disease is described in greater detail on p. 338). The mesolimbic system may possibly be involved in emotional tone and may be the critical area of dysfunction in schizophrenia. Cell bodies arise in the midbrain and supply axons to the limbic system structures.

The best evidence for dopamine excess in schizophrenia comes from pharmacologic studies. These have been mostly inconclusive, but the drugs that are most effective in treating schizophrenia (phenothiazines, butyrophenones) are agents that block dopaminergic transmission. The action of the drugs appears to be through a blocking of postsynaptic dopamine receptors of which there are at least four types. All of these antipsychotic drugs have disturbing extrapyramidal side effects that in many ways are similar to the symptoms and signs of Parkinson's disease, in which cholinergic influence is greater than dopaminergic because of degeneration of the nigrostriatal pathway. Thus the effects of the drugs are to reduce the amount of dopamine available to the neurons and cause cholinergic effects to predominate. The administration of anticholinergic drugs improves these extrapyramidal side effects.

More evidence for dopamine involvement in schizophrenia comes from the effects of amphetamines. These drugs cause many behavioral effects that in some ways resemble the bizarre behaviors of schizophrenia. Large doses in chronic users cause hallucinations, delusions, and stereotyped, repititious, compulsive acts. Included in the latter are acts of grooming, picking at oneself, and taking apart and putting together objects. There is a molecular similarity between amphetamine and dopamine, and its action may be to potentiate dopaminergic neurotransmission. Furthermore, drugs that block dopamine receptors also attenuate the effects of amphetamines.

Dopamine receptors D1 and D2, when bound by dopamine, react either by increasing adenylate cyclase (D1) or by inhibiting its formation (D2) and thus influencing the concentration of postsynaptic cyclic AMP (Fig. 11-2). Although dopaminergic pathways are important in nervous system function, only about 1% of the brain's neurons release dopamine. Excessive amounts of dopamine may not be as significant as alterations in the number or function of dopamine receptors. Recent evidence (Wong et al., 1986) indicates that there is an excess of D2 receptors in schizophrenics that is independent of drug treatment. Excessive dopamine stimulation of postsynaptic neurons is the result of excessive binding due to an increased receptor concentration. Mesolimbic and mesocortical projections that are excessively activated could explain the highly aroused state and some of the most common behavioral and cognitive disturbances in schizophrenia.

A second theory of schizophrenia is that the disorder results from the formation of endogenous psychosis-producing substances within the brain. Many of the endogenous hallucinogenic compounds that have been analyzed are biochemically very similar to known neurotransmitters. Most of them, including lysergic acid diethylamide (LSD) and mescaline, are merely methylated derivatives of dopamine and serotonin. Some studies have shown the existence of small amounts of these methylated hallucinogens in the urine of schizophrenic patients. It is not known whether many normal people also have such substances present but merely utilize them differently. It has recently been shown that LSD and other hallucinogenic drugs act by specific, serotonin receptor binding in the brain (Jacobs, 1987). Other neurotransmitters, such as dopamine, may be influenced by the serotonin receptors.

Another theory of schizophrenia suggests that the symptoms are the result of an imbalance in endorphin metabolism or levels within the brain. This is based on the findings that an increased concentration of endorphin is present in the cerebrospinal fluid of schizophrenics, and hallucinations are alleviated in some schizophrenic patients receiving the opiate antagonist naloxone. It is also known that opiates increase dopamine release in the corpus striatum. However, there is also evidence that a natural endorphin has neuroleptic activity, and some schizophrenics respond to endorphin treatment (Nicol and Gottesman, 1983).

Schizophrenics may have anatomic alterations in the brain. Structural changes have been observed in the cortex and limbic system. Changes in ventricle size, decreased blood flow to the frontal cortex, and asymmetry of the right and left amygdala have all been reported (Barnes, 1987). It is not known how important these alterations are, whether they have any etiologic role, or whether they are secondary to the schizophrenic process or to drug treatment.

Recent research is lending support to a left hemispheric dysfunction in schizophrenia (Gur, 1987). The left hemisphere is generally most involved in reasoning and language, two functions profoundly disturbed in schizophrenia. In this disorder there is possibly more dopamine concentrated in the left hemisphere of the brain than in the right. Both soft and hard studies of the left hemisphere indicate disturbances in normal function. Conversely, depression appears to be more involved with right hemisphere deficit, as does anxiety. The right hemisphere is most involved in emotional processing, particularly perception and expression of emotions. In some studies, anxiety also appears to involve function of the right side of the brain.

Although these hypotheses about the etiology of schizophrenia provide the scientist and clinician with some working approaches to the problem, they are far from conclusive. Many other possible biochemical abnormalities have been suggested or actually shown in schizophrenia. Serotonin, GABA, and acetylcholine receptors may all play some role in the pathophysiology.

ANXIETY

The state of acute, unremitting anxiety is another of the very common psychiatric disorders believed to have a neurochemical basis. Tranquilizers used in the treatment of anxiety are among the most commonly prescribed drugs. Leading the list is the drug Valium, which is in a group of drugs known as benzodiazepines. Other common benzodiazepines are Librium and Dalmane. These drugs are mainly used as tranquilizers, muscle relaxants, and sleeping medications. While the biochemical cause of anxiety is unknown, understanding of the effects of the drugs used to treat it has lead to some speculations as to the etiology of the condition. The benzodiazepines seem to exert their effects on inhibitory systems in the brain, particularly

GABA, which is an inhibitory presynaptic and postsynaptic neurotransmitter. GABA-mediated inhibition is widespread throughout the brain and therefore the effects of benzodiazepines are also very diffuse. There is recent work from many laboratories on the interaction of GABA receptors and benzodiazepine receptors. It appears that the GABA receptors and the benzodiazepine receptors interact in such a way that there is facilitation of binding of one when the other is occupied. It is interesting that the benzodiazepines that normally have some anticonvulsant activity greatly enhance this effect when the GABA receptors are occupied. It is possible that a combination of a GABA-like molecule with a benzodiazepine will be a future drug of choice for treatment of convulsive disorders.

The observation that benzodiazepine receptors exist in biologic tissues is an interesting phenomenon in itself. It could imply that there are endogenous antianxiety molecules normally produced as part of the control of behavior, which interact via initial binding to the benzodiazepine receptors. This type of interaction led to the discovery of the brain opiates such as endorphin and the enkephalins, and presumably it will lead to the discovery of some brain mediator that is similar in molecular structure to the benzodiazepines. Recently, a naturally-occurring, anxiety peptide, which binds to the benzodiazepine receptor, has been discovered. The peptide is concentrated in areas of the brain involved in emotion (Marx, 1985). Purines and nicotinamide are physiologic brain substances that have been suggested to have antianxiety effects.

An animal model with perhaps some relevance to anxiety in humans is a mouse strain with a genetic defect that leads to the degeneration of Purkinje cells within the cerebellum. A behavioral effect of this genetic disease is the production of nervous, staggering mice. Even before the development of the degeneration, the number of benzodiazepine receptors within the cerebellum is very significantly decreased. Another piece of evidence for the significance of benzodiazepine receptors is the existence of a rat strain that is by nature highly fearful and that has a decreased number of benzodiazepine receptors within the brain.

ANOREXIA NERVOSA

Eating disorders have reached epidemic proportions among female adolescents in the United States, and bizarre notions of food needs and an inordinant emphasis on extreme thinness have certainly contributed to this rise in incidence. Anorexia nervosa, the extreme result of relentless dieting, exists in approximately 1 in 200 adolescent girls, and about 1 of every 15 anorexic patients is male. The box on p. 390 lists the Feighner criteria for anorexia nervosa (Feighner, 1972). Bulimia, characterized by periodic binging and gorging, is considered a subgroup of the anorexia diagnosis. These individuals often do not suffer extreme emaciation and malnutrition. However, many classic anorectic patients do produce self-inflicted vomiting and overuse laxatives and purgative agents in their attempts to lose weight. Such overuse leads to fluid and electrolyte disorders that can be life-threatening.

Evidence of hypothalamic dysfunction in anorexia-nervosa is reflected by the disturbed release of gonadotropins, secondary amenorrhea, decreased production of thyroid-stimulating hormone and growth hormone, increased production of corticotrophin-releasing hormone (CRH), and hypercortisolism with abnormal dexamethasone suppression. Many of these problems are believed to be the result of weight loss or decreased caloric consumption rather than being a direct result of the disease process.

FEIGHNER CRITERIA FOR ANOREXIA NERVOSA

1. Onset before age 25
2. Anorexia, with at least 25% weight loss
3. Distorted attitude toward eating, weight, and food (denial of illness, enjoyment of weight loss and thinness, unusual handling or hoarding of food)
4. No known medical condition that could cause the anorexia or weight loss
5. No coexisting psychiatric disease
6. At least two of the following: amenorrhea, lanugo, bradycardia, hyperactive periods, bulimia, vomiting

---

The eating disorders of anorexia-nervosa and bulimia have traditionally been considered psychiatric problems that arise from adolescent conflicts involving self-esteem and self-worth. Newer research implicates a possible biologic basis for these disorders. Many anorectic patients are originally obese, and this may or may not be physiologically important. The biologic effects of self-imposed starvation are devastating, and in many cases it has been difficult to distinguish a physiologic cause from effect. Nevertheless, much evidence has accumulated to suggest a link between depression and anorexia, as evidenced by results of studies of genetic, endocrine, neurotransmitter, and pharmacologic factors which are shared by the two disorders. As in depression, a disruption in the hypothalamic-hypophyseal-adrenocortical axis (HHA) exists, causing hypercortisolism and disordered sleep with early onset

of REM sleep (Katz et al., 1984). Bulimic patients more closely resemble endogenously depressed patients than do anorectic patients without the bulimic feature. Nevertheless, the majority of anorectic patients do not appear to suffer endogenous depression per se. When both conditions do exist, it has been suggested by Katz (1984) that the depressed adolescent is trying to gain some sense of control by beginning to self-restrict food. This is a defense against the depression that is further supported by the release of endogenous endorphins that occurs in starvation. Such a situation might serve to reward the starvation behavior by producing a euphoria that counteracts the depression. Other possibilities for the coexistence of the two conditions are obvious. They may in fact share a similar biochemical basis in terms of etiology. The hypercortisolism is the result of excessive secretion of CRH from the hypothalamus, as seen in depression; however, there is greater hypercortisolism in anorexia. In animal studies, starvation and weight loss can precipitate hyperactivity of the hypothalamic neurons that secrete CRH.

The clinical effects of anorexia nervosa relate to the extent of cachexia and malnutrition that develop and to whether laxative and purgative abuse has occurred. Hormonal changes include decreased LH and FSH, resulting from decreased secretion of releasing hormone from the hypothalamus. This appears to be related to body fat composition and weight. The reproductive system reverts to a prepubertal level of functioning, producing amenorrhea. The amenorrhea usually disappears with weight gain, although it may take a long time for normal reproductive function to resume. Other endocrine functions are disturbed in anorexia. Thyroid hormone output is low; there is a decreased basal metabolic rate, lowered body temperature and cardiac output, and poor peripheral circulation with cold extremities.

In line with the typical carbohydrate starvation, there is an increased resting insulin level, a sustained insulin response to glucose loading, and increased amounts of cholesterol and other lipids in the serum. If the patient is engaging in purging, there is often hypoproteinemia, electrolyte depletion (which can lead to serious cardiac dysfunction and even sudden cardiac death), and epilepsy.

Anorexia nervosa is a disease that exemplifies the interactions between mind and body that can result in disease. Although there may or may not be a biochemical cause for the initial disease, the psychologic parameters tend to reinforce in a positive feedback manner the biologic dimensions. The patient begins to diet, somehow this behavior becomes positively reinforced both by psychologic and physiologic "rewards," and the dieting becomes even more extreme until the weight loss produces an emaciated, lean, prepubertal body. Treatment of anorexia therefore must consider both the mind and the body in order to be successful.

SUBSTANCE ABUSE

One of the most serious problems in Western society is substance abuse by both children and adults. Although drug abuse and drug addiction represent a frightening specter, alcohol is by far the most frequently abused chemical substance. Alcoholism is so common that it results in the seventh leading cause of death in the United States—cirrhosis of the liver (Chapter 21). This section will focus on the research that implicates a biochemical and genetic basis to alcohol abuse, tolerance, and addiction. Understanding all such considerations is important in order to give holistic care to the alcoholic patient and to help in the prevention of alcoholism in people who are at risk.

Genetic background

It is only the human species that voluntarily consumes large amounts of ethanol-containing beverages until they become intoxicated. Animals can be made to consume alcohol through various ingenious, experimental paradigms, but human beings need no such artificial devices. Animals generally have an aversion to alcohol and will not ingest more than they can metabolize. They do not become dependent on alcohol (Pohorecky, 1981). There is compelling evidence for a genetic risk for alcoholism in humans. Most of the studies of dizygotic versus monozygotic twins show a great concordance of alcohol related behaviors for the monozygotic twins (Dietrich and McClearn, 1981). Adoption studies and half sibling studies further support genetic influences. There are genetic differences in alcohol dehydrogenase, the enzyme that converts ethanol to acetaldehyde in the liver (Fig. 11-3), and studies have tried to relate these genetic variations with alcoholism risk. Some assumptions of these studies have included the intriguing possibility that acetaldehyde itself can produce chemicals in the brain that increase alcohol drinking. Thus, the way that alcohol is metabolized, which is influenced by genetic variability, will lead to varying amounts of acetaldehyde. This in turn influences further consumption of alcohol. Animal studies further supporting genetic factors in the development of alcoholism include differential EEG responses to alcohol in humans, which appear to be genetically programmed. Thus, one person's behavioral and neurologic response to ingestion of a certain amount of alcohol is markedly different from another

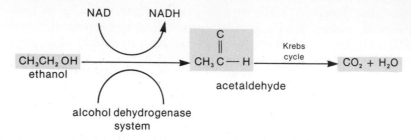

Fig. 11-3. Metabolic handling of ethanol, yielding acetaldehyde.

person's response. Many animal studies also support genetic factors in the central nervous system's response to ethanol. The general conclusion of all studies examining a genetic basis for alcoholism is that there are probably many genes involved. Perhaps there are also many sub-types of alcoholism, and there is a strong interaction of environmental factors with genetics.

Development of alcoholism

Human beings who come to depend on alcohol have both psychologic and physiologic dependency, and the degree of both is observed by the response to alcohol withdrawal. In fact, dependency can only be diagnosed through the reaction of the person to withdrawal. Alcoholism is characterized by dependency and not by the amount of alcohol that is consumed, although these are usually related. The development of tolerance to alcohol is another parameter. The alcoholic individual must ingest more and more alcohol in order to produce the same behavioral effect, and as more is consumed, dependency also increases. Tolerance is manifested at the cellular level by various adaptive mechanisms; enzyme production and membrane functions are altered in order to function in the presence of

ethanol and its metabolic derivatives.

Before we attempt to describe dependency and how it develops, it would be helpful to consider the effects of alcohol on cellular processes. Continued consumption of alcohol damages many organ systems, but those most at risk are the brain, liver, heart, nerves, and pancreas. Ethanol is highly lipid soluble; it quickly passes through the stomach and is absorbed there very quickly. It also passes through other cell membranes and exerts its most immediate effects on the central nervous system. Ethanol may increase the fluidity of the cell membrane, thus altering its electrochemical properties and producing a depression of neurochemical functioning in the brain. Ethanol also acts as a calcium antagonist, thus decreasing calcium transport and intracellular availability. Calcium is important in depolarization, cell membrane receptor function, and many intracellular enzymatic processes. Ethanol also appears to inhibit neurotransmitter function in many ways, leading to central nervous system depression (Littleton, 1981).

The development of alcoholism, which is characterized by tolerance and dependency, requires ingestion of ethanol over time. The amount of time that it takes to develop alcoholism is extremely variable.

People may become psychologically addicted only, physiologically addicted only, or in most cases, both psychologically and physiologically addicted. When tolerance develops, it can be demonstrated at the subcellular and cellular levels and seems to involve membrane and synaptosome lipids and calcium binding. In the liver, metabolism of alcohol is increased as tolerance develops. Dependency on alcohol is also characterized by biochemical changes. For example, fatty acid metabolism is disturbed, and this may contribute to the deposition of triglycerides in organs like the liver. Neurotransmitter metabolism is also altered, particularly that of catecholaminergic neurons. When alcohol is withdrawn from the dependent person, the delirium tremens that result (anxiety, tremors, hallucinations, convulsions) are indicative of responses by an alcohol-adapted central nervous system that can no longer function in the absence of alcohol.

Understanding the biochemical changes that occur as a person becomes dependent on alcohol helps in understanding the symptoms. Eventually, as research in this area continues, prevention and cure may be more realistic goals than they are today. There is no question, however, that psychosocial factors are as important as physiologic ones in the development of an alcohol-abuser from a social and occasional drinker.

SUMMARY

Reviewed in this chapter were behavioral syndromes from a mind-body perspective. The relationships that exist or are speculated to exist between psychology and physiology were clarified. Frank psychosis such as schizophrenia and depressive disorders have strong biologic underpinnings, but even the more neurotic behaviors (anorexia) or dependency disorders (alcoholism) are associated with, and perhaps even caused by, biochemical perturbations. Yet the influence of the environment cannot be factored out, and the nature versus nurture argument still continues. It is clear that even disorders with strong genetic roots may not manifest themselves unless there are psychosocial or environmental disturbances that may alter the brain chemistry and function directly. Certainly the role of stressors and stress in the expression of emotional or psychologic deviations cannot be underemphasized. Nor can the role of positive, supportive, nurturing, and caring environments be ignored in the recovery of the emotionally ill and in the maturation and development of the psyche during childhood.

BIBLIOGRAPHY

Barnes D: Biological issues in schizophrenia, Science 235:430-433, 1987.

Crisp A: Nutritional disorders and the psychiatric state. In Van Praag H, et al, editors: Handbook of biological psychiatry, part IV, Brain mechanisms and abnormal behavior—chemistry, New York, 1981, Marcel Dekker Inc.

Dietrich R and McClearn G: Neurological and genetic aspects of the etiology of alcoholism, Fed Proc 40:2051-2055, 1981.

Feighner JP, et al: Diagnostic criteria for use in psychiatric research, Arch Gen Psychiatry 26:57-63, 1972.

Fox, J: NIMH study finds one in five have disorders, Science 226:324, 1984.

Gilbert P: Depression: from psychology to brain state, New Jersey, 1984, Lawrence Erlbaum Associates, Inc.

Gur, R: Psychiatric disorders as brain dysfunction, National Forum LXVII(no. 2):29-32, 1987.

Holden C: Depression research advances, treatment lags, Science 233:723-726, 1986.

Holzman PS: Eye movement dysfunctions and psychosis, Int Rev Neurobiol 27:179, 1985.

Jacobs, B: How hallucinogenic drugs work, Am Sci 75:386-392, 1987.

Katz J, et al: Is there a relationship between eating

disorder and affective disorder? New evidence from sleep readings, Am J Psychiatry (1984) 141:753-759, 1984.

Kolata G: Manic-depression: is it inherited? Science 232:575-576, 1986.

Littleton J: Biochemical aspects of alcohol tolerance and dependency. In Van Praag H, et al, editors: Handbook of biological psychiatry, part IV, Brain mechanisms and abnormal behavior—chemistry, New York, 1981, Marcel Dekker, Inc.

Marx, J: "Anxiety peptide" found in brain, Science 227:934, 1985.

Marx J: Nerve growth factor acts in brain, Science 232:1341-1342, 1986.

Nicol S and G I: Clues to the genetics and neurobiology of schizophrenia, Am Sci 71:398-404, 1983.

Pohorecky LA: Animal analog of alcohol dependency, Fed Proc 40:2056, 1981.

Rosenthal, D: Genetic aspects of schizophrenia. In Van Praag, H, editor: Handbook of biological psychiatry, part 3, New York, 1980, Marcel Decker, Inc.

Rosenzweig M, Bennett E, and Diamond M: Brain changes in response to experience, Sci Amer 226(2):22-30, 1972.

Spokes E: Biochemical abnormalities in schizophrenia: the dopamine hypothesis. In Curzon, G, editor: The biochemistry of psychiatric disturbances, New York, 1980, John Wiley and Sons, Inc.

Wong DF, et al: Positron emission tomography reveals elevated D2 dopamine receptors in drug-naive schizophrenics, Science 234:1558-1562, 1986.

Wood K and Coppen A: Biochemical abnormalities in depressive illness: tryptophan and 5-hydroxytryptamine. In Curzon G, editor: The biochemistry of psychiatric disturbances, New York, 1980, John Wiley & Sons, Inc. NY: John Wiley & sons, 1980.

UNIT V

Comfort pattern

12

Pain

Pain is a complex, subjective experience that involves physiologic, psychologic, social, cultural, and, for some, spiritual components. Because pain is a symptom of many pathophysiologic conditions, it is a phenomenon that is encountered frequently by the clinician; it may be a response to treatment as well. Pain most often occurs as a response to some health problem; however, in chronic, pathologic pain syndromes it becomes the disease. In many situations pain serves a protective function by alerting the individual to actual or potential tissue damage. It is considered a signal or warning sign in those situations and, as such, indicates the need for action. In other situations, such as with the postoperative patient with incisional pain or the patient with chronic pain syndrome, pain serves no useful purpose.

This chapter will consider current definitions and theories of pain, the neurophysiologic basis for pain, and the physiologic rationale for the treatment of pain. The nursing diagnoses, acute pain and chronic pain are used to organize this discussion of pain as a response to a health problem.

DEFINITIONS AND THEORIES

A variety of definitions of pain are found in the literature. There is probably no one definition of pain that completely describes the concept of pain as a human response to an actual or potential health problem. Pain has been defined as the following:

A subjective experience arising from activity within the brain in response to damage to body tissues, to changes in the function of the brain itself either as a result of damage due to injury or disease, or to changes of a more subtle nature perhaps depending upon biochemical changes which also appear to play a role in producing mental illness (Bond, 1984);

An unpleasant sensory and emotional experience associated with actual or potential tissue damage, or described in terms of such damage (International Association for the Study of Pain Subcommittee on Taxonomy, 1979);

An abstract concept which refers to (1) a personal, private sensation of hurt; (2) a harmful stimulus which signals current and impending tissue damage; (3) a pattern of responses which operates to protect the organism from harm (Sternbach, 1978);

Whatever the experiencing person says it is, existing whenever he says it does (McCaffery, 1979).

Although this list of definitions is not comprehensive, those presented show the variety of types of definitions that have been proposed. Bond's definition is physiologic in nature, whereas Sternbach's tends to be psychologic. The Association's definition is a mix of the two approaches, and McCaffery's definition falls outside of either approach. It is based on the fact that there is a cognitive component to the pain experience and thus it becomes a psychophysiologic phenomenon. Because of this cognitive component, that is determined by past experiences, anticipation, and sociocultural influences among other factors, the pain experience is unique to and, therefore, defined by each person. McCaffery's definition supports the clinical fact that the patient's subjective expression of pain is a more reliable indicator of the presence of pain than more objective indicators such as blood pressure and heart and respiratory rate changes.

Acute and chronic pain must be differentiated from one another, because they represent two different clinical entities. Acute pain is defined as pain of relatively short duration for which there is a specific, identifiable cause. It is also expected to abate as the cause is treated or removed. Acute pain provides a warning about tissue damage or injury, is characterized by sympathetic activation and anxiety, and generally responds to medication and treatment (Carron, 1981). Ischemic pain is an example of acute pain. It serves to warn of impending hypoxic injury and cell necrosis. The cause is identifiable and once blood flow is restored to the affected area, the pain subsides.

Chronic pain is defined as pain that has persisted for longer than 6 months. It may be either intermittent or constant and may be initiated by injury or disease, or it may accompany a chronic disease process. An example of the latter is the pain of rheumatoid arthritis (Gershon, 1986). There may not be an identifiable cause. Chronic pain does not serve as a warning of tissue injury or any other useful purpose. It is characterized by an absence of sympathetic activity in its manifestation, nonresponsiveness to treatment, and changes in

behavior and lifestyle that are probably due to the accompanying insomnia, anxiety, and depression. There is an ongoing debate about whether depression is the result of chronic pain or whether pain is a part of, or an outcome of, depression. The two conditions may be physiologically related because both are hypothesized to be the result of neurotransmitter deficiencies (Ignelzi and Atkinson, 1980; Gershon, 1986). The constellation of signs and symptoms that accompanies chronic, intractable pain is called the chronic pain syndrome.

Theories about the nature of pain have been developed over the years. The purpose of such theories is to explain the concept of pain in such a way that prediction and control of the phenomenon might be achieved in the clinical setting. The theories that will be reviewed here have been synthesized from a variety of sources and include the specificity, pattern, affect, and gate-control theories of pain (Ignelzi and Atkinson, 1980; Melzack and Wall, 1982; Meinhart and McCaffery, 1983).

Specificity

The specificity theory is an extension of the work of Muller. Muller proposed that excitation of a particular receptor and sensory pathway elicited a particular sensation. In the late 1800s a physician by the name of Max von Frey extended Muller's work and proposed a theory of the cutaneous senses in which specific pain receptors and nerve fibers for pain were postulated. The view of pain within the specificity theory is that of a specialized sense that is separate and distinct from all others. Receptors and tracts specific to the sensation of pain were thought to transmit stimuli to and evoke a response from pain centers located in the brain. Such an arrangement would dictate a fixed stimulus-response relationship, which could be interrupted surgically. Phantom limb pain and the failure of surgical interruption of nerve tracts to cure pain are cited as clinical facts that do not support this theory.

Pattern

In this theoretical approach pain was thought to be the result of the pattern of nerve stimulation. Nerve endings and tracts were thought to be shared with other sensations, with pain being signaled by the spatiotemporal patterning of impulses. Physiologic research has not supported this theoretical approach, however, because specific tracts and nerve fibers have been shown to respond to painful stimuli.

Subsumed under this heading are actually several theoretical orientations. Goldscheider first proposed that the critical variables in pain production were stimulus intensity and central summation. Weddell and Sinclair were adherents of the belief that excessive peripheral stimulation produces a pattern of impulse transmission that is interpreted centrally as pain. This approach is known as peripheral pattern theory. In contrast, Livingston emphasized central summation in an attempt to explain phantom limb pain and the pain of causalgia and the neuralgias. He postulated that abnormal spinal cord activity in the form of activation of closed, self-exciting neuron loops (reverberating circuits) is responsible for these unremitting and untreatable pain syndromes. Another proponent of central summation theory was Gerard, who hypothesized that pools of synchronously firing, spinal cord neurons develop in response to loss of sensory control of their firing and account for excessive and abnormally patterned discharges of impulses to the higher centers.

Hebb suggested that pain is the result of such synchronized neural firing within the thalamocortical tract rather than the spinal cord. Related to central summation theory is sensory interaction theory; this theory hypothesized a specialized, input-controlling system that would prevent summation. This approach served as a major foundation for future work. Noordenbos proposed that a change in the ratio of small fibers (those that carry pain-producing nerve impulses) to large fibers (that inhibit such transmission), such that small fibers were favored, would result in increased transmission, summation and, consequently, excessive pain.

Affect

Basically, this theory states that pain has both sensory and affective aspects. Pain is seen not as a purely physical sensation but as one with overtones of feeling or affect as a response.

• • •

Although each of these theories addresses some aspect of pain, none account completely for the totality of the experience. None of these theoretical approaches account for the motivational, cognitive, and cultural dimensions of pain or for the interactions among them that make the experience unique for each individual. The notion of pain as a unidimensional experience was the theme of these approaches rather than that of pain as a multidimensional experience associated with a variety of diverse mechanisms. In response to the deficiencies of these theories a more comprehensive theoretic framework was sought that would account for all of the following:

1. Physiologic specificity of receptor-fiber units and central nervous system pathways

2. The role of spatiotemporal patterning in the transmission of impulses
3. The influence of psychologic variables on pain perception and response
4. Clinical observations related to pain, such as the persistence, spread, and spatiotemporal summation of pain (Melzack and Wall, 1982)

To this end, Melzack and Wall advanced a new theory.

Gate-control

First proposed in 1965, the gate-control theory postulates that a "gating" mechanism allows the modulation of pain impulses and, therefore, pain perception and response. Melzack and Wall (1982) have updated the original conceptual model to incorporate new facts and ideas while maintaining the validity of the conceptual model of "gating" and the underlying propositions. This theory is thought to be the most adequate explanation of the pain phenomenon currently available and, as such, has been very useful in stimulating discussion and research about the nature and treatment of pain (Bishop, 1980).

Propositions of this model include the existence of a spinal gating mechanism that is influenced by the relative activity of the large and small diameter fibers and neural impulses descending from the brain, including some activated by cognitive input. Pain is thought to occur when the output of the spinal cord transmission (T) cells exceeds a critical level. The activity of the T cells depends on the activity of the cells of the substantia gelantinosa (SG). The gate is closed, that is T cell transmission is inhibited, when the SG cells are activated. The gate is opened, that is T cell transmission is facilitated, when the SG cells are inhibited. SG cell function is mediated by input from the periphery and the central nervous system.

Large fiber input activates SG cells, and small fiber input inhibits SG cells. A schematic diagram of the gate-control theory is presented in Fig. 12-1.

Because the substantia gelantinosa runs the length of the spinal cord bilaterally, receives afferent input from both large and small fibers, and influences cells that connect to the brain, it is postulated that the spinal gating mechanism is most probably located in the substantia gelatinosa of the dorsal horn. The cells in lamina V are probably the spinal transmission (T) cells since they receive afferent input from the small fibers of the skin, viscera, and muscles, are influenced by fibers that descend from the brain, respond to a wide range of stimulus intensities, increase their rate of firing in response to increased intensities of stimulation, and have their output influenced by the relative activity in the large and small fibers.

One of the more important points about the gate-control theory is that it allows for integration of all dimensions of the pain experience. The overt behavioral response, which characterizes pain, is determined by sensory, motivational, and cognitive processes that act on motor mechanisms of the central nervous system (Melzack and Wall, 1982). Integration of all these components is postulated to occur through parallel processing systems, which are schematically illustrated in Fig. 12-2.

NEUROPHYSIOLOGY OF PAIN

It should be obvious from the preceding discussion that the pain processing system is made up of large, integrative, neuronal networks. Inherent to this system are receptors, pathways, and neuroregulatory substances that allow the processing of nerve impulses between the peripheral and central nervous systems.

Physiologically, pain is viewed as a re-

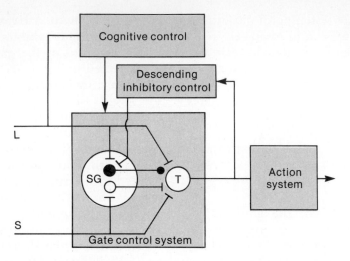

Fig. 12-1. The gate-control theory: Mark II. The new model includes excitatory *(white circle)* and inhibitory *(black circle)* links from the substantia gelatinosa *(SG)* to the transmission *(T)* cells as well as descending inhibitory control from brainstem systems. The round knob at the end of the inhibitory link implies that its action may be presynaptic, postsynaptic, or both. All connections are excitatory, except the inhibitory link from SG to T cell.

(From Melzack R and Wall DD: The challenge of pain, New York, 1982, Penguin Books.)

sponse to some stimulus. The painful stimuli most usually encountered may be placed into any one of three categories: thermal, mechanical, or chemical. These noxious stimuli cause cell damage, allowing the release and activation of chemical substances with algetic (pain producing) properties as part of the inflammatory response to injury. Pathologic mechanisms that give rise to painful stimuli are summarized in Table 12-1.

The pain receptors are chemoceptive and can be stimulated by a variety of chemical substances that are released or activated in response to cell injury, including potassium and hydrogen ions, some amines, and peptides (Bond, 1984). Chemical substances that are most directly involved in the chemical interactions that mediate pain include histamine, serotonin, bradykinin, and prostaglandins (especially of the E series). These substances produce pain directly and increase the sensitivity of the receptors to noxious stimuli. They

exert their effects individually and in combination with one another. Prostaglandins, which are generated from cell phospholipids via the arachidonic acid cascade, potentiate the effects of histamine and bradykinin. Bradykinin itself can stimulate the release of arachidonic acid and thus facilitates the synthesis of prostaglandins. Serotonin increases the vascular and noxious effects of both bradykinin and the prostaglandins and potentiates the action of histamine and bradykinin to decrease the sensory threshold of the nerves (Ignelzi and Atkinson, 1980; Zimmerman, 1981; Bond, 1984).

Aside from the inflammatory response, there is evidence that changes in the nerve tissue occur as part of the reparative process experienced by damaged nerves. These changes include sensitization of the nociceptors in the immediate area of injury (primary hyperalgesia), sensitization of nerves more distant from the site of injury, and changes in the central nervous

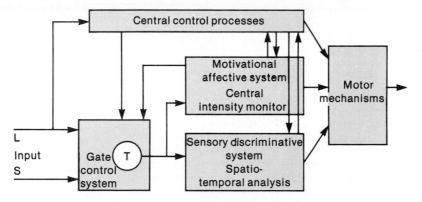

Fig. 12-2. Conceptual model of the sensory, motivational, and central control determinants of pain. The output of the T cells of the gate-control system projects to the sensory-discriminative system (via neospinothalamic fibers) and the motivational-affective system (via the paramedial ascending system). The central control trigger is represented by a line running from the large fiber system to central control processes; these, in turn, project back to the gate-control system and to the sensory-discriminative and motivational-affective systems. All three systems interact with one another and project to the motor system.

(From Melzack R and Wall DD: The challenge of pain, New York, 1982, Penguin Books.)

system such that there is an abnormal response to normal afferent signals (secondary hyperalgesia). Such changes may contribute to acute pain's evolution into a chronic pain state (Wall, 1984), in which nerve injury has occurred.

In the case of the chronic pain syndrome, however, there may be no identifiable stimulus that fits into the categories discussed above. Speculation about the nature of this type of pain is that an imbalance in neurotransmitter substances may provide the stimulus (Gershon, 1986).

Receptors and pathways

The nociceptors or pain receptors are undifferentiated, free nerve endings that arise from unmyelinated or thinly myelinated axons. These receptors are polymodal; that is, they are able to respond to different types of noxious stimuli (heat, cold, chemical irritation, mechanical distortion) with different levels of sensitivity for each. For example, the most common receptor, a high threshold receptor, responds read-

ily to heat and irritant chemicals, whereas mechanical stimuli must be of moderate or greater intensity. Nociceptors demonstrate an augmented response to repetitive stimulation; this is in contrast to other somatic sensory organs that show fatigue after repetitive stimulation (Ignelzi and Atkinson, 1980). This phenomenon, known as *sensitization*, is unique to the sensation of pain (Bishop, 1980).

The neuronal fiber types that have been found to be associated with pain are the large, myelinated, fast-conducting, sensory, class A (alpha and delta) fibers and the small, nonmyelinated, slow-conducting, sensory, class C fibers. The character of the fiber may be important in the differentiation of the type of pain that is experienced. There is some experimental evidence that stimulation of the class A delta fibers results in clearly localized, pricking, or sharp "first" pain, whereas stimulation of the class C fibers results in vague, dull, or aching "second" pain.

These neuronal fibers arise from bipolar

Text continued on p. 405.

Table 12-1. Major causes of pain

Abnormal initiating mechanism	Pathophysiology	Clinical state	Character of pain
Ischemia	Blood supply to involved area is reduced as a result of arteriosclerosis, external pressure on artery, vasospasm, or occlusion; when muscles do not receive an adequate supply of blood and oxygen for aerobic metabolism, have anaerobic metabolism with accumulation of lactic acid and cellular breakdown with release of bradykinin and histamine, which stimulate the nerve endings	Myocardial ischemia, myocardial infarction, angina pectoris, mesenteric infarct/ischemia, pulmonary infarction, chronic arterial occlusion, Reynaud's disease, compartment syndrome, sickle-cell crisis, cerebral thrombosis	Constricting, squeezing, burning, or heaviness that may be provoked by exercise or stress
Increased arterial pulsation	The rhythmic stretch and relaxation of sensitive arterial walls with each systolic impulse stimulates pain receptors in response to the mechanical stretching	Malignant hypertension headache, migraine headache, arteritis, vascular headache	Throbbing and aching localized to involved area and sometimes accompanied by tenderness to pressure on area; pain increased by activity that increases systolic pressure such as exercise, bending over, fever, etc.
Pressure of mass on adjacent structure	Presence of a space-occupying mass exerts pressure on the nerves and displacement and traction on surrounding organs	Intracranial mass, hemorrhage, neoplasm, hiatus hernia, urinary retention, torsion of ovarian cyst	Constant aching, most often severe, intensified by movement of involved area
Spasm of a hollow viscus	Distention of an organ with air or fluid causes pain from overstretch of the tissues and the forcible peristaltic moving of the contents against resistance	Ileus, intestinal colic, intestinal obstruction, impacted stone in bile duct, gastroenteritis, labor, ureteral colic or spasm	Rhythmic cramping that increases to very severe and then subsides; with repetition every few minutes; in late obstructive disease pain becomes continuous as ischemia develops
Chemical irritation	Irritating chemical substances like hydrochloric acid, pancreatic enzymes, and bile come in contact with the naked nerve terminal in the peritoneum or pancreatic bed	Peptic ulcer disease, pancreatitis, heartburn, esophageal reflux, esophagitis	Steady burning or gnawing

Table 12-1. Major causes of pain—cont'd

Abnormal initiating mechanism	Pathophysiology	Clinical state	Character of pain
Inflammatory process	The elaboration of kinins, toxins, and other chemical sustances in response to injury, invasion and multiplication of microorganisms, or other pathology lowers the threshold for pain; additionally the accompanying swelling from collection of exudate or edema puts pressure on nerves of adjacent organs	Chest: Pericarditis, pleuritis, pneumonia, myositis, acute tracheitis Abdomen: Appendicitis, cholecystitis, peritonitis diverticulitis, hepatitis, subphrenic abscess, pyelonephritis Other: Sinusitis, phlebitis, reaction to foreign body, prostatitis, acute pelvic inflammatory disease	Steady aching that frequently radiates and is accentuated with movement or increased abdominal pressure; when more severe, sharp, and penetrating (knife-like) Same as above
Tissue injury External penetration	When tissue is damaged, the pain receptors in the free nerve endings in the skin and deeper structures are stimulated; the tissue reaction of swelling also stimulates the pain receptors responding to mechanical pressure	Surgical incision Wounds: Laceration, bruise, burn	Pricking, burning, aching in area affected
Internal disruption	Rupture or tear of a structure	Dissecting aortic aneurysm, pneumothorax, mediastinal emphysema, rupture of esophagus, perforated duodenal ulcer, perforated viscus Ectopic pregnancy: tubal abortion, tubal rupture Rupture of uterus Rupture of corpus luteum cyst; rupture of graafian follicle	Abrupt onset with quick progression to agonizing severity Abrupt onset but pain of lesser severity than when larger organs are involved; pain gradually subsides instead of becoming more severe
Metabolic or toxic disorder	Metabolic abnormalities resulting in hypercalcemia, porphobilinogen, sodium, and fluid depletion, and/or metabolic acidosis	Hyperparathyroidism, acute intermittent porphyria, adrenal insufficiency, uremia, diabetic ketoacidosis	Abdominal pain of varying degrees of severity, which may be continuous, colicky, or intermittent cramping

Continued.

Table 12-1. Major causes of pain—cont'd

Abnormal initiating mechanism	Pathophysiology	Clinical state	Character of pain
	Pain from toxin ingestion or bite of black widow spider	Heavy metal poisoning, arachnidism, food poisoning	Severe cramping pain in abdomen
Osseous injury or lesion			
Skeletal bones	Disruption of continuity, tension on the periosteum, or alteration in the function of joints and overlying tissue (nerves, ligaments, tendons, or bursae) stimulate the pain receptors; if edema develops, pain is intensified from stimulation of pressure receptors	Fractures, sprains, ruptured tendons, scurvy, rickets, arthritis, bursitis, ostecmyelitis, Paget's disease	Ache or deep pain in general area of lesion that is increased with movement and pressure on area
Vertebral column	Irritation of the fascia, ligaments or tendons of the back, demineralization of the bones, or degenerative or traumatic changes in the disks with softening, loosening, and displacement of the nucleus pulposus, exerting pressure on (or stretching) adjacent ligaments and/or nerve roots	Sciatica, intervertebral disk disease, osteoarthritis of the spine, ankylosing spondylitis, osteoporosis	Backache, which may be accompanied by abnormal posture, limitation of motion of the spine, and if nerve root involved, radiation of pain, sensory alterations, and altered tendon reflexes; nerve root pain is exacerbated by sudden increases in intraspinal pressure as from coughing, sneezing, or straining
	Tumors extending from vertebral bodies or from extraspinal spaces through intervertebral foramens and other osseous lesions cause resorption of normal osseous tissue by production of substances that lyse bone, resulting in bone deformity, pathologic fractures, and destruction and narrowing of the intervertebral disks	Primary extramedullary spinal cord tumors Secondary to neoplastic diseases, lymphoma, tuberculosis	Same as above

Table 12-1. Major causes of pain—cont'd

Abnormal initiating mechanism	Pathophysiology	Clinical state	Character of pain
Muscular spasm or contraction	The contracting muscle compresses the intramuscular blood vessels with a reduction in flow of blood to the area but an increase in the metabolic rate of the muscle, resulting in relative muscle ischemia.	Tension headache, muscle cramp, muscle strain	Spasmodic muscular contraction with knot in muscle sometimes palpable
Nerve root, sensory ganglions, peripheral nerve disorders	Compression, stimulation, traction, or inflammation of nerve roots, sensory ganglions, or peripheral nerves result in pain	Trigeminal neuralgia, glossopharyngeal neuralgia, herpes zoster, tabes dorsalis, entrapment neuropathies, neuritis (intercostal, peripheral, etc.)	Sharp, lancinating, or throbbing occurring in quick succession and frequently triggered by end organ stimulation
Psychogenic, psychologic needs, secondary gain	Various psychologic factors are responsible for pain by precipitation of physiologic changes (vascular changes, muscle tenseness, hyposecretion and hypersecretion of glands), by conversion of an emotional conflict into physical complaint, or by development of delusions	Hysterical pain, hypochondriac pain, phantom pain (in some cases), spastic colon, delusional pain, conversion symptoms, psychosomatic pain, psychologic augmentation of pain	Pain may be of any nature. Most frequently described as a sharp aching in the region of organ to which it is attributed

From Aspinall, MJ and Tanner, CA: Decision making for patient care, New York, 1981, Appleton-Century-Croft.

neurons in the dorsal root ganglion, and the impulse passes through these cells from the periphery to the spinal cord. The afferent axon of these cells synapses in the dorsal horn grey matter, which has been subdivided into 10 concentric layers or laminae. Laminae II and III correspond to the substantia gelatinosa. At this level, synaptic connection can occur with either a spinal neuron, which is a link to motor and sympathetic reflexes, or with a second order neuron within an ascending pathway, which allows passage of the impulse to higher levels of the central nervous system, including the somatosensory cortex, thalamus, reticular formation, and limbic forebrain. There are multiple ascending pathways that are organized with either long intersynaptic distances and few synapses (oligosynaptic) or short intersynaptic distances and many synapses (polysynaptic) (Smith and Covino, 1985). The oligosynaptic pathways allow rapid conduction of the impulse and localization of pain. Conduction is relatively slower via the polysynaptic pathways, and localization is not possible because there is no associated somatotopic organization.

The major ascending pathways for nociceptive afferents include the spinothalamic, spinoreticular, and spinocervical tracts. Anatomically, the spinothalamic tract is considered to have two parts, the neospinothalamic or lateral component and the paleospinothalamic or ventral component. The neospinothalamic tract projects to the posterior thalamic nuclei and is thought to be important in discrimination of spatial and temporal aspects of pain and touch. The paleospinothalamic tract projects to the medial and intralaminar thalamic nuclei and has many collaterals to the brainstem, which allow for interaction, integration, and reflex activity. This branch is thought to participate in the less discriminative aspects of pain and aversive motivation. The spinoreticular tract projects to the brainstem and reticular formation. The spinocervical tract projects to the posterolateral ventral nucleus of the thalamus and may be involved in integration of the motor functions and behavioral responses to pain (Bishop, 1980; Ignelzi and Atkinson, 1980).

Ascending afferent information and spinal reflex activity are subject to selection, modulation, and control through the influence of descending inhibitory pathways (Bishop, 1980; Yaksh, 1984). Experimental evidence obtained using electrical stimulation and pharmacologic agents indicates that there are probably multiple pathways that exert inhibitory influences on nociceptive impulses (Terman, Lewis and Leibeskind, 1984). Brainstem structures are thought to be the site of origin of these pathways, and the function of at least one is believed to include opiate mechanisms (Ignelzi and Atkinson, 1980; Zimmerman, 1981). Naloxone, a narcotic antagonist, only partially reverses stimulation-produced analgesia (SPA), providing evidence that a combination of opioid and nonopioid pathways exist (Meinhart and McCaffery, 1983). Pain and stress are known to activate these pathways, although the opioid and nonopioid pathways may respond to different types of stress (Terman, Lewis and Leibeskind, 1984; Phillips and Cousins, 1986).

Modulation of the afferent information can occur at any point in the path of transmission at which synapses occur. The first point at which modulation occurs, through the integration of ascending and descending input with additional local and peripheral nerve input, is in the substantia gelatinosa in the dorsal horn. Further integration occurs at the level of the brainstem that contains many nuclei and through which all information is transmitted via ascending and descending pathways in the reticular formation. Experimental evidence supports the nucleus raphe magnus in the medulla as the site of origin for at least one inhibitory pathway (Ignelzi and Atkinson, 1980; Phillips and Cousins, 1986). Ascending connections from the brainstem are with the thalamus (the third level of integration), where conscious perception of pain occurs. Thalamic nuclei serve as relays for thalamocortical projections. The final point of integration and perception is within the cortex (Ignelzi and Atkinson, 1980).

An example of how modulation works is seen in the inhibition of the response of the dorsal horn neurons to peripheral pain stimulation by electrical nerve stimulation. The inhibitory effect of nerve stimulation is thought to be the result of activation of both the inhibitory interneurons at the level of the spine and the descending inhibitory systems (Zimmerman, 1981). This is thought to be the mechanism of action of "counter-irritant" techniques for the relief of pain, such as transcutaneous electrical nerve stimulation, massage, and acupuncture.

Neuroregulation

At each synapse there is the possibility either of facilitation or inhibition of the pain impulse (Dodson, 1985). Synaptic activity depends on the availability and function of various chemical neuroregulatory substances; these substances can be functionally subdivided into neurotransmitters and neuromodulators. Neurotransmitters or neurohormones are low–molecular weight substances with a short half-life; they act by binding to receptors of postsynaptic neurons. Neuromodulators are large–molecular weight substances with a relatively longer half-life; they may act by altering the synthesis, release, or activity of presynaptic neurotransmitters or by acting on postsynaptic receptor sites (Ignelzi and Atkinson, 1980).

To qualify as a neurotransmitter, chemical substances must meet several criteria. These criteria include the presence of the substance and mechanisms for its synthesis and metabolism in neural tissue, its release with nerve stimulation, blocking or potentiation of its action by drugs with the same actions, and the same response to exogenous administration of the substance as that elicited by nerve stimulation (Smith, 1985). The two major transmitter systems include the monoamine and cholinergic systems (Ignelzi and Atkinson, 1980). Proven neurotransmitters include norepinephrine, epinephrine, dopamine, and acetylcholine. Other putative (or suspected) neurotransmitters involved in pain perception include substance P, serotonin (5 HT), somatostatin, gamma-aminobutyric acid (GABA), and histamine (Bishop, 1980; Meinhart and McCaffery, 1983; Phillips and Cousins, 1986).

Substance P is thought to be an excitatory transmitter released by the nociceptive afferents, but its activity appears to be dose related. At high doses it excites spinal cord and brain neurons, which are sensitive to nociceptive stimuli; at low doses it causes the release of endorphins and inhibits nociception (Ignelzi and Atkinson, 1980). Substance P has also been found in a descending inhibitory system between the brainstem raphe nuclei and the dorsal horn (Smith, 1985). Opioids inhibit the release and action of substance P (Bond, 1984). The ability of somatostatin to excite neurons in nociceptive pathways and its distribution within the central nervous system is similar to that of substance P (Ignelzi and Atkinson, 1980).

It appears that serotonin plays a dual role as both an excitatory and inhibitory transmitter. Serotonin acts in the peripheral nervous system as an algesic substance that excites and sensitizes nociceptors. Acting on the dorsal horn neurons, serotonin appears to inhibit transmission of the pain impulse and is thought to be a transmitter involved in the descending inhibitory pathways. These paths are thought to be activated through the binding of the opiate receptors by either endogenous or exogenous opioids, and the subsequent stimulation of the descending neurons causes the release of serotonin at synapses within the spinal cord (Zimmerman, 1981; Phillips and Cousins, 1986). Serotonin depletion has been found to decrease stimulation-produced analgesia (SPA). Injection of serotonin directly into the central nervous system, or administration of its precursor—5 hydroxytryptophan (5 HTP), has been found to restore analgesia (Gershon, 1986; Smith, 1985; Ignelzi and Atkinson, 1980). The availability of serotonin also affects the activity of morphine. The effects of morphine are enhanced with the injection of serotonin or with interference with serotonin's reuptake, and the effects of morphine are lessened with serotonin depletion or blocking with drugs (Dodson, 1985; Feinman, 1985).

Norepinephrine acts in the opposite way. Depletion of norepinephrine has been found to enhance antinociception (Ignelzi and Atkinson, 1980). Increased norepinephrine levels can potentially lower the pain threshold and increase pain. Norepinephrine has been found to decrease the effectiveness of morphine (Gershon, 1986).

Dopamine is also thought to have some role in pain transmission and modulation. Administration of L-dopa (a dopamine precursor) increases the pain threshold and produces analgesia, presumably by increasing the dopamine level (Ignelzi and Atkinson, 1980).

Speculation about a mechanism that links depression and chronic pain has focused on abnormal levels of various neurotransmitters. Concentrations of serotonin and norepinephrine in the central nervous system indicates that overlap exists between affective and nociceptive paths. The results of clinical studies of the levels of these neurotransmitters in depressed individuals and the actions of antidepressant medications suggest that decreased concentrations of serotonin and norepinephrine may be a pathogenetic mechanism in depression (see Chapter 11). Evidence supports the existence of mutually interacting feedback loops between serotonin, norepinephrine, and enkephalin (Gershon, 1986).

Neuromodulators include the endogenous, opioid peptides, which are morphine-like in their action. The identification and mapping of opiate receptor sites throughout the nervous system and in the gastrointestinal tract stimulated the search for endogenous substances capable of binding to these receptors. Although referred to generically as endorphins, three families or classes of these opioid peptides, based on their derivation from three distinct precursor molecules, have been recognized: (1) beta-lipotropin, which contains beta-endorphin; (2) enkephalin, which contains Met-enkephalin and Leu-enkephalin and; (3) dynorphin (Meinhart and McCaffery, 1983; Millan, 1986; Phillips and Cousins, 1986). The roles of these substances in the modulation and control of pain are very complex. The effects depend on a number of interacting variables, including the particular substance, the receptor type being affected, whether action is occurring at the level of the brain, spinal cord, or periphery, the type and duration of the stimulus causing pain, the nature of the response, and the conditions of activity (Millan, 1986).

The actions of the endogenous opioids mimic the central and peripheral effects of morphine and other exogenous opioids. The enkephalins, which are subject to rapid enzymatic degradation, have a relatively short half-life as compared to the endorphins. The enkephalins are thought to inhibit the release of excitatory neurotransmitters and have been shown to inhibit the release of substance P. They subsequently inhibit the transmission of noxious impulses when they bind to opiate receptors in the dorsal horn. In contrast, endorphin release can be stimulated by neurons in descending substance P pathways (Ignelzi and Atkinson, 1980). Beta-endorphin has an increased affinity for opiate receptors in the hypothalamus and pituitary gland. The enkephalins are considered weakly analgesic, whereas the dynorphins are considered to have an analgesic potency that is 50 times greater than that of beta-endorphin (Meinhart and McCaffery, 1983).

The endogenous opioids are secreted in response to stress and pain (Meinhart and McCaffery, 1983; Millan, 1986). Elevated levels of these substances have been found following surgery (Cohen, et al. 1981; Dodson, 1985). The effects of counter-irritant, stimulation techniques, such as acupuncture, transcutaneous electrical nerve stimulation, and massage, have been shown to be at least partially mediated through the mechanism of endorphin release (Lewith and Kenyon, 1984). There is some evidence that the placebo response may be mediated by endorphins as well (Levine, Gordon, and Fields, 1978).

At this time, information about the actions of the endogenous opioids is not complete and is the subject of much ongoing research. Elucidation of the mechanisms through which the endogenous opioids exert their effects may provide the means to control these systems to provide more complete pain relief in the clinical setting.

MANIFESTATIONS OF PAIN

The observable behaviors associated with pain include vocalization, a startle response, a flexion reflex, and avoidance movements. Associated with these reflexive responses are the autonomic and learned responses that pain evokes (Abu-Saad and Tesler, 1986). The autonomic, somatic, and affective behaviors associated with pain differ depending on whether the pain is acute or chronic in nature.

Learned responses can be highly individualized, and they often represent coping strategies that a person has used successfully to deal with pain in the past. Complex perceptual and cognitive processes at the higher levels of the central nervous system allow the integration of the nociceptive impulse with emotion, beliefs, expectations, and the present situation. As a result of these processes, the meaning, quality, and intensity of the pain and the psychologic and behavioral responses to it are determined in relation to the individual's personality, cultural background, past learning history, and the present psychosocial context in which the pain is being experienced (Chapman, 1985).

The patient will voluntarily limit movement or activity that becomes associated with causing or increasing pain. Guarding (or splinting) is a protective rigidity that is adopted to limit pain caused by movement. An example is seen in the postoperative patient (see pp 420-423). Lack of or inadequate participation in the "stir-up" regimen (dangling, ambulation, bed exercises, coughing, and deep breathing) results in the following nursing diagnoses: potential for altered tissue perfusion related to thrombophlebitis or embolism, ineffective breathing pattern, and potential for ineffective airway clearance. The classic behavioral response of the chronic pain patient is assumption of an immobile posture of stance with little, if any, facial or verbal expression, as if the least movement will aggravate the pain.

The autonomic response includes input from both the sympathetic and parasympathetic systems. The initial response is that of *activation*, as in the reaction of the body to any stressor. The sympathetic system response is usually predominant in acute pain, and blood will be shunted to the vital organs through peripheral vasoconstriction. The patient's pulse, respiratory rates, and blood pressure will be increased, and the nurse may note pallor, perspiration, and dilated pupils. Sympathetic activation causes increased smooth muscle sphincter tone and decreased intestinal and renal motility. Intestinal secretions are also increased. The patient may experience nausea and vomiting. More serious results of sympathetic activity can include gastric stasis and dilation and urinary retention (Phillips and Cousins, 1986). This sympathoadrenal activation can have negative consequences, especially in a patient with a compromised cardiovascular system. Myocardial ischemia, infarction, or failure may occur in response to the increased systemic resistance, decreased coronary filling time, increased cardiac workload, and increased myocardial oxygen consumption.

With severe, acute pain, inhibition of the vasomotor center rather than sympathetic activation may occur. This *rebound* effect causes peripheral pooling of blood, which is reflected by a decreased blood pressure and, in turn, can result in decreased perfusion and tissue hypoxia. Pain should be prevented or treated as rapidly as possible to minimize these responses.

If pain persists, *adaptation* occurs since the body cannot sustain prolonged sympathetic activation. The signs of sympathetic activation will no longer be present despite the continued presence of pain (Donovan, 1982). This is the case in patients with chronic pain. Adaptation may be a result of parasympathetic system activity, inhibition of the sympathetic system, or central inhibition at the level of

the spinal cord (Abu-Saad and Tesler, 1986). Signs of parasympathetic stimulation may be seen in the patient with chronic pain in contrast to signs of sympathetic activity (Donovan, 1982).

Another consequence of pain is muscle spasm, which is part of the segmental and suprasegmental, reflex responses to pain (Phillips and Cousins, 1986). Segmental reflex responses will be most intense in the areas of the body supplied by the same innervation as the site at which the painful stimulation occurred. Muscle spasms will produce pain directly and reduce gastric and renal motility. They also lead to both voluntary and involuntary immobility, the negative consequences of which are detailed in Chapter 14. Both the reflex muscle spasms and the reflex sympathetic activity that are elicited by pain have the potential to create a vicious cycle of pain since nociceptors can be further stimulated and sensitized by these reflexes (Zimmerman, 1981; Phillips and Cousins, 1986).

Pain will affect every aspect of the individual's wellness. In response to pain, the appetite is depressed, the activity level and ability to concentrate are decreased, the normal sleep pattern is disrupted, social interaction is reduced, and attention may be focused exclusively on the pain problem (Wall, 1984).

Chronic pain syndromes

It was stated previously that pain sometimes becomes a pathologic state in itself. Many conditions are capable of causing severe, prolonged pain—a chronic pain syndrome. Pain may be a direct result of the pathology that is present or a result of the treatment for these conditions. Musculoskeletal disorders, myofascial disorders, and cancer are some examples of such conditions. Often, there is no identifiable cause for the pain. For example, it is estimated that an organic or structural cause can be identified in only 20% of the patients who experience low back pain (Meinhart and McCaffery, 1983). The pain experienced with chronic, intractable, benign (or nonmalignant) pain syndrome is as real as the pain for which a direct cause can be identified.

Pathologic pain has been defined as pain that arises spontaneously from neural tissue without any apparent stimulus. Pathologic pain is characterized by responsiveness to affective states, nonresponsiveness to potent analgesic medication, and reoccurrence, and sometimes even worsening, of the pain after surgical intervention (Ruch, 1979).

Pain syndromes have been classified arbitrarily as peripheral or central, depending on the site of pathologic origin within the nervous system. Presented in Table 12-2 are the various disorders that have been classified within this schema (Meinhart and McCaffery, 1983).

The peripheral pain syndromes are considered *reflex sympathetic dystrophies,* which is a collective term applied to conditions that are the result of injury to a peripheral nerve or extremity. The reflex sympathetic dystrophies are characterized by the following signs and symptoms that occur in varying patterns and degrees in individual patients: severe pain (usually burning in character), extreme sensitivity

Table 12-2. Classification of pathologic pain syndromes

Peripheral	Central
Causalgia	Thalamic syndrome
Postherpetic neuralgia	Trigeminal neuralgia (tic
Phantom limb pain	douloureaux)

to pain (hyperalgesia), altered sensitivity to stimuli (hyperesthesia or hypoesthesia), abnormal responses to stimuli (dyesthesia), an unpleasant affective response (hyperpathia), and sympathetic responses including vasomotor, sudomotor (either the absence of or excessive sweating), trophic, cutaneous, and skeletal muscle changes. The syndrome is exacerbated by stress. Causalgia is a good illustration of these responses. Causalgia is usually characterized by severe, burning pain within 2 weeks of injury to the radial, ulnar, brachial plexus, median, or sciatic nerve. Most often, pain occurs in the palms of the hands, soles of the feet, or the digits. The patient may report that the slightest touch, even that of clothing against the site, stress, or heat, may cause excruciating pain. The chronic phase develops within 3 to 6 months and is characterized by vasomotor changes, edema, and red-purple coloring of the affected area. Joints may swell and stiffen, the skin around the painful area may become shiny and taut in appearance or scaly and discolored, the affected limb may be either cooler or hotter than usual, and excessive sweating in the palms or soles may occur.

The pathologic mechanisms of these pain syndromes are not understood completely, and more than one mechanism may be involved in an individual syndrome. Central pathologic pain syndromes are thought to be the result of spontaneously produced, high-frequency bursts of nociceptive impulses resulting from pathology of central neurons. Peripheral syndromes are thought to be a result of abnormal generation and transmission of nociceptive impulses from injured nerves. For example, postherpetic neuralgia may be the result of degenerative changes in the spinal cord, dorsal root ganglia, or nerve trunks, which are secondary to infection of the dorsal root ganglia by the varicella-zoster virus.

Phantom limb pain presents some unique features that make the explanation of its pathogenesis more complex than the generation and transmission of abnormal impulses. Surgical techniques to interrupt the sensory pathways are not always successful in resolving phantom limb pain. The following associations have been found between the presence of pain and the position of the limb before and after amputation: (1) phantom limb pain is more likely to be present if there was pain in the limb before surgery, and the pain in both conditions will be similar in quality; (2) traumatic amputation is less likely to be followed by phantom limb pain, especially if it is accompanied by a loss of consciousness; (3) the individual may perceive the amputated limb as being in the same position as it was before amputation. For these reasons, pattern-generating mechanisms have been proposed to explain phantom limb pain (Melzack and Loeser, 1978).

Headache is a commonly experienced type of pain. Like other types of pain, headache may be a symptom of underlying pathology or it may be the primary problem. Infection, tumors, abcesses, traumatic injuries, and hypertension represent intracranial pathology that can result in headache pain. Changes in intracranial pressure and dilation and distention of cerebral vessels cause stretching and traction on pain-sensitive, intracerebral structures. Other possible mechanisms of headache resulting from intracerebral pathology include compression and irritation of sensory nerves and inflammation of nerves and blood vessels. Often more than one mechanism is involved. For example, infection and bleeding in the brain can cause increased intracranial pressure,

meningeal irritation, and cerebral vasculitis, all of which result in headache (Meinhart and McCaffery, 1983).

Extracranial pathology in the sinuses, teeth, jaw, eyes, ears, nose, and throat can also cause headache. Headache may be a response to sustained contraction of the skeletal muscles in the face, head, neck, shoulders, and upper back. The underlying pathologic mechanisms are the same as for intracranial pathology with the addition of referred pain. Characteristics of some different types of headaches are summarized in Table 12-3.

ASSESSMENT AND DIAGNOSIS

Concepts that are basic to assessment of the pain experience include threshold and tolerance. *Threshold* refers to a point at which some response to a painful stimulus occurs. There are two thresholds that are relevant to the evaluation of pain. The *pain perception threshold* is the point of initial response—when pain is first perceived in response to a noxious stimulus. The *severe pain threshold* is the point at which pain becomes unbearable. Pain *tolerance* is measured by the interval between the two thresholds and represents the range of perception between these two points. Although the lower threshold (perception) is relatively constant across individuals under laboratory conditions, the upper threshold depends on personal and sociocultural factors and, therefore, varies widely, accounting for individual differences in the level of pain tolerance (Bond, 1984; McMahon and Miller, 1978).

Because pain is, by its very nature, a subjective, multidimensional experience, subjective indicators of its presence must be considered more reliable than objective indicators. Only the patient can indicate the location, radiation, intensity, character, and temporal pattern (duration and

Table 12-3. Characteristics of headache

	Location	Duration	Onset	Associations
Muscle contraction	Temporal, frontal, parietal, occipital, posterior cervical, or generalized	Hours to days (in the present form may be present for years)	Gradual	Emotional stress Head and neck position
Migraine	Any area May be unilateral and repetitive	Hours to days	Gradual or abrupt	Positive family history Aura secondary to vasoconstrictive events
Cluster	Temporal-ocular areas	Hours Groups of attacks 10-120 minutes (usually less than 60 minutes)	Abrupt	Homolateral nasal congestion and lacrimation miosis, ptosis Often nocturnal
Lumbar puncture	Occipital to frontal	Hours to days	Abrupt on standing	Relieved by lying down
Trigeminal neuralgia	One or more divisions of 5th nerve (Unilateral)	Minutes	Abrupt	''Trigger'' areas often present Occur in attacks
Subarachnoid hemorrhage	Postcervical Occipital Frontal	Hours to days	Abrupt	Very severe Nausea, vomiting, lethargy Localizing signs (Partial III nerve paresis)
Meningitis and encephalitis	Postcervical Frontal	Days	Gradual	Fever, lethargy, seizures
Cranial arteritis	Temporal areas or generalized	Days, weeks, or months	Gradual—rarely abrupt	Painful vessels Systemic symptoms Increased E.S.R. Retinal arteritis Anterior optic neuritis
Hypertension	Occipital Frontal	Weeks	Gradual	Worse in AM

(From McKhann GM and Speed III WG: Disorders of sensation: pain and headache. In Harvey AM, et al: The principles and practice of medicine, ed 21, Norwalk, Conn., 1080, Appleton-Century-Crofts, Table 125-2, p 1257.

chronology) of the pain and the factors that precipitate, accompany, aggravate, and/or alleviate it. Harrison and Cotanch (1987) state that the following areas should also be included in assessment: the physical, psychologic, and emotional causes of pain, the availability of support systems, and the meaning of the pain to the patient. It is important to know whether the pain is perceived as a threat to life or continued quality and productivity of life by the patient. Additionally, the patient's usual coping style and past patterns of handling pain need to be assessed. This is information that only the patient and family can provide. The impact of the environment on the pain should also be assessed by the nurse. Assessment of the response of family and support persons to the patient's pain may provide clues as to the meaning of pain behavior in the situation. Assessment of the psychosocial, cultural and contextual, as well as the physical, components of the pain experience allow a holistic approach in the care of the patient.

Anxiety often accompanies pain and may heighten the patient's perception of pain. Its presence will be influenced by whether the pain can be attributed to a physical cause, the patient's understanding of the pain and its cause, the meaning of the pain to the patient, and whether treatment offers hope of relief from the pain. The inability to find a physical cause for pain can be a source of great anxiety for patients as its reality is sometimes viewed with suspicion and doubt by others and the lack of a treatable cause offers little hope for relief from the pain. Anxiety can also be a cause of pain in some conditions. For example, while the pain of colitis can be attributed to tissue damage, an attack can be brought on and sustained by emotional conflict.

The source of the pain may be difficult to assess because of the phenomenon of referred pain. The actual pain sensation is perceived as being in a location that is different than the actual source of the pain and is a result of shared innervation, that is, the location and the source of the pain are innervated by the same spinal segment. Examples include angina pectoris and the pain of a myocardial infarction being perceived in the jaw or arm or an injury to the diaphragm resulting in shoulder pain. Headache is a commonly experienced result of the referred pain of temporomandibular joint (TMJ) syndrome (Meinhart and McCaffery, 1983).

Because of the nature of its innervation, visceral pain is diffuse and poorly localized and, therefore, also difficult to assess. Although the organs are not supplied with nociceptors per se, they can respond to the mechanical pressure of distention or swelling. Examples include abdominal pain resulting from the accumulation of gas and/or fluid in the intestines or flank pain as a result of bleeding in the kidney, which stretches the surrounding capsule.

Clinical assessment of pain needs to be regular, systematic, simple, and quick, yet reliable, and should incorporate the multidimensional aspects of pain. The purpose of this assessment is to provide a basis for treatment by allowing selection of an appropriate intervention for managing the pain. Various instruments have been developed to make the assessment of pain more objective and reliable. Donovan (1987) states that the ideal instrument for such assessment would have to be brief, easy to use, subjective, individualized, and holistic.

Syrjala and Chapman (1984) report that there have been three major approaches to instrumentation for measuring pain; quantification of subjective reports, quantification of behaviors or activities that can be attributed to pain, and identification of physiologic correlates of pain. Instruments or tests may provide a measure of one area (unidimensional perspective) or a combination of these areas (multidimensional perspective). Self-report scales are examples of simple, unidimensional tools by which the patient can rate the intensity of the pain being experienced. An example of a multidimensional measure of the total pain experience is the McGill Pain Questionnaire. The best measure to use must be based on the patient's ability to comprehend and respond to requirements of the instrument. McGuire (1984) provides a comparison of the properties of various instruments that have been designed to measure pain.

The expression of pain by some patients is not always possible. The nurse must learn to anticipate pain, interpret pain signals, and rely on less reliable, objective indicators of pain. The nurse can use anticipatory information related to the pathology and treatment that the patient is experiencing. The nature of the pain associated with different conditions is summarized in Table 12-1. Differing amounts of pain can be anticipated depending on the type of surgery the patient has had. For example, pain should be expected in the patient who has had thoracic or abdominal surgery. Patients who have had intracranial surgery involving the skull and skin may have, at most, moderate pain, whereas those patients in whom neck muscles have been dissected (such as for posterior fossa exploration) may have severe pain (Dodson, 1985). Severe muscle spasms may follow surgery or trauma to the bony skeleton (Phillips and Cousins, 1986). To make the diagnosis of pain, the nurse must often integrate observations of the patient's movements and facial expressions, blood pressure, and heart and respiratory rates with knowledge about the possible causes of pain in the individual patient (Harrison and Cotanch, 1987).

TREATMENT RATIONALE

The expected outcome for a patient in pain is relief of pain such that the patient indicates that he or she is comfortable. Such a goal is only infrequently attained, however. Donovan (1987) reports that inadequate relief of pain continues to be a major clinical problem. This can be attributed to pharmacologic undertreatment and lack of differentiation between acute and chronic pain models. Pharmacologic undertreatment of pain is the consequence of clinicians' lack of understanding about tolerance and the differences between physical dependence, psychologic dependence, and addiction (Coyle, 1987). Application of the acute model of pain to the chronic pain patient results in inappropriate and inadequate treatment. In contrast to acute pain, where physiologic factors may predominate, psychologic, social, cultural, and environmental factors take on equal importance in the pathogenesis of chronic pain. Treatment of chronic pain must go beyond the pain itself to other aspects of the patient's life that impact on the pain state. Even with such a comprehensive approach, chronic pain is often refractory to treatment.

Two general categories of interventions for pain relief include pharmacologic and nonpharmacologic methods. For acute pain, pharmacologic treatment tends to be the more widely used approach. For some patients with chronic pain, nonpharmacologic methods may take on more importance as a form of treatment. Because pain is a subjective sensation, each patient's response to treatment will be different and a combination of analgesic medication with a nonpharmacologic method may be needed by individual patients for the most effective form of pain relief. This is especially true for patients with chronic pain. Nonpharmacologic methods are summarized in Table 12-4. With the exception of transcutaneous electrical nerve stimulation (TENS), these methods do not require a physician's order and pose little, if any, risk to the patient (Donovan, 1982). Related to pharmacologic treatment is the expected outcome that pain relief is achieved without any adverse effects of treatment such as respiratory depresson, hypotension, and decreased level of consciousness (Phillips and Cousins, 1986).

Antidepressant medication has been used in the treatment of chronic pain. Both tricyclic antidepressants and monoamine oxidase inhibitors have been found to relieve chronic pain. This class of medication produces both analgesic and antidepressant effects. The tricyclics block

Table 12-4. Nonpharmacologic methods for controlling pain

Technique	Physiological effect	Comments
Cutaneous stimulation Massage TENS* Heat Cold Vibration Mentholated rubs	Stimulates large fibers; modulates pain at SG-T gate in dorsal horn.	Most effective for local and superficial pain. Moderate stimulation is applied using a powder or lotion to minimize friction or a mentholated rub to increase stimulation. Sites of application include over the pain, around the pain, proximal to the pain, trigger points, acupuncture points, contralaterally. See McCaffery (1979) and Chan P: Finger acupressure. Los Angeles, Price Stern Sloan, 1975.
Auditory stimulation Comedy Music Distraction	Intense stimuli through thalamus, midbrain, and brainstem cause the production of modulating substances (i.e., endorphins and serotonin). Diversion of attention from the pain decreases the aversive nature of the stimulus. The resulting relaxation decreases muscle guarding at the site of the pain.	Most effective when used with headphones. Needs to match patient's taste. Effective for mild to moderate pain.
Breathing techniques	Same as auditory stimuli.	"He-who" breathing most broadly effective. Childbirth education classes are a readily available way to learn some of these techniques.
Relaxation and biofeedback	Increases blood flow and reduces muscle tension, which reduces the concentration of neurotransmitters at the site of pain. Also can be a type of auditory stimulus. May increase endorphins by way of cortical mechanisms.	For specifics, see Donovan MI: Cancer nurs, 3:27-32, 1980, and Donovan MI: Cancer care: a guide for patient education. New York, Appleton-Century-Crofts, 1981.
Imagery and hypnosis	Alters perception of the noxious stimulus in the cerebral cortex. May produce relaxation. May increase endorphins through cortical mechanisms.	For specifics see Barber J: Cancer nurs, 1:361-364, 1978, and Barber J: CA, 30:130-136, 1980; see also Donovan, as cited above.

*Transcutaneous electrical nerve stimulation.
From Donovan M: Cancer pain: you can help! Symposium on oncologic nursing practice, Nurs Clin North Am, 17:718, 1982.

neuronal uptake and thereby increase the levels of serotonin, noradrenaline, and dopamine at the synapse. Tricyclic compounds have also been found to bind to opiate receptors in the brain. The MAO inhibitors increase uptake, which increases the release of these neurotransmitters (Feinmann, 1985; Gershon, 1986).

Analgesic medication can be classified according to the mode of action. Medications that act by inhibiting prostaglandin synthesis include the nonnarcotic analgesics and the nonsteroidal antiinflammatory drugs (NSAID). Aspirin and other NSAIDs inhibit cyclooxygenase, the enzyme necessary for the conversion of arachidonic acid in the prostaglandin cascade. This limits the amount of prostaglandin that can be generated. The opioid or narcotic analgesics alter pain perception by binding to the opiate receptors in the central and peripheral nervous system and by activating descending inhibitory neurons, which inhibit transmission of the impulse at the spinal cord level. The final class of medications, adjuvant analgesic drugs, does not produce analgesia directly but potentiates the effects of other drugs or counteracts their side effects (Coyle, 1987).

The choice of an analgesic most often depends on the intensity of the pain and on the metabolic state of the patient. Conditions that can affect the pharmacodynamics and pharmacokinetics of a drug include renal failure, liver disorders, and preexisting drug or alcohol dependency. In the obese patient, absorption of oral medication can be reduced by decreased gastric emptying, and absorption of injectable medication can be impaired by injection into fatty tissue. In the elderly patient a variety of conditions exist that can affect pharmacodynamics and pharmacokinetics: decreases in blood flow, protein binding, hepatic and renal function and the general ability to adapt to physiologic and pathologic changes; increased sensitivity to CNS depressant drugs and in target organs; and altered respiratory capacity (Dodson, 1985).

In addition to analgesic and antidepressant medication, patients with chronic pain may be treated with other pharmacologic agents, such as muscle relaxants and tranquilizers. Some of these agents may intensify depression and, therefore, also intensify the chronic pain condition (Carron, 1981). Additionally, dependence (both physical and psychologic) on these drugs may develop.

After the correct medication is chosen, decisions regarding the correct timing, dosage, and route of administration must also be made (Donovan, 1982). Although many of these decisions are the responsibility of the physician, the effective use of analgesic medications in the institutional setting is a responsibility of the nurse, who must exercise clinical judgment in administering the right amount at the right intervals for the most effective pain relief in each patient. For patients who will be administering their own medication or whose family members may be administering the medication to them, the nurse has the responsibility for teaching the most effective and safe use of these medications.

The proper amount of medication will need to be assessed for each patient because every individual will respond differently to analgesic drugs. "Average" values are just that; there is no "average" patient. Analgesic medication should be administered before pain reaches its most intense level and before activities that are sure to increase it. For severe pain, a routine schedule for administration, rather than an "as needed" administration, may help to control the pain by providing a more even and constant level of analgesia. The goal should be to prevent as well as treat pain (Bryan-Brown, 1986).

For patients experiencing moderate to severe pain, the most common method of administration of narcotic medication is by intramuscular or intravenous injection (Leib and Hurtig, 1987). The intramuscular method of administration tends to produce a variable pattern rather than a constant level of analgesia. Respiratory depression may be more likely to occur with the high peak plasma levels of opioids caused by intramuscular or bolus intravenous administration (Dodson, 1985). Continuous intravenous infusion of small amounts of a narcotic allows a more constant serum level of the drug to be maintained, which in turn, allows a more constant pattern of analgesia to be achieved. Furthermore, a more constant serum level of a narcotic allows a lesser amount of drug to be used, decreasing the risk of tolerance development and side effects (Harrison and Cotanch, 1987). This method obviously requires close nursing supervision and proper titration of the rate of administration of the drug to alleviate the patient's pain.

Patient controlled analgesia (PCA) is another innovation that allows the patient to administer increments of medication to himself or herself. This method gives the patient more control and independence and allows the maintenance of a more constant level of pain control. Medication is placed in an intravenous line that is connected to a button-switch activated pump. The patient can activate the pump as often as necessary until a predetermined dosage is reached. When the maximum dose is reached, the pump is deactivated until a preset minimal time period elapses (Paice, 1987). This method of analgesia administration may not be appropriate for all patients, but it does represent a viable treatment option for those who are alert and oriented and who could manage such a system safely.

Another innovation is the direct administration of narcotic medication into the intrathecal and epidural spaces of the spinal cord. This method allows a maximum analgesic effect with minimal central depressant effects. Sensory and motor functions also remain intact. Contraindi-cations to this method of narcotic administration include the following: (1) local or systemic infection; (2) bleeding or clotting disorders; (3) musculoskeletal or spinal abnormalities; (4) certain preexisting neurologic disorders; or (5) inability to provide close, continual monitoring of patients (Leib and Hurtig, 1985). The catheter must be placed by an anesthesiologist.

Fear, anxiety, depression, stress, and fatigue are known to negatively affect the perception of pain. The inability to rest and relax leads to feelings of fatigue and weakness. This may blunt the mental capacities needed to use such strategies for coping with pain as distraction or imagination. Anxiety serves to heighten perception of painful stimuli. Cousins and Phillips (1986) propose that pain, anxiety, and sleep deprivation comprise a vicious cycle. If uninterrupted, this cycle can lead to anger and depression as the patient becomes demoralized and loses confidence in the ability of health care professionals to relieve the pain. A feeling of powerlessness may ensue as the patient feels that there is nothing that can be done to alter the situation. The chronic pain state is characterized by what Wall (1984) describes as "disappointment of failure to recover and of failure of treatment." Patients with chronic pain often develop a feeling of hopelessness about their pain. This may become so severe and overwhelming that suicide may be considered by the patient as a treatment option (Meinhart and McCaffery, 1983).

The creation of an atmosphere conducive to pain relief is an intervention that is within the control of the nurse. If pain relief measures are to be maximally effective, nurses must integrate measures for stress reduction, anxiety reduction, and promotion of sleep and rest into the plan of care. The design and decor of the nursing unit can be planned to be aesthetically pleasing, peaceful, and functional. Policies and procedures that allow maximum interaction with family, the presence of familiar objects in the environment, and distractions such as television and radio can be useful in promoting an atmosphere conducive to patient comfort.

This method of care is more difficult for the nurse working with a chronic pain patient in a pain clinic or in the home. Modification of the social and family environment, the unlearning of learned responses, and adoption of effective strategies for coping with pain, and possibly even disability as a result of that pain, may require psychiatric and occupational evaluation and counseling. Consultation with and referral to mental health professionals such as psychiatric clinical nurse specialists, clinical psychologists, psychiatrists, or psychiatric social workers may be necessary. An anesthesiologist may be called on to perform a nerve block, or a surgeon may become involved if treatment is to include surgical intervention. It is generally acknowledged that a multidisciplinary approach in the treatment of chronic pain or complex acute pain problems is necessary and beneficial. The nurse may become the coordinator of the different disciplines involved in the care of the patient. In this situation, the nurse will need to monitor the patient's responses to a variety of interacting treatments, evaluate the effectiveness of that treatment, and communicate those findings to the appropriate person. The importance of this role cannot be emphasized strongly enough because the nurse may be the person with whom the patient communicates most regularly, and only the patient can accurately evaluate the pain being experienced.

Donovan (1982) states that the most ef-fective intervention for the relief of pain is a positive approach by the persons involved in the care of the patient. This conveys to the patient an attitude that the presence of pain is acknowledged and will be treated. The author speculates that this type of approach may be effective, because a placebo response is elicited. Studies have demonstrated greater pain relief in patients whose nurses attempted to communicate with them and apply individualized interventions (McMahon and Miller, 1978). A positive approach will also help to minimize anxiety.

Providing information about and offering positive suggestions during treatments and invasive procedures can also be effective in helping the patient control the acute pain that can be expected as a result of those procedures. Positive suggestions can help the patient focus on distractions or relaxation techniques during procedures. Providing information about how to move and how to splint an incision with a hand, pillow, or folded blanket can help patients ease their own pain. The work of Johnson and associates (as compiled in Horsley, et al, 1981) indicates that patients use sensory and procedural information provided to them about a treatment to develop coping strategies for dealing with the event. Geach (1987) recommends viewing the patient as a partner in "pain work" as a means to increase the patient's understanding of and participation in the treatment of pain.

Patients with chronic pain can be taught biofeedback and relaxation techniques that can give them more control over their pain. A greater sense of control may have the added benefit of improving their morale and outlook on life. Physical therapy may also be useful in the treatment of chronic pain related to a musculoskeletal condition.

For some patients with severe, intractable pain, surgical intervention may be attempted. Surgery is viewed as a last resort and should be attempted with caution, because it may not completely relieve the pain and may even worsen it. The various surgical procedures that are used for pain relief include neurotomy, rhizotomy, cordotomy, and hypophysectomy. The beneficial, analgesic effect of hypophysectomy was a serendipitous effect observed in patients being treated with this procedure for hormone dependent malignancies like breast cancer.

Patients who have been relieved of their pain, even temporarily, will often need acknowledgment that their pain-related behavior was acceptable to others. The role of the nurse is one of support in this situation. At this stage the patient may also be very anxious about the reoccurrence of pain, and the nurse needs to review and reinforce with the patient those strategies that were most helpful in coping with the pain.

Two case studies are presented in the following text. In the first case study the patient is experiencing acute postoperative pain. As has been noted throughout the chapter, postoperative pain can have deleterious effects on other aspects of the patient's recovery. The second features a patient who has chronic pain. The unremitting nature of this pain and the effect it has had on all aspects of the patient's and her family's life should be noted by the reader. These case studies are placed together at the end of the chapter so that the reader can compare the different manifestations of pain and responses to treatment that characterize each pain state.

CASE STUDY: ACUTE PAIN

History

Present illness: RM is a 50-year-old man who had a colon resection for adenocarcinoma of the transverse colon. This is his first postoperative day. He has a midline incision and two drains lateral to the incision. He also has a urinary drainage catheter and an intravenous catheter through which he is receiving fluids as well as antibiotics. RM is currently complaining of severe pain and is requesting medication.

Subjective and Objective Data

RM complains of severe pain superficially around the incision and deeper within the abdomen. When the nurse asks him to quantify the pain using a 0 to 10 numeric rating scale (0 meaning "no pain" and 10 meaning the "worst pain imaginable"), RM responds that his pain is a 10. Upon further questioning he also states that the deep pain is throbbing and dull. The pain around the incision is sharp. He also reveals that the injection he received for pain 6 hours ago (10 mg morphine IM) relieved the pain for about 4 hours. He describes his pain at that time as a 4. He also states that moving about in his bed and coughing cause "excruciating" pain and that it is even difficult to take a deep breath.

RM is grimacing and guarding his abdomen. He is pale, diaphoretic, and tachycardic (110 beats per minute). His blood pressure is 130/90 (his normal pressure is 115/80). Respirations are shallow and frequent (30 per minute). When asked to participate in pulmonary hygiene exercises, he makes an attempt to deep breathe but is overcome with pain and refuses to continue.

Contributed by Judy Paice.

Discussion

Surgical intervention results in trauma to afferent nerve endings. This noxious stimuli results in depolarization of the pain fiber in a process called transduction. These fibers transmit nociceptive (painful) messages to the dorsal horn of the spinal cord through electrical conduction. In acute pain this transmission occurs primarily by way of larger myelinated afferent fibers or A axons. Once this message reaches the spinal cord, neurotransmitters deliver it to the anterolateral side of the cord, where ascending fibers transmit this message to supraspinal centers (including the thalamus and the cortex). This event is termed transmission. It is at this point that the individual actually perceives the sensation of pain.

During episodes of acute pain the autonomic nervous system is activated. The "fight or flight" response occurs, resulting in aberrations in vital signs and other effects. Thus in acute pain experiences such as that experienced by this patient, the individual may exhibit increases in heart rate, blood pressure, and respirations. Because the body cannot maintain this high level of excitation for extended periods however, this response will eventually abate, and vital sign changes will no longer provide information regarding the body's response to pain. Therefore it is unwise for the clinician to depend solely on these objective signs when assessing pain.

Treatment for acute postoperative pain can include both pharmacologic and nonpharmacologic therapeutic interventions. Pharmacologic interventions are used primarily and might include narcotic and nonnarcotic analgesics. Because of the type of surgery and the amount of pain he is experiencing, RM requires narcotic analgesics for effective management of his pain.

He is currently receiving 10 mg of morphine IM every 6 hours. He previously stated that this dose reduced his pain to a 4 after 4 hours but that the pain returned to a 10 after 6 hours. The reduction in pain from a 10 to a 4, coupled with RM's statement that the pain relief only lasted for 4 hours, indicates that the narcotic dose and the frequency of injections must be increased so that more complete relief may be obtained. The recommended dose of narcotic analgesic is morphine, 15 mg IM every 4 hours. Once RM is able to tolerate oral intake, this medication should be converted to an equianalgesic oral dose (10 mg of morphine IM or 60 mg of morphine orally). The pain would be expected to subside after several days. Analgesic therapy must be titrated to meet each patient's needs.

Nonsteroidal antiinflammatory drugs are very effective for mild to moderate pain, particularly pain originating in the muscle or bone. Most of these agents are available in the oral form only. If the postoperative patient with arthritis or related pain requires analgesia for this type of pain, indomethacin (Indocin) is available in the suppository form for rectal administration. RM is not currently complaining of this type of pain, so use of this type of medication as well as other nonnarcotic agents, including anxiolytics, anticonvulsants, and sedatives, would not be appropriate for the current situation.

Transcutaneous electrical nerve stimulation (TENS) has proven effective in treating postoperative pain. Electrical stimulation to large pain fibers reduces pain impulse transmission. Relaxation techniques may assist in reducing muscle tension, which can contribute to pain sensation. Distraction, by listening to enjoyable music for example, has been shown to lower pain perception and result in the use of less pain medication after surgery. As with all other therapeutic interventions for pain, these techniques must be individualized to meet each patient's needs.

An ineffective breathing pattern is seen in the postoperative patient who has had abdominal surgery. This pattern is characterized by shallow breathing and the reduction of diaphragmatic movement. This pattern promotes ventilation at a constant and reduced tidal volume lacking in periodic deep breaths or sighs (Latimer et al, 1971). During normal tidal respiration when the lungs return to a resting position at the end of expiration, some alveoli collapse, and there is a decrease in lung compliance assumed to reflect this collapse. Lung volumes and compliance will continue to decrease during ventilation at a constant tidal volume since the pressures and volumes associated with tidal respiration are insufficient to reexpand the already collapsed alveoli and prevent the collapse of others. Higher than normal pressures and volumes are required to reexpand the collapsed alveoli. In normal respiration very deep breaths or sighs provide such pressures and volumes, promoting expansion of the alveoli with the reversal of the atelectatic changes described above. Caro, Butler, and DuBois (1960) and Ferris and Pollard (1960) demonstrated that the normal pattern of tidal respiration, punctuated by periodic deep breaths, is essential to maintain alveolar inflation. They found that in persons who had normal tidal volume and alveolar ventilation who were prevented from taking deep breaths, functional residual capacity and residual volume decreased, and transpulmonary shunting occurred within 1 hour Deep breaths reversed these changes. Bendixen et al (1964) demonstrated similar findings in anesthetized persons.

This ineffective breathing pattern is generally believed to be the primary mechanism in the development of atelectasis in the postsurgical patient. Atelectasis is the most common postoperative pulmonary complication, and its occurrence has been attributed to a number of factors, including "guarding" or "splinting" due to incisional pain, relative immobility, tightly applied bandages, and the general depression of respiration caused by the use of narcotic, sedative, and anesthetic agents (Shekleton, 1982). Speculation about another possible cause for this pattern of ventilation has been reported recently in the literature. There is some preliminary experimental support for the postulate of Ford and Guenter (1984) that reflex inhibition of inspiratory muscle activity by way of intraabdominal afferent nerves may occur as a direct effect of upper abdominal surgery.

Nursing measures that may be instituted following surgery to treat an ineffective breathing pattern and potential for ineffective airway clearance include coughing and deep breathing exercises, turning the patient or assisting the patient to turn frequently, early ambulation, the administration of various forms of respiratory therapy, the judicious use of analgesics to enhance performance of these activities, and the provision of adequate environmental humidity and systemic hydration to thin secretions. Bartlett, Gazzaniga, and Geraghty (1973) concluded that the ideal respiratory maneuver for preventing and reversing atelectatic changes is one that "emphasizes maximal alveolar inflation and maintenance of a normal functional residual capacity." Such a maneuver requires a high alveolar inflating pressure exerted over a long period of time with the largest possible inhaled volume. Deep breathing provides higher transpulmonary pressures and greater volumes than those seen during normal or tidal respiration. Deep breathing with emphasis on sustained maximal inspiration will promote expansion of all alveoli throughout the lung.

Various devices such as blow bottles, rebreathing tubes, intermittent positive pressure breathing (IPPB), continuous positive airway pressure (CPAP), positive expiratory pressure (PEP), and incentive spirometry have been used to enhance the patient's performance of deep-breathing exercises. There are conflicting reports and an ongoing debate in the literature about the relative efficacy of these devices in promoting postoperative ventilatory function (Belman and Mittman, 1981; Bartlett, 1982; O'Donohue, 1985). Comparison of the results of studies in which these devices were evaluated is difficult because of differences in the samples and definitions of pulmonary complications used across studies (Pontoppidan, 1980). A general conclusion that can be drawn is that deep-breathing exercises alone are as effective in promoting postoperative ventilatory function as other techniques, provided they are done frequently and consistently. Lederer, VanDeWater, and Indech (1980) state that hourly coaching in deep-breathing exercises is more important than any device used to encourage deep breathing.

The nurse has the primary responsibility for helping the patient overcome the effects of an ineffective breathing pattern by performing coughing and deep-breathing exercises. The emphasis should be on sustained maximal inspiration and use of the abdominal muscles to allow diaphragmatic breathing. Specifically, the patient should inhale slowly and deeply through the nose with the mouth closed while expanding the abdomen, hold the breath for 3 to 5 seconds, and then slowly exhale through the mouth while contracting the abdomen. This should be repeated 3 to 5 times, and a deep breath should be followed by a low-pitched, hollow sounding cough from the chest area. During these exercises, which should be repeated on an hourly basis, discomfort can be minimized by supporting the incision with the hands, a pillow, or a folded blanket (Shekleton, 1982). One institution has reported giving surgical patients a "teddy bear" to use as a splint.

The goals of treatment include relief of pain and promotion of an effective breathing pattern and airway clearance. It is very important for RM's complete recovery that his pain be controlled so that he can perform deep-breathing and coughing exercises to prevent the development of pulmonary complications. Ac-

complishment of the second goal depends on the outcome related to the first goal.

The dosage and frequency of RM's morphine was increased. The care plan included a schedule with times assigned for treatments and activities that cause pain. This would allow medication administration to be timed so that its maximum effectiveness could be reached before initiation of painful activities such as deep breathing, coughing, and ambulating. The nurse also instructed RM in the use of relaxation and distraction techniques. His pain was brought under control, and he was able to participate actively in his care after that point. His temperature remained normal, and his lungs remained clear to auscultation. He was discharged on the sixth postoperative day with instructions to continue his breathing exercises and ambulation schedule.

Nursing Diagnoses

1. Acute pain related to surgical procedure, incision, and presence of drains.
2. Ineffective breathing pattern related to surgery and guarding response to pain.
3. Potential for ineffective airway clearance related to reluctance to cough and deep breathe.
4. Potential for infection related to incision and presence of drains and IV.

CASE STUDY: CHRONIC, NONMALIGNANT PAIN SYNDROME

Objective and Subjective Data

AS is a 42-year-old female with a history of multiple illnesses, including chronic, nonclassical migraine headache, chronic, low back pain, peptic ulcer disease, angina, mitral valve stenosis, chronic anxiety, and a reactive depression second-

Contributed by Susan Wright.

ary to chronic illness and pain.

Present illness: AS was admitted to the hospital for treatment of a nonclassical migraine headache. She had been experiencing the headache for 2 years, and there had been significant worsening of symptoms over the previous 2 weeks. Her secondary complaint is low back pain.

General appearance: The patient is lying supine in bed, in some acute distress, and with a somewhat blunted affect.

Physical examination

Vital signs

    Temperature: 98.4

    Pulse: 90

    Respirations: 20

    Blood pressure: 110/70 (lying)

PERRLA: Myopia (corrected with glasses), mild photophobia

Skin: Cool, clammy, and pale

Neck: Normal range of motion with no lymphadenopathy

Lungs: Clear to auscultation with normal chest-X-ray

Cardiovascular: Normal heart sounds and pulses all palpable and equal

Abdomen: Obese with epigastric tenderness with palpation; no guarding or rebound

Neurologic: Alert and oriented; cranial nerves II to XII intact; sensation, proprioception, and cerebellar function intact; toes downgoing; deep tendon reflexes equal

Laboratory studies: All within normal limits

Treatment

Problem 1: Chronic nonclassical migraine headache of 2 year's duration. Unsuccessful trials of ergotamine tartrate Bellergal, indomethacin, Midrin, amitriptyline, Zomax, Cafergot, Ergomar, inderal, biofeedback, acupuncture, and occipital nerve block. Minimally successful trials of oxycodone terephthalate (Percodan), meperidine, and rest.

Problem 2: Chronic low back pain of unknown origin of 5 year's duration. Unsuccessful trials of amitriptyline, indomethacin, ibuprofen, Zomax, ice, heat, acupuncture, and epidural steroid blocks have been attempted 3 times. Minimally successful trials of Percodan and acetominophen with codeine. Reasonably successful trial of corticosteroids. However, this was discontinued because of untolerable side effects.

Problem 3: Chronic anxiety that is reasonably well controlled with diazepam.

Problem 4: Reactive depression secondary to chronic illnesses and pain. Not being treated currently.

Discussion

AS was admitted to the hospital for symptomatic treatment of a chronic migraine headache. Her intractable headache in combination with other chronic pain problems is collectively referred to as chronic, nonmalignant pain syndrome (CNMP). CNMP is a syndrome in which the patient experiences pain from one or more sources for at least 6 months. It is often difficult to locate an organic cause for the pain(s), and just as often the pain is refractory to treatment, including surgery, pharmacotherapy, and behavioral/psychologic modalities. As is typical of CNMP, no direct organic cause could be found in this case. In addition, pain is an invisible problem (unlike a fractured leg for example), and the patient is left with the burden of proving to health care professionals that they have pain. As a part of the burden, patients often adopt "pain behavior," such as guarding, limping, and altered mobility.

The perception of the amount and quality of pain is truly a subjective experience and can only be known fully to the individual who is experiencing it. The same wound or pathology in two people can cause very different pain responses. The reason for this is not known, although several variables—culture, previous experience with pain, and meaning of the pain—may contribute to the difference. However, recent studies suggest that specific neuropeptides and/or neurotransmitters play a role at least in part in the perception and transmission of pain; these include endorphins (meaning endogenous morphine), enkephalins, serotonin, and norepinephrine. In addition, there are probably other neurochemicals not yet known.

Endorphins bind to specific receptors (called opioid receptors) in the brain and spinal cord to block the transmission of the pain message. Chemically, morphine has a very similar structure to endorphins and therefore, is also able to bind to the opioid receptors. The amount of endorphins present at a given time in a given individual can vary significantly. For example, if a person is subjected to a stressful event that results in a painful injury, their body may respond to that by producing large amounts of endorphins. Also, people who run as a form of exercise often experience a "runner's high." This euphoria may result from the production of large amounts of endorphins and may explain why some people become dependent on exercise. It is also possible that other people may not produce enough endorphins or that the endorphins are broken down too quickly. With less endorphin available to bind to the receptors, more pain may be perceived. In the case of AS, it is possible that she does not produce the same amount of endorphins as others and therefore has a greater sensitivity to pain.

Two additional neurotransmitters, serotonin and norepinephrine, are known to be important in the occurrence of some types of depression. They are now being recognized as important in the transmission and modulation of pain, giving pain and depression a neurochemical link. This link may be especially important in chronic, nonmalignant pain. This theory has been tested empirically through the use of specific drugs, which seem to produce improvement in both depression and chronic pain. The drugs are commonly known as tricyclic antidepressants, and they are primarily of two types: sero-

tonergic and noradrenergic. It is hypothesized that these drugs inhibit the breakdown of either serotonin or norepinephrine, thus making more of those chemicals available at the nerve synapse and thereby inhibiting the transmission of pain and or the process that may lead to depression and/or pain. Tricyclic antidepressants have been very successful in treating many people with chronic pain and/or depression. AS showed symptoms of depression that included feelings of sadness, blunted affect, inactivity, and loss of appetite. These symptoms are brought on by the profound limitations that prolonged pain brings, possibly by a neurochemical imbalance, or by a combination of the two. The answer is not known. AS has taken amitriptyline (a serotonergic antidepressant) and imprimine (a noradrenergic antidepressant) without success. It is still possible that AS has a neurochemical imbalance that is resulting in extreme sensitivity to pain but that the imbalance is in some as yet, unidentified chemical.

In addition to depression, both acute and chronic pain are often associated with anxiety. Anxiety may occur for several reasons. First, in anticipation and fear of pain, a person responds by guarding the area of pain by tightening the muscles. Most or all of a person's attention is turned from the outer world to an inner world. In turn, this response heightens the sense of pain, further increasing the anxiety, which further heightens the pain, etc. This becomes a cyclical response. AS was admitted to the hospital so that she could be given opioid analgesics in moderately high doses around the clock. This was done in an attempt to break the cycle of pain in her migraine headache. The doses are given on a scheduled rather than on an as needed basis for several reasons. First, the medication will be more effective if the pain is not allowed to escalate to its original level before the next dose is administered. Second, patients often experience significant anxiety if they call for medication but don't know how soon they will receive it. A schedule treats the pain before it reaches a peak and can reduce anxiety by allowing the patient to know exactly when they will get the medication. In AS's case, a trial of this schedule for 5 days was only minimally successful, possibly because of the complexity of the case.

An additional factor to consider in acute pain, and sometimes in chronic pain, is the possibility of an autonomic nervous system (ANS) response to pain and/or anxiety, which may result in loss of peripheral vasomotor tone and lead to hypotension and tachycardia. It is possible for an individual to go into shock from severe and unrelieved pain. In cases of prolonged acute or chronic pain, the body may adapt so that the symptoms of ANS arousal are not always present with pain. Absence of these signs does not preclude the absence of pain.

Hidden in the focus on treatment of AS's acute pain problem (migraine) were long-standing problems as a result of chronic pain (both from her low back and previous migraines). As a result of spending a great deal of time in bed because of the pain, AS was intolerant of activity. She was able to walk only to the bathroom and back and was exhausted by the time she returned to bed.

AS has been married for 20 years and has no children. Her husband is very supportive and provides encouragement but expressed a need for some help, possibly in the form of a support group. They had given up nearly all social activities, and he was feeling isolated and alone. AS agreed with this; she also expressed a great deal of guilt over "holding him down" but had no insight and was unable to develop a plan for dealing with these problems.

Pain, especially chronic pain, is a multidimensional phenomenon. There are physiologic, neurochemical, psychologic, and social implications to consider. A pa-tient such as AS presents a complex challenge to caregivers and demands a multidisciplinary, multimodality approach to treatment. The needs are many and would include the following:

Nursing Diagnoses

1. Chronic pain
2. Activity intolerance
3. Potential for disuse syndrome
4. Anxiety
5. Body image disturbance
6. Sleep pattern disturbance
7. Powerlessness
8. Ineffective individual coping
9. Social isolation
10. Ineffective family coping: Compromised

SUMMARY

The identification and treatment of both acute and chronic pain is a significant clinical problem. A major nursing responsibility and probably the most important intervention that a nurse can provide is relief from pain and suffering. The nurse often plays a central role in the management of pain. To be most effective in this role, the nurse must examine his or her own beliefs about the meaning of pain, make a commitment to learning about the nature and treatment of pain, and use every means at his or her disposal to alleviate suffering so that healing results.

BIBLIOGRAPHY

Abu-Saad H and Teslar M: Pain. In Carrieri V, Lindsey A, and West C, editors: Pathophysiologic phenomena in nursing, Philadelphia, 1986, WB Saunders Co, pp 235–269.

Bartlett RH: Postoperative pulmonary prophylaxis: breathe deeply and read carefully, Chest 81(1):1–3, 1982.

Bartlett R, Gazzaniga A, and Geraghty T: Respiratory maneuvers to prevent postoperative pulmonary complications, JAMA 224:1017–1021, 1973.

Belman M and Mittman C: Incentive spirometry: the answer is blowing in the wind, Chest 79(3):254–255, 1981.

Bendixen H: Atelectasis and shunting, Anesthesiology 25:595–596, 1964.

Bishop B: Pain: its physiology and rationale for management, Physical Therapy, 60 (1):13-35, 1980.

Bond JJ: Pain: its nature, analysis and treatment, ed 2, New York, Churchill Livingstone, Inc.

Brown RM and Pinkert TM: Mechanisms of pain and analgesia as revealed by opiate research: summary and recommendations, Nat'l Inst Drug Abuse Res Mono Ser 45:70-75, 1983.

Bryan-Brown CW: Development of pain management in critical care. In Cousins M and Phillips G: Acute pain management, New York, 1986, Churchill Livingstone, Inc, pp 1-19.

Caro C, Butler J, and DuBois A: Some effects of restriction of chest cage expansion on pulmonary function in man: an experimental study, J Clin Invest 39:573, 1960.

Carron H: Current concepts of pain mechanisms, Urol Surv 31(1):1-2, 1981.

Chapman R: Psychological factors in postoperative pain. In Smith G and Covino B, editors: Acute pain, London, 1985, Butterworth & Co. Ltd, pp 22-41.

Cohen M, et al: Surgical stress and endorphins, The Lancet, Jan 24, 1981, pp 213-214.

Coyle N: Analgesics and pain, Nursing Clinics of North America 22(3):727-741, 1987.

Dickenson AH: A new approach to pain relief? Nature 320:681-682, 1986.

Dodson ME: The management of postoperative pain, London, 1985, Arnold Edward Publishers Ltd.

Donovan M: Cancer pain: you can help! Nursing Clinics of North America 17(4):713-727, 1982.

Donovan M: Preface to symposium on pain control, Nursing Clinics of North America 22(3):645-648, 1987.

Feinmann C: Pain relief by antidepressants: possible modes of action, Pain 23:1-8, 1985.

Ferris B and Pollard D: Effect of deep and quiet breathing in pulmonary compliance in man, J Clin Invest 39:143, 1960.

Ford GT and Guenter CA: Toward prevention of postoperative pulmonary complications, ARRD 130:4–5, 1984.

Geach B: Pain and coping, Image 19(1):12–15, 1987.

Gershon S: Chronic pain: hypothesized mechanism and rationale for treatment, Neuropsychobiology 15(1):22-27, 1986.

Harrison M and Cotanch PH: Pain: advances and issues in critical care, Nursing Clinics of North America 22(3): 691-697, 1987.

Heft MW and Parker SR: An experimental basis for revising the graphic rating scale for pain, Pain 19:153-161, 1984.

Horsley J, et al: Preoperative sensory preparation to promote recovery, New York, 1981, Grune & Stratton, Inc.

Ignelzi RJ and Atkinson JH: Pain and its modulation, Neurosurgery 6(5):577-590, 1980.

International Association for the Study of Pain; Subcommittee on Taxonomy, 1979.

Jacox A: Pain: a source book for nurses and other health professionals, Boston, 1977, Little, Brown & Co.

Latimer R, et al: Ventilatory patterns and pulmonary complications after upper abdominal surgery determined by preoperative and postoperative computerized spirometry and blood gas analysis, Am J Surg 122:622–632, 1971.

Lederer DH, Van de Water JM, and Indech RB: Which deep breathing device should the postoperative patient use? Chest 79(5):610–613, 1980.

Leib RA and Hurtig JB: Epidural and intrathecal narcotics for pain management, Heart and Lung 14(2):164-174, 1985.

Levine J, Gordon N, and Fields H: Evidence that the analgesic effect of placebo is mediated by endorphins. In Pain abstracts, 1, Seattle, 1978, International Association for the Study of Pain.

Lewith GT and Kenyon JN: Physiological and psychological explanations for the mechanism of acupuncture as a treatment for chronic pain, Soc Sci Med 19(12):1367-1378, 1984.

McCaffery DB: Nursing management of the patient with pain, ed 2, Philadelphia, 1979, JB Lippincott Co.

McGuire DB: The measurement of clinical pain, Nursing Research 33(3):152-156, 1984.

McMahon MA and Miller SrP: Pain response: The influence of psycho-social-cultural factors, Nurs Forum 17(1):59–71, 1978.

Meinhart N and McCaffery M: Neurophysiological aspects. In Meinhart N and McCaffery M, editors: Pain: a nursing approach to assessment and analysis, Norwalk, Conn., 1983, Appleton-Century-Crofts, pp 27-89.

Meinhart N and McCaffery M: Pain syndromes. In Meinhart N and McCaffery M, editors: Pain: a nursing approach to assessment and analysis, Norwalk, Conn., 1983, Appleton-Century-Crofts, pp 213-241.

Melzack R: Concepts of pain measurement. In Melzack R, editor: Pain measurement and assessment, New York, 1983, Raven Press, pp 1-5.

Melzack R and Loeser JD: Phantom body pain in paraplegics: evidence for a central "pattern generating mechanism," Pain 4:195-210, 1978.

Melzack R and Wall DD: The Challenge of pain, New York, 1982, Penguin Books.

Millan MJ: Multiple opioid systems and pain, Pain 27:303-347, 1986.

O'Donohue WJ: Prevention and treatment of postoperative atelectasis, Chest 87(1):1–2, 1985.

Paice J: New delivery systems in pain management, Nursing Clinics of North America 22(3):715-726, 1987.

Phillips GD and Cousins MJ: Neurological mechanisms of pain and the relationship of pain, anxiety and sleep. In Cousins M and Phillips G, editors: Acute pain management, New York, 1986, Churchill Livingstone, Inc, pp 21-48.

Pontoppidan H: Mechanical aids to lung expansion in nonintubated surgical patients, ARRD 122:109–119, 1980.

Ruch TC: Pathophysiology of pain. In Rush T and Patton H, editors: Howell-fulton-physiology and biophysics: the brain and neural function, ed 20, Philadelphia, 1979, WB Saunders Co, pp 272-324.

Shekleton M: The effect of preoperative instruction in coughing and deep breathing exercises on postoperative ventilatory function, Ann Arbor, Mich, 1982, University Microfilms Inc.

Smith G and Covino B: Acute pain, London, 1985, Butterworth & Co, Ltd.

Smith TW: The mechanisms of pain and opioid-induced analgesia, Molecular aspects of medicine 7:509-545, 1985.

Sternbach RA, editor: The psychology of pain, New York, 1978, Raven Press.

Syrjala KL and Chapman CR: Measurement of clinical pain: a review and integration of research findings. In Benedetti C, Chapman CR, and Moricca G, editors: Advances in pain research and therapy 7:71-101, New York, 1984, Raven Press.

Terman G, et al.: Endogenous pain inhibitory substrates and mechanisms. In Benedetti C, Chapman CR, and Moricca G, editors: Advances in pain research and therapy 7:43-56, New York, 1984, Raven Press.

Wall PD: The gate control theory of pain mechanisms: a reexamination and restatement, Brain 101:1-18, 1978.

Wall PD: Neurophysiology of acute and chronic pain. In Benedetti C, Chapman CR, and Morricca G, editors: Advances in pain research and therapy 7:13-25, New York, 1984, Raven Press.

Wall PD and Melzack R, editors: Textbook of pain, New York, 1984, Churchill Livingstone, Inc.

Yaksh TL, Howe JR, and Harty GJ: Pharmacology of spinal pain modulatory systems, Advances in pain research and therapy 7:57-70, 1984.

Zimmerman M: Physiological mechanisms of pain and pain therapy, Triangle 20(½):7-18, 1981.

UNIT VI

Activity-exercise pattern

13

Musculoskeletal pathophysiology

The major functions of the musculoskeletal system are twofold. The first is to provide structure for the body. In so doing the musculoskeletal system serves as a means of support and protection for the vital organs. The second purpose is to provide the mechanical means to allow movement of the various body parts and ultimately of the entire body. The bones play major roles in hematopoiesis and in promoting balance among certain mineral constituents of the body as well.

When the human being is viewed as a system, it seems obvious that through its structural and protective functions the musculoskeletal system contributes to the maintenance of wellness. The musculoskeletal system contributes to maintenance of the steady state in wellness and restoration of the steady state in disease in other ways as well. The roles of bone in promoting balance among minerals and in hematopoiesis allow adaptation to constantly changing conditions in the internal environment. The role of the musculoskeletal system in promoting mobility allows adaptation to constantly changing conditions in the external environment. The ability to adapt to everchanging environmental conditions is an absolute prerequisite to restoration and maintenance of wellness in humans.

The functional components of the musculoskeletal system are the muscles, bones, and joints. In order to facilitate the presentation of material, this chapter has been organized according to these functional components. It must be understood, however, that dysfunction in one area will affect normal function of the other components because of the structural and functional interrelationships that exist within the musculoskeletal system. The bones and joints comprise a framework and lever system, the movement of which is made possible through contraction of the muscles. In most disorders of the bones and joints the muscles are secondarily affected and vice versa.

Normal structure and function of the musculoskeletal system depends upon adequate nutrition, exercise, and the condition of other body systems, especially the nervous system. Many pathophysiologic processes that occur in other body systems or that affect the nutritional status or ability to exercise have the potential for affecting the musculoskeletal system in a secondary but profound way.

The focus of this chapter is on primary musculoskeletal disorders; however, the secondary effects of disorders occurring outside of the musculoskeletal system on its function will also be discussed. The major response to dysfunction of the musculoskeletal system is impaired physical mobility, which is discussed in the following chapter.

PATHOPHYSIOLOGIC MECHANISMS AND DISORDERS OF MUSCLES

The motor unit, by definition, is comprised of a single motor nerve fiber and the muscle fibers it supplies. The physiologic processes involved in the normal function of the motor unit include the following: (1) generation and propagation of the action potential along the membrane of the nerve axon and muscle fiber; (2) neuromuscular or synaptic transmission at the motor endplate; (3) excitation-contraction coupling; and (4) chemicophysical contraction of the muscle. The function of the motor unit is monitored via a feedback loop comprised of the intrafusal muscle fibers with their spindle receptors, the tendon organ receptors, and their afferent connections to the central nervous system (CNS).

There are many points at which pathophysiologic mechanisms may interfere with normal motor unit function and thus disrupt muscular contraction as illustrated in Fig. 13-1. Many of these mechanisms can be caused by disorders outside the musculoskeletal system, and muscular function is affected in a secondary way. These mechanisms are discussed in detail in other chapters. For example, alterations in fluid volume and composition, no matter what the primary cause, have the potential to seriously disrupt normal muscle function by altering the electrical properties of the cell membrane; these are discussed in Chapter 18. Muscle weakness, cramping, and tetany are common manifestations of potassium, sodium, phosphate, and calcium imbalance. Mechanisms that can interfere with the neurologic aspects of motor unit function

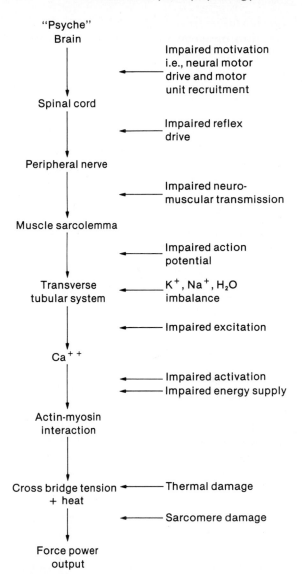

Fig. 13-1. Steps involved in muscular contraction and the possible pathogenetic mechanisms by which it can be disrupted.

(From Edwards RHT: Biochemical bases of fatigue in exercise performance: catastrophe theory of muscular fatigue. In Knuttgen H, Vogen J, and Poortmans J, editors: Biochemistry of exercise, 1983, Champaign, Ill., Human Kinetics Publishers.)

are discussed in Chapter 10. Pathophysiologic mechanisms that interfere with muscular aspects of motor unit function are discussed in this chapter, although the distinction between muscular and neurologic dysfunction is somewhat artificial, since it is known that muscle and nerve exert tropic influences on one another. Evidence of a tropic effect of nerve on muscle is based on experimentally derived data demonstrating that the histochemical reactivity of a muscle fiber is determined by the type of alpha motor neuron by which it is innervated. The exact nature of a tropic substance or substances is unknown at the present time. Many disorders currently thought to be myopathic in origin may actually be neurogenic in origin as a result of a total or partial deficiency in these tropic substances.

The term *myopathy* is applied to diseases of the muscle in which there is no apparent neurologic involvement. While myopathies may occur secondarily to nutritional, endocrine, infectious, toxic or other disturbances of the steady state, the focus of this chapter is on myopathies in which the muscle tissue is primarily affected. Generally, the cause of the primary myopathies is genetic with the immediate problem being the absence or improper construction of certain enzymes or proteins which are necessary for muscle cell structure and function. Since the purpose of the muscle is to generate enough force to allow movement, manifestations of muscle dysfunction will be related to alterations in force or the power output of the muscle.

Manifestations

The major manifestations of muscle dysfunction—muscle weakness and muscle fatigue—are related to the fundamental properties of muscle—strength and endurance. Strength is defined as the maximum force that a muscle can develop with maximal stimulation. Contractile force is determined by the force-length (length-tension), force-velocity, and force-frequency relationships. Strength also depends on the size and number of individual fibers in a given muscle. Loss of strength is manifested as weakness, which is defined as failure to *generate* an expected or required force on the initial attempt at performance (Edwards, 1978).

Endurance is defined as the ability to maintain a contraction against a load and is determined by the relative distribution of fiber types within the muscle and the intensity (or force and duration) of the contraction. Muscle fibers can be differentiated on the basis of their maximal shortening velocity and their ATP synthesizing capability, which, in turn, determines the degree of fatigue resistance present. Oxidative slow fibers (type I) are fatigue resistant, glycolytic fast fibers (type IIa) fatigue rapidly, and oxidative fast fibers (type IIb) have an intermediate capacity to resist fatigue (Vander et al., 1985). The adult human diaphragm, for example, is comprised of chiefly the high-oxidative, fatigue-resistant fibers because the ability to breathe depends on this muscle maintaining activity without interruption. In contrast, the majority of the muscles in the arms are of the glycolytic type, as these muscles are often called upon to perform tasks like lifting or carrying heavy objects, which require the generation of large amounts of tension over a relatively short period of time.

Loss of endurance is manifested as fatigability. Muscle fatigue is defined as failure to *maintain* an expected or required force (power output) with repeated or sustained contraction (Edwards, 1981 and 1983). The term fatigue is used here in reference to a physiologic state of muscle and not in reference to the subjective sensation of overwhelming exhaustion and decreased capacity for physical and mental work (NANDA, 1988). Physiologically, muscle fatigue can be classified as central or peripheral, depending on its site of origin. Central fatigue is the result of impaired neural stimulation, while peripheral fatigue is the failure of response, that is, stimulation is constant but continued force is decreased. Edwards (1983) has proposed that fatigue may serve a protective function in that serious, irreparable damage might occur should a muscle continue its activity beyond a certain critical point.

These properties of muscle can be altered by the use (or lack of use) of the muscles. The strength and endurance of the muscles can be increased through exercise and conditioning of the muscle. Strength training increases the size of the glycolytic fast fibers because those are the fibers recruited during high-intensity (load), short-duration exercises like weight lifting. The diameter of the fibers increases as a result of the formation of new myofibrils, and the concentration of glycolytic enzymes increases. Endurance training increases the mitochondrial capacity of the oxidative slow and fast fibers because these fibers are recruited during low-intensity, long-duration exercises like marathon (long distance) running. Not only does the number of mitochondria increase, but the capillary network increases around these fibers (Vander et al., 1985). If the regular exercise program is stopped, the muscles will revert back to the preexercise condition, a situation known as *deconditioning*. If muscles are not used, a condition known as disuse atrophy will develop.

Other possible manifestations of muscle disorders include alterations in contractility such as myotonia, hypotonia, paralysis, and contracture, which are discussed later in the chapter, and pain and cramping.

Everyone has experienced muscle pain following a vigorous exercise session or the muscular aches that accompany many temporary viral infections. Muscle pain should be evaluated as to whether it is localized or generalized. If it is local, the site should be examined for swelling and induration. If the pain is generalized, it should be determined whether it is accompanied by weakness or any other systemic manifestations. Diffuse, generalized aching pain is the chief manifestation of the *fibrositis syndrome*, which is also called fibrositis or fibromyalgia. The pain is often accompanied by stiffness and weakness. There will be a large number of tender sites located in muscles and over bony prominences and associated with skinfold tenderness and reactive hyperemia. A feeling of overwhelming fatigue to the point of exhaustion is another chief complaint and sleep pattern disturbances are part of the syndrome. Patients with this disorder tend to be perfectionists in their approach to life and are sensitive to cold, noise, environmental irritants, and stress. The pathogenesis is not known and fibrositis is viewed as a pain amplication syndrome. It is believed that there is a quantitative change in otherwise normal pain mechanisms. In true, primary fibrositis there is no evidence of inflammatory changes or other muscle damage. Secondary fibrositis can accompany other rheumatic disorders like rheumatoid arthritis. Estimation of the true incidence of primary fibrositis is complicated by the inclusion of persons with referred pain syndromes (Kelley, Harris, Ruddy and Sledge, 1985).

Muscle cramps are thought to occur as a result of neuronal hyperactivity, specifically of the intramuscular portion of motor nerve terminals. This deduction is supported by a variety of clinical and experimental observations such as the appearance of fasciculations before and after the cramp, precipitation by changes in the composition of the extracellular fluid, occurrence during rest, after trivial effort, or following forceful contraction of a shortened muscle and termination by passive stretching (Engel and Banker, 1986).

Mechanisms

The underlying pathophysiologic mechanisms that may act singly or in combination with one another to disrupt normal muscle structure and function include the following:

1. Alterations in the amount and type (composition) of contractile tissue
2. Alterations in the metabolic and electrochemical functions of the muscle cells
3. Cell damage by inflammation and trauma

Alterations in composition of the contractile tissue. A change in the size (bulk) or composition of muscle tissue is the pathologic defect accompanying many of the more commonly seen muscle disorders. It stands to reason that a change in size or composition will affect the strength of the muscle. An obvious example is the great strength exhibited by weight lifters whose muscles are well developed through exercise and training. A reduction in muscle mass or a loss of some muscle fibers even with a compensatory increase in the size of accompanying normal fibers usually results in a loss of strength. This is a feature of most myopathies and accounts for the clinical manifestations of weakness and to some extent easy fatigability.

The two major alterations in muscle tissue bulk and composition that accompany primary and secondary muscle disorders are atrophy and hypertrophy. *Atrophy*, or a loss or shrinkage of muscle fibers, occurs following interruption of neural input,

with disuse, immobility, malnutrition, steroid use, Cushing's syndrome, and in primary muscle disorders. The morphologic changes that characterize atrophy include the following in order of occurrence.

1. Reduction in the size of fibers
2. Enlargement and dislocation of sarcolemmal nuclei
3. Progressive degeneration of fibers
4. Deposition of fat cells and an increase in endomysial and perimysial connective tissue

The entire muscle will eventually appear shrunken and flabby. The normal red-brown color of the muscle will change to a yellowish brown, and in the most advanced stages the muscle will be a pale gray from deposition of fat and fibrous tissue.

Hypertrophy is an increase in the size or bulk of a tissue without an increase in the number of cells or tissue elements. Individual fibers increase in diameter and length as a result of the formation of new myofibrils, usually in response to increased use. Normal muscle fibers adjacent to abnormal fibers are subject to a greater than normal work load, and hypertrophy of the normal fibers often occurs as a compensatory response to the increased work load when the adjacent fibers are abnormal.

Morphologic changes may not be uniform throughout the muscle but rather may affect certain fiber types preferentially. The following discussion illustrates different patterns of morphologic changes involving the muscle fibers.

The atrophy following loss of nerve supply (denervation atrophy) affects all types of fibers equally while atrophy of a normally innervated muscle affects type II fibers predominantly. The former type of atrophy occurs where the nerve supply has been damaged by a disease process, such as poliomyelitis or a cerebrovascular accident (CVA) (see Chapter 10). The latter type of atrophy accompanies steroid use, disuse or immobility, malnutrition and cachectic states, and primary muscle disorders where the nerve supply is intact. Because of the usual pattern of innervation of motor units, there will be a mix of atrophic and normal-appearing fibers throughout the muscle tissue in denervation atrophy if the total muscle is not completely denervated. The normally innervated fibers adjacent to denervated atrophic fibers may eventually hypertrophy and develop secondary myopathic changes in response to the increased work load as well (Engel and Banker, 1986). Such a pattern is seen in the post-polio syndrome (see Chapter 10).

The simultaneous presence of atrophic and hypertrophic fibers throughout muscle tissue is characteristic of the *muscular dystrophies.* Aside from inflammatory conditions, the most commonly seen primary muscle disorders are those classified as muscular dystrophy. The muscular dystrophies are a group of genetically transmitted diseases characterized by progressive pathologic changes in the skeletal muscles, which result in bilateral, symmetric wasting, and weakness of the muscles while the motor nerves appear intact. Each muscle fiber is affected individually, which leads to a mixture of normal- and abnormal-appearing fibers. Change in size is most apparent in the abnormal fibers, some of which are atrophied and others hypertrophied.

Criteria that define a form of muscular dystrophy include the following:
1. Muscle weakness is a primary cause of symptoms.
2. Results of electromyographic (EMG) and muscle histologic tests are negative for signs of denervation.

3. The disorder is inherited.
4. Weakness becomes progressively more severe.
5. Evidence of abnormal storage of fat or carbohydrates in fibers is lacking.

The various types of muscular dystrophies differ from one another in the manner of genetic transmission, age at onset, progression of the symptoms, and the sites of the affected muscles. The signs and symptoms depend on the muscle groups affected. For instance, in Duchenne muscular dystrophy the muscles of the pelvis and calves are especially affected, resulting in a waddling gait and lordosis, signs pathognomonic to this type. Becker's muscular dystrophy is a less severe disease that maps to the same chromosomal locus and may be an allelic form of Duchenne muscular dystrophy (Nudel et al., 1988). Onset is usually insidious in all types of muscular dystrophy. Presented in Table 13-1 is a summary of the major types. The Duchenne type muscular dystrophy results in the most extreme manifestation of this group of diseases and this disorder will be presented in greater detail.

Disease model: Duchenne muscular dystrophy. Duchenne muscular dystrophy is a sex-linked (x-linked) recessive condition, meaning that it occurs primarily in males and is transmitted by female carriers. It is one of the most common lethal genetic diseases, affecting 1 out of every 3500 live male births (Nudel et al., 1988; Scott et al., 1988). Duchenne muscular dystrophy has occasionally been reported in females with X chromosome anomalies.

Affected boys are usually identified between 2 and 3 years of age. Most often delayed walking is the first sign of abnormality. While most affected boys walk by 2 years of age, most never walk normally and none are able to run or jump normally. The age at which symptoms be-

Table 13-1. Muscular dystrophies

	Inheritance	Age at onset	Major clinical features	Course
Duchenne type	X-linked recessive	Early childhood	Symmetric weakness; initially pelvifemoral; weakness in shoulder girdle later and then trunk muscles; "pseudohypertrophy" of calves; reduced intelligence	Progressive; inability to walk by puberty; death by age 20
Becker type	X-linked recessive	Second decade	Milder variant of Duchenne type	"Benign"; ability to walk into adult life
Facioscapulohumeral	Autosomal dominant	Childhood to late adult life	Usually facial weakness first; scapular weakness; humeral weakness	"Benign" course not progressive
Limb-girdle	Autosomal recessive	Variable onset first to sixth decade	Two variants: (1) pelvifemoral weakness, (2) shoulder girdle weakness	Variable progression; disability within 20 years
Distal myopathy	Autosomal dominant	Middle to late adult life	Weakness in small muscles, hands; weakness in tibialis anterior and gastrocnemius	Slow progression
Ocular myopathy	?Autosomal dominant	Variable	Group of syndromes all having weakness of extraocular muscles initially, sometimes involvement of face, neck, and limbs	Rarely progressive

From Robbins S and Cotran R: Pathologic basis of disease, Philadelphia, 1979, WB Saunders Co.

come apparent has been found to vary between 1 and 10 years, with the mean age at onset being 2.88 years. The time before obvious clinical symptoms appear has been designated as preclinical, since it is believed the disease is present from birth. High serum enzyme activity (creatine phosphokinase, CPK) as well as abnormal muscle histology have been observed during the first year of life.

Clinical manifestations. Early clinical manifestations are related to the symmetric muscular wasting and weakness, which starts in the extensors of the hip and knee joints and spreads to the extensors of the foot. Parents may report developmental delays and falls. The child may walk clumsily and have difficulty climbing steps or keeping up with other children in running games. A characteristic waddling, lordotic gait with a protruding abdomen and toe walking is seen as muscle wasting and weakness progress. When attempting to rise from a supine position, the boy will do so in a characteristic way, climbing up his body by pushing on his thighs to lever his trunk upwards. This action is known as Gower's sign (Fig. 13-2). Some of the proximal muscles become noticeably enlarged, especially those of the calves. The gluteal and deltoid muscles are similarly affected. The infiltration of muscle by adipose and connective tissue contributes to the muscle enlargement, hence use of the term "pseudohypertrophy" to describe these changes. True hypertrophy of normal muscle fibers occurs also (Fig. 13-3).

As the child grows older, between 6 and

Fig. 13-2. Gower's sign. Patient "climbs up" his own body to stand upright. Note enlargement of calf muscles and winging of scapulae.

11 years of age, the muscles of the shoulder girdle, upper arms, and flexors of the neck become involved. At the age of 5 or 6 years, there may appear to be some improvement in the child's condition because of a normally occurring period in which muscle growth exceeds muscle break-

down. This period is short-lived, and usually by the age of 10 years or early adolescence the child becomes unable to walk and is confined to a wheelchair.

Another prominent feature of the disease process is the development of contractures. The muscles permanently shorten

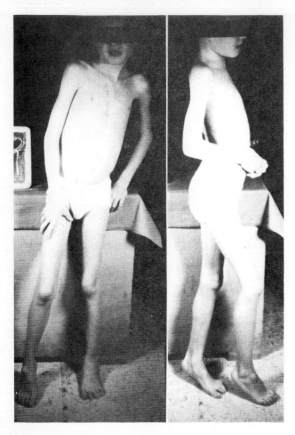

Fig. 13-3. Duchenne's muscular dystrophy. Note well-developed calf muscles, wasting of other muscles, and "toe walking" position of feet.
(Courtesy Shriners Hospital for Crippled Children, Chicago.)

and joints become fixed. Flexion deformities of the hip, knee, and elbow joints develop and the ankle becomes plantar flexed. The deformities rapidly progress once the child is confined to a wheelchair, probably as a result of prolonged immobility in a sitting position. When the exaggerated lordosis of the upright position is replaced by kyphosis in the sitting position and with the patient tending to lean toward the dominant side, scoliosis develops (Fig. 13-4). Two patterns in the development of scoliosis have been noted: in the

first the deformity is rapidly progressive after the patient becomes wheelchair bound; in the second it is more slowly progressive (Bradford et al., 1987). In addition to the physical discomfort it causes, severe scoliosis can also compromise cardiopulmonary function.

Death usually occurs by the age of 20 years (Slater, 1987), most commonly as a result of respiratory infection and failure. Cardiac failure has occasionally been given as a cause of death. Abnormalities of cardiac rate, rhythm, and conduction are common but bear no relationship to the age of the patient or severity of the disease process (Farah et al., 1980).

The potential for both pulmonary infection and impaired gas exchange exists because of the responses that develop as the respiratory muscles are affected by the disease process, that is, ineffective breathing pattern and ineffective airway clearance. The ineffective breathing pattern is related to respiratory muscle weakness and will be exacerbated if scoliosis has developed to a point where lung expansion is further restricted by the bony deformity. Reduced maximal inspiratory and expiratory pressures reflect the decrease in respiratory muscle strength. The loss of muscle strength is related to the inability of the lungs to expand to maximal capacity, and vital and total lung capacities have been found to decrease as muscle strength declines and functional ability is lost (Inkley et al., 1974). Alveolar hypoventilation is the result of this ineffective breathing pattern, and impaired gas exchange occurs when the alveolar hypoventilation becomes severe enough to cause carbon dioxide retention and hypoxemia. There is a corresponding decrease in flow rates and the ability to expel airway secretions as the cough becomes less forceful, which leads to ineffective airway clearance and

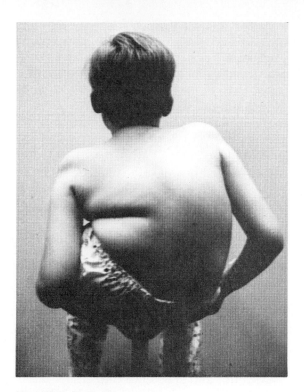

Fig. 13-4. Scoliosis.
(Courtesy Ronald L. DeWald, MD and Mary Faut, RN, Orthopedics and Scoliosis, Ltd., Chicago.)

the potential for pulmonary infection.

The decline in pulmonary function has been suggested as a parameter for monitoring the progression of the disease process. In fact, Rideau et al. (1984) have proposed that patients with Duchenne muscular dystrophy achieve a maximum plateau vital capacity by 10 to 12 years of age, which can be used to determine the prognosis of the restrictive pulmonary disorder. They found that patients with a maximum plateau vital capacity of less than 1200 cc had the poorest prognosis, becoming wheelchair bound prior to 10 years of age and dying before 17 years of age. Those patients with a maximum plateau vital capacity greater than 1700 cc had the best prognosis with the longest life

expectancy. They observed that vital capacity deteriorated rapidly once the vital capacity fell below 40% of predicted and the scoliosis curve had progressed to greater than 23 degrees.

Intellectual impairment is another feature of Duchenne muscular dystrophy that sometimes occurs in Becker's as well (Nudel et al., 1988). This impairment is nonprogressive and does not correlate with the degree of illness. It affects verbal more than practical intelligence. The mean IQ of affected boys is lower than that of nonaffected siblings or boys of comparable age but observed values usually demonstrate a normal distribution (fall within a bell-shaped curve). Approximately 30% of affected children have an IQ below what is accepted as the lower limit of normal. The nature of the relationship between this type of muscular dystrophy and intellectual impairment is unknown. Lack of progression of intellectual impairment over time and the presence of normal and even high levels of intelligence in some affected children make the determination of a clear relationship between the etiologic factors involved and intelligence difficult. In the past it was believed that intellectual impairment was a "social" consequence of the disease in that the affected child had less education or was affected in a unique psychosocial way. However, in families with two or more affected members, the usual finding of similar IQs in the affected children strongly suggests a genetic determination of intellectual ability.

While morphologic abnormalities of the CNS have been found at autopsy, none have been consistently noted. Slight cerebral atrophy is suggested (Engel and Banker, 1986).

Pathogenesis. In the past, before identification of the abnormal gene, many of the cellular abnormalities present in Duchenne muscular dystrophy were examined for their relevance in the pathogenesis of this disorder. The finding of necrotic and regenerating muscle fibers led to speculation about an ischemic pathogenetic mechanism. A disorder of vascular origin was thought plausible, since it is known that female carriers of the disorder exhibit a high incidence (approximately 59%) of Raynaud's phenomenon and a decrease in circulation time, while in patients there is the early appearance of vasomotor disorders of the extremities, a positive response to vasodilator therapy, abnormalities in arm to arm circulation time, and low muscle blood flow and low oxygen consumption at high work loads.

Much speculation centered on cell membrane defects as being pathogenic. Electron microscopic studies have demonstrated abnormalities in the muscle plasma membranes of patients with Duchenne muscular dystrophy and in the erythrocyte membranes in patients with other types of muscular dystrophies. The function of lymphocyte membrane receptors has been found to be altered in some types of dystrophy. Abnormal membrane permeability was suggested by the finding of increased sarcoplasmic enzyme levels in the serum of patients with Duchenne muscular dystrophy.

Since the identification of the gene locus at which the mutation responsible for Duchenne muscular dystrophy occurs, studies have focused on the identification of a protein product of the gene that could explain the pathologic changes which occur in the disease. The gene is located in the middle of the short arm of the X chromosome in band 1 of region 2 (band Xp21) (Kolata, 1986; Monaco et al., 1986). It is large, spanning 1000 to 2000 kb, and encodes a 14 kb mRNA (Koenig et al., 1987). Expression of gene transcripts has been re-

ported in striated, smooth, and cardiac muscle and, most recently, in the brain of rat, mouse, and rabbit (Nudel et al., 1988).

The mutation that results in the pathologic changes characteristic of muscular dystrophy appears to be a deletion of portions of the DNA segment comprising the gene (Kunkel, 1986; Koenig et al., 1987 Roses, 1988; Bobrow et al. 1988). Because of the nature of the mutation, the protein product of the gene would be expected to be absent or markedly reduced (Scott et al., 1988). The protein encoded by this gene has only recently been identified and named *dystrophin* (Slater, 1987; Hoffman et al., 1987a). This protein has been found to be present in normal muscle but missing from the muscle of both patients with Duchenne muscular dystrophy and mice with an X-linked form of mouse muscular dystrophy. Koenig et al. (1988) have identified the complete amino acid sequence of dystrophin and speculate that it is a large, rod-shaped protein that possibly plays a structural role in the cytoskeleton of the cell. Hoffman, et al. (1987b), through a process of subcellular fractionation using antibody probes, have localized the presence of dystrophin to the triadic junction in muscle cells that contains the T tubules and sarcoplasmic reticulum. This is where excitation-contraction coupling takes place and where calcium release from the sarcoplasmic reticulum occurs in response to membrane depolarization and results in myofibrillar contraction. Because the triadic structures are responsible for the release, uptake, and storage of calcium within the muscle fiber, dystrophin is most likely to be necessary for the maintenance of calcium homeostasis. The investigators speculate that the absence of dystrophin in Duchenne muscular dystrophy may disrupt normal calcium homeostasis and allow increased intracellular calcium levels that may activate intracellular phopholipases. This could account for the tissue degeneration and elevated serum sarcoplasmic enzyme levels found in patients with Duchenne muscular dystrophy. Another possibility posed by the investigators is that dystrophin serves to attach the triads to the myofibrillar cytoskeleton by binding with actin filaments. The amino terminus of dystrophin has been noted to be similar to a region on alpha-actinin, another protein known to bind with actin filaments.

There is an interesting difference between the human form of Duchenne muscular dystrophy and mouse muscular dystrophy. While dystrophin seems to be lacking in both, the human form is relentlessly progressive and ultimately fatal, while the mouse form is characterized by near-normal muscle function following an early period of muscle cell degeneration. Investigation of this difference may suggest treatment measures for humans (Slater, 1987).

Treatment rationale. At present there is no treatment or cure for the underlying pathologic process of Duchenne muscular dystrophy. The goal of treatment is to postpone the development for as long as possible and to minimize the progressive manifestations that inexorably occur. The child should be assisted to maintain independence for as long as possible. Obesity should be prevented in order to maintain mobility for as long as possible. Passive exercises and joint stretching to prevent contractures should be taught to the parents (Vignos, 1983). Development of flexion contractures of the hips and shortening of the Achilles tendon (the earliest deformities to develop) can be postponed by regular passive stretching and by having the child lie prone. The latter can be encouraged while the child reads or watches TV. A splint to keep the ankles in a neutral position can be worn at night. Some authorities have recommended the use of lightweight long-leg braces combined with surgical release of lower extremity contractures to maintain ambulatory capability. A major treatment goal at this point is to keep the child ambulatory for as long as possible. A program of active exercise may help to prevent an accelerated deterioration of muscle, although this is not certain (Vignos, 1983).

Once the child requires a wheelchair, flexion contractures of the hips and knees invariably develop. Prevention of footdrop deformity can be attempted through use of boots and by placing the feet on the wheelchair footrest so that a 90-degree angle is maintained at the ankle joint. As mentioned earlier, scoliosis develops rapidly as the child spends more time in the wheelchair. This is the most difficult deformity to prevent. Rigid plastic jackets and braces have been used to prevent spinal deformity, but these are not without certain drawbacks—most notably, physical discomfort and reduction in respiratory excursion. Use of these devices does not guarantee prevention of spinal deformity. A wheelchair with a molded seat designed to support the spine may offer the most likely means of delaying the development of spinal deformities (Fig. 13-5).

Breathing exercises have been advocated as a means of improving ventilatory function (DiMarco et al., 1985). The importance of interventions directed toward minimizing the risk of contracting a respiratory infection, such as avoiding contact with a person who has an upper respiratory tract infection, maintaining an adequate nutritional status, obtaining an adequate amount of rest, and avoiding fatiguing and stressful situations should be taught to the patient and family.

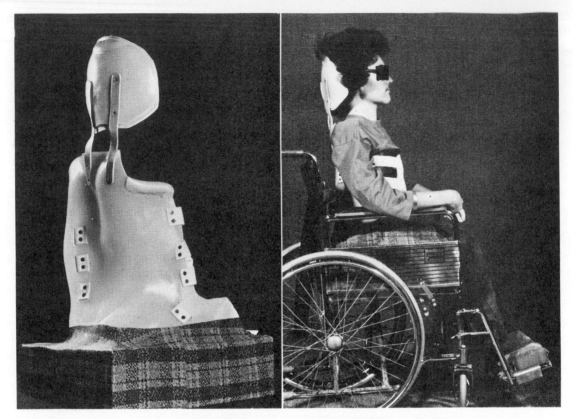

13-5. The "Gillette" Sitting Support Orthosis. Custom molded plastic shell that conforms to the body contours posteriorly and laterally from the knees to the upper thorax. It is mounted on a base that provides support to the shell and allows the unit to be removed from the wheelchair for use in other places. Note the head rest and thoracoabdominal support apron.
(Photo courtesy Orthotics Dept, Gillette Children's Hospital. St. Paul, Minnesota)

Prompt, aggressive treatment of a respiratory tract infection is important, since these children are prone to rapid, progressive pulmonary deterioration with even a minimal insult to the respiratory system.

A major part of treatment of the child and family lies in the realm of psychologic support. Attendance at school should be encouraged for as long as possible. The child with normal intelligence levels can attend a regular school until physically unable and then can be placed in a school for the disabled where any special needs are more likely to be met. Acquisition of cognitive and manual skills will help the child develop a sense of accomplishment and self-worth. If intellectual capacity is diminished, other skills in the areas of art, handcrafts, and music might be stressed instead, and placement in a special school may be indicated from an early age.

The debilitating nature of the disease, as well as the effort required to care for the child, may tax even the strongest family's physical and emotional reserves. The physical demands of care, chronic emotional stress, and the financial strains associated with this disease make coping with it extremely difficult. The child and family require development of a strong support network and its maintenance by the health care team responsible for care. Families that have demonstrated the ability to cope with this disease identify a support group outside the family, open communication between family members, and outside activities for the parents as important. The willingness to cope with one day at a time is also a factor in being able to adjust to the demands of the disease on the family (Buchanan et al., 1979). Because of the nature of the disease and its widespread effects, the health care team should be multidisciplinary and may include physicians, nurses, social workers, psychologists, and physical, occupational, respiratory, and recreational therapists. The local branch of the Muscular Dystrophy Association can be used as a resource for educational materials and support networks.

The parents of a child with Duchenne muscular dystrophy should receive genetic counseling. There are four possible outcomes if a woman who is a carrier becomes pregnant. She may have any of the following:

1. A girl who is normal
2. A girl who is a carrier
3. A boy who is normal
4. A boy who has Duchenne muscular dystrophy

At the present time there is no one test available for identifying carriers with 100% accuracy. Genetic probes cover only a small part of the Duchenne locus (Bobrow et al., 1988). Familial occurrence of the disease is the current method by which different types of Duchenne carriers are classified. A *definite carrier* is the mother of an affected son with an affected brother, maternal uncle, sister's son, or other male relative in the female line of inheritance. A *probable carrier* is the mother of two or more affected sons but no other known affected relatives or a mother of an affected son and one or more affected grandsons. A *possible carrier* is the mother of one affected son with no other affected male relatives, or a woman without an affected son but with an affected male relative in the female inheritance line (Engel and Banker, 1986). Carrier status cannot be determined with greater certainty until more is known about the rate of the gene mutation. If the mutation rate is equal in males and females, then one third of all cases are due to new mutations in the ovum. There is a two-thirds chance that the mother is a carrier. If the mutation rate is unequal, then all mothers of affected boys are carriers. This has obvious implications for genetic counseling and prevention of the disease (Roses, 1988; Bobrow et al., 1988).

Disruption of normal electrochemical and metabolic functions. Other pathophysiologic mechanisms by which muscular function may be altered include disruption of the normal electrochemical and metabolic (energy-producing) functions of the cell. These two mechanisms are related, as energy is required to maintain the normal electrical properties of the cell membrane. Alteration of the electrical properties of the membrane will affect the electrochemical functions of the cell and, subsequently, can disrupt excitation-contraction coupling. In some primary muscle diseases, like the myotonic disorders and the periodic paralyses, the electrical properties of the membrane are altered as a result of changes in the membrane regulatory functions. In some primary muscle diseases, the metabolic capacity is altered, thus affecting the energy available to maintain the normal electrical properties of the membrane and allow excitation-contraction coupling to occur. Metabolic capacity can be inadequate due to an increased demand for energy or a decreased supply of or inability to use substrates and oxygen. The latter is the case in a group of disorders known as the glycogen storage diseases. An example of a disorder in which the demand for energy is increased such that it cannot be met and, in fact, becomes detrimental to the continued viability of the muscle is malignant hyperthermia. Disruption of the electrochemical and metabolic functions of the muscle cell will become apparent through abnormal contractile states of the muscle such as contracture, myotonia, hypotonia, and flaccid paralysis, which are usually accompanied by muscular weakness. Most frequently these disruptions are the result of a genetic or congenital defect.

Myotonia. The term myotonia refers to a condition in which the muscle fibers remain contracted, that is, the muscle is unable to relax following a voluntary, willed contraction. The small muscles of the hands and fingers are those most often affected, and myotonia is clearly demonstrated when the patient is asked to release a clenched fist and cannot do so. Myotonic lid lag is characterized by a patient's inability to lower the eyelids for 10 to 20 seconds when told to look down following a prolonged upward gaze. Patients report the symptom of muscle stiffness or cramping. In some individuals repeated muscle contraction eliminates the stiffness while in others the myotonia is aggravated (myotonia paradoxica). Exposure to cold and tapping a muscle may also elicit a myotonic muscular response.

The pathophysiologic mechanism underlying myotonia appears to be increased excitability of the muscle fiber membrane such that impulses are fired spontaneously (without stimuli) or following stimuli that are normally ineffective. The pathogenesis of this increased muscle fiber excitability has been investigated using an animal model. A certain type of goat that is subject to transient myotonic episodes has provided a valuable animal model for experimental investigation of the phenomenon of myotonia. Using the myotonic goat model, studies have shown evidence of a reduction in chloride permeability of the cell membrane. It is hypothesized that afterpotentials in a normal fiber are smaller because the normally high chloride permeability stabilizes the membrane potential while a reduction in chloride permeability in myotonic fibers allows unusually large afterpotentials, leading to repetitive and seemingly spontaneous firing of action potentials.

The reduced chloride permeability hypothesis is the most plausible for explaining the myotonia seen in goats and in the human myotonic disorder, myotonia congenita. There is a decrease in the number of Cl^- channels and there may be abnormalities in Na^+ channel activation as well. The myotonia seen in other conditions may be the result of hyperexcitability of the membrane induced by other mechanisms. A reduction in resting membrane potential is a possible mechanism and in fact has been demonstrated in muscle fibers of patients with dystrophia myotonica. Abnormal Na^+ channel activity may be a factor, as an abnormally high intracellular Na^+ ion concentration is found in myotonic dystrophy (Engel and Banker, 1986). Other hypotheses that have been speculated on but for which no evidence in humans has been demonstrated include a reduction in the critical membrane potential and a decrease in calcium ion concentration.

Investigators have attempted to discover

some membrane defect that could account for these hypothesized pathophysiologic mechanisms. A difference in the relative amounts of fatty acids between muscle phospholipids from normal and myotonic patients has been found. This finding leads to the question of whether membrane function is altered as a result of the abnormal composition of the membrane itself.

Myotonic disorders. Pathologic disorders characterized by myotonia can be hereditary or acquired. An example of acquired myotonia is that which accompanies hypothyroidism. The myotonic disorder disappears with treatment of the underlying endocrine disorder. True hypertrophy of the muscles and myotonia have been observed in recovery from various types of polyneuritis. Myotonia may also be induced by a variety of drugs which include clofibrate, triparonol, 2,4-dichlorphenoxyacetate, monocarboxylic acids, and 20,25-diazacholesterol. The latter also produces cataracts, a prominent feature in dystrophia myotonica, which is hereditary.

There are a variety of hereditary myotonic disorders. The major ones include dystrophia myotonica and myotonia congenita. Both disorders are inherited as an autosomal dominant trait. Dystrophia myotonica is also known as myotonic dystrophy and Steinert's disease. The name *myotonia atrophica* was used in the past and has again been advanced as a proper one because there is strong belief that the muscle involvement is secondary to chronic lower motor neuron involvement or that there is a decrease in inhibitory influence on the muscle from the lower motor neuron, which manifests as myotonia. Myotonia congenita is also known as Thomsen's disease. There are two different forms of each disorder, which are discussed below.

DYSTROPHIA MYOTONICA. The clinical manifestations of dystrophia myotonica are quite varied and initially appear between the ages of 15 and 35 years. When symptoms are apparent at birth the condition is recognized as a specific clinical syndrome called neonatal or early-onset dystrophia myotonica. Myotonia is not present until 2 years of age in most affected children. The syndrome at birth is characterized by severe generalized hypotonia and muscular weakness, difficult breathing, sucking, and swallowing, and facial diplegia. Prognosis is poor; if the infant survives the neonatal period, motor development will be slow with a high incidence of mental retardation. The mothers of these affected children are always affected with dystrophia myotonica, although usually only mildly.

In the adult form, myotonia is usually not a dominant feature. There is a characteristic facial appearance with hollow cheeks and sagging jaw that is caused by ptosis, facial muscle weakness, and atrophy of the masseter and temporalis muscles. Cataracts may be observed via slit lamp examination in over 90% of the adult patients. Cataracts may occur as early as in the first decade. Baldness (frontoparietal alopecia) is frequently seen in males. Endocrine involvement includes atrophy of the testes in males, menstrual disturbances in females, and abnormalities in glucose tolerance. During pregnancy, symptoms of myotonia and muscle weakness increase with improvement occurring within 2 weeks of delivery.

Cardiac abnormalities have been reported. Cardiac involvement occurs late in the course of the disease and is usually not severe enough to cause symptoms of cardiomyopathy and failure. A majority of patients demonstrate ECG abnormalities, including conduction defects. Sudden death has also been documented (Engel and Banker, 1986).

The effect of dystrophia myotonica on pulmonary function depends on the extent to which the respiratory muscles are involved. Weakness of the musculature may lead to a reduced inspiratory effort and ultimately to alveolar hypoventilation. Manifestations of nervous system involvement include intellectual deterioration, lack of drive or initiative, and an increased need for sleep. Changes in mentation along with increased muscular weakness lead to a steady decline in the patient's social activities.

MYOTONIA CONGENITA. The two main clinical manifestations of myotonia congenita include myotonia and generalized muscle hypertrophy, giving the individual an athletic or well-developed appearance. Muscle stiffness is the predominant feature, but transient weakness also occurs (Engel and Banker, 1986). Myotonia becomes apparent in infancy or early childhood. In another form of myotonia congenita (Becker type), which is inherited as an autosomal recessive trait, onset occurs later than in Thomsen's disease but the myotonia tends to be more severe.

Treatment of the myotonia associated with dystrophia myotonica is usually not indicated, since the myotonia is not disabling. The myotonia of myotonia congenita is disabling and can be abolished or greatly relieved with treatment. The drugs commonly used to treat myotonia include quinine, procainamide, and phenytoin. Because the side effects of these drugs are severe, drug therapy should be used only if the myotonia interferes with activities of daily living.

Hypotonia. The term hypotonia means a loss or defect in the normal tonicity, or tension, of the muscles. Muscle tone refers to the muscle being in a steady state of contraction. Hypotonia is a loss of this steady state of contraction. Hypotonia is a

feature of a group of congenital myopathies named after some distinguishing morphologic abnormality observed in the cell. These disorders differ in mode of hereditary transmission, specific clinical manifestations, and the type of morphologic abnormality present. A listing is presented below:

Central core disease
Centronuclear myopathy
Congenital fiber type disproportion
Congenital lipid storage disease
Congenital mitochondria-lipid-glycogen disease
Congenital muscular dystrophy
Fingerprint body myopathy
Focal loss of cross-striation
Minicore disease
Multicore disease
Myopathy with loss of myobfibrils
Myotubular myopathy
Nemaline (rod) myopathy
Reducing body myopathy
Sarcotubular myopathy
Type I fiber atrophy and myotube-like structures
Type I fiber hypotrophy with central nuclei
Zebra body myopathy

A complete description of each one is beyond the scope of this book; however, these descriptions can be found in references cited at the end of this chapter. Generally, they are relatively nonprogressive disorders, although there are progressive forms of some. Some clinical manifestations are universally present in these disorders and are described in the text to follow (Engel and Banker, 1986).

There is a generalized hypotonia present in the newborn at birth. These neonates are referred to as "floppy" babies. Muscular weakness may be diffuse but proximal weakness is primarily demonstrated. Muscle bulk is normal or slightly decreased, and there is no hypertrophy of muscles. Deep tendon reflexes are either decreased or absent. Skeletal abnormalities such as a highly arched palate, a long face, hip dislocation, pes cavus, or kyphoscoliosis are frequently present. Some of these skeletal abnormalities are probably related to the muscular weakness. Motor development is delayed with some milestones never being met; these children do not run or jump. Serum levels of creatine kinase (CK) are normal or only slightly increased. Motor and sensory nerve velocity studies are normal, and the EMG shows a normal or "myopathic" pattern. The pathogenesis of these disorders is not clearly understood at this time. Some appear to be related to enzyme deficits, whereas others may be due to alterations in the muscle tissue itself. Some may even be due to an abnormality of innervation.

Periodic paralysis. There is a group of disorders known as the periodic paralyses that are characterized by a combination of flaccid muscular paralysis and serum electrolyte disturbances. The entire musculature is affected, although the muscles of the extremities are most noticeably affected. The paralytic episodes are transient, lasting from less than an hour to several days, without permanent effects, although some patients may gradually develop a persistent muscular weakness thought to be related the presence of vacuoles that arise from the proliferation, degeneration, and autophagic destruction of SR and T system–derived membranous organelles (Engel and Banker, 1986). The pathogenesis of vacuolar myopathy is not understood, but the similarity of these changes across the different types of periodic paralyses indicates that a common pathogenetic factor is involved.

These disorders are classified based on the apparent mode of transmission and on the serum potassium abnormality present. A listing of the recognized periodic paralyses by mode of transmission is shown in the box below.

There are both primary and secondary forms of periodic paralysis. In contrast to the primary forms, secondary forms of hypokalemic and hyperkalemic periodic paralysis are not genetically determined, although a genetic predisposition is suggested by the high incidence of thyrotoxic periodic paralysis seen in the Oriental population (Engel and Banker, 1986). Secondary hypokalemic periodic paralyses occur in association with hyperthyroidism, excessive loss of potassium, and barium intoxication. Secondary hyperkalemic periodic paralysis can be precipitated by a serum potassium level greater than 7 mEq/L.

The different primary types of periodic paralysis are distinguished by the presenting clinical manifestations and precipitating features. For example, hypokalemic episodes may be brought on by ingestion of a heavy carbohydrate meal or by glucose and insulin. An incipient attack can sometimes be "walked off." In contrast, hyperkalemic episodes tend to be provoked by administration of potassium but not by heavy meals. Exposure to cold may also provoke weakness in the primary forms of these disorders. The differentiat-

---

Familial, autosomal dominant trait

Hypokalemic periodic paralysis
Hyperkalemic periodic paralysis
Normokalemic periodic paralysis

Nonfamilial, occurs sporadically

Hypokalemic periodic paralysis
Hyperkalemic periodic paralysis

Table 13-2. Typical features of the three types of periodic paralyses

	Hypokalemic	Normokalemic	Hyperkalemic
Age of onset (years)	10-20	0-10	0-10
Intervals between attacks	Weeks or months	Weeks or months	Days
Duration of attacks (hours)	6-24	24	1-3
Time	Night	Night	Day
Carbohydrate meals	+	—	
During heavy exercise	—	—	+
After heavy exercise	+	+	—
Iatrogenic provocation	Glucose + insulin	Potassium	Potassium
Prophylactic treatment	Potassium chloride	High salt diet	Frequent high carbohydrate meals
	Low sodium and low carbohydrate diet	9-alpha-fluoro-hydrocortisone	Avoidance of fasting Avoidance of cold exposure
	Acetazolamide		Chlorthiazide
	Spironolactone		Hydrochlorthiazide
	Avoidance of cold exposure		Acetazolamide Tocainide
Treatment of attack	Potassium chloride	Sodium chloride	Calcium gluconate, glucose, and insulin

Adapted from McComas AJ: Neuromuscular function and disorders, London, 1977, Butterworth (Publishers), Inc. Modified from Pearson (1963).

ing characteristics and forms of treatment according to the type of serum electrolyte abnormality present are given in Table 13-2.

The basic defect responsible for the paralytic episodes appears to be membrane inexcitability. The surface membrane is unable to propagate an action potential. A variety of studies have demonstrated a reduced resting membrane potential during paralytic attacks in the familial types. The etiology of the membrane inexcitability remains a subject of speculation. Two mechanisms that have been hypothesized as being responsible for the paralytic episodes include increased sodium permeability and internal potassium sequestration. Another hypothesis has been that both mechanisms operate together. It does appear that abnormalities of the sodium channels are involved. For example, increased sodium permeability has been shown to be a cause of paralysis in primary hypokalemic paralysis (Rudel et al., 1984).

Contracture. *Malignant hyperthermia* is an uncontrolled hypermetabolic state that can be precipitated in susceptible individuals by certain anesthetic agents. Aerobic and anaerobic metabolism in skeletal muscle increases to such an extent that temperature can rise as quickly as 1° C every 5 minutes, arterial carbon dioxide tension may exceed 100 mm Hg, and pH can fall below 7.0. Most patients also demonstrate muscle contracture, or physiologic rigor, which is a state of muscle contraction not initiated by electrical activity. Severe rhabdomyolysis may occur with excessive release of myoglobin and myoglobinuria, which puts the patient at risk for the development of acute tubular necrosis and renal failure (Engel and Banker, 1986).

The syndrome of malignant hyperthermia was first described and has been studied extensively since in swine that were inbred for muscular development. The swine model and the human form are similar in the changes in vital signs, acid-base balance, biochemical parameters, and metabolic and muscular responses that occur (Gronert, 1980).

The current favored theory regarding its pathogenesis is that the control of intracellular, ionized calcium level is lost and metabolism increases in an attempt to supply enough ATP to pump calcium back into storage sites and decrease the intracellular calcium level. There is experimental evidence obtained from both swine and humans that supports this theory. The occurrence of an acute episode appears to depend on susceptibility, a triggering event, and the absence of inhibitory factors. Susceptibility does appear to be an inherited trait. The most current view is that more than one gene or allele may be involved, making the expression variable between recessive and dominant (Gronert, 1980). Abnormalities have been found in many different organ systems in susceptible individuals, which suggests that there may be a generalized defect in membrane properties or permeability. While a variety of events such as exercise, heat, anoxia, excitement, and ischemia have been found to trigger malignant hyperthermia episodes in swine, the human trigger appears to be more homogeneous, with volatile anesthetic agents being the only recognized

one. Responses similar to malignant hyperthermia have also occurred in humans due to drugs like ketamine, MAO inhibitors, tranquilizers, phencyclidine and tricyclic antidepressants, viral infections, lymphoma, thyroid storm, and exercise stress. As acidosis and temperature increase, the normal control of enzyme activity and cell function is lost. A reduced threshold for thermal inactivation of cellular function has been demonstrated in swine (Engel and Banker, 1986).

The mortality from this disorder was reported to be as high as 70%. With improved early recognition and treatment with dantrolene, a muscle relaxant that acts to decrease calcium release by the SR, it has been reduced to less than 10%.

The *glycogen storage diseases* are a group of rare, inherited disorders in which an enzyme required for the metabolism of glucose or glycogen is missing. These disorders are classified by number, by the missing enzyme, and by the name of the person who first described the condition (see Table 13-3 on p. 450). Muscle contracture during ischemic exercise is a hallmark of some of these metabolic myopathies (Engel and Banker, 1986); however, not all of these disorders affect muscle function.

Type V, or McArdle's disease, is one of the glycogen storage diseases in which muscle function is directly affected. It illustrates a muscle condition in which metabolic function is disrupted. This disorder results from the lack of an enzyme specific to muscle that allows the breakdown of glycogen to lactic acid. Thus the conversion of glycogen to lactic acid is prevented. Severe muscle pain is precipitated by exercise, and muscles may become swollen. Symptoms may persist for as long as a day but are relieved by rest.

Table 13-3. Glycogen storage diseases*

Type	Enzyme deficiency	Other nomenclature	Clinical involvement of muscle
I	Glucose-6-phosphatase	von Gierke's disease	No
II	Acid maltase (acid alpha-1,4-glucosidase)	Pompe's disease	Yes
III	Amylo-1,6-glucosidase (debranching enzyme)	Cori's disease Forbes' disease Limit dextrinosis	Yes
IV	Amylo-1,4 → 1,6-transglucosidase (α-1,4-glucan 6-glycosyl transferase or branching enzyme)	Andersen's disease Amylopectinosis	Yes
V	Muscle phosphorylase	McArdle's disease	Yes
VI	Liver phosphorylase	Hers' disease	No
VII	Phosphofructokinase	Tarui's disease	Yes
VIII	Liver phosphorylase b kinase	—	Possible

*From Bethlem J: Myopathies, ed 2, New York, 1980, Elsevier North-Holland, Inc.

The ingestion of glucose or fructose during exercise may help to increase tolerance for exercise. These patients have a normal life expectancy and can manage with minimal incapacity as long as exercise is restricted.

Acid maltase deficiency is another glycogen storage disease in which muscle function is disrupted. While it is a relatively rare disorder, it does illustrate the effects of generalized body muscle deterioration as seen in the patient in the following case study.

CASE STUDY: ACID MALTASE DEFICIENCY

Subjective and Objective Data

Present illness: TF is a 46-year-old white female with the adult onset form of acid maltase deficiency. Her muscle function has deteriorated to the point that she requires the use of a negative pressure respirator at night to rest her ventilatory muscles. TF participates in a research

Contributed by Maureen Shekleton.

study and is being seen in her home by a nurse on a weekly basis. Her insurance coverage includes a weekly visit by a home health aide who takes her vital signs and helps her take a bath and wash her hair and a monthly visit by a respiratory therapist who checks her respiratory equipment and auscultates her chest.

History

Past medical history: TF was diagnosed with acid maltase deficiency (AMD) at 26 years of age. The diagnosis was difficult to make because there was no previous family history of AMD. A younger sister has since been diagnosed with AMD but presented with symptoms at a much later age than TF. TF began using a negative pressure respirator for nocturnal ventilation 6½ years ago after repeated episodes of respiratory failure that necessitated the use of assisted mechanical positive pressure ventilation and, at one point, she also had a tracheostomy to facilitate mechanical ventilation. TF has not been intubated or maintained on positive pressure ventilation since starting the negative pressure ventilation. She has had repeated episodes of pneumonia and requires antibiotic therapy and increased bronchial hygiene and ventilatory support. One year ago, she fell and fractured her left leg and required several months of physical therapy in order to resume walking.

Social support: TF is married with no children. Both her family and her husband's live nearby and are able to visit and help with errands, chores etc. TF's young niece and nephew stay with her in the summer and on weekends. They help around the house and TF states that they are good company although their bickering sometimes bothers her. Her mother- and father-in-law were killed in an accident last year and TF and her husband miss them a great deal. TF states that they were very good to her and helped a lot. She also has a couple of friends who call and come to visit.

Oxygenation status: TF spends 9 to 13 hours each day on her respirator. She places herself on it at bedtime and sleeps with it on; if she feels tired during the day she will take an early afternoon nap with it on. She does her own positive pressure breathing treatments 2 or 3 times each day, which helps her to expectorate secretions as well as to expand her lungs. She is on 1 L of oxygen by continuous nasal cannula. Without the oxygen, her oxygen saturation level, measured by pulse oximetry, drops to between 85% and 89%. During exercise, her oxygen saturation level drops below 80%, so she increases the flow to 3 L before beginning any activity. Her breathing pattern is exaggerated, with use of accessory muscles and frequent gasping respirations through the mouth. Relevant ventilatory parameters are as follows:

Vital capacity	10% of predicted
Maximal voluntary ventilation	26% of predicted
Maximal inspiratory pressure	10cm H_2O pressure
Maximal expiratory pressure	15cm H_2O pressure

Arterial blood gas results on 32% FiO_2:

pH	7.39 (low normal)
pO_2	88mm Hg (low)
pCO_2	54mm Hg (high)
HCO_3	32 meq/L (high)
Base excess	6.2 (high)

Mobility/activity status: TF can walk short distances using a walker. Her gait appears exaggerated and unsteady. Her grip strength as measured with a dynamometer is very weak. She does develop dyspnea with exertion. She is able to stand at the sink for short periods and do dishes, and she can fold laundered clothes while sitting in a chair. A recently purchased small exercise treadmill allows her to do light walking exercise. She is able to meet her daily hygiene needs, but requires assistance with bathing. She dresses and toilets herself. She requires some assistance with dressing if she is getting dressed up to go out. TF spends most of the day watching television while sitting in a rocking style recliner chair. She rocks constantly in the chair stating it helps her breathing.

Comfort/rest status: TF sleeps approximately 9 hours each night. She takes a nap if tired and if going out or doing something out of the ordinary. She has moderate pain in her left knee and ankle but is unable to tolerate any analgesic medication. She rubs the leg occasionally while talking. She complains of cramping during her regular, monthly menstrual periods.

Nutritional status: She appears thin and emaciated because of muscle wasting. She weighs 99 pounds and is 5 ft 6 in tall. She can feed herself and eats regular meals, many of which are ordered from a local pizza and sandwich shop that delivers to the home. She requires assistance cutting meat and takes a sandwich apart to eat it. She drinks from a cup but is unable to use a straw because she cannot generate enough negative pressure to move liquid up into her mouth. She takes a daily liquid nutritional supplement formulated for patients with pulmonary disease.

Elimination status: Normal patterns are maintained. Does get up once a night to urinate.

Communication pattern: TF's speech is slow and slightly slurred and her voice has a nasal tone quality. She states that the slurring gets worse and she is harder to understand when tired. She speaks slowly so she can be readily understood by others. She frequently stops speaking to take a deeper than normal breath.

Health perception-health management: She manages her respiratory care by herself and is very knowledgeable about her muscle disorder and respiratory needs. She is careful to minimize contact with anyone who has a respiratory tract infection. She is able to suction secretions from her respiratory tract if it becomes necessary. Antibiotics are available and at the first sign of a respiratory tract infection she notifies her physician and starts the antibiotic medication. She sees her pulmonologist at regular visits and as needed. A dental hygienist comes to her home once a year to perform dental prophylaxis and examine her mouth. She has not seen her gynecologist for over a year. She was examined by a home health nurse who made weekly visits until approximately 6 months ago when the insurance coverage would no longer include this service. She takes full responsibility for managing her health needs.

Coping/stress management: TF maintains a very optimistic, positive outlook on life. She has learned to live within the restrictions imposed by the disease process and tries to do whatever she can around the house. She has a very pleasant, easy-going personality and speaks frequently of maintaining a hopeful outlook about life. TF is very attached to her four cats and says that they "keep her company" and enjoys watching them play.

Discussion

Acid maltase is a lysosomal enzyme which is necessary for the release of glucose, oligosaccharides and maltose from glycogen and the incorporation of maltose into glycogen. Accumulation of glycogen and acid mucins occurs in cells which are lacking this enzyme. Its precise metabolic role is unclear at the present time. There is speculation that it is necessary for the regulation of tissue levels of glycogen, an important source of energy for the muscles (Engel and Banker, 1986).

Acid maltase deficiency is inherited as an autosomal recessive trait. There are three recognized forms of this glycogen storage disease that differ by age of onset and death, progression and organ involvement. The infantile form usually presents within the first few months of life. The muscle weakness is rapidly progressive and death occurs by age 2 years, usually of cardiopulmonary failure. The childhood form presents during infancy or early childhood. The child demonstrates delays in motor development and muscle weakness. The respiratory muscles in particular are affected and death is usually due to respiratory failure by the second decade. The adult form presents after the age of 20 years as a slowly progressive myopathy, affecting the torso and limb muscles, as was the case with TF who was originally diagnosed in her mid 20's. Deep tendon reflexes are noted to diminish and eventually disappear. About one-third of the patients present with signs of respiratory insufficiency, however, the respiratory muscles are eventually affected in all cases and the usual cause of death is respiratory failure.

Symptoms of respiratory insufficiency include headache, somnolence, nausea, orthopnea, and dyspnea on exertion. Signs include hypoxemia, hypercapnea, decreased maximal inspiratory, and expiratory pressures at the mouth, reduced transdiaphragmatic pressure during maximal inspiration, and a significant reduction in vital capacity which is further decreased by one-half when the patient assumes the supine position. The diaphragm is disproportionately weak. The respiratory muscle dysfunction results in a restrictive ventilatory defect with basilar atelectasis. TF has exhibited all of these clinical manifestations as her respiratory muscles became involved. TF's respiratory muscle weakness is apparent in the spirometry values and the low maximal inspiratory and expiratory mouth pressures that she demonstrates. The lack of ventilatory reserve is apparent from the low maximal voluntary ventilation measurement. She continues to retain CO_2 as seen in the blood gas results and rapidly develops significant hypoxemia when off oxygen as demonstrated using pulse oximetry. She recalls that the most distressing symptom was the headaches she experienced when she began to develop respiratory insufficiency. The headaches are caused by the cerebral vasodilation that occurs in response to increased levels of carbon dioxide. It is interesting to note that her sister began experiencing headaches 3 months ago and two months later experienced an episode of pneumonia which resulted in respiratory failure and the need for assisted mechanical ventilation.

Medical treatment is supportive as there is no cure for this disorder. Research has provided encouraging results related to acid maltase replacement therapy in vitro. Human applications remain undeveloped at this time (Engel and Banker, 1986). Treatment includes maintaining the highest degree of mobility for as long as possible. Assistive devices can be used and physical therapy and exercise programs can help maintain the remaining muscle function.

Once the respiratory muscles are affected, treatment must include maintaining ventilatory function and preventing respiratory failure. Because of the muscle weakness and the altered energy metabolism caused by AMD, the inspiratory muscles are prone to develop fatigue which in turn contributes to deterioration of respiratory status culminating in ventilatory failure. Avoiding increased demands on and fatigue of the respiratory muscles is important. The muscles can be rested using assisted nocturnal ventilation or an oscillating or rocking bed. At one time TF used such a bed to rest her muscles and assist in achieving full chest excursions. The rocking motion moves the abdominal contents against and away from the diaphragm assisting its movement that, in turn, increases both inspiratory and expiratory capacities. When respiratory function became more compromised she went on the negative pressure respirator. Because AMD patients have trouble coughing forcefully and expectorating secretions, they are prone to develop pneumonia with respiratory tract infections. They must be taught to avoid contact with contagious persons and bronchial hygiene techniques to assist in removing secretions. An infection or any other condition that increases the oxygen demands of the tissues and increases the work of breathing has the potential of worsening the respiratory muscle weakness and promoting the development of muscle fatigue. It is hypothesized that respiratory muscle fatigue represents the final common pathway to ventilatory failure in all conditions in which the respiratory muscles are affected.

Nursing Diagnoses

1. Impaired physical mobility related to muscle weakness
2. Ineffective breathing pattern related to restrictive defect due to muscle weakness
3. Activity intolerance related to hypoxemia
4. Bathing self care deficit

5. Potential for ineffective airway clearance related to muscle weakness and inability to cough forcefully
6. Potential for infection
7. Potential for disuse syndrome
8. Potential for injury related to weakness
9. Potential for social isolation

Cell damage by inflammation. Another pathologic mechanism that disrupts normal muscle function is inflammation. Secondary inflammatory changes in the muscle may occur as the result of an infection such as leprosy, a parasitic invasion such as trichinosis, or in conjunction with another disease process. The term *polymyositis* is applied to nonhereditary, inflammatory myopathies of a primary nature. When a skin rash is also present, the term *dermatomyositis* is applied. Forty percent of the patients with polymyositis present with inflammatory changes in the skin as well as muscle. Pathologic and immunopathologic differences also exist between the two disorders (Engel and Banker, 1986).

Disease model: polymyositis and dermatomyositis. Polymyositis may become apparent through a large variety of differing combinations of signs and symptoms. These inflammatory disorders have been classified in a variety of ways. The following classification was adopted by the Research Group on Neuromuscular Diseases of the World Federation of Neurology:

1. α-Polymyositis; possibly an organ-specific autoimmune disease
2. β-Polymyositis or dermatomysitis; possibly one feature of a non-organ-specific autoimmune disease and associated with systemic lupus erythematosis, rheumatic fever, rheumatoid arthritis, progressive systemic sclerosis, polyarteritis nodosa, and Sjögren's syndrome
3. γ-Polymyositis or dermatomyositis; possibly a conditioned autoimmune response in malignant disease

Polymyositis occurs twice as frequently in females as in males. The peak age of onset in children is between 5 and 15 years. The peak age of onset in adults is between 45 and 55 years. The disease occurs most frequently in adults, however.

A significant association between polymyositis and malignant disease has been noted, although detection of one facilitates detection of the other and, therefore, this relationship may be spurious. Many different types of tumors have been reported. In most cases the manifestations of dermatomyositis or polymyositis preceded manifestations of the tumor, but this is not true in all cases. The incidence of associated malignancy is higher with dermatomyositis than with polymyositis (Engel and Banker, 1986).

The course of polymyositis is highly variable. Some patients present with an insidious but progressive weakness. Others demonstrate a brief but rapidly advancing disorder. Still others present with a disease that varies in intensity at different times.

The muscles of the body are not uniformly affected and the effects of the disease process vary among different muscles as well as among regions within the same muscle. Because of this, histologic examination may be negative, depending on whether the area of muscle biopsied was myositic. Histopathologic changes include the presence of inflammatory cells (lymphocytes and plasma cells), degenerating and regenerating cells, and increased amounts of connective tissue between the fibers. Using electron microscopy researchers have found that the intramuscular capillaries appear abnormal; the endothelial cells and basement membrane appear to be thickened when compared to normal tissue.

Clinical manifestations. A major symptom is symmetrical weakness of the proximal limb muscles and the neck flexors. Patients may complain of difficulty climbing stairs, getting out of the bath, or rising from a sitting position resulting from weakness of hip muscles. Because of shoulder muscle weakness the patient may have difficulty combing hair; neck muscle weakness may cause difficulty lifting the head. Dysphagia and dysphonia may occur as a result of bulbar muscle weakness. Respiratory muscles may also be affected.

Muscular pain and tenderness may be associated with the weakness. The affected muscles may be tender and feel hard on palpation. Muscle atrophy, contractures, and calcification occur later in the disease process. Skin calcifications occur more frequently in children, with 33% of children affected with dermatomyositis developing calcifications. Associated with muscular disturbances may be a feeling of malaise and the presence of a fever.

The skin rash present in dermatomyositis is an erythematous eruption distributed across the nose and cheeks in a characteristic "butterfly" pattern. The skin lesions may also be found on forehead, upper chest, arms, and neck. Heliotrope rash, or a lilac discoloration, of the upper eyelids may be present. Periorbital edema may be associated with the heliotrope rash. Hyperemia at the bases and sides of nails and red streaks over the backs of hands and fingers may be observed. A local vasculitis may be observed in the periungual area.

When polymyositis or dermatomyositis occurs in combination with connective tissue diseases, Raynaud's phenomenon is a frequent manifestation. Raynaud's syndrome is a transient blanching or cyanosis seen in one or several fingers (sometimes in toes) as a result of cooling. When arthralgia or joint pain is severe, an association of rheumatoid arthritis or systemic lupus erythematosus should be considered.

Some patients experience intestinal disorders, and children affected with dermatomyositis may even develop ulcerative lesions of the gastrointestinal tract. A nonproductive cough and dyspnea may be the presenting symptoms in polymyositis or may occur later in the disease process. The underlying pneumonitis and bronchiolitis later progress to interstitial fibrosis. Esophageal hypomotility caused by weakness of the pharyngeal muscles may contribute to the dysphagia.

The erythrocyte sedimentation rate (ESR) will be increased in approximately 50% of the cases in response to the inflammatory process. Elevated serum CPK levels will be found in response to the tissue degeneration that occurs in these disorders. The enzyme serum creatine phosphokinase is abundant in muscle tissue; as the tissue is destroyed this enzyme is released into the serum. However, elevation of CPK levels has not been found to correlate with the degree of weakness and disability reported by the patient. Serial measurements of CPK levels and the ESR provide useful indicators of the response to treatment as well. Electromyographic findings superficially resemble the myotonic response and are indicative of a myopathic process.

Etiology and pathogenesis. The etiology and pathogenesis of these disorders are unknown at the present time. Viruslike particles were believed to have been found via electron microscopy in the sarcoplasm and myonuclei, leading to speculation that these disorders may have a viral etiology. However, these tubular aggregates have been shown experimentally not to cause viral symptoms (Engel and Banker, 1986). Certain viruses are known to precipitate myositis in lower animals. The symptom of muscular tenderness and aching commonly reported by patients with influenza provides indirect evidence that viral disorders can affect muscles. A theory of viral etiology remains unproved, since no virus has been isolated and no epidemiologic evidence of a direct infectious agent has been found.

The possibility that polymyositis may be an autoimmune disorder is suggested by the following:

1. The association of polymyositis and dermatomyositis with connective tissue disorders
2. A positive response to treatment with corticosteroids or immunosuppressive therapy
3. Onset often preceded by viral infections or use of drugs such as penicillin or sulfonamides, suggesting a hypersensitivity mechanism

The finding that lymphocytes from patients with polymyositis destroy human fetal muscle cell cultures provides additional evidence in support of an autoimmune etiology. Granular deposits of IgG, IgM, and C_3 have been found in the walls of blood vessels of patients with polymyositis and dermatomyositis. This is particularly true in cases of childhood dermatomyositis and has led to speculation about the occurrence of immune complex–induced vascular injury in these disorders (Engel and Banker, 1986).

Treatment rationale. Treatment is aimed at suppression of the inflammatory response through the use of corticosteroid drugs. Prednisone is the drug of choice. Control of the side effects of steroid therapy requires daily potassium supplementation, a high protein, low carbohydrate, low sodium diet, and ingestion of antacids between meals. Serial measurement of CPK levels and the ESR are used to monitor the effects of treatment with corticosteroid drugs. Immunosuppressive therapy can be used if there is no response to steroid therapy.

Cell injury by trauma. Trauma to a muscle may result in disruption in the continuity of the muscular tissue via strain, ischemia, or rupture. A *strain* is the result of use of a tissue beyond its functional ability. The muscle becomes "stretched" beyond its normal limits. A strain may be acute (the result of a sudden force) or chronic (the result of repetitious use of a muscle beyond its functional capacity).

The pathologic changes that occur in response to a strain may include hemorrhage and an inflammatory response in the disrupted tissue. (See Chapter 2 for the discussion of tissue repair.) Pain is the major clinical manifestation. Pain from an acute strain is severe, and its onset can usually be associated with the activity that caused the strain. The onset of pain in chronic strain is more gradual and the pain is less severe and more aching in character. The pain will be aggravated by activity in either type of strain.

Treatment involves use of analgesics for pain relief and rest with minimal activity of the injured area at least initially. Cold compresses may be used at first to control edema. As healing proceeds, the return to normal activity of the injured area should be gradual, with care being taken to avoid any subsequent injury to the healing area.

Muscle bundles may rupture when severe tension is suddenly applied to a contracted muscle. A rupture that is extensive and occurs at the musculotendinous junction of a major muscle may require surgical repair.

Altered tissue perfusion because of loss

of arterial blood supply results in ischemic necrosis of muscle within 6 hours. Such a loss may be the result of vascular damage secondary to trauma, or arterial occlusion secondary to thrombosis or embolism. Both the primary and collateral vascular supplies of the muscles are extensive, so infarction of muscle is not a common occurrence. It does occur in diabetes mellitus, atherosclerotic occlusive disease, childhood dermatomyositis, and polyarteritis nodosa (Engel and Banker, 1986). The muscle fibers of necrotic muscle will eventually be replaced by dense fibrous scar tissue. This causes a condition known as fibrous contracture to develop. A contracture is a persistent shortening of the muscle that is resistant to stretching and leads to progressive joint deformity.

A condition known as traumatic myositis ossificans, or posttraumatic ossification, occasionally develops after a bone fracture, dislocation, or isolated muscle injury. Heterotopic ossification (new bone formation in an abnormal site) occurs between the torn muscle fibers, causing a painful, rapidly enlarging mass to develop in the injured tissue. Treatment for this condition consists of rest for the injured area, since the heterotopic bone will be spontaneously resorbed without further aggravation of the injury.

PATHOPHYSIOLOGIC MECHANISMS AND DISORDERS OF BONES

The skeleton serves as a means of structural support and protection for the soft tissues and organs of the body. Bone is a specialized form of connective tissue. It serves as the anchoring tissue for the origin and insertion sites of the muscles. In addition, bone plays a major role in calcium metabolism and blood formation in the body. The pool of calcium in the bone that is exchangeable with the blood is influenced by the activity of calcitonin and parathyroid hormone. The role of bone tissue in chemical homeostasis is discussed in Chapter 18.

The microstructure of the bone consists of cells and mineralized matrix, which form a complex array of haversian canals and osteons. The major bone cells include the osteoblasts, osteocytes, and osteoclasts. The *osteoblast* is the primary cell responsible for the deposition (formation) of bone as it participates in the synthesis of collagen and some of the carbohydrate protein complexes that comprise osteoid. The osteoblast also participates in mineralization of the matrix through its function as the origin of matrix vesicles, its regulation of the movement of calcium in and out of bone fluid, and its capacity to store calcium within the mitochondria (Vaughan, 1981). Alkaline phosphatase, the characteristic enzyme of the osteoblast, is considered to be a marker of active mineralization and participates in raising the calcium and phosphate solution ion product to allow the precipitation of apatite at calcification sites. Osteocalcin or bone Gla protein (BGP), the major noncollagenous protein in the organic matrix of bone, is thought to be produced by the osteoblast. It is a calcium-binding protein that is vitamin K dependent and that may inhibit calcium phosphate precipitation or play some role in bone resorption (Vaughan, 1981). Osteonectin is a phosphoprotein synthesized by the osteoblast that forms a link between calcium and collagen, thus binding the two substances (Raisz and Kream, 1983).

When the osteoblast matures and becomes surrounded by matrix, it becomes an *osteocyte* and is responsible for maintenance of the blood supply and provision of nutrients and oxygen to bone tissue. Osteocyte death results in bone death. Its role in mineral homeostasis has not been proven. It is believed to function in the immediate maintenance of plasma calcium levels through bone resorption (osteocytic osteolysis) in response to parathyroid hormone (Vaughan, 1981; Deftos and Glowacki, 1984).

The *osteoclast* is the primary cell responsible for bone resorption or breakdown, which requires dissolution of the mineral constituents and hydrolysis of the organic constituents. Factors that affect bone resorption, such as parathyroid hormone, calcitonin, and diphosphonates, alter the appearance, number, and behavior of the osteoclasts (Vaughan, 1981).

The mechanical functions of bone are made possible through the combined properties of components of the extracellular matrix (Deftos and Glowacki, 1984). The matrix of bone is comprised of organic osteoid, which is impregnated with calcium hydroxyapatite crystals in a lattice-like structure and amorphous calcium phosphate. The latter probably represents the calcification front or interface between uncalcified osteoid and calcified matrix in the process of mineralization (Vaughan, 1981). The organic component represents approximately one third and the inorganic, mineral component represents two thirds of the matrix of mature bone tissue. The organic osteoid consists primarily of collagen (approximately 85% to 90%) accompanied by small amounts of proteins, proteoglycans, glycoproteins, peptides, and lipids.

Collagen is the major structural protein of most connective tissue, and its genetic expression varies depending on its location (Table 13-4). The collagen in the bone matrix is primarily type I, whereas that contained in cartilage is primarily type II. The synthesis of collagen begins with the synthesis of a larger molecule, procollagen, by the osteoblasts. It is secreted by the osteoblast and processed extracellularly by enzymatic cleavage of propeptides, fibril formation, and cross-linkage to form the collagen molecule, as illustrated

Table 13-4. Structurally and genetically distinct collagens

Type	Tissue distribution	Molecular form	Chemical characteristics
I	*Bone,* tendon, skin, dentin ligament, fascia, arteries, and uterus	$[\alpha 1(I)_2\alpha 2]$	Hybrid composed of two kinds of chains. Low in hydroxylysine and glycosylated hydroxylysine
II	*Hyaline cartilage,* cornea, vitreous body, and neural retinal tissues	$[\alpha 1(II)]_3$	Relatively high in hydroxylysine and glycosylated hydroxylysine
III	Skin, arteries, and uterus	$[\alpha 1(III)]_3$	High in hydroxyproline and low in hydroxylysine; contains interchain disulphide bonds
IV	Basement membranes	$[\alpha 1(IV)]_3$	High in hydroxylysine and glycosylated hydroxylysine; may contain large globular regions
V	Basement membranes and perhaps other tissues	αA and αB	Similar to type 4

From Vaughan J: The physiology of bone, ed 3, Oxford, 1981, Clarendon Press.

in Figure 13-6. The presence of hydroxylysine and hydroxyproline in the protein makes it unique.

The three major functional activities of bone cells include modeling, remodeling, and repair. *Modeling* involves the growth processes that allow the bones of the newborn to develop into the larger, identically shaped bones of the adult. Modeling is dependent on dietary as well as physiologic factors. *Remodeling* occurs in both the growing and grown skeleton and involves coupling of the constantly occurring paired processes of bone resorption and formation. It is estimated that approximately 3.5% of the adult human skeleton is undergoing remodeling at any given point in time (Vaughan, 1981). Net bone mass increases during the first two decades of life and decreases after the third or fourth decade (Raisz and Kream, 1983). It generally peaks at age 30 to 35 years (Avioli, 1987). *Repair* refers to the cellular processes that occur in response to a disruption in the continuity of bone tissue (fracture). Repair is especially significant when a major break in a bone occurs; however, repair may be just as significant under ordinary conditions, since microfractures probably occur all the time as a result of the constant stresses to which bone is subjected.

Disruption of these cellular activities constitutes the underlying pathophysiologic mechanisms of a variety of diseases and disorders of growth and development. Such disruption may also occur as a secondary effect of disease outside of the skeletal system. An example is the renal osteodystrophy discussed in Chapter 20. Other examples include periodontal disease and malignancy. The bone resorption effect of prostaglandins (PGE_2) and parathyroid hormone has been found to be enhanced in vitro by endotoxin. This may help to ex-

plain the loss of bone around the teeth in periodontal disease (Deftos and Glowacki, 1984). Bone is a frequent target site of metastatic spread of malignant cells from a primary cancer site. Two thirds of the malignant lesions found in bone result from metastasis. Primary tumors of the bone, when they do develop, are usually malignant as well. Hypercalcemia is associated with certain types of malignancies (Burkitt's lymphoma, leukemia, and myeloma) and inflammation, and it is now recognized that this depends on the local production of prostaglandins, which stimulate osteoclasts. Those of the E series are the most effective stimulators of bone resorption in vitro. It is thought that macrophages or monocytes synthesize prostaglandin, which activates lymphocytes to produce osteoclast activating factor (OAF) (Vaughan, 1981). Certain pharmacologic agents may also disrupt these functions. In fact, nonsteroidal antiinflammatory agents, because of their inhibition of prostaglandin synthesis, are used to treat the hypercalcemia associated with malignancy discussed previously. Heparin, an anticoagulant, has been found to increase bone resorption by stimulating osteoclast activity and the release of collagenase (Vaughan, 1981; Deftos and Glowacki, 1984). Glucocorticoids also increase bone resorption, and osteoporosis is a side effect of their use. There is speculation that the use of anticoagulants such as dicumarol by a pregnant woman may cause bone abnormalities in the fetus because of interference with the biosynthesis of osteocalcin, which is vitamin K dependent (Vaughan, 1981). In addition, infection and disruption of the blood supply may also serve as mechanisms resulting in pathophysiology of the body's structural integrity.

Bone is generally classified according to

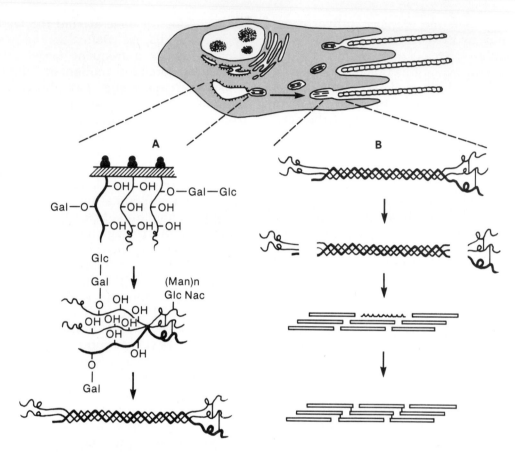

Fig. 13-6. Biosynthesis of type I procollagen and the processing of procollagen to type I collagen fibrils. **A,** intracellular steps in which two pro α1 chains and one pro α2 chain are hydroxylated and glycosylated by posttranslational enzymes. The C-propeptides of the pro α chains associate and become disulfide-bonded, and when approximately 100 prolyl residues are converted to hydroxyprolyl residues, a nucleus of triple-helical conformation forms at the C-terminal end of the collagen domain. The triple-helical conformation then propagates to the N-terminal region. **B,** Conversion of procollagen to collagen fibrils. The N- and C-propeptides are cleaved by 2 specific proteinases. The collagen molecule then spontaneously self-assembles into fibrils. Subsequently, the tensile strength of the fibrils is increased by the formation of intermolecular cross-links.

(From Prockop DJ and Kivirikko KI: Heritable diseases of collagen, NEJM, 311:376-386, 1984.)

structure. Cortical bone is hard, compact bone that is found encasing the shafts of the long bones. Trabecular bone is also called spongy or cancellous bone because of its appearance; it is found in the vertebrae, the ends of long bones, and flat bones. These categories are used to describe mature bone tissue. Another type of bone, woven bone, is that seen in embry-onic development and in the repair of fractures (Vaughan, 1981; Chambers, 1987).

Alteration in skeletal modeling (growth and development)

Over the course of human development, from embryo to adult, the human organism could be considered to have three different skeletons. The first skeleton is cartilaginous and is particularly well suited to intrauterine life and the rigors of birth. Movement and support are not requirements of the organism at this stage of development, and skeletal flexibility allows birth with minimal trauma.

During the infant's first 18 months of life, a fibrous skeleton predominates. This second skeleton is adequate for the activities performed by the young infant. It is also the reason why physical support must be provided within the infant's environment. When support for movement is necessary, the fibrous bone is replaced by the more rigid bone that will be present throughout the life span.

Bone is formed in the body by the process of *ossification*. While there are two types of ossification, the basic process of bone formation is the same: the organic matrix or osteoid is laid down by the osteoblasts and undergoes calcification. *Intramembranous ossification* refers to the formation of osteoid without a preformed frame or "scaffold" of cartilage to shape the resulting osteoid mass. *Endochondral ossification* refers to osteoid production guided by a "map" or framework of preformed, calcified cartilage. The former is primarily responsible for the bulk of the bone mass and the width (cortical) growth of the bones, which imparts strength. The latter along with the forces of stress is responsible for the length of the cylindric bones.

Normal skeletal growth and development depend on dietary and hormonal factors as well as those physiologic factors intrinsic to bone. Adequate amounts of vitamin A are needed for normal epiphyseal cartilage cell growth, maturation, degeneration, and modeling. Vitamin D is essential for absorption of calcium; vitamin C is essential for collagen synthesis. Deficiencies in any of these vitamins and in protein intake will result in impaired skel-

etal growth and development. Endocrine dysfunction as it affects skeletal growth and development is discussed in detail in Chapter 8.

In some disorders characterized by abnormal skeletal growth and development, the production of normal cartilage is affected and thus endochondral ossification is disrupted. In other diseases osteoid production is affected and thus both the endochondral and intramembranous processes are disrupted.

The primary pathologic defect in achondroplasia is faulty cartilage production with the subsequent disruption of endochondral ossification. Dwarfism occurs, with the limbs being disproportionately shorter than the trunk. Cartilage production is normal in the disorder known as osteogenesis imperfecta, but osteoid production is abnormal. In this condition both the endochondral and intramembranous ossification processes are disrupted.

The basic defect is a genetic mutation that causes faulty collagen synthesis. Collagen abnormalities have been implicated in other genetic disorders such as homocystinuria, Ehlers-Danlos syndrome, and Marfan's syndrome. In Marfan's syndrome the mutation is thought to cause defective cross linking of collagen (Vaughan, 1981). The affected individual appears tall and thin with excessively long extremities, marked joint laxity, and a high incidence of cardiovascular disease. All of these disorders are the result of mutations in the structural genes that direct collagen synthesis. The genetic expression of the mutation, that is, the tissue affected and the severity, varies depending on the specific collagen abnormality that results (Fig. 13-7). Generalizations that can be made at this point in time are that mutations that alter the amino acid sequence of the C-terminal half of the procollagen molecule produce weakened, brittle bones, whereas

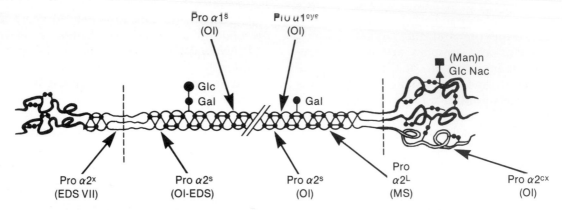

Fig. 13-7. Some of the known mutations that cause synthesis of structurally abnormal type I procollagen. Pro $\alpha1^s$ and pro $\alpha2^s$ mutations cause synthesis of shortened pro $\alpha1$ or pro $\alpha2$ chains; pro $\alpha2^L$ mutation causes synthesis of a longer pro $\alpha2$ chain; pro $\alpha1^{cys}$ mutations introduce a cysteine residue into the pro $\alpha1$ chain; pro $\alpha2^x$ mutation of the N-terminal region of the pro $\alpha2$ chain has not been fully defined; pro $\alpha2^{cx}$ mutation changes the sequence of the last 33 amino acids of the C-propeptide of the pro $\alpha2$ chains. The major phenotypic manifestation of osteogenesis imperfecta (OI) is brittle bones; the major phenotypic manifestation of Ehlers-Danlos syndrome (EDS) is joint laxity; the major phenotypic manifestation of Marfan's syndrome (MS) is a long, thin skeleton.
(From Prockop DJ and Kivirikko KI: Heritable diseases of collagen, NEJM, 311:376-386, 1984.)

mutations that affect the N-terminal portion produce joint laxity and other manifestations, characteristic of the Ehlers-Danlos syndrome (Prockop, 1988). Incomplete bony closure of one or more of the neural arches is the primary defect in a congenital abnormality of the spine known as *spina bifida*, although the clinical manifestations are related to any associated neurologic deficits that may be present.

There are many examples of skeletal dysplasias and congenital and developmental abnormalities related to the musculoskeletal system. Classification of these disorders varies from author to author and can be found in orthopedic textbooks on musculoskeletal disorders. The following disease models are presented to illustrate the effects of abnormal skeletal modeling.

Achondroplasia. A particular type of dwarfism is characteristic of the hereditary disorder known as achondroplasia. Intramembranous ossification is normal;

however, endochondral ossification is disrupted because of altered cartilage development and, consequently, the lengthwise growth of bone will be affected. The ultimate cause of the disorder is unknown.

Achondroplasia is the most common type of dwarfism. It is inherited as an autosomal dominant trait. Approximately 50% of all affected children die in utero, as a result of difficult birth, or in the first few months of infancy.

Clinical manifestations. Because endochondral ossification is affected, the length of bones is altered. The average height of an achondroplastic dwarf is about 50 inches. The long, cylindric bones of the extremities are most severely affected. The fingertips reach the hip joint rather than mid-thigh. Fingers are stubby. The legs are bowed and have the appearance of "duck legs." The trunk growth is not affected to the same degree as the bones of the extremities, which accounts for the disproportion between the trunk and extremities (Fig. 13-8).

A typical facial appearance results from normal intramembranous ossification coupled with early closure of epiphyseal ossification centers in the base of the skull. The brain grows upward and forward because of lack of space in the base. This results in bulging of the forehead and bossing of the frontal bones. The nose has a saddlelike appearance. The mandible is relatively normal in size but appears large because of the skull changes, and prognathism results.

Although trunk length may be near normal, vertebral development is affected. The vertebral body may be wedge shaped. This most commonly occurs between the twelfth dorsal and third lumbar vertebrae. Lordosis occurs with a horizontal tipping of the sacrum giving a characteristic prominence to the buttocks. Intervertebral disks are subject to distortion and abnormal pressure, which cause rupture. A complication seen in adult life is paraplegia and disturbed bladder function resulting from pressure on the cord and nerve roots in the lower spine.

There is no treatment for this condition. Because the expression of the genetic defect is not known at the present time, the course of this condition cannot be altered. Ruptured intervertebral disks may require laminectomy.

Osteogenesis imperfecta. Osteogenesis imperfecta is a hereditary disorder also known as "brittle bones." Patients with osteogenesis imperfecta have been found to have mutations in one of the two structural genes that code for type I procollagen (Prockop, 1988). This disorder is rare but does demonstrate the effect of abnormal osteoid production. Defective collagen synthesis resulting in defective cross-linkage causes skeletal fragility, thin skin,

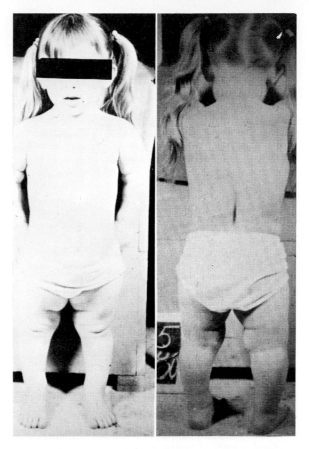

Fig. 13-8. Achrondroplastic dwarf.
(Courtesy Shriners Hospital for Crippled Children, Chicago.)

poor teeth, thin sclera with a blue appearance, a tendency to macular bleeding, and ligamental laxity leading to hypermotility of the joints (Fig. 13-9). The teeth are poor because of malformation of dentin. The ligaments and tendons may be affected. Deafness is often associated with this disorder and is thought to be caused by otosclerosis.

Skeletal fragility allows fractures to occur with even slight trauma. While fractures readily occur, they do heal in the same manner as normal bone, although often with greatly increased callus forma-

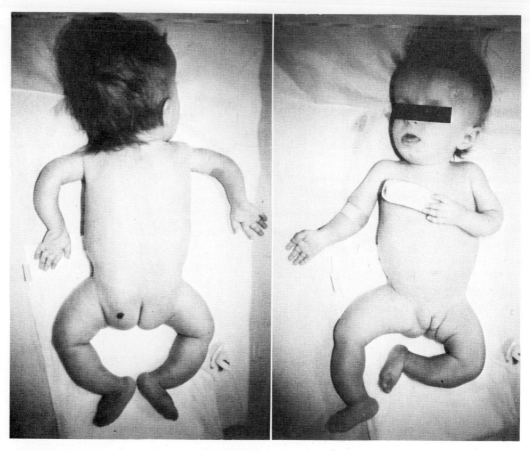

Fig. 13-9. Infant with osteogenesis imperfecta.
(Courtesy Shriners Hospital for Crippled Children, Chicago.)

tion. The entire skeleton is affected.

There are different forms of this disorder that differ in severity and prognosis. These are presented in Table 13-5. These differences are probably related to different genetic mutations (see Fig. 13-7). Treatment is usually directed toward preventing fractures and helping parents and family cope with the demands of protecting and caring for the child.

Fibrous dysplasia. This disorder is characterized by normal bone being replaced by fibrous tissue. Clinical manifestations usually appear in late childhood, although severe cases may be apparent at birth. There are three classifications depending on the extensiveness of skeletal involvement:

1. Monostotic—one bone is involved
2. Polyostotic—more than one bone is involved
3. Polyostotic with associated endocrine disturbances—more than one bone is involved accompanied by precocious puberty, hyperthyroidism, and early rapid growth with premature closure of epiphyseal growth centers

Pathologic fractures are often the pre-

Table 13-5. Classification of osteogenesis imperfecta*

Classification	Characteristics†
I. Fetal or prenatal form: osteogenesis imperfecta congenita	Severe with multiple fractures throughout body at birth
	Skull soft and membranous
	Infant may be stillborn or die at birth or within a few weeks
	Loss of stature
II. Infantile form: osteogenesis imperfecta tarda, gravis form	Less severe
	Multiple fractures during infancy
	Skull thin and globular, may resemble that seen in hydrocephalus
	Loss of stature
	Survival after first few years increases chances of lessening frequency of fractures and continued survival
III. Adolescent form: osteogenesis imperfecta tarda, levis form	Normal at birth
	Fracture due to minimal trauma later in childhood
	Delayed ambulation
	With increasing age, tendency to fracture is lost

*From Hilt NE and Cogburn SB: Manual of orthopedics, St. Louis, 1980, The CV Mosby Co.
†Blue sclerae are usually associated with all types.

senting complaint. Pain is also a feature when fractures and deformity make weight bearing difficult. The physical deformity can be great depending on the area and extent of involvement. The earlier symptoms appear, the greater will be the skeletal deformity. The progress of the disease will be slow when symptoms are mild. Again, there is no treatment for this disorder, which is thought to be developmental or congenital in origin.

Alterations in skeletal remodeling and mineralization

Skeletal tissue is a very dynamic tissue and the process of remodeling is constantly occurring. At many heterogenous sites throughout the skeleton microscopic areas of bone are being resorbed to be replaced by the formation and deposition of new bone. Changes in the balance between the processes of bone resorption and formation, which are under both hormonal control and local regulation (Raisz and Kream, 1983), play a critical role in calcium metabolism (see Chapter 18). Various physiologic factors that influence bone deposition and formation are summarized in Table 13-6.

Normally, there exists a steady state relationship between the processes of bone formation or deposition and resorption. These processes are balanced with one another in order to maintain normal Ca^{++} metabolism and skeletal mass. When the steady state relationship between these two processes is disrupted, the potential exists for both Ca^{++} metabolism and skeletal mass to be affected. The discussion in this chapter is limited to the skeletal effects of disruption of the balance between the processes of bone resorption and formation. Ca^{++} metabolism is discussed in Chapter 18.

When the normal ratio of resorption to formation is balanced and maintained,

Table 13-6. Factors that influence bone deposition and resorption

	Deposition	Resorption
Increase	Exercise, stress on bones	Parathyroid hormone excess
	Growth hormone	Vitamin D hormone [1,25 (OH) · D]†
	Fluoride*	Vitamin A excess
	Vitamin C	Adrenocortical steroid excess
	Thyroid hormones	Calcium deficiency (dietary or malabsorption)
	Insulin	Phosphorus deficiency (dietary, malabsorption, renal loss)
	Androgens	Anabolic steroid deficiency (androgen, estrogen)
	Vitamin D metabolites	Immobilization
	Parathyroid hormone	Acidosis
		Heparin
		Pregnancy and lactation
		Osteolytic neoplasms (including leukemia)
		Prostaglandins (especially PGE_2)
Decrease	Immobilization, disuse, bed rest	Calcium
	Growth hormone deficiency	Phosphorus
	Adrenocortical steroid excess	Parathyroid hormone deficiency
	Anticonvulsants	Calcitonin
		Magnesium deficiency
		Anabolic steroids
		Alkalosis
		Mithramycin
		Diphosphonates (P-O-P)
		Colchicine

*Fluoride in excess causes deposition of uncalcified osteoid and produces osteomalacia.
†Osteolytic effect of parathyroid hormone requires presence of vitamin D hormone.

skeletal mass will remain constant. If the ratio is altered to favor resorption, a loss of bone mass will occur. This is the underlying pathophysiologic mechanism in osteoporosis. Some authorities use the term *osteopenia* to describe a significant deficiency in bone mass and apply the term *osteoporosis* only when structural failure accompanies a deficiency in bone mass (Aitken, 1984). For this discussion, osteoporosis is defined as an absolute loss of bone volume caused by alteration in the normal ratio of bone formation to resorption. It is a decrease in the overall quantity and structural bony material per unit volume of bone, which may affect all the bones of the body but demonstrates a pref-

erence for those of the axial skeleton. The composition of the remaining bone is normal (Vaughan, 1981).

Bone loss is manifested by cortical thinning and trabecular thinning and loss. Bones become fragile and very susceptible to gross and microscopic fractures. The vertebrae (see Fig. 13-10), femoral necks, and wrists are the sites most frequently affected. Bone loss may result in loss of stature. Osteoporosis becomes symptomatic when it is severe enough to cause microfractures and collapse of the vertebral bodies, which produces back pain. It is not usually diagnosed until a fracture occurs or it may be discovered incidentally in a patient being examined for some other

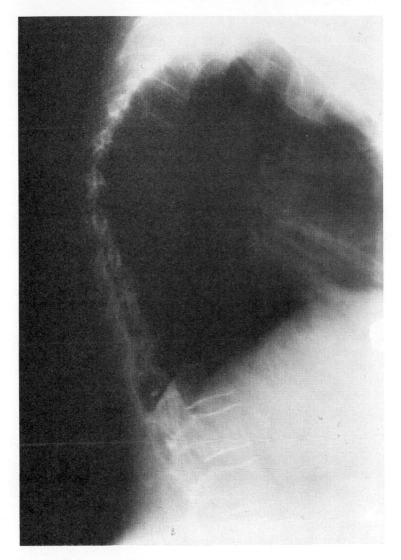

Fig. 13-10. Osteoporosis affecting vertebrae of the spine.
(Courtesy Ronald L. DeWald MD and Mary Faut RN, Orthopedics and Scoliosis, Ltd., Chicago.)

problem (Aitken, 1984; Avioli, 1987).

Conditions and treatments that alter the ratio between bone formation and resorption and place a person at risk for the development of osteoporosis include hormonal disturbances, disuse or immobility, use of corticosteroid and other types of drugs, congenital conditions, and some gastrointestinal disorders. These are listed in the box on p. 468 (Heidrich and Thompson, 1987). Resorption may increase, formation may decrease, or a combination of increased resorption and decreased formation may occur depending on the cause. The manner in which immobility alters the ratio of resorption to formation is discussed in Chapter 14. The osteoporosis that commonly accompanies rheumatoid arthritis is probably related to several factors; immobility (or disuse), steroid therapy, chronic inflammation, and the joint erosion that increases local osteoclastic activity.

Endocrine disorders
  Hyperparathyroidism
  Hyperthyroidism
  Hyperadrenocorticolism
  Premature menopause
    (including surgical) and amenorrhea
Congenital disorders
  Turner's syndrome
  Kleinfelter's syndrome
  Homocystinuria
  Testicular feminization
  Adrenogenital syndrome
Gastrointestinal disorders
  Peptic ulcer disease
  Malabsorption syndrome
  Lactase deficiency
  Postgastrectomy
Medications
  Corticosteroids
  Heparin
  Thyroid hormone
  Aluminum-containing antacids
  Furosemide
  Anticonvulsants
Immobilizing disorders
  Parkinsonism
  Rheumatoid arthritis
  Bed rest
  Paralysis from any cause

A loss of bone mass is also associated with the aging process. This involutional osteoporosis is responsible for 80% of all cases of osteoporosis (Riggs, 1987), and it is the most common metabolic bone disease encountered clinically. It is also referred to as senile and postmenopausal osteoporosis, and it represents a major public health problem. It is estimated that osteoporosis is responsible for the occurrence of over a million fractures at a cost of $6 billion dollars each year. These numbers will increase as the population ages, since osteoporosis associated with the aging process accounts for the majority of cases. By the year 2000 these numbers are expected to double, as twice as many women over 65 years of age will be alive (Riggs, 1987). One of every three women over the age of 65 years is expected to suffer a vertebral fracture. In the group reaching extreme old age, one of every three women and one of every six men are expected to suffer a hip fracture, which can be fatal in up to 20% of all cases (Riggs and Melton, 1986).

Bone mass peaks at 30 to 35 years of age and begins to decline within 5 to 10 years after that point in both sexes. The rate of loss is initially the same for men and women, but women experience a postmenopausal acceleration in the rate of bone loss. Following this period, the rate of bone loss again becomes similar to that of men (Avioli, 1987). The difference in the rate of bone loss is believed to be accompanied by a difference in the type of bone that is predominantly lost, which subsequently affects the type of fracture that occurs. This has led to the description of two types or patterns of involutional osteoporosis by Riggs and Melton (1983, 1986). The type I syndrome is related to menopausal factors and associated with trabecular bone loss and vertebral crush and Colles' fractures. The type II syndrome is related to aging factors and associated with both types of bone loss and fractures of the vertebrae and proximal femur. These patterns are summarized in Table 13-7.

Table 13-7. The two types of involutional osteoporosis

	Type I	Type II
Age (yr)	51-75	>70
Sex ratio (F:M)	6:1	2:1
Type of bone loss	Mainly trabecular	Trabecular and cortical
Rate of bone loss	Accelerated	Not accelerated
Fracture sites	Vertebrae (crush) and distal radius	Vertebrae (multiple wedge) and hip
Parathyroid function	Decreased	Increased
Calcium absorption	Decreased	Decreased
Metabolism of 25-OH-D to 1,25-(OH)$_2$D	Secondary decrease	Primary decrease
Main causes	Factors related to menopause	Factors related to aging

From Riggs BL: Pathogenesis of osteoporosis, Am J Obstet Gynecol 156:1342, 1987.

The mechanism of age-related bone loss seen in the type II syndrome is decreased formation. Osteoblast function is reduced, and there is an abnormality in vitamin D metabolism leading to impaired calcium absorption and secondary hyperparathyroidism (Riggs, 1987). Diminished renal function may also play a role (Avioli, 1987). The bone loss related to menopause seen in the type I syndrome is characterized by a high rate of bone turnover and increased bone resorption. The number and activity of the osteoclasts increase (Riggs and Melton, 1986). Estrogen deficiency is thought to be etiologic; however, the exact effect of estrogen on bone has not been determined. No estrogen receptors have been identified in bone, so its antiresorptive action is probably indirect. Possi-

ble mechanisms of estrogen's action that are being examined currently include the following: (1) stimulation of calcitonin production, (2) increased activation of vitamin D and promotion of calcium absorption, (3) decreased prostaglandin production and blocking of the resorptive action of PTH (Roche, 1986). While supportive evidence exists for each of these, none have been proven (Riggs and Melton, 1983; Lindsay, 1987). Supplemental estrogen therapy has been demonstrated to reduce both trabecular and cortical bone loss after the onset of menopause (Lindsay, 1987).

Risk factors for this disorder have been identified through epidemiologic studies. At greatest risk are white or Asian women who are of slight or slender build and who have had an early menopause or oophorectomy (Lindsay, 1987). Other risk factors include a sedentary life-style or inactivity; low calcium intake; smoking; excessive consumption of alcohol, caffeine, fiber, and protein; small muscle mass; and nulliparity (Lindsay, 1987; Avioli, 1987). The amount of bone present before the onset of age-related bone loss may be the most important determinant of susceptibility, and many of the risk factors that have been identified for osteoporosis can be explained by their relationship to peak bone density (Riggs, 1987). For example, women do not attain as great a peak bone mass as men, blacks have a greater peak bone mass than whites, and genetic factors determine the maximum attainable bone mass for an individual. The possibility of a genetic etiology for osteoporosis has been advanced by Prockop (1988), who identified an early reduction in bone mass in the parents of a child with osteogenesis imperfecta who were found to be heterozygous for the same gene defect. He postulates that "minor" genetic mutations may constitute the genetic predisposition for disorders of connective tissue in later life.

The medical conditions and drugs mentioned previously that predispose a patient to the development of osteoporosis should be considered as risk factors whose effects are additive to these more generic risk factors. Conditions that place a patient at risk for falls also increase the risk of osteoporotic fracture. Medical disorders and drugs that cause dizziness, gait instability, or sensory perceptual impairment can be etiologic for falls. Ninety percent of hip fractures are the result of falls, although fewer that 1% of all falls result in hip fracture. One of the beneficial effects of exercise may be keeping the muscles conditioned enough to preserve protective responses to minimize injury in the event of a fall (Osteoporosis, 1987).

Usually, the patient presents with a fracture before the need for treatment is even recognized. There is no adequate treatment for osteoporosis, although for some patients sodium fluoride has been shown to stimulate bone formation (Riggs and Melton, 1986; Osteoporosis, 1987). Prevention is the most cost-effective approach to the problem given its incidence and its human and monetary costs. The goals of preventive strategies include the promotion of peak bone density by the fourth decade of life and minimization of the rate of bone loss after that point (Heidrich and Thompson, 1987). A listing of these strategies is included in Table 13-8. It is important to note that at this point the administration of estrogen (and progesterone in women with an intact uterus to reduce the risk of endometrial cancer) is the intervention proven most effective for reducing the frequency of osteoporotic fractures (Osteoporosis, 1987; Lindsay, 1987). Calcitonin can be used in women who are unsuitable can-

Table 13-8. Strategies for maximizing bone density and preventing bone loss

Estrogen replacement	Recommended for high-risk women from cessation of menses to 70 years; given as 0.625 mg conjugated estrogen (or equivalent) daily 25 days each month
	For women with intact uteri, add medroxyprogesterone acetate 10 mg daily on days 16 through 25
Calcium intake	Assure adequate intake in all age groups; recommended daily intake (add 400 mg for pregnancy or lactation):
	Children: 800 mg
	Teenagers: 1200 mg
	Men: 800 mg
	Premenopausal women, women taking estrogen: 1000 mg
	Postmenopausal women not taking estrogen: 1500 mg
Exercise	Advisable for all age groups; should be weight bearing, at least 30 minutes three times weekly
Habit modification	Assist with discontinuing smoking and excess alcohol intake
Management of coexisting diseases	Limit use of medicines associated with bone thinning and falls; correct endocrinopathies; minimize immobilization: suggest environmental changes to minimize falls in the disabled or elderly

From Heidrich F and Thompson RS: Osteoporosis prevention: strategies applicable for general population groups, J Fam Pract 25(1):33, 1987.

didates for estrogen therapy, but cost and mode of administration currently limit its applicability. While epidemiologic data indicate that calcium intake helps in achieving maximum bone density, there is insufficient supporting evidence to recommend dietary calcium supplementation alone for minimizing the rate of bone loss (Roche, 1986) or as a substitute for estrogen (Osteoporosis, 1987). Other therapies being evaluated currently include the use of vitamin D and its metabolites, stimulation of bone formation using growth factors produced using recombinant DNA technology, administration of calcitonin plus phosphate, the use of parathyroid hormone, intranasal administration of calcitonin, cyclic administration of estrogen, and sequential resorptive and formative therapy (Roche, 1986; Riggs and Melton, 1986).

Prevention of osteoporosis requires cooperation of the patient and, as in coronary artery disease prevention, life-style modification. It is extremely hard to achieve complete cooperation when the potential onset of the disorder seems quite remote to the individual. Interventions to change health behaviors are important in reducing the incidence of osteoporosis, and there is a growing body of literature on the efficacy of such health behavior interventions. Such interventions should be targeted to those at risk for the development of osteoporosis. Currently, risk assessment is based on family and life-style history, race, body type, and measurement of bone density. More precise delineation of risk and demonstration of the efficacy of preventive measures are considered major areas for research.

In osteoporosis the bone tissue that remains is normally mineralized and its microscopic appearance is normal (Riggs, 1987). This is an important distinction between osteoporosis and osteomalacia. *Osteomalacia* is characterized by inadequate mineralization of newly formed osteoid matrix with the accumulation of excess uncalcified osteoid matrix on the surfaces of remodeled osteons. The excess osteoid is the result of a failure to mineralize newly synthesized matrix. There is a decrease in the radiographic density of the bones. The bones will be weaker than normal, and these "soft" bones gradually bend and become deformed. In osteomalacia the mineral-to-matrix ratio of the bone is disrupted while in osteoporosis it remains normal. Osteoporosis and osteomalacia may coexist as well (Fig. 13-11). A comparison of the different metabolic bone diseases is presented in Table 13-9.

Rickets is the term applied to osteomalacia that occurs in the growing bones of children. In children's bones a zone of uncalcified preosseous cartilage forms at the usual site of calcifying cartilage in the epiphyseal plate. This accounts for the deformities that develop in children with the disorder: bowlegs, knock-knees, small stature, and clinically observable enlargement at the sites of the epiphyseal plates. This enlargement at the costochondral junctions accounts for the physical sign known as "rachitic rosary."

Rickets is most often seen as a result of a nutritional vitamin D deficiency. This type of rickets readily responds to improved diet with vitamin D supplementation. Persons working with lower income, poorly educated populations need to be aware of the signs of this disorder as well as the need for adequate preventive health teaching about good nutrition for the parents of young children. Vitamin D deficiency in adults is rarely the result of inadequate nutritional intake but can occur as a result of defective absorption from the intestinal tract. Other causes of osteomalacia and rickets include renal disease, some inborn errors of metabolism that result in defective tubular reabsorption of phosphate, and certain anticonvulsant drugs that inactivate vitamin D.

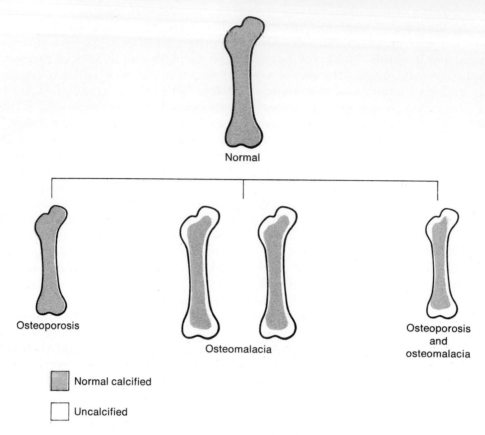

Fig. 13-11. Differences in bone mass and mineralization in osteoporosis and osteomalacia. Osteoporosis results in a smaller but completely calcified bone. Osteomalacia results in normal-sized bones in which bone matrix is not calcified.

Table 13-9. Comparison of the major metabolic bone diseases

	Osteitis fibrosa cystica	Osteoporosis	Osteomalacia
Etiology	Excessive PTH	Varied but usually unknown	Vitamin D deficiency; malabsorption
Serum			
Calcium	Increased	Normal	Decreased or normal
Phosphate	Normal or decreased	Normal	Decreased
Alkaline phosphatase	Normal or increased	Normal	Increased
Pathophysiology	Increased bone resorption	Decreased bone mass (resorption > accretion)	Decreased mineralization
Histopathology	Cysts; fibrosis; "brown" tumor	Normal histology	Increased osteoid tissue
Radiology	Subperiosteal resorption; cysts	Rarefaction of axial skeleton; "codfish" vertebrae; compression fractures	Rarefaction of appendicular skeleton; pseudofractures (Looser's zones)

From Sodeman's Pathologic Physiology, Sodeman WA and Sodeman TM (Eds), 7, Philadelphia, 1985, WB Saunders Co.

Osteopetrosis. Osteopetrosis is a rare hereditary disorder also known as "marble bones." The pathologic defect appears to be a failure of resorption of bone by the osteoclasts. Defects in the monocytes and macrophages have also been demonstrated (Vaughan, 1981). Obviously, normal growth is impeded and skeletal growth will most likely be moderately stunted.

The term *marble bones* was applied in reference to the increased density seen on x-ray films. In most cases, however, the bones are of a chalky consistency and transverse fractures are common. Some problems that frequently accompany this disorder because of bony encroachment on nerve foramina of the skull include hydrocephalus, blindness, deafness, dental caries, and facial palsies. Because of bony encroachment on the hematopoietic marrow space, a progressive aplastic anemia may also be present and often results in early death in infants.

Prognosis depends on age and severity of symptoms at onset. The earlier the symptoms appear, the more severe the manifestations seem to be. This is related to the different forms of genetic transmission. The autosomal recessive form occurs early (in utero and infancy) and is rapidly progressive and fatal. The autosomal dominant form appears in adolescence or early adulthood, and the manifestations are less severe (Deftos and Glowacki, 1984). Sarcoma has been reported as a late complication. Bone marrow transplantation in affected children has been found to restore osteoclast, monocyte, and macrophage function (Vaughan, 1981).

Disease model: Paget's disease of bone. Paget's disease of bone, or *osteitis deformans*, is a disorder characterized by a marked increase in bone remodeling. Bone formation and resorption occur in an accelerated and random manner (Vaughan, 1981). The primary mechanism is increased resorption, with increased deposition occurring secondarily (Deftos and Glowacki, 1984). This disease is characteristically found in middle-aged or elderly patients; the incidence rises with increasing age. The incidence is reported to rise from 3% to 4% at age 45 and 5% to 11% at age 90 years. Men appear to be affected more frequently than women. The disease has been found to occur in more than one member of a family.

The etiology is unknown (Vaughan, 1981). Paget thought the disease was an inflammatory process when he named it osteitis deformans. Familial incidence has led some to speculate on the possibility of a genetic factor being causal. Another theory is that Paget's disease is actually a benign neoplasia of the bone. This theory is supported by the observations that bone tumors occur more frequently in patients with Paget's disease and that the osteoclasts in the affected area assume bizarre shapes with as many as 100 nuclei. There has also been speculation that this disorder has a viral origin, as viruslike particles and viral antigens have been found in osteoclasts (Deftos and Glowacki, 1984). There is no support for a generalized metabolic or biochemical derangement as its cause.

Pathogenesis. There appear to be three phases in the disease process. The first phase involves intensive resorption of existing bone. During this phase the bone is weakened and subject to deformity. The next phase is characterized by accelerated, disorganized deposition of spicules of lamellar bone accompanying the resorption activity. In the final phase, osteoblastic (bone formation) activity becomes dominant, probably as a secondary, compensatory effect, and the enlarged bones become thick and dense. Usually more than one bone is involved, although the pathologic process is a localized one, and in an involved area the numbers of active bone surface cells—osteoblasts and osteoclasts—are greatly increased. The process culminates in a focal and diagnostically significant "mosaic" pattern of lamellar bone associated with increased fibrous tissue in adjacent marrow and increased local vascularity. The bony tissue is structurally weak.

Clinical manifestations. There can be extreme differences among patients with Paget's disease in the extent of skeletal involvement and in the course of the disease process. The disease usually involves the lumbosacral spine, pelvis, skull, tibia, and femurs. The clinical manifestations depend on the extent and site of skeletal involvement. In most cases the disease never progresses to the extreme form and may only involve one bone. Many affected persons remain asymptomatic, with morphologic changes being identified only incidentally. Persons with more severe cases may experience bone pain or may notice bowing of the lower limbs or that their head seems to be larger (for example, hats don't fit as well). Pain in the back and lower limbs is the most common reason patients seek medical attention. Such pain is probably the result of vertebral compression and microfractures. Enlarged vertebrae may cause spinal cord or nerve compression with resultant neurologic manifestations, which in the most extreme form might include paraplegia. Skull involvement may cause face pain and headache. Hearing loss may occur because of bony encroachment on the eighth cranial nerve or pagetic changes in the ossicles of the inner ear. Spinal column involvement will give the appearance of the trunk being bowed forward. The characteristic appearance of a patient with extensive Paget's disease includes a large, low-set, protruding head, long arms, bowed back and legs, and rounded shoulders. The gait is characteristically wobbly. The serum alkaline phosphatase level will be markedly increased in response to the increased skeletal osteoblastic activity.

Pathologic fractures and progressive deformity may occur as a result of the disease process. Other potential complications include osteoarthritis (degeneration of the articular cartilage of the joint) resulting from additional stress placed on the joints, high-output heart failure caused by the increased vascularity of the involved bone tissue, and an increased incidence of bone tumors with metastasis.

Treatment rationale. The goal of treatment is to inhibit bone resorption. Calcitonin and mithramycin are used to inhibit osteoclast activity. Because of their ability to bind to hydroxyapatite, diphosphonates have been used to stabilize bone as well as for their antiosteoclastic effect (Vaughan, 1981).

Disruption of bone tissue continuity

Once the elastic limit of the bone is reached, it will no longer absorb force but will break under the strain. Application of a force exceeding the capacity of the bone to absorb it will result in a fracture.

Bone fractures occur most frequently as a result of external trauma but may also occur as the consequence of some deformity with the bone itself. Fractures that occur in the latter manner are called *pathologic* and are usually seen in disease

Text continued on p. 479.

Table 13-10. Complications of fractures*

Complication	Contributory factors	Signs and symptoms	Treatment	Prevention	Comments
Delayed union	Inappropriate or inaccurate reduction Immobilization that is inadequate or interrupted during healing process Severe traumatization to surrounding tissue structures Disturbances of circulation to bone resulting from surgical intervention or injury Infections, especially in open fractures Loss of bone tissue such as excision of necrotic fragments in open fractures Excessive distraction from traction or internal fixation causing separation of fragments Mobility at fracture site during immobilization period	Healing phase beyond predicted time as evidenced through radiographic examination	Determine cause of delayed union and correct if possible Longer immobilization period	Appropriate implementation of principles of fracture management Early, accurate, gentle reduction Appropriate immobilization Circulation not impaired No unnecessary or repeated traumatization to area Frequent observation of fragment separation Appropriate internal fixation Other	Union accomplished but over longer time May be encountered with any fracture

*From Hilt NE and Cogburn JB: Manual of orthopaedics, St. Louis 1980, The CV Mosby Co.

Continued.

Table 13-10. Complications of fractures—cont'd

Complication	Contributory factors	Signs and symptoms	Treatment	Prevention	Comments
Malunion	Malalignment of fracture site at time of immobilization Mobility at fracture site during period of immobilization	Obvious external deformity at fracture site Deformity or angulation as evidenced on radiographic examination	Determination of degree of angulation Correction of degree of angulation weighed with risk of delayed union or nonunion No treatment may be indicated Severe angulation may require remanipulation, adjustments with immobilization, or surgical intervention	Appropriate reduction Adequate immobilization after reduction Continued monitoring of positioning and alignment Decreased mobility at fracture site during healing phase	Some degree of spontaneous angle correction, especially in children, will occur with growth and healing process
Nonunion	Bone fragment separation of varying degrees Loss of bone tissue resulting from excision or development of necrotic fragments Inadequate internal or external fixation permitting mobility at fracture site Disruption of healing process through repeated manipulations Placement of soft tissue between bone fragments causing disruption of healing process	Excessive mobility in all directions at fracture site Pain on weight bearing and activity (lower extremity) Muscular atrophy Loss of joint motion	Orthotic devices to promote stability and prevent deformity Surgical intervention (bone graft) Cortical graft Cancellous graft Subperiosteal graft Osteoperiosteal graft	Appropriate reduction Adequate immobilization Monitoring of healing process and mobility at fracture site	

	Infection, usually associated with open fractures or surgical intervention		See Chapter 17
	Circulatory impairment resulting from severe soft tissue injury or reduction		
Fat embolism	Skeletal injury	Within 3 days after fracture	Treatment for shock
		Altered level of or disturbance of consciousness	Respiratory support
		Tachycardia	Oxygen
		Dyspnea	Intubation if necessary
		Hypovolemic shock	Controlled volume, ventilation with positive end-expiratory pressure
		Petechial skin hemorrhages (especially over chest, shoulders), petechia in conjunctiva	Corticosteroids
		Fever	
		Platelet count less than 150,000/mm^3	
		PaO_2 less than 60 mm Hg	
		ECG	
		Tachycardia	
		Prominent S wave on lead 1	
		Prominent Q wave on lead 2	
		Shift in transition zone to left	
		Inverted T waves	
		Depressed RST segment	
		Right bundle branch block	
		Increased serum lipase	

Continued.

Table 13-10. Complications of fractures—cont'd

Complication	Contributory factors	Signs and symptoms	Treatment	Prevention	Comments
		Possible patchy pulmonary infiltrates on chest x-ray examination Possible presence of fat in urine			
Nerve compression syndromes	Impingement on nerve structures in specific anatomic area due to: Displacement of bone fragment Soft tissue alteration (such as stretching of nerve) due to injury Fracture management	Pain or discomfort Burning sensation Generalized or specific muscular weakness or paralysis Muscle atrophy Limitation of motion Altered reflexes Altered sensory status	Relief of source of compression Surgical intervention may be required to relieve compression or correct resulting deformity	Appropriate splinting and emergency treatment of fracture Accurate initial and frequent assessment of neurovascular status to detect early alterations	May include: Carpal tunnel syndrome (median nerve entrapment at wrist) Ulnar nerve syndrome (at wrist or elbow) Radial nerve compression (at elbow) Tarsal tunnel syndrome (posterior tibial nerve compression) Common peroneal nerve compression Sciatic nerve compression
Compartmental syndrome	Decrease in size of specific compartment due to constrictive force such as cast or dressing Increase in contents of compartment due to hemorrhage, increased pressure, etc.	Sensory alterations indicative of structures involved Motor alterations Pain on passive motion Tenseness on palpation over area	Decompression within 12 hours after onset of symptoms	Early detection	
Infection	Open fracture Open reduction	Pain Fever Erythema Drainage	Antibiotic therapy intravenously Surgical irradication of infected tissue Immobilization	Appropriate initial wound care of open fractures Strict aseptic techniques during surgical open reduction	See Chapter 2

states in which bone matrix is decalcified or in which there is a general decrease in the total amount and strength of bone tissue. In these states the elastic limit of the bone is reduced and, consequently, the amount of force needed to break a bone is also reduced. Among the disease states that cause weakening of bone tissue are Paget's disease, osteogenesis imperfecta, and metastatic bone disease. Patients experiencing immobility or other conditions leading to osteoporosis are also subject to the occurrence of pathologic fractures.

Fractures can be classified in a variety of ways. A *direct* fracture is one that occurs at the specific site of injury; an *indirect* fracture is one that occurs either above or below the specific site of injury. A *closed*, or *simple*, fracture is one in which the injured bone does not disrupt soft tissue and skin. An *open*, or *compound*, fracture is one in which the injured bone projects through soft tissues and skin. An open fracture carries an increased risk of infection developing. Fractures may be further described by their anatomic location, type, completeness of break, and any other pertinent pathologic features that might apply (Salter, 1983). Complete descriptions of the various types of fractures can be found in orthopedic texts or manuals.

The most common signs and symptoms of a fracture are pain, edema, and excessive motion at a site where motion does not occur normally. The intensity of these clinical manifestations varies depending on the nature and extent of the incurred damage. Spasm of the surrounding muscles can be minimized by keeping the injured part immobilized until treatment can begin.

Fracture healing. Bone tissue repair occurs in a characteristic manner (Heppenstall, 1980). Immediately after the fracture occurs, the vascular supply is disrupted,

hemorrhage occurs, and a hematoma is formed at the site. Bone at the edges of the fracture becomes necrotic and an inflammatory response ensues. Cells in the fracture area are induced to form new bone. As a result of fibroblastic activity, a rich capillary supply, and phagocytosis, the hematoma is replaced by fibrous or cartilaginous granulation tissue. A soft callus is formed that "bridges" the fracture surface and creates a nonosseous union. This callus is gradually converted to fiber bone (hard callus). The final phase of repair occurs when fiber bone is converted to lamellar bone. This is the stage of remodeling. The bones of children have a greater capacity for remodeling than adult bones. A child's bone, originally healed in an angulated state, may regain normal anatomic alignment over time with remodeling (Salter, 1983).

Treatment rationale. The ultimate aim of treatment is to promote the normal repair process and restore function to the injured part. This is accomplished through reduction of the fracture and maintenance of the reduction through immobilization. Reduction means restoration of bone tissue to normal anatomic alignment and length and may be accomplished through closed manipulation, traction, or open surgical reduction. Choice of a type of reduction depends on the severity, type, and location of the fracture. The probability of nerve, vascular, and soft tissue damage also is considered in treatment decisions.

When a satisfactory anatomic position is achieved and confirmed via radiographic examination, the reduction must be maintained. Immobilization of the injured part is required and may be achieved in a variety of ways. External fixation using casts or splints is one of the most common means employed to treat fractures. Traction may be used to maintain and achieve reduction. Open surgical reduction is required for use of internal fixation devices such as plates, nails, screws, and rods. Open fractures are most commonly reduced through open reduction in conjunction with internal fixation. Use of internal fixation devices carries the increased risk of infection, migration of the device, and tissue reaction. Inability to maintain immobilization for the time necessary to permit healing may delay healing or allow improper healing to occur with the subsequent development of a permanent deformity.

As a result of immobilization, a certain amount of muscle atrophy, loss of tone, and joint stiffness will occur (see Chapter 14). After healing has occurred and immobilization is no longer required normal muscle tone and full range of motion must be restored to allow normal functional use of the injured part. This is accomplished through a program of exercise that promotes a gradual increase in activity for the injured part.

Alterations in skeletal repair. The healing process can be disrupted or lengthened by infection, lack of blood supply, disturbances of vitamin D or C and protein intake and/or metabolism, inadequate immobilization, or extensive accompanying tissue injury. *Delayed union* is the term applied when the healing process is lengthened. The term *malunion* refers to healing with angulation or lack of proper alignment at the site. *Nonunion* is a condition in which repair fails and a firm union is not achieved. This condition results in formation of a false joint (pseudarthrosis); motion will be present where there should be none. Nonunion has traditionally been treated with bone grafts but recently investigators have demonstrated a similar success rate using electric current. Application of an electric current at the fracture site has been found to enhance bone formation. The use of electricity in the treatment of nonunion is promising. A cooperative study involving 16 teams is currently being conducted in the United States to evaluate this form of treatment more completely. A complete listing of possible complications of fractures, the signs and symptoms, and contributory factors is presented in Table 13-10.

Fractures are a common sequel to traumatic injury. The general effects of trauma were discussed in Chapter 5. The following case study illustrates the need for appropriate monitoring and intervention to prevent the possible complications of orthopedic trauma.

CASE STUDY: ORTHOPEDIC TRAUMA

History

A ten-year-old boy, Mike, on an errand for his mother, was hit by a truck while crossing the street. A witness at the accident said that the boy was hit on his left side and was thrown to the side of the street striking the edge of the gutter on his right side. The boy did not lose consciousness. He was brought by emergency vehicle to the emergency room where his mother met him.

Subjective and Objective Data

Mike is crying and says, "My leg! My leg! It hurts bad! Will I ever walk again?" His mother keeps repeating to the emergency room personnel, "Oh dear, if only I hadn't sent him to the store."

Physical examination and diagnostic studies revealed the following: a displaced fracture of the left femur, comminuted fracture of the left distal fibula and an incomplete fracture of the clavicle.

Contributed by Judy Trufant.

All other full body x-rays were negative.

Severe contusions of the left thigh and abrasions of the right trunk, arm and face were noted. Circulation, motion and sensation were intact.

Mike was assessed as stable enough to undergo surgical correction of the fractures. Under general anesthesia his fibula was reduced and casted, his femur was reduced and the left extremity was placed in 90-90 traction with Steinman pin. His clavicle was immobilized with a clavicle harness. The abrasions were debrided and cleaned with dressings applied to those on the right arm. Intravenous fluids were started and an in-dwelling urinary drainage catheter was placed. He was stabilized in the recovery room and after injections of morphine sulfate and valium was transferred to the orthopedic unit.

Discussion

During this early period following multiple traumatic fractures and soft tissue injury, monitoring for four potential complications must have high priority in the nursing care plan. These are neurovascular compromise (including paresis and paralysis), fat embolism syndrome, compartmental syndrome, and misalignment (see Table 13-10).

Nursing interventions related to neurovascular compromise include frequent and careful neurovascular assessment at least every hour. This should include comparing the affected left leg to the right for differences in circulation, warmth and color. The toes of the left foot should be checked for temperature, color, capillary refill (blanching sign), sensation, and motion. Documentation of these assessments on a flow sheet and validations of individual nurses' assessments from shift to shift are important.

Signs and symptoms of fat embolism must be kept uppermost in mind during assessment of the respiratory, cardiovascular, and neurologic systems. Interventions that may be helpful in the prevention of or the quick detection of fat embolism include maintaining adequate ventilation by assisting with coughing and deep breathing, and monitoring results of arterial blood gases. Assessment of pre-injury behavior and monitoring of subtle behavior changes and level of consciousness are also important. Careful attention to maintaining immobilization of the fractures is of primary importance. This can be accomplished by keeping traction in place and by frequently checking for effectiveness. Any type of movement, either spontaneous by the patient or as part of nursing care should be kept to a minimum. The urinary drainage catheter eliminates movement and positioning associated with toileting.

Another complication which is possible in the left thigh, that has extensive soft tissue trauma, and in the casted fibula is compartmental syndrome. Assessment and alertness for this complication are important so that measures may be instituted quickly to prevent its occurrence and the possibility of severe nerve and muscle damage. Signs of compartmental syndrome include progressive pain out of proportion to what is anticipated and pain upon passive stretch of the muscles. In addition, motor weakness (a late sign) hypoesthesia and tightness of the compartment (both palpable and experienced by the patient) may be present. Interventions must be immediate and include removing any constrictive dressings, bivalving the cast and splitting all soft dressings to the skin (on doctor's orders). The affected extremity should not be elevated above heart level if compartmental syndrome is suspected, which in this case would require readjustment of the traction. Recognizing and preventing complications from myoglobinuria by testing urine, maintaining intake and output, and administering fluids is also important.

Interventions to prevent misalignment must also be included in the care plan. Misalignment can be prevented by strict maintainence of the traction placement and proper body alignment. Any movement by the patient during care should be planned to prevent any excessive motion at the fracture site. Movement by the patient in this early period is usually deterred by pain. Discouraging excessive movement is also an important intervention for preventing fat embolism.

Nursing Diagnoses

1. Acute pain related to bone and soft tissue injury and to immobilization devices
2. Self-care deficits: Inability to ambulate and decreased ROM of upper extremities related to immobilization devices
3. Fear: Related to pain and loss of body function
4. Potential for infection related to placement of Steinman pin
5. Potential for disuse syndrome
6. Grieving: Guilt, related to perceived role in child's accident (Mother)

Infection

The reaction of bone tissue to an infection is essentially the same as in other tissues (see Chapter 2). The mineral structure of bone, however, causes unique problems in successful treatment. First, infected bone is replaced by fibrous connective tissue. New cortical bone, deposited in response to irritation of the periosteum, can be very dense. This covering of new bone (called the involucrum) envelops the bone destroyed by infection (called the sequestrum). For these reasons, drainage of exudate and attainment of adequate antibiotic concentration at the site of the infection can be difficult.

Many infectious processes affecting bone occur secondarily as a result of more generalized infection or primary infection of some other part of the body. Examples include tuberculosis, syphilis, and leprosy. Skeletal changes can be prevented with adequate treatment of these disorders. Although somewhat controlled in the United States, skeletal tuberculosis remains a problem in developing countries in other parts of the world. U.S. health care providers working with refugee or immigrant populations from these countries need to be alert to its incidence. The presently increasing incidence of tuberculosis in the United States may result in skeletal tuberculosis becoming a more commonly seen disorder in the future. The spine is often involved in tuberculosis with a marked predilection for involvement at the thoracolumbar junction (Bradford et al., 1987).

Disease model: osteomyelitis. Osteomyelitis is the disease model used to illustrate the effects of an infectious process on bone. The bacteria that most commonly cause osteomyelitis include *Staphylococcus aureus*, *Streptococcus*, *Hemophilus influenzae*, and *Escherichia coli*. Less frequently, *Salmonella*, *Proteus*, and *Klebsiella pneumoniae* cause osteomyelitis. *Brucellosis* is endemic to the Midwest, and it is estimated that approximately 10% of the patients with chronic brucellosis develop *Brucella* osteomyelitis.

Osteomyelitis may occur in an acute or chronic form. The acute form is marked by a rapid onset and a systemic, febrile course with local manifestations. The chronic form is a recurrence after an initial acute episode. Chronic osteomyelitis indicates that resistance to treatment has developed. The initial episode may occur as a result of trauma (a penetrating wound or open fracture) or of infection occurring elsewhere in the body. Hematogenous spread may occur as a result of boils, impetigo, sties, or infected lesions elsewhere on the body. Acute osteomyelitis is seen most frequently in infants and young children and is more common in boys.

Clinical manifestations. In acute osteomyelitis all the systemic signs of infection are present (see Chapter 2). In addition, the infected site will be edematous, reddened, and warm to the touch. The patient will complain of pain with movement and will often semiflex the extremity for comfort. In the chronic form, the patient will appear recovered from the initial attack only to experience an exacerbation at a later time. The earliest signs and symptoms tend to be chills and fever and severe pain at the site. A sinus tract may form between the bone and the skin.

Treatment rationale. The infected tissue is excised and drained surgically. Irrigation tubes may be inserted during surgery to provide a means for irrigation of the site with antibiotic solution. Systemic, intravenous antibiotic therapy is begun following surgery. The choice of antibiotic will be determined by the results of the culture and sensitivities of the infecting organism; the length of the course of treatment will be determined by the age and response of the patient. A child is usually treated with IV antibiotics for 2 to 4 weeks followed by oral antibiotic therapy. In the adult, IV antibiotic therapy is maintained for at least 4 to 6 weeks and is followed by prolonged oral antibiotic therapy. The affected area should be immobilized to prevent permanent deformity and aggravation of the condition. Proper anatomic positioning of the limbs and extremities can help prevent contracture deformities from developing. Pain is treated with analgesic medication. Severe bone loss may require bone grafting (Bradford et al., 1987).

Altered tissue perfusion: avascular necrosis

When bone is deprived of its blood supply, the reaction is similar to that of other tissues: ischemia and death of tissue. The blood supply may be disrupted as a result of trauma, thrombosis, or embolism. There is some evidence that mechanisms such as marrow cell hypertrophy, microembolic phenomena, and lipid induced osteocyte necrosis can, either singly or in combination, cause bone necrosis (Cruess, 1986). The subchondral bone at the ends of long bones is most susceptible; the neck of the femur and hip joint are most commonly affected. For example, the head of the femur may undergo necrosis in patients with sickle cell anemia in response to the arterial occlusion by the sickled red blood cells. In Gaucher's disease, a metabolic disorder, abnormal cells accumulate and occlude the blood supply. The *osteochondroses* represent a group of clinical disorders (primarily seen in children) in which the avascular necrosis is idiopathic or without a recognized etiology. Legg-Perthes' disease is an example in which the femoral head undergoes necrosis leading to more serious deformity of the hip joint if left untreated.

In children, posttraumatic avascular necrosis of a pressure epiphysis can lead to retarded growth in the epiphyseal plate and joint incongruity. In adults, avascular necrosis will delay fracture healing and can lead to irreparable joint damage.

PATHOPHYSIOLOGIC MECHANISMS AND DISORDERS OF JOINTS

A joint is a junction between two or more bones. It is a point at which articulation between the bones may occur. There are three types of joints:

1. Fibrous: bones are connected by collagenous tissue

2. Cartilaginous: bones are connected by a mass of cartilage that acts as their growth center (examples include the discovertebral joints of the spine and the sternomanubrial and costochondral junctions)

3. Synovial: junction enclosed by a fibrous capsule, which is lined with a synovial membrane and held together and stabilized by ligaments and tendons (examples include the knee and hip joints)

Synovial fluid is a dialysate of blood plasma plus mucin that contains large amounts of protein-bound hyaluronic acid. The function of the synovial fluid includes lubrication of articular surfaces and nourishment of the articular cartilage. The lubricating quality of the fluid may be altered by any of the following mechanisms:

1. Impairment of secretory capacity of the synovial cells
2. Dilution
3. Mixing with exudates
4. Depolymerization by chemicals, bacteria, or enzymes

The nutrient quality of the fluid may be altered by the following factors:

1. Disruption or changes in the blood supply of the synovia
2. Change in fluid composition
3. Barriers at the cartilage level, such as granulation tissue

It is easy to visualize how an inflammatory or infectious process, bleeding into a joint, or trauma can result in permanent joint damage just by the alterations these conditions may cause in the quantity and quality of the synovial fluid with the result of impairment of either the nutritive or lubricant functions of the fluid.

Cartilage is an essential component of cartilaginous and synovial joints. This tissue contains no blood vessels, lymphatics, or nerves and is incapable of regeneration; therefore damage or degenerative changes will be permanent. Any irregularity or damage of the articular surface leads to progressive degenerative changes of the surrounding cartilage and ultimately to pain and limitation of movement. Even the normal stresses and strains of living cause wear and tear on the cartilage, causing it to be less resilient and more susceptible to injury. Cartilage is especially susceptible to damage by enzymes in the purulent exudates of certain types of infecting organisms.

The fibrous joint capsule of synovial joints with its associated ligaments prevents undesired movement and thus stability of the joint as well as allowing the desired range of motion. Stretching of or increased fluid pressure in the capsule can cause excruciating pain. If the joint capsule is stretched beyond its limits, instability of the joint may ensue. The joint will be "loose" with excessive and abnormal range of motion. Fibrosis and scar formation within the joint and muscle contractures can cause a joint contracture to develop. In this condition the normal range of motion of the joint is lost.

Ehlers-Danlos syndrome was mentioned earlier as a genetic disorder of collagen synthesis (see Fig. 13-7). In addition to the joint laxity seen, retinal detachment, small corneas, and vertebral anomalies also characterize this disorder. The skin is friable and hyperextensible and demonstrates abnormal (hypertrophic) scar formation.

Arthropathies are a major cause of physical disability. Much preventive health teaching is needed for persons and parents of children involved in active exercise and sports programs about the necessity of using protective equipment, proper conditioning and warm-up, and treatment for what seems like even a minor injury. The pathophysiologic mechanisms that can alter joint structure and function include inflammation, degeneration, and articular disruption.

Inflammation

The term *arthritis* literally means inflammation of a joint. The effects of inflammatory reactions in joint tissue are discussed in detail in Chapter 2, and gouty arthritis is presented as a disease model of inflammation. Arthritis may also be the consequence of an infectious process in the joint (septic arthritis) and bleeding into a joint (hemophilic arthritis).

The tissues of the joint structure are mesenchymal in origin and thus will be affected in disorders of mesenchymal tissue function such as the hypersensitivity and collagen disorders. Sustained, chronic tissue inflammation is the hallmark of these disorders, each with its particular pattern of organ involvement. Arthralgia is a common symptom in these disorders. Disorders characterized by immune-mediated inflammatory processes, such as rheumatoid arthritis, are discussed in Chapter 2.

The *seronegative spondylarthropathies* are a group of chronic inflammatory disorders involving the cartilaginous joints. The initial inflammatory lesions are replaced by fibrotic tissue that subsequently undergoes calcification and ossification. This fibrous and bony ankylosis causes a loss of mobility in the joints. Included in this group of disorders are ankylosing spondylitis (Marie-Strumpell disease), Reiter's syndrome, yersiniosis, and psoriatic spondylitis. There is a familial pattern of occurrence in these disorders, which cause pain, stiffness, and loss of joint mobility.

Ankylosing spondylitis has been found to be highly associated with ulcerative colitis and regional enteritis. HLA-B27 has been identified in 90% to 95% of affected patients, leading to speculation that this disorder is an immune response to some infectious agent in genetically predisposed individuals. The pathologic changes in the spine, sacroiliac, hip, and shoulder joints are identical to those found in rheumatoid arthritis. In severe cases, fusion of the vertebral bodies results in immobilization of the spine accompanied by great disability.

Degeneration

The most common arthropathy is that characterized by degenerative alteration of the articular cartilage combined with hypertrophic changes in the articular bone ends. Inflammatory changes are not significant. Both synovial and cartilaginous joints are affected. There are a variety of names applied to this condition, including osteoarthritis, degenerative arthritis, degenerative joint disease (DJD), osteoarthrosis, senescent arthritis, and hypertrophic arthritis. Primary or idiopathic osteoarthritis is viewed as the inevitable effect of the aging process or a lifetime of wear and tear on the joints. DJD that develops in response to a mechanical (as when a minor joint deformity is present), traumatic, or inflammatory initial insult to the cartilage is referred to as secondary osteoarthritis.

Disease model: osteoarthritis. Osteoarthritis—or the more descriptively accurate term, degenerative joint disease—is primarily a disorder of middle and later life that mainly affects the weight-bearing joints. This disorder may occur in younger individuals after previous joint injury as well. The joints most commonly affected include the vertebrae, hips, knees, distal interphalangeal joints of the fingers, great toe, and base of thumb. The term arthritis is somewhat misleading, since the pathologic process is not inflammatory.

Clinical manifestations. The course of osteoarthritis is a slowly progressive and usually insidious one, and pain is the major symptom. The earliest indication of the disorder may be stiffness or achy pain and swelling in one or more joints. The symptoms may be noticed first upon arising in the morning and may be exacerbated by cold, damp weather. The stiffness may be relieved by moderate activity. The pain may also be relieved by moderate activity but is usually relieved by heat and rest. Physical examination reveals no local heat and only mild tenderness. The joints may also demonstrate a restricted range of motion, small effusions, and crepitus. Fragments of cartilage may break loose within the joint and are referred to as "joint mice." The pain, deformity, and limitation of movement may be quite severe in some cases. Osteoarthritis may coexist with other musculoskeletal disorders such as rheumatoid arthritis.

Pathogenesis. The etiology of idiopathic DJD is unknown. It is agreed that trauma (progressive, cumulative, and insidious over the years) probably plays a contributing role similar to secondary DJD. The pathologic changes observed in the involved joints in both types of DJD are a reflection of cartilage injury and repair. Compressive trauma, especially significant in the weight-bearing joints, leads to cartilaginous erosion and osteolytic changes. Laxity or instability of the structural joint components would contribute to abnormal weight-bearing stresses, leading to further cartilage injury. A vicious cycle develops when the consequent repair process is inadequate to keep up with the cartilaginous degeneration. There is speculation that the slowing of the metabolic and restorative capacities of the body tissues, which inevitably accompanies the aging process, contributes to the failure of cartilaginous repair. There is also the possibility that the extent of progressive injury over time just reaches a point at which repair is no longer possible. Increased proteolytic enzyme activity has been observed in osteoarthritic cartilage, and it is unknown whether this is a secondary effect of injury or a primary, initiating event in the pathologic process. Researchers are also trying to determine if the increased water content of osteoarthritic cartilage makes the cartilage more vulnerable to injury. One group of researchers is working on the hypothesis that osteoarthritis is not the result of degeneration but the result of an imbalance in the anabolic and catabolic processes in cartilage (Redeker, 1988). Such abnormal cartilage metabolism causes the loss of proteoglycans from the collagen matrix. The pathologic processes underlying DJD remain a subject of examination and research.

Treatment rationale. Treatment is symptomatic and aimed at retarding the inevitable effects of articular degeneration. Moving to a warm, dry climate may be enough to give relief from symptoms. This may not be a feasible solution for all afflicted and thus use of salicylate and nonsteroidal antiinflammatory drugs for pain relief, ambulatory aids (walkers, canes, etc.), splints or braces, planned exercise and physical therapy regimens, and rest and immobilization of affected joints when necessary may be employed. Surgery for alteration or restoration of the articular surfaces may be necessary when pain and deformity are severe.

While the primary form of this condition has been viewed as one of the inevitable effects of the aging process, it is nonetheless an important one with which health care providers should be familiar. Health care providers will be confronted with treatment of this disorder more and more frequently as life expectancy increases and a greater proportion of our society reaches the older age group.

Articular disruption

Trauma to the joints may result in a sprain, ligamental tears, a meniscal tear in the knee joint, subluxation, or dislocation. A form of arthritis referred to as traumatic arthritis may also result. The manifestations of this type of arthritis are similar to those of osteoarthritis except that involvement is limited to the traumatized joint only. A *sprain* is the incomplete tearing of the articular capsule or ligaments that is the result of a sudden twisting motion to the joint. The continuity of the synovial membrane may be disrupted; however, stability of the joint remains unaffected. The ankle and knee joints are most susceptible to sprains. *Whiplash* is the common term applied to cervical sprain. Swelling, pain, and limitation of movement are the chief manifestations. Treatment is directed toward reducing discomfort and promoting healing through immobilization of the joint and reduction of edema. Application of cold, elevation of the extremity, and use of a compression bandage may be employed to control edema.

Ligamental tears can also be the result of a twisting force or a forceful impact to the joint. The joint will be unstable in addition to the other signs of tissue injury noted earlier. The knee is most commonly the joint affected. Treatment depends on the extent of the tear. Surgical repair is indicated for the most extensive, complete tears. Treatment of mild tears may be only symptomatic, while treatment of moderate tears is directed toward protection of the joint. A *meniscal tear* often accompanies a ligamental tear of the knee. These injuries occur frequently in athletes involved in contact sports. The major function of the menisci is to promote stability of the knee joint. Again, symptoms and treatment depend on the severity of the injury.

A *subluxation* is an incomplete dislocation. A *dislocation* is the separation of articular components such that articular surfaces are no longer in contact with one another. There will be less tissue damage with a subluxation, since the dislocation is only partial. The tissue damage accompanying dislocation may include disruption of the articular capsule, damage to surrounding ligaments, varying degrees of soft tissue damage, and possible neurovascular damage. These injuries are most often the result of trauma but may be congenital as well. It has been found that 1 in 60 infants is born with instability of one or both hip joints. While this instability is resolved in most infants, dislocation persists in many with an incidence of 1.55 per 1000.

Dislocation and malalignment of the joints can also lead to deformity and limitation of movement. There is speculation that even a mild disorder of the joint in early life (one that may even be undetected or cause no problem itself) can contribute to the development of degenerative joint disease in later life.

Malalignment of the spinal joints, such as that seen in scoliosis (a lateral curvature of the spine—see Fig. 13-4), can lead to painful degenerative joint disease of the spine in adults. Bradford et al. (1987) report that the most common problem is pain followed by progressive deformity, which can lead to impaired pulmonary function, body image disturbance, and neurologic deficits. Thoracic deformities most often affect cardiopulmonary function. Based on a review of many studies of the natural history of scoliosis, Bradford et al. (1987) concluded that the observed general trend is that a significant reduction in vital capacity, a twice-normal likelihood of early death from cor pulmonale, back pain, and disturbed self-image inevitably occur with a 90-degree curve or greater. Individual patients with lesser curves can also experience these same problems, but it is not as likely. Also the degree of curvature may progressively increase. Childhood scoliosis often worsens with growth and should be corrected as early as possible.

Other types of spinal deformity that can occur include kyphosis and lordosis, which are abnormal posterior and anterior angulations of the spine. All of these spinal deformities may occur singly or in combination with one another.

SUMMARY

Presented in this chapter were the major pathophysiologic mechanisms and disorders that affect the musculoskeletal system. Disorders of development, nutrition, metabolism, and the nervous system have a profound effect on this system as well. Disorders of the musculoskeletal system are most frequently reflected by some alteration in the individual's mobility level. An alteration in the individual's level of mobility has the potential to disrupt musculoskeletal function even further. The effects of impaired physical mobility as a response to musculoskeletal dysfunction are discussed in the following chapter.

BIBLIOGRAPHY

Aegerter E and Kirkpatrick J: Orthopedic diseases, ed 4, Philadelphia, 1975, WB Saunders Co.

Aitken M: Osteoporosis in clinical practice, Bristol, England, 1984, John Wright & Sons.

Avioli L and Krane S, editors: Metabolic bone disease, vol II, New York, 1978, Academic Press, Inc.

Avioli L and Krane S, editors: Metabolic bone disease, vol I, New York, 1977, Academic Press, Inc.

Avioli LV: The osteoporotic syndrome: detection, prevention and treatment, Orlando, 1987, Grune & Stratton, Inc.

Bethlem J: Myopathies, ed 2, New York, 1980, Elsevier North-Holland, Inc.

Bluestone R: Rheumatology, Boston, 1980, Houghton Mifflin Co.

Bobrow M, Walker A, and Walton J: The parental origin of mutations causing Duchenne muscular dystrophy, Arch Neurol 45:85, 1988.

Bradford DS, Lonstein JE, Moe JH, Ogilvie JW, and Winter RB: Moe's textbook of scoliosis and other spinal deformities, ed 2, Philadelphia, 1987, WB Saunders Co.

Buchanan DC, LaBarbera CJ, Roelofs R, and Olsen W: Reactions of families to children with Duchenne muscular dystrophy, Gen Hosp Psychiatr 1:262, 1979.

Carlson M and Winter R: The "Gillette" sitting support orthosis, Orthot Prosth 32(4):35, 1978.

Chambers J: Metabolic bone disorders: imbalances of calcium and phosphorus, Nurs Clin North Am 22(4):861, 1987.

Cruess RL: Osteonecrosis of bone. Current concepts as to etiology and pathogenesis, Clin Orthop 208:30, 1986.

Deftos LJ and Glowacki J: Mechanisms of bone disease. In Frohlich ED, editor: Pathophysiology: altered regulatory mechanisms in disease, Philadelphia, 1984, JB Lippincott Co.

DiMarco AF, Kelling JS, DiMarco MS, et al.: The effect of inspiratory resistive training on respiratory muscle function in patients with muscular dystrophy, Muscle Nerve 8:284, 1985.

Edwards RHT: Physiological analysis of skeletal muscle weakness and fatigue, Clin Sci Mol Med 54:463, 1978.

Edwards RHT: Human muscle function and fatigue. In Porter R and Whelan J, editors: Human muscle fatigue: physiological mechanisms, Ciba Foundation Symposium #82, London, 1981, Pitman Medical.

Edwards RHT: Biochemical bases of fatigue in exercise performance: catastrophe theory of muscular fatigue. In Knuttgen H, Vogel J, and Poortmans J, editors: Biochemistry of exercise, Champaign, Ill, 1983, Human Kinetics Publishers.

Engel AG and Banker BQ, editors: Myology: basic and clinical, vols 1 and 2, New York, 1986, McGraw-Hill Book Co.

Farah MG, Evans EB, and Vignos PJ: Echocardiographic evaluation of left ventricular function in Duchenne's muscular dystrophy, Am J Med 69:248, 1980.

Gronert GA: Malignant hyperthermia, Anesthesiology 53:395, 1980.

Heidrich F and Thompson RS: Osteoporosis prevention: strategies applicable for general population groups, J Fam Pract 25(1):33, 1987.

Heppenstall RB: Fracture treatment and healing, Philadelphia, 1980, WB Saunders Co.

Hilt N and Cogburn S: Manual of orthopedics, St. Louis, 1980, The CV Mosby Co.

Hoffman EP, Brown RH, and Kunkel LM: Dystrophin, the protein product of the Duchenne muscular dystrophy locus, Cell 51(6):919, 1987a.

Hoffman EP, Knudson CM, Campbell KP, and Kunkel LM: Subcellular fractionation of dystrophin to the triads of skeletal muscle, Nature 330:754, 1987b.

Inkley SR, Oldenburg FC, and Vignos PG: Pulmonary function in Duchenne muscular dystrophy related to stage of disease, Am J Med 56:297, 1974.

Kelley WN, Harris ED, Ruddy S, and Sledge CB: Textbook of rheumatology, ed 2, Philadelphia, 1985, WB Saunders Co.

Koenig M, Hoffman EP, Bertelson CJ, Monaco AP, Feener C, and Kunkel LM: Complete cloning of the Duchenne muscular dystrophy (DMD) cDNA and preliminary genomic organization of the DMD gene in normal and affected individuals, Cell 50(3):509, 1987.

Koenig M, Monaco AP, and Kunkel LM: The complete sequence of dystrophin predicts a rod-shaped cytoskeletal protein, Cell 52(2):219, 1988.

Kolata G: Two disease-causing genes found, Science 234:669, 1986.

Kunkel LM: Analysis of deletions in DNA from patients with Becker and Duchenne muscular dystrophy, Nature 322:73, 1986.

Larson CB and Gould M: Orthopedic nursing, ed 9, St. Louis, 1978, The CV Mosby Co.

Lindsay R: Estrogen therapy in the prevention and management of osteoporosis, Am J Obstet Gynecol 156(5):1347, 1987.

McComas AJ: Neuromuscular function and disorders, London, 1977, Butterworths.

Monaco AP, Neve RL, Colletti-Feener C, Bertelson CJ, Kurnit DM, and Kunkel LM: Isolation of candidate cDNA's for portions of the Duchenne muscular dystrophy gene, Nature 323:646, 1986.

NAON: Core curriculum for orthopaedic nursing, Pitman NJ, 1986, AJ Janetti Inc.

Nudel U, Robzyk K, and Yaffe D: Expression of the putative DMD gene in differentiated myogenic cell cultures and in the brain, Nature 331:635, 1988.

Osteoporosis (editorial), Lancet 2:833, 1987.

Prockop DJ: Osteogenesis imperfecta: a model for genetic causes of osteoporosis and perhaps several other common diseases of connective tissue, Arthritis Rheumatism 31:1, 1988.

Prockop DJ and Kivirikko KI: Heritable diseases of collagen, N Engl J Med 311:376, 1984.

Raisz LG and Kream BE: Regulation of bone formation, N Engl J Med 309:29 (Pt I): 83 (Pt II), 1983.

Redeker M: Osteoarthritis: a little understood crippler, The Magazine (Rush Presbyterian St. Luke's Medical Center), 11:3-8, Summer, 1988.

Rideau Y, Glorion B, DeLaubier A, et al.: The treatment of scoliosis in Duchenne muscular dystrophy, Muscle Nerve 7:281, 1984.

Riggs BL: Pathogenesis of osteoporosis, Am J Obstet Gynecol 156:1342, 1987.

Riggs BL and Melton LJ: Evidence for two distinct syndromes of involutional osteoporosis, Am J Med 75:899, 1983.

Riggs BL and Melton LJ: Involutional osteoporosis, N Engl J Med 314:1676, 1986.

Roche AF, editor: Osteoporosis: current concepts, Report of the 7th Ross Conference on Medical Research, Columbus, Ohio, 1987, Ross Laboratories.

Roses AD: Mutants in Duchenne muscular dystrophy, Arch Neurol 45:84, 1988.

Rüdel R, Lehmann-Horn F, Ricker K, and Küther G: Hypokalemic periodic paralysis: in vitro investigation of muscle membrane parameters, Muscle Nerve 7:110, 1984.

Salter R: Textbook of disorders and injuries of the musculoskeletal system, ed 2, Baltimore, 1983, The Williams & Wilkins Co.

Scott MO, Sylvester JE, Heinman-Patterson T, Shi Y-J, Fieles W, Stedman H, Burghes A, Ray P, Worton R, and Fischbeck K: Duchenne muscular dystrophy gene expression in normal and diseased human muscle, Science 239:1418, 1988.

Slater C: The missing link in DMD? Nature 330:693, 1987.

Vander AJ, Sherman JH, and Luciano DS: Human physiology: the mechanisms of body function, ed 4, New York, 1985, McGraw-Hill Book Co.

Vaughan J: The physiology of bone, ed 3, Oxford, England, 1981, Clarendon Press.

Vignos PJ: Physical models of rehabilitation in neuromuscular disease, Muscle Nerve 6:323, 1983.

14

Impaired physical mobility

Mobility is defined as the ability to move about freely. The term can be used to describe a state of free movement within all aspects of life: physical, psychosocial, political, economic, spiritual, geographic, and occupational. Mobility is highly valued in our transient society and is sometimes equated with freedom. Indeed, a certain sense of freedom does emanate from the ability to move about without restriction. Many individuals use their level of mobility to define their health status; that is, they view the inability to get out or perform their routine daily activities as a manifestation of illness. Discussion of the concept of mobility within this chapter will be limited to the effects of impaired physical mobility on the overall functioning of the person.

Movement of the various parts or of the entire body is essential for the maintenance of both physiologic and psychologic well-being. Movement serves many purposes, such as providing the means for nonverbal communication and the expression of emotion; for self-defense, as an individual can move away from harmful or noxious stimuli; and for satisfaction of basic and secondary needs, as the person participates in activities of daily living that are both life sustaining (eating, drinking, etc.) and wellness enhancing (recreation, work, etc.). The ability of any organism to interact with and react to the various forces and conditions operating within the internal and external environments is in itself considered a basic need. It is a prerequisite to the occurrence of even minimal levels of function as the maintenance of wellness depends on the organism's ability to adapt to changing environmental conditions. The ability to adapt depends to a great extent on the human organism's level of mobility.

In order for the level of physical mobility to be within normal limits, the nervous, muscular, and skeletal systems and the vestibular apparatus and proprioceptor organs must be intact and functioning. Trauma (accidental or surgical), disease, or altered levels of consciousness can result in impaired functioning of these organ systems with the result of altering the normal mobility level. Pathology of these organ systems is not the only condition from which an altered state of mobility may result, since restriction of movement can also be voluntary or proscribed. When any of these conditions are present and result in a departure from the normal level of physical mobility, a state of impaired physical mobility is the response that becomes the focus of treatment.

Impaired physical mobility is defined by the North American Nursing Diagnosis Association as a state in which the individual experiences or is at risk of experiencing limitation of physical movement. It includes any condition in which the ability to move is impaired or restricted. There is a wide spectrum over which this can occur, hence use of the term is relative. The degree of impaired physical imobility can be *absolute*, as in the comatose patient who is incapable of initiating any movement on his own. More frequently seen, however, is a lesser degree of impaired physical mobility or immobility of one body part, as in a patient who is partially paralyzed or who has sustained a bone fracture and has a cast in place. The term takes on a relative meaning in these conditions.

The degree of impairment of physical mobility present can be assessed using four qualitative measures described by Spencer and associates (1965):

1. Physical inactivity, which is manifested by a reduction in body movement
2. Physical restriction or limitation of movement, which is manifested by an imposed reduction of movement
3. Constancy of body posture in relation to gravity, which results in a loss of the body's ability to adapt to changes in position and posture
4. Sensory deprivation, which causes a reduction in the stimulus to move and which is manifested by even greater physical inactivity

A judgment regarding the degree of impaired physical mobility can be made based on how many of the above conditions are present. The more conditions present, the greater will be the degree of impaired physical mobility experienced by the individual. In the comatose patient all four conditions are present, and the degree of impaired physical mobility is total. In comparison a person with a fractured arm and a cast in place to restrict movement of the injured arm is able to continue to participate in activities of daily living, making some minor adjustments to compensate for the temporary loss of use of the injured arm. The degree of impaired physical mobility in this patient is considered minimal since only one condition, physical restriction of movement, is present.

The duration of the immobile state is another important variable to be considered in the clinical situation. Both the duration and degree of the immobility are determined by the primary cause of the disruption and by the individual's response to that disruption. Depending on the cause, the impaired physical mobility can be considered permanent or temporary and the degree either partial or absolute.

No matter what the cause, impaired physical mobility in itself has profound negative effects on all the body systems. The severity, that is, the scope and progression, of these effects is directly proportional to the duration and degree of the immobility. In addition, these effects themselves contribute further to the immobility. Fig. 14-1 illustrates this phenomenon; it is easy to see that the potential for development of a vicious cycle is present. A response to immobility that decreases the duration and the degree of the immobility will also have the result of minimizing the effects of the immobility and thus their potential for further altering the level of mobility to any great extent. Fig. 14-2 illustrates the interrelationship between impaired physical mobility and a response that reduces the duration and degree of the impaired physical mobility.

In this chapter we will discuss the concept of impaired physical mobility, conditions in which some degree of immobility may be expected, and the systemic effects

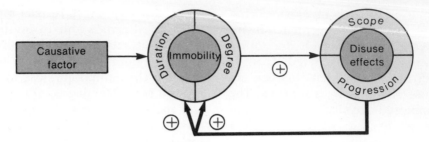

Fig. 14-1. Systems model of feedback relationship between immobility and its effects. The severity (i.e. scope and progression) of disuse effects are proportional to the degree and duration of the immobility being experienced. The disuse effects will also contribute to further immobility, thus a positive feedback relationship exists with the potential for development of a vicious cycle.

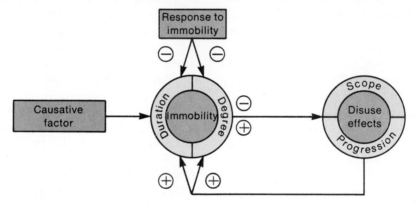

Fig. 14-2. Role of response to immobility. A response which lessens the duration and degree of the immobility will also minimize the scope and progression of the disuse effects.

of impaired physical mobility. The treatment of the effects of immobility will be discussed in terms of a reversal of the pathophysiology that is present.

CAUSATIVE AND PREDISPOSING FACTORS

Impaired physical mobility is an identifiable and treatable response to many different health problems. Alterations in the level of physical mobility can result from prescribed restriction of movement in the form of bed rest, physical restriction of movement through the use of external devices, voluntary restriction of movement,

or impairment or loss of motor function.

Prior to World War II, immobilization in the form of imposed bed rest was considered the treatment of choice for most medical and surgical conditions and was imposed during the period following childbirth as well. This form of treatment was begun in the 1860s under the influence of John Hilton of Guy's Hospital in London. His teachings regarding the benefits of bed rest as medical therapy were a drastic and radical departure from the accepted methods of treatment at that time. Prior to that time, confinement to bed was a sign of approaching death. Once bed rest became recognized as a therapeutic measure, it was prescribed as treatment for most disorders. Pathologic complications that occurred during convalescence were regarded as the inevitable results of the primary disease process rather than the results of the impaired physical mobility caused by bed rest.

The observation that the incidence of complications seemed less in injured soldiers who were rapidly mobilized during World War II led to questions about the real benefit of bed rest as a treatment measure. Research since that time has documented the negative effects of prolonged immobility and the positive effects of early mobilization following illness, injury, surgery, and childbirth. (Birkhead et al., 1963; Kottke, 1966; Browse, 1965; Olson 1967; Carnevali and Brueckner, 1970). As a result of these studies the use of bed rest as acceptable treatment has been modified. Bed rest continues to be an acceptable therapeutic measure for the treatment of conditions such as ischemic coronary disease, in which the increased metabolic demands of increased activity cannot be met and attempts by the body to meet these demands would result in damage to the organ systems. Bed rest is also beneficial in conditions in which organ damage has been sustained, as the reduced workload promotes healing and repair of injured tissue; in conditions in which an anatomic abnormality is aggravated by the effects of gravity; and in conditions in which weight bearing by the muscles, joints, and bones is contraindicated.

Casts, splints, slings, and traction are means by which body parts are immobilized to allow the injured part to rest and heal. These are not the only means by which movement can be physically restricted, however. Sometimes for safety reasons a patient must be physically restrained, which creates an obvious impairment to normal mobility. Drainage devices, intravenous therapy, bulky dressings, and the necessity of being on a ventilator or a monitoring device also physically restrict mobility.

Impairment or loss of motor function can occur as a result of trauma to or disease of the functional components of the motor system: brain, nerves, proprioceptive organs, neuromuscular junction, muscles, joints, or bones. A complete discussion of the effects of trauma is outside the scope of this book; however, impaired physical mobility is a frequent sequela to trauma, either as a primary result of the injury sustained (for example, paralysis) or as a secondary result of the treatment regimen (for example, casts or splints). A discussion of the mechanisms by which disorders of the musculoskeletal and nervous systems disrupt mobility is included in Chapters 10 and 13. A discussion of inflammation as a mechanism that disrupts mobility is included in Chapter 2.

Disease in organ systems not directly involved in motor function can also alter the level of mobility. A feature common to most diseases is a general reduction in physical activity. The more severe the disease, the more severe the reduction. This reduction in physical activity can be attributed to many factors: weakness, loss of endurance, decreased energy production, and reduction in normal organ function. In chronic, progressive disease this reduction in activity may be quite insidious. An example is the emphysemic individual who leaves his second-floor walk-up apartment as little as possible because it is just too difficult to go out anymore.

Voluntary limitation of movement is often the first response to acute, temporary illness; a person just does not feel well and cuts down on usual activities. The general achiness that often accompanies colds, flu, and fever makes the person even more reluctant to move about. The presence of pain or the fear that movement will cause pain also can cause a person to limit movement. The subjective feeling of fatigue and/or weakness will also limit a person's willingness to move. Voluntary restriction of mobility can also be the result of some psychological impairments like depression or a knowledge deficit about the need for physical movement (Creason et al., 1985).

Primary disease processes in organ systems outside the motor system may produce secondary pathologic changes within the functional components of the motor system. An example of this is sickle cell anemia. Degeneration of the heads of the femur and humerus may occur as a result of infarction caused by arterial occlusion by the sickled cells. These bones are most susceptible to infarction because the arterioles supplying them are long and tortuous, collateral circulation is poor, and the rate of blood flow through the marrow is slow. In other words, hypoxia and acidosis, necessary prerequisites to sickling, will be present, especially in the distal portions of the bone. In addition, osteoporosis may occur in the vertebrae and may cause vertebral collapse. Another example is the *renal osteodystrophy* that accompanies renal disease (see Chapter 20). Osteoporotic changes may accompany a number of pathologic conditions that occur outside of the motor system. Among these are hyperthyroidism, Cushing's syndrome, hepatic cirrhosis, hypogonadism, vitamin C deficiency, and gastrectomy.

Pregnancy, especially in the later stages, and obesity are physical conditions in which a voluntary reduction in physical activity often occurs. Obese individuals are more susceptible to the effects of immobility during convalescence and are often more difficult to mobilize. Alterations in the level of consciousness and severe catatonic states can also affect an individual's ability to move independently in a safe manner.

The action of various drugs can alter the individual's level of mobility. Sedatives and some analgesics can make a person very lethargic and unwilling (even physically unable) to participate in any physical activity. Patients who receive chemotherapy treatment for cancer often complain of overwhelming fatigue that keeps them from their usual activities. Other drugs can have a more direct effect on motor function. Both steroid and heparin therapy can cause osteoporosis. Heparin promotes bone resorption by potentiating the action of parathyroid hormone and vitamins A and D and probably through some direct effect on bone as well. Steroid drugs cause osteoporosis through depression of osteoblastic (bone formation) activity, while osteoclastic (bone resorption) activity remains normal. Osteomalacia may result from the excessive intake of aluminum gels, which diminish intestinal phosphate absorption through the formation of insoluble aluminum phosphate. This mechanism serves as the basis for a type of therapy in conditions where serum phosphate levels are high. Osteomalacia may also result from the use of anticonvulsant drugs, which inactivate vitamin D. Ototoxic drugs, such as streptomycin, can impair an individual's sense of balance through damage to the vestibular apparatus.

Sensory deprivation and overload can also affect an individual's mobility level. Studies in which sensory and motor stimuli were reduced or made monotonous have demonstrated that the subjects respond by consistently reducing the level of physical activity. This sets up a positive feedback loop since immobility itself will cause a further reduction in sensory and motor input (Downs, 1974; Zubek et al., 1969).

Another factor that may alter the level of mobility is age. As a consequence of the aging process, older persons generally reduce their physical activity, which is related to both reduced physical ability to move and lack of stimuli to move. Retirement, lack of a substantial income, and loss of social contacts provide little motivation to go out. The physiologic processes involved in aging (see Chapter 9) intrinsically result in a certain degree of motor function impairment. The osteoporosis of aging appears to result from an imbalance between the bone formation and resorption process. Women are more susceptible to the development of osteoporosis than men, especially after menopause. This is most likely because of the loss of estrogen, which inhibits bone resorption to a certain degree, although the finding of increased numbers of mast cells (which synthesize heparin) in the bone marrow of elderly, osteoporotic women indicates that other factors may also play a part (see Chapter 13). In addition, osteoarthritis and decreased sight may also contribute to reduced mobility in the aged individual. These problems are compounded if a chronic disease accompanies the aging process.

EFFECTS OF IMPAIRED PHYSICAL MOBILITY

The effects of impaired physical mobility are both metabolic and functional and reflect a lack of use. Because of the dynamic interaction of all the body components, no system escapes the consequences of immobility. Interestingly, the manifestations of prolonged immobility seen in healthy individuals are identical to those seen in astronauts subjected to weightlessness and relative inactivity during space flight. In fact, studies conducted by the Air Force and the National Aerospace Administration are among those that have increased the body of theoretic knowledge about the consequences and treatment of the effects of prolonged immobility (Fisher and Fisher, 1980; Goode, 1981; Lynch, Jensen, Stevens et al, 1967; Mack and LaChance, 1967; and Ryback, Lewis and Lessard, 1971).

It has already been mentioned that the treatment of injured soldiers during World War II was the impetus for questioning the advisability of prolonged immobility. Prompted by the observation that the more rapidly mobilized soldiers seemed to experience fewer complications, a group of researchers in the middle and late 1940s conducted what is now considered a classic study documenting the effects of prolonged immobility on healthy individuals (Deitrick et al., 1948). The subjects in this study were four young, healthy men. Physiologic parameters such as heart rate, muscle size and strength, response to position change, metabolic rate, and excretion of metabolic products were measured during three separate periods, each approximately 6 weeks in length: before immobilization, during immobilization, and after immobilization. The data from each period were compared to determine the physiologic changes that had occurred and the length of time necessary for recovery from these changes. The results of this study have been consistently replicated in other studies involving normal subjects and in the experiences of astronauts on prolonged space missions.

The effects of impaired physical mobility seen in healthy subjects are a result of deconditioning, which is defined as loss of functional capacity secondary to lack of use (Spencer et al., 1965). The effects produced in healthy subjects include the following:

1. Decreased basal metabolic rate
2. Decreased blood volume and red cell mass
3. Increased urinary excretion of calcium, phosphorus, and nitrogenous waste products
4. Decreased muscle mass
5. Decreased endurance for physical activity
6. Increased pulse rate
7. Inability to tolerate position change

In most clinical situations these effects occur with pathologic conditions, which compound the problem even further. Some of the effects of impaired physical mobility seen in ill persons have not been observed in healthy subjects participating in immobility studies. The effects of impaired physical mobility contribute to the development of certain problems. These problem areas serve as the organizing element in the discussion of the effects of immobilization since they more accurately reflect the effect of immobility on the whole individual. The following problem areas can be expected to occur in the individual who is experiencing immobility in the presence of pathology:

1. Loss of endurance for physical activity
2. Decreased physical stability
3. Impaired oxygenation processes
4. Chemical disequilibrium
5. Disruption of normal elimination processes
6. Impaired tissue integrity

Each problem area will be discussed separately in terms of the effects of immobility that contribute to the problem, the clinical manifestations, and the underlying pathophysiologic mechanisms. These problem areas are preventable but have the potential to develop if treatment to minimize the duration and degree of impaired mobility is inadequate. It cannot be emphasized enough that prevention of the complications of immobility is primarily the responsibility of the nurse. This is the one area where the outcomes depend totally on independent nursing judgment and action.

Loss of endurance

The problem of loss of endurance for physical activity (or activity intolerance) can be attributed to both diminished functional capacity of the muscles and an increased cardiac work load. It is primarily related to the loss of functional capacity of the muscles that accompanies lack of use (deconditioning). The functional capacity is normally determined by the frequency, duration, and intensity of use. The functional capacity of a muscle that is used infrequently or only for short periods of time for nonstrenuous activity will be greatly diminished. This loss of functional capacity is characterized by loss of muscle mass, tone, and strength, which limits the amount of work that can be performed before the physiologic limit is reached.

The loss of muscle mass and strength caused by decreased use is directly related to the principle that catabolic and anabolic processes balance each other: a reduction in catabolic processes leads to a reduction in anabolic processes and thus to a reduction in both cell size and available cellular energy. This reduction in cell size, which occurs secondary to impaired physical mobility, is referred to as *disuse atrophy*. The loss of muscle mass resulting from disuse atrophy is both measurable and observable. In the study conducted by Dietrick, et al. (1948), measurement of limb circumference and creatinine retention and x-ray examination documented a

4% to 10% loss in mass in the thighs, and a 10% to 12.5% loss of mass in the calves. Such a loss can be seen in the obvious difference in size of two limbs following removal of a cast from one.

Loss of muscle strength in the immobilized legs measured between 13% to 20% in the Deitrick study. Deitrick et al. (1948) also concluded that it took 4 to 6 weeks for recovery of preimmobility muscle mass and strength in healthy subjects.

The antigravity muscles of the lower limbs are those most affected, lending support to the theory that the normal stresses of gravity are important in maintaining function and development and therefore mobility. This is also true for muscle tone, a state of constant, partial contraction of the muscles. Standing upright requires a greater degree of muscle tone than does lying in bed. Muscle tone diminishes during the period of time an individual spends in bed or in a recumbent position. This loss of muscle tone further contributes to the loss of mass and strength because it represents a certain degree of disuse.

The problem of loss of endurance for physical activity or activity intolerance can also be attributed in part to an increased cardiac work load. Cardiac function is most affected when the impaired physical mobility involves assumption of the recumbent position and the inability to change position in relation to gravity. Upon assumption of the recumbent position with the head nearly flat, blood that normally pools in the lower extremities is mobilized and thereby increases venous return to the heart. Because of the permissive nature of the heart's pumping function, cardiac stroke volume will be increased to accommodate the increased venous return, which results in an increased work load for the heart.

Inactive or immobilized individuals have a relative tachycardia when compared to active or athletic individuals of the same age and with the same physical characteristics. This is thought to result from a dominance of vagal or parasympathetic effects in the active individual as compared to a dominance of sympathetic effects in the inactive individual. A progressive increase in the resting pulse rate was documented by both Dietrick et al. (1948) and Taylor et al. (1949). This increase in pulse rate was found to be greater in magnitude during exercise and required twice as long to return to pre-exercise levels in the immobilized subjects when compared to active subjects. Results of these studies also demonstrated that the pulse rate did not return to normal (preimmobility) levels for at least 6 to 8 weeks after resumption of regular activity.

Tachycardia contributes to the increased cardiac work load by increasing the amount of work performed per unit of time. Fatigue of the myocardium is a potential consequence of the increased energy expenditure in the presence of a reduced ability to supply energy to the myocardium since tachycardia reduces the diastolic period, which shorten both ventricular and coronary filling times. Tachycardia further contributes to the increased cardiac work load through this inefficient utilization of energy.

The problem of loss of endurance for physical activity can be attributed to both the diminished functional capacity of the muscles and an increased cardiac work load. Manifestations of this problem include weakness, easy fatigability, and an increased pulse rate, especially during exercise or activity. Loss of endurance will lead to a further reduction in physical activity since an individual will match his level of activity to his capacity or tolerance for such activity. Because of this, loss of endurance or activity intolerance becomes a priority problem since it is a central feature in the vicious cycle of impaired physical mobility. Closely related to this problem are those of impaired oxygenation processes and chemical disequilibrium since decreased levels of available oxygen and disruption of normal metabolic processes will affect the amount of energy available for activity.

Decreased physical stability

Various definitions of the term *stability* can be applied to different aspects of normal physical movement: "the capacity to return to equilibrium after having been displaced" refers to a change in position, and "steadiness" refers to balance and coordination. To be "stable" means to be "not likely to give way" or "not easily thrown off balance." Certain results of impaired physical mobility work together to disrupt stability and to reduce the potential for steady movement with the ability to change position readily and without danger of falling off balance or having the body "give way." The immobilized individual will have difficulty maintaining equilibrium while in motion in an upright, weight-bearing position because of the generalized body weakness, loss of joint mobility, osteoporosis, and postural hypotension that occur as sequelae of the immobility being experienced.

Weakness is the result of muscle atrophy and the slowing of metabolic processes that occur as a result of decreased activity. When a muscle atrophies, it can no longer generate the same amount of force; i.e., the strength of the muscle is decreased. The general slowing of metabolic processes means that less energy is available for activity. Stability is affected because it becomes extremely difficult to perform ac-

tivities such as attaining and maintaining the upright posture, which require the use of energy.

Loss of joint mobility is a result of the pathologic changes that occur in the muscles and connective tissues in response to decreased joint movement. New connective tissue, which has a characteristic loose appearance, is constantly being formed around the joints and muscles. This areolar nature of the connective tissue is maintained by its being stretched through normal movement. If movement becomes limited or absent, stretching of this tissue is concomitantly reduced or absent, and the connective tissue becomes denser, fixed, and less resilient, or fibrosed. This fibrosis hinders movement even more. Stiffness of the joints may be the first sign of loss of joint mobility.

The muscles, because of decreased use and loss of tone, become either stretched from being held in a lengthened position, or contracted from being held in a shortened position. Fibrosis of the connective tissue around them will cause them to remain fixed in these positions. Because of these changes, the muscles and connective tissues become progressively more resistant to movement, and eventually the joint may become fixed in one position. This condition is referred to as a *contracture*.

The contracture deformity called *foot-drop* is the result of the foot's not being supported while the individual remains in a non–weight-bearing position for any extended length of time. The foot becomes fixed in a position of plantar flexion since the tendon of the calf muscles will shorten while the anterior muscles of the leg tend to be stretched and will lengthen when the foot is allowed to remain in an unsupported position. Fig. 14-3 illustrates the normal position of the foot and the position that results when the foot is not sup-

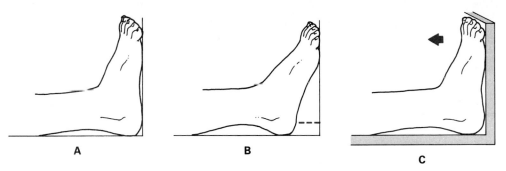

Fig. 14-3. A, Normal position of the foot. **B,** Usual position of foot with individual in supine position. It is this position which promotes the development of a footdrop contracture deformity. **C,** Corrected position. A support should be used that maintains the normal anatomic position of the foot.

ported, which becomes the position of footdrop. Normal use of the foot becomes impossible in the presence of footdrop.

Individuals who remain in bed for an extended period of time are particularly susceptible to the development of contractures. Flexion deformities are those most frequently seen as the use of flexion is one way of relieving discomfort, expecially in the back, hips, and knees, and of maintaining body warmth. Flexion of the hips occurs when the person is in a lying, semireclining, or sitting position in a soft bed. Flexion of the hips is increased when the knees are also flexed. Often the knees are flexed by means of a pillow, rolled blanket, or use of the knee gatch to keep the person from slipping down in the bed. Fig. 14-4, *A*, illustrates the bed-lying position. The head is positioned with the neck flexed. This position obviously discourages functional alignment of the bones and muscles for the weight-bearing position (Fig. 14-4, *B*).

It seems obvious that the presence of contractures will further impair the normal mobility of the individual and that a bedridden individual with a chronic, debilitating disease is especially at risk. Once contractures have begun to form, a greater than normal energy expenditure will be required to move since the added resistance at the joint must be overcome. Contractures may form in less than a week and may require months of steady therapy to reverse. In the meantime the individual is susceptible to all the other consequences of immobility as well. Table 14-1 lists the length of time required for recovery of full range of motion following immobilization for treatment of a shoulder dislocation.

A reduction in bone mass, or osteoporosis, is also a result of impaired physical mobility that works to reduce physical stability. The processes of bone formation and resorption are normally in balance with one another; however, as a result of immobility this balance is disrupted to favor bone resorption, or destruction. The exact mechanism by which activity can stimulate bone growth is not completely understood at this time. It is a fact that the bones of athletic individuals are heavier than those of sedentary individuals. Activity and movement and the resultant mechanical stress on the bones is thought to stimulate bone growth through a *piezoelectric effect*, in which there is an electrical gradient and a flow of current that stimulates bone growth at the site of the

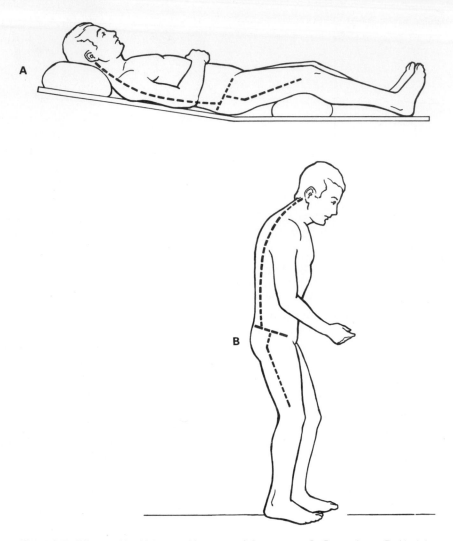

Fig. 14-4. Effects of bed-lying position on upright posture. **A,** Recumbent. **B,** Upright.

stress where a negative potential is thought to exist. Lack of stress on the bones is thought to disrupt the electrical field and thus the stimulus for balanced bone growth and resorption.

There is also disagreement as to the exact effect of immobility on the balance between formation and resorption. Some authorities state that osteoclastic (destruction) activity increases while osteoblastic (formation) activity decreases, and others contend that both osteoblastic and osteoclastic activity increase but that the increase in osteoblastic activity is not as great as that of the osteoclastic cells. In any event, the result is the same: destruction of the matrix and release of the mineral constituents of the bone into the general circulation, with any excesses eventually being excreted in the urine.

Table 14-1. Mobility recovery rate for shoulder dislocation

Period of immobilization	Period of recovery
0 days	18 days
7 days	52 days
14 days	121 days
21 days	300 days

Dietrick et al. (1948) found that the level of calcium in the urine of the immobilized subjects rose on the second to third day after immobility began, indicating that bone resorption begins soon after the level of mobility is reduced. There was no radiologic evidence of osteoporosis in these subjects; however, a loss of approximately 25% to 30% of the total body calcium must occur before x-ray changes are seen. The urinary loss of calcium may also lead to the development of other problems, which are discussed later in this chapter.

Weight bearing with stability in the osteoporotic individual cannot always be achieved since weight bearing can result in the body's "giving way." If osteoporosis is severe enough, pathologic fractures of the bones may occur. The neck of the femur, the ribs, and the lower end of the radius are most susceptible. Vertebral compression can also occur, resulting in back pain, which is a common complaint following long periods of immobility and which can become chronic. Weight bearing under these conditions can become very difficult and, again, an effect of immobility is seen to contribute to further impaired physical mobility. Individuals who are at greatest risk for the development of osteoporosis are postmenopausal females and patients in whom a pathologic process or treatment (e.g. steroid therapy), which also affects the processes

of bone formation and resorption, exist concurrently with the impaired physical mobility.

Postural or *orthostatic hypotension* refers to a fall in blood pressure during a change from the lying or sitting position to the standing position, which manifests itself as a feeling of dizziness or faintness upon rising. Under normal conditions the baroreceptor reflexes elicit an immediate sympathetic response to the reduction in arterial pressure that normally occurs as a person stands up. This sympathetic response causes the splanchnic and peripheral vessels to constrict, thus preventing pooling of blood in the lower extremities and maintaining arterial pressure. Failure of these vessels to constrict, as seen in immobilized individuals, results in rapid pooling of venous blood in the lower extremities, decreased venous return, decreased cardiac output, and reduced arterial pressure, causing dizziness and loss of consciousness (Thomas et al., 1981; Levy and Talbot, 1983). This effect has been consistently observed in all of the studies of immobilized individuals cited thus far.

These studies have also demonstrated that postural hypotension occurs in the presence of intact sympathetic nervous system responses and that it occurs more frequently when the subjects are passively raised to an upright position. These observations have led to the conclusion that postural hypotension in response to immobility is the result of changes in the reactivity of the vessels themselves rather than any change in sympathetic function. This change in the reactivity of the vessels is thought to be a result of disuse similar to the loss of tone in unused muscles; the vessels become acclimated to the lower blood pressure, higher flow, and the increased diameter of the supine position. Another possibility is that the muscle tone and contraction in the lower extremities, which are necessary for actively assuming the upright position, aid in promoting vasoconstriction and inhibiting venous pooling. The muscles prohibit venous pooling by exerting a pumping action on the vessels as they contract. This effect is lost during periods of immobility, when the muscles are not used. Deitrick et al. diminished the fainting response to passive placement in the upright position by wrapping the subjects' legs with elastic bandages, thus simulating the action of the muscles. Deitrick's subjects whose legs were immobilized began to faint in response to passive placement in the upright position after only 1 week of immobilization.

It seems apparent that the loss of physical stability would be detrimental to the maintenance or restoration of normal levels of mobility. Stability promotes and enhances normal mobility. Lack of physical stability further impairs it.

Impaired oxygenation processes

Several of the effects of immobility compound one another to impair oxygenation processes in the immobilized individual. Among these responses to impaired physical mobility are a reduction in blood volume and red cell mass, decreased cardiac output, ineffective breathing pattern and airway clearance, and potential for altered tissue perfusion related to thrombus and embolus formation. Not all these effects have been observed in healthy individuals who are immobilized; however, even in healthy individuals the effects of immobility will alter the oxygenation processes, although not to the same extent as in persons who are ill or debilitated.

A reduction in blood volume and red cell mass alters the oxygen-carrying capacity of the blood, and the decrease in cardiac output that is secondary to venous stasis alters the transport process by which oxygen is delivered to the body tissues. The combination of these two conditions may adversely affect the ability of the body to supply or deliver oxygen to body tissues, which has implications for periods during which the body's oxygen requirements may increase. These effects of immobility are seen in healthy individuals but are potentially more dangerous in ill or debilitated individuals.

Ventilatory ability is also affected by immobility (Tyler, 1984). An ineffective breathing pattern characterized by reduced chest and lung expansion is the result of the pressure created in the supine position by the abdominal organs and the bed against the diaphragm and thoracic cage. This can be compounded in the ill individual by the pattern of breathing caused by anesthesia and surgery, by poor posture in bed, and by the use of constrictive bandages, binders, or clothing.

The reduction in chest and lung expansion and the increased work of breathing are interrelated. Ventilatory activity is affected by the stimulus for respiration, the resistance against which the respiratory muscles have to work, and the strength of the muscles themselves. With a reduction in activity there is also a reduction in the body's energy needs, which is reflected in a lowered BMR, indicating slowing of the metabolic processes. As a result of the slowing of the metabolic processes, less carbon dioxide is produced, removing the stimulus for respiration and causing the respiratory rate to drop. In addition, tidal volume drops as a result of diminished chest expansion, which is caused by weakness of the muscles of respiration and by the pressure of the abdominal organs and the bed against the chest cavity. The combination of the weakness and the added resistance result in an increase in the work of breathing, or the effort a person must put forth to breathe.

The effects described so far occur in anyone experiencing immobility. Ineffective airway clearance related to stasis of respiratory tract secretions has not been a problem in healthy subjects participating in immobility studies. Individuals who are prone to develop ineffective airway clearance during a period of immobility are those in whom ventilatory function is already impaired, the cough reflex is suppressed, and secretions are thicker than normal, or who are unable to move at all. Under normal conditions, mucus produced in the lungs is swept outward by the action of the cilia. When an individual is in the upright position, the bronchioles are in a vertical plane, and the mucus coats them in a fairly uniform manner. In the supine position, the bronchioles are predominantly in a horizontal plane, and the mucus tends to pool on the lower side as a result of the pull of gravity. The mucosa on the upper sides of the bronchioles tends to dry out, and the cilia are damaged by this drying. The cilia on the lower side are unable to move all the mucus that has become pooled. Thus several factors, namely, position, lack of ciliary action, and reduced respiratory excursion, contribute to stasis of the respiratory secretions. The diameter of the lumen of the bronchioles is reduced in the supine position, and this effect is intensified by the pooling of secretions within the bronchioles. Fig. 14-5 illustrates the effect of the pooled secretions on the lumen diameter of the bronchiole.

The conditions just described predispose an individual to the development of hypostatic pneumonia or a mucus plug. Lack of deep breathing can also result in atelectasis (see Chapter 16) caused by "inspiratory failure." *Pneumonia* is an inflammatory process characterized by consolidation due to exudate filling the alveolar spaces. This inflammation can be the result of an infectious process or the aspiration of food, vomitus, or chemical agents. The immobilized patient is at risk for developing pneumonia for two reasons. First, accumulated secretions can act as a medium for the growth of microorganisms and thereby lead to infection. Pneumonia can be caused by a variety of organisms, including the pneumococci, streptococci, staphylococci, various viruses, bacilli, and fungi. Secondly, the supine position predisposes an individual to aspiration.

The signs and symptoms of pneumonia include dyspnea, fever, cough, pallor, malaise, and cyanosis if hypoxemia due to the shunting of pulmonary blood around nonfunctional alveoli is severe. In general they are the signs and symptoms of an acute inflammatory process in which the lung tissue is directly affected. Chest pain is often present and may indicate pleurisy. Consolidation will appear as radiopaque or as a hazy area on the chest x-ray in the dependent areas of the lung fields. Breath sounds over the affected lung tissue will be absent or bronchial in nature (Sanchez, 1986). The color and consistency of the expectorated mucus will depend on the causative organism. Since the secretions pool in the dependent areas of the lung, it is in these areas that the infectious process will occur—the lateral segment of the middle lobe, the apical segment of the lower lobe, and the axillary portions of the anterior and posterior segments.

As stated earlier, the persons most at risk are those who are totally unable to move or in whom ventilatory function is already impaired, mucus secretion is excessive, or the cough reflex is suppressed. Any combination of these factors would also predispose an individual to the devel-

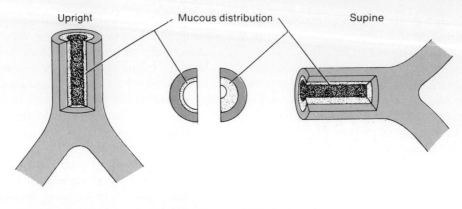

Upright   Mucous distribution   Supine

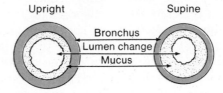

Effects on lumen diameter

Upright   Supine

Bronchus
Lumen change
Mucus

Fig. 14-5. Effect of recumbent position and gravity on distribution of respiratory tract secretions and diameter of bronchiolar lumen.

opment of respiratory problems. An example is the heavily sedated or anesthetized patient in whom the cough reflex is suppressed, respirations are depressed or rapid and shallow, the mucus is thick and tenacious, and the membranes of the upper respiratory tract are dry. These patients are prone to develop stasis of the respiratory tract secretions and hypostatic pneumonia. Poor posture in bed and the use of constrictive bandages or binders and clothing may also impair ventilatory function and cause these patients to be potentially more susceptible to the development of respiratory difficulties. Administration of nonhumidified oxygen will cause drying of the mucous membranes.

Venous thrombosis is another condition that may develop as a result of impaired physical mobility and that contributes to the problem of impaired oxygenation processes by altering tissue perfusion (Moser and Fedullo, 1983). Basically the term *thrombosis* refers to a blood clot that has formed inside a blood vessel. The terms *thrombophlebitis* and *phlebothrombosis* are attempts to classify different types of venous thrombi by the initiating factor. Inflammation of the vein serves as the initiating factor in thrombophlebitis, while the thrombus itself serves as the initiating factor in phlebothrombosis, and an inflammatory response ensues. Clinically the effects are the same no matter what the sequence of events.

Because of the relatively slow flow of venous blood, veins are the most common sites of thrombosis. Thrombi most commonly develop in the deep veins of the legs and can spread the entire length of a vein. A thrombus formed in slow moving blood is comprised of layers of platelet aggregates (pale thrombus) alternating with a fibrin network containing leukocytes and red cells (red thrombus). This arrangement and the sequence of formation of a venous thrombus are illustrated in Fig. 14-6.

Normally blood does not clot within the blood vessels; some abnormal condition or conditions must be present (see Chapter 3). Conditions that enhance the formation of intravascular thrombi include endothelial damage or changes in the vessel, venous stasis, and changes in the clotting tendency of the blood. Of these conditions, only venous stasis is directly influenced by immobility. Immobility contributes to venous stasis through loss of the pumping action of the muscles and by the very nature of the venous structure itself. Blood will pool in the direction of gravity; however, with activity and movement and the constant changing of body position, this

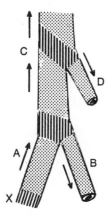

Fig. 14-6. Mode of extension of venous thrombosis. Thrombus occludes a small vein, *A,* at point *X,* and red thrombus (dotted areas) rapidly extends in stagnant column of blood up to entrance of next tributary; *B,* where platelet deposition forms a cap of pale thrombus (lined areas); when this occludes junction of *A* and *B,* red thrombus extends rapidly up to entrance of next tributary, *C,* and so on. Red thrombus also forms in each tributary as its entrance to major channel is occluded (arrows show direction of thrombosis).

(From Muir's textbook of pathology, revised by JR Anderson, London, 1976, Edward Arnold [Publishers] Ltd.)

pooling is reduced to a minimum. During inactivity it is enhanced in the dependent areas of the body. With a lack of muscular activity the pumping action that the muscles exert on the veins and that assists venous return is greatly diminished. The many bifurcations and valve pockets within the veins also contribute to localized areas of stasis during periods of immobility. This has been found to be especially pronounced in older people.

Venous stasis has not been found to be the sole cause of thrombus formation, although stasis in combination with other factors may accelerate thrombus formation. It is believed that stasis may create a local environment in which thrombin is concentrated and sequestered from inactivation by the liver. Hypercoagulability associated with an increase in the number and the adhesiveness of the platelets and a rise in the prothrombin time has been observed following trauma (accidental and surgical), childbirth, and myocardial infarction. These changes are maximal on the tenth day following the injury, which coincides with the time most thromboembolic episodes occur. There is also some evidence that fibrinolysis is inadequate. This effect may be the result of impaired plasminogen activation.

Estimating the amount of endothelial damage in the veins that occurs as a result of immobility is extremely difficult if not impossible. The intimal endothelium of a thrombosed vessel is usually found to be normal. Sites of invasive treatment measures, such as locations where an intravascular cannula have been used, may serve as focal points for a thrombotic process to begin. Whether endothelial damage occurs as a result of prolonged pressure on a vessel is a point of speculation. Kinking of the vessel because of the position of the extremity may do more to create a disturbance of blood flow than to actually damage the intimal lining of the vessel. The turbulent flow that results may predispose to platelet deposition and hence thrombus formation.

The origin of thrombi in the immobilized, ill individual is probably multifactorial, with all the above-mentioned conditions involved. Consider the postsurgical patient who is placed on his side with one leg on top of the other in the recovery room while still under the influence of an anesthetic agent. The fully alert, conscious patient would not tolerate the discomfort and would soon change position. The postsurgical patient cannot readily change position and may even be unaware of any discomfort from the position. Pressure points on the veins may cause venous stasis, and this situation in the presence of increased viscosity caused by a postsurgical reduction in volume and hypercoagulability of the blood may accelerate thrombus formation in this patient.

Signs and symptoms of venous thrombosis depend on whether the pathologic changes occur in the superficial or deep veins. The clinical manifestations of a thrombus of a superficial vein include visible reddening of the affected vein and tenderness and hardness on palpation. A slight elevation in temperature and pulse rate occurs in response to the inflammatory process. Deep vein thrombosis following immobilization after surgery or during illness or bed rest usually occurs in the soleal veins of the calf. Local pain on compression of the calf may be the only symptom. If a major vein is involved and the thrombus is extensive, swelling of the leg because of the blocked venous return may occur. If the thrombus is not extensive, an increase in the circumference of the calf that is measurable but not necessarily visible may occur with redness, warmth, and tenderness in the affected area. The calf pain will be aggravated by movement, and *Homan's sign* (calf and popliteal pain upon dorsiflexion of the foot) is often present. There will also be the systemic manifestations of an inflammatory process: fever, leukocytosis, increased erythrocyte sedimentation rate, and an increased pulse rate.

Thrombus formation is a serious complication of immobility not just because of the disruption of venous circulation but also because of the potential danger of embolism. An embolism is the result of the thrombus or a portion of it detaching from the vein wall into the general circulation and becoming lodged in some other part of the circulation. The site of embolism secondary to thrombosis of the systemic veins is usually the pulmonary arteries and their branches, a condition referred to as *pulmonary embolism*, which can result in sudden death. Thrombosis of the veins of the lower extremities is the most common cause of pulmonary embolism.

The detachment of a thrombus from the wall of a vein may be the result of any number of activities that cause a sudden increase in venous return, for example, increased activity after a period of immobility, straining during a bowel movement, and isometric exercises. The straining associated with defecation, performance of isometric exercises, and even positioning oneself in bed cause what is called *Valsalva's maneuver*, an attempt at forced expiration with the glottis closed. With closure of the glottis, intrathoracic pressure rises, causing a reduction in venous return and ventricular filling. During straining the cardiac output and arterial pressure fall, coronary filling is decreased, and the diameter of the femoral vein increases. With release of the glottis and the consequent drop in intrathoracic pressure, venous return will suddenly and maximally increase and arterial pressure will rise. This drastic change in the velocity of venous blood flow and the increased diameter of the femoral vein may facilitate a clot's becoming detached and passing into the circulation.

The clinical manifestations of pulmonary embolism depend on the size of the embolus and the portion of the pulmonary circulation that it occludes. A large embolus from the femoral or iliac trunk that occludes the pulmonary artery will cause sudden death preceded by a period of intense, severe dyspnea with cyanosis and gross neck vein distension. The effect is that of acute right-sided failure of the heart. Cardiac output and arterial pressure drop. Shock and loss of consciousness rapidly ensue as perfusion of the vital organs decreases. Death occurs within minutes to hours following the embolism (Fig. 14-7).

Smaller emboli can pass through the right side of the heart and pulmonary artery to become lodged in the branches of the pulmonary artery, which become progressively smaller. The patient may experience quite severe dyspnea of sudden onset. Chest pain may also occur similar to that of a myocardial infarction. Other signs and symptoms will be the same as in right-sided heart failure because pulmonary vascular pressure and pulmonary resistance increase. If the reduction in cardiac output is severe, signs of cerebral hypoxia such as restlessness, confusion, or a change in the level of consciousness may also appear.

Infarction of pulmonary tissue may follow embolism, but because the bronchial arteries also supply the lungs, this rarely occurs. The clinical manifestations of infarction include tachycardia, tachypnea, chest pain, cough, hemoptysis, dyspnea, a

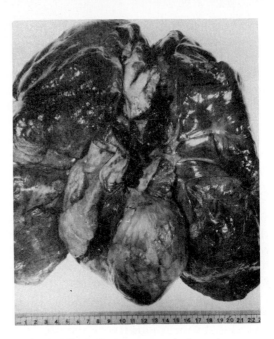

Fig. 14-7. Massive pulmonary embolism after postoperative phlebothrombosis in leg veins. Death occurred suddenly on sixth postoperative day.
(From Anderson WAD and Kissane JM: Pathology, ed. 7, St. Louis, 1977, The C.V. Mosby Co.)

low-grade fever, and leukocytosis. Serum levels of the enzyme lactic dehydrogenase will be elevated, reflecting its loss from damaged tissue.

The treatment of pulmonary embolism is supportive since there is no cure for an embolism once it has occurred. Oxygen is administered to relieve hypoxemia and promote oxygenation of the tissues. Sedation may be used to relieve anxiety and promote rest, which in combination with absolute bed rest serves to reduce the work load of the heart and lungs. Vasopressor agents are used to restore normal arterial blood pressure if hypotension occurs, since administration of large quantities of fluid is contraindicated because of the already existing state of heart failure. Anticoagulant therapy is initiated to prevent other thromboembolic episodes and extension of the already existing clot. Various surgical procedures can also be used for persons in whom anticoagulant therapy is contraindicated or who experience repeated episodes of embolization. Measures to prevent further thrombus formation in the lower extremities should be instituted to lessen the chances of recurrence.

Chemical disequilibrium

The effects of impaired physical mobility that disrupt normal chemical equilibrium of the body include a negative calcium balance, a negative nitrogen balance, and an alteration in compartmental fluid distribution in dependent areas. Calcium loss is promoted by the osteoporotic process induced by immobility. Calcium is released into the extracellular fluid as the bone is resorbed, and urinary excretion of calcium increases in order to maintain normal serum calcium concentrations during immobility. Hypercalcemia may result if immobility occurs concurrently with rapid bone turnover, that is, during growth periods or in the presence of Paget's disease. In these conditions the amount of calcium released because of the increased bone resorption of immobility exceeds the renal capacity for excretion. The renal excretion of calcium during periods of immobility has been found to be greater in men than in women. There is also impaired dietary absorption of calcium during immobility, causing increased fecal excretion. The combination of increased urinary and fecal excretion results in a negative calcium balance when the total amount excreted exceeds that taken in. Increasing the amount of calcium in the diet will have no effect on calcium balance since dietary absorption is impaired (Lerman et al., 1977).

Findings of the study by Deitrick, et al. (1948) demonstrated that urinary excretion of calcium began within the first week of immobility and reached a peak during the fourth to sixth week of immobility. The subjects in the study lost between 1% and 2% of their body calcium during 6 weeks of immobility. It has been estimated that as much as 5% of the total body calcium may be lost in a young man who is immobilized for 3 months with a fractured femur. Urinary excretion of calcium is monitored not only because it is a sign of the degree of osteoporosis that occurs but also because this increased amount of calcium in the urine may negatively affect normal elimination processes.

The nitrogen balance provides a gross measure of protein utilization by the body. A *negative nitrogen balance* is said to exist when excretion of nitrogen from the breakdown of protein exceeds intake. During periods of immobility urinary excretion of nitrogen increases to the extent that negative nitrogen balance results. Urinary excretion of nitrogen in healthy immobilized persons occurs on approximately the fifth or sixth day after immobilization. The loss of nitrogen is thought to reflect the depletion of muscle tissue as atrophy occurs. This is supported by the fact that the sulfur-nitrogen ratio of the urine remains unchanged during immobility, indicating that tissue rich in sulfur (e.g., skeletal muscle) is being broken down.

In certain disease states and as a result of trauma (surgical or accidental) and stress, protein is rapidly catabolized, and the potential for development of a negative nitrogen balance is great. Table 14-2 lists various pathologic conditions in which the protein requirements of the body are altered. The combination of immobility and a pathologic condition in which protein requirements are increased

Table 14-2. Pathologic conditions altering protein requirements*

Condition	Increased	Decreased
Sepsis	x	
Fever	x	
Trauma—injury	x	
Fractures	x	
Burns	x	
Gastrointestinal disorders (ileostomy, colostomy, diarrhea and other malabsorption states, ulcerative colitis)	x	
Respiratory infections	x	
Parasitic infections	x	
Bacterial infections	x	
Viral infections	x	
Hepatic coma		x
Liver disease	x	
Massive hepatic necrosis		x
Proteinuria	x	
Renal disease (glomerulonephrosis)	x	
Renal failure, acute and chronic		x
Cancer	x	
Marasmus (protein-calorie malnutrition)	x	
Kwashiorkor (protein malnutrition)	x	
Pain	x	
Anxiety or other psychologic stress	x	
Profuse sweating	x	

*From Nutrition in Clinical Care by R. Howard and N. Herbold. Copyright 1978 McGraw-Hill Book Co. Used with permission of McGraw-Hill Book Co.

will further enhance the development of a negative nitrogen balance.

Another factor that may contribute to development of a negative nitrogen balance is the individual's nutritional status. The immobilized individual may experience anorexia as a result of disruption of normal GI tract function, a decrease in the BMR, and a probable reduction in social stimuli for eating. Persons experiencing a pathologic process may be anorexic already as a result of the effects of the disease and its treatment. For example, chemotherapy and radiation therapy compound the anorexia already present in cancer patients. An ill individual may be on a restricted therapeutic diet as well. Immobilized individuals who are experiencing a pathologic process are especially at risk for the development of impaired nutritional status and a decreased nutritional status will in turn contribute to the development of a negative nitrogen balance. The decrease in nutritional status and negative nitrogen balance will compound the loss of muscle mass and strength that occurs in immobility, thus a vicious cycle ensues. Fig. 14-8 depicts the central role of nutritional status in this cycle.

The consequence of a state of negative nitrogen balance is a lack of adequate nitrogen for protein synthesis. With severe protein depletion the plasma protein concentration will decrease, although originally these proteins are spared.

Fluid will shift from the intravascular to the interstitial compartments in the dependent areas of the body as a result of the increased hydrostatic pressure secondary to venous stasis. Blood will pool in the dependent areas of the body as a result of the cumulative effect of gravity, the reservoir nature of the veins, and the loss of pumping action of the muscles. As the volume of the pooled blood increases, the hydrostatic pressure of the blood at the venous end of the capillary bed will increase proportionately. An increase in the blood hydrostatic pressure will increase the hydrostatic pressure gradient, and when this gradient becomes higher than the osmotic pressure gradient, the Starling forces will be disrupted, favoring movement of fluid out of the intravascular compartment and pre-

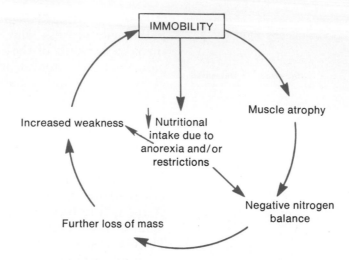

Fig. 14-8. Factors contributing to negative nitrogen balance of immobility and its contributory role, leading to further impairment of mobility.

venting its return. If plasma protein concentration has decreased, plasma osmotic pressure will be less than normal and the Starling forces will be more easily disrupted. Dependent edema will then occur in any body part on a level below that of the heart for any period of time. Edematous tissue may be quite uncomfortable and is more easily injured than normal tissue. Edema of the lower extremities can make standing and walking extremely difficult, inhibiting mobility even more.

Altered patterns of elimination

The effects of impaired physical mobility can disrupt normal elimination patterns of both the bladder and the bowel. Constipation is often seen in the person who is immobilized, but it is not a direct consequence of immobility per se. It is the result of weakened abdominal and perineal muscles and decreased gastric motility, which are the results of immobility. Decreased gastric motility also causes bloating and belching and may contribute to the feeling of anorexia that many im-

mobilized individuals experience. Other factors probably also play a part in constipation. A change in diet, emotional stress, or some other change in activities of daily living can cause constipation in a well individual. The person experiencing illness and immobility is subject to any or all of these factors in addition to the effects of immobility. A person on bed rest in a hospital setting may experience difficulty using a bedpan since the anatomic position one must assume when using a bedpan does not allow maximal use of the muscles in the act of defecation. This person may be embarrassed by the lack of privacy and may suppress the urge to defecate with the eventual result of constipation.

The supine position itself affects stimulation of the urge to defecate. Normally, as stool descends into the lower rectum, stimulation of the anorectal ring results in a desire to defecate. In the upright position this descent of fecal material is sudden, resulting in strong stimulation, whereas in the supine position, rectal filling is slow and stimulation is weak.

Whether the urge to defecate is suppressed, weak, or nonexistent, the results are the same. The fecal material will continue to increase in size, and water will be resorbed, causing it to become hard. Defecation cannot occur at this point without a great deal of difficulty and discomfort. Straining to try to pass a larger than normal, hardened mass of stool will cause a Valsalva maneuver, which is contraindicated in the immobilized individual for reasons already discussed.

Normal patterns of urinary elimination can be disrupted by renal calculi, retention of urine, and urinary tract infection. Like constipation these are not direct consequences of immobility but are the results of the high level of urinary calcium and the recumbent position. The formation of renal calculi, or "recumbency stones," depends on several factors:

1. Urinary concentrations of calcium, citric acid, and phosphate
2. Ratio between the concentrations of calcium and citric acid in the urine
3. pH of the urine
4. Stasis of the urine
5. Presence of infection

Calcium is normally excreted in the urine and is kept in solution by the action of citric acid and the acidic condition of the urine. During periods of immobility, as a result of reduced metabolic activity, fewer acid products of metabolism are formed to be excreted, and the pH of the urine rises. Citric acid concentration remains the same as in the pre-immobility period. The alkalinity of the urine and the altered ratio between citric acid and calcium concentrations favoring the calcium level enhances precipitation of calcium salts within the urine.

The effect of gravity in the upright position favors complete emptying of the bladder as well as the kidneys. The recumbent position causes stasis of the urine in the renal pelvis as well as incomplete emptying of the bladder. In the supine position the effect of gravity causes urine to pool in the dependent calyces of the kidney. This is illustrated in Fig. 14-9. Stasis also favors precipitation of calcium salts out of solution in the urine.

Sometimes individuals are unable to void in a sitting or lying position, and retention of urine occurs. Retention can cause distention of the bladder to such a degree that small tears develop in the mucosa, providing a site for infection. Extreme fullness of the bladder can lead to dribbling of small amounts of urine; the bladder actually overflows. This is called

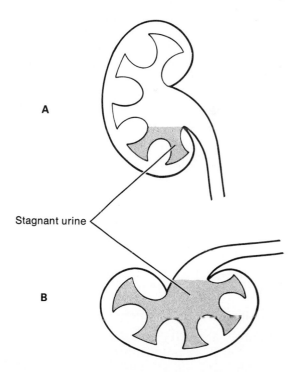

Fig. 14-9. Effect of position and gravity on distribution of urine in calyces of kidneys. **A,** Upright position. **B,** Recumbent (supine) position promotes stasis of urine in dependent calyces and inhibits complete emptying of urine.

retention with overflow. The presence of stagnant urine in the kidneys and bladder also increases the potential for infection to develop. The presence of a urinary tract infection will even further enhance the conditions for renal stone formation; the urine becomes more alkaline, and the cellular debris from the inflammatory process provides nuclei for stone formation.

A reduction in the volume of the urine will also contribute to stone formation. When the individual first lies down, urinary volume will increase because of the increased blood flow to the kidneys. Urinary volume will decrease if fluid intake is reduced for any reason. This is an important point to remember for ill and bedridden persons. Often adequate amounts of fluid are not provided, and the person is unable to get his own. Sometimes there are stringent medical restrictions on the amount of fluid a person is allowed. In this case the quality of the fluid takes on special importance. Fluids and foods that will increase the acidity of the urine are recommended (acid-ash diet).

The signs and symptoms of renal calculi include hematuria, colicky flank pain, backache, and nausea and vomiting. Bloatedness, constipation, urinary retention or infection, and formation of renal calculi are very uncomfortable conditions that may lead to further reduction in the level of mobility. The effects of urinary tract obstruction are discussed more completely in Chapter 20.

Impaired tissue integrity

Impaired integrity of the skin and underlying tissue is not a problem in healthy, immobilized individuals but is a serious and potentially devastating problem in the ill or debilitated individual. The potential for impaired tissue integrity exists in all patients experiencing impaired physical mobility. It is compounded by the presence of a negative, nitrogen balance since tissue synthesis and repair will be retarded.

Various terms are used to describe this problem: *pressure sore, pressure ulcer, decubitus ulcer*, or *bedsore*. These terms all refer to a wound that is the result of ischemic injury to the skin and subcutaneous tissues because of prolonged pressure, shear, and/or friction (Fig. 14-10).

The consequences of a pressure sore to the individual include pain, increased susceptibility to infection, loss of body fluid, discouragement, depression, and further impairment of physical mobility. Any break in the skin will make an individual more susceptible to infection since the skin constitutes the body's first line of defense. A pressure sore, especially a large one, may leak substantial quantities of body fluids that contain protein and other constituents. A pressure sore may be extremely uncomfortable and may make turning and moving very difficult, thus contributing to further immobility. Development of a pressure sore may prolong hospitalization, delay rehabilitation, and impose economic hardship as well (Parish, Witkowski, and Crissey, 1983).

The consequences to the health care system include higher morbidity and mortality rates and increased health care costs related to an increased need for institutionalization and nursing care. In a review of the literature on pressure ulcers, Maklebust (1987) reports the following statistics: approximately 60,000 persons die from complications related to pressure sores each year; the cost estimates to heal each pressure ulcer range between $5000 and $40,000; and the presence of a pressure ulcer can increase nursing care costs by as much as 50%. It is obvious, then, that prevention of pressure ulcer develop-

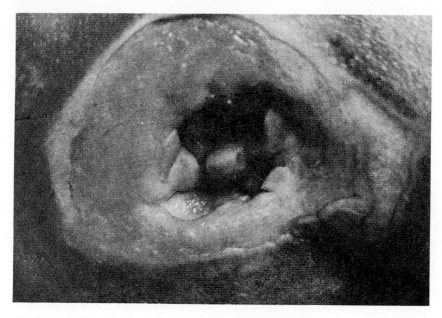

Fig. 14-10. Decubitus ulcer formation in debilitated patient.
(From Beyers, M., and Dudas, S.: The clinical practice of medical surgical nursing, Boston, 1977, Little Brown & Co.)

ment could result in great cost savings to the health care system and could prevent much suffering in already ill and debilitated patients.

Any patient experiencing impaired physical mobility is at risk for the development of pressure sore, although the potential is greater in certain groups of patients. A patient with impaired sensory input or motor function is at greater risk than a patient with intact sensory input and motor function (Sklar, 1985). It is estimated that the incidence of pressure sores is as high as 85% among spinal cord–injured patients and the cause of up to 8% of the deaths in this population (Reuler and Cooney, 1981).

Other factors that place a patient at greater risk for the formation and nonhealing of a pressure sore are malnutrition (protein deficiency, negative nitrogen balance, lack of adequate amounts of vitamin C), anemia, dehydration, hyperglycemia, maceration (moistness and softening of the skin), heat, circulatory impairment, and corticosteroid therapy (catabolism is increased). Edematous tissue is more prone to pressure damage since the blood supply is already impaired and waste products remain as a result of the existing disruption of the Starling forces in the capillary bed. Excessive moisture on the skin can be the result of wound drainage, perspiration, condensation from humidified oxygen delivery systems, and fecal and urinary incontinence. Reuler and Cooney (1981) state that the presence of moisture increases the risk of pressure sore formation fivefold. Heat increases tissue metabolism and the need for oxygen, making already hypoxic tissue even more susceptible to ischemic injury. Age must also be considered in the pathogenesis of a pressure sore; the incidence increases in the elderly.

Obesity can either decrease or increase susceptibility to pressure sore development. Adipose tissue, in small quantities, can serve a protective function by cushioning the bony prominences against the effects of pressure. This function is thought to be most applicable to those persons over 75 years of age. On the other hand, adipose tissue is not as well vascularized or as resilient as other types of body tissue so it is more vulnerable when subjected to sustained pressure and shearing forces (Natow, 1983).

As stated previously, pressure is the essential element in the formation of a pressure sore. Obviously, the skin and subcutaneous tissue can tolerate some pressure or sitting and lying would be impossible. Externally applied pressure that exceeds the pressure of the capillary bed obstructs blood flow and results in tissue hypoxia. Ischemic injury occurs if the hypoxic condition is allowed to persist beyond a critical time threshold. If a tissue pressure greater than 32 mm Hg remains unrelieved beyond this point, the vessels will collapse and thrombose (Maklebust, 1987). If the pressure is relieved prior to reaching this threshold, circulation is restored through the physiologic mechanism of reactive hyperemia. The local histologic changes, documented through both light and electron microscopy, seen in response to pressure are as follows (Constantian, 1980;

1. Gross changes: pallor (early), edema and reactive hyperemia (late)
2. Moderate pressure (100 mm Hg for 2 hours): patchy congestion of the skin vessels, subcutaneous edema, and moderate inflammatory infiltrate
3. Sustained pressure (100 mm Hg for 6 hours): intense inflammatory infiltrate, degenerating muscle fibers, loss of cross-striations, and swelling of myofibrils

Other factors that are important to note in the pathogenesis of a pressure sore are the varying degrees of pressure tolerance that different body tissues exhibit and the gradient and distribution of the pressure. Fat and muscle are more susceptible to ischemic injury than the skin (Cherry and Ryan, 1983). Rather than being distributed and dissipated over large areas of the body surface, pressure is concentrated over bony prominences, which are close to the body surface and have less subcutaneous fat and muscle padding. These are the sites at which pressure ulcers are most likely to develop. Fig. 14-11 illustrates the location of these sites in various body positions. Localized pressure areas can also be created by external devices, such as casts, traction apparatus, catheters, tubing, or loose, foreign objects in the bed that exert a constant pressure.

Subcutaneous tissue damage may be quite extensive; the greatest damage occurs at the bony interface because of the way in which pressure is dissipated across the subcutaneous soft tissues to the bone. Pressure is transmitted between the surface and the bone in a cone-shaped pattern with its base at the bone surface. A wider area of subcutaneous damage may therefore exist than that which is apparent on the skin's surface.

Another type of mechanical stress that can contribute to the formation of a pressure sore is *shearing force*. This occurs when adjacent, parallel surfaces of tissues move in such a way that the end result is displacement of these tissues relative to one another. When a patient is moved or repositioned in bed without being lifted or when the patient is allowed to slide down in the bed, the skin surface may adhere to the bed while the bone slides in the direction of movement. The deeper tissue will slide with the bone and the subcutaneous tissue attached to the dermis remains in

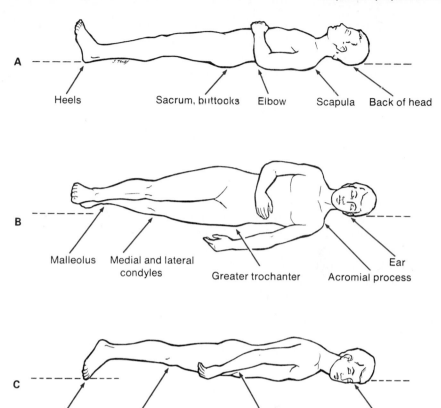

Fig. 14-11. Pressure points in various body positions. **A,** Supine. **B,** Side. **C,** Prone. These are the sites at which pressure sores are most likely to form.

position with the skin. The result is stretching of the tissues and kinking of and damage to the blood vessels. Deep massage over bony prominences can have the same effect. Subcutaneous fat is particularly vulnerable to damage because of its lack of tensile strength (Reuler and Cooney, 1981). Shearing force is thought to be particularly relevant to the development of sacral pressure sores (Maklebust, 1987).

Friction results when two surfaces come into contact with one another while moving in opposite directions. The effect of the friction generated when skin is dragged across sheets can be abrasion or removal of the outermost layer of skin. This effect

is exaggerated by moisture. Removal of the outermost layer of skin enhances the potential for infection and makes the skin more susceptible to pressure damage.

The clinical manifestations of the effects of pressure present on a continuum. Intervention will depend on the stage of pressure-induced damage that is present. The initial change is that of *blanchable erythema*. This appears as a red spot that turns white when compressed and immediately recolors when the compression is relieved. This area may appear slightly elevated and warm to the touch. If sensation to the area is intact, the patient may complain of pain or tenderness. With removal and avoidance of repeated pressure, the skin will return to normal within 24 hours as permanent damage has not occurred. If pressure is unrelieved, the second stage in the formation of a pressure sore will present as *nonblanchable erythema*. The area will be more sharply defined, the color will be more intense (a dark red to cyanotic), and the color will not fade when the area is compressed. The affected area may feel cool and soft to the touch. If sensation is intact, there will be pain and tenderness. With prompt relief of pressure, the damage is reversible, but it may take 1 to 3 weeks for the tissue to return to normal. Treatment of both blanchable and nonblanchable erythema includes avoidance of pressure on the affected area and keeping the area cool and dry until the tissue returns to normal.

If pressure is unrelieved, damage will progress to the third stage, *decubitus* or *pressure dermatitis*. This stage is characterized by disruption of the epidermis. Vesicles, bullae, scaling, and crusting (serous and hemorrhagic) appear. If sensation is intact, there will be pain and tenderness. Pressure must be relieved immediately and unruptured vesicles and bullae should remain intact to prevent contamination. Cool compresses can be used, but to avoid maceration, the site should not be covered with material that holds moisture (e.g., plastic). Heat, which increases the metabolic demands of the tissues, must be avoided. Therefore the use of warm compresses, heat lamps or heating pads is contraindicated (Tepperman and Devlin, 1983). Topical agents that reduce the effects of inflammation can be applied. Healing is possible but will require 2 to 4 weeks. Treatment must be prompt and aggressive, if progression to the next stage is to be prevented.

The fourth stage is the development of a true *pressure ulcer*. The early ulcer appears as a superficial erosion of the epidermis with indistinct borders, an irregular shape, and a glistening erythematous base that is surrounded by an area of decubitus dermatitis or nonblanchable erythema. This is categorized as a Grade I pressure sore (Shea, 1975). If pressure persists, a chronic or true pressure ulcer will develop either Grade II, III, or IV) (Shea, 1975). The base of the chronic ulcer appears flat and dusky red in color. The tissue does not bleed easily, and various tissues (muscle, tendon, bone, etc.) may be exposed depending on the depth of the ulcer. Because of the pressure gradient phenomenon, a relatively small surface opening may expose a much larger necrotic cavity beneath the skin with wide undermining and extensive fat necrosis. The skin surrounding the chronic ulcer is warm, indurated, erythematous, and blanches very little with pressure (Parish et al., 1983).

A pressure sore can form rapidly, and once formed it will continue to deteriorate unless treated aggressively. Pressure must be relieved and avoided; this can be accomplished through frequent repositioning or through the use of a variety of devices that can be used to support specific pressure areas (e.g., gel flotation pads, sheepskin, foam boots), aid in turning or moving a patient (e.g., Stryker frame, CircOLectric bed), or support the entire body surface to change, minimize, or equalize pressure distribution across the body surface (e.g., water bed, air-fluidized bed, foam egg crate mattress) (Maklebust et al., 1986; 1988).

Necrotic tissue must be debrided because it provides a potential site for infection. Infection causes further tissue destruction and retards healing. The organisms that are most frequently involved in infection of a pressure ulcer include the normal microbes found on the skin. Organisms from the gastrointestinal tract most often infect ulcers located below the waist (Gurevich, 1983). Infection and sepsis are potentially life-threatening complications of a pressure ulcer (Reuler and Cooney, 1981).

The ulcerated area must be kept clean, and agents that stimulate granulation tissue formation can be applied. Because of the nature of the injury, healing occurs through *second intention, connective tissue repair*. The site is filled with highly vascular granulation tissue over a matrix of fi-

brin. Collagen fibrils are eventually deposited that serve as the basis for scar formation. Fowler (1987) has provided a review of local wound care that consists of cleansing, possible debriding, and using the appropriate material to dress the wound. In severe ulcers, surgical closure of the wound may be necessary.

Nutrition is especially critical since second intention healing requires more tissue synthesis than primary intention healing. Natow (1983) recommends a diet that is high in protein and carbohydrates with a moderate amount of fat. Vitamin C and

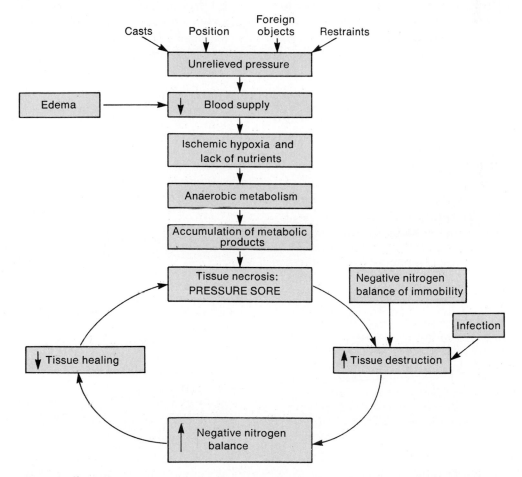

Fig. 14-12. Pathogenesis of pressure sore and resulting cycle once pressure sore has developed.

zinc suppplements are suggested for the diet of patients who have a pressure sore or who are at risk for developing one. In contrast to the normal repair of healthy tissue, in which an 80% growth rate is seen by the third day, a growth rate of less than 70% at 14 days has been observed in biopsied, pressure ulcer tissue (Sieggreen, 1987). Fig. 14-12 illustrates the sequence of events in the formation and perpetuation of a pressure sore.

The following case study illustrates the effects of impaired physical mobility on the integument. In this patient, both the medical condition and mental depression were interactive in causing the impairment of physical mobility that led to impaired tissue integrity.

CASE STUDY: IMPAIRED TISSUE INTEGRITY

History

LG, a 54-year-old woman, was admitted to the hospital because of a 10 day episode of depression and withdrawal. Five years prior to this admission, she was in a car accident that resulted in a spinal cord injury with lower extremity paralysis. Since the accident, LG has experienced episodic periods of depression. There is no other significant past medical history.

LG's family reports that for the past 10 days she has remained in bed or in her wheelchair for long periods of time. Although she has been instructed in a turning regime while in bed and in lifting exercises while in the wheelchair, during her periods of depression she is unable to adhere to the recommended regime. The family also reports that she has not consistently followed her bowel and bladder program.

_____
Contributed by Xavier Smith.

Objective data

On admission, LG's primary nurse notes a 2 × 3 cm, open area over the coccyx. The pressure sore is grade one (partial thickness ulceration limited to the epidermal and dermal layers) with no drainage or foul odors. LG appears well nourished. The remainder of the assessment is unremarkable and consistent with the previous history.

During care the next morning, LG keeps her face turned away from the nurse and does not initiate any verbal interaction. When asked a question she responds slowly with monosyllabic answers. The bed linens are wet and smell of urine. The nurse also notes that LG does not assist when being turned in bed or getting up to her wheelchair.

Discussion

There is a potential for the development of pressure ulcers whenever the blood flow to the skin, subcutaneous tissue, and/or muscle is compromised as a result of externally applied pressure. The bony prominences (e.g., the greater trochanter, heel, coccyx, and malleolus) are the most common sites of pressure ulcer development. There are several factors other than pressure to consider in the etiology of pressure ulcers. "Shearing force" causes the strangulation of blood vessels between the superficial fascia and the deep fascia. There is a potential for this to occur when a patient is placed in a sitting position in bed or in a chair and is unable to maintain a full upright sitting position. As the patient slides down, the blood vessels are stretched and a compromised blood flow and/or ischemia can result.

Moisture reduces the skin's ability to withstand other physical factors such as friction and heat. Prolonged moisture, as occurs with urinary incontinence, may cause the skin to become macerated and thereby contribute to the potential development of breakdown. This may have contributed to LG's developing a pressure ulcer since she has not been adhering to her bowel and bladder program.

Poor nutritional status may result in reduction of muscle mass and subcutaneous tissue loss. As a result, there is a decrease in the padding between the skin and underlying bone, further increasing susceptibility to the effects of externally applied pressure.

Impaired physical mobility is a significant risk factor for the development of pressure ulcers. In a healthy, active person, the discomfort that arises from externally applied pressure is the stimulus for movement or a change in position. In illness the discomfort stimulus may be ineffective or absent. Paralysis, sensory disturbances, a decreased level of consciousness, and apathy may all contribute to a negligible or inadequate movement response when areas of the skin are compressed as is the case with LG.

LG is able to assume responsibility for her own skin care and prevention of impaired tissue integrity when not experiencing a depressive episode. Until her depression and withdrawal are successfully treated, however, her skin care will become the responsibility of the nurse. The care plan must include interventions to prevent further impairment of tissue integrity, prevent infection, and promote healing of the existing pressure sore. Once a pressure sore has developed, an aggressive and consistent treatment regimen is required in order to prevent infection and enhance wound healing. The treatment plan must be individualized based on the grade and size of the pressure ulcer. The following interventions would be incorporated into the care plan for a patient like LG, with a grade one, uncomplicated pressure sore.

Treatment

1. On the first day, measure and grade the pressure sore (Shea, 1975). Grade and measure the ulcer every 3 to 4 days. Inspect the ulcer for drainage and/or foul odor. Medical intervention may be required if drainage or foul odor are present.
2. Cleanse the ulcer with normal saline.
3. Place an occlusive dressing on the ulcer. Follow the manufacturer's recommendations regarding application and length of time the dressing is to remain on the wound. Assess the ulcer every time the dressing is changed.
4. Reposition the patient at least every 2 hours. Consider the use of a foam convoluted mattress or an alternating air mattress. Consider the use of a foam convoluted pad for the wheelchair.
5. Inspect the skin, especially that over the bony prominences, with each position change.
6. Provide perineal hygiene with each episode of incontinence. Maintain bowel and bladder program.
7. Assess nutritional intake. A positive nitrogen balance is necessary. Calories are required for energy and protein for wound repair. Nutritional supplements may be required.

Other aspects of the care plan for LG would address the treatment of her depression and withdrawal. Discharge planning should include instruction of the family regarding recognition of the onset of depression and the need to seek consultation with a mental health professional in the earliest stage possible.

Nursing Diagnoses

1. Impaired tissue integrity related to impaired physical mobility
2. Impaired physical mobility related to paralysis and depression
3. Potential for disuse syndrome
4. Potential for infection related to pressure ulcer
5. Functional incontinence related to spinal cord injury and depression
6. Altered health maintenance related to depression

7. Impaired social interaction related to depression
8. Knowledge deficit related to onset of depression and need for consultation. (family)

Each of the problems caused by the effects of impaired physical mobility has the potential of reducing the level of mobility even further. The reciprocal relationship between the state of immobility and the problems it causes is illustrated in Fig. 14-13, which also summarizes the effects of immobility that contribute to each problem. The problems are related and compound one another.

The following case study provides an ex-

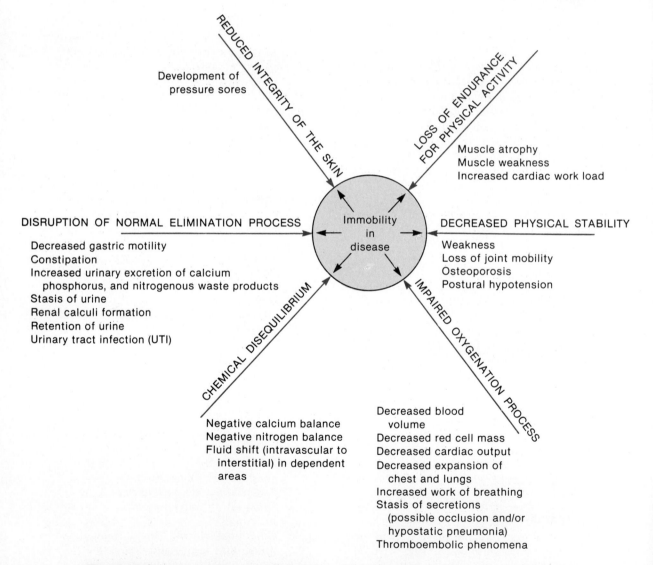

Fig. 14-13. Problems resulting from effects of immobility in ill individuals. Effects of immobility that contribute to each problem are listed. Arrows indicate reciprocal nature of immobility and problems.

ample of how the effects of impaired mobility compound one another. This patient is acutely aware of a progressive downward spiral in his mobility level and how it diminishes his already limited functional ability even further.

CASE STUDY: EFFECTS OF IMPAIRED PHYSICAL MOBILITY

History

RH, a 52-year-old male, suffered a spinal cord injury (level C5-C6) in a car accident 30 years ago. He was left with no movement in his lower extremities and with very limited, gross motor movement in his arms. He has had multiple episodes of pneumonia, urinary tract infection, gastroparesis, and paralytic ileus in the past. After each acute episode, he has had to go through a rehabilitation period to regain his optimal level of mobility and functional ability. However, with each acute episode he has been able to regain only a part of his previous level of mobility.

Since RH's injury, he has lived in a variety of long-term care settings, moving when his insurance status changes or when he becomes dissatisfied with the care he is receiving. He is very knowledgeable about the effects of immobility and how to prevent them, and he becomes very upset if facility staff members do not adhere to the strict schedule he has laid out for turning, exercising, and getting up in his wheelchair. He supervises his hygiene activities and the routines of bowel and bladder management, monitors his diet, and stays away from anyone with an infection or who is not feeling well.

Because of the level of his spinal cord injury, RH's respiratory status is unstable. His respiratory muscles are weak, and he has both an ineffective breathing pattern and ineffective airway clearance. These problems have contributed to the repeated respiratory tract infections and pneumonias that he has experienced in the past. Each episode has been increasingly more severe and difficult to treat. RH developed respiratory failure and has had to be mechanically ventilated during the last three episodes of pneumonia. Since the last episode of pneumonia, 2 years ago, RH has been unable to be weaned from the ventilator completely. He can be off the ventilator completely for about 2 weeks before he develops mild respiratory distress with deterioration of his blood gas status. He then has to be placed back on the ventilator for several hours each day. With each setback, RH becomes withdrawn and irritable with the staff.

Discussion

At this time, RH is living in a facility that specializes in the care of patients with unique, long-term, respiratory needs. He has a permanent tracheostomy and currently spends a minimum of 6 hours each night and 2 to 3 hours each afternoon on the ventilator. The highest inspiratory pressure he is able to generate is $-40cm$ H_2O pressure. Other spirometric measures obtained during spontaneous breathing are as follows:

Vital capacity	1 L
Minute ventilation	3 L/min
Tidal volume	111 ml

Because of the weakness of his respiratory muscles, RH sometimes has difficulty expectorating secretions. He undergoes chest physical therapy treatments twice a day. He occasionally needs to be suctioned when on the ventilator.

During an acute stage of respiratory failure he developed severe contractures of the elbow and wrist joints of each arm, and his hands and arms are "locked" in the flexed position. He will never regain the degree of movement he had in his arms before the onset of this last pneumonia. He is no longer able to assist with

Contributed by Maureen Shekleton.

his transfers and turning in bed. He states that he does not feel as strong as he was 2 years ago. RH has not attained the same weight he was at prior to the last episode of pneumonia. He can feed himself and drink from a glass using specially adapted aids to hold the silverware and glass. He admits that it takes longer to eat than it used to and that sometimes he tires out and doesn't finish the entire meal. He will not allow anyone to feed him. He receives a liquid nutritional supplement each day but does not usually finish the whole amount. He states that drinking the whole amount makes him feel bloated.

RH is able to sit up in his wheelchair for about 2 hours at a time. It is a motorized wheelchair, and he is able to visit with other patients and joins group activities in the community room. After being up for awhile, he needs assistance shifting his weight. He periodically requests this help and repeatedly tells those who come to his aid that he does not want to get another bedsore. There are scars on his elbows, heels, and coccyx from healed pressure ulcers. The nursing staff pay special attention to these areas, inspecting them for signs of irritation, cleaning them, and applying lotion and massage.

RH speaks freely about his accident, recovery, and rehabilitation. He says that he knows that the staff resent his trying to control his care but that he feels he must or risk developing more problems and possibly even dying. He expresses anger when he talks about the contractures developing during his last acute illness and openly blames those who were responsible for his care.

Since his injury, RH has experienced all of the effects of impaired physical mobility discussed in the text with the exception of urinary calculi. He knows that all of the muscles in his body are getting progressively weaker, and he is frustrated because he believes there is little he can do to prevent this from happening.

Nursing Diagnoses

1. Impaired physical mobility related to spinal cord injury and sequelae to immobility
2. Potential for disuse syndrome
3. Ineffective breathing pattern
4. Ineffective airway clearance
5. Anxiety related to further deterioration of condition
6. Powerlessness related to sense of progressive deterioration

It was stated earlier that no body system escapes the consequences of immobility. The effects of immobility on the various systems of the body are summarized in Table 14-3.

The diagnostic category, potential for disuse syndrome, has been approved for clinical use and testing through the 1987-1988 diagnosis review cycle of the North American Nursing Diagnosis Association (NANDA). This category has been defined by NANDA as "the state in which an individual is at risk for deterioration of body systems as a result of prescribed or unavoidable musculoskeletal inactivity." Risk factors include all of the conditions discussed earlier in this chapter that lead to impaired physical mobility. Prevention of all of the potential effects of impaired physical mobility is incorporated within this one category, which is recommended for use in planning the care of an at risk patient (Kim, et al., 1989). If any of the pathologic sequelae of impaired physical mobility should occur, the revised care plan would incorporate the appropriate nursing diagnosis (e.g., impaired tissue integrity or altered tissue perfusion).

It must be remembered that each person will react to immobility in a different way. Not every individual who experiences im-

Table 14-3. Systemic manifestations of impaired physical mobility

Circulatory	Gastrointestinal	Metabolic	Respiratory	Musculoskeletal	Genitourinary	Integument
↓ Maximum cardiac output ↑ Heart rate Postural hypotension Dependent edema Thromboembolism	Anorexia ↓ Gastric motility Belching Bloating Constipation (partially due to muscle weakness)	↓ BMR Negative nitrogen balance	↓ Excursion ↓ Diameter of airways Stasis of secretions → hypostatic pneumonia ↑ Work of breathing	Muscles Atrophy Weakness Shortening ↓ Elasticity of tendons and ligaments Joints ↓ Mobility Contractures Skeletal Osteoporosis	↑ Excretion of calcium (formation of urinary calculi) ↑ Urinary excretion of nitrogen ↑ Urinary excretion of phosphorus Stasis and retention of urine→ urinary tract infection	↑ Susceptibility to breakdown (especially at pressure points and in edematous areas)

paired physical mobility will experience all the potential problems just discussed or in the same way as others might. The extent of the problem depends on how long the immobility is left untreated. The severity of the effects is directly proportional to the duration and degree of the immobility; hence a response to immobility in the form of treatment of both the duration and degree of the immobility is the definitive factor in preventing the problems just discussed (Fig. 14-2).

TREATMENT RATIONALE

Treatment of impaired physical mobility must begin immediately if the degenerative changes that can occur are to be prevented. The effects of immobility are secondary to lack of use of the functional components of the motor system. The longer the immobility is left untreated, the more of these effects will occur, and some changes may become irreversible.

The goal of treatment of impaired physical mobility is prevention of all of the effects of immobility discussed here. The preventive measures that constitute the treatment of impaired physical mobility are all within the realm of independent nursing judgment and action. The clinician must make treatment of impaired physical mobility a priority if the patient is to attain an optimal level of wellness.

Lack of endurance and decreased physical stability can be prevented or at least minimized by range of motion exercises to all joints while in bed, early ambulation and positional changes, and isotonic and isometric exercises (in individuals for whom these types of exercises are not contraindicated) (Lentz, 1981; Winslow and Weber, 1980). Weight-bearing activities will help decrease the amount of calcium lost by increasing bone deposition. Anatomic positioning of the limbs will help to maintain structural as well as functional integrity of the underlying muscles, joints, and connective tissue. The use of elastic stockings to prevent venous pooling in the extremities helps to prevent postural hypotension as well as the development of thromboembolic phenomena. Coughing, deep-breathing exercises, and change of position will prevent ineffective airway clearance and promote a more effective breathing pattern through excursion of the respiratory muscles (Tyler, 1984). Frequent position changes will also prevent stasis of urine and prolonged pressure on body parts. Use of a commode rather than a bedpan and adequate amounts of fluid and roughage in the diet will promote normal elimination patterns. The diet should also include high protein, acid-ash foods to improve the nitrogen balance and maintain the acidity of the urine. These are all relatively simple measures that can be taken to prevent the development of complications.

Prevention of impaired tissue integrity should be a major focus of the nursing care of the immobilized patient. It is important to remember that once a pressure sore has formed, it is extremely difficult to treat. Prevention is the best treatment (Horsley, 1981). When movement is not possible or is extremely restricted, there are a variety of mechanical aids that can be used to relieve pressure and prevent contracture development. Successful prevention begins with an assessment of the potential for impaired tissue integrity based on identification of the risk factors present in each patient with impaired physical mobility. Gosnell (1987) provides a review of the various assessment instruments that are available for use (Williams, 1972; Gosnell, 1973; Gruis and Innes, 1976; Norton, McLaren, and Exton-Smith, 1981; Abruzzese, 1985; Bergstrom, et al.,

1985; Stotts, 1985; Waterlow, 1985; Pritchard, 1986; Bergstrom, Demuth and Braden, 1987). Parish et al. (1983) has outlined five strategies essential to the successful program of pressure sore prevention:

1. Removing pressure at all body support-surface interfaces
2. Minimizing shear forces
3. Maintaining a clean and dry skin surface
4. Implementation of supportive therapy when needed
5. Treatment of concurrent disease

SUMMARY

Impaired physical mobility is an important concept in the study of pathophysiology since some degree of immobility accompanies all illness and can have a significant effect on the progress and treatment of the disease entity. The effects of immobility may accelerate the pathophysiologic processes that are present. They may complicate the treatment of the disease and prolong the convalescent period. Certain consequences of immobility may even result in death.

An understanding of the effects of impaired physical mobility and why they occur will lead to a greater understanding of how to prevent them. Even more critical is the appreciation for the importance of preventing these effects that comes from this understanding.

BIBLIOGRAPHY

Abruzzese RS: Early assessment and prevention of pressure sores. In Lee BY, editor: Chronic ulcers of the skin, New York, 1985, McGraw-Hill, Inc, pp 1-19.

Darbenel JC, Ferguson-Pell MW, Beale AQ: Monitoring the mobility of patients in bed, Med Biol Eng Comput 23(5):466, 1985.

Bergstrom N, Demuth P, and Braden B: A clinical trial of the Braden scale for predicting pressure sore risk, Nurs Clin North Am 22(2):417-428, 1987.

Birkhead H, Haupt G, and Mayers R: Circulatory and metabolic effects of prolonged bed rest in healthy subjects, Fed Proc 22:520, 1963.

Browse N: The physiology and pathology of bedrest, Springfield, 1965, Charles C Thomas, Publisher.

Carnevali D, and Brueckner S: Immobilization –reassessment of a concept, Am J Nurs 70:1502-1507, 1970.

Cherry GW and Ryan TJ: Pathophysiology. In Parish LC, Witkowski JA and Crissey JT, editors: The decubitus ulcer, New York, 1983, Masson Publishing USA, Inc, pp 11-20.

Constantian M, editor: Pressure ulcers: principles and technique of management, Boston, 1980, Little, Brown & Co, Inc.

Creason N, Pogue N, Nelson A, and Hoyt C: Validating the nursing diagnosis of impaired physical mobility, Nurs Clin No Amer 20(4): 669-683, 1985.

Deitrick J, Whedon G, and Schorr G: Effects of immobilization upon various metabolic and physiologic functions of normal men, Am J Med 4:3-36, 1948.

Downs F: Bed rest and sensory disturbances, Am J Nurs 74(3):434-438, 1974.

Fisher W and Fisher A: Medical implications of space, Top Emerg Med 2:137-149, October 1980.

Fowler EM: Equipment and products used in the management and treatment of pressure ulcers, Nurs Clin North Am 22(2):449-461, 1987.

Goode A: Microgravity research: a new dimension in medical science, Lancet 1(8223):767-769, April 1981.

Gosnell D: An assessment tool to identify pressure sores, Nurs Res 22:55-59, 1973.

Gosnell D: Assessment and evaluation of pressure sores, Nurs Clin North Am 22:399-417, 1987.

Gruis M and Innes B: Assessment: essential to prevent pressure sores, Am J Nurs 76(11):1762-1764, 1976.

Gurevich I: Infected decubiti: the problem of patient placement and care, Top Clin Nurs 5(2):55-63, 1983.

Horsley JA: Preventing decubitus ulcers: CURN Project, New York, 1981, Grune & Stratton, Inc.

Kim MJ, McFarland GD, and McLane AM, Pocket Guide to Nursing Diagnoses, ed 3, 1989, CV Mosby.

Kottke FJ: The effects of limitation of activity upon the human body, JAMA 196.117-122, 1966.

Lee BY, editor: Chronic ulcers of the skin, New York, 1985, McGraw-Hill, Inc.

Lentz, M. (1981) Selected aspects of reconditioning secondary to immobilization. Nsg Clin No Amer 16(4), 729-737, 1981.

Lerman S, et al: Parathyroid hormone and the hypercalcemia of immobilization, J Clin Endocrinol Metab 45(3):425-428, 1977.

Levy, T and Talbot, J: Research opportunities in cardiovascular deconditioning. (Contract #NASW-3616) Washington, DC: National Aeronautics and Space Admin, 1983.

Lynch TN, et al: Metabolic effects of prolonged bed rest: their modification by simulated attitude, Aerospace Med 38:10-20, 1967.

Mack P and LaChance P: Effects of recumbency and space flight on the bone density, Am J Clin Nutr 20:1194-1205, 1967.

Maklebust J: Pressure ulcers: etiology and prevention, Nurs Clin North Am 22(2):359-377, 1987.

Maklebust J, Mondoux L, and Sieggreen, M: Pressure relief characteristics of various support surfaces used in prevention and treatment of pressure ulcers. J of Enterostomal Therapy, 13(3):85-89, 1986.

Maklebust J, Sieggreen M, and Mondoux L: Pressure relief capabilities: A comparison of the Sof Care bed cushion and the Clinitron Bed, Decubitus 1(2): May 1988.

Moser, K and Fedullo, P: Venous thromboembolism. Chest, 83, 117-121, 1983.

Natow AB: Nutrition in prevention and treatment of decubitus ulcers, Top Clin Nurs 5(2):39-44, 1983.

Norton D, McLaren R, and Exton-Smith A: Pressure sores. In Horsley JA, editor: Preventing decubitus ulcers: CURN project, New York, 1981, Grune & Stratton, Inc, pp 104-149.

Olson, E, editor: The hazards of immobility, AJN 67(4):780-797, 1967.

Parish LC, Witkowski JA, and Crissey JT: The decubitus ulcer. Masson Publishing USA, Inc, New York, 1981.

Pritchard V, 1986. Pressure sores: Calculating the risk. Nurs Times, February, 59, 1986.

Reuler JB and Cooney TG: The pressure sore: pathophysiology and principles of management, Ann Intern Med 94(5):661-666, 1981.

Ryback R, Lewis O, and Lessard C: Psychobiologic effects of prolonged bed rest (weightless) in young, healthy volunteers (study II), Aerospace Med 42:529-535, 1971.

Sanchez F: Fundamentals of chest x-ray interpretation, Crit Care Nurs 6(5):41-61, 1986.

Seiler WO and Stahelin HB: Recent findings on decubitus ulcer pathology: implications for care, Geriatrics 41(1):47, 1986.

Shea JD Pressure sores: Classification and management. Clin Orthopedics and Related Research, October, (112):89-100, 1985.

Sieggreen MY: Healing of physical wounds, Nurs Clin North Am 22(2):439-447, 1987.

Sklar CG: Pressure ulcer management in the neurologically impaired patient, J Neurosurg Nurs 17(1):30, 1985.

Spencer W, Valbona C, and Carter R, Jr: Physiologic concepts of immobilization, J Phys Med Rehabil 46:89-100, 1965.

Stotts N: Nutritional parameters as predictors of pressure sores in surgical patients. Nsg Research 34(6):383, 1985.

Taylor H, et al.: Affects of bed rest on cardiovascular function and work performance, J Appl Physiol 11:223-239, 1949.

Tepperman, P and Devlin, M: Therapeutic heat and cold. Postgrad. Med, 73(1), 69-76, 1983.

Tompkins ES: Effect of restricted mobility and dominance of perceived duration, Nurs Res 29:333-338, 1980.

Thomas J, Shirger A, Fealey R, and Sheps S: Orthostatic hypotension, Mayo Clin. Proceedings 56:117-125, 1981.

Tyler M: The respiratory effects of body positioning and immobilization, Resp Care 29(5):472-483, 1984.

Verhonick P, Lewis D, and Goller H: Thermography in the study of decubitus ulcers, Nurs Res 21(3):233-237, 1972.

Warren R: Osteoporosis, J Oral Med 32(4):113-119, 1977.

Waterlow J: A risk assessment card. Nurs Times, November, 49, 51, 55, 1985.

Williams A: A study of factors contributing to skin breakdown, Nurs Res 21(3):238-243, 1972.

Winslow E and Weber T: Progressive exercise to combat the hazards of bedrest, Am J Nurs 80(3):440-445, March 1980.

Zubek J, et al: Behavioral and physiologic changes during prolonged immobilization plus perceptual deprivation, J Abnorm Psychol 74:230-236, 1969.

UNIT VII

Sexuality-reproductive pattern

15

Reproductive pathophysiology

The major physiologic function of the reproductive system is the procreation of new life and thus the perpetuation of the species. Reproductive ability is primarily under endocrine control, although it is also influenced by various neural and metabolic factors. Sexuality is one aspect of wellness and requires a healthy reproductive tract.

The female ovary and the male testis serve both exocrine and endocrine functions. The exocrine function is gametogenesis, or the production of ova and sperm. The endocrine function is secretion of the sex hormones, which control sexual development and function. The hormones of the female serve the additional function of preparing the body for and maintaining pregnancy.

The effects of reproductive dysfunction are discussed in this chapter in terms of the manifestations and mechanisms of this dysfunction. Disorders of sexual differentiation are discussed in Chapter 4; endocrine causes of reproductive dysfunction are discussed in Chapter 8.

MANIFESTATIONS OF DISORDERS OF THE REPRODUCTIVE SYSTEM

Disorders of the female reproductive system may become apparent through a variety of clinical manifestations. For example, the menstrual cycle is characterized by the cyclic discharge of blood, mucus, and cellular debris from the uterine mucosa. The presence of pain in the form of abdominal cramps is associated with ovulatory menstrual cycles (Goebelsmann, 1985). The general nature of these manifestations is important, but the characteristics of their occurrence within the menstrual and reproductive cycles are just as important if not more so. Bleeding after the onset of menopause or between menstrual periods is an example of this; what is considered normal in one part of the reproductive cycle may represent dysfunction in another part of the cycle. Polymenorrhea is considered normal in the pubertal adolescent, but in the mature female this symptom may indicate an underlying pathologic condition such as endometrial cancer.

Infertility, abnormal discharge from the breast, vagina, or penis, abnormalities of lactation, and gynecomastia are other potential manifestations of disorders of the reproductive system. Many of these manifestations apply chiefly to disorders of the female reproductive system but the male reproductive system may be affected as well.

Pain

Dysmenorrhea is the term applied to the lower abdominal and pelvic pain that occurs with normal menstruation. *Primary dysmenorrhea* is usually considered a benign condition that occurs principally in young adults and adolescents. In some women, however, the pain is severe enough to be disabling. It tends to decrease with maturity and particularly after the first pregnancy. *Secondary dysmenorrhea* is seen in women in their late 20s and early 30s and is indicative of coexisting organic disease, which may include inflammatory and infectious processes, cervical stenosis, the presence of an ovarian cyst, pelvic congestion, endometriosis, and adenomyosis.

A number of interrelated mechanisms have been implicated in the pathogenesis of primary dysmenorrhea, including mechanical obstruction of the menstrual flow by a small cervical outlet, anxiety, vascular spasm, and uterine hypercontractility. The pain is often described as "laborlike" indicating that excessive uterine contractility is the pathogenetic mechanism most frequently operating in dysmenorrhea. Research has demonstrated that certain prostaglandins (PGE_2 and $PGF_{2\alpha}$) stimulate uterine contractions. These substances are, in fact, used to stimulate labor, and the pain and associated symptoms of diarrhea, nausea, and vomiting associated with exogenous administration of prostaglandins parallels the clinical picture of the patient with severe dysmenorrhea. Other findings implicating prostaglandins in the production of dysmenorrhea include the following:

1. Significantly higher levels of prostaglandins in the endometrium, endometrial washings, and menstrual fluid of women with dysmenorrhea as compared to women experiencing a normal menstrual period
2. The efficacy of prostaglandin synthetase inhibitors in the treatment of primary dysmenorrhea

3. The occurrence of dysmenorrhea in ovulatory cycles only, since in anovulatory cycles in the absence of increased progesterone there is no increase in prostaglandin levels

The increased amount of prostaglandins in the menstrual fluid is postulated to cause the intense, cramping pain by stimulating excessive uterine contractions, which in turn cause uterine ischemia because of reduced blood flow during the contractions. Prostaglandins also act to sensitize the nerve terminals to the physical and chemical stimuli for pain. Why some women have greater than normal levels of prostaglandins in their menstrual fluid is unclear at this point.

While the role of endogenous prostaglandins in the pathogenesis of primary dysmenorrhea is well documented, the role of prostaglandins in secondary dysmenorrhea remains subject to speculation, debate, and further study. Greater than normal concentrations of prostaglandins have been found in the endometrium of women with disorders characterized by painful menstruation such as endometriosis, endometrial carcinoma, and fibromyoma. Increased levels of prostaglandins have been found in animals with an intrauterine contraceptive device in place, leading to speculation as to whether many of the symptoms experienced by women with an IUD may be the result of the action of prostaglandins released in response to the trauma and irritation caused by the IUD itself. There are no data at the present time on the prostaglandin levels in women with pelvic inflammatory disease although, since prostaglandins are mediators in the inflammatory reaction, one might expect these levels to be elevated in the presence of this condition.

Dysmenorrhea is characterized by pain in the lower abdomen, which may be sharp and crampy or dull and constant. It begins approximately 12 to 14 hours before flow begins and lasts for 24 to 48 hours. It is sometimes associated with headache, fatigue, irritability, nausea, vomiting, and diarrhea. The pain may radiate to the thighs, upper legs, and back. Dysmenorrhea occurs only in ovulatory cycles.

The symptom cluster known as *premenstrual syndrome (PMS)* has been discussed for more than 50 years (Frank, 1931). The syndrome is described as a cyclic symptom complex that begins after ovulation and ceases with the onset of menstrual flow. Specific symptoms are unique to each patient in both type and severity. Reported symptoms include, in order of frequency: (1) anxiety and irritability; (2) breast tenderness and weight gain; (3) hypoglycemia; and (4) depression and withdrawal (Reid and Yen, 1981).

Many theories have attempted to explain the pathophysiology of PMS, including estrogen/progesterone imbalance, excess aldosterone, hypoglycemia, hyperprolactinemia, excess prostaglandin activity, and neurotransmitter dysfunction (Strickler, 1987). The neuroendocrine events of the menstrual cycle are indeed mediated by a number of hormones and affected by environmental and internal stressors. There are at present no convincing data to defend any one theoretical explanation of the condition known as PMS. There is no single treatment regimen that is effective for all patients, and care must be individualized for each patient.

Pain is the most universal symptom of *ectopic pregnancy,* which is the result of implantation of the fertilized ovum outside the uterine endometrium. Other signs and symptoms include bleeding, abdominal or pelvic tenderness and shoulder pain, orthostatic symptoms, and CNS complaints such as dizziness, confusion, or fainting. The most common site of ectopic implantation is the fallopian tubes. Two general mechanisms are suspected in ectopic pregnancy: (1) an increase in the receptivity of ectopic tissues (especially tubal tissue) to the fertilized ovum and (2) conditions characterized by tubal pathology that prevent or retard the passage of the fertilized ovum into the uterine cavity. This pregnancy normally cannot go to term, although rare cases of term ovarian pregnancies have been reported. Ectopic pregnancy usually terminates through rupturing, which constitutes an emergency situation.

The most common source of tubal pathology is pelvic inflammatory disease (PID). The risk of ectopic pregnancy is greatly increased following an episode of PID (Farrell, 1986). The inflammatory response to infection results in tubal distortion, scarring, occlusion, and loss of motility and function.

Bleeding

Vaginal bleeding or the lack of it must first be assessed in terms of whether it is occurring in the pregnant or nonpregnant state. As discussed earlier, the age of the patient must also be considered.

Amenorrhea is the absence of menstruation; it is considered normal before menarche, after menopause, and during pregnancy and lactation. *Primary amenorrhea* is the failure of menstruation to begin. It is considered to be present if a girl reaches 18 years of age without having menstruated. *Secondary amenorrhea* is the cessation of menstruation following the initiation of menstruation at the menarche. Primary amenorrhea is usually the result of ovarian dysfunction or hypothalamic-pituitary disorders. Secondary amenorrhea may be the result of endocrine dysfunction but is also frequently a feature in a number of general illnesses. An example of this is the patient with chronic renal disease who has ceased to menstruate with the onset of renal failure but who had previously experienced normal menstrual cycles. Secondary amenorrhea can also be the result of psychologic stress and anxiety, the effects of which are probably mediated via the hypothalamus.

Dysfunctional bleeding in the adolescent is related to immaturity of the pituitary-ovarian axis and the presence of anovulatory menstrual cycles. Progesterone secretion is insufficient, and therefore complete shedding of the endometrium does not occur. The consequence of this is irregular periods of bleeding.

Dysfunctional uterine bleeding in the menopausal or postmenopausal woman may indicate a pelvic malignancy. Cervical erosion and polyps, both benign lesions, are frequent causes of intermenstrual bleeding or excessive menstrual flow. Bleeding usually occurs with no discomfort. Uterine fibroids, which most commonly occur in women of childbearing age, are another form of benign tumor that causes abnormal bleeding, pain, and pressure. Surgical removal of the tumors and often hysterectomy are necessitated by this condition.

Bleeding during pregnancy. Bleeding during pregnancy is often indicative of a serious complication. Potential causes of bleeding during early pregnancy include abortion, ectopic pregnancy, and hydatidiform mole. Bleeding after the 28th week of gestation is considered antepartal hemorrhage resulting from abnormal placental separation.

The term *abortion* implies the termination of pregnancy prior to the time the fetus has sufficiently developed to survive, which is usually at about 20 weeks. The term *miscarriage* is usually applied when

abortion occurs spontaneously. Spontaneous abortion in the early months of pregnancy is usually preceded by the death of the fetus. Early fetal death may be the result of an abnormality in the developing embryo or reproductive tissue or systemic disease of the mother. Genetic abnormalities of development appear to be the most common cause of early fetal death. The mechanisms by which these malformations develop are discussed in Chapter 4.

Clinically, spontaneous abortion can be grouped according to the following classifications: threatened, inevitable, incomplete, complete, and missed, which are summarized in Table 15-1. One half or less of the women who bleed during early pregnancy actually abort. A *threatened* abortion is characterized by vaginal bleeding or bloody vaginal drainage during the first half of pregnancy. This may or may not be accompanied by low back pain and mild abdominal cramping. Slight bleeding at the time the normal menstrual cycle would have occurred is considered physiologic. Most *missed abortions* terminate spontaneously after a period of time with no ill effects to the mother. The incidence of missed abortion is increasing with the use of potent progestational compounds to treat threatened abortion.

Inevitable abortion is characterized by rupture of the membranes and cervical dilation. Prior to the tenth week of pregnancy the fetus and placenta are likely to be expelled together. After the tenth week the placenta is likely to be retained either completely or in part. This causes bleeding, which is the main sign of *incomplete abortion*. Signs of a threatened abortion may appear upon death of the fetus. After this the uterus will no longer enlarge, and mammary changes revert. Occasionally, coagulation defects develop, which are

Table 15-1. Classification of different types of spontaneous abortion

Type of spontaneous abortion	Definition/Description	Symptoms	Signs	Treatment
Threatened	Bleeding in early pregnancy (< 20 weeks)	Uterine bleeding Possibly mild uterine cramping	Cervical os closed Soft cervix consistent with pregnancy Uterine size consistent with dates	Confirm pregnancy to be in the uterus by physical examination or ultrasound (rule out ectopic pregnancy) Rest, observation (50% will go on to spontaneous abortion)
Inevitable	Bleeding with dilation of cervical os and no passage of products of conception	Uterine bleeding Usually moderate uterine cramping	Cervical os open to 8 mm instrument Uterine size consistent with dates	Suction curettage*
Incomplete	Some products of conception have been expelled with some remaining in uterus	Uterine bleeding Usually moderate uterine cramping Possibly passed tissue	Cervical os open Products of conception passed Uterine size may be small for dates	Suction curettage*
Complete	All products of conception have been expelled from uterus	History of bleeding and cramping, now lessened or stopped Passed tissue	Cervical os open Products of conception passed Uterine size small for dates	If unsure whether complete, perform suction curettage* If complete: Oxytocin drip if still bleeding or if uterus soft, boggy Rh sensitization prophylaxis if patient Rh negative
Septic	Infection of tissue products of conception may or may not have been passed	Uterine bleeding Usually moderate uterine cramping May have passed tissue May have fever, chills	Cervical os usually open Uterus is tender to palpation Cervix usually tender to motion Frequently purulent cervical discharge is noted	Parenteral antibiotics (Cefoxitin, 2 g i.v.) Suction curettage* 30 + min after antibiotics
Missed	Following fetal death, products of conception are retained for up to 4 weeks or longer	Frequently loss of symptoms of pregnancy (morning sickness, breast tenderness)	Cervical os closed Uterine size small for dates	Dilitation and curettage

Adapted from Farrell RG: OB/GYN emergencies: the first 60 minutes, Rockville, Md, 1986, Aspen Publishers.
*Suction curettage includes: oxytocin drip, fluid and blood if indicated, Rh sensitization prophylaxis of patient is Rh positive, treatment of any infection, and careful follow-up instructions.

probably mediated by the thromboplastin from the dead and macerated fetus. *Habitual abortion* refers to three or more consecutive abortions. *Septic abortion* refers to an infectious process accompanying abortion.

A *hydatidiform mole* is a benign tumor of the placenta in which some or all of the chorionic villi are converted into a mass of clear vesicles. The incidence of this disorder appears to be quite high in some parts of the world (mainly Asia and Mexico), and it usually affects women in the end of their childbearing years. Persistent bleeding, which can be either spotty or hemorrhagic, and rapid uterine enlargement are characteristic. Additionally, the manifestations of hypertension, absence of fetal activity and heart sounds, hyperemesis gravidarum due to secretion of human chorionic gonadotropin, and increased thyroxine secretion without hyperthyroidism are seen. Treatment involves the immediate termination of the mole and later follow-up for possible malignant changes, since it is the most common lesion preceding choriocarcinoma, a highly malignant trophoblastic neoplasm (Farrell, 1986).

Bleeding that occurs during the later part of pregnancy is usually caused by abnormal separation of the placenta from the uterine site of implantation. There are two conditions in which this mechanism is operative: abruptio placentae and placenta previa. A comparison of the signs and symptoms of these conditions is presented in Table 15-2. In *abruptio placentae* a normally situated placenta becomes separated prematurely. This separation may be partial or complete. It occurs in 0.5% to 2.7% of all pregnancies (Farrell, 1986). Bleeding occurs between the placenta and uterine wall and may result in formation of a decidual hematoma (concealed hemorrhage). External bleeding may or may

not occur. The extreme form, in which at least one half the placenta is separated, presents with pain, uterine rigidity, absent fetal heart tones, and hypovolemic shock. In less severe forms, fetal heart sounds may be audible although abnormal. Acute renal failure and disseminated intravascular coagulation (DIC; see Chapter 3) are complications of this disorder. Abruptio placentae is considered a hemorrhagic emergency. Associated factors that have been identified include trauma, maternal age and gravidity, cigarette smoking, folic acid deficiency, a short umbilical cord, sudden uterine decompression, hypertension, and compression or obstruction of the vena cava, which increases venous hydrostatic pressure distal to the site of compression or obstruction (Farrell, 1986). A recent report has also linked cocaine use to this complication (Acker et al., 1983).

Treatment depends on the condition of the fetus. If the fetus is alive, emergency cesarean section is performed. If the fetus is dead, a vaginal delivery may be elected if the mother's condition is stable (Farrell, 1986).

In *placenta previa* the placenta is abnormally attached to the lower uterine segment over or near the cervical internal os. It occurs in approximately 0.5% of all pregnancies (Farrell, 1986). Multiparity and advancing age seem to predispose women to the development of this disorder, which is characterized by painless hemorrhage in the latter part of pregnancy. Many abortions in early pregnancy may be the result of misplaced placental tissue. In the latter part of pregnancy the lower segment of the uterus stretches and thins out, which results in tearing of the placental attachments. The stretched myometrium is unable to compress the bleeding vessels, and hemorrhage occurs. This

Table 15-2. Differential diagnosis of third trimester bleeding

	Onset of labor	Placenta previa	Abruptio placentae
Bleeding	Dark red, mixed with mucus	Bright red	Dark red
Pain	With contractions	Absent	Constant
Uterus	Soft between contractions	Usually soft	Usually firm, tense
Coagulation	Normal	Normal	Often abnormal
Ultrasound	—	Usually diagnostic	Not reliable

Reprinted from OB/GYN emergencies: the first 60 minutes, R.G. Farrell, p. 65, with permission of Aspen Publishers Inc. © 1986.

hemorrhage occurs without warning in a woman who has previously been in good health. It may occur during sleep, so that she wakes up to find herself in a pool of blood.

The diagnosis of placenta previa usually results in cesarean delivery even when lesser degrees of the disorder are present. Many believe this is the only appropriate method for delivery of the infant. Vaginal delivery is elected only for low-lying placental implantation (Naeye, 1987).

Discharge

Discharge from any body orifice must be assessed in terms of amount, color, consistency, and accompanying odor. The various infectious processes that affect the male and female reproductive systems can often be identified through the discharges they produce. Abnormal changes in the character of the vaginal discharge during the menstrual cycle may be indicative of underlying pathology. Discharge from the male or female breast (other than during lactation) may indicate an underlying pathologic process.

Leukorrhea is the term applied to any vaginal discharge other than blood. The mucous glands of the cervix are the chief source of leukorrheal discharge, which normally is a clear, viscid, alkaline mucus. The amount of this discharge increases, and its consistency changes at the time of ovulation. A change from the normal secretion to a thin, watery, profuse secretion in the menopausal and postmenopausal woman is usually indicative of cell breakdown, which suggests a metastatic process. Vulval irritation and contact dermatitis also may alter the amount and character of the vaginal secretion as can forgotten tampons and other foreign bodies inserted into the vagina.

Infertility

Failure to conceive may be the result of infertility in either of the partners; the incidence of infertility is equally common in both sexes. For conception to occur it is necessary for the ovary to produce an ovum and for viable, motile sperm to be deposited near the cervix. The reproductive tract of the female must permit free passage of the sperm and ovum. For further development to occur, implantation of the fertilized ovum must take place in a suitable uterine endometrium. The deposition of sperm depends on adequate production of sperm and seminal fluid and a patent delivery system. Failure in meeting any of these conditions or failure of the pituitary to secrete gonadotropic hormones or of the gonads to respond to the pituitary stimulus can cause infertility. Fig. 15-1 illustrates the points at which normal fertility in the male and female can be impaired.

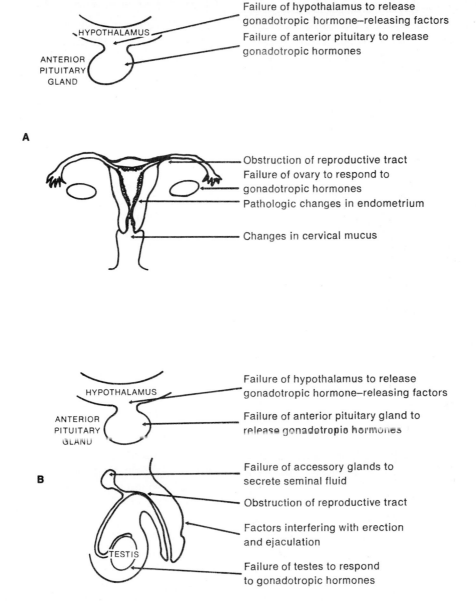

Fig. 15-1. Causes of infertility in female, **A,** and male, **B.**
(Adapted from Roddie IC and Wallace FM: The physiology of disease, London, 1975, Lloyd-Luke [Medical Books] Ltd.)

Mechanical obstruction within the female reproductive tract is the most common cause of female infertility. Obstruction may be the result of inflammatory changes following infection within the reproductive system. This mechanism is responsible for female infertility after an untreated gonorrheal infection. The development of scar tissue and adhesions in the peritoneal cavity as a result of surgical procedures or a peritoneal inflammatory reaction may also cause obstruction of the female reproductive tract. This mechanism accounts for the infertility that often accompanies endometriosis. Other causes of female infertility include alterations in the cervical mucus that may prevent penetration by the sperm, pathologic changes in the endometrium that may prevent implantation, and immunologic reactions to sperm. Approximately 15% of all cases of female infertility are the result of hormonal failure: failure of the pituitary to release gonadotropic hormones or failure of the ovary to respond to them. Examples of these conditions are discussed in Chapter 8.

Spermatogenesis will be impaired by lack of gonadotropic hormones or failure of the testes to descend into the scrotum, since the increased abdominal temperature inhibits sperm production. Damage to the prostate gland and seminiferous vesicles may reduce the volume and alter the composition of seminal fluid. Changes in the seminal fluid will impair the motility of the sperm. The motility of sperm is also affected in a disorder known as immotile cilia syndrome. Sperm are immotile due to structural defects in the tail. This is a congenital disorder of ciliary motility (Center and McFadden, 1985). Inflammatory damage to the seminiferous tubules may occur as a complication of mumps, as well as other infectious processes. Failure to attain an erection and ejaculate is an obvious cause of male infertility. Control of these functions is provided by both psychologic and neurologic factors.

Treatment for infertility depends on the cause. Obstruction may be relieved by various surgical procedures. Ovulation may be induced by hormonal therapy. Hormonal therapy to stimulate spermatogenesis has been tried but has not proved to be very successful.

Disorders of lactation

Female breast development at puberty is the result of the action of estrogen, which stimulates development of the ducts, and progesterone, which stimulates alveolar growth. Prolactin influences the secretion of these hormones and thus promotes breast development. Galactorrhea, or milk production, normally occurs in the female following pregnancy. Galactorrhea in nonparturitional females and in males is abnormal and is inevitably accompanied by increased prolactin secretion. Galactorrhea is frequently associated with a pituitary tumor, although it may accompany endocrine disorders and the administration of certain drugs (L-dopa, rauwolfia, alkaloids, tranquilizers, antidepressants).

During pregnancy the breasts enlarge and develop in response to placental hormones. Milk production is enhanced by suckling, which produces neural stimuli that promote prolactin secretion. The absence of lactation after pregnancy is characteristic of Sheehan's syndrome or pituitary necrosis following delivery. Other disorders which may be experienced include engorgement and infection.

Engorgement. Congestion of the venous and lymphatic system of the breast is a normal precurser of lactation. Exaggeration of this state leads to breast engorgement during the first week postpartum. Moderately severe engorgement results in firm, warm breasts. The lobules of the breast are palpable as tender, irregular masses. Considerable pain and a transient temperature elevation can be present. Frequent, round-the-clock demand feedings, breast support, and massage will alleviate the condition in a few days.

Mastitis. Inflammation of the breast parenchyma occurs most often in primiparous nursing patients. Infection is usually caused by coagulase-positive *Staphylococcus aureus* and may be limited to the subareolar region or may involve an obstructed lactiferous duct and surrounding parenchyma.

The source of the staphylococcus is almost always the nursing infant's mouth and throat, secondary to contamination by nursery personnel. During nursing, the organism enters the breast through the nipple at a site of a fissure or abrasion. Inflammation, pain, and fever result. Pitting edema and fluctuation over the inflamed area are evidence of abscess formation. Continuing breast-feeding is not recommended in the presence of a breast abscess. Appropriate antibiotic therapy and possible surgical incision and drainage of the abscess may be required (Ogle and Alfano, 1987).

Gynecomastia

Gynecomastia, or enlargement of the male breast, is a normal and transitory finding in approximately half of all normal males at puberty. Gynecomastia in the male adolescent must be evaluated in terms of whether development of secondary sex characteristics is also occurring, since puberty is a time when gonadal dysfunction and disorders of sexual differentiation become apparent. Klinefelter's syndrome is a disorder of sexual differentiation in which gynecomastia may occur; the gynecomastia that accompanies this syndrome is usually more severe than that seen in normal males. There is a high correlation between the occurrence of male breast cancer and Klinefelter's syndrome.

Gynecomastia may also occur secondary to testicular tumors. It often accompanies liver disease and is thought to be related to the lack of inactivation of estrogen, which occurs as a result of liver dysfunction. Gynecomastia may be a manifestation of an endocrine disorder or may occur as a side effect to therapy with certain drugs. These drugs include digitalis, steroids, androgens, psychotropics, spironolactone, phenothiazine, and marijuana. Gynecomastia may also occur as an idiopathic disorder.

DISEASE MODEL: ENDOMETRIOSIS

Endometriosis demonstrates some of the manifestations just described, such as pain and abnormal bleeding. Endometriosis is a disease in which endometrial-like tissue, which represents a type of abnormal cellular proliferation, is found in locations other than the uterine lining. While the exact incidence is unknown, it is estimated to be present in 10% to 20% of women of reproductive age, with the incidence doubling to 30% to 40% in infertile women. The ectopic lesions are most frequently found on the peritoneal surfaces of the reproductive organs and surrounding pelvic structures; however, they can occur anywhere in the body (Bayer and Seibel, 1986).

While a number of theories have attempted to explain the cause of endometriosis, none have been able to account for all aspects of the disease (Houston, 1984). When the disease was first described as a clinical entity in the 1920s, the theory of *retrograde menstruation* proposed that viable endometrial cells passed through the fallopian tubes during menstruation. Once in the pelvic cavity, these cells implanted and grew into endometriotic lesions. While this theory explains the occurrence of lesions on adjacent structures within the pelvic cavity, it does not explain the presence of endometriotic lesions in lung, brain, and other soft tissues, in nonmenstruating women, or in men.

Other theories have tried to explain widespread endometriosis via lymphatic or hematogenic routes. The theory of *coelomic metaplasia* suggests that, since both endometrium and peritoneum are derived from the same embryonic tissue, peritoneum undergoes transformation into endometrial tissue under the influence of a stimulus such as cyclic ovarian hormones. These theories, however, cannot explain why all individuals are not affected.

The immune system has been implicated in the disease. A deficiency in cellular immunity would allow menstrual tissue to implant and grow outside the uterus. While genetic relationships seem to exist, as shown by an increased incidence of endometriosis in first-degree female relations of patients, there has been no success in linking endometriosis with a particular HLA antigen.

The association of endometriosis with particular social and personality characteristics (education, intelligence, ambition, anxiety) has not been validated. As surgical diagnosis through laparoscopy increases, the association with such variables decreases. However, the trend to postpone pregnancy until later in life does seem to increase the degree of pathology as endometrial implants are allowed to increase.

Early endometrial implants appear as red, petechial patches that grow into dark brown, black, or blue lesions as menstrual-like debris collects. The surrounding area becomes thickened and scarred with a typical "powder burn" appearance. As the disease progresses, the number and size of lesions increase (Marrp and Vargyas, 1985).

Lesions on the ovary are known as endometriomas or "chocolate cysts" because of the dark brown syrupy contents that remain after the liquid part of the blood is reabsorbed. These cysts may undergo atrophy and fibrosis or may rupture, releasing blood into the peritoneal cavity. The resulting inflammation causes scar tissue and adhesion formation. Rupture of an endometrioma that causes severe bleeding constitutes an emergency situation. Severe disease can distort surrounding organs.

Endometriosis is often associated with pelvic pain, abnormal bleeding, and infertility (Brosens et al., 1986). The severity of the pathology is not, however, always reflected in the severity of the symptoms, and many women with severe disease may be asymptomatic. The mechanisms by which endometriosis causes pelvic pain and infertility are not well documented. Premenstrual pain is thought to be the result of estrogen and progesterone stimulation. Implants enlarge, undergo secretory change, and bleed, but fibrotic tissue around lesions prevents the escape of fluid. Pain is the result of pressure and inflammation. This rationale cannot explain the absence of symptoms in patients with severe pathology.

The relationship of moderate and severe endometriosis to infertility can be explained by the presence of pelvic adhesions that distort anatomic relationships and encase the ovary. Mild endometriosis with little or no anatomic pathology can also result in infertility. Disorders of folliculogenesis and ovulation have been suggested as well as immunologic factors.

Current methods of treatment include pseudopregnancy, pseudomenopause, and surgery (Schneider et al., 1986). High constant levels of estrogen and progesterone, as occurs during pregnancy, have been shown to cause implants to undergo a decidual reaction with fibrosis and necrosis. Pseudopregnancy hormonal regimens involve either constant daily administration of estrogen or progesterone or of an estrogen-progesterone combination oral contraceptive in sufficient doses to eliminate cyclic bleeding. Pelvic pain is usually relieved, but pregnancy rates are lower than after other therapies.

Because endometriosis regresses after surgical castration or menopause, pseudomenopause therapy attempts to reduce estrogen and progesterone stimulation of endometrial implants. Two regimens currently are used: danazol, a mild androgenic compound, and gonadotropin-releasing hormone agonists (GnRHA). Danazol binds to androgen steroid receptors, displaces naturally occurring testosterone and inhibits steroidogenic enzymes in the ovary. Endometrial implant growth is therefore inhibited. Menopausal and androgenic side effects result, which can be a source of discomfort and concern for the patient. GnRHA cause a down-regulation of pituitary gonadotropin receptors and decreases gonadotropin production. Menopausal but no androgenic effects result.

Surgical treatment involves removal of implants or adhesions and reconstruction of anatomic pathology. In severe cases, relief from pain may necessitate hysterectomy and oophorectomy.

Successful management may require use of more than one treatment or repeating treatments. Choice of treatment regimen must take into consideration severity of symptoms, age of the patient, contraindications to certain hormone protocols, and desire for future fertility and childbearing.

MECHANISMS OF REPRODUCTIVE DYSFUNCTION

Reproductive dysfunction can cause a lack of maternal adaptation to pregnancy, disruption of normal fetal growth and maturation, and difficult parturition. Many pathologic processes may develop during the reproductive period that will evoke these conditions. Those processes most commonly encountered in the clinical setting and the role of preexisting maternal disease states in evoking these conditions are discussed in this chapter.

Lack of maternal adaptation to pregnancy

Normally during pregnancy the mother's body adapts to the growing fetus in order to meet its needs as well as her own. This adaptation involves complex physiologic changes in nearly every system of her body. Occasionally a pathophysiologic process develops that prevents complete adaptation of the mother to the new physiologic state of pregnancy. The course of the pregnancy or the life of the mother may be seriously jeopardized, or the symptoms may evoke only minor discomfort. Pathophysiologic conditions that impair maternal adaptation to pregnancy include hyperemesis gravidarum, hypertension, and polyhydramnios. The conditions of abruptio placentae and placenta previa are discussed earlier in this chapter.

Hyperemesis gravidarum. This condition is characterized by excessive nausea or vomiting that may cause severe fluid and electrolyte abnormalities in the pregnant woman. A moderate degree of nausea and vomiting is often experienced by otherwise normal women during the first trimester of pregnancy. The etiology of the nausea and vomiting of pregnancy is unclear but may be related to the presence of chorionic gonadotropin, since the incidence of nausea and vomiting is higher during the periods of pregnancy when the secretion of this hormone normally peaks and in cases of hydatidiform mole in which levels of this hormone remain high.

Uncomplicated nausea and vomiting of pregnancy is usually limited to the first 14 to 16 weeks of the pregnancy and is not accompanied by signs of impaired nutritional status. In contrast, hyperemesis gravidarum is a condition in which the excessive nausea and vomiting is accompanied by impaired nutritional status with altered fluid volume and composition, a

5% or greater reduction in body weight, and more severe signs of potassium loss, dehydration, and ketosis. Endocrine, allergic, metabolic, and neurotic/psychosomatic factors have been proposed as possible etiologic factors in hyperemesis gravidarum. In many cases the psychogenic component may be a major factor.

Other causes of nausea and vomiting, including gastroenteritis, cholecystitis, and pyelonephritis, must also be ruled out in the pregnant woman. Treatment is aimed at restoration of normal fluid and electrolyte levels, improved nutritional status, and control of the nausea and vomiting. Antiemetic drugs may be used with caution as to possible effects on the fetus. Provision of psychologic support should be included in the treatment plan when indicated as well.

Hypertensive disorders. Normal pregnancy causes major changes in hemodynamic and renal function. These changes include an increase in body fluid volume related to increased sodium and water retention, a decrease in systemic blood pressure related to decreased peripheral vascular resistance, and an increase in cardiac output that is related to the increased fluid volume and, in turn, increases renal blood flow and GFR. The decrease in total peripheral vascular resistance is due to impaired responsiveness to vasopressor substances and to the uterine vasculature acting as a low-resistance shunt (Rose, 1987). Vasopressor resistance appears to be related to the enhanced production of vasodilator prostaglandins, most notably, prostaglandin E (PGE_2) and prostacyclin. Sodium and water retention is probably a response to the increased vasodilation and relative hypotension that occur.

Further hemodynamic alterations are able to cause profound disruptions in tissue perfusion and body fluid homeostasis. Hypertensive disorders remain a significant cause of maternal and perinatal morbidity and mortality. In the past the phrase "toxemia of pregnancy" was used to identify such disorders; however, no toxin has ever been identified or implicated in the pathogenesis of these disorders.

Hypertensive disorders that can complicate an otherwise normal pregnancy are classified according to the following scheme*:
  I. Pregnancy-induced hypertension
    A. Preeclampsia
    B. Eclampsia
 II. Chronic hypertension (preceding pregnancy)
III. Chronic hypertension with superimposed pregnancy–induced hypertension
    A. Superimposed preeclampsia
    B. Superimposed eclampsia
 IV. Transient hypertension

Chronic hypertension refers to the presence of persistent blood pressure elevation before the 20th week of gestation. Pregnancy-induced hypertension appears after the 20th week of gestation, and when this is accompanied by proteinuria it is designated as either preeclampsia or superimposed preeclampsia. If convulsions develop, it is designated as eclampsia or superimposed eclampsia.

Preeclampsia and eclampsia must be differentiated from gestational hypertension, which is the relatively late (third trimester) appearance of hypertension without any evidence of proteinuria or any other signs of preeclampsia and no pre-

---

*From Gant N and Worley R: Hypertension in pregnancy: concepts and management, New York, 1980, Appleton-Century-Crofts.

vious history of hypertension. Since hypertension precedes the appearance of proteinuria, these women must be monitored closely for the development of preeclampsia, and the diagnosis of transient or gestational hypertension can be made safely only after delivery. Some of these patients may develop hypertension at some point in the future, especially if the blood pressure remains elevated by the tenth day postpartum (Rose, 1987).

Preeclampsia is defined as a combination of hypertension, proteinuria, and edema during the second half of pregnancy. From 5% to 8% of pregnant women develop preeclampsia (Farrell, 1986). Hypertension is determined by a 15 mm Hg increase in the diastolic and a 30 mm Hg increase in the systolic blood pressure above normal or a systolic pressure of 140 plus a diastolic pressure of at least 90. An acute weight gain or severe edema indicating the retention of fluid suggests the development of preeclampsia.

Eclampsia is defined as preeclampsia plus the occurrence of one or more convulsions. Five percent of the patients who develop preeclampsia will progress to eclampsia (Farrell, 1986). While most will demonstrate manifestations of severe preeclampsia before the onset of seizures, approximately 25% will only have mild preeclampsia, and some will develop seizures without warning signs or symptoms. Seizures most often occur before labor begins but may also occur during labor or within 24 hours after delivery (Schrier, 1986).

Preeclampsia and eclampsia occur most often in a first pregnancy. They may occur in subsequent pregnancies but usually only if a predisposing factor such as chronic vascular disease or diabetes mellitus is present. Multiple fetuses, diabetes mellitus, placental disorders, and dietary deficiencies are predisposing factors to the development of preeclampsia and eclampsia. Social and environmental factors such as poverty, lack of sanitation, lack of prenatal care, and poor health and dietary practices predispose the pregnant woman to the development of preeclampsia. Pregnant teenagers are also more likely to develop preeclampsia. A familial predisposition is also suspect, as it has been observed that daughters and granddaughters of women with eclampsia more often develop preeclampsia.

Clinical manifestations. The usual sequence of events in the development of preeclampsia is rapid weight gain followed by an increase in blood pressure and subsequently proteinuria. Other signs and symptoms depend on the severity of the condition. Signs and symptoms of severe preeclampsia are listed in Table 15-3. Cerebral edema may cause headache and visual disturbances ranging from blurring of vision to blindness in the more severe

Table 15-3. Clinical and laboratory features of severe preeclampsia

Blood pressure greater than 160 mm Hg systolic or greater than 110 mm Hg diastolic or an increase of greater than 60 mm Hg systolic or greater than 30 mm Hg diastolic over baseline levels
Proteinuria greater than 5 gm/24 hr or 3-4* by dipstick
Oliguria (less than 400 ml/24 hr)
Cerebral or visual disturbances, i.e., lethargy, headache, scotomata, blurred vision
Extreme hyperreflexia or clonus
Epigastric or right upper quadrant pain
Abnormal liver function tests
Hemoconcentration
Pulmonary edema
Thrombocytopenia
Microangiopathic hemolysis; disseminated intravascular coagulation (DIC)

From Feinberg LE: Hypertension and preeclampsia. In Abrams RS and Wexler P, editors: Medical care of the pregnant patient, Boston, 1983, Little, Brown and Co.

case. A severe, generalized headache often precedes the onset of convulsions. The deep tendon reflexes may be hyperactive. Epigastric pain and vomiting may occur. The epigastric pain results from hepatomegaly and is considered to be a very serious symptom.

An atypical form of pregnancy-induced hypertension called HELLP syndrome is seen in about 10% of patients with severe preeclampsia/eclampsia. This group of patients have relatively normal early pregnancies. During the second and third trimester, however, they develop epigastric or right upper quadrant pain. Viral symptoms, nausea, and vomiting might also be present. There is no elevation of blood pressure at this time. Laboratory findings usually show hemolysis (H), elevated liver enzymes (EL), and low platelets (LP). Symptoms may result in an incorrect diagnosis of gallbladder disease, viral hepatitis, idiopathic thrombocytopenic purpura, or peptic ulcer. Patients need to be managed as though they have severe preeclampsia (Weinstein, 1982).

Glomerular function is also adversely affected. The glomerular lesions (Fig. 15-2) are a characteristic and constant pathologic finding in preeclampsia. These lesions are reversible and are thought to be responsible for the reduced glomerular filtration rate (GFR), reduced renal blood flow, and loss of protein in the urine. The rate of protein excretion is variable but may approach that seen in the nephrotic syndrome. In fact, preeclampsia is the most common cause of nephrotic syndrome in pregnancy (Schrier, 1986). Sodium and water retention occurs in response to the decreased GFR and increased secretion of ADH, aldosterone, and corticosteroids. Renal failure may develop.

An abnormal responsiveness to vasopressor agents such as angiotensin, norepinephrine, and vasopressin has been observed in women who develop preeclampsia. Under normal conditions, the vascular system of the pregnant woman is relatively resistant to the vasopressor effects of these agents. Research has also demonstrated a rise in diastolic blood pressure upon assumption of the supine position in women who show an exaggerated pressor response (Rose, 1987). The value of this finding as a predictive sign of women in whom pregnancy-induced hypertension is most likely to develop is still being debated. Plasma renin activity and the plasma concentrations of renin substrate and angiotensin are elevated in normal pregnancy, and findings in preeclamptic women are similar.

Maternal death may result from cerebral hemorrhage, acute cardiac failure with pulmonary edema, or hepatic failure. Intravascular platelet thrombi with perivascular hemorrhages have been found in the brain at autopsy. Women with severe preeclampsia and eclampsia are at risk for development of disseminated intravascular coagulation as well (see Chapter 3). Possible maternal complications due to severe preeclampsia are listed in Table 15-4. Chronic fetal distress with intrauterine growth retardation and acute fetal distress may develop as uterine blood flow is decreased in preeclampsia.

Pathogenesis. There is controversy concerning the exact etiology and pathogenesis of preeclampsia. Theories of uterine ischemia, increased vascular reactivity, hypovolemic compensation, and protein-poor diets have been proposed to explain the pathogenesis of eclampsia. The uterine ischemia theory was first proposed in 1939; hypertension results when uterine ischemia is induced in a variety of animals. Additionally, preeclampsia occurs in patients who have diseases more likely to

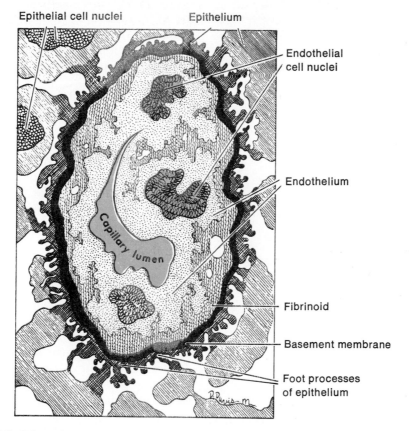

Fig. 15-2. Schematic representation of electron micrograph showing renal glomerular capillary in woman with preeclampsia. Note swelling of endothelial cells and greatly narrowed lumen but normal basement membrane.

(From Sandberg E: Synopsis of obstetrics, ed 10, St. Louis, 1978, The CV Mosby Co.)

be accompanied by decreased placental perfusion (Rose, 1987). Fig. 15-3 presents a possible sequence of events that may constitute a vicious cycle when initiated by ischemia.

Other theories have also been proposed. It was pointed out previously that pregnant women who develop preeclampsia demonstrate an abnormal responsiveness to vasopressor agents such as angiotensin II. This is hypothesized to be related to another difference between the normal and preeclamptic pregnant patient. It appears that the production of prostacyclin in the

preeclamptic patient is less than the increased production seen in normal pregnant patients. Fitzgerald et al. (1987) found an increase in prostacyclin synthesis across four groups that represented normotensive, chronically hypertensive, hypertensive during labor, and pregnancy-induced hypertensive patient types. The latter group, however, displayed a lesser increment of increased synthesis that persisted throughout the pregnancy. Decreased vasodilator synthesis would allow the abnormal responsiveness to pressors as well as promote uterine ischemia

Table 15-4. Maternal consequences of severe preeclampsia

Central nervous system complications
  Eclampsia
    Seizures
    Encephalopathy and coma
    Psychosis, self-limited
  Cerebral hemorrhage
Cardiopulmonary complications
  Pulmonary edema
    Usually noncardiogenic
    Left ventricular failure possible
    Potential for superimposed bacterial or aspiration
      pneumonia
  Pleural, pericardial effusions; ascites
  Cardiovascular collapse (shock)
    Rare complication within first 24 hr postpartum
    Possible contributing role of diuretic therapy and
      unappreciated degree of hemorrhage, fluid loss
Renal disease (major manifestations)
  Acute renal failure
  Nephrotic syndrome
Abruptio placentae
Hematologic complications
  Thrombocytopenia
  Microangiopathic hemolysis
  DIC
Liver disease
  Mild functional abnormalities
  Subcapsular hemorrhage with pain (rare hepatic rupture)
Retinal detachment

DIC = disseminated intravascular coagulation.
From Feinberg LE: Hypertension and preeclampsia. In Abrams RS and Wexler P, editors: Medical care of the pregnant patient. Boston, 1983, Little, Brown, and Co.

through the vasoconstriction that would result (Schrier, 1986). Thromboxane B_2, which is a vasoconstrictor and platelet aggregator, has also been found to be increased in preeclampsia, and since its actions are directly opposite those of prostacyclin, the relative changes in these two substances may also be important in the pathogenesis of preeclampsia (Rose, 1987). Activation of the coagulation pathway is also suspect, as fibrin deposition occurs in the kidneys and other organs and thromboxane may also play a role in this pathology. A possible interactive role for these mechanisms in the pathogenesis of preeclampsia is outlined in Fig. 15-4.

Another possibility is that some kind of immune response is occurring. It has been determined that the risk of developing preeclampsia is greater in the first pregnancy than in subsequent pregnancies with the same father. A subsequent pregnancy that is the first with a new father carries an increased risk of developing preeclampsia. Speculation is that antibodies, which could block a response to paternal antigens in placental tissue, have not been developed because of lack of exposure (Rose, 1987).

Treatment. There is some question whether or not the development of preeclampsia can be completely prevented, although maintenance of maternal health during pregnancy through appropriate prenatal care may reduce the risk of its developing. There are indications that a high-protein, vitamin-supplemented diet in which excessive Na^+ intake is avoided may contribute to a reduced incidence of preeclampsia in high-risk patients. The progression of preeclampsia to eclampsia can be prevented through good prenatal care, early assessment, and close monitoring of pregnant patients who are at risk for this condition. Early detection and treatment can prevent progression to the stage where maternal and fetal well-being are seriously jeopardized.

The objectives of treatment of preeclampsia include prevention of convulsions and delivery of a healthy infant. Treatment includes strict bed rest and mild sedation in less severe cases. Antihypertensive drugs may be used if the hypertension is severe. Magnesium sulfate is used to prevent and control convulsions

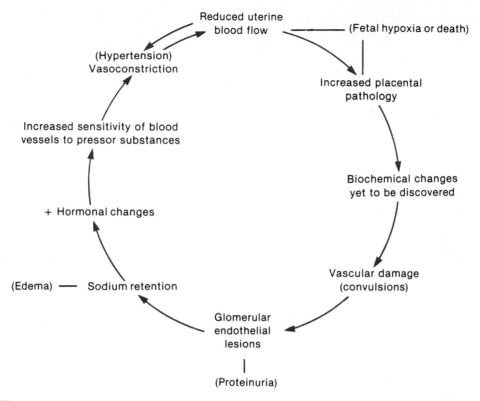

Fig. 15-3. A concept of the sequence of events that may constitute a vicious cycle in the pathogenesis of preeclampsia and eclampsia.

(From Page E and Villee D: Human reproduction: Essentials of reproductive and perinatal medicine, Philadelphia, 1981, WB Saunders Co.)

(Pritchard, 1979). If the preeclampsia is severe or eclampsia occurs, immediate delivery of the baby, either by induction of labor or cesarean section, is indicated. Termination of the pregnancy is the only "cure." Because these conditions develop in the later stages of pregnancy, the risks of premature delivery are somewhat lessened but remain a consideration. If preeclampsia develops during the first half or prior to the twenty-fourth week of pregnancy, a hydatidiform mole is the more probable cause and treatment of that condition (discussed earlier in this chapter) is indicated.

The following case study illustrates the manifestations and typical clinical course of patients who experience pregnancy-induced hypertension. With appropriate and timely intervention the outcome can be positive as it was for this patient.

CASE STUDY: PREGNANCY-INDUCED HYPERTENSION

Objective and Subjective Data

TJ is a 17-year-old single white female, gravida 1, para 0000, 34 weeks pregnant who was seen in the outpatient clinic this

Contributed by Sarah J. Naber.

morning at a regular prenatal visit. Her pregnancy has been followed in the public aid clinic since she registered at 12 weeks' gestation. The prenatal record indicates that her prepregnant weight was 120 pounds and her total weight gain has been 40 pounds with an 8-pound gain in the last 2 weeks. Her blood pressure was 110/70 on registration and remained fairly constant until 24 weeks' gestation when it rose to 125/80. Subsequently, the blood pressure readings were 130/80 at 28 weeks and 135/85 at 30 weeks. She has been seen every week since 30 weeks' gestation, and nutritional counseling to promote adequate protein, fiber, and fluid intake along with frequent rest periods in the left lateral recumbent position have been the main feature of the prenatal management plan. When she was seen by the nurse-midwife this morning, excessive weight gain, nondependent edema, 1+ proteinuria, and a blood pressure of 145/90 were documented. Upon consultation with the clinic obstetrician, a decision to admit TJ to the hospital for medical management was made.

Present illness: TJ was admitted to the high-risk antepartum unit for monitoring of her pregnancy and the superimposed hypertensive state. The initial nursing assessment revealed the following:

General appearance: lying quietly on her back, in no obvious distress.

Vital signs
   Temperature: 98.6°
   Pulse: 88
   Respirations: 22
   Blood pressure (supine): 140/90

HEENT-perrla: no A/V notching

Cardiovascular: normal heart sounds

Abdomen: uterine fundus 33 cm above the symphysis pubis, estimated
   Fetal weight 4½ pounds
   Fetal heart rate 144, heard loudest in the LLQ
   Fetal movements felt by examiner

Neurologic: alert, oriented, DTRs 2+ bilaterally , no ankle clonus

Urine dipstick. 0-1 + protein

TJ told the nurse that her mother also had problems with her blood pressure during her first pregnancy.

Treatment

Bedrest was ordered immediately, and TJ was advised to lie in a lateral position. Blood was drawn for BUN, alkaline phosphatase, SGOT, and hematocrit/hemoglobin determinations. Vital signs were ordered to be checked every 4 hours. An external electronic fetal monitor (EFM) was applied, and a 30-minute strip was run. All of the blood tests and the fetal monitor strip were within normal limits.

Twenty-four hours later, TJ was complaining of a moderate headache and her blood pressure was 150/95. The urine protein was 2+ by dipstick. Repeat BUN, alkaline phosphatase, and SGOT determinations revealed elevated values at this time. The EFM strip was normal. The DTRs were now 3+. A decision was made to start intravenous magnesium sulfate therapy.

Twelve hours later, TJ's clinical condition had not stabilized. Her blood pressure was 155/100, and DTRs were still brisk with two beats for ankle clonus. She was complaining of blurred vision along with persistent headache and upper abdominal pain. Decreased fetal heart rate variability was noted on the EFM strip. A cesarean section was performed on an emergency basis, and a 4-pound, 12-ounce male, Apgar scores 8 and 9, was delivered.

Discussion

TJ was hospitalized with moderate pregnancy-induced hypertension (PIH). Onset of symptoms of PIH occurs after the 20th week of pregnancy with excessive weight gain typically being the first indication of the presence of the disorder. Blood pressure elevation indicated the condition was worsening, and when protein was detected in the urine, the classic triad of symptoms of PIH was present.

The cause of PIH remains obscure. TJ, however, was at higher than usual risk for the disorder in that she is a young primigravida in a lower socioeconomic group. Nutritional deficiencies are much more common in poor teenagers, and protein and calorie deficiencies have been linked to the development of PIH, although the roles of calcium, iron, and vitamin deficiencies, as well as inadequate lipid utilization, have been investigated. The fact that TJ's mother may have had PIH is important to note in that a genetic basis for development of the condition may exist; several studies have shown a high correlation between mothers and daughters who experienced PIH.

Upon admission to the hospital, blood studies of TJ's renal and hepatic functioning were done. Electronic fetal monitoring was done to determine the condition of the fetoplacental unit. Deep tendon reflexes (DTR) were tested to determine CNS status. In PIH an increased vascular sensitivity to angiotensin II develops and blood vessel spasms occur. Constriction of the blood vessels impedes blood flow, and the rise in blood pressure serves to offset the decreased circulation at first. As vasoconstriction persists, blood supply to all organs is impaired, and the placenta, kidneys, liver, and brain are especially affected. Increases in serum BUN, alkaline phosphatase, and SGOT and loss of fetal reactivity along with CNS hyperexcitability indicated that TJ's clinical condition was not responding to magnesium sulfate and rest therapy. When TJ additionally complained of visual blurring (due to retinal arteriolar spasms) and abdominal pain (due to liver distention) and ankle clonus (due to CNS irritability) appeared, the decision to terminate the pregnancy was made. If the disease process is allowed to progress, damage to the blood vessel wall linings occurs and blood clotting factors are deposited at the damaged sites. Thus there is a danger for the devel-opment of disseminated intravascular coagulation (DIC), and timely termination of pregnancy is important to interrupt the disease process.

Both TJ and her baby had satisfactory clinical courses following the cesarean delivery. Twenty-four hours after surgery, TJ's blood pressure was 130/80 and at 48 hours it was 120/75. Her neurologic irritability had disappeared, and there had been a 20-pound weight loss associated with a diuresis in the first 72 hours following delivery.

Nursing Diagnoses

Major nursing diagnoses during the acute PIH episode would include:
1. Altered (renal, hepatic, cerebral and fetoplacental) tissue perfusion
2. Sensory/perceptual, alterations (visual and kinesthetic)
3. Pain
4. Altered family processes related to situational transition and/or crisis

Major diagnoses related to early postpartum care for TJ would include:
1. Pain
2. Potential altered parenting related to prematurity
3. Potential altered family processes related to developmental transition and/or crisis

Hydramnios. Hydramnios, or polyhydramnios, refers to an excessive quantity of amniotic fluid. Hydramnios presents a serious threat to the viability of the fetus, as the incidence of prematurity in cases of hydramnios is twice the overall rate. Fetal malformation accompanies 20% of all cases of hydramnios. Hydramnios is present in nearly all cases of esophageal atresia and in approximately one half the cases of anencephalus.

The effects of hydramnios on the mother

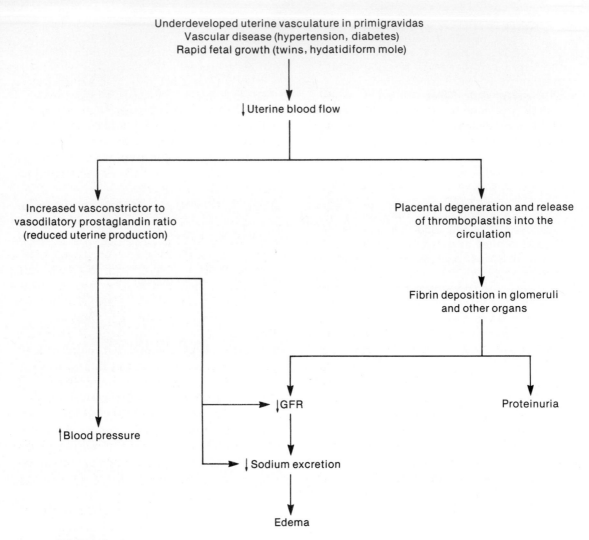

Fig. 15-4. Proposed model of pathogenesis of preeclampsia demonstrating interaction between different proposed mechanisms.
(From Rose BD: Pathophysiology of renal disease, ed 2, New York, 1987, McGraw-Hill Book Co.)

range from discomfort and difficult breathing due to the extreme size of the abdomen to such serious complications as abruptio placentae, postpartum hemorrhage, and uterine dysfunction. Compression of the major veins by the grossly expanded uterus can cause edema of the lower extremities and vulva. The mother usually tolerates hydramnios better if it develops slowly. Rapidly developing hydramnios can cause severe pain and intense dyspnea.

Tenseness of the uterine wall can make palpation of the fetus difficult if not impossible. Difficulty in eliciting fetal heart tones because of the excess fluid and obvious uterine enlargement are other characteristic signs. When hydramnios is diagnosed, further examinations by roent-genogram and ultrasound should be made to determine the presence of multiple fetuses or fetal abnormalities.

The mechanisms that cause this condition may be associated with the fetus's ability to swallow and inspire amniotic fluid and to urinate. Observations regarding the occurrence of abnormal amounts of amniotic fluid with certain types of fetal malformations tend to support this idea. Fetal malformations in which the ability to swallow is impaired are almost always accompanied by hydramnios, while fetal malformations that cause anuria are almost always accompanied by *oligohydramnios*, in which the amount of amniotic fluid is decreased.

Other conditions. Other conditions that may occur and that indicate or precipitate lack of maternal adaptation to pregnancy include anemia, diabetes, and antepartal fetal death. Acquired anemias are caused either by underproduction or by increased loss of red blood cells (see Chapter 3). Presence of an hereditary hemoglobinopathy can seriously complicate pregnancy as well.

Diabetes mellitus requiring insulin administration is the most frequent metabolic disorder of pregnancy. Gestation complicated by diabetes is a complex metabolic state combining the dynamic changes of pregnancy with the alterations of carbohydrate metabolism characteristic of diabetes mellitus.

Maternal insulin does not cross the placental barrier and so does not significantly regulate placental glucose uptake or transport. In the first few weeks of pregnancy, increased levels of estrogen and progesterone result in increased insulin secretion and tissue sensitivity to insulin. These initial changes are anabolic in nature and result in increased storage of tissue glycogen, lowered hepatic glucose production,

and increased peripheral glucose utilization. Fasting blood glucose levels are lowered by 5% to 10% by 10 weeks' gestation. Blood glucose levels remain lower as pregnancy continues, and the lowest fasting blood glucose level is usually seen in the third trimester. Increasing human placental lactogen secretion, free cortisol levels, and glucagon levels in the last half of pregnancy result in the further lowering of fasting blood glucose levels.

Type I diabetic women experience a state of increased starvation ketosis during the early weeks of pregnancy. This is characterized by early morning ketosis and frequent episodes of hypoglycemia as a result of increased sensitivity to previously stable insulin dosages. As the pregnancy continues, however, insulin need increases.

Pregnant women with type II diabetes may suffer insulinopenia from pancreatic beta cell exhaustion. In many cases, however, they may actually have increased levels of circulating insulin but be experiencing functional insulin resistance. Type II diabetic women usually do not have the same significant decreases in fasting blood glucose levels as type I diabetic women experience and, therefore, usually experience less hypoglycemia (Service, 1986).

Fat metabolism in the early months of normal pregnancy is characterized by fat storage, decreased lipolysis, and fat cell hyperplasia. By the middle of pregnancy, increasing levels of hPL result in increased lipolysis and increased free fatty acids with a tendency to ketosis during fasting periods. Plasma cholesterol and triglycerides increase as pregnancy continues. The insulin-dependent pregnant woman is at increased risk for severe ketosis and metabolic acidosis and must receive adequate insulin (Hollingsworth, 1985).

The placenta receives most of its energy from glucose, which diffuses across the placental membrane in direct relationship to maternal glucose levels. Carbohydrate supply to the fetus is also probably increased by aerobic lactate productivity of the placenta. High fetal glucose levels result in increased fetal insulin production with resulting increased fetal somatic growth.

Management of diabetic women during pregnancy is aimed at achieving a metabolic environment that is normal for pregnancy. Frequent monitoring of blood glucose levels, titration of insulin, and careful prenatal care are essential.

Women who experience abnormal carbohydrate metabolism as demonstrated by a 2-hour postprandial glucose level greater than 120 mg/dl are diagnosed as having pregnancy-induced glucose intolerance (Schneider and Curet, 1982). This term is recommended over the more common term of gestational diabetes because it emphasizes that the glucose intolerance is limited to pregnancy and may be managed by diet.

In approximately half the cases of antepartal fetal death the cause is uncertain. Established causes include congenital abnormalities, hypertensive disorders, chronic disease in the mother, erythroblastosis fetalis, and fetal infections. Antepartal fetal death is suspected when previously felt fetal movements cease, when uterine growth is less than expected or stops, and when fetal heart tones cannot be auscultated. If spontaneous labor and delivery do not occur within a month, the chances of maternal coagulopathy developing increase and induction of labor is indicated.

Alterations in normal fetal growth and maturation

Intrauterine growth and development result from both genetic and environmental factors. Standards for normal fetal growth and development consider birth weight, length, head circumference, and gestational age. Abnormal fetal growth is now determined by percentile ranking. Small for gestational age (SGA) infants are in the 10th percentile or below for their gestational age and are sometimes referred to as growth-retarded infants. Large for gestational age (LGA) infants are in the 90th percentile or above for their gestational age.

Term infants are born between 38 and 42 weeks after onset of the last maternal menstrual period. A preterm infant is born prior to 38 weeks' gestation. A postterm infant is born after 42 weeks or more gestation. Infants weighing greater than 4500 gm are of excessive size (macrosomia). Infants weighing less than 2500 gm are considered low birth weight infants. The premature infant is usually considered to be an infant of 1000 to 2500 gm with a gestational age of 28 to 38 weeks (Taylor and Pernoll, 1987).

A variety of mechanisms may be responsible for fetal growth retardation. The influence of maternal factors on fetal growth and development is discussed elsewhere in this chapter and in Chapter 4. Predisposing maternal factors for delivery of a low birth weight infant include smoking, poor nutrition, low socioeconomic status, age, coexistent chronic illness, infection, preeclampsia or eclampsia, and use of alcohol or other addicting drugs. Other factors that influence fetal growth are classified as either fetal or placental in origin. Included among the fetal factors are the presence of multiple fetuses, chromosome disorders, and chronic infection. A placental villitis of unknown etiology has been found in the placentas of fetuses in whom growth retardation was marked. Other placental factors include a small placenta or one in which the blood supply is interrupted.

A problem with fetal growth should be

suspected if during the latter half of pregnancy the mother fails to gain weight or the uterus is smaller than expected for the gestational age of the fetus. Death of the growth-retarded infant is most likely to occur during the last 2 to 3 weeks of pregnancy. The growth-retarded infant may tolerate labor and delivery very poorly, and preterm delivery is often indicated. In the absence of intrinsic disease the prognosis for these infants is generally good with rapid and steady weight gain following delivery.

The duration of pregnancy is normally 40 weeks from the first day of the last menstrual period, which allows enough time for full development of all the fetal tissues and organs. A shorter than normal gestational period causes incomplete structural and functional development of fetal organs and tissues. A longer than normal gestational period may also result in problems for the fetus.

Preterm infant. The preterm infant (or one who has experienced a shorter than normal gestation period) is suceptible to a variety of pathologic conditions because maturation of many of the body's organ systems and tissues is incomplete. Most significantly, respiratory function is compromised because of insufficient surfactant production. Idiopathic respiratory distress syndrome (IRDS) is characterized by atelectasis resulting in hypoventilation, hypoxemia, and acidosis (see Chapter 16).

Not only is the preterm infant susceptible to respiratory acidosis related to inadequate ventilatory function but also it is susceptible to development of metabolic acidosis because of an inability to excrete hydrogen ions and a decreased bicarbonate threshold in the kidneys. Capillary fragility may lead to pulmonary or cerebral hemorrhage. Red blood cells are more rapidly destroyed. Deficiencies of the fat-soluble vitamins may develop because of decreased absorption by an immature gastrointestinal tract. These infants are also prone to hypoglycemia and hypothermia. Hypoglycemia may develop as a result of the low glycogen stores present in these babies. Hypothermia may be the result of a combination of factors. There is minimal body fat in the preterm infant because of underdevelopment of brown adipose tissue. Lack of brown fat, inadequate glycogen reserves, and the relative inability to constrict surface vessels limit the preterm infant's ability to minimize heat loss. The preterm infant is also more susceptible to infection, since the immaturity of the immune system limits the infant's ability to mount an immune response. Necrotizing enterocolitis and persistent patent ductus arteriosus are other complications the preterm infant is more prone to develop.

Prior to birth, unconjugated bilirubin freely transfers across the placenta to the maternal circulation. Normally the liver conjugates bilirubin with glucuronic acid, which is synthesized from uridine disphosphoglucuronic acid in a reaction catalyzed by the enzyme glucuronyl transferase. Some studies have demonstrated a deficiency in both the enzyme and uridine diphosphoglucuronic acid in fetal livers of some mammals. Other substances are also conjugated with glucuronic acid and may compete with bilirubin for conjugation. An increased amount of unconjugated bilirubin in the blood is referred to as *hyperbilirubinemia* and can be observed clinically as jaundice. Unconjugated bilirubin can cause pathologic changes and degeneration of the basal ganglia in the brain, a condition referred to as *kernicterus*. The basal ganglia acquire a yellowish discoloration. Infants who survive demonstrate spasticity and incoordination.

Hyperbilirubinemia may be the result of

increased destruction of red blood cells due to a hemolytic disorder or of increased bleeding in difficult deliveries associated with oxytocin administration. The most common form of hyperbilirubinemia in the neonate is physiologic jaundice. In fully mature, normal infants, jaundice increases for 3 to 4 days after birth because of the following factors: an increased rate of red cell destruction, which is normal; a reduction in hepatic uptake of free bilirubin; a decreased rate of conjugation; and decreased bacteria-mediated conversion of bilirubin to urobilinogen in the intestine, which allows more excreted bilirubin to be absorbed from the gut.

Hyperbilirubinemia more commonly develops in the preterm infant because of the increased rate of red blood cell destruction as well as immaturity of the liver glucuronyl transferase system. The preterm infant is also susceptible to disorders that may further contribute to hyperbilirubinemia. Hypoxia and acidosis reduce the protein-bound bilirubin, while hypothermia and hypoglycemia increase elements that compete with bilirubin for binding sites. Both these mechanisms increase bilirubin toxicity and are more likely to be present in the premature infant. Consequently, physiologic jaundice is more severe and prolonged in these infants and they are more prone to develop kernicterus.

Phototherapy, or exposure to ultraviolet light, is used in the treatment of hyperbilirubinemia. Light increases peripheral blood flow, promotes excretion of bilirubin by the liver, and reduces absorption from the intestine because of shortened intestinal transit time. The exact mechanisms by which these effects occur are not completely clear.

Postmature infant. The effects of postmaturity on the infant are quite variable. Growth may continue, or it may stop, and the infant may actually have a reduced birth weight at the time of delivery. The increased incidence of stillbirths as pregnancy advances beyond term is now generally recognized.

The physical changes that typically appear in the postmature infant are thought to be related to placental insufficiency. The mildest changes include an abundance of scalp hair, long nails, reduced vernix, and loose wrinkled skin with desquamated epithelium. The appearance of these infants has been likened to that of an elderly person. Meconium staining of the fluid, skin, and vernix may indicate more severe fetal distress, and mortality during labor and delivery is likely to be higher in these infants than in those in whom only mild changes have occurred. Hypoglycemia is common. In the infant who has continued to grow, delivery may be difficult because of the large body size, and this infant will be more prone to sustain a birth injury; cesarean section should be considered.

Placental disorders. Even though the placenta is largely fetal in origin, it can be a reflection of maternal, as well as fetal, disease. Maternal diseases can affect the fetus by changing the quality or quantity of maternal blood (Perrin, 1984). Such alterations result in abnormalities that are nonspecific in their association with particular diseases. Maternal conditions such as hypertension and diabetes, which have been discussed previously, result in such nonspecific pathologic changes.

Placental infarction. Placental infarction is an area of ischemic necrosis of the placental villi resulting from obstruction of blood flow following thrombosis of a spiral artery. It is the placental lesion most readily associated with uteroplacental vascular disease. The lesion can occur in any cotyledon, but most commonly is found at the placental margin. When limited to this region, it is not associated with significant risk to the fetus. A fetus may survive infarction of 20% to 30% of the placenta if the remaining placenta continues to have adequate maternal blood supply.

Amniotic band syndrome. Amniotic band syndrome is the result of disrupted and dislocated amnion adhering to the surface of the fetus. These band or stringlike membrane segments appear to result from an amnion tear early in the pregnancy. These bands can produce constriction of developing limbs or other fetal parts and have been known to result in amputation.

Twin-twin transfusion syndrome. Nearly all twins with monochorionic placentas show an anastomosis between blood vessels of the two umbilical circulations. This anastomosis usually involves vessels in the placental surface and results in little pathology. When the communication involves deep arteriovenous vessels, a serious complication may result. Shared lobules of the placenta may be supplied by an umbilical artery from one twin and drained by an umbilical vein branch of the other twin. This occurs in 15% to 20% of monochorionic twins. The twin receiving the transfusion is plethoric and polycythemic and may develop cardiopathy. The other twin is pale and anemic and shows signs of intrauterine starvation (Knuppel and Goodlin, 1987).

Adherent placenta. Placenta accreta, the abnormal adherence of the placenta to the uterine wall, is believed to be the result of inadequate decidual formation by the uterine mucosa. Adherence may be partial or total. In rare instances the placenta may involve the myometrium (placenta increta) or even perforate the uterus (placenta percreta). Attempts to manually remove a placenta accreta results in

hemorrhage that may be severe enough to necessitate immediate hysterectomy (Rushton, 1984).

Abnormal parturition

The process of normal labor begins at approximately the 40th week of gestation, is characterized by progressive cervical dilation secondary to rhythmic uterine contractions and terminates with delivery of the baby and placenta within about 12 hours (Crawford, 1985). There is a decrease in progesterone level associated with the spontaneous onset of labor. A higher perceived intensity of in-labor pain and more emotional feelings toward pregnancy have been found to be correlated with factors such as previous menstrual problems and abortion, unstable emotional feelings, mate's negative or indifferent feelings about the pregnancy, younger age, less education, and unrealistic expectations about pain (Fridh et al., 1988).

Dystocia is the term applied to abnormal or difficult labor characterized by lack of progress. Abnormalities of labor can be related to its onset, duration, and the fetal and maternal outcomes.

Labor may have to be induced, or brought about with pharmacologic agents, in women who go beyond the 42nd week of gestation. The danger with induction results from excessive frequency of contractions that can lead to fetal hypoxia (Crawford, 1985). Premature labor occurs prior to 36 weeks of gestation, most frequently in association with maternal infection or increased uterine size as seen in hydramnios and with multiple births. Other causes include incompetent cervix, trauma, and conditions which induce uterine hypoxia (Farrell, 1986). The risks prematurity poses to the fetus are discussed in a previous section of this chapter. Treatment of prematurity also poses the risk of impaired maternal-infant bonding due to the necessary separation and reliance on health care providers for care of the infant.

Both extremely long and extremely short periods of labor pose maternal and fetal risks. The precipitous delivery due to extremely severe contractions can cause fetal hypoxia. Intense and prolonged contractions disrupt placental blood flow, and the shortened relaxation times between contractions does not allow adequate time for reperfusion and oxygenation. The fetus may also sustain intracranial injury, as the skull may not have enough time to mold to the maternal pelvis. The incidence of traumatic maternal injury, including uterine rupture if the cervix has not dilated and effaced, is also a possible outcome. Postpartal hemorrhage due to atony of the uterus frequently occurs following this type of labor and delivery (Farrell, 1986).

Labor can be prolonged if any of the following conditions exist either singly or in combination:

1. Weak or uncoordinated uterine forces
2. Faulty presentation caused by fetal position or abnormal development.
3. Obstruction of the birth canal by too narrow a pelvic outlet or an extremely large infant

Other factors that can adversely affect the course of labor include excessive amounts of analgesic or anesthetic drugs administered to the mother, especially during the latent phase; primigravidity; and premature rupture of the membranes while the cervix is closed and uneffaced. Psychologic factors such as excessive fear and anxiety can also prolong labor. These factors can act alone or they can act in concert with one another.

Most prolonged labor represents extension of the first stage, and any extension of either the first or second stage of labor results in an increased risk of perinatal death. Other potential dangers to the fetus as a result of prolonged labor include asphyxia and hypoxia because of the long labor itself and an increased incidence of traumatic birth injuries such as cerebral damage due to pressure on the head of the neonate and injury from the use of instruments in difficult rotation and extraction maneuvers. Prolonged hypoxia during a long and difficult labor may also make the neonate less responsive to normal respiratory stimuli. Maternal sedation and anesthesia during labor and delivery also may seriously depress the neonate's respiratory center.

Another complication the infant may suffer is meconium aspiration. Aspiration of normal amniotic fluid is most likely a physiologic event. Fetal distress, a likely event in prolonged labor, may cause a defecation reaction and the subsequent contamination of amniotic fluid with meconium. The contaminated fluid may be quite thick, and aspiration of this fluid may create a mechanical obstruction of the airway, as well as a chemical pneumonitis that may develop in the lung tissue. The resulting respiratory distress may be quite severe. Fetal distress and meconium-stained amniotic fluid are indications that immediate delivery by cesarean section may be necessary. To minimize the extent of the damage caused by aspiration, the neonate's mouth and nares should be suctioned prior to the delivery of the shoulders. Suctioning of the entire airway and endotracheal intubation to allow suctioning of the trachea and bronchi should be carried out as soon as possible after birth.

Fetal distress seems to be best reflected by disturbances in the fetal heart rate pattern. General guidelines for assessing the normalcy of the fetal heart rate pattern include the following:

1. Baseline heart rate of 120 to 160 bpm
2. Baseline variability of 5 to 15 bpm
3. Reactivity or acceleration noted with movement >15 bpm
4. Deceleration with contraction <15 bpm
5. Absence of late deceleration (which is always a sign of fetal hypoxia)

Fetal distress is an indication that the viability of the fetus is at risk and delivery must occur immediately (Crawford, 1985).

At birth the neonate's condition is assessed using the Apgar scoring system (Table 15-5) applied 1 and 5 minutes after birth. The best possible score is 10. The score at 1 minute indicates the need for resuscitation, while the score at 5 minutes is related to long-term morbidity and mortality.

Prolonged labor also represents a danger to the mother. The incidence of traumatic injury to the birth canal, lacerations, hemorrhage, infection, and shock is sharply increased in the mother who experiences prolonged labor. Maternal exhaustion, which depletes energy stores and lengthens convalescence, is also a complication of prolonged labor.

Other potential complications of labor and delivery include prolapse of the umbilical cord, rupture of the uterus, and amniotic fluid embolism. A prolapsed cord is usually the result of maladaptation of the presenting part to the lower portion of the uterus. Breech or shoulder presentations, an unengaged head, and the presence of twins are conditions in which prolapse of the cord is more likely to occur.

Rupture of the uterus may be spontaneous, caused by obstructed labor or overstimulation with oxytoxic drugs, traumatic, or the result of rupture of an old uterine scar from a previous cesarean section or myomectomy. With adequate obstetric care, however, this complication is unlikely to occur.

Amniotic fluid embolism is the most lethal obstetric complication. Amniotic fluid enters the venous system and precipitates severe, sudden cardiopulmonary collapse. Conditions that predispose the patient to development of this complication include those that expose a large area of the venous system such as placenta previa or abruptio, precipitous labor, multiparity, and intrauterine fetal death (Farrell, 1986).

Infection resulting from premature rupture of the membrane is another potential complication of labor and delivery. If membranes have been ruptured for 24

Table 15-5. Apgar scoring for assessing neonatal condition

Physical signs	Score		
	0	1	2
Heart rate	Absent	<100	>100
Respirations	Absent	Weak cry	Strong cry
Muscle tone	Limp	Some flexion	Good flexion
Reflex irritability	None	Some motion	Good motion
Skin color	Blue	Blue limbs, pink body	Pink

hours or more, an ascending infection occurs in one out of four patients. Antibiotic therapy and early delivery can prevent the occurrence of neonatal death.

Following delivery, potential complications include postpartum hemorrhage and puerperal infection. Postpartal hemorrhage may result from uterine atony or lacerations of the cervix and vagina. Puerperal infection is more often the result of self-contamination with the normal bacterial flora of the vagina. The prior occurrence of hemorrhage or trauma or retention of membranous or placental tissue predisposes the postpartum patient to the development of infection. The presence of an elevated temperature when all other possible causes of infection, such as a urinary tract infection or mastitis, have been ruled out is assumed to be caused by infection in the reproductive system. Antibiotic therapy is instituted in all but the very mild cases of puerperal infection.

SUMMARY

This chapter presented an overview of the normal reproductive process and the manifestations of disruption of that process. The mechanisms of reproductive dysfunction that were discussed in this chapter include lack of maternal adaptation to pregnancy, disruption of normal fetal growth and development, and difficult parturition and its effect on the mother and neonate.

BIBLIOGRAPHY

Acker D, Sacks BP, Tracey, KJ, et al.: Abruptio placentae associated with cocaine use, Am J Obstet Gynecol 146:202, 1983.

Bayer SR, and Seibel MM: Endometriosis: clinical symptoms and infertility, Prog. Clin Biol. Res. 225:103, 1986.

Beischer NA and Mackay EV: Obstetrics and the newborn: an illustrated textbook, Philadelphia, 1988, W.B. Saunders Co.

Brosens IA, Cornillie FJ, and Vasquez G: Etiology and pathophysiology of endometriosis, Prog. Clin. Biol. Res. 225:81, 1986.

Burrow GN and Ferris TS: Medical complications during pregnancy, Philadelphia, 1982, W.B. Saunders Co.

Center D and McFadden R: Pulmonary defense mechanisms. In Sodeman W and Sodeman T, editors: Sodeman's pathologic physiology: mechanisms of disease, ed 7, Philadelphia, WB Saunders Co, 1985.

Crawford JW, editor: Risks of labour, New York, 1985, J. Wiley & Sons.

Dawood MY, editor: Dysmenorrhea, Baltimore, 1980, Williams & Wilkins Co.

Farrell RG: OB/GYN emergencies: the first 60 minutes, Rockville, Md, 1986, Aspen Publishers.

Fitzgerald DJ, Entman SS, Mulloy K, and FitzGerald GA: Decreased prostacyclin biosynthesis preceding the clinical manifestation of pregnancy-induced hypertension, Circulation 75(5):956, 1987.

Frank RT: The hormonal basis of premenstrual tension, Arch Neurol Psychiatr 26:1053, 1931.

Fridh G, Kopare T, Gaston-Johansson F, and Norvell KT: Factors associated with more intense labor pain, Res Nurs Health 11(2):117, 1988.

Gant N and Worley R: Hypertension in pregnancy: concepts and management, New York, 1980, Appleton-Century-Crofts.

Gilbert ES and Harmon JS: High-risk pregnancy and delivery: nursing perspectives, St. Louis, 1986, The CV Mosby Co.

Goebelsmann U: The menstrual cycle. In Mishell DR and Davajan V, editors: Infertility, contraception and reproductive endocrinology, NJ, Medical Economics Books, 1985.

Hollingsworth DR: Maternal metabolism in normal pregnancy and pregnancy complicated by diabetes mellitus, Clin Obstet Gynecol 28(3):457, 1985.

Houston DE: Evidence for the risk of pelvic endometriosis by age, race and socioeconomic status, Epidemiol Rev 6:167, 1984.

Knuppel RA and Goodlin RC: Maternal-placental-fetal unit; fetal and early neonatal physiology. In Pernoll ML and Benson RC editors: Current obstetrics and gynecologic diagnosis and treatment, Norwalk, CT, 1987, Appleton-Lange.

Marrp RP and Vargyas JA: Pelvic endometriosis. In Mishell DR and Davajan V, editors: Infertility, contraception and reproductive endocrinology, NJ, Medical Economics Books, 1985.

Naeye RL: Functionally important disorders of the placenta, umbilical cord and fetal membranes, Hum Pathol 18(7):680, 1987.

Ogle KS and Alfano MA: Common problems of initiating breastfeeding. The physician's role in encouraging success for the nursing couple, Postgrad Med 82(6):159, 165, 1987.

Perrin EV, editor: Pathology of the placenta, New York, 1984, Churchill Livingstone.

Pritchard J: The use of magnesium sulfate in preeclampsia-eclampsia, J Reprod. Med 23(3):107-114, 1979.

Reid RL and Yen SS: Premenstrual syndrome, Am J Obstet Gynecol 139:85, 1981.

Rose BD: Pathophysiology of renal disease, ed 2, New York, 1987, McGraw-Hill Book Co.

Rushton DI: Placenta as a reflection of maternal disease. In Perrin EV, editor: Pathology of the placenta, New York, 1984, Churchill Livingstone Inc.

Schneider HP, Schweppe KW, Cerkel U, and Ochs H: Management of endometriosis, Prog Clin Biol Res 225:135, 1986.

Schneider JM and Curet LB: Obstetrical management of the pregnant diabetic. In Sciarra JJ, Depp R, and Eschenbach DA, editors: Gynecology and obstetrics. Vol 3. Maternal and fetal medicine, Hagerstown, MD, 1982, Harper & Row, Publishers.

Schrier R, editor: Renal and electrolyte disorders, ed 3, Boston, 1986, Little, Brown & Co.

Service FJ: What is "tight control of diabetes?" Goals, limitations and evaluation of therapy, Mayo Clin Proc 61(10):792, 1986.

Strickler RC: Endocrine hypothesis for the etiology of premenstrual syndrome, Clin Obstet Gynecol 30(2):377, 1987.

Taylor C and Pernoll ML: Normal pregnancies and prenatal care. In Pernoll ML and Benson RC, editors: Current obstetric and gynecologic diagnosis and treatment, Norwalk, Conn, 1987, Appleton-Lange.

Weinstein L: Syndrome of hemolysis, elevated liver enzymes and low platelet count: a severe consequence of hypertension in pregnancy, Am J Obstet Gynecol 142:159, 1982.

UNIT VIII

Physiological pattern

16

Oxygenation and respiratory pathophysiology

Overview of Oxygenation

The production of energy is necessary for the cell to carry on such metabolic activities as the transport of substances across membranes, the synthesis of substances within the cell, and specialized electrical and mechanical work functions. The generation of *adenosine triphosphate* (ATP), the form of energy utilized by the cell, depends on the availability of oxygen. In the mitochondria of the cell, hydrogen atoms, released from glucose molecules, combine with oxygen in a series of oxidative reactions from which energy is generated to convert adenosine diphosphate (ADP) to ATP. The role of oxygen in ATP production is summarized in the following equation:

$$ADP + CHO + O_2 \rightarrow CO_2 + H_2O + ATP$$
$$\text{\textbf{Simple sugars}}$$

Lack of an adequate supply of oxygen or the inability to use oxygen leads to a state of tissue hypoxia that, if not rapidly corrected, leads to functional impairment and/or death of the cell. Cellular hypoxia seriously impairs the process of cellular energy production, limits the cell's ability to carry on normal cellular functions, and generally disrupts the steady state of the cell. Hypoxia is an important concept in the study of pathophysiology because it can be produced by a variety of disease mechanisms.

Topics that are discussed in this chapter include the role of oxygen in cellular energy production, the causes of and responses to hypoxia, and disorders of ventilation and exchange. Disorders related to perfusion or the transport of oxygen between the lungs and body tissues are covered in the following chapter.

CELLULAR OXYGEN UTILIZATION

ATP is a nucleotide comprising adenine (a nitrogen base), ribose (a sugar), and three phosphate radicals. Two of the phosphate radicals are connected by a high-energy bond. When energy is needed by the cell, a phosphate radical is enzymatically hydrolyzed, releasing the energy from the bond (approximately 8000 calories per mole of ATP) and leaving ADP.

The formation of ATP from nutrients depends on a series of chemical reactions. Enzymes in the cytoplasm of the cell convert glucose into pyruvic acid and fatty acids, and most amino acids into acetoacetic acid. The pyruvic and acetoacetic acids are converted into acetylcoenzyme A (Fig. 16-2, A), which is transported into the mitochondria of the cell. Located within the mitochondria are the enzymes of the Krebs cycle and the enzymes and respiratory pigments that form the electron transport chain.

The mitochondria are active organelles

of the cell, which are constantly changing shape. They are especially active and numerous in highy metabolic tissue such as the liver. The outer membrane separates the mitochondrion from the cytoplasm of the cell. The inner membrane has deep folds within itself, which are called cristae and are lined with spherical particles. It is thought that the enzymes and respiratory pigments of the electron transport chain are arranged along the inner membrane so that the sequential occurrence of reactions and the orderly flow of electrons from one assembly to another are enhanced. Fig. 16-1, *A*, schematically illustrates the normal mitochondrion and the proposed arrangement of the components of the electron transport chain, Fig. 16-1, *B*, presents an electron micrograph of a mitochondrion.

In the mitochondria, hydrogen and carbon dioxide are released from the acetyl portion of acetylcoenzyme A through the sequence of chemical reactions of the Krebs or citric acid cycle (Fig. 16-2, *A* and *B*.) Some ATP is formed as a result of the reactions occurring within the Krebs cycle; however, approximately 90% of the ATP needed by the cell is formed during the subsequent oxidation of the released hydrogen. Hydrogen atoms and electrons are transferred via a series of oxidation-reduction reactions along the electron transport chain to oxygen, the final acceptor, to form water. During these reactions, at different points along the chain, inorganic phosphate becomes coupled with ADP to form ATP. This process of electron transfer from donor to acceptor with the resultant phosphorylation of ADP to form ATP is called *oxidative phosphorylation* (Fig. 16-2,*C*).

Oxidative phosphorylation depends on both a supply of oxygen adequate to meet the cell's requirements and on the cell's ability to utilize the delivered oxygen. Cel-

lular oxygen requirements are determined by the rate of the cell's metabolic reactions. These energy-producing metabolic reactions occur in response to the availability of ADP, and its presence acts as a feedback mechanism to initiate the glycolytic reactions. As the end products of the metabolic reactions accumulate, the hydrogen ion concentration increases (pH decreases), and the respiratory center is stimulated to increase the rate of respiration to make more oxygen available for oxidative phosphorylation. The respiratory rate and depth, the arterial oxygen and carbon dioxide content, and the total blood flow and oxygen-carrying capacity will determine the amount of oxygen delivered to the cell each minute. The intactness of the mitochondria and the enzymes and respiratory pigments of the electron transport chain will determine the cell's ability to utilize the oxygen effectively.

NORMAL OXYGENATION PROCESSES

The term *oxygenation* denotes those processes by which oxygen is delivered to the cell and carbon dioxide (CO_2), a metabolic waste product, is removed from the cell. Oxygenation is effective when a balance exists between the supply of and the demand for oxygen at the cellular level. Delivery of an adequate supply of oxygen to the cells depends on the processes of ventilation, exchange, and perfusion, whereas demand depends on the rate of utilization of oxygen by the cell.

The processes of ventilation, perfusion, and exchange depend primarily on an intact cardiopulmonary system. *Ventilation* refers to the mechanics of inspiration, to deliver oxygen from the atmosphere to the alveoli, and expiration, to expel carbon dioxide from the lungs. Ventilation depends on neurogenic and chemical factors, the respiratory muscles, compliance and

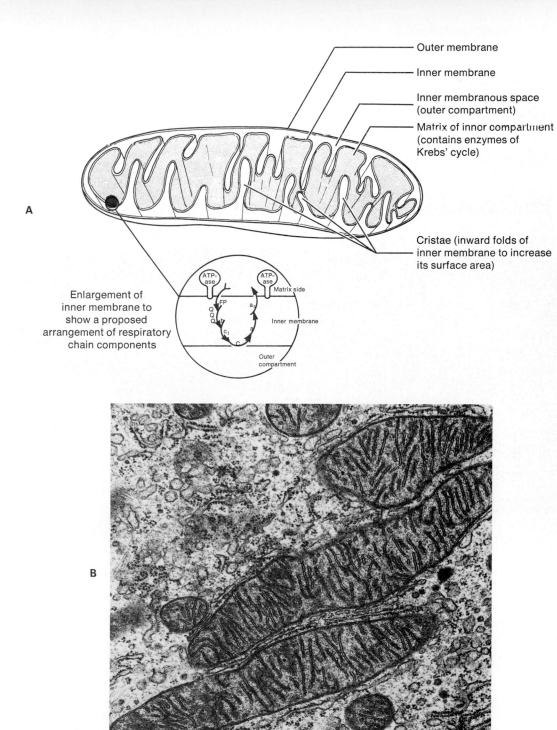

Outer membrane

Inner membrane

Inner membranous space
(outer compartment)

Matrix of inner compartment
(contains enzymes of
Krebs' cycle)

Cristae (inward folds of
inner membrane to increase
its surface area)

A

Enlargement of
inner membrane to
show a proposed
arrangement of respiratory
chain components

ATP-ase

ATP-ase

Matrix side

FP

Q Q

b

a₃

Inner membrane

c₁

a

C

Outer
compartment

B

Fig. 16-1. A, Mitochondrion with enlargement of inner membrane, showing proposed structural arrangement of respiratory chain components. **B,** Mitochondria sectioned both longitudinally and across. (×25,000).

(**B** from Anderson WAD and Kissane JM: Pathology, ed. 8, St. Louis, 1985, The CV Mosby Co.)

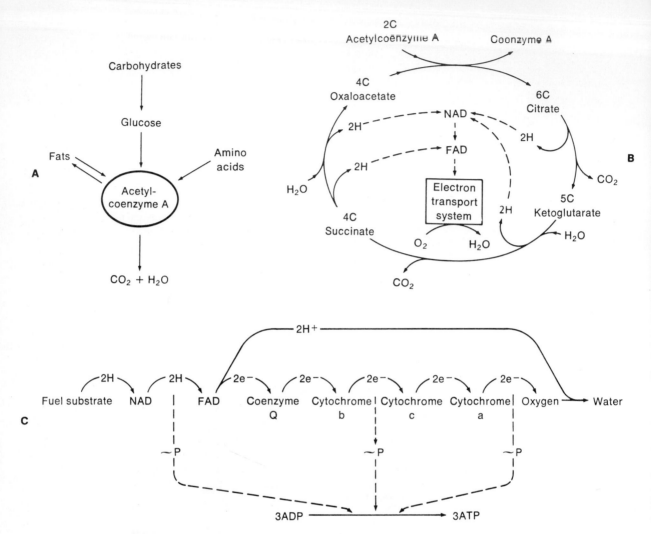

Fig. 16-2. A, Acetylcoenzyme A is an important intermediate in oxidation of carbohydrates, proteins (amino acids), and fats. **B,** Citric acid cycle. **C,** Electron transport system. Electrons are transferred from one carrier to next, terminating with molecular oxygen to form water. A carrier is reduced by accepting electrons and then is reoxidized by donating its electrons to next carrier. ATP is generated at three points in the chain. These electron carriers are located on the inner membranes of the mitochondria (see Fig. 16-1, *A*).

(From Hickman CP, Hickman CP Jr, and Hickman FM: Integrated principles of zoology, ed. 8, St. Louis, 1987, The CV Mosby Co.)

patency of lung tissue, and patency and resistance of the airways. *Exchange* refers to the diffusion of oxygen from the alveoli into the blood and, subsequently, into the body tissues, replacing carbon dioxide, which is removed in the same way. Exchange depends on the integrity, thickness, and surface area of the membrane across which the exchange is to occur, the relative pressure gradients and solubility of gases on each side of the membrane, the affinity between oxygen and hemoglobin, and, at the alveolar membrane, the relative distribution of ventilation and perfusion. *Perfusion* refers to the flow of blood that allows the transport of oxygen and carbon dioxide between the alveoli and the body tissues. Perfusion depends on the pump (heart), intact blood vessels, maintenance of pressure and flow within the vessels, and the oxygen-carrying capacity of the blood. *Utilization* refers to the process by which the cell makes use of oxygen to form ATP. Utilization depends on intact cellular and mitochondrial mechanisms for energy production. The rate of utilization or demand for oxygen is ultimately determined by the metabolic requirements of the cell, or put another way, the rate of the cell's metabolic reactions.

HYPOXIA: A RESPONSE TO ALTERATIONS IN OXYGENATION

Disruption or alteration of these processes can lead to an imbalance between the supply of and demand for oxygen such that the supply and/or utilization of oxygen is insufficient to meet the demands of the body tissues. Oxygenation is no longer effective and is considered to be impaired or inadequate. *Hypoxia* is the term applied to the condition that exists when oxygenation at the cellular level is impaired or inadequate. The tissue Po_2 is reduced. It is the eventual response to an alteration in oxygenation.

When hypoxia occurs, oxidative phosphorylation is impaired, and cellular energy production is severely reduced; 1 minute of anoxia results in a tenfold decrease in the ATP:ADP ratio. Glycolysis, the series of chemical reactions in which glucose is broken down into pyruvic acid and hydrogen, does not require oxygen and can continue in the presence of hy-

poxia but will yield only a relatively small amount of ATP. Under aerobic conditions the accumulation of greater than normal quantities of the products of glycolysis, pyruvic acid and hydrogen, would cause the glycolytic reactions to stop because of feedback inhibition. Under anaerobic conditions, however, the pyruvic acid and hydrogen are converted to lactic acid, which allows glycolysis to continue, since there is no accumulation of the normal end products of glycolysis. Anaerobic glycolysis via the Embden-Meyerhof pathway provides an energy source in the absence of oxygen, but it is an inefficient energy source, and the long-term effects are potentially detrimental to the functioning of most cells.

The presence of increased quantities of lactic acid under hypoxic conditions shifts the pH of the cellular environment to the acid side. A state of metabolic acidosis rapidly develops as the lactic acid is produced and diffuses out of the cell into the extracellular fluids. The Na^+-K^+ pump becomes less effective because of a decrease in the energy available for this active transport process. Na^+ ions move into the cell, and K^+ ions leak out. This results in osmotic swelling of the mitochondria and cell, which gives the cell a swollen, cloudy appearance (Fig. 16-3). This cloudy swelling is especially prevalent in metabolically active tissue and is reversible. Mitochondrial function can be restored with a return of adequate oxygenation even after permanent changes have occurred elsewhere in the cell. Unchecked, however, the reduction in energy production, shift in pH, and loss of cell volume and composition control will lead to release of intracellular enzymes, clumping of intracellular and nuclear components, and further inhibition of chemical reactions until the cell becomes unable to perform any of its

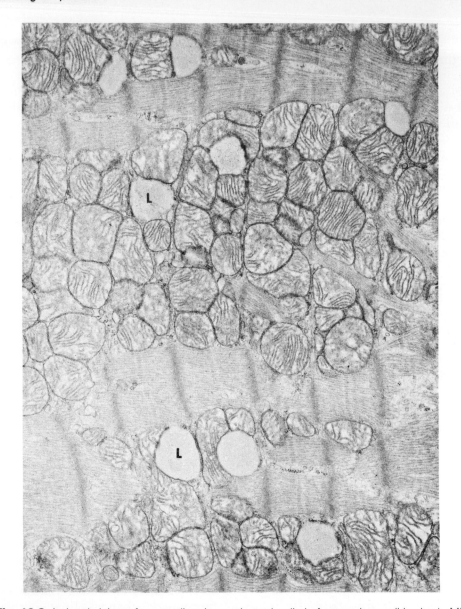

Fig. 16-3. Ischemic injury of myocardium in a patient who died of severe irreversible shock. Mitochondria are swollen and numerous droplets of neutral lipid, L, are present.
(From Scarpelli D and Trump BF: Cell injury, Bethesda, Md, 1974, Universities Associated for Research and Education in Pathology, Inc.)

functions (homeostatic control, motility, uptake of materials, synthesis, export, and reproduction) and is considered dead. Fig. 16-4 schematically illustrates this sequence of events in detail. The cellular effects of hypoxia include a shift to anaerobic metabolic pathways and the production of lactic acid, a reduction in ATP production, loss of cell volume and composition control, and a shift in the pH

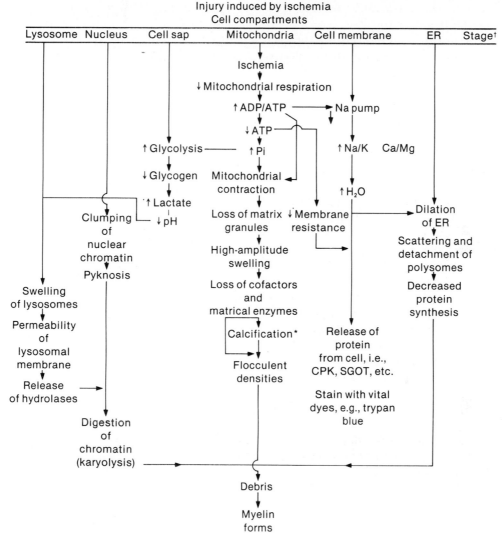

Fig. 16-1. Flow sheet of sequential events that occur in response to impaired oxygenation.
(From Scarpelli D and Trump BF: Cell Injury, Bethesda, Md, 1974, Universities Associated for Research and Education in Pathology, Inc.)

*Calcification does not generally occur in the centers of infarcts unless reflow of blood is permitted.

†Numbers at the right correspond to the temporal sequence of events.

of the body fluids to an acidotic state, with eventual cell death if oxygen does not become available before irreversible changes occur. *Infarction* is the term applied to cell death and necrosis.

Causes

Hypoxia can occur in response to an increased demand for or a decreased supply or utilization of cellular oxygen. Tissue hypoxia related to an inadequate cellular supply of oxygen can result from poor perfusion of the tissue with blood *(stagnant or ischemic hypoxia)*, a reduction in the oxygen-carrying capacity of the blood due to inadequate amounts of either blood or hemoglobin *(anemic hypoxia)*, or a reduction in the arterial oxygen concentration *(hypoxemic hypoxia)*. Tissue hypoxia can be the result of inability of the cell to use the oxygen being delivered to it *(histotoxic hypoxia)* (Vander, Sherman, and Luciano, 1985). Tissue hypoxia, which is related to the cellular demand for oxygen, is the result of increased metabolic requirements for oxygen.

Disorders of ventilation and exchange will lead to the condition of reduced arterial oxygen content, ultimately causing hypoxemic hypoxia. Disorders of perfusion will lead to alterations in the volume, oxygen-carrying capacity, and circulation of the blood, ultimately causing either anemic or stagnant hypoxia. (Diseases that impair the process of perfusion will be discussed in the following chapter.) Disorders of chemical equilibrium and the presence of poisonous chemical substances such as cyanide or arsenic lead to disruption of the cell's enzyme systems and inhibition of electron transport and the oxidation-reducing reactions of oxidative phosphorylation, ultimately causing disruption of utilization and histotoxic hypoxia.

In some disease states the body is able to meet normal cellular oxygen requirements but is unable to increase the supply of oxygen to the cell when oxygen requirements or demands become greater than normal. In the presence of such a disease state any condition that would increase the metabolic rate would also enhance the development of hypoxia. Examples of conditions that increase the metabolic rate include exercise, fever, anxiety, stress, and an increase in the work load expenditure of any organ system. Increased muscular activity resulting from seizures or shivering can also increase the metabolic rate. In some pathologic conditions such as burns, trauma, and sepsis (overwhelming infection), the metabolic rate is increased to such a degree that these patients are at continual risk for the development of tissue hypoxia. Regulation of the metabolic rate is under endocrine control, so endocrine disease can also cause a hypermetabolic state. For example, an increased amount of thyroid hormone has the effect of increasing the metabolic rate and oxygen consumption. The "normal" oxygen requirement for patients with hyperthyroidism is therefore grossly increased, and these patients are susceptible to the development of hypoxia even under normal circumstances.

Systemic effects and clinical manifestations

Hypoxia alters the blood flow to the tissues and results in a shunting of the blood to the major organs. Blood flow through the tissues is determined by the local availability of oxygen as well as other substances in the tissue; the lower the concentration of oxygen in the tissues, the greater the blood flow to those tissues. Two theories have been proposed to explain this phenomenon. The *oxygen demand* or *myogenic theory* is based on the fact that smooth muscle requires oxygen to remain contracted. According to this theory the oxygen concentration in the tissues regulates the contractile state of the precapillary sphincters in the arterioles by affecting the cytosolic Ca^{++} concentration (Vander et al., 1985). When the oxygen concentration in the tissues increases, the precapillary sphincters close and remain closed until oxygen concentrations decrease, causing the sphincters to reopen.

The second theory is the *vasodilator* or *metabolic theory.* According to this theory vasodilator substances affect the precapillary sphincters and arterioles directly, causing vasodilation and increasing the blood flow and oxygen concentration in the tissues. An increase in the metabolic rate or a decrease in the availability of nutrients or oxygen would cause an increase in the rate of formation of the vasodilator substances. One of the postulated vasodilator substances is lactic acid, the product of anaerobic metabolism.

Tissue hypoxia cannot be measured or observed directly. Assessment of oxygenation status must, therefore, focus on indicators of the adequacy of the processes of ventilation, or exchange and perfusion, and on identification of clinical manifestations or signs and symptoms that reflect functional impairment or death of cells due to hypoxia.

Manifestations of hypoxia may appear locally, the result of hypoxia affecting one particular organ, or systemically, the result of hypoxia affecting all the body tissues. Localized hypoxia is usually the result of a condition obstructing the delivery of oxygen to one particular area. The obstruction may be of the blood supply to the area or of the exchange process (the diffusion of oxygen out of the blood) at the cellular level. Generalized hypoxia can result from a variety of conditions affecting ventilation, exchange, and tissue perfusion. These conditions are discussed later in this chapter and in the following chapter.

Manifestations of hypoxia may vary in degree also. Some conditions cause only a slight reduction in the amount of oxygen delivered to the cell; other conditions result in a major reduction in the amount of oxygen; still others result in a total lack of oxygen (anoxia) in the tissues. Manifesta-

tions of hypoxia may indicate that the degree of hypoxia present is so severe that it poses a grave and immediate threat to the patient's survival. Manifestations of hypoxia in some conditions may progressively worsen over a period of time. In these conditions physiologic mechanisms develop that help the body compensate for the chronic hypoxia.

Certain compensatory mechanisms develop in response to chronic hypoxia so that cellular needs can continue to be met. Hypoxia of renal tissue and possibly of other organs stimulates the kidneys to release the enzyme renal erythropoietin factor (REF) into the plasma, where it reacts with a plasma protein produced by the liver to form erythropoietin. Erythropoietin stimulates the bone marrow to increase red blood cell production. Formation of erythropoietin begins immediately in response to the hypoxia, but the peak of its effects is reached after 5 or more days. This mechanism increases the oxygen-carrying capacity of the blood and is demonstrated in persons who live in high altitudes and develop high-altitude polycythemia. Polycythemia is often seen in patients with severe emphysema and congenital heart disease who experience chronic hypoxemia and tissue hypoxia.

Another compensatory response to chronic hypoxia is the development of collateral circulation to areas where the flow of blood and hence oxygen delivery are obstructed. An increase in the vascularity of chronically hypoxic peripheral tissue results in a phenomenon called clubbing (Fig. 16-5). This is an increase in the size of the terminal digits with a loss of the normal nail bed angle. This sign is often present in patients with chronic respiratory and cardiac conditions.

Different tissues and organ systems respond to hypoxia in specific ways. Some

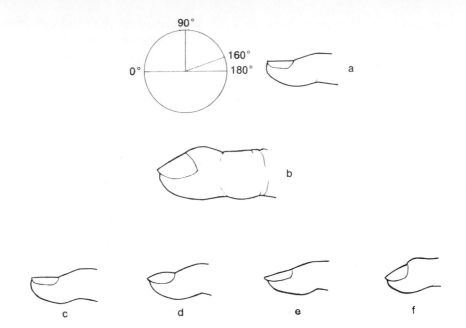

Fig. 16-5. Clubbing: *a, normal base angle; b,* clubbed finger; *c,* normal; *d,* curved nail; *e,* early clubbing (loss of base angle); *f,* advanced clubbing.

are much more susceptible to the effects of ischemia than others. Nerve cells, for example, die after a few minutes of anoxia due to impaired blood flow. In contrast, fibroblasts can survive for a much longer period in the presence of anoxia.

The cells of the central nervous system are particularly sensitive to hypoxia, as the metabolism of simple sugars is the usual source of energy for central nervous system cell function. Oxygen is rapidly utilized by cerebral tissue, and oxygen consumption by the brain accounts for 20% of the basal oxygen consumption. Increased permeability of the cerebral capillaries is a response to hypoxia that contributes to the formation of cerebral edema. The subsequent disruption of the normal function of the cells of the central nervous system caused by hypoxia results in a wide variety of clinically observable signs and symptoms, reflecting physiologic dysfunc-

tion of that system. Sensory/perceptual alterations and changes in behavior such as increased restlessness or uncooperativeness, dizziness or syncope, inability to concentrate, apprehension, or any change in the level of consciousness from lethargy or mild confusion to unconsciousness may be indicative of hypoxia. None of these signs are specific for hypoxia, however, and all possible causes of central nervous system dysfunction must be ruled out.

Hypoxia causes vasoconstriction of the precapillary vessels in the pulmonary vascular bed, which increases pulmonary vascular resistance. When hypoxia is chronic, the normal function of the right side of the heart is impaired because its work load is chronically increased as a result of the increased pulmonary vascular resistance.

The myocardium has a lower capacity for anaerobic energy production than any other tissue. The energy that can be generated anaerobically is inadequate to sustain cardiac function for more than a few minutes. Irreversible injury and death of the cardiac muscle cells in the sequence already described will occur quickly in the absence of oxygen because of the extreme dependence of these cells on aerobic metabolism for ATP production. Anaerobic glycolysis cannot supply adequate amounts of ATP, since myocardial glycogen stores are rapidly depleted, and the content of anaerobic gycolytic enzymes is minimal in cardiac muscle.

Cardiac conduction tissue has a high oxygen consumption rate and the development of dysrhythmias reflects its sensitivity to an oxygen deficit. The automaticity of cardiac cells is affected, and tachycardia (an increased heart rate) will occur early, with bradycardia (a slow heart rate) developing if the hypoxic condition is not corrected. As cell membrane functions deteriorate and sodium and water enter and potassium leaves the myocardial cells, there will be a decrease in the resting potential across the myocardial cell membrane and changes in the action potential. The clinically observable result will be seen as changes on the electrocardiogram.

Renal tubular absorption depends on renal oxygen consumption and will be altered in hypoxic states. Renal ischemia is a known etiologic factor in the development of acute renal failure, the most extreme manifestation of disrupted renal function.

The centrilobular cells of the liver receive a greatly diminished oxygen supply under normal conditions because of the low oxygen concentration of the blood in the portal system and the anatomic structure of the supplying blood vessels. Therefore these cells are particularly susceptible to the effects of hypoxia. Liver dysfunc-

tion, cell death, and centrilobular fibrosis may result.

Pain is often the primary manifestation of tissue hypoxia caused by ischemia. In conditions in which tissue perfusion is decreased, the removal of the products of metabolism as well as the delivery of oxygen becomes a problem. The pain is thought to occur in response to the stimulation of neural receptors by the lactic acid remaining as a result of anaerobic metabolism. The effects of stagnant or ischemic hypoxia are usually local and in peripheral areas may also include abnormal sensations such as numbness and tinging as nerve endings are affected.

When extreme tissue hypoxia results from either hypoxemic or stagnant (ischemic) hypoxia, cyanosis may be present. *Cyanosis* is a dusky bluish or grayish discoloration of the skin and mucous membranes that occurs when increased amounts of reduced hemoglobin are present in the blood. It is not a reliable sign of oxygenation status, however. First, cyanosis is a subjective observation dependent on many factors; for example, lighting, skin thickness and pigmentation, and the examiner's powers of observation. Second, hemoglobin must be present in normal amounts in order for cyanosis to be interpreted meaningfully. Cyanosis is apparent when 5 g of hemoglobin per 100 ml of blood has been reduced to deoxyhemoglobin and has reached the superficial capillaries. This is equivalent to a Pao_2 of 50 mm Hg or less and an oxygen saturation level of 75%, so it is a relatively late sign. A person with a hemoglobin deficiency may be extremely hypoxic before cyanosis becomes apparent. A person who has an overabundance of hemoglobin might appear cyanotic even though oxygen continues to be delivered in sufficient quantities to the cells. The absence or presence of cyanosis is not an absolute indicator of oxygenation status and must be interpreted in light of all other data.

Another symptom commonly reported by patients who experience an alteration in oxygenation status is *dyspnea*, breathlessness or shortness of breath. A distinction should be made between physiologic and pathologic breathlessness (Burki, 1980). Physiologic breathlessness refers to the not unpleasant sensation of breathlessness experienced by healthy persons after exercise or excitement. Pathologic breathlessness refers to the distressing sensation of not being able to completely catch one's breath. It is to the latter description that the terms dyspnea and shortness of breath are applied.

Dyspnea is defined as the subjective sensation of difficult or uncomfortable breathing and includes both the perception of and the reaction to the sensation by the patient (Carrieri and Janson-Bjerklie, 1986). It may be described as air hunger or the inability to get enough air. The term *dyspnea* is used to describe responses on a continuum between the subjective report of breathlessness or difficult breathing to a visible, extremely exaggerated respiratory effort characterized by use of the accessory muscles of respiration, flaring of the nares, and an extreme increase in the rate of respiration. Dyspnea is not a direct reflection of the state of tissue oxygenation but rather is a symptom reflecting the conscious perception of a discrepancy between the need for respiration and the body's ability to meet that need.

The occurrence and description of this symptom are highly variable among individuals, even those who have the same disease. Dyspnea can be constant or episodic, brought on by exertion or states of arousal and excitement. There may be little correlation between the severity of the reported sensation of dyspnea and the actual degree of physiologic dysfunction that is present. A person with advanced, severe respiratory disease may report relatively little dyspnea in comparison to a person with mild respiratory disease who reports severe, disabling dyspnea (Carrieri, Janson-Bjerklie, and Jacobs, 1984). Gift (1987) states that the reported severity is a function of two factors; the intensity of the afferent sensations and the individual's interpretation of and response to these sensations. The response will be shaped by past experience, the level of understanding of the symptom, age, and the response of family and significant others in the environment. Dyspnea, as a response to a health problem, is very similar to pain because both are subjective phenomena for which objective, quantitative measurement parameters may hold little relevance to the individual patient.

For these reasons, the presence of dyspnea must be carefully evaluated. Conditions surrounding the occurrence of dyspnea need to be determined because they provide information about the possible cause. For example, does dyspnea occur at rest or with exertion? Is it brought on by a change in position (orthopnea)? Does it occur only at night (paroxysmal nocturnal dyspnea)? Did it begin suddenly or worsen over time? A person may apply the label *shortness of breath* to other subjective sensations such as pain on breathing, difficult expectoration of secretions, and severe coughing fits during which breath is lost. Anxiety may also cause a person to become acutely aware of the breathing pattern and can exacerbate dyspnea in patients with organic disease. Many patients with cardiopulmonary disease experience the panic-dyspnea cycle in which the feeling of shortness of breath causes fear and arousal, which in turn leads to more dyspnea, and a vicious cycle ensues (Shekleton, 1987).

Various mechanisms have been proposed and examined as being pathogenetic in the development and occurrence of the sensation of dyspnea. These include the work of breathing, rate of oxygen consumption, abnormal respiratory drive, and reduction in ventilatory reserve, to name a few. The currently favored theory is that the actual sensation of dyspnea arises as a result of inappropriate mechanical factors within the respiratory muscles. Afferent impulses from the respiratory muscle spindles are generated as a result of inappropriate length–tension relationships in the respiratory muscle fibers and abnormal chest wall movement during inspiration and expiration. These impulses are sensed as signs of difficult or uncomfortable breathing (Burki, 1980).

Fatigue, weakness, and activity intolerance can also reflect tissue hypoxia as a result of the inadequate energy production that occurs. Fatigue and activity intolerance are diagnostic categories that have been approved by the North American Nursing Diagnosis Association for clinical use and validation. *Fatigue* is defined as an overwhelming sense of exhaustion and decreased capacity for physical and mental work. *Activity intolerance* is defined as a state in which an individual has insufficient physiologic or psychologic energy to endure or complete required or desired daily activities. *Weakness* is defined here as a feeling of lack of strength. As subjective responses to hypoxia, these three phenomena are related to one another. As with dyspnea, they are perceptions that are affected by both physiologic and psychologic factors. Assessment should include questions regarding the severity and the impact of these symptoms on activities of daily living. Such subjective responses

to existing pathophysiology can have a more negative impact on a person's ability to cope with the disease than the actual manifestations of the disease itself.

Clinical indices of the adequacy of oxygenation processes

It is not clinically feasible to measure the state of oxygenation of tissues directly. There are various clinical diagnostic studies that yield information relative to the adequacy of the various processes of oxygenation and thereby allow an approximate determination of the oxygenation status of the cells. The study of arterial blood samples to determine the amounts of oxygen and carbon dioxide present is called *arterial blood gas analysis* and indicates the effectiveness of the ventilatory, exchange, and, to a limited extent, the perfusion processes. Pulmonary function studies measure various lung volumes and capacities and the rate of air flow during ventilation. Measurement of pressures within the cardiovascular system and determination of the presence and rate of pulses throughout the body provide information on the adequacy of perfusion and the oxygen transport process. Measurement of the hematocrit and hemoglobin content of the blood indicates the oxygen-carrying capacity of the blood. Observation of the patient's respiratory rate and rhythm, color, and various body characteristics as well as careful attention to and interpretation of the patient's subjective complaints can provide important information as to the adequacy of the oxygenation processes. Subjective as well as objective data must be considered; often subjective data provide the only means for valid and meaningful interpretation of objective data. This points up the necessity of complete and continual assessment of the patient's condition. Changes in the oxygenation status are frequently reflected in subjective data or data that can be interpreted subjectively. Changes may occur quickly and may require rapid action if the patient is to survive, or they may be insidious and thus difficult to detect.

SUMMARY

Presented so far in this chapter has been a review of the role of oxygen in cellular metabolism and a discussion of the cellular and systemic effects of hypoxia. Tissue hypoxia can be the result of much pathophysiology and, therefore, is a central concept of the study of pathophysiology. It is also a central concept in the clinical practice of nursing because it is a potential sequel to responses to disease that nurses diagnose and treat. In this situation the goal of nursing care is to prevent the development or minimize the effects of hypoxia. The occurrence of hypoxia creates other responses that are also diagnosed and treated by nurses. These relationships are illustrated in Fig. 16-6.

Tissue oxygenation will be most directly affected by disruption of the oxygenation processes; ventilation, exchange, and perfusion. Disease in body systems other than the respiratory and cardiovascular systems can alter these processes as well as the utilization of and demand for oxygen. The focus of the remainder of this chapter and the next will be the cardiopulmonary disorders that disrupt or impair the oxygenation processes of ventilation, exchange, and perfusion. It is important for the student to remember that while a pathologic process may primarily affect either the respiratory or cardiovascular system alone, the other will eventually be affected because of the interdependent function of the two systems in the process of oxygenation.

Overview of Respiration

Roussos and Macklem (1982) support the concept of a two-part respiratory system made up of the lungs, which are the gas-exchanging organs, and a pump that ventilates the lungs. The pump is composed of the chest wall, the respiratory muscles, and the nerves and centers in the nervous system that control its function. This conceptualization allows ventilation and exchange to be viewed as the functional processes of the respiratory system. The focus of the remainder of this chapter is on mechanisms by which disorders of ventilation and exchange occur.

The lungs can be affected by infectious and inflammatory conditions just like other tissues of the body. Infection and inflammation are discussed in Chapter 2. It is important to point out that the incidence of tuberculosis, an infectious disease that causes caseating granulomas and affects lung tissue, is on the rise among groups characterized by malnutrition and substandard living conditions; this includes the poor, the homeless, and chemical abusers. Immigrants from underdeveloped countries have also increased the incidence of this once dreaded but now treatable disease in the United States.

Many persons with AIDS seen in the hospital initially have an opportunistic infection of the lungs, pneumocystis carinii pneumonia (PCP). This condition is discussed in the case study on AIDS which appears in Chapter 2. Persons with AIDS are also at risk for mycobacterial and fungal diseases, which primarily affect the lung.

Lung tissue is a common site for primary cancers as well as for metastatic spread of cancer from another primary site. The process of carcinogenesis and the

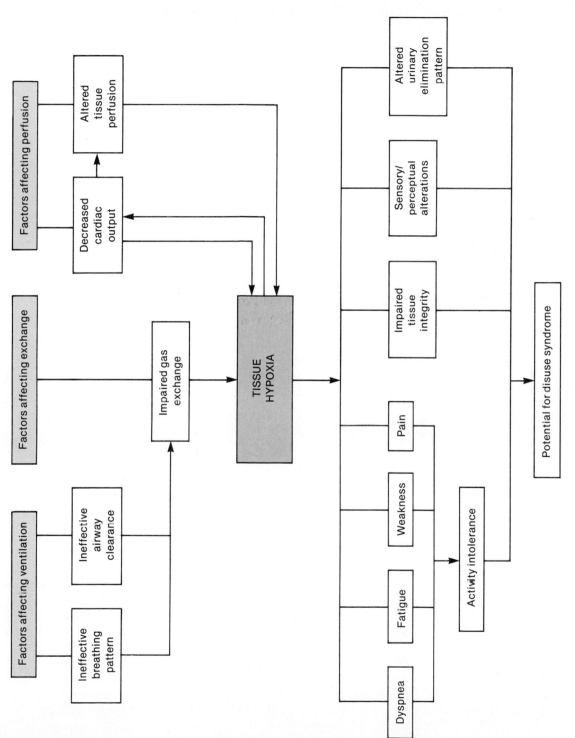

Fig. 16-6. Central role of hypoxia as a sequel to physiologic responses to alterations in the oxygenation processes of ventilation, exchange, and perfusion as a cause of other physiologic responses that are the domain of nursing practice.

effects of cancer of the lung are discussed in detail in Chapter 6.

Inhalation and the direct effect of toxic substances on lung tissue is the mechanism of lung injury associated with tobacco smoke and certain dusts and fibers. Exposure to tobacco smoke and other toxic physical and chemical agents is discussed in detail in Chapter 5. Lung cancer and emphysema are the most devastating results of tobacco smoke. Smokers are also prone to more frequent respiratory tract infections, chronic cough and sputum expectoration, and an increased risk of pulmonary complications should anesthesia and surgery be required. There is evidence that these harmful effects can also occur as a result of passive exposure to environmental tobacco smoke (i.e., the inhalation by nonsmokers of environmental tobacco smoke from smokers) (U.S. Surgeon General, 1987; National Research Council, 1986). This is especially true for children of smokers, among whom increased morbidity and long-term pulmonary functional impairment have been found (Tager, 1988). The recent findings of increased incidence and risk of bronchial hyperresponsiveness and atopy in children of smokers reported by Martinez et al. (1988) support a possible link between environmental tobacco smoke and increased risk and severity of asthma in these children. The known effects of passive exposure to environmental tobacco smoke provide a strong rationale for the enactment and enforcement of antismoking regulations in public areas.

The *pneumoconioses* are forms of interstitial lung disease that result from occupational exposure to dust or fibers that are inhaled and initiate a fibrogenic or carcinogenic process in lung tissue. Examples include black lung disease as a result of the inhalation of coal and silica dust by coal miners, silicosis caused by the inhalation of silica dust by sand blasters and foundry workers, and asbestosis and malignant mesothelioma resulting from asbestos exposure among boiler workers and pipefitters. There is often a long latency period between exposure and the onset of symptoms, and this "at-risk" phase is characterized by the chronic stress of worry about personal susceptibility. Lebovitz (1985) retrospectively confirmed, through a series of studies, that denial was quite prevalent during the at-risk phase in a group of asbestos workers who subsequently developed malignant mesothelioma. He speculated that the long-term coping mechanisms used by the exposed person could be predictive of the ability to cope with the disease should it develop as depression, anxiety, helplessness, fatalistic attitudes, anger, and guilt are reactions that have been observed in patients with industrially acquired pulmonary disease. Some of these observations may apply to smokers and others with lung injury in whom exposure to the causative agent could have been prevented.

Occupational safety laws have done much to protect workers from exposure to these types of harmful inhalants; however, some exposure continues to go unrecognized. For example, the use of asbestos in building materials was quite common before the harmful effects of asbestos were known. Physical deterioration or remodeling in such buildings could have caused unsuspected exposure to occupants and workers. Now all buildings built before the early 1970's should be tested for the presence of asbestos, and, if it is found, special precautions must be taken to protect occupants and workers. Pathologic pulmonary effects of other compounds encountered in the workplace continue to be recognized as well. For example, occupational exposure to low molecular weight compounds like isocyanates; formaldehyde; metals such as nickel, platinum, chromium, and copper; soldering flux; drugs; amines; anhydrides; persulfates; dyes; styrene; cyanoacrylates; and methacrylate has been found to induce asthma (Stankus, Sastre and Salvaggio, 1988). These and other pathologic exposures are constantly being recognized, and occupational safety and disclosure acts need to be reviewed and updated periodically.

It seems obvious that inhalation of the many compounds known to pollute our enviromental air may be responsible for as yet unrecognized pulmonary pathology. Exposure to pollutants, noxious gases, fumes, and dusts are known to cause the exacerbation of symptoms in persons with cardiopulmonary disease. Protection of the environment through clean air legislation enactment and enforcement must be a priority if further deterioration of our air quality is to be prevented.

Respiratory disorders, ranging from the time-limited experience of the common cold to the chronic, progressively worsening experience of chronic obstructive pulmonary disease (COPD), are a major source of morbidity and mortality in the United States. These disorders also impose a large financial burden on society and the health care delivery system. The overall cost of respiratory disease, including both direct and indirect costs, was estimated to be $40.9 billion in 1986 (personal communication, American Lung Association, Statistics Department.)

NORMAL VENTILATORY FUNCTION, DYNAMICS, AND REGULATION

Ventilation is the process by which oxygen is drawn into the lungs and carbon dioxide is expelled from the lungs. As stated earlier, adequate ventilatory function depends on an intact thoracic musculoskeletal system, patent conducting airways, and functioning neurochemical regulatory controls, as well as the patency and integrity of the lung tissue itself.

The primary respiratory unit, or *acinus*, is that portion of the lung distal to the terminal nonrespiratory bronchiole. It comprises the respiratory bronchiole, the alveolar duct, and the terminal alveolar sac (Fig. 16-7). With an increase in the chest cavity size, air is drawn into the alveoli through the conducting airways. The conducting airways (nose, nasopharynx, trachea, bronchi, and bronchioles) warm, humidify, and filter the air. The inspired air is warmed to body temperature, humidified to 100% water vapor, and cleansed of most particulate matter before it reaches the lower trachea. Functional lung tissue is also kept free of the effects of infectious and pollutant materials through various defense mechanisms, which include mucociliary clearance; nervous system reflexes (including cough and bronchoconstriction); the secretion of lactoferrin, lysozyme, and secretory IgA; and the cellular (macrophage) and immune system responses (Kim and Larson, 1987).

For ventilation to occur, the airways must be patent and functioning. Under normal conditions, airway clearance depends primarily on the mechanism of mucociliary transport or clearance. This occurs through the functional combination of ciliary action, mucus secretion, and the production of periciliary fluid, known as the mucociliary system or apparatus. The mucociliary system must be intact and functioning to move mucus in a cephalad direction to the mouth and nose where it can be swallowed or expectorated (Wanner, 1986).

The surface epithelium of the trachea, bronchi, and bronchioles consists of cil-

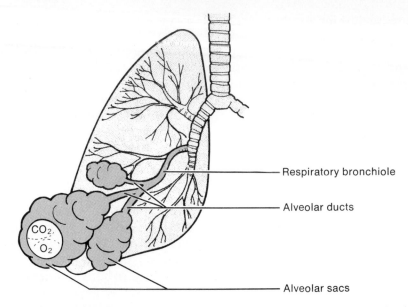

Respiratory bronchiole

Alveolar ducts

Alveolar sacs

Fig. 16-7. Primary respiratory unit, the acinus, includes respiratory bronchiole, alveolar duct, and terminal alveolar sac.

iated, pseudostratified, columnar cells occasionally interrupted by mucus-secreting cells. Airway secretions are produced by mucus-secreting glands (submucosal glands) found in the cartilage-containing airways (trachea and bronchi) and epithelial mucous cells (goblet cells). In the normal adult, approximately 100 ml of mucus is produced each day. Most of this is reabsorbed with only about 10 ml actually being removed (Cosenza and Norton, 1986). The mucus or gel layer of fluid actually "floats" in patches on top of another layer of fluid that surrounds the cilia and is called the periciliary fluid or sol layer. The mucus layer is propelled toward the nasopharynx by coordinated waves of motion caused by the beating action of the cilia (Kim and Larson, 1987; Wanner, 1986).

The function and efficiency of the mucociliary system depend on a functionally and morphologically intact ciliated epithe-

lium and on the interaction between the mucus and cilia, which, in turn, depends on the thickness (depth) and rheologic properties of the mucous and periciliary fluid layers. Transport velocity is slowed as the depth and viscosity of the mucus increase or the elasticity decreases (Wanner, 1986). In other words, the clearance of secretions becomes more difficult if there is an increase in the amount or change in the character of the secretions or if ciliary action is impaired or slowed in any way. These mechanisms can compound one another as well. An example can be seen in the patient with chronic bronchitis who routinely has an increased amount of mucus production caused by the response of the mucus-secreting cells to chronic inflammation. If this patient develops an acute infection, the amount of secretions will be increased even more, the character of the mucus is changed, and it becomes thicker, which may actually cause damage to the cilia or denude the epithelium, causing stasis of the secretions with the potential for mucous plug formation and occlusion of the airway (Cosenza and Norton, 1986).

If the mucociliary system becomes impaired in any way or overwhelmed by the presence of an excessive amount or abnormally thick and tenacious mucus, the cough becomes the major mechanism for airway clearance. An effective cough requires (1) a deep breath that expands the airways so that air will flow distal to any secretions, (2) closure of the glottis, and (3) contraction of the muscles of expiration with a subsequent increase in intrathoracic and intrapulmonary pressures and sudden opening of the glottis. Intrathoracic pressure remains high while central airway pressure drops, causing dynamic compression of the central airways that reduces their diameter and increases airflow velocity. This should result in the forceful expulsion of air and secretions due to the high linear velocity of the airflow (Kim and Larson, 1987; Cosenza and Norton, 1986). The ability to cough forcefully and effectively will be impaired in conditions in which the neuromuscular function of the chest is impaired, the respiratory muscles are weakened, airway resistance is high, or the cough reflex is suppressed.

The two phases of ventilation are inspiration and expiration. *Tidal volume* (V_T) is the measurement used to represent the volume of air inspired or expired with each normal breath. *Minute ventilation* (V_E) is the amount of air that is actually moved in or out of the lungs each minute. It is calculated by multiplying the tidal volume by the number of breaths taken in a minute (f = frequency of breaths/minute):

$$V_E = V_T \times f$$

Minute ventilation is also the sum of the alveolar ventilation (V_A) and the dead space ventilation (V_D):

$$V_E = V_A + V_D$$

The physiologically significant portion of the ventilation is the *alveolar* or *effective ventilation*. This is the portion of the minute ventilation that actually reaches the alveoli and participates in gas exchange. Assessment of the adequacy of alveolar ventilation is not possible through direct measurement or clinical observation of the patient. The physiologic parameter that most directly and accurately reflects the adequacy of alveolar ventilation in relation to the metabolic rate is the partial pressure of carbon dioxide in the arterial blood (P_{CO_2}) (Martin, 1987).

Approximately 150 cc of air remains in the conducting airways and is considered nonfunctional for gas exchange. Any portion of the minute ventilation that does not participate in gas exchange is termed *dead space ventilation*. Changes in the amount of dead space ventilation require a compensatory change in the rate of alveolar ventilation in order to maintain a normal level of alveolar ventilation. The ratio of dead space volume to tidal volume (V_D/V_T) is an important measure of the efficiency of ventilation. A departure from the normal ratio, if uncorrected, will result in abnormal concentrations of blood gases.

Enlargement of the chest cavity is accomplished through muscular contraction. Contraction of the diaphragm causes it to descend, and the downward movement causes the chest cavity to lengthen. Elevation of the sternum and ribs causes an increase in the anteroposterior chest size. The abdominal muscles can also be recruited to further increase chest expansion. For this reason ventilation will be disrupted in pathologic conditions that cause altered musculoskeletal function. While inspiration is an active process, expiration is achieved through passive relaxation of the muscles, which allows the elastic recoil of the thorax and lung, causing chest cavity size to decrease.

The thorax and lungs have a continuous tendency to collapse, which is referred to as recoil tendency. Intrapleural pressure is the amount of negative pressure in the intrapleural spaces necessary to keep the lungs from collapsing and is considered a measure of the recoil tendency. As the lungs expand and the recoil tendency becomes greater, intrapleural pressure becomes more negative (Vander et al. 1985). This recoil tendency results from the presence of elastic fibers throughout the lung tissue, which are constantly attempting to shorten, and the surface tension of the fluid lining the alveoli, which causes the sides of the alveoli to be attracted to one another and therefore causes the alveoli to tend to collapse. Specialized secretory cells in the alveolar epithelium secrete pulmonary *surfactant*, a lipoprotein containing dipalmitoyl lecithin, which reduces the surface tension of the alveolar fluid and prevents the collapse of the alveoli.

The movement of air in and out of the lungs is ultimately the result of pressure changes that occur as the lungs are alternately compressed and distended. During inspiration as the lung volume increases, the intra-alveolar pressure becomes less than atmospheric pressure, and air is pulled into the expanded lungs. During expiration as lung volume increases, the intra-alveolar pressure becomes greater than atmospheric pressure, and air is forced out of the lungs.

During normal tidal respiration when the lungs return to a resting position at the end of expiration, some alveoli do collapse as a result of the recoil tendency and the volume and pressure changes in the lung. The pressures and volumes associated with tidal respiration are insufficient to reexpand the already collapsed alveoli and to prevent the collapse of others. Pressures and volumes higher than normal are needed. The highest intra-alveolar pressure is reached while coughing. In normal respiration very deep breaths and sighs also provide such pressures and volumes, promoting reexpansion of the alveoli. This fact serves as a basis for the use of coughing and deep-breathing exercises following surgery and in other pathologic conditions characterized by alveolar collapse. Research has demonstrated that a sustained maximal inspiration is the respiratory maneuver most suitable for reexpanding alveoli and preventing the collapse of others.

The inherent ability of the lungs and thorax to expand in response to an increase in intra-alveolar pressure is referred to as *compliance*. Pulmonary compliance is expressed as the volume increase in the lungs for each unit increase in the intra-alveolar pressure. For each centimeter increase in pressure the normal lungs can increase in size by approximately 130 cc in the adult. Pulmonary compliance is decreased in the presence of any condition that limits the ability of the lungs to expand.

In addition to the energy expended by contraction of the respiratory muscles, energy must be expended to overcome resistance to air flow and lung expansion. Both the airway and the viscosity of the pulmonary tissues offer resistance to air flow. The resistance caused by the pulmonary tissue is also called nonelastic tissue resistance.

The *work of breathing* is the total amount of effort required to expand and contract the lungs. It is determined by the degree of compliance of the lung tissue, the resistance of the airway, the presence of active expiration (normally a passive process), and use of the accessory muscles of respiration. Decreased pulmonary compliance, increased airway resistance, active expiration, or use of accessory muscles will increase the work of breathing. A change in ventilatory pattern may also affect the work of breathing. There is an optimal ventilatory pattern at which the work of breathing is at a minimum. A slow, deep ventilatory pattern (for example, that seen when carbon dioxide levels are low) or a shallow rapid pattern (for example, that seen with high carbon dioxide levels) has the effect of increasing the total work of breathing.

Any condition in which the work of breathing is increased will also result in an increased energy expenditure by the body. Such an increase accelerates metabolic activity, and consequently the need for oxygen is also increased. In conditions in which the work of breathing is increased a vicious cycle has been set up: an increased need for oxygen occurs in the presence of a reduced ability to meet even normal oxygen demands, which causes a further increase in the work of breathing, requiring an even greater increase in oxygen consumption (Fig. 16-8).

Control of the rate and rhythm of respiration is highy developed, maintaining alveolar ventilation at a level sufficient to meet the oxygen needs of the body even during periods of extreme demand. Control is maintained through both neural and chemical mechanisms.

The respiratory center is located in the medulla oblongata and pons of the brain stem. The rate, rhythm, and depth of the respiration and, subsequently, the level of alveolar ventilation are controlled by this

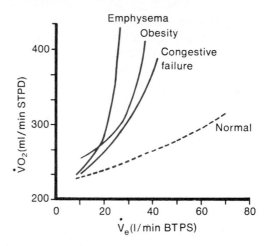

Fig. 16-8. Changes in oxygen consumption ($\dot{V}O_2$) associated with increasing ventilation in a normal person and in patients with congestive heart failure, obesity, and emphysema.

(From Cherniack RM, Cherniack L, and Naimark A: Respiration in health and disease, ed 2, Philadelphia, 1972, WB Saunders Co.)

center. In response to signals from inspiratory and expiratory neurons in this center the respiratory muscles are alternately stimulated and inhibited. Efferent fibers carry impulses away from the center to the respiratory muscles via the phrenic and intercostal nerves.

The respiratory center responds to afferent nerve impulses from pulmonary stretch receptors, central and peripheral chemoreceptors, the cortex and thalamus of the brain, and arterial and venous baroreceptors. Stretch receptors, located throughout lung tissue and especially in the bronchi and bronchioles, are stimulated by inflation of the lungs. When stimulated, these receptors transmit impulses via the vagal afferent fibers to the respiratory center. The respiratory center responds, causing reflex inhibition of inspiration to prevent further inflation. This is called the Hering-Breuer reflex and serves to prevent overdistension of the lungs.

The relative concentrations of oxygen and carbon dioxide in the blood determine the ventilatory requirement, that is, the rate and depth of respiration. The central chemosensitive areas are located in the anterior medulla and are responsive to changes in the carbon dioxide levels and hydrogen ion concentration of the surrounding fluid. Under normal conditions the carbon dioxide level provides the primary stimulus to ventilation. An increase in carbon dioxide levels causes a corresponding increase in the hydrogen ion concentration. This is because carbon dioxide in combination with water yields carbonic acid, which readily dissociates into hydrogen and bicarbonate ions. This is summarized in the following equation:

$$CO_2 + H_2O \leftrightarrow H_2CO_3 \leftrightarrow H^+ + HCO_3^-$$

A rise in carbon dioxide levels and/or hydrogen ion concentration directly stimulates the neurons of the respiratory center, which responds by increasing the rate and depth of respiration to "blow off" carbon dioxide. When the hydrogen ion concentration decreases, the respiratory center inhibits respiration so that carbon dioxide can be retained to maintain the balance between the bicarbonate and carbonic acid content of the body fluids. The hypoxic drive provides a secondary stimulus to ventilation under normal conditions.

Peripheral chemoreceptors located in the carotid and aortic bodies have afferent nerve fibers leading to the respiratory center. In response to both low arterial oxygen levels and (to a lesser extent) high carbon dioxide levels, impulses from these chemoreceptors stimulate the respiratory center. These chemosensitive relationships are schematically illustrated in Fig. 16-9.

The respiratory center is also stimulated by impulses from both the cortex for conscious hyperventilation and the thalamus in response to emotions. In addition, baroreceptors in the aortic and carotid sinuses respond to an increase in blood pressure by inhibition of the respiratory center.

Arterial oxygen levels do not exert the major control over respiration and alveolar ventilation, because changes in alveolar ventilation have little effect on the degree of oxygen saturation of the blood. Alveolar ventilation can decrease to one half the normal rate, and the oxygen saturation of the blood can remain within 10% of normal. However, changes in alveolar ventilation have a profound effect on the level of carbon dioxide in the blood and interstitial fluids. Carbon dioxide is an end product of the metabolic reactions occurring in the cells, and accumulation of carbon dioxide and the resultant change in the hydrogen ion concentration (pH) will adversely affect the course of the metabolic reactions. Pa_{CO_2} is also one determinant of arterial oxygen pressure. For these reasons it is important that the carbon dioxide level be regulated precisely and that it serve as the major feedback mechanism for alveolar ventilation.

Clinical indicators of ventilatory function

Since the rate of removal of carbon dioxide from the alveoli is directly dependent on the rate of alveolar ventilation, measurement of the pressure exerted by carbon dioxide in the blood (P_{CO_2}) yields information on the adequacy of alveolar ventilation. Normal alveolar ventilation is defined as that level of alveolar ventilation sufficient to meet metabolic needs, which is reflected by the ability to maintain a normal arterial carbon dioxide pressure of approximately 40 mm Hg.

Arterial blood gas analysis is the clinical procedure used to obtain information

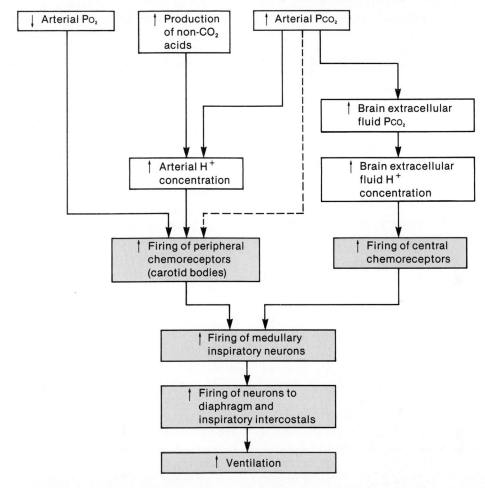

Fig. 16-9. Summary of chemical inputs that stimulate ventilation. Ventilation would be reflexly decreased when arterial P_{O_2} increases or when P_{CO_2} or hydrogen ion concentration decreases. The dashed line from arterial P_{CO_2} denotes the fact that the direct effect of P_{CO_2} on the peripheral chemoreceptors is minor (in contrast to its effect via hydrogen ion).

(From Vander AJ, Sherman JH, and Luciano DS: Human physiology: the mechanisms of body function, New York, 1985, McGraw-Hill Book Co.)

about the tension or pressure being exerted by the gases in the blood. The pressures being measured are actually partial pressures, since each gas exerts a particular amount of pressure. This is based on Dalton's law of partial pressures, which states that the total pressure of a given volume of a gas mixture is equal to the sum of the separate or partial pressures

that each gas would exert if it alone occupied the entire volume. Partial pressure can be calculated using the total amount of pressure exerted by the gas mixture and multiplying it by the percent concentration of the particular gas being evaluated, although electrodes are used that measure blood gas concentrations directly and accurately. The following data can be obtained through arterial blood gas analysis:

Po$_2$: the partial pressure or oxygen tension in the arterial blood. This reflects the amount of oxygen dissolved in the blood. *Hypoxemia* is the term used to describe a decrease in the partial pressure of oxygen in the arterial blood.

Pco$_2$: the partial pressure of carbon dioxide in arterial blood. This value is directly affected by the rate of alveolar ventilation.

pH: the negative logarithm of the hydrogen ion concentration. It is an indicator of the relative acidity and alkalinity of the body fluids.

O$_2$ saturation: the amount of hemoglobin combined with oxygen and expressed as a percentage. This reflects the amount of oxyhemoglobin in the blood.

Blood gas values are interrelated. For this reason, interpretation of the results requires analysis of each value in relation to the others rather than in isolation. Presented in the box below are the normal values obtained through blood gas analysis.

End tidal (expired) levels of carbon dioxide can be examined noninvasively using a capnograph. End tidal carbon dioxide measurements do not provide the same degree of reliability as measurement of the partial pressure of carbon dioxide in the arterial blood. The amount expired may not accurately reflect the metabolic production of carbon dioxide because the end tidal value will be affected by ventilation/perfusion inequality as well as by positional changes and other variables that are not controllable.

Airway patency can be examined through auscultation of lung sounds, which are discussed later in this chapter. Other parameters by which the adequacy of the ventilatory process can be evaluated include the respiratory rate and pattern and the various lung volumes, capacities, and flow rates. Respiratory rate and pattern can be examined using the techniques of inspection and palpation; however, new, noninvasive, computerized monitoring systems that employ inductive plethysmography are available. Information about respiratory rate, tidal volume, ratio of inspiratory time to total breath time (duty cycle), inspiratory flow, and degree of synchrony between chest wall and abdominal movement can be obtained using this type of monitoring.

The adequacy of the ventilatory mechanics can be examined through the various lung volumes and flow rates, which are obtained through spirometry and pulmonary function testing. Commonly obtained parameters are presented in the box on page 589. The relationship between the lung volumes and capacities during resting and maximal ventilation is illustrated in Fig. 16-10. Flow rates are obtained from the flow-volume loop, which is depicted in Fig. 16-11. The flow-volume loop includes both the forced inspiratory and expiratory maneuvers. The peak expiratory flow rate (PEFR) can be measured very simply using a handheld peak flow meter and is the most useful parameter for determining the degree of airflow obstruction present in asthmatic patients, especially during an attack.

The most useful test of ventilatory mechanics is the forced vital capacity (FVC),

---

NORMAL ARTERIAL BLOOD GAS VALUES

pH	7.35-7.45
Pco$_2$	35-45 mm Hg
Po$_2$	95-100 mm Hg
O$_2$ saturation	93-98%

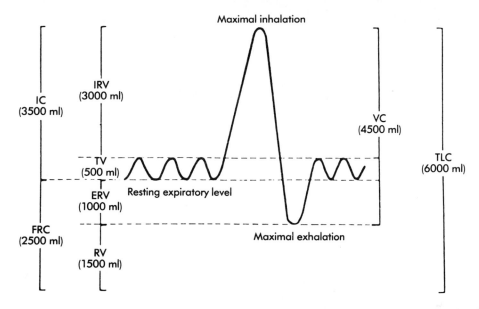

Fig. 16-10. Lung volumes and lung capacities. *Lung volumes:* tidal, expiratory reserve, residual, and inspiratory reserve. *Lung capacities:* functional residual, vital, inspiratory, and total lung. Capacities are composed of two or more volumes. Values shown are for an average-sized young adult.
(From Spearman CB, Sheldon RL, and Eagan DF: Egan's fundamentals of respiratory therapy, ed 4, St. Louis, 1982, The CV Mosby Co.)

which can be obtained very simply using spirometry. This is the total volume of air that can be forcibly exhaled following a maximal inspiration. Measures of the forced expiratory volume (FEV) of air at 1 (FEV_1), 2 (FEV_2), and 3 (FEV_3) second intervals following a maximal inspiration can be obtained as component volumes of the FVC. A normal FEV_1 rules out significant mechanical dysfunction and is, therefore, a good screening parameter. The ratio of FEV_1 to the FVC (FEV_1/FVC) is the best indicator of airway obstruction (Martin, 1987). These parameters are used to grade the degree of pulmonary impairment present in disorders that affect ventilatory function (Table 16-1) as well as aid in the diagnosis of the type of ventilatory dysfunction present (see Table 16-2).

Additionally, an assessment of respiratory muscle strength can be made by measuring the maximum static mouth pressures generated during inspiration (maximal inspiratory pressure [Pi_{max}]), and expiration (maximal expiratory pressure or [Pe_{max}]). A measure of endurance is the maximum sustained ventilation (MSV) or the maximum level of ventilation that can be sustained for 10 to 15 minutes. It is a relatively constant fraction (80%) of the maximum voluntary ventilation (MVV) in normal persons. The MVV is the volume of air, expressed in liters/minute, that a person can breathe with a maximal, repetitive, voluntary effort over 12 to 15 seconds. Another measure of endurance is the sustained inspiratory pressure–endurance time (SIP-ET), which is a measure of the length of time over which a person can generate an inspiratory effort against a maximal threshold load.

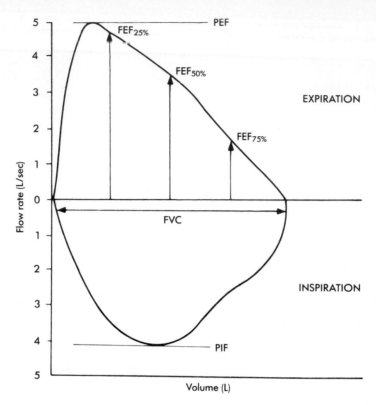

Fig. 16-11. Normal flow-volume loop. The flow-volume loop includes both expiratory and inspiratory flow-volume curves. The FVC can be read directly on the horizontal axis. The peak and other flows can be read directly on the vertical axis. *PEF,* Peak expiratory flow; *PIF,* peak inspiratory flow; FEF$_{25\%}$, FEF$_{50\%}$, and *FEF$_{75\%}$*, forced expiratory flow at 25%, 50%, and 75% of the FVC.
(From Spearman CB, Sheldon RL, and Egan DF: Egan's fundamentals of respiratory therapy, ed 4, St. Louis, 1982, The CV Mosby Co.)

Alterations of Ventilation

A level of alveolar ventilation that is sufficient to meet the body's metabolic demands will be reflected by a partial pressure of carbon dioxide in arterial blood of approximately 40 mm Hg. Ventilation in excess of that required to meet metabolic demands is termed hyperventilation, whereas ventilation at a level insufficient to meet metabolic demands is called hypoventilation. These terms should not be used to describe a patient's breathing pattern. A person whose respiratory rate is very rapid may still be retaining carbon dioxide and thus be experiencing alveolar hypoventilation.

Responses to ventilatory dysfunction, which nurses diagnose and treat, include ineffective breathing pattern and ineffective airway clearance. Some examples of conditions that cause *ineffective breathing pattern,* defined as a state in which the inspiratory and expiratory pattern does not provide adequate or appropriate ventilation, include those characterized by chronic airflow limitation (Lareau and Larson, 1987), decreased lung expansion (Hopp and Williams, 1987), neuromuscu-

Table 16-1. Classification of respiratory impairment

	Class 1 0% (no impairment)	Class 2 10-25% (mild impairment)	Class 3 30-45% (moderate impairment)	Class 4 50-100% (severe impairment)
Dyspnea	If dyspnea is present, it is consistent with the activity	Dyspnea with fast walking on level ground or when walking up a hill; patient can keep pace with persons of same age and body build on level ground but not on hills or stairs	Dyspnea while walking on level ground with person of the same age or walking up one flight of stairs; patient can walk a mile at own pace	Dyspnea after walking more than 100 meters at own pace on level ground; patient sometimes is dyspneic with less exertion or even at rest
	or	or	or	or
Tests of ventilatory function FVC FEV_1 FEV_1/FVC ratio(%)	Above the lower limit of normal for the predicted value as defined by the 95% confidence interval	Below the 95% confidence interval but greater than 60% predicted for FVC, FEV_1, and FEV_1/FVC ratio	Less than 60% predicted, but greater than 50% predicted for FVC 40% predicted for FEV_1 40% actual value for FEV_1/FVC ratio	Less than 50% predicted for FVC 40% predicted for FEV_1 40% actual value for FEV_1/FVC ratio 40% predicted for D_{co}
	or	or	or	or
$\dot{V}O_2$max	Greater than 25 ml/(kg · min)	Between 20-25 ml/(kg · min)	Between 15-20 ml/(kg · min)	Less than 15 ml/(kg · min)

From American Medical Association: Guides to the Evaluation of Permanent Impairment, ed 2, Chicago, 1984, AMA.

lar dysfunction, malnutrition (Openbrier and Covey, 1987), and/or respiratory muscle fatigue (Larson and Kim, 1987). Terms used to describe different breathing patterns are included below.

tachypnea: rapid, shallow pattern of respiration.

hyperpnea: rapid, deep pattern of respiration, which is usually seen after exercise.

eupnea: quiet, ordinary respiration with no exaggerated effort or awareness of the sensation of breathing, usually 16 to 20 respirations per minute.

apnea: cessation of respiration.

bradypnea: pattern of slow breathing, usually fewer than ten respirations per minute.

Cheyne-Stokes: pattern of periodic breathing characterized by initial shallow respirations, which increase in depth, reach a peak, and then decline, and are followed by a period of apnea.

hypopnea: slow, shallow pattern of respiration.

Biot's: Sequence of deep gasps followed by apnea and then deep gasps.

Ineffective airway clearance is a response to conditions characterized by an increased amount of respiratory tract secretions, abnormally thick and tenacious se-

Table 16-2. Altered pulmonary mechanics in restrictive and obstructive lung disease

Clinical example	Spirometric measurements	Nonspirometric lung volumes	Lung compliance	Airway resistance
Restrictive disorders				
Pulmonary fibrosis	Decreased FVC Decreased FEV_1 Increased $\dfrac{FEV_1}{FVC}$	Decreased TLC Decreased FRC Decreased RV	Decreased	Decreased
Neuromuscular disease	Decreased FVC Decreased FEV_1 Normal $\dfrac{FEV_1}{FVC}$	Decreased TLC Normal FRC Increased RV	Normal	Normal
Obstructive disorders				
Asthma (during attack)	Decreased FVC Decreased FEV_1 Decreased $\dfrac{FEV_1}{FVC}$	Increased TLC Increased FRC	Normal	Increased
Emphysema	Same as asthma	Same as asthma	Increased	Increased

From Martin, L: Pulmonary physiology in clinical practice, St. Louis, 1987, The CV Mosby Co.

cretions, impaired ciliary action, and/or ineffective cough. Some examples of conditions that cause ineffective airway clearance, defined as a state in which an individual is unable to clear secretions or obstructions from the respiratory tract to maintain airway patency, include infection (Hanley and Tyler, 1987), chronic airflow limitation (Kim and Larson, 1987), neuromuscular dysfunction (Hoffman, 1987), and the presence of an artificial airway (Shekleton and Nield, 1987).

Presented in the following two sections is an explanation of the pathophysiologic mechanisms by which these responses are brought about in disorders of ventilation. Ventilatory dysfunction can be the result of an impairment or alteration in either respiratory drive or the ventilatory mechanical response. Disorders outside of the respiratory system can also cause disruption of ventilatory control and function (van Lunteren and Cherniack, 1987). These disorders are addressed in other chapters of this book.

HYPERVENTILATION
Pathophysiologic mechanisms and clinical manifestations

The term *alveolar hyperventilation* refers to ventilation in excess of that required to meet metabolic needs and maintain normal carbon dioxide levels in the body tissues. The pressure exerted by the carbon dioxide in the blood will fall below normal levels, since carbon dioxide is expired in greater than normal amounts by the lungs. As a result there is less carbon dioxide available to combine with water and form carbonic acid. There is a deficit of carbonic acid with a subsequent decrease in the hydrogen ion concentration.

The plasma pH (a measure of hydrogen ion concentration) will be alkaline, and

VENTILATORY PARAMETERS

Lung volumes

Tidal volume (V_T)

Volume of air inspired and expired with a normal breath (400-500 cc or 5 cc/kg body weight). Usually about 10% of VC.

Inspiratory reserve volume (IRV)

Maximal volume that can be inspired from the end of a normal inspiration

Expiratory reserve volume (ERV)

Maximal volume that can be exhaled by a forced expiration after a normal expiration

Residual volume (RV)

Volume of gas left in lung after maximal expiration

Lung capacities

Vital capacity (VC)

Maximal amount of air that can be expired after a maximal inspiratory effort (70 cc/kg body weight) (IRV + V_T + ERV); When exhalation is forceful it is called forced vital capacity (FVC)

Inspiratory capacity (IC)

Maximal volume that can be inspired after a normal expiration (V_T + IRV)

Functional residual capacity (FRC)

Volume of air left in lungs after a normal expiration (ERV + RV)

Total lung capacity (TLC)

Total volume of gas in lungs after maximal inspiration (IRV + V_T + ERV + RV) (Men: 3.6-9.4 liters; women; 2.5-6.9 liters)

Flow rates

Forced expiratory flow (FEF_{25}, FEF_{50}, FEF_{75}

Volume of air forcibly exhaled per second or minute at 25%, 50%, and 75% of the FVC

Maximal midflow (MMF_{25-75})

Flow rate (liters/second) measured between the 25% and 75% points of the FVC

Maximal expiratory flow (MEF)

Total amount of air expired per minute, breathing as rapidly as possible

Maximal inspiratory flow (MIF)

Total amount of air inspired per minute, breathing as rapidly as possible

Peak expiratory flow rate (PEFR)

Highest rate of flow sustained for 10 msec or more at which air can be expelled from the lungs

---

the normal ratio of 1 part carbonic acid to 20 parts bicarbonate is decreased on the carbonic acid side. Other terms used to describe this condition include respiratory alkalosis, primary carbonic acid deficit, hypocapnea, and nonmetabolic alkalosis (see Chapter 18).

The renal system attempts to compensate for this abnormality in acid-base balance by excreting bicarbonate ions and retaining hydrogen ions and nonbicarbonate anions. As a result of this homeostatic mechanism the pH (an expression of the hydrogen ion concentration) of the urine will be on the alkaline side, plasma bicarbonate levels will fall below normal, and the normal carbonic acid–base bicarbonate ratio of 1:20 will be restored.

In the presence of alkalosis, calcium ionization is decreased, which causes muscular irritability, since the muscle becomes more responsive because of the altered membrane potential. The decrease in ionized Ca^{++} results from the fact that protein-bound calcium is in equilibrium with H^+ according to the following formula:

$$CaPr + H^+ \leftrightharpoons HPr + Ca^{++}$$

When H^+ decreases, as in alkalosis, the reaction is driven toward the production of bound Ca (CaPr), thus reducing the amount of Ca^{++}. Muscular stiffness, aching, and cramps may be the only symptoms experienced; however, twitching, convulsions, and tetany may also occur. Tetany is more likely to occur only if the alkalosis develops rapidly. Signs that indicate abnormal muscular irritability can be elicited in the presence of respiratory alkalosis. Contraction of the muscles around the mouth in response to tapping the facial nerve in front of the ear is referred to as a *positive Chvostek's sign*. Muscular spasms of the hand and wrist as a result of compression of the brachial artery for 1 to 5 minutes is called a *positive Trousseau's sign*.

Blood flow to the vital organs is decreased as a result of both the vasoconstrictor effect of the low carbon dioxide concentration and the reduced cardiac output. Increased respiratory effort causes an increase in the intrathoracic pressure, which in turn impedes venous return, a major determinant of cardic output. Subjective feelings of shortness of breath and chest pain resulting from the increased thoracic pressure and respiratory effort may be experienced. The alkalotic condition of the plasma inhibits the release of oxygen from oxyhemoglobin. The combination of vasoconstriction, reduced cardiac output, and inhibition of the release of oxygen from oxyhemoglobin results in tissue hypoxia.

The brain, because it utilizes approximately 20% of the total oxygen supply, is extremely sensitive to hypoxia, and symptoms such as dizziness, light-headedness, inability to concentrate, tinnitus, blurred vision, and disorientation may develop; ultimately unconsciousness may occur. Alkalosis also causes increased neuronal excitability. Convulsions are probably partially caused by cerebral ischemia, as well as by the muscular and neuronal irritability.

Etiology and treatment

Alveolar hyperventilation leads to respiratory alkalosis because of the excessive loss of carbon dioxide through the lungs with a resultant decrease in the arterial carbon dioxide concentration. One of the most common causes of alveolar hyperventilation and respiratory alkalosis is the abnormally rapid rate of respiration that accompanies anxiety and extreme emotional states. These persons sometimes hyperventilate to the point of unconsciousness. Treatment is aimed at promoting the accumulation of carbon dioxide by breath-holding and rebreathing expired air. Recurrence is prevented by making the person aware of the effects of his breathing patterns and helping him understand and overcome the cause of anxiety.

Another primary cause of alveolar hyperventilation is increased respiratory drive. High fever and infections such as encephalitis and meningitis cause irritability of the brain tissue, including the tissue of the respiratory center, causing it to become more sensitive than normal to stimuli. The result is an exaggerated respiratory response to even normal stimuli. Salicylate poisoning causes excessive stimulation of the respiratory center (see the case study in Chapter 5). Central nervous system lesions (tumors, trauma, or bleeding) can also alter the sensitivity and response of the respiratory center, causing alveolar hyperventilation. Hyperventilation syndrome is an idiopathic disorder caused by acute or chronic dysregulation of ventilation, and causes respiratory alkalosis and increased adrenosympathetic tone (Stoop et al., 1986).

Mechanical overventilation with a respirator will cause the loss of excessive amounts of carbon dioxide. Readjustment of the rate or addition of dead space to allow the patient to rebreathe greater amounts of his own air will correct the problem.

Alveolar hyperventilation can also occur as a compensatory homeostatic mechanism. In the presence of metabolic acidosis, pulmonary ventilation increases in order to reduce the amount of carbon dioxide available for form carbonic acid. Treatment is directed toward resolving the underlying metabolic acidosis. Alveolar hyperventilation can be caused by hypoxemia. A low arterial oxygen concentration stimulates peripheral chemoreceptors, which in turn stimulate the respiratory center to increase the respiratory effort. Administration of supplemental oxygen will usually increase oxygen saturation and eliminate the stimulus to increased respiratory effort.

Exposure to increased environmental temperatures causes hyperventilation as the lungs attempt to help maintain the normal body temperature. The same mechanism is partially responsible for the hyperventilation that occurs as a result of fever. Increased body temperature causes a 7% increase in the metabolic rate per degree Fahrenheit increase in body temperature. Any condition that increases the body's metabolic rate will also increase production of carbon dioxide, an end product of metabolism and the primary stimulus to respiration.

HYPOVENTILATION
Pathophysiologic mechanisms and clinical manifestations

Alveolar hypoventilation is ventilation at a level insufficient to meet metabolic needs and prevent retention of carbon dioxide. The result of alveolar hypoventilation is carbon dioxide retention, which is accompanied by hypoxemia. As the carbon dioxide concentration increases, oxygen concentrations decrease and carbonic acid levels rise, causing the ratio of 1:20 to increase on the carbonic acid side. Terms used to describe this condition include respiratory acidosis, primary carbon dioxide excess, nonmetabolic acidosis, hypercarbia, and hypercapnia.

The renal system attempts to compensate for the increase in extracellular carbonic acid by conserving base bicarbonate and excreting hydrogen ions and nonbicarbonate anions. This results in excretion of an acid urine and an increase in plasma bicarbonate levels. Before compensation occurs, the plasma pH will decrease. When carbon dioxide retention is chronic, the compensatory action of the kidney will keep changes in plasma pH minimal. Elevated arterial carbon dioxide and decreased arterial oxygen levels stimulate the carotid and aortic chemoreceptors to cause an increase in the rate and force of cardiac contraction, with a corresponding increase in pulse rate, strength of pulse, and blood pressure. Palpitations or a subjective awareness of the heartbeat may be experienced because of increases in the rate and strength of cardiac contraction.

Elevated carbon dioxide levels also

cause cerebral vasodilation and an increase in cerebral blood flow. This causes both an increase in cerebrospinal fluid (CSF) pressure and cerebral edema. Dizziness, headache, confusion, and a feeling of pressure in the head are symptoms. Papilledema, or swelling of the optic nerve, may also result. The headache is usually in the occipital area, is throbbing, and is of greatest intensity when the patient first awakens.

As the extracellular hydrogen ion concentration increases, hydrogen ions begin to enter the cell. Potassium ions leave the cell in order to maintain the normal electrical gradient. Serum potassium levels will be increased at first but will decrease as a deficit in the total body potassium stores develops. Symptoms of low potassium levels (hypokalemia) include generalized muscle weakness and cramping. Long-term potassium loss causes degenerative changes in myocardial cells: loss of striation, nuclear disintegration, and eventually fibrosis. Life-threatening cardiac arrhythmias may occur, since potassium is necessary for normal myocardial performance. These arrhythmias may also be attributed to the direct effects of hypoxia and hypercapnia on myocardial cells.

Changes in behavior in the presence of hypercapnia and hypoxemia are to be expected. Lethargy, disorientation, confusion, and uncooperativeness may occur in varying degrees. *Asterixis,* a flapping motion of the wrist when the hand is extended, may also be present. If the carbon dioxide concentration increases rapidly, convulsions and unconsciousness may result.

In response to the hypoxemia and acidosis, vasoconstriction of the pulmonary vessels and elevation of the pulmonary artery pressure occur as compensatory mechanisms to improve perfusion in the pulmonary vascular bed. This increases the work load of the right side of the heart, causing hypertrophy and predisposition in the patient to the development of right-sided heart failure, or *cor pulmonale.* This is a constant threat to patients with chronic conditions that cause hypoventilation. Compensatory responses to chronic hypoxia, including erythropoiesis and increased vascularity of peripheral tissues, will also occur in the presence of chronic conditions causing hypoventilation.

In patients experiencing chronic carbon dioxide retention, the hypoxic drive becomes the main stimulus for respiration as the central respiratory centers become nonresponsive to the high carbon dioxide levels. This is seen in emphysema where airway obstruction results in chronic hypoventilation and chronically elevated arterial carbon dioxide levels. The hydrogen ion concentration normally increases with a rise in carbon dioxide levels; however, in chronic carbon dioxide retention the change in pH is slight because of the compensatory mechanisms of bicarbonate ion retention and hydrogen ion excretion by the kidneys. Administration of high levels of oxygen to these patients will remove the stimulus of low oxygen levels that causes respiration. As CO_2 levels increase in response to the depressed respirations, a condition referred to as *carbon dioxide narcosis* develops. The effects of this condition vary from a headache and drowsiness to complete disorientation, extreme lethargy, and eventually coma and death.

Collapse of the alveoli is referred to as *atelectasis* and is the result of inadequate expansion of lung tissue. The tendency to develop atelectasis is enhanced in conditions that cause alveolar hypoventilation. Alveolar collapse occurs in obstructive disorders where the flow of inspired air is partially or completely obstructed with the subsequent reabsorption of alveolar air (absorption atelectasis) and as a result of space-occupying lesions or fluid accumulation in the chest, which compresses lung tissue (compression atelectasis). Microatelectasis is often observed by x-ray after surgery and is the result of "inspiratory failure" or respiration at a constant or reduced tidal volume. Microatelectasis can also occur as a result of increased surface tension within the alveoli caused by surfactant deficiency. The collapsed alveoli are no longer functional for gas exchange, and the immediate result of atelectasis is disruption of normal blood gas values. A later result may be superimposed infection and bronchopneumonia due to the anaerobic conditions existing in the collapsed lung tissue.

Etiology and treatment

Alveolar hypoventilation causes respiratory acidosis through retention of carbon dioxide and hypoxemia. Conditions that lead to alveolar hypoventilation and respiratory acidosis can be grouped under two major headings: (1) those that decrease respiratory drive or alter the sensitivity and function of the respiratory center and (2) those that decrease the ventilatory response through impairment of the mechanics of respiration.

Various drugs and anesthetic agents inhibit the sensitivity and function of the respiratory center. Sedatives, narcotics, and certain analgesics and anesthetics depress the sensitivity and function of the respiratory center, which in turn depresses respiration and leads to alveolar hypoventilation. Judicious use of such agents will prevent the development of alveolar hypoventilation.

Oxygen is a drug that can have toxic effects, and it should always be administered accordingly. For patients in whom the hypoxic drive provides the main stimulus for respiration, administration of high concentrations of oxygen will remove the sole stimulus for respiration. Alveolar hypoventilation is already present, and elimination of the stimulus to breathe will further depress ventilatory function. In these patients the sensitivity of the respiratory center is altered, since it is nonresponsive or refractory to chronically elevated levels of carbon dioxide.

The function of the respiratory center may also be depressed as a result of disease processes and direct damage to it. The respiratory center can be damaged by a reduction or loss of its blood supply, trauma (surgical or accidental), or increased intracranial pressure. Blood supply to the medulla can be reduced or "lost" as a result of hemorrhage, narrowing, or obstruction of an artery by clot formation or arteriosclerotic processes. Increased intracranial pressure is the result of an increase in the volume of the intracranial matter and fluids. The volume increase can result from a variety of causes: abnormal tissue growth of a tumor, hemorrhage, overproduction of cerebrospinal fluid, obstruction of the circulation of the cerebrospinal fluid, or the edematous swelling of brain tissue. *Primary idiopathic alveolar hypoventilation* is a disease condition in which there appears to be a primary defect in the functioning of the respiratory centers, leading to hypoventilation.

Alveolar hypoventilation may occur as a result of *sleep apnea*. Two respiratory patterns may emerge during sleep: periodic apnea and regular breathing accompanied by intermittent periods of hypoventilation. Periodic apnea may be central or obstructive in nature. Central apnea is caused by a failure of rhythmogenesis (lack of respiratory drive) for three or more respiratory cycles. This type of apnea commonly occurs at the onset of sleep. It is characterized by absence of chest movement and airflow. Obstructive apnea is a result of complete airway occlusion as oropharyngeal muscles relax. It is characterized by chest movement without airflow and intermittent periods of alveolar hypoventilation. Clinical manifestations include snoring, somnolence, and signs and symptoms of respiratory and/or cardiac failure. Hypersomnia may be the patient's chief complaint. There is some speculation that sudden infant death syndrome (SIDS) may also be caused by disordered neural control of respiration during sleep (see Chapter 4).

The goals of treatment of alveolar hypoventilation include the following:

1. Restoring or maintaining optimal ventilatory function
2. Improving cellular oxygenation
3. Restoring or maintaining normal acid-base balance

Obviously the second and third goals depend on successful achievement of the first. To improve impaired ventilatory function the cause of the impairment must be considered. When the cause of the impairment is decreased respiratory drive, the patient can be ventilated using an artificial respirator set on automatic so it "breathes" for him. This is a temporary, emergency measure. To permanently correct hypoventilation the cause of the decreased respiratory drive must also be treated. When decreased respiratory drive is the result of drugs, dosage or use should be decreased. An antagonist must be given in some cases, and in other cases various procedures to remove the drug from the body will have to be utilized. When the decreased respiratory drive is the result of disease or trauma, surgery to reduce intra-cranial pressure, restore blood supply, or repair damage might be done. Various drugs can be used to reduce cerebral edema and consequently intracranial pressure. If severe damage to the medullary centers has occurred, restoration of normal respiratory function is highly improbable.

Alveolar hypoventilation can also occur in conditions in which the ventilatory response is decreased because of disruption of the normal mechanics of respiration. These conditions, which are discussed in the following sections, can be classified according to the type of impairment that occurs:

1. Obstructive disorders, acute and chronic
2. Restrictive disorders
3. Pulmonary surfactant deficiency

The results of pulmonary function tests reflect both obstructive and restrictive disorders. The type of ventilatory alteration that is demonstrated can be used in making a differential diagnosis (Table 16-2). In obstructive disorders residual volume, and therefore functional residual capacity (FRC), will be increased and expiratory flow rates will be decreased. The ratio of FEV_1/FVC will be decreased. In restrictive disorders the vital capacity will be reduced and the peak flow rate and maximal mid-flow rate may or may not be changed. The FEV_1 will be decreased, but the ratio of FEV_1/FVC will be normal or increased. In some disorders both obstructive and restrictive breathing patterns are demonstrated. For example, tumor growth can cause obstruction to airflow, as well as restriction through a decrease in the size of the chest cavity.

Obstructive disorders

Airway obstruction may be chronic or acute. Acute obstruction may result from aspiration of a foreign object, swelling of the trachea and pharyngeal area, spasm of the larynx or bronchoconstriction, swelling or displacement of the tongue so that it occludes the airway, or ineffective airway clearance and the accumulation of respiratory tract secretions. Swelling or edema of the airway or tongue is an inflammatory response that can be evoked by physical or chemical trauma (e.g. airway obstruction following a burn with smoke inhalation), a hypersensitivity response (e.g., a severe anaphylactic reaction), or an infectious process (e.g., acute epiglottitis or tracheobronchitis).

The potential for ineffective airway clearance and airway occlusion caused by accumulated secretions exists in all conditions marked by impaired mucociliary transport and/or a depressed or ineffective cough mechanism. Mucociliary transport can be impaired by an increase in the amount of secretions, a change in the character of the secretions so that they become thicker and stickier, and a slowing or loss of ciliary action.

A change from the normal amount of character of the respiratory tract secretions is most often the result of infection or chronic pulmonary disease. The alteration in the amount and character of secretions that occurs in the chronic obstructive disorders is discussed later in this chapter. *Young's syndrome* is an inherited disorder in which bronchial and epididymal secretions are abnormal, resulting in chronic sinopulmonary infections, bronchiectasis, and azoospermia (Kueppers, 1987). The disease progresses slowly, and these patients are often identified when they are evaluated for an infertility problem.

Ciliary action can be affected in a number of ways. Ciliary action can be slowed or stopped by pharmacologic and anesthetic agents. The cilia can be damaged by the inhalation of toxic substances that pro-

duce ciliostasis or denude the epithelium. Certain known air pollutants, in sufficiently high concentrations, are ciliotoxic, which helps to explain the detrimental effect of high levels of pollution in exacerbating respiratory symptoms in people with cardiopulmonary problems. Tobacco smoke from cigarettes produces these direct effects on the cilia and, coupled with the increased mucus production that it stimulates, it is easy to understand why smokers must rely on the cough mechanism to maintain a clear airway (Center and McFadden, 1985). Direct trauma, such as that caused by the insertion of instruments or endotracheal or tracheostomy tubes or by suctioning the airway with too high a pressure, can also cause denuded epithelium and ciliary damage (Shekleton, 1987).

Structural abnormalities of the cilia have also been shown to adversely affect their function. A cross section of a normal cilium is illustrated in Fig. 16-12. Both acquired and congenital disorders can result in structural abnormalities that cause ciliary dysmotility. Patients with recurrent respiratory tract infections and bronchitis have been found to have structural defects such as ciliary fusion and missing or extra microtubules that apparently can occur as a result of prolonged bronchial injury or infection (Center and McFadden, 1985). The *immotile cilia syndrome* (ICS) or *ciliary dyskinesia* is an inherited defect in which structural abnormalities occur as the result of a genetic mutation. The mode of transmission has been found to be recessive for the majority of affected families and dominant for some. The most commonly found structural defects in ICS include absence of the outer dynein arms and absence of both dynein arms and nexin links, although all possible alterations have been found (Kueppers, 1987). These patients usually seek medical atten-

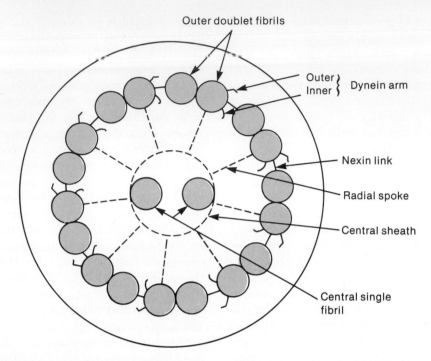

Outer doublet fibrils

Outer ⎫
Inner ⎭ Dynein arm

Nexin link

Radial spoke

Central sheath

Central single fibril

Fig. 16-12. Cross-sectional view of the normal structure of a single cilium. Characteristic 9 + 2 microtubular arrangement is present in which the two single fibrils in the center of the cilium are surrounded by nine coupled pairs of outer fibrils. Dynein arms are the site of ATPase activity. Nexin links and radial spokes provide anchoring between microtubules and limit action of the microtubules as they slide along one another to create unidirectional beating motion with fast downstroke and slow recovery stroke. Approximately 200 cilia are on each columnar epithelial cell, which beat in a coordinated manner, approximately 1000 to 1500 times each minute, to move secretions toward nasopharynx. Ciliary efficiency also depends on rheologic properties of mucus layer.

tion for the pulmonary problems they experience that are the result of impaired mucociliary clearance caused by ciliary stasis or weak or discoordinated ciliary motion. A history of chronic sinusitis, otitis media, and bronchitis with frequent respiratory tract infections, including colds and pneumonia since childhood, is usually given. Bronchiectasis usually develops as a result of the recurrent infections. Adult males are infertile as a result of immotile spermatozoa. In approximately half the patients with ICS, situs inversus is present and is believed to be caused by dysfunction of the cilia that help propel the developing organs through the coelom during embryonic development (Center and McFadden, 1985). When situs inversus is present along with the other signs and symptoms, this condition is called Kartagener's syndrome (Kueppers, 1987).

An ineffective cough can be the result of conditions in which the respiratory muscles are weakened, airway resistance is high, or neuromuscular function is impaired. The cough reflex may be depressed or nonexistent in an altered state of consciousness such as coma or as a result of the direct action of drugs that depress cerebral function.

Surgery provides an example of a common clinical situation in which mucociliary transport is impaired and the normal protective cough mechanism is suppressed. Following anesthesia and surgery, the expectoration of respiratory tract secretions becomes more difficult than it is normally because of the increased viscosity of the secretions, inhibition of ciliary action, pain, and depression of the cough mechanism. Before surgery, anticholinergic drugs are administered to promote smooth muscle relaxation and to decrease body secretions. The mucous membranes of the respiratory tract, nasopharynx, and mouth become very dry, and mucus secretion is reduced. Endotracheal intubation bypasses the normal humidifying mechanisms of the upper airways. Ciliary action is inhibited because of damage to the cilia during endotracheal intubation and lack of proper humidity, and by the direct drug action of narcotic and anesthetic agents. Depression of the cough mechanism after surgery is the result of a combination of direct drug action (i.e., of anesthetic, narcotic, and sedative agents) and the altered level of consciousness. If secretions are allowed to accumulate, crusting and eventually occlusion may occur.

Abnormal breath sounds are the most direct signs of the presence of secretions in the airways. Rales or crackles reflect the presence of secretions, mucus, and fluid in the smaller airways, while rhonchi or wheezes reflect the presence of secretions in the larger airways. Wheezes also reflect narrowing of the airway diameter and are a common finding in chronic obstructive disorders (Martin, 1987). If obstruction of the airway has occurred, the breath sounds will be diminished or absent. The presence of normal breath sounds accompanied by an alteration in the amount or consistency of the respiratory tract secretions and a cough are signs that indicate that the person is not retaining secretions

currently but is at risk for developing ineffective airway clearance (Shekleton and Nield, 1987).

Acute obstruction. The signs and symptoms accompanying total acute obstruction of the airway include marked respiratory effort with extreme sternal, abdominal, and intercostal retractions, sternal rocking movements, extreme anxiety, and cyanosis. The person may be unable to speak or cough and often clutches the neck. Arterial hypoxemia and acidosis rapidly ensue and the tissues are subjected to extreme hypoxia. If the obstruction is not relieved, the person will experience progressive lethargy and decreased respiratory effort and loss of consciousness within minutes. Respiratory efforts cease as hypercapnea and acidosis become extreme.

Partial airway obstruction may also occur, and the manifestations will be somewhat less extreme. The pulse and respiratory rates will rise. Characteristic of partial obstructial is respiratory stridor. Inspiratory stridor indicates a glottic or subglottic obstruction. Expiratory stridor indicates a "ball-valve" type of obstruction below the cords. Mucosal edema results in a barking cough or rough stridor. As hypoxemia develops the patient may exhibit dyspnea, cyanosis, and anxiety.

Treatment rationale. Any degree of acute airway obstruction is serious and requires immediate treatment. A partial obstruction may progressively worsen if left untreated. Other complications of airway obstruction include permanent pulmonary damage, hypoxia damage to the central nervous system, and noncardiogenic pulmonary edema.

The first concern in treating acute obstruction is reestablishing the airway by removing or bypassing the obstruction. The airway must be open for ventilation to occur at all. A foreign body can sometimes be forced out of the airway using the

Heimlich maneuver. Compression of the abdomen causes residual air from the lungs to be forced out, dislodging the foreign body. Bronchoscopy is used to remove a foreign body that has been aspirated and lodged below the vocal cords. Laryngoscopy can be used to remove a foreign body lodged above the vocal cords.

Bypassing an obstruction can be achieved by insertion of an endotracheal or nasotracheal tube or by creation of an external opening to the trachea (tracheostomy). Removal of accumulated secretions can be done by inserting a catheter attached to suction into the airway to remove secretions. Edema of the airway structures can be minimized or reduced through the use of various drugs.

Most frequently the tongue is involved in airway obstruction. The tongue may fall back and occlude the airway in conditions in which the muscles that form the floor of the mouth are allowed to relax. Such conditions include any state of unconsciousness, myasthenia gravis, paralysis resulting from use of muscle relaxants or other drugs, and stroke (cerebral vascular accident). Repositioning the head so that the neck is hyperextended will open the airway. Nasopharyngeal and oropharyngeal airways may also be used to hold the tongue in position and maintain an open airway.

Disease models: acute obstruction. It has already been mentioned that acute airway obstruction may be the result of a variety of pathophysiologic mechanisms. It should also be pointed out that infants and small children are especially at risk for airway obstruction because of the anatomic structure of their respiratory systems. The tongue is larger in proportion to the rest of the mouth, the larynx is higher, cartilaginous support of the airway is less, there are fewer true alveoli, and the airways are

of smaller diameter compared to the adult. The potential for the development of airway edema is great because of the greater proportion of soft tissue present and the looser attachment of mucous membranes lining the airway as well. Respiratory disorders account for approximately half of the acute illnesses of children under 17 years of age. The clinician must therefore always be alert to the possibility of acute airway obstruction developing in the pediatric patient. For this reason, the disease models to be discussed are diseases that affect children. Bronchiolitis is a model of small or lower airway obstruction: laryngotracheobronchitis (croup) and epiglottitis are models of upper airway obstruction.

Bronchiolitis. Inflammation of the bronchiolar mucosa and obstructing secretions characteritize bronchiolitis, a viral disorder. Usually the causative agent is the respiratory syncytial virus (RSV), although adenovirus, parainfluenza, influenza type A, and rhinovirus have also been implicated. High levels of maternal antibodies to RSV during the first month of life and development of endogenous antibody after the first year of life affords protection from RSV (Kirby and Taylor, 1986). Acute bronchiolar obstruction is the result of plugging with mucus, cellular debris, and edema, all sequelae of the inflammatory process that occurs in response to infection. Air is trapped distal to the obstruction, leading to air-trapping, overexpansion of the lungs, and atelectasis. Although the disease in most children is generally benign and self-limiting, in 1% of affected children the obstruction is significant enough to result in respiratory failure. The critical period is the first 24 to 72 hours.

Bronchiolitis affects children under the age of 18 months with the peak incidence occurring before 2 and 5 months. It most commonly occurs during the winter and early spring months. The child usually presents with a history of an upper respiratory infection during the preceding days. Preceding signs and symptoms usually include rhinorrhea, low-grade fever, loss of appetite, and difficulty eating. The signs and symptoms accompanying bronchiolitis are similar to an acute asthmatic attack; however, there is little bronchiolar smooth muscle in the airways of infants, and asthma rarely occurs before 1 year of age. The severity of an episode is likely to be greater in children younger than 6 months of age and with a history of prematurity or congenital heart disease (Kirby and Taylor, 1986).

Increased respiratory effort will be apparent with a prolonged expiratory phase, audible wheezing, nasal flaring, and retractions. Wheezing is the result of turbulent air flow through the obstructed airways. A harsh cough will be present. The chest x-ray film demonstrates hyperinflation, and scattered infiltrate, generalized fine rales are heard on auscultation. The heart and respiratory rates will be increased. Diminished or absent breath sounds in the presence of listlessness, a decreased respiratory rate, pallor, and cyanosis indicate imminent respiratory failure and intervention must be immediate.

Treatment rationale. Goals of treatment include improving the oxygenation status and preventing complications. Children in respiratory failure or immediate danger of such may require endotracheal intubation and ventilatory assistance. In children in whom the disease is not quite so severe, humidified oxygen is administered. Oxygen can be administered via hood, mask, or cannula and is usually given at a concentration no greater than 40%. Extreme flexion of the neck must be avoided to prevent obstruction of the main airway. The child will be more comfortable with the head of the bed elevated. A child in extreme respiratory distress will sit with the head thrust forward. Suction can be used to clear the airway if the child is unable to bring up and expectorate secretions. Chest physiotherapy is generally not used in the acute phase.

Intravenous therapy is initiated to prevent dehydration from insensible loss resulting from fever, tachypnea, and the inability to take fluid and food orally. Handling of the child should be kept to a minimum, since this may overly tire him and further tax his reserves. The parents and siblings will require much explanation, support, and encouragement during the acute phase, since the acute illness can be extremely frightening and overwhelming to parents. Parents may also feel that they could have prevented the illness from occurring. Once the critical period is over, most children recover within a few weeks. Children who are affected most severely will develop long-term abnormalities of pulmonary function as a sequela (Kirby and Taylor, 1986).

Laryngotracheobronchitis. Acute upper airway obstruction in the child may be the result of laryngotracheobronchitis (viral croup) or epiglottitis, both of which can lead to a life-threatening situation. The child with laryngotracheobronchitis (LTB) is especially at risk for obstruction because of the narrow diameter of the trachea. LTB is usually caused by the parainfluenza type I, II, and III viruses, although the adenoviruses, rhinoviruses, and respiratory syncytial viruses may also be implicated. Adenovirus can cause particularly virulent disease (Kirby and Taylor, 1986). Edema of the subglottic area (larynx, trachea, and bronchi) accounts for inspiratory stridor. Edema of the vocal cords accounts for the characteristic harsh barking cough, which is often referred to by both parents and clinicians as "croupy." A history of a cold for the preceding 1 to 2 days will be given by the parents. Boys between the ages of 6 months to 3 years are most frequently affected (Kirby and Taylor, 1986). The parents may also report that symptoms lessen or are absent during the day but worsen at night. A low-grade fever, hoarse voice, and normal white blood cell count are other clinical manifestations. Treatment includes cool mist and hydration for the less acutely ill child and the administration of nebulized racemic epinephrine HCl via intermittent positive pressure breathing (IPPB). There is some evidence that steroids may reduce traumatic upper airway edema and thus may be of some use in the treatment of croup (Kirby and Taylor, 1986).

Acute epiglottitis. Acute epiglottis is a rapidly progressing pediatric medical emergency (Kirby and Taylor, 1986). Inflammation of the epiglottis, aryepiglottic folds, and supraglottic area is caused by *Haemophilus influenzae* type B, which can usually be cultured from both the throat and blood. A small number of cases are caused by *Staphylococcus aureus*. In contrast to viral croup, the onset of epiglottitis is sudden and the child becomes acutely ill immediately. Respiratory difficulties typically increase over a 2- to 4-hour period. There is usually no cough, but an elevated temperature, dysphagia, drooling, and stridor at rest will be present. The child will complain of a severe sore throat and spontaneously assume a sitting position with the neck hyperextended. The epiglottis will appear swollen and "cherry red." Direct visualization should only be attempted by a clinician skilled in the technique using the appropriate equipment. Visualization via incorrect methods, for example, using a tongue depressor, or an attempt to obtain a throat culture may cause sudden obstruction and must be avoided. A positive "thumb sign" indicative of the swollen epiglottis will be observed on a lateral x-ray film of the neck. The white blood cell count will be elevated and shifted to the left.

Treatment includes intubation or tracheostomy to bypass the obstruction and establish a clear airway. The child should remain in an upright, sitting position before treatment, since the epiglottis will further occlude the airway if the child is in a supine position. IV antibiotic therapy is instituted and steroids may be administered, since septicemia is often present. After 48 to 72 hours of antibiotic treatment, the epiglottis will appear normal in size and color and the child can be extubated.

While croup usually occurs during the "flu" season (winter months and early spring) in children between the ages of 3 months to 3 years, epiglottitis has no specific seasonal occurrence and usually affects children between the ages of 3 and 7 years. Another difference between the two disorders is that while there may be recurrent bouts of viral croup, epiglottitis usually is a singular occurrence.

Chronic obstruction. Chronic airway obstruction is the result of a group of diseases that have the ultimate effect of obstructing the flow of air from the lungs, leading to hypercapnea and hypoxemia. This group of diseases is known collectively as chronic obstructive lung disease (COLD) or chronic obstructive pulmonary disease (COPD). Chronic obstructive pulmonary disease is the most common cause of alveolar hypoventilation with associated hypoxemia, chronic hypercapnia, and compensated respiratory acidosis.

Disease models: chronic obstruction. Included in the group of diseases known as COPD are asthma, bronchitis, and emphysema. These disorders are characterized by air flow limitation resulting from obstruction and/or loss of elastic recoil of the lung tissue. These disorders can occur independently or in combination, but most patients diagnosed with COPD exhibit some characteristics of each (Shekleton, 1987). COPD is second to coronary heart disease as a Social Security–compensated disease (Kueppers, 1987). Table 16-3 presents an overview of the differential features of each of these disorders. Also discussed is *cystic fibrosis,* a hereditary disease characterized by production of excessive exocrine gland secretions that can also cause chronic obstruction.

Asthma. Asthma is also known as *reactive airway disease* and is characterized by reversible bronchoconstriction with dyspnea and wheezing during an acute attack. Wheezing is the result of turbulence as air flows through narrowed airways containing excess sputum. Chest tightness without wheezing may occur during an episode of bronchospasm. Airway resistance may be increased 5 to 6 times normal. The forced vital capacity may be as low as 50%

of predicted normal, with flow rates reduced to an even greater extent. The peak expiratory flow rate (PEFR) may be only 15% to 20% of normal (Kirby and Taylor, 1986). During an acute attack, the chest x-ray film may demonstrate hyperinflation and atelectasis. The patient will appear agitated and anxious and may even be confused if the hypoxia is severe enough.

The alteration in blood gases that will occur depends on the extent and length of the attack. Hypoxemia caused by ventilation perfusion mismatching will show up first as a decrease in PO_2, and as the attack persists oxygen saturation will also decrease. The PCO_2 may remain normal or even decrease as a result of the hyperventilation response in mild to moderate attacks. In severe attacks of long duration, PCO_2 levels will increase as carbon dioxide is retained because of alveolar hypoventilation. The work of breathing will be increased, and a combined respiratory and metabolic acidosis may develop (Kirby and Taylor, 1986).

Status asthmaticus is an acute attack that is refractory to treatment and may

Table 16-3. Differential features of COPD

Feature	Emphysema	Chronic bronchitis	Asthma
Family history	Occasional (α_1-antitrypsin deficiency)	Occasional (cystic fibrosis)	Frequent
Atopy	Absent	Absent	Frequent
Smoking history	Usual	Usual	Infrequent
Sputum character	Absent or mucoid	Predominantly neutrophilic	Predominantly eosinophilic
Chest x-ray film	Useful if bullae, hyperinflation, or loss of peripheral vascular markings is present	Often normal; occasional hyperinflation	Often normal; hyperinflation during acute attack
Spirometry	Obstructive pattern unimproved with bronchodilator	Obstructive pattern improved with bronchodilator	Obstructive pattern usually shows good response to bronchodilator

From American Lung Association: Chronic obstructive pulmonary disease, ed. 5, New York, 1981, The Association.

last for hours or even days. Mucus plugging, mucosal edema, and inspissated secretions provide the mechanism for bronchodilator resistance (Kirby and Taylor, 1986). It is considered to be a life-threatening condition. Increased respiratory effort increases intrathoracic pressure and reduces venous return to the heart. This effect, along with the vasocontriction and increased resistance in the pulmonary vascular bed, increases the predisposition to right-sided heart failure. Signs of exhaustion and dehydration may be present in addition to hypoxemia, hypercapnia, and acidosis.

Histologic changes that occur in asthma include the following: an increase in the size and number of the mucosal goblet cells and submucosal mucous glands, thickening of the bronchial basement membrane, hypertrophy of smooth bronchiolar and bronchial muscle, submucosal infiltration of mononuclear inflammatory cells, and usually eosinophils and plugs of mucus blocking small airways.

The obstruction that occurs in asthma, which is intermittent in nature, is caused by narrowing of the bronchioles and bronchi, edema of the mucous membrane, and ineffective airway clearance due to excessive production of abnormally viscous mucus. Asthma can be classified as either extrinsic (allergic) or intrinsic (idiopathic). Extrinsic asthma is characterized by childhood onset and a positive family history of allergy; a positive wheal and flare skin reaction is obtained upon injection of antigens, and high levels of IgE are present. Extrinsic asthma attacks occur as an anaphylactic type of hypersensitivity reaction. An inhaled antigen (allergen) combines with a specific antibody of the IgE immunoglobulin class on an effector cell membrane (usually basophils and mast cells), causing the cell to degranulate and

release mediating substances, which stimulate the responses described earlier (see Chapter 2). The mediators act on specific receptor sites on the smooth muscle cell membranes to reduce the intracellular level of cyclic AMP, which results in smooth muscle contraction. Edema is the result of the increased capillary permeability caused by the mediator substances. These mediator substances include histamine, slow-reacting substance of anaphylaxis (SRS-A), eosinophilic chemotactic factor, prostaglandins, and bradykinin, among others. As a mediator, histamine seems to be of less importance in asthma than SRS-A, which has been found to be a combination of three leukotrienes (LTC, LTD, and LTE). LTC has been shown to be a potent bronchoconstrictor (Bone, et al., 1987b).

Intrinsic asthma is characterized by a negative family history for allergy, normal IgE levels, onset in adolescence or adulthood, and a negative skin test for allergens. The stimulus for asthmatic attacks in persons with intrinsic or idiopathic asthma is nonspecific.

Another mechanism through which asthmatic attacks are thought to occur is a relative imbalance between the intracellular nucleotides cyclic guanosine monophosphate (cGMP) and cyclic adenosine monophosphate (cAMP). cAMP inhibits mediator release and decreases muscle tone while cGMP facilitates mediator release and smooth muscle contraction. There is experimental evidence that cGMP activity increases in the lungs of experimental animals during an anaphylactic bronchospasm. In addition, an increase in the cGMP/cAMP ratio has been demonstrated in asthmatic persons after acetylcholine challenge. In both types of asthma vagally mediated reflex bronchoconstriction results in cholinergic overactivity, which may account for the nonspecific irritant sensitivities in patients with asthma. An additional factor postulated to contribute to the hyperreactivity of the airway is a relative insensitivity of the β-adrenergic receptors of the bronchial smooth muscle with the subsequent loss of epinephrine regulation. In both types of asthma many varying conditions can precipitate an acute attack, including changes in temperature and humidity, worry and stress, exercise, fatigue, exposure to pollutants and smoke, sinusitis and other infections, and pollens.

The occurrence of asthma tends to be familial. Persons with eczema and hay fever have a greater likelihood of developing asthma than persons without those conditions. A respiratory tract infection or insult may precipitate asthma in childhood or in mid-adult or later adult life. Asthma symptoms in children may abate with the onset of puberty but may reappear in later life following some respiratory insult such as general anesthesia. Ingestion of aspirin or other nonsteroidal antiinflammatory drugs may precipitate bronchospasm or worsen asthma.

The course of the disease as well as response to therapeutic treatment is highly individual. Treatment of asthma includes prevention of acute attacks through the avoidance of irritants and immunotherapy for allergies. During acute attacks, treatment consists of the administration of bronchodilating drugs (β-adrenergic agents and methylxanthines) in nebulized form, steroids to decrease swelling, and bronchial hygiene measures to remove secretions and prevent secondary infection.

Bronchitis. The morphologic changes that occur in bronchitis include hypertrophy and hyperplasia of mucus-secreting bronchial glands and mucosal goblet cells, loss and structural defects of cilia, and permanent inflammatory changes in the bronchial epithelium and wall. The enlargement and overactivity of the mucus-secreting glands constitute the primary defect. The airway lumen can be significantly narrowed as a result of hypertrophy and hyperplasia of the mucus-secreting glands and goblet cells, since mucus glands form a large proportion of the bronchial wall (Fig. 16-13). Airway obstruction in bronchitis is related to narrowing of the airway due to mucus gland hyperplasia and increased secretions, which are often extremely viscous in character. Patients are prone to episodes of infectious bronchitis and pneumonia, probably as a result of retention of pathogenic organisms in the lower airways due to impaired mucociliary clearance (Center and McFadden, 1985). Clinically the manifestations of bronchitis include excessive sputum production and coughing. Chronic bronchitis commonly precedes and sometimes accompanies emphysema.

Emphysema. In emphysema the acinus—that portion of the lung distal to the terminal nonrespiratory bronchiole—is involved. The acinus includes the respiratory bronchiole comprised of alveoli and nonalveolated epithelium, the alveolar duct, which is completely alveolated, and the terminal alveolar sac, or blind end of the airway, which is also entirely alveolated. Classification of emphysema depends on the area of the acinus involved. *Centrilobular emphysema* affects the respiratory bronchioles and is also called *centriacinar emphysema*. Involvement of the entire acinus is termed *panlobular* or *panacinar emphysema*. Involvement of the alveolar ducts and sacs is termed *periacinar* or *distal acinar emphysema*. The two principal types of emphysema are centrilobular and panlobular (Fig. 16-14).

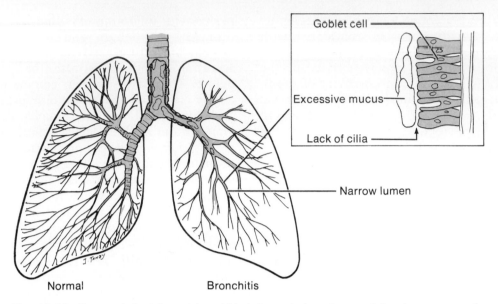

Goblet cell

Excessive mucus

Lack of cilia

Narrow lumen

Normal   Bronchitis

Fig. 16-13. Characteristic defect of bronchitis is hyperplasia and overactivity of mucus-secreting bronchial glands. Airway lumen can be significantly narrowed as a result of this.

Centrilobular emphysema is more prevalent in men than in women and is rarely seen in nonsmokers.

Panlobular emphysema has been found in the lungs of aged persons, in persons with bronchitis who also smoke, and in persons with some degree of preexisting bronchial or bronchiolar obstruction. The incidence is similar in both sexes.

In a small group of emphysema patients the incidence of panlobular emphysema is related to a hereditary deficiency of a normal serum α_1-globulin, α_1-antitrypsin, which is also referred to as α_1-protease inhibitor (PI). This protein appears to function as an antiprotease, which protects the tissues of the respiratory tract from the destructive effects of neutrophil elastase, a proteolytic enzyme or protease. The activity of this protease is regulated by the enzyme-inhibitor combination of neutrophil elastase/α_1-protease inhibitor (Proteases, *Lancet*, 1987). When the levels of the inhib-

itor antiprotease are deficient, connective tissue destruction is unimpeded, leading to emphysemic changes in the lung tissue (Brantly et al., 1988).

This deficiency is transmitted by a single, autosomal recessive gene. The severity of the deficiency is related to the allelic form or the α_1-antitrypsin phenotype that is inherited. These variants are referred to as Pi types and the phenotype most frequently associated with α_1-antitrypsin deficiency is PiZZ (Kueppers, 1987; Brantly et al., 1988).

The disease becomes symptomatic between the third and fifth decades of life. It is accelerated by smoking. This is believed to be caused by the enhanced attraction of macrophages by cigarette smoke that, in turn, attract neutrophils (which release the elastase) and by the inhibition of antiprotease activity by the oxidant radicals generated by cigarette smoke (*Lancet*, 1987). Therapy directed at replacing the

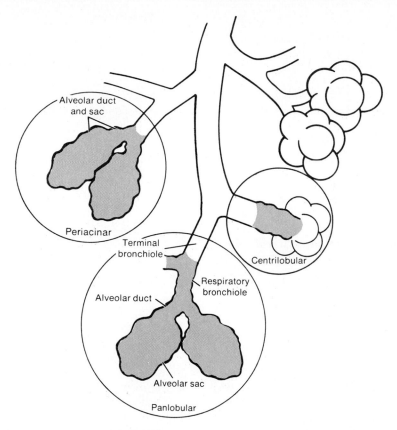

Fig. 16-14. Two principal types of emphysema: panlobular and centrilobular. Atrophic centrilobular emphysema is asymptomatic because peripheral alveoli are available. As centrilobular emphysema advances, periphery of acinus will also be destroyed, and condition becomes similar to panlobular emphysema and is symptomatic.

deficient protein has recently become available and is discussed in the following.

CASE STUDY: α₁-ANTITRYPSIN DEFICIENCY EMPHYSEMA

Objective and Subjective Data History

PP is a 44-year-old white woman with a history of emphysema due to α₁-antitrypsin (A1AT) deficiency, cor pulmonale, and

_____
Contributed by Cynthia A. Gronkiewicz.

bipolar disorder (see Chapter 11). She reports an increase in dyspnea over the last 2 years aggravated by anxiety, humidity, cold air, and greater than 75 feet of ambulation. She has a 40-pack-year history of smoking but quit 4 months ago. PP's history is significant for sinus headaches, occasional paroxysmal nocturnal dyspnea (PND), two-pillow orthopnea, and increasing pedal edema over the past 2 to 3 months.

During the past 7 months, PP has been hospitalized 5 times because of respiratory insufficiency and impending respiratory failure. A1AT deficiency was diagnosed 6 months ago. Current therapy includes bronchodilators (Theodur and Albuterol by nebulizer), diuretics, corticosteroids, supplemental oxygen, and lithium.

Her occupational history is negative for exposure to toxins or asbestos; she has done office work her entire life. PP's husband died following cardiac surgery within the last year. She has a son, daughter, and grandson.

Present illness: PP is referred to a pulmonologist 3 days after moving from Florida to Chicago. Her primary physician felt she was no longer able to function independently. Since her arrival, she reports an increase in shortness of breath, chest tightness, nonproductive cough, wheezing, and pedal edema. PP denies any recent upper respiratory infection, change in medication, increase in fluid intake, or addition of sedatives.

General appearance: A cachectic, anxious woman using portable oxygen; 65 inches tall; weighs 93 pounds

Skin: Warm, clammy

EENT: No nasal polyps or pharyngeal exudate

Cardiovascular: HR regular at 96/minute; S_1 S_2; no S_3, gallop, or murmur; + JVD; + HJR; 3+ pedal edema to the knees; no clubbing

Respiratory: Increase in AP diameter; hyperresonant to percussion; distant breath sounds; bibasilar late inspiratory crackles; fine end-expiratory wheezing

Gastrointestinal: Normoactive bowel sounds; no hepatomegaly

Neurological: Reflexes intact

Chest x-ray film: No infiltrates; flattened diaphragms, slight cardiomegaly, increase in pulmonary vascular markings

Pertinent laboratory values

Arterial blood gases (on room air): Po_2 52; pH 7.32; Pco_2 64; HCO_3^- 34

α_1-antitrypsin level: 37 mg/dl (normal 200 − 400 mg/dl)

Sweat test: Negative

Albumin: 3.2

Treatment

PP was admitted to the hospital for acute respiratory failure and cor pulmonale. The medical therapy plan included:

1. Emphysema
   a. Bronchodilators
   b. Prolastin therapy
   c. Pulmonary rehabilitation
   d. Oxygen therapy
2. Cor pulmonale
   a. Lasix
   b. Intake/output; daily weight; fluid restriction
   c. Oxygen therapy
3. Bipolar disorder
   a. Lithium
   b. Supportive therapy

Discussion

A1AT deficiency is a genetic disorder characterized by low serum levels of A1AT (less than 80 mg/dl) and a high risk for the development of emphysema in the third or fourth decade of life (Brantly et al., 1988). A1AT is a glycoprotein produced by hepatocytes and mononuclear phagocytes. It is the principal inhibitor of neutrophil elastase, a protease capable of destroying alveolar structures as well as bacteria. As A1AT is responsible for more than 90% of antineutrophil elastase defense in the lower respiratory tract, its absence results in chronic destruction of the lung parenchyma. This deficiency leads to loss of alveolar septa and supporting connective tissue within the lungs with subsequent expiratory collapse of the small airways.

A1AT deficiency comprises 2% of all cases of emphysema (Proteases, *Lancet*, 1987). Patients are most commonly affected in middle age with moderate to severe emphysema. Although a slowly progressive disease, the process can be markedly accelerated by cigarette smoking. In patients who smoke, symptoms develop 15 to 20 years earlier than in patients who do not smoke (Proteases, *Lancet*, 1987). PP has a 40-pack-year history of smoking and presents with severe emphysema as demonstrated by pulmonary function tests:

	Actual	Predicted	% of Predicted
FVC	.97	3.37	29%
FEV_1	.42	2.78	15%
FEV_1/FVC	44%	80%	
TLC	1.84	5.20	35%
Diffusing capacity (DLCO)	3.97	21.03	19%

PP's pulmonary function tests and arterial blood gas analysis already demonstrate a severe degree of alveolar destruction with subsequent alteration in gas exchange. She has both a severe obstruction abnormality (FEV_1/FVC = 44%) and a significant loss of functional alveolar capillary bed as evidenced by the reduced diffusing capacity. Her arterial blood gases reflect both hypoxemia and chronic hypercapnea as evidenced by the elevated bicarbonate level. An oxygen assessment study reveals a decrease in the oxygen saturation level to 85% on room air when walking. A 91% saturation can be maintained on 0.5 L/min of oxygen. Similar results were seen in her nocturnal desaturation study.

A1AT deficiency is an autosomal recessive disorder. PP was adopted at the age of 3, so no medical records of her parents are available. Her children, in their twenties, have both tested negative for A1AT deficiency.

Studies have shown A1AT replacement therapy replenishes the missing protease inhibitor to reestablish antineutrophil elastase protection. Weekly infusions of Prolastin (α_1-proteinase inhibitor) at 60 mg/kg of body weight produce levels well above the 80 mg/dl threshold. This is the serum level at which sufficient amounts of A1AT diffuse through the lung parenchyma to provide adequate protection to the epithelial lining and alveolar structures. The serum half-life is 4 to 5 days, but adequate serum levels are maintained through the eighth day.

First commercially available in 1988, replacement therapy with weekly injections of Prolastin safely sustains normal serum and lung fluid levels to prevent continual destruction of lung parenchyma. The A1AT used for infusions is prepared from pooled plasma of normal donors. Although there has been no evidence for hepatitis transmission, PP and all recipients are given both hepatitis B vaccine and anti-hepatitis B immunoglobulin before the first infusion. No adverse side effects have been reported in the 700 infusions to date.

The annual cost of Prolastin therapy in 1988 is approximately $30,000. Most major insurance companies reimburse 80% to 100% of the cost, but the financial aspect needs to be addressed before initiating therapy. PP's insurance carrier provided 100% reimbursement. Replacement therapy along with smoking cessation are critical to halting the destruction of lung parenchyma. It must be emphasized to the patient that A1AT replacement does not reverse the current degree of lung dysfunction, but rather halts further deterioration (Wewers et al., 1987; Hubbard and Crystal, 1988).

In addition to treatment of her acute exacerbation and A1AT replacement therapy, PP was admitted to the pulmonary rehabilitation program. This is a multidisciplinary program involving physical therapy, occupational therapy, dietary planning, psychological evaluation, social services, vocational counseling, and education regarding lung disease and treatment. By incorporating breathing retraining, work simplification, and energy conservation techniques into her daily activities, PP demonstrates an increased level of strength and endurance in her overall exercise tolerance. In addition, rehabilitation programs have been shown to decrease the number of hospitalizations in people with COPD.

Nursing Diagnoses

Patients with A1AT deficiency emphysema have a multitude of physical and psychologic factors affecting their state of health. A number of nursing diagnoses are appropriate for PP. The following are most directly related to the pulmonary disorder she is experiencing.

1. Ineffective airway clearance due to tracheobronchial obstruction and secretions
2. Impaired gas exchange due to an altered oxygen supply and destruction of lung parenchyma
3. Anxiety due to current changes in her health status, socioeconomic status, and environment
4. Alteration in fluid volume due to cor pulmonale and nutritional status

Other genetic factors such as sex, familial prevalence, blood type, and secretor status have been found to be associated with the occurrence of COPD (Kueppers, 1987). Some individuals have been identified who develop intermittent airflow limitation, sometimes called "asthmatic tendency," in response to inhaled exogenous agents. This characteristic of bronchial hyperresponsiveness or airway hyperreactivity may be the pathologic link between acute exposures to inhaled agents like smoke and dust and the development of chronic lung disease in later life. Exposure to environmental and industrial air pollutants does not appear to directly cause chronic obstructive disease to the extent that they cause other respiratory problems. COPD is believed to be a disorder of multifactorial causation with genetic, behavioral, and environmental factors (Table 16-4) all contributing to the development and severity of the disease (Higgins and Thom, 1988; Kueppers, 1987). Such a scheme for the possible pathogenesis of COPD is depicted in Fig. 16-15.

The one environmental factor known positively to be etiologic in the development of bronchitis and emphysema is cigarette smoking. While the effects of passive inhalation of environmental tobacco smoke are less certain, cigarette smoke that is inhaled directly into the lungs affects the respiratory system in a number of ways that can promote the development of obstructive lung disease. For example, mucociliary clearance is impaired because of increased mucus production and ciliary dysfunction, and alveolar macrophages increase their production of superoxide oxygen radicals, which leads to decreased antiprotease activity and, possibly, airway reactivity.

The morphologic changes of lung tissue that occur in emphysema include thickening of the bronchiolar walls due to submucosal edema and cellular infiltration as well as hyperplasia of the mucus-secreting glands and goblet cells and dilation of the distal air spaces with destruction of the alveolar septa. Obstruction occurs because of the narrowing of the bronchiolar lumen, loss of the elastic recoil of the lung tissue, and secretion of excessive amounts of thick, tenacious mucus. This obstruction is greater during expiration than during inspiration and is irreversible, in contrast to the potentially treatable obstruction that accompanies asthma and bronchitis.

In normal lungs expiration is passively achieved through relaxation of the diaphragm and chest muscles, which allows the elastic recoil of the thorax and lungs to reduce the size of the chest cavity. As the lung tissue is compressed, intraalveolar pressure becomes greater than the pressure in the airways, and air is forced out of the alveoli into the airways and into the atmosphere. In emphysemic individuals expiration becomes an active process that increases the work of breathing and the energy expenditure of the body. The

Table 16-4. Established and suspected risk factors for COPD

Factor type	Established	Suspected
Demographic	Age, sex (male)	Low socio-economic status
Genetic	α_1-antitrypsin deficiency	Increased airway reactivity
		ABO, ABH secretor pheno-
		types
		Familial tendency
		Atopy
Environmental/	Tobacco smoke (per-	Tobacco smoke (environmental)
behavioral	sonal)	Air pollution
		Occupational exposure(s)
		Climate
		Poor nutrition

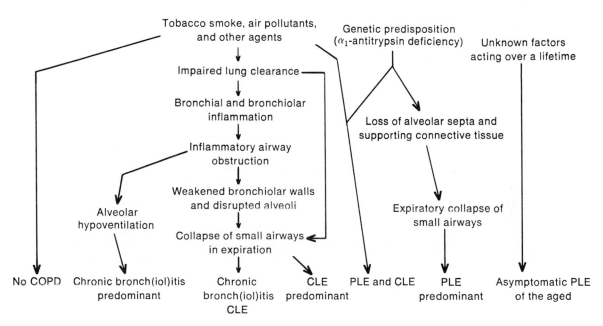

Fig. 16-15. Concept of pathogenesis of chronic obstructive pulmonary disease (COPD). PLE, Pan-lobular emphysema; CLE, centrilobular emphysema.
(From American Lung Association: Chronic obstructive pulmonary disease, ed 5, New York, 1981, The Association.)

airway diameter is already reduced as a result of changes described previously, and during expiration the increased pressure of the surrounding tissue causes further compression and collapse of the airway because of loss of the supporting tissue (Fig. 16-16). Air becomes trapped, causing distension of the distal airways. This airway distension leads to further destruction of the alveolar parenchyma. The elastic recoil of the tissue is reduced as the elastic fibers are destroyed, and surface

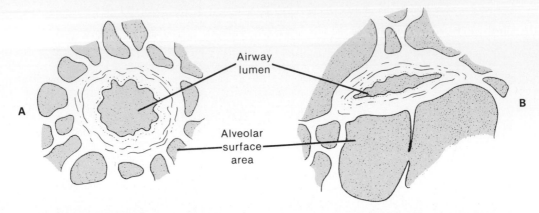

Fig. 16-16. A, Normal terminal bronchiole in cross section. **B,** Emphysematous terminal bronchiole in cross section. Loss of alveolar surface in emphysematous tissue surrounding lung results in partial bronchiolar collapse.

(Adapted from American Lung Association: Chronic obstructive pulmonary disease, ed 5, New York, 1981, The Association.)

tension decreases because of the reduction in alveolar surface area (Fig. 16-17). According to Poiseuille's law, as airway diameter decreases, the resistance to air flow increases. Pursed-lip breathing with use of accessory muscles will develop as the patient tries to exhale more completely and forcefully. In emphysemic individuals, then, the work of breathing is increased as a result of increased resistance to air flow and active expiration. The trapped air causes the lung tissue to become hyperresonant on percussion and residual volume, and consequently, total lung capacity to increase. Eventually the anteroposterior diameter of the chest will increase as a result of the airway distension and respiratory pattern. This causes the chest to become barrel shaped. Patients with emphysema will assume a characteristic position, sitting forward with the elbows flexed and arms extended and resting on a table, the back of another chair, or the knees for support (Frownfelter, 1987).

While the primary effect of these pathologic changes is on expiration, the major muscle of inspiration, the diaphragm, is placed at a mechanical disadvantage by the changes that occur. The hyperinflation of the lungs deforms the chest wall and flattens the diaphragm, shortening its resting length. It is therefore less effective as a force generator. The increased airway resistance acts as an increased load against which it must function. The breathing pattern is changed to one characterized by higher frequency and smaller tidal volume that further increases the work of breathing. The combination of increased load and decreased efficiency of the breathing pattern predisposes the respiratory muscles to the development of muscle fatigue (Lareau and Larson, 1987), which can lead to ventilatory failure.

The onset of emphysema is insidious. Much damage may occur before dyspnea becomes bothersome or flow rates are measurably impaired. The clinical manifestations of emphysema depend on the severity of obstructive processes. Presented in Table 16-5 are the physical findings in progressive chronic obstructive pulmonary diseases (COPD).

In mild obstructive disease the arterial

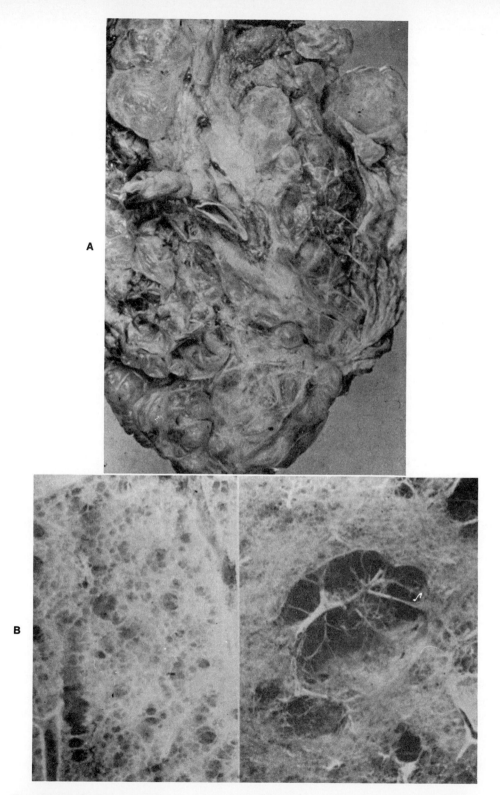

Fig. 16-17. A, Gross pathology of emphysemic lung. **B,** Microscopic view of alveolar tissue in panlobular and centrilobular emphysema.

(Courtesy Department of Pathology, University of Tennessee, Memphis.)

Table 16-5. Physical signs in COPD

Stage	Signs
Early	Examination may be negative or show only slight prolongation of forced expiration (which can be timed while auscultating over the trachea—normally 3 seconds or less), slight diminution of breath sounds at the apices or bases, scattered rhonchi or wheezes, especially on expiration, often best heard over the hila anteriorly (the rhonchi often clear after cough)
Moderate	Above signs are usually present and more pronounced, often with decreased rib expansion, use of the accessory muscles of respiration, retraction of the supraclavicular fossae in inspiration, generalized hyperresonance, decreased area of cardiac dullness, diminished heart sounds at base, increased anteroposterior distance of the chest*
Advanced	Examination usually shows the above findings to a greater degree, and often shows evidence of weight loss, depression of the liver, hyperpnea and tachycardia with mild exertion, low and relatively immobile diaphragm, contraction of abdominal muscles on inspiration, inaudible heart sounds except in the xiphoid area, cyanosis
Cor pulmonale	Increased intensity and splitting of pulmonic second sound, right-sided diastolic gallop, left parasternal heave (right ventricular overactivity), early systolic pulmonary ejection click with or without systolic ejection murmur
	With failure: distended neck veins, functional tricuspid insufficiency, V waves and hepatojugular reflux, hepatomegaly, peripheral edema

From American Lung Association: Chronic obstructive pulmonary disease, New York, 1981, The Association.
*Physicians may put misplaced confidence in relating the shape of the thorax to the presence or absence of obstructive lung disease. It has been shown that the classic "barrel chest" with poor rib separation may be due solely or largely to dorsal kyphosis. In such patients ventilatory function may nonetheless be normal because of good diaphragmatic motion.

oxygen level and oxygen saturation are slightly below normal. The Pco_2 may be normal or slightly below normal because of hyperventilation occurring as a result of stimulation of the hypoxic drive by low oxygen levels. Arterial pH is within normal limits due to renal compensatory mechanisms, which cause selective excretion of bicarbonate ions and retention of hydrogen ions. As a result, the serum bicarbonate levels may fall below normal.

In moderately severe obstructive disorders the reduction in Po_2 and O_2 saturation is more severe, and mild hypercapnia results because of the alveolar hypoventilation. Because the hydrogen ion concentration normally increases with a rise in carbon dioxide levels, the arterial pH becomes slightly acidotic. With chronic carbon dioxide retention, however, arterial pH changes are minimal because of the compensatory mechanisms of selective bicarbonate ion retention and hydrogen ion excretion by the kidneys. Serum bicarbonate levels may be elevated as a result.

In severe obstruction, severe hypoxemia and hypercapnia are present. Severe acidosis is a result of both the greatly increased carbon dioxide levels and the accumulation of lactic acid as metabolism shifts to anaerobic pathways. Summarized in Table 16-6 are the blood gas changes that occur in varying degrees of obstructive disease. Fig 16-18 shows the blood gas changes as the obstructive process proceeds to cause ventilatory failure.

Hypoxemia is the result of the ventilation perfusion inequality that develops as

Table 16-6. Arterial blood gases in obstructive disease

	Normal	Mild	Moderately severe	Severe
P_{O_2}	95-100 mm Hg	60-80 mm Hg	50-60 mm Hg	50 mm Hg
O_2 saturation	93-98%	88%-95%	75%-87%	75%
P_{CO_2}	35-45 mm Hg	32-38 mm Hg	45-55 mm Hg	55 (may be as high as 80) mm Hg
pH	7.35-7.45	7.35-7.45	7.30-7.35	7.25
HCO_3^-	22-26 mEq/L	20-24 mEq/L	26-35 mEq/L	20 mEq/L

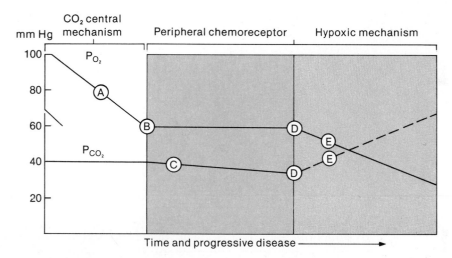

Fig. 16-18. A theory on pathogenesis of ventilatory failure in chronic obstructive pulmonary disease. *A,* Decreasing arterial P_{O_2} due to early disease process. *B,* Peripheral chemoreceptor stimulation begins and becomes primary drive to breathe. *C,* Arterial P_{O_2} level remains fairly constant while arterial P_{CO_2} level may decrease to some degree. *D,* Theoretic points at which work of breathing is so costly that a decreased arterial P_{O_2} is unavoidable. *E,* Arterial P_{O_2} begins to decrease, and arterial P_{CO_2} begins to increase.

(From Shapiro BA, Harrison RA, and Walton JR: Clinical application of blood gases, ed 2. Copyright © 1977 by Year Book Medical Publishers, Inc., Chicago. Used by permission.)

the alveolar-capillary membrane surface is destroyed. Hypoxia and acidosis cause vasoconstriction in the pulmonary vascular bed that, in turn, causes increased pulmonary vascular resistance and pulmonary hypertension. Other possible causes of pulmonary hypertension in COPD include an anatomic reduction in the size of the cap-illary bed, increased cardiac output, increased blood volume, increased blood viscosity, and increased intrathoracic pressure caused by expiratory airflow limitation (Weidemann and Matthay, 1987). As shown in Fig. 16-19, some of these mechanisms are also compensatory in response to hypoxia and acidosis and thus

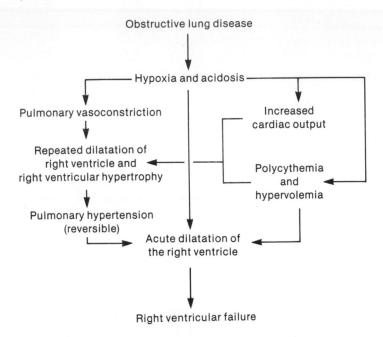

Fig. 16-19. Altered hemodynamics and development of cor pulmonale in obstructive lung disease. (From Ferrer MI: Med Clin North Am 63:1, 1979.)

contribute to the development of a vicious cycle that will cause further deterioration of cardiopulmonary function in the form of *cor pulmonale.* Cor pulmonale is the term applied to the dysfunction and hypertrophy of the right side of the heart that occurs in response to pulmonary hypertension. While it is regarded as a form of heart failure, the cardiac output often is normal or increased. This may indicate, however, an inability to increase cardiac output to the degree that is an appropriate response to hypoxemia (Weidemann and Matthay, 1987).

Secondary polycythemia occurs as a compensatory mechanism in response to hypoxia, which favors reduction of hypoxemia but causes increased blood volume and viscosity. The increased blood volume will increase the work load of the heart. The increased viscosity increases resistance to blood flow in the lungs and heart

and thus also contributes to the increased cardiac work load as well as predisposing the patient to thrombus formation (see Chapter 3).

The degree of hypoxemia and the adequacy of the compensatory mechanisms will determine the type and severity of the clinical signs and symptoms. Two syndromes describing the extremes of the clinical spectrum of emphysema have been identified: the "pink puffer fighter" and the "blue bloater nonfighter." The pink puffers maintain relatively normal blood gas values and show progressive dyspnea and weight loss, no cyanosis, little cardiac enlargement or sputum production, and a large increase in residual volume. They are able to hyperventilate, and therefore hypoxemia is not extreme, and cyanosis does not result, hence the name. The pink puffers show an increase in lung capacity. The blue bloaters show marked cyanosis and the edema of right-sided heart failure, hence their name. Arterial hypoxemia is marked, and compensatory mechanisms are not as effective as in the other group. The heart is hypertrophied, the hematocrit is increased, lung capacity is decreased, and sputum production is increased. These patients experience frequent episodes of right-sided heart failure. The pink puffer syndrome applies to those patients in whom the morphologic changes are predominantly emphysematous (type A). The blue bloater syndrome applies to those patients in whom the morphologic changes are primarily bronchitic (type B). Presented in Table 16-7 is a summary of the features of both syndromes. Most patients demonstrate features of both syndromes in varying combinations (West, 1987).

Treatment rationale. Treatment of obstructive disorders such as bronchitis and emphysema is aimed at maximizing ventilatory function. Bronchodilating drugs can be prescribed. Current research is di-

rected at pharmacologic agents to improve diaphragmatic contractility. Clearing the airways of mucus is of primary importance. Bronchial hygiene and chest physical therapy measures can be used to help clear secretions from the airways.

Breathing exercises and breathing retraining can help maximize ventilation, prevent atelectasis, correct abnormal breathing patterns, and decrease the work of breathing as well as give the patient some degree of control over shortness of breath. The breathing pattern adopted by the COPD patient is an attempt to compensate for the mechanically disadvantaged diaphragm through use of the accessory muscles. The sensation of dyspnea may even cause the patient to initiate inspiration before completing expiration. The result is increased dyspnea and a very inefficient and uncoordinated breathing pattern. A breathing exercise especially suited to the COPD patient is diaphragmatic breathing through pursed lips. The patient must learn to relax the accessory

Table 16-7. Features of types A and B chronic obstructive lung disease.

	Type A	Type B
Clinical features	Dyspnea	Cough, sputum (sometimes purulent)
		Cyanosis, plethoric appearance
		Polycythemia
	Cor pulmonale unusual	Fluid retention, cor pulmonale
	"Pink and puffing"	"Blue and bloated"
	Progressive dyspnea	Progresses to respiratory failure
Radiology	Hyperinflation	Normal or congested lung fields
	Attenuated peripheral vessels	Evidence of previous infection
Physiology	Airway obstruction (low FEV, etc.)	Airway obstruction
	TLC high	May be normal
	Elastic recoil low	Usually normal
	CO diffusing capacity low	May be normal
	Pco_2 normal	Pco_2 raised
	Po_2 often above 65 mm Hg	Po_2 often below 65 mm Hg
Pathology	Widespread emphysema	Severe bronchitis; may have some centrilobular emphysema

From West, JB: Pulmonary pathophysiology—the essentials, Baltimore, 1977, The Williams & Wilkins Co.

muscles and use the diaphragm as the main inspiratory muscle. Pursed lips breathing can decrease air trapping by preventing bronchiolar collapse during expiration. These techniques also help to slow the respiratory rate and relieve the sensation of dyspnea (Frownfelter, 1987).

A promising direction for breathing exercises is conditioning and training the inspiratory muscles for strength and endurance. This may have the twofold effect for patients of improving ventilatory function and enhancing the muscles' resistance to inspiratory muscle fatigue. Two techniques have been used for inspiratory muscle training. Isocapnic hyperventilation (also called isocapnic hyperpnea) is used to increase the endurance of the respiratory muscles. Inspiratory resistive breathing allows both strength and endurance training effects, since it incorporates both isometric and isotonic aspects (Larson and Kim, 1987).

Recently success has been reported in preventing acute respiratory failure in COPD patients by periodically resting the muscles using mechanically assisted ventilation during the night. This is done to allow the muscles to recover from any present or impending muscle fatigue. Muscle reserves are thus replenished or enhanced.

Oxygen can be administered to correct hypoxemia but only at low flow rates. Administration of high levels of oxygen will remove the stimulus to breathe and cause further respiratory depression. Correction of hypoxemia reduces the stimulus for erythrocytosis and ameliorates the progression of pulmonary hypertension. Long-term oxygen therapy has been shown to improve the long-term survival and neuropsychologic function of hypoxemic patients with COPD (Weidemann and Matthay, 1987).

Encouraging the patient to stop smoking is important not only because further tissue damage may occur but also because carbon monoxide is inhaled in the smoke. Carbon monoxide competes with oxygen for combination with the hemoglobin molecule and increases the affinity of the remaining hemoglobin for oxygen, which impairs its release from hemoglobin to the tissues. Smoking directly increases both hypoxemia and hypoxia of the tissues.

The nutritional status of the COPD patient has taken on greater importance with the recognition that weight loss is associated with an increased incidence of acute respiratory failure, the development of cor pulmonale, and high mortality (Openbrier and Covey, 1987). COPD patients often demonstrate decreases in total body mass, to which loss of muscle mass and depleted fat stores are contributory. They often appear cachectic. The causes of weight loss in COPD are not completely understood but are most probably related to decreased intake in the face of increased demand.

COPD patients have increased caloric needs because of the increased work of breathing that they experience. The increased metabolic requirement is reflected by the fact that oxygen consumption rates as high as 150% of normal have been found in patients with chronic air flow limitation. The metabolic requirement of an individual patient will be further increased by infection, acute respiratory failure, or ventilator dependence.

Intake may be deficient for several reasons. Many patients report that eating causes dyspnea. Gastric fullness or distension can impede the downward movement of the diaphragm. Since the degree of dyspnea correlates with the amount of food eaten, smaller, more frequent meals may help alleviate this sensation. Patients also report decreased appetite and gastrointestinal discomfort. Some of these complaints may be related to the effects of the bronchodilating and corticosteroid medications. Alterations in the senses of smell and taste can also blunt the appetite. The effects of medications, mucosal alterations, and increased sputum production can affect these senses.

Malnutrition will contribute to an even more ineffective breathing pattern as respiratory muscle strength and endurance are decreased and muscle tissue is catabolized to provide substrates for energy production. The goal then is to restore and/or maintain an optimal nutritional status for each patient. Nutritional therapy must be individualized for each patient, and consultation with a dietician is recommended. The use of a nutritional supplement may be required to meet the increased caloric needs. The source of calories is also important for the respiratory patient because carbohydrates have a higher respiratory quotient than fats or protein. A high carbohydrate intake will increase CO_2 production in relation to oxygen consumption to a greater degree than would a comparable caloric intake of fat or protein. If the patient's capacity for meeting even normal ventilatory demands is already taxed to the limit, the increased demand in response to increased CO_2 production can precipitate acute respiratory failure. The importance of nutritional intervention in the COPD patient is emphasized in a case study discussed later in this chapter. Fluid intake should be maintained to reduce the possibility of dehydration (due to exaggerated respiratory effort) and to thin secretions.

The patient should also be taught the signs of infection and preventive measures, since infection increases the metabolic rate and need for oxygen. A severe respiratory infection can intensify the hypoventilation and cause acute ventilatory failure superimposed on the already present chronic ventilatory failure. Infections must be treated promptly and aggressively.

Cystic fibrosis. Cystic fibrosis is another disease in which the amount and character of the respiratory tract secretions are affected leading to obstruction. Cystic fibrosis is a hereditary, chronic disease characterized by abnormal secretions of the exocrine glands. It is genetically transmitted as an autosomal recessive trait. It is estimated that 4% to 5% of the general population are carriers, and the incidence of the disease in the United States is approximately 1 in every 1600 to 2000 Caucasian births (Kueppers, 1987). At present no reliable method of detecting a carrier of the abnormal gene exists. The genetic aspects of this disease are discussed in Chapter 2 and are currently a major focus of research.

An abnormally viscous, excessive amount of mucus is secreted from the exocrine glands of the respiratory, gastrointestinal, and reproductive tracts, leading to obstruction of the ducts of these organ systems. The increased viscosity of the secretions has been attributed to a relative lack of water, altered electrolyte composition, and abnormalities in the organic constituents, especially the mucus glycoproteins. The electrolyte concentration of secretions from the salivary and sweat glands has been found to be abnormal. Studies have demonstrated that this is related to impaired chloride permeability in the epithelial cells of sweat ducts, indicating a defect in chloride transport. Frizzell et al. (1986) demonstrated that the defect is not in the conductance mechanism itself but rather is related to its regulation. The findings of this study indicate that the chloride channels and their regulation by calcium are normal, but activation of chloride channels by beta-adrenergic stimulation of the cAMP pathway is abnormal. The inability to stimulate chloride channel activity in CF cells by either epinephrine or cAMP has been demonstrated in other studies as well. The levels of sodium, potassium, and chloride in sweat are abnormally elevated. In fact, a positive sweat chloride test ($Cl^- > 60$ mEq/L) is used to confirm the diagnosis of cystic fibrosis when the history includes any or all of the following: recurrent respiratory tract infections, signs and symptoms of gastrointestinal malabsorption (diarrhea and failure to thrive—see Chapter 21), and a family history of cystic fibrosis.

The clinical manifestations vary among affected individuals depending on the severity of the disease process. Digestive and nutritional problems develop secondary to pancreatic insufficiency and intestinal obstruction and malabsorption. Electrolyte abnormalities occur secondary to the excessive loss in the sweat (see Chapter 18). Infertility, nodular biliary cirrhosis, and gallbladder disease may occur as the result of plugged ducts in the respective organs.

Pulmonary involvement occurs in all persons afflicted with the disease, and in over one half of those diagnosed the presenting problem is usually respiratory in nature. The thick, excessive amount of mucus in the lungs cannot be moved by the cilia and plugs the bronchi and bronchioles, leading to obstruction and, consequently, to air-trapping, mucus stasis, and secondary infection. A characteristic finding is the presence of *Staphylococcus aureus* and *Pseudomonas aeruginosa* in the sputum of patients with cystic fibrosis. The presence of a particular mucoid variant of *Pseudomonas* in cystic fibrosis pa-

tients is a classic finding, and the relationship between the presence of this organism and the occurrence of cystic fibrosis has been the subject of some research about the basic pathologic defect. The presence of potentially pathogenic organisms along with the excessive, thick mucus and anaerobic conditions resulting from plugged airways makes these persons prime candidates for the development of respiratory tract infections. A vicious cycle develops in which mucus obstructs the airways and predisposes the affected person to respiratory infection, which, if it does occur, will cause even greater amounts of mucus to be produced leading to further airway obstruction. The ultimate sequela to this cycle as it is chronically repeated is permanent lung damage in the form of *bronchiectasis*, or dilation of the bronchi and destruction of the bronchial walls. This destruction of the respiratory bronchioles and alveolar ducts leads to connective tissue deposition and interstitial fibrosis. A chief cause of the morbidity associated with cystic fibrosis is chronic pulmonary disease, with respiratory failure and cor pulmonale being the major causes of death (Kirby and Taylor, 1986). A schematic summary of the pulmonary pathophysiologic events that are the result of abnormal mucus production is presented in Fig. 16-20.

Cystic fibrosis has traditionally been viewed as a disease of children. This view is outdated because more affected persons are reaching adulthood as a result of improved case findings, early recognition, and intensive treatment, including pulmonary and antibiotic therapy, and improved nutrition support (Kueppers, 1987; Shekleton, 1987).

Restrictive disorders

Restrictive disorders are those characterized by limited lung expansion. A restric-

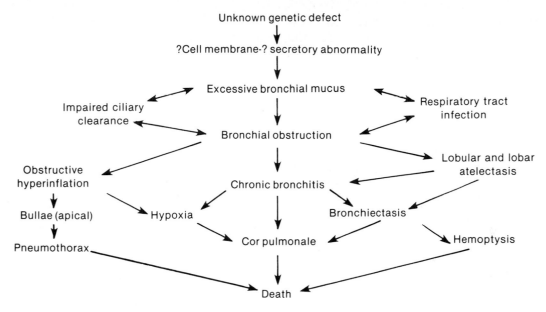

Fig. 16-20. A schematic representation of the interrelated sequence of events involved in the pulmonary pathophysiology of CF.
(From Holsclaw DS: Cystic fibrosis: overview and pulmonary aspects in young adults, Clin Chest Med 1(3):408, Sept, 1980.)

tive disorder can be the result of parenchymal (interstitial) lung disease as well as disorders that affect the chest wall such as those caused by musculoskeletal defects and neuromuscular impairment. Extrathoracic conditions that limit chest wall expansion, such as pregnancy, ascites, or obesity, can also lead to a restrictive defect in the breathing pattern (Hopp and Williams, 1987).

The functional lung volumes and total lung capacity are decreased and alveolar hypoventilation occurs because lung expansion is restricted. There is a decrease in pulmonary compliance and an increase in the elastic recoil of the lung and chest wall. Large changes in pressure result in only small changes in volume. Subsequently, the work of breathing increases. In intrapulmonary disorders such as fibrosis, edema, sarcoidosis, atelectasis, and pneumonia, the primary defect that leads to volume loss is decreased compliance

and increased elastic recoil of the lung tissue. The lungs are said to be "stiff." In extrapulmonary conditions the loss of volume is related to decreased compliance of the chest wall.

Kyphoscoliosis and muscular dystrophy are examples of disorders in which musculoskeletal function is impaired, causing restricted movement and expansion of the thoracic cage. Weakness and paralysis of respiratory muscles are possible complications of Guillain-Barré syndrome and myasthenia gravis, which are both neuromuscular diseases. Respiratory muscle paralysis can also be caused by certain drugs that are used to promote skeletal muscle relaxation, for example, curare and succinylcholine.

Many other conditions may impair ventilation by causing restriction of the size and movement of the thoracic cage. These include obesity, abdominal distension (with gas or fluid), pain, immobility, and tightly applied bandages. When the volume of the abdominal cavity increases, the downward movement of the diaphragm is restricted.

Grossly obese persons may experience the *pickwickian* or *obesity hypoventilation syndrome*, which is characterized by dyspnea, somnolence, hypoventilation, and hypoxemia with the compensatory mechanism of increased pulmonary artery pressure leading to hypertrophy and failure of the right side of the heart (cor pulmonale). Secondary polycythemia causes a ruddy complexion. The pickwickian syndrome is so named after a character described by Dickens in the *Pickwick Papers* who was obese, sleepy, red-faced, and slow. Pathophysiologic mechanisms that appear to affect ventilation in the obese individual include increased work of breathing, reduced chest wall compliance resulting from mechanical restriction of the downward movement of the diaphragm, the compensatory mechanism of increased pulmonary artery pressure, and in some persons sleep apnea.

Not all obese persons develop obesity hypoventilation syndrome (OHS), and when it does develop the severity does not correlate with the degree of obesity. The causative factor in the development of full-blown obesity hypoventilation syndrome is a combination of the mechanical ventilatory effects of obesity and disordered ventilatory control that leads to persistent hypercapnia (Hopp and Williams, 1987). Mechanical ventilatory function is impaired because thoracic movement is impeded by the increased weight on the chest wall and the excessive abdominal fat. All obese persons exhibit impaired ventilatory mechanics, including decreased chest wall compliance and increased work of breathing; however, the degree of this impairment is greater in the person with OHS. The OHS patients also demonstrate respiratory muscle weakness that may be related to fatty infiltrates in the diaphragm and to the mechanical disadvantage at which it is placed by being stretched by the abdominal contents. There is speculation that dyspnea and activity intolerance occur in response to the development of inspiratory muscle fatigue in grossly obese patients.

Abnormal respiratory control or drive is also exhibited by patients with OHS (Hopp and Williams, 1987). They do not respond appropriately to a hypercapnic challenge, that is, they cannot increase their minute ventilation when asked to inhale carbon dioxide. The hypoxic drive has also been found to be decreased in these individuals.

It is hypothesized that hypercapnia may begin with carbon dioxide retention during periods of sleep apnea. The hypersomnolence seen in obese persons during waking hours is a result of the sleep pattern disturbance related to sleep apnea that many experience. Sleep apnea may be central, the result of a central nervous system defect, or obstructive, the result of mechanical blockage of the airway during sleep caused by anatomic factors such as a large tongue, receding or small jaw, a short, thick neck, fatty infiltration or relaxation of the pharynx, and hypertrophy of the adenoids and tonsils. While obstructive sleep apnea occurs frequently in the obese patient, some patients exhibit both types of apnea. Table 16-8 presents an overview of the clinical spectrum of the cardiorespiratory effects of obesity. Treatment consists of weight reduction, use of drugs to increase respiratory drive in central sleep apnea, elevation of the head of the bed, use of a tongue restraining device or tracheostomy in obstructive sleep apnea.

Severe abdominal or chest pain results

Table 16-8.   Comparison of obese normal subjects, obese patients with sleep apnea, and patients with obesity hypoventilation syndrome

	Very obese, but otherwise normal	Very obese with sleep apnea	Fully developed obesity hypoventilation syndrome
Arterial hypoxemia	Often present, due to $\dot{V}/\dot{Q}$* mismatching; diurnal and nocturnal, usually mild	Often present due to both $\dot{V}/\dot{Q}$* mismatching and periodic hypoventilation; diurnal mild; nocturnal often severe during apnea	Present day and night, due to both $\dot{V}/\dot{Q}$* mismatching and alveolar hypoventilation; more severe during sleep-associated apnea
Hypercapnia	Absent	Diurnal, absent; may be present during sleep, usually mild	Present day and night; may be severe, particularly during sleep-associated apnea
Pulmonary hypertension	Absent, except occasionally associated with left ventricular failure	Often present and sometimes severe at night associated with apneic episodes and hypoxia	Usually present day and night; worse at night with apneic episodes; often associated with right ventricular failure
Polycythemia	Absent	Sometimes present, depending on severity and duration of nocturnal hypoxemia	Usually present and sometimes severe
Systemic hypertension	Occasionally present; more frequent than in the non-obese	Frequently present; often accentuated during sleep or present only during sleep	Frequently present; often accentuated during sleep or present only during sleep
Ventilatory response to hypercapnia	Normal, both awake and asleep	Usually normal awake; may be abnormally depressed during sleep	Always depressed, both awake and asleep
Ventilatory response to hypoxia	Normal, both awake and asleep	Usually normal awake; may be abnormally depressed during sleep	Often depressed both awake and asleep
Lung compliance	Generally normal or slightly decreased	Generally normal or slightly decreased	Normal to moderately decreased
Chest wall compliance	Slightly to moderately decreased	Slightly to moderately decreased	Moderately to severely decreased
Ventilatory work	Slightly to moderately increased	Slightly to moderately increased	Moderately to severely increased
Static lung volumes	ERV reduced, often severely; VC slightly to moderately reduced	ERV reduced, often severely; VC slightly to moderately reduced	ERV reduced, often severely; VC typically lower than in obese normals or obese sleep apneics; RV is usually normal
Maximal voluntary ventilation	Slightly to moderately reduced	Slightly to moderately reduced	Moderately to severely reduced
Heart failure	Low output left ventricular failure owing to systemic hypertension or high output failure owing to increased peripheral tissue demands may occasionally occur	Low output left ventricular failure owing to systemic hypertension or high output failure owing to increased peripheral tissue demands may occasionally occur	Although biventricular failure may be present, clinical picture is dominated by right ventricular failure related to hypoxia, acidemia and hypercapnia

From: Sharp J, Barrocas M, and Chokroverty S: The cardiorespiratory effects of obesity, Clin Chest Med **1**(1):113, Jan. 1980.
*V/Q = Ventilation-perfusion ratio.

in *splinting* of respirations in order to avoid any movement that may increase the pain. Splinting refers to a shallow type of respiratory effort with tidal volume at a constant and reduced level. Lung compliance and lung volume will decrease continuously during ventilation at a constant tidal volume, since the pressures and volumes associated with tidal respiration are insufficient to reexpand the already collapsed alveoli and to prevent the collapse of others. This pattern of respiration is seen most frequently after upper abdominal and thoracic surgery (see p. 420).

Conditions that affect the pleurae may also cause restricted thoracic movement. the pleurae are a double-layered serous membrane covering the lungs. The parietal pleura adheres to the chest wall surrounding the lungs. The visceral pleura covers the lungs. The parietal pleura is well supplied with nerve endings. A layer of serous fluid between the two membranes allows them to glide over each other as the lungs expand and contract. *Pleurisy,* or inflammation of the pleurae, impairs this movement. Pleuritic pain can be quite severe. It is usually described as a stabbing, acute pain felt on breathing or moving. Pleuritic pain in the costal or cervical regions is referred to the chest wall and causes tenderness to the touch, while pain in the diaphragm is referred to the shoulder and abdomen. Pleurisy associated with a decrease in the amount of serous fluid between the pleura is called dry, or fibrinous, pleurisy. A pleural friction rub can be heard on auscultation of the chest.

Pleurisy associated with an abnormal accumulation of fluid in the pleural space is called wet, or serofibrinous, pleurisy. The accumulation of fluid is called a *pleural effusion* and can be either a transudate or an exudate, depending on the causative mechanism. A transudate is the result of either an increased hydrostatic pressure or decreased oncotic pressure and has a relatively low protein content. The pleural tissue remains normal. An exudate is the result of disorders in which the pleural surface tissue is altered so that fluid can leak without a change in the hydrostatic or oncotic pressures. This fluid has a relatively high protein content. Exudates are often caused by infectious or inflammatory processes involving the lung tissue. Conditions that can cause pleural effusions are listed in Table 16-9. Accumulation of large amounts of fluid restricts the amount of space in which the lung has to expand and may even cause collapse of the lung.

Introduction of air into the pleural cavity will also cause collapse of the lungs, or *pneumothorax* (see Fig. 16-21). The chest x-ray film will demonstrate partial or complete collapse of lung tissue, overexpansion of the rib cage, depression of the diaphragm on the affected side, and displacement of the mediastinum away from the affected side. Pneumothorax may be the result of trauma or may occur spontaneously.

Spontaneous pneumothorax occurs primarily in two groups of patients. The first group is composed of relatively young (less than 40 years old), healthy persons who have subpleural apical blebs. Cause of the blebs and of their rupture is unknown. The second group is composed of older individuals who have COPD. Many other pulmonary conditions carry an increased risk of spontaneous pneumothorax, and conditions such as endometriosis and Marfan's syndrome are also associated with it. Spontaneous pneumothorax may occur in up to 1% of all live births. Certain conditions such as aspiration of meconium and hyaline membrane disease increase the risk in the newborn.

Males are affected more frequently than

Table 16-9. Diseases associated with exudative and transudative pleural effusions*

Exudates	Transudates
Malignancy	Congestive heart failure
Carcinoma	Hypoproteinemic states, in-
Mesothelioma	cluding
Lymphoma	Nephrotic syndrome
Infection	Liver cirrhosis
Parapneumonic	Pneumothorax
Tuberculosis	Atelectasis
Fungal	Pulmonary embolism (some
Viral	cases)
Collagen-vascular	Peritoneal dialysis
Systemic lupus	Meigs' syndrome (benign
Rheumatoid arthritis	ovarian tumor)
Pulmonary embolism	
(some cases)	
Pancreatitis	
Subphrenic abscess	
Uremia	
Asbestosis	
Chylothorax	
Traumatic hemothorax	
Esophageal rupture	
Drug-induced effusion	
Postradiation therapy	
Sarcoidosis	
Idiopathic (undiagnosed)	

From Martin L: Pulmonary physiology in clinical practice, St. Louis, The CV Mosby Co. 1987

*The majority of diagnosed exudates are caused by malignancy, infection, or pulmonary embolism; approximately 20% of exudative effusions remain undiagnosed after the initial evaluation. The majority of transudates are caused by congestive heart failure and low-protein states.

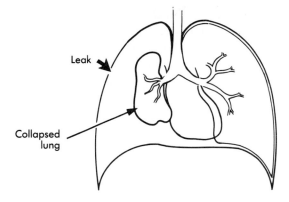

Fig. 16-21. Collapse of one lung from a pneumothorax. Pneumothorax may occur from puncture of the chest wall (as here) or from tear of the lung or of a mediastinal structure contiguous with pleural space (e.g., esophagus). In either case, air enters pleural space, and intrapleural pressure changes from subatmospheric to atmospheric. When this occurs, normal lung elastic recoil is unopposed, and lung collapses. Right and left pleural cavities are physically separated by the mediastinum; thus an air leak on one side does not collapse the other lung.

(From Martin L: Pulmonary physiology in clinical practice, St. Louis, 1987, The CV Mosby Co.)

females. Healthy patients who develop spontaneous pneumothorax tend to smoke more than the average and have a characteristic body build. Tall, thin men with long chests and young women with a short anteroposterior diameter are prone to develop spontaneous pneumothorax. There is speculation that the blebs occur secondary to the mechanical stress placed on the apex of the lung with increased height.

The onset of spontaneous pneumothorax occurs more frequently when the patient is at rest. Signs and symptoms include pleuritic chest pain, dyspnea, and occasionally a cough. Auscultation reveals diminished breath sounds, and percussion demonstrates hyperresonance on the affected side. Chest movement will be asymmetric. The intensity of the clinical manifestations generally depends on the severity of the collapse and the patient's general state of health.

Treatment consists of observation and insertion of a chest tube in most cases. A chest tube allows removal of air or fluid from the pleural space and promotes reexpansion of the collapsed lung tissue by reestablishing the normal negative intrapleural pressure. Use of a chest tube depends on the extent of the collapse, evidence of progression of the collapse, respiratory failure, the severity of the underlying disease (if present), and the general state of the patient's health.

In 1% to 2% of all cases of spontaneous pneumothorax, a condition known as *tension pneumothorax* develops. The leak is a ball-valve type and allows air to enter but not escape from the pleural cavity. With each breath the positive pressure in the pleural cavity increases. The increased pressure causes displacement of the mediastinum (manifested by tracheal deviation toward the unaffected side), reduced venous return because of pressure on the great vessels, reduced cardiac output and blood pressure, and eventually shock. This condition is considered a medical emergency and treatment with insertion of a chest tube must be initiated immediately.

Hemothorax is the term applied when blood enters the pleural cavity. *Catamenial pneumothorax* refers to spontaneous pneumothorax associated with menstruation. Women with this condition usually have had a previous pregnancy and repeated episodes of spontaneous pneumothorax. Endometriosis is often an associated condition. Twenty percent of all persons with spontaneous pneumothorax develop recurrences within a year.

Surfactant deficiency

Surfactant deficiency can also cause a disruption in the mechanics of breathing, which will eventually cause hypoventilation. Pulmonary surfactant is secreted by cuboidal type II cells in the alveolar epithelium and reduces the surface tension of the fluid lining the alveoli, thus reducing the tendency of the alveoli to collapse. In conditions in which the amount of surfactant being secreted is deficient, the alveoli will have a greater than normal tendency to collapse. When alveoli collapse they become nonfunctional for gas exchange, and lung expansion becomes extremely difficult. There is a decrease in pulmonary compliance and an increase in the work of breathing. Surfactant has a half-life of 14 hours, and replacement is dependent on normal ventilation of the alveoli. Surfactant production will be adversely affected in those conditions in which ventilation is impaired, thus setting up a vicious cycle to perpetuate ventilatory impairment.

In the past, pulmonary surfactant deficiency was thought to play a partial role in the development of *adult respiratory distress syndrome* (ARDS). More recent evidence indicates, however, that if surfactant abnormalities exist, they are the result rather than a primary cause of lung dysfunction. Once present, however, a surfactant abnormality could contribute to further deterioration of lung function. The role of surfactant abnormalities in the pathogenesis of ARDS has been the subject of much research.

Respiratory distress syndrome (RDS) of the newborn, or *hyaline membrane disease*, is caused by a lack of adequate amounts of pulmonary surfactant in the lungs of certain neonates. Premature infants of very low birth weight are most susceptible because the surfactant-synthesizing ability of the lungs develops during the later stages of fetal life. The increased incidence of RDS seen as birth weight and gestational age decrease indicates that the primary defect is immaturity of the surfactant-secreting components of lung tissue. Other groups of infants susceptible to the development of RDS include infants of diabetic mothers, the second born of twins, and possibly, infants born by cesarean section without prior labor. In addition to low birth weight and prematurity, the gestational history of infants who develop RDS often includes a fetal stress provoking intrapartal event such as maternal hypotension, vaginal bleeding, or birth asphyxia.

The ability of the unborn infant's lungs to secrete surfactant can be determined prenatally by measuring the lecithin/sphingomyelin ratio of the amniotic fluid or by the amniotic fluid foam test.

Factors other than surfactant deficiency contribute to the pathogenesis of RDS. These include the small alveolar size and the wide range of alveolar diameters. Because of these physical properties and the loss of the surface active alveolar lining layer, the infant with RDS must generate maximal ventilatory pressure to reexpand and prevent further collapse of alveoli and maintain respiratory function. As alveoli collapse, compliance is reduced and the work of breathing is increased. RDS is characterized by atelectasis, which results in hypoxemia, hypercapnia, and acidosis. Pathologic changes include degeneration of the epithelial and endothelial cells of the alveolocapillary membrane and development of a hyaline membrane lining the alveolar sac, causing even greater impairment of gas exchange. The hypoxia causes pulmonary vascular constriction with the sequela of increased pulmonary vascular resistance. The interaction of these pathophysiologic mechanisms is depicted in Fig. 16-22.

The mortality associated with RDS is estimated to be 30% of all neonatal deaths and 50% to 70% of premature infant deaths in the United States. The clinical course of RDS is characterized by increasing respiratory deterioration and dependence on ventilatory support measures until evidence of alveolar type II cell regeneration occurs and surfactant production reappears (Avery, 1987). Clinical manifestations include those of respiratory distress: nasal flaring, retractions, increased apical pulse, cyanosis when breathing 40% oxygen, an expiratory grunt, and a uniform reticulogranular pat-

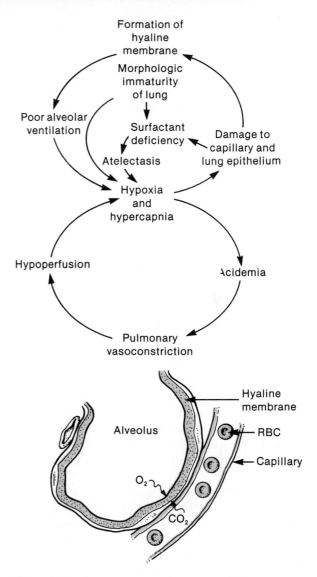

Fig. 16-22. Interdependent relationship of factors involved in pathology of respiratory distress syndrome. (From Pierog SH, and Ferrara A: Medical care of the sick newborn, ed 2, St. Louis, 1976, The CV Mosby Co.)

tern in peripheral lung fields on chest x-ray film. As respiratory distress worsens, there will be a progressive increase in the number of apneic episodes and the infant's color will be extremely cyanotic.

Treatment of RDS is aimed at improving the oxygenation of the tissues through improved ventilation and reexpansion of the alveoli despite the surfactant deficiency. Assisted ventilation and supplemental oxygen are used to promote oxygenation. Continuous positive airway pressure (C-PAP) and positive end-expiratory pressure (PEEP) are two techniques that help reexpand alveoli by providing increased airway pressure and preventing the normal collapse of alveoli at the end of expiration. A dangerous complication of using high distending pressures is barotrauma. Limitation of peak airway pressure with conventional mechanical ventilation can be achieved using low ventilatory rates of long inspiratory duration. Adequate gas exchange often requires the use of dangerously high airway pressures that can damage already distended airways and cause alveolar rupture with the sequelae of pneumothorax and pneumomediastinum (air in the mediastinal space). A new form of ventilatory support being used to treat infants with RDS is high frequency ventilation (HFV). There are different forms of HFV, but essentially the technique involves delivery of small tidal volumes at frequencies greater than 60 breaths per minute (Avery, 1987). This allows maintenance of a relatively constant lung volume and adequate carbon dioxide elimination with small tidal volume and pressure changes, thus minimizing the possibility of barotrauma. Supportive treatment is continued until the infant is able to maintain ventilation and alveolar expansion on its own.

There is experimental evidence that corticosteroids may speed the maturation of the pulmonary surfactant-secreting system. They do, however, potentiate the effects of oxygen toxicity, and their use in the early stages of RDS has been questioned (Kirby and Taylor, 1986). A promising treatment is replacement of the missing surfactant with exogenous synthetic surfactant. Early results indicate that significant early and sustained increases in oxygenation can be achieved in very low birth weight infants, although the effect lasts for only a short time. Controlled clinical trials of the efficacy of such replacement therapy are needed, as many questions regarding the dosage, timing of administration, and method of administration remain unanswered (Avery, 1987). Closure of a patent ductus arteriosus may be required in patients who are resistant to treatment or who experience further deterioration of their respiratory status.

Possible complications of RDS and its treatment include intraventricular cerebral hemorrhage, coagulation defects, cardiac complications, persistent pulmonary hypertension (sometimes called persistent fetal circulation), and secondary infection. A chronic lung dysfunction that can develop in infants treated for RDS is *bronchopulmonary dysplasia* (BPD). It is the leading cause of morbidity and late mortality in neonates who require ventilatory support.

Oxygen toxicity, barotrauma, the severity of RDS, and the degree of lung immaturity have all been cited as etiologic factors in the pathogenesis of BPD. Frank and Sosenko (1988) have further proposed that "the occurrence and severity of BPD very likely depends on the degree of imbalance that is established between lung injury and lung repair capabilities." They postulate that the capability for tissue repair is compromised by the minimal caloric energy reserves of the very low birth weight neonate and that, for this reason, undernutrition should also be considered an etiologic factor. Deficiencies of vitamins A and E have been reported (Avery, 1987;

Kirby and Taylor, 1986). This risk of developing BPD is increased in the presence of other pathologic processes such as patent ductus arteriosus, persistent pulmonary hypertension of the newborn (persistent fetal circulation), and pulmonary infection (Farrell and Palta, 1986). The risk also seems to be greater in infants in whom the onset of diuresis is delayed or who have received an increased fluid load (Avery, 1987; Kirby and Taylor, 1986).

While the etiology is multifactorial, the pathologic changes seen in the lung tissue are most consistent with those of oxygen toxicity and barotrauma, which are thought to be the leading etiologic factors. The terminal airways are the most compliant areas in the lung. Pressures associated with mechanical ventilation cause distension and eventually rupture of these airways, resulting in pulmonary interstitial emphysema (emphysematous coalescence of alveoli) and air leak. The antioxidant enzyme systems that protect lung tissue from the effects of free oxygen radicals mature late in fetal life, paralleling the surfactant-secreting system. This plus the deficiency of vitamin E, which has antioxidant properties, makes the neonate's lung tissue especially susceptible to the cytotoxic effects of high oxygen concentrations.

The pathologic alterations of BPD represent damage and extensive repair of the airways, lung parenchyma, and pulmonary vasculature. Alveolar and bronchiolar epithelial necrosis and repair with bronchial metaplasia and interstitial fibrosis are the predominant pathologic findings. Proliferation of smooth muscle tissue accompanies these changes (Avery, 1987). Vascular changes include thromboses, medial hypertrophy, intimal degeneration, and adventitial fibrosis (Taussig, 1986).

The clinical manifestations reflect the pathologic changes that occur. Pulmonary manifestations of chronic dysfunction, such as airway obstruction with air trapping and hyperinflation of the chest, excessive mucus production with a decreased ability to clear the mucus, and alveolar edema related to increased endothelial permeability, develop. Many of the manifestations seen in RDS continue, including tachypnea, intercostal retractions, hypoxemia, hypercapnia, and compensated respiratory acidosis. The vascular changes are consistent with pulmonary hypertension, which eventually causes right ventricular hypertrophy and dysfunction. Serial chest x-ray films show first diffuse opacification, followed by cyst formation with enlargement of the cysts, and eventually hyperexpansion of the lungs as the disease progresses, and basilar hyperlucency and streaky infiltrates in the apices as resolution occurs. Attempts to feed the infant orally often cause coughing and choking. Feeding difficulties occur because of the respiratory insufficiency and possibly because of impaired swallowing thought to be related to carbon dioxide retention (Kirby and Taylor, 1986). The next case study (see p. 629) demonstrates the potential for both aspiration and impaired growth that can result because of feeding difficulties.

Because the staging (or timing of occurrence) of the pathologic changes and development of chronic dysfunction varies between individual infants, identification of an exact point in time at which transition from the acute disorder of RDS into the chronic lung disorder of BPD is difficult. This has probably contributed to some of the differences of opinion about diagnostic criteria for BPD. Different authors have proposed different sets of criteria for identification of the development of BPD. All include a history of assisted positive pressure ventilation, supplemental oxygen administration, persistence of manifestations of respiratory insufficiency, and progression of the radiographic changes described in the preceding text (Kirby and Taylor, 1986).

The exact incidence of BPD is uncertain because of the historical lack of generally accepted diagnostic criteria and changes in the population of ventilated infants, but it is estimated that between 2.5% and 6% of all infants who receive ventilatory support develop BPD. The incidence is different when one separates out the very low birth weight infants, and it may be as high as 40% in infants who weigh less than 1500 gm at birth. At present it does not usually develop in infants who weigh more than that at birth (Avery, 1987).

A major goal of high risk perinatal treatment is prevention of premature births and the development of RDS. If RDS occurs, a major goal of treatment is prevention of the development of BPD through the use of appropriate levels of pressure-assisted ventilatory support and supplemental oxygen, and then reduction of this support as soon as possible. The use of vitamin E and other antioxidants to minimize oxygen toxicity is currently under investigation as preventive therapy in neonates who require prolonged ventilatory support. Maintenance of an appropriate fluid balance is also part of the preventive treatment. If BPD develops, ventilatory support and oxygen therapy that is adequate to prevent hypoxic pulmonary hypertension will continue. Bronchial hygiene (suctioning and chest physiotherapy) will be needed to maintain effective airway clearance. The smooth muscle proliferation makes possible a positive response to bronchodilator agents, which reduce airway resistance. Corticosteroid medication is used to reduced the inflammatory reaction to injury. Avery

(1987) reports that ventilator-dependent infants with BPD were able to be weaned from the ventilator and showed improved pulmonary function after short-term steroid therapy. Controversy still surrounds the use of steroids because of the increased potential for infection and growth derangement this type of pharmacologic agent can cause. Adequate nutrition must also be provided, as the energy needs of these infants will be increased because of the increased work of breathing and ongoing tissue repair.

The mortality associated with BPD has been reported to be as high as 33% (Avery, 1987). Late deaths are often the result of cardiac dysfunction, a major cause of which is cor pulmonale. Radiographic changes may persist for up to 2 years. During the first year, the infant can experience recurrent infections and may even require reinstitution of ventilatory support. An increased oxygen requirement has been reported to be a more sensitive indicator of impending infection than even chest x-ray changes (Kirby and Taylor, 1986). Avoidance of infection and prompt and aggressive treatment should an infection occur are necessary if further lung damage is to be prevented. Growth and developmental delays also occur. The long-term prognosis is good if the infant survives the first year, and in the majority of the patients who survive, normal pulmonary function eventually returns (Avery, 1987).

Some infants require long-term assisted ventilation and oxygen therapy, and many of these patients can be treated successfully in the home. This allows a significant reduction in both the cost of care and the potential for nosocomial infection. Home care of an infant with BPD does require a supportive and capable family environment, which was, unfortunately, lacking for the child in the following case study. The child has remained hospitalized throughout her young life. Given the extent of her respiratory insufficiency and neurologic deficits, her prognosis is not as good as can be expected for most infants who develop BPD.

CASE STUDY: BRONCHOPULMONARY DYSPLASIA

Objective and Subjective Data
History

BW is a 15-month-old female toddler with a diagnosis of bronchopulmonary dysplasia. She weighed 1000 gm at birth following a 35-week gestation. Born of a 15-year-old, unmarried, white mother from a very deprived background, the infant suffered from respiratory distress syndrome. She was treated with mechanical ventilation and oxygen therapy for 5 days. Subsequently the infant developed all the symptoms of bronchopulmonary dysplasia and has continued to require mechanical ventilation and oxygen. She has a permanent tracheostomy to facilitate this treatment. Repeated attempts to wean her from the respirator have failed. When off the respirator, she becomes extremely tachypneic and exhausted within an hour.

The infant also was diagnosed with hydrocephalus at the age of 1 month and a shunt was performed. This shunt malfunctioned once and was repaired. Neurologically, BW is severely developmentally delayed, unable to walk, does not speak, but does indicate her needs by pointing and grunting.

BW's parents are rarely present, and she has been essentially raised by the intensive care staff. Nurses arrange to spend time with her in play and in supportive activities. She feeds very poorly and chokes and coughs throughout any oral feeding. Total parenteral nutrition is required to maintain her in a well-nour-

Contributed by Maureen Groër.

ished, well-hydrated state. She is in less than the fifth percentile for both height and weight, and the Denver Developmental Screening test indicates that her developmental maturation is at about the 6-month level.

General appearance and physical examination: On physical examination, without assisted ventilation, BW has a respiratory rate of 60, pulse of 150, and moderate intercostal, suprasternal, and substernal retractions. She has been off the ventilator for 5 minutes and appears anxious and fretful. She has a barrel-chested appearance, enlarged head, and is slightly cyanotic, with moderate distal clubbing of the fingers. She is supported by pillows in a sitting position inside a mist tent that delivers 5 L of oxygen per minute. The most remarkable aspect of her appearance is her cushingoid appearance. She had been on steroid medication, which was discontinued at the age of 6 months. Nevertheless she has the typical moon face, wasted limb musculature, and abdominal striae seen in patients on steroid medication. The persistence of this appearance has tentatively been attributed to chronic stress associated with the severe, persistent respiratory distress associated with her disease.

Nursing Diagnoses

1. Ineffective breathing pattern related to B.P.D.
2. Impaired gas exchange related to BPD
3. Ineffective family coping: disabling related to parental abdication of responsibility for child care
4. Altered growth and development related to neurologic defects and parental deprivation
5. Altered nutrition: less than body requirements related to high metabolic requirements and feeding difficulties
6. Potential for aspiration related to feed difficulties

Another possible complication of treatment with supplemental oxygen is *retrolental fibroplasia*. If arterial oxygen tension is raised to levels equal to or greater than 100 mm Hg, retinal vessels and cells may be damaged, causing blindness. The high partial pressure of the oxygen causes destruction of the retinal arteries and hyperplasia of the developing, immature retinal cells. The incidence of retrolental fibroplasia is inversely proportional to birth weight. It is rarely seen in infants who weigh over 1200 to 1500 gm at birth but still occurs in very low birth weight infants (Avery, 1987). This complication can be avoided through careful, frequent monitoring of arterial blood gas levels and inspired oxygen concentrations and adjustment of the latter based on the infant's arterial oxygen pressure levels.

Oxygen toxicity has been alluded to frequently in the preceding discussion. It is really a disorder of exchange because oxygen concentrations greater than normal are toxic to the cells involved in gas exchange—those of the alveolar epithelium and vascular endothelium. The capillary endothelium is damaged in the earliest stages of hyperoxia, reducing the functional area of the capillary bed. This is followed by destruction of alveolar type I cells. Alveolar type II cells and fibroblasts do not appear to be as susceptible to hyperoxic damage. Edema occurs as a result of increased membrane permeability, and atelectasis also occurs. Hypoxemia develops as the alveolar capillary membrane becomes nonfunctional for gas exchange. Alveolar type II cells are able to proliferate and repair the alveolar epithelium, eventually converting to type I cells. If fibroblast proliferation is excessive, fibrosis results and the repair is defective (Massaro, 1987).

The damage of oxygen toxicity is thought to be the result of the activity of free radicals that are formed through oxygen metabolism. Under normal conditions, protection from the effects of free radicals is afforded through the action of enzymes that catalyze their removal like superoxide dismutases, peroxidases, and nonenzymatic antioxidant compounds such as vitamin E, vitamin C, and beta-carotene. It appears that tolerance of oxygen depends on a relative balance existing between the rates of enzyme synthesis and free radical formation. Under hyperoxic conditions, damage occurs because the rate of free radical formation outstrips the rate of enzyme synthesis. Experimental evidence from animal models indicates that while an early increase in enzyme formation is possible, the depletion of substrates for protein synthesis prevents a sustained response. A current direction in experimental work is the identification of pharmacologic agents that increase resistance to the effects of hyperoxia. Enzymes with a prolonged half-life, endotoxin, and antioxidant compounds are being examined currently. The timing of administration of corticosteroid medication also needs to be examined. Administration coinciding with the onset of hyperoxia in rats has been found to exacerbate oxygen toxicity, whereas administration immediately before or at the termination of hyperoxia had beneficial effects on lung function (Massaro, 1987). This apparent temporal variation in the effectiveness of corticosteroids in treating hyperoxic lung injury may be related to the clinical controversies surrounding the use of this medication in the treatment of conditions such as RDS and ARDS, in which oxygen toxicity may be an etiologic or exacerbating factor.

NORMAL EXCHANGE PROCESSES

Exchange is the process by which oxygen diffuses from the alveoli into the blood and from the blood into the tissues. Carbon dioxide is removed in a reversal of the same process. Normal exchange processes require an adequate level of alveolar ventilation and perfusion, appropriate pressure gradients and intact membranes between the areas where exchange occurs, and normal affinity between hemoglobin and oxygen in the blood.

In the lungs there is an extensive network of capillaries, which are close to the thin alveolar walls. The alveolar epithelial lining is composed primarily of squamous type I cells. These cells are especially suited for gas transfer and are, therefore, most easily damaged by toxic inhalants. Following an injury they are unable to regenerate, and alveolar type II cells replace the injured cells and eventually transform into type I cells (Center and McFadden, 1985). The capillary and alveolar walls are separated by a thin interstitial space. This approximation constitutes the alveolocapillary membrane (Fig. 16-23). Diffusion of oxygen and carbon dioxide is continually taking place across the alveolocapillary membrane. Exchange across the membrane depends on several factors:

1. Adequate ventilation to maintain normal gas concentrations and volumes in the alveoli
2. Normal flow of blood through the pulmonary capillary bed (perfusion)
3. The thickness of the membrane itself
4. The surface area of the membrane
5. The relative pressure gradients and solubility of the gases on each side of the membrane (Diffusion is the passive movement of molecules or atoms from an area of higher concentration to one of lower concentration.)
6. Normal affinity between oxygen and hemoglobin

For effective gas exchange to occur, the ventilation and perfusion of alveoli must take place in a fairly uniform way. If ventilation and perfusion are relatively equal, the ratio is about 0.8 to 1.0. When the ratio is above or below this value, ventilation perfusion inequality or mismatch exists. The ratio of ventilation to perfusion ($\dot{V}/\dot{Q}$) controls the concentration of oxygen and carbon dioxide in the alveolar air and in the blood. In other words, perfusion of poorly ventilated alveoli will result in low oxygen and high carbon dioxide tensions in the blood. This is termed a low ventilation-perfusion ratio and a shunt is said to exist. A high ventilation-perfusion ratio occurs when ventilation of alveoli is relatively greater than blood flow around them. This has the effect of increasing dead space ventilation.

Various conditions can affect either ventilation or perfusion in the lungs, resulting in a ventilation-perfusion mismatch. Even in normal lungs there is a certain degree of ventilation-perfusion mismatch. When a person is in an upright position, the apices of the lungs are well ventilated but, because of the effects of gravity, poorly perfused. In the bases of the lung the opposite effect is true; perfusion is greater than ventilation.

The alveolar units with high ventilation-perfusion ratios can compensate for those with low ratios to a limited extent. The amount of oxygen that can combine with hemoglobin is limited so that the total oxygen concentration of the blood will remain low. The carbon dioxide level, however, can be adjusted. In the alveoli with the high ventilation-perfusion ratios more carbon dioxide will be removed from the blood, resulting in a lowered P_{CO_2}. When this blood mixes with the blood from alveolar units having low ventilation-perfusion ratios, the overall effect will be a normal arterial P_{CO_2}.

The pressure gradient between the al-

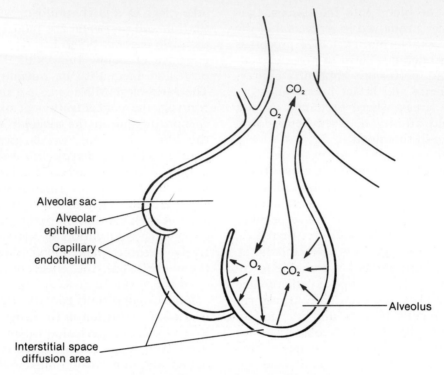

Fig. 16-23. Alveolocapillary membrane.

veoli and the blood causes oxygen molecules to move across the membrane into the blood. These molecules immediately bind with hemoglobin. The ability of hemoglobin to bind with oxygen at different oxygen tensions is expressed graphically by the hemoglobin dissociation curve (Fig. 16-24). This curve shows the percent saturation of hemoglobin that can be expected at different partial pressures of oxygen in the blood. The nonlinear S shape of the curve allows the oxygen saturation of the blood to be relatively high despite low partial pressures of oxygen. For instance, with a Po_2 of 40 mm Hg at a pH of 7.4, the hemoglobin saturation would be approximately 75%. The affinity of hemoglobin for oxygen is dependent upon Po_2, temperature, and red blood cell pH and 2,3-diphos-phoglycerate concentration. Fig. 16-24 illustrates the normal oxyhemoglobin dissociation curve *(A)* and the effect of pH changes on this curve *(B)*. A shift to the right of the curve indicates a decreased affinity of hemoglobin for oxygen, which promotes oxygen unloading in the tissues. A shift to the left of the curve indicates an increased affinity of hemoglobin for oxygen, which impedes oxygen unloading in the tissues. The Bohr effect (the effect of pH on hemoglobin affinity) serves to promote the uptake of oxygen in the lung and to promote the release of oxygen in the tissue, where pH is relatively low.

ALTERATIONS OF EXCHANGE

Impaired gas exchange is defined as a state in which there is an imbalance be-

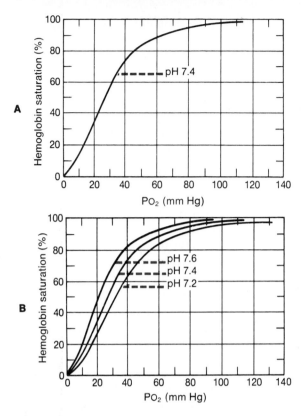

Fig. 16-24. A, Oxyhemoglobin dissociation curve. **B,** Shifts in oxyhemoglobin dissociation curve at various pH levels (Bohr effect).

tween oxygen uptake and carbon dioxide elimination at the capillary membrane level (NANDA definition). Impaired gas exchange can be the result of conditions in which the normal ventilation-perfusion ratio is altered, the functional capacity of the alveolar capillary membrane or capillary membrane beds is reduced, or the normal affinity between hemoglobin and oxygen is altered. Extrapulmonary as well as pulmonary conditions can cause such changes and ultimately disrupt the normal gas exchange process. Conditions that alter the normal ventilatory process and the relative concentrations of gases on either side of the alveolocapillary membrane, the

perfusion of alveoli with arterial blood, or the permeability of the membrane itself will ultimately disrupt the exchange process.

Gas exchange between the atmosphere and the blood is the result of both ventilation and perfusion of the alveoli. Alterations in the normal relationship between these two processes will result in disruption of the normal exchange of gases and consequently of the blood gas concentrations.

Both ineffective breathing pattern and ineffective airway clearance, if allowed to progress untreated, may lead to impaired gas exchange because of the subsequent disruption in the ventilation-perfusion relationship that will eventually develop. Aside from the altered lung volumes and capacities, many of the clinical manifestations of disorders of ventilation that were previously discussed are a reflection of the concomitant disruption of the exchange process, since exchange is dependent on ventilation.

Because the gases diffuse across the alveolocapillary membrane space, changes in the cellular integrity of and fluid pressures around the membrane must also be considered when evaluating alterations of exchange. Alterations of exchange can be caused by alterations in the functional capacity of the alveolocapillary membrane space. Examples of conditions in which the functional area of the alveolocapillary membrane is reduced include pulmonary edema (cardiogenic and noncardiogenic), granulomatous and fibrotic processes, cancer, and oxygen toxicity.

Ventilation-perfusion abnormalities

The alveolus with its associated pulmonary capillary is the basic functional respiratory unit in which gas exchange takes place. Shapiro et al. (1982) state that this unit can theoretically exist in any of four different types of ventilation-perfusion relationships (Fig. 16-25) that affect gas exchange:

1. Normal unit: ventilation and perfusion are relatively equal
2. Dead space unit: alveolus is ventilated, but blood flow through capillary is reduced or nonexistent
3. Shunt unit: alveolus is not ventilated, or ventilation is reduced, but perfusion continues
4. Silent unit: both alveolus and capillary are nonfunctional

An infinite number of ventilation-perfusion relationships may exist on the spectrum between the two extremes of dead space and shunt.

Dead space ventilation is that portion of the total ventilation (tidal volume) that does not participate in gas exchange. There are three possible components of dead space ventilation:

1. Anatomic dead space: the portion of the total ventilation that remains in the conducting airways
2. Alveolar dead space: ventilation in an alveolus that is not being perfused with blood
3. Dead space effect: effect that occurs when ventilation is relatively greater than perfusion, and the excess venti-

lation does not participate in gas exchange; this can result from either overventilation or underperfusion.

A shunt is that portion of the cardiac output that does not participate in gas exchange. The physiologic or total shunt can be divided into three components:

1. Anatomic shunt: approximately 2% to 3% of the cardiac output that normally bypasses the pulmonary circulation and returns to the left side of the heart unoxygenated; this is the blood return from the bronchial, pleural, and part of the coronary circulations (Dantzker, 1986).
2. Capillary shunt: blood that perfuses totally unventilated alveoli; the sum of the anatomic and capillary shunts is called the true, or absolute, shunt; this is refractory or unresponsive to any form of oxygen therapy.
3. Shunt effect: effect that occurs when perfusion is relatively greater than ventilation; this can be the result of either poor ventilation of the alveoli or an excessive rate of blood flow; this results in *venous admixture* and is responsive to oxygen therapy.

Conditions that contribute to dead space or shunting will result in a disruption of the exchange process. The extent of the disruption and the degree to which normal

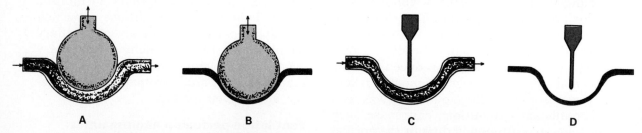

Fig. 16-25. Theoretic respiratory unit. **A,** Normal unit: normal ventilation and normal perfusion. **B,** Dead space unit: normal ventilation and no perfusion. **C,** Shunt unit: no ventilation and normal perfusion. **D,** Silent unit: no ventilation and no perfusion.

(From Shapiro BA, Harrison RA, and Walton JR: Clinical application of blood gases, ed 2. Copyright © 1977 by Year Book Medical Publishers, Inc., Chicago. Used by permission.)

blood gas values are altered will depend on the severity and persistence of the underlying defect. The maldistribution and mismatching of ventilation and perfusion that occur in chronic diffuse bronchopulmonary disease result in an increase in both the dead space and shunting effects throughout the lungs. Initially hypoxemia alone will be present. The carbon dioxide level of the mixed arterial blood will remain normal because alveolar units with high or normal ventilation-perfusion ratios can compensate for the increased carbon dioxide level in the blood coming from alveolar units with low ventilation-perfusion ratios by "blowing off" greater amounts of carbon dioxide. The exchange of oxygen differs from that of carbon dioxide in that it is much more limited. Oxygen is far less soluble than carbon dioxide, and its saturation level in the blood is limited by the amount of hemoglobin available. The compensatory increase in the rate of alveolar ventilation in response to the resultant hypoxemia also helps keep arterial carbon dioxide levels within normal limits. As the disease progresses, however, carbon dioxide retention will also occur as increasingly greater numbers of alveolar units are affected by the disease process (see Fig. 16-18).

An increase in dead space ventilation can be the result of disrupted perfusion or overventilation that does not participate in the exchange process. Pulmonary perfusion can be disrupted by a variety of causes. An embolism in a major vessel, numerous microemboli in smaller vessels (see Chapter 14 for discussion of pulmonary embolism), a decrease in cardiac output, reduction in the area of the pulmonary capillary bed, or increased pulmonary vascular resistence can all have the effect of increasing dead space ventilation.

Alveolar septal destruction reduces the amount of alveolar surface area available for gas exchange, so that the overall effect is ventilation in excess of perfusion, or dead space effect. Use of a volume ventilator without a simultaneous increase in the amount and distribution of the pulmonary blood flow will also enhance the dead space effect. Anatomic dead space increases with a rapid, shallow respiratory pattern; alveolar gas is never completely renewed, and the work of breathing is increased.

Anatomic shunting is a direct flow of blood between the right and left sides of the heart without passing through the pulmonary capillaries to be made available for gas exchange. Congenital heart defects such as septal defects and patent ductus arteriosus are examples of conditions in which a direct anatomic communication exists between the pulmonic and systemic circulations, completely bypassing the lungs. Blood flow through vascular pulmonary tumors may also result in an anatomic shunt as blood flows through the tumor into the pulmonary veins. Blood flowing past collapsed (atelectasis), fluid-filled (pulmonary edema), or pus-filled (pneumonia) alveoli results in a capillary shunt. Underventilation of alveoli and uneven distribution of ventilation within the lungs results in venous admixture because of the shunt effect.

Shunt as a mechanism of hypoxemia bears further discussion. Other mechanisms can lower the partial pressure of oxygen in the blood, as is shown in Fig. 16-26. It is clinically significant as the major mechanism of hypoxemia in pulmonary edema, atelectasis, and pneumonia (Dantzker, 1986). True shunt can be differentiated from ventilation-perfusion abnormality (shunt effect) by the lack of response to increased concentrations of

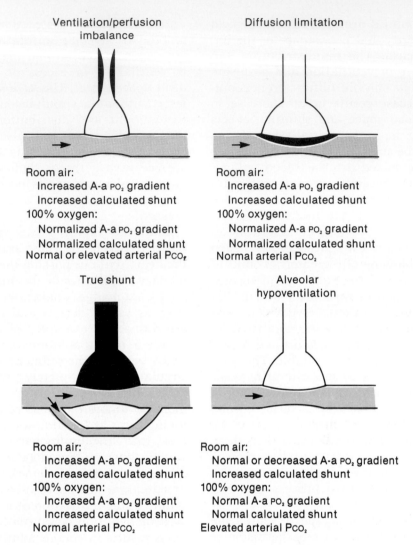

Ventilation/perfusion imbalance

Room air:
  Increased A-a P_{O_2} gradient
  Increased calculated shunt
100% oxygen:
  Normalized A-a P_{O_2} gradient
  Normalized calculated shunt
Normal or elevated arterial P_{CO_2}

Diffusion limitation

Room air:
  Increased A-a P_{O_2} gradient
  Increased calculated shunt
100% oxygen:
  Normalized A-a P_{O_2} gradient
  Normalized calculated shunt
Normal arterial P_{CO_2}

True shunt

Room air:
  Increased A-a P_{O_2} gradient
  Increased calculated shunt
100% oxygen:
  Increased A-a P_{O_2} gradient
  Increased calculated shunt
Normal arterial P_{CO_2}

Alveolar hypoventilation

Room air:
  Normal or decreased A-a P_{O_2} gradient
  Increased calculated shunt
100% oxygen:
  Normal A-a P_{O_2} gradient
  Normal calculated shunt
Elevated arterial P_{CO_2}

Fig. 16-26. Effect of four mechanisms of hypoxemia on A-a P_{O_2} gradient, calculated shunt, and Pa_{CO_2} on normal (room air) and increased concentrations of oxygen.

(Adapted from Miller A, editor: Pulmonary function tests: a guide for the student and house officer, Orlando, 1987, Grune & Stratton, Inc.)

inspired oxygen, especially as the degree of shunt increases. The P_{CO_2} will remain normal as long as minute ventilation is maintained, but CO_2 retention may develop if the shunt is very large (greater than 50%). Even in this situation P_{CO_2} may drop as hypoxia stimulates ventilation.

Another mechanism by which hypoxemia may occur is a reduction in the concentration of inspired oxygen. This occurs at high altitudes and in the cabins of commercial airplanes. Patients with chronic respiratory disorders accompanied by hypoxemia will need to be counseled regarding the appropriate precautions to take when traveling in order to prevent further reductions in their Po_2.

Aveolocapillary membrane alterations

A reduction in functional membrane space through a loss of total surface area will result in disruption of the exchange process. The destruction of the alveolar septa that occurs in emphysema is one example of this. Tuberculosis and pneumoconiosis are others. Changes in the cellular structure of the membrane itself can also adversely affect exchange. This is the primary functional abnormality in conditions such as sarcoidosis, systemic sclerosis, berylliosis, interstitial fibrosing pneumonitis, and oxygen toxicity. Some of these disorders are characterized by simultaneous disruption of ventilation and exchange. One example is *sarcoidosis*, a systemic granulomatous disorder of unknown etiology. Noncaseating granulomas are found in the tissues of the affected organs and the lung is affected in 90% of the cases (Martin, 1987). Many patients remain asymptomatic and require no treatment. Those who become symptomatic demonstrate obstructive and restrictive breathing patterns and impaired gas exchange as a result of a diffusion defect. Symptomatic patients are treated with corticosteroid medication. Another example is *idiopathic pulmonary fibrosis* in which a restrictive pattern of breathing and impaired gas exchange resulting from a diffusion defect are present (Hopp and Williams, 1987). Symptoms of both disorders include dyspnea and cough.

Fluid in the interstitial and alveolar spaces will also limit exchange. A shunt develops as the nonfunctional membrane space continues to be perfused with blood. Shunt is the pathogenetic mechanism of hypoxemia in *pulmonary edema* (Dantzker, 1986). Other clinical manifestations of pulmonary edema include those of respiratory distress (dyspnea, tachypnea, exaggerated respiratory effort, and use of the accessory muscles for breathing), coughing and expectoration of pink-tinged, frothy sputum, and the abnormal lung sounds known as crackles or rales. The patient will appear anxious and frightened and may be restless, agitated, or disoriented as a result of cerebral hypoxia. The chest roentgenogram will show diffuse alveolar infiltrates.

Based on the Starling principles (see Chapter 18), there are two mechanisms that can disrupt pulmonary capillary hemodynamics and cause pulmonary edema: (1) alteration of the normal pressure relationships and (2) increased membrane permeability. Alveolar edema can develop as a result of either of these mechanisms. The pulmonary vasculature is normally a low-pressure system that reduces capillary hydrostatic pressure. In cardiogenic or hydrostatic pulmonary edema, elevated capillary hydrostatic pressure causes the transudation of protein-poor fluid into the interstitium and alveoli. The usual cause is an abnormal postcapillary elevation of pressure in the left side of the heart that is reflected backward into the pulmonary vasculature. As a result, hydrostatic pressure in the pulmonary capillaries rises to favor movement of fluid out of the capillary and into the interstitial space and lung tissue (Ayres, 1982). (Disorders that cause cardiac dysfunction are discussed in the following chapter.) In addition to cardiac causes, hydrostatic pulmonary edema can occur after fluid overload.

Noncardiogenic or permeability pulmonary edema is the result of increased vascular permeability due to damage or injury to the alveolocapillary membrane. The pulmonary capillary pressure remains normal, and the interstitial exudate has a

COMMON CAUSES OF NONCARDIOGENIC PULMONARY EDEMA

Adult respiratory distress
  syndrome
Airway obstruction
CNS lesions
Diabetic ketoacidosis
Drugs
  Narcotics
  Barbiturates
  Propoxyphene
  Ethchlorvynol
  Chlordiazepoxide
  Salicylates
  Thiazides
Fat embolus
Gastric content aspiration
High altitude

Hypoglycemia
Infection/sepsis
Lung reexpansion
Near-drowning
Organophosphate insecticides
Oxygen toxicity
Pancreatitis
Paraquat ingestion
Posttrauma
Pulmonary embolus
Smoke inhalation
Transfusion reaction
Toxic inhalation
Uremia

SYNONYMS FOR ARDS

Adult hyaline membrane disease
Adult respiratory insufficiency syndrome
Congestive atelectasis
DaNang lung
Hemorrhagic atelectasis
Hemorrhagic lung syndrome
Hypoxic hyperventilation
Postperfusion lung
Posttraumatic atelectasis
Posttraumatic pulmonary insufficiency

Progressive pulmonary consolidation
Progressive respiratory distress
Pump lung
Respiratory insufficiency syndrome
Shock lung
Transplant lung
Traumatic wet lung
Wet lung
White lung

higher protein content than the transudate of cardiogenic pulmonary edema (Albert, 1987). The many and varied conditions associated with noncardiogenic pulmonary edema are listed in the box at top of page.

Noncardiogenic pulmonary edema is the major feature of the *adult respiratory distress syndrome* (ARDS). This clinical syndrome is not a disease in itself, but rather the composite of manifestations of acute lung injury that develops as a response to some pathologic event (Murray et al., 1988).

The term ARDS was first used more than 20 years ago to describe a clinical course of patients who developed respiratory distress caused by progressive lung dysfunction. Clinical and pathologic findings were similar to those seen in respiratory distress syndrome in the newborn, hence the name. While the title was new, the deterioration of pulmonary function that followed traumatic events and catastrophic illness had been recognized in the early part of this century; a progressive respiratory failure was described in soldiers who were battlefield casualties in World War I. The Vietnam War provided the circumstances for more complete description of this phenomenon. New techniques of battlefield care allowed the resuscitation and treatment of a very large number of healthy young adults who had sustained traumatic injury and who went on to develop this deterioration of lung function (Petty, 1982). In the past ARDS has been referred to by a variety of other titles, (see the box on p. 638), which reflect the circumstances surrounding the development of progressive respiratory failure following trauma or illness.

Bone et al. (1987b) define ARDS as a diffuse lung injury resulting in noncardiogenic pulmonary edema and acute respiratory failure. This lung injury occurs as a response to some pathologic insult such as trauma or overwhelming infection (sepsis). Many clinical conditions known to precipitate acute lung injury and ARDS are listed in Table 16-10.

The causative mechanism of the injury to the alveolar epithelium and pulmonary vascular endothelium is unknown at the present time and is the subject of much ongoing research. An inflammatory response and perturbations in the coagulation and fibrinolytic systems are characteristic of ARDS, and the role of inflammatory mediators (see Chapter 2) in the pathogenesis of ARDS has been the subject of intense scrutiny (Hyers and Ohar, 1988). The response and interaction of these substances in tissue injury is summarized in Fig. 16-27. Elucidation of the mechanism of injury will allow for treatment that can prevent or ameliorate that injury.

Table 16-10. Conditions associated with ARDS

Condition	Examples
Aspiration	Gastric contents (pH < 2.5) Near-drowning Ethylene glycol Hydrocarbon fluids
Drug related	Heroin Methadone Barbiturates Colchicine Salicylates Thiazides Propoxyphene
Infection	Pneumonia (bacterial, viral, or fungal) Tuberculosis Gram-negative sepsis
Inhalation injury	Smoke Oxygen Phosgene Chlorine Cadmium Ammonia
Metabolic	Diabetic ketoacidosis Uremia Pancreatitis
Obstetric	Eclampsia Amniotic fluid embolism Dead fetus
Shock	All causes
Trauma	Burns Fat embolism Lung contusion Head injury All other traumatic injury
Miscellaneous	Postcardiopulmonary bypass DIC Air embolism Multiple transfusions Bowel infarction Carcinomatosis

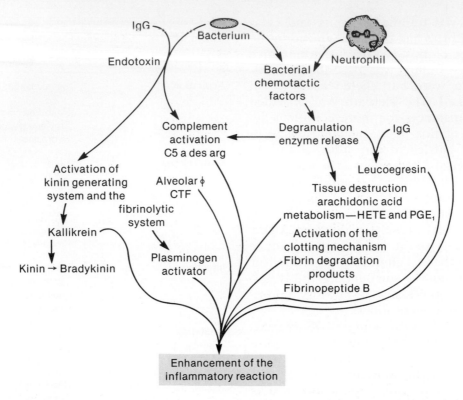

Fig. 16-27. Schematic summary of chemotactic factors that can be generated following tissue injury. Many of these substances have been implicated either directly or indirectly in ARDS. Research is needed to show which substances are initiators or perpetrators of ARDS and which are byproducts of the inflammatory response.

(From Davis JM and Dineen P: Chemoattractants in trauma. In Dineen P and Hildick-Smith G, editors: The surgical wound, Philadelphia, 1981, Lea & Febiger.)

Pathologic findings in ARDS reflect lung injury and include alveolar hemorrhage and the presence of a hyaline membrane. Noncardiogenic pulmonary edema is a central pathophysiologic event in ARDS. Alveoli become nonfunctional for gas exchange because they are filled with fluid as a result of increased membrane permeability. Surfactant defects develop. Lung compliance and functional residual capacity decrease due to atelectasis and edema. Shunting occurs and hypoxemia develops. A proposed scheme of these events following shock is shown in Fig. 16-28. Pulmonary vascular resistance may increase in response to hypoxia, vasoconstriction, in-creased interstitial fluid pressure, or intravascular clotting. Pulmonary hypertension is an unfavorable prognostic sign (Bone et al., 1987). The reader can see that many of these conditions will further perpetuate the pathophysiology that is occurring.

The clinical course of the syndrome develops in a characteristic manner. The stages of development of ARDS are summarized in Table 16-11. As the syndrome progresses and the work of breathing increases, the patient exhibits all the signs of respiratory distress discussed earlier. Acidosis develops in responses to tissue hypoxia and the shift to anaerobic metabolic

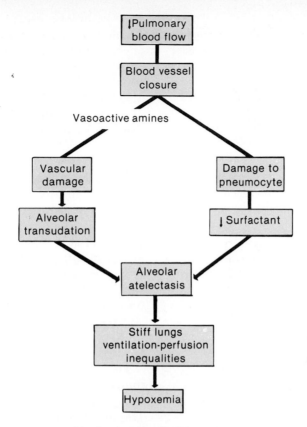

Fig. 16-28. Pathways proposed in the genesis of adult respiratory distress syndrome (ARDS) accompanying shock.

(From Kones RJ: Cardiogenic shock mechanisms and management, New York, 1974, Futura Publishing Co.)

Table 16-11. Clinical stages in ARDS

Stage	Findings
1: Acute injury	Normal physical examination and chest roentgenogram
	Tachycardia, tachypnea, and respiratory alkalosis develop
2: Latent period (apparent stability)	Lasts approximately 6 to 48 hours following injury
	Patient appears clinically stable
	Hyperventilation and hypocapnea persist
	Mild increase in work of breathing
	Widening of the alveolar-arterial oxygen gradient
	Minor abnormalities on physical examination and chest roentgenogram
3: Acute respiratory failure (respiratory insufficiency)	Marked tachypnea and dyspnea
	Decreased lung compliance
	Diffuse infiltrates on chest roentgenogram
	High-pitched crackles heard throughout all lung fields
4: Severe abnormalities (terminal stage)	Severe hypoxemia unresponsive to therapy
	Increased intrapulmonary shunting
	Metabolic and respiratory acidosis

Adapted from Taylor R: Chapter 14, p. 221 in Kirby RR and Taylor RW: Respiratory failure, Chicago, 1986, Year Book Medical Publishers, Inc.

Table 16-12. Criteria for diagnosing the adult respiratory distress syndrome

Parameter	Characteristics
Clinical setting	Catastrophic event
	Pulmonary
	Nonpulmonary, e.g., shock
	Exclusions
	Chronic pulmonary disease
	Left heart abnormalities
	Respiratory distress (judged clinically)
	Tachypnea >20, usually greater
	Labored breathing
X-ray	Diffuse pulmonary infiltrates
	Interstitial (initially)
Physiologic	Alveolar (later)
	Pao_2 <50 with Flo_2 > 0.6
	Overall compliance <50 ml/cm H_2O (usually 20 to 30 ml/cm H_2O)
	Increased shunt fraction $\dot{Q}s/\dot{Q}t$ and deadspace ventilation V_D/V_T
Psathologic	Heavy lungs, usually >1000 gm
	Congestive atelectasis
	Hyaline membranes
	Fibrosis

From Petty T: Adult respiratory distress syndrome: definition and historical perspective, Clin Chest Med 3:3, 1982.

pathways. The classic criteria used to diagnose this syndrome are a compilation of the clinical, physiologic, and pathologic findings discussed so far. These criteria are presented in Table 16-12.

Treatment. Treatment must be aggressive and prompt if the patient is to survive. Gas exchange is facilitated through the use of mechanical ventilation with positive end-expiratory pressure (PEEP) (Ayres, 1982). The use of steroids to reduce inflammatory injury remains controversial. Studies have demonstrated that the efficacy of these drugs varies, depending on the underlying cause of ARDS (Bone et al., 1987a; Murray et al., 1988). Of course, the precipitating condition must also be treated. ARDS must be viewed as a stressor that is overlaid on another disorder, causing further perturbation of the steady state. These patients are cared for in critical care units, which can be an additional source of stress for the patient and family.

Even with aggressive treatment, the mortality remains as high as 50% or greater (Petty, 1988). Many complications are associated with ARDS and its treatment. Multiple organ failure is often associated with ARDS and prognosis is poor (see Chapter 5). In patients who survive, normal lung function does return over time (Lakshminarayan and Hudson, 1981).

The following case study illustrates many of the difficulties encountered in the diagnosis and treatment of ARDS. The patient did not survive despite extremely aggressive treatment. Sepsis is one of the most frequent causes of ARDS, and the reported mortality associated with septic ARDS ranges between 80% and 90% (Jacobs and Bone, 1986). The early recognition and treatment of infection is, therefore, of utmost importance, but, as this case demonstrates, not always possible.

CASE STUDY: ADULT RESPIRATORY DISTRESS SYNDROME

History

MV is a 24-year-old Hispanic male with autoimmune hemolytic anemia diagnosed 3 years before admission, and no other significant health problems.

Contributed by Peggy Covey.

Objective and Subjective Data

MV came to the emergency room complaining of upper abdominal pain after being beaten up 4 days prior. The pain was epigastric, sharp, constant, and through the back. He complained of increased pain with ambulation, two episodes of nausea and vomiting, feeling "full," fatigue, decreased appetite, pruritus, and yellow sclerae.

Physical examination

Vital signs:

Temperature: 99.9° F

Pulse: 100 beats/min

Respiration: 20 breaths/min

Blood pressure: 150/80

Lungs: Clear and resonant

Sclerae: Icteric

Abdomen: Soft; concave with hyperactive bowel sounds; no organomegaly; epigastric tenderness with no guarding or rigidity

The rest of the physical examination was unremarkable

Admitting laboratory data

Hct 31.6

WBC: 17.5

Poly: 54

Bands: 0

Lymphs: 16

Segs: 25.2

PT/PTT: 11.0/28/4

BUN: 5

Creatinine: 0.6

NA^+: 136

K^+: 4.3

Cl^-: 102

CO_2^- 24

Glucose: 90

CA^{++}: 8.9

Bilirubin:

Total: 3.0

Direct: 1.7

LDH: 1300

SGOT: 201

SGPT: 105,

Alkaline phosphatase: 23

Serum amylase: 67

Chest x-ray and abdominal flat plate: Within normal limits

Clinical course: MV was admitted to a surgical unit where the following tests were performed:

Upper GI: Within normal limits

Liver-spleen scan: Few small focal defects; questionable hematoma/laceration

Ultrasound of abdomen: One small gallstone in the gallbladder; kidneys and liver within normal limits; pancreas not visualized

CT scan of abdomen: No intraperitoneal fluid or blood but pancreas was diffusely enlarged

Initial blood cultures: Negative

MV's pain subsided over several days. On the sixth day MV complained of increased pain and he was febrile. Laboratory data at that time:

Bilirubin: 19.5

Hematocrit: 28.7

Platetets: 782,000

Amylase: 137

Exploratory laparotomy revealed only gallbladder with sludge, no evidence of obstruction, and a cholecystectomy was done.

The first 3 postoperative days were uneventful. On the fourth postoperative day, MV was experiencing shortness of breath, increased abdominal girth, increased abdominal pain, anuria and no palpable peripheral pulses. PaO_2 on 40% ventimask = 70 mm Hg, HR = 130, BP = 154/104, WBC was increased, and chest x-ray film was clear. MV was admitted to the ICU were mechanical ventilatory support was initiated with the following settings: 40% *FiO_2, *IMV = 4, *PEEP = +8 cmH_2O, *TV = 800 ml. Repeat cultures of blood,

---

*PEEP, positive end-expiratory pressure; TV, tidal volume; IMV, intermittent mandatory ventilation—a form of ventilatory support wherein the patient can initiate his own breathing pattern and the ventilator is set to "breathe" a minimum number of times should the patient not initiate breathing; FiO_2, fractional concentration of inspired oxygen; O_2, oxygen.

wound, urine, and sputum were negative. Massive fluid resuscitation with hyperalimentation was begun. A pulmonary artery catheter was inserted: pulmonary capillary wedge pressure = 5 mm Hg, cardiac output = 6.5 L/min (normal 3.0 to 5.0), systemic vascular resistance = 1325 (normal = 1500), $\dot{Q}_s/\dot{Q}_t$ (shunt) = 25% (normal = 3.0 to 5.0).

Within 2 days MV's pulmonary function grew worse, with the following arterial blood gas findings: pH = 7.37, Pao_2 = 50 and Pco_2 = 67; on ventilator settings of FiO_2 = 100%; PEEP = +10 cm/H_2O, IMV = 8; and TV = 800 ml. Systemic vascular resistance had dropped to 217 with cardiac output = 17.3 L/min $\dot{Q}_s/\dot{Q}_t$ (shunt) = 36%. Chest x-ray film showed diffuse alveolar infiltrates. MV was restless and disoriented, and was given Pavulon and morphine to promote relaxation and reduce oxygen consumption. His diagnosis was ARDS due to unknown septic focus. A second exploratory laparotomy revealed massive small bowel infarction requiring resection of nearly all of the jejunum and ileum (2½ to 3 feet were left intact).

During the next 4 days MV's pulmonary status was stable with ventilator settings of FiO_2 = 45%, PEEP = +20 cm/H_2O, IMV = 14, TV = 800 ml. Cultures were negative, but he continued in a hyperdynamic state with low systemic vascular resistance.

On the fifth day his shunt increased to 45%, and chest x-ray film showed diffuse, fine granular infiltrates. During the course of the next 5 days MV developed increasing hypoxemia (Pao_2 as low as 35 mm Hg) and required 100% FiO_2 with PEEP of +50 cm H_2O on the ventilator. Lung compliance continued to decrease as reflected by peak pressures reaching +80 to +120 cm H_2O. $PaCO_2$ began to climb as it became more difficult to ventilate the patient, reaching 118 mm Hg. A brief trial of high frequency jet ventilation was attempted, which the patient did not tolerate. Blood pressure and cardiac output dropped accompanied by low pH and increased CO_2 retention. Tham (Tromethamine—a weak base which when given IV combines with carbon dioxide to form bicarbonate and cationic buffer) was started to correct the pH (7.1 to 7.23). Cultures remained negative. Subcutaneous emphysema was noted over the trachea and upper chest. Finally, 25 days after admission MV's heart rate suddenly dropped with no blood pressure. Advanced cardiopulmonary support was begun. The patient did not respond to dopamine, calcium chloride IV push twice, Isuprel, or transthoracic pacing and was pronounced dead.

Discussion

Sepsis is one of the major etiologic factors in ARDS. Despite repeated negative cultures, the septic focus in MV was not found; however, sepsis was the most likely factor in his ARDS. Even though the exact mechanism of the lung injury during ARDS is not yet known, the clinical syndrome has been well described. MV exhibited the hallmark characteristics of ARDS: a catastrophic event, severe dyspnea and hypoxemia with no pulmonary history, and alveolar edema with diffuse bilateral pulmonary infiltrates on chest x-ray film. The chest x-ray examination may be initially normal as MV's was, but rapidly changes to show diffuse alveolar infiltrates. The alveolar endothelial damage that occurs during ARDS results in both surfactant abnormalities and increased alveolar endothelial permeability. As a result, there is impairment of the mechanics of ventilation as well as of gas exchange. The lack of surfactant causes reduced lung compliance ("stiff lungs"), which made it very difficult to mechanically ventilate MV. To deliver the set tidal volume of 800 cc, the ventilator was required to develop peak pressures of +80 to 120 cm H_2O. When peak pressures are that high, there is added risk of further lung injury and pneumothorax due to barotrauma. MV did in fact develop subcutaneous emphysema, indicating pleural rupture. The brief trial with high frequency jet ventilation was attempted to improve ventilation and reduce intrapulmonary pressure.

During ARDS the alveoli collapse, become flooded with fluid, and develop a hyaline membrane. These factors prevent the exchange of oxygen and carbon dioxide in the pulmonary blood; therefore unoxygenated blood is returned to the left heart, a situation known as shunt. As the percentage of shunt increased, MV became refractory to oxygen therapy. Initially an FiO_2 of 40% maintained MV's PaO_2 at 75 mm Hg, but eventually 100% FiO_2 with 45 cm H_2O PEEP was required to maintain a PaO_2 of 71 mm Hg.

In these patients generally a euvolemic fluid balance is desired. The increased cardiac output of 17.3 L/min was in part a compensatory response to the increasing hypoxemia. Hypervolemia can increase hydrostatic forces, causing further alveolar edema, whereas hypovolemia in conjunction with the high PEEP levels required for oxygenation can reduce cardiac output and blood pressure. MV was able to maintain an adequate cardiac output and blood pressure on fluid replacement therapy.

Mortality during ARDS is high, which was the case for MV. Until more is known about the exact mechanism of the lung injury, supportive therapy until the patient's lung injury can heal is the only treatment available, and mortality will therefore remain high. Survivors of ARDS tend to recover with very little impairment of lung function and can resume normal activity.

Nursing Diagnoses

1. Anxiety related to severe dyspnea
2. Ineffective breathing pattern related to decreased lung compliance
3. Potential for decreased cardiac output related to increased intrapulmonary and intrathoracic pressures
4. Impaired verbal communication due to presence of artificial airway and use of
5. Pavulon (a neuromuscular blocking agent used to promote skeletal muscle relaxation)
6. Potential alteration in fluid volume
7. Impaired gas exchange due to alveolar capillary membrane abnormalities and alveolar edema
8. Impaired physical mobility due to use of Pavulon

Alterations in hemoglobin affinity

Changes in the normal affinity of hemoglobin for oxygen also can disrupt exchange by inhibiting oxygen loading and unloading. When affinity is decreased, the oxygen-carrying capacity of hemoglobin is decreased but release of oxygen to the tissues is facilitated. When the affinity between hemoglobin and oxygen is increased, release of oxygen to the tissues is inhibited. The effect of pH on the normal affinity of hemoglobin for oxygen was discussed in a previous section of text. Other conditions that affect the normal affinity between hemoglobin and oxygen are listed in Table 16-13.

Conditions other than decreased pH (increased hydrogen ion concentration or acidosis) that cause a shift to the right of the oxyhemoglobin dissociation curve or decreased affinity include increased PCO_2, increased temperature, and increased amounts of 2,3-diphosphoglycerate (2,3-DPG). This latter substance is an organic phosphate produced by glycolysis that binds hemoglobin in the red blood cell. Under normal circumstances these conditions all occur as a result of increased metabolic activity in the tissue. Enhanced unloading of oxygen in the tissues is obviously an efficient way to ensure a supply of oxygen sufficient to allow the maintenance of metabolic activity. When these

Table 16-13. Conditions associated with alterations of O_2-Hb affinity (O_2-Hb dissociation curve)

Shift to left (increased affinity)	Shift to right (decreased affinity)
Increased pH	Decreased pH
Decreased Pco$_2$	Increased Pco$_2$
Decreased temperature	Increased temperature
Decreased 2,3-DPG due to	Increased 2,3-DPG due to
Decreased pH	Increased pH
Stored blood	Hypoxemia
Increased ADP	Anemia
Phosphate depletion	Phosphate retention
Red cell pyruvate kinase activity	Red cell pyruvate kinase deficiency
Red cell hexokinase deficiency	
Chemical inhibition of glycolysis (e.g., monoiodoacetate)	
Decreased 2,3-DPG binding to Hb due to	
Fetal hemoglobin	
Diabetes mellitus	

Abnormal hereditary hemoglobins

Hb Ranier	Hb Kansas
Hb Barts	Hb Seattle
Hb H	Hb S
Hb Yakima	
Hb J Capetown	
Hb Chesapeake	
Hb Kempsey	
Hb Hiroshima	
Hb Little Rock	

Abnormal acquired hemoglobins

Carboxyhemoglobin
Methemoglobin

Adapted from Frohlich ED: Pathophysiology: altered regulatory mechanisms in disease, ed 2, Philadelphia, 1972, JB Lippincott Co.

conditions are the result of pathology, however, the effect may not be beneficial.

Other conditions besides increased pH (decreased hydrogen ion concentration or alkalosis) that cause a shift to the left of the oxyhemoglobin dissociation curve or increased affinity between hemoglobin and oxygen include decreased Pco$_2$, decreased temperature, and decreased 2,3-DPG. Oxygen unloading in the tissues is inhibited, and the patient is at risk for tissue hypoxia. An example is the surgical patient whose body temperature may be decreased and whose blood losses may have been replaced with a large quantity of stored blood, in which the amount of 2,3-DPG is reduced.

RESPIRATORY FAILURE

Respiratory failure is the clinical state in which gas exchange becomes so impaired as to result in death. The respiratory system is often the first system to be identified as failing in the multiple organ failure syndrome (Hyers and Ohar, 1988). Although definitions vary, respiratory failure is said to occur when the lungs are not adequately oxygenating the blood or preventing the retention of carbon dioxide. Acute respiratory failure is characterized by extreme dyspnea, a low arterial Po$_2$ (50 to 60 mm Hg or less), a high arterial Pco$_2$ (50 mm Hg or more), and a low arterial pH (acidemia). All four of these criteria do not have to be met, but most patients in respiratory failure exhibit at least two of these criteria (Balk and Bone, 1983a). The manifestations of respiratory failure depend on the underlying cause.

Like heart failure, respiratory failure is not a disease in itself but rather a sequel to disease in which the processes of ventilation and/or exchange are disrupted. Accepting the notion of a two-part respiratory system with the lungs as gas exchanging organs and a pump that ventilates the lungs, failure can occur in either part and affect one or the other of these processes (Fig. 16-29) (Roussos and Macklem, 1982). The characteristics of two types of acute respiratory failure that can occur are listed in the box on p. 647. Type

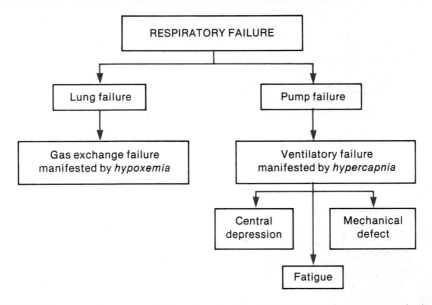

Fig. 16-29. Diagrammatic representation of respiratory failure. The respiratory system is depicted as consisting of two parts: (1) the lung, the gas-exchanging organ, the failure of which is manifested by hypoxemia; and (2) the pump that ventilates the lung, consisting of the chest wall, the respiratory centers that control them, and the nerves. Failure of the pump due to central depression, mechanical defect, or fatigue is manifested mainly by hypercapnia.
(From Roussos C and Macklem PT: The respiratory muscles, N Eng J Med, 307(13), 786-797, 1982.)

I is failure of exchange and can occur with any of the disorders characterized by alteration of the exchange process as the primary pathophysiologic mechanism of disease. Type II is ventilatory failure and can occur with any of the disorders in which alteration of the ventilatory process is the primary pathophysiologic mechanism of disease. While either ventilation or exchange can be the first process to fail, the type of failure can change as the ventilation-perfusion relationships change over the course of the underlying disease, and eventually both processes are affected if the underlying condition worsens or is not corrected (Bone et al., 1987b).

Respiratory failure may also be classified according to its duration (Kirby and Taylor, 1986). Acute respiratory failure has developed rapidly and recently. Chronic

CLASSIFICATION OF RESPIRATORY FAILURE ACCORDING TO PATHOPHYSIOLOGY

Hypoxemic respiratory failure

$PaO_2 < 55\text{-}60$ mm Hg
$PaCO_2 \leq 40$ mm Hg
Synonyms
    Type I respiratory failure
    Nonventilatory respiratory failure

Hypoxemic-hypercapnic respiratory failure

$PaO_2 < 55\text{-}60$ mm Hg
$PaCO_2 > 50$ mm Hg
Synonyms
    Type II respiratory failure
    Ventilatory failure

From Bryan CL: Classification of respiratory failure. In Kirby RR and Taylor RW: Respiratory failure, Chicago, 1986, Year Book Medical Publishers, Inc.

respiratory failure develops slowly, allowing compensatory changes to develop. This often occurs in the patient in whom the primary abnormality is an alteration of ventilation. Ventilatory failure is considered chronic when metabolic compensation for the acidemia has occurred. Chronic ventilatory failure is characterized by a high arterial Pco_2, a near normal pH, and a low arterial Po_2. These patients are usually capable of limited physical activity and must avoid exposure to infection, air pollution, or any other potential respiratory insult. If a patient with chronic ventilatory failure develops an exacerbation of the underlying condition or a respiratory infection or insult of some sort, his or her condition will rapidly worsen because pulmonary reserves are minimal. When this occurs, acute respiratory failure is said to be superimposed upon chronic failure.

Mechanical ventilation and intensive oxygen therapy are usually necessary to restore normal or, in the case of acute failure superimposed on chronic, compensated arterial blood gas levels. Assisted ventilation and intensive oxygen therapy are adjuncts to whatever therapy the underlying condition requires.

PSYCHOPHYSIOLOGIC EFFECTS OF CHRONIC RESPIRATORY DISEASE

Chronic respiratory disease often has an insidious onset and is progressively debilitating. The disease process may be quite advanced before a diagnosis is made. Treatment can help slow the course of the disease but, for the most part, will not reverse the pathophysiologic changes that occur over time. The manifestations of the disease as well as different aspects of treatment can be frightening and overwhelming to the patient and family. Successful rehabilitation of the patient with chronic lung disease depends as much on

improving the individual's ability to cope with the disorder as on treatment of the physical aspects of the disease. Helping the patient and family learn to cope with the effects of chronic respiratory disease, therefore, should be a major goal of treatment and is exemplified in the case study that follows this section. This goal will apply no matter what setting a respiratory patient might be in—hospital, home, or clinic.

As the processes of ventilation and oxygenation are disrupted and tissue hypoxia develops, certain pathophysiologic responses to the disease they are experiencing will become apparent. These are discussed in earlier sections of this chapter and may include fatigue, weakness, activity intolerance, dyspnea or shortness of breath, coughing, and possibly, changes in appearance, such as clubbing of the extremities or development of a barrel-shaped chest. Children may experience stunted growth and development. Normal sleep patterns can be disrupted as a result of dyspnea and coughing spells or the inability to maintain a comfortable supine position. Hypoxia, hypercapnia, and the use of medications may cause temporary states of confusion or delusion or occasional memory dysfunction.

As the disease progressively worsens, these signs and symptoms become more pronounced and the patient's ability to perform the usual activities of daily living is affected. The patient can become increasingly dependent on others to perform activities in which independence was once the norm. The patient may stop participating in some activities altogether. The time span between acute exacerbations of the disease may decrease, and these exacerbations may become more difficult to reverse. Acute respiratory disorders superimposed on the chronic problems are life threatening and can cause further pathologic changes in the respiratory system.

The psychologic and psychosocial effects of this progression of events include many possibilities. The prognosis associated with most chronic respiratory conditions can create feelings of hopelessness and powerlessness within the patient and family. The ever-increasing dependence on others can cause a loss of self-esteem. The patient and family can be expected to grieve over both real and anticipated losses. The increasing dependence on others and feelings of hopelessness, powerlessness, and grief can lead to anxiety and depression. Anxiety and depression can cause changes in behavior that become a source of concern for the family. The patient may be reluctant to express anger with both family members and care providers for fear of alienating the people on whom continued dependence is essential. This can lead to more anger and, subsequently, frustration and despair. Additionally, strong emotional states can cause an increase in respiratory symptoms, so patients will learn to avoid getting angry or upset so as not to precipitate an acute episode. For these reasons, patients with COPD are said to live in an "emotional straitjacket." Because of their inability to express emotion these patients are often thought to be apathetic and withdrawn.

Social isolation can develop as the demands of work or social interaction become too strenuous to be continued. One of the first social roles to change in response to decreasing energy levels is that of the working person. The patient can become homebound as it becomes apparent that extremes of temperature or humidity and exposure to environmental pollutants can cause exacerbations of the more acute manifestations of the disease. Changes in physical appearance and symptoms such as coughing and expectoration of sputum may cause feelings of embarrassment and lead to further social isolation if the patient becomes reluctant to even be seen by others.

Children with chronic respiratory conditions can experience difficulty in achieving independence from their parents as they mature. The completion of developmental tasks may be delayed. These children may be less able to withstand the competitive pressures of school and, as they approach adulthood, the pressures of finding and maintaining employment. Because of an altered self-concept or distorted body image, they can have difficulty forming social relationships and making sexual adjustments.

The coping patterns exhibited by patients with different respiratory conditions have been characterized through descriptive research and are reviewed by Shekleton (1987). A general conclusion based on this review is that the pathologic process of chronic respiratory disease interacts with psychologic and psychosocial factors to determine the respiratory patient's quality of life. Psychosocial adaptation to illness and coping ability are important factors, which are distinct from the severity of disease, in determining the degree of disability and functional impairment seen in patients with chronic respiratory disease. One point for the reader to remember is that coping behaviors are not inherently adaptive or maladaptive but become maladaptive when used in a way that does not facilitate the patient's adaptation to the difficulties imposed by the underlying chronic disease.

Another conclusion that can be drawn, based on reports in the literature, is that psychosocial assets and coping ability can be assessed and strengthened through structured clinical interventions. Many investigators have reported that, as a result of pulmonary rehabilitation programs, indices of functional ability and psychosocial status show improvement while physiologic parameters such as spirometric measures remain unchanged. This demonstrates a strong mind-body interaction that supports the importance of assessing, supporting, and reinforcing the patient's psychosocial assets and coping abilities in the treatment of chronic respiratory disease.

Intervention strategies

The goal of psychosocial care of the patient with chronic respiratory difficulty is to promote effective coping with the disease in order to optimize the patient's quality of life. Effective coping behavior can be maximized through three intervention strategies (Shekleton, 1987). The first strategy is to minimize, to the greatest extent possible, the psychophysiologic impact of the disease on the patient's lifestyle. The second strategy involves providing whatever level of support the patient needs to be able to cope adequately with the disease and its effects. The third strategy involves promoting a sense of hope and optimism in the patient.

The psychophysiologic impact of the disease can be minimized through breathing retraining and the appropriate use of stress management techniques and self-management skills by the patient. The goals of breathing retraining are (1) to slow the frequency of respirations, (2) to enhance a sense of control over breathing, and (3) to promote a feeling of calmness. One exercise involves having the patient count during inhalation and exhalation. This is especially helpful for patients whose dyspnea is related to anxiety.

Stress management techniques that can be taught to the patient and used in unsupervised settings include meditation, guided imagery, relaxation exercises, and biofeedback. Both breathing retraining and stress management techniques may be useful in helping break the panic-dyspnea cycle that many patients with respiratory disease experience. Frownfelter (1987) provides a detailed review of breathing exercises, breathing retraining, and stress management techniques.

Self-management skill depends on the patient becoming aware of which activities and treatments seem to alleviate symptoms and which seem to make the symptoms worse. The patient can be asked to keep a log or diary of daily routines in which feeling states and associated symptoms of the disease are noted during the performance of usual routines or participation in certain activities. The clinician and patient can review the log and determine what activities the patient should avoid to prevent an acute exacerbation of symptoms and what can be done to alleviate an acute episode should it occur. Essential self-management behaviors include work simplification and energy conservation measures that can be taught to the patient and family.

Providing support to the patient involves determining, first, the adequacy and appropriateness of the coping mechanisms already being employed by and, second, the adequacy of the social support system available to the patient and family. If deficiencies in either area exist, recommendations can be made about the need for counseling, therapy, or additional assistance in the home. Support groups have been used to help patients cope with other types of chronic diseases and can be helpful for patients with respiratory disorders. Local lung associations and some hospitals do conduct "Better Breathers Clubs" in which methods to cope with the disease are stressed.

Communicating to the patient a sense of optimism about the disease and its potential impact on life can help to increase the patient's sense of hope. Without minimizing the seriousness of the disease, the clinician should convey a tone of optimism and confidence about the patient's ability to function at an optimal level and respond to treatment. Experts believe that as long as a patient feels that there can be some control over the condition and remains action oriented, the ability to cope will remain intact. If the patient loses confidence in these abilities, a feeling of helplessness ensues.

The patient's sense of optimism and hope will be further enhanced through promoting a sense of self-esteem. Self-esteem can be heightened by the clinician's acknowledging the degree of self-management skill demonstrated by the patient and allowing the patient more control of the treatment process through goal setting. Goals that are mutually agreed on between patient and clinician and represent realistically attainable achievements can provide benchmarks by which progress can be measured.

The following case study highlights the importance of a holistic approach to the care of a patient with COPD. There is no cure for this devastating illness, which is commonly seen among patients being treated in both hospitals and the community. Assisting the patient in dealing with the psychophysiologic aspects of the disease can be the most important part of the total treatment plan, since this can have the greatest impact on enhancing the COPD patient's quality of life.

CASE STUDY: PSYCHOPHYSIOLOGIC EFFECTS OF CHRONIC OBSTRUCTIVE PULMONARY DISEASE

Objective and Subjective Data History

RA is a 55-year-old male who was diagnosed with emphysema 9 years ago. RA has a 30-year history of smoking two

Contributed by Candice Vitalo.

packs of cigarettes per day. He quit smoking completely 8 years ago. Eight months after his initial diagnosis he suffered a respiratory arrest at home, etiology unknown. He was intubated and placed in the ICU, where his condition was stabilized, and he was treated and sent home after a 10-day period. At that time he was placed on a regimen of medications and was able to return to work as an industrial engineer in a print company. He worked up until 2 years ago, when he noticed a progressive worsening of his breathing and exercise tolerance, (i.e., able to walk one block before shortness of breath, climb one flight of stairs before shortness of breath, weakness, fatigue, and insomnia). He was eventually readmitted to the hospital for oxygen evaluation, which was justified based on the results of arterial blood gas analysis, pulmonary function tests, and a low level treadmill test using pulse oximetry. RA was discharged and told to use 1 L of oxygen via nasal cannula for 12 to 18 hours a day. Approximately 1 year ago he was treated for a mild episode of congestive heart failure after having complaints of ankle swelling. Digoxin and Lasix were added to his medications at that time.

Present illness: RA has not been readmitted to the hospital in the past 2 years. He is being followed in the pulmonary outpatient clinic, which he visits every 3 to 4 months. In recent months he began to show signs of worsening COPD (i.e., more shortness of breath and fatigue). After questioning, it was discovered he was only using the oxygen system an average of 10 hours a day because the tank was bulky and too hard to physically manage on his own. He suffers two to three bad colds a year on the average and takes ampicillin as needed, as prescribed per impending cold symptoms. He has been on and off a 10-day course of antibiotics four times within the past 3 months and has not seemed to recover from a lingering respiratory tract infection. Chronic fatigue, shortness of breath, and weakness persist, and he continues to lose weight. RA also expresses much frustration over his inability to perform minimal tasks around the house lately. RA is knowledgeable about his disease and is compliant with his medications and follow-up doctor appointments, which makes him responsible for self-management of his disease.

General appearance: Thin and somewhat fragile, walks very slowly and steadily, and stops for rest periods as needed. Stands erect with rolled shoulder posturing while leaning on desk. Develops mild respiratory distress after walking 100 feet without oxygen use. Height 5'8", weight 129 pounds.

Vital signs
  Temperature: 99.6° F
  Apical pulse: 100 and regular
  Respirations: 24
  Blood pressure: 120/70 sitting, 140/90 lying flat

Allergies
  None

PERRLA, wears corrective eyeglasses for reading only

Skin: Cool and dry to touch, buccal cyanosis noted, as well as purplish cast to nail beds when hands hung dependently without oxygen use, positive capillary refill

Neck: Normal range of motion, throat clear, no lymphadenopathy, no carotid bruits, no jugular vein distention

CV: ECG shows NSR without ectopy, normal heart sounds, no gallop or murmur auscultated

Lungs: Barrel chest, no musculoskeletal deficits, no egophony, vesicular hyperresonant breathing sounds slightly decreased to both bases, occ. sputum production: white, small amounts, no wheezing. Chest x-ray film—emphysematous changes, bullae at both bases, depressed diaphragm, slightly enlarged right side of heart

Abdomen: Soft, bowel sounds positive in all four quadrants, no bruits, masses, or tenderness

Neurological: Alert and oriented, appropriately verbally responsive to questions, cranial nerves II to XII intact, deep tendon reflexes equal, sensation intact, normal gait

Extremities: 3 + all pulses, positive capillary refill, no pedal edema

Laboratory data: Complete blood count slightly elevated WBCs, electrolytes, PT/PTT all within normal limits

Arterial blood gases	On room air	On 1 L O_2 per nasal cannula
Oxygen saturation	88%	91%
pH or pH	7.42	7.44
Pco_2	44.3	46
Po_2	61.2	71
HCO_3	29.3	29
BE	4.7	5.5

Spirometry

8 years ago		10 months ago	
Actual	(% Predicted)	Actual	(% Predicted)
FVC	2.23 (53%)	FVC	2.13 (48%)
FEV$_1$	1.05 (32%)	FEV$_1$	0.77 (24%)
FEV$_1$/ FVC	43	FEV$_1$/ FVC	36
		VC	2.90
		TLC	8.24 (131%)
(no lung volumes done)		RV	5.33 (250%)

12-minute distance walk: Attempted without oxygen using pulse oximetry and percentage oxygen saturation (SaO_2%) dropped from baseline 89% to 77% within 3 minutes. Patient expressed slight to moderate breathlessness. After a 20-minute rest 1 L of oxygen was added and patient was able to complete self-paced test with Sao$_2$% not dropping below 84%, and a pulse rate ranging between 81 and 110 beats/min during walk.

Nutrition: Height 5'8", weight 129 lb. Appetite fair to poor depending on weather and shortness of breath. Ten-pound weight loss over past 3 months noted.

Social history: Korean war veteran (1951-1955) stationed in Germany. Since discharged, returned to night school and obtained industrial engineer degree. Alcohol—occasional social drink, denies regular use. Income—Social Security and disability benefits and wife works part-time.

Family history: Married, owns home in suburbs, has 24-year-old adopted daughter who has a 4-month-old baby. Both daughter and son-in-law live with them for financial reasons at present.

Siblings: Two healthy sisters

Mother: Died at age 70, cervical cancer

Father: Died at age 87, atherosclerotic heart disease

Medications: Ventolin inhaler two puffs every 4 hours, Atrovent inhaler two puffs every 4 hours, digoxin 0.125 mg every morning, Lasix 20 mg every morning, theophylline 300 mg three times a day, Terbutaline 2.5 mg three times a day, KCL 20 mEq every morning.

The medical treatment plan includes the following:

Problem #1: Deterioration of respiratory status
> —Unable to manage current oxygen system
> —Chronic shortness of breath, fatigue, progressive weakness

Problem #2: Chronic respiratory tract infection
> —Unsuccessful trials of ampicillin
> —Lingering cold symptoms, that is, chest congestion, persistent increased sputum production

Problem #3: Activity intolerance
> —Reduced ability to perform household chores

Problem #4: Malnutrition secondary to loss of appetite
> —10-pound weight loss past 3 to 4 months
> —Anthropometric measurements below normal standards

Problem #5: Increased anxiety
> —Loss of control over breathing condition
> —Probable worsening COPD
> —No present treatment

Discussion

RA was brought into the pulmonary clinic by his wife after phoning his physician. Based on his symptoms and test results it was concluded that patient had a respiratory tract infection that was not responding to ampicillin. He was switched to tetracycline and encouraged to rest and drink 2 quarts of fluids a day. After 2 weeks he began to feel stronger and his congestion disappeared. His oxygen system was switched over to liquid oxygen to increase his compliance by easing oxygen transport and allowing greater mobility overall. RA, like many other frail emphysema patients, finds it physically difficult to maneuver the bulky oxygen tank system in and out of his home, car, and clinic setting. The light-weight liquid oxygen system allows the patient more mobility, more freedom of movement, and reduced strain upon his upper arm and chest muscles. This system has also increased client's compliance from 10 to 20 hours of use per day. Commonly this problem is encountered, and patients discover that by using trapezius, intercostal, and pectoral muscle groups less, their ability to breathe is improved and they do not fatigue as quickly.

After 1 month pulmonary function tests

were repeated and RA showed a significant reduction from those tests done 10 months previously.

	Actual	% Predicted	Arterial blood gases (on room air)	
FVC	2.22	(52)	Oxygen saturation	90.9%
FEV$_1$	0.63	(19)		
FEV$_1$/ FVC	28		pH	7.44
VC	2.51	(59)		
TLC	7.02	(112)	Pco$_2$	46.3
RV	4.50	(209)	Po$_2$	64
			Hco$_3$	31.9
			BE	7.3

Blood gases showed (compensated) respiratory alkalosis as well as mild hypoxemia without oxygen use. TLC and RV are increased due to air trapping.

Client was encouraged to perform household chores in moderation with frequent rest periods. It was suggested the family discuss delegating tasks client has difficulty with, for example, lawn care and taking out trash. Information describing life-style changes COPD patients often undergo was provided to the wife to share with other family members. The option of attending some pulmonary rehabilitation sessions that would possibly help patient strengthen daily activity performance was also suggested.

Based on client's current height and weight, it was found he was below normal standards. This is not unusual because so many people with lung disease tend to use up many calories to breathe and store very little in muscle and fat. Dyspnea sometimes makes eating difficult also. RA was told to eat smaller, more frequent meals and make a real attempt not to skip meals. A nutritional supplement was also prescribed for the client, and a dietary consult was set up as well in order to improve nutritional status. Finally, patient's frustration over finances and living arrangement as well as the progressive loss of independence was discussed. To help the patient deal with living and breathing problems better, client was enrolled in a mental hygiene clinic and the phone number for the Better Breathers Club nearest to his home was provided to him.

His wife expressed feelings of social isolation and a desire to go out more, so she decided to work part-time in order to get out of the house regularly as well as help out with limited income. She seemed very supportive and provided a great deal of praise and encouragement to spouse. She said that she does not mind helping him and feels he still does well on his own and is not afraid to ask her for assistance.

COPD is a chronic disabling condition that becomes frustrating and burdensome over time. It places a strain on all family members involved and becomes difficult to cope with when independence is lost. This complex case presents a challenge to all those involved and requires a multidisciplinary approach with constant reevaluation and follow-up care.

Nursing Diagnoses

1. Impaired gas exchange related to COPD
2. Altered tissue perfusion: cardiopulmonary
3. Alteration in comfort related to chronic shortness of breath
4. Alteration in nutritional status: less than body requirements related to loss of appetite
5. Activity intolerance related to chronic shortness of breath
6. Body image disturbance
7. Anxiety related to oxygen dependence
8. Impaired social interaction related to oxygen dependence and sense of social stigma
9. Situational low self-esteem related to loss of independence
10. Sleep pattern disturbance
11. Potential ineffective family coping related to current living arrangement

Summary

An overview of the process of ventilation and exchange and the normal dynamics and compensatory mechanisms that are evoked in response to disruptions is presented in this chapter. The terms *hyperventilation* and *hypoventilation* are used in reference to the adequacy of alveolar ventilation as measured by the removal or retention of carbon dioxide in the arterial blood. The relatively equal distribution of ventilation in relation to perfusion of the alveoli is essential for the exchange of gases to occur normally. Disorders of ventilation will subsequently disrupt exchange, since normal ventilation is a prerequisite for exchange.

The responses to respiratory disease that nurses diagnose and treat include ineffective airway clearance, ineffective breathing pattern, and impaired gas exchange. These diagnostic categories have been approved for clinical use and testing through the NANDA process. Other responses to respiratory disease such as dyspnea await development as diagnostic categories but are treated nonetheless.

BIBLIOGRAPHY

Albert KA: Pulmonary edema: In Simmons DH (Ed), Current pulmonology, Vol 8 (pp. 1-16), Chicago, 1987, Year Book Medical Publishers, Inc.

American Lung Association: Chronic obstructive pulmonary disease ed 5, New York, 1977, The Association.

Anderson FD: Issues in the postresuscitation period, Crit Care Nurs Q 10(4):51-61, 1988.

Avery GB, editor: Neonatology: pathophysiology and management of the newborn, ed 3, Philadelphia, 1987, JB Lippincott Co.

Ayres SM: Mechanisms and consequences of pulmonary edema: cardiac lung, shock lung, and principles of ventilatory therapy in adult respiratory distress syndrome, Am Heart J 103:97, 1982.

Balk R and Bone RC: Classification of acute respiratory failure, Med Clin North Am 67:551, 1983a.

Balk R and Bone RC: The adult respiratory distress syndrome, Med Clin North Am 67:685, 1983b.

Bartlett JG and Gorbach SL: The triple threat of aspiration pneumonia, Chest, 68:560, 1975.

Bone RC: Treatment of severe hypoxemia due to the adult respiratory distress syndrome, Arch Int Med, 140:85, 1980.

Bone RC, Fisher CJ, Clemmer TP, Slotman GJ, Metz CA, and Balk RA: A controlled clinical trial of high dose methylprednisolone in treatment of severe sepsis and septic shock, N Engl J Med 317:653, 1987.

Bone RC, George RB, and Hudson LD, editors: Acute respiratory failure, New York, 1987, Churchill Livingstone, Inc.

Brantly ML, Paul LD, Miller BH, Falk T, Wu M, and Crystal RG: Clinical features and history of the destructive lung disease associated with alpha-1-antitrypsin deficiency of adults with pulmonary symptoms, Am Rev Respir Dis 138:327-336, 1988.

Burki NK: Dyspnea. In Wiliams MH, editor: Disturbances of respiratory control, Clin Chest Med 1(1):47-55, 1980.

Campbell JC and O'Donohue J Jr: Aspiration of gastric contents. In Simmons DH, editor: Current pulmonology, 8:163-174, Chicago, 1987, Year Book Medical Publishers, Inc.

Carrieri V and Janson-Bjerklie S: Dyspnea. In Carrieri V, Lindsey A, and West C, editors: Pathophysiologic phenomena in nursing, pp. 191-218, Philadelphia, 1986, WB Saunders Co.

Carrieri VK, Janson-Bjerklie S, and Jacobs S: The sensation of dyspnea: a review, Heart Lung 13(4):436-447, 1984.

Center D and McFadden R: Pulmonary defense mechanisms. In Sodeman W and Sodeman T, editors: Sodeman's pathologic physiology: mechanisms of disease, ed 7, pp. 460-481, Philadelphia, 1985, WB Saunders Co.

Cosenza J and Norton L Celentano: Secretion clearance: state of the art from a nursing perspective, Crit Care Ns 6(4):23-39, 1986.

Dantzker D, editor: Cardiopulmonary critical care, Orlando, 1986, Grune & Stratton, Inc.

Farrel P and Palta M: Bronchopulmonary dysplasia. In Farrell PM and Taussig LM, editors: Bronchopulmonary dysplasia and related chronic respiratory disorders, Columbus, Ohio, 1986, Ross Laboratories.

Fisher AB: Oxygen therapy: side effects and toxicity, Am Rev Respir Dis 122(5) part 2 of 2:61-69, 1979.

Francis PB: Acute respiratory failure in obstructive lung disease, Med Clin North Am, 67:657, 1983.

Frank L and Sosenko I: Undernutrition as a major contributing factor in the pathogenesis of bronchopulmonary dysplasia, ARRB 138:725-729, 1988.

Frizzell RA, Rechkemmer G, and Shoemaker RL: Altered regulation of airway epithelial cell chloride channels in cystic fibrosis, Science 233:558-560, 1986.

Frownfelter D, editor: Chest physical therapy and pulmonary rehabilitation: an interdisciplinary approach ed 2, Chicago, 1987, Year Book Medical Publishers, Inc.

Gift AG: Dyspnea: a clinical perspective, Scholarly Inquiry Nurs Pract 1(1):73-85, 1987.

Hanley MV, and Tyler ML: Ineffective airway clearance related to airway infection, Nurs Clin North Am 22(1):135-150, 1987.

Higgins M and Thom T: Epidemiology and natural history of COPD. In Simmons DH, editor: Current pulmonology, Vol 9, Chicago, 1988, Year Book Medical Publishers, Inc.

Hodgkin JE and Petty T: Chronic obstructive pulmonary disease: current concepts, Philadelphia, 1987, WB Saunders Co.

Hoffman LA: Ineffective airway clearance related to neuromuscular dysfunction, Nurs Clin North Am 22(1):151-166, 1987.

Hopp LJ and Williams M: Ineffective breathing pattern related to decreased lung expansion, Nurs Clin North Am 22(1):193-206, 1987.

Hubbard R and Crystal R: Alpha-1-antitrypsin augmentation therapy for alpha-1-antitrypsin deficiency, Am J Med 84(6A):52-62, 1988.

Hyers TM and Ohar JM: Inflammation and coagulation in the adult respiratory distress syndrome. In Simmons DH, editor: Current pulmonology, Vol 9, Chicago, 1988, Year Book Medical Publishers, Inc.

Jacobs E and Bone R: Clinical indicators in sepsis and septic adult respiratory distress syndrome, Med Clin North Am 70(4):921-933, 1986.

Janson-Bjerklie SJ and Schnell S: Effect of peak flow information on patterns of self-care in adult asthma, Heart Lung 17(5):543-549, 1988.

Kaplan RL, Sahn IA, and Petty TL: Incidence and outcome of respiratory distress syndrome in gram negative sepsis, Arch Intern Med 139:867, 1979.

Kim MJ and Larson JL: Ineffective airway clearance and ineffective breathing patterns: theoretical and research base for nursing diagnosis, Nurs Clin North Am 22(1):125-134, 1987.

King TKC: Pulmonary gas exchange. In Baum GL and Wolinsky E, editors: Textbook of pulmonary disease, pp. 99-116, Boston, 1983, Little Brown and Co, Inc.

Kirby RR and Taylor RW: Respiratory failure, Chicago, 1986, Year Book Medical Publishers, Inc.

Kueppers F: Genetics and the lung. In Simmons DH, editor: Current pulmonology, Vol. 8 Chicago, 1987, Year Book Medical Publishers, Inc.

Lakshminarayan S and Hudson L: Pulmonary function following adult respiratory distress syndrome, Semin Respir Med 11(3):160-164, 1981.

Lareau S and Larson JL: Ineffective breathing pattern related to airflow limitation, Nurs Clin North Am 22(1):179-191, 1987.

Larson JL and Kim MJ: Ineffective breathing pattern related to respiratory muscle fatigue, Nurs Clin North Am 22(1):207-223, 1987.

Lebovitz AH: Industrially acquired pulmonary disease, Adv Psychosom Med 14:78-92, 1985.

Macklem P and Roussos CS: Respiratory muscle fatigue: a case of respiratory failure? Clin Sci Mol Med 53:419-422, 1977.

Martin L: Pulmonary physiology in clinical practice, St. Louis, 1987, The CV Mosby Co.

Martinez FD, Antognoni G, Macri F, Bonci E, Midulla F, DeCastro G, and Ronchetti R: Parental smoking enhances bronchial responsiveness in nine year old children, Am Rev Respir Dis, 138:518-523, 1988.

Massaro D: Tolerance to hyperoxia. In Simmons DH, editor: Current pulmonology, Vol 8, Chicago, 1987, Year Book Medical Publishers, Inc.

Medoff-Cooper B: The effects of handling on preterm infants with bronchopulmonary dysplasia, Image 20(3):132-134, 1988.

Montgomery R, Dryer RI, Conway TW, and Spector AA: Biochemistry: a case-oriented approach ed. 4, St. Louis, 1983, The CV Mosby Co.

Murray JF, Matthay M, Luce J, and Flick M: An expanded definition of the adult respiratory distress syndrome, Am Rev Respir Dis, 138:720-723, 1988.

National Research Council: Environmental tobacco smoke, Washington, DC, 1986, National Academy Press.

Neilsen L: Assessing patients' respiratory problems, Am J Nurs 80(12):2192-2196, 1980.

Neilsen L: Interpreting arterial blood gases, Am J Nurs 80(12):2197-2201, 1980.

Openbrier DR, and Covey, M: Ineffective breathing pattern related to malnutrition, Nurs Clin North Am 22(1):225-247, 1987.

Pepe PE, Potkin RT, Reus DH: Clinical predictors of acute respiratory distress syndrome, Am J Surg 144:120, 1982.

Petty T: Adult respiratory distress syndrome: definition and historical perspective, Clin Chest Med 3(3):3-7, 1982.

Petty T: ARDS: refinement of concept and redefinition, Am Rev Respir Dis, 138:724, 1988.

Petty T, editor: Chronic obstructive pulmonary disease, ed 2, New York, 1985, Marcel Dekker, Inc.

Proteases, antiproteases, and emphysema, Lancet 2(8563):832-833, 1987.

Pulmonary problems in infants and children, Am J Nurs 81(3):509-531, 1981.

Risser N: Preoperative and postoperative care to prevent pulmonary complications, Heart Lung 9(1):57-67, 1980.

Rothstein R, editor: Respiratory emergencies, Part I, Topics Emerg Med 2(1); 1980.

Rothstein R, editor: Respiratory emergencies, Part II, Topics Emerg Med 2(2), 1980.

Roussos C, and Macklem PT: The respiratory muscles, N Engl J Med 307(13):786-797, 1982.

Sasahara AA, McIntyre KM, Cella G, Palla A, and Sharma GVRK: The clinical and hemodynamic features of acute pulmonary embolism. In Simmons DH, editor: Current pulmonology, Vol. 9, Chicago, 1988, Year Book Medical Publishers, Inc.

Sewell E, editor: Directions in pediatric respiratory disease, Clin Chest Med 1(3), 1980.

Shapiro B, Harrison RA, and Walton JR: Clinical application of blood gases, ed. 3, Chicago, 1982, Year Book Medical Publishers, Inc.

Shekleton ME: Coping with chronic respiratory difficulty, Nurs Clin North Am 22(33):569-581, 1987.

Shekleton ME, and Nield M: Ineffective airway clearance related to artificial airway, Nurs Clin North Am 22(1):167-178, 1987.

Stankus RP, Sastre J, and Salvaggio JE: Asthma induced by exposure to low molecular weight compounds and cigarette smoke. In Simmons DH, editor: Current pulmonology, Vol. 9, Chicago, 1988, Year Book Medical Publishers, Inc.

Stoop A, deBoo T, Lemmens W, and Folgering H: Hyperventilation syndrome: measurement of objective symptoms and subjective complaints, Respiration 49:37-44, 1986.

Tager IB: Passive smoking—bronchial responsiveness and atopy, Am Rev Respir Dis, 138:507-509, 1988.

Talamo RC: Alpha-1 antitrypsin deficiency and emphysema, Chest, 2(4):421, 1977.

Taussig LM: Long term management and pulmonary progress in bronchopulmonary dysplasia in bronchopulmonary dysplasia and related chronic respiratory disorders. Ross Conferences on Pediatric Research, Ross Laboratories, 1986.

US Surgeon General: The health consequences of involuntary smoking, Rockville, Md., 1987. US Department of Health and Human Services (CDC), Publication No. 87-8398.

Vander AJ, Sherman JH, and Luciano DS: Human physiology: the mechanisms of body function, New York, 1985, McGraw-Hill Book Co.

Van Lunteren E, and Cherniack NS: Disorders of the regulation of ventilation in patients with non-respiratory diseases. In Simmons DH, editor: Current pulmonology, Vol. 8, Chicago, 1987, Year Book Medical Publishers, Inc.

Wanner A: Mucociliary clearance in the trachea, Clin Chest Med 7:247-258, 1986.

Weinstein L, and Michel JL: Pulmonary infections from extrapulmonary sources. In Simmons DH, editor: Current pulmonology, Vol. 8, Chicago, 1987, Year Book Medical Publishers, Inc.

West, JB: Pulmonary pathophysiology, ed 3, Baltimore MD, 1987, Williams & Wilkins.

Wewers M, Casolaro M, Sellers S, McPaul K, Wittes J, and Crystal R: Replacement therapy for alpha-1 antitrypsin deficiency associated with emphysema, N Engl J Med 316:1055-1062, 1987.

Wiedemann HP and Matthay: Cor pulmonale in chronic obstructive pulmonary disease: circulatory pathophysiology and new concepts of therapy. In Simmons DH, editor: Current pulmonology, Vol. 8, Chicago, 1987, Year Book Medical Publishers, Inc.

17

Cardiovascular pathophysiology

Adequate tissue perfusion depends on both an intact transport system and an intact transport medium. The transport system is the body's cardiovascular system—the heart and blood vessels. The transport medium is the blood. The steady state of the organism depends on the adequate delivery of oxygen and nutrients to and the removal of the products of metabolism from the tissues. Alterations in the function of the heart or blood vessels and in the volume or composition of the blood affect the oxygenation status of the cells. Delivery of nutrients and other substances to the cells or various parts of the body is also impaired.

Responses to cardiovascular dysfunction that nurses diagnose and treat include decreased cardiac output and altered tissue perfusion. Decreased cardiac output is the result of failure of the pump (heart). Altered tissue perfusion can be the result of altered pressure or flow within the vessels, disrupted vessel patency or integrity, or decreased oxygen-carrying capacity of the blood, as well as decreased cardiac output. The pathophysiologic mechanisms that come into play, the precipitating disease states, and the treatment rationale for each type of disruption will be discussed in this chapter.

REVIEW OF CARDIAC FUNCTION, DYNAMICS, AND REGULATION

Under normal conditions in a healthy adult the heart functions as a pump. With each contraction, blood is ejected into the pulmonary and general circulations with a regular rate, rhythm, force, and volume. The normal rate, force, and volume of blood pumped into the circulation are maintained in a resting state and increased when metabolic demands increase. The cardiac muscle, valves, conduction system, blood supply, and regulatory (neural) mechanisms must be intact and operating for the heart to perform its pumping function efficiently.

The cardiac cycle is divided into two stages: a period of relaxation, diastole, and a period of contraction, systole. During the cardiac cycle, blood continually enters the atria of the heart. The right atrium receives the blood returning from the general circulation via the great veins. The left atrium receives the blood returning from the lungs via the pulmonary veins. During the first part of diastole, approximately 70% of the blood entering the atria flows directly into the ventricles. In the latter part of diastole, atrial contraction forces more blood to flow into the ventricles. As ventricular contraction begins, pressure rises quickly in the ventricles and causes the atrioventricular (AV) valves (mitral and tricuspid) to close and the aortic and pulmonic valves to open. Closure of the AV valves prevents a backflow of blood to the atria during systole. With the opening of the pulmonic and aortic valves, blood in the right ventricle enters the pulmonary artery and is carried to the lungs, and blood in the left ventricle enters the aorta and is carried to the organs and tissues throughout the body. At the end of systole the ventricular muscle relaxes, and intraventricular pressures decrease. During systole the AV valves remain closed, and blood is allowed to accumulate in the atria, causing increased atrial pressures. As a result of the decreased ventricular and increased atrial pressures the AV valves reopen, allowing blood to flow between the atria and ventricles (Fig. 17-1).

Blood is pumped by the right side of the heart into the pulmonary circulation, where it is oxygenated, and by the left side of the heart into the systemic circulation, where it delivers oxygen and nutrients to the tissues, removes the metabolic waste products, and carries various substances throughout the body.

The autonomic nervous system affects cardiac function by altering the strength and rate of the heart's contraction. Parasympathetic simulation slows the rate and slightly decreases the strength of cardiac contraction. Sympathetic stimulation markedly increases the rate and strength of cardiac contraction. Autonomic control is maintained through reflex action, allowing the heart to respond to constantly changing body conditions.

Cardiac function is generally assessed by how adequately the cardiac output is meeting the body's needs. Cardiac output is the product of stroke volume and heart

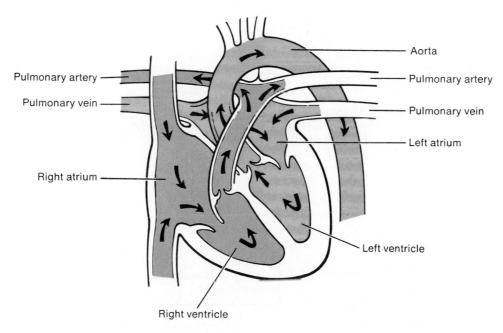

Fig. 17-1. Normal blood flow through heart.

rate (Fig. 17-2). Heart rate is regulated via both intrinsic and extrinsic mechanisms, which will be discussed later in this chapter. Stroke volume is determined by the size of the left ventricle as well as the degree of myocardial fiber shortening. The extent of myocardial fiber shortening is in turn determined by *preload*, or ventricular end diastolic volume; *contractility*, or inotropic state of cardiac tissue, which is the inherent force of ventricular contraction independent of load; and *afterload*, or the ventricular wall tension developed during ejection. The extent of shortening is of great physiologic importance, since it ultimately determines the quantity of blood ejected by the intact ventricle at any given diastolic fiber length. Increases in preload and contractility will increase myocardial fiber shortening, while increases in afterload will decrease it.

Preload, or ventricular end diastolic pressure (synonyms are ventricular end diastolic volume, filling pressure, tension, or wall stress), determines the resting length of the sarcomeres of cardiac muscle fiber. A major principle of cardiac function is that the force of the cardiac contraction will vary from beat to beat as a function of end diastolic size. This principle is also known as Starling's law of the heart or the Frank-Starling phenomenon. It is based on the length–active tension relationship curve, which means that striated muscle fiber responds to increased stretch (length) with an increase in the force of its contrac-

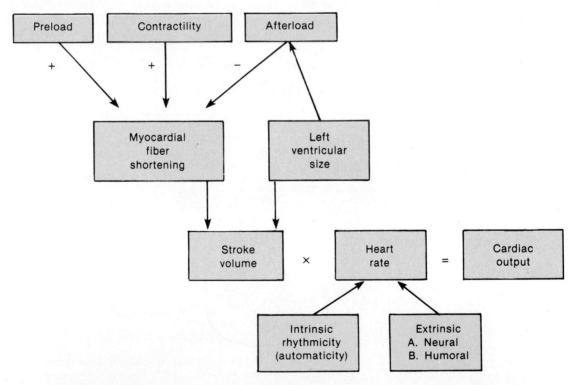

Fig. 17-2. Determinants of cardiac output. Increases in preload and contractility increase myocardial fiber shortening while increases in afterload decrease it.

tion. Stated another way, the force of contraction depends on the extent of development of active tension during isometric contraction, which can be altered by changing initial muscle length. There is a maximal length at which maximal tension occurs that represents the physiologic limit of this mechanism, and it is shown in Fig. 17-3. A muscle length above the maximum will generate less tension, and the force of contraction will be reduced. Physiologic factors determining end diastolic volume include venous return, venous tone, total blood volume and distribution, ventricular compliance, intrapericardial pressure, and atrial performance, since atrial contraction improves ventricular filling.

Contractility, or inotropic force, is affected by sympathetic nerve activity, the level of circulating catecholamines, loss of contractile mass through injury or disease, and the rate and rhythm of the cardiac contraction. A variety of exogenous pharmacologic agents and pathophysiologic conditions such as anoxia, ischemia,

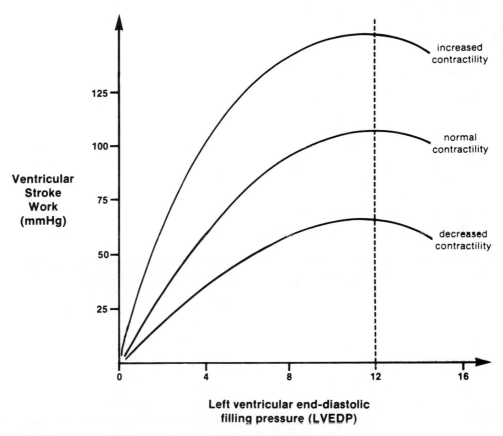

Fig. 17-3. Frank-Starling curve. As left ventricular end-diastolic volume increases, so does ventricular stroke work. When left ventricular end-diastolic filling pressure exceeds a maximal point *(dashed vertical line)*, stroke work, contractility, and cardiac output diminish.

(From Michaelson C: Congestive heart failure, St Louis, 1983, The CV Mosby Co.)

or acidemia can alter contractility. The mechanism responsible for the depression of contractility seen in congestive heart failure has not yet been identified.

Afterload, or intraventricular systolic pressure, is a function of both arterial pressure and left ventricular size. Aortic impedance is a component of afterload that reflects arterial resistance changes. Left ventricular outflow impedance is determined by the compliance or distensibility of the large arteries and total peripheral resistance. It is also related to blood viscosity and intraarterial volume. Afterload will be elevated if compliance is reduced or total peripheral resistance is elevated. Afterload functions as a negative feedback mechanism to reduce myocardial fiber shortening. For example, when increased vasoconstriction occurs, raising arterial pressure, afterload is also increased. As a result of negative feedback (see Fig. 17-2), myocardial fiber shortening is depressed and the stroke volume and consequently cardiac output are also reduced, lowering blood pressure.

The normally functioning heart will pump out all of the blood (minus the end systolic volume) returned to it without any increase in the right atrial pressure. Venous return is the primary factor determining cardiac output as the heart itself plays a permissive role in cardiac output regulation. Intrinsic autoregulation refers to the heart's ability to increase cardiac output in response to an increased amount of blood returning to it.

DECREASED CARDIAC OUTPUT

The heart's ability to perform its pumping function effectively may become impaired as a result of a variety of conditions characterized by some disruption of the physiologic determinants of cardiac output (Fig. 17-2). *Heart failure* and *pump failure* are terms used to describe the condition that exists when cardiac output becomes inadequate to meet the body's needs. Impairment of the heart's pumping function causes a decrease in cardiac output as well as an increase in systemic venous pressure, since the heart is unable to pump all of the blood being returned to it.

Pathophysiologic mechanisms

When cardiac output becomes less than normal for any reason, some acute adjustments are made by the body. Reflex stimulation of the sympathetic nervous system causes arteriolar constriction, which helps raise blood pressure as well as redistribute blood flow to those organs requiring the most oxygen (heart and brain). Sympathetic stimulation of the beta-adrenergic receptors in the heart also results in an increase in the rate and force of cardiac contraction. An increase in heart rate above normal is called *tachycardia*. Stimulation of the sympathetic nervous system is primarily through baroreceptor reflexes, although some response through chemoreceptor reflexes is also thought to occur as the decreased blood supply causes local tissue hypoxia. Baroreceptors located in the vessels respond to decreased arterial pressure (carotid sinus and aortic reflexes) and increased venous pressure (Bainbridge reflex). In response to the increased venous pressure, cardiac filling and therefore preload are increased, and the cardiac muscle fibers are stretched. This stretching of the muscle fibers causes an increase in the force of their contraction (Starling's law of the heart).

The acute responses of vasoconstriction, increased heart rate (tachycardia), and increased force of contraction are short-term adjustments that cannot totally compensate for the effects of heart failure over an extended period. In fact, the long-term effects of these adjustments are detrimental to the heart's pumping action. Vasoconstriction promotes blood return to the heart, further increasing venous pressure, and increases the resistance against which the heart must pump. Wall tension increases as cardiac muscle is stretched with increased filling. The cardiac muscle fibers can be stretched beyond their physiologic limits. An increase in the rate of contraction shortens the diastolic period of the cardiac cycle. This shortens filling time for both the ventricles and coronary arteries. As a result of the reduced ventricular filling time, cardiac output per contraction is actually decreased. As a result of reduced coronary artery filling time, the oxygen requirement of the myocardium cannot be completely met. The increased rate, wall tension, and force of contraction further increase myocardial oxygen requirements. This increased demand for oxygen in the presence of reduced ability to meet the demand further impairs cardiac function and contributes to fatigue of the myocardium. For a short period of time, however, cardiac output can be maintained through these mechanisms.

Expansion of the extracellular fluid volume is another compensatory mechanism evoked by reduced cardiac output. Expansion of extracellular fluid volume occurs as a result of depression of kidney function, the activation of the renin-angiotensin system, and the action of antidiuretic hormone (ADH).

Renal function is depressed in the presence of heart failure because of the negative effect that reduced arterial pressure and sympathetic vasoconstriction of the afferent arterioles in the kidney have on glomerular pressure. Formation of dilute urine is inhibited, since the glomerular filtration rate drops as a result of the decreased glomerular pressure.

When blood flow in the kidneys is below normal, the juxtaglomerular cells of the kidneys are stimulated to release the enzyme renin. Renin catalyzes the conversion of a plasma protein polypeptide, angiotensinogen or renin substrate, into a peptide, angiotensin I. Angiotensin I is converted into angiotensin II by a converting enzyme. Angiotensin II raises arterial pressure directly by causing vasoconstriction of arterioles and veins, which increases peripheral resistance. Angiotensin II indirectly elevates arterial pressure through expansion of extracellular fluid volume. It directly affects the kidneys to retain sodium and subsequently water, and it stimulates the adrenal cortex to release aldosterone, a mineralocorticoid that also causes retention of sodium and subsequently water by the kidneys. It also stimulates thirst.

Secretion of ADH is the body's response to stimulation of the volume receptors in the great vessels and decreased cerebral blood flow and stimulation of osmoreceptors. ADH acts on the collecting tubules of the kidneys to cause reabsorption of water. These compensatory mechanisms (Fig. 17-4) raise arterial pressure through expansion of extracellular fluid volume, but they also increase venous return to the heart from the systemic circulation. Thus a vicious cycle has been set up, further stressing an overburdened heart.

Increased levels of atrial natriuretic peptide have been identified in patients with congestive heart failure. Atrial natriuretic peptide is released from atrial myocyte granules in response to plasma volume expansion and elevated atrial pressure. It is not known at this time what role (if any) this substance may play in the pathogenesis and/or perpetuation of heart failure (Raine et al., 1986).

Other mechanisms that are adaptive ini-

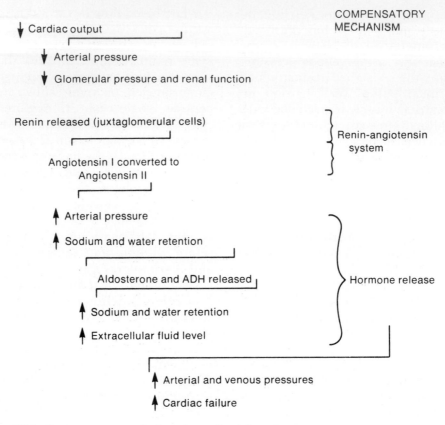

COMPENSATORY
MECHANISM

↓ Cardiac output

↓ Arterial pressure

↓ Glomerular pressure and renal function

Renin released (juxtaglomerular cells)

Angiotensin I converted to
Angiotensin II

} Renin-angiotensin
system

↑ Arterial pressure

↑ Sodium and water retention

Aldosterone and ADH released

↑ Sodium and water retention

↑ Extracellular fluid level

} Hormone release

↑ Arterial and venous pressures

↑ Cardiac failure

Fig. 17-4. Compensatory mechanisms in cardiac failure that promote volume expansion, which increases venous return, thus contributing to further cardiac decompensation and failure.

tially but become self-limiting are cardiac dilation and hypertrophy. Cardiac output of the failing heart is maintained chiefly through the retention of fluid in the body. A persistent increase in the volume of blood entering the ventricles results in a sustained lengthening of their muscle fibers, or *dilation*. This dilation allows the heart to contract more forcefully; however, there is increased tension on individual muscle fibers rather than on cardiac muscle as a whole. This results in increased myocardial oxygen consumption. As dilation increases, cardiac reserve, the maximal percentage that cardiac output can increase above normal, is decreased.

This mechanism is related to Starling's principle of autoregulation, and, as stated previously, it has a physiologic limit. At a critical point further lengthening of cardiac muscle fibers is no longer physiologic, contraction becomes weak, and cardiac output drops.

Dilation is often associated with hypertrophy or enlargement of the muscle mass and a change in the geometric configuration of the heart. There is disagreement as to which condition appears first. Hypertrophy occurs in response to the increased cardiac work load and does result in augmented pumping ability because of the increase in the muscle wall size. However, as muscle mass increases, the blood supply to it does not increase to a comparable degree. As a result, cardiac function in a hypertrophied heart will be severely compromised by even a slight reduction in coronary blood flow. Hypertrophy can further increase cardiac work load through the changes in ventricular compliance and wall tension that it causes.

Physiologic compensation for decreased cardiac output related to cardiac dysfunction is limited. This is graphically illustrated by the left ventricular function curves shown in Fig. 17-5. The initial response to decreased cardiac output actually increases cardiac output above normal levels. Sympathetic activation and increased preload are responsible for the increased rate and contractility that shift the ventricular function curve to the left. As other compensatory mechanisms that increase blood volume and filling pressure are activated, the curve shifts to the right and cardiac output is maintained at near

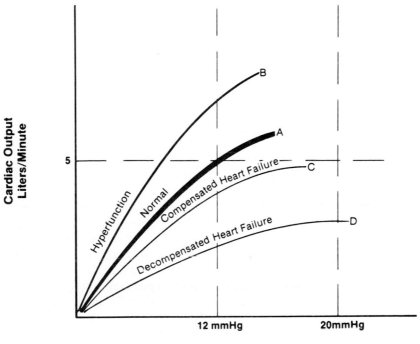

Fig. 17-5. Left ventricular function curves. *Curve A* represents cardiac output at physiologic filling pressures. *Curve B* represents cardiac hyperfunction caused by sympathoadrenergic stimulation yielding a marked increase in cardiac output at physiologic filling pressures. *Curve C* represents compensated heart failure reflecting normal cardiac output with elevated filling pressures. *Curve D* represents decompensated severe heart failure illustrating a marked decrease in cardiac output in spite of high filling pressures. A shift to the left, as occurs when cardiac function moves from curve A to B, represents an increase in ventricular contractility resulting from sympathetic stimulation. A shift to the right, as occurs when ventricular function moves from curve C to D, represents depressed cardiac contractility resulting from hemodynamic burden or intrinsic myocardial dysfunction. (From Michaelson C: Congestive heart failure, St Louis, 1983, The CV Mosby Co.)

normal levels. This stage is often referred to as *compensated heart failure*. Under normal conditions—in a resting state or with limited activity—these mechanisms allow the failing heart to compensate and maintain a normal cardiac output.

Cardiac decompensation *(decompensated heart failure)* occurs when the cardiac dysfunction or hemodynamic load increases. Filling pressures continue to rise, ventricular compliance is decreased, and the physiologic limit of the length-tension relationship is surpassed. Cardiac output drops as the curve shifts further to the right and clinical manifestations of ventricular failure appear (Michaelson, 1983). The same effect occurs during periods of stress or activity because the failing heart is unable to increase cardiac output in response to increased demand. The normal compensatory mechanisms by which cardiac output is increased are already being used just to maintain a cardiac output sufficient to meet routine demands. In other words, there is no cardiac reserve or reserve is minimal at this stage.

Initially only one side of the heart may be considered in failure. Failure of the right and left sides may occur independently, but as the failure progresses, the function of the unaffected side will be compromised, since both sides are part of the same closed system. Most often, heart failure begins with failure of the left ventricle, which worsens until the backward effects of left-sided failure cause such intense tension in the pulmonary circulation that the function of the right side is impaired because of the increased resistance it is pumping against. The clinical manifestations of heart failure are related to the backward and forward effects of right- and left-sided ventricular dysfunction, which are summarized in Table 17-1.

Clinical manifestations

Heart failure can occur as an acute or a chronic condition. When cardiac dysfunction develops slowly over a long period of time, the heart is able to enact compensatory mechanisms that allow an adequate cardiac output to be maintained except during periods of stress or activity. Chronic heart failure refers to the compensated state and usually reflects systemic congestion. Acute heart failure usually occurs in response to acute left ventricular dysfunction, as might occur with massive damage to the myocardium (e.g., acute myocardial infarction) or with an overwhelming hemodynamic load (e.g., fluid overload or acute hypertensive crisis). Acute heart failure may also be an exacerbation of a chronic cardiac condition in response to some stressor that increases cardiac demands and/or causes sudden deterioration of the underlying condition. Pulmonary pressures rise rapidly, and compensatory mechanisms cannot respond effectively. Acute heart failure reflects pulmonary congestion and reduced systemic perfusion and must be treated immediately and aggressively if the patient is to survive.

For the purpose of discussion, the clinical manifestations of failure of the right and left sides of the heart will be examined separately. It should be remembered, however, that in a closed system such as the heart, a totally isolated condition cannot exist for any length of time.

Left-sided heart failure. Left-sided heart failure occurs when the output of the left side of the heart is less than the total volume of blood received from the right side of the heart. More blood is being received from the pulmonary circulation than the left side of the heart can pump out. As a result, pulmonary filling pressure rises while systemic filling pressure falls. Signs and symptoms of left-sided failure result

Table 17-1. Pathophysiologic effects of ventricular dysfunction

Backward effects	Forward effects
Failure of the left ventricle	
Decreased emptying of left ventricle	Decreased cardiac output
Increased volume and end-diastolic pressure in left ventricle	Decreased perfusion of body tissues
Increased volume and pressure in left atrium	Decreased blood flow to kidneys and glands
Increased volume in pulmonary veins	Increased secretion of sodium- and water-retaining hormones
Increased volume and pressure in pulmonary capillary bed	Increased reabsorption of sodium and water
Transudation of fluid from capillaries to alveoli	Increased reabsorption of sodium and water
Filling of alveolar spaces	Increased extracellular fluid volume
Pulmonary congestion	
Decreased emptying of right ventricle	Increased total blood volume
Sometimes referred to as congestive theory or backward theory of heart failure	*Sometimes referred to as low output theory or forward theory of heart failure*
Failure of the right ventricle	
Decreased emptying of right ventricle	Decreased volume from right ventricle to lungs
Increased volume and end-diastolic pressure in right ventricle	Decreased return to left atrium and subsequent decreased cardiac output
Increased volume and pressure in right atrium	All forward effects of left-sided heart failure
Increased volume and pressure in great veins	Expansion of blood volume
Increased volume in systemic venous circulation	
Increased volume in distensible organs (liver, spleen)	
Increased volume and pressure in capillary beds	
Hepatomegaly and splenomegaly	
Dependent edema and serous effusion	

from decreased systemic perfusion (forward effects) and pulmonary congestion (backward effects).

As cardiac output falls, systemic perfusion is also decreased. Hypoxia of the body tissues develops in response to the altered tissue perfusion coupled with the hypoxemia due to pulmonary congestion. Easy fatigability, weakness, and dizziness are clinical manifestations of tissue hypoxia and contribute to activity intolerance. Muscle weakness can be a response to the loss of potassium as well to hypoxia of muscle tissue. Aldosterone, secreted to ex-

pand fluid volume, causes the kidneys to excrete excessive amounts of potassium in addition to retaining sodium and water. Unless potassium is replaced, muscle function, including that of cardiac muscle, will be adversely affected (see Chapter 18). Increased fatigue and weakness are often the earliest symptoms of left-sided heart failure. The brain responds rapidly to hypoxia, hence the dizziness; as failure and the resultant hypoxia worsen, memory loss, disorientation, confusion, and, ultimately, unconsciousness can develop. In response to hypoxia, the work of breathing is increased because of stimulation of the chemoreceptors and respiratory center of the brain. This compounds the effects of pulmonary congestion.

The predominant signs and symptoms of left-sided ventricular dysfunction are those of pulmonary congestion. Under normal conditions, fluid does not move from the pulmonary capillaries into the alveoli because of the pressure gradients that exist in the pulmonary vascular bed and lymphatic clearance of the interstitial space. When either of these mechanisms is disrupted, the potential exists for the development of pulmonary congestion. With left ventricular dysfunction, left end-diastolic pressure rises and is reflected backward into the pulmonary vasculature, eventually causing increased pulmonary capillary hydrostatic pressure. This is the basic pathogenetic mechanism in the formation of *hydrostatic* or *cardiogenic pulmonary edema.*

It is believed that the ensuing disruption of pulmonary pressures and pulmonary congestion occur in stages that reflect the degree of disruption and congestion present (Ingram and Braunwald, 1984). Stage I involves early pulmonary congestion and is characterized by few signs and symptoms because lymphatic drainage increases proportionally to remove any excess fluid accumulating in the interstitial space. During auscultation of the lungs, mild crackles (rales) may be heard on inspiration due to the reopening of small airways. These abnormal breath sounds are heard mainly over the basilar segments because of the effect of gravitational pooling of fluid in the lower lungs. The patient may experience slight shortness of breath (breathlessness or difficult breathing) during strenuous activity, exercise, or stress, and this symptom is referred to as *dyspnea on exertion.* In response to increased cellu-

lar demands for oxygen, the normal heart increases the cardiac output. As blood flow through the lungs increases, the rate of oxygenation of the blood increases. The failing or failure-prone heart is unable to increase cardiac output during exercise, and the rate of oxygen saturation of the blood cannot increase. Exercise increases venous return, and the right side of the heart pumps the total increased volume of returning blood to the left side. The failing left side of the heart is unable to pump the total amount of blood received by it to the systemic circulation. As a result, blood accumulates in the pulmonary vascular bed, and pulmonary vascular pressure rises.

Stage II constitutes the formation of interstitial edema as depicted in Fig. 17-6. Pulmonary capillary pressure at this point usually exceeds 18 mm Hg (normal is 10 to 12 mm Hg), and the rate of fluid leaving the capillaries is greater than can be removed by lymphatic clearance. Lymphatic drainage may also be impaired by elevated systemic venous pressure. Crackles may be heard over more of the lung fields, and generalized haziness and loss of definition may be seen on the chest x-ray film. The accumulation of fluid in the interstitial space causes decreased lung compliance, which increases the work of breathing. Gas exchange will be disrupted, and hypoxemia will develop as a result of shunting as some alveoli close and diffusion is impaired by the fluid at the alveolar capillary interface. As the failure worsens and functional vital capacity is further decreased, dyspnea will occur not only during periods of activity or stress but also during periods of rest.

Orthopnea, or the inability to breathe in a lying position, is also a symptom of left-sided heart failure. In the supine position, blood that had pooled in the lower extremities returns to the heart because of the ef-

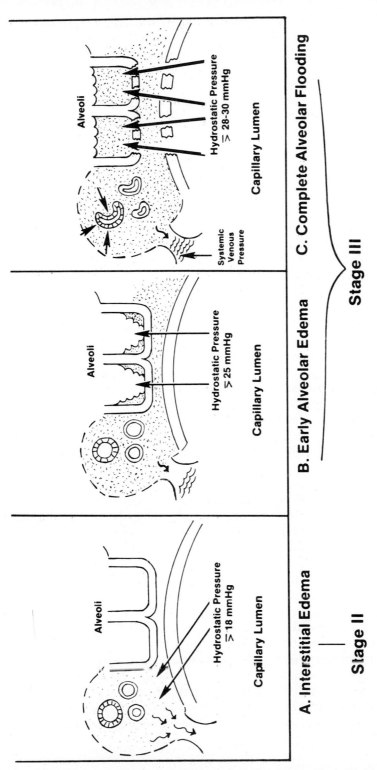

Fig. 17-6. Evolution of cardiogenic pulmonary edema. Graphic representation of cardiogenic pulmonary edema. **A,** Stage II—interstitial edema caused by an increase in net filtration pressure. Fluid pools first in loose perivascular space, causing decreased lung compliance and increased work of breathing. **B,** Stage III—early alveolar edema. Extravasation of fluid across alveolar-capillary membrane has invaded loose perivascular space and tight interstitial space and has pooled in corners of adjacent alveoli. **C,** Stage III—complete alveolar flooding. End-stage of cardiogenic pulmonary edema when disruption of alveolar-capillary membrane allows fluid to flood alveoli and large airways. Note that perivascular edema distorts bronchioles and pulmonary vessels to further compromise ventilation and perfusion.

(From Michaelson, C: Congestive heart failure, St Louis, 1983, The CV Mosby Co.)

fects of hydrostatic pressure and gravity. This sudden increase in venous return cannot be handled by the left side of the heart, and blood accumulates in the pulmonary circulation. The effect is the same as that following exercise. Also, the movement of the diaphragm is mechanically restricted by the abdominal organs pushing against it, and this further contributes to the shortness of breath.

Orthopnea is relieved by sitting because venous blood again pools in the lower extremities, venous return decreases, and vascular pressure in the pulmonary circulation decreases. Pressure on the diaphragm is relieved as the abdominal organs move downward in the abdominal cavity. The onset and increase in severity of orthopnea can be insidious. A person experiencing orthopnea may not realize he is actually having trouble breathing while lying down but knows he feels more comfortable when using several pillows for sleeping. The degree of severity of orthopnea is measured by the number of pillows needed by a person for comfortable sleep. A person who uses four pillows for sleeping is said to be experiencing "four-pillow orthopnea."

Paroxysmal nocturnal dyspnea is another symptom of left-sided heart failure. Periods of difficult breathing or air hunger (dyspnea) occur intermittently during the night. The person experiencing left-sided heart failure will awaken suddenly with severe shortness of breath and coughing spasms. He may open a window and gulp for air in an attempt to catch his breath. It is thought that paroxysmal nocturnal dyspnea (PND) occurs in response to a sudden increase in right ventricular output or a sudden increase in the body's need for oxygen. Possible triggering events include dreams, nightmares, or a full bladder. The attack is self-limiting and usually lasts only a short time. The change in position from lying to standing or sitting probably aids in decreasing the venous return in the same way that relief for orthopnea is achieved. In stage III, fluid filters into the interstitium and alveoli as pulmonary capillary pressure arises above the plasma oncotic pressure, which is normally 25 to 28 mm Hg (Fig. 17-6). Pulmonary edema represents the most extreme form of left-sided ventricular failure. Pulmonary edema is an acute, life-threatening condition that occurs when serum transudation into the pulmonary interstitial space and alveoli becomes rapid and extreme. Functional vital capacity is severely reduced, shunting ensues, and arterial hypoxemia results (see Chapter 16). Cardiac output and consequently systemic arterial pressure are also severely decreased. Signs and symptoms of acute pulmonary edema include intense dyspnea of sudden onset; rapid, gasping, gurgling respirations; use of the accessory breathing muscles, nasal flaring, and inspiratory retraction of the supraclavicular fossae and intercostal spaces; extreme anxiety and restlessness, even combativeness; a rapid, weak, irregular pulse; increased venous pressure; and decreased urinary output. The skin feels cool and damp to the touch and appears ashen gray and cyanotic. Auscultation of the heart reveals the presence of a third heart sound and a very rapid heart rate called a *gallop rhythm*. Auscultation of the lungs reveals wheezes and crackles (rales) throughout the lung fields. The patient appears unable to catch his breath and resists lying flat. A cough accompanied by expectoration of frothy, pink-tinged sputum may also be present. The pallor, sweating, rapid pulse rate, and cold skin result from the sympathetic stimulation that occurs in response to the decreased cardiac output. Kidney function is depressed because of the decreased cardiac output and resultant decrease in arterial pressure in the kidneys. Pulmonary symptoms are the result of pulmonary congestion.

Treatment of pulmonary edema must be rapid if the patient is to survive. Treatment goals include increasing the cardiac output and tissue perfusion, decreasing venous return, and improving oxygenation. Cardiac output is increased through the use of rapid-acting cardiotonic drugs that improve the function of the failing left side of the heart. These drugs are classified as cardiac glycosides and have positive inotropic and negative chronotropic effects. The positive inotropic effect is the increased contractility of the muscle fibers, which augments the strength of contraction and increases stroke volume. The negative chronotropic effect is the slowing of the myocardial contraction rate through an increase in vagal sensitivity and the refractory period of the AV conduction tissue. The net result is an increase in cardiac output, better utilization of available energy (oxygen) by the myocardium, and a lengthening of the period of diastole, which allows the myocardium to rest and increases the filling time for the coronary arteries. The use of the cardiac glycosides must be closely monitored in the presence of low potassium levels, as this enhances the action of these drugs and alterations in the heart's normal rhythm may occur. Additionally, sympathomimetic and vasodilating agents are used to increase tissue perfusion.

Intravascular blood volume is reduced through the use of rapid-acting diuretic drugs to increase urinary output; rotating tourniquets, which trap blood in the extremities; and positioning the patient in a high Fowler's position with the legs dependent. Reduced intravascular blood volume results in a decreased venous return and,

concomitantly, decreased venous pressure. Because less blood is returning to the heart, the output of the right ventricle decreases, and as a result pulmonary vascular pressure also drops. The reduced pulmonary vascular pressure allows the serous fluid in the pulmonary interstitial space and alveoli to filter back (be reabsorbed) into the intravascular compartment.

Oxygenation of the blood is improved by administration of (1) high concentrations of oxygen under positive pressure and (2) the drugs aminophylline and morphine sulfate. Oxygen administered under pressure promotes the rapid formation of oxyhemoglobin, prevents further fluid transudation out of the capillaries, and helps move fluid already in the lung tissue back into the capillaries. Assisted mechanical ventilation may be necessary.

Aminophylline promotes dilation of the bronchioles. Morphine sulfate decreases the work of breathing and reduces metabolic demands for oxygen through two mechanisms. First, it acts as a sedative to relieve feelings of apprehension and anxiety and promote relaxation. Second, morphine directly depresses the respiratory center in the medulla, decreasing the respiratory rate and the work of breathing. It also has a peripheral vasodilating effect, which contributes to the relief of acute pulmonary edema by reducing preload and afterload.

The improved oxygenation and decreased venous return reduce the work load of the heart. Cardiac function is enhanced by both the reduced cardiac work load and the direct effect of the cardiac glycosides. As the circulation improves, the function of the body's various organ systems also improves and potentiates the effects of the treatments just described. As circulation to the kidneys improves, urinary output increases, and renin will no longer be secreted. As liver function improves, aldosterone and ADH are deactivated more rapidly.

Right-sided heart failure. Failure of the right side of the heart occurs when the output of the right ventricle becomes less than the total volume of blood being returned to the heart from the systemic circulation. Right-sided failure can occur independently, but it most often occurs as the sequela to left-sided heart failure (Michaelson, 1983). Isolated right-sided failure is usually the result of pulmonary disease (cor pulmonale) or congenital defects that increase pulmonary vascular resistance or pressure in the pulmonary artery. Defective functioning of the tricuspid valve will also cause isolated right-sided heart failure.

Signs and symptoms of right-sided failure result from decreased systemic perfusion and increased venous pressure and systemic congestion. In response to the decreased cardiac output, urinary output drops, and hypoxia of the tissues causes weakness and fatigue with little exertion. Fluid retention and an increase in the heart rate occur as compensatory mechanisms. Systemic venous pressure rises as a result of the expansion of the intravascular fluid volume and the accumulation of blood in the systemic circulation caused by the inability of the right side of the heart to pump it into the pulmonary circulation. The resultant rise in systemic capillary pressure causes filtration of serous fluid into the interstitial spaces. In the early stages of right-sided heart failure, edema (Fig. 17-7), or the presence of fluid in the interstitial spaces, is visible as the swelling of dependent parts of the body (i.e., the lower extremities where hydrostatic pressure is greatest). As the heart failure worsens, edema occurs in the upper body tissues and affects various organ systems (see Chapter 18 for discussion of edema).

The distensible sinusoids of the liver and spleen expand to act as reservoirs for the excess blood. This results in an enlargement of both these organs, which is referred to as hepatomegaly (liver enlargement) and splenomegaly (spleen enlargement). Palpation of the abdomen reveals tenderness in the right and left upper quadrants where these organs lie and definition of their borders. Inadequate deactivation of aldosterone and ADH because of poor liver function will lead to further fluid volume expansion, contributing to the vicious cycle already set up.

Ascites, or free fluid in the abdominal cavity, occurs as serous fluid filters out of the portal system because of the increased vascular pressure. The function of the gastrointestinal system is adversely affected by the edema and depressed functioning of the intestines and other abdominal organs. Ascites leaves little room for expansion of the stomach and intestines. These conditions lead to such symptoms as anorexia (loss of appetite), indigestion, nausea, and vomiting. The presence of any electrolyte imbalances, drug interactions, or toxicity will further aggravate these symptoms.

Peripheral vein distension allows direct observation of the results of increased venous pressure. With increased venous pressure the jugular vein appears distended or bulging, even with elevation of the head, a state in which the vein is normally flat and unobservable. When the jugular vein is compressed and emptied, it should fill from the top; however, in the presence of increased venous pressure it will fill from the bottom. Distention, or bulging, of the hand veins with the hands raised to heart level is also a sign of increased venous pressure. The severity of the increase in venous pressure can be di-

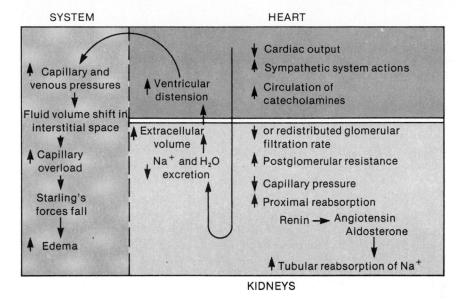

Fig. 17-7. Pathogenesis of cardiac edema.

rectly measured by means of a catheter inserted into the right atrium and attached externally to a manometer. The measurement thus obtained is called *central venous pressure*. Normal central venous pressure is between 0 and 10 cm of water pressure. This value will be elevated in the presence of increased venous pressure.

Heart failure seen clinically is usually a combination of right and left-sided failure. The term *congestive heart failure* is generally used to describe combined failure of the right and left sides of the heart. The forward and backward effects of bilateral ventricular dysfunction and the related clinical manifestations are shown in Fig. 17-8. Other terms used to describe heart failure include cardiac failure, myocardial failure, power failure, low output failure, and high output failure. The last term refers to a situation in which the body's metabolic requirements are increased beyond the capacity to meet them. Cardiac output may be normal or even above normal, but tissue needs are not being met.

Treatment rationale

Goals for the treatment of congestive heart failure are similar to those for pulmonary edema; they include the following:

1. Improvement of cardiac output and circulation throughout the body
2. A decrease in the workload of the heart
3. Prevention of potential complications
4. Promotion of an optimal level of function

Cardiac output is increased through the use of inotropic agents that increase the contractility and decrease the rate of contraction of the myocardium. With increased cardiac output and better circulation to all parts of the body, many of the signs and symptoms of heart failure disappear. Organ function throughout the body improves as tissues once again receive the oxygen and nutrients necessary for metabolism. As the blood supply to the brain is increased, the sensorium improves. Edema fluid will begin to be mobilized as a result of improved circulatory

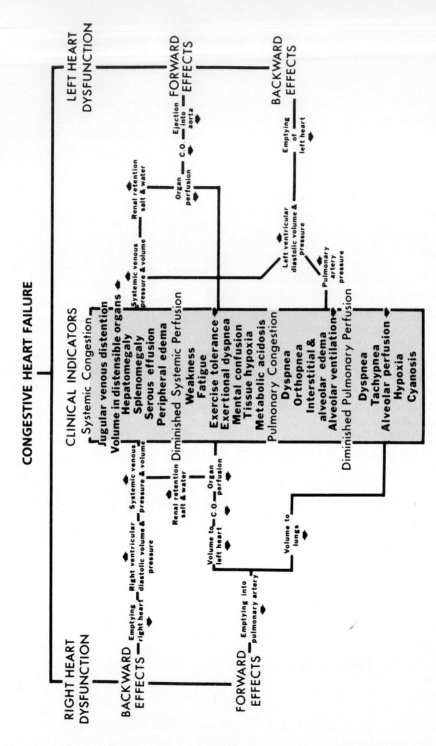

Fig. 17-8. Clinical indicators of congestive heart failure. Schematic representation of complex interaction of forward and backward effects of right and left ventricular dysfunction. Note: These effects all lead to development of one or more groups of clinical indicators characteristic of the syndrome "congestive heart failure." (From Michaelson C: Congestive heart failure, St Louis, 1983, The CV Mosby Co.)

dynamics. Tissue perfusion can also be enhanced through the use of vasodilating agents.

Cardiac workload is decreased by keeping venous return within normal limits (or at a level that the failure-prone heart can manage) and by reducing tissue demands for oxygen. Venous return is reduced through the use of diuretic drugs to in-crease urine output and through restriction of the amount of fluid and sodium allowed in the diet. The actions of pharmacologic agents in interrupting the pathophysiologic mechanisms of heart failure are summarized in Fig. 17-9.

After the acute phase of heart failure when the heart has begun to compensate, venous return from the peripheral, depen-

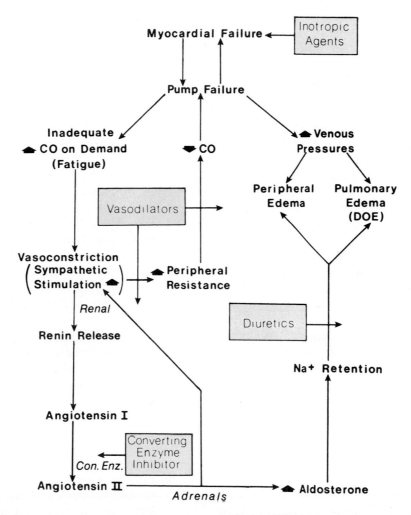

Fig. 17-9. Summary of actions of different types of pharmacologic agents in interrupting the patho-physiologic mechanisms of heart failure. DOE = dyspnea on exertion. CO = cardiac output.

(From Hurst, JW: The heart and arteries. Copyright © 1982 by J.W. Hurst. Used with the permission of McGraw-Hill Book Company.)

dent areas of the body is facilitated through the use of elastic support stockings. These also help prevent any further formation of edema in the tissues and assist circulation to prevent clot formation.

Tissue demands for oxygen are reduced through frequent rest periods, avoidance of fatiguing activities and becoming overtired, and spacing activities to avoid doing too much at one time. Positioning the patient with the head elevated helps reduce the work of breathing, which also helps reduce tissue demands for oxygen. Because of the effects of gravity, the head-elevated position also decreases venous return to the heart. Blood will remain in the lower extremities and pelvic region.

Complications can occur as a result of either the disease process or the treatment. Edematous tissue is easily injured and is prone to the development of infection. Once injured, it heals more slowly than normal tissue. Special skin care and protection should be given to edematous areas to avoid injury. Venous stasis occurs in the presence of a sluggish circulation and predisposes the individual to intravascular clot formation and thrombophlebitis. Bed rest as a treatment measure also contributes to venous stasis. The feet and legs should never be massaged, since a clot may be jarred loose into the circulation. Diet and drug therapy can lead to severe fluid and electrolyte imbalances, which in turn can lead to dehydration or cardiac arrhythmias.

An optimal level of functioning is promoted through rehabilitation and teaching. Increasing the patient's understanding of the disease and its treatment may promote cooperation and consistent compliance with the regimen in the treatment of chronic heart failure. The patient requires information about the disease process in order to assume responsibility for management and to prevent recurrent episodes.

Etiology

Heart failure is not a disease entity in itself but rather the result of disease processes that disrupt the physiologic determinants of cardiac output; preload (cardiac filling), contractility, afterload (cardiac emptying), and heart rate. Examples of the variety of pathologic mechanisms that can lead to heart failure include the following:

1. An overwhelming increase in extracellular fluid volume (e.g., too rapid administration of IV fluids)
2. Damage to or loss of functional myocardial muscle tissue (e.g., myocardial infarction, ischemic heart disease)
3. Aberrations in the rate and rhythm of the heart (e.g., bradycardia and tachycardia dysrhythmias)
4. Incompetence of the cardiac valves (e.g., mitral stenosis)
5. Inflammatory or infectious processes that result in the weakening of myocardial muscle tissue (e.g., myocarditis, endocarditis, pericarditis)
6. Increased resistance to the heart's pumping action (e.g., hypertensive vascular disease, aortic stenosis)
7. Congenital defects of the heart (e.g., patent ductus arteriosus)
8. Constriction of heart tissue resulting in mechanical limitation of the heart's pumping action (e.g., constrictive pericarditis, cardiac tamponade)
9. Conditions in which cardiac output is normal or even high but metabolic requirements of the body are greatly increased, or *high output failure* (e.g., hyperthyroidism, Paget's disease)

Table 17-2.   Conditions causing heart failure

Abnormal volume load	Abnormal pressure load	Myocardial dysfunction	Filling disorders	Increased metabolic demand
Aortic incompetence	Aortic stenosis	Cardiomyopathy	Mitral stenosis	Anemias
Mitral incompetence	Idiopathic hypertrophic	Myocarditis	Tricuspid stenosis	Thyrotoxicosis
Tricuspid incompetence	subaortic stenosis	Coronary artery	Cardiac tamponade	Fever
Overtransfusion	Coarctation of the aorta	disease	Restrictive pericarditis	Beriberi
Left-to-right shunts	Hypertension	Ischemia		Paget's disease
Secondary hypervolemia	Primary	Infarction		Arteriovenous
	Secondary	Dysrhythmias		fistulas
		Toxic disorders		
		Presbycardia		

From Michaelson C: Congestive heart failure, St Louis, 1983, The CV Mosby Co.

10. Conditions in which the oxygen-carrying capacity of the blood is decreased accompanied by compromised cardiac function (e.g., anemia coexisting with coronary artery disease)

11. Cardiomyopathies: a heterogeneous group of chronic myocardial disorders that are not caused by ischemia, hypertension, valve disease, or shunts, and that appear to be noninflammatory in nature (e.g., endomyocardial fibrosis)

A complete analysis of all possible causes of decreased cardiac output is beyond the scope of this book. Listed in Table 17-2 are the conditions that can cause heart failure grouped in broad categories of pathophysiologic mechanisms. Inflammation as a mechanism of pathophysiology is presented in Chapter 4. The following case study demonstrates how an inflammatory process can disrupt cardiac function to such a degree that decreased cardiac output as a result of heart failure occurs. A descriptive survey of some of the other causes of decreased cardiac output such as dysrhythmias and congenital and valvular defects is presented in the follow-

ing section. Ischemic heart disease is discussed later in this chapter.

CASE STUDY: VIRAL MYOCARDITIS

Objective and Subjective Data History

Mr. J is a 46-year-old black male who had a previous abnormal ECG with nonspecific ST-T wave changes. He underwent a cardiac angiogram that showed insignificant coronary artery disease. He had no previous history of angina, hypertension, or diabetes mellitus. Travel history included a fishing trip to Ohio 1 month before admission, but he denied exposure to any known viral or bacterial illness. He has a history of 30 pack-years of smoking.

Present illness: Mr. J was admitted to the medical intensive care unit (MICU) with complaints of chest pain, shortness of breath, and a nonproductive cough. Nine days before admission, he experienced epigastric pain and nausea unrelieved by antacids or laxatives. He did not produce sputum and, at this time, he denied fever, chills, myalgias, or arthral-

Contributed by Lisa Hopp.

gias. Three days before admission, he began to experience burning substernal chest pain that was exacerbated when he took a deep breath or assumed the supine position. At this time, he developed shaking chills and shortness of breath. He came to the emergency room because of increasingly severe chest pain and dyspnea. His chest pain was unrelieved by nitroglycerin or antacids in the emergency room.

Physical examination

General appearance: An acutely ill, but alert well-nourished man in moderate respiratory distress

Vital signs:

Temperature: 101.5° F (PO)

Pulse: 120

Respirations: 28

Blood pressure: 68/54 mm Hg without pulsus paradoxus

Skin: Warm and dry; no edema

Heart: Nonpalpable apical impulse; normal S_1 and S_2 with a two-component pericardial friction rub; no S_3, S_4, or murmurs; jugular venous distention present.

Lungs: Bilateral basilar rales

Abdomen: Soft and not distended; liver enlarged, measuring 12 cm at the MCL, and nontender

Remaining physical examination was unremarkable.

Pertinent laboratory values and diagnostic tests:

Chest x-ray film: Cardiomegaly and right lower lobe infiltrate

ECG: Sinus tachycardia; low QRS amplitude in the frontal leads; diffuse S-T segment elevation; left axis deviation

Echocardiogram: Not definitive for pericardial effusion

Gated blood pool study: Markedly dilated and diffusely hypokinetic ventricles; left ventricular ejection fraction 37%

Impression: dilated cardiomyopathy.

Initial hemodynamic pressures:

	Patient	Normal
Right atrial pressure (mean):	10	0-5 mm Hg
Pulmonary artery pressure (mean):	42	<13 mm Hg
Pulmonary capillary wedge pressure:	30	4-12 mm Hg
Cardiac output:	3.1	4-8 L/min
Arterial pressure:	95/55	
Mean arterial pressure:	68	80-95 mm Hg
Systemic vascular resistance:	1497	800-1200*

Arterial blood gases (on room air):

pH:7.5

P_{CO_2}: 28 mm Hg

P_{O_2}: 68 mm Hg

Blood chemistries

K: 5.8 mEq/L

Cr: 1.9 mg/dl

Na: 128 mEq/L

Bun: 61 mg/dl

CPK: 2640 U/ml (isoenzymes within normal limits)

SGOT: 307 U/ml

SGPT: 45 U/ml

Complete blood count:

Hg: 10.8 gm/dl

Hct: 31.2%

WBC: 28,200

Polys: 64%

Bands: 18%

Treatment

Several problems were identified:

1. Improve cardiac output and tissue perfusion. To treat the decreased

---

*SVR units are dynes/sec/cm

cardiac output related to biventricular failure, the following were instituted:
   —inotropic drugs including dopamine and dobutamine
   —intra-aortic balloon counterpulsation
   —diuretic therapy
   —control of atrial fibrillation and ventricular tachycardia with digoxin, lidocaine, and quinidine
2. Improve oxygenation and relieve pulmonary congestion. To treat the impaired gas exchange related to pulmonary congestion, the following were done:
   —mechanical ventilation with positive end-expiratory pressure
   —diuretic therapy
3. Promote elimination of metabolic waste products and correct acidosis. This involved treatment with:
   —peritoneal dialysis
   —bicarbonate infusion as necessary
4. Relieve chest pain. The patient was given indomethacin.
5. Suspected viral or bacterial infection. This was treated by:
   —erythromycin for broad spectrum bacterial coverage
   —ethambutol and isoniazid for possible tuberculous pericarditis

Discussion

The presumed cause of this patient's biventricular failure was a viral infection of the myocardium and pericardium. The diagnosis of viral myocarditis in this case was based on epidemiologic data, characteristic signs and symptoms, and ECG changes. Although all serum microbiologic and immunologic tests were negative for any viral or bacterial infection, the diagnosis was supported by the sudden onset of pump failure, diffuse S-T segment elevation, absence of significant coronary artery disease by previous angiography, and recent history of flu-like symptoms. Laboratory methods frequently fail to verify infection, since the patient usually seeks medical attention several days into the illness so that the acute phase, when the tests are sensitive, has passed. Since viruses often cause myocarditis in this country, a virus probably induced this patient's heart disease. Therefore antimicrobial agents were prescribed to cover all possible pathogens.

Investigators have been unable to clarify if the virus invades the myocardium directly or if the virus causes an autoimmune mechanism that is responsible for the pathogenesis of the myocardial damage and dysfunction. However, microscopic examination has revealed that polymorphonuclear cells infiltrate the myocardium; subsequently, myofibril inflammation, edema, and necrosis of the tissue occur. The clinical consequences of these changes depend on the size and number of these inflammatory lesions. Some patients experience severe pump failure while others may remain unaware of the infection. (Owens-Jones, and Hopp, 1988).

Chest pain is often the first sign of cardiac involvement. This patient experienced typical pericardial pain that was substernal, burning, and intensified with a deep breath. Since indomethacin, an antiinflammatory drug, improved the pain while antianginals did not, pericarditis and not angina was believed to be the source of his chest pain.

This patient progressed to experience severe, global myocardial dysfunction because of a diffuse inflammatory process. Evidence of left heart failure included symptoms such as dyspnea and a dry cough, signs such as bibasilar rales, and altered hemodynamics like the elevated pulmonary capillary wedge pressure (PCWP), high pulmonary artery pressure

(PAP), and decreased cardiac output. Cardiac tamponade was ruled out because it may accompany pericarditis, and the patient exhibited some evidence of this life-threatening complication including profound hypotension, a narrow pulse pressure, pericardial friction rub, reduced heart sounds, and jugular vein distention. However, the hemodynamic evidence of equalization of diastolic pressures and the lack of pericardial effusion by echocardiogram failed to support the diagnosis.

The elevated pulmonary pressures, dyspnea, and rales occurred when myocardial contractility fell; stroke volume then decreased and blood pooled in the pulmonary vasculature. This increase in pulmonary hydrostatic pressure caused fluid to leak into the interstitium of the lung tissue. Hence the patient became short of breath and rales could be heard as alveoli filled with fluid. Ultimately gas exchange became severely impaired, and the patient required mechanical ventilation and positive end-expiratory pressure to maintain adequate oxygenation and ventilation.

This patient also exhibited signs of right heart failure, including elevated right atrial pressure, jugular vein distention, and an enlarged liver with elevated liver enzymes. These signs result from increased right ventricular pressure, subsequent backup of blood, and congestion of venous side vessels and tissues.

As cardiac output falls, oxygen delivery to the working body tissues decreases. At the same time tissues such as the myocardium, kidneys, and liver consume more oxygen because of increased cellular activity. If adequate oxygen is not delivered to the tissue, anaerobic metabolism ensues, acidosis occurs as lactic acid accumulates, and ultimately the major organs fail and tissue may even become necrotic. This patient experienced renal failure as a result of poor perfusion and impaired oxygen delivery.

Successful treatment of severe pump failure depends on interventions that interrupt the positive feedback mechanisms that failed homeostasis has caused. The balance between oxygen delivery and oxygen demand must be restored. The following interventions were implemented to improve oxygen delivery: mechanical ventilation with PEEP and high FiO_2, inotropic drugs to enhance contractility and cardiac output, antiarrhythmics to improve cardiac output, and intraaortic counterpulsation to improve coronary artery perfusion and systemic perfusion pressure. The following interventions were implemented to decrease oxygen demand: strict, complete bed rest: diuretics to decrease preload; intraaortic balloon counterpulsation to decrease afterload and preload; and antipyretics when needed.

Unfortunately some of the interventions, such as inotropic drugs and vasopressors to improve oxygen delivery, take their toll in oxygen consumption. The balance is delicate and complex. The nurse must help restore this balance by knowledgeably administering and titrating these powerful drugs according to hemodynamic parameters, decreasing oxygen demand by minimizing the patient's muscular and emotional activities and coordinating the complex, multidisciplinary interventions.

The impact of a catastrophic illness on the patient's family is also profound and complex. However, the nurse can provide reassurance and offer hope. This patient regained normal myocardial function after 2 weeks of intensive nursing and medical care and 3 more weeks of rehabilitative care in the hospital. He did require chronic digitalization and antiarrhythmic therapy accompanied by some life-style changes, but he and his family survived a life-threatening ordeal.

Nursing Diagnoses

1. Decreased cardiac output related to biventricular failure

2. Impaired gas exchange related to pulmonary congestion
3. Altered elimination pattern related to renal failure
4. Acute chest pain related to pericardial inflammation
5. Anxiety related to critical illness

Cardiac dysrhythmias. The cardiac cycle is initiated by the spontaneous generation of an electrical impulse in the sinoatrial (SA) node, the heart's pacemaker. *Automaticity* is the property of the cardiac cells that allows their spontaneous repetitive self-stimulation. Self-initiated depolarization is possible because of the unstable resting membrane potential of the pacemaker cells.

The rate and rhythm of cardiac contraction are primarily determined by the self-generated impulse, although the autonomic nervous system can also affect heart rate. Parasympathetic stimulation via the vagus nerve slows the heart rate by decreasing the rate of firing of the SA node and decreasing the speed of conduction through the atrioventricular (AV) node. Sympathetic stimulation increases both the heart rate and the speed of conduction through the AV node.

The pacemaker cells of the sinoatrial node have the fastest rate of spontaneous depolarization and therefore are the primary pacemaker cells of the heart. The impulse or action potential spreads throughout the heart muscle via the conduction system. Cells in this system are highly specialized and provide for rapid excitation and conduction of impulses in the heart. Conduction of the action potential should be differentiated from transmission. *Transmission* refers to the perpetuation of the action potential across the neuroeffector junctions. This process requires the pres-

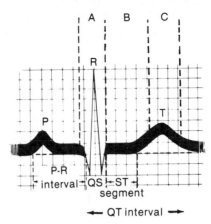

Fig. 17-10. Normal electrocardiographic tracing. The P wave represents atrial depolarization; the P-R Interval represents the spread of the impulse through the atria and AV node, His bundle, and bundle branches, and is normally 0.12-0.20 sec. in duration; the QRS complex, ventricular depolarization and is normally 0.06-0.10 sec. in duration; the QT interval, ventricular depolarization and repolarization and is normally 0.36-0.44 sec. in duration; and the T wave, ventricular repolarization. Area A represents the absolute refractory period, Area B, the relative refractory period and Area C, the vulnerable period.

ence of a neurohumoral substance. *Conduction* refers to a wave of sequential ionic changes that precede the action potential and follow its passage along the nerve fiber. It does not require the presence of a neurohumoral substance but only integrity of the cardiac conducting tissue and normal concentrations of electrolytes.

Fig. 17-10 diagrams the normal electrocardiogram and the sequence of electrical events it represents. The electrical event of depolarization is analogous to the mechanical event of contraction, or systole. Repolarization is synonymous with diastole, or relaxation.

The cardiac action potential has five phases which are illustrated in Fig. 17-11. Phase 0 is the depolarization with an influx of sodium. Phase 1 is a brief change in electrical potential toward repolarization. Phase 2 is a stabilization of the repolariza-

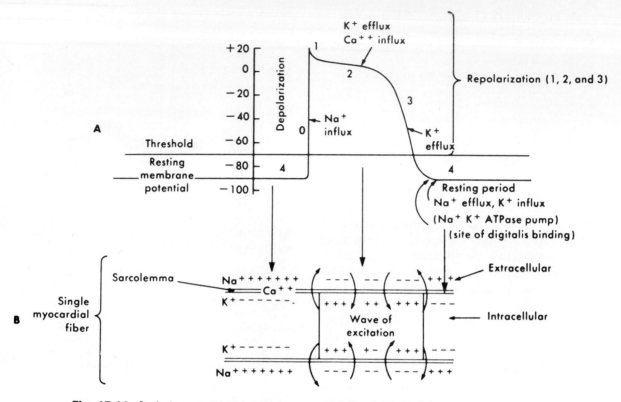

Fig. 17-11. A, Action potential of a single myocardial fiber (cell). **B,** Ionic exchanges that occur across the cell membrane of a single myocardial fiber during action potential.

(From Hahn, AB, Barkin, RL, and Oestreich, SJK: Pharmacology in nursing, ed 16, St Louis, 1986, The CV Mosby Co.)

tion, or a plateau period with calcium and sodium entering and potassium leaving the cell. This allows a sustained cardiac contraction. Phase 3 represents more rapid repolarization. Phase 4 is the resting phase during which the intracellular charge becomes more electropositive, finally reaching threshold level, causing spontaneous depolarization and initiation of the action potential (phase 0).

The various phases of the action potential correspond to the refractory periods of the cardiac muscle which are marked in Fig. 17-10. During depolarization and the beginning of repolarization (phases 0, 1, 2, and the beginning of phase 3) the cell cannot respond to a stimulus because there is essentially no electrical difference between the two sides of the cell membrane. This is called the *absolute refractory* period. During phase 3 the cell again becomes electronegative, and a stronger than threshold stimulus can initiate an action potential. This is called the *relative refractory period.* As phase 4 begins, the cell enters a vulnerable period during which a lower than threshold stimulus can initiate an action potential. During this time a single stimulus can initiate a repetitive series of action potentials, causing the cardiac muscle to contract in a rapid, repetitive, nonfunctional pattern.

A cardiac *arrhythmia* or *dysrhythmia* (since some arrhythmias have definite rhythms) is any deviation from the normal rate and rhythm of cardiac contraction. A cardiac rate that is extremely rapid or slow or a cardiac rhythm that is grossly abnormal results in a decrease in cardiac output. Furthermore, it is indicative of some underlying abnormality in the cardiac tissue, interfering with the normal spontaneous generation or conduction of the cardiac impulse. Criteria constituting "normal" cardiac rate and rhythm (Watanabe et al., 1985) include the following:

1. The impulse originates in the SA node.
2. Contraction occurs at a frequency between 60 and 100 beats per minute in the adult and 130 to 160 beats per minute in the newborn.
3. Contraction occurs at regularly and equally spaced intervals (regular rate).
4. Atrioventricular and intraventricular conduction occurs via the appropriate conduction tissue.
5. Conduction occurs within a constant, normal period of time.

Based on the criteria just listed, dysrhythmias may be the result of disordered impulse formation, conduction, or a combination of both (Moe and Antzelevich, 1984). A variety of pathogenetic mechanisms can disrupt impulse formation or conduction of excitation, and these are listed in Table 17-3. Impulse formation is disrupted through alterations in the automaticity and membrane potential of cardiac cells. Conduction of excitation is disrupted by alterations in the physiologic and anatomic determinants of conductivity. The physiologic determinants include the effectiveness of the stimuli and the excitability of the receiving fibers. Anatomic determinants include the fiber diameter and the geometric arrangement of fibers. An example of how alterations in both the anatomic and physiologic determinants of conductivity disrupt conduction is seen in the mechanism of reentry. *Reentry* or cir-

Table 17-3. Electrophysiologic mechanisms of cardiac arrhythmias

Abnormalities of impulse formation

Alterations of physiologic automaticity in the specialized conducting fibers:
    Enhanced automaticity
    Depressed automaticity
Development of abnormal automaticity in the atrial and ventricular muscle fibers
Other mechanisms of impulse formation:
    Oscillations of membrane potential
    Delayed afterdepolarization (transient depolarization)
    Early afterdepolarization
    Local potential differences causing reexcitation of certain fibers, due to either asynchronous repolarization or partial depolarization

Disturbances of conduction of excitation

Decremental conduction
Inhomogeneous conduction
Conduction delay and block
Unidirectional block
Reentry

Combined disturbances of impulse formation and conduction

Parasystole
Ectopic rhythms with exit block
Fibrillation

From Watanabe Y, Dreifus LS, and Sodeman WA, Sr: Arrhythmias—mechanisms and pathogenesis. In Sodeman WA and Sodeman TM, editors: Sodeman's pathologic physiology,: mechanisms of disease, ed 7, Philadelphia, 1985, WB Saunders Co.

cus movement excitation is postulated to be the underlying pathogenetic mechanism in a variety of types of dysrhythmias, such as tachycardia, flutter, fibrillation, and premature beats. It requires that there be (1) two anatomically separate conduction pathways; (2) unidirectional block at some junctional point in one of the paths; (3) slow propagation over the unblocked path; (4) delayed excitation of the tissue beyond the block; and (5) reexcitation of the tissue proximal to the block (which must be sufficiently recovered following initial depolarization) (Watanabe et al., 1985; Moe and Antzelevitch, 1984).

Dysrhythmias are classified according to the site of origin (sinus if in the SA node, atrial if in the atria, junctional if in the AV node, and ventricular if in the ventricles), the rate, if abnormal (bradycardia for a rate below 60 beats per minute and tachycardia for a rate above 100 beats per minute), and the order, velocity, regularity, and pattern of the rhythm. Premature or escape beats or AV dissociation are examples of disordered rhythms. Velocity refers to the speed of conduction that can be abnormally slow or stopped (blocks) or abnormally fast as occurs in the Wolf-Parkinson-White syndrome resulting from the presence of misplaced conduction tissue. *Paroxysmal* is a term applied to an dysrhythmia that occurs intermittently. Examples of abnormal patterns are flutter and fibrillation. Flutter is an extremely rapid but regular pattern of contraction. Fibrillation is a totally nonfunctional quivering of the myocardial tissue.

Dysrhythmias are detected through changes in the electrocardiogram. For example, a lengthened (>0.20 second) P-R interval indicates a conduction delay in the AV node or His bundle. This arrhythmia is usually referred to as first-degree heart block. Inverted P waves indicative of retrograde conduction, a shortened P-R interval (<0.12 second), and a rate of 40 to 60 indicates an escape pacemaker functioning in the AV junctional tissue. This dysrhythmia is referred to as an AV junctional or nodal rhythm. A premature ventricular contraction (PVC or PVB) is indicated by a widened (>0.12 second) and bizarre-looking QRS complex with no apparent preceding P wave and which is usually followed by a compensatory pause.

Some dysrhythmias are lethal in that the heart beats so erratically that cardiac output and tissue perfusion cease. Other relatively minor dysrhythmias can be tol-erated for longer periods of time. The signs and symptoms of hypotension will be present if cardiac output is diminished without adequate compensation. Heart failure occurs when cardiac output is further diminished and compensatory mechanisms cease.

Congenital heart disease. Congenital heart disease refers to structural defects of the heart that developed in utero. The exact cause of all of these disorders has not been elucidated; however, maternal viral infections, especially rubella, during the first 3 months of pregnancy are known to result in disorders of fetal development. The reader is referred to Chapter 4 for a more complete discussion of disorders of embryonic development and teratogenic mechanisms.

Congenital heart defects can affect oxygenation by causing a reduction in effective cardiac output or by increasing the resistance against which the heart must pump. "Effective" cardiac output is reduced because of the mixing of arterial and venous blood (anatomic shunting) that occurs in many of these defects. The direction of the shunt will determine the type and severity of the manifestations.

Valvular heart disease. Valvular disease is most often the result of rheumatic fever; however, it can be caused by some other conditions as well, for example, syphilis, bacterial endocarditis, and calcific atherosclerosis. Valvular disorders can be of congenital origin as well. Chronic valve deformities result in hemodynamic changes that increase the work load of the heart.

Valvular disorders are of two types that are depicted in Fig. 17-12. In *stenosis* the valve is narrowed and blood flow is obstructed. The valve cusps become thickened and fibrotic and may even become calcified and fused with one another. They cannot open completely. *Insufficiency* or

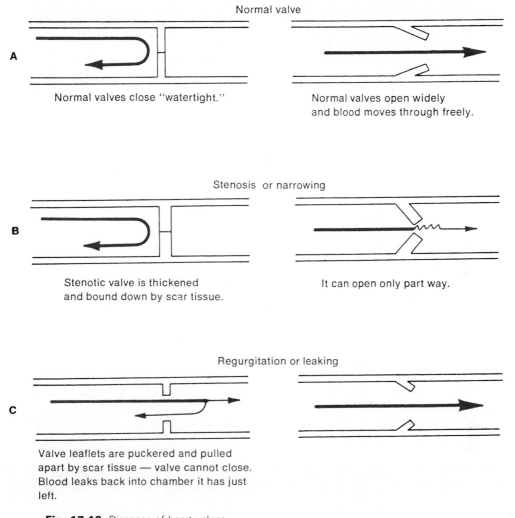

Fig. 17-12. Diseases of heart valves.
(From Phibbs, B.: The human heart: a guide to heart disease, ed. 4, St. Louis, 1979, The C.V. Mosby Co.)

regurgitation occurs when the valve cusps retract and no longer close completely; hence leaking of blood occurs during systole.

With stenosis, pressure in the cardiac chamber antecedent to the affected valve increases because of the resistance against which it is pumping. This increase in pressure is reflected backward throughout the heart, increasing the work load of the heart. The sequelae of events in mitral stenosis illustrate this point. When the mitral valve creates an obstruction to blood flow, cardiac output falls, and pressure increases in the left atrium, which in turn creates increased pressure in the pulmonary veins. As pressure increases in the pulmonary veins, it also increases in the pulmonary vascular bed, with resultant congestion of that vessel system and decreased exchange of oxygen and carbon dioxide. With aortic stenosis there is an additional problem. Blood flow to the coronary arteries is reduced because of decreased pressure in the aorta.

Regurgitation, or leaking of blood, has similar effects. Additionally, cardiac filling is impaired. Cardiac work is increased because the heart never empties completely and must work harder to pump an adequate amount of blood to meet tissue demands. The severity of these effects depends on the extent to which the valve can still function.

Disease model: rheumatic fever and heart disease. Rheumatic fever, the major cause of valvular disease, is an inflammatory condition that in itself is not an infection but the aftermath of an infection of the group A beta-hemolytic streptococci. The course of rheumatic fever is similar to serum sickness and occurs in three phases:

Phase I: Streptococcal infection
Phase II: Latent period (1 to 5 weeks)
Phase III: Acute rheumatic fever

The characteristic lesion is the *Aschoff body* (Fig. 17-13), a collection of reticuloendothelial cells mixed with plasma cells and lymphocytes, surrounding a necrotic, collagenous center. It is actually a "point of inflammation," and many of these points can be found in the heart, lungs, joints, and brain.

Diagnosis of rheumatic fever is made on the basis of major and minor criteria. There is a high probability of rheumatic fever if the presence of two major criteria or one major and two minor criteria are supported by evidence of a preceding group A streptococcal infection (see Table 17-4). The complications of rheumatic fever include congestive heart failure result-

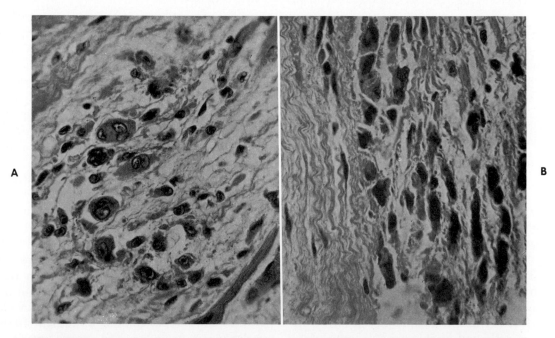

Fig. 17-13. Aschoff bodies in myocardium in 15-year-old boy. **A,** Intermediate phase with distinct Aschoff cells. **B,** More advanced lesion with elongation of cells, pyknosis, and smudging of nuclei.
(From Anderson, W.A.D., and Kissane, J.M.: Pathology, ed. 7, St. Louis, 1977, The C.V. Mosby Co.)

Table 17-4.   Major and minor criteria for the diagnosis of rheumatic fever

Major	Minor
Migratory polyarthritis: swelling, pain, redness, tenderness, heat in one or more joints (not all joints are affected at once, and pain may move from joint to joint)	Arthralgia
	Fever
	Leukocytosis
	Increased erythrocyte sedimentation rate (ESR)
	Increased C-reactive protein (CRP)
Carditis	Prolonged P-R interval (ECG)
Myocarditis, muscle inflamed and dilated	Previous episodes of rheumatic fever
Endocarditis, valves and inner lining affected	Presence of rheumatic heart disease
Pericarditis, outer lining inflamed	
Pancarditis, all layers affected	
Chorea (St. Vitus' dance): purposeless, nonrepetitive movements with grimacing of face	
Erythema marginatum (rash)	
Subcutaneous nodules	

Supporting evidence of streptococcal infection

Increased titer of
  Anti-streptococcal antibodies; Anti-streptolysin 0 (ASO), others
Positive throat culture for group A streptococcus
Recent scarlet fever

From Jones Criteria (revised) for guidance in the Diagnosis of Rheumatic fever, Circulation 69(1):204A-208A, 1984.

ing from valvulitis and rheumatic heart disease. Whether permanent heart damage will occur depends on the area of the heart involved and whether there have been previous episodes of rheumatic fever. Acute carditis occurs in 40% to 50% of patients experiencing their first attack. Permanent scarring of the valves may result from the first episode, but in most instances the first attack does not leave permanent damage.

Valve damage occurs through inflammation and scar tissue formation. During acute rheumatic fever, valvulitis may occur and cause the valves to become thickened with edema. Aschoff bodies cover the valves, especially the free margins (leaflets). As healing takes place, scar tissue forms and causes fusion of the valve cusps and chordae tendineae. Calcification of the affected areas may also occur (Fig. 17-14). The mitral valve is most frequently affected. Persons with valvular damage are

more susceptible to the development of subacute bacterial endocarditis (SBE), as the scars of rheumatic heart disease provide crevices in which bacteria can lodge and multiply. Even bacteria normally present in the body are potentially virulent to these patients. Special precautions for even minor surgical procedures and dental work must be taken to avoid an acute episode of SBE.

The relationship between rheumatic fever and the group A beta-hemolytic streptococci is not certain, but evidence suggests that it is a hypersensitivity or autoimmune disorder. Other areas of research have examined whether rheumatic fever results from persistence of viable streptococci or variants of the organism and whether the lesions of rheumatic fever are the result of toxins or enzymes. These areas of research have not produced positive results.

Studies have shown that many of the

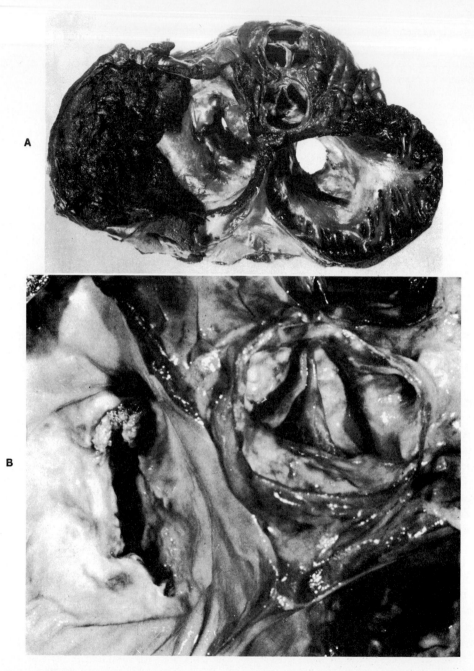

Fig. 17-14. A, Stenosis of mitral, tricuspid, and aortic valves caused by chronic rheumatic endocarditis. Mitral orifice is mere slit. Note large thrombus in dilated left atrium. **B,** Mitral and aortic stenosis with calcification of both valves.

(From Anderson, W.A.D., and Kissane, J.M.: Pathology, ed. 7, St. Louis, 1977, The C.V. Mosby Co.)

factors that seem to predispose a person to the development of rheumatic fever are the same as those factors predisposing a person to the development of a streptococcal infection, including positive familial tendency, worldwide occurrence but a tendency to predominate in temperate zones and to follow the same seasonal variations, environment and life-style (crowded substandard living conditions, poor hygiene, inadequate medical care, inadequate dietary habits), and age (6 to 15 years is the range in most cases; age 8 years seems to be the peak). Since there is a higher incidence of streptococcal infections in families living under acute and chronic stress, this group would appear to be at risk for the development of rheumatic fever.

Primary prevention of rheumatic fever and rheumatic heart disease involves treating all streptococcal infections with antibiotics. A throat culture should be performed on all patients presenting with the complaint of "sore throat" in order to determine the causative organism. Secondary prevention involves preventing the recurrence of streptococcal infections after rheumatic heart disease has occurred. Antibiotics are administered prophylactically on a regular basis throughout the patient's life.

While rheumatic fever has been brought under control in the United States, it has continued to be major public health problem in the world, especially in developing countries. There has been a documented decline in the incidence and severity of rheumatic fever in the United States since 1921. A fourfold increase in this decline has occurred since the advent of antibiotics in the mid-1940s (Massell et al., 1988). The decline before antibiotic treatment and prevention was most probably related to demographic factors reflecting a generally improved standard of living and reduced population density with less crowded living conditions. This overall decline in the incidence of rheumatic fever has occurred without a concomitant decrease in the incidence of group A streptococcal throat infection.

Several outbreaks of rheumatic fever in the United States have been reported since 1985. These outbreaks have not been associated with a concomitant overall increase in group A streptococcal infection. The fact that the incidence of rheumatic fever can change while the relative incidence of group A streptococcal infection does not indicates that some change in the *Streptococcus* organism is responsible for the changes in virulence and rheumatogenicity. In fact, research has demonstrated that the rheumatogenicity of the streptococci appears to depend on the presence of a hyaluronic acid capsule and M protein. Penicillin causes the loss of such a capsule and a decrease in the M protein content. Speculation about the resurgence of rheumatic fever in the United States is that an attitude of complacency about culturing and treating streptococcal throat infection had developed with its near eradication. It is postulated that such complacency may have led to a decrease in the use of penicillin that subsequently allowed the reemergence of a rheumatogenic strain of encapsulated, M protein–laden streptococcal organism and the person to person spread of the organism (Massell et al., 1988).

REVIEW OF NORMAL PERFUSION: BLOOD VESSEL FUNCTION, DYNAMICS, AND REGULATION

Perfusion requires that an intact vessel system be functioning for blood to be carried to the various body organs and tissues. The vascular system is a series of distensible conduits that can be subdivided into arterial, venous, and capillary components. Large-diameter arteries such as the aorta and its main branches have a high elastic fiber content, which allows them to accommodate cardiac stroke volume and convert the intermittent flow of blood to a more even, steady flow. These vessels are often called *Windkessel* vessels after the air compression chambers on old-fashioned, hand-operated fire engines. They are distensible, thus allowing them to accommodate large volumes of blood. This distensibility along with the high resistance offered by the terminal arterioles constitutes a *hydraulic filtering* system, which converts intermittent blood flow to a continuous blood flow to the capillaries. Blood flow during systole is the result of cardiac contraction. Blood flow during diastole is the result of the elastic recoil of the arteries as they discharge the blood that had caused their distension during systole (Fig. 17-15). Reduced distensibility of the arteries results in less efficient hydraulic filtering, reduced capillary blood flow during diastole, and increased cardiac work load.

The nutrient arteries arise from the aorta and its main branches, forming parallel systems that supply various organs and vascular beds (Fig. 17-16). The vascular tone of the small arteries and arterioles can be altered to increase or decrease their diameter and hence resistance to blood flow. For this reason these vessels are called *resistance vessels;* they regulate volume and pressure in the arterial system and blood flow to the capillary bed. According to Poiseuille's law, vascular resistance varies inversely with the fourth power of the radius, therefore seemingly minor changes in the diameter of these vessels can have profound effects on blood pressure.

Capillaries are the *exchange vessels*. Capillary distribution varies among the different types of tissues present in the body. Metabolically active tissue such as skeletal tissue will have a relatively greater concentration of capillaries than does metabolically inactive tissue such as cartilage. The exchange of nutrients and oxygen between the blood and tissues occurs in the capillary bed. Some capillary beds have arteriovenous connections that allow blood to pass directly between the arterial and venous systems. This mechanism allows heat exchange from these vessels. Capillary blood flow throughout the body is not uniform. True capillaries have no smooth muscle tissue. Changes in capillary diameter are passive and caused by changes in precapillary and postcapillary resistance. Capillary flow is under neural as well as local and humoral control. The arterioles and precapillary sphincters are sympathetically innervated and respond to sympathetic stimulation. Local factors such as pH, oxygen, and reduction of available nutrients also affect local blood flow. Humoral control refers to the effect various body substances, hormones, ions, and so on have on local blood flow. *Vasomotion*, rhythmic constriction and relaxation of the precapillary sphincters, results in an intermittent pulsatile flow of blood through the capillaries.

The venules are formed as the capillary network coalesces. The venules are considered exchange vessels because it is felt that there is exchange across the venule wall. The venules converge to form veins of progressively larger diameters. Veins have valves to prevent reflux, and the action of the muscles exerts a milking action to help promote venous return. The veins are referred to as *capacitance vessels* because approximately 75% of the total blood volume can be stored within them.

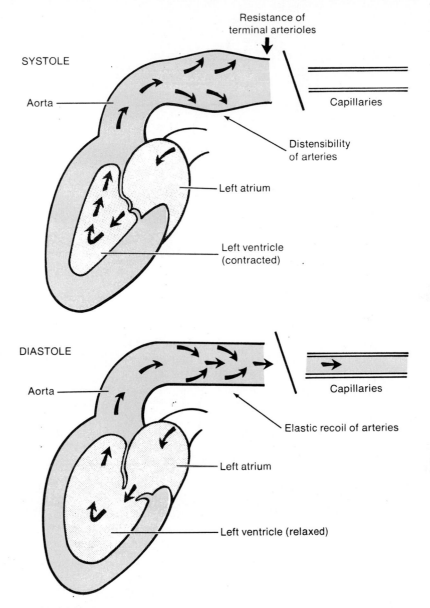

Fig. 17-15. Hydraulic filtering, which converts intermittent blood flow to a more steady, constant flow to capillaries.

Muscular tissue in the venules and small veins, which is innervated by sympathetic fibers, can, through constriction, cause the return the large amounts of "stored" blood to the circulating blood volume.

Arterial blood pressure is a measure of the force that is exerted by the blood against the artery wall. Blood pressure (BP) is dependent on the cardiac output (CO), or volume, and the peripheral resis-

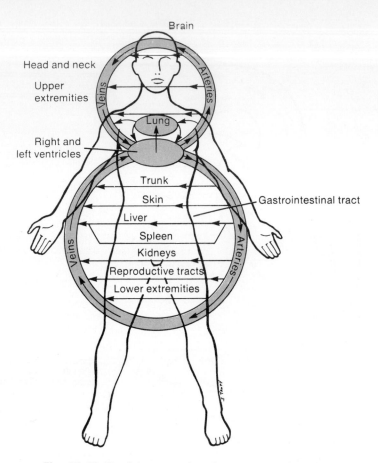

Fig. 17-16. Parallel system of nutrient artery supply routes.

tance (PR). This relationship is summarized by the following equation:

$$BP = CO \times PR$$

From this equation it is apparent that arterial pressure will increase if either cardiac output or peripheral resistance increases without a complementary decrease in the other factor or that pressure will fall if either CO or PR is reduced without a complementary increase in the other factor. A change in one factor necessitates a change in the other to maintain the steady state. Normally the physiologic determi-

nants of cardiac output and peripheral resistance are continually being adjusted via a variety of physiologic mechanisms to maintain a fairly constant arterial pressure despite constantly changing body conditions (Fig. 17-17).

The physiologic determinants of cardiac output have already been discussed (see also Fig. 17-2). It must be pointed out that blood volume (which affects cardiac output) is under renal and hormonal control. Peripheral resistance is determined by local conditions in the tissues, sympathetic nervous system activity, and various hu-

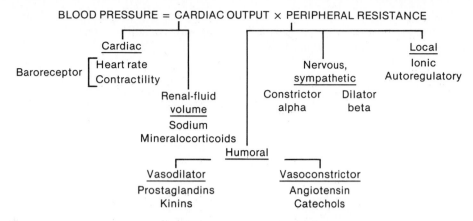

Fig. 17-17. Some of the factors involved in the control of blood pressure that affect the basic equation: Blood pressure = Cardiac output × Peripheral resistance. Catechols = catecholamines. (From Kaplan, NM: Systemic hypertension: mechanisms and diagnosis. In Braunwald, E, Editor: Heart disease: a textbook of cardiovascular medicine, ed. 3, Philadelphia, 1988, WB Saunders Co.)

moral substances. Of importance to local control is autoregulation, which is a property of the resistance vessels that causes vasoconstriction when local blood flow exceeds the requirements of the tissue. Various humoral and hormonal substances have local vasoactive properties as well. Vasoconstricting substances include angiotensin II and the catecholamines; vasodilating substances include histamine, certain prostaglandins, and kinins, among others.

Sympathetic control is the most important single factor related to peripheral resistance. Sympathetic control of peripheral resistance is mediated through baroreceptor reflexes, which constitute a negative feedback mechanism. The blood vessels are in a state of constant partial contraction as a result of the continued transmission of vasoconstrictor impulses from the vasomotor center. This is referred to as *vasomotor tone*. The baroreceptor cells in the carotid and aortic sinuses are sensitive to stretch and send inhibitory impulses to the vasomotor center when stimulated by increased pressure. As a re-

sult, vasodilation occurs. In addition, impulses are sent via the vagus nerve to slow the rate and decrease the contractility of the heart, resulting in decreased cardiac output. As peripheral resistance decreases and cardiac output drops, arterial pressure will also be reduced.

The baroreceptors become relatively inactive in the presence of normal or reduced arterial pressure. Baroreceptors will no longer be stretched, and the inhibitory effect on the vasomotor center is decreased. This allows vasomotor activity to increase, and vasoconstriction results. Heart rate will also increase as a result of decreased stimulation of the cardioinhibitory center and decreased inhibition of the cardioaccelerator center. As peripheral resistance and cardiac output increase, arterial pressure rises. Sympathetic stimulation also causes the adrenal medulla to secrete epinephrine and norepinephrine into the general circulation.

The response of the local vessel systems is determined by the presence of adrenoceptors, or target sites, on the cell membrane. Activation of alpha receptor sites results in vasoconstriction, and activation of beta receptor sites results in vasodilation. Norepinephrine binds with alpha sites, while epinephrine can bind with both alpha and beta receptors. Alpha receptors predominate in the precapillary sphincters of most of the arterioles. Beta receptors predominate in the heart, coronary arteries, brain, and liver. When epinephrine and norepinephrine are secreted, blood is shunted preferentially from the vascular beds where alpha receptors and vasoconstriction predominate to those vascular beds with both alpha and beta receptors and where vasodilation occurs. The parasympathetic system promotes vasodilation, although the mechanism for this action is unclear at this time. The neurotransmitter is acetylcholine, which by itself has a vasodilatory effect.

ALTERED TISSUE PERFUSION

Altered tissue perfusion is defined as the state in which there is a decrease in nutrition and oxygenation at the cellular level due to a deficit in capillary blood supply (NANDA). Alterations in tissue perfusion can occur within specific organ systems (e.g., heart or brain) or, as in the case of shock, throughout the general circulation. Altered tissue perfusion can be a response to decreased cardiac output. In this situation the amount of blood being pumped from the heart to the tissues is decreased. Altered tissue perfusion can also be the result of disruption of the flow of blood through the vessels to the tissues. Blood flow through a vessel depends on the pressure gradient by which it is propelled, the lumen size (radius) and patency, and the length of the vessel through which it is passing, as well as the viscosity of the blood (Poiseuille's law). The pathophysiologic mechanisms of altered pressure and lumen size and patency of the blood vessels have the capacity to disrupt blood flow and, therefore, perfusion of the tissues and will be discussed in the following section.

The response to altered perfusion is ischemia and infarction of the affected tissue. A state of tissue ischemia is said to exist when the oxygen and substrate requirements of the tissue exceed the supply being delivered to and utilized by the cells. West (1986) points out that ischemia represents the reversible cell injury of such an imbalance. Prolonged ischemia leads to tissue hypoxia that, if unrelieved, ultimately causes cell death and necrosis (infarction). The effects of hypoxia are discussed in detail in Chapter 16 and are summarized in Fig. 17-18. Ischemia, as a cause of hypoxia, is different from other causes (see p. 568) because, in addition to a lack of oxygen at the tissue level, impairment of substrate delivery and metabolite removal also occurs. Cell damage occurs not only as a result of hypoxia but also as a result of the buildup of metabolic products and the loss of substrates even for anaerobic energy production.

The tissue response to ischemia depends on the organ system that is affected. For example, certain physiologic characteristics of the mesenteric circulation make it more susceptible to ischemic damage when blood flow is reduced because of a preexisting cardiovascular condition or circulatory problem. For this reason mesenteric ischemic disease is most frequently seen in aged patients with preexisting cardiovascular disease.

In the small vessels of the villi there is a countercurrent exchange mechanism, which allows shunting of oxygen from arteriole to venule. Normally the distal villi do not experience significant oxygen deprivation. However, when mesenteric blood flow is reduced, tissue hypoxia may be-

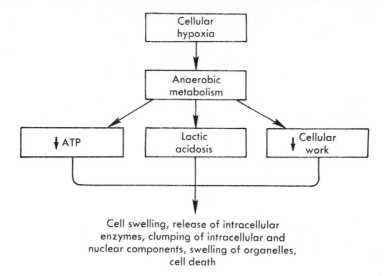

Fig. 17-18. Results of prolonged cellular hypoxia.
(From Groer, M: Physiology and pathophysiology of the body fluids, St Louis, 1981, The CV Mosby Co.)

come marked with subsequent necrosis of the mucosal villous tips. Blood viscosity increases, and microthrombi develop because of the reduced blood flow. In response to hypotension, sympathetic activity increases and the renin-angiotensin system is activated. This causes the release of vasoactive substances such as norepinephrine, dopamine, angiotensin II, and vasopressin, all of which act to constrict the precapillary sphincters in the mesenteric circulation. Resistance to blood flow is further increased as the critical closing pressure in the small vessels is reached. Necrosis of the bowel leads to acute obstruction and allows the release of toxic substances into the general circulation, and toxemia and death rapidly ensue. Fig. 17-19 illustrates the sequence of events just described. Cardiac glycoside drugs may contribute to this condition because of their tendency to constrict the mesenteric arterioles.

Ischemic injury has been extensively studied in the brain, heart and kidneys.

The response to ischemia of the different vital organ systems has been found to vary with the brain appearing to be the most sensitive. This is illustrated in the following discussion of the disease model of cardiac arrest and the postresuscitation syndrome.

Disease model: cardiac arrest and postresuscitation syndrome. All blood flow to the vital organs will stop in the event that a cardiac arrest occurs. In this situation the heart either stops contracting altogether or the contractions are so weak and erratic (as in the case of ventricular fibrillation) that there is no effective cardiac output. When cerebral perfusion stops, the brain uses its remaining oxygen supply within 10 seconds and its glucose supply within 4 minutes (Anderson, 1988). The duration of cerebral ischemia is considered one of the determining factors in resuscitation outcome; that is, if cardiopulmonary resuscitation (CPR) is started very quickly and vital functions are able to be restored within 30 minutes, there is a better

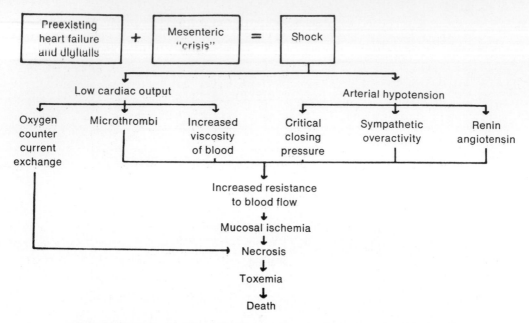

Fig. 17-19. Pathophysiologic mechanisms in nonocclusive mesenteric ischemia.
(From Frohlich, E.D.: Pathophysiology, ed. 2, Philadelphia, 1976, J.B. Lippincott Co.)

chance of recovery without neurologic sequelae because cerebral blood flow decreases and intracranial pressure increases as CPR is continued. Anderson (1988) reports that approximately 50% of resuscitated patients subsequently die of neurologic sequelae and 20% of resuscitated patients sustain chronic neurologic deficits.

The postresuscitation syndrome is the failure of organ systems following "successful" resuscitation or one in which hemodynamic stability of the patient has been achieved. The pathogenesis of this syndrome is related to the pathophysiology of reperfusion following a period of reduced or nonexistent blood flow.

When blood flow stops, hypoxia develops and all of the effects of hypoxia that were described in Chapter 16 occur. In addition to the effects of hypoxia, there will be stagnation of blood in the circulation.

This will lead to increasing viscosity, sludging, aggregation of red blood cells, and the formation of microthrombi as the coagulation pathway is activated (see Chapter 3). This causes occlusion and contributes to preventing reperfusion. The release of prostaglandins, thromboxane, and other local mediators of vasoconstriction may also cause occlusion by causing spasm and vasoconstriction so extreme as to prevent reperfusion (West, 1986). The "no-reflow" phenomenon, in which reperfusion occurs in a nonuniform manner throughout tissue, can also be attributed to swollen cells impinging on the vasculature and preventing flow (Pasternak et al., 1988).

Following the reestablishment of circulation, there is a short period in which the cerebral tissue is hyperfused and an inappropriate hypermetabolic state exists. This is followed by a period of hypoperfusion.

It is at this point that the most deleterious effects of reperfusion occur. Calcium moves into the cell as the membrane mechanisms that maintain normal intracellular and extracellular calcium concentrations break down due to the lack of ATP. Reperfusion injury due to an intracellular shift of calcium has been found to occur in the heart and kidneys as well as the brain. The loss of calcium from the extracellular space and the breakdown of membrane pump functions will allow further disruption of membrane permeability and increased cell swelling. Calcium overloading in vascular tissue causes activation of the calcium-calmodulin complex and the actin-myosin contractile process, which causes vasospasm and increased vascular resistance in the affected organs. This is hypothesized to be a possible initiating event in the development of acute tubular necrosis due to ischemia (Schrier and Conger, 1986) (see Chapter 20). Dysrhythmias and sustained contracture of the myocardium (stone heart) can also result.

Membrane-bound phospholipases are also activated by calcium overloading and cause the liberation of free fatty acids, which then serve as substrates for the formation of prostaglandins and leukotrienes, vasoactive compounds that can perpetuate tissue damage. Oxygen-derived free radical formation is enhanced, further contributing to cell injury. Studies on animals have shown that in reperfused, postischemic brain tissue free radical formation is potentiated by the presence of an increased amount of delocalized iron, which serves as a catalyst for lipid peroxidation (Anderson, 1988) (Fig. 17-20).

Some of these findings point toward possible new modes of therapy following resuscitation. For example, pharmacologic agents that block calcium channels may exert a protective effect on tissue if administered prophylactically. Hemodilution with a plasma volume expander when reperfusion is established may help minimize the effect of vascular sludging. This remains unproven, as does the possibility that the use of agents which scavenge free oxygen radicals and limit leukocyte activation may provide some protection from the effects of such tissue damage mediators.

Ischemia can be a response to other pathophysiologic processes besides altered tissue perfusion. For example, the demand for oxygen and nutrients will exceed the supply in conditions where the tissue requirements are increased beyond the ability of the body to meet those requirements. The potential for tissues to become ischemic is enhanced in conditions in which the metabolic rate is increased or there is a defect in the ability of the tissues to use the substances being delivered. Processes other than altered tissue perfusion that can lead to ischemia are discussed elsewhere in this book. The focus of this section is on altered tissue perfusion due to disrupted blood flow.

Tissue perfusion can be altered by a variety of mechanisms in any given organ system. The same response, ischemia, is elicited, and the clinical manifestations will be similar. The treatment will vary, however, depending on the cause. An example is the clinical entity known as *ischemic heart disease.*

Disease model: ischemic heart disease. Factors that determine myocardial oxygen consumption include the cardiac rate, left-sided ventricular wall tension, and the contractile state of the myocardial fibers. Increases in any of these factors have the effect of increasing myocardial oxygen consumption (Weber et al., 1977). Factors that determine the supply of oxygen to the

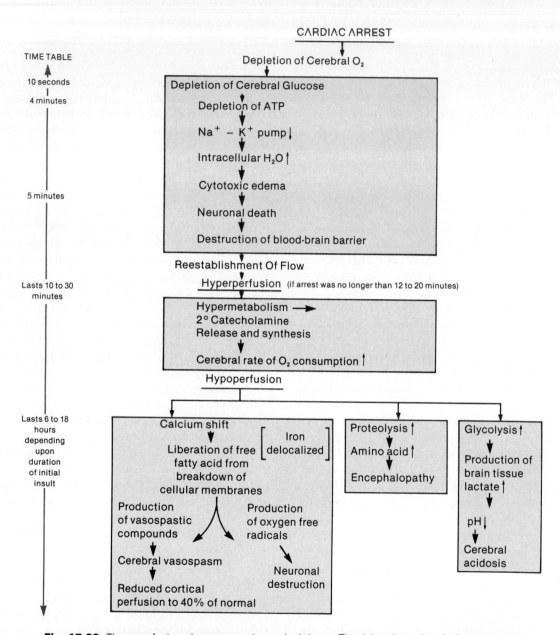

Fig. 17-20. The reperfusion phenomenon in cerebral tissue. The deleterious chemical processes in the hypoperfusion phase actually begin as soon as blood flow is reestablished.

(From Anderson, FD: Issues in the postresuscitation period, Crit Care Nurs O 10(4)51-61, 1988; adapted from Henneman, EA: Brain resuscitation, *Heart Lung* 15(1):3-11, 1986 From Anderson, 1988.)

myocardium include the oxygen content of the blood, coronary blood flow, and coronary vascular resistance, the latter two factors being the most important. Oxygen extraction in myocardial tissue is extremely efficient, and increased coronary blood flow is the only mechanism that can increase oxygen delivery to the myocardium. The distribution of the blood flow is as important as the total flow in providing oxygen and nutrients to the myocardium. Any disease state that alters coronary vascular resistance, total flow, or the distribution of flow has the potential for altering the perfusion of the myocardial tissue.

The most commonly cited cause of altered myocardial tissue perfusion is occlusion of a coronary artery by an atherosclerotic plaque. The pathogenesis of atherosclerosis is discussed later in this chapter. Other mechanisms suspected of causing coronary artery occlusion and thereby altering myocardial tissue perfusion include spasm of the coronary arteries and the formation of fibrin or platelet thrombi. The latter mechanism has been postulated to arise from two possible processes acting either individually or in combination. These processes include platelet adherence to normal or diseased vascular walls and the development of interactive attractive forces between platelets. Besides directly reducing blood flow, it is now hypothesized that spasm may produce intimal damage that can serve as a point of initiation of a thrombotic process. Conversely, spasm may be due to the presence of a vasoconstricting substance, thromboxane A_2, which is released by aggregating platelets at the site of a thrombosis (Pasternak et al., 1988). Illustrated in Fig. 17-21 are the postulated interactions of spasm, thrombosis, and platelet aggregation in causing coronary artery occlusion. These mechanisms usually involve the large coronary arteries; however, small vessel or arteriolar disease may also affect the coronary circulation. The microangiopathy of diabetes mellitus illustrates this mechanism.

As muscle mass increases or hypertrophies in pathologic conditions, the blood supply to it does not increase to a comparable degree. For this reason hypertrophied myocardial tissue lacks the necessary distribution of vessels to supply blood in an amount sufficient to prevent ischemia. This is especially true for conditions in which myocardial oxygen demand is increased. Since cardiac hypertrophy occurs in pathologic conditions such as congestive heart failure and hypertensive vascular disease in which the work load of the heart and therefore the myocardial oxygen demand is chronically increased, the potential for development of myocardial ischemia in these conditions is great.

No matter what the causative mechanism, the clinical manifestations of ischemic heart disease may include chest pain, myocardial infarction, myocardial failure, arrhythmias, and even sudden death. Experimental data suggest that some individuals may suffer from asymptomatic myocardial ischemia (Iskandrian, et al., 1981). Underlying these manifestations is cellular hypoxia, which can be detected in the blood of the coronary sinus as a concentration of lactate exceeding that of the arterial blood. Anginal pain is thought to be caused by neural stimulation by the products of anaerobic metabolism. Arrhythmias reflect cellular dysfunction in the highly oxygen dependent conduction tissue. Depression of the S-T segment on the electrocardiogram is considered to be a classic response to ischemia and results from the altered repolarization of cells.

Contraction of the ischemic myocardial muscle weakens and eventually fails be-

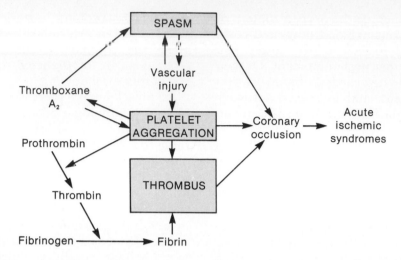

Fig. 17-21. The interrelationship of dynamic mechanisms that may cause or contribute to the clinical presentation of acute ischemic syndromes.

(From Epstein, SE and Palmeri, ST: Mechanisms contributing to precipitation of unstable angina and myocardial infarction: implications regarding therapy, Am J Cardiol 54:1245, 1984.)

cause of lack of ATP for energy and failure of Ca^{++} transport for activation of muscle myosin. Impairment of ventricular function sets up a feedback loop, which perpetuates the ischemia. Left-sided ventricular dysfunction creates a vicious cycle that perpetuates ischemia via three distinct mechanisms, one of which increases myocardial oxygen consumption while the other two act to reduce coronary flow. As the ventricle fails, it dilates, which increases wall tension and thus oxygen consumption, aggravating the ischemic condition. Ventricular dysfunction will lower cardiac output and arterial pressure, thus decreasing coronary perfusion and further aggravating the ischemic condition. The increase in end-diastolic pressure that accompanies ventricular failure also reduces blood flow in the endocardium during diastole, and this tissue becomes extremely susceptible to the effects of ischemia. Shown in Fig. 17-22 are the changes that occur in left ventricular function following myocardial infarction.

Treatment depends on the underlying cause of the ischemia as well as the degree of ischemia present. Treatment of myocardial infarction is different from that of angina pectoris. Vasodilating drugs are used to increase coronary blood flow. Anticoagulant therapy can be used to prevent thrombus formation. An occlusion can be treated by percutaneous transluminal coronary angioplasty, coronary artery bypass graft surgery, or administration of thrombolytic agents such as streptokinase or tissue plasminogen activator. Pharmacologic agents that reduce afterload can be used to reduce the work load of the heart and bring demand in line with the supply of blood. The treatment rationale for the various causes of altered myocardial tissue perfusion is discussed later in this chapter.

Altered vessel pressure

When compensatory mechanisms cannot maintain blood pressure within a normal range, the result may be a persistent increase in blood pressure, *hypertension*, or a

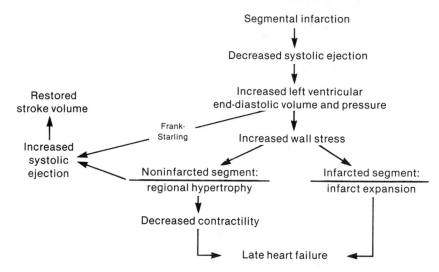

Fig. 17-22. Hypothesis proposed to account for the mechanisms of left ventricular remodeling. (From McKay, RG, et al: Left ventricular remodeling after myocardial infarction: a corollary to infarct expansion. Circulation 74:693, 1986. By permission of the American Heart Association.)

persistent decrease in blood pressure, *hypotension*. Because blood pressure varies among individuals, it is difficult to define a "normal" blood pressure for any group of persons. Also, because of constantly changing conditions to which the body is subjected, blood pressure varies within an individual on a minute-to-minute basis, but a range of the individual's usual pressure can be determined.

Hypotension. Many persons have a chronically low blood pressure, which for them is physiologic. In fact, such a condition may be protective in that there is a reduced work load on the cardiovascular system. Sudden hypotension in a person who does not normally experience it may arise from a variety of pathologic conditions that reduce either cardiac output or total peripheral resistance. Hypotension as a result of reduced cardiac output may be caused by aberrations of the cardiac rate and rhythm, impaired ventricular function, hypovolemia (reduced preload), or

obstruction to flow (increased afterload). Hypotension as a result of diminished peripheral resistance may be caused by neurologic or vascular dysfunction. In the former, sympathetic activity is altered or diminished; in the latter, the vascular response to either local metabolic factors or to sympathetic activity is altered. Hypotension may also be the result of impairment of mechanical factors that normally limit pooling of blood in the veins. Depending on the severity of the hypotension, the patient may experience symptoms of dizziness, presyncope or faintness (sudden weakness and the inability to stand, visual disturbances, and the feeling of impending loss of consciousness) and syncope, or actual loss of consciousness accompanied by pallor and diaphoresis. Loss of consciousness is due to the temporary disruption of cerebral tissue perfusion (Sobel and Roberts, 1988).

Orthostatic or *postural hypotension* is the most commonly experienced episodic type of hypotension. In this condition hypotension occurs when an individual changes from the supine to the upright position. In the resting, supine position, sympathetic discharge to the vasculature is diminished. Compounding this state, venous blood pools in the lower extremities as the individual stands up. In the normal person, compensation for these events occurs rather quickly and there is only a minor, transient decrease in blood pressure. In the person experiencing orthostatic hypotension, such compensation does not readily occur and the reduction in blood pressure is more severe and prolonged and may cause symptoms.

In most of the conditions with which orthostatic hypotension is associated, the ability of the sympathetic system to respond with increased vasoconstriction is impaired. These conditions include chronic idiopathic orthostatic hypotension (a degenerative disorder of the central nervous system in which heart rate is also accelerated), the use of antihypertensive drugs, surgically induced sympathectomy, and a variety of disorders that affect the nervous system and cause secondary orthostatic hypotension (for example, alcoholism, diabetes mellitus, Parkinson's disease, and uremia). In some conditions associated with orthostatic hypotension, including cardiovascular deconditioning such as occurs with prolonged immobility (see Chapter 14), the defect is a reduced ability to respond to sympathetic stimulation. In some conditions the defect is a reduction in cardiac output resulting from decreased venous return. Vein disease that causes pooling of blood in the lower extremities is one example. Another is the supine hypotensive syndrome of pregnancy in which pressure on the inferior vena cava can serve as an obstruction to venous return. Severe, prolonged hypotension can result in *shock*, or circulatory failure or collapse.

Disease model: circulatory failure. Circulatory failure, or *shock*, is a pathophysiologic state in which tissue perfusion is totally inadequate to meet the oxygen or nutritional needs of the cells. Weil et al. (1988) refer to it as failure of tissue perfusion. Shock has been described as "a momentary pause in the act of death" (Warren, 1895). Shock, like cardiac failure, is not a disease entity in itself but a response to some assault or injury the body has experienced. In fact, much of the knowledge about the pathophysiology and treatment of shock has come from observations made on injured soldiers in World Wars I and II (Billhardt and Rosenbush, 1986). No matter what the initiating event, the cause of death in irreversible shock is microcirculatory failure and the subsequent depression of cellular metabolism manifested by disruption of vital organ function.

Etiology. Common to all forms of shock is the insufficient flow of oxygenated and nutrient-enriched blood to the vital organs due to a decrease in cardiac output, maldistribution of blood, or both. Any condition that reduces the heart's ability to pump effectively or decreases venous return has the potential of causing shock. Factors that reduce the heart's ability to pump effectively are discussed in a previous section of this chapter. Factors that decrease venous return include decreased blood volume (hypovolemia), vasomotor dysfunction, and obstruction to the flow of blood. A classification of shock according to the pathophysiologic event that evokes it is presented in Table 17-5. The difference is not in terms of the pathophysiologic response (which is the same in all types of shock) but in terms of etiology. The etiologic factors must be understood if shock is to be prevented or identified in the early stages when recovery is still possible.

Table 17-5.   Classification of shock states

Type of shock	Primary mechanism	Clinical causes

Hypovolemic	Volume loss	Exogenous
		    Blood loss due to hemorrhage
		    Plasma loss due to burn or inflammation
		    Fluid and electrolyte loss due to vomiting, diarrhea, dehydration, osmolal diuresis (diabetes)
		Endogenous
		    Extravasation due to inflammation, trauma, tourniquet, anaphylaxis, snake venom, and adrenergic stimulation (pheochromocytoma)

Cardiogenic	Pump failure	Myocardial infarction Other causes Cardiac arrhythmias Intracardiac obstruction, including valvular stenosis Heart failure
Distributive (vasomotor dysfunction)		
High or normal resistance	Expanded venous capacitance (pooling)	Hypodynamic septic shock due to gram-negative enteric bacillemia Autonomic blockade, spinal shock Tranquilizer, sedative, narcotic overdose
Low resistance	Arteriovenous shunting	Pneumonia, peritonitis, abscess, reactive hyperemia
Obstructive	Extracardiac obstruction of main channel of blood flow	Vena caval obstruction (supine hypotensive syndrome) Pericarditis (tamponade) Pulmonary embolism Dissecting aneurysm or compression of aorta

From Weil MH, von Planta M, and Rackow EC: Acute circulatory failure (shock). In Braunwald, E, editor: Heart disease: A textbook of cardiovascular medicine. Philadelphia, ed. 3, 1988, W.B. Saunders Co.

Hypovolemia, or a decrease in the volume of the intravascular compartment, is the most common cause of diminished systemic blood flow (Weil et al., 1988) and *hypovolemic shock* is the most common form of shock seen clinically (Billhardt and Rosenbush, 1986). Obviously, a decrease in fluid volume leads to diminished venous return, decreased left ventricular filling pressure, reduced cardiac output, and poor tissue perfusion. Volume loss can be the result of either (1) excessive bleeding or hemorrhage, where all the components of the blood are lost, or (2) the loss of plasma only. Hemorrhage can occur as a result of trauma (accidental or surgical), coagulation disorders, delivery of a baby, or carcinoma. When the exception of intracranial bleeding, internal bleeding, or bleeding into a body cavity, can also lead to hypovolemic shock. (The amount of blood loss into the cranium is limited because of the relatively small, fixed, unexpandable size of the cranium.) Crushing injuries may also result in hypovolemic shock. When the pressure is removed, whole blood and plasma leak into the interstitial space as a result of the capillary endothelial damage and the subsequent change in capillary permeability that occurs. Other conditions that may ultimately lead to hypovolemic shock include those characterized by gastrointestinal or renal losses of sodium and water and by altered compartmental distribution (third-space syndromes). Significant fluid and electrolyte losses can also be caused by large exudative skin lesions and burns. These conditions are discussed in Chapter 18. Anaphylactic shock is now viewed as a form of hypovolemic shock due to the massive extravasation of plasma, which occurs in response to an acute hypersensitivity reaction (see Chapter 2) (Weil et al., 1988).

Relative hypovolemia occurs in conditions in which venous return is decreased, although actual total blood volume is not. This is the case for disorders that fall into the category of distributive shock. Vasomotor dysfunction alters the distribution of blood flow without a decrease in the absolute blood volume or impairment of cardiac function. The effective circulating volume is reduced, however, by either increased venous capacitance or shunting. The condition that has traditionally been referred to as *neurogenic shock* falls within this category. Decreased vasomotor tone allows venous pooling of blood, which reduces venous return and, subsequently, cardiac output and tissue perfusion. The reduction in vasomotor tone can occur at the level of the vasomotor center or at the level of the blood vessels themselves. The predisposition to develop this form of shock is enhanced in conditions in which vasomotor tone is reduced or lost. Examples include spinal anesthesia, spinal cord injury, direct damage to the vasomotor center of the medulla or altered function of the vasomotor center in response to low blood glucose levels (insulin shock), severe pain, or the action of tranquilizer, narcotic, or sedative drugs.

Another type of shock now considered to be a form of distributive shock is *septic shock*, which is sometimes also referred to as endotoxic shock. The hyperdynamic state of septic shock is thought to be characterized by low arterial resistance and shunting, while in the more advanced hypodynamic state of gram-negative sepsis with shock there is increased arterial resistance and venous capacity (Weil et al., 1988).

Septic shock is a response to widespread, overwhelming infection. Infections from gram-positive organisms such as staphylococci, streptococci, and pneumococci, or clostridia, or fungi cause approximately one third of the cases of septic shock. The syndrome known as toxic shock syndrome is caused by *Staphylococcus aureus* and presents with a characteristic rash in addition to all the other manifestations of septic shock. The mortality in cases of septic shock as a sequela to infections caused by the gram-positive organisms is approximately 50%.

The cause of the remaining two thirds of cases of septic shock is infection by gram-negative organisms and the enteric coli are responsible for the majority of gram-negative infections that result in septic shock. The mortality in cases of septic shock occurring with infections caused by gram-negative organisms is estimated to range between 25% and 90% (Weil et al., 1988). The incidence of gram-negative sepsis has increased. This is possibly related to the widespread and sometimes indiscriminate use of antibiotic therapy, leading to the development of ever-increasing numbers of virulent, antibiotic-resistant organisms.

Patients at risk for the development of septic shock include persons with indwelling catheters, peritonitis, burns, chronic debilitating disease, or postpartum infection. Patients who have had gastrointestinal or genitourinary tract surgery or a septic abortion, as well as those patients on immunosuppressant therapy or with defects in the function of the immune system, are also at risk.

At the present time, two theories have been postulated for the inception of septic shock. One theory implicates the toxins released from the bacteria, and the other implicates the bacteria themselves as the causative factor. Present in the cell wall of all gram-negative bacteria is endotoxin lipopolysaccharide, which is released when cells die. Experimental studies with animals have demonstrated that administration of this substance results in manifestations similar to those seen in bacteremic, or septic, shock. The value of these studies is questionable, however, because septic shock can also result from infection with gram-positive organisms, which do not contain endotoxin. Through these studies gram-negative bacteria and endotoxin have been shown to bind and activate Hageman factor, which in turn activates the fibrinolytic, clotting, complement, and kinin-generating pathways.

Obstructive shock results when the flow of blood in the great vessels is impeded by mechanical factors. Venous return may be reduced with vena cava constriction or obstruction, cardiac filling and contraction may be impaired with constriction of the heart muscle, or cardiac emptying may be impeded by obstruction in the pulmonary vasculature or aorta. Compression of the vena cava causes an immediate reduction in venous return to the heart. Compression of the vena cava can occur in response to increased thoracic or abdominal pressure. One example is the supine hypotensive syndrome in which the pregnant uterus can exert enough pressure on the vena cava to obstruct venous return when a pregnant patient is in the supine position. Cardiac tamponade is an acute restriction

of the movement of the heart because of fluid or tissue in the pericardial space. Causes include infection (pericarditis), bleeding, trauma, or tumor. Pulmonary embolism, constriction of the aorta, and aortic aneurysm can all obstruct the flow of blood from the heart.

Cardiogenic shock, or low output syndrome, occurs when cardiac function is severely compromised, and cardiac output becomes extremely low. Cardiogenic shock can result from extensive myocardial damage caused by infarction or open heart surgery, as a sequela to heart failure, as a result of prolonged arrhythmias, papillary muscle dysfunction or rupture, septal perforation, pulmonary embolism, or myocardial rupture. The extent of myocardial damage can be correlated with the incidence of cardiogenic shock after myocardial infarction. Cardiogenic shock is more likely to be a complication of myocardial infarction when 40% or more of the myocardium is damaged (Weil et al., 1988). The mortality of patients developing cardiogenic shock continues to be high (approximately 80%) despite new methods of treatment. It is considered a grave complication of myocardial infarction.

It is not known whether cardiogenic shock is related to heart failure or whether they are two entirely different clinical entities. However, therapy to correct heart failure is ineffective in the treatment of cardiogenic shock, indicating that they are different entities.

Pathophysiologic mechanisms and clinical manifestations. As a result of diminished cardiac output, arterial pressure falls. This hypotension is the most immediate antecedent of hypovolemic, cardiogenic, and neurogenic shock. In response to the generalized arterial hypotension, various negative feedback control mechanisms come into play to return arterial pressure and tissue perfusion to normal limits.

Sympathetic stimulation through baroreceptor reflexes provides immediate compensation and results in tachycardia, vasoconstriction, redistribution of blood flow, and increased cardiac contractility. Vasoconstriction of the capacitance vessels results in increased venous return as the blood from these vessels is added to the circulating blood volume. Arteriolar constriction increases total peripheral resistance to help raise arterial pressure but does not occur uniformly in all tissues. Blood flow is shifted to those organ systems in which arteriolar constriction is minimal, such as the heart and brain. Arteriolar constriction is very great in the peripheral tissues and is manifested by cool, pale skin as blood flow is diverted from those areas because of the high resistance.

The increased rate and force of cardiac contraction improves cardiac output. The augmented contractile force results in more complete cardiac emptying, reducing end-systolic ventricular volume. The mobilization of this blood and that previously stored in the capacitance vessels before their constriction is called *autotransfusion* or *intravascular fluid mobilization*.

There is a reduction in capillary filtration pressure as a result of both the decreased arterial pressure and the subsequent constriction of the resistance vessels. Because some arterioles constrict more than venules, the ratio between precapillary and postcapillary resistance increases. As a result of these changes in capillary dynamics there is a net movement of fluid from the interstitial space into the vascular compartment, further augmenting venous return and subsequently cardiac output. This movement of fluid is limited because of the dilution of the plasma proteins, which reduces plasma oncotic pressure. This phenomenon is termed *autoinfusion* or *extravascular fluid mobilization*.

Urine output is reduced because of the negative effect that reduced arterial pressure and vasoconstriction of the kidney arterioles have on glomerular filtration. The reduction in renal afferent arteriolar pressure activates the renin-angiotensin system previously described, which results in the selective retention of sodium and subsequently water by the kidneys. ADH is also secreted, and the thirst mechanism is stimulated in response to a relative decrease in the size of the extracellular volume. These mechanisms act to restore lost fluid volume.

Most of the clinical manifestations to this point are the result of the sympathetic stimulation that has occurred: rapid, thready pulse; decreased pulse pressure; cool, pale skin; oliguria; and increased sweat gland activity. In the presence of fluid volume deficit the skin turgor will be reduced, features may appear sunken, eyeballs may feel "soft," the mouth will be dry, and there will be extreme thirst. Respiratory activity increases as chemoreceptors are activated. As cerebral perfusion becomes inadequate, changes in mental status such as confusion and restlessness occur.

The mechanisms delineated thus far are negative feedback control mechanisms; that is, the drop in arterial pressure serves to stimulate the compensatory mechanisms by which arterial pressure is restored and maintained. This stage is termed *compensated shock*. If the underlying cause of the shock has not been corrected or if the cause is not self-limiting, continued sympathetic stimulation becomes detrimental to the body. Shock at this point is referred to as *progressive*. The response of the body to poor tissue perfusion becomes one of positive feedback, which sets up a vicious cycle in which cardiac output and tissue perfusion will continually decrease until a point is reached where death becomes inevitable. At this point the shock is said to be *irreversible* or *decompensated*.

Vasoconstriction of the arterioles and venules results in decreased blood flow to and through the microcirculation. The surrounding tissues experience ischemic hypoxia. The pH of the tissue fluid becomes acidotic as the products of metabolism accumulate. As a result of the local stimulation provided by the hypoxia and altered pH, the arterioles dilate. The venules, however, remain constricted. Blood can enter the microcirculation but becomes trapped when the venule constricts. Pressures in the capillary bed are altered so that the net movement of fluid is out of the intravascular compartment and into the interstitial space. Plasma proteins are also lost from the intravascular compartment because the permeability of the capillary membrane is altered due to the adverse conditions in the surrounding tissue. The reduction in the flow of blood enhances sludging (the clumping of red cells, leukocytes, and platelets) and intravascular clot formation. In fact, thrombosis of minute vessels has been postulated as one of the causes of progressive shock. Disseminated intravascular coagulation (DIC) that is the result of activation of the coagulation process (see Chapter 3) is a grave complication of shock.

Cellular metabolism becomes anaerobic, leading to formation of increased quantities of lactic acid in addition to the normally produced quantities of organic acids. As progressively greater amounts of acidotic metabolic products form and accumulate, the buffer systems and other compensatory mechanisms that serve to maintain normal acid-base balance become ineffective. Cellular energy production is progressively depressed, and if shock is not corrected, energy production eventually ceases. The cells are unable to perform even the most vital functions. When cellular function is severely depressed or totally stopped, the organ systems fail.

As the myocardium becomes weaker, cardiac output diminishes even further. Impaired cardiac function during shock states is associated with decreased left ventricular compliance and end-diastolic volume. The oxygen demands of the heart are increased due to increased afterload and adrenergic activity. In addition to the lack of oxygen and energy, myocardial depressant factor (MDF), or myocardial toxic factor (MTF), has a direct depressant effect on the myocadium. This substance is thought to interfere with the function of calcium ions in the excitation-contraction coupling mechanism, and as a result cardiac contractility is reduced. It is thought that pancreatic ischemia causes the release of proteolytic enzymes, which serve to either stimulate the release of the toxic factor or alter the plasma proteins to form a new substance with toxic properties.

Also implicated in the progression of shock are various vasoactive substances, including histamine, serotonin, and bradykinin. The plasma kinins act directly on smooth muscle to cause dilation. The prostaglandins are also being investigated for vasodilatory action.

The progression of septic shock in terms of metabolic effects and decompensation is the same as for all other types of shock. However, since the initiating events are quite different from reduced venous return or reduced cardiac output, a discussion of it at this time is appropriate. Two syndromes related to septic shock have been described. One is characterized by high cardiac output, high central venous pressure, a normal urine output, low peripheral resistance, and warm, dry extremities. This is referred to as the *hyperdynamic* type of septic shock. The other is characterized by low cardiac output, high peripheral resistance, and decreased urine output. This is referred to as the *hypodynamic* type of septic shock.

This differentiation has implications in terms of the potential development and recognition of shock. Patients experiencing hyperdynamic septic shock will *not* exhibit the classic signs of shock: decreased pulse pressure; cold, clammy, cyanotic skin (which may also appear blotchy or mottled); oliguria (possibly even anuria); increased respiratory rate (compensatory response to metabolic acidosis); and a weak, rapid (thready) pulse. As cerebral perfusion is diminished, restlessness, coma, convulsion, or other disturbances of behavior may occur.

Measurement of blood pressure is not always useful in the diagnosis of shock. The initiating hypotension is rapidly corrected via reflex control, and when hypotension becomes clinically detectable, compensation is no longer effective, and shock has become progressive. To more accurately monitor cardiac function, placement of a flow-directed, balloon-tipped catheter (Swan-Ganz) into a branch of the pulmonary artery becomes necessary. Through this catheter the pulmonary pressure can be measured. This parameter is a reflection of left atrial pressure and, in the absence of mitral valve disease, of left ventricular diastolic pressure and thus serves as an indicator of left ventricular function. The monitoring of great toe temperature as an indicator of the adequacy of peripheral perfusion has been advocated. Blood lactate levels provide the best indication of systemic perfusion deficits (Weil et al., 1988; Billhardt and Rosenbush, 1986).

Treatment rationale. The goals of treatment include the following:

1. Correction of the underlying cause
2. Improvement of tissue perfusion
3. Correction of acid-base imbalance
4. Prevention of complications

Correction of the underlying cause in septic shock requires intensive antibiotic therapy; in hypovolemic shock, replacement of the effective circulating volume; in neurogenic shock, restoration of vasomotor tone; and in cardiogenic shock, augmentation of cardiac performance. Cardiac function in cardiogenic shock can sometimes be improved by administration of drugs with positive inotropic and chronotropic actions, as well as drugs to counteract peripheral vasoconstriction to reduce resistance to flow and thus reduce cardiac work load. If these fail, mechanical circulatory assistance becomes necessary by means of insertion of a balloon into the aorta (intraaortic balloon counterpulsation). The intraaortic balloon, as it is called, is alternately inflated and deflated, controlling the capacity of the aorta for blood.

Normally correction of the underlying cause of the shock syndrome will also help to increase perfusion as it takes effect. Immediate pharmacologic intervention often is necessary, as these effects take time. Drugs that promote vasodilation and increased cerebral and renal perfusion (for example, isoproterenol, dobutamine, or dopamine) may be indicated. The corticosteroid drugs are used for their positive inotropic effect. The steroids are also thought to help overcome peripheral resistance, as well as to counteract the inflammatory effects of endotoxin in septic shock, although this is controversial at the present time.

Complications of shock include disseminated intravascular coagulation, gastric ulceration, renal insufficiency leading to acute tubular necrosis, and adult respiratory distress syndrome (ARDS, or shock lung). Prevention and early recognition and treatment of complications is a significant part of the care of a patient experiencing circulatory failure.

Hypertension. It is estimated that approximately 58 million people in the United States have systemic hypertension. Hypertension may go undiagnosed and untreated in many of these people, increasing their risk of morbidity and premature mortality (Rocella et al., 1987). Hypertension has an insidious course that may go unrecognized because there are no apparent symptoms and the patient "feels good," hence the nickname the "silent killer." Hypertension is the leading cause of stroke, congestive heart failure, and renal insufficiency (Reis, 1988). In the United States it is also the main reason medical care is sought and the major medical condition for which prescription medication is taken (Kaplan, 1988a).

Definition. Blood pressure varies among and within individuals so that it is hard to define high blood pressure as a specific number of units over "normal." Rather, ranges for different categories of blood pressure have been identified based on epidemiologic studies that evaluated blood pressure measurements in terms of the frequency of occurrence in the population, the association with cardiovascular and other complications, and the relationship to the efficacy and cost-benefit ratios of various treatment modalities (Roccella et al., 1987). The ranges of normal and abnormal blood pressure identified for adults and the upper limits of normal blood pressure for children are included in Table 17-6.

Classification. The commonly used classifications include primary, secondary, benign, and malignant. The classifications of primary and secondary refer to etiology. Hypertension in which a specific cause is unknown is referred to as primary, essen-

Table 17-6. Classification scheme of blood pressure values

In children:

Age (yr)	Arterial blood pressure	
	≥ 95th percentile (mm Hg)	≥ 99th percentile (mm Hg)
Newborns		
7 days	SBP ≥ 96	SBP ≥ 106
8-30 days	SBP ≥ 104	SBP ≥ 110
Infants	SBP ≥ 112	SBP ≥ 118
(≤ 2 years)	DBP ≥ 74	DBP ≥ 82
Children	SBP ≥ 116	SBP ≥ 124
(3-5 years)	DBP ≥ 76	DBP ≥ 84
Children	SBP ≥ 122	SBP ≥ 130
(6-9 years)	DBP ≥ 78	DBP ≥ 86
Children	SBP ≥ 126	SBP ≥ 134
(10-12 years)	DBP ≥ 82	DBP ≥ 90
Children	SBP ≥ 136	SBP ≥ 144
(13-15 years)	DBP ≥ 86	DBP ≥ 92
Adolescents	SBP ≥ 142	SBP ≥ 150
(16-18 years)	DBP ≥ 92	DBP ≥ 98

In adults age 18 years or older:

Range (mm Hg)	Category*
Diastolic:	
<85	Normal blood pressure
85 to 89	High normal
90 to 104	Mild hypertension
105 to 114	Moderate hypertension
≥115	Severe hypertension
Systolic, when diastolic is <90:	
<140	Normal blood pressure
140 to 159	Borderline isolated systolic hypertension
≥160	Isolated systolic hypertension

From the 1988 report of the Joint National Committee on Detection, Evaluation, and Treatment of High Blood Pressure, U.S. Department of Health and Human Services, PHS, NIH Pub. No. 88-1088, May, 1988.
*A classification of borderline isolated systolic hypertension (systolic BP = 140 to 159 mm Hg) or isolated systolic hypertension (systolic BP ≥ 160 mm Hg) takes precedence over a classification of high normal BP (diastolic BP = 85 to 89 mm Hg) when both occur in the same person. A classification of high normal BP (diastolic BP = 85 to 89 mm Hg) takes precedence over a classification of normal BP (systolic BP < 140 mm Hg) when both occur in the same person.

tial, or idiopathic hypertension. Secondary hypertension is elevation of the blood pressure as a result of some other primary disease process. In terms of this classification the most common type of hypertension is primary, which accounts for over 90% of all cases. The remaining 5% to 10% can be classified as secondary. Examples of diseases that cause an elevation of the arterial pressure as part of the disease process include renal disease, pheochromocytoma (a tumor of the adrenal medulla), Cushing's syndrome, and coarctation of the aorta. Treating the primary cause can resolve the elevated blood pressure in these cases.

The following discussion focuses on the pathophysiologic aspects of essential hypertension. The mechanisms by which secondary hypertension is produced are discussed when the causative disease process is discussed elsewhere in this book. A summary of the pathologic mechanisms of secondary hypertension is provided in Table 17-7.

The other two classifications refer to the course of the disease process. Malignant, or accelerated, hypertension is characterized by a rapid and severe increase in blood pressure that causes acute damage to retinal blood vessels (Kaplan, 1988a). Complications occur more frequently and develop more rapidly in malignant hypertension. Benign, or chronic, hypertension refers to a more moderate rise in blood pressure that occurs over a longer period of time. The term *benign* is somewhat of a misnomer because the blood pressure elevation can be quite significant and, if left uncontrolled, can cause complications. In 1% of all cases malignant hypertension occurs as a sequel to benign hypertension (Kaplan, 1988a). Malignant hypertension also occurs without any evidence of preex-

isting benign hypertension and as a sequela to secondary forms of hypertension.

Clinical manifestations and associated conditions. Essential hypertension is most frequently asymptomatic. Some symptoms that are often attributed to hypertension but that occur no more frequently in hypertensive than in normotensive patients are tinnitus, dizziness, fainting, nosebleed, and headache. Headache (especially headache upon awakening) is the symptom most often cited, but there is disagreement as to whether it is related to the disease or is psychogenic in origin. Other symptoms identified in untreated hypertensive patients include nocturia and postural unsteadiness (Kaplan, 1988a).

Obviously the major sign is the alteration in blood pressure that is present. An important point is that the diagnosis of hypertension is not made on one blood pressure measurement but on repeated measurements according to an established protocol for accurate blood pressure measurement. These measurements should be taken not only in a medical clinic or office setting but also on an ambulatory basis as well, since it is well documented that such readings are consistently lower than those found in a clinical setting. An obvious exception to these recommendations is when an initial measurement is so high that immediate treatment is needed to prevent acute deterioration in the patient. Recommendations from the 1988 Joint National Committee on the Detection, Evaluation, and Treatment of High Blood Pressure for follow-up after an initial blood pressure screening in persons age 18 years or older are presented in the box on p. 712.

The diastolic blood pressure reflects the total peripheral resistance, while the systolic blood pressure reflects the compliance of the arteries. An increase in the di-

Table 17-7. Pathologic mechanisms of secondary systemic hypertension

Causes	Mechanisms	Vascular response
Renal dysfunction		
Renovascular disease Renal artery stenosis	Inadequate renal blood flow in post-stenotic vessel triggering renin-angiotensin-aldosterone (RAA) system	↑ Blood volume ↑ Peripheral vascular resistance ↓ Vascular compliance ↑ Afterload
Kimmelstiel-Wilson syndrome	Thickened glomerular basement membrane, causing vascular occlusion, and triggering the RAA and salt and water retention	↑ Blood volume ↑ Peripheral vascular resistance ↓ Vascular compliance ↑ Afterload
Renal parenchymal disease Glomerulonephritis	Cause unknown; thought to be associated with renal autoregulatory mechanisms	↑ Peripheral vascular resistance ↑ Afterload
Pyelonephritis	Interstitial scarring and obstruction of intrarenal vessels, possibly triggering RAA and salt and water retention	↑ Blood volume ↑ Peripheral vascular resistance ↓ Vascular compliance ↑ Afterload
Adrenal dysfunction		
Pheochromocytoma	Increased circulating catecholamines	↑ Alpha stimulation of peripheral vessels ↑ Peripheral vascular resistance
Cushing's syndrome	Increased secretion of mineralocorticoids; increased secretion of cortisol; salt and water retention	↑ Blood volume ↑ Peripheral vascular resistance
Primary and secondary aldosteronism	Inappropriate reabsorption of salt and water from distal tubule and collecting duct in the nephron	↑ Blood volume ↓ Vascular compliance ↑ Blood pressure
Neurologic dysfunction		
Autonomic hyperreflexia (dysreflexia)	Increased and inappropriate reflex sympathetic stimulation causing severe arteriolar constriction	↑ Periphral vascular resistance ↑ Blood pressure

Brain tumors
   Cerebellar
   Posterior hypothalamus
   Brain stem
	Increased catecholamine release	↑ Peripheral vascular resistance
		↑ Blood pressure

Increased intracranial pressure Cushing response	Stimulation of vasomotor center with intense arteriolar vasoconstriction	↑ Peripheral vascular resistance ↑ Blood pressure
Exogenous agents		
Oral contraceptives*	Estrogenic portion of agents may alter renal sodium retention mechanism by unknown process	↑ Peripheral vascular resistance ↑ Blood pressure ↑ Blood volume

Sympathomimetic agents
   Dopamine
   Epinephrine
   Caffeine
   Nicotine
   Amphetamines
	Direct stimulation of sympathetic vasoconstriction of peripheral vessels	↑ Blood pressure
		↑ Peripheral vascular resistance

Steroid therapy	Sodium and water retention	↑ Blood volume ↓ Vascular compliance ↑ Blood pressure

From Michaelson C: Congestive heart failure, St. Louis, 1983, The C.V. Mosby Co.
*Oral contraceptives are the most common cause of secondary hypertension.

GUIDELINES FOR FOLLOW-UP AFTER INITIAL BLOOD PRESSURE SCREENING

Diastolic blood pressure (mm Hg)	Recommended follow-up*
<85	Recheck within 2 yr
85 to 89	Recheck within 1 yr
90 to 104	Confirm promptly (not to exceed 2 months)
105 to 114	Evaluate or refer promptly to source of care (not to exceed 2 weeks)
≥115	Evaluate or refer immediately to a source of care

Systolic blood pressure (mm Hg) when DBP <90 mm Hg:	Recommended follow-up*
<140	Recheck within 2 yr
140 to 199	Confirm promptly (not to exceed 2 months)
≥200	Evaluate or refer promptly to source of care (not to exceed 2 weeks)

From the 1988 report of the Joint National Committee on Detection, Evaluation, and Treatment of High Blood Pressure, U.S. Department of Health and Human Services, PHS, NIH Pub. No 88-1088, May, 1988.
*If recommendations for follow-up of DBP and SBP are different, the shorter recommended time period supersedes, and a referral supersedes a recheck recommendation.

astolic blood pressure reflects increased peripheral resistance to blood flow, which is the most common pathologic finding in essential hypertension. Elevated systolic blood pressure reflects loss of arterial compliance that most probably occurs in response to sclerosis. Isolated systolic hyper-

tension is found more commonly in the elderly, occurring in one third of persons aged 65 years or older. As a greater proportion of the population ages, isolated systolic and combined systolic and diastolic hypertension will be found more frequently (Kaplan, 1988a).

Other manifestations of hypertension are related to the progression of the hypertensive state and the pathophysiology that it causes. An elevation in either the diastolic or systolic blood pressure, although a pathophysiologic response, causes further pathophysiology by the responses of the blood vessels and certain organs to increased pressure. These responses are discussed later in this chapter.

Common findings in patients with elevated blood pressure include a positive family history, a sedentary life-style, obesity, a smoking history, alcohol consumption, increased lipid levels, and excessive salt intake. Hypertension is predictably more severe in patients who smoke. Correlations have been reported between the diastolic blood pressure and obesity, smoking, alcohol, and plasma sodium level and between the systolic blood pressure and body size and psychologic stress (Kaplan, 1988a). Hypertension frequently coexists with diabetes mellitus, and hyperuricemia is found significantly more often in hypertensive patients than in normotensive patients. These associations are not causal but do suggest pathogenetic mechanisms for the development of essential hypertension.

Pathogenesis. Examination of the physiologic determinants of cardiac output and peripheral resistance reveals a number of points at which pathophysiologic mechanisms could disrupt normal blood pressure regulation (see Fig. 17-17). None of these determinant factors is independent of the others, so that a change in any of these factors will precipitate complementary adjustments by the others; a whole new set of relationships will then exist. Hypertension, therefore, can be viewed as a possible compensatory response to altered relationships that could exist in a variety of combinations. Such a response may develop slowly over a long period of time as relationships change and, by the time hypertension appears clinically, the initiating event may no longer exist. It is for these reasons that no single causal mechanism probably will ever be identified for essential hypertension.

The cause of essential hypertension is thought to be multifactorial, with the following mechanisms postulated as having possible contributory roles: (1) increased sympathetic activity; (2) excessive salt intake and abnormal Na^+ metabolism, leading to increased Na^+ and water retention and expansion of extracellular volume (the arterial walls of some hypertensive patients have been found to have an abnormally high Na^+ content); (3) excessive renin secretion and generation of angiotensin II, a potent vasoconstrictor (hyperplasia of the juxtaglomerular cells has been found in severe hypertension); (4) enhanced vascular sensitivity to vasoactive substances and decreased venous distensibility; (5) vasodepressor deficiency (deficiencies of bradykinin and prostaglandins have been found in hypertension); (6) upward shift in baroreceptor response of pressure-natriuresis; and (7) increased intracellular calcium levels.

Goldblatt et al., (1934): showed that renal ischemia, caused by clamping the renal artery, resulted in the activation of the renin-angiotensin-aldosterone system to cause hypertension. Increased sympathetic nervous system activation is also known to increase blood pressure by increasing vascular resistance and cardiac output and by stimulating renin release. Total peripheral resistance is increased by

constriction of the arterioles through the action of norepinephrine. There is supporting evidence in both animals and humans for a pathogenetic role for increased sympathetic responsiveness in the etiology of hypertension (Herd et al., 1987). Such catecholamine hypersensitivity or hyperreactivity may help explain the susceptibility of highly stressed individuals to hypertension. Increased plasma catecholamine levels have been found in some hypertensive patients. Hypertensive individuals have also been found to display greater suppressed hostility on psychometric testing (Shapiro et al., 1987). Hypertension is known to occur more frequently in persons chronically exposed to high levels of psychogenic stress and some hypertensive patients overrespond to stress. Indirect evidence of an enhanced sympathetic response is provided by the fact that pharmacologic agents that inhibit sympathetic activity can be used to lower the blood pressure.

Abnormal metabolism of the cations, sodium and calcium, has been found in hypertension. Increased levels of intracellular sodium have been speculated to be due to inherited defects in sodium transport. There is also believed to be inhibition of a sodium-calcium exchange mechanism, leading to increased intracellular calcium levels. Calcium, in turn, mediates vasoconstriction by its binding to a myofilament regulatory protein and stimulation of myosin phosphorylation (Kaplan, 1988a). Hypertensive patients have been found to exhibit a vasodilator response to calcium channel blocking drugs.

A resetting of the pressure-natriuresis curve also occurs in hypertensive individuals. If this did not occur, the kidneys would continue to excrete fluid until normal pressure was restored. In hypertension, then, some factor has altered the excretory ability of the kidneys so that a higher than normal pressure is necessary to stimulate natriuresis (Guyton, 1988). Evidence of mechanisms that could alter renal excretory ability, such as increased renal efferent arteriolar resistance, inability to modulate renal blood flow in response to sodium loads, and the presence of circulating natriuretic hormones, has been found in hypertensive persons.

Genetic factors are indicated because of observed familial, sexual, and racial predispositions. The incidence of hypertension among blacks is approximately double that found in the white population, and the progression is more severe, leading to higher levels of related morbidity and mortality, in particular renal insufficiency progressing to end-stage renal disease. Women have been found to tolerate hypertension better than men, and before menopause the incidence of hypertension in women is less than in men. Children of hypertensive individuals have been found to demonstrate an increased pressor response to a stressful challenge. The possibility of and the manner in which such hyperresponsiveness might be transformed into hypertension is uncertain at the present time (Herd et al., 1987). The inherited defects Kaplan (1988a) sees as most likely include increased sympathetic nervous system response to stress, a defect of renal excretion of sodium, and a defect of sodium transport across cell membranes.

None of these factors alone results in hypertension. It is most probably the interrelationships between these mechanisms that cause blood pressure to increase. Susceptibility to the effects of environmental mechanisms probably requires genetic predisposition, for example, the interaction of an environmental stressor with an

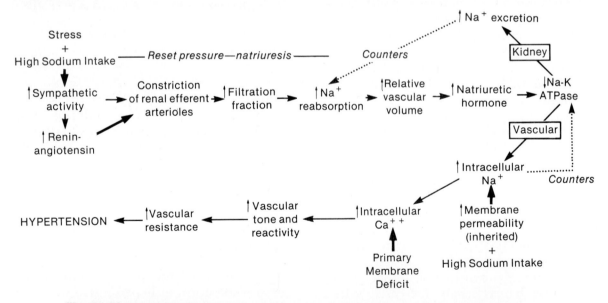

Fig. 17-23. Hypothesis for the pathogenesis of primary (essential) hypertension, starting from two points *(heavy arrows)*. One, starting on the top at left, is the combination of stress and high sodium intake, which induces an increase in natriuretic hormone and thereby inhibits sodium transport. The other, starting at the bottom at right, invokes an inherited defect in sodium transport plus a high sodium intake to induce an increase in intracellular sodium.

(From Kaplan, NM: (1988a): Systemic hypertension: mechanisms and diagnosis, In Braunwald E, editor: Heart disease: a textbook of cardiovascular medicine, ed. 3, Philadelphia, 1988a, WB Saunders Co.

inherited cardiovascular hyperreactivity (Brody et al., 1987). One possible scheme for such interaction that takes into account inherited defects of sodium and calcium transport and the environmental effects of stress and dietary sodium intake is depicted in Fig. 17-23.

Pathophysiologic mechanisms and course. The major defect in essential hypertension is a persistent increase in the total peripheral resistance. The hemodynamic pattern of the changes in cardiac output (CO) and total peripheral resistance (TPR) have been found to vary among patients. An initial pattern of high CO and normal TPR, which, over time, progressively changes so that the CO decreases and TPR rises, has been described. This suggests that the in-creased CO and normal TPR pattern may represent a beginning stage that changes over time. Some patients do not fit this pattern and retain an increased cardiac output in the face of normal resistance or even demonstrate an increased TPR and CO. It should be mentioned, however, that normal resistance in the face of increased cardiac output is not normal. Another consideration is whether different presenting hemodynamic patterns represent qualitatively different forms of disease. No matter what the sequence of events, increased peripheral resistance to blood flow has a variety of effects, which acting together set up and reinforce pathophysiologic mechanisms that perpetuate and aggravate the disease process (Fig. 17-24).

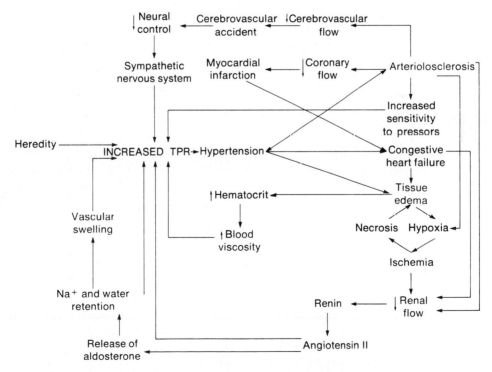

Fig. 17-24. Pathophysiology of hypertension. Increased total peripheral resistance (TPR) may be caused by many factors (vascular disease, hereditary factors, sympathetic nervous system activity, excessive pressor substances or increased sensitivity, and increased blood viscosity). Hypertension itself, acting through a variety of pathophysiologic mechanisms, can further perpetuate increased TPR.

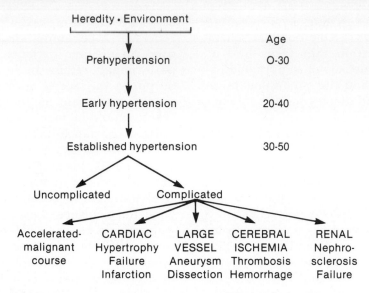

Fig. 17-25. Schematic representation of the natural history of untreated hypertension. (From Kaplan, NM: Clinical hypertension, ed 4, Baltimore, 1986, Williams & Wilkins.)

Hypertension is in itself a risk factor for other types of vascular disease (including coronary, cerebral, and renal) because of the pathophysiologic responses it evokes. Longitudinal studies have demonstrated that untreated hypertension leads to a reduced life expectancy. It is a progressively worsening disorder that commonly coexists with and accelerates the atherosclerotic process. Complications develop as a result of both the hypertensive and atherosclerotic vascular changes that occur. Age is a factor in that hypertension has been observed to increase in frequency and severity with age. Age-related sclerotic vessel changes may contribute to the hypertensive pathology and explain the more frequent occurrence of isolated systolic hypertension in the elderly.

Complications become clinically evident when the underlying vascular damage disrupts tissue perfusion by obstruction or hemorrhage and organ function becomes impaired. The incidence and severity of the complications are positively related to the duration and severity of the hypertensive condition. Of hypertensive patients who remain untreated, 50% die of heart disease, 33% of stroke, and 10% to 15% of renal failure. Presented in Fig. 17-25 is a schematic overview of the natural history of untreated essential hypertension. Presented in Fig. 17-26 is the age-adjusted risk of cardiovascular morbidity in hypertension.

Hypertension leads to vascular damage in two ways; first, by aggravating the atherosclerotic process and, second, by directly stimulating pathologic vascular changes. These pathologic changes include medial smooth muscle hypertrophy (postulated to be an adaptive response to the hypertensive state, which is reversible), fibrinoid necrosis, musculomucoid intimal hyperplasia, and hyaline arteriolosclerosis (Fig. 17-27). The latter two lesions are not specific for hypertension but may occur as a result of other pathologic states as well.

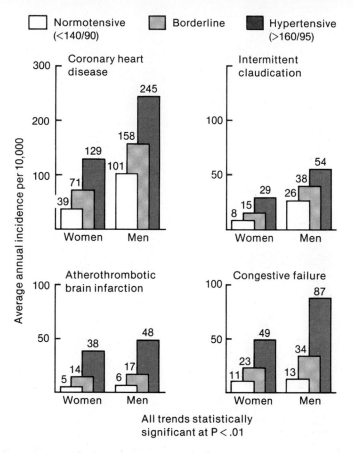

Fig. 17-26. Age-adjusted risk of cardiovascular morbidity according to hypertensive status at each biennial examination in men and women aged 45 to 74 years (Framingham Heart Study cohort, 18-year follow-up.)

(From Castelli, WP and Anderson, K: A population at risk: prevalence of high cholesterol levels in hypertensive patients in the Framingham study, Am J Med 80(suppl 2A):23, 1986.) Also the Framingham Study Monograph, Section 30.

Advanced musculomucoid intimal hyperplasia in the kidney can lead to glomerular ischemia and atrophy of the nephron when no other lesions are present. Hyaline arteriolosclerosis characterized by intimal fibroelastosis (Fig. 17-28) is the most commonly found lesion and is associated with benign nephrosclerosis. This lesion occurs as part of the aging process and in diabetes as well. Speculation about the central role of the smooth muscle changes (mentioned previously as adaptive) in promoting hypertensive vascular disease is schematically diagrammed in Fig. 17-29.

The vascular changes provide a basis for diagnostic evaluation of the severity of the hypertensive process. Through ophthalmoscopy the vasculature of the retina can be visually examined. The earliest change is narrowing of the arteriolar lumen (grade 1), which is followed by sclerosis of the adventitia and/or thickening of the arterial wall (grade 2). This change is visible as arteriovenous nicking. With continuing

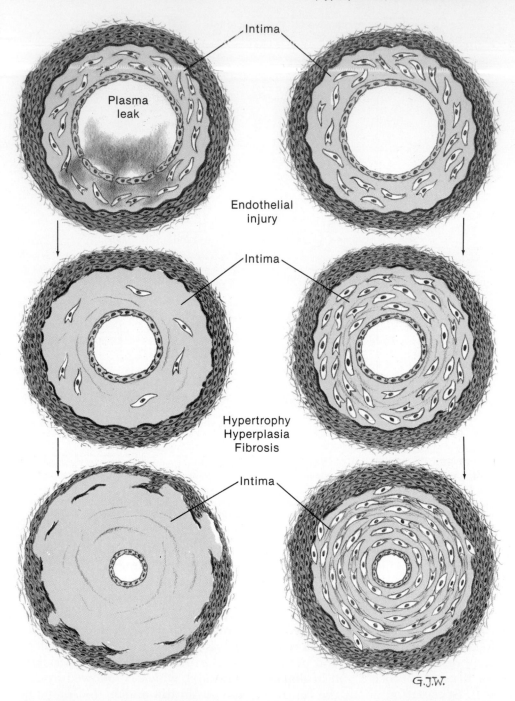

Fig. 17-27. Two types of arteriosclerosis—sclerosis and thickening of walls of arterioles. Hyaline arteriosclerosis is associated with benign nephrosclerosis and proliferative arteriosclerosis may be associated with malignant hypertension, nephrosclerosis and scleroderma.

From Schwartz and Ross: Cellular proliferation in atherosclerosis and hypertension. Prog Cardiovasc Dis, 26:355, 1984.

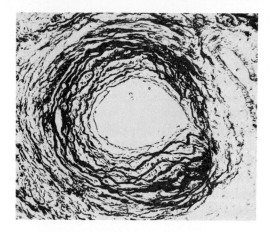

Fig. 17-28. Elastosis in branch of renal artery from case of essential hypertension.

(From Anderson, W.A.D., and Kissane, J.M.: Pathology, ed. 7, St. Louis, 1977, The C.V. Mosby Co.)

hypertension the vein becomes invisible behind the arteriole and is obstructed. As small vessels rupture, hemorrhages and exudates appear (grade 3). Papilledema or edema (swelling) of the optic nerve represents grade 4. The presence of papilledema and a diastolic pressure greater than 140 mm Hg is indicative of malignant hypertension. This is usually preceded by accelerated hypertension that is characterized by retinal hemorrhages and exudates and a sudden increase in blood pressure to a diastolic pressure above 140 mm Hg.

In hypertensive individuals prone to atherogenesis, certain complications more closely related to the atherosclerotic process are more likely to arise as a result of the aggravation of the process by the hypertension. These complications include

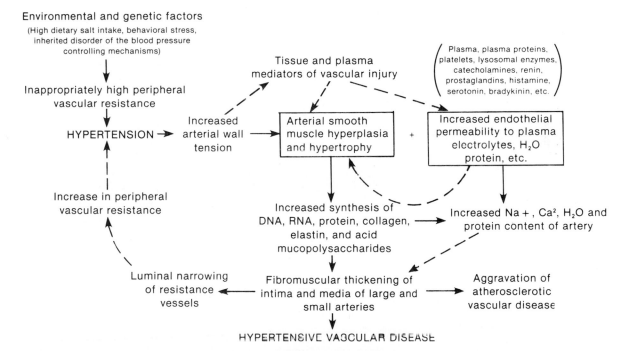

Fig. 17-29. Possible scheme for pathogenesis of hypertensive vascular disease with smooth muscle changes as central in the process. Hypothesized relationships are indicated by broken (dotted) lines. Proven changes are indicated by solid lines.

(From Hollander, W.: Role of hypertension in atherosclerosis and cardiovascular disease, Am. J. Cardiology 38:786, 1976.)

coronary artery disease, thrombotic stroke, abdominal aneurysm, transient ischemic attack, and ischemia of the bowel, kidneys, and extremities.

Cardiac effects include ischemia, hypertrophy and eventually heart failure (Fig. 17-30). The increased resistance to blood flow increases the cardiac work load (increased afterload), which in turn causes left-sided ventricular hypertrophy. The degree of myocardial hypertrophy appears to be positively related to the severity and duration of the hypertension. Hypertrophy makes the myocardium more susceptible to ischemia, as blood supply does not increase to the same degree that muscle mass does, especially when accompanied by atherosclerosis. Angina pectoris, the characteristic pain resulting from cardiac ischemia, may occur. The risk of sudden death is significantly increased (Fig. 17-31). Congestive heart failure occurs when the heart can no longer pump against the increasing resistance (Fig. 17-32). Results of the Framingham study revealed that congestive heart failure was six times more prevalent among hypertensive persons than persons with normal blood pressure, and hypertension was a causative factor in 75% of all cases of congestive heart failure (Kaplan, 1988a).

A life-threatening complication of hypertension is the syndrome known as *hypertensive crisis*. Hypertensive crisis is said to

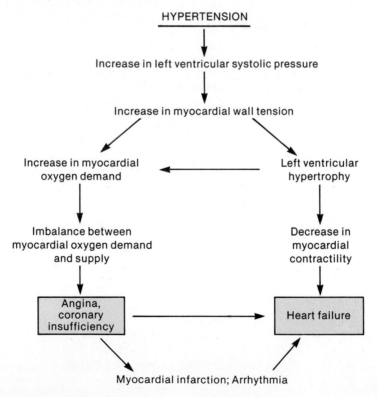

Fig. 17-30. Adverse effects of hypertension on myocardial function.
(From Hollander, W: Role of hypertension in atherosclerosis and cardiovascular disease, Am J Cardiol 38:786, 1976.)

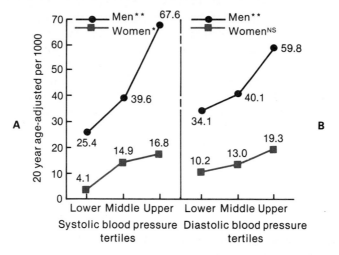

Fig. 17-31. The risk of sudden death over 20 years among the Framingham cohort divided into percentiles of average systolic **(A)** and diastolic **(B)** blood pressure at the initial four biennial examinations. The subjects were aged 35 to 84 and initially were free of overt coronary heart disease. *, $p < 0.05$; **, $p < 0.01$; *NS,* nonsignificant.

(From Kannel, WB, McGee, DL, and Schatzkin, A: An epidemiological perspective of sudden death. 26-year follow-up in the Framingham Study. Drugs 28 (suppl 1):1, 1984a.)

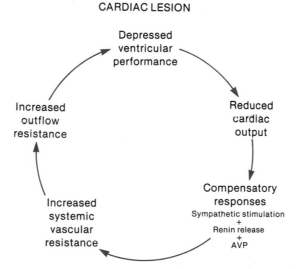

Fig. 17-32. A unifying hypothesis for congestive heart failure. Heart failure results in decreased flow, which activates several biologic systems leading to excessive peripheral vasoconstriction. The failing left ventricle reacts to this as a further impedance to ejection, setting the stage for a vicious cycle. In hypertension, the increased vascular resistance serves as the point of initiation. *AVP,* Arginine vasopressin.

(From Francis, GS, Goldsmith, SR, and Levine, TB, et al: The neurohumoral axis in congestive heart failure, Ann Intern Med 101:370, 1984.)

occur when pressure is so high that immediate vascular necrosis may result. A diastolic pressure greater than 140 mm Hg is considered to be the point at which acute damage occurs. The rapidity of the rise in blood pressure is as important as the degree of severity of the rise. The pathologic changes that occur are of two types. The structural change is fibrinoid necrosis of the arteriolar wall. The functional change is dilation of the cerebral vessels, which promotes excessive blood flow to the brain and leads to cerebral dysfunction.

Fibrinoid necrosis is characterized by a combination of medial smooth muscle necrosis and accumulation of blood products within the vascular wall. Two theories attempt to explain these changes. The first allows that the increased pressure itself forces plasma into the vascular walls, which in turn causes the necrosis. The second theory contends that the increased vascular permeability is a result of the disintegration of the smooth muscle cell. This breakdown is hypothesized to be the result of a state of contraction beyond the physiologic limits of the cells. The changes associated with fibrinoid necrosis are reversible in the earlier stages.

Hypertensive encephalopathy is the term used to describe the signs of cerebral dysfunction caused by a sudden, extreme rise in blood pressure. This includes headache, irritability, confusion, visual loss, altered states of consciousness, seizures, and focal deficits. The cerebral hyperperfusion has been postulated to result from a "breakthrough" of autoregulation in the cerebral vascular bed. Leaking of fluid subsequently causes cerebral edema and produces the observed signs. Other clinical problems that may accompany hypertensive encephalopathy include renal insufficiency manifested by oliguria and azotemia, increased plasma renin activity manifested by hypokalemia due to secondary aldosteronism that results, and microangiopathic hemolytic anemia caused by traumatic red blood cell destruction.

All of the complications of hypertension are summarized in Table 17-8.

Treatment rationale. The goals of treatment include (1) reduction of the elevated blood pressure and maintenance of normal blood pressure levels, and (2) prevention of complications of both the treatment and the disease process. The choice of treatment depends on the degree of hypertension and must be individualized so the maximum benefit with the least amount of side effects is achieved. Treatment can be changed if the target blood pressure is not attained. A general recommendation is that persons with a diastolic blood pressure of 90-94 mm Hg and no other cardiovascular risk factors can be treated initially with nonpharmacologic measures. Other persons with elevated blood pressure will be treated with pharmacologic agents as well. Mild hypertension may be treated by a low-sodium diet and a diuretic drug or other measures cited below. Moderate hypertension may be treated by a diuretic drug in combination with a mild antihypertensive drug. Severe hypertension may be treated by a diuretic drug and a combination of antihypertensive drugs.

Physiologically the disease process can be managed by a combination of diet, diuretic, and antihypertensive drugs. Treatment for less severe forms of hypertension may include weight reduction, life-style changes (e.g., increased frequency of exercise, stress management, restriction of alcohol, and cessation of smoking), biofeedback, and relaxation therapies. The low-sodium diet and the use of diuretic drugs promote the excretion of fluid from the body. This helps to lower blood pressure because venous return and consequently

Table 17-8. Major syndromes associated with hypertension, organs involved, and corresponding pathophysiologic state.

Target organ	Clinical syndrome	Pathophysiologic state
Brain	Hypertensive encephalopathy	Fibrinoid necrosis, edema, hemorrhage
	Transient ischemic attack	Atherosclerosis plus emboli (plaque, platelets, lipids)
	Cerebral infarction	Atherosclerosis
		Lipohyalinosis
		Thromboemboli
		Thrombosis
	Parenchymal hemorrhage	Lipohyalinosis with or without aneurysm
	Subarachnoid hemorrhage	Ruptured congenital aneurysm
		Extension of parenchymal hemorrhage
Heart	Heart failure	Increased afterload
		Hypertrophy
		Increased connective tissue
		Decreased compliance
		Decreased contractility
		Decreased coronary blood supply
	Coronary artery disease	Atherosclerosis
Kidney	Excretory renal failure	Musculomucoid intimal hyperplasia and ischemia
		Fibrinoid necrosis and glomerulitis
		Fibrosis
Aorta	Saccular and fusiform aneurysms	Atherosclerosis
	Dissecting aneurysm	Medial degeneration
Gastrointestinal tract	Ischemia, infarction, and hemorrhage	Musculomucoid intimal hyperplasia
		Fibrinoid necrosis
		Atherosclerosis and thrombosis

From Johnson J and Muirhead E: Vascular complications of the hypertensive state. In Hunt J et al.: Hypertension update: mechanisms, epidemiology, evaluation, management, Bloomfield, NJ, 1980, Health Learning Systems, Inc.

cardiac output are reduced. Antihypertensive drugs block sympathetic innervation, which prevents or reduces vasoconstriction, thus decreasing peripheral resistance. Sedation may also be helpful in terms of reducing the effects of sympathetic stimulation. If renin levels are elevated, a converting enzyme inhibitor can be used. Treatment of hypertensive crisis requires the immediate administration of potent antihypertensive drugs.

The greatest problem in management of the disease process lies in patient compliance with the treatment regimen. Patients must realize that there is no cure for high blood pressure; at best it is controlled. However, once patients begin to feel better and no longer can identify the effects of the disease process, they often stop taking the prescribed medication. Careful teaching about the side effects of any medication and about the disease process will allow patients to actively participate in their care.

Altered lumen size and patency

Various disorders serve to reduce the lumen diameter or the patency and integrity of the blood vessels. Occlusive disorders cause narrowing (stenosis) or complete blockage of the lumen. These include arteriosclerosis, atherosclerosis, thrombus formation, and embolism. A group of disorders known as *peripheral vascular diseases* produce clinical problems by either altering the lumen size or disrupting the patency of the vessel.

When vessel flow is obstructed, for whatever reason, signs of insufficiency depend on the vessel system in which the alteration took place as well as the extent of the flow disruption present. Obstruction of the flow of arterial blood with its resulting hypoxia has two possible effects: creation of a state of *ischemia* or actual *infarction* of tissue. As stated earlier in the chapter, ischemia refers to a state of tissue hypoxia that is reversible when oxygen is again supplied to the tissues. Infarction refers to cell death or necrosis that occurs as a result of oxygen lack. Obstruction of venous flow causes venous distention and edema. The products of metabolism will accumulate and eventually the Starling forces in the capillary bed will be disrupted (see Chapter 18). At this point the delivery of oxygen and nutrients to the tissues is also impaired.

Thrombus and embolus formation. A thrombus is an abnormal clot that develops in and is attached to a blood vessel. An embolus is a clot that has broken loose and is circulating throughout the vascular system. The danger from an embolus is that it can lodge in the vascular beds of vital organs, occluding blood flow and possibly causing infarction. Thrombus formation is enhanced in the presence of a roughened endothelial surface of a vessel. The rough surface serves to activate the clotting process.

Atherosclerotic plaques have thrombogenic properties and often serve as the initiating factor in thrombus and embolus formation. Inflammation of the vessel lining can cause clotting. Stasis of the blood flow also predisposes to thrombus formation as red blood cells settle out of solution and become "sludged." Products of metabolism also accumulate to a greater degree in the presence of stasis of the blood flow, and the presence of these substances causes agglutination of blood cells. (Thrombus and embolism formation are discussed more completely in Chapters 3 and 14.) Embolization may also be the result of other foreign material circulating in the bloodstream in addition to a loose thrombus. Air, bacteria, fat globules, and amniotic fluid may all have the same effects as a dislodged thrombus. Air introduced into the arterial system may be fatal if it reaches the heart or the cerebral circulation. Clumps of bacteria sometimes become dislodged from the primary site of infection. This sometimes is a complication of subacute bacterial endocarditis, in which vegetative colonies of bacteria grow on the valve cusps and are constantly subjected to the flow of blood and the movement of the valves. Amniotic fluid can be introduced into the maternal circulation via the placental circulation. This can occur during the labor and delivery period in normal childbirth but is usually seen only in the presence of obstetric complications.

After severe trauma, usually involving multiple skeletal fractures, a syndrome known as *fat embolism syndrome* may develop. The presence of these microscopic fat emboli is not completely understood, but two theories have been advanced in an attempt to explain this phenomenon. The metabolic theory asserts that fat globules, formed at the time of the injury, combine with platelets to form emboli. The leading hypothesis is the mechanical theory, which asserts that fat globules are released from the marrow of the injured bones and enter the vascular system through damaged vessels at the injury site (Flint, 1987). The fat emboli travel throughout the body, resulting in the appearance of signs and symptoms within a few hours to days after the original injury. The real danger of fat emboli is their effect in the pulmonary vascular bed, where they lodge in capillaries, blocking perfusion and causing an interstitial pneumonitis to develop. Gas exchange at the alveolocapillary membrane is impaired, and a ventilation-perfusion abnormality develops (see Chapter 16). Adult respiratory distress syndrome may develop as the interstitial lung damage worsens.

Most of the clinical manifestations of fat embolism are related to the effects on the respiratory system and the resulting hypoxia. Restlessness and disorientation may be the first signs to appear. The significance of these and other subtle signs and symptoms, such as tachycardia, a temperature elevation, or a feeling of uneasiness or anxiety expressed by the patient, may easily be missed. The presence of dyspnea, wheezing, and rales indicates more extreme respiratory distress. Petechiae may appear on the anterior trunk and axillae and on the soft palate and conjunctiva. These petechiae are thought to be the result of either thrombocytopenia or involvement of the dermal vessels, although the reason for the particular localization is unknown.

Peripheral vascular disease. The peripheral vascular diseases are a group of disorders in which arterial and venous lumen size and patency are affected. Pain and potential impaired skin integrity are two responses that are the major foci of nursing care. Nursing interventions will be directed toward relief of pain, prevention of tissue damage, improving the circulation, and modification of risk factors for the progression of disease. Many of these interventions involve health teaching and helping the client understand the importance of preventive measures such as foot and skin care and life-style alterations. The potential for noncompliance is great in these areas. If impaired skin integrity does occur, the potential for infection is increased and nursing interventions must also be directed toward preventing further tissue damage and infection. The potential for impaired physical mobility and disuse syndrome also must be considered if pain and tissue damage are so great that the patient's abilities to ambulate and move are affected. Depending on the patient's psychologic response to the visible effects of the disease, disturbed body image may also need to be addressed (Herman, 1986; Turner, 1986; Beaver, 1986; Ekers, 1986).

The peripheral circulation may be disrupted by disease processes outside of the vascular system, as well as by those disease processes primarily considered vascular in origin. Diseases such as diabetes, lupus erythematosus, and endocrine disorders may involve the peripheral vasculature.

Venous disorders. Venous disorders may be the result of obstructive or nonobstructive processes. The condition of varicose veins falls into the latter category. The manifestations of venous obstruction depend on how deep the affected vein lies. Thrombosis of a superficial vein may be observed as a red streak that is tender and palpable. Thrombosis of the deeper veins usually results in swelling of the extremity. The danger of venous thrombosis is that it can dislodge and migrate to a vital organ, causing occlusion of its blood supply. Thrombosis can also damage valves in the area, causing them to become incompetent, which allows backflow and pooling of blood in the veins, leading to chronic venous insufficiency (Doyle, 1986).

Varicose veins are tortuous, palpable, distended veins that are usually observable in the lower extremities. An increase in the venous pressure of the lower extremities as a result of nonvascular conditions (pregnancy or a job that requires sitting or standing with the legs in a dependent position for long periods of time) may cause the initial distension and pooling of blood. A health maintenance intervention is teaching persons who are at risk to vary their position and take breaks and put their feet up in a nondependent position occasionally. As veins are stretched, further pooling results, and the valves become incompetent. A vicious cycle is set up that perpetuates the development and progression of varicosities. Pain may be intense and is usually relieved by elevating the affected extremity. The pain is usually of a dull, achy character.

Varicose veins and chronic venous insufficiency (the sequela of obstruction and the resultant valvular incompetence) may both result in serious damage to the skin and soft tissue. Venous insufficiency is characterized by hyperpigmentation and brown indurated skin due to deposits of melanin and hemosiderin secondary to the breakdown of red blood cells in the tissue. The skin appears almost leatherlike. Venous stasis or pooling of venous blood occurs in both disorders and can lead to progressive edema and hypersensitivity, or *stasis dermatitis*. Itching and scratching may cause an infectious process to develop, and the subsequent inflammatory response may result in extensive interstitial fibrosis and cellulitis. Ulceration may be the sequela to even the most minor trauma (Fig. 17-33). Venous ulcers are large and surrounded by hyperpigmentation (Wagner, 1986).

Arterial disorders. Arterial disorders may be the result of two basic mechanisms: obstruction and generalized constriction or dilation of the vessels. Exposure to freezing temperatures may also impair arterial circulation through the mechanisms of vasoconstriction and thrombosis (see Chapter 5).

The absence of palpable pulses, coldness to the touch, a chalk-white pallor alternating with cyanosis, anesthesia or paresthesia, and collapse of superficial veins in the affected extremity are manifestations of an arterial occlusive process. These signs and symptoms will appear suddenly if an embolism is the cause. Complete occlusion, which is the result of a progressive thrombotic phenomenon, may be preceded by intermittent claudication or pain in the legs with exercise, a condition referred to as arterial insufficiency. The pain of intermittent claudication is described as cramping, aching, burning, or squeezing. As the disease process worsens, the pain may even be experienced at rest. Placing the extremity in a dependent position will help restore blood flow and relieve the pain. Burning or shocking pain can be the result of ischemic neuropathy. The patient may also complain of feeling cold in the feet and toes (Wagner, 1986).

Because of the decreased supply of nutrients and oxygen, trophic changes of the tissues occur; loss of hair on the affected extremity, nail deformities, and atrophy of tissue. The skin becomes extremely vulnerable to even minor trauma, and the potential for infection and impaired wound healing is great. The development of gangrene is a particular danger.

Raynaud's disease. Intermittent spasm of the arterioles constitutes the underlying pathologic defect in Raynaud's disease. The etiology of this disorder is unknown but may be related to a defect in

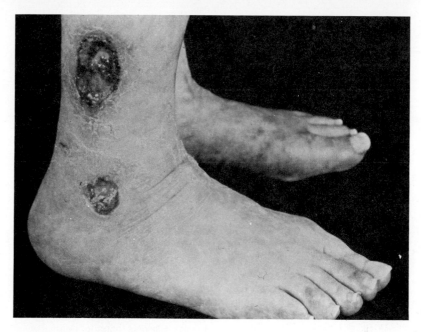

Fig. 17-33. Ulcer formation in patient with venous insufficiency.
(From Beyers, M., and Dudas, S.: The clinical practice of surgical nursing, Boston, 1977, Little, Brown & Co.)

heat production that allows vasodilation. The disease mainly affects women, and onset usually occurs before the age of 40. The tips of fingers, toes, ears, and the nose are most commonly affected. Clinical manifestations include intermittent attacks of numbness and tingling. Severe pain may also occur. At first the affected part will appear pale and feel cold. Pallor is followed by cyanosis. The affected part may become black and gangrenous. Clinical manifestations are precipitated by exposure to cold. The stress response, which causes peripheral vasoconstriction, exacerbates this disorder (Wagner, 1986). Raynaud's phenomenon is the term applied when these manifestations occur secondary to some other disease process.

Treatment includes prevention of attacks by avoidance of cold and careful attention to protective clothing (including the wearing of gloves when handling cold objects such as refrigerated or frozen food). Avoidance of trauma, smoking, vasoconstricting drugs, and careful hygienic care of the affected areas can prevent further tissue damage. Drugs can be used to promote vascular relaxation and decrease pain. Relaxation and biofeedback can be used successfully to promote vasodilation in affected areas as well.

Arteriosclerosis and atherosclerosis. Arteriosclerosis and atherosclerosis refers to a thickening and hardening of the arteries. Muscle and elastic tissue are replaced with fibrous tissue and calcification may occur. The ability of the arteries to change the lumen size is reduced. *Atherosclerosis* refers to a process in which there is deposition of lipids and possibly fibrin in the intimal linings of the medium-sized and large arteries. Subsequent calcification may also occur. This process makes the ar-

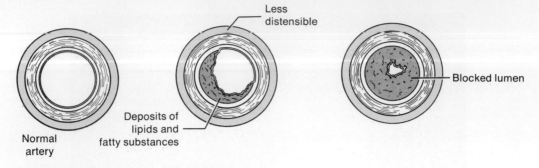

Fig. 17-34. Atherosclerotic vessel changes.

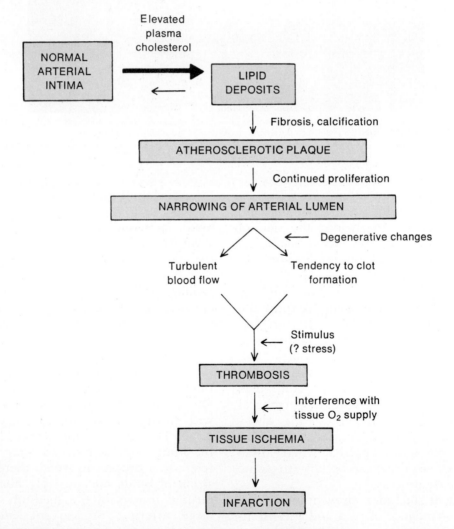

Fig. 17-35. Mechanism producing atherosclerosis and tissue infarction.
(From Montgomery, R., Dryer, R.L., Conway, T.W., and Spector, A.A.: Biochemistry: a case-oriented approach, ed. 3, St. Louis, 1980, The C.V. Mosby Co.)

teries less distensible and most often leads to physical blockage of the lumen and localized stenosis (Fig. 17-34). In some cases the lesion is ulcerated. On the surface of the ulcer, fibrin and thrombi develop, portions of which may break off into the circulation, producing emboli. The clinical effects of atherosclerotic lesions can be attributed to either their stenotic and thrombogenic qualities (Fig. 17-35). Atherosclerosis is the leading cause of death in Western civilization (Ross, 1988).

The characteristic lesion of atherosclerosis is the *atherosclerotic plaque*. The advanced fibrous plaque produces clinical symptoms and comprises a fibrous cap, a cellular layer, and a necrotic center. The fibrous cap is made up of proliferated smooth muscle cells, collagen, and extracellular and intracellular lipids, including foam cells. The necrotic central core contains cell debris, cholesterol esters and crystals, and calcium. The center is soft and of the consistency of a gruel or porridge, hence the use of the Greek stem, *athero*, meaning gruel. When the fibrous plaque becomes calcified or associated with hemorrhage or thrombosis, it is referred to as a complicated lesion (Fig. 17-36).

The pathogenesis of the atherosclerotic lesion has been and continues to be a subject of intensive research and speculation. Over the last two decades research has demonstrated that the predominant cells in the plaque are medial smooth muscle cells with variable numbers of accumulated macrophages (Ross, 1988) and that the cholesterol and cholesterol esters present are derived from low-density lipoprotein (LDL) or very low density lipoprotein (VLDL) from the serum. More recent work has examined the additional mechanisms of arterial endothelial damage and platelet agglutination and disintegration.

Many different types of studies support a strong positive relationship between elevated serum cholesterol levels and the incidence of atherosclerosis. Such an elevation may be the result of endogenous (metabolic disease or genetic) or exogenous (high-fat, high-cholesterol diet) factors.

Familial hypercholesterolemia (FH) is the most prevalent inherited disorder in the United States. The risk of developing heart disease is much greater for persons with FH than for persons in the general population. Persons who inherit the FH trait from one parent are said to be heterozygous, while those who inherit the trait from both parents, a much rarer occurrence, are homozygous for the disorder. The heterozygous condition is found in approximately 1 in 500 persons and is characterized by plasma cholesterol levels in the 300 to 500 mg/dl range. The homozygous condition is characterized by a much more severe elevation of plasma cholesterol levels (up to 1000 mg/dl) that is more refractory to treatment. Patients with FH have been found to lack the gene that codes for certain cell membrane receptors, called LDL receptors, which remove cholesterol-carrying LDL from the blood. One group of researchers has reported restoring the regulation of LDL in cultures of cells from rabbits that are genetically deficient in LDL receptors by linking the human receptor gene to an engineered tumor virus and infecting the cells with the virus. This very beginning work paves the way for future gene replacement therapy in humans. There is experimental evidence that the intact, normal arterial endothelium can admit and discharge limited quantities of macromolecules such as LDLs and fibrinogen, and that both are likely to accumulate in the intima because of their surface charges. Based on these findings, it

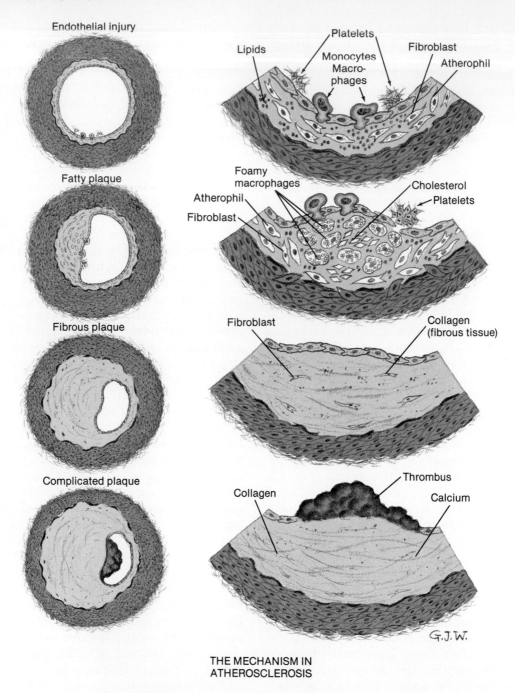

THE MECHANISM IN
ATHEROSCLEROSIS

Fig. 17-36. Formation and progression of the atherosclerotic lesion.

appears that a predominant factor in the development of atherosclerosis is the presence of hyperlipidemic serum with cholesterol-laden LDL.

There are two major hypotheses about the pathogenesis of atherosclerotic lesions. The first views atherogenesis as a response to arterial injury and the second as a form of neoplasia. In the response to injury hypothesis arterial endothelial injury is postulated to act as a stimulus for the release of lipolytic enzymes, vasoactive substances, and growth factors within the endothelial cells. Growth factors such as platelet-derived growth factor (PDGF) are postulated to stimulate the migration of smooth muscle cells from the media to the intima of the artery and promote their subsequent proliferation into an atherosclerotic lesion. This hypothesis allows for the interaction between different cells types that can be activated as a response to injury and releases growth factors. Besides endothelial cells, other cells that have been postulated to play a role in atherogenesis include macrophages and platelets. Some evidence indicates that the smooth muscle cells may themselves release a form of PDGF which influences the cell and its surrounding cells to proliferate. The activated macrophage probably plays a key role in cell proliferation and possibly in causing further cell damage through the release of oxidative metabolites. The mechanism of cell proliferation in response to injury is reversible with a single episode of endothelial damage but is progressive with recurrent episodes of chronic endothelial injury.

Endothelial injury may occur in response to a variety of insults at the cellular level. Many of the identified risk factors have been shown to exert their influence at the cellular level through pro-motion of either endothelial damage or platelet agglutination and disintegration. or example, both hypertension and smoking produce endothelial damage. Vascular spasm in a coronary artery has been hypothesized to cause intimal damage and initiate formation of an atherosclerotic plaque (Pasternak et al., 1988). There is evidence that hypercholesterolemia alone causes increased endothelial permeability and damage and changes in monocyte-endothelial adherence properties. The presence of hypercholesterolemia therefore sets up a vicious cycle perpetuating the progression of the atherosclerotic process.

The second or monoclonal hypothesis views the atherosclerotic lesion as a form of "benign" neoplasia. Some evidence indicates that the lesion may be proliferated from a single smooth muscle cell. The originating cell would have to be transformed by a mutagenic factor such as a virus or chemical that is not yet identified.

Research has also provided clues as to mechanisms promoting prevention of the atherosclerotic process. High-density lipoproteins (HDL), which have a high phospholipid and low cholesterol composition, are hypothesized to exert a protective effect that favors removal of cholesterol from cells. Regular physical exercise has been found to promote more favorable ratios of HDL/LDL in the blood. The plaque growth-stimulating effect of LDL can be blocked by estradiol and by HDL from normal serum. Cigarette smoking is known to decrease plasma HDL levels. Regression of the atherosclerotic plaque through dietary manipulation has been demonstrated in monkeys and swine. Implementation of a low cholesterol or cholesterol-free diet allowed plasma cholesterol levels to normalize and fatty streaks and more advanced lesions to shrink (Ross, 1988). In monkeys the drug cholestyramine has been found to reduce the plaque even without dietary intervention and with a continued elevation in serum cholesterol levels. Recent research indicates that inclusion of fish oil in the diet can lead to a decrease in plasma cholesterol levels and promote the cellular production of prostaglandins, which have antiaggregant, vasodilator effects.

All theories of atherogenesis support the belief that the process begins early in life and continues over a period of many years. There is some debate as to whether the "fatty streak" is a precursor lesion to the atherosclerotic plaque (Fig. 17-37). These streaks are commonly observed in the arteries of infants and young children of all populations around the world, including those populations with a low incidence of atherosclerosis. The fatty streak is known to be composed of lipid-laden macrophages with varying numbers of lipid-filled smooth muscle cells—the same elements that form the more advanced atherosclerotic lesion. Extensive biochemical and immunochemical studies have failed to positively confirm a role for this lesion in the atherosclerotic process; however, observational and epidemiologic data indicate that at certain anatomic sites the fatty streak is most probably a precursor lesion for the more advanced fibrous plaque (Ross, 1988).

Atherosclerosis is a progressive pathologic condition that is unevenly distributed geographically as well as anatomically. It is primarily found in the more industrialized portions of the world. Epidemiologic studies have linked the incidence of atherosclerosis with high serum cholesterol levels and, in turn, to life-style, particularly dietary habits in most persons. High dietary lipid intake has been found to be associated with high serum cholesterol levels, and positive associations have also been found between change in dietary lipid composition and change in serum cholesterol levels. A reduction in elevated serum cholesterol levels can be achieved through diet and maintenance of ideal body weight through

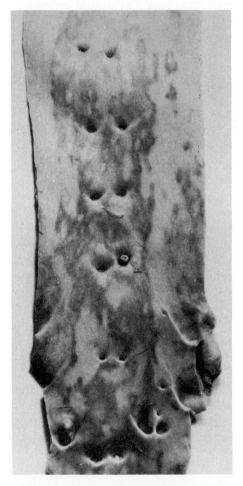

Fig. 17-37. Fatty streaking on posterior wall of aorta from boy aged 11.
(From Anderson, W.A.D., and Kissane, J.M.: Pathology, ed. 7, St. Louis, 1977, The C.V. Mosby Co.)

a program of regular exercise in many persons. In persons whose hypercholesterolemia is refractory to dietary modification (genetic or metabolic etiologies), pharmacologic therapy can be used and might include bile acid–binding resins, nicotinic acid, probucol, or mevinolin. In persons with homozygous familial hypercholesterolemia this type of medical management is not always effective, and weekly plasma exchanges or liver transplantation may be necessary (Bilheimer, 1988).

Other risk factors for the development of atherosclerosis include hypertension, cigarette smoking, diabetes, sedentary lifestyle, sex, age, and genetic influences. A sufficient amount of data exists to support elevated plasma cholesterol levels, cigarette smoking, and elevated blood pressure as independent predictors of risk for developing atherosclerosis within the population (Ross, 1988). Men are affected more frequently than women, except after menopause, when sex distribution becomes equal. Clinical problems caused by atherosclerosis usually become apparent between the fifth and seventh decades but may appear earlier especially in persons with FH.

The anatomic distribution of atherosclerotic lesions will affect the type of clinical condition that results. Ninety percent of all coronary artery and ischemic heart disease is the consequence of atherosclerosis. Atherosclerosis is responsible for much cerebrovascular and peripheral arterial disease and for most abdominal aortic aneurysms as well. The major anatomic sites of involvement include in rank order: (1) the lower (abdominal) aorta and iliacs, (2) the proximal coronaries, (3) the femoral artery, popliteal artery, and thoracic aorta, (4) the internal carotid artery, and (5) the vertebral artery, basilar artery, and circle of Willis.

The abdominal aorta is particularly vulnerable to atherogenesis because of the absence of penetrating vasa vasorum and the extreme physical stress to which it is subjected. While atherosclerosis plays a major role in the pathogenesis of aortic aneurysm, other conditions also can lead to degenerative changes in the aortic wall. These conditions include hypertension, aging, and specific infectious, inflammatory, or autoimmune diseases.

When atherosclerosis is the cause, the aortic wall is weakened in the area of plaque formation because of the erosive nature of the atherosclerotic process. Eventually localized dilation occurs in the area of weakness. In the abdominal aorta this dilation is most commonly circumferential or fusiform (Fig. 17-38); in the thoracic aorta it is more commonly saccular. According to the law of Laplace (wall tension = pressure × radius), aortic wall tension will increase as the vessel expands. A vicious cycle is created as the increased tension contributes to further dilation and even greater wall tension. This condition is further aggravated by the presence of hypertension, which often coexists with atherosclerosis.

The expanding aneurysm may cause pressure on surrounding structures. The signs and symptoms of thoracic aneurysms result from the pressure they place on adjacent structures and can include dyspnea, cough, stridor, wheezing, dysphagia, and recurrent pneumonitis. Abdominal aneurysms are often asymptomatic. Physical examination will reveal abnormal aortic pulsations, and bruits may be heard over the abdomen.

Thrombi often form in the area of stagnant flow within the aneurysm and if released may result in embolization. Pain or

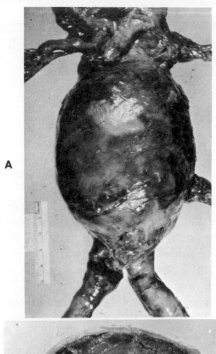

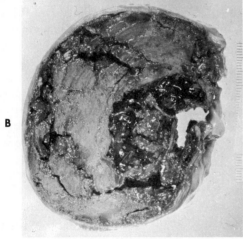

Fig. 17-38. A, Fusiform atherosclerotic aneurysm occupying infrarenal segment of abdominal aorta. **B,** Cross section of aneurysm, showing its lumen mostly occupied by laminated thrombus, but a small blood channel is preserved.

(From Anderson, W.A.D., and Kissane, J.M.: Pathology, ed. 7, St. Louis, 1977, The C.V. Mosby Co.)

tenderness is usually prodromal of impending rupture. Acute rupture is accompanied by extreme pain, hypotension, and usually shock. Rupture without warning is less common in thoracic aneurysms than in abdominal aneurysms because of the usual appearance of symptoms in the former.

CEREBROVASCULAR DISEASE. The brain is extremely dependent on continual, adequate perfusion. Ischemic cerebrovascular disease results when portions of the cerebral vasculature become either narrowed (stenotic) or completely obstructed from thromboembolic or atherosclerotic processes (Gorelick, 1986). Thrombosis and stenosis may reduce the lumen size to the point where arterial insufficiency causes signs of hypoxia such as confusion, slurring of speech, agitation, and forgetfulness. Cerebral emboli can arise in the heart or the cerebral arteries.

A temporary episode of focal cerebral dysfunction, referred to as a *transient ischemic attack* (TIA) if it lasts less than 24 hours and as a *reversible ischemic neurologic deficit* (RIND) if it lasts more than 24 hours, may occur if the ischemic condition does not progress to infarction. Repeated episodes of reversible ischemia may occur, and patients who experience a TIA have a greatly increased risk of suffering a stroke during the following year.

An ischemic stroke (cerebrovascular accident [CVA]) may occur if a vessel becomes completely occluded; the ischemic condition is progressive and nonreversible, and infarction of brain tissue occurs. Lacunar brain infarcts occur in the deeper brain tissue as a result of occlusion of the penetrating branches of the larger cerebral arteries. This is a complication of hypertension that is a degenerative disease of the small cerebral arteries characterized by lipohyalinosis. Atherosclerosis affects the larger arteries and is the most common cause of thrombosis of the extracranial and intracranial cerebral arteries. Ischemic stroke accounts for approximately 80% of all strokes; of this, cerebral embolism causes approximately 14%, and atherothrombotic and lacunar brain infarction cause approximately 66%. Hemorrhagic stroke accounts for the remaining 20% (Gorelick, 1986). The clinical manifestations of alterations in cerebral tissue perfusion are more completely discussed in Chapter 10.

CORONARY ARTERY DISEASE. The findings of many large, well-controlled epidemiologic studies support the notion that the presence of certain risk factors plays a definite role in the development of coronary artery disease. Since atherosclerosis is the causative mechanism in most cases of coronary artery disease (CAD) (Fig. 17-39), it stands to reason that many of the risk factors are the same. These risk factors include family history of cardiovascular disease, a sedentary life-style, obesity, smoking, hypertension, and the presence of various metabolic influences such as diabetes and gout, increased levels of blood cholesterol, hyperlipidemia, abnormal glucose tolerance, and a particular diet pattern (described later). The role of hormonal influences is unclear at the present time; however, in women who have experienced menopause the incidence of CAD is three times greater than in premenopausal women. In women who use oral contraceptives the risk of a myocardial infarction is much greater, especially if another risk factor such as diabetes or hypertension is present. The diet pattern that leads to hypercholesterolemia, hyperlipidemia, and hypertriglyceridemia includes foods high in cholesterol and saturated fats, large amounts of sucrose and glucose, decreased amounts of fiber, more purified foods, and

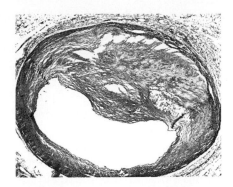

Fig. 17-39. Atherosclerosis of small branch of anterior descending coronary artery. Patient, 47-year-old woman, died of myocardial infarction.
(From Anderson, W.A.D., and Kissane, J.M.: Pathology, ed. 7, St. Louis, 1977, The C.V. Mosby Co.)

high sodium intake. Results of the Framingham Study show that forced vital capacity (a measure of lung function) is predictive of risk: as FVC decreased, the risk of mortality due to cardiovascular disease increased.

There is also strong evidence of behavioral and psychosocial influences on the progression of atherosclerosis and CAD. It appears that interactions exist between biopsychosocial factors and the more physical, traditional risk factors in determining an individual's susceptibility to atherosclerotic heart disease. For example, rabbits fed high cholesterol diets who were petted showed less plaque formation than a comparable group that was not petted. A more human example is a group of accountants whose diet patterns did not change but who showed a rise in serum cholesterol levels between January and April when federal income taxes are due. Smoking behavior and diet patterns are known to change depending on the degree of stress an individual perceives he or she is experiencing (Eliot, 1987). In a review of environmental risk factors in coronary artery or heart disease, Tyroler et al. (1987)

assigned low socioeconomic status the highest priority. In industrialized societies, morbidity and mortality associated with CAD are inversely related to socioeconomic status. This relationship is not completely understood, although it could be linked to other risk factors, since it is known that persons in lower socioeconomic positions smoke more, are more obese, have higher serum cholesterol levels, and have higher blood pressure on the whole when compared to persons in higher socioeconomic positions. It is hypothesized that educational level and social support resources may also affect this variable. Lower education levels, social isolation, and chronic life stress may be characteristic of lower socioeconomic position and affect increased risk as well. An increasing amount of evidence indicates that lack of or minimal levels of social support are linked to increased risk of CAD. Occupations in which workers perceive they have little control and face high demands are associated with increased risk. These associations persist even after controlling for the standard coronary risk factors.

The stress response does appear to play a central mediating role between the physical and behavioral components. Acute stressors have been linked to cardiovascular reactivity. Cardiovascular hyperreactivity has been associated with hypertension and the type A behavior pattern. Recent work with monkeys has demonstrated that the degree of heart rate reactivity is correlated with the severity of coronary atherosclerosis (Shepherd et al., 1987; Manuck et al., 1987). It is postulated that the sympathetic nervous system response to stress and the cardiovascular adjustments that are part of it cause hemodynamic disturbances, such as increased turbulence and mechanical stress on arterial walls, which subsequently lead to endothelial damage. With repetition over time, such damage might set the stage for atherogenesis.

The stress response can also elicit other pathologic changes induced through neurohormonal mechanisms. Increased plasma levels of circulating catecholamines and cortisol have been associated with hypertension and atherosclerosis. Catecholamines have known effects on lipid metabolism and platelet aggregation, both of which are pathologic processes implicated in the development of CAD. Cortisol affects fluid and electrolyte status (specifically sodium retention), influences cholesterol and triglyceride levels, and increases the sensitivity of the arterioles to catecholamines (Eliot, 1987). Manuck et al. (1987) state that catecholamine production is elicited by an active coping response to stress such as a defense reaction, whereas corticosteroid secretion is associated with social subordination and exposure to uncontrollable events, which characterize a passive coping response to stress. Active coping responses to stress in which the individual becomes actively engaged in trying to influence outcomes reflect increased beta-adrenergic activity, whereas passive coping seems to reflect alpha-adrenergic mediation (Shepherd et al., 1987). Such qualitative differences in autonomic responses to stressors do elicit different vascular, endocrine, and cardiac response patterns, which may have important implications for the progression of atherosclerotic pathology and provide clues for different treatment modalities. These biopsychosocial relationships provide a rationale for the use of nonpharmacologic techniques such as relaxation and biofeedback in the treatment of cardiovascular disorders. Eliot (1987) points out that biobehavioral factors often become the triggering mechanism when an acute stress such as emotional shock is superimposed on chronic stress due to constant environmental vigilance. This is certainly well illustrated by the case study of sudden cardiac death in Chapter 5. The mind-body interaction is well characterized by coronary heart disease.

A most interesting association has been demonstrated between behavior patterns and the incidence of coronary artery disease. The coronary disease–prone behavior pattern, dubbed type A behavior, is characterized by extreme aggressiveness, ambitiousness, competitiveness, a strong sense of time urgency, preoccupation with deadlines, and continually striving to complete tasks in the minimal amount of time. This type of personality is particularly well suited to a society of rapid technologic change that functions through large, complex organizations. Indeed, the structure of most business enterprises rewards the type A person with promotions, pay, and incentives, thus reinforcing the behavior. However, in early studies people with type A personality characteristics were found to have twice the risk of developing CAD compared to the type B person, whose personality characteristics are opposite those of type A.

Severeal recent prospective studies have failed to confirm the earlier findings. It now appears that the global type A behavior pattern is not a reliable indicator of subsequent development of CAD and that some aspects of this behavioral pattern may even represent a healthy coping pattern. A subset of this behavior pattern in the domain of hostility/cynicism/anger has been identified as the key behavioral characteristic complex that accounts for the increased risk of CAD associated with type A personality (Williams, 1987). The mode of anger expression also has been found to be related to the occurrence of CAD; patients judged as repressing anger and high in hostility have greater levels of CAD than patients who express anger openly (Costa et al., 1987).

Three risk categories (high, average, and low) have been defined for each sex based on the following variables: systolic blood pressure, serum cholesterol level, smoking, and evidence of glucose intolerance. Each of these factors makes a significant independent contribution to the risk of developing CAD. These effects were combined via a multivariate logistic regression model to determine the three risk categories. An individual's own probability of developing CAD can be estimated using this model.

Alcohol (in moderation) and increased levels of HDLs appear to exert a protective effect against CAD. An inverse relationship between water hardness and cardiovascular mortality has been found; however, the role of trace metals as a protective mechanism has not been clearly elucidated.

Many of these risk factors can be eliminated or modified through changes in lifestyle and dietary patterns (Blackburn et al., 1987). Hyperlipidemia can also be treated with hypolipidemic drugs. Screening for hypertension and diabetes mellitus can identify persons who have these disorders so that they may be treated and the effects thus controlled. The question of whether a person with susceptible personality characteristics can successfully modify his or her behavior is one of considerable current debate and study. Also being studied is the applicability of the concept to females, since most past research has focused on males. Recognition of coronary disease–prone behavior patterns has led many large organizations to offer stress management programs for their executives.

A major thrust of public health education should be toward primary prevention of elevated risk before these factors become operative and require modification.

This requires a population-wide, community-based approach to health education about proper diet, maintenance of ideal body weight and an active life-style, stress, management, and avoidance of smoking at all age levels to minimize the severity and incidence of risk in the general population. Such an approach complements the intensive intervention necessary for risk reduction in susceptible individuals. Carleton and Lasater (1987) note that schools, work sites, and churches are often receptive to health-promotion activities and offer the means to reach large groups of people of all age groups. Attempts at behavioral change must also take into account the fact that behavior occurs within social and cultural contexts that may have an impact on the individual's ability to make life-style changes (Syme, 1987).

The progression of coronary artery disease and manifestation of complications depends on the portion of the coronary circulation that is obstructed and the degree of obstruction. The mildest complication is myocardial ischemia, which is manifested by chest pain of a fairly typical nature called angina pectoris. More severe complications include myocardial infarction and sudden death. Typically angina is triggered by exercise, cold, or anything that increases the work of the heart and consequently myocardial oxygen utilization. The pain is described as a heaviness or fullness that is sharp and stabbing. It usually radiates down the left arm from the chest and intrascapular regions. It goes away spontaneously with rest, usually after 2 to 3 minutes or at the maximum 10 minutes. It frightens the patient so that he stops what he is doing.

Treatment of angina pectoris involves avoidance of precipitating factors, rest, and the use of vasodilating drugs, which increase blood flow to the myocardium. The patient is counseled to stop smoking, since nicotine is a vasoconstrictor. He or she will also be counseled in the prophylactic use of vasodilator drugs before performing physically stressful activity. Pharmacologic agents that block the slow calcium channels are now being used to treat angina, particularly that associated with coronary artery spasm.

Acute myocardial infarction (AMI) is a more severe complication of CAD. It indicates a severe occlusion, either partial or complete, resulting in tissue necrosis of the myocardium. Pasternak, et al. (1988) state that coronary artery occlusion appears to be the final common pathway to AMI in a complex process involving interactions between atherosclerosis, vasospasm, and platelet activation (see Fig. 17-21). While coronary artery thrombosis secondary to atherosclerosis is the most common cause, other pathologic processes can also lead to AMI. Examples include emboli to the coronary vessels, metabolic diseases, congenital anomalies, arteritis, and trauma to the coronary arteries. Cocaine abuse is a recently identified cause of AMI; the mechanism of action involves the effects of increasing myocardial oxygen demand while decreasing coronary blood flow (Pasternak et al., 1988).

A severe, crushing pain that radiates through the chest, to the neck and jaw, down the left arm, and sometimes even to the right arm is the classic type of chest pain. It is not relieved by rest and is accompanied by other symptoms such as nausea, sweating, tachycardia, a drop in blood pressure, and dyspnea. When tissue becomes damaged, cellular substances are released into the blood. When cardiac cells are damaged, enzymes are released into the blood and can be used to make a diagnosis. Table 17-9 summarizes the serum enzymes and their typical responses in myocardial infarction and other diseases. Fig. 17-40 shows the pattern of change following infarction. Because these enzyme changes are nonspecific for myocardial infarction, fractions that are specific for myocardial infarction (referred to as isoenzymes) are used clinically to diagnose this disorder. Changes in the electrocardiogram can also help in the diagnosis of myocardial infarction, as electrical activity is altered in the presence of tissue damage. For example, new Q waves on the electrocardiogram plus a persistent elevation of Ck-MB (an isoenzyme) levels for 12 hours or more indicate that an AMI has occurred (Pasternak et al., 1988).

Complications that can occur include cardiogenic shock, arrhythmias, heart failure, embolism, ventricular aneurysm, and ventricular rupture, any of which may cause death. Postmyocardial infarction syndrome may also occur. This syndrome is characterized by pain, increased white blood cell count, and fever and is self-limiting. The shoulder-hand syndrome, which is characterized by aching pain in the left

Table 17-9. Enzymes evaluated in acute myocardial infarction (AMI)

Enzyme	Normal value (u/ml)*	Elevated value	
		In myocardial infarction	In other conditions
Serum glutamic-oxaloacetic transaminase (SGOT)	8-40	Occurs about 6 hours after AMI; in 18-36 hours reaches peak 2-15 times normal value; usually returns to normal after 3-4 days Nonspecific for AMI Diagnostic value negligible if LDH and CK done.	Occurs in right ventricular failure with hepatic congestion; infarction of kidney, spleen, or intestine; acute pancreatitis; extensive central nervous system damage; primary muscle disease; toxemia of pregnancy; crushing injuries or burns; administration of salicylates, opiates, or coumarin-type anticoagulants; hypothyroidism
Serum lactic dehydrogenase (LDH)	150-300	Occurs 24-48 hours after AMI; in 3-6 days reaches a peak 2-8 times normal; usually returns to normal in 8-14 days	Occurs in a variety of muscle, renal, neoplastic, hepatic, and hemolytic diseases as well as in pulmonary conditions simulating myocardial infarction
Creatine kinase (CPK, CK)	0-4	Occurs within 4-8 hours after AMI; within 24 hours reaches a peak 5-15 times normal but peak may occur anywhere from 8-58 hours after AMI; usually returns to normal in 3 or 4 days Most sensitive for AMI	Occurs in skeletal muscle disease, stroke, hypothyroidism, myopathy associated with chronic alcoholism, clofibrate therapy, electrocardioversion, cardiac catheterization

Adapted from Andreoli K et al.: Comprehensive cardiac care, ed 5, St. Louis, 1979, The CV Mosby Co.
*May vary with different laboratory determinations.

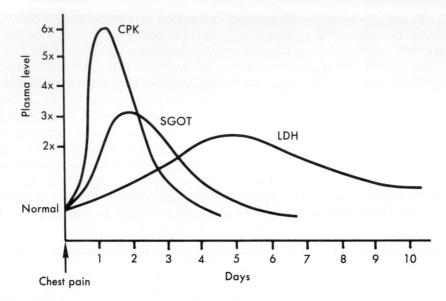

Fig. 17-40. Plot of plasma levels of cardiac enzymes against time after chest pain. Note that CPK (creatine phosphokinase) and SGOT (serum glutamic-oxaloacetic transaminase) peak before LDH (lactate dehydrogenase).

(From Hearse DJ: Myocardial enzyme leakage. J Mol Med 2:185, 1977.

arm and shoulder, may also occur. This is sometimes treated with cortisone to reduce the inflammation.

Treatment rationale. The treatment goals of AMI include the following:

1. Relief of pain
2. Promotion of oxygenation of the tissues
3. Prevention of further tissue damage and promotion of improved coronary circulation
4. Prevention of complications

Analgesic drugs such as meperidine hydrochloride (Demerol) or morphine sulfate are administered for the relief of pain. Supplemental oxygen is administered to improve tissue oxygenation, especially of the myocardium. With improved oxygenation of the body tissues and relaxation that occurs with relief of pain, the cardiac work load is decreased. Anticoagulant therapy is begun and elastic stockings are worn to re-

duce the tendency to develop thromboembolism. Cardiac monitoring is continuous in order to detect the occurence of arrhythmias, and antiarrhythmic drugs are used to prevent and treat any arrhythmias. Intensive treatment is begun at the earliest signs of complications such as heart failure or cardiogenic shock.

The size of the infarct is an important prognostic indicator in patients who have had a myocardial infarction; the larger the infarct, the poorer the prognosis. Following an AMI, the course of recovery may also be complicated by extension of the original infarct or early reinfarction. Prevention of further tissue injury and limitation of the size of the infarct are appropriate goals of treatment for these reasons (Gawlinski, 1987). Interventions aimed at these goals include those which maximize myocardial tissue perfusion and reduce myocardial energy demands. Beta-adrenergic blocking agents are used to reestablish the balance between myocardial oxygen demand and supply. Reperfusion of the myocardium can be achieved by opening or bypassing clogged arteries. Surgery to reestablish perfusion by inserting a new artery to bypass the old has become almost commonplace. The coronary artery bypass graft (CABG) procedure is being performed in community hospitals as well as in tertiary care referral centers. There is currently controversy about the relative efficacy of this procedure in comparison to more conservative medical treatment. The reopening of an occluded artery can also be done with thrombolytic agents, which are injected into the vascular system, or by percutaneous transluminal coronary angioplasty (PTCA). Thrombolytic agents such as streptokinase, urokinase, and tissue plasminogen activator (TPA) activate fibrinolytic processes to lyse the clot (Brooks-Brunn, 1988). This is different from anticoagulant therapy, which prevents the formation of new clots. The value of thrombolytic therapy is its ability to be administered within the critical time period preceding myocardial tissue necrosis. This time period is believed to be somewhere between 3 to 6 hours after the initial infarction has occurred. PTCA is performed using a balloon catheter, which is threaded into the occluded artery and used to cross and compress the occlusion, thereby allowing the free flow of blood past that point.

Rest is important to reduce the energy demands on the myocardium. This means emotional rest as well as physical rest. Any activity that increases heart rate should be avoided, as heart rate is a major determinant of myocardial oxygen consumption. Mild sedation is used to promote rest and relaxation.

Physical activity levels should be kept at a minimum to allow the myocardium to rest and balance oxygen supply and demand. Gradual return to higher levels of activity promotes the regenerative processes. Rehabilitation programs designed to increase activity and exercise tolerance in carefully measured gradients are structured according to the stage of cardiac tissue regeneration that can be expected at given time frames within the convalescent period.

In the short term the best predictors of survival are left ventricular function and the state of the coronary vasculature. A low left ventricular ejection fraction and the presence of stenosis in the left main coronary artery are poor prognostic signs. Over the long term the best prognostic indicators appear to be the progression of chest pain and the extent of coronary atherosclerosis present. The traditional risk factors discussed earlier that are associated with the onset of coronary heart disease do not appear to be useful indicators of the probability of a recurrent ischemic coronary event (Blumenthal and Levenson, 1987).

Secondary prevention includes those interventions targeted at preventing or retarding disease progression in patients diagnosed with coronary heart disease. Nonpharmacologic interventions include dietary restriction of saturated fats and cholesterol, weight reduction and exercise, smoking cessation, stress management, and type A behavior modification (Blumenthal and Levenson, 1987). Pharmacologic intervention includes use of beta-adrenergic blocking agents, hypolipidemic agents, anticoagulant therapy, and platelet inhibitors. The strongest evidence of efficacy exists for the beta blockers, which have been shown to control unstable angina and reduce mortality by preventing recurrent myocardial infarction (Hartley et al., 1987). The beta adrenergic blockers act to reduce myocardial oxygen demands by decreasing heart rate and contractility. Because platelet activity is part of the pathologic processes of atherosclerosis, coronary thrombosis, and spasm, interference with platelet activity would seem to be a necessary intervention. Aspirin, dipyridamole, and sulfinpyrazone are used for this purpose. The potential for noncompliance with any of these interventions exists, and use of a support group like Mended Hearts may help individuals to adhere more closely to a recommended treatment regimen.

REVIEW OF NORMAL BLOOD FUNCTION, DYNAMICS, AND REGULATION

The blood is the transport medium. It helps to maintain wellness not only through its various transport functions but also through its role in maintaining the body defenses, acid-base balance, and normal body temperature. The role of blood in the delivery of oxygen and nutrients is discussed in this chapter. Oxygen delivery to an organ is proportional to the blood flow, the hemoglobin content, and the oxygen unloading in the tissues.

Components of the blood include plasma (the liquid portion), and the blood cells: erythrocytes (red blood cells), leukocytes (white blood cells), and thrombocytes (platelets). The various blood cells are suspended within the plasma portion of the blood. The plasma and the erythrocytes play the greatest role in terms of oxygenation of the tissues.

Plasma is 90% water and 10% solutes. In solution are proteins, which represent the greatest quantity of the solutes, nutrient substances (glucose, amino acids, lipids, fatty acids, etc.), products of metabolism (lactic and pyruvic acids, creatinine, etc.), other humoral substances (hormones, enzymes, etc.), and inorganic chemicals (electrolytes, minerals, etc.). Also in solution in the plasma are the respiratory gases, oxygen and carbon dioxide.

The erythrocytes are cells shaped like biconcave disks. This shape can change readily as the erythrocytes pass through the capillaries. There are approximately 5 million red blood cells per cubic millimeter of blood. Women have fewer red blood cells than men. Red blood cells are produced in the bone marrow. Newly formed erythrocytes, which still contain small amounts of basophilic reticulum interspersed among the hemoglobin, are called *reticulocytes*. Normally reticulocytes make up only 1% of the blood.

The hormone erythropoietin stimulates bone marrow to produce erythrocytes. Hypoxia stimulates the kidneys to release renal erythropoietic factor (REF), which reacts with a plasma protein produced by the liver to form erythropoietin. Androgenic hormones also stimulate erythropoietin production. Red blood cell maturation can be inhibited by lack of either vitamin B_{12} or folic acid.

The major function of the erythrocytes is the transport of hemoglobin. There are two portions to the hemoglobin molecule. The heme portion is made up of an iron atom in the ferrous state in the center of a protoporphyrin ring. Four heme groups are contained within one molecule of hemoglobin. The heme groups give the blood its red color and its ability to combine with oxygen because they contain the oxygen-binding sites. The globin, or protein portion of the hemoglobin molecule, contains two alpha and two beta polypeptide chains. Each of the alpha chains contains 141 amino acid residues, and each of the beta chains contains 146 amino acid residues. The various chains are held together by noncovalent forces to form a three-dimensional, globular protein. Each of the four heme groups is associated with a polypeptide chain.

There is a known structural change that occurs within the hemoglobin molecule when it reacts with oxygen. Of this structural change Perutz (1964) has said, "Hemoglobin's change of shape makes me think of it as a breathing molecule, but paradoxically it expands not when oxygen is taken up but when it is released." When oxygenation of the hemoglobin molecule occurs, the beta chains move approximately 0.7 nm closer to each other and will move apart by the same distance when deoxygenation occurs.

Each iron in the heme portions of the molecule has six potential covalent bonds. Four of the bonds are attached to the pyrrole nitrogens, and the fifth is attached to the globin. The sixth available bond is a weak one that allows oxygen to combine with hemoglobin in a reversible manner. There are four potential oxygen-binding sites on the hemoglobin molecules.

Oxygen is transported in the blood both in chemical combination with hemoglobin and dissolved in the plasma. Normally the amount of oxygen carried in the dissolved state is negligible, only about 3% of the total amount of oxygen being transported. The term *oxygen content* refers to the total amount of oxygen in combination with the blood, that is, the sum of the oxygen in combination with hemoglobin and that dissolved in plasma.

In a normal adult there are 12 to 16 gm (varies by sex) of hemoglobin per 100 ml of blood. Hemoglobin normally exists as either *oxyhemoglobin* (in combination with oxygen: HbO_2) or as reduced hemoglobin (Hb).

Carbon dioxide is also transported in the blood both in chemical combination with hemoglobin as carbaminohemoglobin and dissolved in plasma. Carbon dioxide is also carried by the red blood cells through the bicarbonate ion mechanism. Approximately 25% of the carbon dioxide in the blood is carried as carbaminohemoglobin. Approximately 7% is dissolved in plasma. The rest of the CO_2 is transported through the bicarbonate ion mechanism. Dissolved CO_2 readily diffuses into the red blood cell where it reacts with water to form carbonic acid. This reaction is catalyzed by the enzyme *carbonic anhydrase*. Carbonic acid readily dissociates into hydrogen and bicarbonate ions. This reaction is summarized in the following equation:

$$CO_2 + H_2O \underset{CA}{\rightarrow} H_2CO_3 \rightarrow H^+ + HCO_3^-$$

Bicarbonate ions then move out of the red blood cell into the plasma to reestablish equal concentrations of bicarbonate ions on either side of the cell membrane. Chloride ions must diffuse from the plasma into the erythrocyte to maintain chemical neutrality. This movement of chloride ions from the extracellular to the intracellular compartment is called the *chloride shift*.

Oxygen-carrying capacity is most commonly determined via the measurement of hemoglobin, hematocrit, and red blood cell count. These measurements must always be interpreted in light of other physical signs such as the oxygen saturation, pH (since this has an effect on the affinity between hemoglobin and oxygen), and the reticulocyte count (since this is an indicator of new red cell synthesis). In addition, the bone marrow may be examined to determine the condition of the blood-forming tissues.

Alterations in oxygen-carrying capacity

Oxygen-carrying capacity refers to the blood's ability to bind with oxygen. Since the greatest amount of oxygen is transported in chemical combination with hemoglobin in the erythrocyte, the oxygen-carrying capacity is altered in any condition that affects the red blood cells or hemoglobin. Changes in the volume and in the physical and chemical characteristics of the red blood cells and the hemoglobin molecules are the pathologic, mechanisms underlying anemia and polycythemia, which are discussed more completely in Chapter 3.

Anemia. Anemia is defined as a significant decrease in the red blood cell or hemoglobin concentration in the circulating blood. This is usually detected through measurement of the hemoglobin concentration and the hematocrit.

Etiology and classification. Anemia usually occurs as a result of any hypoproliferative disorder of the blood-forming tissues. Sometimes these tissues are affected secondarily as a result of disease in another organ system. For example, in renal disease the kidney's ability to secrete the enzyme renal erythropoietin factor is depressed and therefore erythropoiesis will also be depressed. There are three types of functional disturbances that lead to anemia:

1. Proliferative disorders, in which production of red blood cells is decreased
2. Maturational disorders with ineffective erythropoiesis (macro- and microcytic)
3. Increased red blood cell breakdown or loss (hemolytic)

Also, blood loss can result in anemia. Hypoproliferative anemias can be the result of bone marrow failure, reduced production of erythropoietin, or iron deficiency. Bone marrow failure can result from the effects of myelotoxic drugs, or the replacement of marrow with malignant cells, or may be congenital. Depressed erythropoietin production accompanies chronic renal disease and certain endocrine disorders.

Erythropoiesis becomes self-limiting in the presence of reduced amounts of iron. An example is the anemia that accompanies inflammation. The primary defect is a decreased supply of iron to the bone marrow because of a block in the release of iron by the reticuloendothelial cells. Another factor in this type of anemia is moderately increased destruction of red blood cells, which is sometimes accompanied by fragmentation due to vasculitis or intravascular clotting. There is also thought to be a relative decrease in the amount of erythropoietin available.

Other iron deficiency anemias are the result of depleted iron stores. The sequence in which an iron deficiency occurs involves first the depletion of body stores accompanied by normal hemoglobin and hematocrit levels. When there is no longer an adequate amount of iron for hemoglobin synthesis, the hemoglobin and hematocrit levels drop. Dietary intake of iron may be insufficient during periods of increased need such as pregnancy and infancy, and dietary supplements become necessary during this time. Iron deficiency anemias can be the result of physiologic losses such as menstruation or pathologic losses such as hemorrhage. They can also be the result of malabsorption states such as sprue or postgastrectomy.

Anemias related to maturational disorders are characterized by normal marrow proliferation not accompanied by a corresponding increase in the concentration of the reticulocytes. This indicates that because of some abnormality in the new red blood cell they are being destroyed before entering the general circulation. There are two types of disorders in this category—macrocytic and microcytic. They are differentiated by the changes in the red blood cell and hemoglobin that occur. Macrocytic anemias include those in which there is some defect in the nucleus of the maturing red cell. The ratio of cellular DNA to RNA is reduced due to enzymatic abnormalities in the pathway of DNA synthesis, which in turn result from deficiency of either vitamin B_{12} or folic acid. A deficiency of vitamin B_{12} is usually not dietary in origin but the result of a disorder in its absorption because of either a lack of the intrinsic factor (pernicious anemia) or disease of the terminal ileum where absorption usually occurs. Folic acid deficiency may be the result of a dietary deficiency, increased need (pregnancy or infection), or some interference with folate metabolism. Drugs, especially alcohol, are usually responsible for the latter.

Hypochromic microcytic anemias reflect some defect in hemoglobin synthesis. Genetically transmitted hemoglobinopathies (discussed in Chapter 2) are included in this group. In the thalassemia and sickle cell disorders the defect is in the globin portion of the hemoglobin molecule. Abnormal porphyrin synthesis results in defects in the heme portion of the hemoglobin molecule.

The hemolytic anemias are characterized by increased destruction of red blood cells, which is manifested by reticulocytosis and hyperplasia of the bone marrow. This destruction may result from abnormal phagocytic activity, increased fragmentation, intravascular lysis, or increased breakdown in the tissues. This classification includes the anemias that occur as a result of increased splenic activity and also those that occur in conjunction with the autoimmune and complement-immune disease.

Clinical manifestations. Generally speaking, anemia is characterized by high cardiac output, tissue hypoxia, and decreased blood viscosity. These latter two effects serve to reduce vascular resistance. The signs and symptoms of anemia are those of oxygen lack and hypoxia of the tissues: easy fatigability, weakness, dyspnea, activity intolerance, pallor, syncope, headache, insomnia, and palpitations. Pallor is observable in the conjunctivae, nail beds, and oral mucosa. In the elderly, local vascular disease may sensitize certain tissues to the effects of anemia. In the presence of preexisting coronary artery disease, anemia may precipitate heart failure or angina. In the presence of central nervous system vascular disease, anemia may produce disturbances in mentation and orthostatic hypotension (a drop in blood pressure when going from a lying to a standing position).

Few, if any, symptoms are apparent with hemoglobin values as low as one fifth of normal. With a drop in hemoglobin below this level cardiac output will fall. The signs and symptoms generally depend on the severity of the anemia (hemoglobin deficit), the rapidity of its development (the more gradually it occurs, the more time for compensatory mechanisms to develop), the patient's activity levels, and the coexistence of cardiopulmonary pathology. With appropriate compensation, chronic anemia can be tolerated well. Compensatory mechanisms include increased cardiac output, redistribution of blood flow, and decreased affinity of hemoglobin for oxygen. If the cardiovascular system cannot respond with these actions, compensation cannot occur.

Treatment rationale. The signs and symptoms of anemia will be relieved with restoration of normal hemoglobin levels. The goals of treatment include the following:

1. Restoration of normal hemoglobin and red blood cell levels
2. Avoidance of conditions that would aggravate symptoms

To permanently restore normal hemoglobin levels, the underlying cause of the anemia must be treated. However, in some cases, such as sickle cell anemia, there is no treatment for the cause. Administration of corticosteroids can increase bone marrow activity and thus blood production in some of the hypoproliferative disorders such as congenital hypoplastic anemia. Transfusions must be given to increase hemoglobin levels when there is no other treatment, when blood volume must be replaced rapidly (such as after a hemorrhage), when hemoglobin levels are dangerously low, or for a relatively minor blood loss when the patient has an inadequate compensatory response due to cardiopulmonary disease. Transfusion therapy carries the following associated risks: transmission of an infectious disease such as hepatitis, deposition of iron in vital organs, and the possibility of a hemolytic or anaphylactic reaction. Achievement of the second goal can be accomplished by encouraging the patient to avoid fatiguing activities and obtain adequate amounts of rest.

The hemoglobin and hematocrit levels and red blood cell count should be routinely monitored in persons at risk for the development of anemia. Some drugs (e.g., phenytoin and isoniazid) have as an inadvertent side effect the development of anemia, so patients receiving them are at risk. Prevention of anemia can be accomplished through administration of iron supplements to persons at risk for development of an iron deficiency anemia, such as menstruating women, infants, or pregnant women. A folate supplement can be used for persons at risk for a folic acid deficiency, such as alcoholic patients.

Polycythemia. Polycythemia is determined by an increase in the hematocrit. Absolute polycythemia is defined as a true increase in the number of red blood cells. Absolute polycythemia represents a normal compensatory response to hypoxia, or it can be the result of some disorder in the regulation of erythropoiesis. An elevated hematocrit can also be the result of a decrease in plasma volume; this is called relative polycythemia. Relative polycythemia can occur as a result of the frank loss of plasma fluid, as in burns, or a shift in fluid from the intravascular to the interstitial space.

Absolute polycythemia may be primary or secondary in origin. Primary polycythemia (polycythemia vera) is considered to be a proliferative disorder. Secondary polycythemias are those under hormonal control and are further classified into two subsets. First are those disorders in which the erythropoietin increase is appropriate. Second are those disorders in which the erythropoietin increase is inappropriate. Examples of the first type are disorders in which hypoxia occurs, such as many of the cardiac and pulmonary problems discussed in Chapter 16 and the early part of this chapter. Examples of the second include various malignant and benign tumors and some renal disorders. Clinical symptoms in primary polycythemia are related to the increased red cell mass and total blood volume, increased blood viscosity, and hypermetabolism. Headache, plethora, bleeding, pruritus, and dyspnea are related to the first mechanism; paresthesias and thrombosis to the second; and weight loss despite good appetite to the third.

SUMMARY

This chapter has presented an overview of the various pathophysiologic mechanisms by which oxygen transport to the body tissues may be disrupted. In many instances these mechanisms can be compensated for during acute episodes as a direct result of medical and nursing intervention. It is therefore important to understand the physiologic basis of restoring normal function as these disease processes may represent a grave threat to the patient's survival.

BIBLIOGRAPHY

Anderson FD: Issues in the postresuscitation period, Crit Care Nurs Q 10(4):51-61, 1988.

Beaver BM: Health education and the patient with peripheral vascular disease, Nurs Clin North Am 21(2):265-272, 1986.

Bilheimer DW: Portacaval shunt surgery and liver transplantation in the treatment of homozygous familial hypercholesterolemia, Prog Clin Biol Res 255:295-304, 1988.

Billhardt RA and Rosenbush SW: Cardiogenic and hypovolemic shock, Med Clin North Am 70(4):853-876, 1986.

Blackburn H, et al.: Task force 5: primary prevention of coronary heart disease, Circulation 76(suppl. I): I164-I167, 1987.

Blumenthal JA and Levenson RM: Behavioral approaches to secondary prevention of coronary heart disease, Circulation 76(suppl. I):I130-I137, 1987.

Braunwald E, editor: Heart disease: a textbook of cardiovascular medicine, ed 3, Philadelphia, 1988, WB Saunders Co.

Brody MJ, et al.: Task force 3: behavioral mechanisms in hypertension, Circulation 76(suppl. I):I95-I100, 1987.

Brooks-Brunn JA, editor: Symposium proceedings: Thrombolytic therapy for acute myocardial infarction: Critical care nursing update, 1988. Heart and Lung 17(6) pt 2:741-792, 1988.

Carleton RA and Lasater TM: Primary prevention of coronary heart disease: a challenge for behavioral medicine, Circulation 76(suppl. I):I124-I129, 1987.

Chesney MA, et al.: Task force 5: nonpharmacologic approaches to the treatment of hypertension, Circulation 76(suppl. I):I104-I109, 1987.

Coronary artery spasm and heart disease, Science 208:1127-1130, 1980.

Costa PT, et al.: Psychological risk factors, Circulation 76(suppl. I):I145-I149, 1987.

Criteria Committee of the New York Heart Association: Nomenclature and criteria for diagnosis of diseases of the heart and great vessels. In Sokolous M and Mellroy MB, editors: Clinical cardiology, Los Altos, 1986, Lange Medical Publishers.

Dantzker D, editor: Cardiopulmonary critical care, Orlando, Fla., 1986, Grune & Stratton, Inc.

Dougherty CM: The nursing diagnosis of decreased cardiac output, Nurs Clin North Am 20(4):787-799, 1985.

Doyle JE: Treatment modalities in peripheral vascular disease, Nurs Clin North Am 21(2):241-253, 1986.

Ekers MA: Psychosocial considerations in peripheral vascular disease: cause or effect? Nurs Clin North Am 21(2):255-263, 1986.

Eliot RS: Coronary artery disease: biobehavioral factors, Circulation 76(suppl. I):I110-I111, 1987.

Flint L: Abdominal injuries. In Richardson J, Polk H, and Flint L, editors: Trauma—clinical care and pathophysiology, Chicago, 1987, Year Book Medical Publishers, Inc.

Gawlinski A, editor: symposium proceedings: Nursing interventions in limiting infarct size in the acute myocardial infarction patient: Nursing implications. Heart and Lung 16(6) pt 2:739-800, 1987.

Goldblatt H, et al: Studies on experimental hypertension, I: The production of persistent elevation of systolic blood pressure by means of renal ischemia, J Exp Med 59:347, 1934.

Gorelick PB: Cerebrovascular disease: pathophysiology and diagnosis, Nurs Clin North Am 21(2):275-288, 1986.

Guyton AC: Hypertension: a neural disease? Arch Neurol 45:178-179, 1988.

Hachinski V: Neurogenic hypertension, Arch Neurol 45:183, 1988.

Hartley LH, et al.: Task force 6: secondary prevention of coronary artery disease, Circulation 76(suppl. I):I168-I173, 1987.

Herd JA, et al.: Task force 2: psychophysiologic factors in hypertension, Circulation 76(suppl. I):I89-I94, 1987.

Herman JA: Nursing assessment and nursing diagnosis in patients with peripheral vascular disease, Nurs Clin North Am 21(2):219-231, 1986.

Ingram RH and Braunwald E: Pulmonary edema: cardiogenic and non cardiogenic. In Braunwald E, editor: Heart disease, a textbook of cardiovascular medicine, ed 2, Philadelphia, 1984, WB Saunders Co.

Iskandrian A, Segal B, and Anderson G: Asymptomatic cardiac ischemia, Arch Intern Med 141(1):95-97, 1981.

Kaplan NM: Systemic hypertension: mechanisms and diagnosis. In Braunwald E, editor: Heart disease: a textbook of cardiovascular medicine, ed 3, Philadelphia, 1988a, WB Saunders Co.

Kaplan NM: Systemic hypertension: therapy. In Braunwald E, editor: Heart disease: a textbook of cardiovascular medicine, ed 3, Philadelphia, 1988b, WB Saunders Co.

Kaplan NM: Clinical hypertension, ed 4, Baltimore, 1986, The Williams & Wilkins Co.

Kottke B and Subbiah M: Pathogenesis of atherosclerosis. Concepts based on animal models, Mayo Clin Proc 53:35-48, 1978.

Manuck SB, et al.: Task force 4: biobehavioral mechanisms in coronary artery disease, Circulation 76(suppl. I):I158-I163, 1987.

Massell BF, et al.: Penicillin and the marked decrease in morbidity from rheumatic fever in the United States, N Engl J Med 318(5):280-286, 1988.

McCall D and O'Rourke RA: Congestive heart failure: biochemistry, pathophysiology, and neuro-humoral mechanisms, Mod Concepts Cardiovasc Dis 54:55, 1985.

Michaelson CR, editor: Congestive heart failure, St. Louis, 1983, The CV Mosby Co.

Moe GK and Antzelevitch C: Mechanisms of cardiac dysrhythmias. In Frohlich ED, editor: Pathophysiology: altered regulatory mechanism in disease, ed 3, Philadelphia, 1984, JB Lippincott Co.

Pasternak RC, Braunwald E, and Sobel BE: Acute myocardial infarction. In Braunwald E, editor: Heart disease: a textbook of cardiovascular medicine, Philadelphia, 1988, WB Saunders Co.

Perutz MF: The hemoglobin molecule, Sci Am 211:67-76, 1964.

Rackley CE, et al.: Modern approach to myocardial infarction: determination of prognosis and therapy, Am Heart J 101:75, 1981.

Raine EG, et al.: Atrial natriuretic peptide and atrial pressure in patients with congestive heart failure, N Engl J Med 315:533-537, 1986.

Reis DJ: The brain and hypertension, Arch Neurol 45:180-182, 1988.

Resnekov L: Cardiogenic shock, Chest 83:893, 1983.

Roccella EJ, Bowler A, and Horan M: Epidemiologic considerations in defining hypertension, Med Clin North Am 71(5):785-801, 1987.

Ross R, et al.: A platelet dependent serum factor that stimulates the proliferation of arterial smooth muscle cells in vitro, Proc Natl Acad Sci USA 7(4):1207-1210, 1974.

Ross EM and Glomset JM: Atherosclerosis and arterial smooth muscle cell, Science 180:1331, 1973.

Ross R: The pathogenesis of artherosclerosis. In Braunwald E, editor: Heart disease: a textbook of cardiovascular medicine, Philadelphia, 1988, WB Saunders Co.

Schrier R and Conger J: Acute renal failure: pathogenesis, diagnosis and management. In Schrier R, editor: Renal and electrolyte disorders, 3, Boston, 1986, Little, Brown & Co.

Shapiro AP, et al.: Task force 4: behavioral consequences of hypertensive therapy, Circulation 76(suppl. I):I101-I103, 1987.

Shekelle R, et al.: Diet, serum cholesterol, and death from coronary heart disease, N Engl J Med 304(2):65-70, 1981.

Shepherd JT, et al.: Task force 3: biobehavioral mechanisms in coronary artery disease, Circulation 76(suppl. I):I150-I157, 1987.

Sobel BE and Roberts R: Hypotension and syncope. In Braunwald E, editor: Heart disease: a textbook of cardiovascular medicine ed 3, Philadelphia, 1988, WB Saunders Co.

Syme SL: Coronary artery disease: a sociocultural perspective, Circulation 76 (suppl. I):I112-I116, 1987.

Turner J: Nursing intervention in patients with peripheral vascular disease, Nurs Clin North Am 21(2):233-240, 1986.

Tyroler HA, et al.: Task force 1: Environmental risk factors in coronary heart disease, Circulation 76(suppl. I):I139-I144, 1987.

Wagner MM: Pathophysiology related to peripheral vascular disease, Nurs Clin North Am 21(2):195-206, 1986.

Warren JC: Surgical pathology and therapeutics, Philadelphia, 1895, WB Saunders Co.

Watanabe Y, Dreifus LS, and Sodeman WA, Sr.: Arrhythmias and pathogenesis. In Sodeman WA and Sodema TM, editors: Sodeman's pathologic physiology: mechanisms of disease, ed 7, Philadelphia, 1985, WB Saunders Co.

Weber K, et al.: Myocardial oxygen consumption: the role of wall force and shortening, Am J Physiol 233(4):21-31, 1977.

Weil MH, Von Planta M, and Rackow EC: Acute circulatory failure (shock). In Braunwald E, editor: Heart disease: a textbook of cardiovascular medicine, ed. 3, Philadelphia, 1988, WB Saunders Co.

West C: Ischemia. In Carrieri VK, Lindsey AM, and West C, editors: Pathophysiological phenomena in nursing: human responses to illness, Philadelphia, WB Saunders, 1986.

Williams RB: Psychological factors in coronary artery disease: epidemiologic evidence, Circulation 76(suppl. I):I117-I123, 1987.

18

Mechanisms of chemical disequilibrium

The body fluid functions in a variety of ways to promote maintenance of wellness in humans. The body fluid constitutes both the external and internal environments of the cell and as such serves many important functions. It serves as the medium for transport of substances to and from the cell and across its membrane. It also serves as the medium in which most metabolic reactions occur, as well as being a necessity for these reactions to occur at all since chemicals must come into contact within a solution to react with one another. The body fluid provides lubrication for moving body parts and assists in heat regulation through evaporation of perspiration. Chemical equilibrium within the body fluid is essential if these functions are to occur normally. This chemical equilibrium is reflected in the normal volume, composition, distribution, and pH of the body fluid and is achieved through fluid, electrolyte, and acid-base balance within the body.

Alterations in the volume, composition, distribution, or pH of the body fluid will cause chemical disequilibrium that will ultimately disrupt wellness. These alterations can occur as a result of primary disorders in the intake, excretion, or regulation of the components of the body fluid or secondarily as part of the pathophysiologic response to other disease states impinging on the steady state. Chemical disequilibrium can also be iatrogenically caused; various treatment modalities have as an inadvertent side effect the loss of fluid, electrolyte, and acid-base equilibrium. Disorders of elimination and its regulation that lead to chemical disequilibrium are discussed in Chapter 20. Disorders of nutrition and the gastrointestinal tract that lead to chemical disequilibrium are discussed in Chapters 19 and 21. Endocrine system disorders that disrupt chemical equilibrium are discussed in Chapter 8.

MAINTENANCE OF NORMAL VOLUME, COMPOSITION, AND COMPARTMENTAL DISTRIBUTION OF THE BODY FLUID

From 45% to 60% of the total body weight in an adult is fluid. The actual proportion in an individual depends on age, sex, weight, and the degree of obesity present (Table 18-1).

The body fluid is comprised of water with various substances in solution (solutes). These solutes are of two major types: electrolytes and nonelectrolytes. Nonelectrolytes are substances that do not dissociate in solution but remain intact and uncharged, for example, dextrose, urea, and creatinine. Electrolytes are substances that dissociate into particles that

Table 18-1. Changes in body fluid with age, sex, and weight

Age/sex/weight	Fluid proportion (%) of kg/wt (approx.)
Premature infant	80
3 months	70
6 months	60
1-5 years	64
11-16 years	58
Adult male	55-60
Adult female	45-50
Obese adult	40-50
Emaciated adult	70-75
Over 65 years	40-50

carry an electric charge. These charged particles are called ions and in solution will conduct an electric current. An ion carrying a positive charge is called a *cation;* an ion carrying a negative charge is called an *anion.* In the normal state these charges are balanced, i.e., electrical neutrality exists. Chemical-combining activity depends on the relative concentrations of anions and cations, which are measured using milliequivalents per liter of solution.

The major body electrolytes are sodium, potassium, calcium, and chloride. Presented in Table 18-2 are the normal concentrations and functions of these electrolytes. Other electrolytes found in the body fluid include magnesium, phosphate, sulfate, bicarbonate, and other trace elements such as zinc. Physiologically important are the concentrations of these substances in the body fluid rather than the absolute total amounts in the body.

Regulation of electrolyte levels is normally provided by the kidneys (which excrete excesses) and hormones. Hormones of the adrenal cortex (aldosterone, cortisone) promote reabsorption of sodium and chloride by the kidneys and allow excre-

tion of potassium, calcium, and magnesium. The parathyroid hormone functions in promoting the absorption of calcium in the intestine and the movement of calcium from bone cells. These actions are accomplished through synergistic action with a metabolite of vitamin D and are activated by low serum calcium levels. Parathyroid hormone also increases renal reabsorption of calcium and clearance of phosphate by the kidney tubules. Thyrocalcitonin is a hormone secreted by the thyroid, which acts synergistically with phosphate levels to lower serum calcium levels. Secretion of this hormone is stimulated by high levels of serum calcium.

Normal water volume is maintained through a balance between water intake and output. Water intake is achieved through drinking and eating and is regulated via the thirst mechanism. Increased plasma osmolarity and decreased plasma volume are the primary stimulants of the hypothalamic thirst center. Psychologic factors, dry oral and pharyngeal mucous membranes and angiotensin II can also stimulate the sensation of thirst. Of course, actual fluid intake depends on the individual's ability to respond to that sen-

24 HOUR FLUID SUMMARY

Intake

Fluids	1,500 ml
Solid food	800 ml
Water of oxidation	300 ml
TOTAL	2,600 ml

Output

Urine	1,500 ml
Perspiration (sensible and insensible)	600 ml
Lungs (vapor) (insensible)	400 ml
Feces	100 ml
TOTAL	2,600 ml

TABLE 18-2. Normal concentrations and functions of the major body electrolytes

Electrolyte	Serum concentration	Function
Sodium (Na)	135-145 mEq/liter	Retention of fluid in body
		Generation and transmission of nerve impulses
		Maintenance of acid-base balance
		Replacement of potassium in cell
		Enzyme activities
		Regulation of osmolarity and electroneutrality of cell
Potassium (K)	3.5-5.0 mEq/liter	Maintenance of regular cardiac rhythm
		Deposition of glycogen in liver cells
		Function of enzyme systems necessary for cell energy production
		Transmission and conduction of nerve impulses
		Regulation of osmolarity and electroneutrality of cell
Calcium (Ca)	4.5-5.5 mEq/liter or 9-11 mg/dl	Formation of bone and teeth (calcium phosphate)
		Transmission of nerve impulse
		Muscular contraction
		Clotting of blood
		Maintenance of cell membrane permeability
Chloride (Cl)	97-104 mEq/liter	Transport of CO_2 (chloride shift) and maintenance of acid-base balance
		Formation of hydrochloric acid in stomach
		Retention of potassium
		Maintenance of osmolarity of cell

sation. The three sources of body water include fluids, solid food, and the water released through oxidative metabolism. Output occurs in the form of urine, perspiration, water vapor from the lungs, and the water content of the feces. Summarized in the box on p. 750 are the average amounts of fluid intake and output for a 24 hour period.

Even if all intake stops, the body still continues to lose water. This is called obligatory loss. This loss occurs through the lungs, skin, and urine; the amount of loss for a 24 hour period is presented in the box in the facing column.

Regulation of the total amount of water excreted by the body is the result of the action of two hormones: antidiuretic hormone (ADH) and aldosterone. ADH increases the permeability of the distal and collecting tubules of the kidneys to water, which results in the reabsorption of water. The posterior pituitary gland releases ADH in response to impulses from osmoreceptors in the hypothalamus. When osmolarity of the body fluid increases, fluid leaves the cells causing them to shrink, which stimulates the hypothalamus to signal the posterior pituitary gland to release the hormone, and subsequently water is reabsorbed by the kidneys. Conversely,

OBLIGATORY LOSS

Lungs	500 ml
Skin	500 ml
Urine	500 ml
TOTAL	1,500 ml

when the osmolarity of the body fluid decreases, the osmoreceptor cells swell, which inhibits secretion of ADH, causing the excretion of water through the kidneys (see Chapter 20).

The volume of extracellular water is also indirectly controlled by the adrenocortical hormone, aldosterone, which is secreted in response to decreased renal blood flow and the subsequent activation of the renin-angiotensin system. Aldosterone causes the retention of sodium by the kidneys, and when sodium is retained, water is also retained.

Another substance known as atrial natriuretic peptide or atrial natriuretic factor (ANF) is also thought to participate in extracellular volume balance through sodium regulation. A group of substances has recently been cloned, sequenced, and described as a family of related peptides or a class of hormones. These peptides are stored in secretory granules found in atrial cells called cardiocytes or myocytes which are more abundant in the right atrium of the heart than in the left. The granularity of these cells is known to change in response to changes in sodium and water balance. Atrial distention is the most probable stimulus for the release of ANF and increased levels of plasma ANF have been described in congestive heart failure and atrial tachycardia. An increase in the circulating volume causes the release of atrial natriuretic factor which, in turn, stimulates a potent and short-lasting diuresis and natriuresis while lowering systemic arterial pressure. The excretion of chloride, potassium, magnesium, calcium and phosphorus have also been found to increase in response to ANF. These effects are mediated through increased renal blood flow and glomerular filtration, inhibition of vasoconstriction and suppression of the release and activity of renin, aldo-

sterone, and ADH. While the physiologic role of ANF is not completely understood at this time, it is thought that ANF may be responsible for the observed loss of sodium that sometimes occurs when levels of salt-retaining hormones (e.g. aldosterone) remain elevated for prolonged periods and for maintaining sodium balance in renal failure (Genest and Cantin, 1987; Laragh, 1985).

Under normal conditions the water and electrolyte levels of the body fluid are maintained within relatively narrow boundaries. The normal constant variation in dietary intake is appropriately matched by alterations in urinary excretion.

It is not only the quantity but also the relative distribution of the body fluid throughout the different fluid compartments that is important in the maintenance of chemical equilibrium. The fluid compartments are structurally and functionally separate and in a state of dynamic equilibrium with one another. The two major compartments are the intracellular fluid (ICF) and the extracellular fluid (ECF).

The fluid in these two compartments accounts for approximately 60% of the total body weight in an adult male who weighs 70 kg. The fluid contained in the intracellular compartment accounts for approximately 35% of the total body weight. The remaining 25% is the fluid contained in the extracellular compartment, which can be further subdivided into the *interstitial* and *intravascular* compartments. The interstitial compartment, the body fluid that bathes the tissue cells, is approximately 12% of the total body weight. The intravascular compartment, that portion of the total body fluid contained in the blood, is approximately 5% of the total body weight. An important conceptual component of the ECF is the effective circulating volume (ECV) or that part of the circulating ECF which is participating effectively in tissue perfusion. The remaining 8% of the body weight represents transcellular fluid and the fluid "trapped" in bone and dense connective tissue.

The fluid in each major compartment has a distinctive electrolyte pattern (Table 18-3). In the intracellular fluid, potassium is the major cation, and phosphate and protein are the major anions. In the extracellular fluid, sodium is the major cation, and chloride is the major anion. Most of the body sodium is outside of the cell, while most of the body potassium is inside the cell. An important difference between the composition of the intravascular and interstitial fluids, which are separated at the capillary membrane, is the greater concentration of the anion protein in the intravascular fluid. The primary extracellular proteins are albumin, globulin and fibrinogen. Intracellularly, proteinate is dominant. The proteins serve many functions, playing a role in the maintenance of intravascular volume as well as preserving the vascular buffering capacity.

Fluid intake or output directly affects the volume and concentration of the intravascular compartment or blood plasma. Changes in the volume and/or concentration of the interstitial and intracellular fluid compartments occur in response to plasma changes.

The fluid compartments are separated from each other by cell membranes. The cell membrane is a structure that is uniquely designed to regulate the move-

Table 18-3. Principal cations and anions of extracellular and intracellular fluid compartments (mEq/L)

Electrolyte	Extracellular fluid		intracellular fluid
	Serum	Interstitial fluid	
Cations of ECF			
Sodium (Na$^+$)	142	145	10
Calcium (Ca^{++})	5	3	10
Cations of ICF			
Potassium (K$^+$)	4.5	4	135
Magnesium (Mg^{++})	2.5	2	25
TOTAL	154	154	180
Anions of ECF			
Bicarbonate (HCO$_3$)	24	27	10
Chloride (Cl$^-$)	104	115	5
Organic acids	6	7	10
Anions of ICF			
Phosphate (HPO$_4^-$)	2	2	100
Sulfate (SO$_4^-$)	1	1	5
Protein	17	2	50
TOTAL	154	154	180

From: Chenevey, B: Nurs Clin North Am *22*(4):749, 1987.
ECF = extracellular fluid
ICF = intracellular fluid

ment of fluids and solutes. Under normal conditions cell membranes are freely permeable to water, selectively permeable to most electrolytes, and relatively impermeable to the plasma proteins and other colloids and large molecules. The cell membrane is a phospholipid bilayer with the molecules oriented in such a way that there is a hydrophobic core. This is the basic building block of the fluid mosaic model in which proteins, which allow specialized functions to occur, are embedded (Figure 18-1). These proteins allow for changes in the structure and function of the membrane, enabling the realization of receptor sites and transport mechanisms. The physicochemical permeability of the membrane and the maintenance of a chemical gradient through active transport processes allow an electrical potential difference to exist across the membrane, which in turn allows cell excitation. Pores and channels that allow for ionic movement also exist within the cell membrane (Groer, 1981).

The movement of water and solutes between compartments is accomplished through both passive and mediated transport processes. Osmosis, simple diffusion, and filtration are passive processes; that is, they are governed by physical laws and require no energy expenditure by the cell. Mediated transport processes are those processes that require a specific transport system to move substances across a cell membrane. Mediated transport processes can be passive or active. Osmosis and filtration are the major forces responsible for water movement across membranes, whereas solutes cross membranes via the processes of simple diffusion and mediated transport.

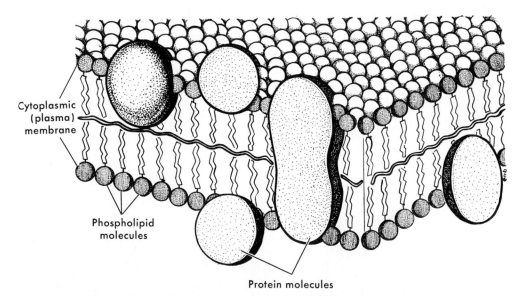

Cytoplasmic
(plasma)
membrane

Phospholipid
molecules

Protein molecules

Fig. 18-1. Fluid mosaic model of cytoplasmic and internal cell membrane. Membrane's molecular structure consists of (1) bilayer of phospolipid molecules arranged with the hydrophilic ends of the molecule oriented toward the outside and the hydrophobic ends pointing toward each other and (2) protein molecules located in all possible positions in relation to phospholipid bilayer—at outer surface, at inner surface, partially penetrating bilayer, and extending completely through membrane.
(From Groer, M: Physiology and pathophysiology of the body fluids, St Louis, 1981, The CV Mosby Co.)

Osmosis

Osmosis is defined as the diffusion of a solvent through a selectively permeable membrane to an area where the concentration of solutes is relatively greater. It is the net movement of water in response to a concentration gradient. Osmotic pressure is the force needed to draw the solvent across the membrane. The osmotic pressure is determined by the relative number of particles in solution on either side of the membrane and is sometimes referred to as *pull pressure,* although this term is technically incorrect. The osmolality of the fluid in the intravascular compartment (plasma) is slightly greater than in the other compartments because of the presence of plasma proteins. The osmotic pressure created by the plasma proteins is also referred to as *oncotic pressure* and is very important in the maintenance of fluid equilibrium. Once an osmotic gradient is established, water will move from the compartment of low osmolality to the compartment of high osmolality until the osmotic pressures are equalized (Fig. 18-2).

When the osmotic pressure is relatively equal on both sides of the membrane (concentrations of solutes are equal) the solutions are *isosmotic* to one another. They are also considered to be isosmotic if no volume change occurs between them. A solution that contains a lesser concentration of solutes than another solution is *hypotonic* or hyposmotic in relation to the other. Water is hypotonic in relation to the body fluids. If a red blood cell is placed in a container of fresh water, water will move into the cell by the process of osmosis, causing the cell to swell and diluting the body fluid inside it. Eventually the cell will burst. A solution that has a higher concentration of solutes than another is *hypertonic* or hyperosmotic in relation to the other. A cell placed in a hypertonic solution will have the water drawn out of it by the process of osmosis, causing it to become crenated (wrinkled and shrunken).

The relative numbers of osmotically active ions in each compartment determine

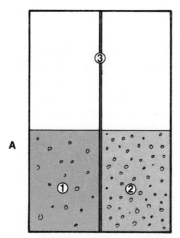

1. Dilute solution
2. Concentrated solution
3. Semipermeable membrane

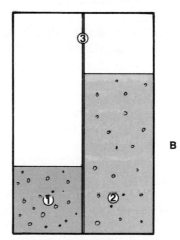

1 and 2. Solutions of equal concentrations

3. Semipermeable membrane

Fig. 18-2. Process of osmosis. **A,** Before. **B,** After.

the distribution of fluid between the extra- and intracellular compartments. For example, sodium ions are partly responsible for extracellular osmolality, while potassium ions are partly responsible for intracellular osmolality. The osmotic activity of these ions is effective because of the Na^+-K^+ pump in the cell membrane, which restricts the movement of these ions between compartments. The Na^+-K^+ pump not only works to maintain intracellular electrolyte concentrations but also serves to regulate cell volume. Because of a greater concentration of nondiffusible anions (protein) in the cells, there tends to be a higher osmotic pressure in the cells than in the interstitial fluid. If the Na^+-K^+ pump became nonfunctional Na^+ would enter the cell down a concentration gradient and either Cl^- would follow or K^+ would leave the cell in order to maintain electroneutrality. The cell would swell in response to the greatly increased osmotic pressure. The activity of this pump appears to be regulated by sodium-potassium-activated ATPase (Na-K-ATPase), an enzyme that hydrolyzes ATP to ADP. The released energy is then utilized to actively transport Na^+ out of the cell and K^+ into the cell. The mechanism by which this energy is coupled to the work is not understood at this time. The osmotic pressure of plasma is higher than that of interstitial fluid because of both the presence of the plasma protein (which for the most part cannot freely cross the capillary membrane) and the greater number of ions in the plasma resulting from the Gibbs-Donnan effect. A solute (for example, urea) able to cross the cell membrane freely and reach equal concentrations on either side is ineffective in generating an osmotic pressure and therefore cannot affect fluid distribution.

Osmotic forces are the prime determinant of water distribution in the body and depend on the relative permeabilities of solutes on either side of a membrane. When a pathologic process causes a membrane to become permeable to a solute to which it is normally impermeable, serious alterations in fluid distribution may occur because of the resultant disruption of osmotic forces.

Diffusion

Simple diffusion is the net passive and random movement of solute particles from an area of higher concentration to an area of lower concentration, or down the concentration gradient, across a membrane that is selectively permeable to the solute. When equilibrium is reached, the random molecular movement will continue but will be equal in all directions because there will no longer be a concentration gradient. Permeable gases and solutes diffuse between the intravascular and interstitial fluid at the capillary membrane.

The rate of diffusion depends on the relative permeability of the membrane to the diffusing solute and the size or steepness of the concentration gradient; that is, the greater the concentration difference, the greater the rate of diffusion (Chenevey, 1987; Groer, 1981). Membrane permeability depends on the nature of the solute and the lipid, protein, and channels within the membrane. Substances that are lipid soluble, such as ethanol and most gases, diffuse through the membrane more readily than substances that are not lipid soluble, such as most ions. Substances that are not readily diffusible through the membrane must move through pores or channels or be transported by carrier molecules, which are discussed in a subsequent section of this chapter.

Small polar molecules like urea and water diffuse more quickly than expected, probably because of a size-related ability to move through small aqueous channels in the cell membrane. Most ionic movement down concentration gradients occurs through channels. Channels behave as if the entry of ions is controlled by a "gate," the state of which (open or closed) varies with changes in the electrical potential difference across the membrane. When open, a channel allows many ions (10^6 to 10^8 per second) to move through. Pores or channels are thought to be specific to one type of ion, and channels have been described for Na, K, Cl, and Ca (Maxwell, Kleeman, and Narins, 1987). The size and charge of the internal lumen of the pore are factors that interact to limit movement through the channel to a specific ion. An example using Na^+ is shown in Fig. 18-3 (Groer, 1981).

The regulation of channel activity may have important implications for clinical therapeutics. In fact, a class of drugs known as calcium channel blockers affects the electrophysiologic and mechanical function of the heart and promotes relaxation of vascular smooth muscle by inhibiting the transmembrane influx of calcium ions into cardiac and vascular smooth muscle. As a result of these actions, calcium channel blockers have a broad range of therapeutic applications, including treatment of certain cardiac dysrhythmias, angina caused by coronary artery spasm, systemic hypertension, and hypertrophic cardiomyopathy (Andreoli et al. 1983).

Although simple diffusion of solute particles is primarily determined by the concentration gradient, the electrochemical and pressure gradients must also be considered. Since oppositely charged ions tend to move toward one another, the presence of an oppositely charged membrane interior will enhance diffusion across the membrane. Diffusion of gases depends on a pressure gradient. The higher the pressure, the greater the number of molecules that will strike and diffuse through the membrane.

Filtration

Filtration is the process by which water and diffusible substances move out of the solution with the greater hydrostatic pressure when a difference in hydrostatic pressure exists on two sides of a membrane. Filtration results from the interaction of forces that serve to promote net fluid movement across the membrane. The following equation describes this interaction:

Net filtration = Kf (forces favoring filtration
− forces opposing filtration)

Where

Kf equals the net permeability of the capillary membrane

In the capillary beds of the body these forces include the hydrostatic pressure,

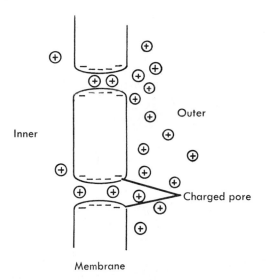

Fig. 18-3. Sodium channel. Negatively charged pores of appropriate diameter for sodium movement may be present in membrane. The atomic diameter of the Na^+ ion is 5 Å (angström) whereas the theoretical Na^+ pore diameter is 7 Å.

(From Groer, M: Physiology and pathophysiology of body fluids, St Louis, 1981, The CV Mosby Co.)

the interstitial fluid pressure, and osmotic pressure. The *hydrostatic pressure* is the force with which the fluid presses against the vessel wall and as such will favor movement out of the capillary. It is the result not only of the weight of the blood against the vessel wall but also of the force with which the blood is propelled by the heart and the effect of gravity. Hydrostatic pressure is higher at the arterial end of the capillary bed than at the venous end. The osmotic force exerted by the plasma proteins is called oncotic pressure and it favors movement of fluid into the capillary. This is the only effective osmotic pressure in the capillary bed since the capillary membrane, unlike the cell membrane, is freely permeable to Na^+ and other electrolytes. Pressures exerted by the interstitial fluid must also be considered. Small amounts of protein will eventually leak out of the plasma into the interstitium; therefore the interstitial fluid will offer some oncotic pressure that favors movement of fluid out of the capillary into the interstitium. There is disagreement about whether the interstitial fluid exerts any hydrostatic pressure against the vessel wall (which would oppose fluid movement out of the capillary) or whether a negative pressure or vacuum exists in the tissues (which would favor movement out of the capillary).

As a result of the various pressure and concentration differences on either side of the membrane, fluid moves out of the capillary into the interstitium at the arterial end and is reabsorbed carrying cellular waste products into the intravascular compartment at the venous end. The filtration-absorption relationships (Fig. 18-4) that are a result of these forces were first

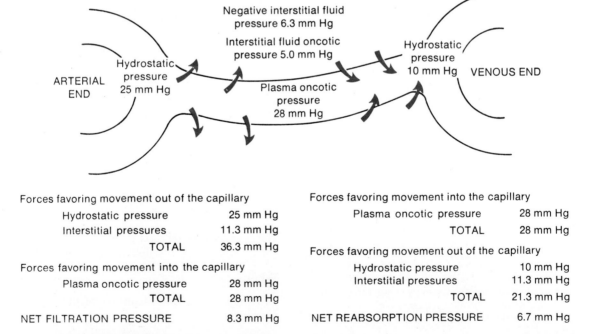

INTERSTITIAL FLUID

Negative interstitial fluid pressure 6.3 mm Hg

Interstitial fluid oncotic pressure 5.0 mm Hg

Hydrostatic pressure 25 mm Hg

Hydrostatic pressure 10 mm Hg   VENOUS END

ARTERIAL END

Plasma oncotic pressure 28 mm Hg

Forces favoring movement out of the capillary	
Hydrostatic pressure	25 mm Hg
Interstitial pressures	11.3 mm Hg
TOTAL	36.3 mm Hg

Forces favoring movement into the capillary	
Plasma oncotic pressure	28 mm Hg
TOTAL	28 mm Hg

NET FILTRATION PRESSURE	8.3 mm Hg

Forces favoring movement into the capillary	
Plasma oncotic pressure	28 mm Hg
TOTAL	28 mm Hg

Forces favoring movement out of the capillary	
Hydrostatic pressure	10 mm Hg
Interstitial pressures	11.3 mm Hg
TOTAL	21.3 mm Hg

NET REABSORPTION PRESSURE	6.7 mm Hg

Fig. 18-4. Capillary bed, illustrating effect of Starling's forces governing movement of fluid between intravascular and interstitial compartments (values shown are arbitrary).

described by Starling in 1896. Assumed in Fig. 18-4 is a negative interstitial fluid pressure as discussed above. Alterations in any of the forces described will result in abnormal filtration-absorption relationships and disrupt the movement of fluid between the plasma and interstitial space.

Mediated transport

Passive diffusion across cell membranes of large polar molecules like sugar and amino acids would occur slowly, if at all. Transport systems that facilitate the movement of these substances across membranes are required. These transport systems exist as proteins or protein complexes (called transporters or translocases) that are integral to the cell membrane. Systems are recognized that can move a single molecule in one direction (uniport mechanism), two molecules in one direction (symport mechanism), or two molecules in opposite directions (antiport mechanism). Basically, these systems allow a process that involves the following steps: (1) recognition of the substance to be transported, (2) translocation or the actual movement of the substance, (3) release of the transported substance, and (4) recovery of the carrier molecule. All transport systems demonstrate saturation kinetics, specificity for a particular substance and the capacity for inhibition. The additional characteristics of movement against a concentration gradient and the coupled input of energy apply to active mediated transport systems as compared with passive mediated transport systems (Devlin, 1986).

Passive mediated transport, or *facilitated diffusion,* allows movement of substances down their concentration gradient much more quickly than expected (Fig 18-5). Initially the rate of transport is much greater than that seen with simple diffusion; however, as the protein transporter becomes

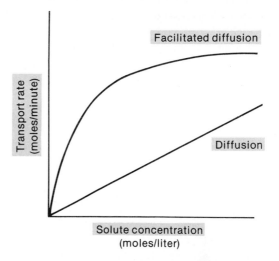

Fig. 18-5. Comparison of rates of simple and facilitated diffusion. Facilitated diffusion demonstrates an initial rapid rate of diffusion, and at low solute concentrations, most transport occurs by facilitated diffusion. The proportion of transport caused by simple diffusion continues to increase while carrier molecules become unavailable because of saturation kinetics.

unavailable (saturated) a maximum rate will be achieved. D-glucose is an example of a molecule transported by facilitated diffusion via a uniport mechanism. The capacity of the transporter appears to be increased to such an extent that glucose uptake increases when insulin is bound to the insulin receptors on the cell membrane. The exchange of Cl^- for HCO_3 in the erythrocyte also occurs as a result of passive mediated transport via an antiport system.

Ionophores are low molecular weight compounds that facilitate ionic movement. Known ionophores include a class of antibiotics of bacterial origin. The existence of ionophores in tissue cells has been proposed (Devlin, 1986).

Active transport systems are also referred to as "pumps" and require the coupled input of energy. Energy can be derived from the hydrolysis of ATP to ADP or from the transmembrane electrochemical gradient of Na⁺. This latter process is also called secondary active transport or Na^+ co-transport (Maxwell et al., 1987). Maintenance of Na^+ and K^+ gradients across membranes is known to be caused by an ATP-driven $Na^+ - K^+$ antiport system. The transporter is $Na^+ - K^+ - ATPase$, an enzyme that is present in all cells and that has a requirement for sodium, potassium, and magnesium ions. Its protein structure has been described, and several conformations of the protein complex have been observed (Devlin, 1986). Other ATPases such as $K^+ - H^+$, Ca^{++} and Mg^{++} are also known to exist (Maxwell et al., 1987). When the electrochemical gradient of Na^+ ions is used to move sugars, amino acids, and other ions, metabolic energy is necessary to maintain the gradient but it is not directly required for transport.

ALTERATIONS IN FLUID VOLUME AND COMPOSITION

Disruption of chemical equilibrium may be the result of changes in the volume and composition of the body fluid. Of particular importance are volume changes in infants, obese individuals, and aged persons. The fluid volume in the infant represents approximately 75% to 80% of the body weight. Although this amount of fluid is relatively greater than that of the adult, the infant has a proportionally greater ratio of surface area to volume and a higher metabolic rate. In addition, the infant's renal system is relatively immature with a limited ability to concentrate urine. The combination of these factors creates the potential for much greater insensible fluid losses than in the adult. Thus the infant is prone to develop serious volume deficits in a relatively short period of time.

Other groups that are considered at risk for the development of excessive fluid loss include the obese and the elderly (Table 17-1). Fat cells contain relatively smaller amounts of water than do other cells, and the percentage of body weight representing fluid is greatly reduced in the obese individual for that reason. A variety of factors contribute to the problem of fluid balance in the elderly. First, the total percentage of fluid body weight decreases with age. In persons over 65 years of age only 40% to 50% of the body weight may be in fluids. Other problems of the elderly that may complicate fluid balance include reduced nutritional intake, an impaired sense of thirst, chronic illness, depressed renal function, and the use of medications that may alter fluid volume and composition.

Possible alterations in the total amount of fluid present in the body include expansion (hypervolemia) or depletion (hypovolemia) of the fluid volume. It is important to assess not only the total amount of fluid lost or gained but also the composition of the fluid itself. Presented in Table 18-4 are the electrolyte concentrations of the various body secretions and excretions. Loss of excessive amounts of any of these body fluids can result not only in a volume deficit but also in electrolyte deficit states. Disruption of the normal patterns of elimination or intake may result in a state of volume expansion or electrolyte excess. In addition, alterations in the amount and composition of the body fluid have the potential for ultimately disrupting the osmolality and pH. Changes in pH are discussed later in the chapter.

Osmolality

Osmolality is a measure of the concentration of solutes within a solution. In plasma and urine it is a measure of the concentration of ions, molecules, and free particles dissolved in water. In plasma the primary osmoles include sodium, glucose, and

TABLE 18-4.   Electrolyte concentration of body excretions and secretions (mEq/liter)

Source	Sodium	Chloride	Potassium	Bicarbonate
Sweat	15-18	15-80	>5	0
Saliva	20-80	20-40	10-20	20-60
Gastric juice	20-100	20-160	5-10	0
Bile	150-250	40-80	5-10	20-40
Pancreatic juices	120-250	10-60	5-10	80-120
Ileum (mean)	129	116	11	29
Cecum (mean)	80	48	21	22

urea. Osmolality is measured as the gram molecular weight of solutes dissolved in 1000 gm of a solvent (Goldberger, 1986).

Serum osmolality. Serum osmolality can be measured directly or calculated. A simple formula for use in the clinical setting is as follows:

Calculated serum mOsm/kg =
$$1.86\ Na^+ + \frac{Glucose}{18} + \frac{BUN}{2.8}$$

This can be further simplified to:

Calculated serum mOsm/kg =
$$2\ Na^+ + \frac{Glucose}{18} + \frac{BUN}{2.8}$$

The effective serum osmolality can also be calculated and is based on the fact that sodium and glucose are the major extracellular solutes. This formula is simply:

$$Effective\ serum\ mOsm/kg = 2\ Na^+ + \frac{Glucose}{18}$$

A change in the concentration of solutes relative to that of the body water will precipitate a movement of water between the ECF and ICF in order to restore osmotic equilibrium. Because water is freely permeable across cell membranes, equilibration of osmolality between the ECF and ICF occurs rather quickly and the body fluid compartments normally exist in a relative state of osmotic equilibrium. The serum osmolality, therefore, reflects the osmolality of the total body fluid.

The serum sodium concentration is responsible for approximately 90% of the osmotic pressure generated by plasma. Because sodium is the principal osmole, osmolality of the body fluid is really a reflection of the relative concentrations of sodium and water. For this reason, the plasma sodium concentration is also considered to be a fairly accurate indicator of the plasma osmolality. It is not an accurate indicator of the total body sodium.

Although sodium and water balance are functionally linked with one another, physiologically they are maintained through separate mechanisms (Kokko & Tannen, 1986). Total body sodium balance is maintained primarily through hormonal and renal mechanisms that control sodium reabsorption and excretion. Total body water balance is regulated via the same feedback loop through which normal serum osmolality is maintained. Plasma osmolality is maintained through variations in water intake and excretion, which are mediated by changes in thirst and ADH secretion. Illustrated in Fig. 18-6 is the feedback mechanism through which plasma osmolality is maintained. The normal quantitative relationships between

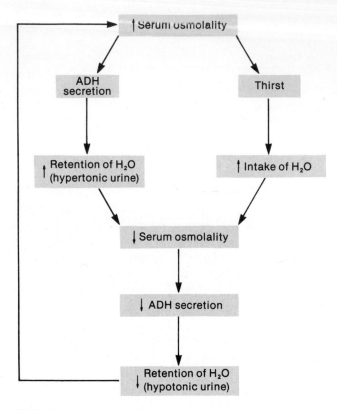

Fig. 18-6. Physiologic mechanisms that maintain normal serum osmolality.

plasma and urine osmolality, plasma ADH level, and thirst are depicted in Fig 18-7.

Alterations in osmolality

Disruption or alteration in the physiologic mechanisms that control sodium and water balance can cause a change in sodium relative to water or a change in water relative to sodium. Either change will alter the osmolality of the body fluid and lead to osmotic shifts of water between the fluid compartments. This has the potential to cause volume changes as well. Because of the relative impermeability of the Na^+ ion and the permeability of H_2O to the cell membrane, the volume (or size) of the ECF depends on sodium regulation, whereas the volume (or size) of the ICF depends on

water regulation (Fig. 18-8). Alterations in sodium balance will be reflected by ECF volume changes, and alterations in water balance will be reflected by ICF volume changes (Humes, 1986).

Clinical syndromes related to alterations in either sodium or water balance will reflect the effects of osmotic and volume changes on the cells and the size of the ECF. Because of the close functional relationship between sodium and water, the plasma sodium concentration can be used as a starting point in clinical decision making about alterations in fluid volume, composition, and distribution related to disorders of sodium and water balance. The serum sodium concentration will be elevated when sodium is present in excess

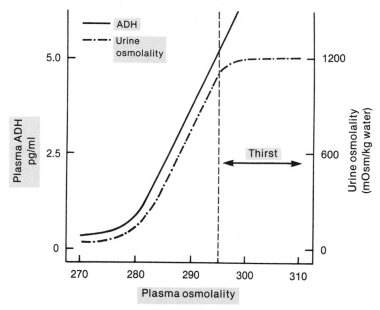

Fig. 18-7. Relationship between plasma ADH, plasma osmolality, urine osmolality, and thirst. ADH release is stimulated when plasma osmolality rises above 280 mosmol/kg water. The effect of ADH on renal water excretion obeys the approximate relationship $\Delta P_{osm} = 95\Delta U_{osm}$ until P_{osm} reaches 295 mosmol/kg water and U_{osm} is maximal. At this point, endogenous water conservation is maximal and thirst is stimulated to provide exogenous addition of water.

(From Humes, HD: Pathophysiology of electrolyte and renal disorders, New York, 1986, Churchill Livingstone.)

of water and decreased when water is present in excess of sodium. Plasma and urine osmolality and the clinical history of the patient will also need to be examined to identify sources of loss or gain of water or sodium.

Hypernatremia. A high serum sodium concentration (hypernatremia) can be the result of either a net sodium excess or a net water deficit (Groer, 1981). Hypernatremia always represents hyperosmolality. However, clinical manifestations will occur only if the hyperosmolar state is also hypertonic. In other words, the hyperosmolality must be the result of an increased concentration of effective osmoles (impermeant solutes) in the ECF that cause an osmotic shift of fluid and net ICF volume depletion or contraction (Humes, 1986).

Development of hypernatremia is also related to the presence of an intact thirst mechanism and the ability to ingest water. Normally, the thirst mechanism is a very effective means of preventing hypernatremia by signaling the need to increase water intake. Consequently, water loss results in hypernatremia only when there is a corresponding decrease in water intake caused by an impaired thirst mechanism or the inability to obtain or ingest water.

There are three possible pathogenetic mechanisms by which hypernatremia occurs: (1) loss of pure water, (2) loss of water and solutes with water being lost in excess of solutes, and (3) gain of sodium. Most commonly seen in the clinical setting is the second or hypotonic fluid loss with the loss of water exceeding that of sodium

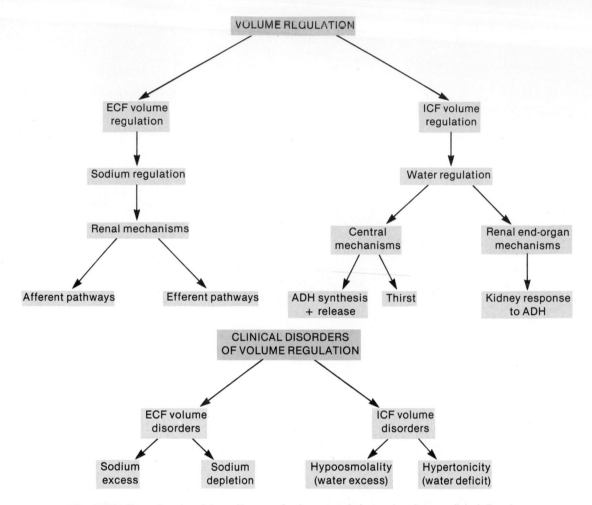

Fig. 18-8. Flow diagram of the pathways of volume regulation and analogous clinical disorders.
(From Humes, HD: Pathophysiology of electrolyte and renal disorders, New York, 1986, Churchill Livingstone.)

(Humes, 1986). Least commonly seen clinically is the third, which may be caused by ingestion of salt tablets or sodium-rich fluid (especially in infants) or may be iatrogenic in origin as a result of parenteral administration of hypertonic saline, therapeutic saline abortion, administration of sodium bicarbonate during cardiopulmonary resuscitation, or dialysis using a hypertonic dialysate (Schrier, 1986). Pathologic conditions that can lead to hypernatremia are classified according to the

operative pathogenetic mechanism in Fig 18-9. These conditions are discussed in more detail in subsequent sections and chapters of text.

Clinical manifestations of hypernatremia are related to the ICF volume contraction and the changes in total body sodium content and ECF volume that occur. The predominance and severity of signs and symptoms will depend on which pathogenetic mechanism has caused the hypernatremia and the rapid-

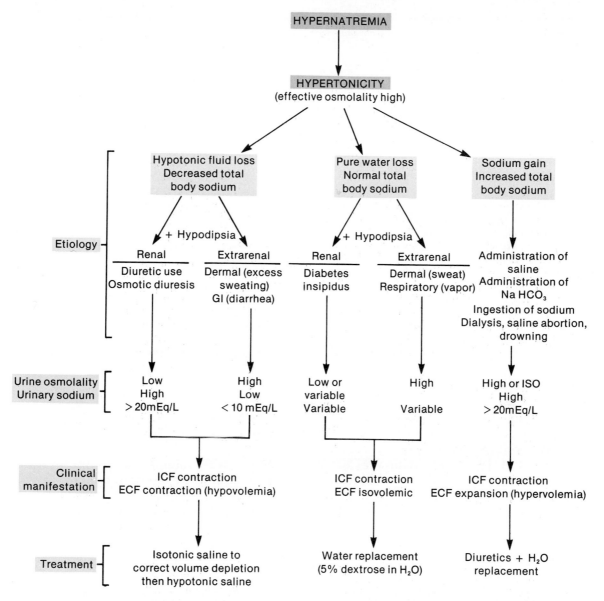

Fig. 18-9. Etiologies, manifestations, and treatment of hypernatremia (hyperosmolality of the body fluid).

(Adapted from Berl, T, Anderson, RJ, McDonald, KM, and Schrier, RW: Kidney Int, 10:117, 1976.)

ity with which it has occurred. Treatment must be tailored to the causative mechanism as well.

Although ICF volume contraction always occurs regardless of the pathogenetic

mechanism operating, the ECF volume and total body sodium level will differ depending on the mechanism causing hypertonicity (Humes, 1986). With the loss of pure water, total body sodium remains

TABLE 18-5. Signs and symptoms of water imbalance (ICF volume changes)

Water deficit (ICF volume contraction)	Water excess (ICF volume expansion)
Symptoms	
Thirst	Headache (rare)
Change in urinary output: oliguria except in solute excess where polyuria is seen	Drowsiness
	Weakness
Weakness	Disorientation
Disorientation	Apathy and lethargy
Signs	
Flushed skin	Weight gain
Scant body secretions	Skin warm and moist
Tongue appears dry and fissured	Cramps
Mucous membranes feel "sticky"	Hematocrit may be slightly low but usually is unchanged
Weight loss (except with solute excess)	Serum sodium concentration is low because of dilution
"Doughy" texture of skin	
Increased temperature	
Hematocrit may be slightly elevated	
Serum sodium concentration is high	
Personality changes	
Hallucinations, delirium, manic behavior, convulsions, and coma may develop	

normal, and the ECF remains isovolemic, and the signs and symptoms of water deficit (ICF volume contraction) will be predominant (Table 18-5). With the loss of water and solutes, total body sodium will be decreased and the ECF will be hypovolemic. In addition to the signs and symptoms of ICF volume contraction, those of ECF volume contraction or deficit will also be present, including tachycardia, orthostatic hypotension, flat neck veins, and poor tissue turgor. With the addition or gain of sodium there will be an increased amount of total body sodium, and ECF hypervolemia will occur. Signs and symptoms of ECF volume expansion or excess such as jugular vein distention, bounding pulse, orthopnea or dyspnea, rales, and increased blood pressure will be predominant. If this develops rapidly, pulmonary edema can occur (Humes, 1986; Schrier,

1986). Clinical manifestations of changes in the ECF volume are summarized in the box on p. 767.

Since ICF volume contraction is the usual sequel to hypernatremia, signs and symptoms of water deficit (Table 18-5) will be part of the clinical presentation regardless of the cause. The signs and symptoms of ICF volume contraction occur as a result of cellular dehydration or loss of water from the tissue cells in response to ECF hypertonicity. The brain cells are particularly sensitive to volume loss, and as cerebral cells shrink, cerebral vessels will tear, leading to bleeding, vascular congestion, and thrombosis. Consequently, many of the clinical manifestations are neurologic, for example, restlessness, lethargy, irritability, hyperreflexia, muscle twitching and spasticity, seizures, and coma leading to death.

EXTRACELLULAR FLUID VOLUME

Contraction	Expansion
	Moderate
Orthostatic hypo-tension	Increased cardiac output
Tachycardia	Bounding pulse
Collapsed veins	Venous distention
Sleepiness, apa-thy, slow re-sponses	Elevated venous pres-sure
Decreased skin turgor	Subcutaneous pitting edema
Soft, small tongue with longitudinal wrinkles	Basilar rales
	Loud heart sounds and S_2
Anorexia	Functional murmurs and gallop
	Severe
Hypovolemic shock	Pulmonary edema
Decreased blood pres-sure	Anasarca
	Moist rales
Absent pulses	Dyspnea or orthopnea
Pallor	Vomiting
Cold extremities	Diarrhea
Distant heart sounds	
Decreased re-flexes	
Stupor, coma	
Nausea, vomit-ing, silent ileus	
Sunken eyes	
Atonic muscles	

As a protective mechanism, the brain is able to generate "idiogenic osmoles" that serve to restore osmolality and subsequently, the water volume of the brain tissue. These "idiogenic osmoles" are thought to be related to intracellular amino acids, particularly taurine (Schrier, 1986). This protective effect takes time to develop, however, and therefore, the rapidity and degree of development of hypernatremia will affect the severity of the clinical manifestations. If hypernatremia develops slowly, allowing time for the generation of idiogenic osmoles and maintenance of brain volume, the clinical manifestations will be less severe than if the hypernatremia develops rapidly. This also has implications for treatment, since rapid correction of hypernatremia in the presence of these idiogenic osmoles sets the stage for an osmotic gradient to develop between the plasma and brain cells, which would allow the net movement of water into the cells causing cellular overhydration and cerebral edema. In order to avoid this complication of treatment, it is recommended that correction of hypernatremia be done slowly at a rate that would reduce the serum sodium concentration by no more than 2 mEq/L/hour over the first 48 hours (Humes, 1986).

Hypotonic fluid loss that results in hypovolemic hypertonicity requires replacement of the ECF volume with isotonic saline followed by hypotonic saline to replace water losses and restore the ICF volume. Pure water loss (isovolemic hypertonicity) requires water replacement, which can be done with a solution of 5% dextrose in water. Hypervolemic hypertonicity requires removal of the excess sodium (which can be done with diuretic agents or dialysis if renal function is impaired) and administration of 5% dextrose in water to correct volume losses that occur (Humes, 1986; Schrier, 1986). These alterations in fluid volume and composition are a response to some underlying pathologic process that must also be treated if normal body fluid volume, composition, and distribution are to be maintained. These etiologic conditions are discussed elsewhere in this text. The identification and management of hypernatremic (hyperosmolal) disturbances of body fluid are summarized in Fig. 18-9.

The following case study shows the effect of fluid loss in an infant. Infants are especially at risk for the development of fluid volume deficit.

CASE STUDY: FLUID VOLUME DEFICIT

History

Baby S was a previously well infant who had received routine well baby care and all immunizations were up-to-date. She had been bottlefed since birth with Similac formula and developing normally. Prior to this illness, she weighed 6.8 kg (15 lbs) on the home scale. Mother reports a normal labor and delivery at another hospital. Baby S is the first child of young parents who recently moved away from their families to a different city when the mother took a new position in a large corporation. The father is responsible for child care.

Present illness: Baby S, a 5-month-old girl accompanied by her parents, was brought to the emergency room by paramedics after suffering a seizure at home. Two days prior to admission Baby S developed a fever and was extremely irritable. She vomited several times and became lethargic in the evening, refusing to drink more than a few ounces of formula. During the next day she began to have profuse green liquid diarrhea and the fever rose to 104° F (40° C). The fever did not respond to acetaminophen. Baby S appeared to drink formula eagerly but vomited it up soon after each feeding, and cried incessantly.

Objective and Subjective Data

The father reports not having called the pediatric clinic because "all babies get sick from time to time and it was just a stomach flu and I didn't want to be any trouble or act like I couldn't handle it." The mother is crying and asks "Will she

Contributed by Maureen Shekleton.

be all right? I didn't realize she was so sick. John's been staying up with her because I have to go to work early in the morning."

Physical examination in the emergency room revealed the following findings:

General findings: Flushed, very lethargic infant with sunken eyes, poor skin turgor, depressed fontanel, dry mouth and skin, dry diaper, no stools at present.

Eyes, ears, and nose: Baby cries without apparent reason.

Neck: Full range of motion, trachea midline, neck veins flat (above clavicle) when infant is both supine and sitting up.

Head: Anterior fontanel depressed; normocephalic; circumference, 43 cm.

Throat: Slightly injected, with no tonsillar hypertrophy. Mucous membranes dry; tongue furrowed.

Thorax: Respirations rapid with regular rate, deep inspirations. Chest clear to auscultation and percussion. Equal expansion and diaphragmatic excursion; no retractions.

Cardiovascular system: Heart rate rapid and thready, with radial pulses barely palpable. Point of maximal impulse (PMI) at fifth intercostal space in midclavicular line. No murmurs.

Abdomen: Soft, sunken; no palpable masses.

Genitalia: Within normal limits (WNL); diaper dry.

Joints and muscles: Good range of motion in all joints, but client irritable when aroused and does not like being handled at present time. Muscle mass normal for age, but motor activity minimal at this time.

Neurologic findings: Client is apparently postictal. Can be aroused fairly easily but is extremely lethargic and sleepy. Reflexes 3+ bilaterally (knee, triceps, biceps, Achilles tendon). Babinski's reflex positive. Sensations intact to touch and pinprick, but responses somewhat sluggish. Pupillary reflex normal, but pupils appear somewhat dilated. Cranial nerves not tested.

Vital signs:

Weight: 6.1 kg

Blood pressure: 90/60

Temperature: 58.1° C (104.6° F)

Pulse: 168 beats/min

Respirations: 45/min

Laboratory data:

White blood cell count: 4300

Lymphocytes, 40%; polymorphonuclear leukocytes, 50%; eosinophils, 1%; monocytes, 8%; basophils, 1%

Hematocrit: 58%

Hemoglobin: 16 gm

Na^+: 150 mEq/liter

K^+: 5.8 mEq/liter

Cl^-: 110 mEq/liter

pH: 7.26

Serum osmolarity: 302 mOsm

Urinalysis: pH 4.0; specific gravity 1.030; no cells or casts

Treatment

Baby S was admitted and hydration was begun intravenously with 5% dextrose in 0.16% saline solution in the amounts indicated below:

1. Maintenance: stool loss = 238 ml, IWL = 354 ml, renal loss = 340 ml (total of 932 ml/24 hr)
2. Repair: 680 ml/36 hr

Baby S recovered quickly and was able to gradually resume oral feedings. She suffered no neurologic sequelae.

Discussion

Baby S had lost both water and solutes because of the severe vomiting and diarrhea she experienced as a result of gastroenteritis. Insensible fluid losses were increased due to the high temperature, rapid respiratory rate, and crying. Laboratory data showed hypernatremia and hyperosmolarity of the serum. The urine was extremely concentrated. The weight loss represented 10% of the body weight. The findings on physical examination demonstrated the clinical manifestations of severe extracellular and intracellular fluid volume deficit, hypernatremia and the early stage of hypovolemic shock.

An infant has a greater fluid requirement because of their rapid metabolic rate and their proportionately greater ratio of surface area to volume as compared to an adult. Therefore, fluid deficits in an infant tend to develop more rapidly and are more severe than in the adult.

Nursing Diagnoses

1. Fluid volume deficit related to vomiting and diarrhea secondary to gastroenteritis. (infant)
2. Altered growth and development related to weight loss. (infant)
3. Knowledge deficit related to prompt identification of need for medical assistance and administration of non-formula fluids. (parents)
4. Altered parenting related to lack of knowledge and nearby social support network. (parents)

Hyponatremia. A low serum sodium concentration (hyponatremia), which also represents an hypoosmolar state, can be the result of either net sodium loss or net water excess (Groër, 1981). In most cases hyponatremia reflects hypoosmolality; however, the serum sodium concentration can be low despite an isotonic or hypertonic condition existing within the body fluid. Isotonic hyponatremia (or pseudohyponatremia), in which plasma osmolality is normal, is the result of protein or lipid in the plasma occupying the volume normally occupied by sodium and water. Hypertonic hyponatremia, in which plasma osmolality is high, is the result of a high concentration of an impermeant solute, such as glucose or mannitol in plasma that causes an osmotic shift of water from the ICF to the ECF, which in turn dilutes the sodium content (Humes, 1986).

Hypotonic hyponatremia, in which plasma osmolality is low, occurs when there is a relative excess of water compared with sodium. Pathogenetic mechanisms by which hypotonic hyponatremia develops include: (1) loss of water and sodium with the loss of sodium being greater than that of water, (2) retention of an excess of body water, and (3) excess body water accompanied by excess total body sodium. Summarized in Fig. 18-10 are the pathologic conditions that can cause hyponatremia through these mechanisms. These conditions are discussed in greater detail elsewhere in this text.

Clinical manifestations will be related to expansion of the ICF and total body sodium content and the related ECF volume. As a result of the decrease in plasma osmolality, water will move from the ECF into the ICF. The effect of overhydration of the brain cells, which causes cerebral swelling and edema, is the presentation of neurologic signs and symptoms. The actual clinical manifestations depend on the degree of hyponatremia present and how quickly it developed. With mild hyponatremia, the patient may complain of nausea and malaise. Headache, apathy, and disorientation develop with moderate hyponatremia (serum Na^+ between 110 and 120 mEq/L). Seizures and coma develop at serum sodium levels below 110 mEq/L. Over time, the brain cells adapt by decreasing their osmolality so that the more slowly hyponatremia develops, the less severe the signs and symptoms will be (Humes, 1986).

The total body sodium content and, consequently, the ECF volume will vary depending on the cause of the hyponatremia. Loss of water and sodium result in decreased total body sodium and ECF hypovolemia. In this situation, ADH will be released because maintenance of an effective circulating blood volume will take precedence over restoration of normal plasma osmolality (the usual stimulus for secretion of ADH). Restoration of an effective circulating blood volume is necessary in order to interrupt the feedback loop in which hypovolemia serves as the nonosmotic stimulus for ADH secretion and water retention. This should be done using isotonic saline or, if volume depletion is severe, some form of collide, like plasma or albumin. Patients with excess body water but a normal total body sodium level will be isovolemic without any edema. Water restriction is indicated for this group of patients. Patients who have excess total body sodium and water will demonstrate hypervolemia and edema. Treatment will include restrictions on the intake of sodium and water, as well as promotion of the excretion of excess water and sodium with diuretic agents (Humes, 1986; Schrier, 1986).

Aggressive treatment to raise the serum osmolality is called for if the serum sodium level is very low and the clinical presentation includes neurologic deterioration. Hypertonic saline or mannitol can be administered but carries the risk of fluid overload. The combined administration of a potent diuretic and hypertonic saline allows water excretion along with electrolyte replacement and results in a safer restoration of plasma osmolality (Humes, 1986; Schrier, 1986). The underlying condition that caused the initial alteration in fluid volume and composition must also be treated. These etiologic conditions are discussed elsewhere in this text. The etiology, manifestations, and treatment of hyponatremic disorders are summarized in Fig. 18-10.

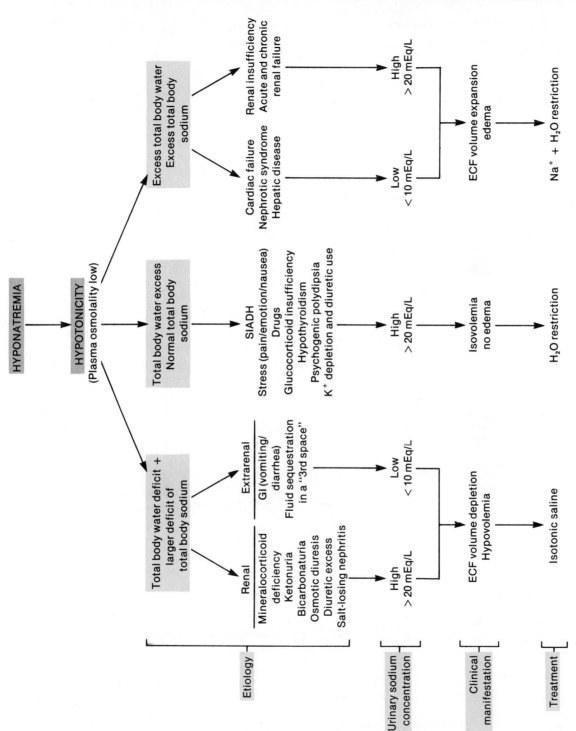

Fig. 18-10. Etiologies, manifestations, and treatment of hyponatremia (hypoosmolality of the body fluid).

(Adapted from Humes, HD, editor: Pathophysiology of electrolyte and renal disorders, New York, 1986, Churchill Livingstone.)

Mechanisms of water imbalance

Water deficit. Water depletion can result from reduced intake, excessive loss, or hyperosmolarity of the body fluid. Reduced intake occurs when water is unavailable or intake is restricted for long periods of time, as might occur when a patient is undergoing diagnostic testing or prior to surgical procedures. Intake can also be reduced because of the inability to swallow, when the sense of thirst is impaired, or in persons who are unable to obtain fluid for themselves, such as an infant or a comatose or paralyzed person. Some aged individuals and psychologically disturbed persons are unable to respond appropriately to the sensation of thirst.

Excessive loss of water via the kidneys can result from a decrease in the concentrating ability of the kidneys either because of primary renal disease or a lack of ADH. Secretion of ADH may be inhibited or impaired by injury to the hypothalamus or by intake of ethyl alcohol. Conditions in which altered ADH secretion is a major feature are discussed in detail in Chapter 20. Because of the effect of alcohol on ADH secretion, alcoholics tend to lose greater than normal amounts of body water.

Excessive loss of water can also occur through the lungs, skin, and gastrointestinal tract. The presence of a tracheostomy or a pattern of rapid respiration results in expiration of a greater than normal amount of water vapor via the lungs. Fever or a hot, dry environment will increase the loss of water through both the lungs and the skin. Mild diarrhea without a proportional electrolyte loss can result in pure water loss, especially in infants and children.

Rapid ingestion or infusion of large amounts of water will cause water loss from diuresis. Water dilutes the extracellular fluid, causing it to become hypoosmolar in relation to the intracellular fluid. This condition inhibits secretion of ADH, which causes water diuresis. The liver participates in this response as an osmoreceptor. Water is absorbed from the gastrointestinal tract into the splanchnic circulation. When the osmolarity of the blood returning to the liver via the portal vein is low, the liver is stimulated to send afferent impulses via the vagus nerve to the hypothalamus, which responds by causing increased excretion of water via the kidneys.

Excretion of excessive amounts of solutes is accompanied by an obligatory water load. These solutes are osmotically active and draw water into the urine to be excreted. Persons with untreated diabetes mellitus excrete large amounts of glucose in the urine. The obligatory water load that is necessary causes the symptom of polyuria and may precipitate a water deficit. This can also be a serious problem in a patient receiving nasogastric tube feedings that contain large amounts of substances such as dextrose and various amino acids in a concentrated form. During water loss that results from solute excess, the patient may gain weight rather than lose and while the water loss is developing will pass large quantities of urine with a low specific gravity. This is different from water loss due to decreased intake, in which the urinary output decreases as the water loss develops, and weight loss is usually quite acute.

Water excess. Water excess is also referred to as water intoxication or overhydration. This condition rarely occurs as a result of increased intake but may in the case of psychotic persons who develop compulsive water-drinking habits. It has occurred as a result of "water diets," in which people ingest large amounts of plain water to maintain the sensation of fullness and to squelch the desire to eat.

Water excess may occur as a result of excessive secretion of ADH and in conditions in which the kidneys do not excrete water normally. Water excess may also develop as a result of iatrogenic causes. For example, dextrose in water solutions may be administered to oliguric patients to increase urinary output when the oliguria results from renal insufficiency. Large amounts of water can be absorbed rectally, and children being treated for congenital megacolon with enemas may develop water excess.

The signs and symptoms of water deficit and excess can be found in Table 18-5. Many of these depend on how rapidly the condition develops. With acute water excess, symptoms appear suddenly and dramatically. Violent behavior may alternate with lethargic behavior. Listed in Table 18-5 are the signs and symptoms that occur with a more slowly developing water excess. Pitting edema is not usually seen with pure water excess, and symptoms do not usually become significant until serum sodium levels drop below 125 mEq/L. It is important to note that *acute* changes in body weight always reflect changes in body fluid balance.

Mechanisms of sodium imbalance

The serum Na^+ concentration reflects more accurately the relative concentrations of Na^+ and H_2O rather than the true or absolute amount of Na^+ in the body. To a great extent the quantity of sodium as the principal cation of the extracellular fluid determines the volume of that compartment. Signs and symptoms associated with excess and deficit states of sodium reflect its role in the regulation of extracellular fluid (ECF) volume. Sodium is osmotically active, and water is drawn along with it. Excess sodium may greatly expand ECF volume, leading to circulatory

congestion and pulmonary edema. Severe sodium deficit leads to ECF volume depletion, which may be to such a degree that circulatory collapse and shock occur.

The sodium balance is closely regulated and maintained within normal limits despite wide variations in dietary intake. The routes of sodium loss include the skin, kidneys, and the gastrointestinal tract. When intake is reduced, regulatory mechanisms operate to minimize the loss of sodium from the body through these routes.

With an increase in sodium intake, plasma volume also increases, which leads to an increase in the rate of glomerular filtration. This increases the amount of sodium filtered and suppresses the release of renin. Consequently aldosterone secretion is inhibited, leading to an increased urinary loss of Na^+. Prostaglandins may also play a role in Na^+ balance because they are antagonists of angiotensin II and adrenergic neurosystem activity. The kinin system also interacts with the prostaglandins and the renin-angiotensin system. Both the prostaglandins and kinins are known to affect Na^+ excretion, but the extent of their roles and interactions between them is not completely clear at this time (Humes, 1986). A third factor, atrial natriuretic hormone is also thought to be released in response to chronic ECF volume expansion; it acts to increase renal Na^+ excretion by increasing the filtered fraction of Na^+ and decreasing tubular reabsorption of Na^+.

When Na^+ intake is decreased, plasma volume also is decreased, causing a drop in the glomerular filtration rate and renal blood flow, which stimulates the release of renin and consequently aldosterone secretion. Sodium will be reabsorbed by the kidneys as a result.

A sodium deficit can be the result of reduced intake or excessive loss. A sodium deficit that is symptomatic is not related to the total exchangeable body sodium but only to the Na^+ of the extracellular fluid. Internal shifts of fluid removing Na^+ from the ECF can produce a serious sodium deficit even when there is an excess amount of total exchangeable Na^+ in the body. A Na^+ deficit is often associated with a deficit of circulating plasma proteins. The reasons for this are not clear, although it is thought to be caused by a reduction in the lymphatic and venous return of the ECF.

As stated earlier, Na^+ is lost through the skin, gastrointestinal tract, and kidneys; excessive loss of Na^+ can occur through any of these routes in the presence of pathologic conditions (see Table 18-4). Sodium may also be lost from the ECF volume because of sequestration in a nonequilibrating compartment in the body. This occurs in burns, in acute venous obstruction, in inflammatory reactions, in peritonitis, and in small bowel obstruction. Fluid can become trapped in these "third spaces," causing a concomitant loss of Na^+.

The Na^+ concentration of fluid entering the colon from the small bowel is similar to that of plasma, and reabsorption of sodium in the colon can reduce the amount of sodium in the feces to very low levels. In the presence of diarrhea, however, this capacity for reabsorption becomes extremely limited, and the concentration of Na^+ in the diarrheal fluid may approximate that of the plasma.

Sweating represents a potential source of great Na^+ loss in the presence of reduced intake. Some sodium will continue to be lost in the sweat in spite of a reduced intake. The mechanisms for reducing the amount of sodium lost are least efficient for sweating (see Chapter 20).

Sodium loss via the kidneys may occur as a result of primary disease of the kidneys and their regulation or as a result of drugs that increase the excretion of sodium ions. Sodium loss via the kidneys may also occur in the presence of diabetic acidosis. The resulting glucose diuresis also causes Na^+ and other electrolytes to be lost in the urine. Measurement of the urinary Na^+ concentration helps differentiate between renal and extrarenal losses.

Sodium deficit may also be the result of severe hemorrhage, loss of bronchial secretions, or as a result of gastric or intestinal drainage and lavage. A sodium deficit may develop if a person's dietary intake of sodium is limited.

Sodium depletion is diagnosed by signs of ECF hypovolemia like poor skin turgor and hypotension. Sodium loss from the ECF causes plasma volume to fall because of the drop in the osmotic pressure of the ECF that occurs. Because of the lowered osmotic pressure, water leaves the ECF for the cells. As the volume of the ECF falls, a concurrent reduction in the plasma volume takes place. When the effective circulating volume becomes so reduced that tissue perfusion does not occur, circulatory failure (shock) ensues. This type of shock will not respond to vasopressor drugs but only to replacement solutions of isotonic or hypertonic saline.

Signs of water excess are more likely to develop with a sodium deficit since the osmotic pressure of the ECF is lower than that of the cells, causing water to flow into the cells. The clinical picture of sodium loss depends on how rapidly this deficit develops. When a sodium deficit develops rapidly, shock is more likely to develop, and the clinical picture is one of acute circulatory failure.

True sodium excess, meaning an increase in the total exchangeable body sodium, is manifested by edema since an excess of Na^+ is always accompanied by a corresponding excess of water. Edema is discussed later in this chapter as a manifestation of an alteration in fluid distribution.

Chloride imbalance

Chloride functions in the body in tandem with sodium as the balancing anion in extracellular fluid. Thus, chloride content affects the osmolality of the ECF and helps regulate fluid volume and distribution between compartments. In addition it helps maintain the resting membrane potential of the cell.

Chloride also plays a role in the acid-base balance of the body. Chloride and bicarbonate, as extracellular anions, compete for sodium binding in the maintenance of electrical neutrality. When chloride concentrations are low, the bicarbonate level is increased by renal reabsorption to maintain ionic balance, and blood pH becomes alkalotic. Excessive circulating chloride levels promote renal excretion of bicarbonate and may alter the pH of the blood toward an acidotic state. In this manner chloride becomes an integral component in maintaining normal acid-base equilibrium. In erythrocytes, Cl^- allows for normal transport of CO_2 by participating electrically in the chloride shift.

Chloride balance is maintained through dietary intake and renal excretion and reabsorption. Renal tubular reabsorption depends on the reabsorption of cations, mostly Na^+. The hormone, aldosterone, causes Cl^- to be retained with Na^+ in exchange for a potassium or H^+ ion. Because of common regulatory paths, disturbances in Na^+ levels will also affect Cl^- in a proportional manner.

Pathologic states that alter the chloride content of the body can occur as a result of sodium disturbances or may be independent of sodium imbalances. In general, chloride elevations, in combination with sodium elevations, are synonymous with hyperosmolal imbalances and should be treated as such. Chloride deficits combined with sodium deficits are approached as hypoosmolal imbalances in terms of recognition and therapeutic interventions. Chloride imbalances occur in relation to acid-base disturbances and are discussed later in this chapter. Potential causes of chloride imbalances are summarized in Table 18-6.

Potassium imbalance

Potassium is responsible for many vital functions in the body. By virtue of its largely intracellular distribution, potassium helps regulate the osmolality of the ECF. Potassium is integral to normal neuromuscular function, influencing the conduction of impulses in nerves and muscles, including the heart. Potassium is also closely tied to the normal acid-base equilibrium. As a cation, potassium can exchange with hydrogen ions across the cell membrane, profoundly influencing pH changes in the ECF.

It is difficult to determine the total exchangeable body potassium because it is an intracellular ion and serum levels do not accurately reflect the real cellular con-

TABLE 18-6. Causes of chloride imbalance

Hyperchloremia (Cl⁻ greater than 105 mEq/L)	Hypochloremia (Cl⁻ less than 95 mEq/L)
Hyperosmolal states in combination with sodium	Hypoosmolal states in combination with sodium
Excessive ingestion or overinfusion of IV solutions	Under ingestion
	GI losses
	Renal disease

From Shekleton M and Litwack K: Critical care nursing of the surgical patient, Philadelphia, PA, WB Saunders Co. (In press).

tent. The terms hyperkalemia and hypokalemia refer to the serum concentrations of potassium. *Hyperkalemia* or *hyperpotassemia*, refers to a greater than normal serum concentration of potassium, while *hypokalemia*, or *hypopotassemia*, refers to a less than normal serum concentration of potassium. Potassium balance is maintained through excretion in the urine, sweat, and feces, while the primary source of potassium is in the diet. Urinary excretion of potassium will be increased whenever increased Na^+ or anion loads are presented to the distal tubules. There is an inverse relationship between tubular H^+ secretion and K^+ excretion. An increase in the output of one will reduce the excretion of the other. This is related also to the renal production of the ammonium ion. Factors that affect K^+ excretion are listed in Table 18-7.

Hyperkalemia does not occur as a result of abnormal retention or accumulation, in contrast to the retention of Na^+ which occurs in a number of pathologic conditions. Hyperkalemia can occur as a result of excessive intake with low urinary output, in the presence of extensive tissue injury as K^+ is liberated from the injured cells, and from administration of a large volume of stored blood. Adrenocortical insufficiency and the presence of respiratory or metabolic acidosis cause the serum K^+ level to rise. Hyperkalemia in the presence of respiratory and metabolic acidosis is a compensatory mechanism. As the hydrogen ion concentration of the ECF increases, K^+ ions move out of the cells and H^+ and Na^+ ions move into them. Increased excretion of K^+ in this situation may eventually lead to hypokalemia.

Hypokalemia may result from dilution after large amounts of K^+-free fluids are ingested or infused. In response to insulin, K^+ moves from the blood into the liver and muscle cells to participate in the con-

TABLE 18-7. Factors influencing potassium excretion

Factor	Effect on potassium excretion
Dietary potassium	
High	Increase
Low	Decrease
Aldosterone	Increase
Sodium excretion	
Low Na concentration in tubular fluid	Decrease
Urine flow	
High (usually associated with high Na^+ excretion)	Increase
Diuretics	
Osmotic	Increase
Loop	Increase
Thiazides	Increase
Cardiac glycosides	Increase
K-sparing	Decrease
Aldosterone inhibitors (spironolactone)	
Amiloride, triamterene	
Acid-base balance	
Alkalosis	
Respiratory	Increase (mild)
Metabolic	Increase (great)
Acidosis	
Respiratory	Decrease initially, then increase (mild)
Metabolic	Increase (great)
Catecholamines	
Epinephrine	Decrease
Norepinephrine	Decrease

From Humes, HD: Pathophysiology of electrolyte and renal disorders, NY, 1986, Churchill Livingstone.

version of glucose to glycogen. An excessive loss of K^+ may occur via the gastrointestinal tract or the kidneys. Gastric and intestinal secretions contain large amounts of K^+, which is usually reabsorbed into the blood (see Table 18-4), and excessive loss of these secretions can result in a serious K^+ deficit. Urinary loss of potassium will be increased by a high sodium load or excess bicarbonate levels, primary renal disease, and the action of various drugs, specifically diuretics and sodium penicillin G. Diuretics cause excretion of chloride, usually with sodium, potassium, or ammonium ions. Since sodium is not always available for excretion and the kidneys may not be able to form ammonium, potassium is excreted with the chloride. Sodium penicillin G apparently acts as an anion, promoting tubular K^+ excretion. The continued normal urinary excretion of K^+ in persons whose intake is reduced and who are malnourished may result in a K^+ deficit. Secretion of ACTH and adrenal mineralocorticoids will increase K^+ excretion in the urine.

Hypokalemia is related to metabolic alkalosis. Potassium loss will cause a metabolic alkalosis, while a metabolic or respiratory alkalosis will cause hypokalemia. When K^+ moves out of the cells, Na^+ and H^+ ions move from the ECF into the cells to replace K^+ and to maintain electroneutrality. Two Na^+ ions and one H^+ ion replace every 3 K^+ ions lost from the cell. As a result the H^+ ion concentration of the ECF falls, and metabolic alkalosis ensues. Further aggravating this condition is the unavailability of K^+ ions for exchange with H^+ in the renal tubules, which results in a urinary loss of H^+ ions.

Conversely, alkalosis (either respiratory or metabolic) causes hypokalemia. K^+ ions from the ECF move into the cells to allow H^+ ions to move out of the cells into the ECF, thus raising the H^+ ion concentration of the ECF. This is a compensatory mechanism that functions to lower pH to normal levels. The various causes of potassium imbalance are summarized in Table 18-8.

Chronic K^+ deficit causes degenerative changes in the renal tubules, which cause hyposthenuria. Large vacuoles develop in the cytoplasm of the proximal convoluted tubules as a result of disordered electro-

TABLE 18-8. Causes of potassium imbalance

Hyperkalemia (serum K^+ greater than 5 mEq/L)	Hypokalemia (serum K^+ less than 3.5 mEq/L)
Increased intake	Decreased intake
Dietary excess	Dietary deficiency
Overinfusion of IV potassium	Alcoholism
Salt substitutes	Anorexia nervosa
Penicillin potassium	
Cellular redistribution	Cellular redistribution
Acidosis	Alkalosis
Hemolysis	Insulin shock
Rhabdomyolysis	Healing process
Crush injuries	
Serious burns	
Infection	
Hyperglycemia	
Decreased excretion	Increased loss
Acute renal failure	a) GI losses
Potassium sparing diuretics (spironolactone, triamterene)	Prolonged vomiting
	Laxatives/enemas
	Diarrhea
Mineralocorticoid deficiency (Addison's disease)	Gastric/intestinal suction
	Fistulas
Factitious	Colostomies, ileostomies
Hemolysis of blood sample	b) Renal losses
Tourniquet cell damage	Diuretics (Furosemide, thiazides, mannitol)
	Mineralocorticoid excess (Cushing's syndrome)
	Interstitial nephritis
	Renal tubular acidosis

From Shekleton, M and Litwack, K: Critical care nursing of the surgical patient, Philadelphia, PA, WB Saunders Co (In press).

lyte pumping in the presence of a chronic K^+ deficit. These structural and functional changes are reversible with K^+ replacement therapy. Degenerative changes of the myocardium may also occur. These changes include loss of striation, karyorrhexis, and karyolysis. Leukocytic infiltration of the myocardium and later fibrosis also occur.

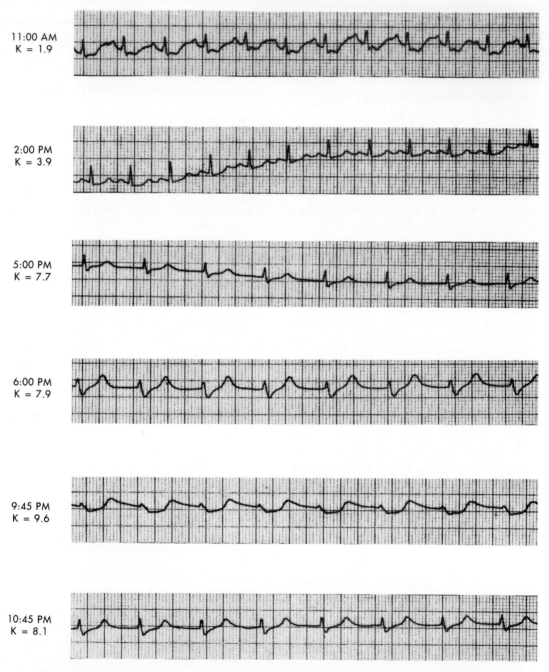

Fig. 18-11. Serial ECG tracings in a patient with marked changes in serum potassium level. In 11:00 AM tracing, depressed ST segment and low amplitude T wave blending into a probable U wave (this cannot be seen with clarity because of superimposed P waves) indicate presence of hypokalemia. Following administration of potassium, 2:00 PM tracing becomes relatively normal. Continued potassium administration results in hyperkalemia with disappearance of atrial activity on ECG and some prolongation of QRS complex. By 7:00 PM QRS complex is more prolonged, and by 9:45 PM QRS complex is greatly prolonged. Secondary ST-T wave changes are present. Improvement follows administration of bicarbonate, glucose, and insulin at 10:45 PM with reduction in serum potassium level; improvement in ECG results.

(From Andreoli et al: Comprehensive cardiac care, ed 5, St Louis, 1983, The CV Mosby Co.)

The muscles of the body are most grossly affected by changes in the potassium balance because of the role of K^+ in depolarization of the cell membranes of the muscle. Changes in the degree of polarization can prevent the initiation and conduction of the impulse along the muscle. A decreased concentration of K^+ outside the cells (hypokalemia) causes *hyperpolarization* so that the degree of depolarization produced by the neurotransmitter is insufficient to initiate an impulse. The cells require more stimulation strength over a longer period to fire, which accounts for the muscle weakness and fatigue that occur (Groer, 1981). An increased concentration of K^+ outside the cells (hyperkalemia), if severe, may initially cause depolarization and cellular excitability. As hyperkalemia worsens, however, the cells become refractory to further stimulation.

The muscle most seriously affected is the heart. The electrocardiogram (Fig. 18-11) reflects the changes in the state of polarization of the cardiac cells that result from potassium excess and deficit.

Muscle weakness is often the first sign of potassium imbalance. A flaccid muscle paralysis may also occur over a period of days as a result of this imbalance. Paresthesias occur with hyperkalemia, probably as a result of the irritation of nerve endings by the potassium. Mental status usually remains unchanged, although the patient may feel apprehensive.

A disorder that is characterized by hypokalemia is known as *familial periodic paralysis* (see Chapter 13). These transient attacks of muscular weakness and paralysis occur in response to situations that reduce the K^+ levels in the body, for example, a large carbohydrate meal, or administration of mineralocorticoids, insulin, or dextrose. The attacks occur at low normal K^+ levels. Other signs and symptoms of K^+ excess and deficit are listed in Table 18-9.

Treatment of deficits of both Na^+ and K^+ is by replacement either through in-

TABLE 18-9.   Clinical manifestations of potassium imbalance

	Mild	Moderate	Severe	Laboratory findings
Hypokalemia	Fatigue Lethargy Decreased deep tendon reflexes	Muscle weakness Abdominal distention Paralytic ileus Hypotension Ventricular dysrythmias ECG: PVCs, decreased T wave amplitude, U waves	Paralysis of smooth and skeletal muscle ECG: ST depression Cardiac arrest	$[K^+] < 3.5$ mEq/L Polyuria
Hyperkalemia	Twitching Hyperreflexia	Muscle weakness Paresthesias ECG: peaked T waves Intestinal colic Vomiting	Muscle paralysis Bradycardia ($K^+ = 7.0$) ECG: wide QRS, sine wave ($K^+ = 9.0$) Death	$[K^+] > 5.0$ mEq/L Oliguria Hyperglycemia

Adapted from Shekleton, M and Litwack, K: Critical care nursing of the surgical patient, Philadelphia, PA, WB Saunders Co (In press).

creased intake of foods containing these electrolytes, oral supplements (K^+ only), or administration of IV fluids containing isotonic saline or K^+ additives or both. Intravenous potassium replacement requires dilution of potassium salts and slow administration to prevent phlebitis or possible cardiac arrest with too rapid an infusion. Adequate renal function must always be assessed before any potassium supplementation to avoid possible rebound hyperkalemia.

Hypokalemia potentiates digitalis preparations, and patients receiving digitalis and diuretics may be at significant risk for digitalis toxicity regardless of the digitalis dosage. The care of patients with potassium imbalance requires thorough knowledge of their medication history and appropriate planning before instituting any therapy aimed at restoring the normal serum potassium concentrations.

Treatment of K^+ excess is aimed at reducing the potassium concentration as rapidly as possible. This can be done by administering agents that facilitate the movement of K^+ out of the ECF and into the cells. Insulin and glucose are effective transfer agents as is sodium bicarbonate when K^+ excess occurs in the presence of acidosis. Removal of the potassium from the body will also reduce serum potassium levels, and this can be accomplished through dialysis or through the use of a cation-exchange resin, which removes K^+ by exchanging it from Na^+ in the gut. The effects of hyperkalemia (especially the cardiac effects) can be minimized through administration of agents antagonistic to the action of K^+ on the cell membrane, for example, calcium.

Calcium and phosphorus imbalances

Calcium exists in the plasma in both bound and ionized forms. The free ionized form is the physiologically active form necessary for blood coagulation, skeletal and cardiac muscle contraction, and nerve function.

Calcium requirements vary with the age and sex of the individual. In general, children, the aged, and lactating and pregnant women require larger amounts of daily calcium than the 0.8 gm/day suggested for normal adults. The usual source of calcium is the diet, primarily in the form of milk and milk products. Once ingested, approximately 50% of the total intake is absorbed by the GI tract in the small intestine. Calcium excretion is both renal and fecal with potential losses through the skin when profuse perspiration occurs. Normally 99% of the filtered calcium is reabsorbed in the kidney, with total excretion dependent on daily intake and effective absorption.

Phosphorus is found in the body in the form of organic and inorganic phosphate salts. However, only the latter is present in the extracellular fluid (Goldberger, 1986). Phosphate balance is maintained through oral intake and renal excretion. The normal phosphorus requirement varies by age and sex and will be increased in anabolic states (Puschett, 1985; Humes, 1986).

Phosphorus is critical to both cell structure and function. It is a constituent of the nucleic acids, phospholipids, and phosphoproteins. It is necessary for cellular oxygen delivery in 2,3-diphosphoglycerate (2,3-DPG) and energy production in adenosine triphosphate (ATP) and creatinine phosphokinase. Phosphorylation of enzymatic proteins is necessary for hormonal regulation of cell function (Humes, 1986). Disorders of phosphate homeostasis can, therefore, have a profound effect on cellular function.

There is a reciprocal relationship between calcium and phosphate. Because the solubility constant of these ions is fixed and they normally exist in a supersaturated state in the serum, a change in the concentration of one will cause an inverse change in the other (Goldberger, 1986). In other words, if the product of the concentrations of calcium and phosphate is to remain constant, a fall in one requires an increase in the other and vice versa.

Hormonal regulation of calcium and phosphorus. Regulation of calcium balance is accomplished primarily through the function of the parathyroids. Normally the rate of secretion of the parathyroid hormone varies inversely with the ionized calcium level of the plasma via a direct feedback mechanism. This hormone increases the plasma calcium level by mobilizing calcium from the readily exchangeable reservoir in bone, increasing renal tubular absorption, and increasing absorption of Ca^{++} in the intestine, but the latter only through a metabolite of vitamin D. The active metabolite of vitamin D that participates in the maintenance of calcium balance is considered to be a hormone because it is produced in the body and transported in the blood to a distant site to produce its effects.

The parathyroid glands secrete parathyroid hormone (PTH) in response to a fall in the serum ionized calcium level. Control of the secretion of parathyroid hormone is via a negative feedback mechanism; a low serum calcium level stimulates parathyroid activity, while high serum calcium levels suppress it. A rise in serum phosphate levels will also stimulate parathyroid activity, but this effect is not a result of the increased phosphate per se but rather of the decreased serum calcium concentration that occurs because of the reciprocal nature of these two ions. Magnesium activates an intermediary in the calcium-mobilizing effects of PTH, and changes in the serum magnesium may affect PTH effectiveness. This may be the basis of the hypocalcemic state

that accompanies low serum magnesium.

The bones and kidneys are the primary target organs of PTH. In the bone tissue, PTH exerts both short- and long-term effects that increase bone resorption and serum calcium levels. First, it stimulates osteocytic osteolysis, which rapidly increases serum calcium. PTH also stimulates bone tissue to increase osteoclast and osteocyte function and inhibits osteoblast function. In the kidneys PTH decreases renal clearance of calcium and magnesium and increases urinary excretion of phosphorus, sodium, potassium, amino acids, and bicarbonate. The mild acidosis that results from excretion of bicarbonate also enhances bone resorption. PTH also stimulates the renal conversion of 25-hydroxycholecalciferol to 1,25-dihydroxycholecalciferol, the active metabolite of vitamin D necessary for PTH to have its full effect on bone and which exerts direct effects on calcium metabolism as well. This hydroxylation is inhibited by calcitonin and high serum phosphate levels, while low serum phosphate levels stimulate it (Maxwell, Kleeman, and Narins, 1987).

The parathyroid hormone also increases urinary phosphate excretion, and elevated levels of plasma phosphate can stimulate its secretion. This is not a direct effect of phosphate on the glands but is a result of the reciprocal nature of the relationship between calcium and phosphate in the plasma. Elevated plasma phosphate levels lower the calcium levels, which in turn stimulate hormone secretion. Compensatory hyperplasia of the parathyroid glands occurs in conditions in which calcium levels are chronically depressed. In renal disease the Ca^{++} level is low because the kidneys retain phosphate and are unable to form 1,25-dihydroxycholecalciferol, and a secondary hyperparathyroidism develops.

Phosphate absorption in the small intestine is stimulated by the active metabolite of vitamin D, 1,25-dihydroxycholecalciferol (Humes, 1986). The excretion of phosphate ions by the kidney is under the influence of parathyroid hormone (PTH), which acts to reduce its reabsorption in the proximal tubule resulting in phosphaturia. The movement of phosphate between bone tissue and the extracellular fluid depends on vitamin D and PTH (Goldberger, 1986).

Other hormones that have a major effect on the plasma Ca^{++} levels include calcitonin, which decreases plasma Ca^{++} by inhibiting bone resorption, and 1,25-dihydroxycholecalciferol, the active metabolite of vitamin D, which increases intestinal absorption of Ca^{++} and mobilizes Ca^{++} from the bone to raise plasma Ca^{++} levels. Fig. 18-12 schematically illustrates the reciprocal nature of calcium and phosphorus and the interrelationship of parathyroid hormone, vitamin D, and calcitonin in maintaining Ca^{++} balance.

In the bone, 1,25-dihydroxycholecalciferol stimulates the formation of osteoclasts and prolongs their life span, effects similar to those of PTH. Both hormones must be present for either to be completely effective in bone tissue. 1,25-Dihydroxycholecalciferol primarily increases calcium reabsorption in the gut and possibly calcium and phosphorus reabsorption in the renal tubules (Fig. 18-12).

Calcitonin is secreted by the C cells of the thyroid gland, and its major effect is to lower serum calcium levels through a reduction of bone resorption activity. The role of calcitonin is closely related to that of parathyroid hormone and vitamin D in the maintenance of calcium, phosphate, and bone metabolism. Obviously, conditions that affect the production of this hormone will have a profound effect on calcium balance. The target organs of calcitonin, which is secreted in response to high serum calcium levels, are similar to those of PTH. The bone effects and the inhibition of the hydroxylation of 25-hydroxycholecalciferol are antagonistic to those of PTH. Calcitonin does increase urinary calcium excretion, but it also has a phosphaturic effect similar to PTH. Calcitonin is currently being utilized as a therapeutic agent in certain hypercalcemic states and in Paget's disease of the bones, in which excessive and abnormal bone resorption and formation take place in a random, uncontrolled manner. Medullary cancer of the thyroid causes hypersecretion of calcitonin; however, serum Ca^{++} levels usually remain within normal limits. Other hormones also can affect calcium balance. These include thyroxine, long-term administration of estrogen, adrenal steroids, and growth hormone.

Alterations in calcium, phosphorus, and skeletal homeostasis can be either manifestations or causes of disruption of the normal action and secretion of these hormonal substances. Disruption of normal parathyroid function sometimes occurs as a secondary, compensatory response to pathology occurring in another part of the body that affects calcium metabolism.

Hypocalcemia. Disturbances of calcium metabolism include hypocalcemia and hypercalcemia. *Hypocalcemia,* or a decrease in extracellular calcium, generally has an excitatory effect on nerve and muscle cells even though it inhibits transmission at the myoneural junction. The increased activity of the motor nerve fibers results in a symptom complex known as *tetany*. The threshold of peripheral sensory nerve receptors to excitation is also lowered, and sensory changes tend to precede motor changes. Tetany can appear with low normal calcium levels in the presence of increased pH because more plasma protein becomes ionized and binds with the calcium in the alkalotic state.

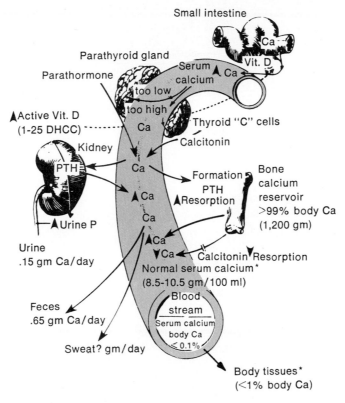

Fig. 18-12. Calcium homeostasis. Control features maintain proper serum calcium that is needed for body tissues. Low serum calcium stimulates absorption of calcium from intestine, retention of calcium by kidney, and release of it from bone. High serum calcium stimulates release of calcitonin, which inhibits calcium resorption from bone.

(From Larson C and Gould M: Orthopedic nursing, ed 9, St Louis, 1978, The CV Mosby Co.)

The neuromuscular irritability of tetany is characterized by paresthesias, carpopedal spasm, Trousseau's sign, Chvostek's sign, and facial muscle spasm. Laryngospasm may be severe enough to cause airway obstruction, and bronchial spasm may simulate an asthma attack. Spasm of the abdominal muscles may mimic an "acute abdomen." Convulsions not relieved by anticonvulsant medications and not accompanied by loss of consciousness or aura may also occur. The symptoms of tetany are more pronounced when there is pressure on the motor nerve such as when the legs are crossed. Tetany may be precipitated by exercise or emotional states possibly because of the resultant hyperventilation and respiratory alkalosis and the release of epinephrine.

Changes in mental status, including psychoneuroses and psychoses, may also occur with hypocalcemia. The electrocardiogram is characteristically normal except for prolongation of the QT interval. Other signs and symptoms are listed in Table 18-10.

Hypocalcemia caused by hypoproteinemia in which the amount of bound Ca^{++}

TABLE 18-10. Major clinical manifestations of calcium imbalance

	Hypercalcemia	Hypocalcemia
Mild	Anorexia	Circumoral or digital paresthe-
	Nausea	sias
	Constipation	Muscle spasms
	Lethargy	Palpitations
Moderate	Skeletal muscle hypotonicity	Hyperactive DTRs
	Bone pain	Cardiac dysrhythmias
	Polyuria	
	Renal calculi	
Severe	Osteomalacia	Tetany
	Pathologic fractures	(Positive Chvostek's, Trosseau's
	Cardiac dysrhythmias	signs)
	Cardiac arrest	Laryngeal stridor
		Coagulopathy
		Seizures
Laboratory findings	$(Ca^{++}) > 11$ mg/dl or 5.5 mEq/l	$(Ca^{++}) < 9$ mg/dl or 4.5 mEq/l
	$(PO_4) < 2.5$ mg/dl	$(PO_4^-) > 4.5$ mg/dl
	Positive Sulkowitch test (urine Ca^{++})	Negative Sulkowitch test (urine Ca^{++})
	X-ray evidence of bone demineralization and renal calculi	

Adapted from Shekleton, M, and Litwack, K: Critical care nursing of the surgical patient, Philadelphia, PA, WB Saunders Co (In press).

is reduced while the ionized Ca^{++} level remains normal is asymptomatic. Hypocalcemia will occur in hyperphosphatemic conditions that result from infusion of phosphate or retention of phosphate such as occurs in renal insufficiency. The administration of large amounts of stored blood may cause hypocalcemia if the excess citrate (added to prevent clotting) binds with calcium. Tetany is more likely to occur if the blood is administered rapidly and if hyperkalemia develops as a result of large amounts of K^+ being released from the stored blood. Certain neoplastic disorders, specifically tumors of the breast, lung, and prostate associated with widespread metastasis, cause increased osteoblastic activity and skeletal uptake of calcium. Tumors that secrete calcitonin also cause hypocalcemia. Hypocalcemia is

a well-documented complication of magnesium deficiency secondary to intestinal malabsorption, alcoholism, primary hypomagnesia, and dietary restriction. Hypocalcemia is seen in patients who have increased amounts of fat in the stool (steatorrhea) resulting from decreased fat absorption because calcium and vitamin D are lost through excretion as calcium salts of fatty acids. This occurs in conditions such as celiac disease, biliary disease, and pancreatic insufficiency (see Chapter 21). A similar mechanism causing hypocalcemia occurs in acute pancreatitis in which large amounts of calcium become fixed by the fatty acids liberated from necrotic mesenteric fat deposits. It has also been postulated that the hypersecretion of glucagon that has been observed in pancreatitis may contribute to hypocalcemia. Hypocalcemia has been reported as a result of glucagon administration.

Tetany is treated by lowering the pH, if alkalosis is present, or by increasing the serum calcium concentration through administration of calcium gluconate. The cause of the hypocalcemia must be treated, though, in addition to treating the hypocalcemic state itself. Where the cause is increased phosphate retention, phosphate-binding antacids are used to promote intestinal excretion of phosphate. Stored blood should be infused at a rate that does not exceed 1,000 to 1,500 ml/hr. Dietary supplementation with calcium and vitamin D may improve hypocalcemia, but this depends on the cause. Hypocalcemia during pregnancy can be prevented by increasing dietary intake.

The following case study demonstrates the clinical manifestations and treatment of hypocalcemia. The calcium imbalance developed in this patient because of increased calcium requirements in the presence of a reduced ability to maintain even normal calcium balance.

CASE STUDY: ALTERATION IN FLUID COMPOSITION: HYPOCALCEMIA

History

The current pregnancy has been complicated by several electrolyte problems including hypomagnesemia, hypocalcemia and hypokalemia for which she has been treated with K^+, Ca^{++}, and Mg^+ supplementation. Previous surgeries include appendectomy, dilation and curettage, thyroidectomy and adenoidectomy. Six years ago, JC had intestinal bypass surgery for control of exogenous obesity. She lost 140 pounds after this surgery.

Present illness: JC, a 38-year-old white

Contributed by June Martin.

female, came to the emergency room with signs and symptoms of tetany. She was complaining of tingling in her hands, face, and arms which had begun approximately 8 hours before coming to the hospital. She decided to seek medical treatment when her hands went into carpal spasm. She is nearly at term in her ninth pregnancy.

Objective and Subjective Data

JC is unable to straighten her hands and cried out in pain when the triage nurse attempted to straighten them.

Physical examination
Within normal limits except for the following:
     Deep tendon reflexes: 3+
     Positive Chvostek's sign
Fetal heartbeat and movements detectable and WNL.
Vital signs
Temperature: 36.1° C (97° F)
Pulse: 100 beats/min
Respirations: 28/min
Blood pressure: 120/88
Laboratory data
Ca^{++} = 6.4 mg/dl
K^+ = 3.4 mEq/liter
Na^+ = 142 mEq/liter
Cl^- = 113 mEq/liter
CO_2 = 19 mM/liter
Albumin = 3.5 gm/dl

Treatment

In the emergency room JC received 2 ampules of calcium gluconate in a solution of 5% dextrose in water. The serum concentration of calcium after this was 7.5 mg/dl. The patient was admitted with an IV solution of 5% dextrose in water. The solution contained six ampules of calcium gluconate in 1 L of solution. Three hours after first having been seen in the emergency room, JC developed generalized tetany, had a grand mal convulsion, and complained of pain with any movement. The IV solution was infusing at a rate of 125 ml/hr. About an hour later JC was able to extend her right forefinger, although her hands were still in carpal spasm. During the next hour she was able to open her hand completely and within the following hour was out of bed and walking about. At this time the concentration of calcium in the IV solution was increased to 10 ampules/1000 ml, and within 3 hours the patient went into labor, delivering a normal baby girl. During the course of the 5-hour labor the serum concentration of calcium was measured and found to be 12.1 mg/dl, and the potassium level decreased to 2.3 mEq/L. The infant's cord blood also indicated hypercalcemia and hypokalemia. The mother was treated with dextrose, 5%, in half-strength normal saline solution, with 40 mEq/L of potassium chloride added. The serum electrolytes returned to normal during the next 24 hours, and JC recovered and was discharged with her baby 4 days later. She was discharged on a regimen of potassium, calcium, and magnesium supplementation and triamterene (Dyrenium).

Discussion

This is a clinical situation in which hypocalcemia developed as a result of several interacting mechanisms rather than because of a single disease state. First of all, pregnancy presents an increased demand to the body. In pregnancy, the calcium requirement is increased by about 50% (Groer, 1981). This patient was unable to meet such a requirement because of an impaired ability to absorb calcium because of her previous intestinal bypass surgery. Calcium uptake from the gastrointestinal tract requires an active metabolite of Vitamin D which is a fat soluble vitamin. After a surgical bypass of the duodenum there is little fat absorption because most absorption takes place in the upper small intestine and is dependent on lipase which is secreted into the duodenum from the pancreas. Hypoalbuminemia is another cause of hypocalcemia which was also present in this patient.

Nursing Diagnoses
1. Altered fluid composition; hypocalcemia related to increased requirement and decreased absorption.
2. Acute pain related to muscle spasms.
3. Potential for injury related to seizure activity.

Hypercalcemia. A greater than normal serum calcium concentration is termed *hypercalcemia*. The level of elevation of the serum Ca^{++} at which symptoms appear varies among individuals. General symptoms include anorexia, nausea, vomiting, weight loss, easy fatigability, lethargy, headaches, and thirst (Table 18-10). Lack of coordination, constipation, and muscle weakness result from decreased tone in smooth and striated muscle. Polyuria caused by impaired renal-concentrating ability is often one of the earliest signs. It has been proposed that an increased calcium ion concentration interferes with active sodium transport across the renal tubule cell membranes by binding with intracellular ATP to form a tight complex calcium-adenosine triphosphate (Ca-ATP). This complex inhibits sodium-potassium-ATPase (Na-K-ATPase), the enzyme necessary for ATP hydrolysis to provide the energy for Na^+ transport. The lesions of metastatic calcification (calcium deposition in various body tissues) tend to first occur in the renal medulla. A characteristic feature of hypercalcemic nephropathy is intrarenal hydronephrosis caused by tubular obstruction. Infection, hypertension, and uremia may be long-term complications. Hypercalcinuria also favors the development of renal calculi.

Other signs of metastatic calcification appear in the cornea and conjunctiva. *Band keratopathy* is a hazy, grayish opacity seen on the cornea concentric with the limbus. Conjunctival lesions appear as glassy particles and impart a gritty sensation in the eyes. Inflammation often develops as a result of these lesions.

Other manifestations include changes in behavior and emotional state. Apathy, depression, and changes in affect and drive are among these. Acute psychoses are common when serum Ca^+ levels rise above 16 mg/100 ml. Neuromuscular excitability is depressed by hypercalcemia. This is characterized by the decreased muscle tone already mentioned, hyporeflexia (hyperreflexia has occasionally been noted), and increased auditory and visual disturbances.

Acute hypercalcemic crisis may occur when the serum calcium level rises above approximately 16 to 18 mg/100 ml. All the signs and symptoms of hypercalcemia will be present. One of the outstanding features will be intractable vomiting with severe volume depletion and electrolyte and acid-base imbalance, fever, altered levels of consciousness including coma or a grossly disturbed mental state, azotemia, and a normal or even above normal serum phosphate level. Death may occur in this state.

The therapy for hypercalcemia is generally aimed at decreasing calcium intake and increasing elimination. However, supportive therapy is often necessary to correct serum values before definitive treatment. Often, isotonic sodium sulfate is administered to create a diuresis and improve excretion. Phosphate preparations may also be given orally or by IV to improve renal calcium elimination. Steroids may be administered to inhibit calcium absorption. Definitive medical or surgical intervention for the underlying cause is often required.

Disease model: hyperparathyroidism. Hyperparathyroidism is characterized by hy-percalcemia and the sequelae to the chronic hypercalcemic condition: renal calculi and skeletal disease related to increased bone resorption. Renal calculi occur in approximately 75% of all patients with hyperparathyroidism, and in many of these patients, renal calculi are the only clinical manifestation of the hyperparathyroid state. In hyperparathyroidism there is an increase in the urinary excretion of calcium and phosphate, and renal calculi form as a result of these substances precipitating out into the urine. Pathologic changes in the kidney (hypercalcemic nephropathy) may progressively worsen.

Skeletal involvement occurs in approximately one third of the patients with hyperparathyroidism. This bone disease is referred to as *osteitis fibrosa cystica generalisata* and is characterized by increased bone resorption, replacement of normal bone tissue with a highly cellular fibrous tissue, and formation of cysts and tumors. The manifestations of this skeletal disorder include pain and pathologic fractures. The pain may be local or diffuse and may become quite severe. The bones may be tender to palpation and the muscles weak and atrophied also.

The other signs and symptoms of hypercalcemia occur in approximately one third of the patients with hyperparathyroidism. Duodenal ulcer and pancreatitis also may be present in the hyperparathyroid state. The incidence of duodenal ulcer is nearly 30% in hyperparathyroid patients. Research has not documented a direct causal relationship, but there does seem to be a direct relationship between the plasma calcium level and the serum gastrin level and gastric secretory rate. The cause of the increased incidence of pancreatitis in hyperparathyroidism is thought to be related to the calcium-dependent conversion of trypsinogen to trypsin. The theory is that the increased calcium content accelerates the conversion reaction, increasing the amount of trypsin, which causes inflammatory changes in the pancreas. Other possible etiologic mechanisms that continue to be examined include direct injury to pancreatic cells by the PTH, obstruction of the pancreatic duct by calculi, and thrombotic or embolic vascular damage associated with the excess PTH or hypercalcemia.

The causes of hyperparathyroidism may

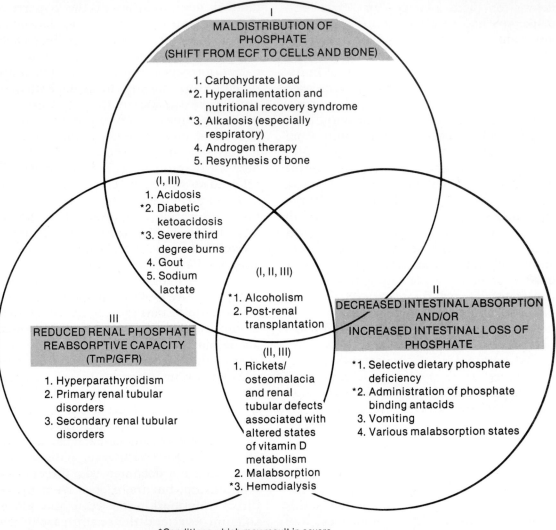

I
MALDISTRIBUTION OF PHOSPHATE
(SHIFT FROM ECF TO CELLS AND BONE)

1. Carbohydrate load
*2. Hyperalimentation and nutritional recovery syndrome
*3. Alkalosis (especially respiratory)
4. Androgen therapy
5. Resynthesis of bone

(I, III)
1. Acidosis
*2. Diabetic ketoacidosis
*3. Severe third degree burns
4. Gout
5. Sodium lactate

(I, II, III)
*1. Alcoholism
2. Post-renal transplantation

III
REDUCED RENAL PHOSPHATE REABSORPTIVE CAPACITY
(TmP/GFR)

1. Hyperparathyroidism
2. Primary renal tubular disorders
3. Secondary renal tubular disorders

II
DECREASED INTESTINAL ABSORPTION AND/OR INCREASED INTESTINAL LOSS OF PHOSPHATE

*1. Selective dietary phosphate deficiency
*2. Administration of phosphate binding antacids
3. Vomiting
4. Various malabsorption states

(II, III)
1. Rickets/ osteomalacia and renal tubular defects associated with altered states of vitamin D metabolism
2. Malabsorption
*3. Hemodialysis

*Conditions which may result in severe hypophosphatemia and other manifestations of the phosphorus depletion syndrome

Fig. 18-13. Clinical disorders associated with hypophosphatemia, classified according to mechanism.

(From Lee DBN, et al: Disorders of phosphorus metabolism. In Bronner F, and Coburn JW, editors: Disorders of mineral metabolism, New York, Academic Press, 1981, vol III, p. 284.)

be classified as primary, secondary, or tertiary. *Primary hyperparathyroidism* applies to conditions in which the pathologic process affects the parathyroid glands directly and the feedback control of PTH secretion is lost so that hypercalcemia develops. Primary hyperparathyroidism may be the result of adenoma, hyperplasia, or carcinoma. Treatment of primary hyperparathyroidism is by surgical removal of the hyperfunctioning tissue.

Secondary hyperparathyroidism refers to conditions in which excessive secretion of PTH and parathyroid gland hyperplasia occur as compensatory mechanisms in response to chronic hypocalcemia. Serum calcium levels remain within normal limits since the feedback mechanism continues to operate effectively. Chronic hypocalcemia is a feature of vitamin D deficiency and calcium deprivation states. It accompanies steatorrhea since calcium and vitamin D are lost through excretion bound to fatty acids. In chronic renal disease, chronic hypocalcemia is the result of the hyperphosphatemia that occurs and its reciprocal effect on the serum calcium.

Hypercalcemia may develop if the normal feedback control is lost; this is referred to as *tertiary hyperparathyroidism*. It can be the result of adenoma formation in the hyperplastic tissue. Tertiary hyperparathyroidism sometimes occurs in patients with chronic renal disease who have been successfully treated with renal transplantation. Parathyroidectomy sometimes becomes necessary in these patients.

Hypophosphatemia. Disturbances of phosphate metabolism include hyperphosphatemia and hypophosphatemia. *Hypophosphatemia,* or a decreased serum phosphate level, can be the result of maldistribution, altered intestinal uptake, impaired renal reabsorption, and combinations of these metabolisms. The underlying mechanisms of clinical conditions associated with hy-

pophosphatemia are presented in Figure 18-13.

A reduction in dietary phosphate intake results in the following: (1) a reduction in fecal elimination and almost complete elimination of urinary phosphate (hypophosphaturia), (2) hypercalciuria and magnesuria and, (3) decreased serum magnesium concentration with no change in serum calcium concentration. These changes are reversible with adequate intake (Dominguez et al., 1976). This represents a state of phosphorus deprivation or mild hypophosphatemia that is asymptomatic. More severe hypophosphatemia in which depletion of phosphorus stores has occurred is accompanied by these same biochemical changes in addition to cellular abnormalities that lead to the clinical manifestations listed in Table 18-11. It is hypothesized that many of the CNS and neuromuscular manifestations are caused by reduction of 2,3 DPG levels and a subsequent reduction in the oxygenation of these tissues.

Muscle weakness is probably the most clinically relevant manifestation of hypophosphatemia (Humes, 1986). Hypophosphatemia may have especially significant effects on respiratory muscle function. There have been reports of respiratory failure (Newman et al., 1977; Aubier et al., 1985), failure to wean from mechanical ventilation (Agusti et al., 1984) and decreased performance following respiratory muscle fatigue (Planas et al., 1981) associated with hypophosphatemia. Clinical manifestations are especially apparent when phosphate levels fall below 1.0 mg/100 ml but may become apparent when the phosphate level falls below 2 mg/100 ml (Puschett, 1985).

Therapy is directed toward correction of the underlying cause of the hypophosphatemia and replacement. Currently, research on the best route, dose, and prepa-

TABLE 18-11. Major clinical manifestations associated with hypophosphatemia

General (systemic)
  Anorexia, malaise, weakness
Neurologic
  Symptoms
    Irritability, paresthesias, confusion, obtundation
      (including coma)
  Signs
    Seizures, dysarthria, intention tremor, anisocoria,
      hyporeflexia, ballismus, ataxia
  Laboratory
    Abnormal EEG
Muscular
  Symptoms
    Muscular weakness
  Signs
    Respiratory failure, myopathy including rhabdomy-
      olysis (especially in alcoholics)
  Laboratory
    Abnormal EMG (decreased nerve conduction veloc-
      ity), elevated CPK
Hematologic
  Red cells
    Increased membrane rigidity leading to spherocyte
      formation and increased destruction
  White cells
    Impaired phagocytic function
  Platelets
    Impaired platelet function and thrombocytopenia
      leading to mucosal bleeding, epistaxis, and mild
      GI hemorrhage
Skeletal
  Symptoms
    Bone pain, joint stiffness, arthralgias
  Signs
    Arthritis
  Laboratory
    Osteomalacia on bone biopsy specimen, osteo-
      penia on x-ray. In patients with hyperparathyroid-
      ism, osteitis fibrosa cystica
Renal
  Symptoms and signs
    Usually none (stone formation is rare)
  Laboratory
    Hypercalciuria, glycosuria, bicarbonaturia, and de-
      creased phosphate excretion

From Puschett, JB: Disorders of fluid and electrolyte balance: Diagnosis and management, New York, 1985, Churchill Livingstone.

ration for replacement therapy is lacking. Prophylactic administration of phosphate is indicated in the patient receiving total parenteral nutrition and in the patient being treated for diabetic ketoacidosis (Puschett, 1985).

Hyperphosphatemia. *Hyperphosphatemia* or an increased serum phosphate level, is most commonly seen as a result of renal insufficiency (decreased glomerular filtration) (Humes, 1986; Maxwell et al., 1987). Other pathogenetic mechanisms include massive phosphate loads and transport defects leading to impaired renal excretion. Conditions associated with these mechanisms are listed in the box on p. 791.

TABLE 18-12. Effects of hyperphosphatemia

Organ or tissue	Symptoms and/or signs
Heart	Conduction disturbances; arrhythmias; forward and backward pump failure leading to progressive hypotension, pulmonary congestion, and shock
Kidneys	Oliguria leading to anuria and progressive azotemia
GI tract	Severe anorexia; nausea; vomiting; paralytic ileus; hematemesis and melena
Lungs and alveolar lining	Dyspnea; impaired O_2 diffusion leading to hypoxemia
Cornea and conjunctiva	Haziness of cornea; conjunctival inflammation producing pain, discomfort, and red eyes
Skin and subcutaneous vessels	Papular eruptions; ischemic necrosis of fingers, toes, and skin at any site

From Maxwell, M, Kleeman, C, and Narins, R: Clinical disorders of fluid and electrolyte metabolism, ed 4, New York, 1987, McGraw-Hill, Inc.

CAUSES OF HYPERPHOSPHATEMIA

Decreased GFR
Renal failure:
   Chronic
   Acute

Increased phosphate loads
Exogenous:
   Enteric:
      Oral ingestion
      Increased phosphorus absorption, e.g., in vitamin D intoxication
      Phosphorus-containing laxatives or enemas
   Parenteral:
      Intravenous phosphorus
      Transfusion of old blood
   Cutaneous:
      White phosphorus burns
Endogenous
   Phosphorus redistribution between cells and ECF:
      Respiratory acidosis
      Diabetic ketoacidosis
      Lactic acidosis and tissue ischemia
   Cell destruction:
      Rhabdomyolysis
      Malignant hyperpyrexia
      Neoplastic disease treated with cytotoxic therapy
      Hemolysis

Increased TmP/GFR
Hypoparathyroidism
PTH resistance:
   Pseudohypoparathyroidism
   Transient resistance of infancy
Abnormal PTH (?)
Other endocrine disorders:
   Hyperthyroidism
   Acromegaly
   Juvenile hypogonadism
   Postmenopausal state
Ambient high temperature
Disodium etidronate

Miscellaneous
Magnesium deficiency
Volume decrease
Tumoral calcinosis
Cortical hyperostosis
Familial intermittent hyperphosphatemia
Factitious hyperphosphatemia

From Maxwell, M, Kleeman, C, Narins, R: Clinical disorders of fluid and electrolyte metabolism, ed 4, New York, 1987, McGraw-Hill, Inc.

Clinical manifestations are related to the reciprocally induced hypocalcemia and deposition of precipitated calcium phosphate salts in the soft tissues and organs. Tetany and convulsions may occur because of the hypocalcemia. Tissue calcification can cause severe organ and tissue dysfunction (Table 18-12). The degree of hyperphosphatemia that develops is related to the balance that exists between the renal capacity for phosphate excretion and the rate at which phosphorus enters the ECF. Calcium phosphate precipitation usually does not occur until the serum phosphate level reaches or exceeds 6 mg/dl. (Maxwell et al., 1987).

Treatment includes removal of phosphate through dialysis and use of phosphate-binding antacids. Treatment of patients with conditions that cause hyperphosphatemia should include prevention as a goal.

Disease model: hypoparathyroidism. Hypoparathyroidism is characterized clinically by hypocalcemia and hyperphosphatemia with decreased bone resorption and increased bone density consequent to the reduction in calcium mobilization from the bones. The clinical manifestations include those of hypocalcemia. These patients frequently suffer ectodermal problems, which include dry skin, brittle nails, and thin hair. Frequent monilial infections of the nails, pharynx, and vagina may occur in patients with idiopathic hypoparathyroidism. Dental abnormalities include softening, late eruption, poor development, and defects in the enamel. Eye problems that may develop are irreversible and include cataracts, conjunctivitis, and photophobia. In chronic hypoparathyroidism, personality changes sometimes occur, including psychoses and mental retardation. Calcification in the basal ganglia, frontal regions, dentate nucleus, and cerebellum of the brain sometimes occurs but is not always related to the signs of parkinsonism that are seen in some patients.

The most frequent cause of hypoparathyroidism is surgical removal of or damage to the parathyroid glands. This may occur inadvertently during thyroid surgery or as a result of interruption of the blood supply to the glands. The hypoparathyroidism that follows is temporary in approximately one third to one half of these patients. A type of latent hypoparathyroidism may also follow thyroid surgery, in which the serum calcium level remains normal, but the return to a normal serum calcium level following a hypocalcemic episode will be extremely slow.

Hypoparathyroidism occurs physiologically in the neonate and is thought to be related to the development of tetany in infants who are fed high-phosphate cow's milk. Hypoparathyroidism during the neonatal period may also occur as a result of maternal hypercalcemia. There is a 25% chance of fetal death and a 50% chance of tetany developing during the first 3 weeks of life in the presence of maternal hyperparathyroidism.

There are two types of idiopathic hypoparathyroidism: early onset and late onset. The early-onset type appears to be an inherited condition that affects males and usually is manifested during the first year of life. It is generally very mild. This condition is different from the hypoparathyroidism that results from congenital absence of the parathyroid and thymus glands (DiGeorge's syndrome), which occurs sporadically in both males and females. The characteristics of this condition include failure to thrive, diarrhea, hypocalcemic tetany, and lymphopenia with increased susceptibility to infection. These infants tend to die early. The other type of idiopathic hypoparathyroidism, which has its onset later in life, occurs more frequently than the early-onset type. This type does not appear to be hereditary in nature, and there is some evidence of an autoimmune etiology. Addison's disease and pernicious anemia have been associated with this condition.

Treatment of hypoparathyroidism involves administration of calcium and vitamin D to correct the hypocalcemia. Hormone replacement therapy is impractical at this time, since it involves frequent intramuscular injection of parathyroid hormone. The hormone extract is ineffective when given orally because it is destroyed by digestive enzymes. Serum calcium levels are usually maintained in the low-normal range. Symptoms are usually absent at this level, and the hypercalciuria that is a common sequela to exogenous calcium administration is kept at a minimum. Formation of renal calculi is sometimes a complication of this form of therapy as is hypervitaminosis D, which causes hypercalcemia to develop. Even with treated hypoparathyroidism in which the serum calcium level is normal, serum phosphate levels remain elevated. Treatment of the hyperphosphatemia by dietary restriction or with either aluminum hydroxide gels, which limit intestinal absorption, or probenecid, which increases urinary phosphate excretion, is not usually necessary.

The condition of *pseudohypoparathyroidism* also bears mentioning. It is a rare, hereditary disorder in which there is no pathologic involvement of the parathyroid glands. The parathyroid hormone level is usually normal but sometimes elevated. The defect is in the target tissue (bone and kidney), which fails to respond to the hormone. A lack of cAMP seems to be the most plausible theory at this time to explain this failure of the target tissue to respond to PTH.

Disease model: aldosteronism

Aldosteronism is a clinical disorder characterized by alterations in fluid volume and composition. Secretion of aldosterone is controlled by the renin-angiotensin system, the potassium concentration of the extracellular fluid, and ACTH. The juxtaglomerular cells of the afferent arteriole of the glomerulus secrete renin in response to renal hypoperfusion. Specialized renal receptor cells participate in the regulation of renin secretion. These include stretch receptors in the afferent arteriole, which respond to lack of stretch, and the cells of the macula densa, which are thought to respond to changes in the sodium chloride load. Stimulation of renin secretion is also mediated by the catecholamines and sympathetic innervation of the kidney. When an individual is in a hypotensive state, less blood is delivered to the kidney, thus stimulating the stretch receptors of the afferent arteriole. The decreased glomerular filtration rate causes less sodium chloride to be delivered to the macula densa, thus stimulating these cells, and sympathetic activity increases because of stimulation of the arterial baroreceptors. Fig. 18-14 illustrates the anatomic arrangements of the juxtaglomerular apparatus and macula densa.

Renin catalyzes the conversion of a plasma protein polypeptide, angiotensinogen or renin substrate, into a peptide, angiotensin I. Angiotensin I is converted into angiotensin II by a converting enzyme. Angiotensin II raises arterial pressure directly by causing vasoconstriction of arterioles and veins, which increases peripheral resistance. Angiotensin II indirectly elevates arterial pressure through expansion of extracellular fluid volume. It may stimulate thirst through centrally acting mechanisms (Humes, 1986). It directly affects the kidneys to retain sodium and water through constriction of the renal efferent arterioles that subsequently increases the filtration fraction. It also stimulates the zona glomerulosa of the adrenal cortex to release aldosterone, a mineralocortiocoid that also causes reabsorption of sodium and subsequently water by the kidney.

Control of further secretion of renin is provided via a negative feedback mechanism in which both angiotensin II and aldosterone participate. Increased systemic pressure results from the vasoconstrictor properties of angiotensin II and the restoration of effective circulating volume by aldosterone. The increase in systemic pressure augments renal perfusion and glomerular filtration rate (with an increased

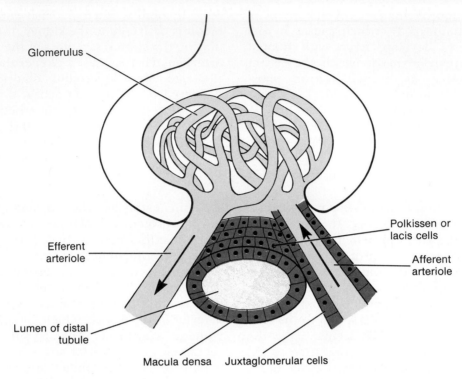

Fig. 18-14. Juxtaglomerular apparatus: specialized renal cells that secrete renin.

glomerular filtration rate, tubular sodium chloride delivery is enhanced), and further secretion of renin is thus inhibited.

Aldosterone's major action is on renal tubular Na^+ reabsorption. However, it is important to point out that other actions may also be caused by the Na^+ effect. Water reabsorption in the tubules is osmotic in nature in response to the Na^+ reabsorption. Aldosterone also stimulates K^+ excretion, since Na^+ reabsorption occurs mainly through a linked pump. Aldosterone also affects acid-base balance, since it causes K^+ excretion, and excesses result in hypokalemia. Hypokalemia causes H^+ to substitute for K^+ on the Na^+-K^+ renal pump. Thus excess H^+ is lost, resulting in a state of metabolic alkalosis. Aldosterone exerts its renal effects through the hor-

monal mechanism of activating protein synthesis. It is metabolized in the liver and, to a lesser extent, in the kidney.

There is a direct relationship between aldosterone secretion and plasma potassium concentration. Elevated plasma K^+ levels will stimulate aldosterone secretion via a direct effect on the zona glomerulosa. This mechanism is also controlled by feedback inhibition. The feedback regulation of aldosterone secretion via the renin-angiotensin system and plasma K^+ concentration is summarized in Fig. 18-15. Angiotensin II and potassium appear to act on adrenal cortical tissue by stimulating conversion of cholesterol to pregnenolone in the zona glomerulosa.

ACTH appears to play a minor role in aldosterone secretion. The permissive nature

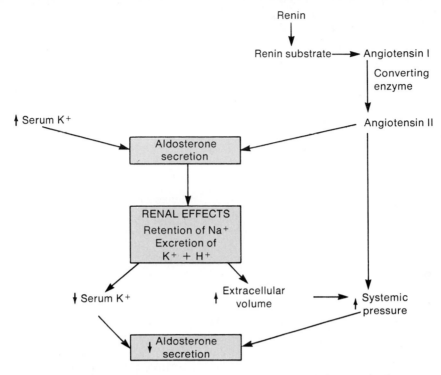

Fig. 18-15. Feedback regulation of aldosterone via two distinct mechanisms.

of this role is demonstrated by the fact that aldosterone secretion in response to volume depletion in hypophysectomized animals is extremely low.

Aldosteronism may be primary or secondary. Primary aldosteronism (Conn's syndrome) results from pathology arising within the adrenal glands, while secondary aldosteronism is caused by pathologic conditions that occur outside the endocrine system and that cause the excessive stimulation of aldosterone secretion.

In primary aldosteronism the secretion of aldosterone is no longer under normal feedback control in that it is not maintained by the appropriate stimuli nor is it inhibited by the factors that normally suppress it. The causes of primary aldosteronism include adrenal hyperplasia in the zona glomerulosa and adrenal adenoma and carcinoma.

Secondary aldosteronism occurs with conditions that decrease renal perfusion and that are sensed by the kidney as a reduction in circulatory volume. Bartter's syndrome is a condition in which excessive renin secretion caused by hyperplasia of the renal juxtaglomerular apparatus causes secondary aldosteronism.

The clinical manifestations of aldosteronism are exaggerations of the normal effects of aldosterone, and are summarized in Fig. 18-16. There is an increased retention of Na^+ and increased urinary excretion of K^+. Metabolic alkalosis is the result of this shift of hydrogen ions into the cells to replace K^+ and maintain electroneutrality. Hypertension develops as a re-

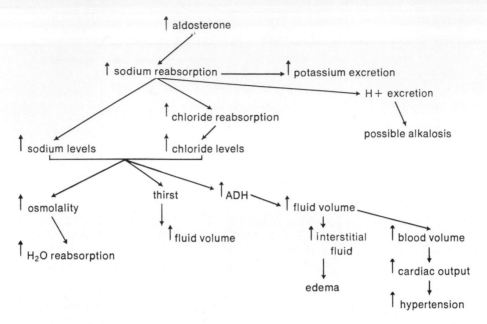

Fig. 18-16. Effects of increased aldosterone.
(From Krueger JA and Ray JC: Endocrine problems in nursing, St Louis, 1976, The CV Mosby Co.)

sult of the increased blood volume and renal changes that occur. Hypertension will not be seen with secondary aldosteronism occurring in response to depletion of the effective circulatory volume. The other manifestations of aldosteronism reflect the electrolyte imbalance that occurs. Muscular weakness, paralysis, paresthesias, and tetany occur in response to hypokalemia and alkalosis.

Renal changes, which cause a loss of renal concentrating ability, occur in response to K^+ depletion. Polyuria and nocturia are symptoms that reflect this loss. The K^+-depleted kidney appears to be susceptible to infection and signs of pyelonephritis may develop.

ALTERATION IN BODY FLUID DISTRIBUTION

Disruption of wellness can be the result of changes in the distribution of the body fluid. A shift of fluid from the intravascu-lar compartment to the interstitial compartment results in *edema*, the visible swelling of the body tissue. In edema the plasma volume is reduced but interstitial volume is increased. A shift of body fluid from the intravascular compartment to a nonequilibrating *third space* results in depletion of the extracellular volume, or hypovolemia. Both conditions may result in reduction of the effective circulating volume of the blood with the effect of reducing tissue perfusion.

Edema

Edema develops as a result of two interacting mechanisms: the alteration of capillary hemodynamics, favoring filtration out of the intravascular compartment, and the accumulation of excess sodium and water in the body. Normally, as fluid begins to accumulate in the interstitium, there is a decrease in the negative interstitial fluid pressure and in the interstitial oncotic pressure caused by dilution. These pressure changes favor reabsorption into the capillary. Lymphatic flow will also increase in order to remove excess fluid from the interstitium. The pressure changes favoring reabsorption and the increased lymph drainage normally prevent any excessive accumulation of interstitial fluid and account for the fact that there must be a 10 to 15 mm Hg increase in the gradient favoring filtration before edema becomes apparent.

Disruption of the Starling forces in a manner that alters capillary hemodynamics to favor the net filtration of fluid out of the capillary into the interstitium can be the result of increases in capillary hydrostatic pressure, capillary permeabil-

ity, or interstitial oncotic pressure, or of a decrease in plasma oncotic pressure (Table 18-13). The capillary hydrostatic pressure remains fairly stable in spite of changes in the arterial pressure because of the resistance provided by the precapillary sphincter. Changes in venous pressure, however, will be reflected by concomitant changes in the capillary hydrostatic pressure since resistance in the venules is not so stringently regulated. Venous pressure can be increased as a result of venous obstruction or an increase in intravascular volume. The edema seen in a limb in which venous thrombosis has occurred results from the increased capillary hydrostatic pressure in the presence of venous obstruction. The edema seen in renal failure is a result of

Table 18-13. Etiology of edema

Etiologic factors	Associated conditions
Increased capillary permeability	Inflammatory reactions
	Burns
	Trauma
	Allergic reactions
	Pulmonary edema (noncardiogenic)
Increased capillary hydrostatic pressure	
Na^+ retention and increased blood volume	Congestive heart failure
	Trauma and stress
	Renal failure
	Refeeding edema
	Adrenocortical hormone secretion
	Drugs; estrogen, phenylbutazone
Venous obstruction	Local obstruction
	Hepatic obstruction
	Pulmonary edema (cardiogenic)
Decreased plasma oncotic pressure	
Decreased synthesis of plasma proteins	Liver disease
	Malnutrition
Increased loss of plasma proteins	Nephrotic syndrome
	Burns
	Protein losing enteropathy
Increased interstitial pressure (plasma protein lost to interstitium)	Lymphatic obstruction
	Increased capillary permeability

the increased capillary hydrostatic pressure caused by the increased intravascular volume.

Any condition favoring the release and accumulation of protein in the interstitial fluid will cause an increase in the interstitial oncotic pressure. The capillary membrane is normally impermeable to all but very small amounts of protein, restricting its presence to the intravascular compartment. The small amount of protein filtered out of the capillary is normally returned to the circulation via the lymphatics. If the lymph flow is obstructed or reduced, this protein will accumulate and cause an increase in interstitial oncotic pressure. A change in capillary permeability that allows free passage of protein will also increase interstitial oncotic pressure. This mechanism characterizes the formation of edema in burns and allergic reactions. If the protein loss from the intravascular compartment is severe, plasma oncotic pressure may also be reduced. The osmotic pressure generated by the plasma proteins (oncotic pressure) plays an important role in promoting reabsorption of fluid into the capillary from the interstitium. This effect is lost when the plasma oncotic pressure is reduced because of lack of protein, and more fluid will continue to enter and remain in the interstitium. Other factors that decrease the plasma oncotic pressure include an increased loss of protein from the body and reduction in the synthesis of plasma proteins by the liver.

The presence of edema also indicates an excess amount of the total body sodium, which is accompanied by an obligatory load of water. The sodium excess may serve as either an initiating or a secondary factor in the pathogenesis of edema. Accumulation of an excess amount of sodium in the body is most frequently caused by either increased retention or reduced ability to eliminate Na^+ in the presence of normal intake. Most commonly the increased retention of sodium and subsequently water is seen in edematous states as a compensatory mechanism to restore and maintain the circulating volume at near-normal levels while fluid accumulates in the interstitial space. Sodium retention following a reduction in intra-vascular volume is thought to result both from a decrease in the glomerular filtration rate reflecting that reduction and an increase in tubular reabsorption. Increased reabsorption along the entire tubule has been demonstrated in edematous states and is affected by several factors: aldosterone secretion, increased sympathetic tone, redistribution of renal blood flow away from the outer cortex, increased peritubular oncotic pressure, and absence of a natriuretic hormone (influencing urinary loss of Na^+). No one of these factors appears to play a primary role in sodium reabsorption, however.

Renal retention of sodium and water as a compensatory mechanism to restore circulating volume is illustrated in conditions such as the nephrotic syndrome, liver disease, and congestive heart failure. With the nephrotic syndrome and liver disease, disruption of capillary hemodynamics is the initiating factor. In both conditions the lack of plasma proteins causes a decrease in the plasma oncotic pressure. In liver disease, synthesis of the plasma proteins is depressed, while in the nephrotic syndrome excessive amounts of the plasma proteins are lost in the urine. As the intravascular volume drops, sodium and water retention increases to maintain the effective circulating volume. In congestive heart failure, both disruption of capillary hemodynamics and renal retention of sodium and water come into play as primary factors in the pathogenesis of cardiac edema. In the presence of heart failure, venous pressure rises because the heart is unable to pump all of the blood being returned to it. The increased venous pressure will cause an increase in capillary hydrostatic pressure (backward theory). As cardiac output falls in the presence of heart failure, various compensatory mechanisms, among them renal retention of sodium and water, come into play. The resulting increase in circulating volume only serves to intensify the already increased venous and capillary hydrostatic pressures. A diagram of the interaction of the disrupted Starling forces and the sodium and water retention that occurs in these conditions is presented in Fig. 18-17.

In contrast to these conditions, increased renal retention of sodium and water plays a primary role in the pathogenesis of cyclic edema seen in menstruating women. The ovarian hormones estrogen and progesterone influence the rate of renal sodium reabsorption. When the rate of the secretion of these hormones increases, sodium and water reabsorption

will also increase. As the total amount of sodium and water increases, venous pressure will continue to rise. When venous pressure increases to the point where the capillary hydrostatic pressure is also increased, fluid will move out of the capillary and remain in the interstitial space. This contributes to the premenstrual edema that many otherwise normal women experience. Birth control pills contain these hormones in varying amounts so that many women taking birth control pills experience edema as an unpleasant side effect. The higher the estrogen content of the pill, the greater the likelihood that edema will develop. Increased levels of these hormones, as well as a reduction in plasma oncotic pressure, interact to promote edema in the pregnant woman.

The kidneys' inability to excrete sodium while normal ingestion continues will result in the accumulation of an excessive amount of sodium. This occurs when renal function is compromised as a result of disease or direct damage to the nephrons. The edema that accompanies renal failure

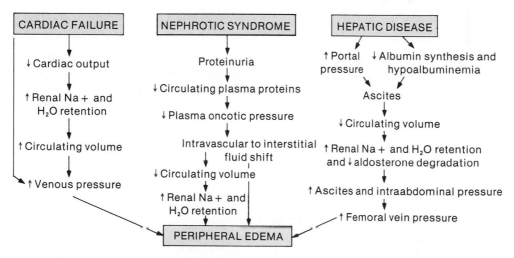

Fig. 18-17. Interaction of disrupted capillary hemodynamics and Na^+ and water retention in three conditions that include edema as a chief manifestation.

occurs when the increased levels of sodium and water increase venous pressure to the point where capillary hemodynamics are altered, favoring filtration out of the capillary. Table 18-13 lists the various etiologic factors and the conditions in which these factors play a primary role in the pathogenesis of edema.

When external pressure on edematous tissue displaces the edema fluid and leaves an indentation, the edema is described as *pitting edema* (Fig. 18-18). The term *brawny edema* describes a type of edema in which the overlying skin is stretched taut and resembles a pig's skin with pronounced

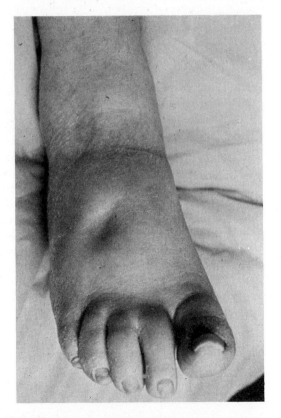

Fig. 18-18. Pitting edema in patient with cardiopulmonary disease.

(From Beyers M and Dudas S: The clinical practice of medical surgical nursing, Boston, 1977, Little, Brown and Co.)

pores. It is hard to the touch, and pressure will not leave an indentation. Brawny edema is characteristic of lymphedema or the edema that accompanies lymphatic obstruction or occurs following removal of lymph nodes (Skov and Muwaswes, 1986). This type of edema is seen in the arm of a woman after a mastectomy with removal of the lymph nodes.

The effects of edema are determined by its location and extent. Edema may be generalized or localized, depending on its cause. For example, hydrostatic or cardiogenic pulmonary edema is the result of the transudation of fluid into the alveoli that occurs when the hydrostatic pressure in the pulmonary capillaries exceeds the plasma oncotic pressure. This occurs when the left side of the heart fails (see Chapter 17). Noncardiogenic pulmonary edema is the result of increased permeability of the alveolocapillary membrane (see Chapter 16). Pulmonary edema constitutes a life-threatening situation because gas exchange is blocked by the presence of fluid at the alveolocapillary membrane. Laryngeal edema, another form of localized edema, results from increased capillary permeability secondary to allergic reactions or burns of the face and neck with smoke inhalation. With severe laryngeal swelling, airway occlusion may occur. This also is a life-threatening situation since oxygen is prevented from reaching the alveolocapillary membrane. In contrast to these conditions is the localized edema of the feet and ankles that may occur after prolonged periods of sitting or standing. This edema usually causes only minor discomfort and is readily relieved by elevation of the extremities.

Edema in an organ such as the brain, which is enclosed in a limited, nonexpandable space, can have serious consequences. As edema increases and brain tissue swells, filling the cranium, intracranial pressure will increase, and cerebral blood flow will be impaired. Signs of the resulting cerebral dysfunction may include restlessness, changes in the level of consciousness from disorientation and lethargy to stupor and coma, irregular pupillary reaction, papilledema, visual disturbances, headache, vomiting, and weakness or paralysis of parts of the body. Changes in the vital signs will reflect the effects of disruption of the cerebral control centers on vital organ function: increased blood pressure, decreased pulse rate, and depressed respirations often with periods of apnea (see Chapter 10).

Generalized edema usually first appears in the dependent, gravity-affected parts of the body; in an ambulatory person, the feet and ankles, and in a bedridden person, the sacrum and buttocks. Aside from discomfort, edematous tissue is susceptible to other problems. The flow of blood to the affected tissue is compromised as a result of the altered capillary hemodynamics. Thus the delivery of oxygen and nutrients and the removal of wastes are impeded, leading to the development of a state of hypoxia and acidosis that will impair cellular function. As a result, the edematous tissue is more prone to breakdown and more susceptible to infection. The effects of even a minor amount of pressure on edematous tissue are intensified because of preexisting hypoxic conditions. Pressure sores that develop in edematous tissue are more extensive and more difficult to heal than those in normal tissue.

The treatment of edema is determined by its effects on the body and its underlying cause. Consideration must be given to the questions of how rapidly the edema fluid can be removed and what the possible consequences of this removal will be to the overall functioning of the body. Obviously, the effects of conditions such as pulmonary and cerebral edema are life threatening, and removal of the edema fluid from the lungs and brain must be done in the most expedient way possible. Sometimes removal of edema fluid has serious consequences, however. Rapid removal of ascitic fluid, for example, can cause a serious depletion of the circulating volume, resulting in hypovolemic shock. It must be remembered that mobilization of the edema fluid through use of diuretic medications is initially at the expense of the plasma volume. Despite this reduction most patients benefit from the use of diuretic medications. However, there are two exceptions: patients with a low effective circulating volume (severe heart failure) and those who have been previously treated excessively with diuretics. In these two groups of patients the reduction in plasma volume is enough to seriously impair tissue perfusion.

It is not enough to treat only the edema; the underlying condition must also be treated; if the underlying condition is not cured or treated the edema will reoccur. Often treatment of the causative condition is enough to initiate mobilization of the edema fluid, for example, the patient experiencing edema secondary to heart failure. With increased cardiac contractility and output as a response to digitalis therapy, both the backward and forward effects of heart failure that lead to edema formation are minimized. Edema caused by venous or lymphatic obstruction will not be relieved until the cause of the obstruction is relieved.

"Third space" syndromes

Third space syndromes in which a significant amount of the ECF becomes unavailable to the effective circulating volume are sometimes referred to as *sequestered edema* or fluid sequestration. This fluid remains in the body and with appropriate treatment may be mobilized to return to the effective ECF. For all intents and purposes a new fluid compartment is formed in addition to the intra- and extracellular compartments, hence the name *third space*.

Conditions that result in large amounts of the ECF becoming trapped outside the extracellular compartment, either in the tissues or in a serous body cavity, include burns, venous obstruction within a major venous system, and intestinal obstruction. The effects of burns on fluid dynamics are discussed later in this chapter. The effects of intestinal obstruction on chemical equilibrium are discussed in Chapter 21. Sequestration of fluid around the site of injury is a feature of trauma, either accidental or surgical, accompanied by extensive tissue damage (e.g., crushing injuries, surgery involving massive tissue resection). Bleeding into a body cavity or tissue can also result in a third space syndrome.

A third space syndrome may also result from *peritonitis*, as inflammatory disorder of the peritoneum that can result from damage by a variety of bacterial and chemical agents. The peritoneal membrane functions in the transport of water and electrolytes between the peritoneal cavity and the circulation. As a result of the inflammatory process this function is disrupted, and large amounts of Na^+ and water may be lost into the peritoneal cavity. Additionally, protein may be lost into the peritoneal cavity, thus increasing the osmotic pull of fluid into this third space. Peritonitis is often a complication of untreated intestinal obstruction, in which the increased permeability of the intestinal wall allows bacteria and their toxins and other substances potentially harmful to mucosal tissue (enzymes, etc.) to move out of the bowel into the peritoneum,

where they initiate an inflammatory response (see Fig. 21-2).

The clinical manifestations of a third space syndrome include those of the pathologic process that originally caused the fluid shift and also the manifestations of depletion of the effective circulating volume. As cardiac output is decreased due to volume depletion, tachycardia and hypotension result. Sympathetic stimulation causes peripheral vasoconstriction, which is manifested by pallor and coldness of the extremities. Oliguria reflects the decreased renal blood flow and the body's attempts to conserve fluid. There will be no weight loss as there is when fluid is lost from the body, however.

The rapidity of the fluid accumulation into the third space is an important variable. If the depletion of the effective circulating volume is severe and acute, hypovolemic shock may develop. If the fluid loss from the ECF occurs slowly, the body can compensate by retaining salt and water. If the fluid loss is quite rapid, there is not enough time for the compensatory mechanisms to begin to function to restore fluid volume in the ECF, and signs of depletion of the effective circulating volume will become apparent. Fluid therapy must be supportive to maintain tissue perfusion until the sequestered fluid can be mobilized from the third space.

Additional signs and symptoms possibly accompanying the hypovolemic state include those of the electrolyte and acid-base disorders that may accompany fluid depletion. These will depend on the composition of the fluid that is lost from the effective circulating volume.

HYDROGEN ION CONCENTRATION (pH)

The pH is an expression of the relative acidity and alkalinity of the body fluid. More specifically it is the negative logarithm of the hydrogen ion concentration. The pH is arrived at using the Henderson-Hasselbalch equation:

$$pH = pK + \log \frac{BHCO_3}{H_2CO_3 + CO_2}$$

where pK = 6.1, B = any cation, HCO_3 = bicarbonate, and $H_2CO_3 + CO_2$ = carbonic acid and dissolved CO_2. Normal pH should be in the range of 7.35 to 7.45.

With the constant addition of the products of metabolism, the maintenance of acid-base balance within normal limits is a constant, dynamic process. The body has three mechanisms by which it can maintain acid-base balance: the buffer systems, the respiratory system, and the renal system.

An acid-base buffer is a solution of two or more chemical compounds that prevents excessive changes in the hydrogen ion concentration when either an acid or a base is added to the solution. A buffer system is made up of a weak acid and its conjugate base. The acid component can neutralize a strong base; however, this will not prevent a departure from the normal acid-base ratio. To illustrate this point, a strong acid added to a buffer system is converted into the weaker buffer acid through interaction with the buffer base, thereby increasing the concentration of the acid component and decreasing the buffer base component. This results in a pH change but not to the extreme that would have occurred in the absence of a buffer system. An example of this is provided by the buffering of hydrochloric acid (a strong acid) by the bicarbonate–carbonic acid buffer pair:

$$HCl + NaHCO_3 \rightarrow H_2CO_3 + NaCl \rightarrow$$
$$H_2O + CO_2$$

Carbonic acid, a much weaker acid, is formed. The pH of the acid varies directly with the buffer base component: as the buffer base increases, pH also increases, and as the buffer base decreases, pH also decreases.

There are several buffer systems in the body, including the phosphate and protein buffer systems, but the bicarbonate–carbonic acid buffer system is the most important physiologically. The components of this system can also be regulated by the lungs and kidneys, which ultimately determine the pH status of the blood. The various buffer systems also work together to minimize pH changes: a change in the base-acid ratio of one system will cause a corresponding change in the other systems.

An additional buffer system is that which operates through the chloride shift mechanism in the red blood cells. This hemoglobin buffering is responsible for pH maintenance despite continuous production of carbon dioxide. Deoxyhemoglobin is a weak acid that is abundant in the venous capillaries and blood. Carbon dioxide from the tissues diffuses into the erythrocytes, which contain a high concentration of the enzyme, carbonic anhydrase (CA), which catalyzes the reaction between carbon dioxide and water shown in Fig. 18-19. The carbon dioxide is quickly hydrated to form carbonic acid, which allows maintenance of a concentration gradient for the diffusion of carbon dioxide into the red blood cells. The carbonic acid dissociates into hydrogen (H^+) and bicarbonate (HCO_3^-) ions. Bicarbonate diffuses out of the cell and into the plasma immediately. Chloride ions then move into the red blood cell to maintain electrical neutrality, hence the name, chloride shift. The remaining intracellular hydrogen ions are buffered by the deoxyhemoglobin. In the pulmonary capillaries, oxygen will diffuse into the cell and bind with hemoglobin to form oxyhemoglobin, a stronger acid that will bind other cations and release hydrogen ions. Bicarbonate ions diffuse into the cell and react with hydrogen to form carbonic acid that readily dissociates into carbon dioxide and water. Again, to maintain electrical neutrality, chloride diffuses out of the cell (Groer, 1981). This sequence of events is depicted in Fig. 18-19.

The respiratory system acts as a feedback system with the carbon dioxide concentration. This is possible because the carbon dioxide concentration is in equilibrium with the hydrogen ion concentration as demonstrated in this equation:

$$H^+ + HCO_3^- \rightleftarrows H_2CO_3 \rightleftarrows H_2O + CO_2$$

When increased amounts of carbon diox-

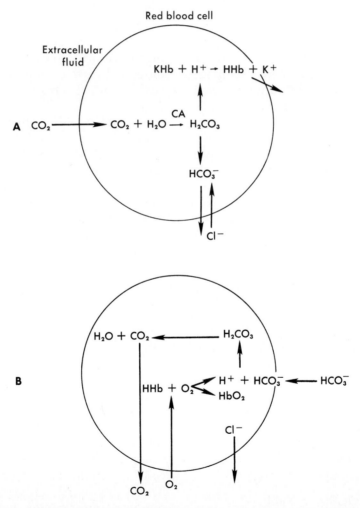

Fig. 18-19. A, Chloride shift and transport of CO_2 into red blood cell at tissue. **B,** Release of CO_2 at lungs. When hemoglobin (Hb) is oxygenated at lungs, it becomes stronger acid, releasing H^+, which results in formation of CO_2. (CA = carbonic anhydrase.)

(From Groer, M: Physiology and pathophysiology of the body fluids, St Louis, 1981, The CV Mosby Co.)

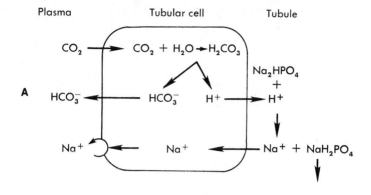

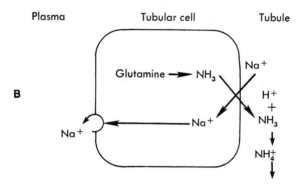

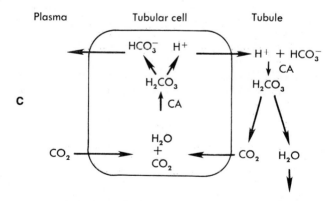

Fig. 18-20. Renal mechanisms in acid-base balance. **A,** Formation of monobasic phosphoric acid, which is measured as titratable acidity in urine. **B,** Ammonia reacts with secreted H^+ and neutralizes it, creating ammonium ion, which is excreted. Na^+ can be reabsorbed because electrical neutrality is not disturbed. **C,** Bicarbonate reabsorption results when carbonic anhydrase (CA) inside cell and on tubular luminal membrane catalyzes formation and breakdown of carbonic acid. Note that filtered HCO_3^- is not directly reabsorbed, but no *net* gain or loss of HCO_3^- occurs through this mechanism.

(From Groer, M: Physiology and pathophysiology of the body fluids, St Louis, 1981, The CV Mosby Co.)

ide are present, the respiratory system becomes more active and "blows off" the excess carbon dioxide, making less available to form carbonic acid. When decreased amounts of carbon dioxide are present, the respiratory system becomes less active and retains carbon dioxide, making more available to form carbonic acid.

The kidneys help regulate acid-base balance through excretion of hydrogen ions in the urine and reabsorption of bicarbonate ions. These mechanisms are illustrated in Fig. 18-20. The kidneys normally excrete an acid urine because the products of metabolism are acid. The urine is normally free of HCO_3^-; however, when there is an excess of bicarbonate ions in the plasma, the kidneys will excrete an alkaline urine. When excess H^+ is present in the plasma, the kidneys will act to conserve an appropriate number of HCO_3^- ions beyond the normal amount (Groer, 1981).

The buffer systems function immediately to prevent drastic changes in hydrogen ion concentration. The respiratory system acts within minutes to correct a sudden change, while the kidneys require a longer period of time in which to readjust the pH. However, renal compensation can return the pH to normal, whereas respiratory compensation generally cannot. The whole aim of compensation is the return to a normal or near-normal pH as rapidly as possible since there is a very narrow limit to the extent of pH change the body can tolerate.

Alterations in acid-base balance

Failure to maintain the hydrogen ion concentration of the body fluid within normal limits so that the pH is maintained at a value between 7.35 and 7.45 results in abnormal conditions known as alkalosis and acidosis. A change in pH indicates a disruption in the normal bicarbonate–car-

bonic acid ratio of 20:1. When the bicarbonate concentration of the blood rises or the carbonic acid concentration falls, the bicarbonate–carbonic acid ratio increases, and the pH becomes greater than 7.45, reflecting a decrease in the hydrogen ion concentration. This state is called *alkalosis*. When bicarbonate concentration of the blood falls or carbonic acid concentration increases, the bicarbonate–carbonic acid ratio decreases, and the pH becomes less than 7.35, reflecting an increase in the hydrogen ion concentration. This is called *acidosis*. Cellular metabolism cannot proceed at excessively high or low pH levels. A pH less than 6.8 or greater than 7.8 is incompatible with survival so that there is a very narrow range in which alterations in pH can be tolerated. Fig. 18-21 schematically illustrates the normal range of pH and the effects of alterations in the bicarbonate–carbonic acid ratio and thus abnormal pH values.

Arterial blood gas analysis is the primary diagnostic tool utilized to assess alterations in acid-base balance. Common parameters obtained from analysis of an arterial blood sample include the partial pressures of oxygen (Po_2) and carbon dioxide (Pco_2) as well as pH, bicarbonate concentration (HCO_3^-), and oxygen saturation. Although oxygen values give clues to the status of oxygenation, the remaining three parameters pH, Pco_2 and HCO_3^- aid directly in the diagnosis of acid-base imbalances.

A systematic approach to arterial blood gases begins with examination of the pH. The pH value helps to determine the existence of an acid-base imbalance; however, it does not indicate the cause of the disturbance. Depending on the etiology, clinical conditions in which the hydrogen ion concentration is outside the normal range are classified as either metabolic or respira-

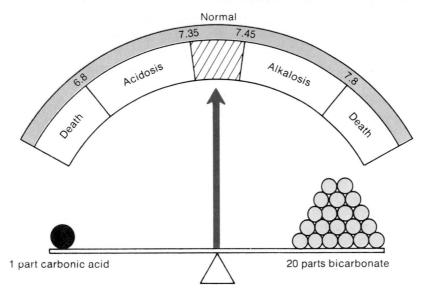

Fig. 18-21. The pH and its relationship to bicarbonate–carbonic acid ratio.

tory. After analyzing the pH to determine if an acid-base disturbance exists, the respiratory or carbonic acid component, the PCO_2, and the metabolic or noncarbonic acid component, the HCO_3^-, must be examined to determine the source of the acid-base imbalance. Disruption of the normal carbonic acid level has a respiratory etiology, while disruption of the normal bicarbonate level has a metabolic etiology. The four primary acid-base disorders include respiratory acidosis, respiratory alkalosis, metabolic acidosis, and metabolic alkalosis. In addition, mixed or combined acid-base disorders may also occur.

Compensation will be attempted through a system not primarily responsible for the acid-base disturbance. Disturbances in the PCO_2 (respiratory parameter) stimulate renal compensation in the form of bicarbonate reclamation and hydrogen ion excretion. Metabolic imbalances primarily affecting the plasma HCO_3^- level produce changes in alveolar ventilation and PCO_2 to accomplish restoration of normal pH. In both instances, compensation tends to direct the measured pH value in the arterial sample toward normal. By virtue of the Henderson-Hasselbach equation, compensation occurs in the same direction as the primary disturbance. Elevations or deficits in the respiratory component obligate elevations or deficits in the renal component of the ratio and, thus, pH remains normal.

The base excess is an additional value reported on arterial blood gas analysis that can help determine the degree of compensation present in an acid-base disturbance. The normal base excess ranges from positive 2 mEq/L to negative 2 mEq/L ($+2$ and -2 mEq/L) and is related to the base (HCO_3^-) content of the sample. Alterations in the normal base deficit indicate that renal compensation is occurring. Bicarbonate levels are changed within the plasma primarily by renal mechanisms; however, hemoglobin buffering also alters bicarbonate levels in exchange for chloride in the chloride shift. If plasma HCO_3 levels are abnormal, with a normal base excess value, the change in bicarbonate is caused by hemoglobin buffering. Thus renal and additional buffering systems are not yet operative. The use of base excess/deficit values, coupled with additional clinical data, can give clues to the time course and source of compensatory mechanisms. Summarized in Table 18-14 are the arterial blood gas values with compensatory changes for primary acid-base disturbances.

Respiratory acidosis and alkalosis. Respiratory acidosis and respiratory alkalosis are the result of disorders of ventilation. Hypoventilation causes CO_2 to be retained leading to respiratory acidosis. Hyperventilation causes CO_2 to be "blown off" leading to respiratory alkalosis. When there is an increase in CO_2, as occurs in respiratory acidosis, the concentrations of both H^+ and HCO_3^- will concomitantly increase. The pH will drop below 7.35, the P_{CO_2} will rise above the normal 40 mm Hg, and the plasma bicarbonate level will increase above the normal 24 mmole/liter. This occurs because when more CO_2 is available to combine with water, more

carbonic acid is formed, which readily dissociates into hydrogen (H^+) and bicarbonate (HCO_3^-) ions. These relationships are summarized in the following equation:

$$H_2O + CO_2 \rightleftarrows H_2CO_3 \rightleftarrows H^+ + HCO_3^-$$

In respiratory alkalosis, with a decrease in CO_2, the converse is true and the concentrations of H^+ and HCO_3^- will decrease. Therefore pH will increase to 7.45 or greater when the buffering capacity of the ECF is exceeded and the P_{CO_2} and the plasma bicarbonate levels will be less than normal. A discussion of the various pathologic processes that disrupt normal ventilation to cause acid-base alterations as well as a detailed description of the clinical manifestations and treatment of both respiratory alkalosis and acidosis are included in Chapter 16.

There is no one set of signs and symptoms that any one patient with either of these disorders will exhibit. Patients with respiratory acidosis will exhibit signs of hypoxia (restlessness, confusion, lethargy, coma) and respiratory difficulty or distress

TABLE 18-14. Arterial blood gas values in the primary acid-base disorders

State	Plasma pH	P_{CO_2} mm Hg	$[HCO_3^-]$ mEq/L	Base excess
Normal	7.35 – 7.45	35 – 45	22 – 26	+2.5 to −2.5
Acidosis				
Respiratory acidosis (uncompensated)	Low	High	Normal	Normal or negative
Respiratory acidosis (compensated)	Low normal	High	High	Positive value
Metabolic acidosis (uncompensated)	Low	Normal	Low	Negative value
Metabolic acidosis (compensated)	Low normal	Low	Low	Negative value
Alkalosis				
Respiratory alkalosis (uncompensated)	High	Low	Normal	Normal
Respiratory alkalosis (compensated)	High normal	Low	Low	Negative value
Metabolic alkalosis (uncompensated)	High	Normal	High	Positive value
Metabolic alkalosis (compensated)	High normal	High	High	Positive value

From Shekleton, M and Litwack, K: Critical care nursing of the surgical patient, Philadelphia, PA, WB Saunders Co (In press).

depending on the underlying condition. Compensation for respiratory acidosis occurs primarily via the kidneys, which act to conserve bicarbonate and excrete an acid urine. Patients with severe chronic obstructive pulmonary disease (COPD) live in a constant state of compensated respiratory acidosis. The pH is near normal and the plasma HCO_3^- level is high as an adaptive response to the high PCO_2 levels (Fig. 18-22). The clinical manifestations of respiratory alkalosis may include paresthe-sias, signs of tetany, vertigo, syncope, and even unconsciousness. Any condition that causes rapid breathing may lead to respiratory alkalosis. Respiratory alkalosis may also occur as a compensatory response to metabolic acidosis. Compensation for respiratory alkalosis occurs primarily via the kidneys, which act to excrete HCO_3^- and retain H^+ (Fig. 18-23).

Metabolic acidosis. Metabolic acid base disorders are the result of an excess or deficit of base bicarbonate in the body. Met-

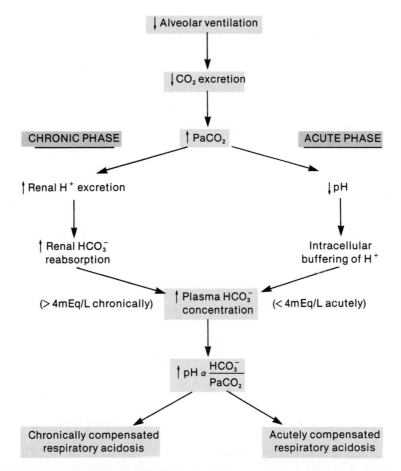

Fig. 18-22. Compensatory pathways initiated in acute and chronic respiratory acidosis. Elevation in $PaCO_2$ promote processes that raise plasma HCO_3^- concentration and thus return pH back toward normal.

(From Humes HD: Pathophysiology of electrolyte and renal disorders, New York, 1986, Churchill Livingstone.)

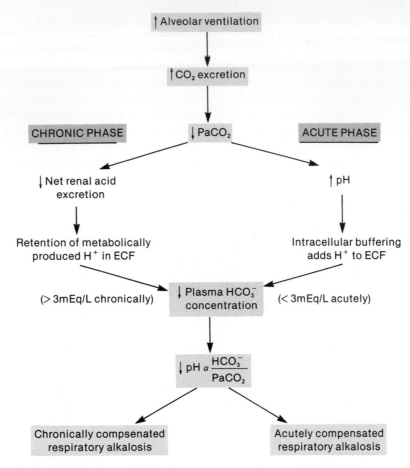

Fig. 18-23. Compensatory pathways initiated in acute and chronic respiratory alkalosis. Decline in $PaCO_2$ promote processes that lower plasma HCO_3^- concentration and thus return pH back toward normal.

(From Humes HD: Pathophysiology of electrolyte and renal disorders, New York, 1986, Churchill Livingstone.)

abolic acidosis is characterized by a deficit of base bicarbonate. The pH will drop below 7.35 and the plasma bicarbonate level will be less than normal. Metabolic acidosis may develop as a result of excess acid being present or a loss of alkali from the body. Excess acid may result when exogenous acid is administered, increased metabolic acid is produced (as in lactic acidosis or ketoacidosis), or the kidneys are unable to excrete a normal endogenous acid load. When excess acid is present, a base bicarbonate deficit develops as bicarbonate reserves are depleted because of the buffering process. When 50% of the total buffer base is used, the acid will no longer be adequately buffered, and the pH will drop.

A loss of alkali, or base, from the body may occur because the kidneys are unable to reabsorb HCO_3^- or alkali-rich body fluid is lost via diarrhea or draining pancreatic

---

TABLE 18-15. Causes of metabolic acidosis

Increased anion gap (normochloremic)	Normal anion gap (hyperchloremic)
Exogenous acid gain	**Loss of base (HCO$_3^-$)**
Methanol ingestion	Renal
Salicylate overdose	Renal tubular acidosis
Paraldehyde ingestion	dosis
Ethylene glycol ingestion	Hypoaldosteronism
tion	Hyperparathyroidism
Solvent inhalation	Carbonic anhydrase
	inhibitors
Increased acid production	Gastrointestinal
	Diarrhea
Ketoacidosis	Small bowel, pancreatic or biliary
Diabetic	drainage or fistulas
Starvation	
Alcoholic	Urinary-intestinal diversion (ureterosigmoidostomy)
Lactic acidosis	
Nonketotic hyperosmolar coma	
Inborn errors of metabolism	
Acid retention (underexcretion)	**Exogenous acid gain**
	Administration of HCl/oral CaCl$_2$/NH$_4$Cl/MgCL$_2$
Renal failure	Hyperalimentation
Acute	Sulfur ingestion
Chronic	**Miscellaneous**
	Anion exchange resins (cholestyramine)
	Dilution
	Recovery from ketoacidosis
	Acute reversal of chronic hypocapnia

---

or duodenal fistulas. Rapid dilution of the extracellular fluid with a base-free solution will also cause a primary base deficit.

Determination of the etiology of the metabolic acidosis is facilitated by calculation of the *anion gap*. The anion gap represents the amount of unmeasured anion present and is calculated by subtracting the sum of the plasma chloride and bicarbonate from the sum of the plasma sodium and potassium:

$$(Na^+ + K^+) - (Cl^- + HCO_3^-) = Anion\ gap$$

The normal anion gap is 16 mEq/L when calculated in this manner (Goldberger, 1986).

The anion gap will be increased if the acidotic condition is caused by an increase in the concentration of nonchloride-containing acid. When the bicarbonate decreases, electrical neutrality must be maintained. If the excess acid is associated with chloride, the anion concentration will be appropriate. If the acid is not associated with chloride, the anion gap may increase to more than 22 mEq/L (Goldberger, 1986; Groër, 1981). Causes of normochloremic metabolic acidosis (increased anion gap) and hyperchloremic metabolic acidosis (normal anion gap) are listed in Table 18-15.

Lactic acidosis provides a good example of normochloremic metabolic acidosis. Lactic acidosis results from conditions that allow or promote an accumulation of pyruvate and lactate, such as cellular hypoxia and anaerobic metabolism, an increased rate of glycolysis and lactic acid synthesis, and diminished renal and hepatic handling of the acid (Maxwell et al., 1987). A representative listing of various conditions that can cause lactic acidosis is included in the box on p. 812. Lactic acid is buffered by sodium bicarbonate, which

CAUSES OF LACTIC ACIDOSIS

Primary decrease in tissue perfusion or oxygenation

Septic shock
Cardiogenic shock
Hypovolemic shock
Mesenteric vascular insufficiency
Hypoxemia ($Pao_2 < 35$ mm Hg)
Anemia
Catecholamine excess

Muscular hyperactivity

Seizures
Long distance running

Systemic disorders or conditions (tissue oxygenation appears normal)

Diabetes mellitus
Hepatic failure
Malignancy
Renal failure
Alkalosis
Pregnancy
Congenital enzymatic defects

Drugs/toxins

Ethanol/methanol
Phenformin
Salicylates
Isoniazid overdose
Iron overdose
Carbon monoxide
Cyanide
Strychnine

Miscellaneous

D-lactic acidosis
Hypoglycemia

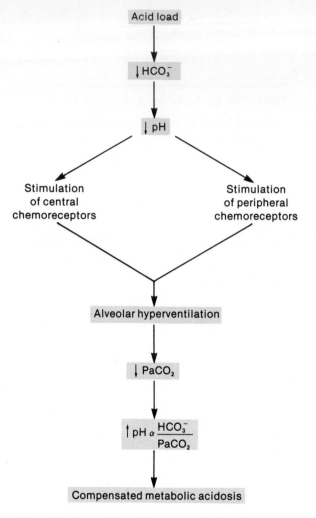

Fig. 18-24. Compensatory pathways initiated in metabolic acidosis.

(From Humes HD: Pathophysiology of electrolyte and renal disorders, New York, 1986, Churchill Livingstone.)

allows the formation of carbonic acid and sodium lactate. The lactate anion is retained and increases the anion gap because it is not associated with chloride (Groër, 1981).

The clinical manifestations of metabolic acidosis are variable and nonspecific. Often the first sign of metabolic acidosis is a characteristic deep, rapid breathing pattern. This respiratory pattern is an indication of a compensatory effort to blow off CO_2 (Figure 18-24). In fact, respiratory alkalosis may even develop. Clinical manifestations of the causative condition may also be present. If the acidotic condition is severe and prolonged without adequate compensation and treatment, coma will ensue. The renal compensatory mechanisms of HCO_3^- reabsorption and H^+ secretion will also be activated but will require 3 to 5 days to restore plasma HCO_3^- levels to normal. There may be a concomitant loss of Na^+ and K^+ in the urine to balance the loss of acid anions. Potassium will move out of the cells to maintain serum K^+ levels. Hypokalemia may develop and, in fact, may be most severe following treatment of the acidosis when the K^+ in the ECF moves back into the ICF.

Correction of the causative condition is the first goal of treatment. If the acidosis is severe or the underlying cause is not treatable, administration of alkali, such as exogenous sodium bicarbonate, will be required.

The following case study demonstrates the manifestation and treatment of metabolic acidosis in an infant. The cause is retention of metabolically produced acids caused by the inability of the kidneys to excrete an acid load.

CASE STUDY: METABOLIC ACIDOSIS

History

The baby's mother is 22 years old and one previous pregnancy had resulted in a stillbirth. Baby J's Apgar scores 1 and 5 minutes after delivery were 5 and 7 respectively. At birth, resuscitation with bag and mask was required and Baby J was immediately transferred to the intensive care nursery. He experienced increasing respiratory distress with intercostal retractions and grunting respirations at a rate of 50 breaths/minute, bilaterally decreased breath sounds, and the following arterial blood gas values indicating respiratory acidosis and hypoxemia:

pH	7.104
pCO_2	62.9 mm Hg
pO_2	20.0 mm Hg
HCO_3	19.7 mEq

The initial chest x-ray showed hyperinflated lungs and fluid in the major fissures. Other abnormal findings on physical examination included poor muscle tone and absent Moro and suck reflexes. Baby J was intubated and placed on assisted mechanical ventilatory support at an FiO_2 of 100%. A tentative diagnosis of persistent fetal circulation was made and he was treated with a tolazoline infusion. A low urinary output was noted during the first 2 days of life which was attributed to renal hypoxia and subsequent renal failure.

Baby J's respiratory status improved over the following 3 days and the fractional inspired oxygen concentration (FiO_2) was able to be decreased and continuous positive airway pressure (CPAP) discontinued. On day 3 the endotracheal tube was removed and oxygen was continued at an FiO_2 of 36%. By day 4 Baby J could breathe room air and began to diurese. Nasogastric tube feedings of Similac 20 were started.

Contributed by Lynda Harrison.

Present illness: Baby J is a 9-day-old male infant who was delivered by cesarean section at 30 weeks gestation because of placenta previa and premature onset of labor. A pattern of slow weight gain over the first 7 days and a 30 gm weight loss between the eighth and ninth days of life led to speculation about the development of late metabolic acidosis which was confirmed with arterial blood gas analysis.

Objective and Subjective Data

On the ninth day of life Baby J's pattern of weight gain was as follows;

Age (days)	Weight (gm)
1	1410
2	1430
3	1450
4	1276
5	1262
6	1247
7	1300
8	1300
9	1270

The following arterial blood gas values confirmed a diagnosis of metabolic acidosis;

pH: 7.30
Pco_2: 29.3 mm Hg
Pao_2: 72.8 mm Hg
HCO_3: 14.5 mEq

Treatment

The baby was treated with a solution of sodium bicarbonate (2 mEq) added to each of two successive feedings. The treatment was considered successful because of the subsequent improvement in the baby's pattern of weight gain, and no further blood gas analyses were done. The infant's weights on the 4 days after treatment were as follows:

Age (days)	Weight (gm)
10	1300
11	1320
12	1360
13	1380

Discussion

Poor weight gain is a primary symptom of late metabolic acidosis in the neonate. The weight gain experienced over the first three days was caused by fluid retention secondary to renal failure. The diuresis which occurred on the fourth day resulted in a weight loss of 174 gm. The slow gain between the fourth and eighth days and the loss of 30 gm between the eighth and ninth days indicated a metabolic problem.

All premature infants are at risk for the development of metabolic acidosis. Baby J's risk was increased because of the many stressors to which he was subjected during the first week of life. The most significant of these stressors in terms of the development of metabolic acidosis was renal hypoxia and the subsequent renal failure. Additionally, the use of high protein formula feedings placed an additional burden on the immature kidneys because of the acid load created by protein catabolism. Breast fed premature infants rarely develop metabolic acidosis.

Blood gas analysis was not routinely done as Baby J's respiratory status had improved. Prevention of unnecessary stress (like that due to blood drawing and blood loss) in premature infants is an important intervention aimed at preventing complications. Evaluation of the growth patterns demonstrated by premature infants takes on additional importance in the care of these infants, as it is a key indicator of underlying problems.

Nursing Diagnoses

Baby J is not experiencing any other problems of prematurity like impaired gas exchange or ineffective thermoregulation at this time. The relevant nursing diagnoses for Baby J's care during the second week of life include:
1. Alteration in acid base balance; metabolic acidosis related to inability to excrete acid load.

2. Altered growth and development related to prematurity and altered metabolism.

The relevant nursing diagnosis for Baby J's parents prior to discharge is:

1. Knowledge deficit related to Baby J's nutritional needs and the need to monitor his weight correctly.

Metabolic alkalosis. Metabolic alkalosis is characterized by an excess of base bicarbonate. The pH is increased above 7.45, and the plasma bicarbonate level will be greater than normal. Metabolic alkalosis may develop as a result of either loss of acid from or the addition of excess bicarbonate to the body. The latter is usually

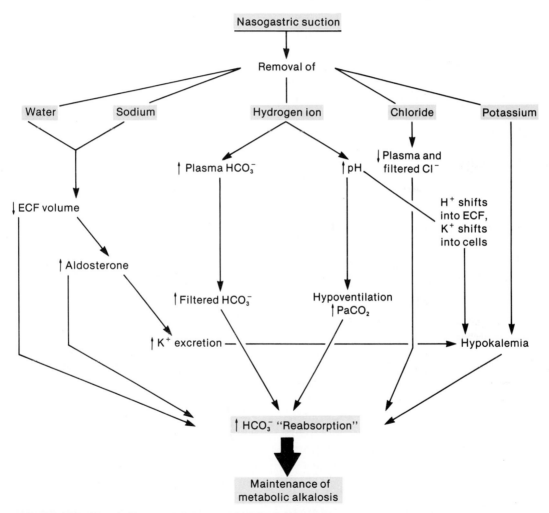

Fig. 10-25. Pathogenesis and maintenance of metabolic alkalosis. In this example of nasogastric suction, metabolic alkalosis is generated by external loss of H^+. Alkalosis is maintained by increased HCO_3^- reclamation by kidney. Kidney is stimulated to increase its rate of HCO_3^- reabsorption (or constrained from dumping excess HCO_3^-) by need to conserve ECF volume. ECF volume depletion per se, secondary increase in aldosterone secretion, relative lack of filtered chloride to accompany sodium reabsorption, hypokalemia, and secondary increase in $PaCO_2$ combine to maintain increased HCO_3^- reabsorption and elevated plasma HCO_3^- concentration. Hypokalemia is caused for the most part by increased urinary excretion. (From Schrier R, editor: Renal and electrolyte disorders, ed 3, Boston, 1986, Little, Brown and Co.)

the result of excessive exogenous alkali ingestion or administration (e.g., milk-alkali syndrome). Excessive acid loss may occur as a result of vomiting or gastric suction (Fig. 18-25). The sustained increase in the plasma HCO_3^- level that occurs in response to this acid loss is stimulated by the loss of Cl^-. Chloride depletion is the most common cause of metabolic alkalosis. Na^+ reabsorption is stimulated. The plasma HCO_3^- is increased as Na^+ and HCO_3^- (since Cl^- is not available) are reabsorbed by the kidneys, and H^+ and K^+ are secreted because of their linkage with Na^+ reabsorption. This mechanism allows electrochemical balance to be achieved and the urine in this case will be acid. Chloride depletion may also be the result of chloride-rich diarrhea. Diuretic therapy with chloriuretic agents involves the same basic mechanism. Metabolic alkalosis is caused by almost all diuretic agents in current use, with the exception of the carbonic anhydrase inhibitors and potassium-sparing agents, which cause metabolic acidosis (Puschett, 1985). Since K^+ is also being lost, a hypochloremic-hypokalemic metabolic alkalosis can develop. Potassium depletion alone can cause metabolic alkalosis as well. Excess mineralocorticoid syndromes are characterized by metabolic alkalosis. Various causes of metabolic alkalosis are summarized in Table 18-16.

There are no specific clinical manifestations of metabolic alkalosis. In fact, this condition is usually identified as the result of a coexisting disease process. In order to diagnose metabolic alkalosis, the clinician must rely heavily on the patient's history and physical examination as well as measurements of plasma levels of electrolytes and blood gases. Respiratory depression (hypopnea and apnea) occurs as a compensatory effect. Signs and symptoms

TABLE 18-16. Causes of metabolic alkalosis

Acid deficit	Excess base (alkali)
Volume depletion with Cl^- deficit	Exogenous sources
NG suction	Milk-alkali syndrome
Prolonged, severe vomiting	Bicarbonate
Diuretic therapy	Administration
Diarrhea	(post treatment of acidosis/cardiac arrest)
Mineralocorticoid excess with K^+ depletion	Transfusions with citrate buffered blood
Hyperaldosteronism	
Cushing's syndrome	Administration of
Bartter's syndrome	acetate buffered
Licorice ingestion	hyperalimentation fluid
Potassium depletion	Overuse of antacids
	Enhanced HCO_3^- reabsorption
	After fasting
	Hypercalcemia and hypoparathyroidism
	After correction of chronic hypercapnia

of associated electrolyte deficit states may be present too. Ionized calcium levels are decreased in alkalosis, which may precipitate twitching, tetany, and convulsions.

As in metabolic acidosis, treatment is directed toward correction of the underlying cause. Provision of Cl^- in Cl^- depletion syndromes will allow HCO_3^- to be lost in the urine. This can be administered in the form of KCl where K^+ loss has also occurred. When excessive mineralocorticoid activity is a cause, treatment must be directed toward interfering with the mineralocorticoid activity. Acetazolamide, the carbonic anhydrase inhibitor Diamox, can

TABLE 18-17.   Primary acid-base disorders

Condition	Other names	Signs and symptoms	Etiologic factors	Compensatory mechanisms
Metabolic				
Primary base bicarbonate deficit. Ketones, chlorides, and/or organic acids replace HCO_3^- ions→deficit of base bicarbonate; ratio of 1 part H_2CO_3 to 20 parts HCO_3^- is ↓ on HCO_3^- side	Metabolic acidosis; Primary alkali deficit; Uncompensated alkali deficit; Nonrespiratory acidosis; Noncarbonic acid excess	Deep, rapid breathing (Kussmaul); Shortness of breath on exertion; Weakness; Stupor; Coma; Laboratory findings: Plasma pH ↓7.35; Urine pH ↓6; Plasma HCO_3^- ↓25 mEq/L in adults and ↓20 mEq/L in children; Anion gap ≥ 16 mEq/L	Gain of strong acid by extracellular fluid; Gain of exogenous acid; Metabolic and organic acid overproduction and/or retention (underexcretion); Loss of base from extracellular fluid; Renal loss; Intestinal loss	Respiratory: ↓ pH stimulates pulmonary ventilation; lungs blow off CO_2, and ↓CO_2 is available to form H_2CO_3; acid side is decreased. Renal: kidneys retain base bicarbonate through preferential excretion of hydrogen ions →acid urine
Primary base bicarbonate excess. Ratio of 1 part H_2CO_3 to 20 parts HCO_3^- is ↑ on HCO_3^- side, resulting in excess of base bicarbonate	Metabolic alkalosis; Primary alkali excess; Uncompensated alkali excess; Nonrespiratory alkalosis; Noncarbonic acid deficit	Depressed breathing (rate and depth); None are specific; Hyperactive reflexes; Muscle hypertonicity; Paresthesias and cramping; Tetany progressing to convulsions; Mental confusion and obtundation; Laboratory findings: Plasma pH ↑7.45; Urine pH ↑7.0; Plasma HCO_3^- ↑25 mEq/L in adults and ↑20 mEq/L in children; Plasma K ↓4 mEq/L	Gain of HCO_3^- from extracellular fluid; Gain of exogenous base; Oxidation of salts of organic acids; Loss of acid from the extracellular fluid; Gastrointestinal loss; Renal loss; Potassium depletion (may be renal or extrarenal); Chloride depletion	Respiratory: lungs hold back CO_2 to build up H_2CO_3 side; breathing may be shallow and irregular; ↑P_{CO_2} of blood stimulates respiratory center. Renal: kidneys excrete HCO_3^- ions and retain H^+ ions and nonbicarbonate anions to aid in restoring ratio and pH to normal range→alkaline urine (exception: Cl^- depletion; see text)

*Respiratory center directly affected.

Continued.

TABLE 18-17. Primary acid-base disorders—cont'd

Condition	Other names	Signs and symptoms	Etiologic factors	Compensatory mechanisms
Respiratory				
Carbonic acid deficit of extracellular fluid CO_2 expelled due to hyperactive breathing; ratio of 1 part H_2CO_3 to 20 parts HCO_3^- decreased on H_2CO_3 side	Respiratory alkalosis Hyperventilation Primary carbonic acid deficit Uncompensated carbonic acid deficit Hypocapnia Nonmetabolic alkalosis	Vertigo/syncope Convulsions Paresthesias Tetany Unconsciousness Laboratory findings pH of plasma ↑ 7.45 pH or urine ↑ 7.0 Plasma HCO_3^- ↓ 25 mEq/L in adults and ↓ 20 mEq/L in children Plasma P_{CO_2} ↓	Anxiety, extreme emotion, hysteria, pain Intentional overbreathing Rapid breathing (hyperpnea) Mechanical overventilation CNS trauma/disease Thiamine deficiency Oxygen lack/deprivation High fever and other hypermetabolic states Encephalitis* Salicylate poisoning*	Renal: kidneys excrete HCO_3^- ions and retain H^+ ions and nonbicarbonate anions; by dropping bicarbonate level proper ratio is nearly restored→alkaline urine.
Carbonic acid excess of extracellular fluid Retention of CO_2 by the lungs causes an excess of carbonic acid; ratio of 1 part H_2CO_3 to 20 parts HCO_3^- increased on H_2CO_3 side	Respiratory acidosis Primary CO_2 excess Uncompensated CO_2 excess Nonmetabolic acidosis Hypoventilation Hypercapnia	Respiratory embarrassment/distress Weakness Restlessness Lethargy/somnolence Disorientation Coma Laboratory findings Plasma pH ↓ 7.35 Urine pH ↓ 6.0 Plasma HCO_3^- ↑ 29 mEq/L in adults and ↑ 25 mEq/L in children Plasma P_{CO_2} ↑	Any condition that causes hypoventilation and retention of carbon dioxide; Chronic pulmonary disease Neuromuscular disease CNS depression with respiratory center involvement Acute respiratory disease or failure Acute airway obstruction Obesity hypoventilation syndrome Pulmonary edema (cardiogenic and noncardiogenic) Trauma	Renal: kidneys conserve base bicarbonate while excreting hydrogen ions and nonbicarbonate anions→acid urine

be used to promote renal bicarbonate excretion. When metabolic alkalosis is severe, administration of an acid such as dilute HCl or ammonium chloride may be indicated. This latter compound is toxic to the central nervous system, however, and can be used only in limited amounts. Oral calcium chloride ($CaCl_2$) can be used as an acidifying agent when hyperammonemia is contraindicated, such as in the patient with hepatic disease (Maxwell et al., 1987). Use of acidifying agents can cause metabolic acidosis and should be used cautiously. When excessive base intake has been a cause, the patient should be taught about the dangers of overuse of antacids. Milk alkali syndrome is no longer a common cause of metabolic alkalosis, however, because use of relatively nonabsorbable antacids has generally replaced the use of more absorbable agents (Puschett, 1985).

The etiologic factors, clinical manifestations, and compensatory mechanisms of the primary acid-base disorders are summarized in Table 18-17. Presented in Fig. 18-26 is the Davenport diagram from which acid-base disorders can be identified. From this diagram it can be seen that respiratory acid-base disorders (points II and III) cause shifts in pH that follow the buffer line while metabolic acid-base disorders (points I and IV) cause shifts in pH that follow the P_{CO_2} isobar. Similarly, compensation involving respiratory mechanisms follows parallel buffer lines while renal mechanisms follow the P_{CO_2} isobars.

Mixed acid-base alterations. Mixed acid-base alterations are characterized by the concurrent existence of two or more of the primary acid-base disorders. The range of mixed disorders includes mixed metabolic and respiratory disorders, mixed metabolic disorders, and triple disorders as

---

I. Mixed metabolic and respiratory disorders
Metabolic acidosis and respiratory acidosis
Metabolic acidosis and respiratory alkalosis
Metabolic alkalosis and respiratory acidosis
Metabolic alkalosis and respiratory alkalosis

II. Mixed metabolic disorders
Metabolic acidosis and metabolic alkalosis

III. Triple disorders
Mixed metabolic and respiratory acidosis
Mixed metabolic and respiratory alkalosis

---

presented in the box above. In the first category, the combination of two similar states (metabolic acidosis and respiratory acidosis or metabolic alkalosis and respiratory alkalosis) represents failure of compensation, whereas the combination of opposite states (metabolic acidosis and respiratory alkalosis or metabolic alkalosis and respiratory acidosis) represents excessive compensation (Schrier, 1986).

A mixed acid-base disorder should be suspected if the pH is opposite that expected or there appears to be a lack of the anticipated response (Table 18-18). Diagnosis depends on a complete history and accurate laboratory data.

Treatment of one acid-base alteration in isolation has the potential for exacerbating the coexisting disorder in some instances. These combined acid-base alterations most often occur in critically ill patients, making diagnosis and restoration of normal acid-base balance extremely difficult. In this population, these acid-base alterations will probably be accompanied by some of the alterations in fluid volume, composition, and distribution that were discussed in preceding sections of this

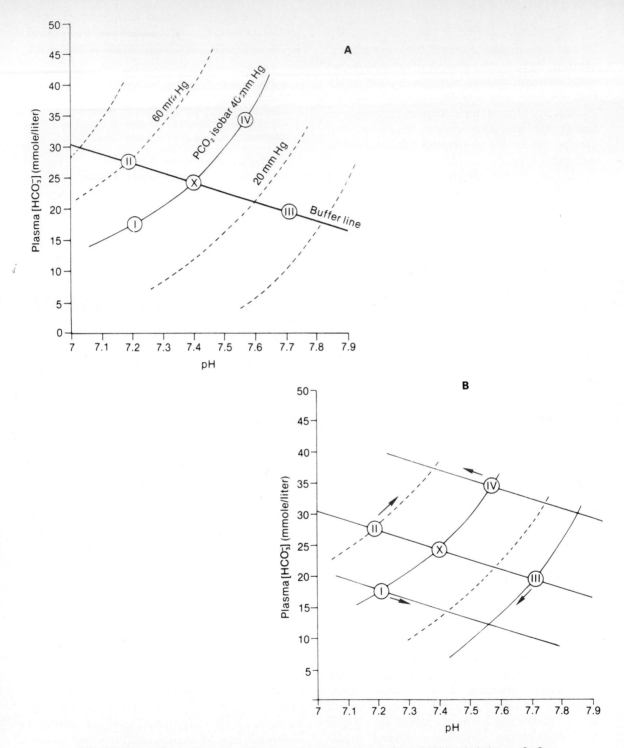

Fig. 18-26. Davenport diagram: classic working diagram for studying acid-base imbalance. **A,** Specific primary acid-base disorders are numbered as follows: I, metabolic acidosis; II, respiratory acidosis; III, respiratory alkalosis; IV, metabolic alkalosis. X refers to normal state. Arrows in **B** indicate compensation for acidosis and alkalosis. Note that arrows point in direction of normal pH.

(From Groer M: Physiology and pathophysiology of the body fluids, St Louis, 1981, The CV Mosby Co.)

TABLE 18-18. Mixed acid-base disorders

Disorder	Compensation	pH
Type 1: Failure of compensation		
Metabolic acidosis and respiratory acidosis	Pa_{CO_2} too high and $[HCO_3^-]$ too low for simple disorders	↓ ↓
Metabolic alkalosis and respiratory alkalosis	Pa_{CO_2} too low and $[HCO_3^-]$ too high for simple disorders	↑ ↑
Type 2: Excessive compensation		
Metabolic acidosis and respiratory alkalosis	Pa_{CO_2} too low and $[HCO_3^-]$ too low for simple disorders	Normal or slightly ↓ or ↑
Metabolic alkalosis and respiratory acidosis	Pa_{CO_2} too high and $[HCO_3^-]$ too high for simple disorders	Normal or slightly ↑ or ↓
Type 3: Triple disorders		
Metabolic alkalosis, respiratory acidosis or alkalosis, and metabolic acidosis	Pa_{CO_2} and $[HCO_3^-]$ not appropriate for simple disorders and anion gap >20 mEq/L	Variable

From Schrier R, editor: Renal and electrolyte disorders, Boston, 1986, Little, Brown & Co.

TABLE 18-19. Clinical situations in which mixed alterations in acid-base balance are likely to occur

Clinical situation	Acid-base disturbance
Sepsis	Acute respiratory alkalosis
	Lactic acidosis
Salicylate overdose	Acute respiratory alkalosis
	Anion gap metabolic acidosis
Renal tubular acidosis or diarrhea with severe hypokalemia	Hyperchloremic metabolic acidosis
	Respiratory acidosis
Drug overdose (carbon monoxide, cyanide, ethylene glycol, methanol)	Metabolic acidosis
	Respiratory acidosis
Cardiopulmonary arrest/cardiogenic shock	Lactic acidosis
	Respiratory acidosis
Liver or cardiac failure plus diuretic therapy	Respiratory alkalosis
	Metabolic alkalosis
Mechanical overventilation plus nasogastric suction	Metabolic alkalosis
	Respiratory alkalosis
Chronic pulmonary disease plus diuretic therapy	Respiratory acidosis or alkalosis
	Metabolic alkalosis
Chronic renal failure plus vomiting	Metabolic acidosis
	Metabolic alkalosis
Surgical or ICU patients	Respiratory alkalosis or acidosis
	Metabolic alkalosis
	Metabolic acidosis

Adapted from Puschett, J: Disorders of fluid and electrolyte balance. Diagnosis and management, New York, 1985, Churchill Livingstone.

chapter. A representative sample of clinical situations in which a mixed alteration in acid-base balance can occur is presented in Table 18-19.

DISEASE MODELS

Many pathologic conditions are characterized by a severe disruption of chemical equilibrium. Examples of such conditions include congestive heart failure, renal failure, diabetic ketoacidosis, and Cushing's syndrome. These disorders are discussed in detail in other chapters. Alterations in fluid volume, composition, distribution, and acid-base balance frequently coexist in the clinical setting. The effects of surgical stress and thermal injury on body fluid homeostasis can be quite profound, and these conditions are presented as examples of clinical conditions in which alterations in fluid volume, composition, distribution, and acid-base balance coexist.

Effect of surgical stress on chemical equilibrium

Maintenance of the steady state is precarious in the surgical patient. Potential departures from the normal chemical equilibrium in the surgical patient can occur anywhere on the spectrum between overhydration and dehydration accompanied by a variety of electrolyte and acid-base disorders. Prior to surgery the patient is allowed nothing by mouth, and if the patient has also been acutely ill during that time it is highly probable that some disruption of chemical equilibrium has already occurred from vomiting, diarrhea, or other causes. Fluid loss during surgery can be quite high because of bleeding and evaporation of fluid from the organs while they are exposed to the environment. On the other hand, overhydration can occur as a result of rapid infusion of IV fluid or infusion of excessive amounts caused by inaccurate estimation of the fluid loss. Basic to the maintenance of chemical equilibrium in the surgical patient, however, is the metabolic response that surgical stress evokes.

First, there is tissue damage, which in extensive surgical procedures may be quite severe. In response to this, metabolic processes accelerate to facilitate repair of the tissue. This causes an increase in the utilization of energy, which must be endogenously supplied because the surgical patient is usually fasting. Fluid not only may be lost from the injured area but also may be sequestered around the damaged tissue, creating a third space, which further contributes to extracellular fluid volume depletion. Additional fluid may be lost via the skin and lungs in response to the rise in body temperature that usually occurs 24 to 48 hours postoperatively as part of the inflammatory response to tissue trauma and the accelerated metabolic processes.

The hormonal and sympathetic responses to surgical trauma (Fig. 18-27) represent protective and restorative mechanisms that allow the body to adapt to the altered physiology and to eventually regain wellness. While these particular responses following surgery do not directly affect acid-base balance, the changes in water and electrolyte balance as well as many of the conditions accompanying surgery (gastric suction, shallow breathing, oxygen therapy, etc.) and primary disease condition may have an effect. For example, respiratory acidosis often occurs as a result of the pattern of shallow breathing seen following surgery. The cause of this hypoventilation is multifactorial: a combination of the effects of pain, drugs, anesthetic agents, positioning, and bandages to name a few. The reduc-

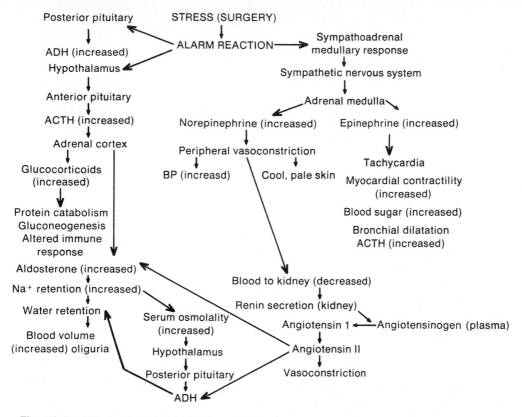

Fig. 18-27. Effects of stress reaction in surgical patient.
(Copyright Nov. 1977, the American Journal of Nursing Co. Reproduced with permission from the American Journal of Nursing, vol. 77, no. 11, Nov. 1977.)

tion in ventilatory capacity is most severe following thoracic and upper abdominal surgery, making these patients more prone to develop respiratory acidosis. Prolonged gastric suction after surgery without adequate fluid and electrolyte replacement may lead to metabolic alkalosis accompanied by severe hypokalemia. Respiratory alkalosis after surgery may be the result of overbreathing because of anxiety or excessive mechanical ventilation either during or after surgery if the patient is placed on a ventilator.

Retention of water, which can be attributed to several factors, is most marked following stimulation of the posterior pi-tuitary, which is responsible for secretion of ADH. The usual regulation of ADH secretion through osmoreceptor control is overridden by the effect of stress, and dilution resulting from water retention may cause hyponatremia, decreased serum osmolality, and signs of water excess or intoxication. Elevated levels of ADH may persist for 2 to 4 days after uncomplicated surgery. Endogenously formed water that is sodium free also figures in postsurgical water retention. Approximately 1 ml of water is formed with each gram of fat or lean tissue oxidized. Tissue catabolism increases after surgery in order to meet the body's caloric requirements so that this water must be considered in calculating the total amount of water in the body.

Stimulation of the sympathetic nervous system and the adrenal medulla causes increased amounts of epinephrine and norepinephrine to be released. This in turn causes vasoconstriction and decreased blood flow to the kidneys where the juxtaglomerular cells are stimulated to release renin, which activates the renin-angiotensin system to cause aldosterone secretion by the adrenal cortex. Aldosterone causes retention of Na^+ and the subsequent retention of water. Aldosterone secretion is further augmented by any reductions in intravascular volume and to a lesser degree by ACTH secretion.

Adrenocorticotropic hormone (ACTH) is secreted by the anterior pituitary gland in response to the hypothalamic hormone, corticotropin-releasing factor (CRF). Stimulation of ACTH secretion consistently occurs as a response to trauma and stress. ACTH stimulates the adrenal cortex to secrete the glucocorticoids and mineralocorticoids, chiefly aldosterone. Increased blood glucose levels and even glycosuria may result from the glycogenolysis and gluconeogenesis that occur in response to the adrenal hormones. The glucocorticoids also cause increased protein catabolism, which leads to a loss of nitrogen and muscle potassium. Serum K^+ levels will increase initially as the K^+ released from the catabolized cells enters the ECF. Eventually negative potassium and nitrogen balances develop, however. The negative nitrogen balance results from a combination of factors: direct tissue damage, protein catabolism, and the effects of starvation (the postoperative patient is usually fasting). Serum K^+ levels will eventually fall after the initial slight increase caused by K^+ mobilized from damaged and catabolized cells. Urinary excretion of K^+ in-

creases in the presence of aldosterone as resorption of Na^+ by the distal tubule is accomplished in exchange for K^+. If excessive losses of K^+ caused by vomiting, diarrhea, or draining fistulas occurred before or after surgery without adequate replacement therapy, the hypokalemia may become quite severe.

Diuresis usually occurs 3 to 4 days postoperatively, and as Na^+ retention continues, serum osmolality tends to increase. At this time the posterior pituitary responds to the increased osmolality and secretes ADH to cause water retention and to restore normal serum osmolality.

The duration of the metabolic response to surgery depends on the extent of the injury and the presence of complications. The development of shock, sepsis, or renal failure will further complicate the return to wellness and the fluid and electrolyte therapy necessary in the interim.

Effect of burns on chemical equilibrium

Thermal trauma, or burns, represents a massive insult to the normal physiologic functioning of the body and especially to body fluid balance. Burns cause a substantial loss of fluid from the effective ECF volume and elicit a maximal systemic response to the decreased circulating volume, tissue destruction, anemia, and electrolyte and acid-base imbalances that occur.

The most significant pathophysiologic event that occurs in the immediate postburn period is a fluid shift from the intravascular compartment into a third space around the burn wound. This burn edema, as it is sometimes called, is a characteristic feature of a thermal injury and is caused by dilation and grossly increased capillary permeability. Formation of the burn edema occurs most rapidly during the first 6 to 8 hours and continues for up to 48 hours after the burn. This 48-hour period is referred to as the stage of *sodium loss and shock.*

The electrolyte composition of this trapped fluid is similar to that of plasma. The plasma protein content of the burn edema is slightly less than that of plasma, but research has documented that the plasma proteins present in the burn edema initially come from the plasma. In severe burns the loss of intravascular oncotic pressure caused by the loss of proteins from the plasma results in fluid leaks into the interstitial spaces at sites remote from the burn injury. The formation of burn edema is augmented by the release of bradykinin produced by tissue proteases.

Fluid loss in burns results not only from the formation and trapping of edema fluid in the third space but may also occur from loss of fluid as exudate (especially in second degree burns) and through vaporization of water from the burn surface. The loss of fluid through vaporization can be very high and is associated with an increased energy expenditure since heat must be generated endogenously to make up for the heat lost from the body surface in order to maintain a normal body temperature. The loss of fluid by vaporization peaks between the fifth and tenth day after a burn.

During the first 48 hours after a burn hypovolemic shock may occur and is thought to be related to the Na^+ deficit rather than to the loss of fluid per se. Na^+ is lost from the ECF into the burn edema and moves into the cells to replace K^+. Hyperkalemia is the result of large amounts of K^+ being released into the ECF from damaged cells. The abnormal movement of Na^+ and K^+ may be caused by injury-related changes in the function and efficiency of the sodium pump. Hemoconcentration occurs because of the loss of fluid in amounts relatively greater than the solid constituents of the blood. This hemoconcentration is re-

flected by an increased hematocrit. Urinary output is reduced because of decreased renal blood flow, increased secretion of ADH and Na^+, and water retention in response to the increased sympathetic, pituitary, and adrenocortical activity caused by stress.

Metabolic acidosis is the result of poor tissue perfusion and release of acidic products of tissue destruction. Blood viscosity is increased as a result of the hemoconcentration, released tissue thromboplastin, and increased platelet adhesion. Widespread thrombosis occurs as a result of damaged vascular endothelium and aggregation of the erythrocytes. Microthrombi develop and block the microcirculation, causing hypoxia of those cells served by that portion of the circulation. Lactic acid will accumulate as a result of anaerobic metabolism. The combination of lactic acid plus the acidic anions released from traumatized tissue (e.g., PO_4^-) increases the H^+ concentration, and pH falls.

There is a fall in cardiac output after a burn that is related to several factors: decreased plasma volume and hypotension, decreased perfusion of the coronary arteries secondary to hypotension, hypothermia caused by evaporative water loss, and acidosis. Acidosis causes reduced cardiac output and increased total peripheral vascular resistance, which increases cardiac work load. The vicious cycle is established since cardiac function will be further impaired, and reduced tissue perfusion will further contribute to the state of acidosis that already exists. In addition, the release of a myocardial toxin by the burned tissue has been documented by research with extensively burned animals. The release of such a factor in humans has been proposed and may be significant in burns involving 80% of the body surface area. This toxin is thought to directly depress cardiac contractility through a negative inotropic effect. The relationship between increased capillary permeability, hemoconcentration, decreased cardiac output, and the edema seen in burns is diagrammed in Fig. 18-28.

Respiratory alkalosis can occur after a burn injury as a result of a rapid pattern of respiration elicited by pain and anxiety in the burn victim. Respiratory acidosis may be the result of hypoventilation caused by swelling or burn damage of the neck, face, or upper respiratory tract, which occludes the airway and prevents normal respiration.

The second stage occurs after the first 48 hours and is called the stage of *sodium and water reabsorption,* or *fluid remobilization.* As fluid returns to the intravascular compartment from the interstitial space, urinary output increases, and the hematocrit drops. Sodium will be lost with the water during the diuresis that occurs in this stage. As fluid reenters the intravascular compartment, the decrease in the number of red blood cells as a result of thermal destruction becomes apparent. The hemoglobinuria that results from the red blood cell destruction can adversely affect renal function and acute renal failure might occur (see Chapter 20). Hypokalemia occurs during this stage as K^+ begins to move back into the cells from the ECF.

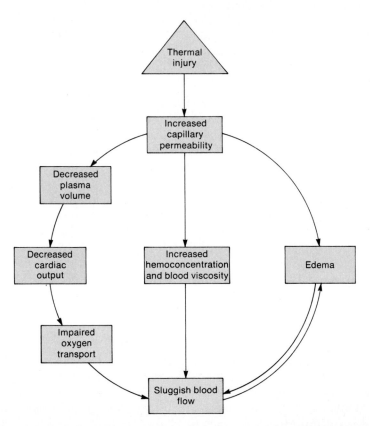

Fig. 18-28. In severe burns, capillary permeability is increased, allowing protein-rich plasma to leak from vascular to extravascular spaces, which causes edema, hemoconcentration, and decrease in cardiac output.

The third stage, *anemia and malnutrition,* or the *convalescent phase,* occurs from the fifth day on. During this stage, signs of calcium deficit may become apparent, although the causative mechanism is not understood. However, calcium is known to be mobilized to damaged tissue. The major concern during this stage is the negative nitrogen balance that has resulted from a combination of factors: protein destruction at the burn, protein losses in the exudate, inadequate protein intake, increased protein catabolism (caused by ACTH secretion), and immobilization. The Na^+ deficit may still be present during this stage also.

Typical changes in serum electrolyte concentrations, fluid intake, body weight, and urinary output that can be expected in a patient who has sustained a thermal injury are presented in Figs. 18-29 and 18-30. Fluid replacement to maintain volume and restore electrolyte levels to normal is critical in the management of the burn patient. Calculation of the amount of fluid lost is based on the surface area and depth of the burn, hence the critical importance of accurate initial assessment of a thermal injury (see also Chapter 5).

Effect of treatment modalities on chemical equilibrium

A variety of treatment measures that are frequently used in the clinical setting have the potential for profoundly disturbing chemical equilibrium. The administration of fluid intravenously is a good example. There are several potential problems that

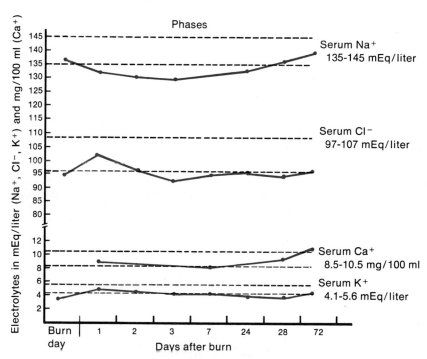

Fig. 18-29. Serum levels of potassium, calcium, chloride, and sodium for 72 days after burn in patient who had second degree (partial-thickness) and third degree (full-thickness) burns over 40% of his body.

(From Beland S and Passos J: Clinical nursing: pathophysiological and psychosocial approaches, ed 3, New York, 1975, Macmillan Publishing Co.)

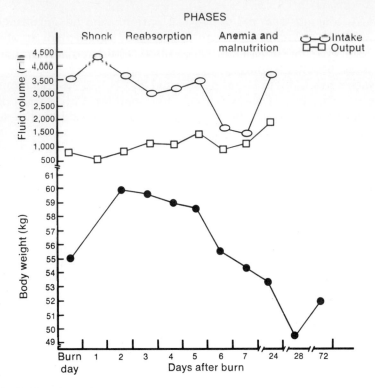

Fig. 18-30. Fluid intake, urinary output, and body weight recordings for 72 days after burn in patient who had second degree (partial-thickness) and third degree (full-thickness) burns over 40% of his body.

(From Beland S and Passos J: Clinical nursing: pathophysiological and psychosocial approaches, ed 3, New York, 1975, Macmillan Publishing Co.)

can arise with the use of parenteral therapy. Rapid administration of fluids can cause fluid overload; administration of too little fluid can cause a state of fluid deficit in the patient. Alterations in the electrolyte levels may also occur, and plasma levels of the electrolytes should be checked frequently when a patient is receiving intravenous fluid.

The parenteral administration of hypertonic dextrose solutions with amino acids and other supplements (electrolytes, vitamins) is called parenteral hyperalimentation, or total parenteral nutrition when used with lipids. The amino acids serve as the nitrogen source, and the dextrose serves as the carbohydrate source. The lipids provide essential fatty acids. This therapy is used to restore and maintain positive nitrogen balance in the patient for whom oral intake is impossible or contraindicated. Fluid volume and electrolyte disturbances may occur in this form of parenteral therapy just as they do in others. Alterations in the serum potassium, magnesium, and phosphorus levels are most likely to occur. Acidosis may develop in patients with an impaired ability to excrete an acid load. Hyperglycemia is common and may cause a hyperosmolar syndrome with dehydration, seizures, coma, and death. A variety of vitamin excess and

TABLE 18-20. Composition of various oral replacement fluids

Solution	Calories (Kcal/30 ml)	HCO_3^- (mEq/L)	Na^+ (mEq/L)	Ca^{++} (mEq/L)	K^+ (mEq/L)	Mg^{++} (mEq/L)	Cl^- (mEq/L)	Predominant carbohydrate
Water								
Pedialyte (oral electro-lyte solution)	6.0		30.0	4.0	20.0	4	30.0	Dextrose
Lytren (oral electro-lyte solution)	9.0 (isotonic)		30.0	4.0	25.0	4	25.0	Glucose
5% glucose in water	6.0							Glucose
10% glucose in water	12.0							Glucose
Pepsi-Cola	13.2	7.3	6.5		0.8			Sucrose
Coca-Cola	14.4	13.4	0.4		12.0			Sucrose
Ginger ale	10.0	3.6	3.5					Sucrose
Gatorade	5.5		23.0		3.0		17.0	Glucose
Lemon-lime soda	9.6		7.5	0.3	0.2			Sucrose
Broth, beef (canned)	6.0		55.0					
Tea, unsweetened	0.25					Trace		

From Groer, M: Physiology and pathophysiology of the body fluids, St. Louis, 1981, The CV Mosby Co

deficiency states may develop as well.

Oral replacement therapy must be appropriately matched to the alterations in fluid volume and composition that have occurred or need to be prevented. Included in Table 18-20 is the composition of various oral replacement fluids. It must be noted that tube feedings and infant formulas have the potential for causing osmotic shifts of fluid as will occur if highly concentrated liquid is absorbed into the circulation. The resulting clincial condition is known as the *dumping syndrome* and is associated with peripheral vasodilation, sweating, tachycardia, flushing, and increased pulse pressure (Goldberger, 1986).

Patients who are being vigorously treated for ulcer with antacids and frequent ingestion of milk products may develop what is referred to as the milk-alkali syndrome. This condition is characterized by hypercalcemia and metabolic alkalosis. Patients with impaired renal function are more prone to develop this syndrome and should be monitored.

The use of gastric or intestinal suction may also lead to fluid, electrolyte, and acid-base disturbances (Fig 18-25). Output via GI suction should be measured for vol-

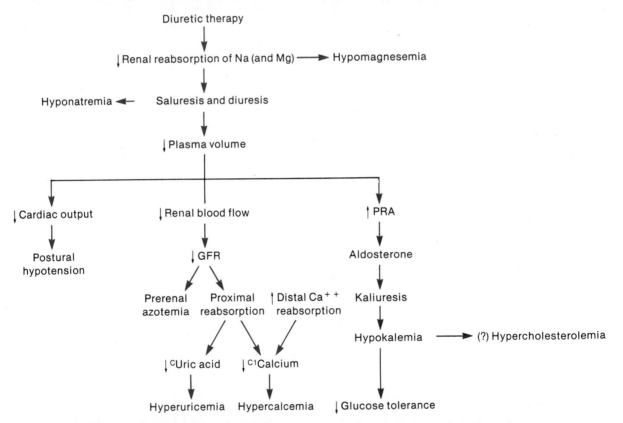

Fig. 18-31. The mechanisms by which chronic diuretic therapy may lead to various complications. The mechanism for hypercholesterolemia remains in question, although it is shown as arising via hypokalemia.

(From Kaplan, NM: Clinical Hypertension, 4th ed. Baltimore, © by Williams and Wilkins, 1986, p. 192.)

ume and described by color and consistency for identification of the type of secretion being lost. Replacement therapy is based on volume and on the electrolyte composition normally found in the type of body fluid being lost. Patients on GI suction are not allowed any oral intake. Any fluid, even small sips of water, will be immediately suctioned out of the stomach and any endogenous electrolytes may be washed out with it.

Medications can have side effects that disrupt normal fluid and electrolyte balance. Diuretic therapy probably presents the greatest potential hazard to the body's chemical equilibrium. Aside from the side effects of the drugs themselves, the diuresis they produce and the mechanisms by which they produce it can lead to severe electrolyte and acid-base disorders and severe volume depletion.

All diuretics act on the renal tubules to increase the urinary excretion of sodium and water. The mechanisms which allow these desired effects can also cause the urinary loss of other electrolytes including chloride and magnesium as well as that most commonly affected, potassium. The mechanisms by which diuretic agents cause alterations in fluid volume and composition are illustrated in Fig. 18-31. The following case study demonstrates some potential side effects of diuretic therapy (Valle and Lemberg, 1988).

CASE STUDY: DIURETIC INDUCED ELECTROLYTE IMBALANCE

History

GL is currently being treated for hypertension with a thiazide diuretic (Hydrochlorothiazide 50 mg) taken once each

---

Contributed by Maureen Shekleton.

day and an oral antihypertensive (Clonidine 0.3 mg) taken 3 times each day. GL gave up smoking 1 year ago when he began to experience angina. He uses a long acting nitrate patch daily and sublingual nitroglycerin as needed. He had smoked up to 1 pack of cigarettes a day for 30 years.

Present illness: GL is a 55-year-old male who was brought to the hospital by ambulance after losing consciousness at home. A Lidocaine infusion and oxygen were started in the field after an ECG showed frequent multifocal premature ventricular beats. He regained consciousness spontaneously.

Objective and Subjective Data

GL tells you that before fainting he felt a heavy sensation and a fluttery feeling in his chest. He denies that this has ever happened before.

General appearance: Alert, slightly obese white male

Vital signs

Blood pressure: 170/110

Pulse: 80 beats/minute, occasional irregularity

Respirations: 22-24 breaths/minute

Physical examination: Unremarkable; heart and lung sounds normal; peripheral pulses palpable and strong.

Arterial blood gases: Normal

Serum electrolytes: Sodium, chloride, and calcium values within low normal range. Potassium; 2.5 mEq/L.

Cardiac rhythm strip shows normal sinus rhythm with frequent multifocal premature ventricular contractions and an occasional couplet.

12 Lead ECG shows lengthened QT interval (0.53 sec.) with evidence of left ventricular hypertrophy.

Treatment

Replacement with oral and parenteral potassium chloride was begun. The ventricular ectopy persisted and blood for a stat determination of serum potassium and magnesium levels was drawn after 4 hours of replacement therapy.

Potassium   3.0 mEq/L
Magnesium   0.9 mEq/L (Normal – 1.4
– 2.2 mEq/L)

An infusion of magnesium sulfate was begun. Over the next several hours the aberrant rhythm gradually disappeared and the QT interval shortened to a normal 0.40 seconds. Repeat serum electrolyte levels the following day showed

Potassium   4.5 mEq/L
Magnesium   1.7 mEq/L

GL continued oral magnesium replacement therapy with magnesium containing antacids for the next 5 days.

Discussion

While the dysrhythmia experienced by GL was generally asymptomatic, it was very serious because of his underlying hypertensive heart disease and because it increased the possibility of a potentially lethal dysrhythmia developing. The occurrence of a cardiac dysrhythmia was related to electrolyte deficits which had developed in response to diuretic therapy in this patient. Hypokalemia may cause dysrhythmias due to enhanced normal automaticity, abnormal automaticity, or slowed conduction. Hypomagnesemia also affects automaticity especially in the presence of other electrolyte imbalances (Roden and Iansmith, 1987). Ventricular ectopy is associated with both hypokalemia and hypomagnesemia (Whang, 1987).

The electrolyte disorders experienced by this patient were the result of his use of a thiazide diuretic. Potassium depletion is the most common complication of therapy with loop or thiazide diuretics, however, these agents can cause significant magnesiuria as well.

It is now recognized that potassium and magnesium deficits often coexist; the reported range of such paired deficiencies is estimated between 38% to 42% (Valle and Lemberg, 1988). Such coexistence is probably due to the fact that there are similarities between potassium and magnesium homeostasis and biochemical interrelationships in their functions. The mechanisms which cause potassium loss are similar to those which cause magnesium loss. Magnesium functions as a cofactor in Na-K ATPase function and therefore helps to control the intracellular compartmentalization of potassium. Effects of hypomagnesemia on cell membrane potential and excitability are similar to those of hypokalemia because of the failure to maintain normal intracellular potassium concentration when magnesium is not available as a cofactor for the membrane pump. Because of these functional interrelationships, the homeostasis of these cations is coupled and a disturbance in one can affect the other. As was seen in this patient, magnesium depletion can cause refractory potassium repletion and must be corrected with magnesium replacement therapy (Whang, 1987).

Nursing Diagnoses

1. Altered fluid composition; hypokalemia and hypomagnesemia related to diuretic induced loss
2. Potential for decreased cardiac output related to ventricular dysrhythmia
3. Knowledge deficit related to maintenance of normal serum potassium and magnesium levels

Chemical disequilibrium may also have adverse effects on drug therapy. For example, in addition to directly causing cardiac dysrhythmias, hypokalemia and hypomagnesemia can interfere with the efficacy or potentiate the toxicity of cardiac drugs like digitalis and quinidine (Roden and Iansmith, 1987). Hypercalcemia, hyponatremia and acid base imbalance can increase individual sensitivity to digitalis and thus also increase the potential risk of digitalis toxicity. This is but one example as most medications require an appropriate chemical environment in order to exert a maximal therapeutic effect with minimal side effects.

SUMMARY

Presented in this chapter was an overview of the effects of alterations in the fluid volume, composition, distribution, and acid-base balance on the physiologic functioning of the body. Chemical processes are basic to this functioning, and disruption of the normal equilibrium of these processes can present a serious threat to life. Pathologic conditions that disrupt chemical equilibrium as a result of abnormal intake, absorption, elimination, or regulation are discussed in other chapters.

BIBLIOGRAPHY

Agusti A, Torres A, Estopa R, and Agusti-Vidal A: Hypophosphatemia as a cause of failed weaning: the importance of metabolic factors, Crit Care Med, 12(2): 142-143, 1984.

Andreoli K, Fowkes V, Zipes D, and Wallace A editors: Comprehensive Cardiac Care, St Louis, 1983, The CV Mosby Co.

Arieff A and DeFronzo R: Fluid, electrolyte and acid-base disorders, New York, 1985, Churchill Livingstone.

Aubier M, et al: Effect of hypophosphatemia on diaphragmatic contractility in patients with acute respiratory failure, New Engl J Med 313: 420–424, 1985.

Baltarowich L: Chloride, Emerg Med Clin North Am 4(1): 175-183, 1986.

Chenevey B: Overview of fluids and electrolytes, Nurs Clin North Am 22(4): 749-759, 1987.

Devlin TM: Textbook of biochemistry with clinical correlations, ed 2, New York, 1986, Wiley.

Dominguez JH, et al: Dietary phosphate deprivation in women and men: effects on mineral and acid balances, parathyroid hormone, and the metabolism of 25-OH-vitamin D, J Clin Endocrinol Metab 48: 1056, 1976.

Genest J and Cantin M: Atrial natriurectic factor, Circulation 75(suppl I):I118-I124, Jan, 1987.

Goldberger E: A primer of water, electrolyte, and acid-base syndromes, ed 7, Philadelphia, 1986, Lea and Febiger.

Groer M: Physiology and pathophysiology of the body fluids, St Louis, 1981, The CV Mosby Co.

Humes HD: Pathophysiology of electrolyte and renal disorders, New York, 1986, Churchill Livingstone.

Jacobson H and Seldin D: On the generation, maintenance, and correction of metabolic alkalosis, Am J Physiol 235(4): 425-432, 1983.

Kaehny W: Respiratory acid-base disorders, Med Clin North Am 67(4): 915-928, 1983.

Keyes J: Fluid, electrolyte, and acid-base regulation, Monterey, 1985, Wadsworth, Inc.

Kokko JP and Tannen RL editors: Fluids and electrolytes, Philadelphia, 1986, WB Saunders Co.

Laragh J: Atrial natriuretic hormone, the renin-aldosterone axis, and blood pressure-electrolyte homeostasis, New Engl J Med 313(21): 1330-1340, 1985.

Littrell K: Arterial blood gas analysis: the matching game, Focus Crit Care 10: 49-51, 1983.

Luke R and Galla J: Chloride-depletion alkalosis with a normal extracellular fluid volume, Am J Physiol 245(4): 419-424, 1983.

Marcinek M: Stress in the surgical patient, Am J Nurs 77(11): 1809-1811, 1977.

Maxwell M, Kleeman C, and Narins R: Clinical disorders of fluid and electrolyte metabolism, ed 4, New York, 1987, McGraw-Hill, Inc.

McFadden E, Zaloga G, and Chernow B: Hypocalcemia: a medical emergency, Am J Nurs 83: 227-230, 1983.

Metheny N and Snively W: Nurse's handbook of fluid balance, Philadelphia, 1983, JB Lippincott Co.

Newman JH, Neff TA, and Siporin P: Acute respiratory failure associated with hypophosphatemia, New Engl J Med 296:1101, 1977.

Nielsen O and Engell H: The importance of plasma colloid osmotic pressure for interstitial fluid volume and fluid balance after elective abdominal vascular surgery, Ann Surg 203(1): 25-29, 1986.

Planas RF, et al: Effects of hypophosphatemia on pulmonary muscle performance. In Massry, SG, et al, editors: Advances in experimental biology and medicine, New York, 1981, Plenum Press.

Puschett J and Greenberg A: Disorders of fluid and electrolyte balance: diagnosis and management, New York, 1985, Churchill Livingstone

Reid I: The renin-angiotensin system and body function, Arch Inter Med 145(8): 1475-1479, 1985.

Roden DM and Iansmith DH: Effects of low potassium or magnesium on isolated cardiac tissue, Am J Med 82(3A): 18-23, March 1987.

Rognes P and Maylan JM: Restoring fluid balance in the patient with severe burns, Am J Nurs 76(12): 1953-1957, 1976.

Rose BD: Clinical physiology of acid-base and electrolyte disorders, ed 2, New York, 1984, McGraw-Hill, Inc.

Schrier R, editor: Renal and electrolyte disorders, ed 3, Boston, 1986, Little, Brown & Co, Inc.

Severinghaus J and Astrup P: History of blood gas analysis, J Clin Monit 1(4): 259-277, 1985.

Shapiro B, Harrison R, and Walton J: Clinical application of blood gases, Chicago, 1982, Year Book Medical Publishers, Inc.

Skov P and Muwaswes M: Edema. In Carrieri V,

Lindsey A and West C, editors: Pathophysiological phenomena in nursing: human responses to illness, Philadelphia PA, 1986, WB Saunders Co.

Valle GA and Lemberg L: Electrolyte imbalances in cardiovascular disease: the forgotten factor, Heart and Lung 17(3):324-329.

Vanatta J and Fogelman M: Moyer's fluid balance: a clinical manual, Chicago, Year Book Medical Publishers Inc, 1982.

Ventrigeia W: Arterial blood gases, Emerg Med Clin North Am 4(2): 235-251, 1986.

Whang R: Magnesium deficiency: pathogenesis, prevalence, and clinical implications, Am J Med 82(3A):24-29, March 1987.

York K: The lung and fluid-electrolyte and acid-base imbalances, Nurs Clin North Am 22(4): 805-814, 1987.

19

Mechanisms of nutritional disequilibrium

This chapter will focus on pathophysiologic disturbances of nutritional integrity. Nutritional integrity implies that normal intake, digestion, absorption, metabolism, and elimination of food proceed without interruption or abnormality. Many systems of the body must be functioning normally for this to occur. The integrity of the brain and nervous system is required for regulation of food intake in proper amounts when the organism requires caloric energy. Patency and normal physiology of the gastrointestinal (GI) tract are required for food to be digested and absorbed. The circulatory system, as the main transport system in movement of nutrients from the GI tract to the liver, adipose tissue, and cells and tissues throughout the body, also plays a critical role in nutritional integrity. The liver and adipose tissue are the major metabolic organs regulating body nutrition and storage of excess calories, and they provide for equilibrium in the open system of food intake, metabolism, and waste disposal. At the cellular level the genetic enzyme complement and the endocrine system appear to predominate in the control of food metabolism. Thus the maintenance of nutrition is a function of all the systems and involves complex mechanisms resulting from

the interaction of a great variety of influences.

This chapter will cover various pathophysiologic mechanisms by which nutritional status can be disturbed. These include disorders of food intake and metabolism; some disease models of various nutritional disorders will also be discussed. Specific diseases of the GI tract will be covered in Chapter 21.

METABOLISM

The total processes by which ingested food molecules are used either for work by the organism or in the synthesis of new organic compounds is summarized by the term *metabolism*. Human beings interact extensively with the environment and in fact depend on the external environment for energy in the form of food calories. Energy in the molecular bonds of food molecules is converted to work energy, or it may be stored in glycogen, lipid, and protein. Ultimately, all energy that is taken in is returned to the environment, so that the second law of thermodynamics is not violated by living organisms. Energy must be supplied by the ingestion, digestion, absorption, and metabolism of food molecules for any physiologic function to proceed. The ultimate source of this energy is, of course, derived from the photons of sunlight, which are converted into food molecules by photosynthesis in green plants. Therefore it is the task of metabolism to release in a usable form the energy contained in the carbon-hydrogen bonds of food molecules. The way that the released energy is coupled to function in the cell is determined by the genetic and environmental factors of the particular cell, tissue, or organ. These factors are usually dynamic in nature, since the constantly changing expression of DNA in all cells in response to the external influences will determine the ultimate metabolism of food molecules and the way they are used for energy.

Catabolism and anabolism are the metabolic processes. *Catabolism* is the release of energy in carbon-hydrogen bonds, with some energy being given off as heat and some being coupled to work by the cell. Most functions that require energy for work in the cell such as movement, cell division, ion transport, and growth, are driven by catabolic reactions. *Anabolic* (synthetic) reactions require energy as well, which is provided by the catabolism of other molecules. Thus both anabolism and catabolism are inevitably linked, and both require the breakdown of carbon-hydrogen bonds in food molecules.

For the energy from food molecules to be used by the cell for work, coupling of this extracted energy to the specific function must take place. The ATP (adenosine triphosphate) molecule is the form in which energy from metabolism is used by the cell. ATP contains high-energy bonds, which, when hydrolyzed, yield large amounts of free energy. Through oxidative phosphorylation energy originally present in the food molecule is transformed into ATP energy. This is accomplished by oxidation of glucose to CO_2 and water through the series of metabolic reactions that comprise the Embden-Meyerhof pathway, the Krebs cycle, and the electron transport chain. The latter two reaction sequences take place in the cytoplasmic mitochondria, organelles whose characteristics were described in Chapter 16.

The actual coupling of the ATP molecule to cellular work involves intermediate molecules, which are phosphorylated by ATP. The mechanics of such coupling and the identification of intermediate molecules have not been clarified.

The food that is ingested by humans normally consists of 40% fats, 45% to 50% carbohydrates, and 12% to 24% proteins. Other molecules that are part of the normal diet (e.g., vitamins, minerals, and nucleotides) are also necessary for metabolism to proceed but are not directly hydrolyzed or oxidized by body tissue for extraction of chemical bond energy. The bonds between carbon and hydrogen determine the structure and the energy content of the food molecule; the mechanism by which this energy is extracted is through the biochemical pathways of the cells, which are mediated by enzymes and regulated by the energy needs of the body.

The food molecules contain a standard amount of extractable energy, which is measured in *kilocalories*. A kilocalorie is a measure of heat energy. It is the amount of heat needed to raise the temperature of 1 kg of water 1° C.

The oxidation of 1 g of fat releases 9.3 kcal, 1 g of carbohydrate, 4.1 kcal, and 1 g of protein, 4.4 kcal. Determination of the caloric value of different foodstuffs is made by burning appropriate amounts of food and measuring the heat produced in a device known as a *bomb calorimeter*. Another method is determination of oxygen by the oxidation of the food. Animals can be placed in bomb calorimeters to determine the amount of heat liberated by their bodies in the oxidation of their food, or the indirect method may be used, in which case the oxygen and the carbon dioxide release are measured. From these values the *respiratory quotient* can be calculated:

$$RQ = \frac{\text{Volume of } CO_2 \text{ released}}{\text{Volume of } O_2 \text{ consumed}} \Big/ \text{Unit time}$$

Different food molecules will be metabolized in a living organism with different respiratory quotients. The RQ is in a sense the measure of efficiency of metabolism of the different food molecules. Since the metabolism of glucose requires 6 mol of O_2 and produces 6 mol of CO_2 and 6 moles of water, the ratio in the equation is 1. Fat oxidation and protein breakdown are less "efficient" in that the RQ for fats is 0.703 and that for proteins is 0.802. RQ is useful, but it should not lead the reader to think that the body oxidizes one compound at a time, even if this compound is presented to the body through ingestion of a meal to the exclusion of other food molecules. The RQ measured in humans is the sum of all the metabolism occurring in a unit of time. There is a metabolic pool of usable interconvertible food molecules in the body, and the liver plays the major role in maintaining the metabolic pool. The RQ does change with disease states, indicating the effect of disease on metabolism. For example, RQ is increased in hyperventilation and alkalosis and decreased in hypoventilation and acidosis. In hyperventilation large amounts of CO_2 are released, thus increasing the numerator of the RQ equation.

Basal metabolic rate (BMR)

When environmental variables such as temperature, nutrition, muscular movement, emotions, and disease states are excluded from the testing conditions, it is possible to measure the basal metabolism of a human being, a value that indicates the minimal energy state of that person in the waking state. It is reported as kilocalories per square meter of body surface per hour. Generally the value for males is higher than that for females; the approximate value for a 20-year-old man is 41.4 and for a 20-year-old woman, 36.2. The BMR increases when food is ingested, in fever, during muscular exercise, with sympathetic stimulation, and with hyperactivity of the thyroid gland. It is decreased with sleep, prolonged malnutrition, age, and underactivity of the thyroid gland. In hyperthyroidism the BMR may be increased by 40% to 80% of normal, and with hypothyroidism it may be decreased from 25% to 40% of normal. The metabolism of food molecules in the body constantly supplies heat, which is, of course, required for thermoregulation, and the excess is given off to the environment. (A human can increase the BMR to produce heat [thermogenesis] in a cold environment by shivering but is not able to effectively lower the BMR in a hot environment.) Seventy percent of the energy in food becomes heat energy in the formation and coupling of ATP, and even more is lost when ATP hydrolysis and cellular work occur. Thus large amounts of the energy in food molecules are returned directly to the environment as heat, emphasizing the open system nature of metabolism.

The metabolism of food molecules is regulated by many control systems in different cells and tissues. The central roles of the liver, the adipose tissue, and the hormones have been known for many years. However, many new and exciting discoveries are being made on the biochemical mechanisms by which carbohydrate, lipid, and protein metabolism proceeds. The rates of the separate reaction sequences are regulated by many finely tuned hormonal, enzymatic, and negative-feedback controls. The effects of hormones on metabolism are summarized in the box on p. 839.

The central role of the Krebs cycle in intermediary metabolism can be seen in Fig. 19-1, which shows the catabolic functions of this mitochondrial reaction series, leading ultimately to the production of high-

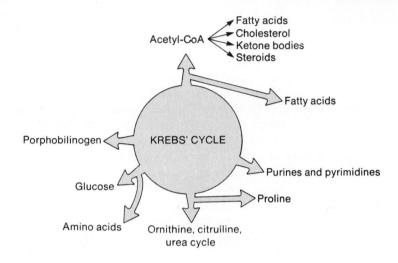

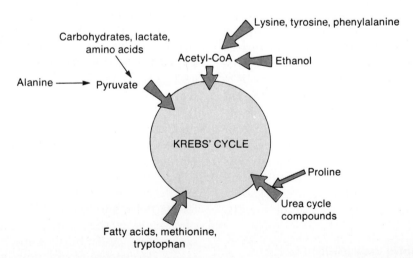

Fig. 19-1. Krebs cycle plays central role in intermediary metabolism either in **A,** anabolic synthesis of fatty acids, ketone bodies, cholesterol, steroids, glucose, purines, and pyrimidines or in **B,** catabolic breakdown of molecules such as glucose, lactate, ethanol, and amino acids for energy. Reactions that are favored are determined by body needs, which in turn influences cellular environment through hormonal and other actions.

EFFECTS OF HORMONES ON METABOLISM

Insulin: Synergistic with growth hormone on protein anabolism
Increases transmembrane transfer of glucose
Stimulates hexokinase reaction
Increases glycolysis and hexose monophosphate shunt
Stimulates fat storage

Growth hormone: Fat catabolism stimulated
Diabetogenic (opposes insulin's action on hexokinase)
Stimulates protein anabolism (in presence of insulin)

Cortisol: Diabetogenic (opposes insulin action on hexokinase)
Increases gluconeogenesis and glycogenolysis; increases blood glucose
Stimulates protein catabolism

Estrogen: Antiinsulinic

Thyroid hormone: Increases carbohydrate absorption from the gut; increases glucose utilization

Somatostatin: Inhibits both insulin and glucagon

Glucagon: Stimulates glycogenolysis

---

energy molecules of ATP and formation of water. Glucose metabolism is primarily responsible for ATP production, but both proteins and fatty acids can be used in intermediary metabolism for energy through conversion into compounds that can enter the Krebs cycle. The Krebs cycle can also be used by the cell for anabolic pathways such as lipogenesis, cholesterol production, porphyrin synthesis, and purine and pyrimidine synthesis. In these situations the substrates of the Krebs cycle are used in early steps of the various biochemical, anabolic pathways.

Source of glucose

Before metabolism of glucose can proceed, this monosaccharide must enter the cell through the cell membrane from the bloodstream. Glucose does not appear to enter cells by simple diffusion but must be facilitated by a carrier-mediated process, which delivers the glucose to the interior cytoplasm of the cell. It has been known for years that insulin is required in certain tissues (especially muscle and adipose tissue) for this carrier-mediated diffusion to occur. Recent identification of both insulin and glucagon receptor molecules on many different types of cell membranes is providing a molecular basis for understanding the actions of these hormones. The central role of glucagon in blood sugar regulation is an area of great scientific debate and inquiry, but evidence is accumulating to indicate that it may be as important as insulin. This evidence and its implications will be elaborated on in the section on diabetes in Chapter 19.

The glucose that enters the cytoplasm is first metabolized by a series of anaerobic reactions that comprise the Embden-Meyerhof pathway, or anaerobic glycolysis. This pathway converts glucose into pyruvate; depending on the oxygenation requirements of the cells and tissues, pyruvate will either form lactate, which accumulates, or *acetyl CoA*, which enters the mitochondrial Krebs cycle. The cell must, of course, be endowed with the appropriate enzymes that catalyze the various steps of these metabolic pathways. The enzyme kind and amount are determined by the genetic constitution of the individual cell, and a great variety of genetic enzymatic deficiency diseases has been described. Normal fat and protein metabolism also require enzymatic degradation before these molecules can be used in energy production. Again, the enzymes required may be deficient, resulting in a variety of diseases.

Regulation of food intake

The intake of food molecules of most animals is regulated so that the energy needs are met. The purpose of the GI tract is basically to provide a mechanism by which the organism can take in, process, and ab-

sorb food molecules, often in excess of what it needs. Cells take up what they need, with the excess then being stored in the body in the form of fat. The regulation of food supply then is mainly at the level of *food intake*, with the hypothalamus playing an important part in the regulation of feeding and satiety. Certain nuclei in the hypothalamus have been identified as centers of mediation for food intake (Fig. 19-2). The *ventromedial nucleus* has been identified as the *satiety center*, and stimulation of this area results in cessation of appetite; the *ventrolateral area* appears to initiate feeding behavior and has been termed the *feeder center*. The two centers inhibit each other reciprocally, so that when one is stimulated, the other becomes inhibited. Destruction of the ventromedial area of the hypothalamus leads to excessive hyperphagia and obesity in experimental animals, whereas destruction of the ventrolateral area leads to aphagia and wasting. These areas of the hypothalamus are nerve centers, and many nerve

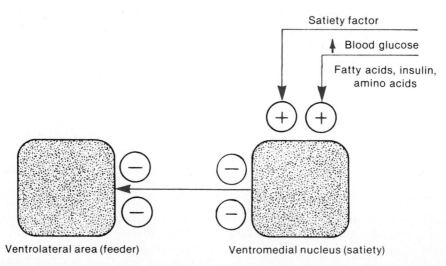

Fig. 19-2. Hypothalamic feeding and satiety center. When the ventromedial nucleus is stimulated, it inhibits ventrolateral feeding center. While satiety center is active, organism does not experience hunger or drive to find and consume food.

pathways pass through the hypothalamus. Thus it seems probable that many other centers in the brain are responsible for input into the hypothalamic appestat; for example, direct autonomic connections have been demonstrated, implicating a role particularly for catecholamines in feeding and satiety. The actual sensing of the state of nutrition, the gastrointestinal tract status, and the amount of food molecules present and available in the body somehow exert regulatory effects on the two centers, but the mechanism is poorly understood. *Blood glucose concentration* is thought to be a major regulator of activities of the centers, but fatty acids, amino acids, and insulin have also been implicated. Perhaps some factor is present in the nourished and alimented animal that acts on the satiety center, activating it and thus in turn depressing the firing rate of the feeder center. When food is needed, the satiety factor is no longer present, and the feeder center turns on. The animal feels hunger and will search for food and eat if food is available.

OBESITY

Obesity is defined as that condition in which the body weight is greater than 20% of the ideal weight for the individual's age, sex, and height. This assumes that the muscle-to-fat ratio is normal. Certainly many athletes exceed their ideal body weight according to the standard charts. However, their lean muscle mass is proprotionately greater than the nonathlete's. Muscle does in fact weigh more per unit volume than adipose tissue. Therefore a better parameter of obesity is the proportion of the body weight comprised of fat. The normal male body is 15% to 16% fat, compared to the female, which is 19% to 22% fat. Athletes may reduce this percentage to less than 9% and still have a normal weight.

The incidence of obesity in affluent societies has been estimated to be as high as 49%. Obesity has increased in prevalence in direct relationship to the amount of highly refined, high-sugar food that is readily available to Western society. Advertising plays a role in the psychologic conditioning to eat sugar-containing, high-calorie foods. Also, in affluent societies infants are often given high-caloric cereals, sugars, and milk even when they do not particularly want them, creating a pattern of food intake and a condition of infantile obesity that has been shown to be related to later obesity.

The causes of obesity are summarized in Table 19-1. Obesity may develop (1) in patients with hypothalamic tumors as a sequela to brain trauma or with inflammatory or other disorders affecting the hypothalamus; (2) in patients with a variety of endocrine diseases such as Cushing's syndrome; (3) in some rare genetic diseases and in type II diabetes; (4) as the aftermath of drug therapy with phenothiazines or oral hypoglycemic agents; (5) as the result of excessive dietary intake of

Table 19-1. Causes of obesity

Nature	Causal associations
Essential	Cause unknown
Genetic	In animals such as the Zucker rat, "Fatty"
Ventromedial hypothalamic injury	Physical: tumors, trauma, neurological disorders affecting hypothalamus
	?Physiologic: disturbances in regulation
Hyperphagia	Force feeding in lean volunteers
Endocrine disease	Hypothyroidism, diabetes, Cushing's syndrome
Psychosocial	Habit, culture, food "cues"

food; or (6) as the result of inactivity. Animal models for the study of obesity include the *yellow obese mouse* and the *Zucker genetically obese rat, "Fatty."* Human models include lean volunteers who force feed themselves to the point of gaining 20% to 25% extra body weight. Some studies have also been done on rats with ventromedial hypothalamic lesions and on humans who have hypothalamic injury caused by trauma or tumors with subsequent hyperphagia and obesity. A number of theories of obesity have been developed from the results of this research. The pathophysiology of obesity is still far from clear, and only certain highlights can be presented here.

Metabolic "efficiency"

Obese mice are metabolically "efficient" in that the food calories that they ingest are more readily stored as fat and less readily used for thermogenesis as compared to their lean counterparts. This also implies that cold sensitivity related to the deficient heat production of the obese mouse is a characteristic, a fact borne out by experimental evidence (Romsos, 1981). Another interesting fact is the increase in energy expenditure associated with an increase in energy (calorie) intake. Thus in nonobese humans a large, short-term increase in caloric intake may cause some weight increase, but a disproportionate amount of the excess calories may be lost as heat. It is certainly important to remember that the processes of digestion, absorption, and metabolism are energy-requiring mechanisms. Therefore, if these mechanisms are "overworked," there will be use of excess calories just for these processes alone. However, as obesity occurs the metabolic efficiency appears to change and that less and less energy goes toward these processes and thermogenesis. The

heart of the defect has been postulated to be related to alterations in the Na^+-K^+-ATPase concentrations in critical tissues. Chapter 8 describes how thyroid hormone appears to act mainly through stimulation of the production of this enzyme. The central role of the Na^+-K^+-ATPase system in overall metabolic efficiency is becoming more apparent. Several studies (Lin et al., 1980) have shown that genetically obese mice are deficient in Na^+-K^+-ATPase in skeletal muscle and liver. It will be recalled that this enzyme is essential for maintaining the electrochemical gradients across cell membranes and for controlling the osmotic pressures of many cells. It is necessary for the pumping of sodium out of cells and potassium into cells. Hypermetabolism resulting from excess thyroid hormone is believed to be caused by excessive amounts of the enzyme. Conversely, it is possible that the hypometabolism of obesity results from decreased amounts of available enzyme.

The most recent research (Hirsch and Leibel, 1988) points to few differences in human thermogenesis in the obese and nonobese state. However, important familial differences do exist in basal metabolic rate, and those with a lower energy expenditure have a much greater chance of gaining weight (Ravussin et al., 1988).

Adipocytes

Adipocytes (fat cells) are found predominantly in the subcutaneous tissues and mesentery, although they occur throughout the body in collections called *adipose tissue*, which ordinarily comprises 10 to 20 kg of body weight. This tissue has been described physiologically as an organ, acting as it does in a fairly uniform way toward stimuli such as hormones, blood concentration of substances, and sympathetic nervous stimulation. The adipose tissue acts as a storage center for excess ingested calories. When the energy needs of the body are less than the calorie intake, the food molecules are converted to fatty acids, which are carried from the liver as lipoproteins and are taken up by the adipocytes. The absolute amount of adipose tissue can increase in either of two ways. Tissue hypertrophy can occur as the individual adipocytes enlarge up to 10 times, becoming full of lipid (up to a one thousandfold volume increase) in which case the cells divide and increase in total number.

It was formerly believed that well-defined critical periods in fat cell development existed during infancy and early childhood and during early adolescence and pregnancy. Adipocyte hyperplasia would occur only during these periods and only in response to excess caloric intake. These cells would then exist for the life of the individual and would always be available to store excess fat. Early childhood overnutrition would thus predict adult obesity, since the presence of this excess fat organ would make accumulation of fat in the adipocytes more likely. This hyperplasia of childhood was thought to be irreversible. Later work has shown that dipocyte hyperplasia can occur at any time in the life cycle (Bjoerntorp, 1983). For fat cells to divide, however, they must reach a critical volume through triglyceride accumulation and probably require some as yet unknown adipogenic signals. In the development of obesity, adipocyte hypertrophy occurs first. If the individual continues to consume excessive calories beyond what is needed for energy balance, these cells then divide. Once formed, they appear to remain for life, although they can reduce their size through fat mobilization into the serum. Some individuals may be more prone to obesity as a result of genet-

ically different propensities of the adipocytes to divide. It also appears that during early childhood and adolescence, adipocyte hyperplasia is more likely to occur than at other times, so the sensitive-period hypothesis is not completely refuted. The association between infantile obesity and later adult obesity still is a reasonably strong association, as is underweight during childhood and later adult leanness.

The hyperplasia that develops in response to overeating during childhood appears to require an intact, functioning pituitary gland. This gland is also required by the embryo in the formation and maturation of the primordial adipoblasts.

In the obese adult the adipose tissue generally appears to respond to excess calories mainly by hypertrophy of the existing adipocytes. Fig. 19-3 shows the direct correlations between fat cell weight and degree of obesity. Microscopic examination of individual adipocytes shows that these cells bulge with single large droplets of triglycerides surrounded by a cell membrane. The cell can only reach a maximum of lipid content (~ 1 μg lipid per cell), and this occurs in moderately severe obesity. In a sense, if hyperplasia did not occur, the

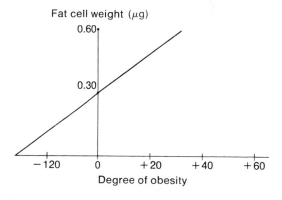

Fig. 19-3. With increasing degree of obesity, adipocytes contain more and more stored lipid.

total degree of obesity would be determined by the number of cells available to store fat. Adults with ventromedial hypothalamic damage generally gain up to a maximum of 136 kg (300 lb), whereas early onset obesity often results in a much greater weight plateau. Adipocytes do not behave uniformly, and there are marked differences in structure and function, dependent on anatomical location. There are also gender differences in fat distribution that may be important; men collect fat in the upper body and abdomen, and women generally store fat peripherally in the thighs, arms, and buttocks. The central fat distribution leads to higher blood lipids, sugar, and insulin levels, effects that are independent of gender (Smith, 1985). The typical female fat distribution appears to be related to sex hormones and has a role in normal human physiology. For example, thigh fat does not participate in fat metabolism to any great degree, except during lactation. At that time it releases fatty acids, under hormonal control, as substrate for milk production. Hormonally, then, fat differs, depending on site. Regardless of gender, when fat is upper body and abdominal, it is metabolically more active and contributes to the risk of many of the diseases associated with obesity.

Hyperlipidemia

Increased serum lipids (triglycerides, cholesterol, and fatty acids) are a common finding in obesity. The metabolism of food is directed toward use of caloric intake for energy and for storage as fat for later use if excess is ingested. When fatty acids are needed for energy, they are released from the adipose tissue as albumin-bound molecules, which are taken up by the liver, skeletal muscle, and myocardium. These fatty acids are liberated or mobilized from triglyceride molecules in the adipocyte through the action of a hormone-sensitive lipase, which is activated in the cell. Fatty acid mobilization is stimulated by epinephrine, thyroid hormone, glucocorticoids, glucagon, and growth hormone and is inhibited chiefly by insulin. The fatty acids in the blood are taken up mainly by the liver between meals for possible use in energy production, ketone body formation, or triglyceride synthesis.

The triglyceride molecules formed in the liver are released into the blood attached to protein as structures known as very low–, low–, and high–density lipoproteins. The source of the liver triglyceride, which is carried on lipoproteins, is mobilized fatty acids from the adipose tissue and fat ingested in the diet. The lipid is loosely bound to protein in these structures and can be easily cleaved away from the lipoproteins. Lipids are used by many tissues other than adipose tissue, liver, and muscle. For example, they are the building blocks of many hormones, and they form the matrix of all biologic cell membranes. Lipid is also important in thermal insulation and as a protective layer around vulnerable internal organs. Cells and tissue that require lipid have ready access to it because of this unique transport system. A blood and tissue enzyme, lipoprotein lipase, facilitates the removal of triglyceride from the lipoproteins. This enzyme is activated by heparin and is concentrated in various parts of the body, particularly adipose tissue, heart, and skeletal muscle. Fig. 19-4 shows the liver in fat metabolism and the carriage of lipid.

In obesity the normal regulation of free fatty acid mobilization in response to the needs of the body is greatly disturbed. Two major defects contribute to the ele-

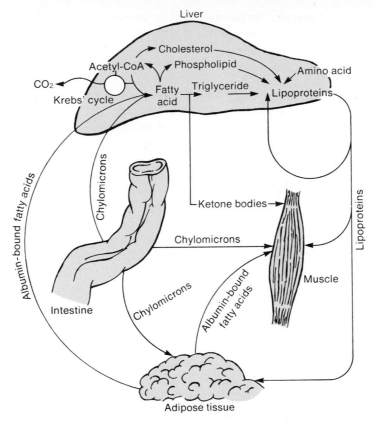

Fig. 19-4. Lipid transport. Lipids are absorbed from intestine as chylomicrons and taken up by liver, adipose tissue, and muscle. In the liver lipids are broken down to fatty acids, which are then either used in energy pathways or converted to phospholipids and triglycerides. Triglycerides are transported as lipoproteins from liver to muscle and adipose tissue. Adipose tissue serves as a lipid storage and can release fatty acids either as free molecules or more commonly as albumin-bound molecules when energy needs of the body demand it.

vated free fatty acid and triglyceride concentration in the obese individual. First, total lipid breakdown (lipolysis) in the adipocytes is increased, thus causing excessive mobilization of fatty acids; second, the regulation of lipolysis and esterification of fatty acids to form triglycerides is abnormal in obesity. Various enzymatic disturbances have also been reported in the adipocytes of obese persons. Normal individuals will experience an elevation of

free fatty acids in the blood in response to fasting. This response is minimal or absent in the obese, although the basal level of free fatty acids is increased above normal. The net synthesis of triglycerides from fatty acids in the liver is also increased and poorly regulated in the obese, and insulin regulation of triglyceride formation is disturbed. The obese person appears to make more lipid from ingested carbohydrate than does the normal person, and some reports indicate that the triglyceride that is formed is not removed normally from the plasma by lipoprotein lipase.

Some believe that the obese have a "ponderostat" mechanism, implying that they have a greatly elevated satiety set point, and the elevated fatty acids result from the fact that the obese person is always "starving." Others suggest that satiety is not involved at all, and that the obese have rare hunger and are responsive to cues, eating on cue as we all do. The obese however have many more cues to eat than the lean person. The lipid defects may be the result of insulin resistance and hyperinsulinism.

Hyperinsulinemia

The finding of increased insulin concentration in the blood in all forms of human obesity is extremely interesting. Some authorities feel that hyperinsulinemia is the primary defect that causes obesity, whereas others consider it to be a physiologic response to obesity. The elevated insulin concentration is present concurrently with insulin resistance. The pancreas may possibly respond initially in a compensatory way to primary insulin resistance at the cellular level by increasing its output of insulin. The normal role of insulin in lipid metabolism is to promote lipogenesis and fat storage; thus, if insulin resistance is present, there may be an increased uptake of free fatty acids by the liver and increased production of tryglycerides, which cannot then be taken up normally by the liver, adipose tissue, and muscle. The normal stimulatory effect of insulin on lipoprotein lipase activity is depressed in obesity. Therefore the hyperlipidemia of obesity may actually be caused by the insulin resistance that is commonly found. High-carbohydrate diets aggravate this situation, and physical exercise improves it.

The mechanism of insulin resistance is not known, although abnormal insulin cell membrane receptors have been described. It is possible too that insulin antagonists may exert an effect in obesity. Glucagon and growth hormone are the likely antagonists, but they have both been reported to decrease in obesity in the Zucker rat. Liver clearance of insulin is depressed in obesity, contributing to hyperinsulinemia.

Because of the resistance to insulin, some obese individuals have a basal hyperglycemia and an abnormal glucose tolerance test, indicating a diabetic predisposition. Cortisol may be important in insulin resistance, and, although its plasma concentration is usually normal in obesity, its production and total turnover are increased.

The beta cells of the pancreas are hypertrophied in obesity, and, if the beta cells are chemically destroyed by streptozocin in rats with ventromedial nucleus injuries, the expected obesity and hyperphagia are almost completely abolished. Vagotomy also abolishes obesity development in the ventromedial nucleus–injured rat. A causal relationship between the hypothalamus and the hyperinsulinism of obesity is suggested by this experiment. It would appear here at least that excessive deposition of fat requires hyperinsulinism. The development of insulin resistance then would be a secondary response of the tissues to constant exposure to high levels of insulin, so that the tissue becomes more and more tolerant of insulin. Conversely, the presence of an increased fat organ in the obese may cause an increased need for insulin for maintenance of the increased adipose tissue mass, thus secondarily creating hyperinsulinemia.

Reversal of the metabolic and hormonal

factors (hyperinsulinism, hypertriglyceridemia, hyperglycemia, and glucose intolerance) that are commonly found in obesity can be accomplished by significant weight reduction. Thus the excessive ingestion of food and the way the body metabolizes this food must be considered the primary cause of most obesity. The reduction of hyperinsulinism in obesity can be accomplished by reduction in the total amount of calories ingested and specifically by a decrease in the ingestion of carbohydrates. Carbohydrates are insulinogenic; in part they also determine or permit the basal response of the pancreatic beta cells to a great variety of other normal stimuli to insulin production. These stimuli include the gastrointestinal hormones gastrin, secretin, and cholecystikinin and other gastric peptides, which are all released when food is present in the gastrointestinal tract (Fig. 19-5).

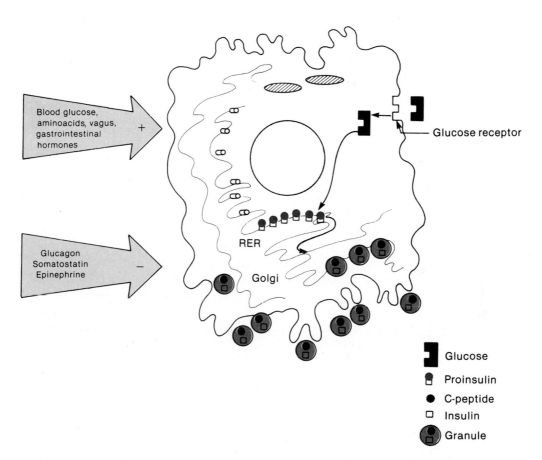

Fig. 19-5. Production of insulin. Pancreatic beta cell is illustrated as possessing a membrane glucose receptor site. When glucose is present, it attaches first to receptor, and then moves into cell. Glucose itself is required in insulin production, which proceeds by protein synthesis along rough endoplasmic reticulum (RER) with formation of proinsulin, which is packaged by Golgi apparatus into granules. Proinsulin is split into insulin and C-peptide. Beta cell is also stimulated by factors other than a rising blood glucose concentration and may be inhibited as well by other factors as shown.

The presence of hyperinsulinemia and insulin resistance in the obese individual clarifies the predisposition of the obese toward the eventual development of diabetes mellitus and thus provides excellent rationale for weight control, particularly in the genetically susceptible adult. The distribution of fat in the body is another risk factor, with increasing abdominal and upper body fat increasing the chance for the development of diabetes. Apparently, the anatomical location of fat is important. Abdominal fat cells are larger and behave differently than fat cells from the thighs, buttocks, or elsewhere.

Hyperphagia

The fatty rat, the animal with ventromedial injury, and obese humans generally are characterized as hyperphagic. They eat voraciously, and their pattern of eating may be altered. The obese person often claims a morning anorexia and may eat fewer meals than the nonobese person. However, the absolute amount of food at a meal is increased, and the intake of sweet-tasting, nonnutritive substances may also be increased. When 3000 calories are ingested at once instead of over the course of the day, an overall elevation of serum lipids occurs. Furthermore, the obese are generally sedentary, a factor that contributes not only to the maintenance of their obesity but also to the metabolic and hormonal alterations that perpetuate the obese state. Nevertheless, obese persons tend to maintain a fixed weight, as do lean people. They really do not consume more calories when they reach this stable weight (Hirsch and Leibel, 1988).

The role of early environmental factors in the attainment and maintenance of ultimate body size seems to be very significant. The roles of overfeeding and underfeeding have already been discussed. Much evidence implicates other early environmental factors and early learning experiences in many species. One example of these influences is the observation made by Capretti and Rawls (1974) that newly weaned rats will choose foods that their mothers consumed during the lactation period. Le Magnen (1972) demonstrated that exposure to food odors during lactation caused the newly weaned rats to preferentially choose foods with these odors in the postweaning period. Continuous exposure to these odors reinforced the desire for these foods as the rats matured. Another example in the human experience is the early family and cultural environment, which largely influences the eating patterns and behaviors that develop for life.

The hyperphagia of obesity may have many causes. Psychologic conditioning and habit certainly play important roles. Genetic factors may be operative, as evidenced by identical twin studies that show that weight gain over the life span is not markedly different in identical twins. Physiologic abnormalities in the regulation of the feeder and satiety centers of the hypothalamus may be present and yet be almost impossible to demonstrate. Parabiotic experiments in mice show that circulating satiety factors are present but are not able to "turn off" the feeder center and "turn on" the satiety center in spontaneous obesity. The hypothalamus is thus unresponsive. There is further evidence that the hypothalamus of the obese person is less sensitive to blood glucose and thus is a defective "glucostat." Obesity is extremely difficult to treat, although recent success has been obtained with behavior modification techniques. Most obese people can be made to lose weight by reduction in caloric intake, but in as much as 80% of this population, the obesity eventually returns.

Food attitudes and behaviors are extraordinarily complex in humans. Some researchers have suggested that in the obese food intake is associated with increased levels of endorphins. This suggests that obesity is the result of an internally conditioned food addiction. However, the limited research that has been done does not support this speculation (Schteingart, Butcher, and Noonan, 1983).

In volunteers who force-feed themselves to gain weight in obesity studies, all the metabolic and hormonal patterns of spontaneous obesity develop, and all parameters return to normal when the excess weight is lost. Weight loss occurs naturally when the diet is self-selected. One interesting factor in these individuals is the requirement that they have to eat a great *excess* of calories to *maintain* obesity once it develops. The fate of these excess calories is not known. It is possible that the excess calories go toward thermogenesis (heat production), which produces a stable body weight even in the face of excess calorie ingestion. Thus each individual has a "programmed" weight, and excess calories beyond those required to (1) maintain that weight and (2) allow for storage of a certain amount of excess calories in adipose tissue are removed from the body as heat. It is certainly commonplace to find individuals who can eat enormous amounts of food without weight gain, as well as the converse. This has also been shown experimentally in human subjects. Furthermore, in periods of undernutrition, thermogenesis may be decreased so that energy from available calories is directed toward maintenance of nutritional and metabolic status.

Association of obesity with disease

Obesity is associated with many disease processes, either through endocrine and metabolic links or through the actual physical effects of excessive fat. Cardiovascular disease and obesity are clearly related, as determined in many ways through many studies. Obesity is associated with increased serum cholesterol, low-density lipoprotein, and triglyceride levels, all of which could contribute to atherosclerotic placque formation. This relationship is strongest for younger people, increasing their risk of premature coronary artery disease. Adult onset diabetes (type II) is also more prevalent in the obese, as is hypertension, gall bladder disease, digestive diseases, kidney stones, cancer (breast, biliary tract, and reproductive organs), respiratory disorders, and arthritis (Brunzell, 1983). When obesity is a risk factor for a disease, the relationship between the two is almost linear; as obesity increases, risk for a particular disease increases. Fatter adults have higher blood pressures, serum lipids, and higher hemoglobin and hematocrit levels. The cause of the hematological abnormalities remains unknown, although it could mainly be a result of excessive food consumption. Longevity is also significantly decreased in the obese. Weight reduction must be considered a medical strategy in obese adults with any of the following conditions: 20% excess weight, family history for type II diabetes, high blood pressure, hypertriglyceridemia or hypercholesterolemia, atherosclerotic disease, gout, heart disease, chronic obstructive pulmonary disease or osteoarthritis, and history of childhood obesity (Burton et al., 1985). Health risk is apparent even at rather low levels of obesity, and statistics show that weight reduction significantly reduces risk. Unfortunately, obesity is not decreasing in the United States, and in middle-aged black women between the ages of 45 and 55 obesity is present in epidemic proportions

(60% compared to 30% in Caucasian women) (Kolata, 1985).

Probably no system is spared the stress of maintaining this excess tissue. The respiratory system is compromised, as evidenced by the pickwickian syndrome, which develops in some extremely obese individuals. This condition is characterized by high Pco_2, somnolence, massive obesity, and hypoventilation. Studies indicate that a number of mechanisms operate to depress respiraton. There is the mechanical effect of obesity on the ability of the respiratory muscles to function normally (decreased chest cage compliance), and there are biochemical effects on respiratory sensitivity.

Cardiovascular function is affected in obesity because of the excess burden on the heart to supply blood to additional tissue. Stroke volume and circulating blood volume are both increased. Congestive heart failure, hypertension, stasis ulcerations, and dyspnea are all commonly found in the morbidly obese individual. The hyperlipidemia associated with obesity also appears to predispose these individuals to atherosclerosis, thrombus and emboli formation, and myocardial infarctions. Hyperlipemic blood is more viscous and coagulable. Obesity also is associated with gallstone development. In the genetically susceptible individual, obesity in adult life is related to the onset and severity of diabetes. Degenerative arthritis may develop as a mechanical complication of obesity.

Increased cortisol production and turnover rate may play a role in the predisposition of the obese to a variety of disorders, and therefore in a sense obesity can be considered a stressor, resulting in adrenocortical activation. Fig. 19-6 illustrates the metabolic responses to overeating and the mechanisms whereby various pathophysiological processes are perpetuated.

PATHOPHYSIOLOGICAL EFFECTS OF DIETING

Although the previous section of this book has focused on the pathophysiology of obesity and has pointed out how obesity contributes to many disease processes, a caution should be noted in terms of dieting. Since so many people do diet, including even very young preadolescent girls, health practitioners should use guidelines for appropriate dieting. Inappropriate, excessive dieting can lead to very serious pathological disturbances and may even cause death. The extreme situation is that of self-imposed starvation as seen in anorexia nervosa (described in detail in Chapter 11). Short-term fasting or very low–calorie diets can produce somewhat similar effects. One principle is that energy expenditure may become markedly reduced when food intake is reduced. The tendency of metabolic changes to conserve energy when food intake is decreased is obviously a coping mechanism. When food intake is increased, metabolic processes cause energy expenditure to increase. During marked food deprivation, to preserve serum glucose, amino acids are required to maintain this new metabolic rate and to provide adequate fuel to glucose requiring organs. Fat is also used as an energy source, leading to fatty acid and triglyceride mobilization from the adipose tissue stores and ultimately to a state of ketosis as these fatty acids are converted to ketone bodies in the liver. Initially these metabolic changes are associated with decreased metabolic water formation, and diuresis, so that a significant percentage of early weight loss (about 60% in the first 5 days) on a very low–calorie diet is water weight (Schemmel, 1980). When caloric restriction is extreme, below 1000 calories per day, the protein use for energy can be significant and can lead to a loss of lean

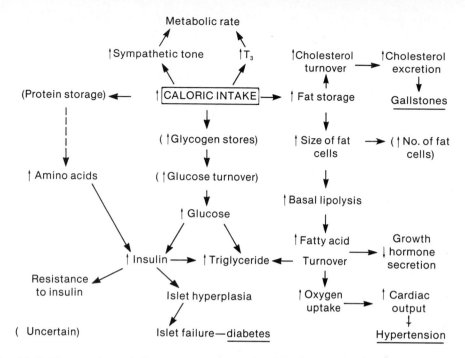

Fig. 19-6. Diagram of metabolic response to overeating. This diagram shows some of the effects of excess caloric intake on the metabolism of lipids, carbohydrates, and proteins on the control of the thyroid hormones and the automonic nervous system.

(From Bray, G: Metabolic responses to positive energy balance. In Hansen, B, editor: Controversies in obesity, 1983, New York Praeger Publishers.)

body mass (mostly muscle) rather than fat loss. Other risks associated with very low–calorie or total fasting diets are decreased serum glucose, ketosis, hyperuricemia, hair loss (possibly resulting from lack of protein), potassium loss and hypokalemia, hyponatremia, hypocalcemia, and hypomagnesemia, decreased glomerular filtration rate (GRF), decreased systolic blood pressure leading to postural hypotension, decreased serum iron, and gastrointestinal villi alterations (Schemmel, 1980). It is generally recommended that dieting subjects consume at least 1000 calories per day to avoid these physiological perturbations. Protein-sparing, low-calorie diets also help avoid

these effects. Such diets generally contain 70% calories from protein and 30% from fat (Wadden et al., 1987). Such diets do cause significant weight loss, although controversy surrounds them. Many weight loss experts recommend a diet of about 1200 calories, with the normal proportions of carbohydrates, proteins, and fats that are recommended for the healthy American diet. If caution is not used in the type of diet chosen, weight gain after a weight reduction diet can result in excess weight gain above the predieting weight. Another concern in dieting is age, because very young, usually lean adolescent girls generally diet excessively and have a preoccupation with weight. Dieting during this period may lead to behavioral changes in food attitudes and in growth and sexual maturation delays.

STARVATION

The result of overingestion is accumulation of fat deposits and gain in weight, whereas undernutrition leads to loss of these energy stores and eventual wasting, or *cachexia*. Undernutrition may result from inadequate or absent intake of food or from inability to absorb or metabolize the calories provided by the food that is eaten. Although the person with juvenile-onset diabetes eats adequate amounts of food (in fact is often voracious), the absolute lack of circulating insulin causes a cellular "starvation," and these children often appear wasted and thin. Cancer, infection, and severe malabsorption can result in a clinical state of starvation. Some infants also respond to emotional and sensory deprivation by the *failure to thrive syndrome* and are in fact starving to death, even though they may eat what are considered adequate amounts of food. *Marasmus* is a clinical term for starvation and cachexia in the infant under 2 years of age; it is seen most often in children who have been totally deprived during their early life. Neglected children of severely disturbed mothers, children growing up in severe poverty, and children suffering from pronounced gastrointestinal tract infections or enzyme deficiencies are all at risk. The child with marasmus often appears to be little more than a skeleton covered with thin flesh and wasted muscles. Generally the dietary deficiency is total, and no one specific nutrient is lacking, as usually occurs in other types of deficiency diseases.

Starvation may occur in anorexia nervosa, a psychiatric disease in which food is utterly refused; and, of course, it can occur when individuals are isolated without food.

Metabolism

As the body adapts to a prolonged fast, the metabolic processes are aimed at sparing carbohydrate and protein reserves and using fats. The length of time that humans can totally abstain from food depends partly on the amount of storage lipid that has been accumulated. Obviously obese people can fast for many weeks longer than their lean counterparts. The average length of time that a human being can go without food intake is 5 to 6 weeks. During this period most of the energy required for normal metabolism comes from fatty acids and ketone bodies. Certain organs of the body require glucose under normal conditions and are unable to use other sources of energy. Other organs (e.g., muscle) normally use fatty acids quite freely in the postabsorptive state after a meal. However, during starvation the glucose-requiring organs can adapt and begin to use ketone bodies and fatty acids. The brain and heart are the most remarkable in this regard. Furthermore, the liver is stimulated by increased glucagon output from the pancreas, which occurs in response to the lowered blood glucose, to produce glucose from available precursors, i.e., amino acids. This process is termed *gluconeogenesis*. Fatty acids are removed from the adipose tissue reserves also through the action of glucagon and other stimuli. Thus almost throughout a starvation fast the liver acts to maintain blood glucose concentration at the normal level, first through glycogenolysis and then through gluconeogenesis. Essentially the same type of response occurs after the ingestion of a very-low-carbohydrate meal, which acts through the intestinal hormones to turn on the production of glucagon, which stimulates gluconeogenesis and also release of insulin. Insulin in turn stimulates lipogenesis, and some fat eaten in such a diet will be used for energy, with the excess being stored by the insulin-stimulated adipose tissue. The insulin produced is not enough to inhibit the production of glucagon in this situation; but, if the meal contained sufficient carbohydrates, a proportionately greater rate of insulin production would ensue. This would depress glucagon production, thus stopping the signal for the liver to split glycogen and produce glucose.

Blood glucose concentration is extremely well regulated, and a variety of sensing mechanisms exist to ensure the maintenance of a fairly constant blood sugar level. The liver itself does not require insulin for glucose entry into the cells, so that the blood glucose is more or less equilibrated with liver glucose, which is rapidly phosphorylated on entering the liver cells. The glucose molecules may be used for glycogen synthesis or for liver energy metabolism. Glycogen synthesis or breakdown by the liver depends in large part on the insulin:glucagon ratio. Figs. 19-7 and 19-8 diagram the normal liver metabolism when food is constantly being supplied and when fasting is taking place. The metabolic pathways that predominate during prolonged fasting are geared toward the breakdown of glycogen, gluconeogenesis, and ketone body formation, as compared to glycogen synthesis and glucose use for energy in the fed state.

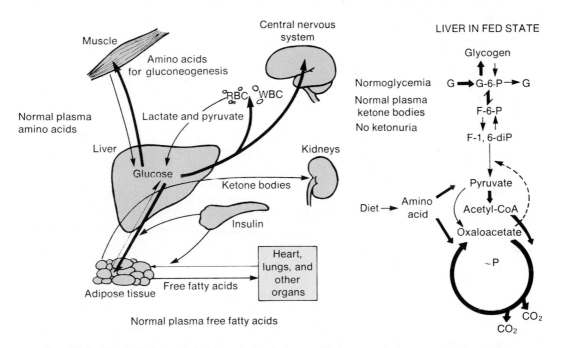

Fig. 19-7. Metabolic interrelationships during fed state. Under normal circumstances insulin is released when carbohydrate is ingested, promoting glucose use and metabolism. Role of Krebs cycle is indicated to right with glucose entering metabolism through Embden-Meyerhof pathway as pyruvate or being used for glycogenesis. Glycogenolysis and gluconeogenesis are not active at this time. (From Bacchus, H: Essentials of metabolic disease and endocrinology, Baltimore, 1976, University Park Press.)

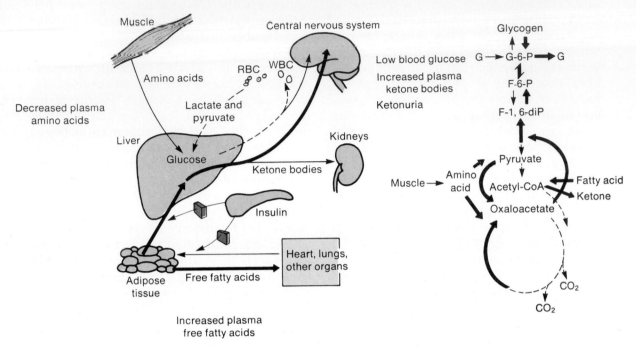

Fig. 19-8. Metabolic interrelationships during fasted state. In starvation due to prolonged fasting, insulin release is inhibited, with fatty acids released from adipose tissue and transported to liver for ketone body formation. Gluconeogenesis and glycogenolysis are both active.

(From Bacchus, H: Essential of metabolic disease and endocrinology, Baltimore, 1976, University Park Press.)

Metabolic stages

There are metabolic stages in starvation, which are determined by the fuel available for the body to burn for energy. The first 24 hours of a fast are characterized by liver and muscle glycogenolysis, which provides glucose. Free fatty acids are also released from adipose tissue and used by muscle as a predominant fuel source. These processes are stimulated by low blood levels of insulin and a high level of glucagon.

As the liver and muscle glycogen is removed, the second stage begins, and gluconeogenesis is stimulated. Both amino acids (mainly from muscle protein) and fatty acids are taken up by the liver, and

glucose use in most tissue of the body progressively decreases. The liver increases the use of fatty acids for energy by forming ketone bodies, which are then sent to all the tissues of the body. Ketone body production occurs as the result of a decreased oxaloacetate concentration in the liver cells, which is caused by a decreased anaerobic glycolysis of glucose and increased utilization of oxaloacetate for gluconeogenesis. Thus the fatty acids that enter the liver from the adipose tissue are dehydrogenated and split into acetyl-CoA fragments; these are then used to form acetoacetate or β-hydroxybutyrate, the ketone bodies. It is thought that fatty acid oxidation in the liver results in high levels of

NADH and acetyl-CoA, which drives the carboxylation of pyruvate to oxaloacetate, which then forms phosphoenolpyruvate, thus proceeding toward gluconeogenesis. Amino acids (and thus protein) are spared from use for energy production by peripheral tissues. They are used for some degree of gluconeogenesis by the liver, so that the blood glucose level is maintained, but the tissues of the body do not take up and use glucose at the normally high rate, having switched to fatty acids and ketone body use for their energy needs. Muscle wasting does, of course, occur, since muscle protein must be hydrolyzed to provide amino acids for gluconeogenesis. Muscle protein breakdown appears to be regulated by the insulin : glucagon ratio, being stimulated when the ratio is decreased. The major amino acids released from the muscle are alanine and glutamine, which are then used by the liver and also the kidney for gluconeogenesis. The muscle must metabolize its endogenous amino acids to provide these substrates, but the energy needs of the muscle for these mechanisms, as well as its contractility needs, can be met through use of fatty acids taken up from the blood. This spares the ketone bodies in the blood, which are the main fuel sources of the brain and myocardium in prolonged starvation.

The development of the terminal phase in starvation is determined by the amount of fat present in the body. The starving individual has a compensated metabolic acidosis because of the keto acids present in the blood. Calcium and phosphorus are depleted, and osteoporosis ensues as the body attempts to maintain these ion stores. Liver failure may occur because of fatty infiltration and is most common in individuals with previous hepatic disease. The basal metabolic rate decreases, and the levels of triiodothyronine decrease, although thyroxine remains at the normal level. Intellectual function is not affected significantly until late in the fast. The hypothalamic satiety center is, however, affected and remains active, and appetite is usually absent during a prolonged fast. (This phenomenon has also been observed in obese individuals on a low-carbohydrate diet and may be a result of ketosis.) Emotional stability is also decreased during a prolonged fast.

All these mechanisms may contribute to death, but the primary cause appears to be the loss of all lipid stores and the subsequent massive use of protein for energy. The terminal phase of starvation is extremely rapid once it appears. Protein in muscle, cell membranes, and blood is rapidly depleted, causing death within about 24 hours after the lipid reserves are gone. This occurs between 5 and 6 weeks after the start of the starvation fast in a normal lean individual with 15% body fat. People are often reported to suddenly fall down and die during the terminal phase of starvation.

MALNUTRITION STATES
Protein-calorie malnutritions of early childhood

Protein-calorie malnutrition of early childhood is prevalent in economically deprived and underdeveloped areas. *Kwashiorkor* (meaning in Ghandian "the disease that comes after the second child") develops when the total quantity and quality of protein in the diet are deficient. Children who are breast fed are protected from this disease in areas where it is prevalent; but, when they are displaced at the breast by a younger sibling and thus forced to eat the common diet, kwashiorkor may result. The diet is characteristically low in protein, with the major source of calories being carbohydrates. Essential amino acids are missing, the protein often being derived from cornmeal rather than animal protein sources. The symptoms and signs that develop may vary from mild to severe. An important contributing factor to the morbidity is the presence of concurrent parasitic infestation and chronic infections in these children. Kwashiorkor can be contrasted with nutritional marasmus, which also is a common finding in deprived children or in children with chronic diarrhea. In this condition, both protein and calories are deficient, leading to the clinical state of cachexia and starvation previously discussed. Figs. 19-9 and 19-10 show the dramatic contrast between these two deficiency diseases. The child with kwashiorkor is usually characterized by edema, muscle wasting, and growth retardation, and often massive ascites may be present. The infant with marasmus does not have edema and appears wizened and wasted. Other variable findings of kwashiorkor include desquamation (Fig. 19-11), diarrhea, anemia, vitamin deficiencies, hepatomegaly, and graying of the hair, which may alternate with normal pigmentation along the hair shaft indicating periods of normal and deficient nutrition.

The pathophysiology of protein-calorie deficiency is related to the normal role of proteins. Protein is required for energy, growth, formation of antibodies and enzymes, repair of tissues, and maintenance of blood colloid osmotic pressure and capillary filtration. A certain amount of adaptation and compensation for decreased

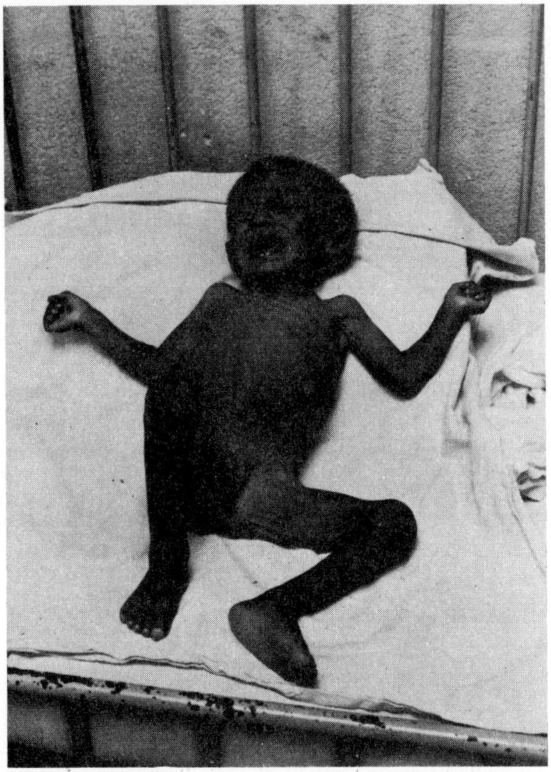

Fig. 19-9. Child in Guatemala suffering from acute malnutrition. There is severe cachexia and no obvious edema.

(FAO photograph Courtesy Y. Nagata.)

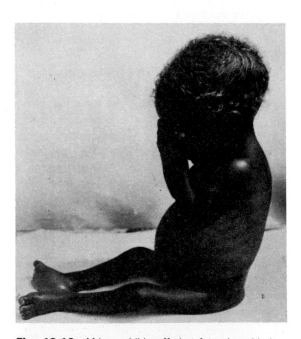

Fig. 19-10. African child suffering from kwashiorkor. Note uncurled graying hair, edema, and skin lesions.

(FAO photograph Courtesy M. Autret.)

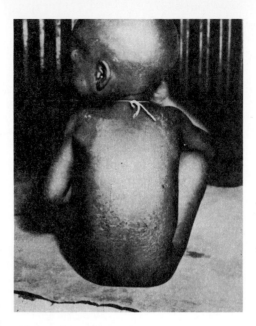

Fig. 19-11. Characteristic "flaky paint": dermatosis of kwashiorkor.

(From Williams, SR: Nutrition and diet therapy, ed 4, St Louis, 1981, The C.V. Mosby Co.)

protein intake will occur. For example, basal metabolic rate, decreased oxygen consumption, decreased nitrogen excretion, and decreased spontaneous activity may all help to maintain the steady state for a certain period. However, over a prolonged period of time, disorders in normal functioning are inevitable. Decreased colloid osmotic pressure accounts for the generalized subcutaneous edema and ascites that are common. Hyponatremia also is common. The edema predisposes the skin to injury and slow healing, and ulcers often occur because of a lack of protein for repair. The edema may actually mask a severe weight retardation, and in fact the moon face and edema are sometimes interpreted as a healthy plumpness. The lack of protein causes protein catabolism with severe muscle wasting. The liver often becomes infiltrated with lipid, but the development of cirrhosis is not common. The

pathogenesis of fatty liver in kwashiorkor is not known, but lipoprotein synthesis by the liver may be impaired. The jejunal mucosa also is affected in the disease, becoming flattened and atrophic, and malabsorption and diarrhea occur.

The long-term effects of kwashiorkor are growth retardation throughout life and possibly some intellectual impairment, particularly if the child was affected in the first 6 months of life. The other signs and symptoms of kwashiorkor can be eradicated with treatment of the underlying disorder and adequate nutrition.

Variations of marasmus and kwashiorkor with signs and symptoms of both conditions are also common; these are considered "intermediate" forms of the two diseases. Since marasmus usually occurs during the first year of life, the effects on brain growth and intellectual development are more profound than in kwaskiorkor, which typically occurs during the toddler years.

Vitamin deficiencies

Deficiencies in one or more vitamins are common even in Western societies. Vitamin deficiencies also occur secondarily in many disease states. A common role of vitamins in physiologic function is participation as cofactors in enzymatic reactions. Enzyme-mediated reactions are of many different types and are involved in all the metabolic activities of the organism. Therefore the signs and symptoms of the various vitamin deficiencies (Tables 19-2 and 19-3) are often extremely variable, depending on which functions are most compromised.

Other nutritional deficiencies

In addition to deficiencies in the intake of calories (as proteins, carbohydrates, and lipids) and vitamins, a great variety of other nutritional deficiencies is possible.

Table 19-2. Requirements, functions, and deficiencies of fat-soluble vitamins*

Vitamin	Physiologic functions	Results of deficiency	Requirement	Food sources
A (retinol)	Production of rhodopsin (visual purple)	Xerophthalmia	Adult: male—5000 IU female—4000 IU	Liver Cream, butter, whole milk Egg yolk
Provitamin A (carotene)	Formation and maintenance of epithelial tissue Toxic in large amounts	Night blindness Keratinization of epithelium Follicular hyperkeratosis Skin and mucous membrane infections Faulty tooth formation	Pregnancy: 5000 IU Lactation: 6000 IU Children: 1500 to 5000 IU depending on age	Green and yellow vegetables Yellow fruits Fortified margarine
D (calciferol)	Absorption of calcium and phosphorus Calcification of bones Renal phosphate clearance Toxic in large amounts	Rickets Faulty bone growth Osteomalacia in adults	400 IU (children; pregnant or lactating women)	Fish oils Fortified or irradiated milk
E (tocopherol)	Related to action of selenium Antioxidant with vitamin A and unsaturated fatty acids Hematopoiesis Reproduction (in animals)	Hemolysis of red blood cells; anemia Possible protection of unsaturated fatty acids Sterility (in rats)	Adult: 12 to 15 IU	Vegetable oils
K (menadione)	Blood clotting, necessary for synthesis of prothrombin Possible coenzyme in oxidative phosphorylation Toxic in large amounts Deficiency in intestinal malabsorption (sprue, celiac disease, colitis) Prolonged antibiotic therapy Anticoagulant therapy (dicumarol counteracts)	Hemorrhagic disease of the newborn Bleeding tendencies in biliary disease or surgical procedures	Unknown	Green leafy vegetables Cheese Egg yolk Liver

*From Williams SR: Nutrition and diet therapy, ed 3, St Louis, 1981, The CV Mosby Co.

Table 19-3. Requirements, functions, and deficiencies of B complex vitamins

Vitamin	Physiologic functions	Clinical applications	Requirement	Food sources
Thiamine (B$_1$)	Coenzyme in carbohydrate metabolism TPP—decarboxylation TDP—transketolation	Beriberi (deficiency) GI†: anorexia, gastric atony, indigestion, deficient hydrochloric acid CNS†: fatigue, apathy, neuritis, paralysis CV†: cardiac failure, peripheral vasodilation, edema of extremities	0.5 mg per 1000 calories	Pork, beef, liver, whole or enriched grains, legumes
Riboflavin (B$_2$)	Coenzyme in protein of energy metabolism (flavoproteins) FMN (flavin mononucleotide) FAD (flavin adenine dinucleotide)	Wound aggravation Cheilosis (cracks at corners of mouth) Glossitis Eye irritation; photophobia Seborrheic dermatitis	0.6 mg per 1000 calories	Milk, liver, enriched cereals
Niacin (nicotinic acid) (precursor—tryptophan)	Coenzyme in tissue oxidation to produce energy (ATP) NAD (nicotinamide-adenine dinucleotide) NADP (nicotinamide-adenine dinucleotide phosphate)	Pellagra (deficiency) Weakness, lassitude, anorexia Skin: scaly dermatitis CNS: neuritis, confusion	14-20 mg (niacin equivalent)	Meat, peanuts, enriched grains
Pyridoxine (B$_6$)	Coenzyme in amino acid metabolism Decarboxylation Deamination Transamination Transsulfuration Niacin formation from tryptophan Heme formation Amino acid absorption	Anemia (hypochromic microcytic) CNS: hyperirritability, convulsions, neuritis Isoniazid is an antagonist for pyridoxine Pregnancy: anemia	2 mg	Wheat, corn, meat, liver
Pantothenic acid	Coenzyme in formation of active acetate (CoA)—acetylation	Contributes to: Lipogenesis Amino acid activation Formation of cholesterol Formation of steroid hormones Formation of heme Excretion of drugs		Liver, egg, skimmed milk
Lipoic acid (sulfur-containing fatty acid)	Coenzyme (with thiamine) in carbohydrate metabolism to reduce pyruvate to active acetate Oxidative decarboxylation	Undetermined (see Thiamine)		Liver, yeast
Biotin	Coenzyme in decarboxylation (synthesis of fatty acids, amino acids, purines); deamination	Undetermined		Egg yolk, liver

*From Williams SR: Nutrition and diet therapy, ed 4, St Louis, 1981, The CV Mosby Co.
†GI, gastrointestinal; CNS, central nervous system; CV, cardiovascular.

Continued.

Table 19-3. Requirements, functions, and deficiencies of B complex vitamins—cont'd

Vitamin	Physiologic functions	Clinical applications	Requirement	Food sources
Folic acid	Coenzyme for single carbon transfer—purines, thymine, hemoglobin Transmethylation	Blood cell regeneration in pernicious anemia but not control of its neurologic problems Megaloblastic anemia Macrocytic anemia of pregnancy Sprue treatment Aminopterin is folic acid antagonist	100 μg Pregnancy: 800 μg Lactation: 600 μg	Liver, green leafy vegetables, as asparagus
PABA (part of folic acid)		Treatment of rickettsial diseases Anemias (see Folic acid)		Same as folic acid
Cobalamin (B_{12})	Coenzyme in protein synthesis Formation of nucleic acid and cell proteins—red blood cells Transmethylation	Extrinsic factor in pernicious anemia—combines with intrinsic factor of gastric secretions for absorption, forms red blood cells (with folic acid) Sprue treatment (with folic acid)	3 μg	Liver, meat, milk, eggs, cheese
Inositol	Lipotropic agent (?)	Undetermined		Citrus fruit, grains, meat, milk
Choline	Lipotropic agent Forms nerve mediator—acetylcholine	Fatty liver—hepatitis, cirrhosis (undetermined in human nutrition)		Meat, cereals, egg yolk

The minerals in the diet are essential for normal function in many cases; and, if they are deficient, disease may result. Again, the body will compensate for as long as possible by a variety of adaptive mechanisms. However, prolonged mineral deficiencies can cause serious disease (e.g., anemias). Table 19-4 describes common trace metals and their functions.

Iron. Hypochromic anemia, or iron deficiency, is the most common anemia, particularly among children, women, and during pregnancy. Iron is normally required in hemoglobin manufacture, form-

ing the heme portion of this molecule. When the hemoglobin concentration in the blood decreases to less than 10 g/100 ml, anemia results. The organism adapts to the anemia, which threatens oxygenation of the cells and tissues, by manufacturing more erythrocytes and by decreasing metabolism and activity. Pallor and fatigue, dyspnea on exertion, tachycardia, and neurologic manifestations are all signs of anemia (see Chapter 3).

Vitamin deficiencies may also produce megaloblastic anemia in folic acid or vitamin B_{12} deficiencies. Failure to absorb vi-

Table 19-4. Common trace metals and their functions

Trace metal	Function	Normal concentrations	Daily requirements	Physiologic effects	
				Excesses	**Deficiencies**
Iron	80% in molecules of hemoglobin; also a cofactor or component of several enzymes	35 mg/kg 50 mg/kg	5-10 mg/24 hr	Hemosiderosis in genetically susceptible individuals	Iron deficiency anemia
Copper	Requires for many enzymatic functions Used in melanin formation, bone development, myelin production, phospholipid synthesis, erythrocyte maturation	75-150 mg	2 mg/24 hr	Rare (can occur in Wilson's disease) Causes liver damage, lenticular degeneration, neurologic and renal pathology	Anemia Ataxia
Zinc	Cofactor or component of several enzymes (including carbonic anhydrase) Required for normal embryonic organogenesis Required for insulin release Involved in retinal function	2 gm	10-15 mg/24 hr	None known	Skin lesions Skeletal anomalies Decreased wound healing Dwarfism Hepatomegaly Hypogonadism
Manganese	Cofactor for several enzymes Required for normal bone growth, nervous irritability, lipid metabolism		6-8 mg/24 hr		
Iodine	Required in formation of thyroid hormones	25-50 mg	100-140 µg/24 hr	None known	Goiters Cretinism Thyrotoxicosis Thyroid tumors

tamin B_{12} in the ileum when gastric intrinsic factor is lacking results in pernicious anemia. The red blood cells are large, and many reticulocytes are present as well. Vitamin B_{12} and folic acid are required in the normal maturation of the erythrocyte in the bone marrow.

Hemolytic anemia of the premature infant may result if there is inadequate vitamin E intake in formulas; it is reversible when these infants are treated with vitamin E preparations.

Calcium. Calcium is an essential mineral required for muscle contraction, bone formation, and many enzyme-mediated reactions. Its absorption requires vitamin D and parathyroid hormone, and its absence either through dietary deficiency or by disordered absorption (e.g., vitamin D deficiency) causes rickets, osteomalacia, and tetany.

Magnesium. A deficiency in magnesium may be brought about by decreased intake, increased output (diuretics), or impaired absorption. It is fairly common in poorly nourished alcoholics, as are most of the other deficiencies. Magnesium activates numerous enzyme reactions and deficiency is associated with neuromuscular abnormalities. It has been suggested that hypomagnesemia in combination with alkalosis is the cause of the delirium tremors of alcohol withdrawal, although the mechanism is not as yet clearly defined.

Zinc. Zinc is an essential mineral, which functions in combination with enzymes, such as carbonic anhydrase. It is required for protein synthesis by certain tissues and for wound healing; it may function in vitamin A metabolism. Zinc deficiency may develop when intake is decreased, such as in the alcoholic, or when malabsorption occurs (e.g., cystic fibrosis). Zinc may be removed from the blood by the action of certain medications (penicillamine), which act as chelating agents. Oral contraceptives also have been reported to lower zinc levels. The symptoms of deficiency are extremely variable, from impairment of growth to abnormalities in the sensation of taste. The following case study illustrates the clinical presentation of zinc deficiency.

CASE STUDY: ZINC DEFICIENCY

Subjective and Objective Data

Identifying data: Mr. L, a 35-year-old white male was the victim of polycystic kidney disease. Both kidneys had been surgically removed 5 years before this episode. Mr. L was maintained on a regimen of renal dialysis, which was done three times weekly in the community dialysis center.

Present illness: Mr. L has been slowly losing weight for about 6 months and complaining of anorexia. He stated that food tasted bitter or bland and was generally unappetizing. He would force himself to eat but occasionally was not able to eat at all. His wife had tried various ways of preparing his salt-free diet but was becoming increasingly frustrated, stating that the food tasted fine to her.

Mr. L underwent tests of various types for possible malignant disease, but these were negative. He had complained of frequent upper respiratory infections and general fatigue as well. When no active disease was found, serum and hair zinc determinations were made. The values for zinc concentration are given below:

Hair: 125 ppm (normal, 180 ppm)
Serum: 60 mg/dl (normal, 75 mg/dl)
The physical examination was within

Contributed by Maureen Groër.

normal limits for all systems; however, there was slight hepatomegaly.

Treatment: Mr. L began taking an oral zinc preparation (ZnSo$_4$ capsules, 220 mg daily). Within 3 weeks he began to increase his caloric intake as well as the amount of meat eaten daily. His taste sensation had returned to normal after a month, and he described eating as once again an enjoyable undertaking. His hair and serum zinc levels were normal, and he continued receiving zinc supplementation.

Discussion

This case study describes the rare phenomenon of zinc deficiency. There are populations at risk for the development of such a deficiency even in the United States. Included are groups with very poor diets, in which the food contains less than 11 mg of zinc daily. Also at risk for the development of zinc deficiency are patients receiving total parenteral nutrition; patients with various disorders, including liver disease, malabsorption syndromes, and sickle cell disease; and some patients who have undergone intestinal bypass surgery. The deficiency has been recognized as causing hypogeuesthesia, or a decrease in taste, as one of the major manifestations. Decreased cellular immunity, anorexia, and poor growth are other problems that may develop.

Implications of the case study are that many groups of nursing clients should be assessed for hypogeuethesia or dysgeuethesia. The elderly in particular may suffer from a borderline deficiency because of dietary and metabolic inadequacies. A simple assessment technique is the preparation of salty, sweet, sour, and bitter solutions of at least four different concentrations. The solutions are then dropped on the patient's tongue, alternating with drops of water, and the patient is asked to describe the taste sensation. A complete nutritional assessment and dietary history should also be part of the evaluation.

Nursing Diagnoses

1. Altered nutrition, less than body requirements related to zinc deficiency.

Other minerals. Numerous other minerals may be ingested in the diet in decreased or excessive amounts. When excessive amounts of such minerals as lead, copper, or iron are present either in the blood or stored in tissue, numerous pathophysiologic disturbances may occur. Some of the effects of environmental chemical agents are discussed in Chapter 5.

GENETIC AND METABOLIC DISTURBANCES
Carbohydrates

Carbohydrates are essential components of the human diet, being used for energy production in every cell of the body in the form of glucose. Indeed, if intake is inadequate, the body's metabolism gears toward the production of glucose from other dietary constituents. Defective absorption in the GI tract, inadequate intake, or abnormal metabolism of glucose all will lead to pathophysiology of nutritional integrity. The problems involved in inadequate intake, such as occurs in starvation or prolonged fasting, have already been discussed. Inadequate absorption may occur in gastrointestinal diseases, such as malabsorption or diarrhea. Certain gastrointestinal enzymes may be deficient, causing poor polysaccharide or disaccharide breakdown in the gut, which then leads to decreased absorption. Lactase deficiency, a common occurrence in the Black population and in the elderly, will result in inefficient hydrolysis of lactose to glucose and galactose, and therefore uptake of this disaccharide cannot occur.

Enzymatic deficiencies. The most common disturbances in carbohydrate metabolism are related to the cellular metabolism of these compounds. Cellular enzymatic deficiencies, which are most commonly genetic in nature, are well described in erythrocytes and lead to anemia. Hemolytic disease results in these anemias with hepatomegaly, splenomegaly, hematuria, and jaundice. The two major enzyme deficiencies that have been described in erythrocytes are of pyruvate kinase and glucose-6-phosphate dehydrogenase (G6PD). Both conditions are quite rare, but a mild form of the latter has been described in 35% of the American black population. This type is essentially asymptomatic except when the erythrocytes are severely stressed by administration of certain oxidant-like drugs (primaquine and sulfa drugs) or by infection. Then hemolytic anemia will develop. The worldwide distribution of G6PD deficiency parallels the distribution of falciparum malaria, as do sickle cell anemia and thalassemia, and thus is thought to provide a selective advantage to those who carry the mutated gene. The malarial protozoan requires certain metabolic and protein characteristics, which are decreased in the G6PD-deficient erythrocyte.

Other enzymatic deficiencies that interfere with carbohydrate metabolism are the glycogen storage diseases, resulting from defective breakdown of glycogen into glucose subunits. Glycogen therefore accumulates in various tissues of the body, particularly liver, kidney, and muscle. There are a number of forms, all genetic in nature, with a variety of symptoms and prognoses. Muscle weakness and growth retardation are major symptoms in most forms.

Another condition of disturbed carbohydrate metabolism is *galactosemia*, which is caused by the accumulation of large amounts of the sugar galactose or its products of metabolism, in particular galactitol, within the blood and tissues. The congenital form has been associated with mental retardation, kidney damage, and lens cataracts. All described forms of this disease are as a result of deficiencies in the enzymes normally involved in galactose metabolism.

Hypoglycemia. Hypoglycemia is an abnormally low blood glucose concentration that can be symptomatic of many disorders. The symptoms of acute hypoglycemia reflect the effects of widespread sympathetic nervous system activation, which is stimulated by low blood glucose concentration and which activates glycogenolysis. When the blood glucose falls to less than 40 mg/100 ml (normal is 80 to 120 mg/100 ml), the individual experiences palpitations, weakness, sweating, dizziness, and hunger. Prolonged hypoglycemia may result in serious central nervous system dysfunction, leading to convulsions and coma.

The cause of spontaneous hypoglycemia is generally an abnormal regulation of insulin production in response to stimuli. It is a common finding in prediabetics in the postprandial state and is caused by production of excess insulin in response to the meal. This causes the blood glucose levels to drop markedly after the meal has been absorbed and the products of digestion and absorption have been distributed to the blood and tissues. This response occurs typically 3 hours after a meal, particularly one high in carbohydrates, if no other nourishment has been taken since the meal. The development of hypoglycemia can be averted in these patients by providing a low-carbohydrate, high-protein meal with a snack just before the third hour after the meal.

Hypoglycemia may occur in conditions

in which the output of insulin in the unstimulated, as well as stimulated, state is extremely high. This might occur in patients with insulinomas, or insulin-producing tumors. The treatment is surgical extirpation when possible. Insulin reactions in the diabetic are also a common cause of hypoglycemia, and immediate ingestion of carbohydrates alleviates the condition.

Postprandial hypoglycemia also occurs in many postgastroenterostomy patients. The cause of this disorder is believed to be rapid absorption of nutrients resulting from rapid gastric emptying into the duodenum through an impaired or absent pylorus. The excessive absorption stimulates the pancreas to produce large amounts of insulin, which results in a lowered blood sugar. This form of hypoglycemia may also be treated by a low-carbohydrate, high-protein diet.

Hypoglycemia may develop from certain genetic enzyme deficiencies that interfere with the metabolism of glucose by the liver. It is also a symptom of hypopituitarism and Addison's disease, in which there is hypofunction of the pituitary and adrenal cortex and reduced corticosteroid production. Corticosteroids are normally antagonistic to the actions of insulin.

Proteins

Abnormalities in the absorption and metabolism of proteins are less common than the disorders of carbohydrates just discussed. Amino acid absorption can be impaired in malabsorption syndromes, and metabolism of amino acids is also affected by certain genetic enzymatic deficiencies. It will be recalled that dietary protein is broken down into small peptides and amino acids in the digestive tract by peptidases and removed from the GI tract through the mucosal cells and into the portal vein. Amino acids are then carried to the liver and other tissues for use. Fig. 19-1 illustrated the entrance of amino acids into anabolic and catabolic reactions via the Krebs cycle. The amino group is removed from the amino acid by transamination or deamination, reactions that are enzymatically mediated. The nitrogen is metabolized as ammonia, which may then enter the urea cycle or may be taken up by glutamine, which is acted upon by glutaminase in the kidney, releasing the ammonia into the urine. Certain amino acids are considered essential, since they cannot be synthesized in the body. These are isoleucine, leucine, lysine, methionine, phenylalanine, threonine, tryptophan, and valine.

A deficiency of protein whether as the result of malabsorption, inadequate intake, or excessive loss (burns, renal disease, excessive catabolism, neoplasms) leads to clinical states associated with negative nitrogen balance. Inadequate intake, exemplified by kwashiorkor, has been previously described. Protein deficiency is associated with decreased resistance to infection, stressors, and traumatic agents. Protein may be lost from the gut in protein-losing enteropathies such as are seen in cancer, ulcers, colitis, and tuberculosis, or it may be lost through the action of catabolic hormones such as cortisol, thyroid hormone, and estrogens and in cachectic wasting associated with malignant tumors (see Chapter 14, Table 14-2). Defective enzymes may result from genetic disease, or alteration in the amount and nature of proteins may be observed. Abnormalities in plasma proteins are associated with a great variety of diseases, including multiple myeloma, cirrhosis, kidney disease, muscular dystrophy, protein-calorie deficiency, and hereditary disorders.

Abnormalities in the metabolic pathways in which the various amino acids are involved can lead to a great variety of clinical manifestations.

The diverse nature of these diseases is due to the multiple roles of protein in cellular metabolism, division, growth, movement, ion transport, buffering, and indeed almost any function. Protein serves structural, enzymatic, and immune functions, and both the nature and the amount of available protein are determined by the availability of amino acids and by genetic regulation of the metabolic pathways.

Lipids

Disorders of intestine-to-liver lipid transport. Fat is required in the diet and is essential for energy production, hormone and bile salt synthesis, and cell membrane integrity. The absorption of fat and the role of lipid in energy maintenance have already been described. Certain clinical disorders exist in which intestinal lipid metabolism is disturbed. Pancreatic diseases in which decreased pancreatic lipases are released into the bowel will result in malabsorption of lipid. This is seen in cystic fibrosis, in which the pancreatic ducts become blocked with thick mucus, and pancreatic degeneration and fibrosis thus ensue. Release of adequate lipase, which is then inactivated by excessive acid, also may occur (e.g., in Zollinger-Ellison syndrome). Micelle formation in the intestinal lumen may also be interrupted in various disorders of bile salt metabolism. These include bile duct obstruction, bowel surgery such that the enterohepatic circulation of bile salts is interrupted, and ingestion of the drug cholestyramine.

Inefficient absorption of lipid micelles also may occur in various disease processes, including celiac disease. Celiac disease is associated with fat malabsorption, steatorrhea, diarrhea, and protein-losing enteropathy, to such a degree that sometimes the blood albumin levels are decreased. Other processes that affect this aspect of lipid absorption include bowel ischemia caused by mesenteric artery occlusion, hookworm, or the drug neomycin.

The synthesis of triglycerides inside the intestinal mucosal cell may be disrupted if the activity of the required cellular enzymes is impaired. This phenomenon occurs in Addison's disease. The formation of chylomicrons, which transport the lipid formed inside the intestinal cell to the liver and other tissues, may also be disturbed. This is observed in congenital abetalipoproteinemia, in which the formation of globulin, which is required in the formation of chylomicrons and lipoproteins, is disturbed. Hypobetalipoproteinemia, may be seen in conjunction with some malabsorption syndromes and in severe debilitation.

Whipple's disease interferes with the transport of lipid from the intestinal cell. The disease process involves infiltration of the lamina propria of the small intestine and distortion of the intestinal villi. This represents a barrier through which nutrients cannot easily pass, thus causing malabsorption.

Obstruction of the intestinal lymphatic drainage may occur in a great variety of diseases and may be severe enough to impede the absorption of chylomicrons into the intestinal lacteals. Lymphatic flow can be impaired by such factors as tumors, tuberculosis, Whipple's disease, trauma, and infection.

Disorders of lipid transport in serum. The normal pathways of lipid transport have previously been discussed. Triglycerides and cholesterol are mainly carried from the liver to the peripheral tissues as lipoproteins. Fatty acids are also transported in the plasma from the adipose tissue to the liver and other tissues as albumin-bound molecules.

Disorders of lipid transport include hyperlipoproteinemias and hypolipoproteinemias. The hyperlipoproteinemias may be either inherited or acquired. Among the inherited forms include diseases in which lipoprotein lipase is deficient, hyperbetalipoproteinemia with normal triglycerides occurs, or hyperprebetalipoproteinemia is present. Acquired hyperlipoproteinemias may also be found in pregnancy, diabetes, pancreatitis, hypothyroidism, nephrosis, liver disease, and multiple myeloma. The symptoms associated with hyperlipoproteinemia depend on which lipoproteins are involved. Abdominal pain, premature atherosclerosis, xanthomas, and pancreatitis are sometimes found.

The *hypolipoproteinemias* are mainly inherited disorders such as congenital β-lipoprotein deficiency, hypobetalipoproteinemia, and familial high-density lipoprotein deficiency (Tangier's disease). The signs and symptoms of these disorders include malabsorption, retinitis, neuropathy, abnormally shaped erythrocytes (acanthocytes) in abetalipoproteinemia, and acanthocytes and orange discoloration of the tonsils in Tangier disease. The abetalipoproteinemias are remarkably asymptomatic.

Purines and pyrimidines

This chapter would not be complete without some mention of the various conditions that can disturb the metabolism of purines and pyrimidines, the nitrogenous bases that are the backbone of DNA and RNA. These bases are derived both from dietary intake and from cellular synthetic pathways. The most common disorder of purine synthesis is gouty arthritis, in which excessive uric acid accumulates in the blood and tissues (see Chapter 2). Excess uric acid develops either as the result of increased synthesis or decreased excretion of purine compounds. Approximately 0.3% of the population have this abnormality, which is thought to be genetic. Pyrimidine metabolism involves the formation of orotic acid, and a hereditary orotic aciduria has been described. This condition is associated with megaloblastic anemia, growth and developmental retardation, and renal disease. Treatment is aimed at administration of uridine, which is deficient in this disease.

NUTRITIONAL DISEASE MODEL: DIABETES MELLITUS

Diabetes mellitus is a common disorder of carbohydrate metabolism caused by either an absolute lack of circulating insulin or an inability to use available endogenous insulin, leading to hyperglycemia and a variety of other metabolic, tissue, and cardiovascular effects. Inheritance is thought to be multifactorial, rather than simply recessive, and the influence of environmental factors (i.e., obesity) on the development of the adult-onset type is critical in the *penetrance* of the genes that determine the expression of diabetes. First degree relatives of persons with type II diabetes have a high lifetime risk. The degree and nature of diabetes are extremely variable, and, although it is possible to identify prediabetics in the population, it is very difficult to predict the possibility of diabetes among populations of genetically "susceptible" individuals.

Insulin production

Fig. 19-5 shows the functional morphology of the insulin-secreting beta cell of islands of Langerhans in the pancreas. Insulin is produced by these cells in response to the stimuli indicated. Normally, insulin is delivered in a pulsatile manner. Probably the major stimulus is increased blood glucose concentration, but the effects of the vagus nerve, gastrointestinal peptides, glucagon, and somatostatin are all considered important in regulation of the response. The release of insulin by the beta cell requires calcium, zinc, and glucose itself. The packaging and extrusion of insulin-containing granules by the beta cell is termed *emiocytosis*.

The beta cell is thought to possess glucose receptors on its membrane, which allow glucose to initially attach to the cell and then move through the membrane and become metabolized. This initiates the formation by the endoplasmic reticulum of *proinsulin*. The Golgi complex is thought to then somehow cleave away a section of proinsulin, known as the C-peptide, leaving insulin. Both molecules are then released by emiocytosis in beta granules. The insulin becomes active in the bloodstream and is free to act on muscle, adipose tissue, and other insulin-dependent sites, facilitating the entry of blood glucose into these cells, and to act on liver glucose metabolism.

The mechanism by which insulin facilitates glucose entry into cells is not completely understood. The entry appears to be facilitated by diffusion, which requires a membrane-bound carrier mechanism. Insulin receptors have been identified in many cells and appear to be membrane glycoproteins. Binding of insulin to these receptors may in some way activate the glucose-carrier system, perhaps by dramatically altering the mosaic structure of the lipoprotein membrane. Not all cells require insulin for glucose entry, although some of them nevertheless appear to have receptor sites. The liver, blood cells, and brain do not need insulin in order for rapid glucose entry to occur.

Glucose use by the body is much more complex than simple dependence on glucose entry into cells. Insulin is known to have both profound and subtle effects (Table 19-5) on metabolism generally, most of which contribute in some way to the maintenance of normoglycemia. The whole direction of insulin function appears to be toward glucose use, fat storage, and protein anabolism. These actions are opposed by several other hormones. Metabolic balance is ultimately determined by hormonal balance.

Type I and type II diabetes mellitus

There are at least two distinct diseases that are classified as diabetes mellitus. *Type I diabetes mellitus* was formerly known as juvenile diabetes, since it most commonly appears during childhood. Only 10% of all diabetes mellitus is type I, and it is characterized by a true lack of insulin production by the pancreas. Type I diabetes is commonly associated with weight loss, rather sudden onset, growth retardation, and volatile, poorly regulated metabolism. Frequent swings in blood glucose levels are common, and ketoacidosis is often observed. Although children are most commonly affected, lean adults do develop the disease as well.

The evidence that a viral infection or possibly an autoimmune response to a viral illness is responsible for type I diabetes has largely been circumstantial. There is an association of its occurrence with viral epidemics, and there is a seasonal pattern to its occurrence. The onset is usually extremely abrupt and occurs in previously well individuals (usually children). However, it is now apparent that the onset is preceded by a long, latent period during which pancreatic beta cells are lost. Viruses that have been possibly implicated include mumps virus, rubella virus, and coxsackievirus. These viruses have been shown to cause type I diabetes in laboratory animals. Children with rubella syndrome have a higher than normal incidence of type I diabetes. There has been a reported increase in the incidence of diabetes in Baltimore following a mumps vaccination program.

Table 19-5. Effects of insulin on tissues (summary of the three major target organs of insulin)

Liver	Adipose tissue	Muscle
Increased glycogen synthesis	Increased glucose transport	Increased glucose transport
Decreased gluconeogenesis	Increased formation of a α glycerophos-phate and triglyceride synthesis	Increased oxidative metabolism of glucose
Increased triglyceride synthesis	Increased fatty acid transport into adi-pocytes by activation of lipoprotein li-pase on adipocyte membrane	Increased glycogen synthesis
Increased very low–density li-poproteins	Decreased cyclic AMP, decreased ac-tivity of hormone-sensitive lipase in adipocyte, and decreased triglyceride mobilization	Increased amino acid transport and protein synthesis
Decreased glycogenolysis		Decreased amino acid release from muscle cell

Pathogenesis

Type I diabetes is associated with inflammatory changes in the islets, an insulitis that appears to have an autoimmune component. The genetics of type I diabetes involve the HLA antigens. As was discussed in Chapter 2, the mechanisms of autoimmunological attack involve T lymphocytes, which respond to antigen once it is processed by antigen-presenting cells with the same histocompatibility antigens as themselves. Expression of these antigens is influenced by physiological factors. It is possible that a class of histocompatibility antigens, the class II MHC antigens, become inappropriately expressed by pancreatic insulin-producing cells. The cell surface antigens are then presented to T cells, which react to them as foreign, and an autoimmunological destruction of the islet cells ensues. Class I MHC antigens are also hyperexpressed on islet cells, and this may be the initial event leading to type I diabetes. All the cells in the islet show this phenomenon, including glucagon and somatostatin-secreting cells (Foulis, 1987). It is possible that some immunological mediator such as interferon may be involved in this initial MHC hyperexpression, and the most likely candidate for stimulating interferon secretion is viral infection. Evi-

dence for a viral involvement in type I diabetes has come from several sources. Pancreatic specimens obtained at autopsy from diabetics have cultured out coxsackie virus B. The other evidence is that some patients with diabetes have serological titers to this virus. Pancreatic infection could cause insulitis and in susceptible patients with the HLA-DP, DQ, DR subtype of the class II MHC, a resultant inflammatory response could cause first the class I MHC hyperexpression, which then secondarily results in class II MHC expression on the beta cells. The inappropriate expression causes T cells bearing these same antigens to commence an autoimmunological attack on the beta cells, with destruction over time of the islets. This sequence is diagrammed in Fig. 19-12 and combines the current thinking of HLA genotype, viral infection, and autoimmunity.

The treatment rationale for type I diabetes has been altered in recent years on the basis of this research. Since these mechanisms involving autoimmunological attack probably take considerable time before complete ablation of pancreatic beta cells is present, immunological suppression is a new approach to treatment. The rationale is that T cell suppression may inhibit the progression of insulitis, and per-

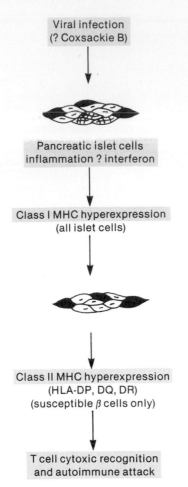

Viral infection
(? Coxsackie B)

Pancreatic islet cells
inflammation ? interferon

Class I MHC hyperexpression
(all islet cells)

Class II MHC hyperexpression
(HLA-DP, DQ, DR)
(susceptible β cells only)

T cell cytoxic recognition
and autoimmune attack

Fig. 19-12. Sequence of inflammatory changes following an initial viral infection in pancreatic islet cells.

haps some insulin-secreting capacity can be maintained. Pancreatic transplants, along with immunological suppression, are also used. However, in monozygotic twin transplants it has been observed that autoimmunological attack of the transplanted pancreas occurs when immunological suppression does not accompany the transplant (Foulis, 1987). This implies that specific cytotoxic T cells are long lived and are capable of recognizing and attacking pancreatic beta cells. Relatives of diabetics who are at risk because of the specific HLA genotype can be screened for genotype, for metabolic abnormalities, and for islet cell antibodies, which may be present for years before any signs of diabetes are detectable. However, about 40% to 50% of the general population has at least one of the HLA subtypes that are associated with diabetes.

Type II diabetes mellitus is noninsulin-dependent diabetes, formerly known as maturity- or adult-onset diabetes. This disorder develops slowly, is usually seen in obese, sedentary adults, and is by far the most prevalent form of diabetes (affecting 9 to 10 million people or 90% of diabetics). There is usually no true lack of insulin secretion. The disease is apparently totally different than type I diabetes. Nevertheless, there is a refractoriness to insulin at the cell membrane receptor level. The development of type II diabetes is an extension of all of the pathophysiological changes seen in obesity with one important difference. In obesity, insulin-resistance at the cellular level is compensated for by hypersecretion of insulin. In diabetes the pancreas does not make up for insulin resistance by enough insulin secretion, and the liver produces excess glucose—causing significant hyperglycemia (Kolata, 1987). Type II diabetes is also characterized by an abnormally regulated or decreased insulin release in response to increased blood glucose levels. Therefore some researchers have suggested that the primary defect is at the level of the pancreatic glucostat's sensing of blood glucose level, which would normally be the initial step in the release of insulin by the pancreas. However, it is equally possible that the initial step in the pathogenesis of the disease is the high level of circulating insulin that occurs in obesity. This "insulinizes" the cells, making them more resistant to the action of insulin, and further increases the demands on an already overburdened pancreas. The phenomenon of "down-regulation" may be important in the refractoriness that develops at the membrane level. Endocrine-dependent cells often respond to increases in hormone concentration by a decrease in the number of available membrane receptors. In type II diabetes, there is an inverse correlation between the insulin concentration in the blood and the number of available cell membrane receptors. Therefore it would appear that the increased blood insulin concentration causes the insulin-dependent cells to become less and less responsive to insulin. Eventually a state is reached in which clinical diabetes appears. It is characterized by inappropriate hyperglycemia, glucosuria, and an abnormal glucose tolerance test. Only rarely does ketoacidosis appear as a complication in type II diabetes.

Type II diabetes is much more accessible to treatment or even cure compared to type I. Type I diabetes essentially requires life-long insulin administration, since the pancreas is unable to produce insulin. Type II diabetes is largely an environmental disease, in that obesity is largely its cause in the genetically susceptible adult. Therefore weight loss, exercise, and proper nutrition can result in a cure. Weight loss by itself has been shown to increase the number of insulin receptors. In addition, oral hypoglycemia agents, traditionally used to treat type II diabetes, may act by increasing both the number of receptors and the insulin binding to cells. Treatment of both diseases will be discussed later in this section.

Diagnosis

The signs and symptoms of diabetes mellitus may develop insidiously. The major symptoms are polydipsia, polyphagia, and polyuria. The individual may complain of headaches and weakness and have other vague feelings of malaise. There is often a family history of diabetes, and obesity may be present, particularly in females. Women often have a history of repeated miscarriages and report having extremely large infants, often in excess of 4500 g (10 lbs) in birth weight. Patients may also report postprandial hypoglycemia. Occasionally cataracts and xanthomas may be present, and some patients may show early signs of vascular disease, particularly in the feet. Intermittent claudication is frequently present, and the feet are cold and hairless, all signs that indicte atherosclerotic changes in leg vessels. Ophthalmoscopic examination may show vascular changes in eyegrounds, and neurologic examination may show neuropathy. Signs of infection or a history of suceptibility to infection may be present as well.

Diagnosis is done on the basis of a glucose tolerance test, since the blood glucose may not be particularly elevated at the time of blood sampling, and the urinary glucose and ketones are absent in most cases. The normal and diabetic glucose tolerance tests are diagramed in Fig. 19-13. The diabetic blood glucose concentration remains over 160 mg/100 ml at 1 hour following the glucose meal and is over 120 mg/100 ml at 2 hours after the glucose meal. If the test is continued, hypoglycemia may develop in certain individuals. The deficiency in the diabetic appears to be a delayed peak insulin secretion in response to elevated blood glucose, occurring about 2 hours after a meal in the diabetic and much earlier, usually within 30 minutes after a meal, in the normal individual. Thus the diabetic remains hyperglycemic after a meal for a much longer period than normal. It has recently been shown that pulsatile insulin secretion is

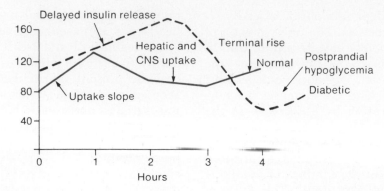

Fig. 19-13. Dotted line indicates a diabetic glucose tolerance test (GTT), and unbroken line shows normal response to glucose "meal." As a result of delay in insulin release following glucose ingestion, prediabetic and diabetic patients experience prolonged period of postprandial hyperglycemia.

disordered in early type II diabetes and that this may be an important pathogenic feature (O'Rahilly, Turner, and Matthews, 1988).

The effects of excess glucose in the blood are still being investigated in many laboratories, but the idea that the glucose molecule itself, in excess, does not have a toxic effect on cells is gradually being discarded. Glucose, for example, has been shown to have an effect on the polyol pathway (in which glucose is metabolized to sorbitol and then to fructose) in the walls of vessels and in the lens of the eye. These effects may contribute to atherosclerosis and cataracts, both of which are serious complications of diabetes. Excess glucose may increase glycosylation of various proteins. The nature and function of protein would be seriously altered by such a chemical reaction. Hemoglobin glycosylation is now used clinically as an index of diabetic control.

Pathophysiologic manifestations

Diuresis. Glucose causes osmotic diuresis when the blood glucose is elevated to levels that exceed the capacity of the kidney to reabsorb it. Glucose remains in the tubular filtrate and is excreted in the urine. Establishment of hyperosmolarity by excess glucose molecules in the tubular filtrate causes water to osmose from the interstitium through the tubular cells to reach an isosmotic concentration. Electrolytes also are present and retained in the tubular filtrate. The increased water drawn to the tubular filtrate will dilute Na^+ ions and cause the reabsorption of Na^+ to be diminished. The loss of water and electrolytes results in increased extracellular osmolarity and cellular dehydration. Thus these patients will have an extreme thirst (polydipsia) to replace the fluid that has been lost through the polyuria of osmotic diuresis.

Metabolism. Figs. 19-7, 19-8, and 19-14 show the patterns of metabolism in the fed state, the fasted state, and the diabetic state. Diabetes resembles starvation in that fatty acids by necessity become the major source of energy when glucose cannot be taken up in the insulin-dependent cells. Thus ketone bodies are formed in the liver and carried through the bloodstream to the heart, lungs, and other organs for use. This produces a state of ketonemia, along with the hyperglycemia and meta-

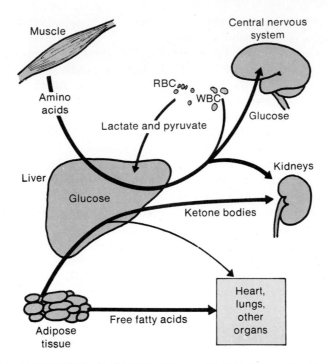

Fig. 19-14. Diabetic ketoacidosis. In diabetes, absence of insulin or presence of cellular refractoriness to insulin results in use of fatty acids for ketone body formation and amino acids for gluconeogenesis. Central nervous system requires glucose for energy and is supplied with glucose at expense of muscle protein. Insulin is not required for glucose transport in brain. Other tissues can use fatty acids and ketone bodies, but increased concentration of these substances in plasma leads to metabolic acidosis.

(From Bacchus, H: Essentials of metabolic disease and endocrinology, Baltimore, 1976, University Park Press.)

bolic acidosis, since the ketone bodies are acidic. The development of ketoacidosis may be precipitated by a number of factors in the diabetic, including infection, stress, surgery, emotional disturbance, and pregnancy; in fact, the prediabetic may show overt diabetes at these times, and thus the penetrance of the disease is precipitated by such factors. The most common cause of diabetic ketoacidosis, however, is omission of insulin in the diabetic patient.

Diabetic ketoacidosis. The signs and symptoms of ketoacidosis include ketonuria, dehydration following polyuria, dry skin, acetone odor on the breath, tachycar-

dia, hypotension, central nervous system depression, and Kussmaul breathing, which is a pattern of respiration in which heavy, labored hyperpnea occurs. Other more variable signs include abdominal pain, anorexia, nausea, and vomiting. The appearance of diabetic ketoacidosis constitutes a medical emergency requiring immediate treatment. Ketosis without acidosis can usually be treated outside the hospital and can be differentiated from metabolic acidosis by a blood pH of over 7.3 and a HCO_3^- of over 15 mEq/L. Since the dehydration that develops in this state contributes markedly to the pathophysiology of increasing ketoacid concentration and cardiovascular effects of hypovolemia, an immediate measure is hydration to correct the hypovolemia and hypotension. Other goals of therapy are to block lipolysis and promote lipogenesis. Therefore insulin is administered promptly, usually intravenously in the crystalline zinc form. The acidosis will be corrected by the rehydration and insulin administration if renal function is not impaired, but alkali is often given during the acute stage in the form of sodium bicarbonate when the pH is 7 or below. Electrolytes are also replaced as soon as the patient is rehydrated and kidney function is normal. Potassium chloride (20 to 30 mEq/hour) is usually added to the intravenous infusion. The patient in diabetic coma should become stabilized about 8 hours after therapy is instituted. If untreated, the diabetic in ketoacidosis will eventually drop into a deeply stuporous and then comatose state, and respiratory and cardiac failure will cause death.

Other forms of diabetic coma. It has become apparent that ketoacidosis is not the only possible cause of central nervous system depression and coma production in the diabetic. Two other major etiologies have been identified: *hyperosmolar nonketotic coma* and *lactic acidosis.*

Hyperosmolar nonketotic coma (Fig. 19-15) develops most frequently in diabetics with sufficient insulin production to depress excessive lipolysis but not enough to permit glucose use and transport across cell membranes. Thus hyperglycemia is present and induces osmotic diuresis, leading to thirst and subsequent ingestion of fluid, most of which often contains large amounts of sugar. The plasma osmolarity is often in excess of 350 mosmol/kg, and the blood glucose is often greater than 600 mg/100 ml. These abnormalities produce a major change in the sensorium and lead often to a condition of increased fluid in-

take, thus aggravating the hyperosmolarity and hyperglycemia. The blood and urine tests for ketones are negative or show a slight increase in concentration. The osmotic diuresis, which dilutes the sodium and other ions present in the tubular filtrate of the kidney, will increase the concentration gradient against which sodium is reabsorbed, so that absolute hyponatremia develops. However, in terms of the extracellular fluid, hyperosmolarity is present, since water is being lost in excess of solute through the kidney. The glomerular filtration rate will decrease drastically as the hyperosmolarity develops, and both azotemia and further increases in blood glucose result. This condition may develop quite slowly, in contrast to ketoacidosis, and may be precipitated by renal disease, cerebrovascular accidents, cardiovascular disease, infections, sepsis, and stress. The mortality rate approaches 40%. The treatment is rehydration, administration of small, spaced doses of insulin, and replacement of potassium, as hypokalemia is a serious problem in these individuals and is exacerbated by the restoration of glucose metabolism.

Lactic acidosis in diabetics can cause a comatose state that carries with it a high mortality rate. The blood sugar level may be normal, whereas blood ketoacids are often increased. There is often dehydration, hypotension, and hyperventilation. Lactic acid is produced normally in amounts of 1500 mmole per day in adults but is equally used to form pyruvate. Generation of excess lactic acid is an effect of cellular hypoxia, which results in increased anaerobic glycolysis, a high $NADH:NAD$ ratio, and defective oxidative metabolism. Cellular hypoxia is, of course, a condition found in a number of disease states, as well as being a normal occurrence following muscular exercise. Diabetics often have chronic disease conditions that pre-

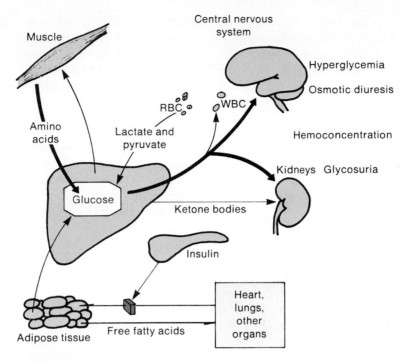

Fig. 19-15. Hyperosmolar nonketotic coma. There is enough insulin for lipogenesis but not enough to permit glucose transport across cell membranes. Thus hyperglycemia occurs without ketosis. Dehydration can lead to hypovolemic shock.

(From Bacchus, H: Essentials of metabolic disease and endocrinology, Baltimore, 1976, University Park Press.)

dispose them to cellular hypoxia. These include cerebrovascular and cardiovascular disease, which may produce tissue ischemia. The treatment of lactic acidosis is aimed at alleviating the acidosis and treating the underlying cause of the excessive lactic acid production, which, of course, may be multifactorial and complex.

It should be mentioned that a coma may also occur in severe hypoglycemia, which may be induced in the diabetic by insulin overdose. Therefore the differential diagnosis of coma in the diabetic must also include the possibility of insulin reaction. The treatment is infusion of a bolus of glucose, which has a dramatic and immediate arousing effect.

Chronic complications of diabetes. Although most diabetics can be maintained by diet and oral hypoglycemic agents or insulin, the development of long-term chronic pathologic changes in many tissues and organs is frequently a concomitant of the disease. In general, the type I diabetic with an absolute loss of insulin production capability is most susceptible to complications, but all diabetics may exhibit the following complications to some degree: retinopathy, neuropathy, peripheral vascular disease, atherosclerotic heart disease, and nephropathy. To a large degree all these conditions can be in part or fully explained by characteristic changes that occur in small and larger blood vessels, i.e., diabetic microangiopathy and macroangiopathy. The pathogenesis of these vascular conditions is a matter of much debate at the present time, and the basic etiology is unknown. Nevertheless, these vascular changes account for most of the mortality directly caused by diabetes.

The primary lesion in microangiopathy is thought by some to be capillary basement membrane thickening and biochemical changes in the glucoprotein composition of this structure. These changes appear to occur slowly over the life span of the diabetic, leading eventually to interruption in the patency of the vessels involved and thus to hypoxia and ischemia of the area supplied by these vessels. It is possible that the cells that produce the basement membrane are at fault in the diabetic and that some abnormal metabolic functioning is responsible for basement membrane alterations. The hyperglycemia present in diabetes may cause these cellular alterations, as might the insulin resistance. Another possibility is the increased growth hormone and irregular fluctuations in its concentration that often are observed in diabetes. Hypophysectomy delays the development of diabetic microangiopathy when patients are provided with all the pituitary hormones except growth hormone.

Diabetic *macroangiopathy* also occurs, but it is not well characterized. Medial calcification, which is correlated with the degree of glucose intolerance, has been observed, and roughening of the contours of the vessels occurs. These specific changes are to be differentiated from atherosclerosis, which arises in the intima and is also common in the diabetic; atherosclerosis is most likely related to hyperlipidemia. However, all of the vascular changes will act together to cause a deficient oxygenation of tissues and specific changes related to hypoxia and ischemia of various organs.

Nephropathy. A specific and distinctive lesion occurs in the kidney of the diabetic and may develop even before the diabetes is overtly manifested. It is a round hyaline mass in the glomerulus, the Kimmelstiel-Wilson nodule. Other nonspecific changes in the vessels of the kidney also occur and are the result of thickening of the basement membrane of the capillaries. Ischemia of the glomeruli result from this microangiopathy, and the disease process is termed *diffuse intercapillary glomerulosclerosis.* The kidney is often hypertrophied, and both kidneys are usually involved. The incidence of renal involvement in diabetes appears to be extremely high, but overt kidney disease such as nephrosis and renal failure may not result. The manifestation of renal involvement usually begins with proteinuria. Edema may also develop, and hypertension may be aggravated. Frank nephrosis is not common but can develop. The eventual outcome of progressive renal nephropathy is azotemia, uremia, and eventually death in kidney failure. The treatment of diabetic nephropathy usually is symptomatic and often involves reduction in insulin because of a decreased degradation of circulating insulin by the damaged kidney. Renal hemodialysis and transplantation are also possible treatments.

Retinopathy. Diabetic retinopathy develops with time, and 80% of those diabetics known to have the disease for 20 years have some degree of retinopathy. Occasionally in type I diabetes, retinopathy develops rapidly, causing blindness by late adolescence. There is a positive correlation between the severity of retinopathy and the degree of vascular disease in general. There are a number of types of retinopathy, the two most common being caused by progressive accumulation of hard, lipidlike exudates or by obstruction of the retinal circulation. Diabetic retinopathy causes more blindness in the United States than does any other condition.

Neuropathy. Diabetic neuropathies are of three major types (1) symmetric sensory disturbances, (2) asymmetric sensory and motor disturbances, and (3) autonomic neuropathies. Neuropathy of one sort or another is common in all diabetics. The signs and symptoms can be extremely variable, and the differential diagnosis quite complicated. Many times peripheral polyneuropathy of a predominantly sensory nature occurs, and the diabetic may have peculiar sensations in both the upper and lower extremities. Eventually motor impairment may also result, causing weakness. Usually these processes are bilateral, but asymmetric neuropathy may also occur. Autonomic neuropathy often is found in conjunction with peripheral neuropathy and is most frequently exhibited by postural hypotension. Other possible effects of autonomic neuropathy include impotence, gastrointestinal disturbances, paralytic bladder, and extraocular muscle paralysis. The pathophysiologic basis of neuropathy was traditionally based on ischemic changes in the nerves caused by angiopathy of the vessels that supply them. Research on glucose metabolism implicates accumulation of sorbitol in the pathogenesis of neuropathy. Sorbitol retention may lead to injury and decreased nerve conduction velocity and may also interfere with the metabolism of Schwann cells, which produce myelin. Segmental demyelination of the nerves is a common finding in diabetic neuropathy.

Atherosclerotic coronary artery disease. The diabetic is more at risk, at least in Western societies, to develop coronary artery disease, and the same factors that predispose the normal individual to atherosclerosis also operate in the diabetic. Coronary artery disease and myocardial infarctions occur with high incidence among diabetics, irrespective of sex, and

at an earlier age than in the normal population. The pathophysiology of atherosclerosis is no clearer in the diabetic than in the nondiabetic. Multiple factors appear to be involved, including hyperglycemia, hyperlipidemia with hypertriglyceridemia, high cholesterol level, hypertension, obesity, physical inactivity, behavior pattern type A, and smoking. There is no question that the development of atherosclerosis and the associated coronary artery disease, cerebrovascular disease, and peripheral vascular disease is accelerated markedly in the diabetic. Furthermore, evidence is accumulating to suggest that reduction of hyperglycemia and a diet low in simple carbohydrates and saturated fats with weight reduction, stress reduction, and exercise can all contribute to an amelioration of atherosclerotic disease.

The signs and symptoms of atherosclerosis are related to the degree of plaque deposition and the anatomic location of the involved vessels. The incidence of myocardial infarction and cerebrovascular accidents is high, and atherosclerosis contributes to the peripheral vascular disease.

Peripheral vascular disease. The diabetic patient often suffers greatly from impaired circulation, particularly of the extremities. Such individuals often show evidence of ulceration, infection, and eventually gangrene, phenomena that develop most commonly in the feet. Signs of peripheral vascular disease of the lower extremity include pallor on elevation of the foot and rubor or hyperemia upon dependence of the limb. Venous filling time is a good test of the adequacy of tissue perfusion in the leg. When major arterial occlusion occurs in an extremity, the patient is extremely susceptible to infection, and ulceration may eventually progress to abscess and cellulitis and ultimately to necrosis and gangrene. Amputation of the part is the only recourse at that time. Surgical revascularization can be performed when the tissue ischemic process is in a fairly early stage. A significant percentage of the diabetic patients with venous stasis and ulceration do not have peripheral vascular disease per se. They often have a history of minor trauma to the part, which rapidly develops into the progressive ulcerative process just described. It is not understood exactly what mechanisms are operative in this situation, but neuropathy and angiopathy may both play roles. These patients obviously cannot benefit from revascularization surgery, and treatment is aimed at alleviating discomfort, avoiding further trauma, and maintaining factors that aid in wound healing.

Diabetics also often have an associated dermopathy, which may be related to peripheral vascular disease, to insulin, or to the diabetic disease process itself. Furthermore, the diabetic is more susceptible to infections of the skin and all other tissues, and a constant vigilance must be maintained so that early treatment can be instituted. Prevention of infection is a major factor for those who care for diabetics.

Treatment rationale

Type I diabetes. Treatments of the two major forms of diabetes differ greatly. Obviously, type I diabetics must be supplied with a source of insulin. Generally insulin is injected parenterally according to the patient's needs. Both long-acting and short-acting insulins are commonly used to control the blood glucose levels. Individuals may titrate the amount of insulin that is needed on a daily basis, depending on diet, exercise, and stress. Newer approaches to therapy include the artificial pancreas, which is a device permitting constant intravenous infusion of insulin into the body fluids, in response to changing blood glucose. This mechanism has been dubbed the "artificial pancreas" since it basically acts like the pancreas in its ability to sense blood glucose levels. However the device requires a computer to calculate the proper dosage, and because of its large size the patient essentially must be bedridden. The glucose sensors currently used have a short period of usefulness and must be changed every few hours. Another device, the insulin pump, does not have all the features of the artificial pancreas, but it permits much greater mobility. This device infuses insulin subcutaneously rather than intravenously, and it can be taped to the abdominal wall since it is about the size of a small tape recorder. It can be programmed to deliver a basal insulin release as well as a higher rate of release following meals. Insulin pumps control the blood glucose level more accurately than do discontinuous insulin injections, but they are not without fault. For example, for the pump to produce best results, the patient must adhere to a strict regimen of diet and exercise. Unfortunately not all diabetics are able to do this consistently.

An experimental approach to diabetes control is an attempt to produce a living culture of pancreatic beta cells that can be transplanted into the body and against which no immunity would develop. Pancreatic cells have been cultured in vitro on hollow, selectively permeable, polymer fibers. In the future these pancreatic cell transplants may be introduced into a diabetic's body in such a way that they will function as a replacement for the damaged pancreas.

Another future approach to type I diabetes therapy is the possibility of pancreatic transplants from an appropriate donor. Some attempts have also been made to transplant suspensions of beta cells into various parts of the body. The greatest problem with such approaches is immunologic rejection.

Type II diabetes. The treatment of type II diabetes is entirely different from that for type I. Traditionally these diabetics have been treated with oral hypoglycemic agents, diet, weight loss, and exercise. Occasionally insulin will also be administered. The question of administration of the oral hypoglycemic agents or insulin to type II diabetics is a matter of serious consideration since the findings of the University Group Diabetes Program (UGDP) have been made available. This study of the long-range problems of diabetics on insulin or oral hypoglycemic agents showed that treatment of hyperglycemic, obese adults with either insulin or oral hypoglycemic agents did not reduce the mortality or affect the incidence of microangiopathy. In fact, the UGDP studies indicated that cardiovascular disease-related mortality was higher in patients receiving tolbutamide and phenformin than in patients receiving placebos or insulin. This occurred despite the fact that the fasting blood glucose concentration in these individuals was on the average 112 mg/100 ml. Therefore it would seem that treatment of type II diabetics with drugs might not be warranted and that diet alone could be used to maintain these individuals.

The diabetic diet has traditionally been low in carbohydrates and high in fat. The observation that diabetics in Asia and Latin America have a much lower incidence of cardiovascular disease than do those in North America implicates exogenous factors, most probably dietary. The diet that now appears most protective of cardiovascular disease is *high in starch, low in refined sugars, and low in saturated animal fats.* This diet derives 25% to 35% of its calories from fat, one third of which is polyunsaturated. Between 40% and 55% of the calories are derived from carbohydrates, which are mainly starch, with the rest of the sugars being derived from fruits, vegetables, and milk. This limits the total cholesterol intake to 300 to 400 mg per day. The aim of this diet is not only to control refined sugar and saturated fats but also to control calories. Apparently when the calories are controlled, a diet high in starch does not produce uncontrolled hyperglycemia or hyperlipidemia. The addition of rather large amounts of dietary fiber has also been recently shown to control type II diabetes. This diet, which is recommended by both the American Diabetes Association and the American Heart Association, is controversial since a high carbohydrate diet results in an increased insulin secretion in both nondiabetics and type I diabetics, and high levels of insulin are associated with low levels of very low–density lipoproteins, which increases heart disease risk.

Use of insulin is also under scrutiny for type II diabetics and presents a problem when the adult diabetic with fasting hyperglycemia does not lose weight. These patients often require insulin to control hyperglycemia, since they do not limit their calories, control their weight, and follow prescribed diets.

Normally 30 to 50 units of insulin are released daily into the portal vein from the pancreas and thus are immediately removed in large part by the liver, providing for hepatic control mechanisms on blood insulin concentration. This is not the case when insulin is injected parenterally and therefore is absorbed irrespective of need. Pulsatile delivery of insulin is believed to be much more physiologic than single injections or parenteral infusion. It is recommended that the diabetic be administered the least possible amount of insulin to control fasting hyperglycemia. Certain situations may arise that will increase the need for insulin. These include surgery, pregnancy, infections, and glucocorticoid administration. Exercise may decrease the need for insulin, as will significant weight loss in the obese individual.

The following case study is a fairly typical presentation of type I diabetes. The subject is an 8-year-old child, who has had the disease for 4 years.

CASE STUDY: TYPE I DIABETES

History

AL is an 8-year-old female with a history of insulin-dependent diabetes mellitus (type I). AL has no other history of significant illness, and she is developmentally appropriate according to the Denver Developmental Screening Test. Despite her young age AL is compliant with her diabetic regime and is responsible for a large part of her diabetic management. She performs her own Chemstrips and insulin injections, and is involved with her mother in planning her dietary regime. Since AL was first diagnosed at age 4, her diabetes has been relatively well controlled. Her mother reports only 2 incidents, both associated with upper respiratory infections, requiring hospitalization to stabilize her blood glucose (BG) level. However, in the month preceding the current hospital admission, AL experienced three episodes of diabetic ketoacidosis (DKA), all of which resulted in emergency hospitalization.

Present illness: AL was admitted to the hospital through the emergency room, only 3 days following discharge from her previous DKA-related hospitalization. According to her mother, AL complained of stomach cramps and vomited three times during the afternoon. She had taken her usual insulin dosages, but ate little of her

Contributed by Elizabeth Wharton.

lunch and dinner. Initial examination revealed the following:

Physical examination

General appearance: mildly lethargic, arouseable

Subjective and Objective Data

Vital signs

Temperature: 99.2° F
Pulse: 160
Respiration: 42
Blood pressure: 103/55

Skin: Cool, clammy, pink

PERRLA

Respiratory: Slightly Kussmaul, with acetone breath

Cardiovascular: Normal sinus rhythm with tachycardia peripheral pulses + 1; capillary refill > 3 seconds.

Neurological

DTRS 3+, otherwise WNL

Significant laboratory values

SMA-6	K	5.4
	Na	140
	Cl	101
	BUN	15
	Glucose	632
ABG	pH	7.162
	pCO2	13
	pO2	80
	HCO3	4.6

Dextrostix (urine): 1000 mg/dl glucose trace acetone pH 6.5

Urine specific gravity: 1.03

Intake/Output - 24 hrs. following admission: 3789 cc/1670 cc.

Treatment

AL was diagnosed to be in diabetic ketoacidosis (DKA) and was treated with insulin and fluid and electrolyte replacement.

2 U/hour regular Humulin insulin in normal saline at 14.5 cc/hr.

D5 in ½ NS with 15 mEq/L KCl and 15 mEq/L KPO4 at 330 cc/hr. She was transferred to the Pediatric Intensive Care Unit so that cardiac monitoring could be done.

Pathophysiology

Difficulties in glucose regulation of type I diabetes arise as a result of patient compliance and normal growth demands of childhood and stress and activity level.

AL was admitted to the hospital in a state of marked hyperglycemia, as evidenced by a blood glucose level of 632 mg/dl. One consequence of this is an increased intracellular fluid shift to the extracellular spaces, resulting in cellular dehydration. In addition, as osmolarity exceeds the renal threshold, osmotic diuresis and glucose spilling ensue. In this situation the excess solute load exceeds the pumping capacity of the renal tubules, so that solutes such as glucose and electrolytes remain in the renal filtrate and are excreted. As the tubular osmotic load is increased, the countercurrent exchange mechanism for water conservation becomes ineffective, and excess fluid is excreted through the urine. This is true despite the presence of ADH, which is secreted in response to high serum osmolarity. In this way, fluid, glucose, and electrolytes are lost from the body. These mechanisms account for many signs and symptoms of hyperglycemia such as polyuria, polydipsia, and electrolyte depletion. AL presented symptoms of dehydration, including lethargy and cool clammy skin. Accurate records of AL's fluid intake and output were not kept before admission.

Following admission, AL's intake exceeded output indicating rehydration was occurring. Dextrostix urine testing on admission indicated glucosuria (1000 mg/dl glucose). Urine specific gravity was high at 1.03. Serum electrolyte levels were normal at admission, but this could be a result of the concentrating effect of dehydration, since hyponatremia and hypokalemia are often present.

In addition to the osmotic effects of hyperglycemia, insulin deficiency results in cellular starvation. The body mobilizes lipids and amino acids to use as alternative fuel sources. A reversal of triglyceride storage occurs so that free fatty acids are released into circulation. Perhaps the most powerful catabolic mechanism is the secretion of ACTH which stimulates of the adrenal cortex to release glucocorticoids. This normally protective mechanism, which helps to prepare the body to deal with a stressor, becomes pathological in insulin deficiency. Glucocorticoids enhance gluconeogenesis through direct stimulation of liver enzymes. In addition, glucocorticoids provide substrate for gluconeogenesis as they act to mobilize amino acids and lipids from extrahepatic tissue. These effects exacerbate the preexisting hyperglycemic states and cause the deleterious symptoms of DKA.

Free fatty acids, released into the circulation in response to glucocorticosteroids, are converted to ketones such as acetoacetic acid in the liver. Acetoacetic acid can enter the Krebs cycle in most cells, thus providing fuel for the cell. However, cells have a limited capacity for ketone use; so that ketones accumulate in the blood resulting in ketoacidosis. AL exhibited several classic signs and symptoms of ketoacidosis upon admission. AL's breath had a typically fruity or acetone odor, indicating the presence of excess ketones in the blood. Urine also showed a trace of acetone. Blood pH was 7.162, indicating severe acidemia. Despite significant dehydration, AL's skin color was pink. This could be attributed to local vasodilation in response to acidosis. Her skin felt cool and clammy as a result of lack of perfusion. AL's anorexia and abdominal pain are symptoms often associated with DKA, but their cause is not clear.

Both the kidneys and lungs have compensatory mechanisms that function to normalize pH. Decreasing serum pH stimulates the respiratory center, so that breathing becomes abnormally fast and deep, as was noted at AL's admission. In this way extra CO_2 is expelled, partially compensating for the metabolic acidosis. As CO_2 is lost, HCO_3 levels are also re duced. This is clearly demonstrated in AL's ABG results.

pH 7.162
P_{CO_2} 13
P_{O_2} 80
HCO_3 4.6

Renal compensation occurs by means of increased excretion of H^+ through the renal tubules. This is accompanied by increased chloride and decreased potassium excretion. Whereas respiratory compensation is an immediate response, renal compensation does not take effect for 2 to 3 days. AL's SMA-6 values do not reflect any significant electrolyte disturbances at the time of admission.

It is important to note the effect of hyperglycemia on potassium. Potassium is lost through several routes, including tissue breakdown related to amino acid mobilization, loss through osmotic diuresis, and loss due to vomiting. In addition, potassium is excreted in response to aldosterone. Paradoxically, elevated serum potassium levels are not uncommon in the untreated patient. However this may not accurately reflect total body potassium status and instead may be the result of plasma volume contraction and metabolic acidosis, which causes potassium to shift to the extracellular spaces as $H+$ is buffered intracellularly. As fluid replacement and insulin therapy is begun, potassium deficiency generally becomes apparent. The most serious consequences of hypokalemia are related to changes in cardiac excitability potentially leading to atrial and ventricular arrythmias.

The 3+ DTRs noted in AL's admission history could possibly be accounted for by neuronal cell dehydration with resultant irritability.

Nursing Diagnoses

AL's overall history indicates compliance with the diabetic care regime. However, with a history of several recent ketoacidotic episodes it would be important to ascertain compliance more carefully, because of this child's age and developmental level. Therefore the following nursing diagnoses are suggested:
1. Potential for noncompliance related to maturational or situational factors
2. Potential fluid volume deficit related to decreased fluid intake and abnormal fluid loss
3. Altered peripheral tissue perfusion: related to hypovolemia
4. Altered body fluid composition: hyperkalemia related to dehydration
5. Potential for altered body fluid composition; hypokalemia related to depletion of total body K^+ and rehydration
6. Potential altered nutrition; less than body requirements due to diabetes

SUMMARY

This chapter has described the patterns of abnormal nutrition that may develop under diverse conditions of pathophysiology. These range from absolute lack of nutrients causing starvation to abnormalities in the metabolism of required nutrients, leading to absolute or relative excess or deficit. The possibilities of abnormalities in these thousands of processes by which the body maintains wellness are overwhelming. There has been no attempt to provide a comprehensive catalogue of these conditions. Rather, it is hoped that the mechanisms through which possible abnormalities may occur have been clarified, so that the student will be able to conceptualize and transfer this knowledge.

REFERENCES

Bacchus H: Essentials of metabolic diseases and endocrinology, Baltimore, 1976, University Park Press.

Bjoerntorp P, Vahouny G and Kritchevsky D: Dietary fiber and obesity, 1985, Alan R Liss.

Bjoerntorp P: The role of adipose tissue in human obesity. Greenwood M, editor. In Obesity, New York, Churchill Livingstone, Inc.

Bray G: Metabolism in positive energy balance. Hansen B, editor: In Controversies in obesity, 1933, Praeger Publishers.

Brownell K and Wadden T: Behavioral and self-help treatments. Greenwood M, editor: Obesity, New York, 1983, Churchill Livingston Inc.

Brunzell J: Obesity and risk for cardiovascular disease. In Greenwood M, editor: Obesity, New York, 1983, Churchill Livingstone Inc.

Burton RT, et al: Health implications of obesity: an NIH consensus, Int J Obes 9:155, 1985.

Capretti PJ, and Rawls LH: Establishment of flavor preference in rats: importance of nursing and weaning experience, J Comp Physiol Psychol 86:670, 1974.

Caro J, and Amatrudo J: Insulin receptors in hepatocytes: post receptor events mediate down regulation, Science, 210:1029, 1980.

Foulis A: The pathogenesis of beta cell destruction in Type I (insulin dependent) diabetes mellitus, J of Path, 152:141-148 (1987).

Garn S: Some consequences of being obese. In Hansen B, editor: Controversies in Obesity, 1983, Praeger Publishers New York.

Hirsch J, and Liebel R: New light on obesity, New Engl J Med 318, 509, 1988.

Hodgson P: Environmental sabotage. In Behavioral management of obesity, Storli J, and Jordan H, editors, Chicago, 1984, Life Enhancement Publications.

Kolata G: Obesity declared a disease, Science 227:1019, 1985.

Kolata G: Diabetics should lose weight, avoid diet fads, Science 235:163, 1987.

Le Magnen T: Regulation of food intake physiological-biochemical aspects (peripheral regulatory factors), Adv Psychosom Med 7:73, 1972.

Lin MH, et al: Heat production and Na^+-K^+ ATPase enzyme units in lean and obese (ob/ob) mice, Am J Physiol 238:E193, 1980.

Levine R, and Luft R, editors: Advances in metabolic disorders, vol 7, New York, 1974, Academic Press, Inc.

Levine R and Pfeifeer E, editors: Lipid metabolism, obesity, and diabetes: impact upon atherosclerosis, Stuttgart, 1974, George Thieme Verlag KG.

O'Rakilly S, Turner R, and Matthews D: Impaired pulsatile secretion of insulin in relatives of patients with non-insulin dependent diabetes, New Engl J Med 318:1225, 1988.

Ravussin E, et al: Reduced rate of energy expenditure as a risk factor for body-weight gain, New Engl J Med 318:467, 1988.

Romsos D: Efficiency of energy retention in genetically obese animals and in dietary-induced thermogenesis, Fed Proc 40(10):2524, 1981.

Schemmel R: Sources of energy during low intake and treatment of morbid obesity by complete or partial fasting, Nutr Physiol Obes 185, 1980.

Schteingart D, Butcher B, and Noonan R: Endorphins and obesity. In Hansen B, editor: Controversies in obesity, 1983, Praeger Publishers, New York.

Smith U: The adipose tissue and the metabolic complications of obesity. In Bjoerntorp P, Vahouny G, and Kritchevsky D, editors: Dietary fiber and obesity, 1985, Alan R. Liss.

Wadden T, et al: Less food, less hunger. Reports of appetite and symptoms in a controlled study of a protein-sparing modified fast, Int J Obes 11:239, 1987.

Elimination pattern

20

Altered elimination patterns and renal pathophysiology

Wellness depends on maintenance of chemical equilibrium, which in turn depends on the function of elimination. Through the skin, lungs, and genitourinary and gastrointestinal tracts the body selectively excretes the products of metabolism and any excess substances for which it has no need. Regulation of elimination is the key to the body's retention of those substances vital to its functioning and excretion of unnecessary toxic substances.

Presented in this chapter is an overview of the process and its regulation for each of the major routes of elimination, as well as a discussion of the effects of disruption of the normal processes of elimination on the chemical equilibrium and various organ systems of the body. Abnormal routes of elimination seen in the clinical situation will also be discussed.

The reader is referred to Chapter 16 for a discussion of the elimination of carbon dioxide and water via the lungs. This chapter deals chiefly with the skin and kidneys as organs of elimination. Altered patterns of elimination via the gastrointestinal tract are only introduced in this

chapter; specific disorders causing these disruptions are discussed in detail in Chapter 21.

THE SKIN

The skin serves many important functions in maintaining the steady state. First and foremost, the skin serves a protective function. It protects the internal organs from the effects of radiation, heat, cold, pressure, chemicals, and microorganisms. Specialized nerve endings in the skin provide cutaneous sensation, which makes an individual aware of potentially harmful conditions. The skin also is important in the retention of body fluids and temperature regulation.

The skin serves as an organ of elimination through perspiration. Under normal conditions, perspiration is more important in terms of body temperature regulation than as a process of elimination per se; however, significant disruption of the body's chemical equilibrium can occur as a result of alterations in the pattern of elimination via the skin.

Perspiration helps to regulate not only

body temperature but also excretion of fluid, sodium, and chloride. The excretory function of the skin can be observed directly when renal failure and uremia occur. The concentration of urea in the perspiration increases. As evaporation takes place and drying occurs, crystals of urea form and appear as a white powder on the skin, usually referred to as *uremic frost.*

Insensible perspiration is mainly composed of water, while sensible perspiration is a hypotonic solution containing primarily sodium and chloride but also lesser amounts of potassium, magnesium, ammonia, and urea. The concentration of the solutes is variable, as is the total amount of perspiration excreted. The rate of excretion depends on environmental temperature and humidity, the amount of clothing worn, the metabolic rate and body temperature, and athletic or physical conditioning to extreme temperature. The normal electrolyte concentration in the sweat is higher in adults than in children. Persons who have become acclimated to a hot environment have a more efficient sweat mechanism; they sweat more, but the concentration of electrolytes in the sweat is less than that of the sweat of a person who has not become acclimated to a hot environment.

Stimulation of the temperature-regulating center of the hypothalamus results in impulse transmission via the sympathetic system to the sweat glands. When stimulated the sweat glands secrete a precursor substance from which various substances are reabsorbed as the precursor substance flows through the duct portion of the glands. When sweat production is slow, for example, in the basal state, the concentrations of sodium and chloride are also low, probably as a result of the reabsorption of these substances from the precursor secretion before it reaches the surface of the

skin. As the rate of sweating increases, the rate of sodium and chloride reabsorption does not increase to a commensurate degree, and consequently the concentrations of sodium and chloride in the sweat increase. This is reflected in the difference between the electrolyte compositions of insensible and sensible perspiration. Reabsorption of sodium in the sweat glands is also under the control of aldosterone, which increases reabsorption of sodium in the ducts of the sweat glands in the same manner as it affects the kidney tubules. Chloride is reabsorbed along with the sodium in order to maintain electroneutrality.

The sodium concentration in perspiration normally is related to dietary intake, but even in the presence of a reduced or nonexistent intake of dietary sodium some sodium will continue to be lost in the sweat. Hence a great sodium loss can occur as a result of sweating in the normal individual who has a reduced intake of sodium.

The electrolyte composition of perspiration may also be related to the presence of some underlying disease state. For example, excess sodium and chloride in the sweat is an important feature of cystic fibrosis. Parents of children with cystic fibrosis have also been found to have greater than normal concentrations of electrolytes in their sweat; however, these differences are of no diagnostic importance since the difference is relatively small. A higher than normal concentration of electrolytes in the sweat, which is nonspecific, may also occur in the presence of chronic pulmonary disease.

Altered elimination patterns

Excessive perspiration. Excessive perspiration can be the result of a variety of conditions, including a hot, dry environment, heavy clothing, vigorous activity or exercise, fever, and fear or anxiety. Sweating occurs in pathologic conditions accompanied by sympathetic stimulation. Sweat is hypotonic to plasma; therefore relatively greater amounts of water than electrolytes will be lost. However, serious depletion of both body water and sodium may occur if the dietary intake of fluid and sodium is restricted or impaired during periods of excessive perspiration. Persons with high electrolyte levels in their sweat are especially susceptible to the development of a sodium deficit. Children with cystic fibrosis, for example, must be given supplemental salt during the summer months, and their parents should be advised to watch for signs of sodium depletion. Perhaps the results of excessive perspiration without adequate replacement of water and sodium are best exemplified by the disorder known as heat exhaustion (see Chapter 5). Excesssive sweating without water or salt replacement results in hypertonic contraction of the body fluid because water is lost in excess of solute (sodium). Excessive sweating with water replacement but without adequate salt replacement results in hypotonic contraction of the body fluid. The signs and symptoms of these disorders are discussed in Chapter 18.

Cessation of perspiration. Heat stroke is a serious disorder that results from the cessation of sweating following exposure to a hot and usually humid environment. The body is unable to dissipate heat, and the body temperature rises. If heat stroke is not treated, the body temperature will continue to rise, and cell death throughout the body will occur. Central nervous system dysfunction is a feature of this disorder in its prodromal stage; however, most victims are comatose before they receive medical attention (see Chapter 5).

Abnormal elimination resulting from impaired skin integrity

Under normal conditions the skin functions as a barrier to prevent the loss of body fluid to the external environment. When the integrity of the skin is broken, the body may lose significant amounts of body fluid. The fluid lost as a result of open, draining wounds, bedsores, abrasions, or skin lesions such as those seen in exfoliative dermatitis and pemphigus is similar to plasma in terms of electrolyte composition and protein content. A significant disruption of body fluid balance occurs when skin integrity is impaired due to a thermal injury (see Chapters 5 and 8). In severe burns, fluid is lost until the burn wound heals or is grafted; therefore emphasis is placed on maintaining adequate fluid and electrolyte replacement, especially in the immediate postburn period.

THE GENITOURINARY TRACT

The organs of the genitourinary system include the kidneys, ureters, bladder, and urethra. The excretory production of this system is urine, which contains metabolic end products, notably the nitrogenous waste products, urea and creatinine.

The kidneys have excretory, regulatory, metabolic, and endocrine functions and are largely responsible for the control of chemical equilibrium of the body fluid. The kidneys can produce glucose under certain conditions. The endocrine functions include the secretion of erythropoietin, prostaglandin, bradykinin, and renin. The hydroxylation of 25-hydroxycholecalciferol (25-OH vitamin D_3) to 1,25-dihy-

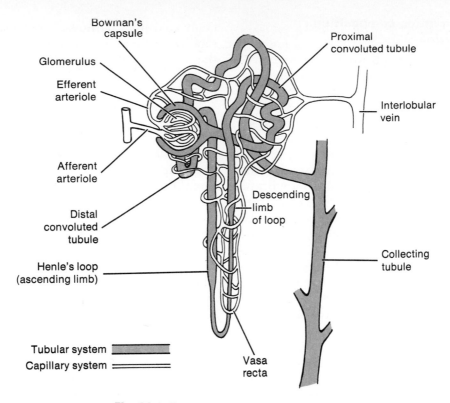

Fig. 20-1. Functional unit of kidney—nephron.

droxycholecalciferol $(1,25[OH]_2D_3)$, the active metabolite of vitamin D, also takes place in the kidney. The presence of this substance is necessary for the parathyroid hormone to have any effect on bone resorption in the maintenance of calcium homeostasis. Maintenance of a constant volume and composition of the body fluids depends greatly on renal response to neural or humoral mediators. For this to occur, renal receptor and effector sites must be intact and functioning.

Regulation of body fluid volume, composition, and pH by the kidneys is achieved through selective excretion, which involves the processes of filtration, reabsorption, and secretion in the functional unit of the kidney, the nephron. The nephron contains the glomerulus in Bowman's capsule, the proximal tubule, Henle's loop, the distal tubule, and the collecting tubule. The nephron is supplied with two capillary beds: the glomerular, which is a high pressure system, and the peritubular, which is a low pressure system that incorporates the vasa recta. Illustrated in Fig. 20-1 is the functional anatomy of the nephron.

Urine formation, composition, and excretion

As blood circulates through the glomerular capillary bed, *filtration*, the first step in urine formation, takes place across the glomerular membrane. Filtration (see Chapter 18) is enhanced and occurs more rapidly here than in other capillary beds because of the high-pressure system that exists and the unique construction of the glomerulus and the glomerular membrane (Fig. 20-2). The glomerular filtration rate (GFR) across the membrane is governed by the Starling forces and therefore is the difference between the sum of the hydrostatic and oncotic forces favoring filtration and the sum of those opposing it in proportion to the relatively permeability of the membrane. This relationship is expressed by the following equation:

$$GFR = K_f \text{ (favoring forces} - \text{opposing forces)}$$

The favoring forces include the hydrostatic pressure of the glomerular capillary and the oncotic pressure of Bowman's capsule, while the opposing forces include the hydrostatic pressure of Bowman's capsule and the oncotic pressure of the plasma within the capillary. K_f is the filtration coefficient, which normally is a constant, and is a function of the area across which filtration occurs and the permeability of the membrane itself. Both the area and the permeability of the glomerular capillary membrane are greater than that of any other capillary bed within the body.

Changes in the glomerular filtration rate, then, can be the result of changes in the permeability and/or surface area of the membrane, in the hydrostatic pressure on either side of the membrane, or in the oncotic pressure on either side of the membrane. The potential for alteration of the K_f exists when the glomerular membrane is affected by a pathologic process that alters its permeability or the surface area of the capillary bed is reduced due to destruction of glomerular tissue or surgical removal of part of the kidney.

The permeability of the membrane is related to its structure. It is composed of three layers (see Fig. 20-2): fenestrated endothelium, the basement membrane, and epithelial cells attached to the basement membrane by foot processes. Slit pores exist between the foot processes and are closed by a thin membrane, the slit diaphragm. The basement membrane is believed to be the major filtration barrier, with the slit diaphragm also believed to play a barrier role (Humes, 1986). Alteration of the structure of the membrane due to injury will affect its function through disruption of its intrinsic barrier properties.

The glomerular membrane is highly permeable to water and small solutes but demonstrates a selective permeability to larger solutes such as protein. There is an inverse relationship between molecular size and filtration rate: the larger the molecule, the lower the filtration rate (Brenner et al., 1978). This relative impermeability to the larger molecules accounts for the normal protein-free composition of the glomerular filtrate, which is similar to plasma in all other respects, and is important also in the maintenance of the plasma volume.

The molecular charge of the larger molecules is also responsible for this differential permeability. Filtration rates of negatively charged macromolecules are less than those of electrically neutral molecules of similar size while filtration rates of positively charged macromolecules are greater. An example of this concept is seen in the difference between the filtration ra-

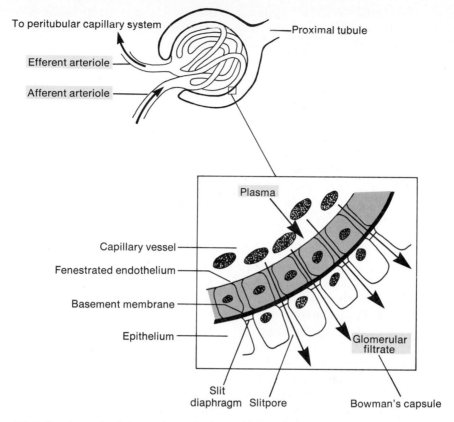

Fig. 20-2. Blood supply of glomerulus and schematic view of cellular structure of glomerular membrane. The mesangial matrix fills the core of the capillary network.

tios of albumin and dextran, two molecules of approximately equal size. Albumin normally carries a negative charge, while dextran carries no charge. The filtration rate of dextran is much greater than that of albumin under normal conditions. Dextran sulfate, which is the negatively charged form of dextran, is filtered in amounts similar to albumin, however. This effect is thought to result from the presence of negatively charged proteins in the glomerular capillary wall. These acidic glycoproteins, called sialoproteins, cause electrostatic repulsion of anions in the plasma (Brenner et al., 1978; Venkatachalam and Rennke, 1978). The loss of these negatively charged proteins from the capillary wall has been implicated as a causative mechanism in some renal diseases accompanied by the increased filtration and urinary loss of protein (Vernier et al., 1983; Kerjaschki et al., 1985).

The capillary hydrostatic pressure is determined by the systemic (aortic) pressure and the resistance afforded by the renal arterioles. Aortic pressure is not dissipated as readily in this system as it is in other capillary systems because of the anatomic structure of the renal arterial system. There are few subdivisions between the aorta and the glomerular capillary bed, and the arterial branches that do exist are short with relatively large diameters, allowing pressure to remain high within the system. The glomerular capillary bed, unlike others, is situated between two arterioles, and resistance to blood flow can be increased or decreased at either end, altering the hydrostatic pressure. Arteriolar resistance is intrinsically and sympathetically controlled in addition to being under hormonal control (angiotensin II and prostaglandins). Constriction of the afferent arteriole retards the flow of blood into the glomerular capillary, and both pressure and GFR decrease as a result. Constriction of the efferent arteriole retards blood flow out of the capillary bed, causing an increase in pressure and GFR. Dilation of the respective arterioles has the opposite effect. Intracapsular hydrostatic pressure may be disrupted by obstruction within the urinary tract. The back pressure from the obstruction will increase the hydrostatic pressure within Bowman's capsule, increasing the total of the forces opposing filtration.

As blood moves through the glomerular capillary bed and protein-free fluid is filtered from it, the plasma oncotic pressure rises as the plasma protein concentration increases. At the efferent arteriole, filtration equilibrium is reached, and the filtration gradient equals zero. The filtration gradient is directly related to the plasma oncotic pressure; thus changes in the concentration of plasma proteins may alter the GFR. Loss of glomerular impermeability to protein will also alter the process of glomerular filtration.

The rate of glomerular filtration is an important initial determinant of solute and water excretion. Studies comparing diseased and normal kidneys on the basis of excretion of Na^+, uric acid, and H^+, and reabsorption of HCO_3^-, glucose, and phosphate found no difference when corrected for the reduced GFR in the diseased kidney. These data suggest that each nephron contributes to excretion in proportion to its GFR. Thus each nephron functions as an independent unit and the total GFR is equal to the sum of the filtration rates of the individual nephrons. For this reason determination of the GFR can be used to estimate the amount of functional renal tissue—in others words, renal function. Determination of the GFR is used clinically to diagnose, determine the severity, and to monitor response to treatment. Measurement of the GFR is also clinically useful for determination of the proper dosage of drugs that are excreted by the kidney. Such drugs can reach toxic levels in the body when renal function (GFR) is impaired.

The glomerular filtrate, an isotonic solution similar to plasma in its composition, is formed at the rate of 120 to 125 ml per minute. It is apparent, then, that large quantities of water and solutes are reabsorbed in the second step of urine formation, which involves modification of the glomerular filtrate through selective reabsorption and secretion across the tubular membranes of the nephron. Examples of tubular function include the following: 98% or more of the filtered water, Na^+, Cl^-, and HCO_3^- are reabsorbed within the tubular segments of the nephron, in contrast to a reabsorption rate of only 40% to 50% for filtered urea, a waste product (Rose, 1984). Secretion of H^+ is necessary for acidification of the urine. Within the tubules, the kidneys also concentrate and dilute the urine and in this way help to maintain the normal osmolality of the body fluid. The osmolality of the urine can be varied within a range of 300 to 1200 mOsm/L (Lancaster, 1987).

Segmental functions of the tubules are fairly specific and are summarized in Table 20-1. The greatest portion of the filtrate is reabsorbed across the membranes of the proximal tubule and the loop of Henle. Approximately 60% to 70% of the glomerular filtrate is reabsorbed in the proximal tubule, and the tubular fluid leaves the proximal tubule as a solution that is isosmotic to plasma. Proximal Na^+ reabsorption creates the electrical and osmotic gradients for the passive transport

of Cl^-, water, and urea and provides the mechanism for Na^+ cotransport of other substances such as bicarbonate, phosphate, glucose, and amino acids. Since the fraction of filtered Na^+ and water will be increased in states of volume depletion and decreased in states of volume expansion, the proximal transport of these other solutes will be altered in the same way as Na^+ (Rose, 1984).

In the loop of Henle, solute in excess of water is reabsorbed. The descending limb of the loop of Henle is permeable to water and to a lesser degree solutes. As the isos-

Table 20-1. Segmental functions of the renal tubules

Segment	Functions

Proximal tubule	Reabsorption
	  70% filtered H_2O and NaCl
	  100% glucose
	  Urea
	  Uric acid
	  Amino acids
	  K^+, Mg^{++}, Ca^{++}
	  HPO^- (depends on parathyroid hormone)
	  90% HCO_3^- (reabsorbed and regenerated; accomplished through secretion of H^+)
	Secretion
	  Organic acids and bases
	  H^+ and NH_3^-

Loop of Henle	Reabsorption
	  NaCl in excess of H_2O
	  Most Mg^{++}

Distal tubule + connecting segment	Reabsorption
	  Filtered H_2O and NaCl (small fraction only)
	  Ca^{++} (depends on parathyroid hormone and calcitonin?)
	  HCO_3^-
	Secretion
	  H^+, NH_3^-, K^+ (depends on aldosterone concentration)

Collecting tubules	Reabsorption
	  NaCl
	  H_2O + urea (depends on ADH)
	  HCO_3^-
	Secretion
	  H^+, NH_3^- (pH of urine may be reduced to 4.5-5.0)
	  K^+ (depends on aldosterone concentration)

motic fluid from the proximal tubule moves through the descending limb, water is reabsorbed and the tubular fluid becomes hyperosmotic as the osmolality of the filtrate equilibrates with that of the medullary interstitium. The ascending limb is impermeable to water, and NaCl is actively reabsorbed from the filtrate in excess of water in this segment. This has two effects. First, it results in a tubular fluid that leaves the loop of Henle as a solution hypoosmotic to plasma. Second, the active reabsorption of NaCl from the ascending limb of the loop of Henle contributes to the production of medullary interstitial hypertonicity and, thus, is critical to the generation of the countercurrent multiplication effect, which allows a gradient of increasingly greater osmolarity to be produced throughout the renal medulla (Fig. 20-3). Hypertonicity is greatest in the inner medulla. The increased osmolarity of the medullary interstitium is also due to the presence of urea as well as NaCl and is maintained through the countercurrent exchanger arrangement of the vasa recta, which minimizes removal of the solutes from the interstitium.

The distal portion of the nephron, which consists of the distal tubule and connecting segment and the cortical and medullary collecting tubules or ducts, is respon-

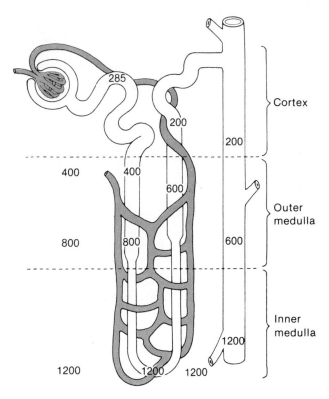

Fig. 20-3. Juxtamedullary nephron. Numbers refer to osmolarity of tubular and interstitial fluid as measured in milliosmoles. Note increased osmolarity of inner medulla as compared to cortex and outer medulla.

(From Groer M: Physiology and pathophysiology of the body fluids, St. Louis, 1981, The C.V. Mosby Co.)

sible for the final qualitative changes in the composition of the urine. This distal tubule is responsible for acidification, aldosterone responsiveness, and precise regulation of Na^+ and K^+ balance. The collecting tubules are responsible for concentrating or diluting the urine. It is believed that the nephron functions most effectively when the major portion of the glomerular filtrate is reabsorbed in the proximal tubule and the loop of Henle, with minimal reabsorptive activity related to changes in intake reserved for the distal portion. The collecting tubules in particular have a limited capacity for reabsorption, and an increase in fluid delivery to the distal portion could exceed this capacity and cause great losses of water and NaCl (Rose, 1984). Intrarenal mechanisms that act to keep distal delivery at a relatively constant rate include autoregulation, glomerulotubular balance, and tubuloglomerular feedback. Autoregulation helps maintain the GFR at a fairly constant rate despite changes in systemic pressure. Glomerulotubular balance allows changes in tubular reabsorption to occur in response to changes in the GFR such that fractional tubular reabsorption remains relatively constant. Tubuloglomerular feedback allows the GFR to change in response to changes in the load delivered to the macula densa, a group of specialized cells in the distal tubule. GFR will decrease in response to an increase in macula densa flow, thus allowing fluid delivery to the distal nephron to return to normal levels (Rose, 1984).

The concentrating and diluting functions of the nephron depend on the presence of antidiuretic hormone (ADH), which renders the membrane of the collecting duct permeable to water (Morel, 1981). The ultimate effect of the water permeability controlled by the presence of ADH is to allow the concentration of urine to be regulated as a function of the osmotic gradient produced by the countercurrent multiplier and exchanger system. The countercurrent mechanism allows a hypotonic urine to be delivered to the distal tubule and provides an increasing osmotic gradient with which the osmolality of the fluid in the collecting tubules can equilibrate if the membrane permeability to water is increased by the presence of ADH (Fig. 20-4). Thus a small amount of concentrated urine will be excreted when ADH is present. In the absence of ADH, a large amount of dilute urine will be excreted. A small amount of ADH is continuously present so that the tendency is always toward antidiuresis.

The active portion of ADH is arginine vasopressin. Cells in the supraoptic and paraventricular nuclei of the hypothalamus synthesize a prohormone, propressophysin, which is packaged in secretory vesicles and transported down axons to the nerve endings (terminal bulbs) in the neurohypophysis (posterior pituitary gland). During transport the prohormone is processed by enzymatic action to form vasopressin, its carrier protein neurophysin, and some small peptide cleavage products, all of which are stored in secretory granules until needed. Depolarization of the plasma membrane of the terminal bulb causes an increase in membrane permeability to Ca^+, which is a critical activator of the release of ADH, through the process of exocytosis. As a result of this process, the neurosecretory granules release their contents directly into the extracellular space through fusion of the membrane of the secretory granule with that of the cell (Kokko and Tannen, 1986; Maxwell et al., 1987). There is no identified physiologic role for neurophysin; however, it does appear to neutralize the negative

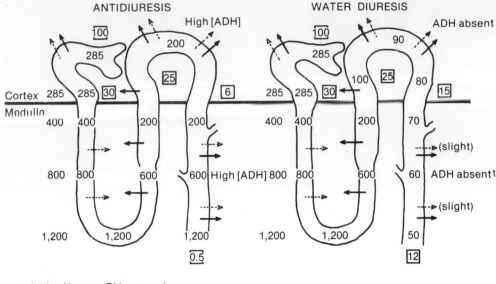

Fig. 20-4. Sodium chloride and water transport in nephron during antidiuresis and water diuresis. Tubular fluid and interstitial concentrations are expressed in milliosmoles per kilogram: large boxed numbers represent percentage of glomerular filtrate remaining in tubule at each site. Note that composition and volume of tubular fluid are essentially the same at the end of the loop of Henle because excretion of a concentrated or diluted urine is determined primarily in collecting ducts.

(From Clinical physiology of acid-base and electrolyte disorders by Rose, D. Copyright 1984 McGraw-Hill Book Co. Used with permission of McGraw-Hill Book Co.)

charge of vasopressin (Schrier, 1986).

The primary stimulus to the release of ADH is a rise in plasma osmolarity; however, nonosmotic stimuli can also cause its release. An increase in the electrical activity of the supraoptic neurons is considered an indication of ADH secretion. Such an increase in electrical activity has been found to occur in response to an osmotic and a nonosmotic stimulus but not in response to a nonspecific stimulus (Kannan and Yagi, 1978).

Osmoreceptors, or specialized cells that are sensitive to osmotic changes (probably due to the resultant change in cell volume), are located in the anterior hypothalamus in or near the nuclei where synthesis occurs (Humes, 1986). ADH secretion is suppressed at low levels of plasma osmolality and begins when a certain setpoint is reached (approximately 280 mOsm/kg). The osmoreceptors are very sensitive to even small increases in the plasma osmolality. As little as a 1% to 2% increase in plasma osmolality will cause a corresponding rise in ADH secretion. The increase in plasma ADH concentration is in direct proportion to the rise in plasma osmolality, that is, the relationship is a linear one (Fig. 20-5).

The sensitivity of the osmoreceptors is affected by the rate of osmolar change, the type of solute, age, and pregnancy. The more rapid the rate of increase, the greater will be the increase in vasopressin secretion. Other solutes besides Na^+, like man-

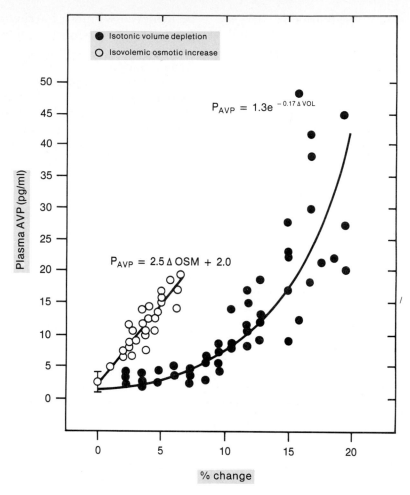

Fig. 20-5. The relationship between plasma vasopressin (AVP) and either the percent increase in plasma osmolality (○; PAVP = 2.5 △ osm + 2.0) or decrease in blood volume [●; PAVP = 1.3 exp (1.7 △ vol)] in conscious rats.

(From Dunn FL et al.: The role of blood osmolality and volume in regulating vasopressin secretion in the rat. J Clin Invest 52:3212, 1973.)

nitol and sucrose, can cause an osmotic gradient capable of stimulating ADH secretion. Glucose has not been found to be an effective osmotic stimulus of ADH secretion, although this remains a matter of ongoing debate and study. Age does not appear to affect the osmotic threshold, but higher plasma vasopressin levels have been observed in older healthy persons in response to an osmotic challenge when compared to younger persons given the same challenge. The osmotic threshold appears to be lowered in pregnancy, resulting in a 2% to 4% decrease in plasma osmolality that reverts to normal on delivery (Maxwell et al., 1987).

The most important nonosmotic factors that affect ADH secretion are hemodynamic in nature. A decrease in the effective circulating blood volume (hypovolemia) or hypotension, each alone or together, will stimulate the release of

ADH. Hemodynamic regulation of ADH release is mediated through the parasympathetic nervous system. Stretch receptors in the wall of the left atrium are low-pressure receptors thought to detect small to moderate changes in blood volume, while baroreceptors in the aortic arch and carotid sinus are high-pressure receptors thought to detect blood pressure changes. Stimulation of these receptors travels via the afferent vagal and glossopharyngeal nerves to ascending pathways that project to the supraoptic nucleus of the hypothalamus (Schrier, 1986; Maxwell et al., 1987). The baroreceptor projections are thought to be near but anatomically separate from the osmoreceptors (Kokko and Tannen, 1986).

This nonosmotic pathway is less sensitive than the osmotic pathway and necessitates a decrease in blood volume or pressure of approximately 5% to 10% before ADH release occurs. Once this point is reached, however, the effects of the nonosmotic pathway will predominate over the osmotic pathway in such a way that a volume-depleted patient can become hyponatremic. The relationship between hemodynamic stimuli and the vasopressin response is exponential in nature as compared to the linear relationship between osmotic stimuli and vasopressin release (Fig. 20-5), and plasma vasopressin levels will rise significantly above those caused by osmotic stimuli with a 15% or greater decrease in blood volume or pressure.

The different stimulus-response relationships of the osmotic and nonosmotic pathways reflect the different physiologic roles each plays and provide an example of the remarkable efficiency of the various physiologic mechanisms involved in the maintenance of homeostasis in the body. Osmotic control is necessary for the purpose of maintaining normal water balance, which is a constant requirement and can be achieved within a narrow range of low levels of ADH. Osmotic regulation of ADH secretion is extremely precise. In contrast, hemodynamic regulation becomes operative when the vasopressor and volume-expanding effects of ADH are needed in order to restore blood pressure and circulating blood volume and thus maintain tissue perfusion. Higher levels of ADH are appropriate in this setting, which becomes a priority over osmotic balance (Humes, 1986).

It is believed that the two pathways operate in parallel with one another such that ADH release continues to occur in response to both osmotic and nonosmotic stimuli. The mechanism of interaction between the two systems is thought to be a shift in the osmotic threshold in response to hemodynamic alterations. The osmotic threshold is shifted to the left in response to hypovolemia and hypotension (Fig. 20-6) and is, therefore, lower and more sensitive to changes in plasma osmolality. The effect of this change is that the normal inhibition of ADH release in response to low plasma osmolarity occurs at a much lower point than normal and the response to increased osmolarity is potentiated (Rose, 1984). The opposite effect occurs in the presence of hypervolemia and hypertension (Fig. 20-7).

Other nonosmotic factors, such as nausea, pain, stress, heat, glucopenia, and surgery stimulate the release of ADH, whereas cold and alcohol inhibit its release (Groer, 1981). With the exceptions of nausea and glucopenia, the nonosmotic stimulatory factors are believed to affect ADH secretion indirectly through their effect on the hemodynamic pathways. Pain and intense emotion (stress) could produce nausea and hypotension through a vasovagal response and thus effect ADH scretion. The stimulation of ADH by nausea is

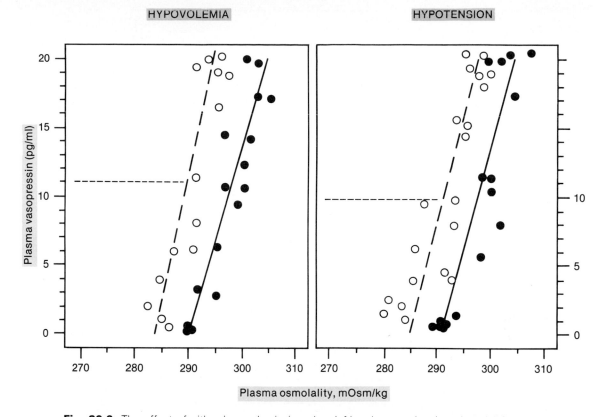

Fig. 20-6. The effect of either hypovolemia *(panel to left)* or hypotension *(panel to right)* on the osmotic regulation of vasopressin levels in conscious rats. Blood volume was reduced approximately 15% by intraperitoneal injection of polyethylene glycol, and mean arterial pressure was reduced approximately 15% by subcutaneous injection of isoproterenol hydrocholoride. Changes in plasma osmolality were induced by intraperitoneal injection of hypotonic, isotonic, or hypertonic saline. Experimental and normal rats are represented by open (○) and closed (●) circles, respectively.

(From Robertson GL, et al.: Osmotic control of vasopressin function. In Andreoli TE et al. editors: Disturbances in body fluid osmolality, Bethesda, 1977, American Physiological Society.)

believed to be mediated through the emetic center independent of osmotic and hemodynamic stimuli (Maxwell et al., 1987). Listed in Table 20-2 are some biologic substances believed to affect ADH release. The sequence of events in ADH release and the stimulatory and inhibitory factors are summarized in Fig. 20-8.

At the cellular level, ADH exerts its effect of increasing the permeability of the luminal membrane of renal tubular epithelial cells by first binding with a specific receptor on the basolateral membrane, which activates adenylate cyclase. Adenylate cyclase is a membrane-bound enzyme that, provided magnesium is present, catalyzes the conversion of cyclic AMP from ATP. Cyclic AMP serves as a intracellular second messenger. The mechanisms of the cellular response to ADH after the generation of cyclic AMP is the subject of much ongoing research. The activity of protein kinase, an enzyme responsible for protein phosphorylation, increases in re-

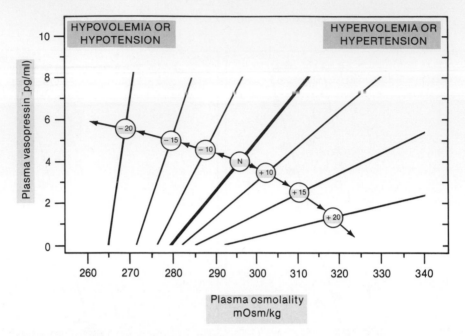

Fig. 20-7. Effect of acute changes in blood volume or pressure on the osmoregulation of vasopressin. The heavy oblique line in the center represents the relationship between plasma vasopressin and osmolality under normovolemic, normotensive conditions. The families of lines to the left and right show the shift in the relationship observed when blood volume or blood pressure is acutely decreased or increased by the percentages indicated within the circles.

(From Robertson GL: Thirst and vasopressin function in normal and disordered states of water balance. J Lab Clin Med 101:351, 1983.)

sponse to cyclic AMP; however, a specific phosphorylated protein has not been identified at this time.

Intramembranous particle aggregates (IMPA), which have been identified through freeze fracture electron microscopy, are believed to contain the actual channels through which water can cross the membrane (Kachadorian et al., 1977; Ripoche et al., 1982). These aggregates are thought to exist within the membrane structure of cell organelles and, in response to ADH, move to and fuse with the luminal membrane (Muller et al., 1980). The movement and maintenance of the aggregates appear to require the presence of microtubules and microfilaments in the cytoskeleton (Kachadorian et al., 1979).

Table 20-2. Putative mediators of vasopressin release

Biogenic mono-amines	Peptides
Norepinephrine	Angiotensin II
Dopamine	Endogenous opioids
Serotonin	Substance P
Acetylcholine	Arginine vasopres-sin
γ-Aminobutyric acid	
Glycine	Electrolytes
Histamine	Potassium
Lipids	Calcium
Prostaglandins	

From Sklar AH and Schrier RW: Physiol Rev 63:1243, 1983.

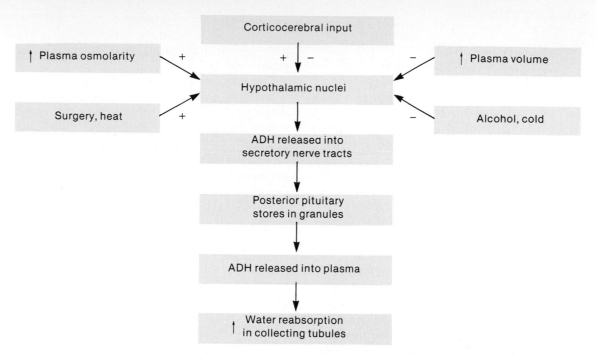

Fig. 20-8. ADH production and release are regulated through plasma volume and plasma osmolarity; increases in plasma volume are inhibitory; decreases are stimulatory. Increased plasma osmolarity will stimulate production, and decreased osmolarity inhibits ADH. Other inputs are also indicated.

(Adapted from Groer, M: Physiology and pathophysiology of the body fluids, St. Louis, 1981, the CV Mosby Co.)

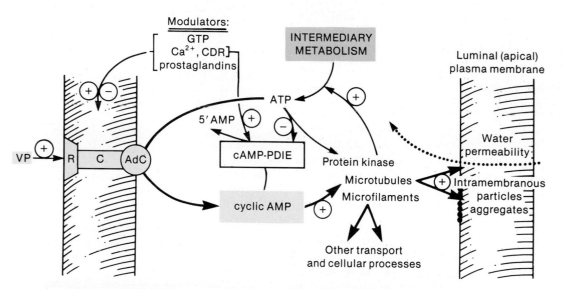

Fig. 20-9. Schematic representation of the cellular action of vasopressin. *GTP,* guanosine triphosphate; *CDR,* calcium-dependent regulator (calmodulin); *ATP,* adenosine triphosphate; *cAMP,* cyclic adenosine monophosphate; *VP,* vasopressin; *R,* receptor; *C,* coupling mechanism; *AC,* adenylate cyclase; *PDIE,* phosphodiesterase. See text for details.

(From Dousa TP: Cellular action of antidiuretic hormone. Mineral Electrolyte Metab 5:144, 1981.)

There is speculation that the action of the microtubules and microfilaments may depend on the phosphorylation of protein by protein kinase. There is also evidence that Ca^+ and calmodulin (complexed together as Ca^{++}-calmodulin) influence the function of the microfilaments and microtubules in the movement of the aggregates (Levine et al., 1981). There is a rise in intracellular Ca^+ in response to ADH secretion; calcium and Ca^{++}-calmodulin are believed to act as intracellular second messengers and as regulators of the enzymatic generation and degradation of cyclic AMP (Petersen and Edelman, 1964). The proposed cellular action of vasopressin is schematically diagrammed in Fig. 20-9.

ADH provides potent, dose-dependent diuretic activity that allows a high degree of precision in osmotic regulation. Another characteristic that makes it ideally suited for this role is its rapid clearance rate. It is metabolized by the liver and kidneys and has a half-life of 15 to 20 minutes. Obviously, any factor which affects the synthesis, release, and degradation of ADH or its action on the renal receptor or effector mechanisms can have a profound effect on body water balance.

Altered urinary elimination patterns

The major functions of the kidneys that become impaired in renal disease include the excretion of waste products, excretion of excess electrolytes and water derived from the diet and endogenous tissue breakdown, and the secretion of hormones. Depending on the underlying cause, any one or all of these functions can be affected. For example, only the excretion of water and maintenance of normal water balance is affected by disorders of ADH regulation. In contrast, all these functions are affected in chronic renal failure, which has progressed to end-stage renal disease.

The stage of progression of renal disease is also another factor that affects the remaining level of renal function. In mild renal disease or in the early stages of chronic renal disease, renal function may be relatively unchanged owing to the compensatory increase in solute and water excretion that occurs in the remaining functional nephrons. As chronic renal disease progressively worsens, the excretory and secretory functions of the kidneys will become increasingly impaired as the function of the remaining nephrons is affected. The progressive impairment of renal function over time occurs in a characteristic

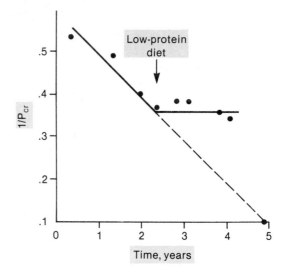

Fig. 20-10. Plot of the reciprocal of the P_{cr} versus time in a man with chronic pyelonephritis. There was a progressive and uniform decline in renal function during the first 2 years of observation. If this course had continued (dashed line), end-stage renal disease ($P_{cr} = 10$ mg/dl, $1/P_{cr} = 0.1$) would have occurred within the next 3 years. However, the institution of a low-protein diet resulted in a stabilization of the P_{cr} and, since muscle mass was constant, the total GFR. P_{cr} = Plasma creatinine, an indicator of renal function.
(From Rose BD: Pathophysiology of renal disease, ed 2, New York, 1987, McGraw-Hill Book Co.)

and predictable linear fashion, as depicted in Fig. 20-10. Progressive renal impairment is also seen in some patients where the disease process has been treated or is no longer active (Rose, 1987).

As damaged or diseased nephrons no longer contribute to overall renal function, the remaining healthy and undamaged nephrons are able to increase their filtration rate as an adaptive, compensatory response. As a result, the total GFR remains at a normal or near normal level. This adaptive hyperfiltration does have limits and reaches the maximum for maintaining the total GFR when approximately one fourth to one third of the nephrons are impaired. Further loss of functioning nephrons will be accompanied by a decrease in the total GFR and the apparent loss of renal function, although not to the same extent as the loss of nephrons. An example is seen in the renal transplant donor who loses half of the functional renal tissue but whose GFR decreases to 70% to 80% of baseline.

While the compensatory hyperfiltration in normal nephrons is initially adaptive and therefore beneficial, the underlying hemodynamic response is thought to cause degenerative changes that eventually alter the function of these nephrons as well. The hemodynamic changes that allow hyperfiltration include dilation of the arterioles (the efferent to a lesser degree than the afferent) with a resultant increase in glomerular plasma flow and hydrostatic pressure (Brenner, 1985). The increase in glomerular capillary pressure appears to be the major factor in the mechanical disruption of the size and charge-selective properties of the glomerular capillary membrane resulting in proteinuria and increased mesangial deposition, which causes expansion of the mesangium. The histologic changes that are seen include glomerular hypertro-

phy, fusion of the foot processes, and mesangial expansion, which leads to capillary collapse and glomerular sclerosis.

The mechanism by which the compensatory response of hyperfiltration occurs is not well understood. It is thought to be related to the presence of protein (amino acids or protein metabolites), which accumulates due to the reduction in GFR. It is known that dietary protein loading increases the GFR (Bosch et al., 1984) and that the hemodynamic changes caused by hyperfiltration can be lessened by dietary protein restriction. Many studies have demonstrated slowing and even cessation of the decline in GFR with dietary protein restriction (see Fig. 20-10) (Rose, 1987). It is even possible that the normal decline seen in renal function with advancing age in healthy persons is a response to the protein-rich diet typically consumed in modern society.

The presence of systemic hypertension will intensify and accelerate the damage caused by compensatory hyperfiltration. The increase in pressure is transferred to the glomeruli because of the vasodilation that occurs. Control of systemic hypertension is absolutely critical in slowing the progression of renal disease for this reason. Pharmacologic agents known as angiotensin-converting enzyme inhibitors are particularly effective for reducing the risk of glomerular injury, since they exert their antihypertensive effect by reversing the efferent arteriolar constriction, which is mediated by angiotensin II. This allows a dissipation of pressure across the glomerular capillary bed.

Other explanations for the progressive nature of renal disease continue to be examined. Mechanisms that may mediate progressive renal disease for which there is some experimental evidence include an immune response, renal deposition of calcium phosphate, abnormalities of lipid metabolism, prostaglandin activity, and vascular coagulation (Rose, 1987). In some patients, it is possible that a combination of these mechanisms is responsible for deterioration of renal function.

Manifestations. Disruption of urine formation and excretion will have profound effects on wellness. Manifestations of this disruption may include changes in the clearance rates of substances, changes in the amount, composition, and specific gravity of the urine and the pattern of its excretion, elevated blood pressure, and the more extreme manifestations of the nephrotic syndrome and renal failure.

Information about the amount, color, specific gravity, pH, and constituents of the urine can be obtained through a simple noninvasive urinalysis. This type of information helps in arriving at a diagnosis but is often inconclusive and offers little help in determining the severity or progression of the disease or the response to treatment. Microscopic examination of the urine sediment can provide important clues as to the nature of renal disease. For example, casts are formed within the lumen of the tubules and indicate the site of nephronal pathology. The presence of protein, blood, and certain types of cells, crystals, and casts may indicate renal dysfunction and, therefore, further testing is required to confirm or rule out a specific disease entity (Table 20-3). Benign, transient changes in the urine of healthy persons can be caused by exercise and standing erect and can occur for no apparent reason. Fever and other pathologic processes besides renal disease can also affect the urinary composition.

Hematuria, or blood in the urine, can arise from any site within the urinary tract. It is often a benign, transient finding and can occur following long-distance running. In the latter, bladder trauma was hypothesized to be the causative mechanism, but the findings of dysmorphic red cells, red cell casts, and mild proteinuria suggest glomerular involvement (Fassett et al, 1982). Hematuria is often seen in association with urinary tract infection. In adults it can also accompany obstruction due to calculus formation, malignancy, prostate disease, or trauma. In children it may accompany perineal irritation, trauma, glomerular disease, or hypercalciuria (Rose, 1987).

Proteinuria should be evaluated in terms of the type and quantity of protein being excreted, as well as the pattern of that excretion. Identification of the type of protein (either albumin or low molecular weight proteins) being excreted can help indicate the site and mechanism of the loss. Albumin is lost in the urine when increased glomerular permeability occurs (glomerular proteinuria). Increased glomerular permeability in humans has been found to occur as a result of three mechanisms: (1) Loss of the negative charge of the glomerular basement membrane; (2) an increase in the size or number of pores in the membrane due to structural damage or change; and (3) the hemodynamic effects of norepinephrine and angiotensin II (Meyers et al., 1982). Low molecular weight protein is usually filtered and reabsorbed in the proximal tubule. The presence of these proteins in the urine (tubular proteinuria) indicates that either tubular function is impaired or the number of these proteins is increased beyond the reabsorptive capacity of the tubules. The latter mechanism is responsible for the proteinuria seen in multiple myeloma and leukemia. Tubulointerstitial disease, tubular damage, the Fanconi syndrome, and sepsis can cause impaired tubular function.

Table 20-3.   Correlation between urinalysis and causes of renal dysfunction

Urinary findings	Etiology
Hematuria with red blood cell casts Heavy proteinuria ($>$3.5 gm day or 50 mg/kg per day) Lipiduria	Any of these findings, singly or in combination, is virtually diagnostic of glomerular disease or vasculitis. The absence of these findings, however, does not exclude these diagnoses.
Renal tubular epithelial cells with granular and epithelial cell casts	In acute renal failure, strongly suggestive of acute tubular necrosis, although marked hyperbilirubinemia alone can produce similar changes.
Pyuria with white blood cell and granular or waxy casts and no or mild proteinuria ($<$1.5 gm/day)	Suggestive of tubular or interstitial disease or obstruction.
Hematuria and pyuria with no or variable casts or proteinuria	May be seen with glomerular disease, vasculitis, infection, obstruction, renal infarction, or acute, usually drug-induced, interstitial nephritis. The presence of eosinophils in the urine usually indicates the last diagnosis.
Hematuria alone	In acute renal failure, suggestive of vasculitis or obstruction.
Normal or near normal (few cells with little or no proteinuria or casts); hyaline casts *not considered* an abnormal finding	Acute: may be seen with prerenal disease obstruction, hypercalcemia, multiple myeloma,* some cases of acute tubular necrosis, or vascular diseases in which glomerular ischemia but not necrosis occurs (including scleroderma, atheroemboli, and rare cases of polyarteritis nodosa). Chronic: may be seen with prerenal disease, obstruction, tubular or interstitial diseases, and nephrosclerosis.

From Rose BD: Pathophysiology of renal disease, ed. 2, New York, 1987, McGraw-Hill Book Co.
*Although the dipstick is likely to be negative (detecting primarily albuminuria), the sulfosalicyclic acid test will be very positive in multiple myeloma, since it will detect the presence of immunoglobulin light chains.

Excretion of more than 2 gm per day of protein is usually indicative of renal disease (Humes, 1986). Excretion of more than 3.5 gm per day is usually accompanied by hypoalbuminemia, hyperlipidemia, and edema and constitutes the nephrotic syndrome (Rose, 1987), which is discussed in more detail later in this chapter.

Transient proteinuria can occur in otherwise normal persons. Exercise can induce both glomerular and tubular proteinuria (Poortmans, 1985) as can fever, infection, and heart failure. The mecha-

nism by which proteinuria occurs in these conditions is unknown but may be hormonally mediated or occur as a result of mild tubular ischemia. Orthostatic proteinuria or increased protein excretion when the individual is in the upright position but not when lying down is also thought to be neurohormonally mediated due to venous pooling that occurs on assuming the standing position. Persons older than 25 years of age with persistent proteinuria (at levels between 1 and 2 gm per day) are more likely to have renal or cardiovascular dysfunction than those persons with transient or orthostatic protein-uria (Rose, 1987).

Pyuria, or white cells in the urine, accompanied by bacteria, cloudiness, alkaline pH, and complaints of dysuria and frequency point to the presence of a urinary tract infection. Culture and sensitivity testing must be done to identify the causative organism and the antibiotic to which it will respond. The presence of white blood cells may also indicate other disease processes, including tubulointerstitial disease, acute interstitial nephritis, and rejection of a transplanted kidney.

Clearance is a technique that allows assessment of renal function through comparison of the excretion rates of urinary substances with the plasma concentrations. Clearance values of substances for which excretion rates remain relatively constant or fixed, such as urea and creatinine, provide information on the overall functional capacity of the kidney. Clearance values for substances whose excretion rates vary greatly from day to day depending on the body's needs reflect the adequacy of the kidneys' regulatory function.

Creatinine clearance, employing a 24-hour urine collection technique, is the most widely used method to estimate GFR, which in turn provides an estimation of the level of remaining renal function. Because creatinine excretion normally equals creatinine production in the steady state, the plasma creatinine level can also be used to detect changes in the GFR. This is a simpler test to perform than creatinine clearance. The plasma creatinine level will vary inversely with the GFR in the steady state. Because of this relationship, serial measurements of plasma creatinine can be used to monitor renal disease progression. As nephron function is lost, the GFR will decrease and the plasma

creatinine will increase. Plasma creatinine will double as the GFR is reduced to half its original value. As can be seen in Fig. 20-11, the relationship is not linear but rather is hyperbolic in nature. In early renal disease, there will be small increases in plasma creatinine levels with large reductions in the GFR. A relatively minor increase in plasma creatinine can represent a significant decrease in the GFR. In more advanced renal disease, there will be large increases in plasma creatinine levels with small reductions in the GFR (Humes, 1986). Because of the inverse relationship, the reciprocal of the plasma creatinine level $1/P_{cr}$ is also used to reflect the decline in GFR (see Fig. 20-10).

The plasma creatinine level also depends on creatinine production. In states where creatinine production is increased (those characterized by muscle tissue breakdown), the plasma creatinine will not accurately indicate renal function, since it will increase out of proportion to any change in the GFR. Evaluation of the plasma creatinine must also take into account the muscle mass, which, in turn, is determined by age, weight, and sex (Rose, 1987).

Another clinical indicator of changes in GFR is the concentration of urea in the plasma, which is measured as the blood urea nitrogen (BUN) level. Urea is similar to creatinine in that it is excreted primarily by filtration. However, since it is also reabsorbed in the tubules, it does underestimate the GFR (Humes, 1986). The normal value is 10-20 mg/dl and changes in the BUN correlate well with the clinical manifestations of renal dysfunction. Like the plasma creatinine level, the BUN level will vary inversely with the GFR (Fig. 20-11). The BUN level can also be altered by the dietary protein load, liver disease, catabolism, or gastrointestinal bleeding.

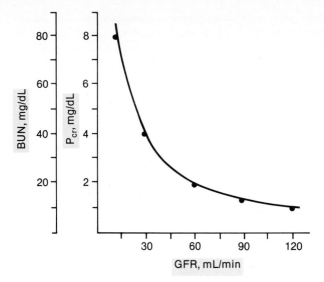

Fig. 20-11. Steady-state relationship between the plasma creatinine concentration (P_{cr}), blood urea nitrogen (BUN), and GFR.
(From Rose BD: Pathophysiology of renal disease, ed 2, New York, 1987, McGraw-Hill Book Co.)

The principal mechanisms for renal regulation of the composition of the body fluid include tubular reabsorption of Na^+, Cl^-, and bicarbonate, and tubular secretion of H^+ and K^+. Clinical manifestations will reflect the tubular segment wherein function has been disrupted. For example, glycosuria, phosphaturia, aminoaciduria, and bicarbonate wasting (proximal renal tubular acidosis) are seen with proximal tubular dysfunction. Dysfunction of the distal tubule may cause distal renal tubular acidosis and aldosterone resistance with loss of Na^+ and retention of K^+.

Tubular function is most frequently assessed by measuring the kidney's ability to conserve sodium and to concentrate the urine. There is a high correlation between the plasma Na^+ concentration and the rate of Na^+ excretion. The plasma Na^+ concentration is the principal determinant of the extracellular fluid volume, the relative constancy of which is maintained through variations in urinary Na^+ and water excretion. The rate of Na^+ excretion will be altered in the presence of renal disease. Changes in the GFR can affect Na^+ excretion; glomerulonephritis is characterized by a reduction in the amount of Na^+ filtered. In some primary renal disease there is retention of Na^+; retention of Na^+ and water occurs as a compensatory mechanism to restore plasma volume in the patient with nephrotic syndrome. A salt-losing nephritis may also occur in renal disease where there is selective damage to the Na^+-reabsorbing mechanisms, such as obstructive nephropathy or medullary cystic disease. The ability to decrease Na^+ excretion in response to decreased intake or hypovolemia is impaired in chronic tubulointerstitial disease to a greater extent than in other forms of chronic renal insufficiency. The kidney is not responsive to mineralocorticoids, and the clinical picture will resemble that of hypovolemia.

Impairment of the ability to concentrate

or dilute the urine may be a manifestation of primary renal disease as well as some other conditions. The inability to concentrate the urine is manifested by polyuria, thirst, and a decreased urine specific gravity. If water intake is inadequate, there may also be signs of water deficit (see Chapter 18). The inability to dilute the urine may result in water retention if water ingestion is not restricted. Hypotonic hyponatremia will develop. If the positive water balance develops rapidly or is great enough, water intoxication will ensue. The concentrating and diluting abilities of the kidney are related to the permeability of the tubules to water, which is controlled by ADH. Syndromes associated with alterations in ADH secretion are discussed later in this chapter. Concentrating ability also depends on medullary hypertonicity, and diluting ability also depends on the delivery of the filtrate to the distal diluting site and sodium transport by the diluting segments.

Osmotic diuresis is the result of an obligatory water load for excretion of substances that are nonreabsorbable (for example, mannitol) or that are present in concentrations that exceed tubular reabsorptive capacity. The diuresis causes an increased loss of sodium chloride and water and is manifested by polyuria. In diabetes mellitus, glucose is present in concentrations that exceed tubular reabsorptive capacity so that it acts as an osmotic diuretic, causing one of the classic manifestations of that disease, polyuria. Where loss of nephron function has occurred, the solute load of remaining nephrons increases, causing an osmotic diuresis.

An increase in blood pressure may also be a manifestation of renal disorders. The secondary hypertension that occurs in renal disease is not completely understood. It is felt that structural damage and changes in the kidney contribute to reduced renal blood flow, which activates compensatory mechanisms that increase blood pressure. The renin-angiotensin system is activated, and both renin and angiotensin II have vasoconstrictive actions. The subsequent sodium and water retention increases blood volume, which contributes to hypertension. Marked activation of the renin-angiotensin system, juxtaglomerular hyperplasia, and excessively high renin levels are the results of renal arterial obstruction. Conversely, the kidney may sustain damage as a result of primary hypertension. Moderate hypertension causes "benign" nephrosclerosis, which is characterized by tubular atrophy and glomerular sclerosis (see Chapter 17). Renal function usually remains fairly in-

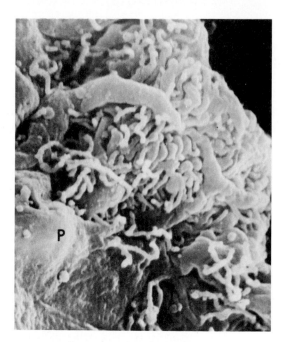

Fig. 20-12. Scanning electron micrograph of glomerulus in severely hypertensive person. Microvilli indicate some injury of podocytes, *P.* (× 7,000).
(From Anderson WAD and Kissane JM: Pathology, ed 7, St. Louis, 1977, The CV Mosby Co.)

tact. Malignant hypertension causes malignant nephrosclerosis. Acute degenerative changes in the arteries and arterioles of the kidney lead to hemorrhagic lesions and basement membrane thickening in the glomerulus. Scarring occurs as the hemorrhagic lesions heal. Obstruction of the vascular bed results from the progressive arterial changes and the scarring. Tubular atrophy and interstitial fibrosis eventually develop (Figs. 20-12 and 20-13). In the more advanced stage, nephrosclerosis impairs renal blood flow and GFR. Hypertension may also stimulate the development of the nephrotic syndrome in the pregnant woman, leading to the condition known as *preeclampsia* (see Chapter 15).

Renal failure. As stated earlier, the major function of the kidneys is the mainte-

nance of body fluid chemical equilibrium, that is, maintaining the volume, composition, and pH of the body fluid within normal limits. Disruption of all these aspects is demonstrated in the most extreme manifestation of kidney dysfunction, renal failure. The term *renal failure* indicates a loss of renal ability to respond to the ever-changing physiologic conditions within the body. The loss of this ability is characterized by alterations in fluid volume, composition, distribution, and acid-base balance, as well as retention of metabolic waste products.

Renal failure may either be acute or chronic. Acute renal failure (ARF) develops suddenly and is usually reversible. More specifically, it is characterized by a rise in plasma creatinine of 0.5 mg per dl per day

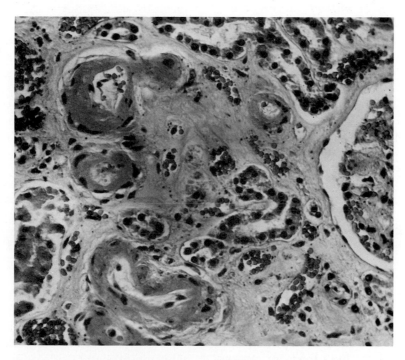

Fig. 20-13. Necrotizing arteriolitis in kidney from case of malignant hypertension. There is fibrinoid necrosis of walls of arterioles, which are swollen and eosinophilic. (Hematoxylin and eosin; ×280.)
(From Anderson WAD and Kissane JM: Pathology, ed 7, St. Louis, 1977, The CV Mosby Co.)

and a rise in BUN of 10 mg per dl per day over several days. Adaptive mechanisms are not seen in ARF. Chronic renal failure (CRF) develops slowly and is irreversible because of progressive destruction of the renal parenchyma. The slow, progressive nature of chronic renal insufficiency and CRF allows adaptive mechanisms to develop, which help to maintain homeostasis until renal function deteriorates to the point where this is no longer possible (Humes, 1986).

The term *renal failure* should be differentiated from the terms *azotemia* and *uremia*, which describe clinical conditions that accompany renal failure.

Azotemia. Azotemia refers to the accumulation of nitrogenous waste products (urea, creatinine, and uric acid) within the body. Azotemia may occur as a result of either circulatory or kidney failure. In circulatory failure these waste products are not delivered to the kidneys, and in kidney failure they are delivered to impaired kidneys, which cannot excrete them. The elevated plasma levels of these substances are reflected in the high BUN and serum creatinine values. The retention of nitrogenous waste products is believed to be responsible for some of the symptomatology seen in renal failure.

Uremia. Uremia is the term applied to the clinical syndrome accompanying renal failure when the metabolic and biochemical changes caused by renal failure become grossly symptomatic. Renal function is so compromised that adaptation and compensation cannot correct the abnormalities which occur. Impaired volume regulation, electrolyte and acid-base imbalances, and the retention of nitrogenous wastes form the basis of these pathophysiologic changes that affect every organ system in the body.

The type and severity of the manifesta-tions of uremia may differ, depending on whether the renal failure is acute or chronic; those of ARF occur at lower levels of the BUN and in a more fulminant manner than those of CRF (Maxwell et al., 1987). The progression to uremia with CRF may be quite insidious due to the adaptation that can occur. When uremia is severe and progressive, no matter what the cause, death is the ultimate result. The BUN and creatinine levels will be high and are often used as an index of the severity of anemia. The systemic toxicity seen in uremia, which resembles a metabolic intoxication, is thought to be related to the presence of substances that have a toxic effect on the body and that, through the process of dialysis, can be removed. These toxic substances are believed to be produced through protein metabolism and normally excreted via the kidneys. While specific toxins remain unidentified at this time (Humes, 1986), it is most likely that several compounds act as toxins via different pathogenetic mechanisms (Schrier, 1986) and are discussed later in this chapter.

The clinical manifestations of uremia reveal the widespread effect of the loss of normal renal function on every system of the body. The signs and symptoms of uremia are often classified according to whether they are correctable by dialysis (Table 20-4). Some of the signs and symptoms are related to the loss of renal control and regulation of fluid volume and composition. Polyuria and nocturia are experienced because the renal concentrating ability is impaired. This usually develops even before the onset of uremia, when the GFR falls below 30 ml per minute (Humes, 1986). Another example includes the contribution of water and sodium retention to hypervolemia and the development of heart failure and pulmonary edema. Pul-

Table 20-4.   Systemic clinical manifestations of uremia

System	Dialyzable	Nondialyzable
Integumentary	Pruritus due to uremia Uremic frost	Pruritus due to Ca^{++} deposition Pallor
Cardiopulmonary	Volume related hypertension Pericarditis Congestive heart failure Pulmonary edema Pleuritis	Hyperreninemic hypertension Accelerated atherogenesis
Neurologic	Early peripheral neuropathy Encephalopathy	Late peripheral neuropathy
Endocrine (metabolic)	Malnutrition Carbohydrate intolerance Sexual dysfunction Amenorrhea	Thyroid dysfunction Infertility (female) Hyperlipidemia Hyperparathyroidism Vitamin D deficiency
Gastrointestinal	Anorexia Nausea and vomiting Colitis Uremic breath	Peptic ulcer
Musculoskeletal	None	Renal osteodystrophy Reduced growth rate Muscle weakness Calcification of tissue
Blood and immune	Platelet dysfunction White blood cell dysfunction Decreased immune response (increased susceptibility to infection)	Anemia

monary congestion in the uremic patient has been labeled uremic pneumonitis. It should be noted that other pathogenetic mechanisms that are brought about by renal dysfunction, including hypertension, cardiomyopathy, anemia, and atherosclerosis, probably also contribute to heart failure (Humes, 1986).

Metastatic calcification is another example of a clinical manifestation of uremia related to altered fluid composition. An increased plasma calcium and phosphate product is hypothesized to cause calcium phosphate deposition in blood vessels, joints, and soft tissue; these deposits can cause cutaneous ulcer formation due to ischemia, conjunctival inflam

mation, and periarthritis (Schrier, 1986; Humes, 1986; Maxwell et al., 1987). Calcium deposition in the skin and hair follicles is believed to contribute to pruritus, a source of extreme discomfort for the uremic patient. Disorders of calcium and phosphate metabolism are related not only to loss of renal regulation and control but also to the derangement in vitamin D metabolism and parathyroid hormone control that occurs. The improvement in pruritus and skin lesions following partial parathyroidectomy lends support to elevated parathyroid hormone levels as a pathogenetic mechanism for these problems.

Some of the signs and symptoms are related to the inability to excrete the products of tissue metabolism. The subsequent accumulation of organic and inorganic compounds can lead to the development of symptoms. Acidosis develops because the kidney can no longer excrete the daily nonvolatile acid load as the ability to acidify the urine through the secretion of hydrogen ions, the generation of ammonia, and the reabsorption and regeneration of bicarbonate becomes increasingly impaired (Kokko and Tannen, 1986). Impaired renal function also allows the accumulation of anions (phosphate and sulfate), which further contributes to the development of acidosis (see Chapter 18).

There is some evidence that accumulation of certain nitrogenous waste products may cause uremic symptoms. The level of urea, as measured by the BUN, is known to correlate with the clinical manifestations of uremia. The pale yellowish skin color characteristic of uremic patients is due to the dermal accumulation of chromogens (Humes, 1986).

Defective platelet function may be related to the increased levels of guanidinosuccinic acid and cyclic AMP found in uremia (Schrier, 1986). Platelet dysfunction is thought to be the cause of the bleeding tendency seen in uremic patients. Purpuric lesions, bruising, and increased oozing from puncture sites may be observed on the skin of the uremic patient. Bleeding in the gastrointestinal tract may also occur. Other commonly seen gastrointestinal problems include anorexia, nausea, vomiting, and diarrhea, as well as a nonspecific gastritis. Anorexia, nausea, stomatitis, and possibly colitis are thought to be at least partly due to the presence of urea (Schrier, 1986). Pancreatitis may also develop. As a result of these gastrointestinal problems and poor dietary intake, uremic patients can develop a negative nitrogen

balance and protein-calorie malnutrition (Schrier, 1986).

The pathogenesis of uremic neuropathy has been postulated to be related to increased levels of myoinositol, an organic compound shown experimentally to be a neurotoxin (Liveson et al., 1977). Aside from being irritating to the patient, neuropathies can also cause disability. A commonly seen neuropathy is that of "restless legs," in which the patient avoids lower extremity inactivity due to numbness that progresses to paresthesias and hypalgesia, which in turn progress upward from the toes and feet. Motor neuropathy and footdrop may develop, and fingers and hands can be involved if deterioration goes untreated (Schrier, 1986). Parathyroid hormone may also play a role in the pathogenesis of neuropathies.

Some of the signs and symptoms of uremia are related to the kidney's inability to perform metabolic functions, including the functions of producing, stimulating, and responding to hormones appropriately (Table 20-5). The levels of some hormones the kidneys normally excrete or degrade will be increased. For this reason, both insulin and glucagon levels are increased; however, uremic patients are glucose intolerant, apparently due to peripheral resistance to insulin (Schrier, 1986). Some hormone levels are increased because of inappropriate stimulation. Renal ischemia may cause renin secretion, which in turn stimulates aldosterone release, which will contribute to hypertension and alterations in fluid volume and sodium balance. As a trade-off for maintaining phosphate metabolism, the level of parathyroid hormone is elevated, leading to secondary hyperparathyroidism (Bricker, 1972). The levels of some hormones decrease due to decreased production. Erythropoiesis is depressed as the damaged kidneys can no

Table 20-5. Hormonal alterations in uremia

Hormone	Potential metabolic consequences
Increased	
Prolactin	Lactation
Luteinizing hormone	Gynecomastia
Gastrin	Gastritis
Renin-aldosterone	Hypertension
Glucagon	Glucose intolerance
Growth hormone	—
Parathyroid hormone	Osteitis fibrosa, pruritus, and others
Insulin	Glucose intolerance
Decreased	
1,25-$(OH)_2$ vitamin D_3	Osteomalacia, osteitis fibrosa
Erythropoietin	Anemia
Somatomedin	Decreased linear growth in children
Testosterone	Reduced libido and impotence
Follicle-stimulating hormone	?Impotence

From Schrier, R: Renal and electrolyte disorders, ed 3, Boston, 1986, Little, Brown & Co.

longer produce normal amounts of erythropoietin. The action of some hormones is altered as the renal response to the hormone is impaired. For example, the renal hydroxylation of 25-hydroxycholecalciferol to 1,25-dihydroxycholecalciferol, the active metabolite of vitamin D necessary for calcium absorption from the gut, is impaired. This contributes to the development of hypocalcemia and, subsequently, to the development of secondary hyperparathyroidism.

As can be seen from the preceding examples, often more than one pathogenetic mechanism is responsible for a clinical manifestation of uremia. Anemia develops due to decreased red blood cell production, shortened red cell life span, and bleeding (which was discussed previously).

Erythrocyte production is limited not only by a deficit of erythropoietin but also by a decreased bone marrow response to it (Schrier, 1986). Increased red blood cell destruction may be a direct effect of toxic substances in the blood but may also result from mechanical factors, as the renal lesions may physically damage the red cells as they pass through the renal vasculature.

Bone disease, or *renal osteodystrophy*, is a fairly common finding in patients with chronic renal failure and uremia and develops via several interacting mechanisms. Phosphate retention is postulated to be the primary pathogenetic factor. Even in early renal failure, a transient, slight hyperphosphatemia is believed to occur in response to the decreased renal function. This causes a reciprocal decrease in the plasma concentration of ionized calcium, which stimulates the secretion of parathyroid hormone (PTH). Other factors that contribute to hypocalcemia (and thus to increased parathyroid hormone secretion) include defective calcium absorption from the gastrointestinal tract because the kidneys cannot convert vitamin D to its active form, a decreased calcemic response to PTH, and an altered feedback relationship between serum calcium and PTH secretions. These latter two factors may be related to the impaired vitamin D metabolism (Maxwell et al., 1987).

Parathyroid hormone returns the concentrations of phosphate and calcium to normal by its actions on the bones and kidneys. Parathyroid hormone increases the calcium level by stimulating osteocytic osteolysis of bone; osteoclastic resorption is increased. Renal excretion of phosphate is enhanced and renal clearance of calcium is reduced. A "trade-off" occurs: higher levels of circulating parathyroid hormone for a normal serum phosphate level (Bricker, 1972). In response to continued stimulation, hyperplasia of the parathyroid glands and secondary hyperparathyroidism develop. Impaired renal degradation of parathyroid hormone also contributes to the development of secondary hyperparathyroidism (Maxwell et al., 1987).

Over time, the bone effects of parathyroid hormone and the impaired vitamin D metabolism cause a variety of skeletal diseases, including osteitis fibrosa, osteomalacia, and, less commonly, osteosclerosis and osteoporosis. This sequence of events is summarized in Fig. 20-14. Osteitis fi-

brosa is due to increased bone resorption, which is characterized radiologically by subperiosteal resorption, reduced cortical thickness, and cyst formation. Endosteal fibrosis and a disordered collagen structure are features. Osteitis fibrosa occurs in response to the hyperparathyroidism. Osteomalacia is due to deficient bone mineralization and is characterized radiologically by increased osteoid width. Osteomalacia occurs primarily in response to the impaired vitamin D metabolism. Its occurrence has also been found to correlate highly with aluminum intoxication (see subsequent discussion). Most patients

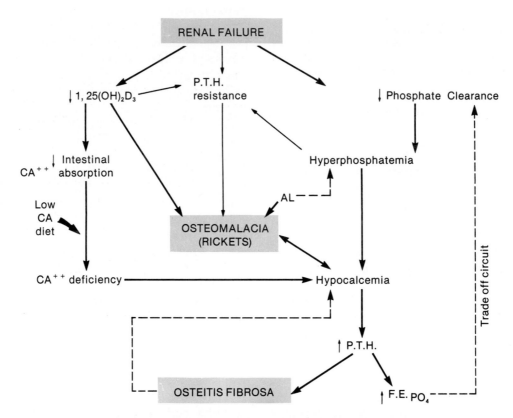

Fig. 20-14. Schematic presentation of the development of renal osteodystrophy in chronic renal failure. The dashed lines indicate negative feedback. Secondary hyperparathyroidism and bone disease occur in renal failure when there is retention of phosphorus, decreased absorption of calcium, and impaired vitamin D metabolism. AL = aluminum, PTH = parathyroid hormone.
(From Humes HD: Pathophysiology of electrolyte and renal disorders, New York, 1986, Churchill Livingstone Inc.)

will have some combination of these two disorders, with the features of one usually predominating over the other (Humes, 1986; Maxwell et al., 1987).

The clinical manifestations of renal osteodystrophy depend on the type of skeletal disease present, the severity and duration of the underlying renal insufficiency, and the stage of skeletal development at which it began. Because children are experiencing the processes of skeletal growth, modeling, and remodeling, as opposed to adults in whom only the process of remodeling is occurring, children are prone to the development of skeletal deformities such as bowing of the long bones and "knock-knees." Osteomalacia usually predominates in children, leading to "renal rickets." Children also experience retarded growth, which is probably due not only to the impaired calcium and phosphorus metabolism present but also to the malnutrition and hormonal aberrations that accompany renal disease. Other clinical manifestations of renal osteodystrophy include bone pain, fractures, spontaneous tendon rupture, and proximal muscle weakness. Alterations in gait may occur, leading to impaired physical mobility. Associated nursing diagnoses may include activity intolerance and potential for injury (Chambers, 1987).

Conversely, one pathogenetic mechanism may cause multiple clinical manifestations of uremia. A good example is the elevated level of parathyroid hormone, which seems to act as a uremic toxin. In addition to its pathogenetic role in hyperparathyroid bone disease, there are indications that parathyroid hormone may also be involved in the pathogenesis of numerous uremic abnormalities, including pruritus, metastatic calcification, neuropathy, anemia, impotence, and alterations in lipid and carbohydrate metabolism (Massry, 1983). Both cardiomyopathy and

encephalopathy are believed to be related to the direct effects of increased PTH and increased calcium content found in the heart and brain tissue of uremic patients. Partial parathyroidectomy and dialysis have been observed to improve both left ventricular function and mental function, providing support for a pathogenetic role for parathyroid hormone in cardiomyopathy and encephalopathy.

The central nervous system manifestations of uremia (uremic encephalopathy) resemble those of other metabolic encephalopathies. A whole spectrum of signs and symptoms, which may appear as apathy, lethargy, inability to concentrate, slurred speech, insomnia, and impaired cognition, can progress to confusion, hallucinations, stupor, seizures, and coma. The onset of encephalopathy may be quite insidious in the patient with CRF. Complaints of headache, restlessness, inability to focus attention and express ideas, activity intolerance and fatigue, memory loss and feeling cold may be heard from the patient, while others may observe personality changes such as irritability, withdrawal, depression, and paranoid delusions. Periods of lucidity may alternate with periods of disorientation. Neurologic manifestations will progress more rapidly in the patient with acute renal failure. Lethargy can rapidly change to confusion and agitation. If untreated, coma, cranial nerve signs, and hyperreflexia will develop. EEG changes have been identified in both CRF and ARF patients, although the EEG changes seen in CRF are milder than those seen in ARF. Following resolution of ARF, EEG changes have been found to persist for up to 3 weeks (Maxwell et al., 1987).

Other causes of CNS dysfunction must also be considered in the uremic patient. Many of these same signs and symptoms can be caused by electrolyte disorders, drug effects, acidosis and the rapid correction of acidosis, hypertension, cardiac arrhythmias, and cerebral hemorrhage (Humes, 1986). Patients who are being treated with hemodialysis may experience the dialysis disequilibrium syndrome. The accompanying neurologic signs and symptoms are similar to those seen in hyponosmolar states (see Chapter 18). Cellular dysfunction occurs as fluid moves into the cells in response to the decreased plasma osmolality brought about by dialysis. Another dialysis-related disorder with neurologic manifestations is called dialysis dementia or dialysis encephalopathy. This lethal disorder is thought to be related to aluminum intoxication. Aluminum, from the dialysis solution or from aluminum containing phosphate binding agents, accumulates in the brain tissue and causes neurologic symptoms (Maxwell et al., 1987).

Not all of the signs and symptoms seen in uremia can be completely explained. The immune system is thought to be depressed, which is evidenced by an impaired ability to reject transplanted tissue and an increased susceptibility to infection. Infection in the uremic patient may be overwhelming. Another example is serositis, which may appear as pericarditis or pleuritis and can be improved by dialysis. (Schrier, 1986). The fact that some of the clinical manifestations are improved by dialysis provides some evidence that a removable substance is the causative mechanism, and, therefore, the search for a uremic toxin continues.

Acute renal failure. Acute renal failure (ARF), the abrupt cessation of renal function, most often presents with a sudden onset of azotemia. Blood urea nitrogen (BUN) and creatinine levels progressively rise. Although it is usually manifested by oliguria, a urinary output of less than 400 ml per 24-hour period, the urinary output can vary from total anuria to polyuria (output > 1000 to 2000 ml per day; Maxwell et al., 1987). The nonoliguric form may represent a less severe form of ARF than the oliguric (Rose, 1987). Complete anuria is seldom seen, and after 1 to 3 weeks (10 to 12 days is typically seen), the oliguric or true failure phase of ARF ends and the diuretic or recovery phase begins.

Because of the loss of renal function the patient experiences alterations in fluid volume, composition, and acid base balance. The specific alterations vary somewhat depending on the underlying cause of acute renal failure (Table 20-6). During the oliguric phase these alterations generally include fluid overload (hypervolemia), hyperkalemia, hyperphosphatemia, hypocalcemia, hyponatremia, and acidosis. Hyperkalemia can be a lethal complication of ARF (Maxwell et al., 1987) and must be treated promptly and aggressively. Uremic signs and symptoms may be present, including lethargy and impaired cognitive function, dysarthria, slurred speech, and bleeding (Rose, 1987). Nausea and vomiting, due to the accumulation of metabolic wastes and any existing electrolyte imbalances, may exacerbate the existing alterations or cause the development of new ones. Infection may be a significant problem and is a common cause of death (Rose, 1987). During the diuretic phase there is an inability to conserve fluid and electrolytes and the patient is at risk for fluid deficit and hypovolemia, as well as the loss of sodium and potassium. The severity of the clinical manifestations and the length of the ARF episode also depend on the underlying cause.

The severity of ARF is highly variable. When the course of ARF is more benign, only mild reductions in renal function might be seen. In other patients the uremic syndrome develops quite rapidly.

Table 20-6.   Fluid and electrolyte abnormalities associated with acute renal failure

Anatomic classification	Etiologies	Fluid/electrolyte abnormality
Prerenal	Hemorrhage, gastrointestinal loss, burns, trauma, sepsis, diabetic ketoacidosis	Hypovolemia, hypotension
	Congestive heart failure, nephrotic syndrome, hepatorenal syndrome	Hypervolemia, edema
Postrenal	Postobstructive diuresis	Polyuria, hypovolemia, hypernatremia
Renal		
Vascular	One-kidney renovascular hypertension, malignant hypertension, scleroderma kidney, polyarteritis, cholesterol emboli, nonsteroidal anti-inflammatory agents, cyclosporin therapy	Hypervolemia, hypertension, hyponatremia, hypokalemia
Glomerular	Acute nephrotic syndrome, rapidly progressive glomerulonephritis	Hypervolemia, hypertension, edema
Tubular;		
Ischemic acute tubular necrosis	Disseminated intravascular coagulation, sepsis, heatstroke	Severe hyperkalemia, severe anion gap metabolic acidosis, respiratory alkalosis, hypophosphatemia
	Cardiac arrest	Hypernatremia
	Severe hyperglycemia	Hyponatremia or hypernatremia
	Acute hemorrhagic pancreatitis	Severe hypocalcemia and high anion gap metabolic acidosis
	Hepatorenal syndrome	Respiratory alkalosis, renal tubular acidosis
Endogenous nephrotoxins	Rhabdomyolysis (myoglobin)	Hyperphosphatemia, hypocalcemia, hypercalcemia, severe high anion gap metabolic acidosis
	Myeloma	Hypercalcemia, renal tubular acidosis, Fanconi syndrome
	Solid tumors	Hypercalcemia
	Acute lymphatic leukemia, lymphosarcoma, Burkitt's lymphoma	Hyperphosphatemia, hypocalcemia
Exogenous nephrotoxins	Heavy metals (Hg, Bi, U)	Renal tubular acidosis, Fanconi syndrome
	Methoxyflurane	Hypernatremia, polyuria
	Amphotericin B	Hypokalemia
	Polymyxin B	Normal anion gap metabolic acidosis
	Streptozotocin	Renal tubular acidosis, Fanconi syndrome
	Mithromycin	Hypocalcemia
	Cisplatin	Hypomagnesemia
	Cyclosporin	Hyperkalemia
	Glycols, snake venom	Severe high anion gap metabolic acidosis

From Maxwell M, Kleeman C, and Narins R, editors: Clinical disorders of fluid and electrolyte metabolism, ed 4, New York, 1987, McGraw-Hill Book Co.

Regardless of severity, most forms of ARF are reversible. Dialysis treatment will be necessary until renal function returns to normal.

Acute renal failure may be the result of a diverse array of diseases and physiologic insults to the body. The causes are sometimes classified as prerenal, renal, or postrenal. *Prerenal* causes include those conditions in which blood flow to the kidneys is disturbed or in which systemic changes affect kidney function indirectly. *Postrenal* causes include conditions in which the function of the urinary tract is disrupted (obstruction). *Renal* causes are those conditions in which the primary pathologic process occurs within the kidney itself. Included in Table 20-7 is a general listing of conditions and the mechanisms by which they act to precipitate ARF.

The most common cause of acute renal failure is *acute tubular necrosis (ATN),* which is a syndrome caused by a variety of disease processes and physiologic insults (Maxwell et al., 1987). The mechanisms by which ATN occurs include isch-

Table 20-7. Causes of acute renal failure

Prerenal	Postrenal	Renal
Hypotension	Obstruction	Glomerular impairment
Shock	Calculi	Glomerulonephritis
Excessive treatment of hypertension	Prostatic hypertrophy	Postinfectious nephritis
	Carcinoma	Lupus nephritis
	Ligation	Polyarteritis nodosa
	Hematoma	Goodpasture's syndrome
True volume depletion	Edema	Wegener's granulomatosis
Gastrointestinal loss through vomiting, diarrhea, or bleeding	Retroperitoneal fibrosis	Henoch-Schönlein purpura
Skin loss through burns or sweating		Vascular alterations
Renal loss through excessive use of diuretics, osmotic diuresis, diabetes insipidus, adrenal insufficiency, or salt wasting nephropathy		Vasculitis
		Malignant nephrosclerosis
		Arterial or venous occlusion
		Hemolytic-uremic syndrome
		Preeclampsia
		Postpartum renal failure
		Renal cortical necrosis
		Progressive systemic sclerosis
Volume depletion		Tubular impairment
Third space sequestrations		Acute tubular necrosis (ischemic and nephrotoxic)
Edematous conditions		Intratubular obstruction (multiple myeloma)
		Uric acid nephropathy
Selective renal ischemia		Hypercalcemia
Hepatorenal syndrome		Reaction to radiocontrast media
Bilateral renal artery stenosis		Interstitial damage
Drugs:		Diffuse pyelonephritis
Nonsteroidal antiinflammatory drugs (NSAIDs)		Acute interstitial nephritis
Ca^{++} channel blockers		Papillary necrosis

emia and direct toxic damage. Etiologies of ATN are listed according to the operative pathogenetic mechanism in Table 20-8. Often both mechanisms interact in the pathogenesis of ATN. Various drugs and poisons, for example, mercury, carbon tetrachloride, and ethylene glycol, are known to exert a toxic effect on the renal tubules. Mercuric chloride damages tubules directly, but the effects of poisoning on the whole body cause decreased renal perfusion due to vasomotor collapse, and the resulting ischemic damage of the tubules is also thought to play a role in the development of ATN. Other examples include a hypovolemic, hypotensive patient who is also septic and being treated with an aminoglycoside antibiotic. The ischemia and nephrotoxicity can potentiate one another (Rose, 1987).

The term *acute tubular necrosis* reflects the pathologic histology present. The extent and location of the lesion differ somewhat depending on the pathogenetic mechanism. ATN of ischemic origin tends to be patchy and most severe in the outer medulla. The medulla is particularly susceptible to ischemia because of the nature of the blood supply, which is low in oxygen, and the high metabolic rate of the tubular cells. In contrast, ATN of nephrotoxic origin tends to be more uniform and occurs in those nephron segments where uptake of the injurious agent is most likely to occur—the proximal convoluted and straight tubules (Rose, 1987).

It should be noted that many of the prerenal causes of ARF cause renal hypoperfusion and tissue ischemia and therefore can also cause ATN of ischemic origin. It is a matter of progression; ATN represents hypoxic injury in response to the ischemia, which often accompanies the prerenal disorders listed in Table 20-7. This is most likely to occur if the ischemia is prolonged or severe. Prevention of the development

of ATN through rapid correction of all hypotensive and hypovolemic conditions must be a priority of care. Renal function must be carefully monitored and dosages carefully adjusted when pharmacologic agents that are known nephrotoxins are administered.

Together, prerenal disorders and ATN account for up to 75% of all cases of ARF. The distinction between prerenal disease and ATN is an important one, as the treatment will differ. Volume replacement can help to restore renal function in prerenal disease, while dialysis is necessary in ATN (Rose, 1987). Despite the use of dialysis, the mortality from ARF remains high and depends on the cause of the renal failure and the general health of the patient. The mortality associated with ARF following trauma or surgery is estimated to be as high as 70% to 80%, while the mortality associated with other causes is estimated to be about 25%. (Schrier, 1986; Rose, 1987).

Various theories have been advanced to explain the severe reduction of GFR characteristic of ARF after the causative event has occurred. These theories include:

1. *The back leak theory:* The glomerular filtrate, because of the disrupted integrity of the tubular epithelium, is totally reabsorbed into the renal capillaries.

2. *Tubular obstruction:* Obstruction occurs as a result of tubular edema or intraluminal debris such as casts and breakdown products of hemoglobin and myoglobin. The resulting increase in tubular pressure would reduce the GFR. This theory applies to ARF seen after severe crush injury or burns, in which myoglobin is released in large amounts.

3. *Vascular theory:* Vascular events that can decrease GFR include vasoconstriction of the afferent arteriole, vasodilation of the efferent arteriole, and de-

Table 20-8. Classification of etiologies and agents of ATN

Acute ischemic renal failure

Surgery
 Major abdominal surgery (2)* (1)
 Aortic surgery (1) (2)
 Open-heart surgery (1) (2) (3)
 Transurethral prostatectomy (water irrigation) (3)
Diagnostic radiology (2)
Obstetrics
 Septic abortion (5) (2) (4)
 Postpartum hemorrhage (1) (2)
 Placenta previa (1) (2)
 Abruptio placentae (1) (2)
 Uterine rupture (1) (2)
 Intrauterine fetal death (1) (2) (4)
 Severe toxemia (1) (2) (4)
Trauma
 Crush injuries (2) (3) (1) (4)
 Fractures (1) (2)
Hemoglobin release (3)
 Infections (septicemia, endotoxins, *Clostridium welshii,* (1) (2) (4) (5); epidemic hemorrhagic fever, (2) (4) (5); malaria (1) (4) (5)
 Mismatched transfusion (3) (4)
 Hemolytic-uremic syndrome (4)
 Glucose-6-phosphate dehydrogenase deficiency (2) (1) (5)

Valvular heart disease (2) (4)
Venomous snake bites (2) (1) (4)
Glycerol therapy (3) (4)
Fresh water submersion (1) (2) (3)
Myoglobin release
 Rhabdomyolysis (excessive exercise† (2) (1) (4); crush injury (2) (1) (4); electric shock, burns (2) (3) (1) (4); heatstroke (2) (4); Hoff's disease (epidemic myoglobinuria) (2); potassium depletion (2); idiopathic, primary, paroxysmal (2); acute polymyositis (2)
 McArdle's syndrome (2)
Proteinuria
 Multiple myeloma with Bence Jones proteinuria (2) (1)
 Waldenström's macroglobulinemia (2) (1)
 Nephrotic syndrome (2) (1)
 Low molecular weight dextran therapy (2) (1)
Miscellaneous
 Major hemorrhage (2)
 Vomiting or diarrhea (severe) (2)
 Myocardial infarction (1)
 (?) Hepatorenal syndrome (2) (4)

Acute nephrotoxic renal failure

Heavy metals
 Mercury (organic and inorganic), bismuth, uranium, cadmium, arsenic, arsine, lithium
Organic solvents
 Carbon tetrachloride, tetrachloroethylene, ethoxyethanol, methanol, toluene, chloroform, trichloromethane, trichloroethylene
Glycols
 Ethylene glycol, diethylene glycol, diglycolic acid, oxalic acid

Antibiotics
 Neomycin, kanamycin, gentamicin, polymyxin, colistin, bacitracin, phenazopyridine, co-trimoxazole, amphotericin, rifampin
Chlorinated hydrocarbon pesticides
 Chlordane, paraquat
Miscellaneous
 Cisplatin, carbon monoxide, mushroom poison, creosol, aniline and other methemoglobin-producing chemicals, phenylbutazone, lysol, phenols, sodium chlorate, diesel fuel, methoxyflurane, radiocontrast media

From: Maxwell M, Kleeman C, and Nahrins R, editors: Clinical disorders of fluid and electrolyte metabolism, ed. 4, New York, 1987, McGraw-Hill Book Co.
*Note: Numbers in parentheses indicate contributing factors, in order of importance: (1) hypotension, (2) ECF loss, (3) release of pigments (hemoglobin, myoglobin), (4) DIC, (5) infection.
†Includes march myoglobinuria, anterior tibia syndrome, karate.

creased permeability of the glomerular membrane.

4. *Cell swelling and dysfunction:* An ischemic event reduces the amount of metabolic energy available for the active transport process of sodium pumping out of the cell. Because cell membranes are permeable to Na^+, Na^+ would diffuse into the cell and the resultant rise in cellular osmolarity would cause an osmotic movement of water into the cell. This swelling has been associated with decreased blood flow, which promotes the persistence of ischemia.

5. *Renin-angiotensin:* According to this theory, tubular dysfunction resulting from ischemia or toxic injury causes an increased intraluminal Na^+ concentration. Sensed at the macula densa (see Chapter 18), the increased Na^+ concentration stimulates the release of renin, and thus the renin-angiotensin system is activated. Renin and angiotensin II cause constriction of the afferent arteriole, which causes a reduction in GFR.

Schrier (1986) provides a complete review of supporting and contradictory data for each theory. The following case study demonstrates the clinical course of acute renal failure.

CASE STUDY: ACUTE RENAL FAILURE

Present illness: BA is a 20-year-old male construction worker who suffered a massive crushing injury to his right thigh in an accident on a construction job. When he arrived at the emergency room yesterday afternoon his vital signs were:

Blood pressure: 94/56

Contributed by Maureen Shekleton.

Pulse: 120 beats/min and weak
Respirations: 28 breaths/min

His skin was noted to be cool and clammy. He was alert and complaining of pain. Despite the pressure dressing, the bleeding could not be controlled and vital signs could not be stabilized. Under local anesthesia, the wound was cleansed, debrided, large vessels were tied off, and small bleeders cauterized. The wound was sutured closed. X-rays were negative for fractures.

BA was brought to the unit with stable vital signs, a dry, intact dressing on his right leg, and a urinary drainage catheter in place. A unit of whole blood was infusing and he was complaining of being thirsty.

History

BA has previously experienced good health. He had all immunizations and a recent tetanus antitoxin when he cut himself while on another construction job about 6 months before this accident. This is his first hospitalization. He had his last complete physical examination when he played high school sports 3 years ago.

Objective and Subjective Data

During morning report, the night nurse tells you that for the last 4 to 5 hours his urine output has been averaging 20 to 35 cc/hr and the total output has been 600 cc since admission including 100 cc of vomitus. He has received 2500 cc of IV fluid and blood. His blood pressure has remained stable at 110-120/60-70 and his pulse rate has ranged between 80-90 beats/min. Blood was drawn for a stat BUN and electrolytes and the laboratory is expected to be calling with the results momentarily.

Upon entering BA's room you note that there is only about 10 cc of dark brownish yellow urine in the collection receptacle. The leg dressing is dry and intact and the toes are warm and dry with good color and capillary refill. BA appears healthy and well nourished. Muscles in the extremities are defined and well developed.

You introduce yourself and BA asks you how long he has been in the hospital. When you ask him to wiggle the toes on his right foot, he does not appear to understand right away. When you ask how he is feeling he says he awoke with a headache and says, "I never get headaches, I guess I hurt my head." When asked if his leg hurts he denies all but a "little soreness."

You ask the resident to come and examine the patient and for the laboratory to supply the blood chemistries. The results are:

BUN: 38 mg/dL
K^+: 5.5 mEq/L
Na^+: 120 mEq/L
Ca^{++}: 3.2 mEq/L

Discussion

BA is experiencing acute renal failure secondary to hypovolemia and hypotension. He is in the oliguric phase which is characterized by the decreased urine output, increased BUN, hyperkalemia, hypocalcemia, and hyponatremia. He is demonstrating the early stages of disorientation and confusion due to hypotonic hyponatremia and the resultant increase in cellular fluid volume. He also has complained of nausea and vomiting.

Renal ischemia was most probably the primary etiologic mechanism for this patient's renal failure. With a crush injury, large amounts of blood can be lost, both externally and through bleeding into the muscles. The injury to the muscles will also result in large amounts of myoglobin being released which can also cause acute renal failure to develop. The mechanism by which heme pigments lead to renal failure is not understood although myoglobin is not directly nephrotoxic since either renal vasoconstriction or volume depletion must also be present for renal failure to develop in this situation (Rose, 1987). It is speculated that decreased renal perfusion leads to a slowing of tubular flow which allows the precipitation of heme pigment casts that subsequently cause tubular obstruction. A triad of findings characteristic of rhabdomyolysis includes pigmented granular casts in the urine, a positive urine Hematest (due to the presence of heme), and an elevated level of serum creatine phosphokinase, an enzyme released from damaged muscle cells. Other findings that indicate cellular damage and the release of cellular constituents include hyperkalemia, hypocalcemia (due to precipitation of calcium phosphate in the damaged muscle tissue), hyperphosphatemia, hyperuricemia, and a high anion gap metabolic acidosis. The plasma creatinine level also rises out of proportion to the degree of renal dysfunction present.

Treatment

Medical treatment will include dialysis for this patient. The hyperkalemia needs to be treated immediately as this can be a lethal complication. The prognosis for complete recovery of renal function is good given the patient's age and general condition of good health.

Nursing Diagnoses

1. Fluid volume excess and altered fluid composition related to ARF
2. Altered patterns of urinary elimination related to ARF
3. Pain related to leg injury
4. Potential for infection related to wound, IV insertion site, urinary drainage catheter, renal failure and anemia
5. Fatigue related to anemia and tissue repair
6. Impaired physical mobility related to leg injury
7. Activity intolerance due to fatigue and leg injury
8. Knowledge deficit related to relationship of injury to renal failure

Chronic renal failure. Chronic renal failure (CRF), or renal insufficiency, develops more slowly than acute renal failure. The causes of CRF include pathologic processes that result in a progressive loss of renal function over time. This renal insufficiency is typified by the gradual loss of functioning nephrons, which increases the solute load and GFR of the remaining functional nephrons. The adaptive response of compensatory hyperfiltration by individual, normal, remaining nephrons in order to maintain the highest total GFR possible is discussed earlier in this chapter. Further adaptation by the remaining nephrons for the decrease in total GFR that progressively occurs includes the allowance for higher plasma levels of substances and the maintenance of daily excretion rates through a decrease in tubular reabsorption of some substances (phosphate and sodium) and an increase in tubular secretion of others (potassium and ammonium) (Humes, 1986). Bricker et al. (1978) described the continual increase in the adaptive functions of the remaining nephrons, as the total number of such nephrons decreases, as a "magnification phenomenon."

The manifestations of chronic renal failure become apparent as the total GFR is reduced due to the progressive loss of functional nephrons. An early manifestation of renal failure is loss of concentrating ability (Humes, 1986). As the GFR declines, there will be an increase in BUN and plasma creatinine levels (see Fig. 20-11). Hyperparathyroidism also develops. In moderately severe renal failure, where the GFR is equal to 20 to 50 ml per minute, anemia and electrolyte disorders appear. The full spectrum of uremic manifestations appears when the GFR has dropped to 10 to 15 ml per minute or less. This sequence of events is illustrated in Fig. 20-15. Conditions such as hyperten-

sion, hypovolemia, obstruction, infection, heart failure, electrolyte abnormalities, and administration of nephrotoxic agents can cause an acute deterioration of renal function superimposed on the CRF as well.

The treatment of renal failure includes dietary restrictions, fluid restriction, dialysis, and transplantation. Dietary Na^+ and water intake will be limited if edema, increased blood pressure, or low serum Na^+ levels (dilutional) are present. Increased Na^+ and water intake may actually be beneficial in removing more waste products if excretion also increases. Dietary K^+ will be restricted if hyperkalemia or oliguria develops. Elimination of dietary protein and exercise restriction reduce the amount of nitrogenous waste products that have to be excreted in the urine. Increased serum phosphate is common and antacids containing aluminum, which bind phosphate, are administered to reduce the plasma phosphate levels. Magnesium-containing compounds are avoided. Anemia is now being treated with recombinant human erythropoietin (Raine, 1988).

Dialysis is used to remove toxic substances and excess fluid and electrolytes from the blood. Dialysis is defined as diffusion of solutes and water through a passive, semipermeable membrane placed between two solutions, wherein the rate of diffusion is increased by either the continuous or intermittent replacement of the partially equilibrated blood and dialysate (Kokko and Tannen, 1986; Maxwell et al., 1987). *Hemodialysis* is a process in which the blood is removed and pumped through an extracorporeal system that contains the dialyzer membrane in a dialysate bath. The process of *peritoneal dialysis* makes use of the body's own membranes as the dialysate is infused into the peritoneal cavity, allowed time to equilibrate with the body fluids, and then drained from the peritoneal cavity. Dialysis will be

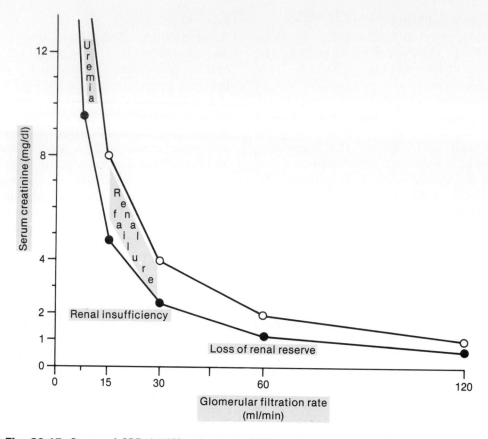

Fig. 20-15. Stages of CRF. A 50% reduction in GFR doubles the serum creatinine concentration from a normal value of 0.6 mg per dl *(closed circles)* or 1.0 mg per dl *(open circles)* in a progressive fashion.

(From Humes HD: Pathophysiology of electrolyte and renal disorders, New York, 1986, Churchill Livingstone Inc.)

needed in 50% of CRF patients within 5 months of the creatinine clearance dropping below 10 ml per minute. (Humes, 1986).

Possible complications of dialysis include overcorrection and the development of hypotension or new electrolyte abnormalities. Bleeding may occur due to the use of heparin in hemodialysis. As dialysis is an invasive procedure, the nursing diagnosis potential for infection is also appropriate (Humes, 1986). Dialysis disequilibrium syndrome and dialysis encepha-

lopathy were discussed previously. Over the long term, renal transplantation may be indicated and beneficial, as it offers the patient an opportunity for better renal function than can be achieved through dialysis, minimizes the long-term sequelae of renal dysfunction, and allows a more normal life-style without reliance on dialysis treatments.

The following case study demonstrates the features of chronic renal failure. The manifestations of systemic lupus erythematosis are described in Chapter 2.

CASE STUDY: CHRONIC RENAL FAILURE

Present illness: DS is an 18-year-old white female with systemic lupus erythematosis (SLE), chronic renal failure (CRF), and chronic pericarditis. She has been readmitted to the hospital for complaints of increased chest and joint pain, edema, weakness, dizziness, thirst, headache, and decreased urinary output.

History

The SLE was diagnosed when DS was 15 years old. She has required dialysis twice a week for the last year and a half due to renal failure secondary to lupus nephritis. She has been readmitted to the hospital on numerous occasions usually as her symptoms worsen. Last year she was able to obtain her high school diploma with a home tutor. She becomes fatigued very easily and does not participate in any social activities other than with her family. She spends most of her time watching TV. She exhibits all of the signs and symptoms of SLE including arthralgias, arthritis, malar rash, fever, malaise, increased ANA titer, and pericarditis (see Chapter 2). She has been amenorrheic since developing renal failure. She maintains a low protein, low sodium, low potassium diet, with a fluid restriction. She continues on corticosteroid, diuretic, and antihypertensive medication. The patient and family are very knowledgeable about the treatment regime and claim to adhere to it scrupulously.

Objective and Subjective Data

DS's general appearance is that of a thin, underdeveloped young woman with a rounded, puffy red face and protruding eyes. Her skin is pale with a yellowish cast and appears dry with obvious flakes of dead skin. There are red marks on her forearms from scratching. Her lips appear

Contributed by Maureen Shekleton.

chapped and slightly cyanotic. Her extremities appear thin and wasted and her fingers are red. Her feet and sacral area are swollen with pitting edema. She has a nonproductive cough.

Height: 5 feet 3 inches
Weight: 98 pounds
Blood pressure: 132-170/70-110 (range)
Pulse: 80-100, regular and strong
Respirations: 20-24 breaths/minute
Laboratory data:
  BUN: 98 mg/dL
  Creatinine: 8.5 mg/dL
  Hemoglobin: 6.4 gm/dL
Urinary output: 300 cc/ 24 hours; dark, yellowish brown, foul smelling urine.

DS complains of severe pruritis, weakness and fatigue. She tells you that she really dislikes dialysis because she gets bored and feels so tired and "out of it" afterwards. She also complains frequently of an upset stomach and lack of appetite. She never talks about future plans or hopes.

Discussion

Lupus nephritis is the result of immune-mediated glomerular damage; immune complex deposition and activation of the complement system occur causing damage to the basement membrane. This patient has diffuse, proliferative glomerular disease. Her renal disease is obviously advanced and she exhibits many uremic signs and symptoms (Table 20-4) such as fatigue, anorexia, anemia, muscle weakness, pruritis, and amenorrhea. The malaise and pericarditis could be caused by either the SLE or CRF. The hypertension may be partly volume related since she is retaining fluid.

Treatment

Control of systemic hypertension and restriction of dietary protein are the most important aspects of treatment since the hemodynamic changes can exacerbate the glomerular damage. Her prognosis is uncertain because of the rapidity of deterioration and inability to control the hypertension. Immunosuppressant therapy may also be tried, however, the previous lack of response to anti-inflammatory therapy is not encouraging.

Nursing Diagnoses

1. Altered urinary elimination pattern related to CRF
2. Powerlessness and hopelessness related to disease progression
3. Body image disturbance related to disease manifestations
4. Altered growth and development related to disease and social restrictions
5. Fatigue related to renal failure and anemia
6. Activity intolerance related to fatigue and weakness
7. Social isolation related to activity intolerance and possible embarrassment about disease manifestations
8. Potential for infection related to renal failure, hemodialysis, corticosteroid therapy and anemia

Nephrotic syndrome. *Nephrotic syndrome* is the term applied to a complex of signs and symptoms related to protein loss via the kidneys. The presence of protein in the urine is a fairly consistent manifestation of diffuse renal disease. Regardless of the primary disease process, the signs and symptoms that comprise the nephrotic syndrome are ultimately related to the loss of protein from the body. The pathogenesis of proteinuria was discussed earlier.

The severity of the clinical manifestations is related to the extent of the protein loss. As protein stores are depleted, the resulting aggregate of clinical signs known as the nephrotic syndrome develops: proteinuria, hypoalbuminemia, edema, a hypercoagulable state, hyperlipidemia, and lipiduria. The urine appears foamy. Nephrotic crises, which are episodes of severe hypoalbuminemia and anasarca associated with anorexia, nausea, vomiting, and abdominal pain, occur occasionally, but their cause is unknown. A urinary protein loss of 3.5 gm or 50 mg per kg per day or more will precipitate the nephrotic syndrome (Rose, 1987).

As body protein stores are depleted, hepatic synthesis of albumin is reduced, which reduces the albumin content of the blood. This results in a decreased plasma oncotic pressure, which favors the transudation of fluid into the interstitial spaces. Edema formation in the nephrotic syndrome is discussed in Chapter 18. In patients with the nephrotic syndrome there is a generalized, soft, pitting edema with periorbital swelling. Circulating plasma volume is reduced, and sodium retention is stimulated. Lymph flow increases, and in patients with gross fluid retention, dilated lymphatics can often be identified over the flanks and buttocks.

Because low molecular weight plasma proteins (e.g., albumin) are lost preferentially in the urine, high molecular weight proteins such as the lipoproteins remain in the plasma. This contributes to the hyperlipidemia and hypercholesterolemia. The liver also increases its production of cholesterol. The lipiduria is probably the result of increased filtration of some of the smaller lipoprotein molecules and cholesterol esters.

Nephrotic syndrome accompanies those primary renal diseases characterized by glomerular damage, especially membranous nephropathy and focal glomerulosclerosis. The nephrotic syndrome is seen in approximately 5% of patients with systemic lupus erythematosus (SLE) and in 10% to 20% of patients with diabetes mellitus. Diabetic patients with the nephrotic syndrome usually exhibit retinal microaneurysms, diastolic hypertension, azotemia caused by reduced renal function, and superimposed congestive heart failure.

The causes of nephrotic syndrome can be categorized as follows:

1. Immune complex, autoantibody, or hypersensitivity disease
2. Hereditary or congenital conditions
3. Metabolic disease (sarcoidosis and diabetes mellitus)
4. Pregnancy-induced preeclampsia
5. Circulatory disease (bilateral renal vein thrombosis)

Treatment of the nephrotic syndrome caused by primary renal disease is directed toward relief of edema and correction of the hypoproteinemia. Increased dietary protein will provide the nitrogen necessary for protein synthesis and build up depleted nitrogen stores (restore positive nitrogen balance). Depending on the cause of the nephrotic syndrome, corticosteroid therapy may be successful.

The term *nephrosis* should be differentiated from the nephrotic syndrome. Nephrosis is applied to a variety of lesions that are pathologically unrelated. Hence its meaning in general is quite ambiguous, and it is not used synonymously with the nephrotic syndrome.

Etiologic mechanisms. The major mechanisms by which primary disruption of genitourinary elimination occurs include inflammation, obstruction, altered tissue perfusion, and impairment of the ability to concentrate and dilute the urine. These mechanisms are discussed in terms of the renal pathology and alterations in renal function they cause. Renal function can be disrupted by diseases outside the genitourinary system as well as within. In fact, causes of altered renal function are usually classified as being prerenal, postrenal, or renal (intrinsic kidney disease). Prerenal causes include diseases outside of the genitourinary system that can secondarily affect renal function. Intrinsic renal disease can be further classified according to the affected structure: glomerular or nonglomerular, the latter including the tubular, interstitial, and vascular components of the kidneys (Figure 20-16). Conditions outside the genitourinary system in which renal function is altered as a secondary effect of the disease are discussed in greater detail in other chapters.

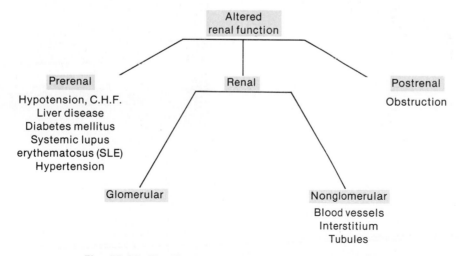

Fig. 20-16. Classification of causes of altered renal function.

Inflammation. Inflammation induced by immunologic processes is the basis of the glomerular damage that occurs in a group of diseases classified as *glomerulonephritis.* The primary lesions are glomerular, and other anatomic changes in the kidney occur secondary to them. Glomerular damage has been demonstrated experimentally to be the result of two major immunologic processes: the deposition of antigen-antibody complexes in the glomerular walls and an antibody reaction with antigens in the glomerular basement membrane (Figs. 20-17 and 20-18). Glomerular damage can be due to immune complexes alone or the mediators activated by the immune response such as complement, vasoactive peptides, platelets, neutrophils, fibrin, and macrophages (Rose, 1987).

Acute, diffuse, proliferative glomerulonephritis is also referred to as acute poststreptococcal glomerulonephritis; it is the most commonly seen type of glomerulonephritis. The immunologic mechanism in this disorder appears to be the deposition of antigen-antibody complexes within the glomerular walls. This inflammatory disorder occurs at all ages but is frequently seen in children and young adults. It usually follows an acute respiratory or skin infection caused by group A hemolytic streptococci. There is often a latent period between the acute infection and the onset of the glomerulonephritis, which usually develops within 1 to 4 weeks after the onset of the infection. The factors that pre-

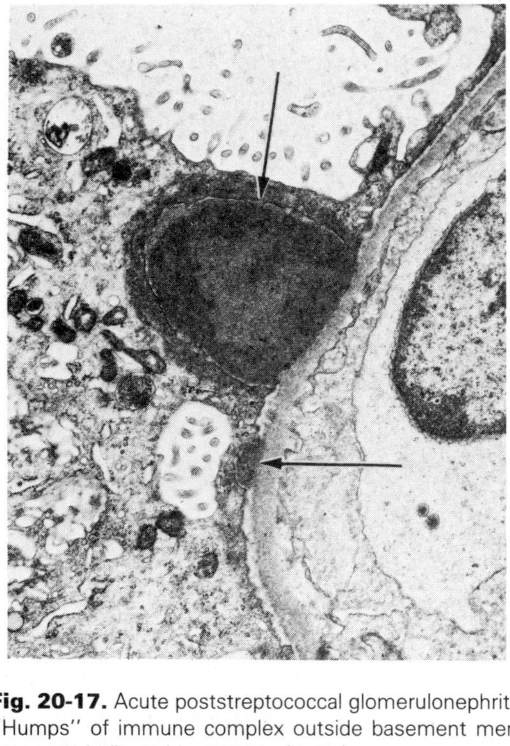

Fig. 20-17. Acute poststreptococcal glomerulonephritis. ''Humps'' of immune complex outside basement membrane are indicated by arrows. (×60.)

(From Anderson WAD, and Kissane JM: Pathology, ed 7, St. Louis, 1977, The CV Mosby Co.)

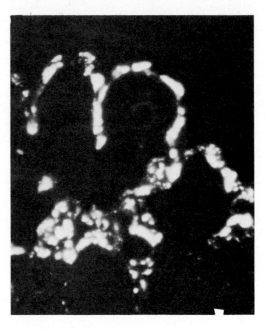

Fig. 20-18. Acute poststreptococcal glomerulonephritis. ''Humps'' of immune complex stained with fluorescent antihuman complement (C3). (×1,000.)

(Courtesy Dr. C. Cornwall, Syracuse, N.Y. From Anderson WAD, and Kissane JM: Pathology, ed 7, St. Louis, 1977, The CV Mosby Co.)

dispose an individual to the development of streptococcal infection are discussed in Chapter 17.

Glomerular permeability is increased in glomerulonephritis allowing the escape of protein and red blood cells from the plasma into the urine. There is also a loss of functional glomerular surface area. Inflammatory cells accumulate within the glomerular capillaries and mesangium (Humes, 1986). The net effect is a reduction in the GFR. There may, however, be marked proximal tubular reabsorption of the filtered water and sodium, which is a feature of the *acute nephritic syndrome*, a common occurrence in poststreptococcal glomerulonephritis (Humes, 1986).

The clinical manifestations of the acute nephritic syndrome include a reduction in urinary volume (oliguria) and excretion of a brownish, smoky urine with a high specific gravity, reflecting the proteinuria, hematuria, and presence of red blood cell casts. There is usually a slight to moderate increase in blood pressure (although it can be quite severe), which is thought to result from decreased renal blood flow and the subsequent activation of the renin-angiotensin system. Fluid volume expands as a compensatory mechanism. Edema occurs and is usually seen as puffiness of the eyelids in the morning that gradually subsides during the day. Edema sometimes becomes severe and generalized. Headache may also be a complaint.

Treatment is symptomatic, and prevention of complications is of utmost concern. Bed rest is indicated during the acute phase. Sodium and fluid restriction and the use of diuretic and antihypertensive agents may be needed if the edema and hypertension are severe. When edema and hematuria are resolved, BUN levels return to normal.

Ninety-five percent of the children who develop this disease recover completely. In adults the condition is usually more serious, with only 60% to 70% recovering completely. Death may occur from complications, including acute heart failure or acute renal failure. In others the glomerular lesions persist and progressively worsen, usually causing death from hypertension and renal failure within 2 years. These patients are then classified as having rapidly progressive glomerulonephritis, which also sometimes occurs for no apparent cause.

Proteinuria that persists for several months is consistent with recovery. However, when proteinuria persists for a year or more, the glomerular damage is most likely progressing, although there may be no other clinical manifestation of this. The possibility of progressive glomerular damage is increased if there are also red blood cells and leukocytes in the urine. These patients are most likely to develop chronic glomerulonephritis. There are other types of glomerulonephritis, all of which may eventually reach an end stage in which glomerular function is so depressed that chronic renal failure characterized by uremia and hypertension develops. The rate of progression to this end stage is determined by the type and severity of the preceding glomerulonephritis syndrome. This end stage is referred to as *chronic glomerulonephritis*.

Most patients who develop chronic glomerulonephritis are between 40 and 50 years old. In 70% of the patients there is no clinical history of prior renal disease. In these cases it is often impossible to decide what type of silent glomerulonephritis was present. Pathologic changes in the kidneys in this syndrome include a uniform and equal reduction in size with diffuse thinning of the cortex. The surface may be highly granular, and the renal ar teries and branches show arteriosclerotic thickening. If hypertension is present, cortical mottling and hemorrhage may be superimposed on the other pathologic changes.

Severe hypertension accompanying chronic glomerulonephritis will aggravate renal destruction, and renal failure will progress rapidly to death. Where hypertension is less severe, the progress of the renal failure will be much slower, and chronic glomerulonephritis will continue for years.

Another inflammatory process that appears to be immunologically mediated is *acute tubulointerstitial nephropathy or nephritis*. In adults the most common cause of this disorder is a hypersensitivity reaction to a drug, most notably methicillin. Other antibiotics, including penicillin, ampicillin, rifampin, the sulfonamides, and the cephalosporins, as well as other diverse drugs including the nonsteroidal anti-inflammatory drugs, certain diuretics, interferon, and cimetidine, can also cause this condition (Adler et al., 1985). In children infection seems to be a more common cause. Streptococcal infection is most significant, but acute interstitial nephritis also has been seen as a complication following diphtheria, leptospirosis, Legionnaires' disease, and some viral infections (Humes, 1986). An idiopathic form also occurs. Antitubular basement membrane (TBM) antibodies have been identified in methicillin-induced and idiopathic interstitial nephritis (Rose, 1987).

Patients usually have an acute deterioration in renal function, which sometimes progresses to acute renal failure, following a systemic infection or after beginning a new medication. A latent period of about 10 days usually intervenes. Mild proteinuria and hematuria may be present. White blood cell casts may also be found in the urine. In the case of drug sensitivity acute tubulointerstitial nephritis, signs of an allergic process such as fever, eosinophilia, and/or a maculopapular skin rash may also be present.

Treatment involves discontinuation of the drug or treatment of the infection. The degree of recovery of renal function depends on the severity of renal impairment that occurred due to the acute interstitial nephritis (Rose, 1987).

Inflammation may also occur as a result of an infectious process. *Acute pyelonephritis* is a bacteria-induced inflammatory disorder involving the renal pelvis, calices, and parenchyma. It usually occurs secondary to lower urinary tract infection that has ascended but may also occur due to hematogenous spread secondary to infection at another site in the body (Humes, 1986). The most common causative organism is *Escherichia coli*, although other organisms from the gastrointestinal flora are common. Once the bacteria reach the kidney, they proliferate, and an inflammatory response ensues, often with abscess formation (Fig. 20-19). The irregular and patchy renal lesions seen are characteristic of the random manner in which the bacteria spread from the infected calyces.

The most common site of urinary tract infection is the bladder, and it is highly likely that cystitis is a factor in most cases of pyelonephritis. Clinical manifestations of cystitis include dysuria, frequency with small amounts of urine, and visible cloudiness in the urine. There is evidence that occurrence of the vesicoureteral reflex (reflux of urine from the bladder into the ureters) is enhanced in cystitis. As a result of the inflammatory process, swelling of the ureterovesical valves may cause them to function incompetently and allow urine to flow back into the kidneys.

Bacteriuria of over 100,000 organisms

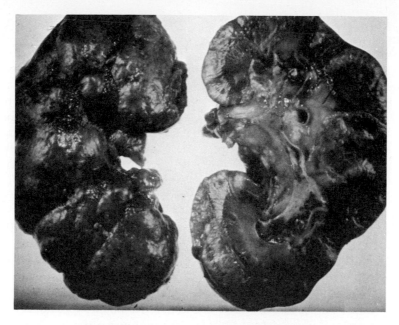

Fig. 20-19. The effects of acute pyelonephritis.

per milliliter of urine usually indicates a urinary tract infection. This can reflect infection at any point along the urinary tract. An important determination is whether the renal parenchyma has been involved. A high titer of serum antibody to the infecting bacteria and cellular casts in the urine are fairly accurate indications that the kidneys have been affected. Pyuria can be the result of infection along any portion of the urinary tract.

Significant bacteriuria in the absence of symptoms of urinary tract infection has been found in the aged and in approximately 1% of healthy schoolgirls and 5% of pregnant women. Urinary tract infections occur most frequently in females. Some of the factors that predispose a person to the development of urinary tract infection include urinary tract obstruction, structural abnormalities, certain disease states in which resistance to infection is reduced, diabetes mellitus with a general

susceptibility to infection, and pregnancy in which urethral dilation and stasis of urine occur.

The clinical manifestations of acute pyelonephritis include frequency of urination, dysuria, flank pain and tenderness in the lumbar area, and fever and other systemic signs of an inflammatory process. Uncomplicated acute pyelonephritis is not usually associated with ARF (Humes, 1986). Treatment involves an antibiotic to which the infecting organism is sensitive.

Chronic pyelonephritis is a form of chronic tubulointerstitial nephropathy that results from recurrent infection in the presence of some underlying anatomic abnormality. Humes (1986) states that chronic renal insufficiency does not occur as a result of infection unaccompanied by underlying urinary tract pathology. Infection in the presence of obstruction, renal calculi, or vesicoureteral reflux (VUR) can result in chronic pyelonephritis and eventually chronic renal insufficiency and failure if initiation of treatment is delayed.

Chronic pyelonephritis due to VUR, which is also called reflux nephropathy, is the second most common cause of chronic tubulointerstitial nephropathy (Humes, 1986). Cortical scarring appears to be associated with the incidence of intrarenal reflux or the retrograde movement of urine into the renal parenchyma. If urine is infected, this will initiate an inflammatory process in the tissue. There is speculation that normal urine may also cause damage through the initiation of an immune response. VUR most often is seen in children who have a congenital or developmental abnormality of the ureterovesical valve. Neurogenic bladder can also cause VUR.

The clinical picture of chronic pyelonephritis includes a history of recurrent urinary tract infection and hypertension. Reflux nephropathy is a common cause of juvenile hypertension and accounts for 20% to 30% of the end-stage renal disease seen in children. Progressive renal deterioration is seen if treatment is not initiated before significant renal damage has occurred. Medical treatment consists of continuous prophylactic administration of an antimicrobial agent. There is controversy regarding the usefulness of surgical correction of the underlying abnormality (Rose, 1987).

Obstruction. The major effect of urinary tract obstruction is interference with the flow of urine. An obstruction can occur anywhere along the urinary tract, and the effects depend on the degree, duration, and site of the obstruction, as well as whether one or both kidneys are involved. If the obstruction is complete and bilateral, anuria will be a manifestation, with eventual development of renal failure if the obstruction is not relieved. Obstruction may be acute or chronic also.

Obstruction results in dilation of the collecting system proximal to the site of the obstruction. Back pressure from the obstruction is eventually transmitted to the kidney, and dilation of the pelvis and calyces will occur. These anatomic changes can be visualized radiographically and are used to diagnose obstruction. This enlargement of the collecting system and the atrophy of the renal parenchyma that accompanies it is termed *hydronephrosis*. Mechanisms thought to be responsible for the parenchymal atrophy include intrarenal reflux, ischemia, the direct effect of pressure (pressure atrophy), and infection (Schrier, 1986). Prolonged obstruction is considered to be a primary cause of chronic tubulointerstitial nephropathy (Humes, 1986). As intracapsular hydrostatic pressure increases, the gradient favoring filtration is reduced, and the GFR decreases. Other alterations in renal function that may occur reflect tubular dysfunction and include progressive azotemia, decreased urinary concentrating ability, changes in urinary sodium excretion, and inability to acidify the urine and excrete potassium (Schrier, 1986).

The possible causes of obstruction are many and varied (Schrier, 1986). Obstruction can result from congenital defects in the urinary tract. The position or structure of the organs may be such that urine flow is impeded. This is most frequently seen in children. Obstruction can result from tumor growth within or outside the urinary tract. Pressure from growth of a tumor in the tissue surrounding the urinary tract may be enough to impair the free drainage of urine. Tumors and calculi are the most common causes of obstruction of the upper urinary tract (Rose, 1987). Calculi may form and become lodged in the ureters or bladder neck. This is a major cause of obstruction in young adult males (Humes,

1986). With increasing age, prostatic hypertrophy, tumors, and calculi become more frequent causes in men. Cervical cancer is a leading cause in older women. Strictures of the ureters or urethra may result from inflammatory damage secondary to infection. Strictures may also occur as a result of trauma. Pregnancy may cause ureteral obstruction because of the pressure of the uterine contents. In the Black population, sickle cell disease must be considered.

The two most common causes of obstruction are urinary calculi and bladder neck obstruction resulting from benign prostatic hypertrophy. The appearance of renal calculi is often related to the presence of an excessive amount of calcium in the urine. Hypercalciuria may occur as a result of hyperparathyroidism. Infection predisposes to stone formation, since calcium and phosphate are more soluble at a lower pH, and infection causes urinary pH to rise. The incidence of calculi is increased in patients with hyperuricemia. Patients experiencing immobility are also more susceptible to development of renal calculi (see Chapter 14).

Benign prostatic hypertrophy occurs in men after the age of 50. Hypertrophy may take place in the muscular or glandular structures or both. The reason for the hypertrophy is not completely clear but is thought to be related to changes in the relative amounts of estrogen and androgen that occur with aging. The hypertrophy may impinge on the urethra, the bladder, or both, depending on the portion of the gland that is hypertrophied. The urethra becomes distorted and displaced, and urine flow is impeded. If the bladder wall is also affected so that the normal contour of the bladder is changed, allowing the development of dependent areas within it, complete emptying of the bladder will also be impaired, and urinary stasis will occur in these areas. Stasis predisposes to calculi formation and the development of infection. A complication of prostate hypertrophy is chronic prostatitis, the development of inflammation or infection within the glandular tissues themselves.

The clinical manifestations of obstruction depend on the cause, extent, and anatomic location of the obstruction (Table 20-9). Anuria will be present with complete bilateral obstruction. With lesser degrees of obstruction, dysuria, hematuria,

Table 20-9. Clinical manifestations of urinary tract obstruction

Location	Acute obstruction	Chronic obstruction
Bladder neck, urethra	Anuria (if complete) Intensity of urinary stream decreased Suprapubic pain Distended, palpable bladder	Frequency Dribbling Urgency Nocturia Incontinence Hesitancy Intensity of urinary stream decreased
Kidney, ureter	Renal colic (ureteral obstruction) Flank pain, tenderness Hematuria (occasional) Paralytic ileus	Often asymptomatic Vague back, flank, or abdominal discomfort Hematuria (occasional) Polyuria, nocturia (if partial and bilateral)

frequency, dribbling, and nocturia may occur and alter the normal pattern of elimination. If an infectious process is present, the temperature may be elevated. Renal colic is usually intermittent but severe and may radiate from the flank. This pain is thought to be related to the abnormal increase in pressure distal to the obstruction in the renal pelvis. These patients appear pale and anxious, and sometimes they are afraid to move for fear that movement will aggravate the pain. If a renal calculus was the source of the obstruction and it is suddenly dislodged, relief from the pain will be immediate.

Complications of urinary tract obstruction include infection, hypertension, renal calculi, renal failure, and papillary necrosis. Calculus formation is enhanced by the stasis of urine and the presence of infection. Papillary necrosis may result from severe obstruction and is thought to be caused by ischemia induced by reduced medullary blood flow.

Patients with urinary tract obstruction are more likely to develop a urinary tract infection for the following reasons: (1) the stagnant urine serves as a culture medium for bacterial growth; (2) obstruction, in the absence of structural changes, predisposes to intermittent intrarenal reflux, and prolonged, partial obstruction causes thickening and dilation of the ureters, which often allows free reflux of urine; (3) obstruction appears to reduce the kidneys' ability to resist infection; and (4) obstruction may lead to renal failure, a condition in which general susceptibility to infection is increased.

The incidence of hypertension and the development of renal failure are related to the duration and type of obstruction. With the exception of chronic unilateral obstruction, relief of the obstruction will return the blood pressure to normal.

Progressive renal failure only develops as a result of bilateral obstruction. In patients with partial obstruction, renal failure and irreversible renal damage will not develop as rapidly as in patients experiencing complete obstruction.

Recovery of renal function is possible if the obstruction is relieved relatively soon after onset. It appears that the longer the duration of obstruction, the less likely are the chances of complete recovery of renal function. Recovery is better when obstruction is partial and when infection has not occurred (Schrier, 1986).

Treatment of obstruction is aimed at restoring the normal flow of urine, which sometimes must be done surgically. Another goal of treatment is restoration of normal fluid and electrolyte balance, which may have been disrupted by the obstructive process. Diuresis occurs following relief of obstruction, and while this may be physiologic to an extent, prolonged and severe diuresis can lead to extreme fluid and electrolyte deficits, especially of water and Na^+ (Rose, 1987).

Not only can obstruction within the urinary tract be a problem but obstruction can also occur within the tubules of the nephron. Intratubular obstruction with cellular debris and casts is part of the characteristic picture of acute tubular necrosis, which is a major cause of acute renal failure. Acute renal failure due to obstruction of the collecting tubules by uric acid crystal precipitation characterizes *acute uric acid nephropathy*. An acute onset of oliguria or anuria is seen in the setting of increased tissue breakdown, which is associated with increased purine metabolism and uric acid production. This condition often occurs in patients with an underlying lymphoproliferative or myeloproliferative disorder after the initiation of chemotherapy and may also accompany seizures, ischemia, and some cases of primary gout. Uric acid precipitation requires a high urinary uric acid concentration and an acid pH and, therefore, can be prevented by increasing the urine volume through adequate hydration, alkalinization of the urine, and administration of allopurinol, which decreases uric acid production by inhibiting the enzyme xanthine oxidase, which is necessary for conversion of uric acid from precursor nucleic acid metabolites.

Uric acid stones can also form outside the tubules in the urinary tract in a form of uric acid renal disease known as *uric acid nephrolithiasis*. A third renal disorder resulting from abnormal uric acid metabolism is *chronic urate nephropathy or chronic gouty nephropathy*. This is characterized by interstitial urate deposition with little effect on long-term renal function and is thought to be relatively uncommon. It is now believed that many patients who were previously diagnosed with this disorder in actuality have chronic lead nephropathy (Humes, 1986; Rose, 1987).

Altered tissue perfusion. As with all other tissues in the body, adequate renal perfusion is necessary for the delivery of oxygen and nutrients and the removal of metabolic wastes. The renal circulation is especially critical, as it is the point of final removal of metabolic wastes. Because of its excretory functions, renal tissue is highly metabolic and therefore highly susceptible to the effects of ischemia.

Renal perfusion can be altered by changes in either pressure or flow. The effects of hypotension and hypertension on the kidneys are discussed in a previous section of this chapter. Flow can be disrupted by either partial or complete occlusion of a blood vessel, which may be the result of an immunogenic or nonimmunogenic process. Nonimmunogenic processes include vasospasm, mechanical disruption, thromboembolic phenomena, intravascular coagulation, and platelet deposition.

A group of disorders that affect renal function fall within the classification of systemic vasculitis. These disorders are generally believed to result from immunologic processes because circulating immune complexes have been identified in patients with active vasculitis (Rose, 1987). It is thought that deposition of these complexes in the vascular wall initiates complement and neutrophil activation, causing increased vascular permeability and vascular injury. The disorders that most commonly affect the kidney, causing glomerular dysfunction, include polyarteritis nodosa, Wegener's granulomatosis, and a type of hypersensitivity vasculitis, Henoch-Schönlein purpura (Humes, 1986). The glomerular pathology seen in polyarteritis nodosa and Wegener's granulomatosis includes areas of fibrinoid necrosis and sclerosis due to ischemic damage, which occurs as vascular integrity is disrupted by inflammatory changes. Progressive renal deterioration often occurs. Respiratory failure and renal failure are the major causes of death in Wegener's granulomatosis (Rose, 1987). Henoch-Schonlein purpura usually begins as a mild glomerulonephritis; however, in severe cases, fibrinoid necrosis and crescent formation are found. Progressive renal deterioration is uncommon.

The formation of small vessel platelet thrombi is the pathogenetic mechanism that causes disorders classified as *hemolytic-uremic syndromes* (HUS). In the acute stage, platelet and fibrin thrombi occlude the glomerular capillaries, arterioles, and small interlobular arteries, which also show intimal thickening. The subsequent ischemia causes necrosis in the arterioles and glomeruli. In severe cases, cortical necrosis also occurs. The predominant site of pathology has prognostic implications. Glomerular changes are reversible, as is demonstrated by the spontaneous, complete recovery seen in childhood HUS. Arterial involvement occurs more frequently in adult HUS and is associated with a greater degree of hypertension and less complete recovery of renal function, probably due to persistent ischemia and necrosis (Rose, 1987).

The disorders caused by this platelet thrombi formation are characterized by acute renal failure, hemolytic anemia, and thrombocytopenia. The clinical characteristics of these disorders are summarized in Table 20-10.

Thrombotic thrombocytopenic purpura is a relatively rare disorder, and adult HUS is relatively uncommon. Childhood HUS occurs more frequently and is one of the more common causes of ARF in children (Humes, 1986). In children, it most often occurs within 3 weeks after an episode of viral or bacterial gastroenteritis (Drummond, 1985), whereas in adults it is often idiopathic. Its onset is marked by pallor, oliguria or anuria, petechiae, purpura, or other bleeding. Hypertension and hepatosplenomegaly will be present in approximately half the affected patients. More infrequent findings include abdominal pain, fever, altered mental status, convulsions, and coma. The latter symptoms may reflect the uremia and electrolyte disorders more than any primary pathologic findings (Rose, 1987).

HUS appears to be the result of isolated platelet consumption, in contrast to the generalized activation of the coagulation pathway seen in disseminated intravascular coagulation (DIC). Two theories have been proposed to explain the isolated

Table 20-10. Clinical characteristics of the HUS

Disorder	Clinical setting	Clinical features
Thrombotic thrombocytopenic purpura (TTP)	Most often affects females between the ages of 10 and 50; usually idiopathic	Characteristic pentad; fever, microangiopathic hemolytic anemia, thrombocytopenic purpura, renal failure (usually slowly progressive), and neurologic abnormalities
Childhood HUS	Primarily affects children under the age of 4 following an episode of gastroenteritis or, less often, an upper respiratory infection	Acute renal failure, microangiopathic hemolytic anemia, and thrombocytopenia
Adult HUS	May rarely follow gastroenteritis as in children, but most common in women postpartum or in those taking oral contraceptives, in cancer patients (if treated with mitomycin C or the combination of cisplatin and bleomycin), or in transplant patients taking cyclosporine	Acute renal failure, microangiopathic hemolytic anemia, and thrombocytopenia, but fever, neurologic abnormalities, and a cardiomyopathy may also be present

From Rose BD: Pathophysiology of renal disease, New York, ed. 2, 1987, McGraw-Hill Book Co.

platelet consumption. The first theory is that platelet aggregation and platelet thrombus formation occur secondarily, in response to vascular endothelial injury. Endothelial cell damage in the glomerular capillaries is the most consistent histologic lesion found in HUS and has been observed to occur before platelet aggregation in the experimental setting (Cattell, 1985). The second theory is that these events occur as primary phenomena in response to either the presence of a platelet-aggregating factor (PAF) or a deficiency of a platelet-aggregating inhibitor in the plasma (Rose, 1987).

Sickle cell anemia is a disease in which altered renal function is common due to the renal vascular disruption caused by sickling of the erythrocytes (see Chapter 3). Sickling, a characteristic change in the shape of the red blood cell, occurs in response to hypoxia, hypertonicity, and acidity. These conditions are prevalent in the medulla due to the countercurrent exchange mechanism, and the resultant sickling causes increased blood viscosity with sludging and stasis of blood in the capillaries of the vasa recta. This in turn causes microthrombi formation and medullary ischemia, which leads to papillary necrosis with tubular dysfunction and defective countercurrent exchange as the eventual results. Clinical manifestations such as hyposthenuria, intermittent nocturia, urinary pH remaining above 5.3, and occasional hyperkalemia reflect the impaired urinary acidification and decreased ability to concentrate the urine and excrete potassium due to the impaired tubular function and countercurrent exchange (Rose, 1987). Hematuria is thought to be the result of the physical destruction of blood vessels and papillary necrosis (Buckalew and Someren, 1974).

The glomerulus is also affected. In the earlier decades of life, the GFR is elevated. The increase in GFR and renal blood flow are thought to be mediated by vasodilator prostaglandins in response to the medullary ischemia. The development of glomerulosclerosis is probably related to the glomerular hyperfiltration and perfusion that occur. Proximal tubular reabsorption is markedly increased, most probably as an adaptive response to the increased GFR and dysfunction of other tubular segments (de Jong and Statius van Eps, 1985). The pathogenetic mechanisms of the altered renal function seen in sickle cell disease are diagrammed in Fig. 20-20.

The GFR does fall below normal at approximately 30 years of age, and a progressive loss of renal function occurs. The nephrotic syndrome can develop in those patients who demonstrate glomerular pathology associated with immune complex deposition (de Jong and Statius van Eps, 1985). Renal failure is a major cause of death in sickle cell disease (Thomas et al., 1982).

Occlusive changes in the vasa recta leading to papillary necrosis constitute the underlying pathology found in *analgesic abuse nephropathy*. This disorder is caused by the long-term ingestion of analgesics containing aspirin, acetaminophen, or phenacetin and especially those with the combination of aspirin and phenacetin (Rose, 1987). Whether the origin of this disorder is truly vascular is a matter of ongoing study. The hyaline thickening of the vasa recta capillaries and early medullary ischemia support a vascular pathogenesis (Rose, 1987). Medullary ischemia can be promoted by aspirin through inhibition of vasodilating prostaglandin production. A direct nephrotoxic mechanism of injury has also been proposed (Duggin, 1980).

Impaired concentrating and diluting ability. The ability to concentrate the urine

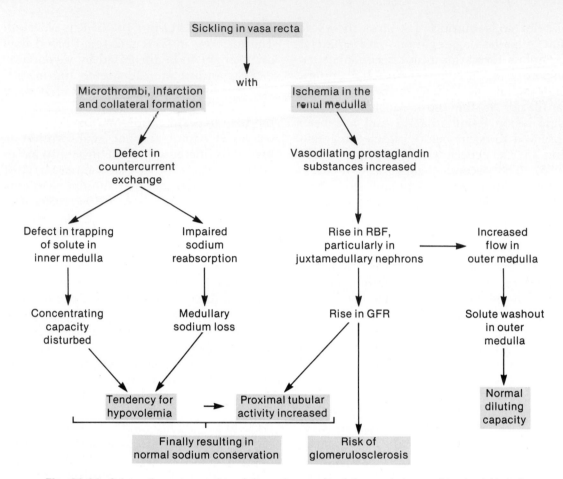

Fig. 20-20. Schematic representation of the pathogenesis of the renal abnormalities in sickle cell anemia.
(From de Jong PE and Statius van Eps LW: Kidney Int 27:711, 1985. Reprinted by permission from Kidney International.)

depends on the presence of ADH, the appropriate renal response to ADH, and medullary hypertonicity. Both concentrating and diluting abilities depend on delivery of a hypotonic filtrate to the distal segment. The ability to excrete a dilute urine depends on the appropriate absence of ADH. Alterations in ADH secretion, the renal responsiveness to ADH, medullary hypertonicity, blood flow, and delivery of an appropriate solute load to the distal segment can all impair the concentrating or diluting functions of the kidneys.

Diabetes insipidus is the term applied to a clinical syndrome characterized by excretion of an extremely dilute urine. The renal concentrating ability is reduced because of a failure of ADH secretion (central or neurogenic diabetes insipidus) or lack of renal response to ADH secretion (nephrogenic diabetes insipidus). Patients with central diabetes insipidus have low levels of circulating ADH, and their polyuria is vasopressin responsive, which constitutes a basis for therapy. This is in contrast to patients with nephrogenic diabetes insipidus, who have normal circulating levels of ADH and vasopressin-resistant polyuria. An extra 1200 ml of water or more can be lost in the urine each day as a result of this diuresis. A person with an intact thirst mechanism will maintain normal water balance by increasing intake. A defect in the thirst mechanism or the inability to ingest water in the presence of diabetes insipidus may result in excessive water loss and an increase in plasma osmolality.

Central diabetes insipidus is characterized by loss of renal concentrating ability related to insufficient ADH secretion. Conditions in which the function of the hypothalamus and its tract is disrupted cause central diabetes insipidus. Loss of the posterior pituitary may produce a transient polyuric period. Half of the cases of central diabetes insipidus are idiopathic in origin and are thought to reflect cellular degeneration in the hypothalamic nuclei. Other causes include trauma (accidental or surgical, especially hypophysectomy), neoplasms, and hypoxemic encephalopathy.

Symptoms of polyuria and polydipsia begin abruptly in the majority of cases. The urine will be hypoosmotic. There is a typical triphasic response following trauma, which is seen clinically after hypophysectomy. During the first 4 to 5 days after the trauma a polyuric state exists that probably represents inhibition of the release of the stored ADH due to hypothalamic dysfunction. This is followed by a 5-day antidiuretic phase, which represents the release of stored ADH from the posterior pituitary. Permanent central diabetes insipidus follows the antidiuretic phase.

Nephrogenic diabetes insipidus is characterized by loss of renal concentrating ability because of loss of the normal renal response to ADH. Nephrogenic diabetes insipidus may be congenital or acquired, although the congenital form is rare. Acquired nephrogenic diabetes insipidus can be the result of a variety of conditions. The mechanisms through which the lack of renal response to ADH occurs include decreased generation of cyclic AMP, reduced cyclic AMP effect, and interference with the countercurrent function and renal medullary hypertonicity. For example, impaired renal concentrating ability is seen in hypercalcemia and hypokalemia regardless of the cause of the electrolyte imbalance. Research with animals has demonstrated both impaired cyclic AMP generation and reduction of medullary hypertonicity in these electrolyte disorders. In sickle cell anemia the countercurrent mechanism is impaired because of the sickling of red blood cells in the vasa recta. Hyposthenuria is common, since the hypertonicity and low P_{O_2} of the blood and tortuosity of the vessels in this system favor the sickling process. In renal failure, anatomic changes as well as increased solute excretion per nephron contribute to the loss of renal concentrating ability; however, polyuria in patients with renal insufficiency is limited by the loss of functioning nephrons. Various drugs can also impair the kidney's ability to respond to ADH. Listed in Table 20-11 are disorders that cause nephrogenic diabetes insipidus and mechanisms by which they act to limit the renal response to ADH.

Diabetes insipidus can be treated with fluid intake as long as the thirst mechanism and the ability to respond are intact. If this is not possible, then pharmacologic replacement of ADH can be used in moderate to severe central diabetes insipidus, and pharmacologic agents that stimulate or potentiate ADH action like anticonvulsants, oral hypoglycemic agents, and hypolipidemic agents can be used. In nephrogenic diabetes, a state of mild hypovolemia is induced through the use of diuretics and sodium restriction (Germon, 1987). The effects of this treatment are diagrammed in Fig. 20-21.

In contrast to diabetes insipidus, inappropriate secretion of ADH may also occur in which the ability to maximally dilute the urine is lost. In the *syndrome of inappropriate ADH secretion* (SIADH), water is retained because of enhanced tubular reabsorption, and expansion and dilution

of the body fluid will occur if normal water intake continues.

The net effect of dilution of the ECF is that water will move osmotically into the ICF, causing cellular swelling. The neurologic symptoms of water excess, restlessness and disorientation, are indicative of this osmotic swelling in brain cells. Other signs of water excess caused by SIADH include weight gain (rapid), reduced urinary output, increased urine specific gravity, and reduced plasma Na^+ and Cl^- levels. The effects of dilution of the plasma protein concentration will also occur.

In aged, severely debilitated, or seriously ill patients the effects of this water excess may be quite severe. Severity of signs and symptoms is also determined by the rapidity with which the water excess develops; the more rapidly it develops, the more severe the effects and manifestations. Another term used to describe this condition is water intoxication (see Chapter 18).

If the water intake is restricted, water retention will not occur, and the plasma Na^+ concentration will remain normal. Even though plasma sodium concentra-

Table 20-11. Conditions associated with the etiologic mechanisms of nephrogenic diabetes insipidus

Mechanism	Conditions
Decreased permeability of collecting ducts through decreased cyclic AMP generation and effect	Hypokalemia Hypercalcemia Congenital (rare) Drugs (lithium, phenytoin, dimethyl chlortetracycline)
Impaired countercurrent function	Renal failure Hypokalemia Hypercalcemia Sickle cell anemia Osmotic diuresis Drugs (Lasix, Edecrin)

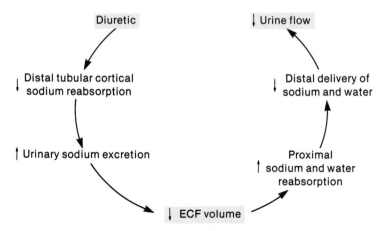

Fig. 20-21. Mechanism of antidiuretic effect of diuretics in nephrogenic diabetes insipidus.
(From Schrier RW, editor: Renal and electrolyte disorders, ed 3, 1986, Boston, Little, Brown and Co.)

tion might be lowered by dilution, the plasma bicarbonate remains unaffected for the most part. Maintenance of HCO_3^- concentration appears to be related to the movement of H^+ into the cells and excretion of H^+ in the urine. Intracellular K^+ moves out of the cells to maintain plasma K^+ levels and is probably linked to the H^+ movement. A mild hypokalemia may develop.

The mechanisms by which SIADH occurs include increased hypothalamic secretion, ectopic production of ADH, potentiation of the ADH effect, and exogenous administration of ADH. Listed in Tables 20-12 and 20-13 are the conditions associated with these mechanisms.

The enhanced hypothalamic secretion of ADH seen in certain neural disorders is not completely understood. Essential hyponatremia has been described in patients with cerebral disorders and certain chronic diseases. It is thought that defective cell metabolism causes a decrease in cell osmolality, which causes the osmoreceptors to signal ADH secretion at a different level of plasma osmolality than normally signals the secretion of ADH. This resetting of the "osmostat" results in a lower plasma Na^+ concentration, which is considered normal for these patients.

Mild SIADH may be treated with fluid restriction. In more severe forms of SIADH, the diuretic furosemide (Lasix) may be administered along with an infusion of hypertonic saline solution. Chronic SIADH is treated with pharmacologic agents, which interfere with the generation of cyclic AMP (see Table 20-11). In effect, a "nephrogenic diabetes insipidus" is created (Germon, 1987).

Other. There are other mechanisms by which urinary elimination patterns are altered. Abnormal cell growth and development is one. The mechanisms underlying neoplastic disease and congenital defects are discussed in Chapters 4 and 6. An example of a hereditary defect in normal renal growth and development is polycystic kidney disease. The kidneys are enlarged due to the presence of cysts. The disorder is usually identified in patients between the ages of 30 and 50 years and presents with flank pain, abdominal complaints, hematuria, signs of a urinary tract infection, and hypertension. The progression to renal failure can be slowed considerably with adequate control of the hypertension. From 10% to 13% of the patients with polycystic kidney disease experience rupture of a cerebral aneurysm (Rose, 1987).

Another mechanism by which normal urinary elimination can be disrupted is direct toxic damage to renal tissue. The heavy metals are examples of this. For example, gold and mercury can cause the

Table 20-12. Conditions associated with the etiologic mechanisms of SIADH secretion

Mechanism	Conditions
Increased production of ADH by hypothalamus	Stress
	Idiopathic conditions
	Central nervous system disorders*
	Pulmonary disorders*
	Drugs (Diabinese, Navane, Cytoxan)
	Miscellaneous—Guillain-Barré syndrome
	Endocrine disorders
Ectopic production of ADH by nonhypothalamic tissue	Hormone-secreting carcinoma*—lungs, bronchi, duodenum, pancreas
Potentiation of effect	Drugs (oral hypoglycemic agents, diuretics)

*See Table 20-13 for more complete listing.

Table 20-13. Disorders associated with SIADH secretion

Carcinomas	Pulmonary disorders	Central nervous system disorders
Bronchogenic carcinoma	Viral pneumonia	Encephalitis (viral or bacterial)
Carcinoma of the duodenum	Bacterial pneumonia	Meningitis (viral, bacterial, tuberculous, and fungal)
Carcinoma of the pancreas	Pulmonary abscess	Head trauma
Thymoma	Tuberculosis	Brain abscess
Carcinoma of the ureter	Aspergillosis	Brain tumors
Lymphoma	Positive pressure breathing	Guillain-Barré syndrome
Ewing's sarcoma	Asthma	Acute intermittent porphyria
Mesothelioma	Pneumothorax	Subarachnoid hemorrhage or subdural hematoma
Carcinoma of the bladder	Cystic fibrosis	Cerebellar and cerebral atrophy
Prostatic carcinoma		Cavernous sinus thrombosis
		Neonatal hypoxia
		Hydrocephalus
		Shy-Drager syndrome
		Rocky Mountain spotted fever
		Delirium tremens
		Cerebrovascular accident (cerebral thrombosis or hemorrhage)
		Acute psychosis
		Peripheral neuropathy
		Multiple sclerosis

From Levi M and Berl T: Water metabolism. In Gonick HC, editor. Current nephrology, vol. 5, p. 45. Copyright © 1982 by Year Book Medical Publishers, Inc., Chicago.

nephrotic syndrome; cisplatin, arsenic, mercury, and uranium can cause acute tubular necrosis; and lead or cadmium can cause chronic tubulointerstitial nephritis (Rose, 1987).

Sometimes the mechanisms that have been discussed in the previous sections interact to cause renal disease. For example, hypercalcemia causes a chronic tubulointerstitial nephropathy, hypercalcemic nephropathy. The mechanisms by which this nephropathy develops include tubular obstruction by cellular debris, calcium deposition, and casts and altered tissue perfusion as the direct effect of calcium on vascular tone leads to renal vasoconstriction and decreased renal blood flow and GFR.

The renal disease that develops in the presence of multiple myeloma provides another example. The development of the interstitial disorder referred to as myeloma kidney is related to the excretion of Bence Jones proteins (immunoglobulin light chains) in the urine. The precipitation of casts of these proteins causes tubular obstruction, but it is also believed that these proteins may be nephrotoxic as well (Rose, 1987).

THE GASTROINTESTINAL TRACT

The normal function of the gastrointestinal (GI) tract in terms of the body's elimination processes involves the formation and excretion of feces. This is accomplished through the mechanisms of ingestion, motility, secretion, digestion, and absorption, which are regulated and integrated by neural and hormonal factors. The membranes of the GI tract are highly specialized and allow an equilibrium to exist between the extracellular fluid and the secretions of the GI tract. Disruption of the normal cycling of body fluid between the extracellular compartment and the GI tract may result in a significant departure from the body's chemical equilibrium. The abnormal loss of GI secretions must be considered in terms of the relative concentrations of electrolytes within the fluid in order to predict the ultimate effect of that loss on the body's chemical equilibrium (see Table 18-4 for a listing of the electrolytic composition of various GI secretions). Abnormal elimination through the GI tract may occur via the mechanisms of vomiting, diarrhea, fistulas, and gastric suction. The fluid lost is usually isotonic, and the most important deficits involve water and Na^+, with K^+ loss occurring in chronic or more severe diarrhea. Acid-base imbalances may also occur.

Abnormal elimination of gastric secretions

Gastric juice is the most acid of all the gastrointestinal secretions. Its chief ions are hydrogen, sodium, chloride, and potassium. Loss of gastric juice is most frequently associated with metabolic alkalosis and deficits of sodium, potassium, and occasionally magnesium. The most common causes of a loss of gastric secretions include vomiting and gastric suction. The mechanisms of vomiting are discussed in Chapter 21.

If excessive loss occurs, fluid volume deficit may develop, as well as the ketosis of starvation, since these patients are usually either unable to eat or are allowed nothing to eat. Ketosis is the result of excessive ketone body production due to metabolism of fat. In the absence of carbohydrate intake a magnesium deficit can also occur. The effects of starvation are discussed in detail in Chapter 19.

Abnormal elimination of intestinal secretions

Intestinal juice is alkaline and contains a relatively large amount of K^+. Loss of intestinal juice is most often associated with metabolic acidosis and deficits of sodium, potassium, and bicarbonate. Intestinal secretions can be lost as a result of diarrhea, externally applied intestinal suction, or pathologic or surgically created fistulas. A fistula is an abnormal passage or opening between the intestines and some body cavity or the external environment. Some disease processes cause fistula formation and are discussed in detail in Chapter 21. An *ileostomy* is a surgically created fistula between the ileum and abdominal wall that allows the contents of the small intestine to drain.

The term *diarrhea* is usually applied to a condition characterized by the frequent excretion of loose, runny stools. The basic mechanisms underlying the development of diarrhea are impaired absorption or increased secretion or a combination of these two mechanisms. Normally only 150 ml of water is lost in the stools daily, but this amount will be greatly increased in diarrhea because of its increased fluid content. Severe diarrhea can lead to daily loss of 5 to 10 L of fluid, and diarrhea in the child can lead to severe fluid and electrolyte imbalances more rapidly than in the adult because of the relatively greater volume of body water in children (see Chapter 21).

SUMMARY

Presented in this chapter was an overview of the processes of elimination that occur via various routes in the body and the mechanisms by which disruption of the normal elimination processes and patterns may occur. Elimination processes constitute a major means of maintaining wellness. It should be apparent that the loss of this control through disruption of normal elimination processes results in profound chemical disequilibrium, the effects and manifestations of which are discussed in Chapter 18. Restoration of chemical equilibrium is the primary goal of treatment in disorders of elimination; however, correction of the underlying cause of the altered elimination process is necessary to prevent the recurrence of chemical disequilibrium. The reliance on artificial means of maintaining chemical equilibrium becomes necessary in chronic states in which elimination processes are permanently impaired.

BIBLIOGRAPHY

Adler SG, Cohen AH, and Border WA: Hypersensitivity phenomena and the kidney: role of drugs and environmental agents, Am J Kid Dis 5:75, 1985.

Bosch J, Lauer A, and Glabman S: Short term protein loading in assessment of patients with renal disease, Am J Med 77:873, 1984.

Brenner B, Hostetter T, and Humes H: Molecular basis of proteinuria of glomerular origin, N Engl J Med 298:826, 1978.

Brenner BM: Nephron adaptation to renal injury or ablation, Am J Physiol 249:F324, 1985.

Bricker NS: On the pathogenesis of the uremic state: an exposition of the "trade off hypothesis," N Engl J Med 286:1093, 1972.

Bricker NS, Fine LG, Kaplan M, et al: "Magnification phenomenon" in chronic renal disease, N Engl J Med 229:1287, 1978.

Buckalew VM and Someren A: Renal manifestations of sickle cell disease, Arch Intern Med 133:660, 1974.

Cattell V: Mitomycin induced hemolytic uremic kidney, Am J Pathol 121:88, 1985.

Chambers J: Fluid and electrolyte problems in renal and urologic disorders, Nurs Clin North Am 22(4):815, 1987.

Chambers J: Metabolic bone disorders: imbalances of calcium and phosphorus, Nurs Clin North Am 22(4):861, 1987.

de Jong PE and Statius van Eps LW: Sickle cell nephropathy: new insights into its pathophysiology, Kidney Int 27:711, 1985.

Drummond KN: Hemolytic—uremic syndrome—then and now, N Engl J Med 312:116, 1985.

Duggin GG: Mechanisms in the development of analgesic nephropathy, Kidney Int 18:553, 1980.

Fasset R, Owen J, Fairley J, Birch D, and Fairley K: Urinary red cell morphology during exercise, Br Med J 285:1455, 1982.

Germon K: Fluid and electrolyte problems associated with diabetes insipidus and syndrome of inappropriate antidiuretic hormone, Nurs Clin North Am 22(4):785, 1987.

Groer M: Physiology and pathophysiology of the body fluids, St. Louis, 1981, The CV Mosby Co.

Humes HD: Pathophysiology of electrolyte and renal disorders, New York, 1986, Churchill Livingstone, Inc.

Kachadorian W, Ellis S, Muller J: Possible roles for microtubules and microfilaments in ADH action on toad urinary bladder, Am J Physiol 236:F14, 1979.

Kachadorian W, Levine S, Wade J, Discala V, and Hayes R: Relationship of aggregated intramembranous particles to water permeability in vasopressin-treated toad urinary bladder, J Clin Invest 59:576, 1977.

Kannan H, Yagi R: Supraoptic neurosecretory neurons: evidence for the existence of converging inputs both from carotid baroreceptors and osmorectors, Brain Res 145:385, 1978.

Kerjaschki D, Vernillo A, and Farquhar H: Reduced sialation of podocalyxin—the major sialoprotein of the rat kidney glomerulus—in aminonucleoside nephrosis, Am J Pathol 118:343, 1983.

Kokko J and Tannen R, editors: Fluids and electrolytes, Philadelphia, 1986, WB Saunders Co.

Lancaster L: Renal and endocrine regulation of water and electrolyte balance, Nurs Clin North Am 22(4):761, 1987.

Leaf A and Cotran R: Renal pathophysiology, ed 3, New York, 1985, Oxford University Press.

Levine S, Kachadorian W, Levin D, Scholondorff D: Effects of trifluoperazine on function and structure of toad urinary bladder. Role of calmodulin in vasopressin stimulation of water permeability, J Clin Invest 67:662, 1981.

Liveson J, Gardner J, and Bornstein M: Tissue culture studies of possible uremic neurotoxins: myoinositol, Kidney Int 12:131, 1977.

Llach F: Focusing on the nephrotic syndrome, Drug Ther (hospital edition) 3(2):15, 1978.

Massry S: Parathyroid hormone as a uremic toxin. In Massry SG and Glassock RS, editors: Textbook of nephrology, Baltimore, 1983, Williams and Wilkins Co.

Maxwell M, Kleeman C, and Narins R, editors: Clinical disorders of fluid and electrolyte metabolism, ed 4, New York, 1987, McGraw-Hill Book Co.

Meyers B, Okarma T, Friedman S, Bridges C, Ross J, Asseff S, and Deen W: Mechanisms of proteinuria in human glomerulonephritis, J Clin Invest 70:732, 1982.

Michelis M: Treatment strategy for the nephrotic syndrome, Drug Ther 3(2):pp 13-14, 1978.

Morel F: Sites of hormone action in the mammalian nephron, Am J Physiol 240:F159, 1981.

Muller J, Kachadorian W, Discala V: Evidence that ADH stimulated intramembrane particle aggregates are transferred from cytoplasmic to luminal membranes in toad bladder epithelial cells, J Cell Biol 85:83, 1980.

Petersen M and Edelman I: Calcium inhibition on the action of vasopressin on the urinary bladder of the toad, J Clin Invest 43:583, 1964.

Poortmans J: Post-exercise proteinuria in humans. Facts and mechanisms, JAMA 253:236, 1985.

Raine AE: Hypertension, blood viscosity, and cardiovascular morbidity in renal failure: implications of erythropoietin therapy. Lancet (1)8577:97-100, 1988.

Ripoche P, et al: Detergent extraction of membrane proteins related to the action of antidiuretic hormone, Biochim Biophys Acta 693:497, 1982.

Rose B: Pathophysiology of renal disease, ed 2, New York, 1987, McGraw-Hill Book Co.

Rose BD: Clinical physiology of acid-base and electrolyte disorders, ed 2, New York, 1984, McGraw-Hill Book Co.

Schrier RW, editor: Renal and electrolyte disorders, ed 3, Boston, 1986, Little, Brown and Co.

Sywed J: Pathophysiology of ARF: rationale for signs and symptoms, Crit Care Q 1(2):1-9, 1978.

Thomas AN, Pattison C, and Serjeant GR: Causes of death in sickle cell disease in Jamaica, Br Med J 285:633, 1982.

Venkatachalam M and Rennke H: The structure and molecular basis of glomerular filtration, Circ Res 43:337, 1978.

Vernier R, Klein D, Sisson S, Mahan J, Oegema T, and Brown D: Heparin sulfate–rich anionic sites in the human glomerular basement membrane. Decreased concentration in congenital nephrotic syndrome, N Engl J Med 309:1001, 1983.

21

Gastrointestinal pathophysiology

This chapter will describe the various gastrointestinal (GI) system disorders (1) in terms of abnormalities in motility, absorption, or secretion or (2) as inflammatory disorders. The GI system is strongly influenced by psychologic factors, and people often describe emotional stressors in terms of the responses of this system. Some examples are "It was a gut reaction," "It made me sick to my stomach," "My stomach turned over," and "My bowels turned to water." These phrases show that the GI system and the brain are interconnected and influence each other. The interconnections involve actual physical nervous system links, neuroendocrine secretions, and GI hormones. There are differences in how much people react to stress with GI upset or with actual physical disease, but there is no question that emotional phenomena influence the functioning of the GI system. Therefore, as we examine the pathophysiologic mechanisms by which GI disease occurs, it is important to consider physical, psychologic, and social stressors as potentiating or even etiologic influences. Although there appear to be psychosomatic associations for many major GI tract disorders, such as gastric ulcers, duodenal ulcers, and inflammatory bowel diseases, these relationships are complex. Distinctive personality types

have been explored, as well as the responsiveness of the person to stressors. These areas of research will be discussed in the appropriate sections of this chapter.

DISORDERS OF MOTILITY

The motility of the GI tract is regulated through many nervous and hormonal mechanisms, which act in response to such variables as distension, food content and amount, pH, activity, metabolism, and blood supply. It should be recalled that the function of a motile GI tract is to grind and mix the food with digestive secretions, disperse it into an absorbable state, and move it caudally through the digestive tract.

Esophagus

Obstruction, either physical or physiologic, and inflammation are two important causes of impaired esophageal motility. The upper esophagus consists of striated and skeletal muscle, while the lower esophagus is smooth muscle. Peristaltic waves move through the esophageal wall, propelling the bolus of food mixed with secretions from the upper esophageal sphincter to the stomach in about 5 seconds. When *dysphagia*, or difficulty in swallowing, develops as a sign of disease, the individual cannot propel the bolus at the normal rate and complains that the food "sticks in his throat"; he may gag in the attempt to swallow the food. Dysphagia is the most common symptom of esophageal disease, but is also seen in other conditions such as goiter, hiatal hernia, and certain neuromuscular conditions. It is also found in psychiatric patients and is termed *globus hystericus*. The most common cause of dysphagia in infants is obstruction caused by congenital malformations of the esophagus, including atresia and tracheoesophageal fistula.

When dysphagia develops, it is often associated with obstruction of the esophagus, such as might occur with esophageal carcinoma, hiatal hernia, or goiter. A physiologic obstruction is one in which the cause is a functional disruption rather than a purely physical barrier, for example, *achalasia*, a disorder in which the esophagus becomes dilated and hypertrophied. Achalasia results from degeneration of the ganglionic nerve supply of the esophagus. Patients who have suffered damage to the swallowing center in the medulla may also have a physiologic obstruction. Other neuromuscular conditions that interrupt swallowing include poliomyelitis, polymyositis, and scleroderma.

Inflammation of the esophageal lining can occur whenever irritation is present, such as would be caused by reflux of gastric acid into the esophagus, or as the sequelae to ingestion of toxic or highly irritating substances such as lye. As with inflammation elsewhere in the body, fibrosis can eventually result, causing strictures in the lumen. The esophagus also reacts to irritation by spasm, thus creating an obstruction to the passage of the bolus. Reflux of acid from the stomach can occur when the cardiac sphincter muscle tone is poor and in *hiatal hernia*, which is a herniation of a portion of the stomach through the opening in the diaphragm through which the esophagus passes; it is common but asymptomatic in the majority of those individuals discovered to have one. In others the predominant symptoms appear to be related to pressure and acid reflux.

Stomach

The musculature and nervous supply of the stomach provide resting muscle tone for the fundus and corpus of the stomach. The pyloric antrum also has muscle tone and can contract actively, as can the rest of the stomach when a peristaltic wave passes over it. Peristalsis at a rate of three waves per minute allows for emptying of food from the stomach into the duodenum. The innervation of the stomach is of two types: *extrinsic*, through both vagal and sympathetic fibers, and *intrinsic*, through ganglionic plexuses, which can be stimulated by the vagus nerve or can become inherently active, much like a primitive, independent nervous net. Furthermore, the smooth muscle of the stomach, and indeed of the entire GI tract, is capable of rhythmic automaticity and is controlled by pacemaker cells that can initiate peristaltic waves, which are conducted through the gut in a one-way direction by the smooth muscle. The intestine appears to have an irreversible cephalocaudal polarity, so that peristalsis can be conducted in only one direction even when a segment of intestine is removed, reversed, and then inserted back into the GI tract.

Distension of the stomach stimulates receptors in the wall, activating vagal afferent fibers, which transmit the signal to the brain and then to efferent vagal fibers, which when fired will cause muscle contraction in the muscularis layer of the stomach. The major slowing down of the contraction wave is at the duodenum. Hormonal mechanisms such as the enterogastric reflex or enterogastrone release also inhibit gastric emptying. Important disorders of stomach motility are vomiting, hypermotility, and disorders of gastric emptying.

Vomiting. Vomiting and the often associated sensation of nausea are the most commonly experienced phenomena related to disordered gastric motility. These are symptoms of a great many disorders, ranging from overindulgence in rich and abundant food, to labyrinthine disease, or to mental illness. The mechanism by which vomiting occurs is forcible contraction of abdominal muscles, expiration against a closed glottis, and a reverse peristaltic wave, which originates in the pyloric antrum. Increased heart rate, pallor, salivation, sweating, faintness, and other signs of generalized autonomic nervous system arousal are often associated with a vomiting episode. The pathway by which vomiting is effected is illustrated in Fig. 21-1. Initiation of the vomiting pathway can be either through stimulation of afferent fibers by irritating substances, which are conveyed to the vomiting center of the brain, or through stimulation of the vomiting center by pathways of nerve fibers from other areas of the brain, such as the hypothalamus or cerebral cortex.

Hypermotility. Gastric hypermotility is often associated with emotional states of anxiety and fear; this is also true for the rest of the GI tract. Hypermotility of this type is caused by excessive parasympathetic firing. Irritation of the stomach lining may also cause hypermotility.

Disorders of gastric emptying. Normally the emptying of chyme into the duodenum is regulated by waves of peristalsis, which occur at a rate of three per minute and sweep across the pyloric antrum, the pylorus, and the duodenum, causing the expulsion of fluid chyme in spurts from the stomach into the duodenum. Obstruction to the flow of chyme can occur, resulting in an increase of gastric pressure and eventually vomiting. Any condition that obstructs the stomach outlet, such as tumors, ulcers, edema, or fibrosis resulting in stenosis, will inhibit the rate and degree of gastric emptying. However, the development of symptoms may be quite slow, as the stomach is able to compensate for obstruction to outflow as long as the antral musculature remains intact and functional. The enterogastric reflex and the release of the hormone enterogastrone inhibit gastric emptying and may be stimulated by irritation of the duodenum.

A major disorder of gastric emptying in infants is *congenital pyloric stenosis*. In this condition the pyloric sphincter is hypertrophied and may actually be cartilaginous in consistency, causing a narrowing of the lumen of the pylorus and dilation of the stomach. The pylorus may be enlarged enough to be palpated; it feels like an olive and is located midway between the umbilicus and the left costal margin. The muscle of the pylorus may go into spasm, contributing to the most dramatic sign of this condition, projectile vomiting after feeding, which in some cases may be extremely forceful. The disorder is usually manifested by the third week of life and is more common in males occuring in a polygenic inheritance pattern. The treatment may be surgical, but the condition resolves itself in many cases. However, dehydration, electrolyte imbalances, and malnutrition may develop and be severe enough to demand surgical intervention (pylorotomy).

The *dumping syndrome* is another disorder of gastric emptying; it is seen in individuals after pyloric surgery or vagotomy.

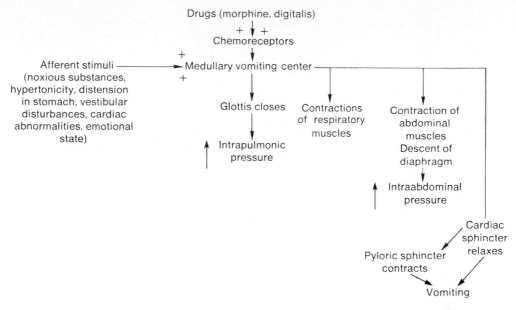

Fig. 21-1. Vomiting pathway. Medullary vomiting center causes chain of events, which increase intra-abdominal pressure, increase intrapulmonic pressure (thus compressing esophagus), and relax cardiac sphincter while pylorus contracts. Thus chyme moves in antiperistaltic direction.

There appears to be either an anatomic or physiologic loss of antral control over gastric emptying. The rate of gastric emptying is markedly increased, with the signs and symptoms, such as sudden weakness, nausea, diarrhea, and hypermotility of the GI tract, appearing after meals.

Intestine

The normal motility of the GI tract is characterized by peristalsis and rhythmic segmentation in the small intestine and mass movements, haustral churning, and pendular movements in the large intestine, as well as defecation, which is primarily a function of the distal colon, rectum, and anus.

Decreased motility. *Obstruction,* either acute or chronic, is the major cause of abnormally decreased motility of the intestines. The causes of intestinal obstruction are many, including tumors, foreign bodies, inflammatory conditions, adhesions, strangulated hernias, and congenital defects.

Acute intestinal obstruction can be so severe as to compromise life in as short a period as 24 hours. Weakness, prostration, and finally irreversible shock ensue. The pathophysiology of intestinal obstruction is illustrated in Fig. 21-2. The prominent symptoms are pain caused by stretching of the gut (the gut can stand cutting and tearing without pain but not stretching), nausea, and vomiting, constipation, distension, and absence of motility. The location of the obstruction is important in predicting the pattern of electrolyte changes that will be observed. A low obstruction can cause an initial period of vomiting, which depletes the body of water, H^+, and Cl^-, causing a metabolic alkalosis. However, the usual outcome is a metabolic acidosis, as the obstruction will eventually

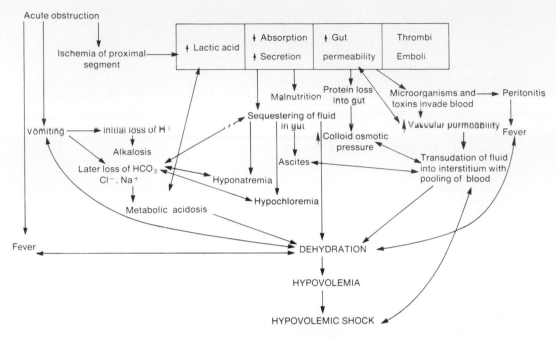

Fig. 21-2. Pathophysiology of acute intestinal obstruction. End results of numerous pathophysiologic mechanisms that are perpetuated by acute intestinal obstruction are vascular dehydration, hypovolemia, septicemia, and shock.

cause vomiting of highly alkaline fecal material.

Obstruction is often mechanical in nature, such as might occur when a loop of bowel is strangulated, which not only causes a mechanical impediment to the flow of intestinal material but also results in ischemia of the strangulated loop of bowel due to impairment of the local blood supply. The small intestine becomes ischemic more quickly than the large intestine but is also able to recover and repair more rapidly. Generally, gastrointestinal ischemia that lasts longer than 2 hours will cause irreversible damage. This will result in the rapid development of septic shock, as the ischemic bowel permeability is drastically increased.

An obstruction of the intestines results in distension of the intestine above the obstruction, and large amounts of gas accumulate. The normal absorptive functions of that segment are greatly impaired within 6 to 12 hours, with the secretion of Na^+ and water into the ischemic segment increasing until up to 50% of the plasma volume may be sequestered in the proximal segment of intestine. The major effect of such a net increase in secretion over absorption is the development of hypovolemic shock, hyponatremia, hypochloremia, and acidosis. The mucosa that suffers occlusion of its blood supply allows plasma proteins to leak into the gut lumen, and toxins and bacteria of the normal flora pass from the gut into the bloodstream. Septic shock ensues and aggravates the severe cardiovascular effects of the hypovolemia. The pressure in the proximal segment of the obstructed bowel may increase to the point that perforation results, and peritonitis is inevitable. Furthermore, the ischemic gut, besides being a prime site for infection, may also become thrombosed, and emboli may be thrown off to other organs.

Fig. 21-2 also shows how one effect of acute intestinal obstruction will aggravate and perpetuate another effect—examples of pathologic positive feedback loops that act to disrupt coping mechanisms and disrupt wellness. For example, the dehydration that is a common sign of intestinal obstruction is the result of a number of mechanisms such as fever, sequestration of fluid in the ischemic gut, vomiting, and pooling of blood. As dehydration continues, the development of hypovolemic shock is also perpetuated, and the shock state itself, with its profound decrease in cardiac output and blood pressure, only aggravates the gut ischemia further, thus promulgating continuing dehydration.

Fifty percent of all acute small intestine obstructions in adults are caused by *strangulated hernias*. A loop of bowel becomes caught as it protrudes through a weak area in the abdominal wall, such as an inguinal ring, and rapidly becomes ischemic and then hypoxic, resulting in obstruction to the passage of material through the tract.

Other important causes of acute obstruction, particularly in the large intestine, are volvulus, diverticulosis, and paralytic ileus in adults and intussusception in children. *Volvulus* is a condition in which the intestine becomes twisted on itself. Infarction of the bowel is a common sequel. *Diverticulosis* is characterized by the presence of hypertrophic rings, which then alternate with herniations of the mucosa and submucosa through sacs in the muscularis, usually in the colon. This condition may be either congenital or ac-

quired, and it is believed that a low residue diet of the type found in most industrialized societies is etiologic. *Meckel's diverticulum* is a special congenital case in which a single outpouching of the small intestine results from the vestigial remnant of an embryonic duct. Diverticula in general are prone to inflammation, impaction with fecal material or foreign bodies, fibrosis, and fistula development. Spastic, colicky pain is common, and acute obstruction occasionally develops.

Paralytic ileus is a common cause of intestinal obstruction following abdominal surgery. It is also seen in hypokalemia. The small intestine becomes atonic, and peristalsis is absent. Distension, pain, and absence of bowel sounds are important symptoms, and if it does not resolve itself, not only is the flow of gastrointestinal contents interrupted but also the vascular supply can become compromised by the increasing distension. Any handling or manipulation of the peritoneum, the abdominal organs, and the gut itself may set up this reflex response. Anesthesia also contributes to decreased peristalsis. In some patients it can be avoided or relieved in part by diet and activity.

Intussusception is a condition found most commonly in children under 2 years of age and is caused by the telescoping of a segment of the small intestine upon itself, usually near the ileocecal valve. The symptoms are quite characteristic, and the condition usually appears suddenly in an otherwise healthy child. The major symptoms are paroxysms of acute abdominal pain, which are then followed by periods of normal activity. Gradually, however, vomiting begins and may proceed until fecal material is vomited, blood is passed rectally, and the child becomes more and more lethargic. Intussusception often will suddenly reduce itself spontaneously or following an enema, and in these instances surgery can be avoided.

Motility of the gut may also be compromised by more chronic obstructive conditions, such as might be caused by slowly growing tumors or interruptions in the myenteric plexuses, which are involved in normal peristalsis, or in the vagal or sympathetic extrinsic controls over normal motility. *Hirschsprung's disease* is an excellent example of neuromuscular obstruction. It is a congenital condition, also called congenital megacolon, in which the ganglia of Auerbach's and Meissner's plexuses are absent from birth in the distal colon. This results in enormous distension of the proximal segment of the colon with fecal material, as the muscle cells of the affected segment are unable to contract normally to permit defecation because mass-movement peristaltic waves are inhibited. Adhesions may result in obstruction of the intestines. These are bands of fibrotic, scarred tissue that sometimes develop after surgery and that can constrict the lumen of the gut.

An extremely common disorder of motility is constipation. Constipation may be caused by destruction of any of the nervous elements in the normal defecation reflex, which over a long period of time produces atony of the rectum and colon and thus a progressively weaker defecation reflex. This phenomenon is observed in individuals who rely on laxatives and stool softeners for regular bowel movements, some of which are known to destroy nervous elements in the gut, and in individuals who continually suppress the urge to defecate. Constipation may also be a primary abnormality of the motility of the sigmoid and descending colon, such that the gastrocolic and duodenocolic reflexes cannot operate. These disorders of defecation do not often result in acute intestinal

obstruction, as described previously. Low obstruction of this nature does not result in proximal ischemia, and absorption and secretion are not impaired. Individuals are known to have been constipated for over a year without apparent adverse effects on their general health. Up to 100 pounds of accumulated feces may burden such rare individuals, but no toxic effects on their physiology have been observed.

Increased motility. Certain susceptible individuals will respond to a variety of stressful stimuli by intestinal hypermotility. Emotional stress may cause irritability of the colon, and *diarrhea* characterized by frequent, watery, mucus-filled stools occurs.

Diarrhea is not always accompanied by hypermotility of the GI tract, however. Most common causes of diarrhea, such as infection, toxic foods, and emotional anxiety, actually are accompanied by a decreased colonic luminal pressure and depressed motility, so that any small increase in colonic pressure will set up a mass movement of feces in the caudal direction. When the diarrhea is caused by hypermotility and cramping, the condition is known as a *spastic irritable colon.*

DISORDERS OF SECRETION

Different parts of the GI tract have different secretory and absorptive functions (Table 21-1). Pathophysiology of any one of these functions can occur, and in many cases, disruption of one function can have a profound effect on another.

Gastric secretion

Peptic ulcers. The major disorder of secretion of the gastrointestinal tract is peptic ulcer disease (PUD) of the stomach or more commonly the duodenum (Figs. 21-3 and 21-4). This is a common condition of

Table 21-1. Secretory, digestive, and absorptive functions of gastrointestinal GI tract

	pH	Secretion	Digestion	Absorption
Mouth		Saliva	Carbohydrates	
Esophagus		Mucus		
Stomach	2-4	HCl; pepsinogen; intrinsic factor; mucus	Begins protein digestion	Alcohol
Small intestine	Duodenum, 6; ileum, 8	Pancreatic enzymes; HCO_3^-; bile; Na^+; water; K^+	Most digestion of proteins, carbohydrates, lipids	Minerals; amino acids; Na^+; glucose; lipids; vitamins; water
Large intestine	8	HCO_3^-, Na^+; Cl^-; K^+; water		Water; Na^+; K^+; HCO_3^-; Cl^-

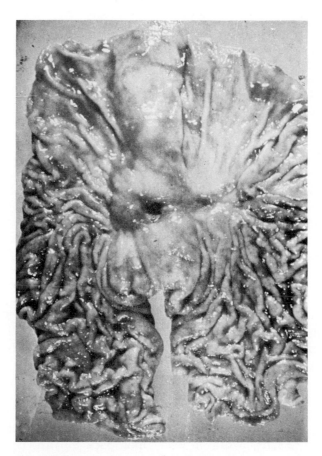

Fig. 21-3. Very well circumscribed peptic ulcer.
(Courtesy Department of Pathology, University of Tennessee, Memphis.)

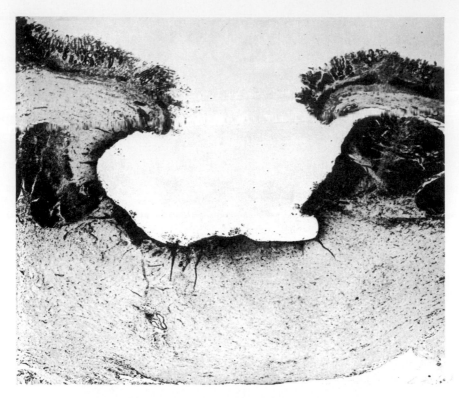

Fig. 21-4. Peptic ulcer. A chronic ulcer extending through muscularis mucosa. Fibrosis of submucosa and base of ulcer provides evidence of continuing process. (×8.)
(From Anderson WAD and Kissane JM: Pathology, ed 7, St. Louis, 1977, The CV Mosby Co.)

the twentieth century (affecting 10% of all Americans) with an increased incidence in men, particularly under the age of 50. It has been associated with increased levels of stress and anxiety in many cases. Estrogen may protect against PUD. There is some evidence of a hereditary predisposition, with the duodenal type occurring more commonly in individuals with blood group O and the gastric type in individuals with blood group A. The gastric peptic ulcer appears to be associated with a breakdown in the normal stomach mucosal defenses to the highly acid stomach secretions, while duodenal peptic ulcer pathogenesis implicates a primary increased acid secretion. Increased HCl secretion causes a break-

down in the mucosa, which then ulcerates.

Stomach. The acidity of stomach gastric juice is very high, the pH becoming as low as 2.0 when acid is being actively secreted. This acid is certainly capable of totally digesting and destroying the epithelial lining of the stomach. The fact that it does not is remarkable. The protective mechanism whereby autodigestion is prevented is through (1) the secretion of a slightly alkaline layer of mucus that coats the surface of the gastric epithelium, (2) dilution of the acid by food and secretions, (3) prevention of diffusion of the HCl from the lumen back into the cells, and (4) regulation of gastric pH by negative feedback mechanisms that act mainly on the gastrin-releasing antral cells. It should be recalled that a marked diffusion gradient for HCl exists between the gastric lumen and the epithelial cells. Diffusion of HCl down this gradient is prevented in part by the presence of nonpermeable tight junctions between adjacent epithelial cells. The gradient for diffusion across the epithelial cell membrane will also increase as HCl concentration in the lumen is increased. If the barriers to diffusion are broken down in any way, there is a tendency, governed by purely physical laws, for the HCl to diffuse back down its gradient into the epithelial cells. There is speculation that a *gastric peptic ulcer*, which is often associated with a lower than normal basal HCl concentration, is caused by such a breakdown in the epithelium, rather than by a hypersecretion of HCl. The diffusion barrier may be interrupted by aspirin, alcohol, inflammation, and perhaps regurgitated bile salts. The detergent-like properties of bile salts, which may be regurgitated into the stomach from the duodenum, may cause the barrier to break down. These substances strip away the surface mucus and can solubilize the membrane lipids, thus increasing the permeability of these cells, allowing massive back diffusion to take place. The pathophysiologic mechanism by which the ulcerative process is perpetuated is illustrated in Fig. 21-5. The refluxed bile salts cause damage and H^+ back diffusion, which further aggravates the mucosal damage, resulting in ulceration. The primary disorder may then be a delay in gastric emptying and motility of the stomach, a process that is in large part mediated by duodenal receptors, which may be CO_2 sensors and which respond to acid stimuli by decreasing the rate of emptying. The actual mechanism by which bile is refluxed forward into the antrum is not well understood, however.

Chronic aspirin users are subject to the development of gastritis, bleeding, and PUD. Aspirin is known to damage the mucosa, causing slight bleeding (around 2 ml) in almost all people and massive hemorrhage in those who for some reason are susceptible. Damage to the mucosa occurs when the aspirin is unbuffered and thus present in the un-ionized state, for it is most soluble in membrane lipids then and can rapidly diffuse through the cell membrane into the mucosal epithelial cells. There it ionizes at the neutral pH of the interior of the cell, so that the un-ionized form is removed almost as soon as it enters the cells. This sets up a steep downhill diffusion gradient for the un-ionized form from the lumen into the cells. The ionized form of aspirin can damage the mucosa, and once this occurs HCl can back diffuse, and hemorrhage may eventually result from the damage. Alcohol is another substance that can be absorbed by the stomach mucosal cells, because of its great lipid solubility, and it is known to enhance the damaging effect of aspirin.

It is believed that slight damage to the stomach mucosa may actually occur in normal individuals with every meal, but the continuous renewal of the gastric epithelium counteracts this process, so that the effect is minor.

Duodenum. While breakdown in the normal mucosa appears to be the major cause of stomach PUD, hypersecretion of acid appears most important in the etiology of *duodenal PUD.* Evidence for this theory comes from the observation that vagal activity is increased, especially during fasting and at night in ulcer patients. The vagus, it will be recalled, increases the release of HCl by stimulating pyloric antrum cells, which produce the hormone gastrin; *gastrin* acts via the bloodstream on the parietal cells of the stomach, causing them to respond by secreting HCl. The vagus is normally stimulated by distension, the presence of food in the stomach,

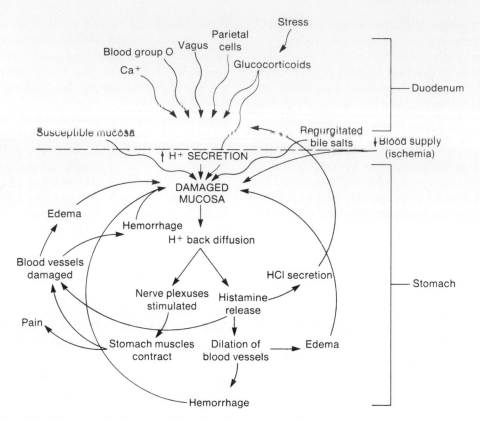

Fig. 21-5. Duodenal and gastric ulcer pathophysiology. In duodenal ulcer, an increased H^+ secretion is implicated; in gastric ulcer, a normal H^+ secretion in the presence of a damaged mucosal barrier is etiologic. Either mechanism results in ulceration, a process that sets up positive-feedback situations so that ulceration is further perpetuated.

higher centers of the brain such as the cortex, and the feeding- and satiety-regulating centers of the hypothalamus. Its basal rate of firing appears to be increased in ulcer patients even when these normal stimulating factors are absent. PUD can be produced experimentally by the administration of excess acid or excessive gastrin release. The Zollinger-Ellison syndrome, which is characterized by the presence of peptic ulceration in patients with a gastrin-secreting pancreatic tumor, also points to the importance of acid hypersecretion. Individuals with blood group O are often found to have an increased secretion of HCl, and further evidence is found

in the association of PUD with an increased parietal cell mass.

It has recently been recognized that duodenal ulcers are not the result of a single etiology. Familial factors are important, but the role of genetics is not fully understood. From 20% to 50% of duodenal ulcer patients have a family history of the disease, which is much higher than nonulcer control populations (Soll and Isenberg, 1983). The stomach mucosa is sensitive to damage by aspirin and other nonsteroidal antiinflammatory drugs; smoking also appears to increase risk.

Some of the more common abnormalities observed include increased pepsin secretion, hyperactivity of gastric antral cells, and increased gastric emptying. The most common symptom of peptic duodenal ulcer is intermittent epigastric pain, which is usually most pronounced when the stomach is empty. The pain is thought to result from increased irritation of the damaged and hyperemic mucosa by HCl, leading to stimulation of the nerve plexuses in the stomach, which causes local muscular contraction. The pain is relieved by eating. The pain that typifies gastric ulceration is often present after a meal, but this is a variable finding.

• • •

The major complication of peptic ulceration of either the stomach or duodenum is hemorrhage, which may be sudden and life threatening. Ulcers may also become chronic inflammatory sites, which can fibrose and cause obstruction. The ulcer may become so excavated that perforation through the gut or stomach wall occurs, leading to massive hemorrhage, peritonitis, and shock. Ulcer symptoms are characteristically episodic, and long periods of time may occur between them. Histamine receptor antagonists, gastric acid inhibitors, a bland, high-fat diet, complete alcohol abstinence, and frequent small meals are generally recommended for the treatment of ulcer. There is however, no good evidence that a bland diet can alleviate this disease.

Surgical treatment is subtotal distal gastric resection and occasionally vagotomy for duodenal ulcers with removal of a large part of the gastrin-secreting pyloric antrum and the parietal cell mass. The surgical treatment for gastric ulcers is the same, but the parietal cell mass is usually preserved.

Personality factors, stressors, and psychodynamics. The pathophysiologic mechanisms by which ulceration occurs are partially mediated through the nervous and endocrine systems. These are in turn greatly influenced by mental state, biologic determinants, and stress responses. The existence of a variety of influences on peptic ulceration has been speculated upon since the 1800s. Animal studies also have confirmed that environmental stressors can cause duodenal ulcers, as in monkeys trained to avoid electrical shock. Human studies include epidemiologic observations on increasing peptic ulcer disease after acute stressors (the London blitzkrieg, for example), or in air traffic controllers (who have increased incidence of hypertension and dyspepsia, but not PUD). Some studies have failed to find an association between life stressors and PUD (Soll and Isenberg, 1983). In work done by Magni et al. (1986) the personality patterns of patients with either gastric ulcers or duodenal ulcers appear similar. Ulcer patients appear to have tendencies toward introspection, anxiety, and conflicts related to dependence-independence; in addition, they are taciturn, adaptable, and lacking in paranoid tendencies.

The pathophysiologic mechanisms by which the mind might influence the development of PUD may be through increased acid secretion, which clearly occurs in response to emotional states; through pepsin and mucus secretion; or through impaired circulation and resultant hypoxia of the gastric or duodenal mucosa. The gastrointestinal "responsiveness" differs for individuals and requires an adequate parietal cell mass to produce sufficient or excessive acid. Ulceration does not occur in individuals lacking in hydrochloric acid secretion.

Stress ulcers. The pathophysiology of stress ulcers has never been clearly described. The occurrence of an acute gastritis and the almost immediate appearance of multiple, well-circumscribed gastric ulcers following head injury, surgery, trauma, burns, and sepsis have led to numerous postulates for their occurrence. Circulating peptides, corticosteroids, and acid hypersecretion have all been suggested. Recent research, however, has led to the suggestion that three factors must exist for this phenomenon to occur. These are the presence of acid, the presence of bile salts or other agents that will increase H^+ permeability through the mucosal cells, and the occurrence of a period of decreased mucosal blood flow, such as might occur during a period of profound hypotension associated with a shock state. Menguy and associates (1974) have shown that hemorrhagic shock in rats is associated with diffuse foci of mucosal necrosis within 15 minutes and with gross ulceration leading to gastric hemorrhage within 45 to 60 minutes. They suggest that a sudden cellular energy deficit causing cellular necrosis, such as is observed in hypovolemic shock induced by hemorrhage, results in damage to the mucosa, leading to stress ulcer formation. Furthermore, it is apparent that the lesions formed during the initial period of gastric hypoxia will be aggravated by the HCl, which continues to form when gastric function is returned to basal levels. Thus the gastric permeability to H^+ must be considered not as a static barrier but rather as a dynamic and changing tolerance of the mucosa that depends on the maintenance of a variety of factors at steady state values.

Achlorhydria. Achlorhydria is depression or total absence of hydrochloric acid and pepsinogen secretion by the stomach caused by atrophy of the gastric mucosa. The stomach pH that results is usually between 7.0 and 8.0. The absence of an acidic stomach environment is not an insurmountable impairment to normal digestion, but the absence of intrinsic factor production in achlorhydria does result in

major pathophysiology. *Intrinsic factor* is produced by the stomach mucosa; it is a proteinaceous substance required by the ileum to absorb vitamin B_{12}. The intrinsic factor is thought to bind the highly charged vitamin complex as the first step in its subsequent pinocytosis by intestinal epithelial cells. It is of interest that both intrinsic factor and vitamin B_{12} are rather large molecules, and when bound together they form an unusually massive complex for the cell membrane to transport. It is the opposite for most other digestive and absorptive processes, where larger molecules are broken down into smaller fragments to facilitate their absorption by the mucosa. When vitamin B_{12} absorption is inhibited in the absence of intrinsic factor, red blood cell maturation is delayed and deficient, so that anemia results. This is termed *pernicious anemia* and is treated by injections of the needed vitamin B_{12}, which delivers the vitamin directly into the bloodstream, thus bypassing the gut entirely.

Achlorhydria is associated with atrophic gastritis in less than 20% of the cases. Atrophic gastritis is present in about half of the individuals with gastric peptic ulcers and is also associated with an increased incidence of gastric carcinoma.

Intestinal secretion

The major function of the small intestine is to disperse and digest the larger molecules of food substances into readily absorbable forms, which mainly occurs in the duodenum, and to then absorb these molecules through the intestinal lining cells and into the capillary blood or lymphatic fluid of the intestinal lacteals. This process is a major function of the jejunum. The small and large intestines participate in both the secretion and later reabsorption of tremendous amounts of fluids and electrolytes, which aid the digestive and absorptive processes. In a sense there is a circulation of about 9,000 ml of isotonic fluid from the blood, through the intestinal lining cells, into the lumen of the gut, back out through the cells, and eventually a return of this fluid to the blood. Only 1,500 ml of fluid is taken in through the diet, and only 150 ml is normally excreted in the feces.

Disorders of secretion can originate at many levels of the gut and can involve fluid or mucus secretion. For example, disordered gastric emptying, such as might occur with the dumping syndrome, results in the sudden influx of a large amount of highly acid and often hypertonic fluid from the stomach into the duodenum. This will result in osmosis of water into the duodenum, and this rush of chyme may overwhelm the limited capacity of the colon to absorb water and electrolytes, so that fluid diarrhea may result. This excessive secretion has occurred in response to the loss of regulation of gastric emptying that occurs in the dumping syndrome. A low, unbuffered gastrointestinal tract pH can by itself inhibit the absorption of water and Na^+ as well, thus further contributing to the net secretion.

Another condition that can result in abnormal fluid secretion has been described in individuals with secretin-releasing pancreatic tumors. Large amounts of secretin are released and cause excessive secretion of highly alkaline fluid from the pancreas, which is poured into the duodenum. Net secretion and Na^+ and water reabsorption impairment result. Increased mucus secretion in the lower bowel is a common response both to a variety of bowel inflammations and in certain tumors.

Disease model: cholera. The best-described disorder of intestinal fluid secretion is the infectious disease *cholera*, which is caused by *Vibrio cholerae*. Individuals with cholera may lose up to 16 liters of diarrhea fluid per day from the gastrointestinal tract as massive secretion of fluid from mainly the jejunum and ileum into the lumen occurs. The mechanism of action for cholera toxin is currently under investigation, but considerable evidence has accumulated to implicate the adenyl cyclase system of the mucosal cells as the site of action for cholera toxin. Adenyl cyclase, converts ATP to cyclic AMP, is required in the control of Na^+ and Cl^- secretion into the bowel lumen. Prostaglandins may be mediators of this process. The increased concentration of sodium in the gut is the result of depressed Na^+ absorption rather than an actual secretion of Na^+. Considerable evidence does exist for stimulation of HCO_3^- and Cl^- active transport into the lumen by cholera toxin, which has an extremely protracted action. The result of such activation is a reversal of the normal direction of fluid and electrolyte movement in the intestine. The colon is presented with large amounts of fluid containing Na^+, Cl^-, and HCO_3^- and is unable to absorb these ions and fluids efficiently. Thus cholera stool composition is approximately the same as ileal fluid. Glucose and amino acid absorption, which are sodium dependent, are normal in cholera, even in the presence of a large amount of fluid being secreted into the gut lumen. Oral fluid replacement in cholera therefore is often high in amino acids and glucose, as their transport mechanisms may actually increase absorption of Na^+, water, and other electrolytes.

It would appear that the many forms of infectious gastroenteritis that afflict humans may actually mimic the interference with normal water and electrolyte movements that is observed in cholera. A number of other organisms elaborate entero-toxins and appear able to act on intestinal secretion. The most noteworthy among these are *Escherichia coli* and *Staphylococcus aureus*, which are known to be common agents for diarrheal diseases.

DISORDERS OF ABSORPTION

Of all the gastrointestinal functions, the function of the jejunum is the most compromised by the various clinical malabsorption syndromes common in humans, as most foods are absorbed in this segment of the small intestine. When protein and carbohydrate digestive products are not absorbed in the jejunum because of some disease process, the osmotic pressure of the jejunum increases, and Na^+ and water reabsorption are impaired, resulting in an increased flow and load of liquid material into the ileum and colon. Malabsorption may be caused by disease of organs such as the liver, gallbladder, or pancreas, such that digestive enzymes or bile is deficient, or it may be caused by primary disorders of the intestinal tract itself.

A primary malabsorption syndrome is *lactose intolerance*, which is caused by a genetically determined lack of lactase, an enzyme required to break down lactose in milk into a form that can be readily absorbed by the gut mucosa. It also acts to cause an osmotic diarrhea (Fig. 21-6). It can be seen that the absence of the enzyme required to break down the ingested food molecules results in a large concentration of these molecules in the lumen of the in-

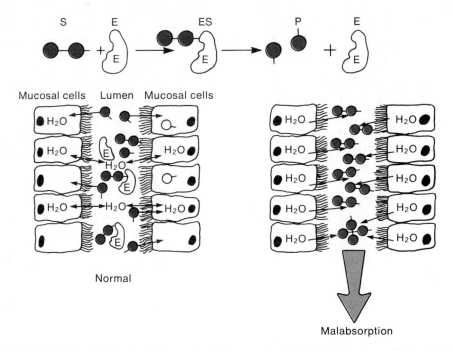

Fig. 21-6. Osmotic diarrhea in malabsorption. When a normally absorbable substance that is broken down by an intestinal enzyme into smaller units so as to be able to pass through mucosal cells remains in lumen due to a deficiency of enzyme, an osmotic gradient is created. Substance accumulates and creates a hypertonic luminal fluid, with water moving into lumen, causing a fluid diarrhea. *S,* Substance; *E,* enzyme; *ES,* enzyme substrate complex; *P,* products.

testinal tract, which acts to osmotically pull water from the luminal cells into the gut, thus causing a large volume of fluid and gas to move through the tract and be expelled as diarrhea. Lactase deficiency may develop in the aged as well. It can be treated by addition of the enzyme to milk or elimination of milk products from the diet.

Other malabsorption syndromes may act differently to cause the characteristic diarrhea, malnutrition, weight loss, and other signs of starvation that are common to all malabsorption disorders. *Celiac disease*, for example, may result in the formation of toxic products, which then act directly on the gut mucosa to damage it and diminish its normal regulatory capacity for secretion and absorption. Celiac disease in children and *nontropical sprue** in adults appear to be the same disease process. There is evidence that a genetic predisposition to these conditions is present.

The most outstanding finding in these disorders is an inability to digest gluten and gliadin, proteins found mainly in wheat, barley, and oats. Toxic peptides may be produced when these large molecules are not broken down completely, and these peptides may then act on the small intestinal mucosa to cause characteristic damage. There are generally hypertrophic changes associated with inflammation in this condition. Flattening and atrophy of the jejunal villi are also common, the surface epithelium is disorganized, and the

ability of the intestinal cells to secrete intestinal hormones, such as cholecystokinin and secretin, is affected. This results in impaired fat absorption, causing a common sign of malabsorption: *steatorrhea*, or fat in the stools. Many abnormal enzyme activities of the intestinal cells have been reported as well. Fermentation of undigested food by large intestine bacteria gives rise to large amounts of flatus and frothy, offensive stools. The major signs and symptoms of celiac disease and nontropical sprue are diarrhea, steatorrhea, malnutrition, weight loss in the presence of an increased appetite, abdominal distension and bloating, hypocalcemia, anemia, and edema. These histologic and physiologic changes revert to normal when a gluten-free diet is administered.

This disorder may have an immune hypersensitivity etiology, or it may be accompanied by an increased gut permeability to antigens normally sequestered in the GI tract. One variation of celiac disease has an associated skin rash, with IgA deposition, presumably an allergic-like dermatitis in response to dietary gluten.

This disease has an immunologic basis, associated with hyperreactivity to gliadin, that is genetically based. Patients with the disease are much more likely than the general population to have HLA-B8, HLA-DR3 and HLA-DR7 (Strobel and James, 1987). It is likely that T cell–mediated immune mechanisms cause the mucosal changes. Interestingly, there is homology between gliadin and a protein product of adenovirus 12, normally a nonpathogenic gastrointestinal virus. This would suggest a possible cross-reactivity mechanism of the host to the viral protein, which in turn would produce an immune response to gliadin in susceptible individuals.

Many other malabsorption conditions cause morphologic changes in the intes-

---

*Tropical sprue, another disorder of absorption, may be caused by bacterial overgrowth secondary to mucosal injury. It is acquired in the tropics but may actually appear 20 years after an individual has migrated from the tropics. It is characterized by sugar, fat, and vitamin B_{12} malabsorption and steatorrhea. It should be differentiated from nontropical sprue, as its etiology and pathogenesis are entirely different.

tinal structure. Kwashiorkor, caused by a protein-calorie deficiency, is usually accompanied by a chronic diarrhea. Atrophic changes in the jejunal mucosa, with resultant malabsorption of glucose and disaccharides, and diarrhea result, further debilitating an already severely malnourished child.

Malabsorption of Na^+ and water has also been described in association with scleroderma, Crohn's disease, and ulcerative colitis. Increased secretion of K^+ into the lumen may also occur in these conditions. The extensive use of laxatives may result in Na^+ and water depletion, which may become chronic and debilitating. Certain laxatives (senna and cascara) also can cause atonia of the colon by irreversible damage to the myenteric nerve plexuses. Defects of intestinal amino acid transport such as in cystinuria and tryptophan malabsorption can occur, and protein malabsorption is often observed in pancreatic disease, stasis of the small intestine, gastrectomy, celiac disease, and Crohn's disease.

Fat malabsorption resulting in steatorrhea is common in many gastrointestinal conditions; it is particularly common in cystic fibrosis, celiac disease, ileal resection (in which the overall absorptive surface is decreased), and in any condition that results in the loss of bile salts (cholelithiasis, hepatic disease). When large amounts of fat are retained in the gut, hypocalcemia may develop, with signs of tetany, since the fatty acids form insoluble calcium soaps, resulting in GI calcium loss.

Vitamin and mineral deficiencies are common in most malabsorption syndromes, and specific vitamin malabsorption also may occur (pernicious anemia). Endocrine disease, diet, drugs, surgery, intestinal factors, and systemic influences may all interfere with absorption of vitamins, minerals, and other food molecules.

Inflammation and infection of the gut have been alluded to previously as being responsible for disorders of secretion, motility, and absorption. There are a number of disease models that illustrate the pathophysiology of gastrointestinal inflammation.

INFLAMMATORY AND INFECTIOUS DISORDERS
Mouth

The teeth are required for digestion of food in that they act to grind and break apart food in preparation for the action of digestive enzymatic degradation.

Dental caries. Probably the most ubiquitous disorder of the human GI tract is dental caries. The cause of carious lesions is largely dietary and results from excessive ingestion of refined sugar, but dental caries must also be considered an infectious disease. Plaque, which accumulates on the tooth surface, is loaded with bacteria that basically feed on sucrose, glucose, and fructose, fermenting these sugars and producing acid, which causes the pH to drop. Acidification of the plaque on the tooth surface produces the first lesion characteristic of developing caries, demineralization. This begins at a pH of about 5.5. Over time (around 18 months) the demineralization proceeds to produce a white or brown area. Underneath this area mineral loss and production of microscopic spaces within the enamel of the tooth occur. Eventually enough of this occurs to cause the actual cavity to form. Once this has developed, bacterial invasion of the tooth proceeds at a faster rate, and the cavity enlarges.

It has been conclusively established that bacteria are essential to the development of carious lesions. The organism best known for this effect is *Streptococcus mutans*, which is gram positive and very strongly acid forming. Other organisms are also suspected in human caries, but *Streptococcus mutans* is the most common agent.

With the development of carious lesions, normal digestive functioning can be definitely impaired. This is best seen in human groups who do not have access to restorative dental care. Even when dental care is available, tooth decay and gum disease, as a concomitant of the aging process, may ultimately lead to alterations in nutritional integrity.

Once a carious lesion occurs, there is usually little that can be done to halt its progress other than dental filling. Much research is directed toward the development of a vaccine against the responsible cariogenic organism, and such a vaccine seems to be a good future possibility. The optimal approach would be prevention of the development of caries through dietary manipulation. The incidence of caries in the human population was very low in ancestral man and before the cultivation of sugar cane and the sugar beet. A return to a more natural diet without the addition of highly sugared foods seems to be highly desirable. Topical application of fluoride and tooth flossing are two additional approaches that help prevent decay. The act of tooth brushing in and of itself probably does nothing to prevent caries.

Stomach

Inflammatory disorders of the stomach may be either acute or chronic.

Acute gastritis. Acute gastritis is so common among the human population that the signs and symptoms need hardly be mentioned. It can occur in response to ingestion of highly irritating or toxic substances, such as aspirin or alcohol, or it can be the result of infection of the stomach by *Staphylococcus* or *Clostridium botulinum*. Stress, burns, and head injuries also provoke a gastritis-like response that may lead to the development of numerous gastric ulcers (e.g., Curling's and Cushing's ulcers). The stomach mucosa responds to all of the above agents by increasing the rate of cell turnover of the epithelial lining, and thus the disease process may be self-limiting, with the renewal of the epithelium providing an adequate surface, and the damaged, necrotic cells produced by the gastritis being sloughed away. If the exposure is particularly intense or long, the mucosa may respond with an acute inflammatory response characterized by hyperemia, edema, infiltration, and occasionally by hemorrhage.

The symptoms of acute gastritis are nausea, pain, vomiting, and often diarrhea if the intestine is involved. A severe but fairly common response is hematemesis, which may lead to a significant loss of blood. Acute gastritis may predispose the individual to the further development of ulceration of the gastric mucosa.

Chronic gastritis. Chronic gastritis is associated with atrophy of the gastric mucosa and the possible development of pernicious anemia. The etiology of this disorder is not well understood at this time, but the incidence does increase with age. An autoimmune background has been suggested, as chronic thyroiditis, an autoimmune disease of the thyroid gland, is often found in individuals with pernicious anemia.

Intestine

Intestinal disorders caused by infection or inflammation are common, and may be acute or chronic. Infectious diarrhea kills 5 to 10 million people per year, mostly in undeveloped countries.

Acute gastroenteritis. This infectious or inflammatory response of the GI tract is common to all who have traveled to foreign countries or have eaten contaminated food. It is also seen frequently among infants, in whom it can be extremely virulent. Generally the condition is mild and self-resolving, causing diarrhea, nausea, vomiting, cramping, and often systemic symtoms such as malaise and fever. Acute gastroenteritis can be caused either by the direct infection of the GI tract lining by a pathogenic organism such as *Salmonella* or *Shigella*, or indirectly by the ingestion of bacteria that produce toxins, such as the neurotoxin of *Clostridium botulinum*. The latter is the cause of the most severe form of food poisoning. Gastroenteritis may also be caused by imbalance in the normal bacterial flora of the gut. Most travelers' diarrhea probably occurs through the latter mechanism. Local strains of gut flora, such as *Escherichia coli*, may be acquired by the traveler, and a temporary upset in the normal flora may occur, causing the signs and symptoms of acute gastroenteritis.

Traveler's diarrhea. The most common cause of diarrhea in developing countries, and the usual cause of diarrhea that develops in travelers to developing countries, is infection with either *Salmonella* (about 10%) or *Escherichia coli*. *E. coli* is, of course, a major and ordinary populant of the gut, but enterotoxigenic strains of the organism exist and cause disease. Travelers exposed to this organism through food or water contamination have a generally mild, watery diarrheal disease less than a week in duration. Infants and children with enterotoxigenic *E. coli* infection can be seriously ill for much longer. The organism secretes an enterotoxin that is able to activate adenylate cyclase, causing excessive fluid secretion into the gut (Quinn et al., 1986). Other strains of *E. coli* that are important pathogens in diarrheal disease include enteropathogenic *E. coli*, enteroadherent *E. coli*, enteroinvasive *E. coli*, and a new strain, found in contaminated hamburger meat in the United States and Canada, *E. coli* 0157:H7 (Quinn et al., 1986). Enteropathogenic *E. coli* infections are usually observed in infants and very young children, and the pathophysiologic mechanism by which diarrhea is produced is not known. Enterotoxic *E. coli* infections usually do not persist longer than 7 days and are generally seen in older children and adults. Enteroadherent *E. coli* attaches to the cell membranes, and enteroinvasive *E. coli* organisms actually invade the enterocytes lining the intestinal tract, and produce a dysentery-like illness. These latter forms of infection produce diarrheal illness through denudation of the absorptive surface of the intestinal mucosa. Osmotic pressure increases as chyme reaches the ileum, since lactose and other food molecules are not broken down by intestinal enzymes. The unabsorbed lactose becomes fermented by colonic bacteria, producing fatty acids, carbon dioxide, and hydrogen, so that a watery diarrhea containing bicarbonate, potassium, and sodium is produced, and metabolic acidosis and dehydration ensue. Representative organisms that produce diarrhea in this manner are *E. coli*, *Salmonella*, *Shigella*, Norwalk virus and rotavirus (the most common gastroenteritis in infants and children), and *Giardia* (a protozoan) (Mitchell and Skelton, 1988).

Other organisms produce diarrhea through the elaboration of toxins. The organism responsible for botulism acts by elaborating a neurotoxin that affects motor nerve synapses and causes abnormal GI tract motility in this manner. The *Clostridium botulinum* neurotoxin causes an early severe diarrhea, but this is later followed by a prolonged constipation. Entero-toxins have a specific action on the gas-trointestinal mucosa, first adhering to en-terocytes and then releasing toxins that stimulate adenyl cyclase activity. This re-sults in a net reduction in sodium reab-sorption and a net increase in electrolyte and water secretion into the gut, a mech-anism previously described for cholera. Microorganisms that produce their effects in this manner include *Vibrio cholera, Ba-cillus cereus, Clostridium difficile* and *per-fringens, E. coli* (enterotoxic strains), *Shi-gella dysenteriae,* and *Staphylococcus aureus* (Mitchell and Skelton, 1988).

Generally pathogens invading the GI tract tend to localize in a particular seg-ment of the gut and accumulate there in amounts of 10^7 to 10^8/g of tissue. This phe-nomenon may be peculiar to the specific pathogen or may be related to the anat-omy and physiology of the gut. Most or-ganisms require at least a concentrated ingestion of 10^2 to 10^3 before infection be-comes established.

Many pathogenic organisms cause gas-troenteritis by actual binding with the mucosal cells of the GI tract, causing an effect similar to cholera, which results in increased secretion of electrolytes and wa-ter into the gut lumen. Other organisms may act by causing a rush of chyme from the small intestine, which contains large amounts of undigested foods that can act osmotically to increase water secretion into the gut and can also result in fermen-tation by large intestinal flora. Large amounts of gas and foul-smelling liquid stool result.

Viruses have been implicated as causa-tive agents of acute infantile gastroenteri-tis. Causative viruses include rotaviruses, reoviruses, picornaviruses, parvoviruses, adenoviruses, and astroviruses.

Giardia lamblia deserves mention as an important agent of gastroenteritis, due to its increasing incidence in immunodefi-cient individuals and in children, particu-larly those in the hospital or nursery school. The organism is a flagellated pro-tozoan that infects by transmission of cysts through contaminated water or di-rect contact. Diarrhea in children that lasts longer than 2 weeks should be inves-tigated for *Giardia,* and nursery school hy-giene should be emphasized. Gastrointes-tinal disease spread in day care settings has become a significant public health problem.

The causes of fluid diarrhea are listed according to the pathogenetic mechanism in the box below. The normal physiology of water and solute balance requires that the 7500 ml of water, 1000 mEq Na^+, 40 mEq K^+, and 750 mEq Cl^- secreted into

---

CAUSES OF DIARRHEA*

Normal gut mucosa
  Increased gastric emptying
  Abnormal upper GI tract secretions
  Hypertonic load
  Increased motility

Abnormal gut mucosa
  Disorders of absorption
    Celiac disease
    Acute gastroenteritis
    Sugar malabsorption
    Laxatives (?)
    Inflammatory diseases
  Disorders of secretion
    Celiac disease
    Mucus-secreting tumors
    Unabsorbable bile acids
    Cholera

*Modified from McColl, I., and Sladen, G.: Intestinal ab-sorption in man, London, 1975, Academic Press, Inc.

the gut each day be reabsorbed by the intestinal epithelium, so that the final output of these substances will be small. This reabsorption mainly occurs in the jejunum, ileum, and colon. If it is not complete, either because the mechanisms for reabsorption are impaired, interfered with, or overcome, or because the transit time of this fluid in the gut is shortened, fluid diarrhea may result. Sodium reabsorption appears to involve sodium diffusion into the cells and active transport at the lateral cell membranes of the mucosal cells (Fig. 21-7). Movement of Na$^+$ into the mucosal cells from the lumen is passive but appears to be coupled to glucose and amino acid absorption. Therefore any defect that interferes significantly with Na$^+$ reabsorption may also deplete the body of

energy-producing food molecules and water.

Whenever the load in the intestine is increased over the ability of the intestine to reabsorb, malabsorption and diarrhea are possible. Osmotic diarrhea occurs when the number of osmotically active particles increases, such as might be seen in malabsorption of specific nutrients, which are therefore left behind in the gut. This causes hypertonicity of the luminal contents, driving excess water into the lumen. The gut may also be defective in absorption of food, fluid, and electrolytes. When either of these processes occurs, the colon is overwhelmed by fluid and electrolytes that it cannot absorb, and fluid diarrhea results. Diarrhea may result from increased motility of the small intestine,

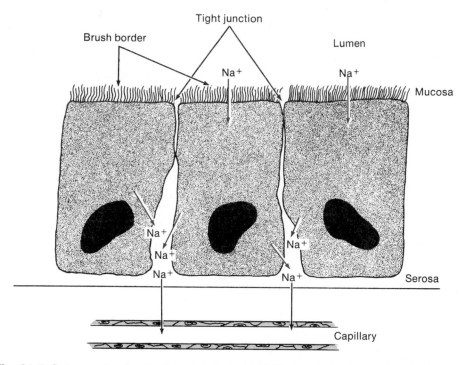

Fig. 21-7. Pathway of molecules through intestinal wall. Na$^+$ and other ions and molecules move through intestinal epithelial cells at brush border and then are actively transported at lateral cell surfaces. Na$^+$, glucose, and amino acid transport are all believed to be linked.

which causes an osmotic rush of fluid fecal material through the large intestine; this rush of fecal material may be aided by the accumulation of the products of fermentation of undigested food by the large intestine bacteria. Some invading organisms that cause gastroenteritis may destroy the colonic mucosa, and decreased water reabsorption may result, contributing to the development of diarrhea. Volume overload of this type may not be accompanied by increased gut motility.

Superinfection. The normal intestinal flora may become imbalanced by antibiotics, such as ampicillin, which are broad spectrum in nature. These drugs may act on components of the normal flora, destroying an innocuous species and thus removing a source of competition for food molecules in the gut. Populations of pathogens that are normally very small or absent then begin to grow and may invade the mucosa, causing *mucous enterocolitis*. The organism *Clostridium difficile* is the most common bacteria responsible for overcolonization and toxigenic effect during antibiotic therapy (Mitchell and Skelton, 1988).

Another common causative organism that may invade and cause ulceration and necrosis of the colon wall is *Staphylococcus aureus*. The enteritis that occurs in this case is prolonged rather than acute. It has been suggested that consumption of sour milk products high in lactobacilli may counteract this effect of the broad-spectrum antibiotics. The problem of superinfection also may occur in the oral cavity and the vagina.

Ulcerative colitis. Ulcerative colitis is classified along with Crohn's disease as an inflammatory bowel disease. However, there are some important differences between them in terms of location and characteristic lesions (Table 21-2).

Table 21-2. Differences between ulcerative colitis and Crohn's disease

Signs and symptoms	Ulcerative colitis	Crohn's disease
Ulcerations	Usually superficial, involving only mucosa	Deep; may invade many layers
Strictures and fistulas	Rare	Common
Involvement of small intestine	Rare	Extensive
Granulomas	Rare	40%-80%
Continuity	Contiguous	Often skips areas
Thickening of bowel wall	Occasionally slightly increased	Thickened
Anal and perianal lesions	Rare	Common
Cancer incidence	Increased risk	Normal risk

Ulcerative colitis is more common under the age of 30 and is occasionally associated with certain behavior patterns and stress states. There is a familial nature to the disease also. Individuals with ulcerative colitis sometimes have attitudes of hopelessness and hidden hostility. They are usually overachievers and will attempt impossible tasks. These psychosomatic factors are not believed to be causative but rather facilitative in ulcerative colitis pathogenesis. Some recent studies refute a serious role for stress or personality in the disease, but many other studies suggest that ulcerative colitis patients tend toward obsessional traits and dysrhythmic states (Arapakis et al., 1986). In a study of personality factors, ulcerative colitis patients exhibit "low dominance," which indicates a decreased tendency toward having a domineering attitude or committing hostile acts. The patients also scored high in intrapunitiveness, indicating a lack of self-confidence and overdependence on others. In the study by Arapakis et al. (1986), both the irritable bowel syndrome and the ulcerative colitis patients exhibited tendencies toward low dominance and high intrapunitiveness. It is not known if these personality factors are reactive to the disease process itself or are etiologic in its causation. These characteristics are considered to be highly neurotic and, if reactive, are certainly not adaptive.

The disorder is characterized by chronic hemorrhagic ulceration of the colon and usually the rectum, which is commonly associated with diarrhea, melena, pain, and fever. Occasionally systemic manifestations appear, including arthritis, liver disease, uveitis, and skin lesions. The cause of ulcerative colitis is unknown, but increasingly the theory that an immunologic abnormality is etiologic is being accepted. In many ways the disease appears to be the result of an initial infection, but no organisms have been identified. Diet has also been implicated as a factor. One theory of pathogenesis suggests that *cross-reactivity* of normal gut antigens with bacterial floral antigens results in the destruction and erosion of the normal mucosa. The bacteria present in the gut may invade a damaged mucosa more easily, thus perpetuating the disease process. Evidence for an immunologic component is also given by the fact that T cell function is disturbed in patients with ulcerative colitis.

The disease typically arises in the left colon, and the earliest sign is tiny abscesses in the crypts of Lieberkühn, which cause the mucosal cells to slough away from the surface, leaving behind ulcerations that eventually coalesce and occasionally invade deep into the muscular coatings of the intestine. Intense hyperemia may be present as an accompaniment to ulcerative changes. The inflammation that is part of this process often takes on the characteristics of a chronic process. However, fibrosis is rare in this condition. Chronic loss of blood and fluids through bloody diarrhea often results in anemia and debilitation. Defects in fluid and electrolyte absorption may be present. Morphologic abnormalities of the mucosa include the development of pseudopolyps and fistulas. The course of ulcerative colitis is characterized by periods of remission and exacerbation. Treatment includes management of diarrhea, fluid and electrolyte losses, bleeding, and anemia; prevention and treatment of secondary infection through drug therapy, such as sulfasalazine; suppression of inflammation by corticosteroid therapy; and surgical colostomy or ileostomy (depending on the degree of involvement of the colon and rectum). It has been previously noted that long-standing chronic ulcerative colitis is associated with an increased incidence of colon carcinoma. A further complication may be the development of *toxic megacolon*, which results from the destruction of the myenteric nerve plexus. Massive dilation and obstruction of the colon may occur and require emergency intervention.

Crohn's disease. This condition should be contrasted to ulcerative colitis, although both are considered inflammatory bowel diseases. It is much less common than ulcerative colitis, and the etiology, the area of bowel involved, and the pathologic changes are different, but the two conditions are often confused, particularly if Crohn's disease is present in the left colon. Crohn's disease can affect both the small and large intestine, and it is characterized by a chronic hyperemic granulomatous response of the mucosa of unknown etiology. The acute condition is usually a regional ileitis that is self-resolving in the majority of cases. The chronic regional enteritis is characterized by intermittent diarrhea, anorexia, abdominal pain, and weight loss. The lesions that develop in the GI tract are likely to become suppurative and transmural, and fistulas frequently form communicating channels from one section of the intestine to another. There are often intermittent patches of enteritis so that areas of affected bowel are followed by disease-free areas. The disease is also one in which remissions and exacerbations occur over the course of many years, and most of the treatment during acute stages is symptomatic. Antibiotics and corticosteroids are the major drugs used in the treatment of Crohn's disease, and surgical intervention is often necessary to excise diseased segments of bowel.

The following case study illustrates the clinical presentation of Crohn's disease.

CASE STUDY: CROHN'S DISEASE

History

Brandon is a 13-year-old male who is brought to the pediatrician's office for evaluation of chronic diarrhea. His appetite has been variable, with frequent bloating and cramping after eating. His parents have noticed for several years that he has diarrhea more often than most people (5 to 6 stools/day). This has been investigated by his family physician, and no pathogens were found. On further questioning it is discovered that he has episodes of diarrhea, slight fever, and severe bloating for 1 to 2 weeks, followed by several weeks to months without diarrhea. Brandon's mother states that he has not increased in height or weight for the past 2 years. He is developing some sec-

Contributed by Kay Bultemeir.

ondary sex characteristics, and she is concerned that he may not grow. Recently he has felt self-conscious about his smallness and has missed 8 days of school in 6 weeks because of the diarrhea.

Social history: Child is the oldest of three children. Presently in the 8th grade and doing very well in school. He is involved in swimming and baseball.

Past history: Normal pregnancy and delivery—birth weight 7 lb. 8 oz., height 20 inches

Childhood illnesses: Chickenpox and occasional sore throats

Hospitalizations: None

Allergies: None known

Medications: None. Denies use of alcohol, tobacco, or controlled drugs

Family history: Negative for diabetes, cancer, hypertension, tuberculosis, autoimmune disease.

Subjective and Objective Data

Physical examination

Weight and height: below 5th percentile.

Temperature: 99.6°.

Hct.: 35%

General appearance: Alert smiling male, who appears younger than stated age

HEENT: No abnormalities except for three aphthous ulcers on lower buccal mucosa

Neck: No thyromegaly

Chest: Clear

Heart: Regular rhythm without murmur

Abdomen: Distended, increased bowel sounds, slightly tender in right lower quadrant to palpation. No masses palpated

Genitalia: Few pubic hairs noted, slight increase in penile size

Child was admitted for work-up of chronic diarrhea and failure to thrive. Positive findings included mucus-containing and blood-tinged diarrhea, negative for ova and parasites. Negative stool cultures. Epiphyseal plates not closed. Barium enema and flexible sigmoidoscopy revealed segmental mucosal inflammation with granular appearance of the mucosa at several sites. No fistulas or strictures found.

Probable diagnosis: Crohn's disease.

Treatment

Vitamin and mineral supplement
Increased calorie and protein diet
Low-residue diet with restricted milk products

Patient was maintained on this regimen for 1 week, but the diarrhea persisted, temperature remained slightly elevated, and patient lost 1 pound during hospitalization.

It was elected to start the child on hyperalimentation to try to optimize nutrition to foster growth. Child tolerated the treatment well and was sent home 6 days after implementation with 12 hours per day of hyperalimentation. He was symptom free on release, and no further weight loss was noted.

Three months after hospitalization, 2-inch increase in height and 5-pound increase in weight were recorded. Hct 38%; no recurrence of diarrhea. Child feeling well and beginning to enjoy activities again.

Pathophysiology

Crohn's disease is an incurable discontinuous granulomatous inflammatory disease of the bowel mucosa, intermixed with normal bowel. It can affect any part of the alimentary canal. It is a chronic, relapsing disease of the inflamed bowel. The process can progress through all layers of the bowel. Submucosal thickening with lymphedema, lymphoid hyperplasia, and nonspecific granuloma develops. Often the process leads to the development of strictures, fistulas, and abscesses. Commonly affected sites are the distal ileum and the ascending colon. When noted in children, a significant failure to thrive secondary to the nutritional deficiency often occurs. The onset may be insidious or stormy. With children the treatment goal must include optimal nutritional supplementation to foster optimal growth.

Signs and symptoms are diarrhea, often intermittent; abdominal pain; weight loss; low-grade fever; and rectal bleeding. Coexisting symptoms often include arthritis, ankylosing spondylitis, uveitis, erythema nodosum, and aphthous oral ulcers. Long-term prognosis is not favorable; 70% of affected individuals will eventually require surgery.

Nursing Diagnoses

1. Diarrhea
2. Altered nutrition: less than body requirement
3. Impaired social interaction
4. Altered growth and development

Acute appendicitis. A discussion of inflammatory conditions of the intestine would not be complete without inclusion of acute appendicitis, which is the most common cause for emergency surgery of the abdomen but which has been steadily declining in incidence in recent years. Acute appendicitis is the result of obstruction and inflammation leading to ischemia of the vermiform appendix, which may result in necrosis and perforation of the appendix and subsequent abscess formation or peritonitis. The earliest and most significant symptom of appendicitis is pain, which is caused by distension of the serosa due to inflammatory edema. Obstruction of the appendix (e.g., by a foreign body or fecolith or even by lymphatic hypertrophy resulting from systemic infection) will result in edema, which can compromise the vascular supply to the appendix. This will increase the permeability of this segment of the intestines, and bacterial invasion of the wall of the appendix by organisms of the normal flora then results in infection and inflammation. The appendix may rupture, causing either a local or generalized peritonitis.

The symptoms of acute appendicitis are pain and rebound tenderness, which usually eventually localize over McBurney's point; nausea and vomiting; anorexia; diarrhea; and systemic signs of inflammation such as leukocytosis and fever. If perforation of the appendix occurs, the pain becomes generalized, and the patient will lie very still and rigid. Many conditions simulate the symptoms of appendicitis, making this condition surprisingly difficult to diagnose. Other conditions that will cause an "acute abdomen" include ruptured gallbladder, perforated duodenal ulcer, pancreatitis, a ruptured tubal pregnancy, sickle cell crisis, and gastrointestinal conditions such as diverticulitis.

DISORDERS OF THE GALLBLADDER

The gallbladder's function is to store and concentrate the bile produced in the liver and then to release it into the duodenum through a physiologic "sphincter," the sphincter of Oddi, when it is required for fat digestion. The major stimulus to release of bile from the gallbladder is mediated through the intestinal hormone cholecystokinin, which is a product of endocrine cells in the duodenum that are activated by fats, proteins, and hypertonic solutions. Cholecystokinin has a stronger effect on gallbladder contraction than does stimulation by the vagus nerve, but both mechanisms act to contract the gallbladder and relax the sphincter of Oddi, allowing bile to squirt into the duodenum at the ampulla of Vater. The gallbladder can store as much as 500 ml of bile between meals, which the organ concentrates by reabsorbing fluid and salt through its mucosal lining. Many organisms do not have a gallbladder, and humans are quite easily able to adapt to the accidental or surgical loss of the gallbladder. In this case the bile ducts themselves dilate and can actually compensate for the absence of the gallbladder by concentrating the bile.

Bile is required in the absorption of lipids that have been taken in and digested in the small intestine. Bile contains salts, acids, and pigments that serve to provide a medium for emulsification of dispersed fatty acids, mixtures of glycerides, and cholesterol. This is necessary for the preliminary absorption of these molecules by the intestinal epithelial cells. When the gallbladder's release of bile is obstructed by gallstones or stenosis of the ducts, the gallbladder often enlarges and may become inflamed and eventually fibrotic. The formation of gallstones with or without overt disease occurs in about 10% of the population. Stones may vary in size from a gravelly mixture to those large enough to totally fill the lumen of the gallbladder. Stones may form when the blood cholesterol is significantly increased, such as might occur in diabetes or during pregnancy; when hemolytic anemia occurs and results in hyperbilirubinemia; when biliary stasis occurs; or when the gallbladder is inflamed or infected. Gallstones are generally of a mixed nature, containing cholesterol, bilirubin, and calcium, and are multifaceted and brown. When bile acids are somehow decreased in the bile, the constituents can precipitate and coalesce, thus forming a stone.

Cholelithiasis

Cholelithiasis is the clinical term for gallstones (Fig. 21-8), accretions that form in the gallbladder. The signs and symptoms of cholelithiasis vary. Whenever gallstones form, they are often free to move into the

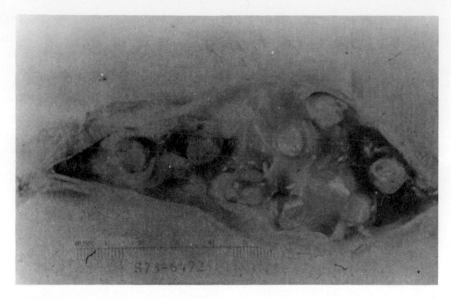

Fig. 21-8. Gallstones. Entire gallbladder is filled with stones and purulent material. (Courtesy Department of Pathology, University of Tennessee, Memphis.)

cystic duct, the common bile duct, and even into the liver via the hepatic ducts. Pancreatitis may also result from obstruction of the pancreatic duct. The most common symptom of gallstones is a colicky pain, believed to be caused by spasm of the sphincter of Oddi, which is a reflex response to gallbladder epithelium irritation or obstruction of the cystic or common bile duct by a gallstone. Obstruction of the common bile duct, if not relieved, will lead to jaundice, a yellowish discoloration of the skin caused by the accumulation of bile pigments in the liver, which then "spill over" into the blood. Before it is apparent, there may be a pruritus. Jaundice is also associated with acholic stools and dark, frothy urine. Jaundice is often first observed in the sclera of the eye but may eventually be evident on all skin surfaces. Obstruction of the bile duct also leads to swelling of the gallbladder with accumulated mucous secretions and eventually inflammation and infection, which often is purulent. The gallbladder may become

gangrenous even when symptoms are absent, and the presence of gallstones will usually result in acute or chronic cholecystitis.

Cholecystitis

Inflammation of the gallbladder, or cholecystitis, may be either acute or chronic. An acute inflammation begins in the mucosal layer of the organ; it may develop as a primary infection, although more commonly it is superimposed on a preexisting chronic cholecystitis that was initially caused by gallstones. The gallbladder becomes dilated and filled with bile, blood, and pus. Infarction of the organ may result from vascular occlusion. The major symptoms are intense pain, malaise, nausea and vomiting, and if perforation has occurred, signs of local or diffuse peritonitis. Chronic cholecystitis may be the sequela of an acute attack of cholecystitis and is almost always associated with the presence of gallstones of either the pure or mulberry type. The major symptoms are vague pain in the upper right quadrant of the abdomen and fat intolerance. The gallbladder may be large enough to palpate, and if the stones contain sufficient calcium salts, they may be visualized by roentgenography. If obstruction is present, jaundice may be another important sign.

Although most cholecystitis is caused by cholelithiasis, a primary infection or inflammation of the gallbladder can itself result in stone formation. Common infective organisms include *Staphylococcus*, *Streptococcus*, and enteric organisms, which may reach the gallbladder through the blood or lymph or by contact with infected neighboring organs. *Salmonella* may be carried in a chronically inflamed gallbladder and excreted in the feces, serving as a source of contagion.

Abnormal bile constituents may themselves be found in the bile and they may injure the gallbladder mucosa, resulting in inflammation and occasionally secondary infection.

The usual treatment for cholecystitis is removal of the gallbladder, particularly if gallstones are present, after the acute inflammation has been relieved by medical intervention.

CASE STUDY: CHOLELITHIASIS

Objective and Subjective Data

Present illness: MY, a 43-year-old widow, was admitted to the hospital after seeing a nurse practitioner at the family health clinic. MY complains of increasing intolerance to fatty foods for the past 5 or 6 months with increasing abdominal pain in the right upper quadrant that radiates to the midepigastric area, tip of the right scapula, and right chest wall.

Contributed by Mildred Fenske.

History

MY's mother and two maternal aunts have had gallbladder disease and her mother has high cholesterol. MY describes herself as "fat all my life."

General appearance: Moderately obese; in acute pain

Skin: Warm

Vital signs
  Temperature: 100° F
  Pulse: 100
  Respirations: 24
  Blood pressure: 140/88
  Weight: 192 pounds
  Height: 5 feet 8 inches

Pertinent laboratory values
  Hgb: 12 g/100 ml
  Hct: 40%
  WBC: 14,000/mm^3
    Bands: 6%
    Segs: 66%
    Lymphs: 38%
  Platelets: 220,500/mm^3
  PTT: 35 seconds
  Bilirubin (total): 1.3 mg/dl
  SGPT: 24 U/L
  SGOT: 28 U/L
  Serum amylase: 28 U/L
  Alkaline phosphatase: 5.2 Bodansky units

Urine: Specific gravity: 1.025

Treatment

On the basis of her subjective symptoms, physical examination, laboratory values, and x-ray films, MY is diagnosed as having acute cholecystitis. An abdominal x-ray film indicated calcified stones in the upper right quadrant of the abdomen, and an intravenous cholangiogram indicated calcified stones in the gallbladder with one or more stones in the common bile duct.

Her orders include:
  NPO
  Nasogastric tube to low suction
  Promethazine 25 mg IM as needed every 3 to 4 hours for nausea and vomiting
  Meperidine 50 to 75 mg IM as needed every 3 hours for pain
  Skin prep for cholecystectomy

D5 1/2 NS IV at 100 ml/hr
Type and cross-match for 2 units whole blood when ordered
Glycopyrrolate 0.2 mg IM
Have patient sign an operative permit for cholecystectomy and exploration of the common bile duct.

Discussion

The gallbladder stores and concentrates bile produced in the liver. The presence of fat stimulates the sphincter of Oddi to release bile into the duodenum. When obstructions prevent the release of bile from the gallbladder, the gallbladder enlarges and becomes inflamed. Prolonged obstruction of the common bile duct leads to jaundice, an elevated bilirubin, swelling of the gallbladder, and, ultimately, inflammation and infection. Gallstones usually contain a combination of cholesterol, calcium, and bilirubin, or they may be composed of bile acids. Pain associated with cholelithiasis and/or cholecystitis is believed to result from spasms of the sphincter of Oddi, a reflex response triggered by obstruction or inflammation. Biliary disease, unlike peptic ulcer disease, is often associated with pain referred to the tip of the right scapula. This pain is transmitted through the sympathetic afferent fibers that enter the ninth thoracic segment of the spinal cord.

MY's slightly elevated SGPT, SGOT, total bilirubin, and alkaline phosphatase values indicate some liver involvement associated with her cholelithiasis; her elevated serum amylase corresponds to some pancreatic effects.

An elevated hematocrit and urine specific gravity are associated with dehydration related to the nausea and vomiting. Increased percentages of band and segmented white cells reflect the body's defence against bacterial infection. Normal PTT and platelet values indicate that a bleeding tendency or an increased risk of thrombus formation during the perioperative period are unlikely.

Nursing Diagnoses

1. Altered nutrition: more than body requirements
2. Fluid volume deficit related to pain, nausea, and vomiting
3. Altered health maintenance related to high dietary fat intake and obesity
4. Acute pain related to gallbladder disease

Cancer

While gallbladder cancer is not common, when it is present it may be overlooked by the patients as causing signs and symptoms of gallstones. The great majority of these tumors are columnar cell carcinomas, and they cause symptoms of inflammation and obstruction.

Congenital anomalies

Surgeons have often observed that the common bile duct, hepatic ducts, cystic duct, and pancreatic duct show great anatomic variety. Occasionally the gallbladder is absent or is found encapsulated by hepatic tissue. The ducts may be abnormally joined to each other or present in a duplicated form. The presence of stenosis or atresia of the common bile duct in the newborn represents the most serious of these anomalies.

DISORDERS OF THE PANCREAS

The pancreas has both exocrine and endocrine functions, but its role in gastrointestinal physiology is basically as an exocrine gland, providing a volume of bicarbonate-containing fluid and a separately regulated juice containing a high concentration of digestive enzymes. The innervation of the pancreas is through the vagus nerve and sympathetic fibers, and the hormonal regulation, which is most important, is via cholecystokinin and secretin release by duodenal endocrine cells. The pancreas provides its secretion to the duodenum via the pancreatic duct, and the patency of this duct is an absolute requirement for the functional integrity of the pancreas and also for normal digestion to take place. The function of the gland may also be compromised by insufficiency, inflammation, or carcinoma.

Pancreatic insufficiency

Cystic fibrosis. This hereditary recessive homozygous condition is a disorder of most if not all exocrine glands and was previously described in terms of genetic factors in Chapter 2. However, its primary manifestations are related to respiratory and digestive tract dysfunction. The mucus secreted in these tracts is more viscous than normal, and 80% of affected children have pancreatic insufficiency. The respiratory effects are described in Chapter 16. The cause of pancreatic dysfunction is related to obstruction of the pancreatic ductules and ducts, causing the lobules of the pancreas to atrophy, with eventual development of fatty infiltration and loss of function. The pancreatic secretions in cystic fibrosis have a greatly lowered enzyme concentration, HCO_3^- level, and fluid composition. Twenty percent of the affected newborns develop *meconium ileus,* caused by the accumulation of viscous meconium in the small intestine, which leads to obstruction. Surgical correction is usually required, but the general development of the infant will continue to be impaired. Malabsorption results from the pancreatic insufficiency, and steatorrhea is common. These children also appear undernourished and usually have symptoms of chronic obstructive lung disease, which may lead to cor pulmonale and heart failure. Most of the signs and symptoms of cystic fibrosis can be directly attributed to

obstruction of the pancreas, intestines, respiratory tract, liver, and reproductive tract by highly viscous, abnormally composed mucus. The treatment is then symptomatic, and pancreatic enzymes are usually administered to aid digestion. Vigorous treatment from infancy onward has led to the survival of some patients into adulthood.

Other causes. A number of diseases have been described that are directly caused by a specific pancreatic enzyme deficiency. These conditions are rare and seem to be associated with genetic defects. Included in this category are pancreatic lipase deficiency, amylase deficiency, and trypsinogen deficiency. All these conditions are associated with maldigestion and often steatorrhea.

Inflammation

Acute pancreatitis. Acute pancreatitis has a mortality higher than 20%; it is found in conjunction with biliary tract disease in more than 50% of the patients and in conjunction with alcoholism in about 30%. The actual etiology of acute pancreatitis is not clear, although whatever the cause, the primary lesion is a chemical inflammation caused by pancreatic enzymes and secretions, which leads to autodigestion and necrosis of the cells of the organ. The presence of gallstones in the pancreatic duct, reflux of bile into the glands, toxins, and direct infecting organisms have all been suggested. (See the box that follows.) Acute pancreatitis thus appears to be associated with either duct obstruction or increased pancreatic secretions. It is often hemorrhagic and typically has an acute onset characterized by nausea and vomiting, severe left-sided radiating pain, and a rigid, tender abdomen. These symptoms may follow the ingestion of large amounts of food or alcohol. The white blood cell

CAUSES OF ACUTE PANCREATITIS

Biliary tract disease
Alcohol
Peptic ulcer
Trauma, surgery, pregnancy
Vascular factors
Hyperlipoproteinemias
Scorpion bites
Carcinoma
Hypercalcemia, infections
Rare causes: cardiopulmonary bypass, Legionnaire's disease, hypotensive shock

Modified from Kaufman D: Symposium on Critical Care Medicine, Acute Pancreatitis, Las Vegas, 1987.

count may be elevated, and pancreatic enzymes such as amylase may appear in high concentration in the blood. Up to 20% of the affected patients develop pulmonary problems.

The pathophysiology of acute pancreatitis is associated with the possibility of irreversible shock in the early stages of the disease process and with the possibility of autodigestion of the gland in later stages. The pancreas responds to the chemical inflammation initially by edema, and as much as 30% of the plasma volume may become entrapped in the gland, leading to hypovolemia. The possibility of shock is even greater if hemorrhage, ischemia, and cellular necrosis develop, as the tissue sloughs off the organ, and infection, abscess, and gangrene are probable. Furthermore, the glandular cell membranes become autodigested by the pancreatic enzymes, which have escaped into the interstitium. These enzymes become activated and perpetuate the inflammatory response, causing more enzymes to be released into the interstitium, a pathophysiologic positive feedback mechanism. Enzymes can then act on other organs and

tissue around the pancreas, and grayish discoloration around the loin or umbilical area is a late and serious sign of tissue autodigestion by pancreatic enzymes. The enzymes released into the bloodstream from the pancreas may themselves promote a systemic vasodilation through the kallikrein-kallidin-bradykinin system (see Chapter 2). This activation contributes to the development of shock, which then may rapidly become irreversible. Shock has been prevented in experimental animals by the administration of a kallikrien inhibitor, aprotinin (not available in the United States).

A major diagnostic test for acute pancreatitis is elevation of serum amylase over 200 Somogyi units which will remain high for 1 to 3 days. This enzyme does not appear to have any dangerous side effects when it is present in the blood but is released by damaged pancreatic tissue. Other conditions such as mumps and renal failure can result in an elevated serum amylase, however, so the test is not conclusive.

Elevated lipase does present problems, a major one being fat necrosis of the pancreas. Furthermore, the liberation of large amounts of free fatty acids by pancreatic lipase will result in hypocalcemia, as Ca^{++} is taken up by the free fatty acids, which then form calcium soaps. Trypsin may increase in the blood and interfere with the coagulation cascade, leading to a prolonged prothrombin time. The gland apparently "shuts down" almost completely during an attack of acute pancreatitis so that although anticholinergics are commonly administered, the need for them is questionable. Other treatment is aimed at fluid and electrolyte replacement, antibiotic therapy, and pain relief. The course of acute pancreatitis is generally short, unless a chronic inflammation of the gland develops. Figure 21-9 indi-

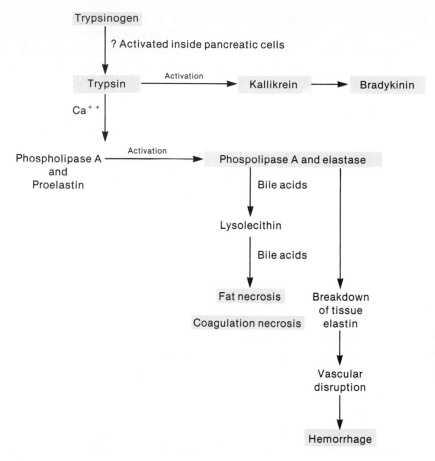

Fig. 21-9. Pathophysiologic mechanisms in acute pancreatitis.
(Modified from Soergel K: Acute pancreatitis. Symposium on Critical Care Medicine, Las Vegas, 1987.)

cates the major pathophysiologic mechanisms by which damage occurs in acute pancreatitis.

Chronic pancreatitis. Chronic pancreatitis is caused by residual damage from the acute disease. Dull persistent pain is characteristic, and acute attacks may recur. Pancreatic secretion is minimal, and malabsorption and steatorrhea are common. Jaundice, caused by stricture of the common bile duct, and diabetes mellitus are also often found. The chronically inflammed pancreas may become fibrotic and calcified, and calculi may form in the gland. Why some individuals experience chronic or relapsing pancreatitis is obscure, but alcoholism appears to be an important contributing factor, being present in at least a third of the patients. Relapse may be prevented in some patients by complete avoidance of alcohol.

Cancer

Cancer of the pancreas is increasing in incidence, being the fourth most common cause of cancer mortality in men. The tumor may be present as a primary cancer or may be the result of metastases from cancers of the lung, breast, thyroid, kidney, or skin melanoma. Primary pancreatic tumors are generally adenocarcinomas and are extremely malignant, metastatic, and invasive. The signs and symptoms are associated with obstruction of the lobules, ductules, and pancreatic duct, which is often obstructed early in the growth of the tumor, as most pancreatic cancer arises in the head of the gland. The symptoms (epigastric pain, flatulence, nausea, malaise) may be so vague in the early stages of the disease that a diagnosis is not made until extensive invasion and metastases have occurred. The treatment therefore is usually only palliative.

DISORDERS OF THE LIVER

The liver is essential for life and functions as a regulator to preserve the steady state (Fig. 21-10). It also is able to withstand and repair damage in a remarkable way. The liver is subject to viral infection, to metastases, and to toxic effects.

Viral hepatitis

Three viruses are known to be associated with viral hepatitis: hepatitis A virus, hep-

atitis B virus, hepatitis D (delta) and a non-A, non-B virus. The A virus is known to cause the short-incubation, low-mortality infectious hepatitis; the B virus has been associated with what was formerly termed *serum hepatitis;* the D virus has only recently been identified, and the non-A, non-B virus is associated with a small percentage of hepatitis. The short-incubation (1 month) form of viral hepatitis (A hepatitis) has been associated with outbreaks in institutions where a large number of people and unsanitary conditions coexist. B or serum hepatitis was so named because it was thought to be transmitted solely through the infected serum, a supposition that has been shown to be untrue. The incubation of this form of hepatitis is usually about 3 months, and the mortality associated with it is much higher than with hepatitis A.

Both hepatitis A and hepatitis B usually have an associated *icterus,* or jaundice, a staining of the skin, mucous membranes, and body fluids with bile pigments, particularly bilirubin. It is often first observed in the sclera of the eye, and even before that it can be detected by exami-

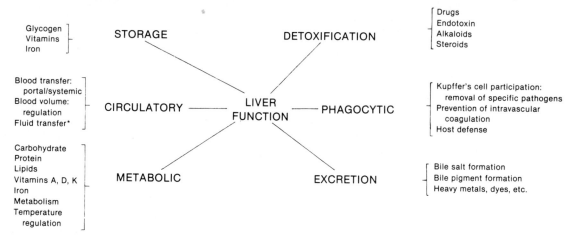

Fig. 21-10. Physiologic functions of liver can be divided into metabolic, excretory, phagocytic, detoxification, storage, and circulatory categories.

Table 21-3.   Mechanisms of jaundice production (normal blood bilirubin is 0.5 mg/100 ml)

Mechanism	Signs	Urine	Feces	van den Bergh test*
Increased breakdown of erythrocytes	Anemia, reticulocytosis, abnormal erythrocytes in blood	Normal (acholuric)	Fecal urobilinogen increased	Indirect positive
Infection or toxic damage to liver cells	Decreased hepatic function	Contains bile salts and bilirubin	Fecal urobilinogen decreased	Direct positive
Bile duct obstruction	Digestive disturbances, high fecal fat	Contains bile salts and bilirubin	Fecal urobilinogen often absent	Direct positive

*The direct van den Bergh test is for conjugated bilirubin, whereas the indirect one tests for bilirubin or bilirubin-protein complexes.

nation of the tympanic membrane.

Bilirubin is formed from hemoglobin breakdown in reticuloendothelial cells. It is conjugated to plasma protein in a form that cannot be excreted in the urine. In the liver the complex is bound to glucuronic acid and forms water-soluble complexes, which are excreted through the bile. The complexes are degraded by intestinal bacteria into stercobilinogen (urobilinogen). Most of this is excreted, some is recirculated, and urobilinogen can than be filtered and excreted by the kidneys.

The appearance of a dark and frothy urine also may precede the clinical appearance of jaundice, and the stools may be acholic if the primary cause of the jaundice is obstruction of the flow of bile into the small intestine. In 29% to 40% of patients with hepatitis, stools may be gray during the first week of jaundice. Jaundice can be produced by hemolytic processes, by obstruction to the flow and release of bile, and by primary hepatocellular disease (Table 21-3).

Hepatitis A. Infection with hepatitis A virus is indicated by virus particles in the feces and other body secretions, and antibodies to the viral capsid protein even before a clinical infection is apparent. The infection is usually transmitted through the fecal-oral route, although poorly cooked mollusks from polluted water have been reported to be fomites and have caused several epidemics. Populations most at risk are the institutionalized, promiscuous homosexual males, the military, infected families, and children in day care centers (Friedman and Dienstag, 1986). The signs and symptoms appear at the end of a prodromal period, with fatigue, weakness, and mild gastrointestinal disturbances being common. A striking aversion to cigarettes also occurs, and patients may complain of pruritus even before jaundice is present; some may have systemic signs such as joint pain, which may reflect the presence of circulating immune complexes. There may be fever, lymphadenopathy, hepatomegaly, and jaundice (which reflects liver cell disruption in bile production). The time during which the patient is contagious is usually just before these symptoms appear. The fundamental lesion in both common types of hepatitis is cellular necrosis. The liver is capable of remarkable regeneration, a process that occurs by budding of remaining liver lobules, and complete regeneration may take place when even as much as 70% of the liver is destroyed. Recovery from hepatitis is then dependent on a balance between cell loss and cell regenerative capability and also on loss of hepatic function. When all the cells become necrotic, death is inevitable. Hepatitis A is associated with a high recovery rate, and usually has a 6-week course. Chronic hepatitis does not follow this infection, nor is there a carrier state. About 40% to 50% of urban Americans have evidence of previous infection.

Hepatitis B. The incidence of this form of viral hepatitis increases in populations of individuals who have received blood transfusions and in drug addicts who may commonly use and share infected needles and syringes. It is much more common in males than females. A large number of asymptomatic hepatitis B carriers exist, particularly in the tropics, and the virus may be found in the blood, as well as in saliva, tears, nasal secretions, and menstrual fluid and in blood-sucking insects that have picked up the virus from infected individuals.

The B virus has been difficult to isolate and characterize and appears in the blood as a virion, called the *Dane particle*, which contains the hepatitis B surface antigen on its outer shell. This viral antigen was termed the *Australian antigen*, since it was originally described in the blood of an Australian aborigine, but is now known as the hepatitis B surface antigen (HBsAg). The central core of the Dane particle contains viral RNA and a DNA polymerase, which is required for the particle to be infective. The surface antigen is also present in the free form in the blood in spherical and tubular shapes.

These HBsAgs appear to be synthesized in hepatic cells. Blood from infected carriers has been shown to contain this antigen, and its presence in even a very small concentration indicates that the blood is potently infective. The presence of surface antigen in the blood is a diagnostic test for hepatitis B, and blood donors are screened for its presence. The virus is now classified into a new and unique viral family, the hepatotropic DNA viruses (Friedman and Dienstag, 1986).

Hepatitis B presents as a more virulent liver disease than hepatitis A and is sometimes associated with the development of chronic hepatitis in those who recover. The prodromal period is characterized by general malaise, joint swelling, rash, pruritus, gastrointestinal symptoms, and hepatomegaly. The appearance of jaundice is accompanied by more marked nausea and vomiting, but occasional cases are anicteric, and the diagnosis may be quite difficult.

Pathologic damage. Hepatocellular necrosis is associated with abnormal elevation of liver enzymes in the serum, as well as impaired liver function in regard to storage and excretion (Fig. 21-10). The degree of liver parenchymal cell damage may be evaluated by the degree of elevation of serum aminotransferase activity—SGOT (serum glutamic-oxaloacetic transaminase) and SGPT (serum glutamic-pyruvic transaminase). Necrosis of only 1% of the liver cells will result in a doubling of the normal serum enzyme activity. Activation of these enzymes is achieved by the liver cell membrane as the enzymes are released. The ratio of SGOT to SGPT is an important indicator of viral hepatitis; this ratio is decreased in early liver damage, although both enzymes increase in absolute amount and activity. The SGPT is normally found in liver cell cytoplasm only, while the SGOT is present in both cytoplasm and mitochondria and is not released at the same rate as SGPT. Other enzymes increase in concentration and activity in the plasma, indicating liver cell damage, but their measurement is not widely used in diagnosis of liver disease.

Necrosis of the parenchymal liver cells is not the only pathologic feature of hepatitis. Inflammation and leukocyte infiltration are certainly prominent signs, occurring in the portal tracts, periportal space, and in the lobules of the liver (Fig. 21-11).

The bile canaliculi and ductules can become dilated and filled with bile-containing material, which may be related to mi-

crovilli damage in the canaliculi or to a disorder of the bile-secreting hepatocyte.

Both forms of hepatitis may result in a cirrhotic process of liver destruction, leading eventually to liver failure. Cirrhosis results from massive necrosis, which leads to fibrosis (Fig. 21-12). Chronic hepatitis may also result in 5% to 10% of acute infections. Chronic hepatitis is associated with active, low-grade B viral infection of the liver. This is twice as common in males, as are all the major complications of chronic hepatitis, cirrhosis, and hepato-

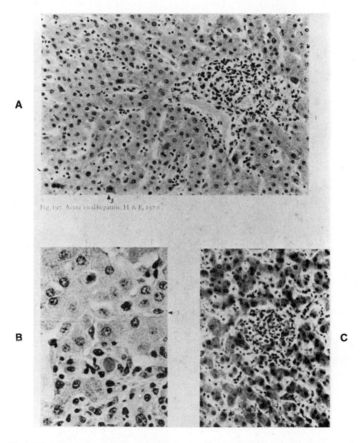

Fig. 21-11. Hepatitis. **A,** Inflammation of acute viral hepatitis. **B,** Inflammatory cells and necrosis of infected parenchymal cells at higher magnification. **C,** Chronic hepatitis in which chronic inflammatory cellular infiltrate and fibrotic scarring are present.
(Courtesy Department of Pathology, University of Tennessee, Memphis.)

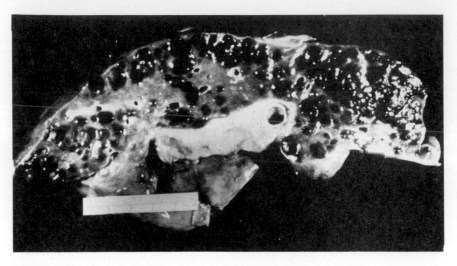

Fig. 21-12. Postnecrotic cirrhosis. Hemorrhagic damaged liver results from acute liver infection. (Courtesy Department of Pathology, University of Tennessee, Memphis.)

cellular carcinoma. There is a very high incidence of this cancer in individuals with chronic hepatitis, with a latency period of about 15 years being common.

Chronic hepatitis. The chronic liver injury produced by persistent hepatitis B infection eventually results in vascular anomalies and liver atrophy as collagen deposition occurs. The liver attempts to regenerate, forming nodules that further disrupt the vasculature and contribute to the eventual development of portal hypertension. These alterations take time to develop, perhaps years, and chronic hepatitis is defined as persistent hepatic inflammation lasting at least 6 months (Payne, 1988). Immune mechanisms may be important in the propagation of chronic disease. Infants infected at birth usually develop a persistent carrier state in which hepatocytes contain virus and are protected from immune attack. The mechanism by which acute infections become chronic hepatitis is not known, although it may be that antiviral antibodies attach to the infected cells and interfere with recog-

nition by T cells. Use of alpha interferons in chronic hepatitis may prove to be effective, since they suppress intracellular viral replication and enhance cell surface HLA-I antigen expression. This will provide a signal to cytotoxic T cells to recognize and attack viral infected cells (Payne, 1988).

Non-A, non-B hepatitis. Numerous cases of hepatitis are not clearly identifiable as either A or B. This form of hepatitis is caused by either the hepatitis D virus or NANB (unknown viral cause). It is commonly seen as a cause for posttranfusion hepatitis, which was formerly largely caused by hepatitis B. Screening of blood donors for HBsAg has nearly eliminated the very serious hepatitis B. Nevertheless, posttransfusion hepatitis is a problem in 3% to 10% of the people who receive blood transfusions. The carrier state for NANB hepatitis is not identifiable with the routine blood screenings now available, and more than a third of those infected develop chronic hepatitis, which may be associated with liver cancer and cirrhosis. Many laboratories are searching for a screening test for NANB hepatitis, and it appears that more than one NANB virus exists. Based on the incidence after transfusion, it is possible that the carrier incidence for NANB hepatitis in the United States is 30 to 70 times greater than that for hepatitis B virus (Friedman and Dienstag, 1986).

Cirrhosis

In cirrhosis the normal liver parenchyma becomes replaced with fibrous, collagenous tissue, eventually resulting in loss of hepatic function. The major types of cirrhosis include cardiac cirrhosis, which is caused by backward congestive heart failure; postnecrotic cirrhosis (Fig. 21-12), biliary cirrhosis, which is caused by bile tract obstruction leading to hepatocellular damage; and portal or Laennec's cirrhosis, which is usually associated with chronic alcoholism.

Cirrhosis is often but not always preceded by fatty infiltration of the liver (steatosis). Fatty liver and sometimes cirrhosis can be caused by the following:

1. Nutritional disorders resulting from, for example, starvation, kwashiorkor, obesity, or surgical jejunoileal bypass.
2. Obstruction in the biliary system
3. An apparently autoimmune disorder that causes infiltration of the biliary system with immune complexes
4. Sequelae of infections and poisons (e.g., carbon tetrachloride)
5. Iron storage disorders (e.g., hemochromatosis) that lead to tremendously elevated iron concentrations; copper storage disease (Wilson disease)
6. Ethanol ingestion

While cirrhosis caused by agents other than alcohol may differ somewhat from Laennec's cirrhosis, all these conditions share many common features. Laennec's cirrhosis, being by far the most prevelent form, will be discussed in detail in this chapter.

Laennec's (portal) cirrhosis. Cirrhosis is the second most common cause of death among persons age 25 to 44 years and the third in those between 45 and 64 (Lieber, 1984). While alcohol is the major etiologic factor, only 8% to 20% of chronic alcoholics develop cirrhosis (Pimstone and Ferich, 1984). There are about 10 million alcoholics in the United States alone, and in nearly one third of these individuals there is the possibility of liver cirrhosis. Several sections of this book have discussed alcohol as a toxic substance, as a teratogen, and in terms of psychopathology and abuse.

Cirrhosis is usually preceded by a theoretically reversible fatty infiltration of the liver cells, which is possibly caused by a fundamental defect in lipid metabolism or secretion and storage. The lipid may represent as much as 40% of the liver weight, as compared to a normal value of 3%. The composition of the lipid is mainly triglycerides and free fatty acids. Triglycerides are normally found in liver cells in small amounts and appear to be present in two "compartments." One compartment is in free exchange with the plasma, while the other compartment seems to hold the lipid and turn it over to the plasma at a very slow rate. It is possible that in fatty liver this second compartment enlarges and sequesters much of the liver cell lipid, thus causing an increased cellular concentration of lipid. The liver appears yellow and greasy and enlarges significantly.

Fatty liver (steatosis). Fatty liver is present in the majority of moderate drinkers (20 to 40 gm per day), and precedes alcoholic hepatitis in most alcoholics. Serum triglycerides are normally taken up by the liver cells and hydrolyzed there into glycerol and free fatty acids. Triglycerides, which are synthesized in the liver, and which may accumulate in huge amounts in steatosis, may be derived from lipid in the diet or in the body fat reserves. The liver may utilize the free fatty acids formed from triglyceride hydrolysis for energy or may convert them to phospholipids, cholesterol esters, or triglycerides once again. The lipids formed in the liver cells are packaged into lipoproteins, which circulate in the blood, delivering the lipids to cells throughout the body, including adipose tissue. Fatty acids may be mobilized from adipose tissue into the blood in a variety of circumstances. The fatty acids become bound to albumin in the blood, and about one third of these fatty acids are taken up by the liver and handled as previously described. Fatty acid mobilization from the adipose tissue is stimulated by lowered blood glucose concentration, glucagon, corticosteroids, somatotropin, thyroid hormone, sympathetic nervous system activation, or epinephrine and norepinephrine. A decrease in blood glucose, which stimulates release of fatty acids from the adipose tissue, may be important in the etiology of fatty liver associated with starvation or malnutrition states. A decrease in fat mobilization may be accomplished by agents that block the stimulators and by insulin. Possible mechanisms whereby fatty liver may be produced are (1) increased fatty acid concentration in the blood and thus increased delivery to and uptake by the liver, (2) increased liver triglyceride formation, (3) decreased release of lipoproteins, and decreased lipid oxidation.

In alcoholics the development of fatty liver precedes the necrotic and fibrotic secondary changes of cirrhosis. It was long held that the cause of fatty liver in alcoholics was primarily the severe nutritional impairment commonly found in the chronic alcoholic. The discovery that alcohol was a direct hepatoxin established the idea that both malnutrition and hepatotoxic effects synergistically acted to produce fatty liver. However, it was believed that fatty liver and cirrhosis caused by the chronic ingestion of alcohol could be prevented by the ingestion of a nutritionally adequate diet. It has since been shown that the administration of ethanol in a total liquid diet that was nutritionally adequate produced fatty liver but not cirrhosis. The baboon has been studied by Leiber and De Carli (1975) who showed that it will develop not only fatty liver but also cirrhosis when fed an adequate diet with large amounts of alcohol over time. The development of cirrhosis occurred in less than a year in some animals. This species is genetically close to humans and lives much longer than most laboratory animals. The development of cirrhosis in baboons indicates that malnutrition is not the primary cause of cirrhosis in alcoholics.

The actual mechanism by which alcohol induces increased liver triglyceride is not well understood. Most of alcohol metabolism does occur in the liver. Nonalcoholic volunteers who ingest large amounts of alcohol over a period of 1 or 2 days are noted to have increased liver triglycerides as an almost immediate effect of the imbibition. Ethanol may act primarily by stimulating the sympathetic nervous system to activate lipid mobilization from the adipose tissue, but its major effect is at the level of the liver cell, inducing enzymatic reactions, some of which act to detoxify alcohol and to perhaps interrupt other enzymatic reactions, leading to eventual triglyceride accumulation in the liver. Alcohol may inhibit reactions that lead to fatty acid oxidation or may interfere with the incorporation of fatty acids into phospholipids and cholesterol, thus leading to an increased yield of triglycerides.

Alcohol appears to be preferentially used as a fuel substrate when it is present, instead of fatty acids, which are the normal energy substrates. Since alcohol produces acetyl-CoA through a series of enzymatic reactions that use nicotinamide adenine dinucleotide (NAD) and produce $NADH_2$, a disruption in the balance of this important coenzyme occurs, at the expense of many of the other liver metabolic processes. The metabolic effects of alcohol include lactic acid accumulation, hypoglycemia, increased serum uric acid accumulation (leading to exacerbations of gout), and trace mineral and vitamin deficiencies. There is an overall increased NADH/NAD ratio, and the citric acid cycle becomes bypassed as the NADH shuttles hydrogens to the electron transport system. The fatty acids that normally would enter the Kreb's cycle instead are deposited as fat. The accumulated lipid of the fatty liver originates from dietary fat, with fatty acids being derived from adipose tissue and lipids synthesized in the liver (Lieber, 1984).

Acetaldehyde is produced by alcohol oxidation and may cause pathologic effects on its own by binding to proteins. Structural disorganization of hepatocyte cytoskeleton, swelling, and increased intracellular protein are all observed early in alcoholic liver injury, possibly due to direct effects of acetaldehyde. These changes may be present in an asymptomatic alcoholic, as studies have shown liver derangement in many alcoholic individuals, even to the point of irreversibility, while clinical symptoms may be absent (Pimstone and French, 1984).

Fatty liver itself may cause severe signs and symptoms, such as hepatomegaly, abdominal pain, ingestion, and anorexia. Necrosis of the cells may develop in an acute manner in this clinical entity, leading to *acute alcoholic hepatitis*, a precirrhotic lesion.

Alcoholic hepatitis develops slowly, and the symptoms are rather general—malaise, fever, anorexia, vomiting, abdominal pain, and jaundice. This disease can progress to hepatic encephalopathy and coma, and can cause portal hypertension, ascites, and esophageal varices. Diagnosis can be difficult, and the disease course quite variable. It may resolve, or it may progress to Laennec's cirrhosis.

The development of fatty liver prefaces the eventual development of cirrhosis if the individual continues to imbibe alcohol. If alcohol ingestion is stopped, the fatty liver can revert to normal, usually in 4 to 6 weeks, and cirrhosis can be avoided. The progression of fatty liver to cirrhosis appears to require that significant cell necrosis occur. The types of fatty liver that are due to causes other than alcohol and that do not develop into cirrhosis are associated with very little or no necrosis. Therefore it has been suggested that the underlying pathologic process that leads to fatty liver in the alcoholic may also result in cirrhosis, since fat accumulation in liver cells is not in itself the cause of necrosis (Fig. 21-13).

Pathophysiologic effects. The liver in portal cirrhosis is generally golden yellow, and the surface is often stippled and nodular, resembling the surface of a football, which is caused by destruction of parenchyma and later repair. The absolute amount of connective tissue is increased, and fibrosis is diffuse. Alcohol causes a net increase in serum proline and hydroxyproline, amino acids required for the biosynthesis of collagen by fibroblasts. This may

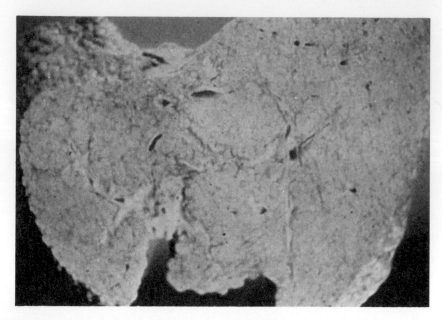

Fig. 21-13. Fatty liver. Extensive fatty infiltration is first event in sequelae leading to Laennec's cirrhosis.
(Courtesy Department of Pathology, University of Tennessee, Memphis.)

either reflect a primary effect of ethanol on proline metabolism and collagen synthesis or may be the result of increased collagen synthesis and deposition in the diseased liver. The fibrosis is also directly related to the necrosis and represents repair of the liver by connective tissue replacement. Infiltration and deposition of hemosiderin in the parenchymal cells are other features.

The major signs and symptoms of cirrhosis are related to the pathophysiologic process perpetuated by a fibrotic, necrotic, functionally impaired liver. The normal function of the intact healthy liver was depicted in Fig. 21-10, and the essential nature of these functions is quite apparent. Failure of the liver to adequately perform these functions can result in a great variety of signs and symptoms. The cirrhotic patient will suffer general ill health, as evidenced by easy fatigability, frequent infections, weight loss, and general malaise.

While muscle wasting is an important development, weight loss is not always apparent, if ascites is present. Aside from generally poor health, specific symptoms are usually present from which a diagnosis of cirrhosis can be made.

Jaundice. Jaundice is not invariably present in cirrhosis but is relatively common, particularly in the later stages of the disease. Many conditions cause jaundice (see Table 21-3). In cirrhosis, hepatic parenchymal cells fail to metabolize bilirubin, and the increased serum bilirubin stains the elastic tissue, causing jaundice. Localized edema may give rise to pigmented areas, particularly if the edema fluid contains protein, since bilirubin is normally albumin bound.

Portal hypertension. Portal hypertension is the most significant complication contributing to mortality from liver cirrhosis. The liver in cirrhosis is usually enlarged, but in advanced disease associated with severe portal hypertension the liver may be shrunken and hardened. The absolute amount of fibrous tissue, however, is invariably increased. The nodules of regenerative tissue and the increased fibrous nature of the liver both act to compress blood vessels, and general narrowing of portal venules occurs. This results in increased back pressure in the portal vein. Increased hepatic artery flow and mass, which causes abnormal communications to form between the hepatic artery and the portal vein, may also occur, and both factors contribute to the development of portal hypertension, as the absolute amount of blood will increase in the portal vein, and there will be increased resistance to blood flow from the portal vein into the portal venules and sinusoids of the liver. Increased back pressure in the portal system will contribute to elevated hydrostatic pressure not only in the portal vein but also in the vessels that feed into this vein—the coronary vein, pyloric vein, su-perior and inferior mesenteric veins, and splenic vein. These veins all receive multiple tributaries before emptying into the portal vein (Fig. 21-14).

The liver, it will be recalled, is a relatively hypoxic organ, receiving arterial blood via the hepatic artery, and venous blood from the gastrointestinal tract and many abdominal organs. The liver microcirculation is arranged so that low-pressure portal blood and high-pressure arterial blood mix in the liver sinusoids, which are drained by hepatic venules. The parenchymal cells that make up the bulk of the liver cell mass form lobules from which a central vein emerges. The sinusoids themselves are lined with phagocytic reticuloendothelial cells such as Kupffer's cells. The blood flow through the liver is regulated by respiration (increasing on inspiration) and by sympathetic innervation of the vessels. The flow through the liver in different areas is highly variable, and generally the splanchnic bed circulation will be profoundly decreased during stress, ex-

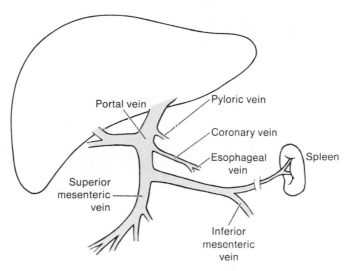

Fig. 21-14. The splanchnic veins. Venous drainage of splanchnic organs. When portal hypertension develops, other vessels can become engorged, leading to stasis and hypoxia of respective organs.

ercise, shock states, and any other phenomenon that will propagate sympathetic nervous system firing. The general adequacy of splanchnic circulation is ultimately dependent on the ability of the liver circulation to handle the portal venous blood. If acute obstruction occurs in the portal vein, due to a thrombus or injury, death follows almost immediately. This effect was shown by a Russian surgeon, Nicolai Eck, who devised the now famous Eck fistula, a portacaval shunt. When portal blood flow is suddenly occluded, rapid hypovolemic shock ensues due to an enormous increase in filtration forces that causes massive extravasation of fluid into the abdominal cavity and throughout the splanchnic bed.

More slowly developing portal occlusion is compatible with life, because the cardiovascular system can form collateral vessels, which are able to shunt the high-pressure portal blood into lower pressure veins, "decompressing" the portal circulation.

Canalization of collateral vessels is particularly prominent (1) in the esophagus, where fragile collateral vessels shunt

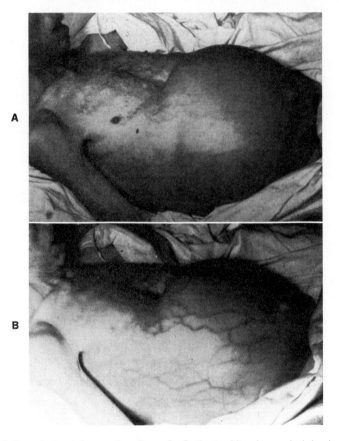

Fig. 21-15. Collateral circulation and ascites. **A,** Patient with advanced cirrhosis of liver shows marked ascites. **B,** Infrared photography is used to demonstrate multiple collateral vessels that are present.
(From Schiff, L: Diseases of the liver, Philadelphia, 1975, JB Lippincott Co.)

blood from the coronary vein into the azygos vein, which drains into the superior vena cava; (2) in the rectum, where collateral vessels connect the middle and superior hemorrhoidal veins to the inferior hemorrhoidal vein, which drains into the inferior vena cava; (3) in the splenic vein, which forms anastomoses into the left renal vein; and (4) in the portal vein itself, which forms connections into the epigastric veins. The cirrhotic patient often will demonstrate the presence of multiple, large collateral abdominal veins, which are grossly visible on the abdomen (Fig. 21-15). A consequence of this sometimes massive collateralization is dilation of the walls of the collateral vessels, which are themselves not particularly strong, and also of the veins, which were not designed to carry the extra volume of blood and higher pressures that are imposed by the cirrhotic liver disease. These vessels then out-pouch, forming local areas of dilation called *varices* as illustrated in Fig. 21-16. Pressure in these varices is increased even above that in the vein of which they are a part as shown by the modified Laplace equation, which states that the tension, *T*, in a tube is proportional to the pressure, *P*, times the radius, *R*, divided by the wall thickness, *h:*

$$T = PR/h$$

Thus factors that cause a decrease in vessel elasticity or increase in radius result in decreased distensibility of the vessel and therefore a rise in pressure. While veins are much more distensible than arteries, the degree of stretching that takes place when varices are formed is probably significant enough to account for the tendency of varices to rupture. When esophageal or more commonly, gastric varices rupture, blood under great pressure, resulting from the concomitant portal hy-

Fig. 21-16. Esophageal varices. Swollen varices and extensive collateral circulation are evident in this segment of esophagus from patient with Laennec's cirrhosis.
(Courtesy Department of Pathology, University of Tennessee, Memphis.)

pertension, is poured out, and a life-threatening hemorrhagic emergency is present. Furthermore, clotting factors produced by the liver may be deficient, and prothrombin time is often increased, contributing to the hemorrhagic state. The treatment of such hemorrhage is aimed at attempting to stop the bleeding either directly by insertion of ballooning tubes or physiologically by administration of vasopressin. The balloon tubes can be pulled so as to exert pressure on the bleeding gastric varices and laterally on the esophageal walls if bleeding is occurring from esophageal varices. The first hemorrhage from bleeding varices has a high associated mortality. There is some evidence that massive upper gastrointestinal bleeding in cirrhosis can also occur from gastric erosion and ulceration.

Surgical decompression shunts are performed to alleviate the portal hypertension that is commonly associated with cirrhosis and that results in varices. The portacaval shunt has been the most common surgical procedure, although other techniques are presently being used. The portal vein is dissected away from the liver and inserted into the inferior vena cava, an operation that will prolong life in many cirrhotics, although the death rate associated with hepatic failure in these individuals is still very high.

Ascites. The common finding of ascites in Laennec's cirrhosis, which is usually found in conjunction with portal hypertension, suggests that the two processes are related, a conjecture that has much experimental backing. It is thought that hepatic lymph formation occurs in excess of what the hepatic lymphatics can remove, because of sinusoidal hypertension. The same phenomenon probably occurs in mesenteric and intestinal capillaries. Another possible factor contributing to ascites formation in cirrhosis is abnormal albumin metabolism, acting to cause hypoalbuminemia and a resultant decrease in colloid osmotic pressure. Loss of protein into the ascites fluid accounts at least partially for hypoalbuminemia. Ascitic pressure forces on renal perfusion may also initiate renin release with subsequent aldosterone-produced Na^+ and water retention. Hyperaldosteronism can occur through impaired degradation of the hormone by the diseased liver, and plasma

volume may actually be expanded in cirrhosis, further accounting for the hypoalbuminism. These positive feedback mechanisms are diagramed in Fig. 21-17.

Treatment of ascites is aimed at removal of the excess fluid by paracentesis, dietary restriction of Na^+ and sometimes fluid, and a high-calorie diet that contains a moderate restriction of protein (no greater than 50 gm per day). The diseased liver is not able to metabolize proteins well, and excess protein can precipitate the development of hepatic coma. Diuretics may be administered as well if the ascites fails to respond to medical management. In general the development of ascites indicates that serious pathophysiologic processes are being perpetuated, and the prognosis is poor, with about 25% of cirrhotic patients with ascites dying within a year. Most do not die from fluid loss caused by ascites but from hepatic coma or gastrointestinal bleeding, complications associated with the liver pathology.

Other signs and symptoms. The individual suffering from Laennec's cirrhosis may have a great variety of symptoms related to the multisystemic effects of liver disease. Fever, neuropathy, cardiovascular disturbances, renal failure, and endocrine imbalance have all been reported in this disease. There is also a tendency to bleed because of a decreased capacity to form clotting factors.

Treatment rationale. The most obvious therapy for alcoholic liver disease is complete abstinence of alcohol, which can result in total reversal of fatty liver and, if enough parenchymal cells are present, reversal of cirrhosis by regeneration of these cells. The architecture of the liver will change with regeneration of new parenchyma, but functional capacity is preserved. The mechanisms by which budding of new regenerative parenchyma

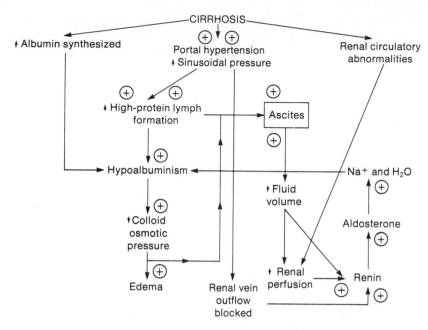

Fig. 21-17. Pathophysiology of ascites formation in cirrhosis. Ascites is caused by many factors that are present in advanced cirrhosis. Edema is also perpetuated by interaction of these factors.

occurs are not known, but a blood-borne factor may be involved. Unfortunately, abstinence is generally not observed by cirrhotic patients, and so the true potential for recovery from this disease is not known.

The complications of cirrhosis must be treated vigorously as patients with this disease are susceptible to many problems that can interact and produce rapid deterioration. These complications include hypokalemia caused by the presence of hyperaldosteronism, hypoxia, renal disease (the hepatorenal syndrome), infection, and encephalopathy, as well as jaundice, portal hypertension, gastrointestinal hemorrhage, and ascites, the hallmarks of the disease. In general the course of cirrhosis is marked by many crises, which require emergency management.

The patient's diet may be an important part of daily management; it is generally

high in carbohydrates, moderate or restricted in protein, low in sodium, and supplemented by vitamins. Attention to fluid and electrolyte status is important, particularly since many cirrhotic patients are given diuretics.

Corticosteroids have been used in the care of the cirrhotic patient. The physiology of corticosteroid action in Laennec's cirrhosis may be based on interference with fibrosis in the diseased liver. Corticosteroids decrease the activity of protocollagen proline hydroxylase and induce the activity of the enzyme collagenase in fibroblasts, increase the collagenolytic activity of hepatic cell lysosomes, and decrease the absolute amount of endoplasmic reticulum in fibroblasts. All these actions may inhibit the deposition of collagen fibers in the liver, thus slowing down the development of hepatic fibrosis. The long-term treatment of cirrhotics by corticosteroids is, however, limited because of their side effects, which may aggravate other pathophysiologic mechanisms operating in the disease.

Hepatic coma

The terminal stage of most liver disease is the development of hepatic coma resulting from liver failure. Hepatic coma can also develop as an acute phase in an otherwise reversible liver disease. Encephalopathy is observed in advanced cirrhosis and can be considered an early stage of hepatic coma. Thirty-six percent of individuals with cirrhosis die in hepatic coma. The onset is insidious, with major symptoms related to encephalopathy causing a diminished level of conscousness, which is often indicated by drowsiness and confusion, irritability, and a characteristic flapping tremor (asterixis). A comatose state follows, from which most patients do not recover. Anatomic changes in the morphology and number of nerve cells have been reported.

The pathogenesis of encephalopathy and hepatic coma traditionally has been thought to be the result of ammonia intoxication. Ammonia ingested in the diet or that arises from the action of gut bacteria normally is removed from the portal blood by the liver and is used in the formation of urea. Urea is then released into the bloodstream and excreted by the kidney. Blood ammonia levels are elevated in hepatic coma, but the degree of elevation cannot be correlated with the degree of encephalopathy. Ammonia has been shown experimentally to have a direct toxic action on brain cells and possibly may act by inhibiting acetylcholine synthesis or by causing the accumulation of GABA (gamma-aminobutyric acid), an inhibitory brain neurotransmitter. Ammonia may also inhibit cerebral energy metabolism. Common precipitating factors in the development of hepatic coma include increased dietary protein, which would give rise to increased ammonia, and gastrointestinal bleeding, which results in deposition of large amounts of blood in the gut. This blood is high in aromatic amino acids and would also give rise to increased ammonia resulting from bacterial breakdown of blood protein. Other precipitating factors include azotemia, sedatives, tranquilizers, and analgesics.

There are, however, several features of hepatic coma that cannot be explained by ammonia intoxication. These incude the increase in brain serotonin and tryptophan levels found experimentally in hepatic coma. It is possible that "false neurotransmitters" are formed in coma, leading to the development of encephalopathy. L-dopa has been occasionally reported to wake people from hepatic coma in a dramatic manner. Another possible factor in the pathogenesis of hepatic coma is *alpha-ketoglutaramate*, which is elevated in the cerebrospinal fluid during coma, and also short-chain fatty acids, which are increased and which may act synergistically with ammonia. The pathogenesis of hepatic coma is therefore an area of continuing research.

Treatment rationale. Treatment of the patient in hepatic coma is complicated by the impairment of drug metabolism and detoxification that commonly occurs in liver damage. Thus administration of hypnotics, analgesics, and sedatives must be carefully considered. Morphine, which is conjugated by the liver, can precipitate hepatic coma, while meperidine hydrochloride (Demerol) can be administered without serious side effects (in terms of liver function), since it is not handled by the liver. Long-acting short-chain barbiturates are normally excreted by the kidney and can be given to patients with liver disease, while the short-acting long-chain barbiturates are metabolized by the liver. Therefore phenobarbital can be administered to patients with liver disease, albeit with caution. Paraldehyde is an extremely potent sedative, which is also metabolized by the liver, and its odor can be present on the breath of a cirrhotic patient for several days after its administration. Anesthesia may provoke serious effects in the cirrhotic patient. Chloroform in particular is extremely toxic to an already damaged liver.

Antibiotics may be administered to the patient in hepatic coma, particularly neomycin, 4 gm per day, to sterilize the lower GI tract. This is an attempt to remove a major source of ammonia. Dietary protein is restricted for the same reason. If upper GI tract bleeding has occurred, the stomach may be aspirated to remove blood, which can serve as a source of amino acids and therefore ammonia. Corticosteroids are also administered frequently.

Removing ammonia from the circulation has been attempted both pharmacologically and physically with exchange transfusions and hemodialysis. This has met with limited success. More radical procedures have included colonic surgery for intractable cases.

Prognosis. The nature of the coma varies from patient to patient. Individuals may go in and out of deep stuporous states, and treatment may result in complete awakening and loss of all signs of encephalopathy. Occasionally death will occur as the result of bronchopneumonia, sepsis, or gastrointestinal hemorrhage, or death may occur naturally in the deep comatose state. The longer and deeper the coma, the less likely it is that the patient will recover.

SUMMARY

This chapter has presented gastrointestinal tract, pancreatic, liver, and gallbladder disease mechanisms. We have viewed the pathophysiology as deviations from normal and have highlighted the psychosomatic influences as well. The roles of life-style, stress, and personality are obviously important in many of the common disorders involving this system. Diet and nutritional status, substance abuse (especially alcohol), and stress management strategies are exogenous influences on gastrointestinal health, while peptides and hormones, nervous connections, and immune status act internally.

Recognition of both the external and internal mechanisms in the pathophysiology of gastrointestinal diseases is important, since treatment strategies and nursing interventions should address both. One of the authors of this book, for example, provides nursing consultation to ulcerative colitis patients in the arena of stress management, positive imagery, and visualization.

BIBLIOGRAPHY

Anderson WAD and Kissane JM: Pathology, ed 7, St. Louis, 1977, The CV Mosby Co.

Arapakis G, Lyketsos C, Gerolymatos K, Richardson S, and Lyketsos G: Low dominance and high intrapunitiveness in ulcerative colitis and irritable bowel syndrome, Psychotherapy 46:171, 1986.

Baer C and Williams B: Clinical pharmacology and nursing, Springhouse, PA, 1988, Springhouse Corp.

Corbett J: (1987). Laboratory tests and diagnostic procedures with nursing diagnoses, Norwalk, CT, 1987, Appleton & Lange.

Friedman L and Dienstag J: Recent developments in viral hepatitis, Disease-a-Month 32:314, 1986.

Guyton A: (1983). Textbood of medical physiology, Philadelphia, 1983, WB Saunders Co.

Kaufman D: Symposium on Critical Care Medicine, Acute Pancreatitis, Las Vegas, 1987.

Lieber C: Metabolism and metabolic effects of alcohol, Med Clin North Am 68:3, 1984.

Lieber C: To drink (moderately) or not to drink? N Engl J Med 310:846, 1984.

Lieber CS and Carli DLM: Alcoholic liver injury: experimental models in rats and baboons, Adv Exp Med Biol 59:379, 1975.

McColl I and Sladen G: Intestinal absorption in man, London, 1975, Academic Press, Ltd.

Menguy R, Desbaillets L, and Masters Y: Mechanism of stress ulcer: influence of hypovolemic shock on energy metabolism in the gastric mucosa, Gastroenterology 66:46, 1974.

Mitchell J and Skelton M: Diarrheal infections, Am Fam Phys 37:195, 1988.

Payne J: Chronic hepatitis: pathogenesis and treatment, Disease-a-Month 34:113, 1988.

Pimstone N and French S: Alcoholic liver disease, Med Clin North Am 68:39, 1984.

Quinn T, Bender B, and Bartlett J: New developments in infectious diarrhea, Disease-a-Month 34:165, 1986.

Schiff L, editor: Disease of the liver, Philadelphia, 1985, JB Lippincott Co.

Sleisenger M and Fordtran J: Gastrointestinal disease, ed 3, Philadelphia, 1983, WB Saunders Co.

Soergel K: Acute pancreatitis. in Symposium on Critical Care Medicine, Las Vegas, 1987, Ch. 91.

Soll A and Isenberg J: Duodenal ulcer disease, In Sleisenger M and Fordtran J, editors, Gastrointestinal disease, Philadelphia, 1983, WB Saunders Co.

Strobel W and James S: The immunopathogenesis of gastrointestinal and hepatobiliary diseases, JAMA 258:2962, 1987.

Glossary

acanthocyte an abnormal erythrocyte characterized by spiny projections that give it a thorny appearance.

aerobic oxygen dependent.

allele two or more genes that occupy the same locus of a chromosome, only one of which will be expressed for a particular trait.

anabolism metabolic chemical reactions involved in the synthesis of body components; the process by which nutrients are taken up by the cell and converted into complex cellular constituents.

anaerobic not dependent on oxygen.

anasarca severe generalized edema.

anencephalic absence of central nervous system structures specifically, the brain.

anisocoria unequal diameters of the pupils.

ankylosing spondylitis a chronic disease involving the spine, that produces changes similar to those seen in rheumatoid arthritis; it is characterized by inflammation of the sacroiliac, costovertebral, and intervertebral joints with ossification and fixation of the spinal joints, which may result in complete immobilization of the spine and thorax.

antichalones agents that reverse the action of chalones.

antitrypsin substance that inhibits trypsin.

arteriosclerosis thickening, hardening, and loss of elasticity of the walls of the blood vessels; these changes may occur in either the intima or media. Arteriosclerosis occurs in the small arteries.

arthropathy joint disease.

Arthus reaction the development of a severe localized inflammatory reaction soon after interdermal injection of an antigenic substance; it is thought to be an immediate hypersensitivity reaction.

aspiration entry of secretions, fluids, or solids into the tracheobronchial passages.

asterixis flapping tremor characterized by involuntary jerking movements, especially in the hands; best elicited by having patient extend his arms, dorsiflex his wrists, and spread his fingers. It is also called *liver flap* because of its frequent occurrence in patients with impending hepatic coma, although it may be seen in other forms of encephalopathy.

ataxia muscular incoordination

atheroma fatty degeneration or thickening of the arterial wall.

atherosclerosis a form of arteriosclerosis in which there are localized accumulations of lipid-containing material (atheroma) within or beneath the intimal surfaces of blood vessels; a common cause of arterial occlusion.

autocatalysis progressive catalysis of a reaction by its own products.

autosomes any ordinary paired chromosome other than the sex chromosomes.

azotemia excess of urea or other nitrogenous compounds in the blood.

ballismus condition in which twisting and jerking movements occur.

bradycardia slow heart rate, below 60 beats per minute in adult and 70 beats per minute in child.

bronchiectasis bronchial dilatation due to with bronchial wall destruction due to chronic obstruction or infection.

carotenemia carotene in the blood; characterized by yellowing of the skin.

carpopedal spasm characteristic flexion and adduction spasm of muscles in hands and feet.

catabolism reactions of metabolism by which complex cellular substances are broken down into smaller simpler compounds.

cataract clouding of the lens of capsule of the eye that obstructs vision, this condition can be caused by aging, injury, or infection.

centromere clear region of the chromosome, which marks the junction of two chromatids and location of attachment to the spindle during cell division.

chalone substance that regulates specific intracellular activity, including cell proliferation.

chelating agent chemical agents known as ligands, which form a ring structure surrounding a metallic ion by firmly binding it with coordinate bonds; the entire complex is termed *chelate, metal complex,* or *coordination compounds.*

chromogen a substance producing color or pigment.

chronotropic affecting the rate of rhythmic movements such as the heart beat.

Chvostek's sign contraction of muscles around the mouth in response to tapping the facial nerve in front of the ear.

chyme semiliquid partially digested food found in the stomach and small intestine during digestion.

cleavage mitotic divisions of the fertilized egg cell.

clone a strain of cells descended from a single cell in tissue culture; this cell population is not only genetically identical but also genetically distinct from similar cells.

conjunctivitis inflammation of the mucous membrane that lines the eyelid.

contracture persistent shortening of the muscle that is resistant to stretching and causes joint deformity.

cor pulmonale 1. chronic: hypertrophy of the right ventricle due to disease of the lungs; 2. acute: dilation and failure of the right side of the heart.

Cori cycle pathway in carbohydrate metabolism; the breakdown of muscle glycogen with the formation of lactic acid, which is reconverted to glycogen in the liver, catabolized to glucose, carried back to the muscles, and again converted into muscle glycogen.

cotyledon portion of the uterine surface of the placenta.

cystic mastitis inflammation of the breast characterized by stromal and epithelial hyperplasia and cystic dilation of the ducts; the affected breast has a diffuse nodular texture.

cytoskeleton structural elements that form an elastic framework of the cell.

deamination removal of an amino group, $-NH_2$, from amino compounds.

dermatoglyphics a study of the surface markings of the skin of palms, fingers, toes, and soles; used in law enforcement for identification and in medicine as a genetic indicator.

dialdehydes chemical compounds containing two aldehyde groups.

differentiation process of acquiring functionally specific characteristics through the cellular diversification of embryologic development.

diploid having one complete set of homologous chromosomes or twice the haploid number, as seen in normal somatic cells of higher organisms.

diurnal occurring during the day.

dysphagia difficult swallowing.

dystocia difficult labor or childbirth.

endergonic reaction that requires energy.

endotracheal intubation insertion of a tube into the trachea, which bypasses the upper airways and allows direct ventilation of bronchi and smaller airways.

entropy measure of the randomness or disorder in a system; a state of maximum probability.

equifinality phenomenon by which a final state may be reached through many different pathways.

exergonic reaction that liberates energy.

exophthalmos abnormal protrusion of the eyeball.

exudate substances such as cells, protein, cellular debris, and fluid that escape from blood vessels into surrounding tissue, usually as result of inflammation.

falciparum malaria infection caused by the organism *Plasmodium falciparum,* one of the most virulent malaria parasites; transmitted only by the bite of the female anopheline mosquito, the disease is characterized by high fever, chills, convulsions, shock, and death.

fibroblast flat, elongated cell with cytoplasmic processes at each end, from which connective tissue is developed.

free radical atom or group of atoms having at least one unpaired electron; their existence is brief because of their extreme reactivity.

gamete basic reproductive cell whose union in sexual reproduction initiates a new individual; a mature female or male reproductive cell: the ovum or spermatozoon.

genotype collection of genes that make up the genetic apparatus of an organism.

glia supporting structure of the brain and nervous tissue; also used to denote a gluelike tissue.

glucose-6-phosphate dehydrogenase specific enzyme that catalyzes the release of two hydrogen ions from glucose-6-phosphate.

glycogenolysis catabolism of glycogen in body tissue to glucose.

glycoproteins conjugated proteins in which the nonprotein groups are carbohydrates; for example, the mucins, mucoids, and chondroproteins.

haploid possessing one complete set of nonhomologous chromosomes or half the number of chromosomes in somatic cells of higher organisms; normal state of gamete cells after reduction division of gametogenesis; the haploid number in humans is 23.

haversian canal central unit of haversian system, which is surrounded by concentrically arranged layers of matrix and cells; it carries blood vessels, which transmit nutrient material to the bone.

hemosiderin iron-containing pigment derived from the hemoglobin of red cell breakdown; functions as a storage form of iron.

hepatoma tumor of the liver; also transition stage between adenoma and carcinoma of the liver.

hepatomegaly enlargement of the liver.

heterozygous having corresponding genes on two different genomes.

homozygous having corresponding genes on two identical genomes.

hyaline crystalline and nearly transparent.

hypercapnia increased concentration of carbon dioxide in the arterial blood; syn. hypercarbia; increased P_{CO_2}.

hyperphagia abnormally increased consumption of food sometimes symptomatic of hypothalamic injury.

hyperplasia increase in mass due to increased number of cells in a tissue or organ.

hypertrophy overgrowth: generally an increase in bulk; use may be restricted due to increase in mass through increase in size but not in number of individual tissue elements.

hypocapnia decreased concentration of carbon dioxide in the arterial blood; syn. hypocarbia; decreased P_{CO_2}.

hypolipoproteinemia deficiency of lipoproteins in the serum; seen in hypobetalipoproteinemia and Tangier disease.

hypophysectomy removal of the pituitary gland.

hyposthenuria excretion of an extremely dilute urine of low specific gravity, indicative of loss of concentrating ability.

hypoxemia insufficient oxygenation of the blood; a lower than normal concentration (or partial pressure) of oxygen in the arterial blood; decreased P_{O_2}.

hypoxia inadequate cellular oxgenation, which can result from deficiency in either the delivery or utilization of oxygen at the cellular level.

iatrogenic induced by treatment; literally, "physician caused."

icterus jaundice yellowish discoloration due to deposition of bile pigments in tissues and secretions; due to liver disease, obstruction of bile ducts or excessive destruction of red blood cells.

immunization process of gaining protection from a specific pathogenic entity through exposure to antigenic substances while infected by disease or by injection of a vaccine that stimulates antibody production.

inotropic influencing the contractility of the muscular tissue, especially myocardium.

intermittent claudication pain, tenderness, and weakness of the calf, which occurs with exercise and subsides after a period of rest; may be due to occlusion of the arterial blood supply, arteriosclerosis, or atherosclerosis.

ischemia reversible tissue injury due to disrupted blood flow.

karyolysis destruction of the cell nucleus.

karyorrhexis fragmentation of the chromatin in cellular nuclear disintegration.

kernicterus deposition of bile pigments in the nuclear masses of the brain, which results in pathologic changes in the tissue.

kinins biologically active small polypeptides generated in plasma during the first phase of the inflammatory response; their effects include vasodilation, increased permeability to proteins, and attraction of neutrophils.

lactase intestinal enzyme that hydrolyzes lactose and other β-galactosides.

micelle 1. ultramicroscopic colloid particle; 2. living unit made up of one or more molecules and capable of growth and division.

microsome ultramicroscopic granular particle of the endoplasmic reticulum observed after cells are broken by centrifugation.

microvilli microscopic hairlike projections from the free surface of a cell, which greatly increase its surface area.

myelogenous originating in the bone marrow.

oligodendrocyte cell that forms part of the neuroglia of the central nervous system; processes from these cells form a partial investment for some myelin sheaths.

omphalomesenteric duct narrow tube, which, in the embryo, connects the umbilical vesicle (yolk sac) with the mid gut of the embryo.

oogenesis formation and development of female gametes (ova).

operon gene in genetics, a portion of a chromosome consisting of an operator region (at the initial end of the gene where the synthesis of mRNA is indicated) and closely linked structural genes or clusters; the cluster is controlled by the operator through the action of inducer and repressor proteins.

orthopnea difficult breathing when laying down.

osseous relating to or having the properties of bone.

osteoblast bone cell that is responsible for the formation of one tissue.

osteoclast bone cell that is responsible for resorption (tearing down) of bone.

osteomalacia condition in which the bone matrix is not calcified.

osteoporosis loss of bone mass.

oxidative phosphorylation electron transfer from donor to acceptor with resultant phosphorylation of ADP to form ATP; occurs in the mitochondrion of the cell via the respiratory pigments of the electron transport chain.

papilledema edema and inflammation (swelling) of the optic nerve at its point of entrance into the eyeball.

parabiotic 1. anatomic and physiologic union of two organisms as of joined twins or experimental union of laboratory animals; 2. reversible suspension of conduction through a nerve fiber.

paresthesia abnormal cutaneous sensation such as numbness, tingling, or prickling: heightened sensitivity.

paroxysmal nocturnal dyspnea difficult breathing that awakens one from sleep.

penetrance in genetics, the frequency of phenotypic manifestation of a trait present in the genotype of an individual.

pes cavus abnormal hollowness of the sole of the foot.

phenotype observable characteristics of an organism; the expression of a given genotype.

photophobia unusual intolerance or sensitivity to light.

piezoelectric effect stimulation of bone growth by an electrical gradient and flow of current, with growth occurring at the site of compressional stress because of the negative potential caused by compressional stress.

pinocytosis cellular process of actively engulfing liquid; a phenomenon in which minute incuppings or invaginations are formed in the surface of the cell membrane and close to form fluid-filled vesicles.

plasmid group of genetic elements that never become integrated into the host chromosome but remain as independent, self-replicating units, including bioblasts, plasmagenes, plastids, and viruses; some plasmids are responsible for the resistance transfer factors, which confer resistance to antibiotics.

pneumothorax collection of air in the pleural cavity, which causes pressure changes that collapse the lung tissue.

polar body cell that separates from an oocyte during the first or second meiotic division; contains little cytoplasm and consists mostly of nuclear material.

polycythemia excessive number of red cells in the blood.

polydipsia frequent drinking due to thirst.

polyphagia eating excessive amounts of food; eating voraciously.

polyuria frequent, excessive urination.

postprandial occurring after a meal.

postural hypotension fall in blood pressure that occurs during a change from a lying or sitting position.

progeny descendants of animals; offspring of plants.

progressive multifocal leukoencephalitis rare disease present usually in patients with another underlying disorder or those who have been given immunosuppressive drugs; characterized by multifocal demyelination of the white matter of the brain with loss of oligodendroglia, cells that elaborate and support myelin sheath.

proprioception awareness of posture, movement, changes in equilibrium and the knowledge of position, weight, and resistance of objects in relation to the body.

prostaglandins group of chemically related, long-chain hydroxy fatty acids present in most body tissue; their specific actions are not fully established, but they do affect smooth muscle, nerves, liver, adipose tissue, circulation, and reproductive organs.

protease protein-splitting enzyme.

pruritus severe itching.

pyruvate kinase enzyme that catalyzes the reaction of phosphopyruvic acid with ADP to form ATP and pyruvic acid, which completes glycolysis.

repressor gene regulatory gene that contains the coded information for the synthesis of repressor protein; combines with an operator gene to prevent RNA synthesis, which inhibits enzyme synthesis.

retrolental fibroplasia formation of an opaque fibrous membrane behind the lens of the eye; usually occurs in premature infants exposed to high oxygen concentration for a long period of time.

rhabdomyolisis excessive destruction of muscle tissue.

Schwann cells cells around certain nerve fibers that deposit lipid insulator sheath (myelin).

sclerosis hardening of an organ or tissue; especially a hardening caused by excessive fibrous tissue formation from inflammation or disease of the interstitial tissue.

scotoma blind spot in visual field; *pl.* scotomata.

sebaceous producing or pertaining to sebum, an oily, fatty secretion.

secretagogue agent that stimulates secretion.

shearing force pressure that results from subcutaneous tissue and bone sliding with movement while the skin remains stationary.

sinus tract abnormal passage or opening to an abscess site.

situs inversus abnormal position of organs on opposite side of body.

spermatogenesis formation and development of male gametes (spermatozoa).

splenomegaly enlargement of the spleen.

steatorrhea excess fat in the stools, seen in malabsorption syndromes.

steroid hormone secreted from the adrenal cortex, which is derived from cholesterol via similar synthetic pathways.

stratification ordered, layered system.

synovial membrane membrane lining the capsule of a joint that secretes synovia, a clear lubricating fluid.

tachycardia rapid heart rate; heart rate over 100 beats per minute in adult and 120 beats per minute in child.

Tangier disease familial disease characterized by a deficit of serum lipoprotein and abnormal cholesterol storage.

tetany condition characterized by intermittent tonic spasms that usually involve the extremities.

thermoregulation maintenance of a body at a specific temperature regardless of fluctuations in its environmental temperature.

tracheostomy or tracheotomy incision of trachea with insertion of a tube to permit ventilation past an obstruction.

transamination reversible transfer of an amino group, $-NH_2$, from one compound to another or transposition of an amino group within a compound.

Trousseau's sign muscular spasms of the hands and wrist as a result of compression of the brachial artery for 1 to 5 minutes.

uremia syndrome of clinical signs and symptoms that occur as a result of renal dysfunction.

vagotomy break in the continuity of the impulses carried by the vagus nerve.

Valsalva's maneuver attempt at forced expiration with the glottis closed, which causes increased intrathoracic pressure.

vasculitis inflammation of a blood vessel.

vernix caseosa sebaceous deposit covering fetus.

xanthoma rounded yellowish lipid plaque found usually on the eyelids.

Index

Page numbers in *italics* indicate boxes and illustrations.
Page numbers followed by *t* indicate tables.

Also Available!

MOSBY'S MANUAL OF CLINICAL NURSING, 2nd Edition
By June M. Thompson, R.N., M.S.; Gertrude K. McFarland, R.N.,
D.N.Sc., F.A.A.N.; Jane E. Hirsch, R.N., M.S.; Susan M. Tucker, R.N.,
B.S.N.; and Arden C. Bowers, R.N., M.S.
(5157-3) 1989

The first edition of MOSBY'S MANUAL OF CLINICAL NURSING was voted
nursing's "#1 most indispensible reference" in an American Journal of Nursing
poll, and the second edition is even better than the first. No student should be
without this comprehensive reference for planning nursing care.

- Part I, "Clinical Nursing Practice," is organized by body systems and covers virtually every condition,
  disease, or disorder you are likely to encounter. Complete nursing care is presented for all medical
  conditions and medical interventions.
- NEW! Part II, "Diagnostic Procedures," contains nursing care associated with every significant diagnostic
  test. The tests are presented by category and are also alphabetically indexed for easy access.
- Part III, "Nursing Diagnoses," has all NANDA-accepted nursing diagnoses including the 16 new diagnoses
  accepted at the Eighth NANDA Conference held in March 1988.
- Nursing care is concisely organized according to the nursing process.
- An assessment for each disease provides a checklist to ensure comprehensive nursing assessment.
- Comprehensive nursing interventions with rationales are linked to every possible nursing diagnosis for every
  disease to allow for individualization of care.
- Patient teaching in the nursing care of each disease encourages you to build teaching interventions right into
  care plans.
- An evaluation section for each disease provides specific data to help determine when your nursing goals
  have been met, or when they need to be revised.

 Mosby

*This useful text provides nurses and students with everything they need to plan and implement high
quality nursing care. To order, ask your bookstore manager or call toll-free 800-221-7700, ext. 15A.
We look forward to hearing from you!*